40/=

HANDBOOK OF TANGANYIKA

(Second edition)

Edited by

J. P. MOFFETT

(Commissioner for Social Development)

This Handbook, although published by the Government of Tanganyika and in part compiled from official records, is not an official publication.

First Published
1958

PRINTED AND BOUND BY THE GOVERNMENT PRINTER
DAR ES SALAAM

FOREWORD

BY

HIS EXCELLENCY THE GOVERNOR OF TANGANYIKA

I have long felt that Tanganyika required some really accurate handbooks designed to give the enquiring scholar, business man or politician a clear and objective picture of the country. In 1955, "Tanganyika: A Review of its Resources and Their Development" was published. This dealt primarily with the economic aspect of the country. This new edition of the *Handbook of Tanganyika* is mainly an historical and descriptive account of the territory. The two books are, therefore, complementary and together afford an unrivalled source of information on the country.

With present rates of development such handbooks lose their value quickly. I hope, therefore, that new editions will keep pace with the country's development, and I am confident that these reference books will achieve a reputation for accurate and up-to-date factual presentation of the many aspects of Tanganyika.

Although this book is the product of many authors, I am particularly indebted to Mr. John Moffett who has found time to collate and edit the material for this new edition of the *Handbook of Tanganyika*.

GOVERNMENT HOUSE,
DAR ES SALAAM.

E. F. TWINING

EDITOR'S PREFACE

The first edition of the *Handbook of Tanganyika* was published in 1930 and is of course long since both out of print and out of date.   One criticism made of it was that it contained very little description either of the country or of the people.   In compiling the second edition an attempt has been made to rectify these omissions, and fairly full descriptions have been given of each of the eight provinces and of their inhabitants.   The second edition is an entirely new work and has been planned on rather different lines. [1] It aims at being supplementary to "Tanganyika: A Review of its Resources and their Development". [2]   As His Excellency the Governor points out in his foreword, it is thus largely historical and descriptive, and the two books together are designed to provide that background of knowledge which is indispensable to a proper appraisal of events in the territory and without which it is virtually impossible to appreciate the information provided, for example, in annual reports of various kinds.   The *Handbook* contains a fairly exhaustive bibliography which should be of permanent value to those seeking further information about any aspect of the territory's affairs, but it may be convenient to list here the main publications wherein further information may be sought.

These are: the annual report on the territory, submitted to the United Nations Organization, the annual reports of the Provincial Commissioners, of the various departments of Government and of the High Commission, the weekly official *Gazette*, the local "Hansard" and the yearly Statistical Abstract.   All these, except the reports of the High Commission (which are obtainable from the Government Printer, Nairobi) are obtainable from the Government Printer, Dar es Salaam.   In addition, there are special reports (usually advertised in the *Gazette*), local newspapers such as the *Tanganyika Standard*, the quarterly journal of the Tanganyika Society—*Tanganyika Notes and Records*[3]—and the *Tanganyika Guide*. [4]

Much of the contents of this book has been compiled from official records and I gratefully acknowledge the assistance of many fellow officers.   But it could not have been compiled from official records alone, and I am indebted to a number of others for contributions which I feel enhance very considerably the value and interest of the book: to Dr. L. S. B. Leakey of the Coryndon Museum, Nairobi, for the section on pre-history; to Dr. A. G. Matthew, Lecturer in African Archæology at Oxford University, for the section on the archæology of the coast; to Sir John Gray, former Chief Justice of Zanzibar, for the chapters on the history of the territory up to the end of the 1914–18 campaign and on missions; to Lieut.-Colonel H. Moyse-Bartlett, M.B.E., M.A., of the School of Oriental and African Studies of London University, for the history of the 6th Battalion, King's African Rifles; to P. J. Greenway, O.B.E., F.L.S., Botanist-in-Charge of the East African Herbarium, Nairobi, for the section on vegetation

---

[1] Suggestions for amendments or additions, for use in future editions, will be welcomed.

[2] Obtainable either from the Crown Agents for Oversea Governments and Administrations, or from the Government Printer, Dar es Salaam, 924 pages, price Shs. 42/- plus postage.   For contents table see Appendix A herein, pp. 531 to 540

[3] Obtainable from the Secretary, The Tanganyika Society, P.O. Box 511, Dar es Salaam.

[4] Obtainable from the Public Relations Office, Dar es Salaam, or from the East African Office, Grand Buildings, Trafalgar Square, price Shs. 2/-.

and flora; to A. Loveridge of the Museum of Comparative Zoology, Harvard, for the section on reptiles and amphibians; to Elliot Pinhey of the National Museum, Bulawayo, for the section on insects, and to G. L. Boedeker for the section on photography. In addition I am indebted to Sir John Gray, to the Secretary of the International African Institute in London and to the Director of the East African Institute of Social Research in Kampala for assistance with the compilation of the bibliography.

CONTENTS

Chapter 1

GENERAL DESCRIPTION OF THE COUNTRY

SITUATION AND BOUNDARIES

Tanganyika is a large compact block of land in eastern Africa lying between the Great Lakes—Lake Victoria, Lake Tanganyika and Lake Nyasa—and the Indian Ocean. It is just below the equator and is bounded on the north by Kenya and Uganda, on the west by the Congo, on the south-west by Northern Rhodesia and Nyasaland, and on the south by Portuguese East Africa. Generally speaking, the boundaries follow natural features, except in the the north, where it is an arbitrary line drawn from the mouth of the Umba River on the Indian Ocean to Lake Jipe, thence round the north of Mount Kilimanjaro, and from there in a straight line to the middle of Lake Victoria and along the first degree of south latitude. In the west it follows a series of lakes and then of high points from the Uganda border to the Malagarasi River, along that river to Lake Tanganyika, and then down the middle of the lake. In the south the boundary goes from the foot of Lake Tanganyika to the head of Lake Nyasa, follows the lake edge half-way down its eastern shore and then the line of the Ruvuma River to the sea.[1]

The territory extends from 1° S. to 11°45' S. and from 29°21' E. to 40°25' E. and is some 740 miles long and 760 miles broad, with a coast-line of about 550 miles.

Its area is 362,688 square miles, which includes 19,982 square miles of inland water. It is thus almost the size of France, Germany and Belgium combined, or more than six times the size of England. It is the second largest dependency under British administration, Nigeria being slightly larger.

It seems that, in the remote past, Tanganyika formed part of a vast flat plain sloping gently to the sea. This plain was dislocated at many points by tectonic action so that whole blocks of country were in some places elevated above the surrounding terrain, while in others the land was either tilted or thrown down, or both tilted and thrown down. The effect of these dislocations on the original drainage system is shown in the abrupt changes of direction of some of the main rivers. (See map on page 151).

As it contains no true deserts and all of it except a narrow belt along the coast lies at an altitude of over 1,000 feet (the great bulk of the country forming a plateau from 3,000 to 4,000 feet in height) Tanganyika is far from being either the Sahara-like wilderness or the steamy jungle so often associated with the tropics. Although so near the equator the effect of its tropical situation is greatly mitigated, over the greater part of it, by the cooling influence of altitude. While most of it is not so "temperate" as the greater part of Kenya, very little is as humidly hot as the central Congo. It is a land of tremendous variety and cannot be called typically tropical.

---

[1]The exact boundaries are to be found in the attachments to the Text of the Trusteeship Agreement at pp. 7-11, Vol. V. of the Laws of Tanganyika.

1

MOUNTAINS

The mountain systems are widely extended over the country, the more important ranges being in the north and south, but perhaps the best way to obtain an immediate picture of their situation is to envisage them as taking the shape of a great figure **9**, the loop encircling the Masai Steppe in the north and the tail extending south and west in a great arc, from near Kilosa on the Central Railway Line through Iringa and Mbeya to the Ufipa Plateau. With the exception of the Matengo highlands in the Songea District of the Southern Province all the territory's mountain ranges worthy of the name lie on or near this great **9**. Encircling the Masai Steppe—an area of some 20,000 square miles—are the Usambara and Pare mountains running up in a north-westerly direction from near Tanga on the coast, then Mounts Kilimanjaro and Meru, the "Winter Highlands" farther to the west merging into the Mbulu and Kondoa ranges, the Gogoland hills in the south leading to the Mpwapwa, Uluguru and Nguru mountains, and finally the Handeni hills closing the gap. Southwards from Mpwapwa and Kilosa there extends the bulk of the Rubeho mountain system, leading into the Iringa highlands and thence to the great cluster of ranges near the head of Lake Nyasa: the Njombe highlands, the Livingstone mountains rising sheer from the shores of the lake, the Kipengere range, the Porotos and Mount Rungwe. Thence the Mbeya range and the hills to the south of it connect with the massif of the Ufipa Plateau. To the west of this great figure **9** lies the vast Central Plateau, while to the east are the coastal plains and the lower-lying lands of the Southern Province.

THE RIFT VALLEY

Mention must also be made of an outstanding natural feature even more important in some respects than the mountains; the Great Rift Valley. This runs northwards from near the mouth of the Zambezi through Tanganyika, Kenya, Abyssinia and the Red Sea to Palestine. It is one of the more remarkable geographical phenomena of the world. Just north of Lake Nyasa it forks, forming the Eastern and Western Rifts. The former is scarcely discernible until it approaches the Central Railway Line, but between Dodoma and Manyoni there is a splendid view of one wall of it near the station of Saranda. Thence it continues northwards and is for long stretches a notable feature of the landscape. Lake Manyara lies at the bottom of it and so does Lake Natron. The western fork is the more important and is responsible for the formation of lakes Tanganyika, Kivu, Edward and Albert. (Lake Victoria lies in a huge shallow depression and is not thought to be the result of tectonic action).

THE CENTRAL PLATEAU

Between the Eastern and Western Rifts lies the Central Plateau, an immense peneplain lying at an average height of nearly 4,000 feet, and covered, for the most part, by *miombo* woodland, that is, by a fairly open cover of trees, *Brachystegia* predominating, with grass below. If any one type of country can be chosen as typical of Tanganyika it is probable that this *miombo* country, with the more open wooded grassland so often found fringing it, would have pride of place. In both types are found those rocky outcrops of granite, often in the form of huge boulders piled one on top of another, which are such a striking feature of the lands to the west of the main mountain ranges. The monotony of the land-

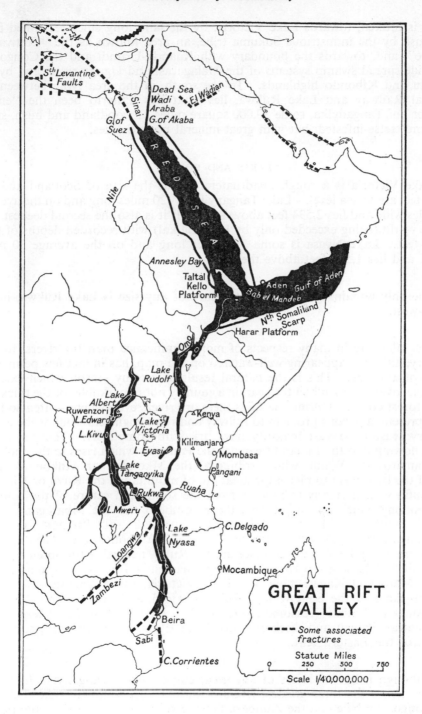

S.th Levantine Faults

Dead Sea
Wadi
Araba
El Wadian

Sinai

G. of Akaba

G. of Suez

Nile

R E D   S E A

Annesley Bay

Taltal
Kello
Platform

Aden   Gulf of Aden

Bab el Mandeb

Nth Somaliland
Scarp

Harar Platform

Omo

Lake
Rudolf

Lake
Albert
Ruwenzori
L. Edward

L. Kivu

Lake
Victoria

L. Eyasi

Kenya

Kilimanjaro

Mombasa

Pangani

Lake
Tanganyika

L. Rukwa

Ruaha

L. Mweru

Loangwa

Lake
Nyasa

C. Delgado

Mocambique

Zambezi

Beira

Sabi

C. Corrientes

GREAT RIFT VALLEY

- - - - *Some associated fractures*

Statute Miles

0   250   500   750

Scale 1/40,000,000

scape is broken, towards Lake Victoria, by the land long since reclaimed from the bush by the industrious Sukuma tribe, an area known as the "Cultivation Steppe", and, towards the boundary with Ruanda-Urundi and the Congo, by the wide-spread swamp systems of the Malagarasi and Ugalla rivers and by the Kasulu and Kibondo highlands. To the south, in the area lying between the Central Railway and Lake Rukwa, lies what has hitherto been the "empty quarter" of Tanganyika, some 30,000 square miles of woodland and bush, semi-arid and tsetse-infested, but with great mineral potentialities.

LAKES AND RIVERS

Lake Victoria is a rough quadrilateral about the size of Scotland and lies 3,717 feet above sea level. Lake Tanganyika is 420 miles long and on the average 30 miles wide and lies 2,534 feet above sea level; it is also the second deepest lake in the world (being exceeded only by Lake Baikal) with recorded depths of over 4,700 feet. Lake Nyasa is some 310 miles long and on the average 30 miles broad and lies 1,568 feet above the sea.

The only remaining lake in the territory of any size is Lake Rukwa, in the south-west.

The lakes are in many respects of more significance than the rivers, for the country, although appearing well-watered on the map, has in fact few permanent rivers of any size. This is the natural result of a rainy season which extends, as a rule, over less than half the year, in a country not remarkable for the thickness of its forest cover. During the rains there are rivers everywhere—often so large as to present a serious problem to railway and road engineers—but at the end of the dry season the vast majority have dried up completely. The permanent rivers flowing into the Indian Ocean are the Pangani, which rises in the snows of Kilimanjaro; the Wami, whose tributary, the Mkondoa or Mukondokwa, is one of the two rivers to pierce the great arc of mountains; the Ruvu or Kingani; the Rufiji with its many tributaries from the south and centre of the country, chief among which are the Ruaha, the Kilombero and the Mbaragandu; and further south the Matandu, Mbemkuru, Lukuledi and Ruvuma, the last-mentioned forming almost the whole of the southern boundary. The only ones which are navigable for any distance are the Rufiji, navigable for about 60 miles by small vessels, and the Kagera, similarly navigable for about 90 miles. The Mori, Mara and Kagera flow into Lake Victoria, the Malagarasi into Lake Tanganyika and the Songwe and Ruhuhu into Lake Nyasa. The Wembere, Manyonga and Sibiti—seasonal rivers—drain a large part of the eastern side of the Central Plateau and discharge into Lake Eyasi, which lies in a subsidiary fissure of the Eastern Rift.

Although it has no rivers of any great consequence, Tanganyika forms the divide whence the three greatest rivers of the African continent take their rise, the Congo, the Nile and the Zambezi, flowing respectively into the Atlantic, the Mediterranean and the Indian Ocean; but strange to say the watersheds of these three systems never meet at any one point—they are separated by a large depression (in the Central Plateau) which has no outlet to the sea.

GENERAL ASPECT[1]

Miombo woodland and the kind of bushland and thicket associated with it occupy more than half of the territory's 343,000 square miles of dry land, forming two huge areas in the west of the Central Plateau and to the south-east of the main arc of mountains. Most of this type of country is tsetse-infested. Wooded grassland—grass with scattered trees and bushes—occupies another one-quarter and is found all over the territory in patches. Grassland proper, where trees and shrubs take up not more than ten per cent of the ground, occupy some 34,000 square miles, mostly in the northern and southern highlands. Closed forests cover only some 4,000 square miles and "deserts" or semi-deserts (including the upper slopes of mountains, salt-pans and country sometimes flooded, as in the neighbourhood of Lake Rukwa) account for about 2,000. The balance, some 30,000 square miles, consists of agricultural country, both that at present cultivated and—a considerable acreage anywhere in East Africa—that formerly cultivated and now abandoned. Such cultivated areas are widely scattered and the population map on p. 306 shows their distribution at a glance. Nearly two-thirds of the territory is entirely uninhabited; on the other hand, two-thirds of the population is concentrated on one-tenth of its surface. (Full details of land, water and vegetation type areas are given in Table 2 at the end of this chapter.)

In so far as any generalization can be made about the appearance of the country, it may be said that, although there is singularly little true forest, there is no lack of trees. The ground is nearly everywhere well covered and even in the wide open spaces the ubiquitous "umbrella thorn" or flat-topped acacia is to be found, very often in association with the grotesque baobab and the symmetrical *candelabra euphorbia:* these give those characteristic touches of local colour to the up-country scene in the same way as the coconut palm, the mangrove and the casuarina do at the coast.

The difficulty of drawing any sort of true picture of the general aspect of this greatly diversified country is enhanced by the astonishing transformation that occurs in it once a year at the onset of the rains. Land which was then a forbidding arid waste of brown bare earth becomes in a few weeks—almost in a few days—an inviting expanse of green grass and vivid flowers. The change is most startling in the areas of least rainfall, for example, near Dodoma, where a visitor during the dry season would find it impossible to believe that the country could ever be green again. In these regions the failure of the rains is catastrophic and the influence of the monsoons is thus of cardinal importance.

CLIMATE: MAIN CHARACTERISTICS AND CAUSATIVE FACTORS

A large part of the territory is subject to the influence of two monsoons annually, the north-east monsoon during the period October/November to January/February and the south-east monsoon for the greater part of the rest of the year.

This is a bald and very generalized statement of the most noticeable characteristic of the climate of Tanganyika, and at this stage it is customary to proceed to a more detailed account of the climate of the different regions into which the

---

[1]For further details of vegetation see chapter 14, pp 401-410.

territory can be divided climatically. It seems that, hitherto, the attempt has not been made to explain in non-technical language why it is that Tanganyika has the climate it does have, why, for instance, it seldom rains in the months of July and August, although the south-east monsoon is blowing hard then and it is commonly supposed that it is this monsoon which brings the bulk of the rain. In the belief that some such explanation is now required an attempt will be made to give reasons for the annual cycle of events.

The causes of the weather in Tanganyika (as elsewhere) are many and complex but some of the more important are as follows. First, there are the two fundamental factors which affect weather anywhere in the world: the fact that the earth goes round the sun once a year and that, in doing so, its axis is tilted, so that the position of any given place on the earth's surface differs in relation to the sun as day succeeds day. Secondly, there are the effects, direct or indirect, of the heat of the sun, of which three are of prime importance for our present study: (a) the fact that, generally speaking, air tends to flow from colder regions, where the cold heavy air is at a comparatively high pressure, to warmer regions where the heated air is at a lower pressure; (b) a sort of consequence of the first, the fact that there normally exists a broad belt of warm low-pressure air beneath the sun, i.e. at the thermal equator, which moves north and south of the actual Equator line seasonally; and (c) the fact that if warm moisture-laden air rises into cooler regions higher up in the atmosphere it tends to discharge its moisture in the form of rain.

It is to the interaction of these factors that we must look for an explanation, even if only a partial one, of the weather we experience in Tanganyika. If we take the south-east monsoon and follow it in its course we may perhaps get some idea of how the factors mentioned interact. The south-east monsoon that affects East Africa originates in the cold latitudes somewhere in the Indian Ocean to the east of Madagascar. The cool, heavy air there flows towards the tropical region of warmer, lighter air. The spinning of the earth on its axis means that as this current of air moves northwards it is deflected and becomes a south-easterly wind. Then, as it enters the equatorial region of low pressure, it turns north again and, still subject to the influence of the earth's rotation, veers round and becomes the Indian Ocean monsoon. It thus describes a huge arc from somewhere to the east of Madagascar through the eastern part of Africa to Arabia and western India.

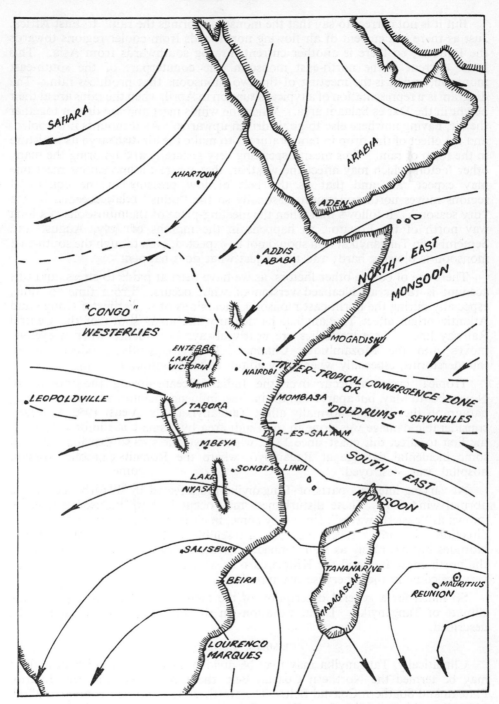

SAHARA

ARABIA

KHARTOUM

ADEN

ADDIS ABABA

NORTH - EAST MONSOON

"CONGO" WESTERLIES

ENTEBBE LAKE VICTORIA

NAIROBI

MOGADISHU

INTER-TROPICAL CONVERGENCE ZONE OR "DOLDRUMS" SEYCHELLES

LEOPOLDVILLE

TABORA

MOMBASA

MBEYA

DAR-ES-SALAAM

SOUTH - EAST MONSOON

SONGEA LINDI

LAKE NYASA

SALISBURY

TANANARIVE

BEIRA

MADAGASCAR

MAURITIUS REUNION

LOURENCO MARQUES

Chart showing a typical wind distribution during the month of April in East Africa

But it is not correct to say that the monsoon "brings the rain" to East Africa. Just as there is a current of air flowing northwards from cooler regions towards the Equator, so there is another current flowing southwards from Asia. This latter current is the north-east monsoon, the counterpart of the south-east monsoon, and it is the meeting of the two monsoons that produces rain. The diagram is a representation of a typical situation in April, when the rains are at their height in the Dar es Salaam area. When the winds meet and are driven together the air, having nowhere else to go, is driven upwards. As it mounts it is cooled, and the effect of this drop in temperature is to make the air discharge its moisture in the form of rain. This means, speaking very generally and ignoring the many other factors which may affect the weather, that where the monsoons meet one may expect rain and that as the belt of low pressure in the equatorial regions moves north and south seasonally so the "rains" are succeeded by the "dry season". It follows that when the meeting-place of the monsoons is a long way north of the Equator, as happens in the months of July, August and September in Tanganyika, rain should not be expected, even though the south-east monsoon is blowing hard; and this is just what does happen.

There are of course other factors, as we have been at pains to stress, and this account is rather an idealized version of what occurs. From time to time, especially during the north-east monsoon, incursions of westerlies of Congo and Atlantic origin affect Tanganyika, particularly the areas south of the Central Railway line. These westerlies are nearly always in evidence when a cyclone moves into the Mozambique Channel. They frequently produce violent thunderstorms, especially where they adjoin either monsoon.

Tropical cyclones occur over the Indian Ocean during the months of November to May, but apart from the indirect influence mentioned in the previous paragraph they do not normally affect Tanganyika. In April, 1952, however, considerable damage was done in the Lindi area by a small but intense cyclone, the first to affect this coast since 1872, when a cyclone struck Zanzibar and did some incidental damage at Bagamoyo, where the Roman Catholic Mission hospital was destroyed.

At varying intervals parts of Tanganyika are affected by disturbances in the normal wind flow. These disturbances may occur in both monsoons and are known as "easterly waves", since they come, in either monsoon, from an easterly direction. In some respects they bear a resemblance to the fronts of temperate latitudes but are rarely as well defined. To the regions they affect (principally the north coast area and the Kilimanjaro area) they occasionally bring showers very welcome in the otherwise dry months.

So much for a general description of the factors which go to make up the climate of Tanganyika. Local variations in the general pattern must now be described.

CLIMATIC ZONES

Climatically, Tanganyika may may be divided into three broad zones which may be termed the Northern Coastal Belt, the Lake Area, and the Interior Plateau and Southern Coastal Belt. The Northern Coastal Belt is an area about 100 miles wide extending from Dar es Salaam northwards to the Kenya border. The Lake Area is the area within approximately 50 miles of the shores of Lake Victoria, mainly at a height of 3,700 to 4,000 feet. The Interior Plateau constitutes the remainder of Tanganyika and includes the coastal area south of

Dar es Salaam. Most of this last area is about 4,000 feet high, but there are marked topographic variations; it includes Mt. Kilimanjaro which rises to 19,340 feet and the Poroto and Uhehe mountains of the Southern Highlands with peaks over 9,700 feet high; in the south-east there is a gradual descent to the sea.

CLIMATOLOGICAL TABLE

Climatological statistics for a number of stations in each province are given on p. 12. This table gives information on atmospheric pressure, temperature, humidity and rainfall.

THE NORTHERN COASTAL BELT

The hot season lasts from December to March and is a period of high relative humidity along the coast. When the thermometer rises above 90° conditions become oppressive. The cool season extends from June to mid-September.

Although showers occur in all months, over half the annual rainfall normally falls during March, April and May, and there is also usually a secondary maximum between October and December. The wettest months are April and May, the rain then being associated with the passage northwards of what is technically known as the "Inter-tropical Convergence Zone" and the onset of the south-east monsoon. The rain is generally in the form of showers, although occasionally continuous light or moderate rain, extending at times along the whole coast, persists for twenty-four hours or more. The beginning of the main rainy season is usually marked by squally weather and thunderstorms. The rainfall may vary considerably from year to year, but generally it is greater in the north, Amani averaging 76 inches per annum, Tanga 53 inches and Dar es Salaam 42 inches. Once either monsoon is well established, falls average only two or three inches a month, the frequency of rain days varying from six days a month in the south to ten in the north.

Although the Northern Coastal Belt is generally sunny, cloud amounts are appreciable with the sky generally half-covered or more. At the onset of the south-east monsoon, however, overcast skies persisting for one or two days at a time are not unusual.

Winds are mainly light to moderate north-easterly or south-easterly, depending upon the monsoon season. On the whole the south-easterlies are the stronger and more persistent, but both monsoons vary appreciably in strength and in time of onset. Squalls occur fairly frequently during the change of season, gusts up to 60 knots having been observed on a few occasions. Nocturnal off-shore breezes sometimes overcome the easterly component of the monsoon and a westerly wind results, but more usually their effect is to reduce the wind almost to calm.

Fogs and mist are unknown on the coast, but are common during the south-east monsoon in the higher parts of the Usambaras.

Further details on the climate of the Northern Coastal Belt may be deduced from the readings for Dar es Salaam, Tanga and Amani included in the climatological table on p. 12

THE LAKE AREA

As already stated, Lake Victoria is an inland sea of an area approximately equal to that of Scotland. The climatic modifications it exerts may be considered as extending to perhaps 50 miles from its shores. This modification is particularly well shown in regard to the diurnal variation of temperature; at most inland stations a diurnal variation of 25° to 30° F. occurs, while on the lake shores the corresponding value is 13° to 14° F. Seasonal variations in temperature are not great, the mean monthly maximum temperature usually being 80°–82°F.

The lake displays the customary sea-board characteristics of on- and off-shore winds and, at the same time, under the influence of the sun, evaporates into the air a continuous supply of water which corresponds to a lowering of the water surface of the lake by about 0·2 inches each day.

Although, on the average, nearly forty per cent of the annual rainfall occurs in March, April and May, there is no really definite "rainy season", the rainfall being fairly well distributed throughout the year. The western parts of the lake hinterland receive some of the heaviest rainfall in East Africa—80 inches to 90 inches—associated in the main with morning thunderstorms. Due to the fact that the predominant wind drift across the lake is east to west, the eastern parts are by contrast very much drier, annual falls being only 30 to 40 inches on average.

Winds are usually light to moderate but thunderstorm squalls are not uncommon. Velocities exceeding 70 knots have been recorded from time to time and these are quite sufficient to cause serious damage.

Detailed information in respect of five stations in the Lake Province is given in the climatological table on p. 12.

THE INTERIOR PLATEAU AND SOUTHERN COASTAL BELT

Throughout this extensive area there is only one rainy season, extending from November or December to April or May, and a dry season for the remaining months of the year. Over most of the area the annual rainfall is between 30 inches and 40 inches, with much of central Tanganyika experiencing less than 30 inches. Over a small area to the north of Lake Nyasa, however, very heavy rains are experienced, the annual fall being about 100 inches.

In the single rainy season the rainfall occurs in the form of afternoon and evening thunderstorms or thundery showers, but sometimes light rain persists through the night and into the next forenoon. At other times such scanty rain as there is occurs in the form of occasional and very localized afternoon showers.

During the dry season nights and mornings are relatively cloudless except in the Kilimanjaro-Mbulu region, where overcast conditions sometimes persist for several hours and occasionally for two or three days at a time without a break. Afternoon skies are usually not more than half clouded. During the wet season very cloudy and thundery conditions rapidly form over very large areas early in the day.

Inland winds are usually light easterly, whichever monsoon is blowing, the ultimate origin of the air being betokened by the relative humidity. Coastal winds are appreciably stronger, and in the event of a cyclone reaching the

Mozambique Channel, they tend to approach gale force. Thunderstorms, which are rare on the coast compared with inland areas, produce occasional squalls in which wind gusts of up to 50 or 60 knots are recorded.

Valley mist and fog occur in the early mornings at any time of year; very occasionally low-lying fog is observed in the estuaries of the Rufiji and Ruvuma rivers.

Temperatures are to a large extent governed by height above sea level and thus cover a wide range. Temperatures over 90°F. are not infrequent in the lower districts, while, at the other extreme, the top of Kilimanjaro is permanently covered with snow and ice.

The climatological table overleaf gives further details for a large number of stations in this area.

Table 1

LAND, WATER AND VEGETATION TYPE AREAS, TANGANYIKA (SQ. MILES)

(1) LAND, SWAMP AND WATER AREAS

Province	Land Area			Open Water	Total Land and Water Area
	Dry Land	Permanent Swamp	Total		
Lake	38,212	922	39,134	13,414	52,548
Western	76,562	1,843	78,405	5,198	83,603
Northern	31,792	373	32,165	798	32,963
Tanga	13,684	119	13,803	—	13,803
Eastern	41,663	431	42,094	—	42,094
Central	36,233	177	36,410	—	36,410
Southern	54,960	263	55,223	—	55,223
Southern Highlands	45,219	253	45,472	572	46,044
Total ...	338,325	4,381	342,706	19,982	362,688

Table 2

(2) VEGETATION TYPES COMPRISING THE DRY LAND AREA

Closed Forest	Forest Woodland Intermediate	Woodland (*Miombo*)	Woodland Bushland Intermediate	Bushland and Thicket	Wooded Grassland	Grassland	Desert and Semi Desert	Vegn. actively induced by Man	Total Dry Land Area
319	214	3,128	555	3,486	16,556	5,602	146	8,206	38,212
160	40	47,431	677	1,920	15,138	6,538	428	4,230	76,562
1,000	—	757	70	12,812	8,548	6,809	464	1,332	31,792
772	101	1,701	954	5,249	2,388	511	505	1,503	13,684
475	287	12,963	4,026	770	16,582	3,767	—	2,793	41,663
32	—	7,278	2,302	10,080	8,353	3,060	221	4,907	36,233
173	743	28,824	3,949	813	15,153	645	—	4,660	54,960
1,048	205	16,880	2,283	4,023	11,078	7,177	274	2,251	45,219
3,979	1,590	118,962	14,816	39,153	93,796	34,109	2,038	29,882	338,325
(4,000)	(1,600)	(119,000)	(14,800)	(39,200)	(93,800)	(34,100)	(2,000)	(29,900)	(338,400)

(1) *Woodland* is land with an open cover of trees, the crowns often in close proximity but not interlaced.
(2) *Bushland and Thicket* is land carrying a cover of more than 50% of densely growing shrubs or small trees.
(3) *In Wooded Grassland*, trees and bushes occupy less than 50% of the ground.
(4) *In Grassland*, trees and shrubs occupy not more than 10% of the ground.
(5) The figures in brackets in the last line of the second table are rounded figures quite sufficiently accurate for reference purposes.

CLIMATOLOGICAL STATISTICS FOR STATIONS IN TANGANYIKA

Units: Pressure in MBS; Temperatures and Dew Point in °F; Rainfall in Ins.; Relative Humidity in %; Cloud Amount in Tenths.

No.	Station / Province	Lat. S (°′)	Long. E (°′)	Alt.	Mean Atmos. Press. 0830	1430	Mean Dry Bulb 0830	1430	Mean Dew Pt 0830	1430	Highest Max	Date	Lowest Min	Date	Mean Max	Mean Min	Mean Temp	Mean Range	Mean R.H. 0830	1430	Avge Total	Max Fall 24 hrs	Date	Mean No. days rain	Mean Cloud 0830	1430	Yrs Press	Yrs Temp	Yrs Hum	Yrs Rain	Yrs Cloud
	CENTRAL PROVINCE																														
(1)	DODOMA	6 10	35 46	3675	891·7	888·2	68·0	81·8	58·3	60·5	97·5	Dec. 1954	45·7	July 1951	84·1	61·6	72·7	22·5	77	45	22·17	3·93	Jan. 1938	55	5·8	5·9	23	23	13	27	22
(2)	MPWAPWA	6 20	36 30	3700	—	—	68·0	78·8	59·5	60·3	95·0	Nov. 1942	46·4	July 1943	81·6	60·3	71·0	21·3	77	52	26·33	4·96	Mar. 1945	86	5·9	5·5	13	13	23	27	12
(3)	KONDOA	4 55	35 47	4547	865·2	861·9	66·5	79·6	58·7	58·8	95·0	Nov. 1954	41·5	July 1937	81·8	59·7	70·7	22·1	77	50	24·95	3·43	Feb. 1935	61	5·3	5·4	22	22	22	25	21
	EASTERN PROVINCE																														
(4)	DAR ES SALAAM	6 50	39 18	47	1013·1	1010·3	77·6	88·3	72·3	72·7	95·5	Mar. 1943	59·0	Aug. 1947	85·5	71·3	78·4	14·2	85	69	42·35	5·99	May 1946	129	5·9	6·1	10	14	14	14	14
(5)	MOROGORO	6 51	37 40	1900	—	—	72·1	84·0	66·8	67·6	98·0	Feb. 1953	48·6	Aug. 1953	86·1	65·5	75·8	20·6	83	57	35·01	3·66	May 1941	124	6·7	6·9	—	10	9	37	10
	LAKE PROVINCE																														
(6)	BUKOBA	1 20	31 49	3753	—	—	68·9	76·4	63·7	66·0	88·3	Mar. 1939	50·0	Aug. 1951	79·5	60·8	70·1	18·7	84	71	80·46	5·45	May 1942	166	8·2	6·5	—	20	17	34	17
(7)	BIHARAMULO	2 38	31 19	4850	—	—	66·5	75·4	58·3	58·4	87·2	Mar. 1953	52·0	July 1954	78·5	61·5	70·0	17·0	75	56	38·13	3·57	Apr. 1948	108	4·6	5·9	18	19	13	33	19
(8)	MUSOMA	1 30	33 48	3764	887·0	884·3	70·7	79·6	61·6	64·7	95·0	Apr. 1943	54·0	July 1945	82·5	65·4	73·9	17·1	73	61	30·14	6·27	Apr. 1954	110	6·5	6·1	18	13	18	33	11
(9)	MWANZA	2 31	32 54	3709	—	—	71·5	81·2	62·2	62·3	95·0	Oct. 1942	52·5	July 1941	83·5	64·2	73·9	19·3	73	55	39·39	4·82	Mar. 1944	111	5·1	4·7	7	6	6	29	11
(10)	UKIRIGURU	2 42	33 01	3933	881·2	878·7	68·9	80·7	60·3	58·6	93·4	Mar. 1942	51·9	July 1946	83·7	63·4	73·5	20·3	74	47	31·87	3·65	Nov. 1951	106	6·8	7·2	6	13	6	18	6
	NORTHERN PROVINCE																														
(11)	ARUSHA	3 23	36 41	4500	—	—	62·0	74·3	57·5	57·8	90·0	Sept. 1952	40·5	Feb. 1953	77·4	54·7	66·1	22·7	86	57	48·61	7·50	Apr. 1949	132	7·5	6·1	—	8	8	32	8
(12)	MBULU	3 52	35 33	5700	—	—	59·7	71·7	56·0	55·4	85·0	July 1946	40·0	July 1951	74·2	54·8	64·5	19·4	59	59	31·65	4·65	Nov. 1941	90	8·2	5·9	10	10	9	36	9
(13)	MOSHI	3 21	37 20	2668	923·9	919·7	70·4	83·4	62·2	63·1	100·2	Mar. 1935	47·5	Mar. 1946	85·5	62·8	74·1	22·7	78	50	34·28	5·78	Apr. 1937	83	7·0	6·0	13	16	15	33	15
(14)	LYAMUNGU	3 14	37 15	4100	—	—	64·1	75·0	59·9	59·5	92·5	Sept. 1943	46·0	Sept. 1946	77·1	57·2	67·1	19·9	86	61	67·46	9·91	Nov. 1942	164	7·1	6·9	—	15	15	20	12
	SOUTHERN PROVINCE																														
(15)	LINDI	10 00	39 42	133	1011·0	1007·9	76·9	84·2	72·0	71·2	97·1	Mar. 1945	57·0	June 1952	87·0	71·1	79·1	15·9	82	67	35·34	4·47	Feb. 1955	98	5·5	5·7	17	20	20	17	19
(16)	SONGEA	10 41	35 40	3783	891·7	889·2	66·1	75·9	59·9	59·9	91·8	Nov. 1945	45·2	June 1946	78·2	60·9	69·5	17·3	80	57	44·31	4·04	Dec. 1944	103	7·0	7·5	15	15	15	41	15
(17)	KILWA	8 45	39 25	30	—	—	80·0	84·1	72·4	74·5	94·5	—	—	—	87·0	73·5	80·3	13·5	78	70	35·71	7·52	Mar. 1938	71	4·9	4·6	—	3	3	44	3
	SOUTHERN HIGHLANDS PROVINCE																														
(18)	IRINGA	7 47	35 42	5380	840·6	838·4	64·2	73·5	54·7	54·6	89·8	Nov. 1943	41·8	July 1935	76·3	56·7	66·5	19·6	71	53	29·18	3·63	Dec. 1936	96	4·3	6·8	16	23	23	26	23
(19)	MBEYA	8 56	33 28	5768	830·0	827·9	62·2	71·0	55·9	54·1	91·0	Nov. 1944	35·7	July 1940	74·0	53·3	63·7	20·7	74	60	33·56	3·45	Apr. 1936	117	5·4	7·0	23	23	8	23	23
(20)	SAO HILL	8 20	35 12	6500	—	—	57·2	67·5	52·9	53·6	85·3	Nov. 1949	38·0	Aug. 1949	70·9	51·4	60·7	19·5	87	59	36·85	3·15	Mar. 1943	164	7·0	7·0	—	8	8	17	7
(21)	CHUNYA	8 32	33 25	4900	—	—	64·7	77·7	55·6	56·0	91·2	Nov. 1953	43·0	July 1949	80·3	59·5	69·9	20·8	73	47	30·61	3·23	Feb. 1955	79	4·1	6·1	—	9	9	20	9
	TANGA PROVINCE																														
(22)	AMANI	5 06	38 38	2989	913·8	911·2	68·1	74·7	64·4	65·6	91·0	Mar. 1943	49·5	Aug. 1946	76·8	61·7	69·3	15·1	88	74	75·65	6·56	Sept. 1946	198	7·5	7·6	12	14	14	41	14
(23)	TANGA	5 04	39 06	30	—	—	78·2	83·5	72·1	72·1	92·7	Jan. 1947	65·1	Aug. 1947	85·6	73·1	79·3	12·5	82	68	52·89	7·49	Oct. 1938	129	6·9	5·6	5	5	3	26	3
	WESTERN PROVINCE																														
(24)	KIGOMA	4 53	29 38	2903	914·6	912·4	71·5	79·3	64·8	66·6	96·3	Oct. 1949	53·1	July 1935	82·0	66·5	74·3	15·5	74	66	37·46	3·81	Jan. 1950	118	6·9	5·8	21	21	21	17	21
(25)	TABORA	5 02	32 49	4151	876·1	873·3	68·1	81·9	58·5	57·8	95·4	Oct. 1941	50·9	July 1937	84·0	62·6	73·3	21·4	66	45	34·63	3·41	Dec. 1941	100	5·3	6·4	24	24	24	46	22

Chapter 2
PALÆONTOLOGY AND PREHISTORY
FOSSIL VERTEBRATE COLLECTIONS

A separate account follows of the general palæontology of the sedimentary rocks of the territory but special mention is necessary of fossil vertebrate remains found there, chiefly bones of extinct reptiles.

Particular interest in Tanganyika was aroused in scientific circles over the discovery there, in the early years of the century, of fossil bones of gigantic reptiles in rocks of Upper Jurassic age (perhaps 125–135 million years old).

The discovery of the fossil bones was due to a Herr Sattler, an engineer attached to a German prospecting company, who in 1907 brought the find to the notice of Professor Frass, an authority on East African geology then working in the territory. The bone-bearing deposits were located in the Tendaguru region just south of the Mbemkuru River, inland about 30 miles from Mchinja in the southern coastal area of the territory. Only in the western part of North America (parts of Montana, Wyoming, Utah, etc.), have comparable fossil remains of this age been found.

Tendaguru was the centre of operations of German expeditions in the years immediately before the 1914–18 war (terminated by the outbreak of war), and of an expedition that was sent to the area by the British Museum, which collected there during the years 1924-29.

A great collection of well preserved bones, mainly of dinosaurs, but including other reptilian and mammalian remains, was assembled by the expeditions and even now is still under study. Among the remains are those of what is believed to have been the largest land-animal yet known to have existed.

It is thought that the dinosaurs lived in the neighbourhood of a large river, which in time of flood, overwhelmed individuals and in some cases groups of the animals; the carcases of these were buried in the silts deposited by the receding floodwaters, or occasionally carried right to the sea and the skeletons preserved, along with marine shells, in sediment laid down just off-shore. It is the occurrence of marine shells, the relative age of which is generally more definitely known than is that of the vertebrate land animals, in closely associated strata, that has helped to establish the age of the reptilian remains.

Further important discoveries of remains of land animals, in this case in Karroo strata (animals living perhaps 175-185 million years ago), were made in 1930 during a reconnaissance survey in the Ruhuhu River depression near Lake Nyasa. No full-scale collecting expedition to the area has been made, but the interest aroused by the original finds, which include types of reptiles occurring also in Karroo rocks in South Africa, led to the area being visited by a British palæontologist in 1936 and a German in 1937. Work on the collections continues both in Britain and Germany.

The work of the several expeditions that have studied and collected vertebrate fossil remains from the Pleistocene deposits (probably less than ½ million years old) of Oldoway *Gorge to the east of the Serengeti Plain, is discussed in the section on Pre-History.

---

*Also spelled Olduvai.

PALÆONTOLOGY

Research on fossils discovered in Tanganyika has been carried on since the end of the nineteenth century and much of the literature refers to material collected during the German administration of the country.

Fossils have been described from rocks of Karroo age onwards and the organic origin of structures found in rocks of the Bukoban System has been suspected.

A short account of the stratigraphy of the fossiliferous sedimentary formations in Tanganyika was given by Stockley (1948(2))[1]; Teale (1937) discussed individual stratigraphical terms. Stratigraphical accounts were also given by several earlier authors (e.g. Dacqué and Krenkel, 1909; Koert, 1913; Behrend, 1918; Gregory, 1921; Krenkel, 1925).

The Bukoban System.—There have been recorded from rocks of the Bukoban System, mainly from limestones near Kigoma, but also from the neighbourhood of Chimala in northernmost Njombe District, specimens doubtfully of organic (algal) origin, described under the name *Collenia*. These were dealt with by Dietrich (1932).

The Karroo System.—The Karroo System in Tanganyika is for the most part non-marine and is generally characterized by the presence of fossil remains of the plant genus *Glossopteris*, though the occurrence of this in the northern part of the territory is not fully established. The *Glossopteris* flora of this age is known throughout most of the southern hemisphere. An account of the palæontology of the Tanganyika Karroo can be dealt with conveniently as concerning the three regions—south-western, central and north-eastern.

Investigations in the south-western region, consisting of areas adjacent to Lakes Nyasa and Rukwa, have yielded plant and animal fossils (vertebrate and invertebrate) that have been examined by a number of authorities. No marine fossils occur in the region. All the Karroo rocks in this area have been related to the various members (K1-K8) of the Songea Series (see Stockley and Oates, 1931(1)). Plant fossils (*Glossopteris, Schizoneura, Noeggerathiopsis, Gangamopteris*, etc.) have been recorded in several members of the Karroo sequence, and described particularly by Potonié (1900) and Walton (in Stockley and Walton, 1932; in Harkin, 1953). Silicified wood, mainly *Dadoxylon* and *Rhexoxylon* is common in upper members of the series, and of particular interest is the report of the occurrence of *Tubicaulis* (Dr. W. N. Edwards *in litt.* to G. M. Stockley).

Cox (1932) described several species of the non-marine lamellibranch genus *Palæomutela* from K5 and a species of *Unio* from K8. He has also examined lamellibranchs from K4 (see Harkin, 1953) which were not identifiable. Harkin (1952) recorded a specimen, possibly of the genus *Kidodia*, from K5, and Nowack (1937) mentioned fresh-water shells in K6. Ostracods have been reported from the K2 (McConnell, 1950).

Vertebrate remains, that include reptiles and amphibia, have been studied extensively and provide correlation with the South African Karroo (Haughton, 1924, 1932, 1953; Huene, 1938(1), 1938(2), 1939(1), 1939(2), 1939(3), 1942, 1944, 1950; Boonstra, 1953(2)).

Several records of the occurrence of plant fossils in the central region of Karroo outcrop in the area of the Ruaha, Ruvu and Rufiji Rivers, south-east.

---

[1]For references see Bibliography.

south-west and south of the Uluguru Mountains, date from the time of the German administration (Lieder, 1892; Bornhardt, 1900; Potonié, 1900; Dantz, 1903; Scholz, 1914(2); Brehmer, 1914). Potonié and Brehmer described a *Glossopteris* flora from the area, including *Glossopteris*, *Schizoneura*, *Noeggera-thiopsis*, *Carpolithes*, *Cardiocarpus*, and *Sphenophyllum*, as well as equisetalean and conifer fragments, also discussed by Janensch (1927), Gothan (1927(2)), Robertson (1934), Stockley (1936(1)) and Spence (1955).

Non-marine lamellibranchs from the central region including species of the genera *Kidodia*, *Palæomutela*, *Palæonodonta* and *"Carbonicola"* have been described by Cox (1936), who was not able to accept all the identifications of material from the area previously made by Woodward (see Teale, 1922), which he re-examined. Cox also gave an account of small marine lamellibranchs of the genera *Gervillia*, *Liebea*, *Myalina*, *Modiolopsis* and *Pteria*. According to Spence (1955) the same genera were also recorded in a collection recently examined by Mr. S. Ware of the British Museum (Natural History). Janensch (1927), Stockley (1936) and Spence (1955) also recorded crustacea.

Vertebrate remains recorded are confined to those of fish. A small collection was described by Haughton (1936), containing *Australosomus* and *Acrolepis*, and Woodward (in Teale, 1922) has recorded *Colobodus*. Janensch (1927), Stockley (1936(1), 1943(1)) and Spence (1955) also mentioned the occurrence of fish remains.

In the north-eastern Karroo region plant fragments have been recorded throughout the succession, but published descriptions refer only to examples from the middle portion of the sequence. Potonié (1900) mentioned *Voltziopsis* and Seward (1922, 1934) listed species of the genera *Ullmania*, *Cupressionocladus*, *Voltziopsis*, *Desmiophyllum* and *Baiera*. There has been difference of opinion as to whether *Glossopteris* occurs at all, and it must certainly be uncommon.

Haughton (1924) described the small reptile *Tangasaurus mennelli* (see also Nopcsa (1924)), also from the middle portion of the series, and Reck is recorded (Janensch, 1927) as having found reptilian bone fragments. No invertebrate fossil remains have been described.

Outside the three Karroo areas mentioned, near Tunduru in southern Tanganyika, Boonstra (1953(1)) has described rhynchosaurian remains to which he assigned a Karroo age, first recorded by Stockley (1947(1)). Other evidence has suggested that the bulk of the sediments in the area are of Cretaceous age (Spence, 1955), and if this is so, it is supposed that the fossil bones came from a Triassic inlier in the Tunduru Beds, or that they are derived fossils.

Harkin, McKinlay and Spence (1954) gave a brief summary of the palæon-tology of the Karroo System in Tanganyika.

The Jurassic System.—The literature contains a considerable amount of descriptive material on Jurassic fossils, and genera and species are too numerous to allow of individual mention. The oldest marine Jurassic invertebrates that have been obtained are of Aalenian or Bajocian age, and fossils from most later stages of the Jurassic have been recorded. Jurassic fossils have been described mainly from localities in the Tanga–Pangani–Wami River area, the vicinity of the Central Railway eastwards from Ngerengere, the Matumbi Highlands and the Kiswere hinterland.

The northern area, from which only marine invertebrates have been recorded, was dealt with by Baumann (1891), Tornquist (1893), Jaekel (1893), Futterer (1894), Weissermel (1900), Koert (1904) and Dacqué (1910), who described ammonites and other fossils of Callovian, Oxfordian and Kimmeridgian age. A fairly extensive ammonite fauna recently collected near Kwa Dikwaso on the Wami River by the Department of Geological Survey, was determined by Dr. W. J. Arkell (Sedgwick Museum, Cambridge) as being of Lower Oxfordian age, but otherwise little has been added to the knowledge of the Jurassic faunas of the area in recent years. Jurassic fossils from the area adjacent to the Central Railway were dealt with by Müller (1900), Menzel in Dantz (1902), Fraas (1908(1)), Dacqué (1910) and Reck (1921). Hennig (1924(1)) summarized previous work in the area and made further palæontological contributions. More recently, Cox (1937) has described a number of Jurassic lamellibranchs from near Tarawanda and Magindu and Drs. L. R. Cox (British Museum (Natural History)) and W. J. Arkell *in litt.*, have recently determined respectively, lamellibranchs and ammonites from Kidugallo.

From the calcareous Mtumbei beds of the Matumbi Hills area, Müller (1900) described Jurassic lamellibranchs and brachiopods, and his list of fossils of these groups was extended by Hennig (1937) and Stockley (1943(1)). Weissermel (1900) described Jurassic corals from this area. As well as named lamellibranchs and brachiopods, echinoid and bryozoan fossils have been observed in the area, but no ammonites, which might allow precise dating of the strata, have been found.

By far the richest marine Jurassic invertebrate assemblages described from Tanganyika have come from the Kiswere hinterland, from the Mbemkuru River depression and from the Mandawa–Mahokondo area to the north. For the most part these were collected during the German Tendaguru Expedition of 1909-1912 which investigated vertebrate fossil localities in the area (mentioned below), and during the subsequent British Museum Tendaguru Expedition of 1924-29. The collections of the British Museum Tendaguru Expedition are for the most part undescribed and other invertebrate collections recently made by the Department of Geological Survey from both of these areas are in process of study. Invertebrate fossil collections from the area were described earlier, however, by Müller (1900) and Krenkel (1910(2)). The work of the German Tendaguru Expedition was described by numerous authors, of whom the following made the more important contributions on Jurassic invertebrates: Hennig (1914(2))—mainly lamellibranchs; Lange (1914)—lamellibranchs; Zwierzycki (1914)—cephalopods; Dietrich (1914)—gastropods, (1925(1))—cephalopods (Mahokondo), (1926)—corals, (1933(2))—cephalopods, gastropods, lamellibranchs; Beurlen (1933)—crustacea; Janensch (1933)—crustacea. Hennig (1937) gave some account of the palæontology of the area, based mainly on collections made during a return visit to the area in 1934, describing cephalopods, lamellibranchs, brachiopods and crustacea. Sieverts-Doreck (1939) has described crinoid remains collected during the German Tendaguru Expedition and during Hennig's subsequent survey. Kitchin (1929) discussed the invertebrate faunas, but his main thesis as to the age relations is not now accepted.

The oldest dated Jurassic fossils in the Mandawa–Mahokondo area are Callovian. In the north of the Mbemkuru River depression the Pindiro Beds, with which, strata underlying the Mandawa–Mahokondo Callovian are correlated, which have yielded to Hennig (1916(2), 1937) a few lamellibranch and gastropod fossils, ante-date this. The bulk of the Jurassic fossils from the Mbemkuru River depression however, are Kimmeridgian–Tithonian in age.

The relations of the Tanganyika Jurassic invertebrate fossil assemblages appear to be largely with the Pakistan and Indian areas, apart from the natural similarities to those from Madagascar, Kenya, Somaliland, etc. There are some similarities also, however, especially in the case of certain ammonites, with European assemblages.

As noted above, it was mainly for the purpose of investigating vertebrate fossil remains that the German and British Museum Tendaguru Expeditions were made. Fraas (1908(2)) first described such remains in the Tendaguru area of the Mbemkuru River depression and his discoveries led to the subsequent expeditions, of which the first was the bigger. Work on vertebrate fossil collections, made by the German Tendaguru Expedition is still in progress and is described by a number of authors as follows: Hennig (1914(2))—fish; Branca (1914(3))—reptiles; Janensch (1914(3), 1924, 1925, 1929(1), 1929(2), 1929(3), 1929(4), 1935, 1936(1), 1936(2), 1936(3), 1947, 1950(1), 1950(2))—reptiles; Hennig (1924(2))—reptiles.

The dinosaurs of the Tendaguru area were mentioned by Hobley (1925) and Parkinson (1928); a popular account of the British Museum Tendaguru Expedition was given by Parkinson (1930(3)), but a complete description of the collection made is not yet available.

There has been some dispute as to the exact age of the various strata yielding fossil bones in the Tendaguru area. It was supposed by the German Tendaguru Expedition that the topmost of three Dinosaur Beds was Lower Cretaceous in age (see Hennig, 1914(1)) but later authors (e.g., Schuchert, 1918; Spath, 1933) consider all of them to be Jurassic. Schuchert (1918, 1934), Mathew (1924) and Simpson (1926) have discussed the relations of the Tendaguru dinosaurs to similar forms occurring in North America.

Gothan (1927(1)) has described a plant fossil (a conifer) from the Jurassic of the Tendaguru area.

The Cretaceous System.—Only from the southern part of Tanganyika have Lower Cretaceous faunas been described, but an isolated occurrence near Mombasa of fossiliferous Lower Cretaceous limestone suggests that strata yielding faunas of this age may yet be found elsewhere in the Tanganyika coastal belt.

Again it is mainly work on material collected during the German Tendaguru Expedition that has been recorded: Dietrich (1914)—gastropods, (1925(2))—foraminifera, (1926)—corals, (1933(2))—mainly lamellibranchs; Lange (1914)—brachiopods, lamellibranchs, annelids; Zwierzycki (1914)—cephalopods. Hennig (1937) described representatives of several groups of fossils collected during a later survey (1934) in the southern coastal area of Tanganyika. Fahrion (1937) gave an account of foraminifera collected then by Hennig, and Sieverts-Doreck (1939) dealt with crinoids collected during the German Tendaguru Expedition and Hennig's later survey.

Previously, Müller (1900), Weissermel (1900) and Krenkel (1910(2)) had described Lower Cretaceous faunas from the area.

It was the belief of the German workers that there is essentially an unbroken upward succession from the Jurassic to the Cretaceous in the strata of the area. Spath (1933), however, has pointed out that there appears to be a complete palæontological break between uppermost Jurassic strata and the lowest Cretaceous bed in the series, the *Trigonia schwarzi* bed, which he believed to be Hauterivian to Aptian, i.e. not lowermost Cretaceous; from this came the bulk of the forms described in the references noted above.

From the upper reaches of the Kilwa creek near the mouth of the Mavudyi River, Hennig (1937) has recorded Albian ammonites. Fahrion (1937) has described Senonian microfossils from near Kilwa and from the Lindi area, where a few Senonian macrofossils were also recorded by Hennig (1937). Outside the southern coastal area of Tanganyika, Müller (1900) has recorded as Cenomanian (i.e. Upper Cretaceous), fossils from Kigua, about 25 miles west of Bagamoyo, and also as Upper Cretaceous, specimens from Mtunha, fifty miles south-west of Dar es Salaam. Reck and Dietrich (1921) also, recorded Senonian fossils from Uzaramo.

Almost no work has been done on vertebrate fossils known to occur in continental sandstones near the southern end of the Rukwa Trough and at the northern end of Lake Nyasa (in Tanganyika). From Nyasaland, Dixey (1928) recorded Dinosaur Beds of Cretaceous age with which the Tanganyika occurrences are correlated (Spence, 1954). Swinton (1950) described fossil eggs, presumed to be dinosaurian, discovered by the Department of Geological Survey in the sandstones of the southern area of the Rukwa Trough.

Silicified wood is known to occur in the Lower Cretaceous Makonde Beds of southern Tanganyika (Bornhardt, 1900), and coalified tree trunks have also been recorded. Potonié (1902) has also described Cretaceous fossil wood. Fossil wood is also common in the Tunduru Beds. (Although these beds are shown on the latest geological map of East Africa (1952) as of Karroo age, as indicated by Krenkel (1925) and Stockley (1947(1)), latest opinion (Spence, 1956) which agrees with that of earlier authors (e.g. Bornhardt, 1900; Dantz, 1903) is that they are Cretaceous.)

Tertiary and Quaternary (*Marine*).—Comparatively little work has been done on Tertiary and Quaternary marine fossils from Tanganyika.

Early Tertiary fossils have been described from the southern coastal region of Tanganyika (Lindi–Kilwa areas) by Wolff (1900(1)), Scholz (1911), Oppenheim (1916), Hennig (1937) and Fahrion (1937). For the most part only foraminifera, large species of which are particularly abundant in the area, have been dealt with, but lamellibranchs, brachiopods and echinoids are also recorded. Paleocene to Lower Miocene (Aquitanian) faunas occur.

Tertiary marine faunas younger than Lower Miocene are not well known in the Tanganyika coastal area, and the discrimination of uppermost Tertiary from Quaternary faunas is not certain. Wolff (1900(2)) recognized as Pliocene, molluscan fossils in a deep borehole at Dar es Salaam, and Wolff (1900(1)) also considered molluscs obtained from Mafia Island to be young Tertiary, but both occurrences have also been considered as Pleistocene (Krenkel, 1925). Koert and Tornau (1910) recorded lamellibranchs from Tanga as Pliocene, but the basis for this age determination could be questioned, and a Pleistocene age for this and a similar fauna from near Dar es Salaam could also be considered. Pliocene lamellibranchs have also been recorded near Pangani. The faunas of Quaternary marine deposits were discussed by Wolff (1900(2)) and by Koert and Tornau (1910) in reference to the Dar es Salaam and Tanga areas, and by Werth (1915). Weissermel (1900) makes reference to "sub-fossil" corals and Wolff (1900(1)) to other "sub-fossils". Cox (1927) discussed the discrimination of Pliocene and Pleistocene molluscan faunas from the East African area.

Quaternary (Non-Marine).—From lake beds to the north of Lake Rukwa, Cox (1939) has described a number of fresh-water and terrestrial molluscan fossils, several new, of Quaternary age. According to McConnell (1950), a further series of mollusca, all Recent forms but differing from those described by Cox (1939), has been recorded by Dr. W. Adam of the Brussels Natural History Museum, also from the Rukwa area. Similar beds to the south of the lake have yielded to Aitken (1950(2)), remains of several aquatic species, and Spence (1954) recorded crustacea from the lake beds of this area. The Middle Pleistocene Bed IV of the Oldoway Series exposed in the eastern Serengeti area has yielded fresh-water lamellibranchs.

Oldoway Gorge is the most notable area from which terrestrial vertebrate fossils of Quaternary age have been recorded. Research has been described both by German authors (e.g. Reck, 1914, 1933, 1935; Reck and Dietrich, 1925) and by British (e.g. Hopwood, 1932, 1934, 1936). Information on the faunas has recently been summarized by Leakey *et al.* (1951), who also lists important previous references. A variety of mammalian remains (over 100 species are recorded, many extinct), is associated with a series of hand-axe cultures dating from Middle Pleistocene. It was at one time believed (Reck, 1914) that a skeleton of *Homo sapiens* discovered in Bed II of the Oldoway Series was *in situ* and therefore of Middle Pleistocene age, but it has been shown (Reeve, 1938; Leakey *et al.*, 1951) to have been buried into this bed and to post-date Bed IV but to ante-date Bed V.

From the Lake Eyasi region a specimen of the hominid *Palæanthropus* associated with other mammalian remains has been described by Reck and Kohl-Larsen (1936), and also mentioned by Reeve (1938).

A Quaternary vertebrate fauna has also been recorded from near the village of Tinde about twenty-five miles south-west of Shinyanga. Hopwood (1931) described mammalian remains and Grace and Stockley (1931) have also mentioned fish and reptilian fossils. A similar assemblage was recorded by Williams (1939) near Shoshamagai about twenty-five miles south-east of Shinyanga. Spence (1954) recorded vertebrate remains (fish and mammalian) from lake beds in the Rukwa area, and Teale (1932) fossil bones from the Songeli-Mtawira Beds of the Iramba Plateau west of Singida.

The occurrence of plant fossils (unidentified) in the Songeli-Mtawira Beds is recorded by Teale (1932). Plant remains are also known from tuffs (possibly Tertiary not Quaternary) in the Arusha area.

The foregoing account outlines the considerable volume of palæontological work that has been done on material from Tanganyika. Sufficient has been accomplished to show that the area is in some respects of unique interest, and to emphasize the great amount of research that yet remains to be undertaken.

PRE-HISTORY

Although the study of pre-history in Tanganyika has not been carried out on such a wide scale as in Kenya and Uganda, the territory can boast of a number of prehistoric sites of world-wide interest and importance.

By far the most important is the famous Oldoway or Olduvai Gorge at the south-east corner of the Serengeti plains, some thirty-seven miles from the Ngorongoro Crater in the Northern Province. Olduvai Gorge was discovered in 1911 and was the scene of important work by German scientific expeditions before the first world war, under the late Professor Hans Reck. This early work led to the finding of fossilized remains of vast numbers of extinct species of animals in deposits of Middle Pleistocene age—a time when early Stone Age man was certainly present. No remains of Stone Age tools were, however, found and the human skeleton which was found at that time, and for which an age contemporary with that of the fossil animals was claimed, was afterwards proved to be of considerably later date, although still belonging to the Stone Age. (See page 19 above.)

In 1931–1932, and during several subsequent years, further detailed work was carried out by a British expedition, and this led to the discovery of Stone Age cultures at all levels throughout the 300 feet of ancient lake deposits exposed in the sides of the gorge. As a result it proved possible to work out the most complete sequence of evolutionary stages of the great hand-axe (or Chelles-Acheul) culture ever found anywhere; a fact which has led to Olduvai becoming the type site for the study of the evolution of this culture, which is found over the greater part of the African continent, over all south-west Europe, and in parts of Asia.

Recently a detailed study of the culture sequence there has been published by the Cambridge University Press.[1]

The fossil fauna also proved to be of the greatest possible interest and included remains of such strange creatures as *Sivatherium*, an extinct giraffe with antlers; *Dinotherium*, an extinct elephant which had tusks in its lower jaw, curving downwards like those of a walrus, instead of in the upper jaw and curving upwards as in the elephant of today; *Stylohipparion*, a little three-toed horse; *Hippopotamus gorgops*, a hippopotamus with periscopic eye-sockets; and many other strange extinct species. The site is now protected by Government, and can be visited with comparative ease from the Ngorongoro camp in the Serengeti National Park.

Another discovery of great importance to pre-history was that made by Dr. Kohl-Larsen on the eastern shore of Lake Eyasi[2]. It consisted of parts of a fossilized human skull of an extinct type of man, in some ways resembling the famous extinct Java and Pekin skulls. With it were associated Stone Age tools of the Levalloisian culture, a culture which is also found in parts of Europe in association with Neanderthal man. Unfortunately it is reported that the original fragments of the Eyasi skull disappeared in Germany during the war, but plaster casts had fortunately been made before the war broke out. The discovery of this skull was of the utmost importance, since it showed that in

---

[1]"Olduvai Gorge: A Report on the Evolution of the Hand-Axe Culture in Beds I-IV", by L. S. B. Leakey. Cambridge University Press, 1951.

[2]Leakey, L. S. B. "A New Fossil Skull from Eyasi, East Africa". *Nature*, December 26th, 1936, p. 1084 "Report on a visit to the site of the Eyasi Skull found by Dr. Kohl-Larsen". *Journal of East African Natural History Society* (1946).

East Africa, during the latter part of the Pleistocene period, the population included this strange and now extinct species of *Homo*, as well as men of our own type (known from discoveries in Kenya of the same geological period).

Excavations by a British expedition at Apis Rock on the Serengeti plains in 1932 revealed a series of Stone Age cultural levels in a large rock shelter, and proved for the first time the presence of the Magosian and Stillbay cultures in Tanganyika. This site has also been protected by Government.

From the point of view of the general public, perhaps the most interesting prehistoric sites in the territory are the very numerous rock shelters with prehistoric art in the Central Province, and especially round Kondoa-Irangi. These sites were first reported by a Government officer, Mr. Bagshawe, in 1923, and further discoveries were made from time to time. A preliminary report and guide was issued recently in *Tanganyika Notes and Records*,[1] by H. A. Fosbrooke, and a detailed survey by Dr. and Mrs. Leakey has been carried out. While a proportion of the paintings are of very recent date, and probably later than the Stone Age, the majority are truly prehistoric and some of the earliest probably are as old as the famous French and Spanish prehistoric art. Most of the sites are rather inaccessible, but those that can be reached by tracks and roads have now been fenced and opened to the public.

The style of these paintings varies from naturalistic reproductions of game animals to fantastic reproductions of the human form. The main characteristics of these latter are the elongated nature of the body, the head-dresses, masks or hair styles which frequently obscure the shape of the head, and the arm and leg ornaments such as can be observed in, for instance, some dancing scenes. Crudely drawn animals are sometimes mistaken by the uninitiated for representations of extinct species, but expert examination has invariably revealed these to be examples of the degraded art forms practised by the immediate predecessors of the present-day inhabitants during (probably) the last two or three centuries.

Owing to the fact that the prehistoric artists used the same rock face again and again as their "canvas" it is not always easy to decipher the early paintings upon which many later paintings are superimposed, but the time spent in doing so is always worth while as the earlier styles of painting are far more beautifully executed and naturalistic. It is hoped that a series of detailed reports with colour illustrations will be published when the survey now being carried out is complete. Of the sites at present open to the public that known as Cheke III, near Kondoa, is the most interesting, and has hundreds of paintings of a large number of different periods, ranging from the earliest to the latest.

Some preliminary excavations at one or two of the sites with prehistoric art show that a very long period of time is involved, and quantities of the colouring materials used for the paintings occur down to a depth of seventeen feet in the accumulations that have formed through the use of the sites for habitation over many hundreds of years.

Another prehistoric site of considerable interest is the neolithic habitation site and cemetery on the floor of the Ngorongoro Crater at the north end. This was first discovered by the Germans in 1913, and more detailed work was carried out by a British expedition in 1941. The Late Neolithic people who inhabited

---

[1]"Tanganyika Rock Paintings". *Tanganyika Notes and Records*, No. 29, July 1950.

this site, perhaps a few hundred years B.C., were early pastoralists who also, probably, practised a little agriculture. A report on the site is being prepared for publication.

A very great deal of work remains to be done in Tanganyika, but what has already been done makes it outstandingly clear that this territory is a rich storehouse of prehistoric remains.

THE ARCHÆOLOGY OF THE COAST

The archæology of the coast of Tanganyika presents quite different problems from that of the interior of the territory. Historically and culturally the East African coast long formed a single unit, curiously in contrast with its own hinterland, but closely linked with the Indian Ocean shores of south Arabia. It is becoming possible to reconstruct a pottery sequence for the Tanganyika coast, at least from the end of the thirteenth century A.D. This sequence can be dated with some exactness owing to the stratographic record of dateable imports found among the local shards. It closely corresponds with a pottery sequence that has been reconstructed from a site on the south Arabian coast. The resemblance is apparent, not only in the unglazed pottery and fragments of glass, but more significantly in the exact proportions of the glazed import wares from the Middle and the Far East. Before the end of the nineteenth century, six civilizations in turn dominated the East African littoral, each has left characteristic traces in Tanganyika and each was linked with the other shores of the Indian Ocean. Behind each there was a permanent factor, the monsoons.

The most recent of these civilizations was formed in the late eighteenth century when the Sultans of Oman gained control of the Tanganyika coast and islands and used them to develop the economic predominance of Zanzibar. This was a composite culture which first clearly takes its very characteristic shape in the early nineteenth century under the Sultan Seyyid Said. Primarily it was derived from eighteenth century Muscat but it had been deeply affected by influences from eighteenth century India. Persian elements had entered into it both through India and through Muscat, Portuguese elements had been retained in it from an earlier period. It presents some curious parallels with the contemporary court culture of the Egypt of Mehemet Ali. The artistic achievement of this Zanzibar culture was considerable. It created a new type of palace architecture, it developed new forms of the rich merchant's house, it was marked throughout by a strong sense of rhythm and of intricate pattern and design, notable in ceramics and metal work and above all in wood carving and lettering. In what is now Tanganyika, Bagamoyo and a number of lesser centres like Kilwa Kivinje contain admirable specimens of Zanzibari domestic architecture and woodwork. The ruined town on Chole island is partly German and partly Zanzibari.

The empire of Zanzibar had been preceded in the late sixteenth, seventeenth and eighteenth centuries by a number of smaller island states, ruled by independent sultans but normally essentially oligarchic in their social structure. Many of the ruins in Kenya and Tanganyika once ascribed to some early medieval Persian settlement were built during this period. Both in Kenya and Tanganyika they represent a single culture, marked by the common use of blue and white Chinese porcelain of seventeenth and eighteenth century types, apparently re-exported from south Arabia. There are similar forms of mosque and house and pillar-tomb and fortification. Dated funerary inscriptions have recently been found in considerable number, normally they are in Swahili. The deserted city of Kua in the Mafia islands is the most perfect specimen of this Swahili culture.

These small sultanates traded in slaves and ivory and grain and used a currency of beads and rolls of cloth, but they were probably economically self-subsisting, using slave-labour on the plantations that stretched outside each city wall. Theirs was again a composite culture, nominally at least it was always Islamic, but it seems clear that it was progressively Africanized even in religious conceptions. It is possible to trace sporadic influences from inner Africa, and there is considerable archæological evidence for forms of phallic worship and of animal sacrifice. The Kaole tombs near Bagamoyo, like the Wasin island ruins, were built during this period as well as the greater part of the Kilwa palace. This culture had come into existence as the Portuguese power faded along the coast and, at least during its earlier phase, Portuguese influence remained apparent in stone carving and design and in fortification.

The sixteenth century had been the period of Portuguese dominance along the Tanganyika coast. Archæologically it left its mark in a considerable number of Portuguese coins discovered there with imports from the sixteenth century West; zecchins from the Venice mint and imitation Venetian zecchins and beads in red Venetian glass. But the Portuguese monuments so far recorded in Tanganyika seem limited to fortifications like the guard-house on Songo Mnara island, the square fort of Santiago which still survives concealed beneath the Arab crenellations of Kilwa castle and, perhaps, the very elaborate fortress in European style which remains practically intact on the Husuni Mkuba site on Kilwa.

This last example may have been built at the orders of some Arab ruler, for Portugal provides the first example of European indirect rule in Africa. The African coast was administered from Goa as part of the *Estado da India*, but it was administered largely through a system of alliances with native sultans. Thus the elaborate civilization of the island kingdoms that had been discovered by the Portuguese at the end of the fifteenth century remained apparently intact for nearly a hundred years after their coming, even though it had been doomed economically by the Portuguese severance of the sea trade routes that had created it. It only finally collapsed and vanished in the anarchy of the late sixteenth and early seventeenth centuries.

It is now becoming possible to reconstruct the civilization of these island sultanates in the fourteenth and fifteenth centuries. They were Islamic merchant cities grown wealthy through trade in ivory and gold and iron, and possessing contacts throughout the Middle and Far East. Preliminary excavations in the deserted palace town on the coral island of Songo Mnara have yielded broken glazed pottery from Egypt, Syria and the Persian area, fragments of brown glazed stoneware from Siam, and a mass of Chinese porcelain: sea-green opaque glaze with a granular grey body, thin-coated bowls of olive-brown celadon, and early Ming in white or tinted honey-brown. A recent expedition to Kilwa discovered pierced carnelians from India, pierced amber and crystal and broken topaz.

By the fifteenth century this island culture had evolved its own characteristic architecture. At Songo Mnara fluted demi-domes rest on fluted pilasters and there is an elaborate vaulted chamber with a barrel roofing inset with a hundred circular cavities. In the palace doorways each pointed arch with its thin stone edging is recessed within a rectangle of cut stone. Within the palace there is an intricate system of sanitation, with stone piping. Everywhere there is an evident delight in geometrical precision and in the exact use of the square. In its present form most of the Friday Mosque on Kilwa Kisiwani is certainly later than 1410 and earlier than 1505, a very possible date would be about 1470, which the coin evidence suggests as the climax of the prosperity of the town. The identity in style between it and the smaller domed mosque at Kilwa suggests that they are of the same period, were probably for the same patron and are possibly by the same architect. The closest parallels to this elaborately ornate mosque architecture are to be found in the Islamic India of the fifteenth century. The closest parallel to the coins from the Kilwa mint, with their rhymed verse inscription, is to be found in the coins from the Indian mint of the Bahmanid kings. These resemblances are significant, for it seems probable that late medieval Kilwa came to greatness primarily through the Indian trade. Yet in itself this Kilwa civilization forms a distinct variant among medieval Islamic cultures, and the extent of its trade contacts to the north as well as to the east give it a particular significance in art history.

During the late medieval period the Kilwa kings would seem to have exercised a vague hegemony along the East African littoral and the "Kilwa" culture seems to have stretched for nearly 600 miles among the scattered islands. A quantity of Kilwa coins has been reported from Italian Somalia, while, southward, Kilwa was linked with Sofala (in what is now Portuguese East Africa), and it was through Sofala that Kilwa gained its gold. At least two sites of crucial importance, apparently belonging to this period, still wait to be adequately explored. Both are in Tanganyika. The first is that of Kisimani in the Mafia island group; the second is Tongoni, on the mainland a little to the south of Tanga. The two most important of the medieval coin-hordes have been reported from the Mafia group and scientific excavation at Kisimani might enable us to reconstruct the history of this period, for at present we are forced to rely primarily on the coin inscriptions. The traditions recorded in the variants of the Kilwa Chronicle are of historic value for the fifteenth and late fourteenth centuries, but they would seem to be interpenetrated by mythological elements and to exaggerate the age of the Kilwa culture on the coast. No archæological evidence has yet been found that could bring back the origins of the Kilwa culture to an earlier date than the second half of the thirteenth century. The earliest coin from the Kilwa mint so far recorded was struck by a Sultan Hasan ibn Talut, who probably reigned some time between 1285 and 1302. The earliest dateable pottery seems derivative from thirteenth century Persian ware of the Rakka type. Preliminary excavation trenches sunk in four sites of this culture showed that the lowest inhabited level was approximately 14th century. Nothing has been found so far to support the tradition that the Kilwa culture was of direct Persian origin. Archæologically it is more likely that its provenance was south Arabian, and its growth stimulated by trade contacts with Islamic India and indirectly with China.

Yet it is clear that there was an earlier Islamic culture in the islands, represented by eight sites which stretch from the Coiama group off the coast of Somalia through Kizimikazi and Unguja Kuu on Zanzibar to the south of Kilwa. None of these sites would seem to correspond exactly to the late medieval cities, and none of them would seem to have been more than a small trading station, marked now by some fragments of a mosque normally built in coral rag, by traces of rough fortification, by broken sgraffito ware and by an occasional coin from the Khalifa's mint at Baghdad. The earliest of such coins to be reported are of the ninth century A.D. Perhaps the settlements were beginning then. Traces of four such settlements have been recorded along the Tanganyika coast. The whole period awaits further archæological excavation. It is even possible that there was a contemporary indigenous non-Islamic town culture on the mainland coast, with which these Arab island settlements traded. There are curious references in early Arab geographers to such towns. El Idrisi wrote in the 12th century of El Banes; it was rich and populous, and its people worshipped a great drum whose sound carried for three miles. The distance that he gives from Malindi suggests that it may have been on the Tanganyika–Kenya border. South of it lay the rich and populous city of Tohnet, which was perhaps the predecessor of Tongoni, and ultimately, therefore, of Tanga. Two market towns are mentioned, further south again. All that can so far be said is that some traces have been found which may be associated with two such great African settlements.

It is just becoming possible to trace an earlier culture still. The way to the East African islands had been known in the East Mediterranean world from the late Hellenistic period to the time of Justinian. In the first century A.D. the route is described in considerable detail by the author of the "Periplus of the Erythræan Sea". A considerable horde of Roman coins has been reported from Port Durnford, and though this is 218 miles north of Mombasa there was Græco-Roman penetration as far south as "Rhapta", possibly an area including both Kilwa and Mafia. Ptolemaic silver coins have been reported from as far down the coast as Msasani near Dar es Salaam, and the "Periplus" provides evidence of constant trade contacts between south Arabia and the Rhapta area which had apparently already existed for some centuries before it was written. Traces of two cultures have been found in islands which may possibly belong to this pre-Islamic period; culture "A" is best represented by the site on Sanje ya Kati island to the south of Kilwa. The people of this culture lived in small oblong houses of carefully dressed masonry, grouped round a central citadel and covering about twenty acres. They knew the use of iron, and used a thin red pottery. Their walls are at times polygonal. They are possibly the same as the people who built towers "ziggurat" fashion from dressed blocks of sandstone; one such tower has been found within four miles of the settlement of the culture "A" people on Sanje ya Kati. The extensive ruins of a settlement of the same type have been reported from the other side of Songo Mnara, and it is possible that these were trading posts of a south Arabian people. But no archæologist would dare to speak in any terms except those of possibility until one of these sites has been scientifically excavated. It is necessary to be still more hesitant about the people of culture "B", who built their small square houses and low walls from lumps of undressed coral and used very rough handmade brown pottery. They were more primitive than the people of culture "A" but in Africa it does not necessarily follow that they belonged to an earlier period or even to a different one. Culture "B" sites have been reported from Gondal in Somalia south to Songo Mnara. All that can be said of these people with certainty is that they must ultimately be fitted in somewhere in the sequence of the cultures of the Tanganyika coast. Scientific archæology in Africa is still only in its preliminary phase. Few areas are as likely to yield so many unexpected discoveries as the Tanganyika coastline and islands.

KILWA *circa* 1591

QVILOA.

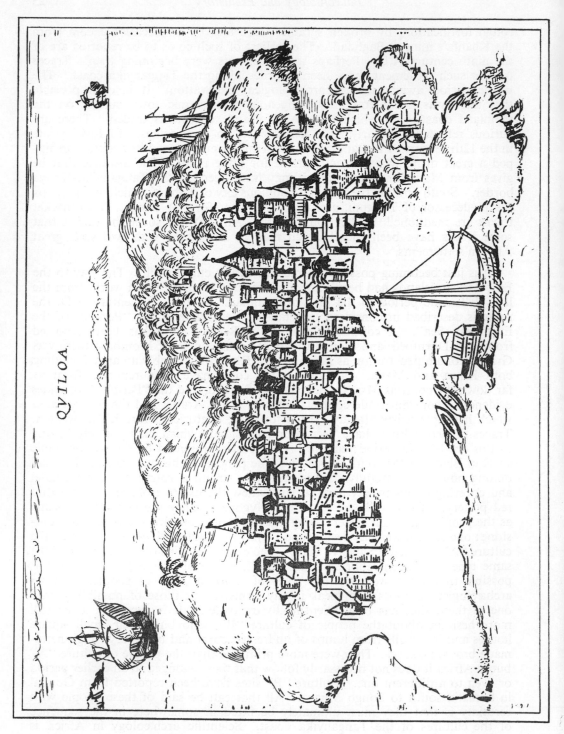

26

Chapter 3

HISTORY UP TO THE END OF THE 1914-18 WAR

EARLY DAYS

The first contact between East Africa and the outside world took place in the remote past. The prevalence of certain trade winds made this comparatively easy even for vessels of a very primitive type. Ever since the day when men first began to go down to the sea in ships and occupy their business in great waters the dwellers on the coasts of Arabia and India have been encouraged by the monsoons to venture across the Indian Ocean. The north-east monsoon, which begins to blow in November or December and continues to blow with remarkable steadiness until the end of February, made the voyage from Asia to Africa one of comparative ease. The south-west monsoon1, which blows with the same steadiness from April to September, made the return journey equally easy. The date at which this intercourse began cannot be fixed with any certainty, but it can be safely said that it must have been several centuries before the Christian era. It was certainly established by the first century A.D., when an anonymous Greek merchant seaman wrote the *Periplus of the Erythræan Sea.*

No doubt these merchant adventurers were originally engaged on purely trading ventures, sailing to Africa with one monsoon and returning with the other, without any attempt at colonization or settlement. Nevertheless in the course of years there was a tendency for some adventurers to remain behind and establish trading posts resembling the "factories" which European merchants were later to establish in India. Some of these trading posts eventually took on a permanent character and, as the the settlers increased in numbers, substantial buildings began to be constructed and many cultural amenities introduced from the settlers' countries of origin. For strategic reasons most of these settlements were established on the numerous islands and islets which are to be found up and down the East African coast. Even on the mainland the tendency was to select a site capable of all-round defence.

The oldest known of these settlements would appear to be those at Kilwa Kisiwani ("Kilwa on the Island") and on other islands nearby. Of these the very earliest is perhaps that on Sanje ya Kati, a small island to the south of Kilwa Kisiwani, where there are ruins of small oblong two-roomed houses grouped round a rectangular citadel. No traces of any mosque have so far been found on this site and it may well be that this settlement dates back to pre-Islamic times.

Kilwa Kisiwani itself has an Arabic chronicle which gives its history from the tenth century of the Christian era down to the time of the arrival of the Portuguese in the first years of the sixteenth century. A translation into English of one version of that chronicle was published by the late Professor S. A. Strong in the *Journal of the Royal Asiatic Society* for 1895. Another version was translated into Portuguese by the historian, John de Barros, and has been printed in his *Decadas da Asia.* Two Swahili versions of the chronicle were printed by C. Velten in *Prosa und Poetrie der Suaheli.* According to these versions settlers

---

1 South of the seasonal equator it blows from the south-east, but as it goes north it veers round until it blows from the south-west.

from Shiraz in Persia reached Kilwa in about 975 A.D. At the time of their arrival there were already other settlements of "Moors" at places called "Songo" and "Xanga", which would appear to be identifiable with the adjacent islands of Songo Mnara and Sanje ya Kati.

The early history of Kilwa has a good deal to say about wars with Songo and Xanga, from which Kilwa eventually emerged triumphant. In those early days the people of Kilwa also subjugated the island of Mafia, which had likewise been settled by people from Shiraz. Though the chronicle records intervals during which Mafia apparently seceded temporarily from Kilwa, the island remained an appanage of Kilwa more or less continuously until the end of the eighteenth century.

The famous Arab traveller, Ibn Batuta, visited Kilwa in 1332. At that time the town appears to have been built principally of wood, though archæological remains show that there must by that date already have been at least one mosque and other stone buildings in existence. The chronicle shows that some two centuries earlier the people of Kilwa obtained a foothold at Sofala (near Beira in what is now Portuguese East Africa), whence they were able to obtain gold from the mines of Monomotapa in what is now Southern Rhodesia. It was said that "Moors" from Mogadishu in what is now Italian Somaliland had originally had the monopoly of this trade, but that the people of Kilwa succeeded in supplanting them. What is certain is that Sofala remained an appanage of Kilwa until the last days of the fifteenth century, when the local governor took advantage of civil discord in Kilwa to declare himself independent. Whilst this connection between Kilwa and Sofala lasted, the former place enjoyed an almost undisputed commercial and political supremacy along the whole of the East African coast. The Kilwans gained a foothold at Mozambique as well as at the mouths of the Angosha and Zambezi rivers. At about the end of the twelfth century they appear to have raided Zanzibar and there are local traditions that about the same time settlers from Kilwa colonized a number of places on the mainland opposite to Zanzibar. Kilwa itself became an entrepôt, where gold was exchanged for other commodities such as cloth. There was a large coastal trade and in addition the north-east monsoon brought ships from Cambay and other parts of India, the Persian Gulf, and Southern Arabia, bringing the commodities of those lands and taking back with them, when the south-west monsoon began blowing, gold, ivory, tortoise-shell, ambergris and slaves.

In this connection it is perhaps of interest to mention that there was a certain amount of indirect commercial intercourse between East Africa and China. A Chinese geographical treatise of 1060 A.D. (*H'Sing T'angshu*) gives a somewhat uncomplimentary description of the land and people of Ma-lin (Malindi) just to the north of Mombasa. At the beginning of the fifteenth century several expeditions were sent from China to East Africa. One which took place between 1417 and 1419 appears to have got as far south as Malindi, and another (from 1421 to 1422) reached Barawa and Mogadishu on the Somali coast. In 1413 another expedition sailed to Bengal, where it was presented with a giraffe from the land of Malindi, which in due course was presented to the Chinese Emperor. Though none of these expeditions proceeded any further south than Malindi, Chinese coins dating as far back as 713 A.D. and Chinese ware have been discovered not only at Kilwa, but also at many other byegone coast settlements along the coast of Tanganyika*

*See "Chinese Porcelain in Tanganyika" by G. S. P. Freeman-Grenville, in *Tanganyika Notes and Records* No. 41 for Dec. 1955.

As already stated, Kilwa was during most of this period the leading port on the East African coast, but scattered up and down that coast between Mikindani further to the south of it and Tanga to the north there are still to be seen a number of Shirazian and Arab remains, which indicate settlements by immigrants and the descendants of immigrants from Asia at varying dates between the tenth and the sixteenth centuries. The most extensive and the most interesting of these are to be found at Tongoni (near Tanga), Kaole (near Bagamoyo), Kunduchi and Msasani (near Dar es Salaam). Traditions regarding Tongoni attribute the colonization of that place at one stage of its history to a tribe called the Wadebuli. Pemba, Zanzibar and Mafia also have traditions of colonization by members of this tribe. A certain Muhammad bin Rukn ad Din al Dabuli, who figures largely in the history of Kilwa at the time of the advent of the Portuguese, would appear to have belonged to this tribe. Tradition suggests that these people were of Asiatic origin. In addition to the resemblance of the name there is a certain amount of archæological evidence which suggests that they may have hailed from Dabhol on the west coast of India, which during the fifteenth century was a seaport belonging to the Bahmani rulers of the Deccan.

The authentic history of Tanganyika may be said to begin with the advent of the Portuguese. In 1498 Vasco da Gama rounded the Cape of Good Hope and made his way to Mozambique. On his departure thence he had intended to call at Kilwa, but was carried past the place and, after calling at Mombasa and Malindi, made his way across the Indian Ocean to Calicut. The first Portuguese to call at Kilwa was the discoverer of Brazil, Pedro Alvares Cabral, who arrived in the harbour with six ships on July 16, 1500. Though there was no open rupture, it was clear that both inhabitants and visitors viewed each other with the utmost suspicion. Cabral continued his voyage for India, leaving on shore a ship's carpenter named Antonio Fernandes to spy out the land. Another fleet arrived from Lisbon in 1501 and met with a similar reception. Like Cabral, the commander, John da Nova, continued his journey by way of Malindi to India.

On July 12, 1502, Vasco da Gama anchored in front of Kilwa with a very large fleet. At this date owing to internal dissensions there was an interregnum in Kilwa and the reins of government were in the hands of an Amir named Muhammad Kiwabi. Vasco da Gama managed by violation of a safe conduct to get the Amir into his hands as a prisoner, and to extort from him a promise to acknowledge the King of Portugal as his overlord and also to pay a tribute of 5,000 crusados (or over £2,000 of contemporary English money). When Vasco da Gama returned to Lisbon the gold which he had received as tribute was worked into a monstrance for the Church of Our Lady at Belem. This monstrance can now be seen in the Museum of Ancient Art at Lisbon.

In February, 1505, two vessels called at Kilwa on their return voyage from India to Portugal to demand the arrears of tribute money, but the commander was met with a flat refusal. As they lacked the necessary force to use compulsion, they had to leave without obtaining payment. But on July 22 in the same year Francis d'Almeida arrived before Kilwa with a powerful fleet. The Amir tried to stave off Almeida's demands by procrastination, but on July 24 Almeida landed his men and took the town and royal palace by force of arms. The Amir Ibrahim fled to the mainland and the Portuguese set up Muhammad bin Rukn ad Din al Dabuli, of whom mention has already been made and who is known to

Portuguese chroniclers as Muhammad "Ankoni", as Sultan in his place. Almeida also set about constructing a fort, to which he gave the name of Santiago. Leaving behind him a garrison of 100 or 150 soldiers, a number of civil officers, and some Franciscan friars, he set sail for Mombasa, to which place he meted out the same punishment as that which he had inflicted upon Kilwa, before crossing over to India.

The Portuguese occupation of Kilwa lasted just over seven years. Muhammad Ankoni was murdered shortly after his appointment as Sultan. None of his successors proved satisfactory. There was much friction between the local inhabitants and the Portuguese, who suffered many losses from disease. Eventually in 1513 the Viceroy of India, Affonso d'Albuquerque, who had never approved of the occupation of Kilwa, ordered the garrison to be withdrawn and the fort to be dismantled. On the eve of their withdrawal the Portuguese allowed the fugitive Amir, Muhammad Kiwabi, to resume the reins of government.

After its evacuation by the Portuguese Kilwa never recovered its former supremacy. The Portuguese had occupied Sofala and had build a fort there in 1505. They also built another fort at Mozambique in 1507, and have continuously occupied both these places until the present day. The immediate result was that Kilwa lost its monopoly of the gold trade and became reduced in importance to the same level as such places as Lindi, Mikindani, and other seaports along the coast.

Despite the severe chastisement which it received at the hands of Almeida in 1505 Mombasa appears to have increased in importance as Kilwa declined. For some eight years more it was the focal point of all resistance to the Portuguese invaders. It appears to have extended its influence, or at any rate to have made its power felt, as far down the coast as Utondwe, a few miles to the south of Sadani. Some time before 1528 the "lord" (*senhor*) of that place gave offence to the ruler of Mombasa and was made a prisoner by him. After he had managed to obtain his release, he vowed vengeance against the people of Mombasa. Accordingly he came to the assistance of Nunho da Cunha, who in 1528 attacked and destroyed Mombasa The Sultan of Mtangata, who also bore the people of Mombasa a grudge, sent two hundred men to assist the Portuguese in these operations. After this second punishment of Mombasa we hear little more of Portuguese activity on the East African coast for some sixty years. The majority of Portuguese vessels sailing to and from India struck across the Indian Ocean in a north-easterly direction after making the Comoro Islands and no longer hugged the East African coast. During all these years the only footholds which they had on that coast were at Malindi, Pemba, and Zanzibar, where they had been allowed by the local rulers to establish factories. In 1585, however, their interest in East Africa was once more revived by the raids on the coast of a Turkish corsair named Mirale Bey.

These Turkish raids more or less coincided with a land invasion of the interior of Tanganyika by a cannibal tribe known as the Zimba. This tribe made its way from the region of Sena on the Zambezi in a north-easterly direction across the Ruvuma into what is now Tanganyika. They are said to have entirely devastated everything which lay in their path. When a quarter of a century later a Portuguese traveller named Gaspar Bocarro passed through these regions, he was shown large tracts of territory which had remained desolate ever since the Zimba had passed that way.   In 1587 they reached Kilwa and, owing to the treachery of one of the inhabitants, managed to make their way by night across the narrow channel which separates that island from the mainland.   They proceeded to sack the town, and, according to one account, to kill three thousand of its inhabitants.

From Kilwa the Zimba made their way slowly northwards.   By 1589 they had reached the mainland opposite to Mombasa, but were prevented from crossing over to the island by the fleet commanded by the Turkish corsair, Mirale Bey.   Eventually, Mirale Bey's fleet was attacked and destroyed by a Portuguese fleet which had been sent against him from Goa.   Thereafter, with the consent and approval of the Portuguese, the Zimba crossed over on to the island and wrought the same havoc and destruction as they had at Kilwa.   Very shortly afterwards however the Zimba met with disaster when endeavouring to take Malindi by assault.   The inhabitants of that place, aided by some Portuguese, put up a stout defence and the Zimba were eventually attacked in the rear by a warlike tribe known as the Segeju.   Very few of the Zimba escaped from the field of slaughter, and their march of destruction was stayed once and for all.   It is not without interest to note that their conquerors, the Segeju, moved during the course of the next century from their original home near Malindi to their present territory near Tanga.

In 1592 the Segeju captured Mombasa, which they handed over to the Sultan of Malindi.   The Sultan in his turn handed it over to the Portuguese, who began erecting Fort Jesus in the following year.   For a century thereafter the commanders of that fort claimed that the whole of the coast between Cape Delgado and Cape Guardafui was subject to their control as representatives of the King of Portugal.

In actual fact the captains of Mombasa exercised very little real authority on the mainland to the south of Fort Jesus.   Letters of instruction which were issued by the Viceroy of India to the commander of the fort in 1598 show that there apparently were Portuguese settlers at Kilwa and Utondwe as well as on the island of Mafia, but it was clear that they resided at these places only by leave of the local rulers.   There was a Portuguese factory at Kilwa in 1616. It was still there in 1667, but an English captain reported then that the place only had a coasting trade with Mombasa, in "small boats", consisting of gold, ambergris, ivory, and slaves, all of which commodities were evidently obtained "at inconsiderable rates" from the interior of the continent.   As already mentioned, Mafia formed part of the dominions of the Sultan of Kilwa, who in about 1634 had allowed the Portuguese to erect a blockhouse on the island for occupation in time of war.

Though there is evidence to show that their imports found their way well into the interior of Tanganyika at this period, there is with one exception no evidence of any serious attempt on the part of the Portuguese to explore the interior of Tanganyika.   The one exception is the Gaspar Bocarro already mentioned, who in 1616 made the journey overland from Tete on the banks of the Zambezi to Kilwa.   He must have passed very close to Lake Nyasa, but he appears to have failed to realise how close he was to it.   He entered Tanganyika somewhere in the upper reaches of the Ruvuma, but it is difficult to identify any of the places through which he passed with places named on modern maps of Tanganyika.   It is interesting to know that he was well received by all the chiefs through whose lands he passed, and also to learn that he did not come across any outpost of "Moorish" settlers until he was only some six hours' march from Kilwa. Shortly after crossing the Ruvuma into Tanganyika and when he was still many days' journey from Kilwa he was shown cloth which had been obtained from "the coast of Malindi".

In 1631 the Sultan of Malindi rose in rebellion against the Portuguese. He managed to surprise the garrison at Mombasa and to capture Fort Jesus. After that he massacred almost all the Portuguese inhabitants of the town. Though he had been brought up as a Christian, he now proclaimed himself to be a Muslim and preached a *jehad*, or holy war, against the Portuguese. Many of the rulers of the coast towns made common cause with him, including those of Mtangata, Tanga, and Utondwe. It took several years for the Portuguese to suppress this rising. As an inscription over the gateway of Fort Jesus at Mombasa shows, it was ruthlessly suppressed "with a chastisement not expected in the Indies." The same inscription records the fact that the ruler of Utondwe was made tributary to the King of Portugal. Other records inform us that severe punishment was meted out at Mtangata and Tanga because many Christians had been slain at those places.

The Portuguese, however, never entirely recovered from the aftermath of this rising. During the next sixty years one coast town after another was constantly rising in rebellion, but none of the towns to the south of Tanganyika appears to have been recalcitrant until 1652 when the Arabs of Oman raided the island of Zanzibar. In that year the "king" of Utondwe, who according to Portuguese records was the son of the "queen" of Zanzibar, gave the raiders some assistance. In the following year the "king" of Pemba, who had also allied himself to the Omanis, raided Mafia, Kwale and Kilwa. A Portuguese expedition failed to intercept the Omani raiders, but drove the "king" of Utondwe and his mother out of Zanzibar, after destroying the latter's town. The Portuguese also intercepted the Pemba raiders as they were returning from Mafia. Half the raiders' vessels were destroyed and the remainder forced on shore at Zanzibar, where their crews were attacked and heavy losses inflicted upon them.

In 1686 a "prince" (*principe*) of Quendoa on the mainland (? Kendwa Island near Dar es Salaam) was reported to have stirred up trouble in Pemba, which had resulted in the expulsion of the "queen" of that island, who was friendly to the Portuguese and who had become a Christian.

In March, 1696, the Arabs of Oman laid siege to Fort Jesus at Mombasa. They finally captured the fort in December, 1698. During the thirty-three months' siege more than one attempt was made to supply the beleaguered garrison with food by friendly rulers along the coast. Amongst these was the ruler of Tanga, whose name is given by the Portuguese as Guaba de Muizabo, but his vessels were intercepted by the besiegers. Utondwe, on the other hand, continued to show its hostility towards the Portuguese and paid for it in 1699 when the last Portuguese relieving squadron, which passed that way after an abortive effort to relieve Fort Jesus, raided the town.

After the fall of Mombasa every island and town on the East African coast appears to have made its submission to the Sultan of Oman. Kilwa is said to have been captured by the Omanis in 1698 and evidence that the Sultan's palace was about this date partially destroyed by fire would seem to confirm this

Giraffe presented to Chinese Emperor in 1414.

From a contemporary drawing. Reproduced from "China's discovery of Africa", by J. J. L. Duyvendak, by kind permission of the publishers, Arthur Probsthain, London.

Entrance to the Old Fort, Kilwa Kisiwani.

statement.   In 1710 a spy reported to the Portuguese Viceroy at Goa that the Omani had converted a house at Kilwa belonging to one Mwana Bakari into a fortress, which was garrisoned by fifty Arabs.   Sixteen years later the Sultan of Kilwa sent a request to the Portuguese at Mozambique for assistance to expel the Omani garrison.   In 1728 the Portuguese took advantage of dissensions amongst the Arabs on the coast to expel the Omani garrison from Mombasa and to re-occupy Fort Jesus.   Shortly after this success a number of local rulers tendered their submission to the Portuguese.   These included Muhinha Maccuma (? Mwinyi Makumba) of Pangani, Macamarumbe (? Makame Irumba) of Mtangata and Ben Sultan Alauya (? the son of Sultan Alawi) of Tanga.   But the Portuguese were expelled from Mombasa in 1729.   Thereafter they never regained their foothold anywhere on the coast to the north of Cape Delgado.

In 1741 the Yorubi dynasty in Oman was supplanted by that of the Busaidi. On the east coast of Africa a number of local governors took advantage of the internal dissensions which led up to this revolution to shake off the overlordship of Oman.   The foremost amongst these seceders were the Mazrui, who persistently asserted the independence of Mombasa.   They did not confine their claims to the island of Mombasa, but asserted their claim to overlordship of a large extent of the coast strip both to the north and south of that island.   The strip to the south extended as far as the Pangani River.

Kilwa appears to have followed Mombasa's example.   In 1745 the Portuguese Governor of Mozambique reported that the civil war in Oman had extended to East Africa and that Kilwa and Mafia, as well as certain other places, "more or less" recognized the Portuguese as their legitimate overlords.   Between 1760 and 1769 a number of communications passed between Hassan bin Ibrahim bin Yusuf, Sultan of Kilwa, and the Governor of Mozambique regarding a plan, which eventually proved abortive, for the recovery of Mombasa.

A new power now appears on the scene.   In the latter half of the eighteenth century the demand for labour for the plantations on the Ile de France (Mauritius) and Bourbon (Réunion) led the French to seek for slaves on the East African coast.   On December 14, 1776, a French trader named Morice entered into a treaty with the Sultan of Kilwa whereby the latter agreed to supply Morice with one thousand slaves annually and to allow him to occupy the fortress at Kilwa.   Morice made over his rights under the treaty to the French Government, who set up a factory at Kilwa.   The French sent a frigate to try to negotiate a more satisfactory treaty and a number of other French vessels called at Kilwa to load cargoes of slaves.   But shortly afterwards—most probably in 1784—the Sultan of Oman sent a fleet to reassert his sovereignty along the East African coast.   The fleet reduced Zanzibar and Mafia into possession, and finally Kilwa, where the Sultan was allowed to remain in nominal control under the close supervision of an Arab governor and garrison.   The French accepted this *fait accompli* and continued to trade for slaves with the new regime.

Though the Sultans of Oman managed to retain their hold of Kilwa and Mafia, the Mazrui held out against them further to the north for another half century. No serious attempts were made further to consolidate the Omani position in East Africa until the accession in 1805 of Said bin Sultan.   For rather more than fifteen years affairs in Oman and the Persian Gulf prevented the new Sultan from paying great attention to Africa.   In 1822 an expedition from Zanzibar wrested

4

Pemba from the Mazrui and thus deprived them of their principal granary.   In 1828 Said bin Sultan personally led an expedition against Mombasa, but the power of the Mazrui was not finally broken until 1837.

In January, 1828, after having patched up a temporary peace with the Mazrui at Mombasa, Said bin Sultan proceeded to Zanzibar, where he decided to make his second home.   In the words of a British naval officer, writing seven years later, his "very respectable naval force" became "with Zanzibar, his principal care and study."   From time to time affairs in Oman and the Persian Gulf dragged him most reluctantly back to his original home in Asia, but he made a point of returning to Zanzibar whenever opportunity offered.   His first visit was a hurried one, as Asiatic affairs recalled him to Oman.   He left Zanzibar in nominal charge of his favourite son, Khalid, who predeceased his father in 1854.   As Khalid was only some thirteen years old, the actual government was entrusted to a distant relative of the Sultan, named Suleman bin Ahmed.   Some years later a British Consul described this individual as "not a clever man, but a kind, good sort of a person; . . . (who) has much influence with the pagan chiefs on the coast of Africa."   There can be no doubt that it was largely owing to Suleman's tactful handling of the inhabitants of the mainland that Said bin Sultan and his two sons succeeded in obtaining in a peaceful manner a firm foothold at many points along the coast of what is now Tanganyika.

It was Said bin Sultan's efforts to foster and promote commerce that led to the opening up of the interior.   There always had been some commercial intercourse between the people of the coast and those of the interior even in Portuguese times, but it appears to have been on a somewhat limited scale.   The principal exports were slaves and ivory, which were brought to the coast and exchanged for commodities from the East, of which Indian cloth was one of the most important.   Some of these imports travelled a very long way inland.   Thus cups and plates are said to have reached Buganda by way of Karagwe during the reign of Kyabagu, who died in about 1780.   Dark blue kaniki cloth, copper wire, and cowry shells first made their appearance in the same country during the rule of Semakokiro, who reigned in the early years of the nineteenth century.   During the latter part of the eighteenth century the demand for slaves in the French colonies of Ile de France (Mauritius) and Bourbon (Réunion) and in South America appears to have led to a considerable increase in intercourse between coast towns such as Mikindani, Lindi, Mchinga, Kiswere and Kilwa and the regions of Lake Nyasa, but communication between the coast and the other central African lakes appears to have developed more slowly.

In the early days of Said bin Sultan's reign this commerce appears still to have been carried on for the most part by ivory hunters and slave traders from the interior.   In 1828 an American merchant named Edmund Roberts reported that he had frequently seen in Zanzibar elephant hunters whose homes were thirty days' march away in the interior, and that the Governor of Zanzibar "occasionally sent presents to the negro kings a long distance inland".   Probably these gifts were sent with the design of keeping certain trade routes open so that traders from the coast might pass and repass without molestation.   There is evidence that by about that date Arab and Swahili traders were beginning to lead caravans well into the interior.   In 1789 the Portuguese explorer Lacerda reported that ivory from Cazembe in what is now Northern Rhodesia was being exported to Zanzibar in exchange for dry goods.   Musa Mazuri, a Khoja from Surat.

informed Burton at a later date that he had reached Unyanyembe (Tabora) in about 1825. At a much later date an Arab named Ahmed bin Ibrahim el Amuri informed Emin Pasha that he had reached Karagwe and Buganda in 1844. At Ujiji on the shores of Lake Tanganyika Burton was informed that the Arabs had first reached that spot in 1840.

When Captain Smee of the *Ternate* visited Zanzibar in 1811 there was a small colony of "Banyan" traders there, but they appear to have been only very temporary residents, who never brought their families with them and who confined their sojourn to one or two trading seasons. One or two decades later traders from Cutch and elsewhere began to bring their families with them and to settle permanently in Zanzibar. In course of time a few of them crossed over to the mainland and set up in business at most of the coast towns which tapped the trade from the interior. Few of them followed the example of the Khoja Musa Mazuri by making their way into the interior, but a number of them financed Arab, Baluchi and Swahili caravans which penetrated to the central lakes and thus enabled trade with the interior to develop on a much larger scale than might otherwise have been the case. In the latter part of his reign Said bin Sultan made a practice of farming out the collection of the customs revenue to one or other of the leading Indian firms in Zanzibar and these farmers of the customs used to send their compatriots to take charge of the customs posts which began to be established along the mainland coast.[1]

It is difficult to say how far Said bin Sultan was directly responsible for the development of trade in the interior of the continent. He certainly encouraged exploitation of those regions and it is equally certain that in his time commercial operations expanded far beyond the more or less casual and haphazard operations in which the coast people had hitherto indulged. To the south of the Rufiji delta the trade routes continued as before to be from the coast towns to the shores of Lake Nyasa. The most northerly was Kilwa Kivinje, which in the 1830's supplanted Kilwa Kisiwani as the principal terminus of the trade with Lake Nyasa. The coastal termini of the trade with Lakes Tanganyika and Victoria extended from Bagamoyo southwards to Mboamaji (near Dar es Salaam) and included such places as Kunduchi, Msasani, Mzizima (near the site of Government House at Dar es Salaam) and Magogoni. A third route led from Pangani, Mtangata, and Tanga to the south of Mount Kilimanjaro towards Lake Victoria but it appears to have been less frequented and eventually to have become more or less closed owing to the hostility of the tribes of the interior, though it was still used by caravans proceeding as far as Usambara.

By 1839, Seyyid Said was regularly sending trading caravans yearly into the interior. Other traders were in the habit of joining these caravans in order to obtain military protection. This practice was continued by Said's son Majid, who in 1869 despatched a caravan by way of Unyanyembe to Mutesa of Buganda. In or about 1839 a caravan leader who had been sent by Seyyid Said "for the express purpose of exploring" returned to Zanzibar with an emissary from the paramount chief of Unyamwezi, "who had come at the request of the Sultan for to make some forms of treaty for the safety and success of his subjects when on trading expeditions." The nature and contents of the treaty (if any) which may have been thus concluded have not been recorded. Doubtless it followed the pattern of similar treaties in other parts of Africa, namely, an undertaking by the

---

[1]See also pp. 298 to 301 for an account of Indian immigration.

Sultans of Zanzibar to pay an annual sum in cash or in kind in consideration of the chief concerned agreeing to grant the right to caravans to trade in or pass through his territory without molestation and to exempt them from exorbitant payments of *hongo* (customary dues) in respect of their merchandise.

The principal trade route was that leading to Tabora.   With certain deviations it followed more or less the line of the present railway from Dar es Salaam.   In those early days, however, there was nothing at Tabora which was worthy of the name of "town".   It consisted of a number of separate little groups of Arab and Swahili houses scattered here and there, round each of which clustered a number of huts.   This large straggling village was known in Said bin Sultan's days, and for many years thereafter, as Unyanyembe.   The average number of Arab and Swahili traders rarely exceeded twenty-five and at certain seasons of the year would be reduced to no more than three or four, the rest being engaged on trading expeditions further into the interior.   Tabora owed its importance to the fact it was the natural junction of two trade routes.   One such route continued west-wards to Ujiji on Lake Tanganyika.   The other turned northwards and reached the south bank of the Kagera river in Karagwe, whence caravans made their way from time to time into Buganda.   When during the reign of Said bin Sultan's son, Barghash (1870–1888), Arabs and Swahilis began to build dhows on Lake Victoria, traffic on this northern route was diverted to a considerable extent to Kageyi and Mwanza on the southern shores of that lake, whence goods were conveyed by water to and from Uganda.

There were small trading centres at the internal termini of those trade routes, but they very rarely contained more than half a dozen Arabs and Swahilis. There were also similar trading centres scattered up and down the trade routes, consisting as a rule of one, and never more than two or three, Arab or Swahili traders, who were ready at an extortionate price to supply the deficiencies of the passing trader's caravan, such as cloth, beads, and wire for the purposes of barter and powder and shot for purposes of defence.   The red flag of the Sultans of Zanzibar was generally to be seen flying at these settlements as well as at the head of every caravan winding its way along the narrow tracks through forest, jungle, and high grass.   The caravan leaders and the settlers at these trading posts claimed, and as often as not were permitted to enjoy, a certain measure of extra-territoriality which exempted them from the jurisdiction of the local chiefs, but this extra-territoriality depended upon the goodwill and sufferance of those chiefs, who expected a large payment of *hongo* (tribute or customary payments, but often a form of blackmail) in exchange for the concession.   That goodwill was by no means always forthcoming.   More than one caravan was waylaid and plundered and its leaders killed and a number of the smaller trade centres also met with a similar fate.

Said bin Sultan's son, Barghash, used to appoint a Liwali (or governor) of Tabora, but this official was in reality no more than a headman of an alien community and the mouthpiece of the Sultan of Zanzibar.   At times he had little authority over even his own compatriots and he had none whatever over the local chiefs.   At the end of Said bin Sultan's reign, Fundikira was *Mtemi* (or ruler) of Unyamwezi.   The Arabs alleged that they had made certain "treaties" with him whereby he had exempted them from taxation of every description.   This allegation was disputed by Fundikira's successor, Manwa Sera.   Whether it was true or not, it was in itself an admission that the Arabs made no claim to sovereignty. Thereafter Manwa Sera and the Arabs of Tabora lived in a state of war with one another which continued until 1865 when Manwa Sera was captured and executed. But this did not bring about peace in those regions. In 1871 Mirambo[1] of Urambo, to the west of Tabora, took the field against the Arabs and at the same time proclaimed himself rightful ruler of Unyamwezi. By 1873 he had so effectively closed the road between Tabora and Ujiji that Bargash bin Said, Sultan of Zanzibar, had to send a force of three thousand Baluchi soldiers to Tabora. But there were divided opinions as to what should be the plan of campaign, with the consequence that nothing whatever was achieved. As the cost of these troops proved a considerable drain upon the revenues of Zanzibar they were eventually recalled at the end of 1874. Thus the one and only serious attempt by Bargash to make his power felt in Unyamwezi proved a complete failure. Mirambo maintained his independence and proved a source of trouble to caravans of all nationalities for many years.

Said bin Sultan was, however, able more effectively to assert his authority on the coastal belt of Tanganyika. Between 1841 and 1843 persistent reports reached him that at Kilwa Kisiwani the Sultan was imitating his predecessor of 1776 by trying to enter into treaty relations with the French. Whether or not those rumours had any foundation in fact, the Sultan of Zanzibar put an end to any possibility of any future rapprochement by deporting the Sultan of Kilwa to Muscat. Further up the coast judicious presents to local chiefs resulted in the recognition of his sovereignty without demur. There was, however, one exception to this as a general statement. In Usambara the local ruler, Kimweri, had managed to build up for himself a compact little kingdom containing about half a million inhabitants and extending from the slopes of Kilimanjaro to the sea coast between Vanga and Pangani, where he appears to have succeeded in supplanting the Mazrui of Mombasa in the days when their fortunes declined. In these regions Said bin Sultan and Kimweri came to a tacit compromise, whereby a dual system of government was established.[2] The coast towns in these regions were governed by officials called Diwans, who were appointed by Kimweri, but the appointment had to be confirmed by the Sultan of Zanzibar, "who makes the candidate a present so that he may not lose sight of the Sultan's interests should they run counter to those of the King of Usambara." This sort of condominium lasted until Kimweri's death in about 1870, when his kingdom was temporarily disrupted by the strife and anarchy arising from a dispute as to his successor. Thereafter the Sultans of Zanzibar acquired sole control over this coastal strip.

In 1862 the attention of Said bin Sultan's son and successor, Majid bin Said (1856–1870), had been called to the land-locked harbour which is now known as Dar es Salaam, as a potential outlet for the trade with the central lakes. In 1866 he started to build on the banks of the harbour, to which he gave the name of Dar es Salaam and to which he intended to transfer his capital. Majid, however, died in 1870 before his plans had reached completion and his brother and successor, Barghash bin Said (1870–1888) discontinued the work. The result was that the buildings erected or partially erected in Majid's time fell into disrepair through neglect and the trade which had begun to concentrate there was diverted to other places on the coast. There was a slight temporary revival of

---

[1]See pages 269–270 below for a fuller description.
[2]See also page 250 below.

the fortunes of the place in 1877 when Mr. (afterwards Sir) William Mackinnon and Sir Thomas Fowell Buxton inaugurated work on the construction of a road for wheeled traffic between Dar es Salaam and Lake Nyasa. But the construction of the road proceeded very slowly and the coastal area was found to be infested with fly, which made the use of transport animals impossible. In 1881 work was abandoned after the road had reached its seventy-third mile. After that Dar es Salaam relapsed again into its former state of decay.

By 1887 the Sultans had a number of customs posts scattered up and down the coast between Tungwe, to the south of Cape Delgado, and Mombasa. Practically every inlet, which might be a potential port for the embarkation of goods from the interior, had its customs post. At the smaller of these posts there were only two or three soldiers, acting as customs guards. In the larger places there was a customs-master, who was invariably a "Banyan". He was appointed by the farmer of the customs from the Sultan of Zanzibar and was expected to make periodical inspection of the smaller posts under his control. The larger of the coast towns was governed by an Arab Liwali, who was generally supported by a garrison of half a dozen to one hundred soldiers. The larger garrisons were commanded by an officer known as an Akida. The more important coast towns had Kadhis for the administration of justice. Where there was no Kadhi the Liwali acted as judge and his jurisdiction often extended, by the consent of the parties, to disputes amongst members of the adjacent African tribes. The Liwalis, Akidas, and Kadhis were all of them Arabs appointed by the Sultan of Zanzibar. The majority of the chiefs living in the immediate vicinity of the principal coast towns were ready to acknowledge the sovereignty of the Sultans of Zanzibar. They were in the habit of going each year to Zanzibar to renew their promises of allegiance and to receive in exchange a present from their overlord. Except for these annual visits to Zanzibar the chiefs were, however, left very much to their own devices and Arab officials rarely attempted to interfere in purely African affairs.

At Pangani there was an exception to the general rule that on the coast the sphere of influence of the Sultan of Zanzibar was limited to a small perimeter round a coast town or customs port. In 1852 or 1853 the caravan route from Usambara and the interior was interrupted by a raid of the Zigua. Kimweri of Usambara was apparently unable to cope with the matter and it was eventually agreed that Said bin Sultan of Zanzibar should protect the coastal end of the trade route by establishing garrisons of his own. Accordingly one such post was established about ten miles up the Pangani River at Chogwe and another a further ten miles to the north-west on a hill called Tongwe. When Burton and Speke visited these two posts in 1857 they found each of them consisted of twenty-five Baluchi soldiers under the command of a *jemadar*. That at Tongwe was a crenellated stone blockhouse built in Arab style. The Baluchi garrison remained at Tongwe until the Sultan of Zanzibar ceded to Germany his sovereign rights over this sector of the coast.

After the Mackinnon Road had been pushed some distance into the interior a similar post was established some miles inland at a place on the road which is referred to in British official correspondence as "the bungalow," but it appears to have been of little military value. In 1873 a British naval officer reported that the Baluchi soldiers were afraid to penetrate more than thirty miles into the interior and that their relations with the surrounding Zaramu people "flavour somewhat of armed neutrality". The garrison made no effort whatever to fulfil the Sultan of Zanzibar's treaty obligations by endeavouring to intercept slave caravans proceeding overland from Kilwa Kivinje to Pangani and Tanga.

There was the same story to be told further to the south. In 1868 a band of marauders known as the Mavite appeared in the neighbourhood of Kilwa Kivinje and blocked its trade with the interior. When a force comprising the Sultan's troops and some armed slaves attempted to dislodge the marauders they were ignominiously defeated. More than once members of the same marauding tribe blocked the road between Ujiji and Tabora. When in 1873 Sir Bartle Frere visited Lindi, he learned that the outskirts of that town had more than once been raided with impunity.

In contrast to this, missionaries and explorers were able to testify that a letter under the hand and seal of the Sultan of Zanzibar in the majority of cases assured them of a safe conduct in regions well within the interior. On one occasion in 1860, when that safe conduct was violated and a German explorer named Roscher was murdered in the vicinity of Lake Nyasa, Seyyid Majid bin Said was able to procure the arrest of the offenders and to have them brought to Zanzibar for punishment.[1] In Usukuma Sultan Barghash's name was held in such reverence by certain clans that he was regarded as a deity to be propitiated at the time of seed sowing. Nevertheless such facts as these merely go to show that the Sultans of Zanzibar were treated with respect by the chiefs of the interior and that their requests were not infrequently acceded to with great deference; they do not in any way prove the Sultan's claims to sovereignty or overlordship. It cannot be said that the Sultan's writ really ran beyond the immediate vicinity of his garrisons and his customs posts and the larger trading centres which were occupied by his subjects. It certainly cannot be said that his writ ran along the caravan routes to the central lakes, which were all of them at different dates obstructed by hostile African tribes, who thereby seriously interrupted communications.

From time to time the Sultan or subjects of the Sultan intervened in matters relating to local tribal politics, but such interventions met with varying measures of success. Near the coast, where local chiefs were in the habit of visiting Zanzibar to receive presents in exchange for their homage, the Sultan's influence appears to have been fairly considerable, but such was by no means always the case further inland. Away from Arab and Swahili trading centres and caravan routes local government was carried on by tribal organizations, which were little, if at all, influenced by the activities of alien immigrants from Zanzibar or the adjacent mainland coast.

In one respect practically the whole of Tanganyika was greatly influenced by the arrival of Arab and Swahili subjects of the Sultan of Zanzibar. The slave trade carried on by these persons profoundly affected the lives of nearly all the natives of Tanganyika. In some places it completely disrupted tribal institutions and organizations and reduced districts to a state bordering on anarchy. Even in districts to which the slave trader rarely came it often had a considerable effect on tribal economy and the ordinary ways of tribal life.

When Said bin Sultan took up his residence in Zanzibar, he was brought into closer contact than hitherto with a number of European powers, with whom he and his sons concluded a series of treaties. The first of these treaties was with the United States of America in 1833. This was followed by treaties with Great

---

[1] See pages 42–43 below.

Britain (1839), France (1844) and the Hanseatic League (1859). These last three treaties contained clauses which reserved to the Sultans of Zanzibar the monopoly of all trade in ivory and gum copal between Mtangata and Kilwa Kisiwani. Though the earlier treaty with the United States contained no such clause, in deference to Said bin Sultan's expressed wishes no Americans attempted to indulge in trade between these two points. But, as already seen, Indians were allowed to trade in this sector of the coast and some of them acted more or less openly as agents for European trading firms in Zanzibar. The restrictions of the Sultan were, however, confined solely to traders. Europeans following callings other than that of commerce were not refused admission to the continent.

EXPLORATION OF THE INTERIOR

Though there are no early written records of journeys into the hinterland of Tanganyika, there can be little doubt that communication between the East African coast and the central African lakes began several centuries before the Christian era. In the very early days of that era a Greek merchant named Diogenes informed a Syrian geographer named Marinus of Tyre that on his return from a voyage to India he landed on the East African coast at a place which he called Rhaptum and which may be identifiable with Pangani. He alleged that he travelled thence "inland for a twenty-five days' journey, and arrived in the vicinity of the two great lakes and the snowy range of mountains whence the Nile draws its twin sources." Marinus of Tyre incorporated this information in a geographical treatise, which is no longer extant. In 150 A.D. however, Ptolemy quoted this statement *in extenso* in another geographical treatise, which has survived. One doubts if Diogenes approached anywhere close to Lake Tanganyika or any other of the central lakes. It would most certainly have taken more than twenty-five days for him to have arrived anywhere in their vicinity. He may have journeyed inland, but his information as to the mountains and lakes must have been derived from conversation with traders who had actually made the journey to those regions.

Except for the journey which Gaspar Bocarro took in 1616 from Tete on the banks of the Zambezi to Kilwa Kisiwani, we hear nothing of attempts by the Portuguese to penetrate into the interior, though they knew of the central African lakes from the works of Ptolemy and Christian and other geographers, and possibly also from traders who had actually visited them.

Medieval Arab geographers wrote a fair amount about the East African coast, but their knowledge of the interior was very limited. It was not until the middle of the nineteenth century that Arab traders appear to have ventured far inland. In about 1850 an Arab named Said bin Habib bin Salim Lafifi left Zanzibar and did not return again to that island for more than sixteen years. During that time he thrice visited Loanda on the west coast of Africa, being in all probability the first traveller to cross the continent at so high a latitude.

Some five years before Said bin Habib set out on his travels a French naval officer named Maizan tried to anticipate his achievement, but his journey soon ended in disaster. Disregarding all advice, he set out from Bagamoyo at the wrong season of the year, having declined the guides and the military escort which were supplied to him and taking with him equipment in heavily laden boxes, which were an obvious temptation to any predatory tribes which he might encounter. He had penetrated a bare fifty miles inland when he was murdered near the Mafisi ferry to the south of the present Ruvu station on the Central Railway.

Said Sultan.

Barghash.

Majid.

Kirk.

Krapf.

Burton.

Speke.

Grant.

Livingstone.

Stanley.

Livingstone's Servants.

Susi.

Chumah.

Von Der Decken.

Cameron.

Elton.

Thomson.

....
....

THE "SLUG" MAP, 1856

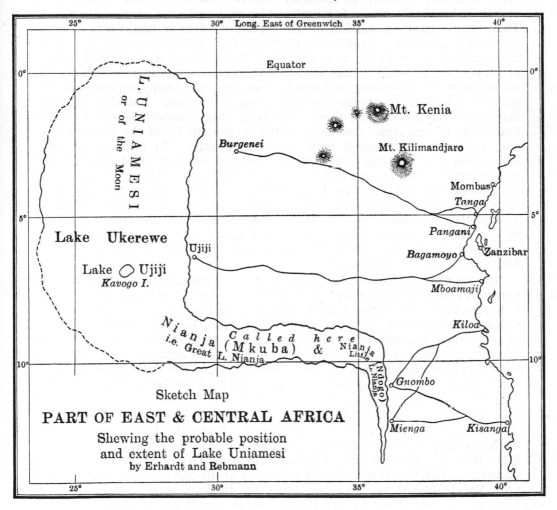

The next Europeans to attempt to explore the interior of what is now Tanganyika were two Germans in the service of the Church Missionary Society, who were in search of a field for their evangelical labours. In 1848, setting out from Rabai, near Mombasa, Johann Rebmann reached the Chagga country and on May 11 in that year set eyes on Kilimanjaro. In July of the same year his colleague, Johann Ludwig Krapf, set out from Mombasa and, travelling overland, reached Usambara, where he met with a friendly reception from the paramount chief, Kimweri. It might be said that both of these Missionaries were almost entirely lacking in the physical aptitudes which go to make the successful explorer. They were even more lacking in the necessary scientific equipment. Krapf carried a gun, which was constantly meeting with extraordinary accidents. His riding animals generally ran away with him. In fact the most remarkable article of his equipment would appear to have been his umbrella, under which he and his men slept in wet weather, and which, when opened suddenly, on one occasion drove off a lion and on another occasion a band of robbers. But whatever their deficiences may have been, these were more than counterbalanced by their knowledge of languages, their sympathetic understanding of the local people, and above all their dogged pertinacity and courage. In addition to their discoveries, they obtained circumstantial information from Arab and Swahili traders regarding the existence of large lakes in the heart of Africa, which in 1855 their compatriot and colleague, James Erhardt, published in a map, which came to be known as the "Slug map" from the shape of the single lake delineated on it. Though their discoveries and their information were derided and even discredited by a number of armchair geographers in England, they were deemed to be sufficiently reliable to give the impetus to the exploratory expeditions which followed very shortly afterwards.

In June, 1857, Richard Burton and John Hanning Speke set out from Bagamoyo to try to discover the lakes of which these two missionaries had heard so much. In February, 1858, they reached Lake Tanganyika. In June that year they were back at Kaze in Unyanyembe, in the vicinity of the modern Tabora. Burton, who was ill at the time, was induced to allow Speke to go in search of a more northerly lake, the existence of which they had learned from an Arab trader. Marching north, Speke reached a creek, and on August 3, 1858, he saw this inlet open northwards into the waters of a great lake, which extended to the horizon and which he named Victoria Nyanza (Lake Victoria). He felt no doubt in his own mind that this lake was the source of the Nile, but Burton refused to accept his theories.

Speke, however, obtained the support of Sir Roderick Murchison, President of the Royal Geographical Society, under whose direction a new expedition was fitted out. Accompanied now by James Augustus Grant, Speke set out from Zanzibar in October, 1860. Kaze was reached at the beginning of the following year, but it was not until October, 1861, that the two explorers reached Lake Victoria. Following the western shores, they eventually reached Karagwe. On January 16, 1862, Speke crossed the Kagera River and entered the Kingdom of Buganda, where on July 28 he stood above the falls where the Nile issues from Lake Victoria. After being detained some time at the courts of the native rulers of Buganda and Bunyoro, Speke and Grant arrived on February 15, 1863, at Gondokoro, whence they made their way down the Nile to Cairo.

Between the dates of these two expeditions other explorers had been in the field to the south of the route which had been taken. When Burton and Speke had returned to the coast in 1859, they found a native of Hamburg, named Albrecht

Roscher, about to set out into the interior. A thesis on the subject of Ptolemy and the Central African trade routes had not only earned him a doctorate, but had also attracted the attention of Ludwig I, the exiled King of Bavaria, who commissioned him to solve the mystery of the "inland seas." He proceeded overland southwards from Kunduchi. On February 10, 1859, he reached Mzizima on the site of the modern town of Dar es Salaam. Three days later he crossed the harbour mouth and continued his journey southwards to the Rufiji. In August, 1859, he joined an Arab caravan at Kilwa Kivinje which was proceeding to Lake Nyasa. In October he reached the eastern shore of the lake. Early in 1860 he decided to make his way northwards, accompanied by only two servants and two porters. He had only been three days out on this journey when he was murdered, for no other reason apparently than greed for his very scanty baggage.

Roscher had in fact been anticipated in his discovery of Lake Nyasa by David Livingstone, who had been appointed in 1858 "Her Majesty's Consul at Quilimane for the eastern coast and independent districts in the interior, and commander of an expedition for exploring Eastern and Central Africa." In accordance with his instructions he proceeded up the Zambezi and, travelling northwards from Tete, reached Lake Nyasa in September, 1859, a few weeks before Roscher. Two years before at the Senate House at Cambridge he had made his famous appeal to the members of that university to help in the evangelization of Africa. In response to that appeal the Universities Mission to Central Africa had come into being. In the early days of 1861 the first contingent of missionaries reached Cape Town, and Livingstone undertook to lead them to the region of Lake Nyasa. The steamer *Pioneer* was available for the purpose and on Livingstone's advice it was decided to make the approach to the proposed mission field up the Ruvuma River, as the vessel was of too deep a draught to negotiate the Shire. But after the vessel had proceeded some thirty miles up the Ruvuma difficulties of navigation showed that the project was impracticable and the missionary party proceeded to the Zambezi instead.

In the latter part of 1862 Livingstone returned to the Ruvuma with a new steamer, the *Lady Nyassa*. On this occasion he managed to get about one hundred and fifty miles up the river, but then found further progress barred by rocks[1]. He therefore returned once more to the Zambezi.

In the meantime Baron Carl Claus von der Decken, an officer in the Hanoverian army, had reached Zanzibar with the intention of joining Roscher. A few days before his arrival Roscher's servant had reached Zanzibar with news of his master's murder. Von der Decken decided to proceed without delay to the scene of the crime in the hope of recovering the dead man's journal and notes. He accordingly proceeded to Kilwa Kivinje to organize his expedition, but owing to the obstruction of the local Arabs he was unable to set out until November, 1860. He met with further difficulties on his way due to the desertion of many of his porters, the insubordinate conduct of his Baluchi escort and the hostile attitude of the local tribes. He reached Mesuli, about 160 miles south-west of Kilwa Kivinje, and then decided to turn back. He reached Zanzibar in the early days of 1861. In October of that year he set out again with Dr. Otto Kersten from Mombasa to explore Kilimanjaro, which he ascended to a height of 14,000 feet. He had intended to proceed thence to Lake Victoria but, finding the Masai opposed his advance, he returned to Zanzibar.

[1] See page 220 for a fuller description.

In 1865 Livingstone was once more in East Africa, having been commissioned by the Royal Geographical Society to make another attack on the Central Lakes. On April 6, 1866, he landed at Mikindani and proceeded to Lake Nyasa, where he arrived in the following August. He pushed on thence into what is now Northern Rhodesia and finally reached the southern end of Lake Tanganyika in March, 1867. Thence he proceeded westwards to Lake Mweru and the Lualaba River. Turning southwards he discovered Lake Bangweulu[1]. In all these journeyings he had suffered constantly from fever and other ailments, which were aggravated by the desertion of a porter with the load containing his medicine chest. From Lake Bangweulu he turned northwards again and, proceeding up the west coast of Lake Tanganyika, reached Ujiji on March, 14, 1869, "a ruckle of bones".

Before he set out on his expedition, Livingstone had arranged for the establishment of a kind of supply depot at Ujiji and had arranged for an Indian trader at Zanzibar to send up stocks of provisions to await him there. On arrival at Ujiji he found that most of the goods which he had ordered had been stolen and others had been dumped 250 miles away at Tabora. He had been without news from Europe or Zanzibar for over three years, but no letters or papers were waiting for him at Ujiji and communication between that place and Tabora was blocked owing to a raid by the Angoni. So after three months' rest Livingstone left Ujiji, crossed Lake Tanganyika and proceeded to explore the Manyema country and the upper reaches of the River Congo. Once again he suffered from frequent bouts of illness. On October 13, 1871, he once more returned to Ujiji, a weary and very sick man.

During these five years of wandering no news of Livingstone had reached Europe and great anxiety was felt regarding his fate. At one time, thanks to a false story spread by some porters who had deserted him, the report got abroad that he had been murdered. In 1870 James Gordon Bennett of the *New York Herald* commissioned Henry Morton Stanley "to find Livingstone". Stanley reached Zanzibar at the beginning of 1871, set out for the interior on March 21 and on November 10 reached Ujiji, four weeks after Livingstone's return to that place, bringing him much needed supplies. With Stanley, Livingstone explored the north end of Lake Tanganyika. After that he accompanied Stanley back to Tabora, where they arrived on February 18, 1872. Stanley tried to persuade Livingstone to return to Europe, but the latter was bent on finishing his task of delimitation of the watersheds of the Nile and Congo. He hoped that the task would take him little more than six months. Stanley therefore left a large quantity of supplies with him and agreed to send up more from Zanzibar, as well as fifty porters.

Several months elapsed before the promised reinforcement of porters reached Livingstone at Tabora. At length, on August 15, 1872, he set out for Lake Bangweulu, proceeding to the east of Lake Tanganyika. His old enemy, dysentery, attacked him once again. He eventually became so ill that he had to be carried in a roughly made litter. On April 17, 1873, at Chitambo's village near the south shore of Lake Bangweulu, he wrote for the last time in his diary that he was "knocked up quite." Early on the morning of May 1 he was found kneeling beside his bed, dead. His faithful servants preserved their master's

---

[1] Livingstone called it Bangweolo.

body as best they could. Then, wrapping it carefully up, they carried it, together with all his papers and instruments, from the heart of Africa to Bagamoyo on the coast, whence it was taken to Zanzibar and finally to its last resting place in Westminster Abbey. James Chuma and Abdulla Susi, the two servants of the dead man, who took chief charge of their precious burden, were later to act as guides to more than one party belonging to the Universities Mission to Central Africa in their journeys.

As Sir Reginald Coupland has said, the great period of East African exploration came to an end on the death of Livingstone. In the brief period of a quarter of a century the mystery of the vast inland sea had been solved and a system of great lakes had been revealed, and the snow-capped peaks of Kilimanjaro and Kenya had been discovered. There were still a great many details to be filled in, but the broad outlines had been traced.

In 1873 a naval officer, Lovett Cameron, was sent out by the Royal Geographical Society to the relief of Livingstone. He followed the well trodden trade route from the coast to Tabora, where he met Livingstone's servants carrying their master's body down to the coast. Cameron decided to push on to Lake Tanganyika, which he mapped accurately for the first time. Thence he made his way across Africa to the west coast.

In 1879 Stanley was once more back in East Africa, under the aegis of the proprietors of the *New York Herald* and the *Daily Telegraph*. Making his way *via* Mpwapwa to the southern shores of Lake Victoria, which he circumnavigated, he not only ascertained the approximate area and shape of the lake, but he was also able to define with a fair measure of accuracy its principal islands and archipelagoes. After spending some time at the court of Mutesa, Kabaka of Buganda, he made his way to Lake Edward, whence, turning southwards through Kasagare and Urambo, he finally proceeded westwards and for the second time arrived at Ujiji. Thence, crossing Lake Tanganyika, he eventually reached the mouth of the River Congo.

James Elton, who had been an officer in the Indian Army, was in 1873 appointed British Vice-Consul at Zanzibar. Soon after his arrival he was despatched from Zanzibar to the mainland to inquire into the extent of slave holding by British Indian subjects and to take the necessary steps for the emancipation of all slaves whom he found in their possession. For this purpose he travelled overland from Dar es Salaam to Kilwa Kivinje, gathering much useful information about the economic potentialities of the districts through which he travelled. In 1875 he was made British Consul at Mozambique. In 1877 he set out to track the slave trade to its source. He made his way to the northern end of Lake Nyasa, whence he went to Tukuyu. Proceeding to the east of Rungwe mountain on to what is now known as the Elton Plateau, he began to descend into the plains at the headwaters of the Great Ruaha river, where he found his progress delayed by inter-tribal warfare. Eventually he was able to push on to the north and finally reached Usoke about fifty miles south-south-west of Dodoma. Here he succumbed to dysentery. His European companions buried him a few miles from the spot where he had died, at the foot of a large baobab tree in the Ugogo country. For more than sixty years afterwards his grave was carefully tended by the local inhabitants. Finally, in November, 1938, a more permanent memorial in stone was erected over his mortal remains.

Much of the plotting of the details of the map of Tanganyika was undertaken at this date by the members of various missionary societies, who performed the task, not as explorers, but as evangelists in search of fields for the propagation of Christianity.   In 1875 a party of missionaries belonging to the Universities Mission to Central Africa set out under the leadership of Bishop Edward Steere, with Livingstone's servant, Chuma, in charge of the porters.   The Bishop reached Mwembe, four days' journey from Lake Nyasa, whence he returned to the coast. Next year he led another expedition from Lindi to Masasi, where he established a mission station.

When Stanley was in Buganda in 1875 he sent to the *Daily Telegraph* an appeal for missionaries to be sent out to that country.   During the course of the next few years various missionary societies in Europe sent out bands of missionaries to work in the interior of Africa.   Most of these parties made use of the recognized trade route from Bagamoyo to Tabora, but some of them diverted from the well beaten track in search of fresh fields for their labours.   Thus Shergold Smith, a former naval officer who led the first party sent out by the Church Missionary Society, explored the Wami and Kingani Rivers in 1876 in the hope of being able to solve the problems of transport by means of water carriage.   Later he proceeded to Lake Victoria, where he did some useful charting of its southern regions including the southern inlet known as Smith Sound.   Alexander Mackay of the same society, who had accompanied Smith in his exploration of the Wami and Kingani Rivers, also did much useful charting of Lake Victoria at a later date. To him must be attributed the first discovery of the inlet to that lake which is now known as the Emin Pasha Gulf.

A party of missionaries of the London Missionary Society under the leadership of John Boden Thomson reached Ujiji in 1878.   With it was Edward Coode Hore, a former officer of the Peninsular and Oriental line, who was responsible for the launching of the first steamer on Lake Tanganyika and whose subsequent voyages added materially to previous knowledge of that lake.

Mention must also be made of Antoine Horner of the Fathers of the Holy Ghost, who arrived in Zanzibar in 1863 and who within a few months was across on the mainland in search of pastures new.   An exploratory journey took him to the Uluguru Mountains, where he established a station at Mhonda.   He also on other occasions explored much of Ukami, Ukaguru and Uzigua.

Further to the north, C. A. Alington of the Universities Mission had already explored the possibility of establishing a mission station in the Usambara country. He had visited Kimweri, the paramount chief, in 1867 and found him well disposed.   In the following year he returned and established a station at Magila. J. P. Farler, who succeeded to the charge of the station in 1875, expanded the work and added considerably to previous knowledge of the Usambara country.

At a somewhat later date much of the *terra incognita* between the northern end of Lake Nyasa and the southern end of Lake Tanganyika was explored by the members of two German missionary societies.   Both parties arrived in 1891. One comprised members of the Berlin Missionary Society led by Alexander Merensky.   The other consisted of four Moravians—Theopile Richard, Theodor Meyer, George Martin (who died in September, 1891) and Johannes Haefner.

As regards other explorers, mention should be made of William Beardall, who was originally lay superintendent at the U.M.C.A. station when it was first established at Masasi.   In 1877 he took charge of the construction of the

Mackinnon Road,[1] which was intended to open up effective communication for wheeled traffic from Dar es Salaam to Lake Nyasa and by that means to help to eradicate the slave trade through the development of legitimate forms of commerce. A year previously Beardall had explored the Rufiji River on the instructions of the Sultan of Zanzibar with a view to examining its potentialities as a means of communication with the interior.

In 1879 Joseph Thomson set out on the first of several explorations into the heart of Africa. On this occasion he was second in command of an expedition which was organized by the Royal Geographical Society under the leadership of Keith Johnston to explore the hitherto unvisited region between Dar es Salaam and Lake Nyasa in the hope of discovering a better line of communication than that hitherto connecting the lake with the coast. After a preliminary excursion into the Usambara country the expedition set out from Dar es Salaam, with Chuma as headman, in a south-westerly direction towards the upper reaches of the Rufiji. Shortly after leaving that river and striking out in a westerly direction, Keith Johnston died. Thomson then took charge of the expedition and, crossing the Mahenge plateau, eventually reached the northern end of Lake Nyasa. Thence he made his way across to the southern end of Lake Tanganyika. Proceeding along its western shore with a small party, he reached the Lukuga outlet from the lake, whence he crossed to Ujiji. After an exploratory journey thence into the Congo, he returned by water from the Lukuga outlet to the southern end of Lake Tanganyika. Picking up his main body of porters there, he proceeded to Tabora and thence to Bagamoyo.

In 1881 Thomson was commissioned by the Sultan of Zanzibar "to determine and report upon the nature, extent and economic value" of some coal formations which had been reported as existing in the upper reaches of the Ruvuma. Once again with Chuma as headman, he set out from Mikindani on July 17, 1881. The expedition reached a point in the Makua country about 270 miles from the mouth of the Ruvuma, but Thomson was unable to discover anything more than bituminous shale, though coal fields have since been discovered up that river.

In 1883 Thomson was back in East Africa, having been commissioned by the Royal Geographical Society to discover a more direct route to Lake Victoria than that by Tabora. Setting out from Mombasa, he made for the Chagga country. Though he experienced some trouble with Mandara, the ruler of that land, he was able to visit the eastern, southern and western slopes of the Kilimanjaro *massif*. Thereafter, proceeding to the east and north of Kilimanjaro, he headed north for Dagoretti in what is now Kenya and so by Lakes Naivasha and Baringo to the shores of Lake Victoria.

Only the barest outline has been given here of the routes covered by Thomson during his travels in what is now Tanganyika and nothing has been said of the numerous trials and difficulties which he encountered. He was the last, and at the same time one of the most successful, of the great geographical pioneers in East Africa. Until the days of mechanical propulsion by land and air few people had visited so many parts of East Africa as he had.

In parts of the route of the early stages of his expedition to Lake Victoria Thomson had been preceded by Dr. G. A. Fischer, who had visited the Chagga country and Masailand in 1882. Fischer was a German physician who had set up in practice in Zanzibar but whose real bent was geographical and zoological exploration. In 1885 he was commissioned by the brother of Dr. Wilhelm Junker to rescue the latter, who had been exploring Central Africa at the time of the Mahdi's rebellion in the Sudan and who was taking refuge with Emin Pasha in the Equatorial Province. Setting out from Pangani, he reached Kageyi at the southern end of Lake Victoria at the end of 1885, but was warned by the Christian missionaries in Buganda that it would be dangerous for him to attempt to pass through Uganda owing to the hostility of Mwanga, Kabaka of Buganda. He therefore decided to make his way round the east side of Lake Victoria to Kavirondo and to try to reach Junker by way of Mount Elgon. On the journey round the lake Fischer and his caravan suffered the greatest possible hardships owing to the difficulty of procuring food. He therefore had to abandon his project and return to the coast. On the way he suffered still further hardships, which led to his premature death shortly after the journey's end. Fischer was anything but a prolific writer, which is all the more to be regretted as his few published works show him to have been a careful observer and an industrious collector.

In 1884 Henry Hamilton Johnston—better known in later years as Sir Harry Johnston—was sent by the British Association and the Royal Geographical Society to make an intensive study of the flora and fauna of Kilimanjaro. He spent five months at three different spots on the side of the mountain, collecting specimens and making notes. He also obtained from the local chief Mandara a written conveyance of a piece of land. Later on he obtained other conveyances in the region of Taveta. On his return he urged the British Foreign Office to proclaim a protectorate over the Chagga country. For reasons which it would be too long to set out here Sir John Kirk, the British Consul-General, advised against the recommendation and his advice was adopted.

As this very brief account of Johnston's Kilimanjaro expedition indicates, by 1884 the "Scramble for Africa" had begun. During that scramble a number of persons were in the field collecting documents from local chiefs who thereby purported to place themselves under German protection. In so far as Tanganyika was concerned, though political agents, and later administrative officers, were to travel far and wide in the territory and into places where hitherto no other European had penetrated, the period of geographical exploration purely and solely for the purpose of exploration may be said to have ended.

THE GERMAN OCCUPATION

Though German merchants had established business houses in Zanzibar in the 1840's and German explorers in the persons of Roscher and von der Decken had begun to explore East Africa as early as 1859, governments in Germany had shown no interest whatever in acquiring a foothold in those regions. So lacking indeed was their interest that when in 1870 the German Consul at Zanzibar informed his home government that Seyyid Barghash, Sultan of Zanzibar, asked to be placed under German protection, no answer was returned. In those days the German Empire had only just come into being and its makers were far too pre-occupied with affairs in Europe to have any thought for any political venture so far afield as East Africa; Bismarck, in particular, for a long time poured cold water on any schemes for German expansion outside Europe.

Nonetheless there was a certain amount of public opinion in Germany which was eager to acquire territorial interests overseas. Prominent amongst those concerned was Otto Kersten, von der Decken's travelling companion. Advocates

Tippoo Tib.

Bushiri.

of the policy of colonial expansion gradually increased in numbers. In 1876 their movement received a fresh impetus when Leopold II of the Belgians summoned to Brussels a conference of geographical experts, which led to the foundation of the International Association for the Exploration and Civilization of Africa, having for its object the acquisition of the Congo basin. The Association's first line of approach to its objective was from the east. In 1877 an expedition commanded by a Belgian, Captain Crespel, arrived in Zanzibar. Crespel died within six weeks of the expedition's arrival; the ranks of the European officers were further thinned by more deaths and the return to the coast of others on account of illness or for other causes. The expedition encountered many other trials and setbacks and it was not until August, 1879, that the sole surviving European, Lieutenant Cambier, reached Lake Tanganyika and established a post on its shores at Karema. A second expedition set out in 1879. This had amongst other equipment four Indian elephants intended for transport purposes. Three of these animals died at an early stage of the journey and the fourth died very shortly after it reached Karema. Two other expeditions set out in 1880 and 1882 respectively. A fifth was recalled in 1884 before it had started inland, as by that date Leopold II had decided that the best line of approach was from the west coast. In 1885 the Association's posts at Karema and Tabora were given up and handed over to the White Fathers' Mission. The achievements of these Belgian expeditions were never at any time of any great value to the Association, but they were enough to arouse in German advocates of colonial expansion an increasing fear that Germany might be forestalled in acquiring commercial and territorial interests outside Europe.

In 1873 a German Society for the Exploration of Equatorial Africa had been founded. This was followed in 1876 by the foundation of the German African Society as a national branch of Leopold II's International Association. In 1880 both organizations combined to form the German African Society of Berlin, which in that year sent out Count von Schoeler in charge of an expedition to prepare for the occupation of the territory between Mpwapwa and Karema. In 1881 the Society sent out three more persons to assist Schoeler in establishing a station near Tabora. A site was selected at Kakoma but, as it proved unhealthy, members of the expedition moved on to the shores of Lake Tanganyika and crossed over into the Congo. The party suffered a number of casualties from death and other causes and with the return in 1884 of these two parties to Europe this first attempt at German settlement in East Africa came to an end.

The year 1884 saw the foundation of the German Colonization Society. It was a year in which schemes for the colonization of East Africa were very much in the air. Public opinion in Germany was becoming more and more insistent that their country should partake in these schemes before it was too late. It was with this knowledge of what might be in the wind that Henry Hamilton Johnston set out under the aegis of the Royal Geographical Society to make a study of the flora and fauna on the slopes of Kilimanjaro. He arrived at Moshi in the middle of 1884 and entered into friendly relations with Mandara, the paramount chief of "Chagga." He obtained from that chief a conveyance of a piece of land near Moshi and later made similar purchases of two other pieces of land on the slopes of Kilimanjaro and of another at Taveta just over the present Tanganyika-Kenya boundary. At Kitimbiri, about two miles north-east of Mandara's capital at Moshi, he established a settlement, which at a later date he transferred to the land acquired by him at Taveta. On July

5

10, 1884, he wrote to the Foreign Office to say that Mandara was anxious for British protection and had asked for a Union Jack. This proposal was referred by the Foreign Office to Sir John Kirk at Zanzibar, who had never been informed by Johnston of the latter's activities. Though Kirk was alive to the fact that "some other Power, less scrupulous, may step in and forestall us," he was unable to see how "Chagga" could be administered as a British protectorate without possession of a port on the coast, either at Mombasa or Tanga. He also felt that any attempt at occupation of Chagga would alter British relations with the Sultan of Zanzibar and would be "the signal for a general scramble and there would be little left of Zanzibar." This opinion was eventually allowed to prevail at the Foreign Office.

The correspondence between Kirk and the Foreign Office was conducted by both sides in complete ignorance of what was actually happening in the regions recently visited by Johnston, who had returned to England at the end of the year 1884. In September, 1884, Carl Peters, one of the founders of the German Colonization Society, accompanied by Count Otto Pfeil, Dr. Carl Juhlke, and August Otto set out from Trieste, disguised as mechanics, under false names and with third-class tickets. They arrived at Zanzibar on November 4, where they were met by a telegram from Bismarck warning them not to expect any protection in their enterprise from the German Government. Nevertheless, six days later they crossed over to Sadani. On December 17, 1884, Peters and Juhlke were back in Zanzibar. Otto had died in Usagara. Pfeil had remained in that country. Peters had arrived back with a bundle of "contracts" concluded with chiefs in Usagara, Uzeguha (Uzigua) and Ukami. Each of these purported to amount to a cession of territory "for all time" to Peters, on behalf of the German Society for Colonization, who "undertook to give special attention" to the grantors "when colonising" those territories. In one treaty with "Sultana Mbumi, Lady of the province of Mukondokwa in Usagara", Peters deemed it wise to insert a clause that the lady "declared that she was not and never had been dependent in any way on the Sultan of Zanzibar." Another signed by Manganga, Sultan of Msovero, contained a similar declaration. In each case it amounted to a tacit admission on the part of Peters that at the very least the Sultan of Zanzibar had a claim of some sort to suzerainty in the districts concerned. An even more astonishing document was a declaration signed on November 26, 1884, wherein it was stated that a certain Salim bin Hamed, who for four years had been the First Minister plenipotentiary of the Sultan of Zanzibar in Nguru, had declared, in the presence of legal witnesses, that the Sultan of Zanzibar did not possess suzerainty or protectorate on the continent of Zanzibar, and especially not in Nguru or Usagara; that Dr. Peters was his friend, and that the Governor promised to support the endeavours of the German Colonization Society as much as he could. The right to the rank and post, which Peters ascribed to Salim bin Hamed, is quite unknown and it goes without saying that Salim bin Hamed had no authority whatever to make any such declaration which could be binding on the Sultan of Zanzibar.

When Peters brought his treaties back to Germany, there was a complete change in Bismarck's attitude towards German schemes of colonization. In part this was no doubt induced by the representations of certain north German firms which had East African interests and which had the support of the very influential Hamburg Senate, to the effect that they were in danger of being deprived of their business in East Africa. Doubtless also he found it increasingly hard to run counter to ever growing public opinion as voiced by the

German Colonization Society. It would also appear that this change was induced by considerations affecting the European political scene. In Bismarck's eyes colonies had a nuisance value, which might make them useful pawns on the international chessboard. The upshot was that on February 27, 1885, the German Emperor issued to the German Colonization Society a Charter of Protection (*Schutzbrief*) declaring that he had placed the territories under his suzerainty and protection and granted to the society the management thereof subject to the superintendence of, and further regulations by, the German Government.

The contents of this Charter of Protection were communicated to Seyyid Barghash, Sultan of Zanzibar, who on April 25, 1885, addressed the following telegram to the German Emperor:—

"We have received from Consul-General Rohlf a copy of your Majesty's proclamation of the 27th February, according to which the countries Usagara, Nguru and Ukami, of which it is said that they lie west of our possessions, are placed under your protection and German rule. We protest against this, because these territories belong to us and we have military stations there, and the chiefs who offer to surrender rights of sovereignty to the agents of the Company are not empowered to do so; these places have belonged to us since the time of our fathers."

Whilst the Sultan had had for six years past a garrison of regular troops at Mamboya, near Mpwapwa, as well as two other garrisons of irregular troops at places in the near vicinity, he had no such military posts in Usambara or Uchagga. On May 1, General Lloyd Mathews was despatched with 180 men to effect a military occupation of those regions. On June 18 he reached Moshi, where he hoisted the Sultan's flag with the consent of Mandara, the paramount chief. Mandara and twenty-four other chiefs from Arusha, Pare, and Taveta signed an acknowledgment that they were the subjects of the Sultan of Zanzibar and in recognition thereof they had hoisted his flags in the towns of their country. Thereafter Mathews brought some of Mandara's elders and other chiefs with him to Zanzibar to confirm their acknowledgment of the Sultan's suzerainty.

In the meantime Peters' companion, Juhlke, who had remained on the mainland after Peters' departure, had decided to get busy. After Mathews' departure from Kilimanjaro, he set out for the same regions. On May 16 he had concluded a treaty with a chief in the Bondei country adjoining Tongwe, "the last possession of the Sultan of Zanzibar." Thence, concluding treaties on his way, he entered the south-eastern portions of Usambara. After that he made for Taveta, where he obtained another treaty on June 13. Six days later he was in Uchagga, where he concluded more treaties. He finally returned to the southern portion of Bondei, having concluded eight treaties in all in the course of his peregrinations.

Mandara of Uchagga, a party to one of these treaties, was alleged by Juhlke to have told him that he had been bribed by Mathews to hoist the Sultan's flag. Mandara subsequently denied this. Juhlke's assertion that he had said, "I love the Germans above other people and in particular above Englishmen and Arabs", if true, shows the small value which could be accorded to any document to which Mandara was a party. Juhlke's further statement that he was ready to hoist the German flag, if Juhlke would bring him a better flagstaff than Mathews had set up, shows that Mandara had little or no notion of what he had given away. Archdeacon Farler of the U.M.C.A., who had been in Usambara for ten years, said that the so-called "Sultans" who had concluded treaties with Juhlke were persons of no consequence. One was not even a village headman. Another was head of a village of only 30 huts, which was directly under the Sultan's fort at Tongwe and was peopled only by members of his own family and slaves. A third was a brother of the two real chiefs, who had both openly acknowledged the Sultan's suzerainty and had never authorized their brother to conclude a treaty on their behalf. But this was one of those occasions when Bismarck was ready to recognize that scraps of paper might be of some value.

On August 7, 1885, five German warships commanded by Commodore Paschen dropped anchor off Zanzibar. Four days later the Commodore submitted to Seyyid Barghash a formal document in which he declared his imperial master's desire to establish friendly relations with the Sultan and to negotiate certain treaties with him, but that negotiations could not begin unless and until he received "the clear and unevasive declaration of Your Highness that You withdraw your protest against the treaties made with the free and legal Sultans of the lands of Usagara, Nguru, Useguha and Ukami . . . and recall your troops and agents from those regions." As this demand was followed by the clearing of the decks of the German warships for action, Barghash could not choose but hear. Eventually he submitted "in consequence of the demand which comes to us from His Majesty the Emperor of Germany as an Ultimatum and as indispensable to the commencement of friendly negotiations."

The result of the Sultan's submission was that Germany acquired certain territories in the hinterland of the continent, but these lacked a suitable port, because the Germans were forced to admit that the coastal strip formed part of the Sultan's dominions. The obtaining of such an outlet formed part of the further negotiations which were now to be carried on, under the cover of the guns of the German squadron, by Admiral Knorr, who had arrived on August 19 to take over from Commodore Paschen. Once again Barghash could not choose but hear. The Germans said they wanted Dar es Salaam and the Sultan had perforce to agree, stipulating only that it should not be fortified or garrisoned by German troops.

Before this ultimatum had been issued to Seyyid Barghash, negotiations had been going on between Great Britain, France and Germany, "with a view to the appointment of a joint commission for the purpose of enquiring into the claims of the Sultan of Zanzibar to sovereignty over certain territories in East Africa, and of ascertaining their precise limits." An agreement on the subject was eventually reached and a Delimitation Commission was appointed consisting of three representatives, from Great Britain, France and Germany respectively. The British representative was Colonel H. H. (afterwards Field Marshal Earl) Kitchener. The Sultan of Zanzibar was not represented on the Commission and, despite Kitchener's dissentient voice, was not allowed to send General Lloyd Mathews to present his case to the Commissioners.

In January, 1886, the Commission began its work at Tungi just to the south of Cape Delgado and, visiting on their way Mikindani, Lindi, Kilwa Kivinje, and Kikunya, eventually reached Kisiju about forty miles to the south of Dar es Salaam. At each place they took evidence which was embodied in a *procès-verbal*. From Kisiju they returned to Zanzibar.

In the meantime the German Colonization Society had become merged in the German East Africa Company, which had been formed to take over the administration of the territories comprised in the treaties of Peters and his colleagues. In addition to this the Company had set about making fresh acquisitions. Count Pfeil, who had remained in Usagara after the departure of Peters, had left that country and gone south to the upper reaches of the Rufiji. He then turned east and proceeded to the coast. In June, 1885, he again left Usagara and marched through Uhehe, Ubena, and Mahenge. By the end of the year he and his European companions had secured a whole collection of treaties in most of the interior westwards to Lake Nyasa and southwards to the Ruvuma River. In August, 1885, Lieutenant Schmidt and a merchant named Sohnge got to work nearer the coast and concluded twenty-one treaties. Seven of these were made between Usagara and Bagamoyo and the remainder in Uzaramo and the country between Ukami and the Rufiji. In the course of their operations they fell foul of the natives of Usagara. Schmidt was wounded and lay for two days in the bush, where he was found by C.M.S. missionaries from Mamboya and brought by them down to the coast. Later, some of the Sultan's regular troops, who were still occupying the post at Mamboya pending demarcation of the frontier, went to the scene and punished Schmidt's assailants.

In February, 1886, the Delimitation Commission recommenced its inquiries on the mainland. Starting at Sadani, they visited Pangani, Tanga and Vanga and thence proceeded northwards to Mombasa. Kitchener later reported that in these regions "the Sultan's government was found everywhere firmly established, and the Commission was unable to find any contrary tendency, although it visited some people secretly in their houses so that they might be perfectly free to make any declaration without fear of the consequences. . . . There are, I believe, very few coastlines in the world where there are so many governors, garrisoned places, and customs houses as are found on the Zanzibar coastline examined by the Commission up to the present." As his ship proceeded up the coast, he was able to see that "at small villages and sometimes at single houses red Sultan's flags were frequently displayed."

Evidence as to the Sultan's powers inland was more general and vague and possibly not wholly reliable, but it is interesting to note that the Governor of Tanga had been able to collect debts from tribesmen living three days inland. When Kitchener proposed a visit to Kilimanjaro, his German colleague, Schmidt, alleged that the journey would be useless, as the Sultan had sufficient influence in those regions to ensure that all the evidence would be in his favour, an allegation which strongly recalls the maxim *qui s'excuse s'accuse*.

As the work of the Delimitation Commission proceeded, it became perfectly clear that the German Commissioner's opinions diverged considerably from those of his British and French colleagues. He refused to be bound by the evidence contained in the *procès-verbal* or to defer to the opinions of his colleagues and reported his differences to Bismarck. The Chancellor got in touch with the British and French governments with the result that eventually, for reasons of international diplomacy which are too lengthy to set out here, instructions went out to Kitchener and his French colleague that none but the unanimous findings of the three Commissioners should be considered. In other words, where the British and French Commissioners considered that the Sultan should have a strip of coast-land 40 miles wide, and the German Commissioner said it should be no more than 10 miles wide, the Commissioners were to give in their report the "unanimous" opinion that the strip should be 10 miles wide! In other words, the joint Anglo-French recommendations were to be omitted from the Report, which by a remarkable *suppressio veri suggestio falsi* was to go out as the unanimous verdict of all three Commissioners, and not as a minority verdict.

The so-called "unanimous" Report recognized the Sultan's sovereign rights over Zanzibar, Pemba, Mafia and the adjacent islets. With regard to the Sultan's sovereignty on the mainland, the Report held that it comprised a ten-mile coastal belt from Mikindani Bay to Kilwa Kivinje, whence it ran to the coast, leaving a ten-mile radius round this last point. After that the coastal belt came to an end. At Samanga, Kikunya, Kisiju and Dar es Salaam there was conceded to the Sultan sovereign rights within a radius of ten miles of each of those three points. After that the Report allowed the Sultan a three-mile coastal belt between the Dar es Salaam perimeter and the perimeter allotted to Sadani. At Sadani and Pangani the Sultan's sovereignty was held to be within a radius of five miles of each town. Between Sadani and Pangani the coastal belt once more became a ten-mile strip, but between Pangani and Vanga it was reduced to a five-mile belt. Kitchener had signed this document in accordance with the instructions which he had received from London, but in so doing he informed Lord Rosebery that he deeply regretted "that the last act of the Commission should have necessarily been the recording of one member's, to my mind, biased opinion as the unanimous one of the Commission. I hope Your Lordship will bear in mind, whatever use the German Government may make of this document, that the French Commissioner and myself are fully impressed with the truth of our original statements recorded in the *procès-verbaux* of the Commission." He further submitted his views as to what the limits of the Sultan of Zanzibar's dominions should be. These included:

(a) The country within a twenty-five miles radius of Tabora and Ujiji respectively.

(b) The well established caravan routes leading into the interior.

(c) The Kilimanjaro regions covered by the treaties concluded by General Lloyd Mathews.

(d) A coastal belt extending forty miles inland.

In the words of Sir Reginald Coupland, "there were to be many further stages in his (Kitchener's) varied career, but none of them was to be embellished by quite so queer an episode as that of the Zanzibar Commission."

Looking in retrospect at the evidence regarding the work of the Commission—and in particular at the *procès-verbal*—it is perfectly clear that Dr. Schmidt, the German Commissioner, was thoroughly biased and unscrupulous and never once willing to make a single concession to the views expressed by his two colleagues. His blustering, interspersed with clumsy attempts at cajolery, led to friction with his colleagues almost from the very start. His refusal to accord the Sultan of Zanzibar the slightest semblance of a fair deal not unnaturally aroused the resentment of Kitchener and the French Commissioner and serves to explain why Kitchener would appear somewhat to have overstated the Sultan's claims to sovereignty. Looking at the *procès-verbal*, one reaches the conclusion that whilst Schmidt's ten-mile coastal belt is not a fair representation of the actual facts, Kitchener's forty-mile belt is an overestimate. Schmidt of course ignored entirely any claim to sovereignty which the Sultan might have beyond this ten-mile belt. Both time and his instructions prevented Kitchener from going into the interior of the continent, consequently his estimates as to the Sultan's sovereignty beyond the coastal belt were purely conjectural. The military posts at Mamboya and Tongwe certainly established the Sultan's claim to sovereignty in those regions, but it is difficult to see how he could be held to exercise sovereignty over the whole length of the caravan routes leading to the lakes. At the best his subjects merely had a right of way along those routes—a right, moreover, which was somewhat precariously enjoyed at the caprice of the local inhabitants. It is true the Sultan appointed local governors at Tabora and Ujiji, but those places were no more than trade enclaves resembling the Hanseatic Steelyard in London and the seventeenth century European factories in India. Even assuming that the local chiefs had absolutely and unequivocally ceded their sovereignty of those two places, the radius of their respective independent territories was certainly very much less than the twenty-five miles ascribed to them by Kitchener. With regard to Kilimanjaro, the treaties of Carl Peters and Juhlke were no doubt not worth the paper they were written upon, but Lloyd Mathew's flying visit to those regions certainly did not bring them under the Sultan's effective administration. That certainly was the view of Mandara with regard to Uchagga. At the same time it is quite easy to understand how the palpable dishonesty of the German claims blinded Kitchener to the weakness of the Sultan's claims.

As was to be expected, the German Government was quick to follow up the tactical advantage secured to them by this "unanimity" on the part of the Delimitation Commission. On November 1, 1886, an Agreement was concluded between the British and German Governments respecting Zanzibar and the opposite mainland, which amongst other matters contained articles to the following effect:—

(1) the Sovereignty of the Sultan of Zanzibar over the islands of Zanzibar, Pemba, and Mafia was recognized.

(2) The coast line from Meningani Bay to Kipini (in what is now Kenya Protectorate) was recognized as forming part of the Sultan's possessions to an internal depth of ten sea miles.

(3) Great Britain engaged to support negotiations for a lease to the German East Africa Company of the customs dues at Dar es Salaam and Pangani.

(4) Germany's sphere of influence was to extend from the Ruvuma River to the River Vanga and thence inland to Lake Jipe, north of Kilimanjaro, and from there in a straight line to Lake Victoria, at its point of intersection by the first degree of south latitude.

(5) Great Britain undertook to use her offices to promote a friendly arrangement of the rival claims of the Sultan and the German East Africa Company to the Kilimanjaro districts.

Only one thing further was required to complete this settlement of East African affairs, namely, the assent of the Sultan of Zanzibar.

On December 3, 1886, Mr. Frederic Holmwood, Acting British Consul-General, on the instructions of the British Government, wrote to him acquainting him with the terms of the Anglo-German Agreement and adding that "Great Britain supports the wish of Germany that Your Highness should withdraw, by means of an official declaration, Your claims to the sovereignty of the Kilimanjaro district, which Your Highness has never exercised, and should make the fact known to the chiefs of that District."

The letter then proceeded to express the hope that the Sultan would "recognise the friendly spirit in which this Agreement had been arrived at" and to advise him that "by a ready adhesion to its terms, Your Highness will assist in bringing about a satisfactory solution of questions which cannot otherwise fail to jeopardise the interests of the Sultanate". At the time that he was presented with this *fait accompli* Seyyid Barghash was a very sick man. In the circumstances he once again could not choose but hear. He replied to the letter the following day. He agreed to grant a lease of the customs at Dar es Salaam and Pangani and he agreed to withdraw his protection from the district of Kilimanjaro, and in addition not to "put our hand towards acquiring any fresh place" in the German sphere of influence without the consent of the German Government. In conclusion, Seyyid Barghash wrote that "with regard to our accepting that this part of our Kingdom should be taken from us and given to Germany, we hope that the two governments will do what is just according to this Agreement, namely, to protect our Kingdom from being divided among them by other nations, and then, in consequence of the friendly way in which the two governments of Great Britain and Germany have asked us to adhere to this Agreement, we are ready to give our adhesion."

In pursuance of this agreement Captain Leue ("Bwana Loya") arrived in Dar es Salaam on May 25, 1887, with seven German assistants and a bodyguard of twelve Arabs sent by the Sultan of Zanzibar for protection. The Germans met with a very cold reception. The Arab governor was the reverse of helpful. He refused to surrender his quarters to Leue. According to local tradition, he even refused to hand over the reins of government and had to be recalled to Zanzibar by the Sultan. Shortly after the appearance of this German vanguard Lutheran missionaries arrived and founded a station on the promontory on the north side of the entrance to the harbour. They were followed in 1888 by the Benedictines of St. Ottilien, who were at first housed in an old Arab building still standing at the corner of Main Avenue and Mission Street. Mortality amongst the devoted members of this Order must have been exceedingly high, as is witnessed by a well filled graveyard in Magazine Street. Shortly afterwards they built the first church in Dar es Salaam on the shores of Kurasini Creek.

The German East Africa Company was naturally interested in the opening up of trade with the interior, but in these early days very little was achieved. Ever since the days when Seyyid Majid began to build at Dar es Salaam there had been a certain amount of trade between the town and the immediate hinterland in gum copal and agricultural produce. This trade had somewhat increased when the Buxton–Mackinnon road was constructed into the interior. It had been almost entirely in the hands of Indian traders. Except for the erection of a plant for washing and sorting the copal, the Company would appear to have done little at this date to encourage or to develop that or any other trade.

REVOLT OF BUSHIRI, 1888–1889

It was hardly to be expected that either the German Government or the German East Africa Company would remain long content with the two narrow footholds on the coast at Dar es Salaam and Pangani. Negotiations were soon afoot to obtain a much larger trading concession. There was no longer any need for the display of the mailed fist and the negotiations were conducted in a more peaceful manner. They were delayed by the illness of Seyyid Barghash. At the beginning of 1888 he visited Oman to take sulphur baths at a village near

Muscat.   On March 26 he arrived back in Zanzibar, a dying man.   He was carried ashore and died five hours later.   It was therefore left to his brother and successor, Seyyid Khalifa bin Said, to conclude the new agreement with the German East Africa Company.

On April 28, 1888, Seyyid Khalifa signed an agreement whereby he made over to the German East African Company for a term of fifty years "all the power which he possesses on the Mrima (mainland) and in all his territories and dependencies south of the Vumba River" stipulating nevertheless that the administration of these territories was "to be carried out in His Highness' name and under his flag and subject to His Highness' sovereign rights."

This concession was no more popular with the Sultan's subjects on the mainland than had been the previous concessions in respect of Dar es Salaam and Pangani.   It was only to be expected that they would resent strongly the intrusion of German merchants into places in which they had hitherto enjoyed a trading monopoly.

The concession included the management of the levying of customs and the control of all customs posts along the coast.   As many of the local chiefs at the principal posts and in the adjacent hinterland had for many years been tacitly allowed to levy *hongo* on goods passing through their territories, this change of management was far from popular.   In pursuance of his agreement the Sultan despatched Suleiman bin Nassor el Lemki (who afterwards became Liwali of Dar es Salaam) to all the chiefs ports at Tanga, Pangani, Bagamoyo, Dar es Salaam, Kilwa Kivinje, Lindi and Mikindani with instructions to his officials to hand over the customs posts to the German authorities.

Although there was no mention of the fact in the agreement itself, a letter which Seyyid Khalifa sent to the Liwali of Kilwa stated that the Germans should be allowed to hoist their flag alongside that of the Sultan of Zanzibar.   It was this question of the flag which served as an igniting spark to a widespread revolt. Though at Dar es Salaam, Lindi and Mikindani no protest was made, the strongest possible resentment was displayed at Tanga, Pangani, Bagamoyo and Kilwa.   So intense was the feeling shown at Pangani that the Company's flag could not be hoisted there until the German gunboat *Moewe* arrived.   Several days after the vessel departed trouble broke out again and shots were fired at the Company's representatives by some of the Sultan's irregular troops.   A similar state of affairs prevailed at Tanga, where a boat from the *Moewe* was fired on when proceeding to the shore and the Company's flag could only be hoisted after a landing party from the gunboat had driven the hostile elements out of the town.   The Company then invoked the aid of the Sultan, who sent General Lloyd Mathews to deal with the situation, but despite his great influence on the coast he had to beat a retreat.   On September 29, 1888, he wrote to Sir John Kirk, who had recently retired, to inform him that "the feeling is against all Europeans. The whole coast and interior is in a ferment."

The leader of the revolt was an Arab named Bushiri bin Salim el Harthi, who had already shown himself to be a somewhat turbulent subject of the Sultan of Zanzibar.   Under his leadership the revolt spread not only up and down the coast, but even as far into the interior as the Southern Highlands, where Mkwawa, the paramount chief of the Hehe, gave his powerful aid.   In November, 1888, the Sultan of Zanzibar, at the request of the British Consul-General, sent a party of Arab soldiers to escort the British missionaries in Usambara to the coast, but the rebels refused to allow the troops to land.   Bishop Smythies then resolved to get in touch personally with the missionaries.   The steamer in which he proceeded to Pangani was fired upon but he managed to land, only to be beset by an excited mob, from whom he was personally rescued by Bushiri.   Next day Bushiri, who at this stage of the warfare displayed a certain amount of chivalry, sent the Bishop with Susi, Livingstone's old servant, under escort to Mkuzi.   From that place the five ladies on the U.M.C.A.[1] staff at Magila, under the escort of three male members of the staff, were able to proceed under Bushiri's protection to Pangani and thence to safety in Zanzibar.[2]

A month or so later the warfare became more embittered.   Dar es Salaam was attacked on the last day of 1888 and again ten days later, but was successfully defended by a small garrison with the assistance of a German man-of-war.   On the second occasion part of the town was gutted and the Lutheran missionary and his family narrowly escaped death whilst fleeing to the warship from their isolated dwelling at the harbour mouth.

After this second defeat the rebels made their way to the Benedictine Mission at Pugu twelve miles west of Dar es Salaam.[3]   Here on January 13, 1889, two brothers and one sister were murdered; two brothers made their escape; and three brothers and one sister were made prisoners; these last were eventually ransomed by the Fathers of the Holy Ghost at Bagamoyo.   Four days later the rebels made an unsuccessful night attack on the fort which had been erected in Dar es Salaam.   On January 25 the menace to Dar es Salaam was finally ended by the defeat with heavy loss of a band of eighty rebels at Ras Chokir, where the Ocean Road Hospital now stands.

Further down the coast the German Company's representative had had to evacuate Mikindani and Lindi.   At Kilwa the Arabs, reinforced by a band of Yao, said to number several thousand, besieged the two German representatives in their house.   The gunboat *Moewe* arrived off the place, but failed to get in touch with them and eventually sailed away, leaving them to their fate.

As the German Company had shown itself incapable of putting down the revolt, the German Government decided to intervene.   The explorer Hermann von Wissmann was appointed Imperial Commissioner and provided with a military staff.   Troops were recruited in Egypt from the ranks of the Sudanese and from the Zulus in Portuguese East Africa.   In the meantime, the Germans in East Africa had persuaded Bushiri to enter into an armistice with a view to conclusion of a treaty of peace.   When Wissmann arrived, he denounced these proceedings and at once resumed hostilities.   It would appear that Bushiri believed that he had been tricked into agreeing to the armistice so as to give time to the Germans to build up their forces.   In any event from thence onwards he became a bitter and implacable foe without any remaining spark of chivalry.

Wissmann made Bagamoyo his base, Bushiri being encamped about six miles away in a strongly fortified position.   In May Wissmann attacked and took Bushiri's fortress, whereupon the latter retreated about forty miles further inland, where he fortified himself again.   In July Sadani was attacked and completely destroyed.   Very shortly afterwards Wissmann recovered Pangani and Tanga.

[1]Universities' Mission to Central Africa.

[2]See also page 382

[3]See page 381 for further details

Bushiri, however, was still at large in the interior. On one occasion he tried to capture some French Fathers of the Holy Ghost at their mission station at Simea; but the Fathers were able to escape to Morogoro, where the local chief Kingo took them under his protection and refused to surrender them to Bushiri. Hearing that Bushiri was threatening the German Company's station at Mpwapwa, Wissmann led a punitive expedition there, only to find that the bird had flown. After building a new station and leaving a garrison there, Wissmann returned to the coast.

In the middle of October, 1888, Bushiri reappeared and encamped about six hours' march from Bagamoyo with a force of five or six thousand Mafiti, or Masitu, a tribe related to the Yao, but was attacked and utterly defeated by von Gravenreuth with a force of one hundred and twenty men.

After this disastrous defeat Bushiri fled to Usagara and disappeared until December, when the news was received that he had been captured in Kwamkoro. A detachment sent to bring him in found him starving and half naked in a hut. He was bound and led to Pangani, where he was hanged on 15th December, 1889.

ASSUMPTION OF CONTROL BY THE IMPERIAL GERMAN GOVERNMENT

Whilst Wissmann was engaged in stamping out the rebellion in East Africa, the Governments of Great Britain and Germany had been engaged in arriving at a settlement of their rival claims in various parts of the globe. On July 1, 1890, an agreement was signed which adjusted the disputes of the two countries regarding their spheres of interest in many parts of East, West and South-West Africa. In the penultimate article of the agreement Great Britain undertook "to use all her influence to facilitate a friendly arrangement, by which the Sultan of Zanzibar shall cede absolutely to Germany, his possessions on the mainland comprised in the existing concession to the German East Africa Company, and their dependencies, as well as the Island of Mafia" in exchange for "an equitable indemnity for the loss of revenue resulting from such cession." In subsequent correspondence which passed between the representatives of the two governments it was eventually agreed that this sum should be four million marks in gold (£200,000). On September 25, 1890, Seyyid Ali bin Said, who had succeeded his brother Khalifa as Sultan of Zanzibar, reluctantly gave his consent to the cession. It is not without interest to note that, at the time of giving his assent, he expressed to the British Consul-General at Zanzibar the opinion that, if his brother and predecessor, Barghash, had been wiser, the whole of the Zanzibar dominions might have been safely brought under British protection and that he himself might have been spared the necessity of signing away more than half his heritage. He also ventured to prophesy that, before many years had passed, the Germans would be compelled to part with what they were then securing. The criticism of Seyyid Barghash was hardly just. The prophesy was in course of time fulfilled.

On April 1, 1891, the German Government took over control from the German East Africa Company. The new proprietors did not enter into entirely peaceful possession. Much of the interior was still in a very disturbed state and there were many other parts in which the arrival of administrators from an alien race was viewed with suspicion, if not with active obstruction or even hostility.

THE WAR AGAINST MKWAWA

One of the first tasks attempted by the new administration was the subjugation of the Hehe. According to their traditions members of this tribe arrived in their present homes about the beginning of the eighteenth century. Though by the middle of the nineteenth century they had become amalgamated into a single political organization, they belonged originally to a number of independent tribal groups, of which it is still possible to recognize some twenty-nine. They owed their consolidation into a single political group to the leadership of one Muyugamba, from whom the present ruling chief of the Hehe is descended. Muyugamba and his son and successor, Mkwawa, built up between them a strong political organization[1]. Mkwawa soon showed himself as an able military commander. The Angoni were utterly defeated in 1882 and the Nyamwezi in the following year. Thereafter he led expeditions against the Gogo, the Sagara, and the Sangu. After ten years of fighting he had built himself up a kingdom extending from Usangu in what is now Mbeya District to Ulaya about twenty miles from Kilosa on the Central Railway line. During that time the Masai had overrun Ugogo and invaded Uhehe, only to be defeated in a decisive battle, in which the Hehe were led by Mkwawa's sister, who was one of his sub-chiefs.

During these ten successful years Mkwawa had levied tribute on all trading caravans passing through his dominions and had attacked those caravans which attempted to evade payment. It was obvious that this practice would soon bring him into conflict with the Germans, especially when they started to penetrate inland and built a fort at Mpwapwa. In view of his father's experience at the time of Elton's visit to Usangu, Mkwawa realized the dangers which he was likely to encounter. It was for that reason that he allied himself with Bushiri at the time of the latter's rebellion, hoping that his ally would be able to expel the Germans from their foothold on the coast. When Bushiri failed him, he sent two envoys to Bagamoyo to try to make his peace with the Germans. Wissmann sent him an invitation to come and see him personally, but Mkwawa was unwilling to do so. In the meantime his people continued to raid caravans passing through his territory.

In 1891 Wissmann's successor, Lieutenant von Zelewsky, decided to put a stop to this practice. In the middle of June of that year he left Kilosa with a force of about one thousand men. Mkwawa got wind of his advance and sent a party with presents to try to placate the German commander, but the party was fired on and only one survivor returned to Mkwawa to report the incident. On learning this, Mkwawa decided to lay an ambush for his invaders. The Germans had to advance up the Katinga valley, which was hemmed in by steep, thickly wooded slopes on either side, and afforded ideal cover for the Hehe. The ambush was accordingly laid in this valley near Lugalo, about twelve miles north-east of Iringa on the present Iringa–Kilosa road. The German force fell completely into the trap and was very nearly annihilated. Zelewsky escaped, but ten Germans were killed as well as two hundred and fifty African soldiers. Some three hundred rifles, three field guns and a large quantity of ammunition fell into the hands of the Hehe.

For over three years more Mkwawa continued to raid caravans and surrounding tribes with impunity. Then in 1894 it was decided to send another strong punitive expedition against him. By this time Mkwawa had built himself

[1]See page 236 for further details.

a strongly fortified post at Kalenga, a few miles to the west of Iringa. On
October 30, 1894, this position was bombarded and then taken by storm after
fierce fighting from hut to hut. Mkwawa himself managed to escape. Thereafter he was fighting a losing battle, but despite all attempts by the Germans
to detach his subjects from their loyalty to him he continued to wage a constant
guerilla warfare which made him a thorn in the side of the Germans. The
following report from a German officer shows the remarkable hold which he
had over his people even in the hour of defeat:

"Mkwawa always moved between our patrols. He was supplied with
information and food in the very localities where our troops operated, but the
inhabitants declined to give our forces any information and denied all knowledge
of his presence. When we were hot on Mkwawa's trail, food and liquor would
often be found placed in the pathless bush; his people always knew where to
find him, the direction he had taken and the points he would traverse.
Altogether, it was certain that Mkwawa exercised an inexplicable influence
over the natives, who, when the pursuing troops surprised his camp, would,
time after time, blindly hurl themselves on the soldiers, sacrificing themselves
merely to give Mkwawa the chance of escape. No scheme for his capture was
possible and no one ever knew even what he looked like."

The end came in 1898 when General von Liebert, Governor of German
East Africa, offered a reward of five thousand rupees for Mkwawa's head. As
was inevitable, the inducement was too tempting to be ignored. On June 14 in
that year an African gave information as to the fugitive's whereabouts and
Sergeant-Major Merkl was sent in pursuit. On June 19 after a hot pursuit
they captured a boy at Pawaga, who admitted that he was Mkwawa's servant
and that his master was lying sick in the bush three hours away. They were led
to a spot near the village of Humbwe on the lesser Ruaha River, where they
saw two figures apparently asleep. Crawling up to the spot and firing at the
figures in case they were being led into a trap, they found that the figures were
those of two dead men, Mkwawa and his servant Mwenyiowala. Sergeant-
Major Merkl's bullet had struck Mkwawa on the head, but both bodies were
cold and the two had evidently been dead for some time. Mkwawa had evidently
shot his companion first, as the body was stiff, and had then shot himself in the
stomach. Sergeant-Major Merkl handed over the body of their dead chief
to the Hehe for burial, having first of all cut off Mkwawa's head, which he handed
over to his superior officer, Captain von Prince. Eventually the skull was sent
to the Anthropological Museum at Bremen.

Though Mkwawa was dead and his head had been severed from his body,
his voice yet spoke. The headless body was ceremoniously laid to rest by his
people and thereafter he became a national hero. In 1904 a German officer
reported that the anniversary of Mkwawa's death was still being celebrated
throughout Uhehe by songs in his praise. In that year it was deemed necessary
to banish his sons to the coast because of the royal ovations which they received
in honour of their father.

When at the close of the German East African campaign the British assumed
administrative charge at Iringa, almost the very first request of the Hehe was
that Mkwawa's skull might be handed back to them. In November, 1918,
Sir Horace Byatt, the British Administrator, urged on the Secretary of State

that an endeavour should be made to recover the skull and to have it returned to Uhehe. Representations were made to the German authorities, who maintained that the skull was not in Germany. The Hehe nonetheless insisted that the skull had been taken there and that they had been told so by Captain von Prince. Eventually in 1949 Sir Edward Twining, the present Governor of Tanganyika, took the matter up and ascertained that the skull was probably in the Anthropological Museum at Bremen. In 1953 he personally visited the Museum and was able with the data in his possession and the assistance of the forensic surgeon of the German police to identify the bullet-shattered skull of the dead hero. Dr. Wagner, the Director of the Museum, agreed to return the skull to the Hehe and on June 19, 1954, fifty-six years to a day after Mkwawa's death, Sir Edward Twining was able to hand it over to Chief Adam Sapi, the grandson of the dead man and the present Chief of the Hehe, and thus to gratify their long-felt yearnings.

OTHER EARLY GERMAN PUNITIVE EXPEDITIONS

The German Government found that they had to deal with other trouble spots besides Uhehe.

As already seen, Tabora, which then as now was situated at the junction of the two trade routes leading from Lakes Tanganyika and Victoria respectively to the coast, was obviously a point of great commercial and strategic importance. At the time of assumption of control by the German Government there was an Arab colony at this place in the nominal control of a Liwali (governor) appointed by the Sultan of Zanzibar, but his writ did not run very far even amongst his somewhat turbulent compatriots and still less amongst the Africans living within the confines of the Arab settlement. Nearby at Kipalapala was a fortified building, which had been originally erected by the Belgian members of the African International Association and had been handed over by them to the White Fathers Mission. Three miles away lived Siki, who after Mirambo's death in 1884 had become paramount chief in Unyamwezi. He also lived in a strongly fortified post and had at his beck and call a well-organized and well-armed military following.

When the Russian explorer, Dr. Junker, arrived at Tabora on September 22, 1886, on his way from Uganda down to the coast, he found a German named Giesecke settled there as agent of a Hamburg firm. Giesecke told Junker that he had been recently fired at. A day or two later he was again attacked and died as the result of his injuries. Four years later an Arab was arrested at the coast for his murder, tried and executed. Siki took advantage of his death to seize all his property. That property included some ivory, which the murdered man had purchased for his firm, and some arms and ammunition, which included a machine gun. Apparently Siki claimed this property by way of some sort of an escheat to himself. At any rate he refused to part with it. Thereafter Siki's people attacked and robbed passing caravans with impunity.

In 1889, when news of the cession of the coast belt to the Germans reached Tabora, his attitude towards the White Fathers became so markedly hostile that at the end of June they decided to abandon their station at Kipalapala and to proceed with the ransomed slave children in their care to their station at the southern end of Lake Victoria.

Emin Pasha, who had recently taken service under the German Government, arrived at Tabora on July 29, 1890[1].   He at once entered into friendly relations with the Arab community and accorded to the Sultan's Liwali recognition as Liwali of the German Government.   At the same time he sent an ultimatum to Siki to deliver up Giesecke's property.   Emin had an escort of about 130 men with him and Siki decided to comply with the request.   Shortly afterwards Emin moved on towards Lake Victoria and Siki returned to his former predatory habits.

In April, 1892, Siki's son attacked a German column, in retaliation for which his fortified *boma* at Ipuli was attacked and destroyed.   In the following June it was reported that Siki was assembling the whole tribe with the intention of exterminating the Europeans.   Two unsuccessful attempts were made with inadequate forces to take his place by storm.   These setbacks added greatly to the prestige of Siki, who now assumed the offensive and very nearly annihilated a column under the command of Lieutenant von Prince.   Thereafter the caravan routes to and from Tabora became completely closed.   On January 9, 1893, a strong German column attacked Siki's fort.   The inmates held out for two days.   The fort was finally stormed and taken.   Siki and his family fled to the powder magazine, which he blew up, destroying himself and them.

In these early days there was also constantly recurring trouble with the Gogo on the caravan route between Tabora and the coast.   The activities of these people were confined to raiding caravans and necessitated the despatch of more than one minor punitive expedition.

Nearer the coast there was some trouble in the areas behind Kilwa and Lindi. Many of the inhabitants of those regions had taken part in Bushiri's rebellion in 1889.   Though Wissmann had been able to recover possession of Kilwa, Lindi, and Mikindani with comparative ease, it took some time to reduce the hinterland to law and order.   Sultan Hassan bin Omar, who ruled the territory to the west of Kilwa, went so far in 1894 as to make an attempt to take that town. The attempt was unsuccessful and in the following year he was captured by a punitive expedition.

Machemba, a Yao chief living on the Makonde plateau to the south-west of Lindi, made his submission after Bushiri's overthrow, but in 1895 he and his people declined to pay hut tax.   Owing to his inaccessibility he and they were able to persist in their refusal until 1899, when a punitive expedition was sent against them.   Machemba took refuge over the border in Portuguese territory. Many of his principal supporters were rounded up and imprisoned.

CARL PETERS IN UCHAGGA

The early treaty-making exploits of Carl Peters have already been recorded. After his return to Europe in 1884 he had been largely instrumental in the founding of the German East Africa Company.   In 1888 he reappeared in East Africa as the head of the German Emin Pasha Relief Expedition.   He has given an account of his exploits on this occasion in a book which has been translated into English under the title of *New Light on Dark Africa*.   That book speaks for itself.   The gospel of *shrecklichkeit* (frightfulness) never had a stauncher advocate than the writer.   The expedition was not sanctioned by the German Government and was rightly regarded by the British Government

---

[1]See also pp. 65 to 69 for a fuller description of Emin Pasha's exploits.

as no more than a filibustering expedition the real object of which was to try
to jump claims in the spheres in which the Imperial British East Africa Company
was working.   Landing in Kwaihu Bay to the north of Patta Island, he proceeded
inland, carrying fire and sword and treaty forms with him, until he reached
Uganda early in 1890.   There he made a treaty with Mwanga, ruler of Buganda,
but left shortly after its conclusion, because he was running short of supplies
and more particularly of ammunition.   From Buganda he proceeded across
Lake Victoria to the White Fathers' Mission at Bukumbi in the Mwanza Gulf,
where he hoisted the German flag.

From Bukumbi Peters proceeded to Iramba, where the Sultan, who was being
harassed by the Masai, agreed to accept the German flag.   A few days later
Peters hoisted the flag at Usure, which was at this date ruled by a Sultana, whom
he never saw and whose personal acquaintance he dispensed with because he
learned that she was in a state of complete intoxication.   When he reached Ugogo,
he was attacked by the local inhabitants, whom he managed to beat off.   His
reply to a request from the Sultan to make peace was that, "It shall be the eternal
peace.   I will show the Gogo what the Germans are."   He then set fire to a
number of their villages.   On arrival at Mpwapwa he met Emin Pasha, who
was proceeding in the opposite direction and about whom more will be said
later on.   Between Mpwapwa and Bagamoyo the countryside had already
been brought under effective German administration.   Consequently there
was no further need for the exhibition of *shrecklichkeit* on his part.   At the
coast Peters learned that his treaties in Uganda and the British sphere of influence
were useless, inasmuch as the Anglo-German Agreement of 1890 left those
territories in the British sphere.

When Peters arrived back in Germany he was received with great honour.
In 1891 he was back again in East Africa as Imperial High Commissioner for the
Kilimanjaro District.   As recounted on a previous page, Wissmann had managed
to conciliate Mandara, who claimed to be the paramount chief of the Chagga,
and to establish peace and good order there.   Shortly after Wissmann's departure
Mandara had died.   He had been succeeded by his son Meli, who according
to all accounts lacked the shrewdness and farsightedness of his father.   It was
additionally unfortunate for the son that he was brought up against Carl Peters.
Presently ugly rumours began to filter through from the slopes of Kilimanjaro
to German headquarters.   Stories were told of terrorism, plunder, the flogging
and chaining of women and children, forced concubinage and even of murder.
One of the worst reports was that of a native youth, who had been hanged
ostensibly for stealing cigarettes but in reality for visiting Peters' African concu-
bines.   One of these women had fled for protection to a neighbouring chief.
She was hailed back and after being frequently and unmercifully flogged was
finally hanged.   It was impossible for all these reports to be ignored by higher
German authority.   Peters was recalled in 1893 and eventually after three
investigations he was deprived in 1897 of his commission for "misuse of official
power."   It is only right to say that at the time of these investigations there
were members of the Reichstag who were outspoken in their condemnation of
Peters, but in the course of time there was a revulsion of public opinion in his
favour and he was regarded as a pioneer empire builder.   In 1906 he was restored
to his previous rank and a statue in his honour was erected at Dar es Salaam.
Later still Adolf Hilter described him as "a model, if stern, administrator".
In 1934 the Nazi Government formally rehabilitated him and made him figure

Peters.

Emin Pasha.

Stuhlman.

Von Lettow-Vorbeck.

as a colonial hero in a set of propaganda postage stamps. The full tale of his cruelties has not been told here because it would be a mistake to regard him as typical of all the old German colonists. Unfortunately for his country and the reputation of his countrymen he was given the opportunity to undo within the space of a few months all that had been achieved with an infinite amount of patience and a thoroughly conciliatory spirit by Wissmann, and by Lieutenant Ehlers, who had arrived at Moshi and hoisted the German flag in 1890.

Peters was succeeded in the Kilimanjaro district by Baron Bülow, of whom Bishop Tucker has written that his "administration was hardly more successful, though doubtless more humane." Relations between Peters and Meli had for obvious reasons been very much strained. They did not improve when Bülow succeeded Peters. On April 26, 1892, a German soldier, who appears to have been on marauding bent, was killed by some of Meli's subjects. Bülow thereupon decided to attack Meli. The plan of campaign was ill-conceived. It ended in the complete defeat of the Germans; Bülow and his second-in-command, Lieutenant Wulfram, being killed. The next Imperial Commissioner was Captain Johannes, to whom Bishop Tucker pays a high tribute as a just and sympathetic administrator. He did his best to arrange a peaceful settlement with Meli, but he had arrived too late to put matters to rights in the Chagga country. If Wissmann's plans for the country had been followed and if a more conciliatory spirit had been displayed towards Mandara's son, a more unified system of administration might well have been established at a very early date. As it was, punitive expeditions led to the complete disruption of anything which Wissmann had achieved, with the result that, at the close of the German period of administration, Uchagga was divided into no less than nineteen chiefdoms, separated from each other by the deep ravines on the slopes of Kilimanjaro as well as by clan feuds and mutual rivalries.

To this lack of unity must also be attributed to some extent the ringing round of large parts of the Chagga country by non-native settlements on the lower slopes of Kilimanjaro. The lands, which were occupied by German settlers, were apparently reduced into their possession without any serious opposition from the local inhabitants, because the Chagga attached greater value to the land higher up the slopes of the mountain. The result was that the tribal lands became more or less entirely enclosed by an outer ring of non-native properties, which were mostly held on terms corresponding to freehold. The gradual increase of the population naturally led to a desire on the part of the Chagga to come down and occupy the lower slopes of the mountain which had thus been alienated to Germans. After the First World War this land hunger led to one of the very pressing problems which had to be solved by the British administration.[1]

EMIN PASHA AND OTHER EARLY ADMINISTRATORS

Emin Pasha was originally Edward Schnitzler, born of a Jewish father at Oppeln in Silesia in 1840. After studying medicine at Breslau and Berlin he practised at Scutari in Albania, where he embraced Islam and assumed the name of Emin. In 1876 he entered the Egyptian service as Emin Effendi and rose to the ranks of Bey and finally, of Pasha. He was engaged by Gordon, first of all as chief medical officer of the Equatorial Province, but was soon employed in diplomacy and administration. In 1878 Gordon appointed him

[1] See page 205

Governor of the Equatorial Province. He held that post until 1889. After the Mahdist revolt in 1883 he was completely cut off from the rest of the world. During his Egyptian service he proved himself to be a skilful linguist and an authority on anthropology, zoology, botany and meteorology.

In 1887 an expedition was organized in Great Britain for his relief. H. M. Stanley was placed in command of it. In 1889, after a mutiny of his Sudanese troops, Emin left the Equatorial Province in company with Stanley and proceeded by way of Lake Edward, Ankole and Karagwe to the east coast at Bagamoyo. On the day of his arrival at Bagamoyo he met with a serious accident, which was due to a fall from a window and which completely incapacitated him for several months. On his recovery he took service with the German authorities.

He was instructed by Wissmann (prior to the conclusion of the Anglo-German Agreement) to proceed to Lake Victoria and forestall any attempts by the English to gain an influence in those regions. The conclusion of the Anglo-German Agreement of July 1, 1890, naturally led to a modification of his original instructions. On April 26, 1890, his expedition set out from Bagamoyo. He was accompanied by two other officers. Franz Stuhlmann went with him as medical officer. He shared all Emin's tastes regarding anthropology, zoology and botany and was destined to make a number of valuable contributions on these subjects in respect of German East Africa. The military escort was under the command of Captain Wilhelm Langheld, who was to remain in East Africa until 1900 and to be responsible for the establishment of law and order and good government in what is now the Lake Province. The party also included a German sergeant named Kuhne, 50 Swahili enlisted as soldiers and 400 armed porters. Two White Fathers took advantage of the protection afforded by the military escort.

At the time of Emin's departure from Bagamoyo the furthest German station was at Mpwapwa. On the way there Langheld was detached with a small party to the Arab settlement at Kondoa-Irangi, where the German flag was hoisted without opposition and the leading Arab appointed as Liwali. Mpwapwa was not reached until June 3, 1890. It was in charge of Baron von Bülow, who, as has been recounted above, was none too favourably reported upon by Bishop Tucker. In justice, however, to his memory it should be here recorded that Emin reported that his treatment of the local inhabitants in the vicinity of Mpwapwa had so far inspired their confidence that large numbers had come to the station and built their huts there.

Emin made a long stay at Mpwapwa, partly because he was waiting for further reinforcements from the coast and partly because Stuhlmann fell seriously ill. It was here that he met Carl Peters.

Emin left Mpwapwa on June 22, 1890. On July 2 two of his Zulu soldiers went off on a marauding expedition and were killed by the Gogo. Next day Emin and Langheld proceeded to burn eleven *tembes* (huts), killed the local chief and some of his people, and carried off a number of cattle. "Now", reported Emin, "quiet reigns everywhere, and the Gogo are coming in from all quarters, asking for letters of protection and flags." Tabora was reached on July 29. Emin met with a friendly reception from the local Arabs, one of whom he appointed as Liwali of the German Government. On August 4 he hoisted the German flag. He also sent an ultimatum to the Nyamwezi chief Siki, demanding the surrender of the property of the German trader Giesecke, who had been murdered by an Arab at Tabora four years previously. After some delay the property was handed over.[1]

Whilst at Tabora Emin sent a party of soldiers to Urambo, where the London Missionary Society had established a station. Kapera, the chief of that place, was being threatened by the Angoni, and was only too glad to receive German protection. Langheld was sent to deal with the Angoni. With the assistance of the local and two of the neighbouring chiefs the Angoni were twice driven off. After their defeat Langheld rejoined Emin. Baron von Bülow, who had joined Emin's expedition at Mpwapwa and had contracted typhoid fever on the way to Tabora, was left in charge at Urambo with a small party of soldiers.

Emin left Tabora on August 26. Four days later he reached Uyui and made a treaty there with the local chief. It was not until September 27 that he reached Lake Victoria at the White Father's Mission station at Bukumbi. By this time information had reached him regarding the Anglo-German Agreement, by the terms of which the first degree of south latitude was fixed as the dividing line of the spheres of interest of the two countries in the region of Lake Victoria. This of course entailed a change in his previous plans.

Whilst at Bukumbi Emin was informed that there were Arabs in the vicinity at Masanga, who were carrying on an extensive slave trade and importing large quantities of arms and ammunition into the country. After the Arabs had failed to comply with an order to present themselves before him, Emin sent Stuhlmann to investigate the matter. Stuhlmann arrived to find that the Arabs had fled, taking most of their possessions with them. Some slaves were, however, left behind. These Stuhlmann brought back and handed over to the care of the White Fathers at Bukumbi. As Emin reported, Stuhlmann's proceedings had put a definite stop to the slave trade at least for the time being. They had also been hailed with delight by the Sukuma, who were very glad to be relieved of Arab oppression. Rwoma, the paramount chief, asked Emin for his protection against a rival. Emin described him as "quite incapable and very unpopular." Kollmann afterwards reported that he "injured his country by almost incredible measures. Later he leagued himself against the German rule with several other chiefs on the lake and fell in battle against Lieutenant von Kolben in the autumn of 1895." In 1890 Emin was far too anxious to move up towards the Anglo-German boundary to be ready to fight Rwoma's battles for him.

On October 19 Emin set out by canoe to cross Lake Victoria, leaving it to Stuhlmann to come round the lake by land. Eleven days later he reached Bukoba Bay, where he was met and given a friendly reception by the local chief Mukotani, who complained of piratical raids by the Baganda and readily agreed to give Emin land where he could build a station. Here Stuhlmann joined him on November 15.

Stuhlmann had met with trouble on the way. Near the C.M.S. station at Usambiro the local chief, Kalemera by name, tried to bar the way and Stuhlmann sent Sergeant-Major Kuhne to deal with the situation with some German troops and friendly natives. Later the Sergeant-Major reported that he had taken and destroyed two *bomas*, that the enemy had lost 163 killed and wounded out

---

[1]See also page 62 above.

of a total of 500 or 600 fighting men, that he had captured 145 women and children and 135 head of cattle, and that the German casualties were two killed and a few wounded.   After that no further difficulties were encountered on the way.

For a little more than three months after his arrival at Bukoba Emin was engaged in building the station.   He was also detained owing to the non-arrival of Langheld, who had been fully employed in dealing with the Angoni in Urambo and Unyamwezi.   After the Angoni had been driven away from Urambo they seized and destroyed a nearby village and Langheld was detained by the necessity of undertaking further operations against them.   Consequently he did not reach Bukoba until January 26, 1891.

In the meantime Emin had been consolidating the German position on the western shores of Lake Victoria by entering into treaties with certain of the leading chiefs in Ihangiro, Kianja, Kiamtwara, Kiziba and Bugabo as well as into an agreement restricting the importation of arms from Uganda into German territory and *vice versa*.

On February 12, 1891, leaving Langheld in charge at Bukoba, Emin set out in company with Stuhlmann for Karagwe, whence he crossed the Anglo-German boundary into Uganda.   Whilst in Mpororo there was trouble between the local inhabitants and four armed porters belonging to the rear party, which was in charge of Stuhlmann.   There was a dispute as to the price of provisions, which ended in the killing of the porters and the seizure of their guns.   On April 5, 1891, whilst he was in Uganda, Emin received from Wissmann a letter of recall, in which he was rebuked for hoisting the German flag at Tabora, for sending Langheld on an expedition against the Angoni, and failing to co-operate with Charles Stokes, an Irish trader who had taken service under the German Government.   Emin decided to disregard the order of recall and proceeded into what is now the Belgian Congo, accompanied by Stuhlmann.   At the end of the year smallpox broke out in the caravan.   On December 6 Emin instructed Stuhlmann to return to a place called Tenga Tenga with the healthy members of the caravan, whilst he himself remained with the sick.   Stuhlmann was informed that, if he received no further instructions within a month, he was to return to Bukoba.   Stuhlmann left Emin four days later.   On January 19, 1892, he received a letter from Emin saying he would follow him back to Bukoba by easy stages as soon as he could.   Stuhlmann accordingly returned to Bukoba. Emin however, did not follow him.   On the contrary during the following March he continued his journey into the Congo.   On October 23 or 24, 1892, he was murdered at the instigation of some Arab slave traders.

After Emin's departure Langheld set about the further consolidation of the German position on the shores of Lake Victoria.   Early in 1892 he sent Sergeant-Major Hoffmann to establish a station at Mwanza on the southern shores of the lake.   He also frequently toured in person the country to the west of the lake. He was instrumental in intercepting a number of slave traders and in securing the release of their captives.   In March, 1892, during Langheld's absence from Bukoba, Stuhlmann successfully intercepted one such caravan, which included eighty-three women and children, who had been made captive in the civil wars in Uganda and who after their rescue were handed over to the White Fathers, who had established themselves close to Bukoba.   Langheld was also responsible for the peaceful settlement in German territory of some two thousand Baganda, who crossed over from their own country into German territory during the same civil wars.

Emin had proved a somewhat undisciplined civil servant. He was also a non-Aryan. For that reason Adolf Hitler never had him commemorated on Nazi colonial postage stamps.[1] Nonetheless he and his colleagues Stuhlmann and Langheld proved far more able and successful colonial pioneers than Peters had ever been. They made their mistakes and some of the hostilities in which they indulged appear to have been unnecessary and uncalled for, but they had at least realised that fire and sword alone could never bring about the establishment of peace and good order in the lands entrusted to their charge. Despite his disobedience to Wissmann's orders Emin had by conciliatory means brought under effective German administration a far greater extent of territory than Carl Peters ever succeeded in doing by the use of *schrecklichkeit*.

Emin and his colleagues were by no means isolated examples of the better type of German colonial administrator. Amongst others may be mentioned Baron von Eltz, who toured the regions between Lakes Nyasa and Tanganyika and in 1893 captured a slave caravan just north of the former lake and handed over the women and children, over a hundred in number, to the Berlin and Moravian missions. There were undoubtedly many others whose unostentatious labours have no memorial. Unfortunately, working side by side with these were others who tended to emulate Carl Peters.

Oscar Baumann may be cited as a typical example of this latter class. He came out under the auspices of the German Anti-Slavery Society and undoubtedly showed himself to be an intrepid and able explorer as well as a sound anthropologist, botanist and naturalist. But there was another, less pleasant side to his character. His own account of his journey from Pangani through the Masai country to Lake Victoria and the sources of the Kagera river is interspersed with numerous details of fights between his escort and the tribes through whose territories he passed. Hostilities began on the slopes of Kilimanjaro. Shortly afterwards he had two brushes with the Masai. When he reached Lake Victoria, his escort fired on the inhabitants of Ukara Island when they refused to let him land. In Sukumaland he twice more came to blows with the local inhabitants, the first occasion being in retaliation for the murder of one of his Sudanese escort, who had wandered away from the caravan on a marauding expedition. After a brush with the Batusi in Urundi he made his way to Tabora. At Usongo, sixty miles to the east of Tabora, he once more had a fight with the inhabitants, to be followed a few days later by another fight with the Nyaturu. Turning to the north again he had a final fight amongst the foothills of Kilimanjaro. We have only Baumann's version of these incidents. Some of this fighting may have been unavoidable, but most certainly not all. It contrasts greatly with the explorations of Speke and Grant, which were made without a shot being fired in anger—and in particular with the conduct of Grant, who recorded with profound relief that he had avoided bloodshed by parleying with certain inhabitants on the western shores of Lake Victoria, whose hostility had been roused by the misdeeds of certain members of his escort.

With his military training and his considerable experience as an explorer in West Africa, Hermann von Wissmann fully realised that the pace could not

---

[1] See page 65 above.

be forced and that the bringing of German East Africa under effective administration must necessarily be a slow process, which could not be achieved merely by a succession of punitive expeditions. It was evidently for that reason that he rebuked Emin for hoisting the German flag at Tabora and for sanctioning attacks on the Angoni. He was soldier enough to realise that with the long and tenuous line of communication between the coast and Unyamwezi any permanent foothold in those regions must be precarious until such time as peace, order and good government had been established throughout the intervening countries. His considerable African experience had further taught him that law and order could not be established in those regions unless a conciliatory attitude had been adopted towards the local inhabitants. Unfortunately for him his strategy was dictated to him by politicians in Europe. Both in London and in Berlin the air was full of mutual suspicion. In each country there was the lurking fear that some citizen of the rival state would emulate Carl Peters by pegging out a claim in the regions behind the other country's recognized sphere of influence, thus presenting his own country with a *fait accompli* which might induce it to go behind existing international agreements. It was for that reason that Emin was instructed to push ahead and consolidate the German position on Lake Victoria and that Baron von Eltz was sent to the plateau between Lakes Nyasa and Tanganyika. But neither of these areas could be securely held if they remained completely isolated from the coast. Something rather more had of necessity to be done, and to be done quickly, than establish a chain of military posts along far-flung and narrow lines of communication. The whole of the intervening country had to be reduced into possession and, if that was to be achieved quickly with the limited staff available, punitive expeditions became almost inevitable.

Germany was the last European state to embark on a policy of overseas expansion and owing to international rivalries was perforce in a hurry to obtain as extensive and as secure a foothold in Africa and elsewhere as she could in as short a time as possible. The result was that she had to depend for the carrying of her plans into execution upon personnel who were very often completely incapable of adapting themselves to local circumstances. The great majority of her early colonial officials, including medical officers and officials employed upon technical work, were army officers largely imbued with the traditional militarism of the service in which they had been trained. Certain of the senior officers, such as Hermann von Wissmann, fully realised that there were fresh lessons to be learned in East Africa and that the regimentation prevailing in Germany was not necessarily suitable to conditions existing in their colony. But the great majority of the officers were subalterns with two or three years' experience of regimental duty, many of whom were quite incapable or else quite unwilling to learn anything outside the ordinary scope of their military duties. Still more unsatisfactory were the German non-commissioned officers, who had been brought up in a hidebound militarism, in which most of their time had been spent in licking conscripts into shape and who, long before the days of Adolf Hitler, held the same opinion of the African as did the author of *Mein Kampf*. Much of the evil that was perpetrated by these people tarred their superiors in the eyes of the inhabitants with the same brush.

It was equally unfortunate for the reputation of the German administration that they almost entirely depended for the recruitment of their rank and file upon Africans who belonged to races which were alien to German East Africa, such as Zulus, Sudanese, and Swahilis from the coast. These mercenaries took full advantage of the protection of the German uniform to prey upon the inhabitants of the countries in which they were stationed and through which they passed. Their superiors very often turned a blind eye to their depredations and rarely took any measures to see that justice was done to their victims. As accounts given by German writers show, more than one clash between the Germans and the local inhabitants arose from the practice of one or more individual Sudanese or Zulu soldiers wandering off, as often as not without permission, on a marauding expedition and being set upon and killed by his intended victims. The attitude of the dead man's superior officer to this form of retaliation was frequently embodied in the saying—*cet animal est très méchant—quand on l'attaque, il se defend.* A party of soldiers was almost invariably sent to attack and set fire to the village and, if possible, to carry off the cattle.

It is only right and fair to say that, as the bibliography of German literature on the subject of their former territories in East Africa shows, many of their officials took a great interest in the people whom they administered and adopted a sympathetic, understanding and conciliatory spirit towards them. It may perhaps be wrong to say that such persons were in a relatively small minority. But whatever their number, the unfortunate result of the blunderings and the misdeeds of the remainder led their victims to believe that their leaven leavened the whole lump.

THE MAJI MAJI RISING, 1905-1907

The rising, which is now called the Maji Maji rising, took its name from the alleged protection which could be given against the Europeans' rifle fire by a concoction of maize, sorghum seed and water. The whole business would appear to have been linked up with a serpent cult. Prior to the rebellion, reports had spread that at Ngarambi on the Lungonya, a southern tributary of the Rufiji River, there was a water monster, whose mediums were able to compound and dispense this medicine as a prophylactic against disease, famine and many other kinds of evil. The medicine could be sprinkled over the body or taken internally. Its reputation spread far and wide and many Africans made pilgrimages to obtain the wonderful panacea. These pilgrimages were conducted in a perfectly open manner and roused no suspicion in the minds of the Germans. In all probability there was originally nothing sinister about the properties which the compounders attributed to the medicine, but later when smouldering embers of discontent with German rule were about to burst into flame the medicine men were induced to attribute to their concoctions the power either to make European rifles spurt water instead of bullets or else to make the bullets trickle off a man's body like drops of water. Even if the water failed to work this miracle forthwith it was alleged that those who had apparently succumbed to the bullets would rise again in three weeks' time.

The magic water was, however, not a cause of the rebellion. It provided the bond of union which led to concerted action by many tribes between whom any such combination had hitherto been believed to be impossible. The main causes of the rebellion were the misdeeds and acts of oppression of certain German officials and of many more of their Arab, Sudanese and Swahili subordinates. Count von Götzen, who was Governor of German East Africa at the time, attributed it to "the radical changes which foreign rule had introduced into their old way of life . . . a heathen and barbaric reaction against a superior and overwhelming culture and its necessary accompaniment of an unaccustomed form of discipline." Götzen was seeking to gloss over the misdeeds of his compatriots and the shortcomings of his own administration, but his words were to a certain extent not far wrong. As the Bishop of Zanzibar, Monseigneur de Courmont of the Holy Ghost Mission, had prophesied many years before, the Germans were always "unfurling *their* flag, talking of *their* judges, *their* governors, *their* taxes, and *their* regulations. The population, being taken by surprise, supports them, but little by little discontent increases, spreads, and blazes up." To the unwilling recruit the drill sergeant is not a popular taskmaster. If he and others of his kind are allowed to employ brutal methods of instruction with impunity and without rebuke, their methods may eventually lead to a mutiny.

Though Götzen afterwards alleged that the rising was the result of a widespread underground movement, which had been laying deep plans for a simultaneous revolt in many parts of the country, there is no really reliable evidence to support the allegation. The rebellion undoubtedly came as a bolt from the blue to the Germans and spread far afield very rapidly, but the evidence goes to show that it was the initial local successes of the original insurgents which encouraged malcontents in other parts of the country to take up arms against the Germans. The revolt began over what at first sight appeared to be nothing more than a labour dispute. There was a Government cotton plantation at Kibata, about forty miles north-west of Kilwa Kivinje, which was maintained by means of compulsory labour. In July, 1905, the Arab *Akida* at Kibata reported that a medicine man was inciting the people to disobey his orders for picking cotton. His warning of possible trouble was, however, disregarded. Shortly afterwards the *Akida* fled for his life and on August 2 the first clash of arms took place when the coast town at Samanga was attacked and set on fire. Thereafter the revolt spread rapidly over an area which may roughly be defined as the country south of the Central Railway and east of a line drawn from Kilosa to the north point of Lake Nyasa.

The attack on Samanga was followed by the murder of a number of solitary Arab and Sudanese traders living in outlying places and the looting of their stores. After these successes the number of the insurgents increased and they proceeded in a large body to the trading centre at Madaba about one hundred miles due east of Kilwa Kivinje. Here they did to death two Swahili overseers of the Government cotton plantation, who had made themselves particularly obnoxious by the exaction of forced labour for cotton picking. Two Arabs and one Swahili trader shared their fate. The rebels, however, spared not only the lives but also the property of two Indian traders. The shops of their other victims were looted.

After this success it was decided to attack the Government station at Liwale, which was situated about one hundred and twenty miles from Kilwa Kivinje on the road to Songea. By this time, if not earlier, the command of the insurgents had been assumed by an elephant hunter named Abdulla Mpanda, who after a visit to Ngarambi to "take the waters" had returned home to find there two askaris from the Liwale *boma*, whose throats he caused to be cut. Thereafter he had the war drums beaten and, after mustering the people, set out for Liwale. At Kingwichiro, fourteen miles from Liwale on the Kilwa Road, they attacked a trading post, the inhabitants of which included a number of discharged askaris. With one exception all these ex-soldiers were killed, their shops being looted and burned to the ground.   A former Sudanese soldier managed to escape and make his way to Liwale.

The station at Liwale was in charge of a sergeant named Faupel.   The only other European at the place was a trader named Aimer.   The station was incapable of any long-sustained defence.   With the aid of the African police the two Europeans put up a spirited defence of the *boma* and inflicted many casualties on their assailants, but eventually sheer weight of numbers prevailed. Incendiary arrows were fired at the thatched roof of the *boma* and set fire to it. Most of the police askaris and their wives and children were trapped in the burning building.   Faupel was shot and killed with poisoned arrows as he tried to escape.   Aimer made his escape, but was captured in his hiding place a few days later and shot to death with poisoned arrows.

About twelve days before the fall of Liwale a party of Benedictine missionaries set out from Kilwa Kivinje for Peramiho near Songea.   The leader of the party was Bishop Cassian Spiess, who was accompanied by two Brothers and two Sisters, three native servants and some Angoni porters.   The Bishop had been warned at Kilwa that he might be running grave risks and had been advised to postpone his journey, but he decided to continue with his original plans. The officer in command at Kilwa was unable to spare an escort for the party, but supplied them with some rifles and ammunition.   On the way the Angoni porters deserted the party, which was eventually waylaid by the rebels at Mikuku-yumbu about forty miles east of Liwale.   The missionaries were at the time unarmed and unaccompanied by any natives.   They were at once shot by the rebels with muzzle-loaders.[1]

Some of the insurgents now turned south to attack other mission stations. Once again it was the Benedictines who were to suffer.   Two brothers at Lukuledi received sufficient warning to enable them to escape to the U.M.C.A. station at Masasi, but those at Nyangao, about forty miles south-west of Lindi, were less fortunate.   A Priest and three Sisters were captured by the rebels but managed to make their escape to Lindi; one of the Sisters, however, became separated from the others on the way and was never seen again.

After finding that their intended victims had fled from Lukuledi, one band of insurgents made for the Universities Mission station at Masasi, where the two Benedictine Brothers had taken refuge.   The European missionaries on the station at the time comprised three ladies and five men, one of whom was so ill at the time as to be unable to walk.   Archdeacon Alfred Carnon, who was in charge of the station, wisely decided that for himself and his compatriots to remain at Masasi might have been heroic, but would most certainly have been useless and could only have imperilled the lives of their African followers as well as their own.   He accordingly decided to evacuate the station.   Eventually, after a long and perilous journey of over one hundred miles, he and his companions together with the two Benedictines from Lukuledi reached Lindi in safety.

After the departure of the Europeans the rebels swooped down on Masasi. The church was set on fire, but the Christian Africans had managed to remove the church plate and other fittings and valuables.   The rebels also set fire to

---

[1]See also page 383 below.

most of the houses on the station, but in the midst of their exultation they met with a wholly unexpected shock.   The followers of the mission were for the most part ex-slaves, who had been rescued from slave dhows by British men of war and were hardly the people one would expect to show any warlike spirit. On this occasion they falsified all expectations by rising and attacking the raiders and driving them off after they had killed no less than twenty-eight of them. The rebels received yet another shock when they started off in pursuit of the fleeing Europeans.   At Chiwata, twenty miles east of Masasi, there was a missionary outstation, at which Barnaba Nakaam, the local Yao Chief, had supplied the fugitives with porters—an unforgivable sin in the eyes of the rebels. Doubtless the rebels intended to make him pay the penalty for that assistance, but once again they found themselves opposed by African Christians.   After their unexpected reverse at Masasi, they decided that discretion was the better part of valour and withdrew.   It was probably due to the bold front thus shown at Chiwata that the hard-pressed European missionaries, including one very sick man who had to be carried in a hastily improvised hammock, managed to read Lindi in safety.

In the meantime the rising was spreading westwards from Liwale towards Songea and thence on to the plateau between Lakes Nyasa and Tanganyika. A force which was despatched from Songea to intercept them was routed at Nakatupe, but not until the government troops had inflicted heavy losses upon the rebels.   On September 19, 1905, the Berlin Missionary Society's station at Jakobi (Pangire) was attacked by a combined force of Sangu, Pangwa, Bena and Kinga which was said to have numbered two thousand, but the missionaries Gröschel and Hahn managed with the help of their followers to drive the enemy off.   Later both missionaries were decorated by the Kaiser for their bravery. At the same time it became clear that neither Jakobi nor the nearby station of Milo could be held for any length of time.   Both stations were accordingly evacuated.   They were afterwards levelled to the ground by the insurgents.

The defeat of the rebels at Jakobi was the first indication that they had over-reached themselves.   The heavy casualties, which had been suffered in more than one engagement, had badly shaken the belief of many of them in the efficacy of the waters of Ngarambi.   There had been no co-ordination of strategy amongst the numerous scattered bands which roamed the countryside.   They had taken the German authorities completely by surprise.   The killing of a number of German subjects and of their unpopular Arab and African subordinates in isolated places had been a very easy matter.   The capture and destruction of the badly sited and weakly garrisoned government station at Liwale had been achieved by fanaticism and sheer weight of numbers.   Generally speaking, the rebels were poorly armed.   Most of their firearms were muzzle-loaders and for their bullets they depended upon telegraph wire and glass stoppers from soda water bottles.   Many of them were solely equipped with bows and poisonous arrows.   Together with the element of surprise and the fanaticism bred of their faith in the potency of the waters from Ngarambi these weapons had sufficed to give them their initial successes against such feeble resistance as could be offered to them in the early days of the revolt.   When the German authorities had had time to recover from their surprise and to organize a plan of campaign to be undertaken by disciplined forces, which were armed with the latest modern weapons of precision, it became merely a question of the time it would take to stamp out the rebellion.

There were a number of surprising features about the rising. Though Count von Götzen described it as the result of a widespread underground conspiracy, in which the sacred water was carried like the fiery cross of Scotland far and wide as the signal for a simultaneous rising throughout the country, it appears to be perfectly clear that no such conspiracy ever existed. The leaders of the revolt came from the ranks of the minor chiefs and medicine men of the Ngindo and the Pogoro, tribes which had hitherto been regarded as not being of a markedly bellicose character. After their initial successes they were joined in the south-east corner of German East Africa by the Magangwara, a predatory tribe which had been a constant source of trouble and danger to coast towns such as Lindi and Kilwa Kivinje during the days of the Sultans of Zanzibar. They were, however, typical badmashes, who might be expected to join in any civil disturbance in order to share in the loot. What was remarkable was that none of the tribes who had given the Germans the most trouble in their efforts at subjugation of the country, such as the Hehe, Nyamwezi and Gogo, participated in the revolt. With their very recent experiences the two last named tribes may have been overawed by German garrisons in their midst. There is also reason to believe that the Hehe, who were momentarily leaderless, were influenced by the counsels of members of the Berlin Mission, who had entered their country as peace-makers after Mkwawa's death.

Despite Götzen's assertions, the picture one gets of the rising is that of a series of riotous disturbances by ill-armed and ill-disciplined bands of Africans, who, on learning of the early successes of the insurgents who had partaken of the waters of Ngarambi, rose in rebellion more or less simultaneously throughout the country to avenge their own personal grievances. Their principal band of union was their hatred of German rule. The waters of Ngarambi imbued them temporarily with a spirit of fanaticism, but that fanaticism began to evaporate as soon as heavy casualty lists showed that the water lacked the potency which the medicine men attributed to it. The insurgents also lacked a leader of the calibre of Bushiri, Siki or Mkwawa and the ease with which they were repulsed by the adherents of the U.M.C.A. at Masasi and those of the Berlin Mission at Jakobi shows what little stomach many of them had for any real fighting. It was easy enough to surprise, loot and kill a few unpopular government officials and their supporters in outlying districts, but never at any time during the revolt does there appear to have been a well concerted plan for the wholesale expulsion of the Germans from the land. In other parts of Africa, where revolts of a similar character have occurred, there has usually been a loyalist element in the native population, which has assisted the government in the suppression of the revolt. Admittedly, there were such people in German East Africa, of whom the Christian adherents of the Universities' Mission at Masasi were a notable example not only at the beginning of the rising but also in the later stages, but they appear to have been few and far between. The attitude of most of the tribes was one of non-belligerency and non-co-operation with either side.

As soon as the news of the murder of Bishop Spiess and his companions reached Germany, two light cruisers and a company of marines were despatched from the Fatherland as well as Papuan and Melanesian soldiers from the German possessions in the Pacific. Counter operations began in October, 1905. They consisted mainly of drives through the disturbed areas by detached columns with the object of rounding up and encircling the rebel forces but, as so frequently has happened in similar operations in tropical Africa, the enemy managed frequently to slip through the net before it could be tightly drawn. Throughout most of the country the rising had been largely suppressed by the spring of 1906, but the ringleaders amongst the Ngindo and the Ndonde held out in the region of Songea until the beginning of the following year. Most of these fought desperately, either being killed in battle or preferring suicide to surrender. Abdulla Mpanda, who would appear to have been one of the original instigators of the revolt and was one of the bravest and most intelligent of its leaders, was killed in January, 1907. With his death the last smouldering embers of the rebellion were virtually stamped out.

The long delay in suppression of the revolt was due in no small measure to the attitude adopted by the inhabitants of the disturbed areas. To some extent that attitude may have been due to intimidation by the insurgents. To a larger extent it was due to latent hostility to the German regime. Although the number who gave armed assistance to the insurgents was relatively small, very many of them gave valuable passive assistance in the shape of supplies and information. For this they were destined to pay dearly. In the words once used by Tacitus of his fellow-countrymen in Germany, the Germans in East Africa made a solitude and called it peace. Villages and crops were ruthlessly destroyed, cattle were carried off, and the German askaris were granted absolute licence to rob, kill or enslave the inhabitants. Famine inevitably ensued amongst the survivors and the numbers who died as a result of it and in actual warfare are said to have reached the figure of 120,000.

THE LAST YEARS OF THE GERMAN OCCUPATION 1907-1914

The Maji Maji rising, following close upon the Herero rising in South-West Africa, came as a great shock to public opinion in Germany. It was realised that there must be something rotten in the state of German colonial administration. In deference to public opinion as voiced by members of the Reichstag it was resolved that drastic reforms were needed. The first step necessary was the creation of a colonial department. As already indicated, Bismarck regarded Germany's overseas possessions as useful pawns on the European international chess board. The result was that, even after William II had dropped the pilot, colonial affairs remained under the control of the Imperial Chancellor. Public opinion in Germany was, however, growing increasingly dissatisfied with such a state of affairs. For them it was a question of *lebensraum*, or the right to "a place in the sun." Great Britain, France and the Netherlands had acquired territories all over the globe to which their surplus populations could emigrate and settle. Germany had been left badly behind in the race. Except for some islands in the tropical Pacific Ocean all that Germany had acquired were certain territories in East, West, and South-West Africa. It was reported that there were considerable tracts of territory in all three of these regions which were suitable for European settlement, but if such things as the Herero or the Maji Maji rising were to occur, it was very evident that none of these territories could be regarded as safe. Something clearly had got to be done, and done quickly, to introduce peace, order and good government into those countries.

Despite Count von Götzen's attempts to explain that the Maji Maji rebellion was the last fling of African paganism against the Christian culture of Germany, and his predecessor, General von Liebert's dictum that "it was impossible in Africa to get on without cruelty", it was beginning to be felt that there was something wrong about the opinion expressed a year before the Maji Maji rising by Herr Schleitwein that "the sentiments of Christianity and philanthropy with which the missionaries work must be repudiated with all energy." It was therefore decided in 1907 that colonial affairs should cease to be the concern of a sub-department of the Chancellor's office and should be transferred to a newly created ministry.

Bernhard Dernburg, the first Colonial Secretary, decided that his first task must be a personal tour of inspection of the territories entrusted to his charge. He returned to Germany somewhat appalled by certain things which he had seen or which had been brought to his notice. In February, 1908, he told the Budget Committee of the Reichstag that "the planters are at war with everybody—with myself, with the Government, with the local officials and, finally, with the natives. It makes a very unfavourable impression on one to see so many white people go about with negro whips. . . . Labourers are obtained under circumstances which could not be distinguished from slave hunts." Despite outcries of indignation from many quarters he set about the task of putting colonial administration to rights. In the face of opposition from militarist and other circles he boldly advocated the adoption of British methods of colonial administration. It was slow work but bit by bit he managed to secure much of his own way. He was succeeded in his post in 1911 by Wilhelm Solf, a Sanskrit scholar, who had had some practical experience of colonial administration in Samoa and who did much to further the policy initiated by his predecessor.

Until there has been a full and exhaustive examination of the German archives, it will never be easy to appraise at their proper worth the labours of the German administration to set their house in proper order during the seven brief years which were left to them after the final suppression of the Maji Maji rising. It is, moreover, unreasonable to draw any comparison between the outlook on African administration as enunciated in 1920 by the League of Nations and such principles as underlay the German policy before the outbreak of the First World War. As already stated, the Germans were late-comers in the field of colonial enterprise. They lacked experience in dealing with African races and the very varied population which inhabited German East Africa. Moreover, to the very end of their rule their primary concern was not so much with the problem of African administration as with the economic development of their territories. There are, and probably always will be, different views as to the merits and shortcomings of their native administration in its latter days. From the very inadequate data which exist at the present time, the conclusion one reaches is that a great deal depended upon the individual administrative officer, whose power for good or for evil was very extensive. As is only too well known, the evil that men do lives after them. The remembrance of the good that they have achieved does not long survive them. Furthermore, Germany had made an exceedingly bad start in the field of African administration and it obviously needed many years of patient labour to live down that past and to re-establish her in the eyes of other nations.

As the result of Dr. Dernburg's inquiries on the spot, a number of administrative changes were made in German East Africa. The Governor remained the supreme civil and military authority, but the tendency now was to confer the post upon a civilian instead of a military man. The troops were placed under a separate commander. The Governor was assisted by an advisory council, which was required to meet at least three times a year and to which financial estimates and all proposed legislation had to be submitted.

As the result of the innumerable punitive expeditions which had preceded Dr. Dernburg's reforms, the pre-German tribal organization had broken down more or less completely in many parts of the territory. But it still remained intact in Ruanda and Urundi (which were mandated to Belgium after the First World War) and in Bukoba, which since Emin Pasha's day had been administered by a succession of conciliatory officers in the persons of Langheld, Kalben, Kollmann and Stuemer. All these three areas were created "Residencies", where the inhabitants still continued to be ruled by their own rulers under the supervision and direction of a German Resident. The remainder of the country was divided into twenty-one districts. Two of these were left in military charge. The remainder were handed over to the charge of a civilian officer, known as the *Bezirksamtmann* (District Commissioner), who was responsible to the Governor for the maintenance of law and order in his district as well as for the collection of taxes. These District Commissioners adopted the system which had been created by the Sultan of Zanzibar, who had left native affairs in the hands of quasi-military officers known as *Akidas*. Under the German rule these *Akidas* were vested with certain magisterial powers and were held responsible for law and order over groups of villages. Subordinate to the *Akidas* were a number of the more influential village headmen, each bearing the title of *Jumbe*. These were given magisterial powers over the villages over which they presided and were likewise responsible for the maintenance of law and order within their respective jurisdictions. Many of the *Akidas* were undoubtedly competent officers and in some instances were later employed by the British Administration. But they were almost without exception imbued with an Islamic culture, which tended to result in their riding rough-shod over native custom. Owing to the vast areas of each of the twenty-one districts it was, moreover, impossible for the European administrative staff, which in 1914 numbered only seventy-nine, to travel in their districts and to exercise effective control over their subordinates. As the local inhabitants were liable to be conscripted for communal labour on works of a public nature and were expected to render certain personal services to their chiefs, in the absence of constant supervision the opportunities for corruption and abuse of authority were manifold.

As has been pointed out, the economic development of the country was the primary concern of the German administration. This led to the alienation at a very early date of certain tracts of land to Europeans for the purpose of planting of economic crops. By a decree passed in 1895 the Government declared all land to be Crown Land. Thereafter some 3,115 square miles were in course of time alienated to Europeans. As the total area of German East Africa comprised roughly some 370,000 square miles, the extent of this alienation was rather less than one per cent, but it included some of the best land. This was especially the case in the neighbourhood of Kilimanjaro, where the local inhabitants were confined largely to the upper slopes and were more or less ringed off from the lower ground by a circle of European plantations. The Germans themselves realised that allocations of land were giving rise to a legitimate cause of complaint and a possible source of unrest. Following on a report of two commissions which were appointed to inquire into the matter, they set apart 175 areas in those regions for the exclusive occupation of Africans.

One of the problems which confronted the German authorities was that of slavery, which was a legally recognized institution in the coastal strip which had previously formed part of the territories of the Sultan of Zanzibar and was likewise accorded similar recognition by the native customary law of the African tribes of the interior. From the very outset of their occupation the Germans adopted a determined attitude towards the slave trade. One of the many causes of Bushiri's revolt had been the resentment of Arab and African slave dealers at German interference with the traffic on the coast and along the recognized slave caravan routes. As already shown, German administrative officers opposed the trade on the shores of Lake Victoria and in other districts in the interior.

Public opinion in Germany fully supported their endeavours and in 1892 the German Anti-Slavery Committee sent out its representatives to assist in the suppression of the traffic and the after-care of the rescued slaves. The explorer Oscar Baumann made his journey from Pangani through Masailand to Ruanda and Urundi as an agent of this committee. But it is to be feared that the committee had little to show in the way of successful achievement during their brief operations. They received considerable financial support from the Fatherland and arrived in the country with equipment and funds which must have excited the envy of the local administrative staff. They built themselves large stations ostensibly as strategic posts for the interception of slave caravans, and constructed a large flotilla for patrolling the central lakes; but in the upshot they achieved rather less than had been achieved before their arrival by such administrative officers as Langheld at Bukoba and Wissmann in the south-west corner of the territory. The French traveller Lionel Decle visited their post on Ukerewe Island in Lake Victoria. He reported that the committee "had built a magnificent station there, but it is not difficult to build magnificent stations if you have four or five hundred men always at forced labour." Baumann's frequent clashes with the inhabitants on his line of march have already been recorded. The committee's African subordinates were many of them guilty of the same acts of extortion and depredation as the native soldiery. Those of the rescued slaves who stood in need of after-care and protection were usually handed over to the local missionaries, and in particular to the White Fathers at Tabora and on the shores of Lakes Victoria and Tanganyika. The work of the agents of the Anti-Slavery Committee therefore overlapped that of the administration and the missionaries and was really superfluous. Consequently after a little more than a year the committee withdrew its agents and sold its stations and equipment to the administration and to the White Fathers.

The slave trade could be extirpated in the course of time but the abolition of the status of slavery presented a more difficult problem. There was in Germany, as in England, a large body of public opinion which clamoured for its immediate abolition. It was, however, very obvious that without the requisite machinery for the enforcement of suitable legislation the status of slavery could not be abolished by a mere stroke of the pen. In addition, domestic slavery had grown up with and formed part of the social life of the inhabitants of German East Africa and peremptory measures for its immediate suppression might have led to serious economic as well as political disturbances. Accordingly in 1907 the Germans enacted a decree for the protection of slaves. The law further declared that all children born after 1906 of slave parents were *ipso facto* free and that slaves born prior to that date could purchase their freedom at prices to be determined by courts of law. Though the intention of the decree was that domestic slavery should gradually be extinguished by effluxion of time, actually very little progress had been made in this respect at the time of the outbreak of the First World War.

In comparison with the neighbouring Protectorates of British East Africa and Zanzibar, the rate of progress was exceedingly slow. Legislation similar to that passed by the Germans in 1907 had been passed in both those protectorates in 1890, but public opinion in the United Kingdom, as voiced by the Anti-Slavery and more than one missionary society, was not content to let the matter rest there. The status of slavery was completely abolished in the very same year as German legislation made this partial attempt to tackle the problem. At the same time it has to be remembered that in the British Protectorates compensation was paid to slave owners and that for many subsequent years aged and sick ex-slaves had to be maintained at the public expense and that, without a special subvention from the home government, the local revenues could hardly have met such an expenditure in German East Africa. Furthermore, in British East Africa the Mazrui rebellion of 1895-1896 had, like Bushiri's revolt a few years earlier, been in a large measure due to the anti-slavery measures of the British authorities. There was therefore reason for caution in regard to the tempo of emancipation in German East Africa, though over-caution may have rather unnecessarily slowed that tempo down.

The only form of direct taxation which the German authorities imposed upon the native inhabitants was a poll tax of three rupees payable by all adult males. Its imposition may not have been a very heavy burden in districts where there was no congestion and where there were reasonable opportunities for earning the necessary money, but in other districts, where the cash resources of the inhabitants were very low and sometimes more or less non-existent, it caused a great deal of very real hardship. Moreover, lack of supervision of the tax collectors led to employment of methods and abuses which gave rise to very justifiable discontent.

One of the objects of the poll tax was indirectly to compel the African to seek employment in the labour market in order to obtain the wherewithal to pay it. Such tribes as the Nyamwezi, Sukuma, and Iramba, who had become wage earners in the days of the Arab or Swahili caravan, began to seek employment on German plantations, but the supply of labour never came up to the demand. The great majority had their own plots, which they cultivated sufficiently to supply their relatively few wants, and they had no inducement to leave their own houses to work for a European in some distant plantation. Attempts at recruitment of indentured labour never satisfied demands.

In his "Thirty Years of German East Africa," Hans Zache has said: "It is a falsely reasoned and falsely proved humanitarianism which seeks to take no cognizance of the education of the native for manual labour. Work is provided so that the colony may benefit by increased production, and not least also it is provided for the blessing of the negro." The blessing accruing to the African from humanitarianism as practised upon him by a German plantation owner would appear at times to have been of a somewhat mixed character, but credit must be given to the German administration for the measures taken by them for

German machine-gun, 1914-18 Campaign.

Photo: Col. W. S. Knox-Gore

The "Koenigsberg".

One of the guns from the "Koenigsberg" being transported up-country.

the promotion of African education, which contrasted quite favourably with the measures taken in the adjacent British protectorates. As a report published by the German Colonial Institute in 1911 shows, there were at that date over one thousand schools in the colony with 287 European and 1,256 African teachers and 66,647 pupils. Most of these schools were in the hands of the missionary societies, only 83 schools with 3,192 pupils being financed by the Government. The vast majority of these schools were elementary schools. The Government maintained two and the missions 29 higher schools with 161 and 1,196 pupils respectively. There were also 3 government and 14 missionary industrial schools with 137 and 149 pupils respectively. There were 17 additional "schools for practical work", the objects of which were "to turn out artisans for the Europeans, and women for domestic work, to develop old Arab handicrafts, and introduce new culture." The cost of educational work was borne entirely by the government and the missions for their respective schools, as attempts to obtain fees from the pupils had not been very successful. Unlike the administration in South-West Africa, there was no insistence on the compulsory learning of German in German East Africa.

In the economic development of the colony the Germans showed considerable activity. Except for cotton cultivation, where endeavours were made on the shores of Lake Victoria and on the coast to encourage African cultivation by free distribution of cotton seed and by the establishment of experimental farms and instruction in crop treatment, the emphasis was on the development of European plantation cultivation. There were three important plantation regions, namely, Usambara in the north, the line of the Central Railway, and the hinterland served by the port of Lindi. There were also more isolated areas on the Mahenge plateau and the district of Iringa, the shores of Lake Victoria, and the vicinity of Kilimanjaro. The most important economic crops raised were sisal, which was introduced from Florida in 1892 by Doctor Richard Hindorf, and rubber, which was planted mainly between Tanga and Korogwe and also in the districts of Handeni and Morogoro. This latter crop dated back for the most part to the boom years 1909-1910, but the yield of latex was so disappointing that many trees were seldom tapped. Other European plantation crops were coffee, cotton, coconuts (for copra) and kapok.

In 1902 the Germans established a biological and agricultural institute at Amani, in the hills behind Tanga, where a series of laboratories and experimental nurseries for plants, shrubs, trees and potential economic crops were laid out and much valuable work was done by the Principal, Dr. A. Zimmermann and his staff. During the First World War the Institute was taken over by British troops in 1916, but the German staff was allowed to remain until after the armistice in 1918, when they were repatriated. Three of the staff remained voluntarily until August, 1920, when Mr. A. Leechman took charge of the station as Director. Later Amani became a long-range research station, with all British territories in East and Central Africa contributing to its maintenance.

In order to foster plantation development the Usambara Railway was started from Tanga in 1896 by a private company, which however had to stop work owing to lack of funds. The Government then took over the line, which reached Korogwe in 1902, Mombo two years later and Moshi in 1912. The Central Line was begun in 1907 and reached Kigoma on Lake Tanganyika in February, 1914. Nominally, the administration of this line was in the hands of a private company, but the Government acquired nine-tenths of the shares and the line was therefore to all intents and purposes a State railway.   In 1914 the Reichstag agreed to finance the construction of a branch line from Tabora to the regions of Ruanda and Urundi, but the First World War put an end to the project.

In the meantime trade had been steadily progressing.   In 1900 exports were valued at £214,682.   In 1906, despite the dislocations caused by the Maji Maji rebellion, that figure had risen to over half a million pounds and six years later it had reached the million pound figure.   In 1900 imports had been valued at £601,527, in 1906 at £1,697,085 and in 1912 at £2,515,000.

In early years the ordinary revenue had been largely assisted by an annual contribution from the Imperial Government on account of military expenditure, but after the suppression of the Maji Maji rebellion that contribution was gradually reduced until in 1914 it had reached the figure of £165,000.   In the meantime ordinary revenue, which had amounted to £296,900 in 1904, had been steadily increasing.   It first exceeded half a million pounds in 1909 and in 1914 had reached the figure of £823,900.

THE EAST AFRICA CAMPAIGN, 1914-1918

Paul von Lettow-Vorbeck assumed command of the colonial troops in German East Africa in January, 1914.   He had seen fighting in the Boxer Rising in China in 1900 and had been wounded in the Herero Rising in South-West Africa in 1903.   In 1911 he had been appointed to command the colonial troops in the Cameroons.   Most of his military service had therefore been spent overseas and had made him eminently qualified for the task which lay before him little more than six months after his arrival in East Africa.

International affairs for some time past had shown that there was the distinct possibility of an outbreak in the none too remote future of a universal war, in which Germany and Great Britain might be found fighting on opposite sides. Von Lettow realized that in any such war the troops under his command could only play a subsidiary part and that the fate of the colony would be decided on the battlefields in Europe.   All that he could hope to achieve with the forces at his disposal was to divert considerable numbers of the enemy from intervening in Europe or some other theatre of war and to endeavour, whenever and wherever possible, to inflict upon the enemy some fairly substantial loss either of men or of potential war material.   In considering how best to employ the troops at his disposal for the above purposes the German commander had to bear in mind two other important matters.   Firstly, unless the British Navy met with some serious disaster or succession of disasters at sea, he could have little or no hope of receiving any material assistance in either men or war materials from the Fatherland and must be prepared to rely almost entirely on local resources for keeping his end up.   Secondly, whatever the issue on the European battlefield, it was all-important that German East Africa should not fall into enemy hands and thereby become a pawn for bargaining with at a peace conference.

At the outset of the war the armed forces in the German East African Protectorate consisted of approximately 250 German officers and N.C.O.'s and 2,500 Africans.   In addition there were about three thousand adult male Germans in the colony of military age.   Some of these were retired naval and military officers and almost without exception all the rest had undergone military training.   In many parts of the colony these reservists had maintained their efficiency as members of local volunteer defence corps. In addition to the military forces there was an armed African police force of 2,200, as well as some three thousand time-expired soldiers capable of recall to the colours. According to a German account the highest total of German forces on the German side at any time during the war was 3,300 Europeans and 15,000 Africans, but owing to the vast extent of territory which had to be garrisoned and protected many of these were in scattered detachments spread throughout the country. Some of these, moreover, were little more than raw recruits.

When hostilities broke out on August 4, 1914, Germany found herself at war with Great Britain and Belgium. Three days later Portugal proclaimed her loyalty to her ancient British ally in all military operations. This meant that on her northern, western and southern land frontiers German East Africa was threatened with the prospect of invasion. Unless Germany could obtain the command of the sea in home waters, there was the obvious risk that the coast might be subjected to a rigorous blockade as well as the danger of enemy landings being effected at Dar es Salaam or Tanga and other vital arteries on the lines of communication with the interior.

The naval side of the ensuing warfare centred largely round the German light cruiser *Königsberg*. This was a vessel of 3,350 tons with a speed of 24½ knots. She carried ten 4·1 inch guns of a modern pattern. The only other German naval vessel in East African waters at the time was the survey vessel *Moewe*. She was in Dar es Salaam harbour at the time of the outbreak of war, but carried no guns. As no satisfactory armament could be obtained locally, her commander scuttled her so as to prevent her from falling into British hands. Her complement of 102 men joined the land forces and later some of them were employed in the amphibious warfare which took place on Lake Tanganyika.

The *Königsberg* put to sea from Dar es Salaam on July 31, 1914, in anticipation of hostilities. There were at that date three British cruisers in East African waters—the *Astrea*, *Hyacinth* and *Pegasus*. With the exception of the last named all these vessels had a heavier armament than the *Königsberg* but were slower. The *Pegasus* was a light cruiser of only 2,135 tons with a speed of 20 knots and armed with eight 4-inch guns. The *Königsberg* managed to evade the vigilance of all three vessels and on August 6—two days after the outbreak of war—to coal from the German collier *Somali* off Ras Hafun. She then disappeared from her opponents' ken. On September 2 she again coaled from the *Somali* off the British island of Aldabra between the Seychelles and Madagascar. Next day she entered the Rufiji River. On September 20 she appeared off Zanzibar and shelled the *Pegasus*, which was lying there with fires drawn, cleaning her boilers. The *Pegasus* was hopelessly outranged by the enemy's guns and was soon reduced to a wreck after suffering heavy casualties. The *Königsberg* then steamed back to the Rufiji. Her hiding place was soon located and the river delta was blockaded. Owing to her shallow draught the *Königsberg* was able to make her way some twenty miles upstream to a point where she could not be approached by the deeper draught British men-of-war. Her armament was too heavy to allow any light craft to approach her and owing to thick jungle her position was exceedingly difficult to locate. It became necessary to attack her with heavy howitzers after aerial observation. For this purpose, two shallow draught monitors, the *Severn* and the *Mersey* were brought out from England and on July 11, 1915, the *Königsberg* was bombarded and blown up. Her crew survived and joined the land forces. Her guns and her ammunition were removed and made a valuable addition to the armament of the land forces. Her commander, Captain Max Loof, was severely wounded but on recovery took command of the German land forces in the Lindi area, where he maintained a stout resistance until forced to surrender to superior odds in 1917. When he abandoned his ship in the Rufiji, he at least had the satisfaction of knowing that he had directed against himself and contained a vastly superior British naval force, which might otherwise have been effectively employed in other theatres of war.

The destruction of the *Königsberg* brought to an end naval warfare in East African waters, but until the British land forces had effectively occupied the harbours along the coast of the colony it was still necessary to retain a large number of men-of-war for the purpose of blockading the four-hundred-mile coastal strip. As in the case of other naval blockades, it was never possible to draw the meshes of the net so close as to make it impossible for the occasional blockade runner to slip through. There were two cases of breaking in and two of breaking out. In 1915 the captured British merchant vessel *Rubens* reached Manza Bay from Germany after being re-christened the *Kronborg*. She was spotted and shelled by British warships and had to be beached, but she was able to deliver an invaluable and much needed cargo of arms and ammunition. An even more successful blockade runner was the *Marie*, which in early 1916 not only landed three batteries of howitzers and mountain guns as well as small arms and ammunition at Sudi Bay between Lindi and Mikindani, but also managed to make her escape to Batavia. The other break-out was made by some members of the crew of the *Königsberg* in 1917, who after an adventurous odyssey reached their Fatherland by way of Arabia and Turkey. There can be little doubt that the successes of the two blockade runners enabled the German land forces to hold out far longer than might otherwise have been the case.

The land warfare in and on the borders of German East Africa lasted from the day of the oubreak of war in 1914 until two days after the conclusion of the Armistice on November 11, 1918. In the opening months of the campaign the Germans were constantly raiding along the coast, on the railway line from Mombasa to Nairobi, and into the frontier districts of Uganda, the Belgian Congo, Rhodesia and Nyasaland. Whilst most of these raids were of the hit-and-run variety, it soon became apparent that the British Protectorate forces would have more than enough to do to hold their own. It was therefore decided to send an expeditionary force from India to deal with the situation. This force, with the exception of a battalion of the Loyal North Lancashire Regiment, consisted of 7,000 Indian troops. It reached Mombasa at the end of August, 1914. It was deployed for an invasion of German East Africa on a line extending from Moshi to Tanga. Part of the invading force proceeded overland to Longido. The rest were embarked in transports to effect a landing at Tanga. The operations began in November, 1914. Von Lettow had prior intelligence of these movements and was able to inflict a heavy defeat on the force which landed at Tanga. The British and Indian troops were compelled to re-embark and the other column received a serious check at Longido and was compelled to retire.

Von Lettow's successes put an end for the time being to any general offensive against his forces and it was not until 1916 that any large-scale attack was resumed. In the meantime the warfare had resumed its previous character of occasional raiding by both forces with varying successes on either side. The most serious reverse encountered by the Germans at this stage of the operations was the capture of Bukoba on Lake Victoria in June, 1915.

After the conquest of German South-West Africa troops from the Union of South Africa became available for service against von Lettow. In February, 1916, the supreme command in East Africa was assumed by General Jan Christian Smuts, who had at his disposal a large body of British, South African, Rhodesian and Indian troops as well as an ever-increasing number of African troops. The new offensive began with an attack by General Jacob van Deventer on Taveta, an outpost in British territory which had been held by the Germans since the early days of the war. Taveta was retaken and Moshi, in German territory, was occupied in March, 1916. Shortly afterwards heavy rains brought about a temporary lull in the operations. When they were resumed in April, van Deventer struck south into Irangi, whilst Smuts advanced from Moshi down the valley of the Pangani River towards the coast. At the same time a Belgian force began an advance on Tabora. Von Lettow was now outflanked both to the west as well as to the north. He was compelled to evacuate the Kilimanjaro and Usambara regions and fall back southwards. Between July and August, with assistance from the British Navy, the whole of the coast line from Tanga to Bagamoyo was occupied by the invading forces. Dar es Salaam fell into their hands on September 4, 1916.

Meanwhile Belgian troops (mostly African) were carrying out successful operations from the Congo. By the end of May they were in possession of Ruanda. Some well-planned amphibious operations enabled them to occupy Kigoma and Ujiji on the shores of Lake Tanganyika by the beginning of August. Co-operating with them was a British column under Brigadier-General Crewe which captured Mwanza on July 14, 1916. Tabora was occupied by the Belgians on September 19.

In the meantime a British force under General Northey had moved north into German territory from Rhodesia and occupied Iringa on August 29. In order to avoid encirclement the Germans had to fall back from the Central Line, which they did their best to render unserviceable by the destruction of important bridges and other railway works, locomotives and rolling stock.

By the end of the year the German forces were split up into three groups. Von Lettow was in the region of Kilwa. To the south of him in the Lindi area was another force under Major-General Wahle, a retired officer who happened to be in East Africa at the outbreak of war on a visit to his son. The third force under Captain Tafel was on the Mahenge plateau.

Smuts relinquished the command of the British forces early in 1917 and proceeded to England. He had been greatly hampered in bringing his operations to a successful conclusion by the heavy incidence of malaria amongst his European troops. By the beginning of 1917 no less than 12,000 out of the 15,000 South African troops had had to be evacuated because of disease. They were replaced by a brigade of Nigerian troops under Brigadier-General Cunliffe and freshly raised battalions of the King's African Rifles.

In addition to disease, rains seriously delayed operations at the beginning of 1917 and it was not until after General van Deventer had assumed supreme command at the end of May that a large-scale offensive was resumed.

Tafel on the Mahenge plateau was threatened both from the north and the south. Being in distinct danger of encirclement, he fell back to the south, hoping to join forces with von Lettow. He managed to reach the Ruvuma, but being unable to procure food, was compelled on November 28, 1917, to surrender with his entire force.

Tafel's surrender left only the German forces in the south-west corner of the colony to contend with. These were not only threatened to the south by Portuguese troops but also by British troops converging on them from the north and west. They were also cut off from the sea and all possible hope of replenishment of their munitions and other supplies by British troops which had with naval assistance occupied Kilwa, Lindi, Sudi and Mikindani in September, 1916. In addition the troops under General Wahle in the Lindi area were being greatly harassed by hostile Makonde. They had consequently been forced up the Lukuledi River and eventually joined forces with von Lettow, who had likewise been compelled to retreat southwards. This last remnant of the German forces under von Lettow crossed the Ruvuma on the night of November 25-26, 1917, into Portuguese territory.

For the next ten months von Lettow held out in Portuguese territory. Without any bases, short of ammunition and other supplies, and without hope of reinforcement or replenishment of his equipment, he maintained a highly successful form of guerilla warfare against a vastly superior enemy force and managed to evade all attempts to encircle him. On September 28 he re-crossed the Ruvuma into German territory, but he had to be constantly on the move to evade capture. On October 17 he quitted Ubena, where he was forced to leave behind a number of sick and wounded, including General Wahle. By the end of that month he had been compelled to retreat into Northern Rhodesia, where he made an unsuccessful attack on Fife. On November 13 he learned that an armistice had been concluded two days previously. He accepted the terms on the following day, and on November 25 formally surrendered to General Edwards at Abercorn.

An eye-witness gave the following description of the surrender to the *Bulawayo Chronicle:*

"Von Lettow, whose striking presence is a good index of what must be a wonderful personality, came in at the head of his first detachment. . . . After these troops had been quickly formed into three lines in close formation, von Lettow advanced a few paces, saluted the flag, then taking out a pocket book, read therefrom a formal statement of surrender in German. He repeated it in English, whereupon General Edwards replied, accepting his surrender on behalf of His Majesty King George V. Von Lettow was then presented to the officers present, and in turn introduced his own officers. . . . Ex-Governor Schnee was also there. Then followed the most dramatic moment of the proceedings, when von Lettow called upon his troops to lay down their arms, the Europeans alone being allowed to retain theirs in recognition of the splendid fight they had put up. The *askaris* laid down their rifles, took off and deposited their equipment and were then marched off by companies to the internment camp. . . . The whole force surrendering numbered 30 officers, 25 other Europeans, 1,165 *askaris*, 482 Portuguese natives acting as porters, 282 followers, 13 headmen, 819 women, making a total of 155 Europeans and 4,277 natives. . . . It was a most impressive spectacle. The long motley column, Europeans and *askaris,* all veterans of a hundred fights, the latter clothed in every kind of headgear, women who had stuck to their husbands through all these years of hardship, carrying huge loads, some with children born during the campaign, carriers coming in singing in undisguised joy at the thought that their labours were ended at last."

No tribute in the hour of victory from victor to vanquished was ever better deserved. As von Lettow said, there was not a single modern pattern rifle amongst those which were laid down by his men. Yet they had on many occasions been brought face to face with the latest weapons of modern warfare. The rights and wrongs of the quarrel in which they were engaged were things which they could hardly be expected to understand. They had been hopelessly outnumbered by their opponents and for many months had been engaged more or less continuously in the difficult task of fighting rearguard actions. Their pay was many months in arrears. Yet they had not been found wanting in personal courage or in devotion to their officers.

Much of this remarkable achievement of a small fighting force must be attributed to the inspiration and leadership of their commanding officer, whose first anxiety after the surrender was to see that his African followers obtained their arrears of pay. In the words of Major-General J. J. Collyer, "If it is remembered how keenly sensitive the native soldier is to any shortcomings in his superior and that von Lettow had only been with his command for six months when hostilities began and kept that command efficient and formidable through four years of steadily declining fortune, some idea may be formed of the resolute nature and soldierly qualities of the German commander-in-chief. His operations consistently bore the imprint of his skill and personality." ("*Operations in East Africa*" in the *Encyclopaedia Britannica* (14th Ed.) Vol. 7, p. 854).

The esteem in which the British held a brave and chivalrous foe was best shown after the war, when General von Lettow-Vorbeck was invited to London as the principal guest at a re-union of members of the services who had participated in the campaign against him.

Whilst every credit must be given to him for the manner in which he fought what was almost from the very start a losing battle, the achievements of his opponents must not be underrated. It is no denigration of von Lettow to say that he possessed certain advantages, other than courage and a sound sense of strategy, which greatly assisted him. The country in which most of the fighting took place was ideal for guerilla warfare. His opponents had to contend with dense tropical bush and jungle and with wholesale inundations of large tracts of the country during the rainy season. They also were confronted by tropical diseases which wrought havoc amongst the European and Indian troops as well as amongst the transport animals. The element of surprise was often out of the question for the attackers, as the defenders were forewarned by the necessarily laborious approach of their adversaries, who had to cut roads and bridge rivers and swamps. Thus, as General Collyer has said, "many good cards were in the hand of the German commander, and he rarely failed to play them with good effect."

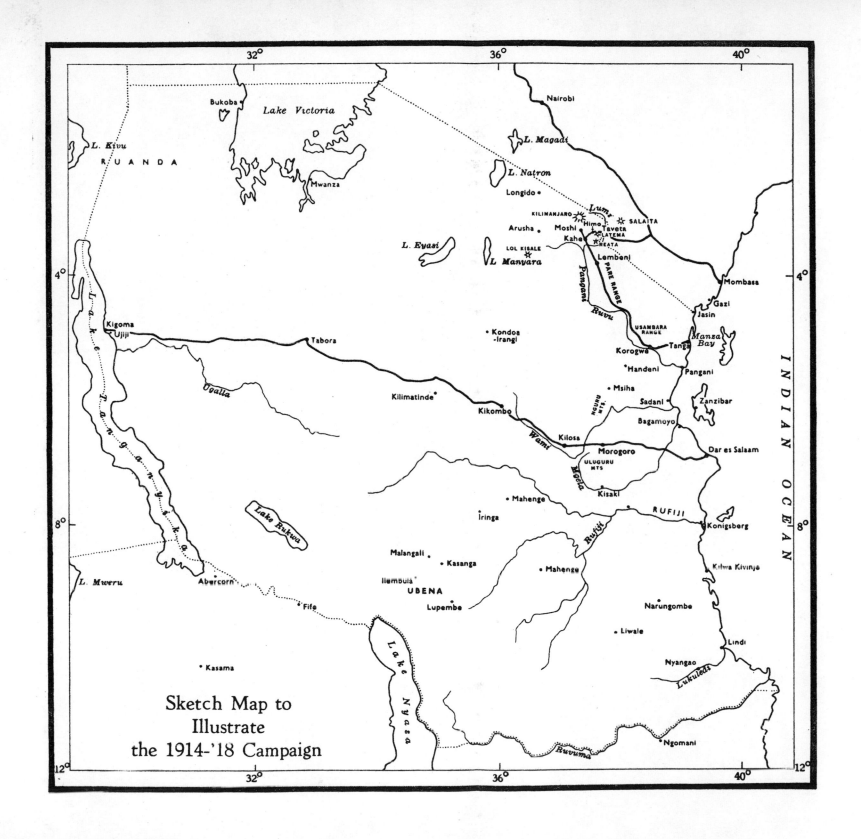

Sketch Map to
Illustrate
the 1914-'18 Campaign

Sketch Map to
Illustrate
the 1914-18 Campaign

Chapter 4

BRITISH RULE, 1919-1954

From the end of the 1914-1918 war period until the year 1954 the history of Tanganyika divides itself with some precision into approximate quinquenniads. The first of these, 1920-1924, was a necessary period of consolidation after the disruptions of the war. Then, in 1925-1929, there was a period of rapid expansion, reflected not only in expansion of the budget, but also in optimistic, sometimes over-optimistic, private investment. By the Autumn of 1930 the cold winds of the depression were starting to blow in Tanganyika, and it was not until 1934 that the country's barometer started again to rise. From 1935 to 1939, Tanganyika experienced a period of great uncertainty, during which, in spite of public assurances given both locally and in the United Kingdom, the impression was abroad that the territory was being used as a political pawn, with the result that public and private investment were both hesitant.

The war of 1939-1945 involved no fighting within the territory and Tanganyika was able to concentrate upon assistance towards the prosecution of the war. Nor should it be forgotten that before the outbreak of war, and in part as a substantial gesture of official confidence in the future of the territory, a Development Plan had been initiated, so that even before the end of the war it was possible to think in terms of post-war development on the basis of those initial plannings. In the period 1945-1949 the territory was engaged in post-war settlement and planning, while in 1950-1954 it engaged in a programme of such rapid development as would have been outside the wildest hopes of those in charge of the administration of the territory at the outset of British rule.

After the foregoing brief summary of the history of the territory in the period 1920-1954 it will now be convenient to examine more closely such of the occurrences in the respective phases as are relevant to the proper presentation of the Tanganyika picture. Before doing so, however, it is necessary to give some account of the determination of the boundaries of the Tanganyika Territory, as that part of German East Africa which passed into the control of the British Government was named[1]; and of the abolition of slavery, which was one of the first tasks before the new British Administration.

TANGANYIKA BOUNDARIES

The end of hostilities found the British Civil Administration in process of taking over control from the military authorities, and at the same time, the Belgian Authorities were in actual occupation of a considerable part of the former German East Africa consisting of the whole of Ruanda-Urundi and areas approximating to the present Kigoma and Biharamulo Districts. On January 31st, 1919, a Royal Commission was issued appointing Sir Horace

[1] At the end of the 1914-1918 War it was clearly necessary to choose a new name for the former German East Africa, and to differentiate that country from the East African Protectorate. A distinguished civil servant, Sir Cosmo Parkinson, in proposing the name Kenia (note the spelling) for the latter, offered the names Tanganyika or Tabora for the ex-German Territory. The former was preferred, and "Tanganyika Territory" was used in the text of the Peace Treaty. A proposal to substitute "Tanganyika Protectorate" in the Mandate negotiations was not pursued. The territory remained as "Tanganyika Territory", (T.T. for short was already foreseen in 1919) until after the 1939-1945 War when "Territory" was dropped from its official name, and the country became entitled "Tanganyika".

Byatt, who had late in 1916 been seconded as a civil administrator from the Malta Administration, to be Administrator of that portion of German East Africa which was occupied by H.M. Forces.   The Peace Treaty with Germany on January 10th, 1920, included provision for the administration by Great Britain of what is now Tanganyika under Mandate from the League of Nations, the Belgian Government assuming similar responsibility for Ruanda-Urundi. Though the land areas thus divided were vastly different in size, there was no such great difference in the division of population, some four million persons in Tanganyika coming under British Administration, while the much smaller area of Ruanda-Urundi contained some three million souls.   The areas of Tanganyika which had been under temporary Belgian occupation were handed over on March 22nd, 1921, and in September, 1922, the Commission charged with the final settlement of the Tanganyika/Ruanda-Urundi boundary started work.   The boundary as originally proposed by the "Milner-Orts" Agreement was intended to provide a corridor for the possible construction of a railway on the west side of the Kagera River to connect Tanganyika with Uganda. But this line would have cut off a portion of the Kingdom of Ruanda from Belgian administration, and by agreement between the British and Belgian Governments and with the approval of the League of Nations, the mid-stream of the Kagera River was taken instead as the international boundary.   This completed the determination of the boundaries of Tanganyika, except that it was not until 1922 that the administration of Mafia Island was taken over, this island having been administered temporarily until then from Zanzibar.

ABOLITION OF SLAVERY

One of the more urgent duties facing the British Administration was the abolition of slavery, a duty which was specifically imposed by Article Five of the Mandate.   As a signatory to the General Act of the Anti-Slavery Conference of Brussels, 1890, and to other international treaties relating to the suppression of slavery, Germany took steps to prohibit slave trading in her East African Protectorate, but permitted the existence of domestic slavery. Whereas Great Britain abolished the legal status of slavery in Zanzibar in 1897 and in the East Africa Protectorate in 1907, Germany had contented herself with introducing legislation to ameliorate the conditions of the slaves' existence and to make it easier for them to obtain their liberty than formerly.   For some years before the war Germany had contemplated the possibility of emancipating all slaves by one stroke of the pen, but she shrank from the great expense which might have to be incurred in compensating slave owners, and she feared the serious political disturbances which might ensue.   The most important step taken was to decree that all slaves born after 1905 should be free; and it was thus thought that, even if the extreme step of abolishing slavery were never taken, slavery would in due course die a natural death and would cease to exist after 1930 or 1940.   It is only just, however, to say that the form of slavery in existence in German East Africa was of a mild kind, which might be described as domestic servitude rather than domestic slavery.   It had indeed been customary since 1899 for the Germans to refer to slaves as retainers, and to owners as masters.   Slave-raiding and slave-trading, with their attendant horrors, were things of the past and under German law no slave might be sold without consenting to the transaction himself.   Married couples might not be separated, and children under twelve years of age might not be taken from their parents.   A slave had various privileges: religious freedom had to be accorded to him; marriage could not be denied him; he could claim, from his master, food, board and lodging and two free days every week; he possessed his own property (but as the master had the right to inherit from his slave, he could claim to supervise the management of the property); he had certain limited rights of inheritance from his master; and his master was bound to support him when he was too old to work.

Under the German law a slave might obtain his freedom by ransom, manu-mission, official grant of letters of freedom (in the case of ill-treatment), passing five years without working as a slave, and failure of heirs on the death of an owner. A female slave also became free if she married a free-man and the latter paid the bridal price to the owner, and when an owner acknowledged a child by his slave as his offspring.

A general survey of conditions in the territory was undertaken by the British Administration. It was found that the figures accepted by the Germans in 1913 relating to the number of slaves were inaccurate and, further, that their estimates appear to have been framed upon a misinterpretation of the status of slavery. For example, in the district of Ujiji, formerly the greatest slave depot in Central Africa, which was credited by the Germans with no less than 20,000 slaves, it was discovered that slavery was practically non-existent. Similarly, in the Districts of Songea and Iringa, where some 15,000 natives were recorded as under the ownership of pagan masters, former war captives had been absorbed into the tribes on terms of equality and were not even spoken of as "slaves". But while slavery was practically non-existent among the pagan tribes of the interior, domestic servitude was still prevalent in the coastal belt, possibly owing to long association with Zanzibar and to Islamic tradition, though deaths and the opportunities afforded to natives by the war to sever their connection with unpopular masters had materially reduced the figures presented to the German Government in 1913.

After this survey, legislation was quickly enacted in 1922 for the abolition of slavery in the shape of the Involuntary Servitude (Abolition) Ordinance and after the non-committal but unfriendly attitude of the Germans towards this institution, and following the occupation of the territory by the British whose attitude to slavery was well known, slavery disappeared without any of the political disturbances which had been feared by the German Administration. The only difficulty was financial, when some of the former slave-owners on Mafia Island experienced temporary difficulty in paying for that labour on their coconut plantations which had formerly been provided by slaves.

THE YEARS OF CONSOLIDATION, 1920-1924

It will be difficult for those of today to visualize the state of the territory after the 1914-1918 war. The territory's economy, its communications and its inhabitants had been disrupted by the East African Campaign, and Tanganyika did not escape the influenza epidemics of 1917-1919 which were estimated at the time to have caused between 50,000 and 80,000 African deaths. In addition, failure of the rains in 1919 caused a disastrous famine in what is now the Central Province, so that even in 1924 there were nearly as many human skulls scattered over the countryside between Kondoa-Irangi and Dodoma, the remains of some of those who had tried to walk to the Central Line to fetch the food there provided by Government, as there were skulls of the horses which had been so freely used by the South African Forces and which had died of trypanosomiasis and other diseases. The only reliable permanent communications consisted of the two railway lines from Dar es Salaam to Kigoma and from Tanga to Moshi. The Great North Road did not exist. In the realization that good communications with the areas south of the Central Line were a necessity, the earliest major road improvement was undertaken on the military track between Kilosa and Iringa. Although this road was the first to be made serviceable, it passed through tsetse country, and the earliest conception of the necessity for a main road from Dodoma to Iringa and Lake Nyasa derived from the need to provide a fly-free route to the south. Even in 1925, the new Governor, Sir Donald Cameron, commented adversely on the lack of reliable communications south of the Central Railway Line, and officers posted to such places as Tukuyu and Songea usually travelled via Beira and Nyasaland.

SITE OF THE CAPITAL

Civil Administration had been started piece-meal as the territory was brought under control during the 1914-1918 war, from the German station of Wilhelmstal, now Lushoto. It was only natural that as soon as war conditions permitted, the seat of Government should be moved to the head of the main transport artery at Dar es Salaam where building investment from that time onwards has steadily removed all likelihood of shifting the capital to a cooler site.

CIVIL LIST

The year 1919 saw the publication of the first annual civil list containing the names, apart from Railways officials, of 356 European Government officers of whom 121 had been seconded to the territory from elsewhere. This small nucleus consisted largely of members of the Administration, Police, and Posts and Telegraphs, and had been expanded to a wholly Tanganyika cadre of 575 by 1924 (apart from Railways and Military staff).

PUBLIC HEALTH

Though small in numbers, the Medical Department was of obvious importance in a situation where the disruptions of war might have been expected to result in serious epidemics. A particular watch was kept for plague, smallpox, cerebro-spinal meningitis and influenza, but of these smallpox alone was difficult to control, owing to deterioration of the imported vaccine, until the territory started to produce its own.

SLEEPING SICKNESS

German records had indicated that sleeping sickness occurred in three separate areas, and a careful watch was therefore kept for this disease. It was not until 1922 that any significant number of cases was detected. A small incidence was discovered in the then Mwanza District, which was brought under reasonable control within two years by the policy of concentrating a scattered but tractable population into close settlements where regular medical examination and treatment could be given. The disease was definitely diagnosed in 1924 in the other two areas reported by the Germans, when small numbers of cases were found in the Liwale area, and near the Ugalla River in the Tabora District, both incidences being forerunners of much more serious things to come.

THE YAWS CAMPAIGN

By 1924 the Medical Department was in a position to organize a territory-wide yaws campaign. Before this, deformities resulting from yaws had been much in evidence, while the cost of salvarsan had been prohibitive. This medical campaign relied on the use of the much cheaper Bismuth Sodium Tartrate (B.S.T.) which, while it did not eradicate the disease owing to the reluctance of patients to undergo the full course of treatment, neverthless resulted in the spectacular disappearance of open lesions and, more significantly, established once and for all the reputation of European medicine amongst Africans and in particular, their confidence in injections. The use of B.S.T. was a medical innovation. It was recorded that in a campaign at that time against yaws in Java the Dutch Authorities had made available for sale a quantity of Neo-salvarsan which would have cost about £250,000. The cost of B.S.T. in 1924 was Shs. 16/- per pound, and this drug, for a similar campaign to that in Java, would have cost a sum of £500.

EDUCATION

It will be of particular interest that the Education Department started literally from scratch, with one officer appointed in 1920, and could only boast six European officers by the end of 1924. By 1914 the German Administration had had a staff of 14 Europeans in its Education Department with 99 Government schools having an enrolment of 6,100 pupils. Little more could be done at first by the British Education Department than to re-open those of the German schools for which the former teachers could be found, an obvious necessity existing for the training of new teachers under a British curriculum. It was noted in the first British annual report for the territory that a fair number of Africans knew how to read and write in Swahili, but any greater degree of education than this was virtually non-existent.

THE TSETSE PROBLEM

In those early post-war years, outsiders were apt to regard Tanganyika mainly as a big game hunter's paradise, but the territory was fortunate in one of its earliest Game Officers, the late C. F. M. Swynnerton, who possessed an inquiring mind which he concentrated upon the tsetse problem. It was this officer, later to die in an air crash on duty, who identified *Glossina Swynnertoni*, one of the more widespread of the tsetse species in Tanganyika, as being distinct from *G. morsitans*, and who initiated study of the differing habits of these "fly" species and of possible methods for their control.

ENEMY PROPERTY

In the meantime, private development was not idle. An early decision had been taken to honour titles to land granted by the former German Government. A full department of Government, that of the Custodian of Enemy Property, was established to realize on these titles, and in the absence of permission for the former German settlers to return to the territory (permission was only granted late in 1925) many opportunities existed, and were taken, for the acquisition of former German holdings by private individuals of other nationalities, chiefly British, Indian and Greek. Since a large number of these holdings were sisal estates, the way was thus clear for the early re-establishment, after war neglect, of the territory's chief plantation industry. This, however, was not the end of the settlement which occurred at this time.

GOLD DISCOVERY

In addition to the re-establishment of coffee plantations in the Northern and Tanga Provinces, there was the discovery in 1922 of alluvial gold in the hilly region immediately to the east of Lake Rukwa, and initially on the Lupa River, resulting in a gold rush to that area and causing some attention to be given to the vast undeveloped tracts of what is now the Southern Highlands Province.

WHITE SETTLEMENT

Lord Delamere, who had for long been a leading settler figure in Kenya, was the moving spirit in attempting to establish "white settlement" in the highlands around Iringa. After a personal visit to that area, which he thought, on defective evidence, was ideal mixed farming country, he encouraged settlers to apply for land in the almost uninhabited downs between Iringa and Sao Hill and sponsored the erection of a bacon factory at Ulete as a focal point. Thus was born "white settlement" in the Iringa District which, radiating from the barely suitable Delamere area, was later to discover better opportunities further afield in that district.

AFRICAN CROP POLICY

In this period, the possibilities of African economic agriculture were at once appreciated, and the numbers of Arabica coffee trees in the Chagga area around Kilimanjaro increased spectacularly. The Robusta coffee of the Bukoba District, thought to be indigenous, already yielded a large and increasing crop, while official efforts to encourage African economic agriculture were concentrated on cotton, particularly in the Lake Victoria Basin and in the eastern districts of the territory. On the other side of the African agricultural picture, this period saw another of the recurrent famines in Ugogo resulting from defective rainfall. This famine, in 1924, saw no repetition of the deaths that had occurred in 1919 since the area had reaped bountiful crops in 1921 and 1922 and this time, with rough tracks open and lorries starting to appear, was able to draw on the Kondoa-Irangi District in addition to using its own reserves.

CIVIL DISTRICTS

For administrative purposes, the territory was divided into 22 districts, many of which contained sub-stations. The pattern of population, disrupted by the war, was not at first clear, and very many of the sub-stations which had been considered a military necessity by the German Civil Administration were quickly found to be ill-sited or redundant and were abandoned.

MASAILAND

The greatest change in the pattern of districts in this period occurred in 1923, when was created what was described as a "reserve" for the Masai tribe whose members had hitherto roamed at will in parts of no less than six administrative districts. The Masai areas were excised from these districts by consent of all interested parties to facilitate a closer administration of these nomads.

THE MANDATE

In the general political sphere the territory was placed under the Mandate of the League of Nations. This meant, in fact, that while responsibility for its administration rested squarely on H.M. Government, reports were made to the League of Nations and were then examined by a permanent panel of international experts, amongst whom Lord Lugard early became prominent. The first annual report was made for the year 1920, and the often academic but usually practical criticisms of the Permanent Mandates Commission were generally helpful while the Mandate lasted.

EAST AFRICAN COMMISSION, 1924

The end of the period of consolidation within the Territory was signalized by the sending from England in 1924 of the East African Commission, better known as the "Ormsby-Gore" Commission, which came to East Africa to examine the political situation. The report of this Commission (Cmd. 2,387) focused attention on the fact that East Africa as a whole differed from West Africa, where there is no non-African settlement of any consequence, and from South Africa where spheres of influence are separated, in that a degree of non-African settlement not only existed, side by side with the indigenous peoples, but even afforded "the main stimulus in the economic progress of the Territories". The subject of closer union in East Africa was already local politics, and such a degree of misapprehension existed in some quarters at the time of the Ormsby-Gore Commission's visit that the Government of Tanganyika found it necessary to include the following paragraph in its report for 1924.

"There appears to be an impression abroad that the population of the Territory includes large numbers of unemployed labourers who form a useful reservoir from which to draw for the development of adjoining territories. The contrary is the case; in many districts the native population is fully employed in economic production on their own account and the less advanced areas are being fully drawn upon by planters for labourers on their estates. Apart altogether from any objections to the employment of natives of the Territory at high altitudes or in places where they are removed from the supervision of their own Government the depletion of the local labour supply cannot be justified on any grounds and therefore, while no obstacles are placed in the way of natives who wish to migrate in search of employment, the Government is unable to take any active measures calculated to support or encourage the supply of native labour for employment outside the Territory."

EARLY LAWS

Notable among the early laws enacted by the British Administration were three Ordinances of which the Involuntary Servitude (Abolition) Ordinance dated June 16th, 1922, has been mentioned elsewhere. Two other Ordinances were to have a profound effect on Tanganyika up to the present time. It is difficult to imagine the disadvantage which would have accrued if the Credit to Natives (Restriction) Ordinance had not been enacted on April 1st, 1923, for it has resulted in the virtually complete absence of indebtedness by Africans to members of other races, and has thus been of inestimable social benefit. The Land Ordinance, dated January 26th, 1923, was a short and uncomplicated piece of legislation designed to validate the granting by the Governor of titles to land, which has remained in force until now with only minor modifications.[1]

THE ECONOMY

The financial position of the territory underwent a remarkable change in this period. As regards public finance, recurring deficits from 1919 onwards,

---

[1]The despatch which defined the nature of this Ordinance was signed on 18.8.22 by the Secretary of State for the Colonies, Mr. Winston S. Churchill.

met in two financial years by free grants from the British Treasury, were replaced by a first surplus in the financial year 1923/24 if Railways figures are excluded. The value of both imports and exports was rising rapidly, and it can be said that, after the trade depression of 1922, the position had been restored by the end of 1924 to such an extent that the interruption of the economy by the war had been fully discounted. Nearly all domestic exports in 1924 were, for the first time significantly greater than in 1913, and in particular exports of sisal had recovered. The only big difference in the pattern of exports as between 1913 and 1924 consisted in the elimination of rubber, which had been in value the third German export crop, deriving from large plantations which by 1924 were derelict. The Bukoba African coffee crop in 1924, of which four-fifths consisted of Robusta, amounted to 3,535 tons giving an income to the Africans of that district exceeding £100,000. In the same year a count of Arabica coffee trees grown by Africans on Kilimanjaro showed over 700,000, of which 140,000 were in bearing; while gold production in the Lupa Goldfield jumped from 1,639 oz. in 1923 to 6,805 oz. in 1924.

THE POPULATION

A record of this phase (1920-1924) would be incomplete without reference to the numbers of the African population. A German "census" had been taken in 1913, and an estimate of the population was made by Government in 1920 which suggested that the population had slightly decreased over the war period. The period of consolidation gave an opportunity to Africans to recover in numbers. Facilities were still inadequate for a full census in 1925, but a further estimate of the population made in that year indicated that there was an upward trend in numbers, a trend which has been shown to have been a fact by later enumerations.

THE BOOM YEARS, 1925-1929

The second quinquenniad of British rule was a period in which great administrative and political changes occurred, uncomplicated by any financial anxiety. The territory and its inhabitants were in so happy a financial position as to mollify criticism of the administrative reforms introduced by Sir Donald Cameron, and of the political changes both present, in the shape of a first Legislative Council, and future, as foreshadowed by the visit of the Hilton Young Closer Union Commission. Even the pointers towards the Depression, which became evident in 1929, were dismissed as being negligible. The ordinary revenue of the territory, which had for the first time exceeded one million pounds in 1923/24, rose steadily each year to only just under two million pounds in 1928/29. The Civil List, 575 European names in 1924, contained 950 in 1930 excluding Railways staff and the Military. Sisal exports, 20,834 tons in 1913, 18,276 tons in 1925, rose to 45,728 tons in 1929. Coffee, 1,059 tons in 1913 and 6,009 tons in 1925, rose to over 10,000 tons for the first time in 1928 and only dropped to 8,857 tons in 1929 owing to poor rains. (Of the 8,857 tons in 1929, no less than 6,666 tons were produced by the Africans of the Bukoba District.) The Lupa Goldfield was producing between 9,000 and 12,000 oz. of alluvial gold annually, and the Mabuki gravels in the Lake Province, yielding nearly 23,000 carats of diamonds in 1929, raised hopes, a pipe-dream in the event, that a new Kimberley had been found. The value of petrol imported in 1929 was five times that imported in 1925.

RAILWAYS DEVELOPMENT

The branch railway line northwards form Tabora reached Mwanza in 1928, that from Moshi reached Arusha at the end of 1929, and in the same year the decision was taken to construct another branch line northwards from Manyoni into the populated areas of Singida and Mkalama, it being considered that this line would be justified by the groundnuts grown by the Iramba and Turu tribes. Yet another railway project was contemplated, in the shape of a line southwards from Dodoma and its location survey was completed in 1928. (This last project would have been considerably more expensive than those which were actually undertaken, and in consequence a Commission was established under the chairmanship of a British expert, Sir Sydney Henn. This Commission examined the areas to be surveyed in 1930, by which time not only the fact that the railway would have passed through many miles of unproductive country, but also the onset of the depression, caused the project to be abandoned.)

Railways were not the only form of communication where development was occurring. New road tracks were being cleared to open up the country, after an initial impetus had been provided by the visit of the Governor himself to Songea and Tukuyu by road in 1925, an undertaking which had been regarded as foolhardy by the unimaginative. The first surveys for proper roads to replace the earlier tracks from Iringa to Mwenzo on the Northern Rhodesian border and from Dodoma to Arusha were undertaken in 1927. It is illuminating that there should have been controversy about the alignment of a road to connect the capital with the interior. In fact the first "Select Committee" of Legislative Council was appointed to decide between an alignment from Dar es Salaam to Morogoro, to connect via Kilosa and Korogwe with the Tanga railway line, and a much shorter alignment from Dar es Salaam through Bagamoyo and Turiani to Korogwe. This Committee, despite its obsession with the bogy of competition with the parallel railway, decided with some reluctance on the Morogoro route. It should be noted that until 1929 railways accounts were incorporated with those of the territory, and that since they had generally involved deficits, the legislature was reluctant to approve of any project which might result in reduction of railway receipts.

AVIATION

It will seem strange, today, to learn that from the end of the 1914–1918 war until 1926 there was no aviation in Tanganyika, though the territory maintained two landing grounds at Mwanza and Tabora, which were reported as suitable for aircraft provided that seven days' notice was given to allow for grass clearing. In 1926 a Royal Air Force Flight passed over the Territory, landing at Tabora, while Sir Alan Cobham also landed there in that year on a trial flight to the Cape. The Government of Tanganyika bought its first aeroplane in 1928 for air survey purposes and in 1929 Imperial Airways were making plans to call at certain intermediate Tanganyika landing grounds on their first trans-continental service.

YAWS

The Medical Department continued its spectacular campaign against yaws. At the start of this campaign, cases treated had jumped from an annual handful to over 20,000 in 1924. By the end of the boom period the authorities were treating over 120,000 cases a year, and new patients presenting themselves for treatment had started to decline in numbers.

8

SLEEPING SICKNESS

The significance of the sleeping sickness situation was not appreciated at this time by the general public. The policy of concentrating scattered population was in operation in the Ugalla River area where by 1926 seven concentrations had been completed and two more were in preparation, to accommodate 14,500 people from an infected area extending to 7,500 square miles. But in 1927 sleeping sickness was discovered north of the Central Line in what was then the Tabora District, an area which would more correctly be described today as the Kahama District with part of Nzega. Over 1,000 new cases were diagnosed in the Kahama area in 1928, an incidence the spread of which could not be satisfactorily controlled in the existing enormous contiguous areas of very thinly populated tsetse bush.

THE TSETSE PROBLEM

In the general field of tsetse control, the department of Government concerned, which had early been separated from the Game Department, was again split in 1927 into Departments of Tsetse Reclamation and Tsetse Research. While the former concentrated on the sheer clearing of shade, without which the tsetse cannot survive, in order to free much needed grazing areas, chiefly in the present Shinyanga District, the latter from headquarters in the Kondoa-Irangi District divided its work into two parts, the survey of fly belts and of their threatening expansion, and the search for more selective methods of tsetse eradication. It having been established that the pupae of tsetse, which are found just underground, cannot survive without shade, research was undertaken into the discriminative clearing of bush, to discover whether the removal of only certain tree species, rather than the more expensive sheer clearing, would control the fly. To illustrate the lengths to which Swynnerton's researches went, he even attempted to introduce a microscopic ichneumon by the million into a restricted area; this reduced tsetse to very small numbers, but unhappily did not completely eradicate it. These abstruse researches could not be expected, except with the greatest of good fortune, to result in the immediate discovery of a technical means for eradicating a pest which had existed in Africa for centuries, and Standing Finance Committee was understandably doubtful about providing the funds required by Swynnerton for these researches as a permanent recurrent commitment. Funds were eventually granted over this period with some reluctance.

EDUCATION

In 1925, education policy had been sufficiently established for it to be possible to hold an initial conference between Government and interested missionary representatives. At this conference Government accepted the responsibility for financial assistance to voluntary agency schools which fulfilled certain conditions as to curriculum and suitable staff. The first of such grants were actually paid in 1927, a year which also saw the first thin trickle of British-trained African teachers. It is of interest that, in face of the desirability that the coming generation of chiefs should be educated so that they could administer more efficiently the policy of indirect rule, one of Government's first central schools, at Tabora, was designed for the reception of the sons of chiefs. (At this time, research into the the line of succession of tribal chiefships had been incomplete and it was not realized that the eldest son of a chief was not necessarily his customary successor. The arbitrary selection of chiefs' sons for the Tabora Central School was thus found likely to result in some administrative embarrassment, and the exclusive use of this school for chiefs' sons was not of long duration.)

ENEMY PROPERTY

The work of the Custodian of Enemy Property was virtually complete by 1928. The total realized by the sale of all land properties was £1,344,604 in respect of estates covering 1,870 square miles. The Germans had, before the war, admitted to having alienated more land in certain areas than was desirable if due regard were to be paid to future native requirements, and no fewer than 107 German properties, chiefly in the present Tanga and Northern Provinces, were retained by Government for African use instead of being re-leased. In these cases the purchase price paid to the Custodian was not subject to public auction as was the case with re-alienated estates, but was determined by the High Court.

CENSUS, 1928

The census of 1928, advertised at the time as a trial for a more formal census to be held in 1931, indicated that the African population was increasing with some rapidity. The census result was known to be inaccurate (for example the female population in one district was found, later, to have been included twice in the published territorial total) but the result gave a correct general indication that an increase of population was occurring.

THE FIRST ROYAL VISIT

To add to the foregoing encouraging picture, Tanganyika was included in 1928 in the itinerary of T.R.H. the Prince of Wales and the Duke of Gloucester. The latter spent some time in the territory shooting big game, while the Prince of Wales had reached Dodoma on his way south when news came of the serious illness of H.M. the King. The Royal party interrupted their programme and embarked at Dar es Salaam on a fast cruiser bound for England.

Against such a picture of development and prosperity, falls in the prices of coffee and diamonds which occurred in 1929 passed almost unnoticed, and a considerable locust invasion, at the end of the period, was regarded as only a temporary, though irritating, interruption to the "tempo" of expansion.

LAND

Before embarking on an account of the administrative and political changes which occurred in this period, it is advisable to explain what happened with regard to land as a result of the atmosphere of prosperity and optimism. Demand for land by immigrants was heavy not so much in areas which already contained a substantial degree of alienation as in new areas made accessible by the development of communications. In particular the removal of the ban on German settlers which had operated until the end of 1925 resulted in the arrival of considerable numbers of these persons who, finding that their pre-war holdings had in so many cases been disposed of to members of other nationalities, applied for land in the Iringa and Mbulu areas. There were a number of these Germans who were content to develop holdings as mixed farms, but others were obsessed by the coffee "bug" and invested what capital they had in planting large acreages of these trees without sufficient trial of the suitability of the soil, or knowledge of the crop's management. (The parlous straits into which many of these coffee farmers in the Southern Highlands Province had got by 1939 will be noted in a later section of this record.) In face of the extensive demand for land, and in the knowledge that the Germans had considered that over-alienation had occurred in the Tanga and Northern areas, the British

Government decided that it was better to indicate areas in which room for alienation appeared to exist than to continue the system whereby individuals applied for parcels of land wherever they pleased.

THE LAND DEVELOPMENT SURVEY

A survey team was put into the field, consisting of three senior officers, one administrative, one agricultural and one surveyor, to investigate, initially, the Southern Highlands Province.   Later this Land Development Survey extended its activities to the Mbulu District and to certain areas in the Eastern Province. On the basis of such knowledge as was then available of population and African agricultural potential, this team made recommendations as to the areas where there appeared to be room for further alienation, recommendations which were accepted by Government and which remained in force for the next decade.

INDIRECT RULE

As regards administrative and political change, if Tanganyika's first Governor, Sir Horace Byatt, had succeeded in making some satisfactory bricks without very much straw, the next, Sir Donald Cameron, was thought at first to be bent on making straw without a solid foundation of bricks.   While such element of the population as was vocal could accept the inauguration of a Legislative Council, with nominated unofficial members, as a necessary first step towards the mirage of autonomy, it at first found itself sceptical in the extreme of "indirect rule", the Tanganyika version of that Nigerian system which Sir Donald Cameron knew so well, and a great part of this formidable man's energies and of the energies of one of his enthusiastic lieutenants, P. E. Mitchell (eventually Governor of Kenya) were taken up with the establishment in the field, and the justification to the public, of local rule by the traditional indigenous authorities.   Before the arrival of Sir Donald Cameron as Governor a tendency had appeared for reliance to be placed to a limited extent upon the indigenous leaders of the people. A Native Authority Ordinance, based upon the existence of chiefship, had been passed in 1923, and in certain administrative districts where strong chiefships existed, native courts had been empowered to determine petty cases.   These tentative arrangements were quickly transformed by Sir Donald Cameron into the full system of Indirect Rule.

The basic objects of this system were first to provide a form of local government, close to the people, which the people themselves understood, using traditional leaders of the people as administrators, and second, to initiate participation by the indigenous people in the Government of the country, such as could be expanded with their increasing education and experience into full integration.   It was clear that the Government had neither the men nor the money to administer such a large territory directly, and that, for example, means must be found for the efficient settlement of petty disputes between Africans. The system as introduced by Sir Donald Cameron involved three institutions. It involved in the first place the recognition of the status of chiefs, and an authorization to enact local by-laws.   This was effected through the medium of a revision of the Native Authority Ordinance of 1923, the new law being passed in 1926.   Secondly it involved the establishment everywhere of Native Courts.   This step will be noted further when the operations of the new Legislative Council are described.   Thirdly it involved the establishment of Native Treasuries which were in effect embryonic Local Government treasuries.   In this connection, an examination of existing African institutions had shown that a system of tribute to Chiefs and Headmen was in existence. It was thought necessary to define the obligations of the individual to his newly recognized authority, and an attempt was made to substitute native treasury salaries to Chiefs and Headmen, calculated at the value of the tribute which was to be abolished. The Germans had had a system whereby a proportion of every tax collected was refunded, in place of salary, to their *Akidas*. This system provided a basis for the calculation of the commutation of tribute, and it was agreed at the start that Poll taxes must include an element of tribute and that native treasuries should receive this proportion of these taxes (the whole being collected by the Native Authorities) as the nucleus of their annual incomes. It was not realized at the time that in the case of many tribes, tribute in kind had been paid in the shape of food, as a form of community self-help, for storage and for distribution by Chief or Headman in case of need. Commutation of tribute thus shifted the onus from the individual Chief or Headman to the native treasury for relieving distress and in particular for alleviation of famine resulting from crop failure.

The transition to Indirect Rule, among the many separate tribes of the territory, could not be expected to pass without some set-backs, and before much time had passed the territory was shocked at the prosecution of one of its leading chiefs for misappropriation of tax moneys. The case was reported in the following terms in the Annual Report for 1929. "A report was received of serious defalcations of Hut and Poll Tax money by an important Chief in the Tabora District amounting to some £10,062. The Chief was brought to trial before the High Court and sentenced to two years' imprisonment, but the conviction was quashed in the Court of Appeal for Eastern Africa on the ground that the trial Court had not been given jurisdiction. The Chief was deposed and has been required to reside at the coast, receiving for the support of himself and his family a small allowance from the Native Treasury of his unit. The defalcations were due to the neglect by local officials to carry out the instructions of the Government with regard to the control of tax books and the remittance of tax. In so far as the taxpayers were concerned, enquiries have revealed no irregularities; no man was required to pay tax twice, or in excess of the amount due from him. It may be of interest to record here that from the inception of indirect rule in 1925 down to the 31st March, 1929, Hut and Poll Tax to the amount of nearly two million pounds was collected by the Native Administration with a total loss from fraud and theft (apart from the loss mentioned above) of £967."

But the general effect of the introduction of Indirect Rule was highly beneficial both as to public order, and as to the eventual evolution of a modern system of local government. As regards this latter aspect, while the original system was based on the selection and encouragement of traditional chiefs, who in accordance with intrinsic African practice functioned with the advice of their Elders, it did not at first provide patently for a "Chief in Council" as distinct from a Chief "sole", such as would conform with modern democratic ideas. The introduction of the new system was such an innovation in Tanganyika that it was clearly necessary to allow it to find its feet before the introduction of such patent democratization. It may here be noted that whatever may have been Sir Donald Cameron's idea of the period which would be necessary before such modification became possible, his system underwent in effect a trial period lasting for 20 years, being called upon in that period to withstand the stresses of, first, the depression, and then the war, both of which for their duration took its modification outside the realms of practical politics. That the system withstood these strains, and lasted effectively, in virtually its original form, for so long, is the measure of its quality.

THE PROVINCIAL SYSTEM

From January 1st, 1926, the territory was divided for administrative purposes into eleven provinces. In such a vast area, with such scattered centres of population, this division was a compromise between the requirements of close administration and the restrictions of the public purse. The eleven provinces were to last until the period of depression, when they were reduced in number to eight, their present figure. At whichever number was current, the Provincial Commissioner, the new post evolved at the creation of provinces, became the Governor's representative in the field directly responsible to the Governor for the peace and good order of each province.

LEGISLATIVE COUNCIL

While the administration of the territory was being reorganized on the foregoing lines, Sir Donald Cameron effected another reorganization at the centre. Stating that "quite frankly and bluntly I declare here that I have had the strongest objection to the extremely difficult—and, I may say, at times almost perilous—task which has fallen to me of having had to administer the affairs of this territory during the last eighteen months without the assistance of a constitutional assembly such as this Council", on the 7th December, 1926, he inaugurated the first Legislative Council for the territory, in which thirteen senior officials of Government sat under his chairmanship with seven nominated unofficials of whom five were Europeans and two Asians. The Governor had considered the matter of African representation on this Council and at the inaugural meeting made the following statement, "The native community cannot be directly represented because for the present a native cannot be found with sufficient command of the English language to take part in the debates of the Council; indeed to understand what is being said. I speak now, of course, of natives of standing who could speak on behalf of the various tribes of the country. But I do not by any means regard the large body of natives as being altogether unrepresented on the Council. Their interests are directly in the hands of the Secretary for Native Affairs, the Chief Secretary, and the Governor himself." It is of interest that even at this inaugural meeting, one of the European unofficial members was Major W. C. Lead, M.C. (later Sir William Lead) who was to serve the Council and Tanganyika for so long and to take such a distinguished place as a leading protagonist of the sisal industry.

The early meetings of Legislative Council were more informal than is now the case, a notable difference being that the Governor himself intervened in debates from the chair. Unofficial members were understandably unused to council procedure but, after the first session which was naturally taken up with inaugural subjects, and an explanation of his policy by the Governor, they quickly adapted themselves to conditions and in the period under review took full part in the proceedings of Standing Finance Committee (which examined the annual Budgets) and in three notable debates. These concerned the supply of labour, the question of Closer Union in East Africa, and the new Native Courts Ordinance of 1929.

LABOUR POLICY

As regards the supply of labour a Labour Department had been formed in 1926, the first Commissioner being Major G. St. J. Orde-Brown, who was later to become Labour Adviser to the Secretary of State. On the analogy of Southern Rhodesia, it was hoped by employers that Government would undertake the recruitment and supply of labour, and it was but a short step from this position for it to be argued that, in the absence of any territorial recruiting agencies, or any means whereby labourers from undeveloped areas could be assisted to seek employment where it was offered, Government should in some way guarantee supplies of the labourers which it had recruited. In face of the very strong terms used by the Governor in an address to Legislative Council, the unofficial members were unable to support, even had they wished to do so, the suggestions which had been made at public meetings in the employment areas that labour should be "forced", and Government resolutely opposed the suggestion that it should organize the supply of voluntary labour, indicating that, instead, industry should organize its own recruitment.

CLOSER UNION

As regards Closer Union, this subject was raised in Legislative Council before the visit of the Hilton Young Commission. The nominated European members unequivocally supported federation, provided that the autonomy of Tanganyika should not be infringed except as regards those services which would be amalgamated. This position was, perhaps more realistically, opposed by the Asian members, who, being no more in a position to anticipate the precise conclusions of the Hilton Young Commission than their European colleagues, drew attention to the probability of equal representation of the three East African Territories in any form of Closer Union which might be arranged, and the consequent possibility that Tanganyika might be out-voted.

NATIVE COURTS

The third of the three notable debates, in April, 1929, concerned the Native Courts Ordinance, and in particular the proposals, novel to Tanganyika, that the Native Courts system should be outside the control of the High Court, and that advocates should be excluded from appearance before native courts. Though the debate revealed lack of knowledge in the minds of unofficial members of the nature of the vast majority of cases, both criminal and civil, brought before native courts, it was advantageous that the subject should be ventilated and that Government should have been enabled to explain the system of appeal which was proposed (with appeal, finally to the Governor himself) and the fact that cases were to be settled either by existing native custom where this was unobjectionable, or by custom introduced by the medium of Rules or Orders under the Native Authority Ordinance. The presence of advocates who could not be expected to know tribal law would in these circumstances have been of no assistance quite apart from any undue influence which they, with their superior educational status, might have exercised over the courts.

THE HILTON YOUNG COMMISSION

Although Tanganyika was taking in this period the foregoing steps to improve its own administration, it must not be thought that its status vis-à-vis the other

East African territories had been finally decided. It was an unprecedented situation that there should be a Colony, Kenya, a Protectorate, Uganda, and a Mandated Territory, Tanganyika, concerned in a political discussion of this nature. Following the Ormsby-Gore Commission which has been mentioned above, a Conference of East African Governors was held in Nairobi early in 1926 to discuss what was then known as the dual policy in East Africa, a policy consisting in the complementary development of non-native and native interests. This conference in its turn was followed by a Colonial Conference in London and these examinations of the East African position resulted in July, 1927, in the presentation to Parliament of Cmd. 2,904, a White Paper announcing a Commission of Enquiry for East and Central Africa to examine the position in its broadest aspects. The terms of reference of this "Commission on Closer Union of the Dependencies in Eastern and Central Africa" can correctly be inferred from its title. The Commission was appointed in November, 1927, under the chairmanship of Sir E. Hilton Young and a voluminous report was made in October, 1928, containing general recommendations, with subsidiary reports from the Chairman and from the other three members. This Hilton Young Report advocated, broadly speaking, the East Africa High Commission and Central Legislative Assembly of today, but with the difference that there would be an East African Governor-General resident at Mombasa. It emphasized the advantages of co-ordination in such matters as transport, customs and scientific research and it stipulated that native policy must be clarified as a preliminary to the proper development of local government, of machinery for consultation with Africans, and of the development of their indigenous institutions.

The report had a bad reception in East Africa. Sir Samuel Wilson, Permanent Under Secretary of State, sent by the Secretary of State to visit East Africa in early 1929 to discuss the recommendations of the report with all interested parties, and to ascertain on what lines a scheme for closer union would be administratively workable, could only say (Cmd. 3378) that there was a serious degree of opposition, which so far as Tanganyika was concerned was centred on objection by the Governor himself to any scheme of closer union until native policy had been further examined; while Asian objections, centred admittedly in Kenya, which were so strong as to necessitate their representation before Sir Samuel Wilson by an Indian Privy Councillor from Simla, served to emphasize that the problems were not confined only to Africans and Europeans.

Lest it be thought that there was a degree of contradiction in the attitude, in Tanganyika, to this question, and of procrastination in England before the final decision was given (in 1930), it should be explained that it was feared in East Africa that the British Labour Party might be indifferent to the continuance of the Mandated Territory of Tanganyika within the Empire, an indifference which Closer Union would have negatived; while changes of Government at this time in England did not contribute to a speedy and unequivocal solution following such protracted, and at times acrimonious, enquiries.

THE YEARS OF DEPRESSION, 1930-1934

Government publications do not often include passages of outstandingly imaginative interest, but the Tanganyika Report for 1933 contained one such passage which is remarkable in that it was written in the middle and not at the end of the period and which provides an excellent introduction to an account of the Depression.   It reads as follows:—

"The trade of the Territory during 1933 presents certain aspects which seem to promise an ending to an economic cycle characterized by a phase of prosperity from 1925 to 1929 and a phase of depression beginning in 1930. In the statistics for the year 1930 there is evidence that the signs of changing conditions were not fully appreciated.   Costly and wasteful methods and habits acquired during the period of unexampled prosperity were not easily given up, and there was a general tendency either to regard the depression as temporary or to hope that the position would be restored by fortuitous developments in America, Europe and elsewhere.   It was a year in which optimism was preferred to reorganization, with the result that the adverse trade balance reached the considerable amount of £1,080,000.

The following year, 1931, emphasized the urgent need for readjustment to meet what was at last recognized as a permanent change in the economic situation, and retrenchment became the order of the day.   To avoid complete disorganization, retrenchment was of necessity gradual and was carried on into 1932 and 1933.   In 1931 it helped to reduce by a million and a half pounds the import requirements of the Territory.   At the same time the concurrent need for an increased output, which would assist in counteracting the collapse in values, was apparent, but the campaign then initiated could not show results until 1932.   Consequently, although there was such a large decrease in the imports there was also a serious decrease in the value of exports, and the year closed with an adverse balance of £600,000.

It was in the year 1932 that the trade figures first contained evidence of the capacity of the community to adapt itself to the new order of things. In spite of low prices the value of the exports increased by one-third, while imports fell to the lowest figure on record since 1921.   Development, and in some cases even proper maintenance, of estates and industrial enterprises unquestionably suffered through compulsory economy, while the continued fall in customs import revenue added to the problems of Government and prevented the adoption of supplementary measures to increase or conserve the natural resources of the Territory.   The favourable trade balance of nearly half a million pounds allowed, however, the liquidation of part of the losses and liabilities of the two preceding years.

In the year under review a further advance towards economic stability on the new basis was recorded.   Trade imports increased by nearly seven per cent, in value, mainly as a result of increased importations of "development" goods such as machinery, building materials, iron and steel manufactures, tools and implements and gunny bags.   The exports increased by 16 per cent over those of 1932 and by £900,000, or nearly 55 per cent, over the 1931 total.   Record production figures were reached for sisal, coffee, gold, groundnuts, rice and beeswax, which are among the main products of the Territory.   In a year marked by adverse weather conditions, generally lower prices, and some locust damage, this is a striking achievement. On the whole year's trading the balance available to redeem the economic overdraft was £780,000 representing a 40 per cent surplus over the value of the imports.

Granting the necessity for maintenance and increase in the quantity of production, the most important care of the future should be improvement and standardization of quality. In the boom period of high prices and active demand the penalty for inferior quality was merely a reduced price, which still showed a handsome return; under the present conditions of supply and demand it is becoming more and more difficult to find a market at any price for low grade produce."

As this indicates, Tanganyika had been slow to realize the magnitude of the depression, and to appreciate that an economic blizzard in consuming countries in 1929 would later have its repercussions in producing countries such as Tanganyika. The depression lasted in Tanganyika until the end of 1934, by which time, although prices for produce showed no substantial rise, the increase in the volume of Tanganyika's exports, and a partial recovery in the value of her imports, showed clearly that things were on the mend. This was so much the case that although the territorial budget for 1935 still provided for a regime of strict economy, Government announced that if improvement was as expected in 1935, public expenditure would be adjusted upwards during the course of that year through supplementary votes.

MATERIAL EFFECTS OF THE DEPRESSION

The material effect of the depression was severe. Excluding re-exports the total value of Tanganyika's imports and exports, which stood at £6,880,543 in 1930, fell to £4,228,954 in 1932 and had only risen to £5,199,774 in 1934. The value of the principal export crop, sisal, had averaged £23 per ton in 1930 and was scarcely more than £12 in 1934. The price of coffee which as already recorded had fallen in 1929, averaged £35 per ton in 1930, and £34 in 1934. For these, the chief non-native export crops, such prices meant at best the bare recovery of production costs, with no margin for replanting, replacements of machinery, or profits. In so far as Africans were producers of coffee, prices still kept growers' heads above the economic level of those who did not plant this crop, but other African crop prices fell disastrously. The f.o.b. price of groundnuts even in 1930 was but £11 per ton, a yield to upcountry producers so small as to curtail production. When this price fell to rather less than £7 10s. 0d. in 1934 there was no incentive whatever to produce. Even the most valuable of what may be called the African products fell seriously in value, beeswax which had averaged £107 per ton in 1930 realizing only £80 in 1934. The territory relied at this time for over 30 per cent of its public revenue on customs duties. These had produced £739,670 in 1929/30, fell to £411,354 in 1931/32 and had recovered by 1934 only so far as to promise the sum of £445,000 at the time when the 1935 Budget was prepared. In 1930 the value of the import and export transit trade handled by the Railways, chiefly to the Congo, had exceeded £2½ million, the Central Line being geared to convey nearly 25,000 tons of copper a year from Kigoma to Dar es Salaam. Almost the whole of this transit trade had disappeared by 1932. There was a slight recovery in 1933 on account of the popularity of Japanese textiles in the Congo, a recovery which continued in 1934, but it did not result in the reappearance of Congo copper. Moreover the Central Line had been seriously disorganized early in 1930 by floods. The German alignment has been described as "the line of least resistance". It included a section between Kidete and Godegode which closely followed a river, and in 1930 for weeks on end passengers and goods were transported over this section by motor boat. There was no other course open to the Railway Authorities than to re-align this section on higher ground at a cost almost as great as that of either the Moshi–Arusha or the Manyoni–Kinyangiri branch lines.

COMMUNICATIONS CAPITAL WORKS

The Railways, in this period of depression, were fully committed to the completion of the branch line to Kinyangiri. Actual construction began in 1930. The line reached Singida in July, 1932, and was completed in 1933 and, in the event, was never operated at a profit. While on the subject of communications, it may be recorded that the construction of the Great North Road between the northern and southern boundaries of Tanganyika was completed in 1932, and it must be admitted that, because of the depression, expenditure on the final section, between Iringa and Mwenzo on the Northern Rhodesian boundary, was curtailed. (The total length of this road in Tanganyika is rather more than 800 miles).

LOCUSTS

To add to the depression, locusts were present in greater or lesser numbers throughout the period. The previous cycle of infestation by the Desert Locust from the north was abating by the beginning of 1930, but in that year the Red Locust from the south made its appearance, and both these species caused damage to food crops resulting in some places in famine conditions throughout this period.

DIAMONDS

In 1930 the production of diamonds, an export item which yielded considerable duty to the revenue, had fallen to 13,107 carats. In effect the gravels which had produced these diamonds were exhausted and production fell in 1931 to 7,790 and in 1932 to only 1,387 carats.

INCREASING PRODUCTION OF GOLD

As against these depressing statistics, there were only two that appeared encouraging. The territory's production of gold, standing at 12,966 oz. in 1930 was steadily rising and reached the figure of 54,541 oz. in 1934, resulting in a situation which will be discussed later in this survey.

CHAGGA COFFEE

A more parochial encouragement was seen on Kilimanjaro, where African production of Arabica coffee, rising annually, exceeded 1,000 tons for the first time in 1932 and fetched a slightly better price than the territorial average noted above. (The territorial average is found from both Arabica and the cheaper Robusta coffees). The coffee growers of the Chagga tribe earned over £50,000 in 1933.

THE "PLANT MORE CROPS" CAMPAIGN

In a mainly agricultural country the positive steps taken by Tanganyika to offset the depression were agricultural, and could be summarized in the slogan "Plant More Crops". It was argued that if crop prices had dropped, for example by half, the prosperity of the territory would be unaffected if the volume of crops could be doubled, and there is no doubt that the financial effect of the depression would have been more severe but for the "Plant More Crops" campaign which was started in 1931. As regards sisal, extensions of plantings in the boom period were coming into production in the period of depression, and tonnages produced increased so consistently that by 1934 considerable quantities were often left temporarily unsold in the hands of producers. The same conditions of temporary over-production appeared to apply to others of Tanganyika's exports, and this was perhaps nowhere more apparent than in the case of the infant tea industry. Almost before this industry had been born in Tanganyika the subject of restriction of acreage and thus of production, in order to maintain price levels, was raised and although production by 1934 had amounted to only 45,617 lb. the tea enterprises in the Usambara and Mufindi areas were given a limit of 2,900 acres, a limit which held good until 1938.

GOVERNMENT ECONOMIES

Faced by a sudden drop of some quarter of its revenue, the Government of Tanganyika was compelled to adopt a policy of the most rigid economy. Quite apart from more obvious economies such as the abandonment of new capital works (and even the abolition of travelling allowances for its officials) it was thought necessary to reduce the staffs which had been built up during the boom period, and to impose a levy on the salaries of those whose services were retained. By the end of 1932, 157 Europeans and 87 Asians in the permanent Government service, and 107 Europeans and 493 Asians employed in the Railways had been retrenched. The Civil Service List, containing the names of 950 officers excluding Railways and Military in 1930, contained only 795 names in 1933. As a measure of economy, the number of provinces was reduced from eleven to eight. On January 1st, 1932, a levy on official salaries was introduced at 5 per cent on the first £480, 7½ per cent on the next £440, and 10 per cent thereafter. This levy was to last until November, 1935, and it was loyally but resignedly accepted by the civil service.

INTRODUCTION OF NON-NATIVE POLL TAX

Among the revenue measures designed to reduce the margin between receipts and payments was the introduction of a graduated Non-Native Poll Tax. The main sources of public revenue had always been customs duties and the African poll tax, non-Africans paying no direct taxes unless their education tax could be so considered. Debate on the proposal to introduce a Non-Native Poll Tax reflected little credit on some of the European unofficial members of Legislative Council. They ignored the fact that Government servants, who did not benefit financially in periods of prosperity, would be subject to this tax in addition to the levy on official salaries, and opposed the proposal only on the grounds that the unofficial community were not in a position to pay the small amounts involved. The argument even degenerated into an assertion on their part that a Non-Native Poll Tax, graduated in accordance with the income of the payer was the thin edge of the income tax wedge, and that it represented an income tax of approximately 2½d. in the £.

PACKAGE TAX

One of the more remarkable of the temporary petty revenue measures at this time was the imposition of a 3d. tax on all imported packages.

GOVERNMENT'S CASH BALANCE

The estimates for 1933, being unbalanced, would have reduced the territory's cash balance to a dangerously low level and loan funds were appropriated as a reinforcement, it being argued that this source of cash represented a refund to the territory of previous railway losses which had been carried in the general account. The Budget for 1934 was only balanced by the agreement of the British Treasury to suspend loan interest payments amounting to £100,000.

REDUCTION IN AFRICAN TAX

The low produce prices obtainable by Africans in this period made it difficult for them to satisfy their tax obligations, and a serious degree of default in the African Poll Tax was soon apparent. Government realized that payment in full at reduced rates of tax was preferable to the indiscipline which would have resulted from wholesale default, and considered it advisable to send a special commissioner to investigate tax rates in certain areas. As a result, rates of taxes in three of the eight provinces were drastically reduced and default was largely eliminated. Estimates for native tax which had stood at £750,000 in 1929/30 appeared at £628,000 in the estimates for 1935.

ROAD COMPETITION WITH RAILWAYS CONTROLLED

As regards the railways, while it was inevitable that the system should be run at a loss on account of the disappearance of Congo traffic, and the start of interest payments on loans, efforts were made to reduce this loss as far as possible, and the protection of the railways against competition by road transport was thought inescapable. Goods rates on the railways varied on both sides of a figure yielding an economic return, high rates on luxury and more valuable goods being designed to offset sub-economic rates on cheap bulk goods. The principle was accepted that lorries, carrying higher rated goods on roads competing with the railways and leaving for the railways only the produce traffic at sub-economic rates, should be charged very high tolls as a discouragement. The Carriage of Goods by Motor (Control) Ordinance, 1931, was passed into law, and a schedule of tolls was introduced which in effect restricted lorry transport to short feeder services.

POSTAL AMALGAMATION

In face of the degree of mistrust of Kenya which existed at the time in Tanganyika, it is probable that the first real amalgamation of services, that of the Posts and Telegraphs, which occurred in 1933, would have been more vigorously opposed but for the depression. But it was shown that this amalgamation, with Posts and Telegraphs headquarters in Kenya, would result in a financial saving to Tanganyika, and the step was approved for that reason.

The stark effect of the depression, and the counter measures taken to off-set it, tended to divert attention in this period from other matters, but some account of the latter must be given in the interests of continuity.

NATIVE ADMINISTRATION, AMALGAMATION AND FEDERATION

Indirect Rule had at first meant the recognition of a host of petty independent Native Authorities, and the establishment of many Native Treasuries so small as to make them financially weak. But once these small units had been established, it became possible to think in terms of amalgamation or federation in the interests of political and financial solidity. A notable example of federation occurred in the Sukuma areas of the Lake Province. Shinyanga, a Sukuma district, was transferred from the Western Province to the

Lake Province, and in all four of the Sukuma districts, Mwanza, Kwimba, Maswa and Shinyanga, the independent chiefdoms amalgamated their treasuries at district level. More than this, in 1932, the first annual informal meeting of all the Sukuma Chiefs was convened at Mwanza and the 52 Native Authorities debated matters of concern to the whole of Sukumaland, an area then containing some 700,000 souls.

CLOSER UNION

As regards territorial politics, the decision of the British Government on the question of Closer Union was at last given in June, 1930. It was agreed that a High Commissioner should be established but in an advisory and not in an executive capacity as had been recommended in the Hilton Young Report. The High Commissioner would be chief adviser on native policy to the Secretary of State, permanent chairman of the Conference of East African Governors, and Administrator of the following common services—Transport, Customs, Defence, Posts and Telegraphs, Extradition, Central Research and the East African Dependencies Trade and Information Office in London.

WHITE PAPER ON NATIVE POLICY

At the same time Lord Passfield also issued a White Paper on native policy which resulted (no doubt in conjunction with the fact of the depression) in such an uproar amongst the white settlers of East Africa as to obscure the decision on Closer Union. This White Paper did no more than to restate British policy as regards the place necessarily occupied by the indigenous peoples of East Africa vis-à-vis non-African immigrants. Reference to the "paramountcy" of native interests were interpreted by white settlers as a threat to the permanency of their settlement, such as they thought would never have been possible had a different political party been in power in England. In the debate on policy for the 1935 Budget, settler members of Tanganyika's Legislative Council voiced forthright opposition to the terms of the White Paper. It was only natural that on account of the depression the influx of new settlers, which had been such a feature of the boom period, should have decreased, thus adding to settler feelings of uncertainty.

EROSION

It has been seen that Tanganyika's solution to the problem of economic depression was to grow more crops. To an existing policy which encouraged Africans to improve their dietary by better agriculture was added a territorial campaign to increase crops for sale, and the result was that by 1932 the problem of erosion had come right into the foreground. The census of 1931 showed that the population was increasing with some rapidity, and more intensive agriculture, by a population which was unaccustomed to taking any precautions against erosion, had started to produce in many places such scars on the countryside as could not escape the notice of the most casual observer. A Standing Committee on erosion under the chairmanship of the Director of the East African Agricultural Research Station, Amani, was established in 1933. More practical perhaps was Government's instruction that at the end of 1934 each province should give an account of the steps which had specifically been taken against erosion during that year. It would be idle to claim that those steps were adequate, but attention had at last been focused on what is perhaps the most serious basic agricultural problem in Tanganyika.

CENSUS, 1931

Mention has been made of the 1931 census. It was undertaken without extra cost or special staff. Methods employed were somewhat primitive, when for example headmen were required to produce seeds of four different plants to indicate the men, women, boys and girls respectively in their areas. The result showed a population exceeding five million, revealing *prima facie* an increase of nearly 2 per cent per annum since 1928. It is now known that the enumerations of both 1928 and 1931 were inaccurate, but the indication that the population was increasing was correct.

TRIBAL DISPENSARIES

Growing reliance on European medicine by an increasing population made no easier the problems of the medical authorities in these times, particularly when, on account of the depression, they had had a 30 per cent cut in expenditure imposed upon them. But it was at this time that the medical side of Native Treasury activities made its presence felt. Slowly but surely a Native Treasury dispensary system was being built up as funds became available for buildings, drugs and suitable dispensers. While in 1929 these Native Treasury dispensaries had treated 190,545 patients, by 1934 the number of patients had reached nearly half a million in a year and there were 310 dispensaries in operation spread throughout the country.

SLEEPING SICKNESS: THE KAHAMA OUTBREAK

In 1927 there had been started a special medical investigation of a typically rural African community in what is now the Kahama District. It has already been recorded that sleeping sickness infection had been discovered there, and during the depression the spread of sleeping sickness in that area became such an acute problem that the special medical investigation had to be abandoned in favour of a sleeping sickness campaign. The infection of tsetse with *T. Rhodesiense* spread, in the huge western fly belt, with great rapidity and by the end of the depression it had been necessary to establish human concentrations against this disease not only in the Kahama District but also over the greater part of the Kibondo and Biharamulo Districts. In the meantime the Tsetse Research Department made possible a more accurate study of the natural spread of the fly belts which threaten so much of Tanganyika. Attention during the depression was concentrated particularly on the Mbulu District of the Northern Province and on the Central Province, and a feature of the period was the large voluntary tribal turn-out in many areas to clear bush and thus bar the way to further fly advances.

AVIATION

As regards aviation, it was considered in 1930 that emergency landing grounds every 50 miles along air routes were essential for purposes of safety. By 1930, 28 landing grounds and emergency strips had been established while by 1934 this number had been increased to 44. A local company, Messrs. Wilson Airways started operations in 1930 in East Africa, in which year the Government aircraft first started to carry Government passengers as a routine. In 1932 Imperial Airways extended their trans-continental service from Kisumu southwards to the Cape, and started regular calls at Moshi, Dodoma and Mbeya.

THE DEPRESSION LIFTS

By the end of 1934, and as a result of the sustained efforts of its producers, Tanganyika had emerged from the slough of the depression as was to be proved by results in 1935. The way in which she had emerged was not precisely as was expected at the time, because the optimistic note evident at the end of 1934 was due not so much to the basic reason for returning prosperity, agriculture, as to a spurious optimism resulting from the increase in gold production. It was thought, erroneously, that increasing gold mining activity, showing results which derived largely from alluvial production, must foreshadow the discovery of many substantial and valuable reefs. The following is an extract from the speech of the Chief Secretary to Legislative Council explaining the reorganization and expansion of the Departments of Lands, Mines, Surveys and Geology which was to take place at the beginning of 1935:—

"Each report which I have received confirms me in the view that this country is at the commencement of gold-mining developments on a very large scale. New discoveries are being continuously made, and in those which are being developed the more work that is done the better the prospects seem. We have indeed passed the state in which there could be any reasonable doubt, and can say with as much certainty as is ever possible in connection with mining that we possess important gold resources and that they are about to be exploited to the full."

Private utterances were even more optimistic, and it was freely claimed that Tanganyika was another Witwatersrand.

THE YEARS OF UNCERTAINTY, 1935-1939

Though for a variety of reasons commodity prices suffered considerable fluctuations in the period between 1935 and the outbreak of war, they showed a significant improvement over those in the depression, and it may fairly be claimed that the lessons of the depression, and the reorganization which had been necessary had put the economy of the history of the territory on to a sufficiently stable basis to off-set not only price fluctuations, but also those temporary reductions in production, resulting from rainfall deficiencies, which are such a feature of Tanganyika. In 1937 the trade barometer was back to the point it had reached in 1929, and had it not been for a complex of uncertainties, the outlook would have been fair indeed. The uncertainties in question were, first, the world political situation with its indication that Tanganyika might become a pawn on the international chess-board; second, the question of Closer Union in East Africa, and third, the local financial anxiety in Tanganyika about the railways budget. Before describing these three uncertainties, it will perhaps be as well to examine the economic atmosphere in which these uncertainties were faced.

IMPROVEMENT IN PUBLIC FINANCES

The improvement in the territory's finances which had been hoped for at the end of 1934 duly materialized. It has already been noted that though the budget for 1935 was still an economy budget, Government had stated that if the financial position improved, expenditure would be increased by supplementary provision. During 1935, interest on loans which had been suspended in order to balance the last of the depression budgets was paid. Before the end of the financial year, the levy on official salaries was abandoned. It has previously been noted that the amalgamation of the Posts and Telegraphs with headquarters in Kenya resulted in economy to Tanganyika. These services started to contribute a surplus to Tanganyika's revenue from 1935.

EXPORTS

The price of sisal reached £29 at the end of 1935, and the value of sisal exported was over £1 million for the first time in that year. In 1937, the volume of trade in Tanganyika exceeded in value the totals of the years 1932 and 1933 together. The production of gold exceeded 100,000 oz. for the first time in 1938, and the value of gold produced in 1939 reached nearly £1 million. The 1939 cotton crop, 65,145 bales valued at £557,358, was a record, and in the same year the coffee crop amounted to 16,599 tons valued at £466,026 including 10,901 tons of Robusta coffee from Bukoba. The production of tea exceeded half a million pounds for the first time in 1938 and in that year Tanganyika was allotted a further tea acreage of 2,050 acres for the period starting in 1939. Against these favourable figures it should be recorded that the value of coffee over this period was depressed (it will be remembered that at this time there was heavy over-production of coffee in Brazil), while the export of groundnuts which had reached 22,251 tons in 1937, fell to 3,579 tons in 1938 and 4,496 tons in 1939 as a result of two unfavourable seasons.

The foregoing figures show that on the whole had it not been for the uncertainties which will now be discussed, Tanganyika's state would have been a happy one.

POLITICAL UNCERTAINTY

As regards the world political situation, it had been necessary for the Governor of Tanganyika to make the following comment in his budget speech of 1936:—

"One factor in the life of Tanganyika of which we have all been uneasily conscious during the present year is that of its political future. While it is unquestionable that the publicity given in Europe to doubts expressed upon this matter have a certain effect in checking the investment of capital in the country, it is easy to exaggerate the force of that effect by disassociating it—as one cannot, I venture to suggest, legitimately do—from the general state of political uncertainty, created by the recent upheaval in Abyssinia, which is also, in a sense, a part of East Africa."

The feeling of uncertainty to which he referred gradually mounted until the time of the Munich crisis. By then the British Government was openly describing its policy as one of appeasement. German spokesmen were making frequent references to the return to Germany of her former colonies, and even suggested that it would be only equitable to undertake a general redistribution of colonial territories among the great powers in the light of Germany's revival. Shortly after the Munich crisis, the Governor of Tanganyika thought it necessary to make another reference to the situation in his opening address at the budget session of Legislative Council, inviting those present to make a public declaration on behalf of the inhabitants of Tanganyika. He said:—

"The maintenance of British rule in Tanganyika Territory has been thought by many to be in jeopardy, and those of us who have no such misgivings realise, nevertheless, that the subject is one on which it would be wrong to keep silence. It is a subject on which it is fitting that this Council should give public expression to the wishes of the inhabitants

9

of the country. It is a subject on which we should ourselves express our confidence and strive to communicate that confidence to others. For at this moment confidence is the most vital and compelling need of every interest in Tanganyika."

The declaration which he sought was unanimously made, but not without an expression of disquiet from the nominated members at the indefinite assurances obtainable from His Majesty's Government. They considered that these assurances ought to have extended to an expression of determination that Tanganyika would remain within the Empire, whereas they were confined to a statement that the status of Tanganyika was not a subject which had been raised internationally. It was, then, fortunate that before the end of the Tanganyika budget session a Private Member's Motion was raised in the House of Commons which enabled the Secretary of State for the Colonies to intervene with a statement of the British Government's view. Mr. Malcolm McDonald, discussing the misgivings which were admitted to exist in Tanganyika, used the following words which were duly reproduced in Tanganyika's Legislative Council:—

"Such misgivings ought to be removed. In order to remove them I do not need to express opinions; I do not need to marshal argument; I only have to state a simple fact. I do not believe there is today any section of opinion in this country that is disposed to hand over to any other country the care of any of the territories or the people for whose government we are responsible either as a Colonial or as a Mandatory Power. That view has been expressed this afternoon in every part of the House and it is a view which is shared by H.M. Government. We are not discussing this matter; we are not considering it; it is not now an issue in practical politics."

THE CENTRAL DEVELOPMENT COMMITTEE ESTABLISHED

These words which today may still seem indefinite were taken at the time to constitute a valuable reassurance. There was still something that could be done in Tanganyika and the Leader of the Nominated Members of Legislative Council, Sir William Lead (he had been knighted for public services to Tanganyika in 1935) requested the Governor to establish machinery for a large scale development programme in the territory not only in the interests of its inhabitants but also as a substantial expression of confidence in its future. This suggestion was immediately accepted by the Governor and a Central Development Committee with ancillary provincial committees was inaugurated. Though the work of this Committee, which proceeded at high pressure for the next eight months, was then interrupted by the outbreak of war, this does not detract from its significance. It will perhaps be relevant to record here that, as a result of the increasing influence of Legislative Council on the affairs of Tanganyika, it became possible in 1939 to add four of its unofficial members to the Governor's Executive Council. They consisted of one Asian and three European members, and included Sir William Lead.

CLOSER UNION

As regards Closer Union in East Africa, this controversy had originally been notable for a conflict of views between the purist, insisting on the independent mandatory status of Tanganyika and the imperialist who wished to retain Tanganyika within the Empire. To illustrate the purist point of view, it may be recorded that the Permanent Mandates Commission of the League of Nations questioned the use of a common postage stamp in East Africa suggesting that this, which was an obvious measure of economy, constituted an infringement of Tanganyika's independent mandatory status. The imperialist on the other hand was shaken in his confidence by the obvious conflict of interest resulting from the disappearance of Congo traffic, between the Kenya and Uganda Railways and that of Tanganyika. It was a shorter haul for Lake Victoria produce from Kisumu to Mombasa than from Mwanza to Dar es Salaam, and produce from Tanganyika's Northern Province enjoyed superior port facilities at Mombasa to those offering at Tanga.

The practical application of the British Government's decision about Closer Union was shelved for the time being in this period of uncertainty and Tanganyika came to the conclusion that she could well afford to abstain from the initiative because, with her expanding prosperity she was all the time quietly attaining her proper status as the senior and not the junior partner in the East African triad.

RAILWAY FINANCES

As regards the local financial anxiety about the railways budget, while railways accounts had been separated from those of the territory in 1929, the railway balance was counted in with that of the territory, so that any deficits were a matter of great public concern. In this period, traffic with the Belgian Congo, which had amounted to 64,374 metric tons in 1930, stabilized itself at a figure of approximately 6,000 tons p.a. In addition the railways became liable to considerable debt charges. For example, in 1934 the railways were run at a cost of £366,177, but had to pay in addition £323,919 in the shape of interest. To add to these disabilities, it was at last realized that there existed no reserve or renewals fund in the railway accounts, so that a decided improvement which actually occurred in their finances over the period did not appear so favourable in their budgets when (admittedly small) provision for renewals had been made.

LABOUR DEPARTMENT RE-ESTABLISHED

As regards domestic affairs, several matters of interest occurred during this period. It was notable that at this time members of the Permanent Mandates Commission had questions arising from one year's annual report answered as a routine in the report for the following year. For example in 1936 the Commission suggested that an effective and specialized labour service should be re-established. This was agreed, and a Chief Inspector of Labour was appointed and arrived in the territory early in 1938.

INCOME TAX ENQUIRY

Again, in 1937, at the instigation of the Permanent Mandates Commission, an enquiry was undertaken as to the advisability of instituting an income tax. After full enquiry, Tanganyika decided against this proposal on the grounds that there were very few people with high incomes in the territory and that the yield from an income tax might well be less than the yield from the Non-Native Poll Tax.

TSETSE RESEARCH

It has already been noted that the legislature was reluctant to provide funds for tsetse research. In 1938 the Colonial Development Fund, which had since its inception contributed small amounts for a large number of projects in the territory, made a substantial grant for tsetse research in East Africa, amounting to £207,974 spread over a seven-year period. In connection with tsetse research, it was learned in 1936 that a trap which it was claimed would catch all tsetse from an infested area had been made and patented in Zululand. This "Harris" trap was used experimentally by a member of the Tanganyika Tsetse Research Department on one of the Kenya Islands in Lake Victoria, but it failed to come up to expectations.

SLEEPING SICKNESS

As regards sleeping sickness, while the Kahama outbreak appeared by 1937 to have been brought within controlled dimensions by the policy of concentration, a new flare-up occurred in 1936 in the third of the areas which had been reported as infected by the former German Government. There had been sporadic cases in this area for some years but over 100 were diagnosed in 1936 in the Liwale area, necessitating a further, and difficult campaign of human concentrations in this inaccessible region. Another small outbreak which was more easily met, was discovered on Ukerewe Island by an African microscopist in 1939. The Medical Department had been conducting research and investigation into sleeping sickness from a centre at Tinde in the Lake Province and in 1939, upon the retirement of its specialist officer, sought the co-operation of the Department of Tsetse Research in the further maintenance of the local strain of *T. Rhodesiense* to ascertain how long it was likely to remain pathogenic to man when maintained solely in game or domestic animals with tsetse as cyclical transmitters. The specialist officer concerned, Dr. J. F. Corson, retired aged over 60, in 1939 after 14 years of devoted service to sleeping sickness research, in the course of which he suffered himself four times from that disease.

TRIBAL DISPENSARIES

It may here be mentioned that in the general medical field the numbers of out-patients treated at the tribal dispensaries in the territory exceeded three-quarters of a million in 1938 and that in that year and in the following year, when 834,408 cases were treated, these numbers exceeded those of out-patients at Government hospitals.

EDUCATION

As regards education, it will be clear that the British curriculum inaugurated in 1926 was starting by 1938 to produce candidates for secondary education who had received their primary training in a single regime. It may be useful then to compare numbers of pupils and staff with those as already recorded[1] which had been achieved in a roughly similar length of time by the former German Government. In 1938 there were 916 European pupils, 4,812 Asian pupils and 35,896 male African pupils in Government or state-aided schools and a much larger number of boys in unassisted mission schools. In addition there were 772 African girls in Government schools and 21,165 girls in assisted and unassisted mission schools. The Government Education staff in 1938 comprised 38 Europeans including three females, and 429 African teachers including 49 females, while mission teaching staffs comprised 212 Europeans including 137 females and 317 Africans including 110 females. Attention was starting to be paid to the matter of female education, and a woman education officer was added to the Headquarters staff of the Education Department early in 1939. The Conference of East African Governors included in 1938 in their deliberations the question of a post-secondary foundation, and it was agreed that Tanganyika should contribute £100,000 to the new Makerere College in 1939.

---

[1] See page 81.

PYRETHRUM

In the field of economics a new plantation crop made its first appearance in the shape of pyrethrum. This was recorded as a notable advance in the search for crops suitable for such marginal areas as that which had been earlier chosen by Lord Delamere. Indeed in a speech by the Governor in 1938 he announced that while a harvest of only 25 tons was expected in that year, it was also expected that a crop of 2,000 tons would be achieved within a period of two years with a value of about £200,000.

SOUTHERN HIGHLANDS ESTATES

At this time also Government agreed to alienate no less than 110,000 acres in one block in the marginal areas of the Iringa District, for a scheme of development by European settlers who were to sub-lease from the principal lessee.

THE CO-OPERATIVE MOVEMENT

The expansion of African economic production necessitated some attention to organized marketing, and it was in this period that attention was first directed to the proper organization of the co-operative movement to that end. In 1935 Government made a senior officer available as a co-operative consultant. Though there was no spectacular increase in this period in the numbers of co-operative societies, it is noteworthy that by 1939, the leading co-operative body in Tanganyika, the Kilimanjaro Native Co-operative Union included 27 primary co-operative societies with 25,728 members within its organization. Besides collecting and selling a crop of coffee in that year worth over £70,000, this Union also organized the collection and sale of other African produce such as maize and hides.

RINDERPEST

In the field of animal husbandry, since the start of British rule, most of the activities of the Veterinary Department had been marshalled against rinderpest. There was no year without this disease in cattle, and its elimination was the more difficult since it is transmitted from place to place by infected game. In 1938 the disease appeared in threatening form south of the Central Railway Line and it was feared in consequence that infection might spread to countries to the south of Tanganyika where the disease was not then present. By 1939 rinderpest and, in consequence, the campaign against it, had spread to the south of Tanganyika, and to within a few miles of Lake Nyasa. Representatives not only from British territories to the south but also from the Congo and Portuguese colonies attended veterinary conferences on this subject in 1938 and 1939.

MINING

Gold production continued to expand, and Government undertook considerable expenditure on the construction of a road of access to the Lupa Goldfield. This road from Itigi to Chunya, some 250 miles in length was completed in 1937. In 1938 a new mineral field was found in the Ukonongo area of the Western Province, the site of the present Mpanda Lead Mine

JEWISH REFUGEES

To end this account of the pre-war period, it may be mentioned that in 1938 Tanganyika had been asked by His Majesty's Government to consider receiving a limited number of Jewish refugees from Germany. A land survey was actually undertaken which was later found useful not for Jewish refugees (who never in fact materialized) but for an expansion of the pyrethrum industry during the war period.

WAR POTENTIAL

Tanganyika was not behindhand in local preparation for the war which was so clearly inevitable, and it may now be useful to summarize her condition and to examine the assets or liabilities which she would contribute to the struggle. In 1939, there were, in Tanganyika, 4,054 British persons including 2,440 males and 3,205 Germans including 1,858 males, the only other considerable European national community being the Greek with 893 persons including 616 males. There were 499 agricultural estates in British, 277 in British Indian, 558 in German and 216 in Greek hands. The elimination of enemy aliens, but the continuation of their industry was clearly the immediate concern. The public economy was properly balanced and, with care, might be expected to withstand war stresses, but the absence of anything more than token direct taxation on non-Africans, in an Empire fighting for its life, was an anomaly that could not continue. As regards production of war supplies, Tanganyika was a producer in 1939 of some 100,000 tons of sisal each year and of some 13,000 tons of cotton, 10,000 tons each of rice and oil seeds, and 16,000 tons of coffee as the other main export crops while, as noted above, production of pyrethrum had started. Except for sisal, the list is not formidable unless an output of 130,373 oz. of fine gold in 1939 is so considered, and it will be seen later how this lost its significance. But there is one war asset missing from the foregoing list, an asset which Tanganyika, far from probable scenes of battle, could indeed provide. How Tanganyika sent thousands of men to the war, made special efforts to feed those men in Abyssinia, Madagascar, the Middle East and in Burma, and tightened her belt so as to make the least possible demand on the rest of the Empire and its allies, will be recounted in the next section of this account.

THE WAR PERIOD, 1939-1945

There was no fighting in Tanganyika during the war. Pre-war preparations for the internment of enemy aliens had been complete, and the Germans in the territory offered no resistance although a few individuals escaped to Portuguese East Africa. For the remainder of the war, Tanganyika was an onlooker so far as war-like operations were concerned though she occupied a position on lines of communication which was at times close to military operations. The failure of Italy to enter the war in 1939 made it possible for large numbers of German ineffectives to be repatriated to Germany from Tanganyika through Italy. Italy's entry into the war in 1940 made her armies in Abyssinia a potential menace to East Africa, but they were entirely defeated in 1941 in a campaign in which Tanganyika troops played a part. The entry of Japan into the war to some extent intensified the danger to allied and neutral shipping in East African waters. One result was the occupation of Madagascar, where Tanganyika troops again distinguished themselves, and finally there came the campaigns in India and Burma where the always cheerful "Jambo" boys (*Jambo* is the usual Swahili greeting) won further laurels. An account of the war service of the Tanganyika battalions of the King's African Rifles appears elsewhere in this handbook.[1]

---

[1]See chapter 13.

ENEMY ALIENS

There were over 3,000 German and Italian nationals in the territory on the outbreak of war, of whom 1,470 were adult males. During the first six months of 1940, 572 German males and 780 women and children were repatriated to Germany. After the fall of France and the entry of Italy into the war over 500 Germans and Italians were transferred to the Union of South Africa for internment. This left some 1,700 enemy subjects in the territory and of these 656 were missionaries, the remainder being accommodated in internment centres on parole.

ENEMY PROPERTY

A full department of Government, that of the Custodian of Enemy Property, had been arranged in great secrecy before the outbreak of war, so that it was possible within a few days to take over enemy estates and businesses. Such of those as were uneconomic were closed down, but the remainder were kept in operation either directly by the officers of the Custodian, or by lessees. The Custodian of Enemy Property continued to operate throughout the war and for some years thereafter.

It may here be noted that the outbreak of war revealed the attitude of German immigrants, and their organization in a way which had previously been only suspect. It was not, perhaps, surprising that a portrait of the German Chancellor should have been discovered curtained behind an altar in a German mission building in Dar es Salaam. It was more surprising that German settlers had apparently been instructed by their local leaders to offer no resistance to internment, assuming no doubt that Germany would very shortly resume possession of Tanganyika without violence. Reputedly the most militant of the local German leaders, one Troost, was actually intercepted in the course of a placid motor drive in the afternoon after the outbreak of war, when he said that he was unaware that war had been declared. The extent to which German settlers had been subsidized by the German Government was discovered when the Custodian of Enemy Property took over their assets. The main German commercial house, the Usagara Company, which derived its capital from the Reich, exercised a strangle-hold on German settlers in its insistence that both their produce and their requirements should remain exclusively in German hands, and at the same time subsidized those settlers who were financially unsound. This particularly applied to numbers of farmers in the Southern Highlands Province who had mortgaged their coffee farms to the Uhehe Trading Company, a subsidiary of the Usagara Company, and who lived on a standard cash allowance of Shs. 400/- per month, any surplus due on coffee deliveries being paid in kind. In fact, one of the few successful German coffee farmers in the Mbozi area was well known as having the finest set of farm buildings in Tanganyika while he himself lived miserably on the above cash allowance, having failed to obtain further funds in return for his coffee, but having been supplied with cement and corrugated iron far in excess of his needs.

SIR MARK YOUNG

In 1941, Sir Mark Young, Governor of Tanganyika, who had imperturbably led the country through the crisis of the outbreak of war, was transferred to Hong Kong, where he arrived shortly before the entry of Japan into the the war. The territory was justifiably concerned to learn of his subsequent capture by the Japanese (an ordeal which he fortunately survived).

SIR WILLIAM LEAD

A notable casualty in Tanganyika occurred during the war in the death of Sir William Lead in January, 1942. A sisal planter by trade, he had been continuously a most valuable member of Legislative Council from its inception, and a member of Executive Council from the time (1939) when unofficials were first appointed to that body. In addition, at the outbreak of war, he volunteered for extra duty as Director of Manpower and Sisal Controller. His memory is now perpetuated by the Lead Memorial Hall in Tanga, the capital of the province which produces the major part of Tanganyika's sisal.

INTERNEES AND REFUGEES

The part which Tanganyika could play towards the prosecution of the war consisted of an effort to provide men and materials, and an effort to make as little demand as possible on the rest of the Empire. In the meantime, Tanganyika, lying on lines of communication, facilitated the passage of South African and Rhodesian troops northwards (travelling in the early war years to Abyssinia and the Middle East in approximately equal proportions by land and sea) and received considerable numbers of Italian internees from Abyssinia, Italian Somaliland and Eritrea, and of some thousands of war refugees, of whom 6,500 Poles from East Poland were a heavy responsibility. These unfortunate people, evacuated from their homes by the Russians, eventually arrived in Tanganyika via Persia and were accommodated in special refugee camps where they could recover from the inevitable hardships which they had suffered during their travels in lands where war and not refugees was the overriding preoccupation.

ARMY RECRUITMENT

The approximate number of men of all races recruited for the forces in Tanganyika up to the end of the war with Japan was some 92,000 of whom, of course, by far the greatest number were African. About half went to combatant and ancillary units, and half to the Pioneer and Labour Corps. A Compulsory Service Ordinance was enacted in July, 1940. The combatant units always attracted volunteers and, although technically conscripts, the number of volunteers steadily increased with the demand as Africans became more accustomed to the idea of military service and learned something about it from friends on leave. The same applied to the African Pioneer Corps once it became known.

It was not long before Africans on leave from the Army could show their friends considerable cash savings from their Army wages and could demonstrate in themselves the remarkable improvement in general health and even in physique which quickly resulted from discipline in the Army and a regular balanced diet.

CIVILIAN CONSCRIPTION

A comparatively small number of labourers was conscripted in 1940/41 for essential public services. In March, 1942, conscription for work on private enterprise began on a very limited scale for the production of foodstuffs; and later for the harvesting of those crops and also for pyrethrum. At the end of the year conscript labour was used for rubber production. Demand continued to increase in 1943, when conscript labour was supplied to sisal estates. The total number of men conscripted for production work and for civil purposes from 1940 to the end of September, 1945, was 84,501; of these some 34,800 were

Ancient and modern.

Photo: Public Relations Department

in respect of public services or Government-controlled production (rubber, minerals and foodstuffs grown by the Custodian of Enemy Property and by the Wheat Scheme). The percentage of conscripts to the total force employed varied from 3·3 to 8·4 per cent, and the corresponding figures for those employed by private enterprise from 1·5 to 4 per cent. Periods of conscription varied from two months to a year. The native labour censuses held in 1944 and 1945 showed some 320,000 adult males in civil employment who, separately from Africans serving in the forces, represented about 38 per cent of the adult able-bodied males of the territory (reckoned at 840,000 for inter-territorial manpower purposes). Of these 320,000, some 100,000 were employed in the sisal industry and 21,000 on rubber, 57,000 on essential foodstuffs, pyrethrum and other agricultural undertakings, and 63,000 in the public services, including Native Administration.

CIVIL LIST

In 1943 the Civil List, excluding Railways, contained 940 names of whom 141 were absent serving with the forces. In 1945 the establishment, including Railways, was 1,483 of whom only 982 were actually on duty and of these 316 were due or over-due for retirement. In 1945 the numbers in the Provincial Administration were 215, while the effective strength was 131 of whom 47 were due or over-due for retirement before the end of 1946.

PUBLIC FINANCES

On the economic side it is difficult to describe the true state of public finance owing to the large number of special accounts which came to be included in the territory's budget (such as those for refugees) and owing to the fact that while at the beginning of the war a railways deficit appeared in the accounts this disappeared as railways results became more favourable and the railways budget was enabled to stand on its own. But to generalize, the revenue of the territory increased from £2,308,108 in 1940 to £4,768,465 in 1945, while expenditure increased proportionately, there being no war year in which a small surplus was not secured. The main sources of revenue before the war had been the customs import duties and the African Hut Tax. While the latter remained steady throughout the war, customs revenue, as a result of war imports, increased from just over £½ million in 1940, to just under £1 million in 1945 and new excise duties were producing some £360,000 per annum by the end of the war. The Non-Native Poll Tax increased from £51,408 in 1940 to £55,716. Income Tax, introduced in 1940 produced £26,803 in that year and by 1945 the annual yield was just under £½ million. It may be noted that while income tax had already been in force before the war in Kenya, it was introduced in Tanganyika as a specific war measure, and on the understanding that it would be abolished after the end of the war.

In effect, the existing levels of taxation together with war increases particularly on customs and excise, added to greatly increased railway revenues resulting from war traffic, produced a buoyant treasury. The incidence of the financial year involved the presentation of budgets late in each calendar year and the buoyant situation was masked by this very fact. The budget for 1940, presented in November, 1939, was prepared at a time when the effects of war could not easily be forecast; that for 1941, presented in 1940, was prepared while the Battle of Britain was scarcely over; that for 1942, presented in late 1941, coincided with Pearl Harbour and in the next year the budget was presented at the time of the battles of El Alamein and Stalingrad. The presentation to Britain early in the war of the whole of Tanganyika's small reserve fund (£200,000) was regarded at the time as a grave though justifiable financial risk but would not have been so regarded had actual financial trends been known. In the later war years it was even possible to undertake certain deferred capital works out of surplus balances, and to tackle some of the arrears of maintenance which had built up as a result of earlier war austerity.

TRADE IN WAR TIME

As regards imports and exports, while the war at sea resulted inevitably in some dislocation, shipping generally was sufficient to keep Tanganyika's trade alive, and indeed was responsible for the remarkable achievement of increasing annual imports of both motor spirit and kerosene by the end of the war period to approximately twice the amounts which were imported in 1940. There were, naturally, some acute local shortages of imported goods. For example, only 5,100 tons of cement were imported in 1943 as against a normal pre-war consumption of over four times that quantity. More serious was the shortage of motor vehicles and of tyres and tubes particularly in a situation where, owing to lack of private transport, the Railways were forced to inaugurate bus and lorry services of considerable dimensions. Imports of tyres and tubes for the whole territory fell to the phenomenally low figure of 1,387 cwt. in 1942 and had only recovered to 6,130 cwt. in 1945 as against a figure of over 12,000 cwt. in 1947. One further illustration of restricted imports may be given. The supply of matches was quite unable to meet the demand, and by the end of the war the individual domestic buyer was restricted to one or at most two boxes at a time.

AGRICULTURE IN WAR TIME

It has been noted that Tanganyika was endeavouring to make as small a demand as possible on other countries during the war. It was then unfortunate that owing to unfavourable seasons, to the extra demands of refugees and internees and to the absence of so many thousands of able-bodied males in the forces, the supply of staple foodstuffs was inadequate in four of the six war seasons. It was necessary to import maize in 1941 and 1942 and again in 1944 and 1945. As against this, the Tanganyika Government itself undertook the production of wheat in order to reduce demand on shipping and to relieve a general shortage of this commodity in the eastern half of Africa. In 1942 it started the Northern Province Wheat Scheme on some very marginal land on the Ardai plain in Masailand, and on some less marginal but more inaccessible land in the Mbulu District. These operations continued until 1945 and if the paper value of wheat produced was high (for example Shs. 66/69 per bag including Shs. 23/56 depreciation on 45,707 bags produced in 1944) this could be offset against a saving of shipping space to which it was impossible to give a money value.

The war caused considerable alteration in the pattern of production in Tanganyika. The main export crop had always been sisal and this was subject to export restriction until the entry of Japan made Phillipine and Java supplies unavailable to the Allies. From 1942 onwards sisal was a war priority crop and production was maintained at approximately 100,000 tons per annum, its value increasing from £1½ million in 1940 to £5½ million in 1945. The production of cotton was another war priority, but the same reasons as had caused the importation of maize into Tanganyika during the war resulted in a reduction in the amount of cotton produced, though increasing prices maintained the incomes of producers. Coffee was not a top priority crop, but its production was of importance to the Tanganyika economy. Exports were maintained at approximately 15,000 tons per annum throughout the war, the value to producers doubling over this period. Two more of the crops which were important to Tanganyika showed heavy declines in quantities exported. These were rice and groundnuts. By the end of the war Tanganyika rice, strictly rationed, was nearly all being consumed in Tanganyika and Zanzibar, while groundnuts, likewise subject to local consumption, were disastrously affected by the poor agricultural season in 1943, and did not recover in 1944 and 1945.

RUBBER AND PYRETHRUM

Though production of ceara rubber from the derelict pre-1914 German estates is in normal times uneconomic, the disappearance of Malaya as a producer, as a result of Japan's entry into the war, made it necessary to comb all possible sources. Production of rubber from the former German estates started in 1942 and had been increased by 1945 to 52,272 centals in that year, an item of export which duly disappeared as soon as the war was over. It may be of interest that the use of thousands of knives for rubber tapping necessitated the provision of suitable hones, and that these hones were all made locally at short notice by the Department of Geological Survey from graphite found in the Morogoro District. Pyrethrum became a priority crop during the war (the powder being required as an insecticide on account of its knock-down properties alongside the slower acting D.D.T.) particularly in the far eastern campaigns. Production increased in consequence from 244 tons in 1940 to 697 tons in 1945.

MEAT SUPPLIES

As a part of the effort to make East Africa self-contained for food, Tanganyika provided cattle for canning in Kenya. Over the whole period more than 400,000 cattle were sent to Kenya for this purpose.

GOLD

Until the introduction of Lease-Lend, the production of gold was of the greatest importance and over £1 million worth was produced in both of the years 1940 and 1941. Lease-lend, however, resulted in the disappearance of priority for gold, and lack of interest, and of machinery, had resulted by 1945 in a reduction of the annual value of gold produced to little more than £400,000.

DIAMONDS

It may be noted that during the war an important new item of production appeared on the Tanganyika scene. Dr. Williamson's discovery of the Mwadui Mine near Shinyanga resulted in a sudden jump in the value of diamond production to £12,600 in 1940. Annual output increased regularly to a value of £638,383 in 1945 and his discovery was to have an even greater effect on the territory after the war.

PAPAIN

Yet another new product, though of small proportions, evolved during the war was papain, the dried milk of pawpaw, which was in demand in America as a "tenderizer" in canning. In 1945, 101 tons were exported.

PRODUCTION OF STAPLE FOOD

The imperative necessity to produce foodstuffs resulted in an alteration in the nature of the agricultural effort in remote areas. Where before the war production of food for sale had been uneconomic owing to the transport factor, it became the regular practice during the war under a system of price control and price averaging, and the same prices were paid for staple foodstuffs grown 500 miles from the railway as were paid to producers in consuming areas. This situation applied particularly to the Southern Highlands Province which had not been a producer of bulk foodstuffs except for its own consumption before the war. The fact that this province could contribute maize and rice to the East African pool was one of the reasons for the establishment by the Railways Administration of road services in that area. In fact, war-time production at controlled prices, with evacuation by public transport, had resulted by the end of the war in a similar pattern of production to that which would have obtained had this remote province been served by a railway. (The territorial policy of self-sufficiency in food has maintained after the war a type of production which is uneconomic without this transport subsidy.)

WAR FUNDS AND CHARITIES

Another feature of the war period in Tanganyika was the contribution by private individuals to various war funds and war charities. A sum of £347,094 was subscribed, including £116,288 to the War Relief and Welfare Fund, £65,914 to the Tanganyika War Fund and £57,576 to the Red Cross, while interest-free loans to His Majesty's Government were made to a total of £74,292, and the war-time excess profits tax amounting to £368,000 was offered "en bloc" to His Majesty's Government. In addition, there were some notable donations for war purposes, including a gift of coffee by the Chagga tribe and gifts of cattle by the Masai. The foregoing figures should not obscure the great amount of voluntary work undertaken by members of the public such as service at soldiers' canteens and assistance to Allied refugees.

EFFECT OF THE WAR ON AFRICAN LIFE

The foregoing are but extracts from a mass of data covering an immense and diversified effort by the whole territory. Speaking in Legislative Council at the end of 1944 the Governor said:—

"In turning our attention to the future I think it is due to those who have borne the burden that we should not forget the past or under-rate the extent of the effort that the war has demanded from them. The chief contribution by this . . . territory to the general war effort has . . . been the provision of manpower for the maintenance of a considerable army which has played and is playing an important role in the operations of war in the African and Eastern theatres. . . . This has involved the withdrawal for the duration of the war from the ordinary native life of the territory of a proportion of the younger men which taken together with the expanded demands of industry has been nearly double that ordinarily required in peace-time. This may not sound very large compared with the ratios in Europe, but it must be remembered that under African conditions where the first call on the activities of the individual is production for his own subsistence and that of his family, the withdrawal of a large percentage of the able-bodied men involves a serious disruption in social and economic life. The proportion of men furnished to the Forces by this territory has been among the highest ratios in the African territories."

MEDICAL

At the outbreak of war the Medical Department had furnished staff and equipment for a casualty clearing station, a field ambulance and a motor ambulance convoy while staff had been detailed and equipment set aside for a general hospital and an ambulance train which were not actually mobilized. Fifteen Medical Officers served in the forces and in the Somaliland and Abyssinian campaigns. It follows that those who remained on civilian duty were under high pressure. Demand for medical help from the general population continued to increase, and it may be noted that in 1944, 1,311,316 patients attended the territory's Native Treasury dispensaries. The war did not result in heavy civilian casualties such as had resulted from the influenza outbreaks at the end of the 1914–18 war, but by 1945 Tanganyika was suffering from a wide sporadic incidence of a mild type of smallpox and, owing to the large outbreak of yellow fever in the Nuba Mountains of the Sudan during the war, she was very much "on her toes" to discover whether the territory was in fact infected. The wartime production of rubber (wherein the normally unemployable semi-nomad Wagogo from the Central Province demonstrated an unexpected aptitude) involved the Medical Department in the establishment of a large temporary hospital at Muheza.

SLEEPING SICKNESS

As regards sleeping sickness, it has already been noted that cases were discovered in the Liwale area before the outbreak of war. These continued during the war as did measures to concentrate the people involved, but the most spectacular development of sleeping sickness during the war occurred in an entirely new area. In October, 1943, the disease was discovered in the hitherto uninfected "fly" belt centred at Babati in the Mbulu District. In this small area over 300 cases were discovered in 1944 and 1945, and, as a measure of control, it was found necessary to evacuate the population from a locality known as Kiru which had been the source of a part of the production of the new crop, papain, which has been mentioned above.

RINDERPEST

By 1940 the rinderpest outbreak in the Southern Highlands Province was under control, but it was considered essential to be absolutely sure that the disease did not spread southwards through infection carried by game. A game-free belt was, therefore, established along the Tanganyika/Northern Rhodesian border which was paid for by the governments interested and patrolled by a force of game scouts and other volunteers with the object of preventing the southward passage of game animals.

CIVIL ORDER

There were no changes in the constitution or position of Tanganyika during the war, and no civil disturbances. At the outbreak of war there had been nearly 20,000 African labourers employed on the Lupa Goldfield. A rumour, fostered by German alluvial diggers that African property would be confiscated by Government on the outbreak of war, caused about 11,000 Africans to rush back to their homes, but the uneventful arrest of enemy aliens soon countered this rumour and the majority of these Africans quickly returned to work. The only other semblance of unrest in the whole of the war period occurred in the Moshi District among Somali troops who were unused to beef in their diet.

The district then enjoyed the unprecedented experience of seeing herds of camels which were imported to feed those troops, and thus to remove their main source of discontent.

POST-WAR PLANNING

By 1944 the favourable course of the war made it possible to start post-war planning. The immediate domestic problem was the re-absorption into civilian life of the thousands of Africans who had served with the Forces. It was thought, erroneously in the event, that these men would be dissatisfied to return to civilian life, and a programme was undertaken of construction of what were called Welfare Centres in the larger townships throughout the territory, it being hoped that these buildings would provide social and cultural facilities for all, but chiefly for ex-servicemen. But the main post-war planning was in connection with development, not "development" as understood by the English speculative builder but development of the territory in the interest of its inhabitants through the medium of large capital works and programmes for expansion of public services. The basis for the planning which was started in 1944 was the report of the Central Development Committee which had functioned before the outbreak of war. Though those responsible could have no more than conjectural knowledge of the post-war financial position, and were in fact considerably alarmed at the financial implications of the post-war plan, a significant amount of work on it had been completed even before the end of hostilities.

RECONSTRUCTION AND PLANNING, 1945-1949

For the sake of convenience the post-war years 1945-1954 are divided in this survey into two quinquenniads, 1945-1949 and 1950-1954 to conform with the original, and the revised official post-war Development Plans. Expenditure by Government on these plans, which totalled over £2,100,000 in the years 1947-1949, did not get into its full stride until 1950 and it is, therefore, thought convenient to regard the period 1945-1949 as being one of preparation.

It will be seen that in this account much emphasis has been given hitherto to the question of the economy. The altered value of money which began to be evident during the war period transformed the financial picture and for this reason comparative financial statistics between the pre-war and the post-war periods are of little value.

POST-WAR PROSPERITY

But even if pre-war and war-time standards are ignored, Tanganyika's financial position in 1945-1949 presents a startling picture. With only slightly increased output, the annual value of sisal increased from under £4 million in 1946 to over £11 million in 1949. Without any increased output, coffee income rose from £675,580 to £1,460,768 in the same period. Annual cotton production increased nearly threefold in bulk and more than five times in value. Diamonds, paying royalty at 15 per cent, were exported to the value of over £1 million in 1948 and £1½ million in 1949 while gold exports showed a revival in 1948/49 after exports of only 47,427 oz. in 1947. The total volume of trade rose from about £17½ million in 1946 to nearly £52½ million in 1949. Small wonder that public revenue increased enormously in the same period, and that by the end of 1949 there was a general revenue balance exceeding £2 million and a reserve fund of £1 million.

THE POST-WAR DEVELOPMENT PLAN

It was not, then, unrealistic to adopt and modify the pre-war development plan, and to envisage a programme of comprehensive development to cover the period 1947-1956 at a cost of just over £19 million particularly when account is taken of Colonial Development and Welfare Funds. It is notable that this plan got slowly into gear. When the plan was approved Tanganyika was still suffering from the disorganization caused by the war-time conditions. There was a severe shortage of staff particularly in the technical departments. There was little equipment or plant with which to get started, particularly with major constructional works on roads, railways, aerodromes, hospitals and schools. The Tanganyika development plan in its slow start was then in marked contrast with, for example, the groundnut scheme which, as recounted hereafter. suffered from inadequate planning and over-hasty approach.

TRUSTEESHIP

At the end of the 1914-1918 war, the British Government had been at pains to avoid any accusation of territorial aggrandisement, and it is said that an unsuccessful attempt had even been made to persuade Italy to accept a Mandate for the southern half of Tanganyika. The final acceptance of the Mandate by His Majesty's Government, its operation for more than a quarter of a century, and the desuetude of the League of Nations made the British Government anxious to substitute a realistic title for Tanganyika after the war of 1939-1945. Only five months after V.J. Day, the following statement was made by Mr. E. Bevin, the Foreign Secretary, to U.N.O. on 17th January, 1946:—

"Another instrument which we welcome is the Trusteeship Council. We made our contribution to its creation at San Francisco and in the Preparatory Commission. At the end of the last war the mandatory system was devised. We have given careful consideration to our own position in connection with the mandates for which we are responsible; and I take this opportunity of informing the Assembly of our intentions.

"We have decided to enter forthwith into negotiations for placing Tanganyika, the Cameroons and Togoland under the Trusteeship system. Preliminary negotiations have already started. I must make it clear that our willingness to place these territories under the Trusteeship system naturally depends upon our being able to negotiate terms which in our view are generally satisfactory, and which achieve the objectives of the Charter and are in the best interests of the inhabitants of the territories concerned.

"These territories have been administered by us for over twenty-five years. We have fulfilled our obligations under the Covenant of the League and to the best of our ability administered and developed them in the interests of their inhabitants. We intend to continue this policy under the Trusteeship system. We are ready to accept the obligation which will rest upon us as the administering authority under this new system. Now, if this is to be achieved, it is most important that the people of the territories themselves and the world at large should be left in no doubt that the continuity of administration will be maintained, until the ultimate objective of the Trusteeship system, self-government or independence, as the case may be, is attained."

The fact that no reference had first been made to the public of Tanganyika before the above statement had been issued occasioned some surprise locally, and a question in Legislative Council was quickly put. It was thought at that time that a Motion would be raised on the question of Trusteeship, and a final official answer was therefore postponed, but in the event, the Motion was withdrawn and the matter was actually never debated. This was not the case with the proposal to establish a High Commission and Central Legislative Assembly for East Africa, which provoked a most lively debate at the end of which a Motion was supported by all official and unofficial European members and was opposed only by the two Asian members present, while the African members abstained from voting.

In 1948 the first U.N.O. Visiting Mission travelled round the territory. It consisted of four delegates representing those member nations of the Trusteeship Council which had been selected by the ballot to make nominations. The report of the Commission was duly considered and adopted by the Trusteeship Council.

THE HIGH COMMISSION AND CENTRAL LEGISLATIVE ASSEMBLY

The actual procedure whereby Lord Passfield's decision on the question of Closer Union had been shelved during the depression was through adoption of the advice of a Select Committee of both Houses of Parliament, given in 1931, against any far-reaching steps involving any form of close political union. That Committee, however, advised in favour of regular Governors' Conferences, and these which had been started in 1926 as a result of the Ormsby-Gore Commission continued until the end of the war. Regular meetings of the Governors were supplemented by frequent technical conferences in order to co-ordinate scientific research and by the end of the war the numbers of inter-territorially controlled common services had been increased as a result of war needs. One of the great drawbacks of the Governors' Conference was that it had been established by an administrative direction from the Secretary of State and had no juridical or constitutional basis. During the war executive responsibility for common services devolved upon the Secretariat of the Governors' Conference. Through it relations with Navy, Army and Air Force were conducted. It carried out functions on behalf of the Ministries of Supply, Food and War Transport and performed many other extraneous duties.

In 1945 proposals were made in England for a change in the inter-territorial organization, to provide for a High Commission consisting of the Governors of Kenya, Uganda and Tanganyika and for a Central Legislature with powers to control certain strictly defined subjects. Discussions on this proposal lasted for more than a year (the debate in Legislative Council on this subject has already been noted) but finally in 1947 an Order in Council was made under the Foreign Jurisdiction Act to implement the proposals as modified and agreed. Briefly stated, the purpose of these proposals was to give a constitutional and juridical frame-work for the administration of departments and services which were by their nature inter-territorial. H.M. Government made two important stipulations, first that the new organization did not diminish the final responsibility of Parliament for the administration of the three East African territories, and second, that the proposal involved neither closer political union of the territories nor the fusion of the territorial Governments. As regards Tanganyika, it must be remembered that assurance was given by H.M. Government to the Fourth Committee of the United

Nations Assembly in December, 1946, that it had not considered that the terms of Article 5 (b) of the Trusteeship Agreement gave any power to an Administering Authority to establish any form of political association between a Trust Territory and an adjacent territory which would involve the annexation of the Trust Territory or would have the effect of extinguishing its status as a Trust Territory. It may also be re-emphasized that the proposal to convert Tanganyika's previous mandatory status into a trust status was made by H.M.Government without any reference to the wishes of the inhabitants of Tanganyika nor prior notice to its Legislature. Such reference or notice would in fact have been difficult owing to the very short time which elapsed between the end of the war and the proposals in question.

As a precaution, it was stipulated that the High Commission and Central Legislative Assembly were to be instituted for a trial period of four years, during which no additional common services were to be transferred to it without a unanimous expression of approval by the three territorial legislatures concerned. (In the event, the original four-year trial period was extended for a further four-year period, and at the time of writing the status of the institution is not yet permanent.)

THE FIRST AFRICAN MEMBERS OF LEGISLATIVE COUNCIL

At the December, 1945, meeting of Legislative Council, the first two Africans to be nominated as members took their seats. In view of what Sir Donald Cameron said about direct African representation it is of interest that one of these Africans had studied at Makerere and had then attended a year's course in agriculture at Lincoln College, Oxford, while the other had, by home study, acquired a working knowledge of the English language, without which the mass of paper which has to be studied by members of Legislative Council would have meant little to him. Both these members were Chiefs, though not Chiefs of complete tribes. It was the former who in his maiden speech said, "I have to apologize for the fact that English is not my mother tongue and if I make mistakes at all, members should then be sympathetic to me." A third African member was nominated in 1947, this time a commoner.

DEVELOPMENT OF LOCAL GOVERNMENT

At Local Government level, while the return to their homes of ex-servicemen introduced no such political activities as had been expected, the very fact that so many persons had had their outlook enlarged by travel during the war focused attention on what may be called the democratization of Native Authorities. It has already been noted that when the time was ripe this process would follow the institution of Indirect Rule and in the period under review, the attention of the Administration began to be directed towards the recognition and democratic multiplication of those hitherto unrecognized advisers who are an integral part of the Bantu administrative organization. This process was not forced, nor was any attempt made at uniformity, but, particularly in 1948 and 1949, there was considerable progress in openly substituting the "Chief in Council" for the "Chief" as the Native Authority. In two provinces trials were started of Provincial Councils, the enlargement of the existing conference of officials by the addition of unofficial Europeans, Asians and Africans. In the Lake Province, the Provincial Council tended to be an off-shoot of central government while in the Southern Highlands Province the tendency was rather in the direction of what is known as Local Government in England. Both Provincial Councils were regarded as "guinea pigs", and the experience gained in them was

10

of particular interest to a Committee on Constitutional Development which was appointed by Government late in 1949 to study the reform of the territorial constitution, and in particular the organization of local government. At the beginning of 1949, a further step in this process was taken when the Township of Dar es Salaam became a Municipality as defined by law, which constituted a considerable step on the road towards municipal autonomy.

THE DEVELOPMENT PLAN

The Ten-Year Development Plan for the territory, formulated in 1946, was estimated to cost over £19 million. It was approved by H.M. Government in January, 1947, financed as follows:—

	£
Colonial Development and Welfare Allocations ...	6,775,000
Territorial Revenue	2,510,000
Surplus Balances	500,000
Loans	5,725,000
Excess Profits Tax Fund	350,000
Agricultural Development Fund	1,250,000
Native Treasuries	500,000

The above sources of funds left a deficit of just over £1½ million to be found from other sources. A word of explanation is necessary about these items of finance. The large sum made available from Colonial Development and Welfare Funds, which had been first mentioned (in the sum of £5¼ million) as early as December, 1945, and which was justly described in Tanganyika's Legislative Council as "astonishing generosity" by a country which had only just emerged from a financially crippling war, was directly responsible for the perpetuation, after the war, of income tax in Tanganyika, it being argued that the territory would not deserve such assistance unless it was prepared to tax itself to an extent which would make a substantial contribution to its own development programme. It will be remembered that the war-time Excess Profits Tax had been offered to H.M. Government. This money was, however, never paid over, since H.M. Government made it available instead for the development of Tanganyika. The Agricultural Development Fund consisted of margins realized by Government between prices paid to producers for certain items of produce and prices realized on subsequent bulk sales to the Ministry of Supply.

The Development Plan included a large number of projects in all fields of activity. Space prevents a detailed account of the proposals, but it may be mentioned that due attention was paid to the necessity for the technical training of African personnel.

The territorial Development Plan included a considerable number of local schemes for agricultural rehabilitation and development. The most notable of these local schemes were sited in the Mbulu District, the Uluguru Mountains and a small area in the Usambara Mountains known as the Mlalo Basin. At the same time a very large scheme of reorganization was undertaken in Sukumaland. Here the grouping of local government institutions at district level was replaced in 1948 by a federation comprising the five Sukuma districts, and construction was started of a federal headquarters at Malya.

AMALGAMATION OF THE EAST AFRICAN RAILWAYS SYSTEMS

The amalgamation of the East African Railways and Harbours took effect from May 1st, 1948, from which date the Railways accounts ceased to be of direct anxiety to the Tanganyika taxpayer though they remained of indirect concern since the East African territories severally guarantee the railways loans which subsequently became necessary for post-war development. At the time of the amalgamation, Tanganyika's railways had already embarked on three extensions. Two of these were necessitated by the groundnut scheme. The larger involved the construction of a deep water port in the Southern Province and of a railway from this port, Mtwara, to Nachingwea, the groundnuts centre. The second consisted of a short branch line from Msagali on the Central Line to Hogoro near Kongwa. The third extension, from Kaliua on the Central Line led to Mpanda, 135 miles distant to the south, the site of an important proposed mining enterprise, and use was made here of the rails salvaged from the abandoned Manyoni–Kinyangiri extension. Though the new line in the Southern Province, which was expected to run for 145 miles, was primarily necessitated by the groundnut scheme, it was also intended to facilitate and develop other production in this hitherto remote and rail-less area.

TEN-YEAR EDUCATION PLAN

In 1946 and in conjunction with the territorial Development Plan, Tanganyika adopted a ten-year plan for the expansion of education costed at over £4¾ million, it being also intended that Native Treasuries should contribute more than £½ million. The primary target in this plan was to provide schools for thirty-six per cent of the children of school age. The census of 1948 showed that the population was larger than that on which the plan had been based, and it was decided in 1949 that it would therefore be necessary to re-cast it in 1950. It is of interest that in 1939 the estimates of the Education Department amounted to £121,716, while in 1949 they amounted to £906,070.

LEPROSY

A notable advance in medical treatment occurred in this period following the discovery of a positive cure for leprosy in place of the palliatives which had previously been used. The first big orders for sulphetrone were placed in 1949, and although the cost was comparatively high at some £6 per patient per annum, considerable use of this drug was started in those of the territory's many leper settlements where technical observation of patients' reactions were possible.

ANIMAL PROTEIN

By 1947 it was clear that it was necessary to maintain and even to extend the take-off of cattle which had been effected during the war for war purposes, in order to prevent over-stocking. A company was formed, Tanganyika Packers, in which Government retained a 51 per cent interest, and the factory in Dar es Salaam was nearing completion in 1949. Plans were also made for another undertaking with similar Government interest, at Arusha, providing an abattoir with cold storage facilities so that frozen carcasses could be sent to Tanga for the feeding of the population of that province, instead of animals being sent on the hoof through the tsetse areas en route.

CENSUS, 1948

In 1948 a general census of the population was undertaken. By contrast with that of 1931, this census involved the employment of specific temporary field staff, while the census report was collated by the Statistical Branch of the High Commission. This census, which it is known was comparatively accurate, and which was accompanied by a subsequent 10 per cent sample census for purposes of check, showed that the population of Tanganyika in the gross was increasing with some rapidity. It is of interest that it was found that of the total Asian population in Tanganyika over half were born in the territory.

LABOUR

The rapid expansion of the territory's economy after the war was reflected by the results of the annual census of employed labour. In 1949 this census showed that over 400,000 Africans were in paid employment out of a total of just over 1,850,000 adult males (including the aged and infirm) found in the 1948 census. The importance of a suitable labour force to the sisal industry induced the Tanganyika Sisal Growers' Association to establish their own labour recruiting agency after the war instead of relying on individual private recruiters, and from this time the initials SILABU, standing for the Sisal Labour Bureau, became a common sight on notice boards and camp signs in the labour recruiting areas.

EX-ENEMY SUBJECTS

After the end of the war, a decision was quickly reached as to the future of ex-enemy subjects. In addition to the 396 missionaries who remained in the territory, 101 of those who had been interned in Southern Rhodesia were allowed to return and 268 of those who had been interned in Tanganyika were allowed to remain.

THE WILSON REPORT

The disposal by the Custodian of Enemy Property of those ex-enemy estates which were not revested brought to the fore the suggestion that over-alienation had occurred in certain areas and could be rectified by the reversion of estates from non-African occupation. The situation was particularly important in the Arusha and Moshi Districts of the Northern Province, and a one-man commission was appointed to settle the matter. The Commissioner was a Judge of the High Court and his report, commonly known as the Wilson Report, gave a basis to the decision as to which ex-enemy estates should be re-leased and which should revert. His recommendations for the creation of a homogenous leased block between Mts. Meru and Kilimanjaro involved the shifting of some members of the Meru tribe to a disconnected expansion area. This recommendation was not at all popular among the tribesmen concerned and formed the subject of their subsequent representations to the United Nations Organization.

LAND

There was considerable interest after the war by immigrants in land, and in the period under review, Government established a Land Settlement Board with the intention that settlement should be rationalized. (The title of this board was later changed to that of the Land Utilization Board in order to demonstrate that settlement was not its only concern. These successive boards dealt with the spate of post-war projects for agricultural development, which had exhausted itself by 1954. Reference has already been made to the lease of a very large block of marginal land, before the war, in the Iringa District. The project that this land should be divided amongst sub-lessees by the principal lessee was a failure and those sub-leases which had been effected were taken over by Government, the balance of the land being transferred to a new lessee for his own development, there being no apparent other demand for it.)

THE GROUNDNUT SCHEME

It is said that the idea of the Groundnut Scheme originated in a suggestion made in Dar es Salaam by the Director of Agriculture to the Managing Director of the United Africa Company, one of the components of the Unilever group, to the effect that an area of 20,000 acres might be planted with groundnuts in order to relieve to some extent the shortage of margarine fats in heavily rationed England. As a result and at the instance of the Colonial Office, a party was sent from England in 1946 which included a former Director of Agriculture in Tanganyika, and it was this party which made proposals for a scheme covering not 20,000 but some three million acres, divided into units of 30,000 acres each, in certain places in East and Central Africa of which the greatest were in three areas in Tanganyika. There is no doubt that the shape of this scheme owed much to the army mentality, closely following as it did the triumph of logistics in the war. It seemed that a scheme had only to be big enough for it to overcome all obstacles.

It was decided in England to proceed with the scheme under the direction not of the Colonial Office but of the Ministry of Food. In great haste, and without preliminary agricultural experimentation, parties were sent from England from the beginning of 1947 to start operations not so much in the two more agriculturally attractive Tanganyika areas but mainly in that area, the Mpwapwa District, which was the least attractive agriculturally and which offered as its only advantage its comparative proximity to the railway. The target for the first year's operations (1947) was 150,000 acres, a target which in the existing state of shortage of implements and resources of all kinds was quite unattainable. In the first year of operations the scheme was under the control of the United Africa Company through a subsidiary Company which was appointed "Managing Agents".

In February, 1948, the Overseas Resources Development Bill became law in England, creating the Colonial Development Corporation with a capital of £100 million and the Overseas Food Corporation with a capital of £50 million. It was the intention that the latter should control the groundnut scheme, the estimate for which was in the region of £25 million. By the end of March, 1948, the scheme had already spent nearly £7¾ million and was spending about £1 million a month. The O.F.C. assumed charge of the groundnut scheme in April, 1948 and in its first annual report for the period ending in March, 1949, it recorded that it had been found necessary to introduce a proper accounting system, to recruit accounting staff, to set up its own internal audit and to set up a financial control of expenditure (H.M.S.O. 252).

The operations of the groundnut scheme in 1947 were characterized by a sense of urgency regardless of cost. Second-hand machinery, scarcely any of which was really suitable for African conditions was bought wholesale from War Disposals, largely in the Phillipines and Middle East. A consignment of Sherman tanks, which Messrs. Vickers Armstrong had been asked to convert into agricultural tractors without preliminary experimentation under African conditions was landed in the Southern Province without proper facilities for delivery at the scene of operations. For about the first year under the O.F.C., the scheme was managed in Tanganyika by an Army General. Such was the expenditure, that the capital limits of the O.F.C. very soon became a practical consideration, particularly since out of the capital limit, another agricultural scheme had been undertaken in Queensland for the production of pigs and pig food.

In view of the huge scale of operations, the fact that there had been no preliminary agricultural experimentation was disastrous. The essence of the scheme was mechanization and although the partially mechanized production of groundnuts had been practised in favourable soil and climatic conditions in the United States, there was no experience of mechanical needs under African conditions. Very quickly it was proved that the areas which the O.F.C. hoped to clear could not possibly be cleared within the time limits proposed, that machinery for land development and agriculture was inadequate and that the very soil, particularly at Kongwa in the Mpwapwa District, did not lend itself to the wholesale production of groundnuts by mechanized means in existing rainfall conditions. The partial failure of the rains in 1949—an all too common experience in the Central Province of Tanganyika—added to the confusion and failure which became apparent.

In 1949 there were troubles with personnel. The Army General mentioned had to resign for reasons of health, and after an interim period wherein the Chairman of the O.F.C., whose headquarters were in London, acted as General Manager in Tanganyika, a joint General Managership was established in the field. The Chairman in question had until his appointment been Assistant General Manager of the *Daily Express* group. Previously he had been associated with the Minister of Food in connection with the publication of a periodical entitled *The Miner*, produced shortly after the General Strike in England. He was knighted in mid-1949 after he had been Chairman of the O.F.C. for little more than a year, and before the end of 1949 both he and the Minister of Food were subject to severe criticism on account of the scheme's failure to achieve its agricultural targets.

By the end of 1949 the groundnut scheme as originally envisaged had largely failed. Particularly was this the case at Kongwa since a start only had been made in the other two, and more agriculturally favourable, areas. In Urambo, where bush clearing was easier than at Kongwa, and where the ground organization was markedly superior, a certain amount of success on a small scale had been achieved, while at Nachingwea, a remote area served at first by neither port nor railway, there were only the small beginnings of agriculture in a more generally fertile area, beginnings which tended to be obscured by disputes as to the siting of a pipeline and fuel tank farm, a new township at Noli which was in fact never built, and a saw mill (at some distance from the centre of the supplies of timber which it was hoped to use for building purposes).

The scheme itself had been conceived on comprehensive lines and was to include not only the production of groundnuts but also their delivery at the coast, social amenities for employees of all races and an increase in Tanganyika's standards of prosperity, efficiency and transport. It was announced from the first that the scheme would later be handed over to the Government of Tanganyika as an interim step towards its final transfer to the people of the territory on a co-operative or other suitable basis. By the end of 1949, as the stocks of groundnuts sold by peasant producers piled up awaiting transport in Northern Nigeria, signs were not lacking in Tanganyika that if the groundnut scheme had a salvage value, this would derive from its experiments to find out how to make unattractive bush lands productive, rather than in the production of groundnuts.

As a result of control of this scheme in the initial years by the Ministry of Food, not by the Colonial Office, the effects on Tanganyika were remarkably small. Though good relations between existing inhabitants and the newcomers were maintained, the lack of staff interchange produced a situation like that which would have arisen had the Army conducted land manoeuvres on the otherwise empty decks of a battleship at sea, the latter representing the established order of things in Tanganyika.

GRAIN STORAGE

By the end of 1949, the impetus and enthusiasm which had been evident at the start of the scheme were waning, just at the time when any consequent reduction in Tanganyika's morale could be discounted by the successes of her own post-war development. In fact, there was only one major cloud on the local horizon. As a result of war-time experiences a system had been started after the war for the storage of surplus grain to meet any later deficits due to poor harvests. As a result of defective rainfall, stocks of grain were depleted in 1948, and entirely exhausted in 1949 when it became necessary to import no less than 70,000 tons of grain, and to offset a part of the high cost by charging users with a levy.

THE YEARS OF RAPID DEVELOPMENT, 1950-1954

The last period to be covered in the present review was characterized by important constitutional changes made in an atmosphere of economic prosperity. It has been seen how the attention of the Administration began to concentrate after the war on demonstrable improvement to the Native Authority structure. This was in conformity with the policy of training a backward people to take a due part in local government in their home areas, before expecting them to make a significant contribution as members of government bodies at higher levels. By the end of 1949 it had become desirable to forecast the progressive changes in the constitution which would be necessitated by increased integration of the indigenous people into the Government of the territory.

THE COMMITTEE ON CONSTITUTIONAL DEVELOPMENT

The Committee on Constitutional Development which had been appointed late in 1949, consisting of Government's Attorney-General and Member for Local Government and all the unofficial members of Legislative Council, was asked "to review the present constitutional structure in the territory, both local and territorial, and to make recommendations for future constitutional developments." The value of the work of this Committee lay not only in its report or in debate on this report in Legislative Council (the nominated members of the Council could scarcely be expected to add much in debate to their own unanimous report) but also in the opportunity which the travels of the sub-committees gave for the general public to air its views. In presenting the report the Chairman made the following comments: "Not as much interest was shown by the general public . . . as had been expected . . . in respect of the Africans it must be recorded that, even among their leaders the political conceptions of most are limited to local units . . . there is no insistent clamour for reform . . . the pace of political and constitutional development must be matched with the capacity of the bulk of the population to absorb change . . ."

The report was completed early in 1951. Those of the recommendations which were acceptable referred to the desirability that the membership of Legislative Council should be enlarged, and that a system of local government should be instituted for both county and urban areas. It recommended that an expert enquiry should be made in the territory to consider the practical applications of these proposals, and whether and if so how the elective principle should be applied. A minor recommendation that an African should be appointed to Executive Council was accepted and implemented in 1951, in the person of the original African member of Legislative Council who had ended his studies at Oxford University.

THE LOCAL GOVERNMENT POSITION

It may be useful at this point briefly to describe the situation with which it was necessary to deal. At the centre, the territory was administered by the Governor, with an Executive Council containing eight official and four, later five (following the addition of an African) unofficial members, while Legislative Council consisted of the Governor sitting with fifteen official and fourteen unofficial members, the latter consisting of seven Europeans, three Asians and four Africans, all appointed on tests of availability and personal suitability and without marked attention to geographical origin. (A Speaker replaced the Governor in 1953.) In the field of local government the Native Authorities, except in certain mainly coastal areas, were the hereditary or partly hereditary rulers of the people under traditional tribal systems. There were 435 Native Authorities in the territory, varying from the Chief of Heru with over 57,000 taxpayers to the Headman of Butandula with 25, from the Chief of Ihangiro who received a salary of £1,100 per annum to the Mwami of Lusaba who received Shs. 10/-, from the Iringa District with one Authority to the Tunduru District with 44. There were 28 Township Authorities in the territory with populations ranging from 20,000 to 1,000 and in Dar es Salaam which had a population of about 70,000 there was a Municipal Council which however relied for some two-thirds of its income on Government grants. There were the two trial Provincial Councils which have been described earlier in this review, while in the remaining six provinces periodical meetings of advisory councils were held with varying degrees of unofficial participation.

LOCAL GOVERNMENT: THE SPECIAL COMMISSIONER

The report of the Special Commissioner on matters arising from that of the Committee on Constitutional Development was signed in 1952 but did not arrive in Tanganyika until April, 1953. The Special Commissioner, Professor W. J. M. Mackenzie from Manchester University, had been assisted in its preparation by the head of the African Studies Branch of the Colonial Office. In the interim, work was well forward in Tanganyika on the preparation of a revised and enlarged Native Authority Ordinance designed to define those administrative, judicial and financial functions which had been largely controlled hitherto only by administrative direction. It had been proposed to introduce the revised Ordinance into Legislative Council early in 1953 but it was withdrawn by Government on the argument that it would have tended to anticipate and possibly to conflict with the implementation of constitutional reform resulting from the Mackenzie Report.

THE LOCAL GOVERNMENT ORDINANCE

Instead, in mid-1953 a complete Local Government Bill was presented to Legislative Council providing for the three types of local government council which had been thought desirable by Professor Mackenzie. He had advocated not only the county and town councils which had been recommended by the Committee on Constitutional Development, but also the local council, which can best be described as the democratized version of a Native Authority.

THE CHIEFS ORDINANCE

To allay any fears which might have arisen from the introduction of this legislation another Ordinance was also passed, the Chiefs Ordinance, in order to demonstrate that it was not part of Government's policy to abolish the office of Chief. The passing of the Local Government Ordinance was accompanied by an assurance from Government that the measure was a blue-print for the future rather than one of immediate wholesale application, and that no County, Town or Local Councils would be instituted, with powers and functions precisely defined by Instrument under the statute, against the wishes of the people affected.

The Local Government Ordinance remains, as stated, a blue-print for the future. Under its provisions, it was clear that while membership of Local Councils might be confined to Africans, that of Town and County Councils would be mixed. By the end of 1954 it was evident that the first Local Council with mixed membership would shortly emerge in the Newala District, that several towns were inclined to apply for the necessary Instrument, and that the first County Council, in the area south and east of Lake Victoria and including the Sukuma organization was a probability. It is not possible to foretell how long it will take to apply the Ordinance throughout the territory, and he would be a rash man who made the attempt since even Professor Mackenzie was unable to include the whole of the territory in a network of proposed county councils, there being certain areas where such an institution appears as yet inappropriate for lack of common interests.

THE ELECTIVE PRINCIPLE

There remains to record Professor Mackenzie's recommendations on the elective principle. The Committee on Constitutional Development had recommended the retention of an official majority on Legislative Council, and parity of representation between Europeans, Asians and Africans on the unofficial side, together with enlargement of numbers. Parity and enlargement had been accepted by Government and Professor Mackenzie recorded that in a country having diversity of numbers as between its three main racial groups, the common roll was preferred generally to the communal, that the time was not yet ripe for Africans to participate in common roll elections, but that elections were desired by Europeans and were feasible for Asians. In recommending the retention of the existing number of administrative provinces, as against the Committee's proposal for a small number of regions, he advocated that the unofficial membership of Legislative Council should consist of 27 persons, i.e. one European, one Asian and one African from each of the eight provinces and from Dar es Salaam.

LEGISLATIVE COUNCIL ENLARGED

The enlargement of the membership of Legislative Council was actually effected in 1955, when 30 unofficial members were nominated, being the 27 recommended by Professor Mackenzie and three members at large to represent special interests. To secure a Government majority over this number of unofficials, Government added 14 unofficials to its own revised bench, consisting of members selected for suitability who were free to speak and vote on any subject except when the Government Whip was in operation.[1]

THE FIRST LADY MEMBERS

It is noteworthy that in this new Council lady members appeared for the first time. The wife of an Asian advocate, a member of the Dodoma Township Authority, was one of the nominated provincial representatives, while a European lady with previous experience as a member of the Dar es Salaam Municipal Council, and the wife of one of the most important tribal chiefs in Tanganyika, who had completed a course of social welfare study in the United Kingdom, took their seats as unofficials on the Government bench.

INTER-TERRITORIAL RELATIONS

The achievement of Central African Federation passed almost unnoticed in Tanganyika, there being no possibility of a similar process in East Africa owing to the political situations in Kenya and Uganda. Though the extension of the original four-year trial period for the East Africa High Commission and Central Legislative Assembly was accepted by the legislature in 1951, the reluctance of Tanganyika for closer association with Kenya persisted, the fact that Kenya derives financial advantage from the siting of High Commission Services Headquarters in Kenya not passing unnoticed. An unfortunate incident occurred in connection with Tanganyika's budget for 1952, when the Member for Finance was forced to admit that certain proposed increased duties on spirits, beer and tobacco were not necessary at that moment to Tanganyika's economy but had been introduced only in the interests of conformity with Kenya rates. As a result the duties were made operative only for 1952; but were perpetuated from 1953 to satisfy the normal and inescapable annual increase in Tanganyika's salaries and pensions bills.

THE U.N.O. VISITING MISSION, 1954

While the U.N.O. Visiting Missions of 1948 and 1951 had attracted little attention, that of 1954 caused some commotion, owing to the attitude of some of its members who appeared to over-emphasize their private theories at the expense of public policy and practicability. It was unprecedented that the Chairman of the 1954 Visiting Mission should have refused to sign its report, and that even after the report had been modified, it should be adopted by a minority of the Trusteeship Council, a majority of members abstaining from the vote. The contretemps will, however, have had its value if it results in better appreciation of the fact that Tanganyika, while ready to consider informed advice, is administered solely by H.M. Government in the interests of her population, and that the ultimate aim of this administration, as of that of other British colonial territories, is self-government when internal development makes this appropriate.

[1] DOUBLE INTERPRETATION

(In view of the mass of official papers, written in English, which are furnished to members of Legislative Council, it may well be asked how it was possible to nominate suitable Africans in these increased numbers. By the end of 1954, only 146 Tanganyika Africans had passed through Makerere and of these no fewer than 94 were in Government or Mission employment (65 of these as teachers), 14 had left Makerere with courses incomplete and four had died. A partial answer lies in the institution of simultaneous English/Swahili interpretation during the sittings of Legislative Council, which was introduced in 1955, members being also permitted to speak in Swahili where the Speaker is satisfied that they would otherwise be hampered.)

ROYAL COMMISSION ON LAND AND POPULATION

In 1951 the retiring Governor of Kenya, Sir Phillip Mitchell, who had held high office in Tanganyika some 20 years previously and had then become Governor of Uganda, suggested to H.M.Government that it would be advisable to appoint a Royal Commission to enquire into land and population problems in East Africa. The Commission which he had suggested was appointed by Royal Warrant on 1st January, 1953, and was charged with an examination of the three East African Territories including Tanganyika. It visited the territory during the months of May and October/November, 1953, and travelled widely in its search for information. It is notable that the members of the Commission included only one East African, and that he was that one of Tanganyika's first two African members of Legislative Council who had been appointed to Executive Council as previously recorded. The report of the Commission was not issued until July, 1955, and does not therefore come within the purview of this record but it may be stated that in view of the distinguished and erudite membership of the Commission and of the care with which its comprehensive report was prepared, it is bound to have an important long-term influence on Tanganyika's agrarian policy.

REVISED POST-WAR DEVELOPMENT PLAN

As regards the Development Plan, the totals of expenditure proposed in 1946 for the period 1947-1956 had not been regarded as immutable for it had been realized that variations in costs and priorities would probably occur during the period of the plan. By 1950 the situation had changed to an extent which made it necessary to recast the plan. As an example of altered costs, it had been thought in 1946 that a bituminized road would cost £2,500 per mile. By 1950 the cost was nearer £10,000. As an example of altered priority it had been decided by 1950 that a large part of the proposed development expenditure on Social Services should be transferred to the recurrent territorial budget. Moreover the original Development Plan had included provision for certain railways capital expenditure and this had been excised from the plan upon the amalgamation in 1948 of the Tanganyika Railways with those of Kenya and Uganda. The costed total of all development plan works which were thought desirable by 1950 came to some £36½ million. The revised plan, adopted in 1950, at some £24½ million represented a realistic estimate both of what the territory could probably afford and of what there was works capacity to execute.

THE ECONOMY

The economy of the territory in the period 1950-1954 was sufficiently buoyant to promise a local share of finance for the revised development plan from loan funds and from surpluses. As a result of a progressively increasing volume of trade (over £69½ million in 1954 after a record of nearly £85 million in 1952 owing to high sisal prices) the exchequer was in a good position. Whereas public revenue in 1949 had amounted to just over £9 million it exceeded £15½ million in 1953, largely as a result of the increased revenue from income tax and excise duties, and remained at that figure in 1954. During this period the price of first quality sisal reached £245 per ton (in 1951) and though it subsequently fell to less than £100 the effect of that rise on collections of income tax, and on revenue resulting from a temporary export tax to raise money for development purposes, was significant. Coffee maintained and even increased its production over the period, with greatly increasing prices. Record prices were realized for this product in 1954, no less than £816 per ton being the top price paid at the Nairobi auctions and £742 in Moshi. As a result, an export tax similar to that on sisal assisted development funds. As a final example of the effect of production on public revenue, it may be noted that over the period 1951-1954 export of diamonds amounted to 840,420 carats, of which the Williamson Mine exported 791,206 carats to a gross value exceeding £8½ million and paying royalty at 15 per cent.

DEVELOPMENT

It would be wearisome to detail the actual annual expenditure on the revised development plan. Suffice it to say that by the middle of 1954 total expenditure had exceeded £20½ million and that it was expected that more than £3½ million would be spent in the financial year 1954-1955. It has been mentioned that large provision for Social Services in the original development plan was transferred to the recurrent territorial budget as a result of the revision of the plan in 1950. In 1949, recurrent expenditure on Education amounted to £404,738 and on Medical Services to £638,030. By 1954-55, these recurrent figures had increased to £1,625,971 in the case of Education and £1,326,026 in the case of Medical Services, quite apart from those sums which were spent on works of a capital nature in the development plan and apart from substantial expenditure by Native Treasuries on these two services.

DAR ES SALAAM AIRPORT

One of the more striking achievements of the Development Plan was the completion of a Class C international airport near Dar es Salaam. This airport was opened ceremonially by the Governor in 1954 in the presence of the Secretary of State for the Colonies.

WATER DEVELOPMENT

Another aspect of the plan worth mention is the increasing importance which it attaches to water development. Those who suffered from restricted domestic supplies in 1953 on the Central Line, particularly in Dodoma and Tabora, will not quickly forget how the Railways had to provide water trains over long distances, but by the end of 1954 the list of completed dams was growing and the first irrigation works had been completed by the Department of Water Development and Irrigation.

THE REVISED TEN-YEAR EDUCATION PLAN

The Development Plan itself was not the only ten-year Plan which needed revision during the period. The ten-year Education Plan needed revision, as has been noted, as a result of the 1948 Census, if the target that one-third of all children of school age should be provided with education was to be attained. The revised plan, formulated in 1950, included the development of what were termed Middle Schools, a separate class of school between the primary and secondary stages. Progress in this revised plan continued rather in advance of schedule and by the end of 1954 the following was the situation as regards the education of Africans. There were 28 teacher training establishments with 2,122 teachers in training; 2,136 primary schools with an enrolment of 189,031 boys and 81,584 girls; 232 middle schools with an enrolment of 19,653 boys and 4,175 girls; 24 secondary schools, including one girls' school, with an enrolment of 2,813 boys and 143 girls; and 10 industrial or vocational schools with an enrolment of 667 pupils. The foregoing figures refer to Government and Government-aided schools only. The Education Department has not, of course, neglected the education of non-Africans but these are financed largely from the proceeds of non-native education taxes and of loans.

It can be inferred that the ten-year Education Plan, dealing with an educationally backward population of some eight million persons, was intended rather to build, staff and fill with pupils a substantial network of primary schools, than to seek out a large number of candidates for higher education from an uneducated population. It is resulting in the provision of an elementary education for many thousands of young people and in the opening of an avenue to higher education, which can be enlarged in future, for the more promising. The Education Department already pays fees for Tanganyika pupils at Makerere University College, this being justified by the very severe selection provided by the present pattern of schools.

IMPROVED STANDARD OF PRIVATE BUILDING

Before the war, it had commonly been held by a number of persons that the Asian community in Tanganyika, far from ploughing back profits into the territory, exported these to India. Political events in India since the war altered this situation if it ever existed, and such alteration became particularly evident upon the issue by the Aga Khan of advice to his many followers in Tanganyika that they must become good Tanganyikans. From that time, a transformation started in the standard of commercial and other buildings owned by the Asian community throughout the territory. An outstanding example of this was completed in 1954 at Dodoma in the shape of a magnificent Jamatkhana. More diffused but no less striking change has occurred in all townships, and particularly in Dar es Salaam where multi-storied buildings are now the rule in the commercial areas.

THE GROUNDNUT SCHEME

At the beginning of 1950, there were three matters weighing heavily upon the promoters of the groundnut scheme—finance, the appearance of large scale plant diseases, and doubt as to whether Kongwa which had been the area of first considerable development was indeed suitable for groundnuts. As regards finance, the resources of the O.F.C. were limited to £50 million, which included expenditure on the Queensland Scheme. By the end of March, 1951, the O.F.C. consolidated balance sheet showed that more than £35 million had been drawn. Expenditure was thus running ahead of estimates. As regards plant disease, this factor assumed importance as soon as significant quantities of crops had been planted. In particular, the rosette and black spot diseases of groundnuts had been found to be so severe that they could ruin plantings unless some control could be found. To add to the financial and disease worries, it became necessary to send a working party to Kongwa to make a realistic appraisal of a situation which had there been further complicated by erratic rainfall. As a result of these troubles, H.M. Government announced the abandonment of the original scheme for growing groundnuts wholesale in Tanganyika and in its place introduced an experimental scheme for investigating the economics of tropical farming, to be managed by the OF.C. in the areas of the previous scheme. The purpose of the new plan was stated to be to establish by large scale experiment the economics of clearing and mechanized or partially mechanized agriculture in tropical conditions. Over a 6½-year period ending in September, 1957, the revised scheme was expected to cost £6 million altogether, including provision for guarantees and commitments incurred in the earlier scheme. This change of emphasis and scope introduced a major complication in that construction of a port and railway in the Southern Province had already started.

The following is an extract from Cmd. 9158:—

"When the groundnuts scheme was adopted in 1947 it was considered that progress in the major areas of production in the Southern Province of Tanganyika would be considerably hampered by the lack of a railway and a first-class port in that region. As it was then thought that the Southern Province would be exporting annually more than 400,000 tons of groundnuts alone by 1952 it was decided that a new port and railway should be built as quickly as possible. The contracts for their construction were signed on behalf of His Majesty's Government by the then managing agency and were taken over by the Overseas Food Corporation when it was set up in 1948.

"It was realized from the outset that it would be anomalous for the Overseas Food Corporation to retain ownership of such an important public utility in East Africa. Accordingly an agreement was negotiated with the newly amalgamated East African Railways and Harbours Administration whereby that Administration undertook to buy out the Corporation after completion of the project and in the meantime to supervise construction on behalf of the Corporation who made the necessary capital advances as required. The Administration were to repay the advances as soon as they were in a position to raise a public loan for the purpose. In return the Overseas Food Corporation undertook to guarantee the interest and sinking fund on the loan to the extent that these were not covered by revenue from local traffic. This guarantee was revised in January, 1950, to cover operating losses as well.

"With the collapse of the groundnut scheme in 1950-51 the future of the port and railway was immediately in jeopardy and was jointly reviewed by the Tanganyika Government, the East African Railways and Harbours Administration, the Overseas Food Corporation and His Majesty's Government. Notwithstanding the severe fall in the Corporation's traffic to be expected in that area, with a consequent fall in the expected revenue of the port and railway, it was decided that construction already well under way should be completed. At that time, it was calculated that the capital cost of the port and railway would amount to £4,550,000 and while it was reckoned that annual deficits would be inevitable for at least the first 10 years it was considered that there was a reasonable expectation that the Tanganyika Government's plans for the accelerated development of the province, together with traffic expected to arise at some future date from the new mineral areas under exploration in the Southern Highlands, would yield revenues sufficient to balance the deficits within a reasonable period of time.

"Since that time rising costs have raised the capital cost of the port and railway to approximately £6 million. This is far beyond the capital investment which can be supported by the present day expectation of traffic. The existing financial arrangements have therefore had to be reconsidered once more by all the parties concerned. Subject to Parliament's approval, a new settlement has been agreed whereby

"Her Majesty's Government will forgo repayment of capital advances made by the Overseas Food Corporation prior to the 1st April, 1953, amounting to £3,691,403 and interest thereon, in order to reduce the capital investment to a reasonable figure, estimated to be about £2,500,000;

"the Tanganyika Government will assume responsibility for the whole of the net operating deficits on the recapitalized structure; and "the East African Railways and Harbours Administration will find, without advances from the Overseas Food Corporation, the further capital required to complete the project and will forgo fixed annual renewal charges (at present standing at £95,000 a year) for so long as there are deficits."

The reduced scope of the scheme was accompanied by its transfer from control by the Ministry of Food to that of the Colonial Office. This transfer resulted in a more individual agricultural approach than had been possible with the large scale operations by the O.F.C., and it may briefly be stated that by the end of 1954 the scheme had proved that groundnuts are a feasible crop in the Nachingwea area, that the basic economic crop in Urambo appears to be tobacco, while Kongwa is only really suitable for ranching (a decision which provoked a local African headman to remark that this was the same use as had been made of the Kongwa area before the groundnut scheme started). It became increasingly obvious that the main beneficiary of the revised scheme would be Tanganyika, and that it was therefore desirable to associate the Government of Tanganyika with it. It was therefore decided to convert the independent O.F.C. insofar as it existed in Tanganyika, into a corporation, half British and half Tanganyikan, under the name of the Tanganyika Agricultural Corporation. This conversion was completed in 1954, whereupon the O.F.C. as such ceased to exist.

By the end of 1954 field operations in Kongwa, Urambo and Nachingwea were confined to quite small acreages, these being divided in all three areas into farms of varying sizes so that it could be ascertained what was the optimum size of an individual's farm. This was the case not only with the African Tenant Farmers' Schemes at Nachingwea and Urambo, where promising trials continued of properly costed mechanical and other assistance to individual Africans, but also with larger farms managed by individual trained farmers from the O.F.C. staff who operated independently, but under financial control, to ascertain the prospects of larger-scale mixed farming.

COLONIAL DEVELOPMENT CORPORATION

If the story of the O.F.C. in Tanganyika is one of failure, that of the Colonial Development Corporation is so far one of success. The C.D.C. has undertaken two projects in the territory. The first consisted of the Tanganyika Wattle Estates Ltd., a subsidiary company formed to grow wattle on 30,000 acres of formerly unproductive land in Ubena, in the Njombe District, and to export extract from the wattle bark in due course. The scheme has progressed strictly to its time schedule, and although the factory is not yet erected, the stand of wattle trees promises that when they have grown to maturity the factory will be fully occupied not only with bark from C.D.C. plantations but also from trees grown by neighbouring farmers, including Africans. The other project, a non-profit making conception, has been completed. This consisted of the examination of coal and iron deposits in the area to the north-east and close to the north end of Lake Nyasa, to ascertain both quality and extent. The C.D.C. has shown that in this broken and unaccessible country there are millions of tons of useful coal and of magnetite iron. This investigation was completed contemporaneously with technical surveys of new railway possibilities in the south and south-west of the territory. A rail link from the Central Line to the railways of Northern Rhodesia or an extension of Tanganyika's Southern Province Railway to the west would approach but not reach the very broken country in which these coal and iron deposits lie.

CIVIL LIST

By contrast with 1919 when the only women in the Government Service were a few nursing and health visitor employees in the Medical Department, the civil list in 1954, containing the names of 2,485 persons, included those of 483 women of whom 158 were in the Medical Department in various capacities.

REVISED STRUCTURE OF THE CIVIL SERVICE

Here it may be mentioned that in the post-war period, and owing to the increased cost of living, there were two salaries revisions in the Government Service. The first, which divided the service into three sections, Senior, Junior and Subordinate, took effect from the beginning of 1946. The second, which established a single service for the territory, took effect from the beginning of 1954. It had been necessary before the end of the war to pay allowances to Government staff in compensation for the increased cost of living. By paying these allowances, and then by consolidating them into salary, Government's policy anticipated discontent, just as in a rather parallel way, Government's policy as regards constitutional reform, as exemplified by the passing of the Local Government Bill, anticipated political demand.

THE QUEEN'S DIAMOND

It is of interest that the most striking diamond found so far at Mwadui has been a pink stone weighing 54½ carats. It is not possible to guess the value of this stone, since it was a unique specimen. Its future was decided when Dr. Williamson was permitted to present it to the Queen, then Princess Elizabeth, on the occasion of her marriage. It was cut into a magnificent pink brilliant weighing 23·6 carats and was set by Messrs. Cartier of London as the centre stone of a clip brooch of floral design, studded with over 100 smaller brilliants from the Williamson Mine.

MKWAWA'S SKULL

There had been included in the Treaty of Versailles a clause requiring the return from Germany to Tanganyika of the skull of Mkwawa, a famous tribal chief who had been foremost in opposition to German penetration in the last decade of the 19th Century. This requirement had not been satisfied, but as a result of enquiries in Germany after the war of 1939-1945, the skull was located in a museum store. It was retrieved by the Governor of Tanganyika in person and presented to the tribe by him in 1954, much to their satisfaction. The chief of the tribe sent certain tribal trophies to the German museum in return for his grandfather's skull.

PROSPERITY ON KILIMANJARO

The foregoing record of the salient happenings of the period 1950-1954, must not obscure the fact of Tanganyika's diversity, a diversity of peoples, soils and climates resulting in an immense diversity of social, political and economic conditions and requirements. The territory exhibits gradations in all these spheres which go to make up its territorial entity, and this record may appropriately end with an account of a contrast to illustrate its diversity. The K.N.C.U. is now salesman for nearly all African-grown mild coffee in Tanganyika. At the end of 1952, with over thirty affiliated societies and over 35,000 members, it started its own coffee auction floor. In 1953/54 its own crop exceeded 6,000 tons of hulled coffee, and realized £3,720,000. The K.N.C.U. is drawn from the members of the Chagga tribe. This tribe, seventh in numbers out of more than 100 distinct tribes in the territory, relatively prosperous as the above figures show, and politically conscious to an extent which created an unified Chiefship in the period under review, was honoured by the selection of its new Chief as an official guest by H.M. Government for the Queen's Coronation.

FAMINE IN THE CENTRAL PROVINCE

By contrast, let us take the Gogo tribe. The foregoing account of British rule in Tanganyika since the end of the 1914-1918 war began with mention of a disastrous famine in their area and it can end with mention of another. As a result of defective rainfall there was an insignificant staple crop in Ugogo in 1953, and a crop sufficient to feed the populace for only some three months in 1954. So severe were the effects on grazing that it is estimated that three-quarters of the domestic livestock in Ugogo were eaten, sold or died of starvation in the two-year period. But the people, under famine conditions, were in a far better state in 1953 and 1954 than they had been in 1919. Then, there were no roads worthy of the name. Lorries were few and inefficient. Contact with a people scattered and terrified by the war scarcely existed. It was a matter of great difficulty to persuade Africans to come, in many cases as far as 100 miles, to the depots on the Central Railway Line to fetch the food there provided by Government and to carry it back to their homes by head porterage. In 1953/54, a network of roads existed, transport was adequate, and the confidence of the people was undoubted. Distribution of famine relief food on a pattern evolved over the years during the recurrent food shortages in this area, was therefore highly efficient, and it may be noted that to the staple foods made available by Government was added a substantial contribution of dried milk made by UNICEF, part of which was fed to the children for whom it was primarily intended, and part of which was mixed with staple flour to add to its nutritive value. The Gogo, fifth in numbers of Tanganyika's tribes, are not the most advanced of tribesmen, but in spite of their recurrent food shortages they are certainly among the most cheerful, and it is not inappropriate that an account of 35 years of British rule should end by recording this fact.

CONCLUSION, 1919-1954

If an account has now been given of events which were of importance to Tanganyika in the period of British rule to date, it is still necessary to put some of those events and their consequences into perspective so that a balanced picture may emerge.

The best estimate of population, at the start of British rule, showed that there were just over four million Africans in the territory. Today there are some eight million, as a result of natural increase and of immigration, the latter being of considerable weight. If numbers have increased, the size of the territory is the same, and, with more varied dietetic demands, the agrarian system on which the economy of the country largely depends must also cater increasingly for the proper subsistence of the people. Against this background the sleeping-sickness menace, the end-product of the groundnut scheme and the new Department of Water Development come into perspective.

SLEEPING SICKNESS

The infection of tsetse with the human strains of trypanosome has become in the period a major consideration over a large part of the Western Province, in that part of the Southern Province which became infected from the Liwale outbreak and to a lesser extent in parts of the Lake and Central Provinces and of the Mbulu District. Though human mortality is controlled by the policy which has been described, and is now of negligible proportions, nevertheless infection is perpetuated in game animals, and the danger of its presence has a sobering effect on agricultural initiative in thousands of square miles of country.

URAMBO, NACHINGWEA AND KONGWA

Population increase results in increasing pressure on the land. There are three extensive areas in the territory where agriculture by primitive methods is unrewarding, the steppe area in the Western Province, the area centred on the Nachingwea District in the Southern Province, and Ugogo, the two former being sited in sleeping sickness country. If the experiments of the Tanganyika Agricultural Corporation can find a use for these areas which is permanently productive and socially attractive, then the Groundnut Scheme will have finally provided a form of safety-valve against over-population in tribal cradle areas.

WATER SUPPLIES

Apart from a continuing effort in Masailand to provide and improve supplies of water for cattle, the development of artificial water supplies, so as to open otherwise unusable land was started systematically in Tanganyika in the early thirties, mainly in the Lake Province in face of a local problem of population density. It was only after the war, however, as more money became available for development, that it became possible to think in terms of a service of technicians big enough in all respects to tackle the problem, and even by 1954 though some progress had been made, the service had not been sufficiently expanded to meet the territory's needs, but was being expanded as rapidly as possible.

THE PATTERN OF EXPORTS

As to economic as distinct from subsistence production, it should be explained that the territory's aim is to increase the variety of its products to a point where depression in a few markets, as occurred in 1930-1934, does not constitute a territorial disaster. Up to 1914, economic production was almost entirely non-African, and if there were the beginnings of an African coffee industry in Bukoba, the only really important territorial output consisted of sisal, cotton and rubber from German estates. Sisal is still Tanganyika's main crop, and the only product (save perhaps beeswax and diamonds) where the volume sold is of world significance. It is produced from marginal land (of which there is ample in Tanganyika) and it requires heavy capital backing. Production in 1954 amounted to 167,642 tons and the industry was employing over 140,000 labourers out of some 218,000 employed in agriculture in the territory, and out of a total of some 439,000 in all occupations. But signs were not lacking by 1954 of the necessary diversification of production.

In that year, owing to exceptional prices, the value of a record coffee crop amounting to 19,382 tons came within £1 million of the value of sisal. A record cotton crop, grown largely by Africans in the Lake Province, brought in over £3½ million. Over the years, much attention has been given to the better preparation for export of hides and skins and in 1954 these yielded £1,302,954. In addition there were a number of valuable exports which had not been thought of in 1919 such as cashew nuts (£554,009), castor seed (£396,518), papain

(£154,864), pyrethrum (£40,472), sunflower seed (£322,550), tea (£503,917) and wattle bark (£44,309), all of which help to spread the risk of any recession in commodity prices.

THE PATTERN OF AGRICULTURE

The pattern of agriculture, as between plantation and peasant, has greatly altered under British rule. Plantation agriculture is still of great importance. It occupies about one per cent of the territory's area, including the large areas of marginal land under sisal and, with its capital backing, is better able to withstand the effects of a poor harvest than is peasant agriculture. But the latter earned in 1954 a greater sum than the former (even when the value of sisal is included), a reward of effort to which must be added the fact that it also fed some eight million mouths throughout the season.

RINDERPEST

Mention has been made both of the tsetse problem and of rinderpest. Research has yet to reveal an economic method for the wholesale eradication of tsetse, and the attack is still based on discriminate bush clearing, with immediate settlement to prevent regeneration of the bush. No cheap prophylactic has been found for scrub cattle, to assist this process, but the Veterinary Department has maintained dairy herds in clearings in "fly" country, and (in a large scale experiment) on the Mkata plains, and the O.F.C., now the T.A.C., at both Urambo and Nachingwea, have demonstrated already that with the aid of modern drugs more valuable cattle can be kept in close proximity to "fly". As to rinderpest, the veterinary authorities, prevented from eradicating it both by the cost and by the transmission of this disease by infection in game, have nevertheless confined it to areas north of the Central Railway Line, an achievement which provides, instead of the game-free belt of the war period, a 250-mile belt of susceptible cattle between the disease and Northern Rhodesia, a belt in which any outbreak would be very quickly detected and controlled.

NATIVE TREASURY FINANCE

No mention has yet been made of local government finance, that is, of the finances of the Native Treasuries inaugurated by Sir Donald Cameron. From the start these Treasuries were most carefully controlled by Administrative Officers with the result that, over the years, they have been built up into a formidable force in rural affairs. Amalgamated or federated where necessary to a point of financial stability, these treasuries carried forward surplus cash balances of over £1¼ million at the end of 1954, expected in 1955 to collect over £2½ million from local rates, produce cesses and local fees and dues, and to spend over £1 million on their own internal administration, over £850,000 on Social Services, over £300,000 on Natural Resources services and nearly £1 million on "Development" or capital works. This result has not been achieved at pre-war tax rates. Commonly, the pre-war tax rate had by 1954 been doubled, one half going to Central Government and the other to Native Treasuries, an increase in total tax which, with increasing economic production, the African population could well afford. But it is an interesting commentary on increased prosperity, increased activity by African administrations, and the decreased value of money that in 1954 the Native Treasuries spent £2,354,000 and carried forward a greater balance at the ned of it, than were raised as public revenue or carried forward by the Central Government of the territory in any of the pre-war years.

PROGRESS OF THE TERRITORY

The foregoing figures, and those relating to public finance must be read in their proper context. Tanganyika is a vast country, only just second in size to Nigeria among the colonial territories in the British Commonwealth of Nations, but the population is comparatively small and at that, a peasant population whose training in soil conservation and agricultural production, even in production of staple crops for subsistence, is difficult. A Development Plan costing £24 million and divided among numerous projects of all types may look large, but looks smaller when read in 1954 against a territorial road mileage of 18,440, or a main road mileage of 7,101. It is necessary to go outside Tanganyika for a comparison to find out whether expansion of the economy is keeping pace with that of other comparable countries. One then finds a remarkable parallel in that Tanganyika with a current annual public revenue of some £15 million and a volume of trade in the region of £60 million is matched almost exactly by Nigeria where the last available figures showed a revenue of some £59 million (Estimates 1953/54) and a volume of trade at £233 million (1953) with a population just four times as large as that of Tanganyika.

THE TEMPER OF THE PEOPLE

To complete the Tanganyika picture, it remains to make specific mention of the "temper" of the people. In these days of catchwords and publicity, it is necessary to discuss Tanganyika's position as regards the bogy of "racial discrimination", the spectre of "emergent nationalism" and the ideal of a "multi-racial society".

RACIAL DISCRIMINATION

A degree of racial discrimination is to be found in the Laws of Tanganyika but this, as distinct from the common implementation of the phrase, operates generally in favour of and not against the backward section of the population. The Credit to Natives (Restriction) Ordinance has already been noted. An African uses land in his tribal areas free of charge whereas a non-African not only pays rent but is subject to defined development conditions. The African receives free medical attention at Government Hospitals while the non-African pays. An African shopkeeper pays a trading licence fee much lower than the lowest fee chargeable to a non-African, and the African can set up shop where he likes without paying rent (unless he leases a site in a demarcated trading centre) whereas a non-African must lease a plot and is normally restricted to sites in trading centres. As against such instances, the 1954 Local Government Ordinance contains no differentiation nor mention of race, and the town planners zone townships into high, medium and low density zones instead of into European, bazaar and African quarters. The latest Annual Reports for Tanganyika state categorically that no racial discrimination exists. This must be qualified as indicated above, but it means that there is no colour bar. A bar exists, but, as in all countries, it is a culture bar.

TRIBALISM

An underlying factor of the first importance in the history, not only of the period under review, but of the whole period since the arrival of the first "invaders" (to use the late Sir Reginald Coupland's term), is the strength of tribalism and the importance of the tribe; in fact, no account of conditions in the country would be complete without mention of this factor nor can a proper assessment be made of trends and developments without an appreciation of its fundamental significance. The tribe is still "the sheet-anchor" of the African in Tanganyika*. The fact that the country contains so many tribes—about 120 in all—does not affect this contention. It is remarkable to what extent each tribe still lives within the tribal boundaries shown on map facing page 298. True, representatives of almost all tribes such as the Nyamwezi, Pare, Haya and Nyakyusa have a reputation as travellers and many do not return home at the end of their wanderings but settle down far from home; nevertheless the great majority of tribesmen are still to be found living together in their own tribal areas. Such areas are not of course static, and tribal expansion tends to disregard district boundaries (witness the infiltration of the Nyakyusa from the Rungwe District into neighbouring districts) but within a given area about 90 per cent or more of the inhabitants will usually be found to belong to the local tribe.

The significance of this fact will be at once apparent in connection with the development of local government, but it has a much wider significance and is a basic consideration which cannot be ignored in considering any form of development or of economic, political or social advancement.

A MULTI-RACIAL SOCIETY

It is no disparagement either of the efforts of Government or of the Africans themselves to say that the indigenous peoples of Tanganyika are more backward today than their counterparts in several other African territories. The potential is there, but it is an inescapable historical fact that while tutelage of Africans started elsewhere at an earlier date, it started in Tanganyika in a systematic way only on January 1st, 1926, with the formal inauguration of Indirect Rule. If progress, in nearly thirty years, has been steady, and in some periods spectacular (such as with the current revised ten-year Education Plan), this progress could not have occurred at all without expatriate help in men and money, nor can it continue without such help. This is only another way of saying that if Tanganyika is to prosper a multi-racial society is a necessity. It has been seen how the Ormsby-Gore Commission found that, in 1924, non-African settlement provided the main stimulus in the economic progress of the territory. No calculation has ever been undertaken of the annual cash value to the territory of the sisal industry and to a lesser extent of gold mining or of non-African coffee production but it is clear that without their stimulus, in the shape of imports, wages, exports and resulting taxes paid, the financial position of the territory, particularly in the years between the two wars when African response to production encouragement was hesitant, would have been as untenable as it would have been had there existed no immigrants to take retail trade and produce buying into the farthest backblocks.

To preserve a proper balance, in the interests of the development of the territory, between African and non-African interests is the responsibility of the Government of Tanganyika no less than its obligation to educate the primitive tribesman. There are no individual African capitalists so that capital for new enterprises depends largely upon the maintenance of a multi-racial society, African investment taking the form of co-operative subscription. There have been notable African achievements. The K.N.C.U. for example has been mentioned, while in 1954 there were outstanding achievements in the Newala District in the shape

---

*Address by the Governor to Legislative Council on 20th April, 1955.

of an African subscribed water-works scheme, and in the Njombe District in the shape of a co-operative wattle-planting plan. But the African is mainly, and naturally, preoccupied with his own subsistence and, lacking capital as has been stated, he leaves the risk of proving a new crop to the non-African, just as, with his agricultural tradition, he usually leaves the business of shopkeeping to people who are better trained than he is in that vocation.

If Tanganyika is to be efficient a multi-racial society is even more necessary on the technical than on the farming side. It will be clear, from what has been recorded, that the indigenous people must needs rely almost exclusively on members of other races for technical help whether in commerce, industry or in the professions. African society nursed in a tradition of subsistence agriculture is not as yet a particularly fruitful source of suitable candidates for technical training at advanced levels, and is even less likely to find men who will spare time for training in the liberal arts. The basic fact of the multi-racial situation is all too liable to be overlooked when, in argument, such catch-phrases as "paramountcy of native interests" or "white leadership" are bandied about. From the point of view of trusteeship, of a responsibility for the advancement of the indigenous peoples, it would be a disaster of the first magnitude if a multi-racial society ceased to exist.

(*This book goes to press in the middle of the quinquenniad 1955-1959 but a short account of the main events of the years 1955-1957 is given in Appendix D*)

Chapter 5

THE CENTRAL PROVINCE

SITUATION

The Central Province, as its name implies, is situated in the centre of the territory, astride the central railway line, with the Great North Road passing through the middle of it. It consists of the eastern portion of the great central plateau, together with a portion of the main north-south arc of mountainous country, and lies between the Northern, Eastern, Southern Highlands, Western and Lake Provinces. In the south it is separated from the Southern Highlands Province by the Njombe River, which lower down becomes the Kisigo and is one of the tributaries of the Great Ruaha River. In the west the boundary is again a natural one for most of its length and is composed of the Wembere River which, after entering Lake Kitangiri, emerges as the Sibiti and flows into Lake Eyasi. These two boundaries run through remote and very thinly populated country. In the south-west the boundary runs through country of a similar nature but for much of its length it is not far from the line of the Itigi-Rungwa-Mbeya Road. In the north the Mbulu District forms a great peninsula which extends into the province almost as far south as the district headquarters at Kondoa. On the east the boundary is the great Masai appendix for much of its length, and, further south, the Kilosa District of the Eastern Province. The total area is approximately 35,000 square miles and the province has a population of about 820,000.

DISTRICTS

The province contains, at the time of writing, five districts, with provincial headquarters at Dodoma, but it is probable that by the time this Handbook appears in print the former Mkalama District will have been separated from the Singida District. The Mpwapwa District, 4,200 square miles and with a population of 102,000, adjoins the Kilosa District of the Eastern Province and is a continuation of the long appendix of Masailand. It extends from the Masai border to the Great Ruaha River and contains, in the north-west, the former Kongwa District—the scene of the main part of the Groundnut Scheme. The Dodoma District has an area of about 6,600 square miles and contains 217,000 people. Most of the Manyoni District, 10,800 square miles and containing 152,000 people, extends to the south of the railway and much of the more southerly part of it is very thinly populated. The Kondoa District has an area of about 5,000 square miles and a population of some 146,000 people; for the whole of its western border it marches with Masailand. The Singida District (including the former Mkalama District) has an area of about 8,000 square miles and is the most thickly populated of the five districts, having a population of over 302,000.

PHYSICAL FEATURES

The greater part of the province, as will be apparent from the physical map opposite, is situated between the 3,000 and 5,000 ft. contour lines and much of this area consists of partly wooded plains studded with the granitic boulders which are so characteristic of the great central plateau. In what is now the Mpwapwa District the northern part, formerly known as the Kongwa District, is a prolongation of the Masai steppe.   Further south, but still to the north of the railway, there is the Kiboriani massif, on the southern slopes of which is situated the district headquarters of Mpwapwa.   The railway passes along the valley of the Mukondokwa or Mkondoa River and separates this massif from the imposing Rubeho Mountains, which occupy the whole of the southern part of the district and connect up with the Iringa Highlands.   In the Dodoma District there are no mountains to break the monotony of the plain and few hills worthy of the name, except perhaps the Chenene Hills in the north which, through the Sandawi Hills in the south of the Kondoa District, connect up with the mountainous region forming an offshoot from the Mbulu Range.   In the Singida District the Durumo River separates two mountainous areas, that to the east forming an extension of the Mbulu mountain area and that to the west containing an isolated range known as the Iramba Plateau.

The province is well known for its aridity and the average rainfall throughout is not more than 25 inches per annum.   In consequence, although it may appear comparatively well watered on the map, there are only two rivers which do not dry up completely during the dry season—these are the Kinyasungwe-Mukondo-kwa in its lower reaches and the Njombe-Kisigo system near where it joins the Great Ruaha.   The centre of the province is drained by the Bubu and Mponde rivers, which flow into the great Bahi swamp just to the south of the Central Line between Dodoma and Manyoni.   The Wembere-Durumo system which drains the western part of the Singida District has already been mentioned.   Apart from the Bahi swamp and lakes Kitangiri and Eyasi, the province contains no lakes of any great size but there are several permanent waters of importance.   In the Mpwapwa District there are the small lakes Kimagai and Gombo, both of which are skirted by the Central Line; in Dodoma there are lakes such as that at Mvumi; near Kondoa on the Great North Road one passes another small lake and there are still others in the vicinity; the district headquarters at Singida are situated between lakes Singida and Kindai.

The old caravan route between the coast and the Great Lakes led through the province and some of the early explorers have left vivid accounts of how the country looked to them in those days—and of course in outward appearance it has changed hardly at all since then.   All were glad to reach Mpwapwa, whether travelling west along the valley of the Mukondokwa River or eastwards from the dreaded "Mgunda Mkali" (Fiery Plain) and Ugogo.   Thus Cotterill, Consul Elton's companion on his ill-fated journey from Lake Nyasa to Useke in what is now the Manyoni District, describes Mpwapwa in these words:—

> "The village of Mpwapwa lies on the lower slopes of a hill conspicuous for its beauty even amid that lovely scenery.   Rich forest and grassy glades, with here and there a jutting crag, lead the eye upwards to a crown of precipices.   A green fertile valley at its base, filled with grazing cattle and dotted with hamlets, is sundered by a broad stream—the Mukondokwa, or one of its larger affluents.   On its northern bank we pitched our camp, and in a short time realized the fact that we were among another people. Provisions began to pour in.   Groups of natives gathered about the camp with friendly looks of recognition, and a head-man brought a present." [1]

---

[1] "Travels and Researches among the Lakes and Mountains of Eastern and Central Africa" from the journals of J. F. Elton, 1879.   p. 401.

The Rubeho Mountains to the south of Mpwapwa contain some magnificent country, including the Wota Plateau, which at one time was considered a possible site for a new capital. These mountains form one of the few well-watered upland areas which do not suffer from overcrowding of both the human and the stock population.

To the north of the Kiboriani range, "the other side of the hill" from Mpwapwa township, the Kongwa area presents a very different aspect, being one large rather arid plain, the monotony relieved by low hills in a few places only, st etching away to the vast open spaces of Masailand.

To the west lies the Dodoma District, the heart of Ugogo, the country dreaded by all early travellers, both because of the difficulty of travelling through it and because of the rapacity of the Gogo chieftains along the route (see page 156). Burton, with his well-known meticulous attention to detail, thus describes this region:—

"The general aspect is a glaring yellow flat, darkened by long growths of acrid, saline, and succulent plants, thorny bush, and stunted trees, and the colouring is monotonous in the extreme. It is sprinkled with isolated dwarf cones bristling with rocks and boulders, from whose interstices springs a thin forest of gums, thorns and mimosas.

The surface is in rare places a brown vegetable humus, extending but a few inches in depth, or more generally a hard yellow-reddish ferruginous clay covered with quartz nodules of many colours, and lumps of carbonate of lime, or white and siliceous sand, rather resembling a well-metalled road or an untidy expanse of gravel-walk than the rich moulds which belong to the fertile African belt. In many parts are conical anthills of pale red earth; in others iron-stone crops out of the plain; and everywhere fine and coarse grits abound. The land is in parts condemned to perpetual drought, and nowhere is water either good or plentiful.

There is no Vuli (short rains), and thus the climate is unrefreshed by the copious tropical rains. About the middle of November the country is visited by a few preliminary showers, and towards the end of December the Masika, or rainy season, commences with the wind shifting from the east to the north and north-east, blowing steadily from the high grounds eastward and westward of the Nyanza Lake, which have been saturated by heavy falls beginning in September. The winter seldom exceeds the third month, and the downfall is desultory and uncertain, causing frequent droughts and famine. For this reason the land is much inferior in fertility to the other regions, and the cotton and tobacco, which flourish from the coast to the Tanganyika Lake, are deficient in Ugogo, whilst rice is supplanted by the rugged sorghum and maize." [1]

But of course the whole of Ugogo is not like the region traversed by Burton, and had he seen it a few months later in the year he would doubtless have painted a very different picture of it.

Much of the land to the south of the railway line in the Manyoni District (i.e. the greater part of the district) is very similar to that in the Dodoma District, but north of the railway, and extending into the Singida District, is the remarkable "Itigi Thicket", the "Mgunda Mkali" of the explorers, a dense, fully closed

---

[1] R. F. Burton "The Lake Regions of Central Africa", pp. 282-5, 1860.

thicket of coppicing shrubs, 8 to 15 feet high, covering over 2,000 square miles. Burton, as usual, gives a full description of this forbidding region and as it contains a vivid picture of the granitic outcrops which are such a noticeable feature of the whole of the central plateau, extending over so much of the Central and Western Provinces, it is worth reproducing:—

"From east to west the diagonal breadth of Mgunda Mk'hali is 140 miles. The general aspect is a dull uniform bush, emerald-coloured during the rains, and in the heats a network of dry and broom-like twigs. Except upon the banks of nullahs—"rivers" that are not rivers—the trees, wanting nutriment, never afford timber, and even the calabash (baobab) appears stunted. . . . Upon the rolling surface, and towering high above the tallest trees, are based huge granitic outcrops. These outcrops of gray granite and syenite are principally of two different shapes, the hog's back and the turret. The former usually appears as a low lumpy dome of various dimensions; here a few feet long, there extending a mile and a half in diameter: the outer coat scales off under the action of the atmosphere, and in places it is worn away by a network of paths. The turret is a more picturesque and changing feature. Tall rounded blocks and conical or cylindrical boulders, here single, there in piles or ridges, some straight and stiff as giant ninepins, others split as if an alley or a gateway passed between them, rise abruptly and perpendicularly almost without foundationary elevation. . . . One when struck was observed to give forth a metallic clink, and not a few, balanced upon points, reminded me of the tradition-bearing rocking stones. At a distance in the forest, the larger masses might be mistaken for Cyclopean walls, towers, steeples, minarets, loggans, dwelling houses, and ruined castles. They are often overgrown with a soft grass, which decaying, forms with the degradation of the granite a thin cap of soil; their summits are crowned with tufty cactus, a stomatiferous plant which imbibes nourishment from the oxygen of the air; whilst huge creepers, imitating trees, project gnarled trunks from the deeper crevices in their flanks. Seen through the forest these rocks are an effective feature in the landscape, especially when the sunbeams fall warm and bright upon their rounded summits and their smooth sides, here clothed with a mildew-like lichen of the tenderest leek-green, there yellowed like Italian marbles by the burning rays. . . ." [1]

In the Kondoa District the people of the Rangi tribe occupy the hills in the north and the Burungi and Sandawi the lower lands. Parts of the highland country are most attractive and the Great North Road reaches a height of nearly 6,000 feet above sea level between Kondoa and Babati, on the way to Arusha. These hills were once thickly covered with forest and had a great depth of soil, but when the forests were felled and the earth laid bare the very depth of the friable soil made it the more easily eroded and now nothing remains in many places but the rocky sub-soil, split by innumerable channels, great and small, down which the rain courses during the wet season. In places these channels are as much as fifty feet deep—veritable canyons—making reclamation of the land exceedingly difficult if not virtually impossible.

In the Singida District the erosion problem is not so formidable, despite the dense population, because the soil is not quite so friable nor, generally speaking, are the slopes so steep. The parts of the district near its western and northern

---

[1] R. F. Burton "The Lake Regions of Central Africa", pp. 282-5, 1860.

border are very thinly inhabited and are for the most part wooded grasslands, merging into the swamps along the Wembere and Sibiti rivers. In the south there is a large fairly compact block of woodland which adjoins the Itigi Thicket. Many parts of the inhabited areas present much the same appearance as the cultivated regions of Ugogo, but are on the whole more fertile.

CLIMATE

The outstanding feature of the climate of the Central Province is its scanty and uncertain rainfall. The average over a period of about 20 years has been some 25 inches per annum, but the rainfall varies greatly from year to year and there is often a gap in the rains during the planting season which results in very considerable losses and sometimes necessitates the complete replanting of crops. Figures for rainfall over the years 1950-1956 are given in the table below:—

Station	Altitude	Average	1950	1951	1952	1953	1954	1955	1956
Mpwapwa	3,700	26·25 (29 years)	23·5	23·6	23·1	18·43	18·05	19·63	30·70
Dodoma	3,675	22·24 (29 years)	18·9	25·4	17·7	16·25	14·31	20·53	25·93
Manyoni	4,100	25·15 (25 years)	30·3	42·3	29·7	21·54	17·93	19·36	*
Kondoa	4,547	24·74 (27 years)	24·9	44·0	22·9	*	15·76	19·72	24·59
Singida	4,900	24·97 (28 years)	23·6	40·6	20·3	19·19	27·04	24·63	25·36

*Records incomplete.

From this it will be seen that the Mpwapwa District is, by a small margin, the most favoured district, doubtless due to the effect of the Kiboriani and Rubeho mountain ranges. Dodoma, in the middle of the vast Ugogo plain, receives only some twenty-two inches a year, and in the year 1948 only a little over half this amount fell. Throughout the province the first rains are expected in October/November and continue, intermittently, until April/May. It is usual for the dry season to last for six months, sometimes longer, and at the end of the season the degree of desiccation is indeed remarkable and is a factor of fundamental importance in the formulation of any plans for development.

Further details regarding the climate at certain stations in the province are given in the climatological table on page 12.

POPULATION

The combined results of the 1948 census, a complete one, and the 1952 census, a partial one only, are given below:—

Station	European	Indian	Goan	Arab	Somali	Coloured	Other	Total Non-African	African	Total Population
Mpwapwa	641	292	16	146	131	17	67	1,310	100,673	101,983
Dodoma	386	2,154	59	512	168	23	35	3,337	216,602	219,939
Manyoni	24	149	4	160	7	8	1	353	52,247	52,600
Kondoa	81	117	4	254	90	12	7	565	145,366	145,931
Singida	102	582	–	517	177	31	30	1,439	301,053	302,492
	1,234	3,294	83	1,589	573	91	140	7,004	815,941	822,945

It will be seen that the European population of the province is very small and that over half is found in the Mpwapwa District; this is accounted for by the fact that the Overseas Food Corporation holdings (now the Tanganyika Agricultural

Corporation) and a European secondary school are both situated in the district. Most of those in the Dodoma District are Government officials stationed at provincial headquarters. There are only six settlers in the province. Of these five have estates in the north-eastern parts of the Mpwapwa District and one in the Manyoni District.

The European population in the Singida District is made up of officials, missionaries and miners.

Most of the 3,000 Asians live in the towns, but there is a number of petty traders in smaller trading settlements throughout the area, and in both the Dodoma and Singida Districts the number of Arabs and Somalis is notable. The last-named are mostly engaged in the cattle trade.

There are six main tribes in the province, the Gogo, Nyaturu, Iramba, Irangi, Sandawi and Burungi, and these are briefly described below.

THE GOGO

The Gogo, according to the 1948 census, constitute the fifth largest tribe in the territory, numbering, at that time, over 271,000. They are thought to have increased to about 300,000 since then. They are found mostly in the Dodoma and Manyoni Districts, where they form about 80 per cent of the population, and in the Mpwapwa District, where they account for nearly 50 per cent. It seems that in origin they were a tribe of pastoralists who, of necessity, have now become cattle-keeping agriculturists, although cattle remain their great source of wealth and, indeed, in their arid and climatically unfavoured country, the very staff of life.

In the old days they were dreaded by the early explorers and by the Arab traders for their grasping ways and for the unmerciful fleecing which each caravan had to suffer as it passed through the country. Tribute (*hongo*) had to be paid to every chief in turn before he would grant the caravan passage through his dominions and of course the object was to secure the maximum amount which it was thought the travellers could be made to pay. Nevertheless the chiefs did not wish to put a stop completely to all such traffic, since they had considerable stores of ivory which they could only dispose of at the coast with the assistance of the Arabs.

All the early travellers give some account of the Wagogo, usually varying only in degree as regards their unfavourable nature. Perhaps the least biased is Stanley's which remains a not inapt description of many of them today.[1]

"They are, physically and intellectually, the best of the races between Unyamwezi and the sea. Their colour is a rich dark brown. There is something in their frontal aspect which is almost leonine. Their faces are broad and intelligent. Their eyes are large and round. Their noses are flat, and their mouths are very large; but their lips, though thick, are not so monstrously thick as those our exaggerated ideal of a negro has. For all this, though the Mgogo is a ferocious man, capable of proceeding to any length upon the slightest temptation, he is an attractive figure to a white traveller. He is proud of his chief, proud of his country, sterile and unlovable though it be; he is proud of himself, his prowess, his weapons and his belongings; he is vain, egotistic, and a tyrant, yet the Mgogo is capable of forming friendships, and of exerting himself for friendship's sake. One grand

---

[1] "How I Found Livingstone", by H. M. Stanley, pp. 250-1.

vice in his character, which places him in a hostile light to travellers, is his exceeding avarice, and greed for riches, and if the traveller suffers by this, he is not likely to be amiably disposed towards him.

The Mgogo warrior carries as his weapons a bow, and a sheaf of murderous-looking arrows, pointed, pronged, and barbed; a couple of light, beautifully-made assegais, a broad sword-like spear, with a blade over two feet long; a battle-axe, and a rungu, or knob-club. He has also a shield, painted with designs in black and white, oval-shaped, sometimes of rhinoceros, or elephant, or bull-hide."

But the Gogo have not remained completely untouched by the impact of European civilization. During the 1939-45 war many of them were conscripted as labourers on some of the old German ceara rubber estates and proved to be apt pupils at the art of tapping. They were also engaged by the Overseas Food Corporation as labourers on the Groundnut Scheme but did not prove so satisfactory for this work. Nevertheless the numbers offering themselves as labourers on estates in the neighbouring districts to the east and north are increasing. As the Gogo Development Plan (see page 160) is implemented the way of life of these still somewhat primitive tribesmen will change, but as the tribe is a large one and custom dies hard it may be a considerable time before much change is noticeable.

A pleasing characteristic of the Gogo is their love of music, especially of singing. Hugh Tracey, the well-known authority of African music, made some recordings of Gogo songs and wrote:[1]

"My impressions of that day's work are filled with superlatives. In all my experience of Africa I had not heard better chanting than we recorded that afternoon and late into the evening, as the red-ochred, pig-tailed, decorative young men sang and danced for us while their young women gave brilliant performances on the drums."

THE NYATURU

The Nyaturu or Arimi occupy a large part of the Singida District and the northern portion of the Manyoni District. There were over 180,000 of them in 1948. They belong to the Bantu group of tribes and are supposedly a mixture of various people who entered this area some 250 years ago. The area was then sparsely populated by the Taturu, a nomadic or semi-nomadic branch of the Tatoga tribe, other branches of which are the Barabaig of the Mbulu District and the Burungi of the Kondoa District. The immigrants are thought to have been mostly Kimbu (now found between Manyoni and Lake Rukwa), with some Fipa (now found in the Sumbawanga District); most of the larger clans seem to be of Kimbu origin.

Like the Gogo, the Arimi may be described as cattle-keeping agriculturists.

It was in their country that the disturbing series of "lion-man" murders took place in 1946-7, when unscrupulous malefactors (including quite a number of women) took advantage of the presence in the area of man-eating lions, and of the general belief that certain persons could at will turn themselves into lions, to perpetrate murders by trained dupes dressed in lion-skins.[2]

---

[1] "A Recording Tour in East Africa" *Tanganyika Notes and Records*, No. 32 for January 1952.

[2] See "The Lion-Men of Singida" by A. W. Wyatt in *Tanganyika Notes and Records*, No. 28, page 3; January 1950.

THE IRAMBA AND IAMBI

The people of the Iramba tribe have inhabited for about the last two hundred years the area comprising the Iramba Plateau, the Wembere Steppe and the Dulumo Valley.   Little is know for certain of the earliest history of this people, but it seems that at one time the clans now comprising the Iramba (who call themselves *Aniramba*) were part of the Kimbu tribe.   There is a legend that many clans originally came from the coast, but from which part of the coast is not known; one of the clans maintains that it came from the vicinity of Bagamoyo, but there is no evidence to bear out this contention.   Tradition states that about two hundred years ago there was a split amongst the Kimbu and that the clans now comprising the Iramba and Iambi were either driven out of their country or left voluntarily.   As far as can be ascertained there were two large migrations which apparently were almost simultaneous and took the form of parallel columns.   The first and larger body eventually reached the Iramba Plateau, having spent some years in the Ushora area on the way.   In the meantime, the second column had selected a route to the east and parallel to the first column. This route lay through Ugogo and Turu, and after meeting with resistance during the march the column finally arrived at and stayed in the area now known as Iambi.

When the Aniramba arrived on the Iramba Plateau tradition states that the area was uninhabited and that the clans settled down and began to establish themselves by cultivating their fields and raising stock.   Cattle were not, however, brought with them originally, but were obtained later.

On the arrival of the second column, it was agreed that the latter should inhabit the country to the east of the Dulumo Valley, known as Iambi, and that the first column should remain in Iramba.   Thus it came about that the two clans, originally part of one tribe, the Kimbu, constituted themselves into separate tribes and were named Iramba and Iambi.

THE IRANGI

The Irangi are a Bantu tribe surrounded by non-Bantu people, the Masai and Barabaig (Nilo-Hamitic) and the Sandawi (Khoisaniform).   They are primarily agriculturists, but most have a few cattle and some small stock.   As has been stated, the country they inhabit contains, in places, some of the worst examples of erosion to be seen anywhere in Tanganyika.   There were 95,000 Rangi in 1948.   An account of the Irangi Development Scheme is given on page 160.

THE SANDAWI

The members of the Sandawi tribe occupy the south-western part of the Kondoa District and have as their neighbours the Nyaturu to the west, the Barabaig and Irangi to the north, the Burungi to the east and the Gogo to the south.   With none of these other tribes except the Nyaturu can they be said to have much affinity.   Like the Masai, they stand apart, even to the eye of the stranger, being much lighter in hue than their neighbours, and their speech also betrays them—an unusual tongue abounding in gutturals and clicks.   Because of these peculiarities they have long been thought to be related to the Bushmen, and those who have studied them have noted, besides their "click" language, the existence in their country of rock paintings, the veneration in which they hold the aphis, and other points of similarity.   According to the tribe's own traditions they are an aboriginal race, at one time hunters, without stock or agriculture, collectors of honey and edible roots. Later they were taught stock-keeping by the Nyaturu and Tatoga, from whom they acquired cattle, sheep and goats in exchange for their women (who are still famous for their fecundity). In the latest study of the tribe[1] a comparison is made between certain physical characteristics of South African Bushmen, Hottentots, Dahomeans, Nyaturu and Sandawi and the conclusion is reached that "the evidence . . . is clearly to the effect that the Hottentots and Sandawi are of the same stock and do not merely possess affinities in language; that the traditions of the Sandawi covering their contacts with the neighbouring Nyaturu are confirmed by the degree of the physical resemblance between them and that the Bantu-speaking Nyaturu and the distant Dahomeans received their racial make-up partly from the same source. The evidence makes it possible to place, with some confidence, among the Khoisan, or at least the Khoisaniforms, the Sandawi . . . "

THE BURUNGI

The Burungi are a Hamitic people, belonging to the same group as the Gorowa (from whom they are separated by the Irangi) and the Iraqw. They numbered 9,700 at the time of the 1948 census.

AGRICULTURAL RESOURCES

The wealth of the province, generally speaking, lies in its cattle. Of these, in 1956, there were some 987,263, and small stock numbered 1,350,664. Large numbers of cattle, small stock and hides and skins are marketed every year. In 1956, 85,621 cattle fetched £421,747 on the markets and 97,096 small stock £57,697. [2] The clarified butter industry is described on page 162.

A considerable amount of beeswax and honey is also produced. Gum is collected from a species of acacia and is marketed in considerable quantities (193 tons in 1954) and there are small fishing and salt-making industries at the Bahi swamp.

As one would expect, the province, being largely a "rain-shadow" area and receiving such a small and uncertain rainfall, is subject to frequent food shortages and famines. Ecologically it may be divided into two areas, the plains area and the uplands plateaux. In the plains the altitude ranges from 3,200 to 4,600 feet above sea-level and a great part is covered with deciduous scrub—impenetrable in many parts but more open in others. These plains contain extensive areas of "sunk-lands" where communities of acacia with tall grass and ground flora are found. The upland plateaux are situated at an altitude of 4,600 to 5,900 feet. The vegetation of these higher areas is of many types, ranging from deciduous scrub, open woodland, *miombo* forests, to "evergreen" forest, but in both areas the same crops tend to be grown and throughout the province it is notable what little variety is seen in the staple food crops. These are bullrush millet, sorghum, maize and groundnuts. The main cash crop in the past has been groundnuts but there is now increasing cultivation of castor, for which very good prices have recently been received. Other crops grown are beans, rice, onions and cassava. There is a remarkable absence of fruit trees and bananas and, hitherto, damp

---

[1] See "The Physical Characters of the Sandawi" by J. C. Trevor. *Journal of the Royal Anthropological Institute* Vol. LXXVII, Part 1, 1947.

[2] In 1955 the corresponding figures were 872,899 cattle and 1,266,672 small stock, 80,287 cattle marketed for £418,189 and 71,650 small stock for £52,248.

valley bottoms and lake sides have not been cultivated in the dry season as in other parts of the territory. There is also a surprising lack of short-term cash crops normally planted with the first rains, such as cowpea and gram.

GOGO DEVELOPMENT SCHEME

In 1952 a Development Scheme was prepared for Ugogo, an area which covers about 15,000 square miles in the Mpwapwa, Dodoma and Manyoni Districts. Although the Gogo have been described as cattle-keeping agriculturists, only some 60 per cent of them own cattle; at that time these numbered about 900,000 head and in addition there were about 1,500,000 small stock. Owing to the uncertain rainfall, settlements have grown up round the permanent waters and in many places considerable overstocking has resulted. The Gogo are not at all politically conscious and although a system of democratic councils has been worked out for them there has so far been little response. The Gogo remain very much today as they have been for many generations and are markedly conservative in outlook.

The implementation of the scheme received an immediate setback as a result of the severe famines that occurred in 1953 and 1954 and considerable revisions was necessary. It was decided that with the plan in existence, famine relief works should so far as was practicable be in implementation of the plan but measures for the immediate alleviation of famine conditions naturally took priority. Apart from those aspects of the plan which dealt with overstocking and its concomitant evils, the majority of recommendations therein were fulfilled by 1957. Sixty-two dams and hafirs and 38 anti-erosion projects were undertaken and completed. An increase in the number of grain silos, improvements to communications and extra village roads were other recommendations fulfilled.

The problem of overstocking solved itself as a result of the two famine years. The cattle and small stock population dropped by roughly a third and despite two excellent seasons in 1956 and 1957 stock populations are still considerably less than they were in 1952, i.e. 750,000 head of cattle as compared with 900,000 in 1952, and 1,250,000 goats and sheep as compared with 1,500,000.

IRANGI DEVELOPMENT SCHEME

In 1948 a scheme was prepared and financed from local development funds for the Kolo area of the Irangi Highlands. This was in the nature of a pilot scheme and was confined to a limited area, 16 square miles, carrying a population of some 370 families and 3,000 head of stock, and rapidly deteriorating in fertility. It was designed to ascertain how the land was used, what the crop yields were and how the stock was kept, to assess to what extent the land could be improved by a reduction in stock numbers and by better agricultural methods, and to estimate the maximum carrying capacity of the area in humans and stock. It was, in effect, an attempt to find out how correct land usage principles could be applied in local circumstances.

The results of this survey have been used in the preparation of a larger scheme, made necessary by the accelerating deterioration of land conditions in the highlands as a whole, and the Irangi Development Scheme was prepared.

The Irangi Highlands cover an area of approximately 1,250 square miles and contain 100,000 people, 90,000 head of cattle and 215,000 sheep and goats. The soil is friable and more easily eroded than most, and this, combined with over-cropping and over-grazing, has brought about a serious situation.

The scheme involves, briefly, an attempt to relieve the pressure on the highlands by the development of the only expansion area available—that in the plains to the east below the great escarpment which so abruptly marks the eastern edge of the Irangi tribal area. Here, on the border of Masailand, in country some 1,000-1,500 feet below, and in rather different climatic conditions, there would appear to exist large areas (some 500 square miles in all) of open grazing land of good quality, but these are separated from one another by belts of thick bush heavily infested with tsetse fly. A considerable amount of settlement has already taken place in favourable areas at the foot of the escarpment and on the fan slopes between it and the plains. The main obstacles to the spread of such settlement are three: the lack of suitable agricultural land, the lack of water and the presence of tsetse fly. It is clear that the first obstacle cannot be overcome except to the extent that small pockets of suitable land may become available with the clearing of the bush. Such clearing is of course necessary in order to get rid of the third obstacle, the fly, and to open up the ridges between the grassy plains to grazing. The remaining obstacle, lack of water, has to a certain extent been overcome by the provision of boreholes and piped supplies from springs on the escarpment to various points in the plains. Government funds came to an end in 1956, by which time most of the plan had been implemented. In 1957 the Local Authority provided funds for the continuation of the scheme and it is hoped that it will be complete by 1959.

The scheme is thus primarily aimed at the provision of grazing grounds to relieve the pressure of stock on the highlands, where a culling scheme has already been in operation; the lack of suitable agricultural land in the plains makes it impossible to open up the area for settlement in the ordinary way but at the same time reinforces the need for better land usage methods in the hills. With the removal of stock from the hills the limitation of the number permitted to remain will be made easier and the land given a chance to recover.

MINERALS

The province was well known in the past as a producer of gold and it was from Sekenke Mine that the gold for the "Tabora Sovereigns", much prized by numismatists, was obtained and minted by the Germans during their East African military operations in the first World War. In common with a number of other gold mines, production was suspended at Sekenke during the last war and has received little attention since. At present, a large area is being tested for the existence of alluvial gold.

Copper, graphite and mica have been found in the Mpwapwa District; corundum and nickel in the Dodoma District and garnets at various places. Up to date the province does not appear to be a promising mineralised area, but it is regarded as one well worth further investigation by modern methods, particularly for base metals. The United Kingdom Atomic Energy Authority has opened an office in Dodoma in order to assist in the prospecting for and development of uranium deposits in East Africa generally.

INDUSTRIES

The most important industry in the province is the production of clarified butter. The first factory was set up by Government at Isabe in the Kondoa District in 1932 and in normal times there are about eighty centres where milk is collected and the product prepared. In 1952 the total production amounted to 224,085 kilos, in 1953 to 143,296 kilos, and in 1954 to 55,150 kilos.[1] The effects of the two famine years, 1953 and 1954, will be apparent from these figures.

The preparation of hides and skins, and the salt-making and fish-drying "industries" have already been mentioned on page 159.

ADMINISTRATIVE STATIONS[2]

Dodoma[3].—The Provincial headquarters is situated at Dodoma where the Great North Road crosses the Central Line, 285 miles from Dar es Salaam. The altitude is 3,700 feet above sea level and the town is situated in the middle of a somewhat featureless plain and has grown up with the construction of the railway and the road; it did not exist at all in pre-European times. It has an excellent aerodrome and is on the route Entebbe-Mwanza-Tabora-Dodoma-Dar es Salaam. Dodoma is also a district headquarters, and here there are normally stationed a District Commissioner and three district officers. In addition, a Resident Magistrate and officers of the Agricultural, Education, Forest, Game, Labour, Medical, Prison, Public Works and Water Development Departments, and of the Police Force are normally stationed there. The town contains the headquarters of the Geological Survey Department and there are also representatives of the East African Posts and Telecommunications Department of the High Commission. At the time of the census in 1952 the Dodoma township contained 9,375 Africans, 311 Arabs, 58 Somalis, 2,113 Indians and Goans and 360 Europeans.

Mpwapwa[4].—The District Headquarters at Mpwapwa are pleasantly situated at the foot of the Kiboriani Range, with one of the province's few perennial streams flowing by. As we have seen, Mpwapwa receives slightly better rainfall than any other district in the province and this, combined with its situation in the lee of the mountain, has made it a pleasantly green oasis in the general aridity of the Ugogo country. With the advent of the Overseas Food Corporation and the development of the Groundnut Scheme in the Kongwa[5] area to the north, a new district headquarters was established there, but now that there is a

---

[1] In 1955, 49,344 kilos; in 1956, 49,752 kilos.

[2] For further information see the table on page 542.

[3] Additional particulars are also given in "Tanganyika: A Review of its Resources and their Development" p. 809. The name *Dodoma* is properly *Idodoma*, meaning, in Chigogo, "a place where something bogged down". The Gogo tribe is a composite one and the Gogo living in the Dodoma area are supposed originally to have come from Uhehe. When they came north as far as a spot near the present site of Dodoma, the area then being uninhabited, it is said that one of their cattle became bogged down in some soft ground. The migrants stopped there, dug a well and obtained water. They then decided to settle in the area and gradually spread to the areas around Dodoma so that the name *Idodoma* became common to the neighbourhood.

[4] *Mpwapwa* is said to be the closest the Germans and Swahili could get to the actual Chigogo name for the place in question, which is *Mhamvwa*, a name still used by the majority of the local people. Mhamvwa was a prominent early settler in the area whose name was adopted for the place.

[5] From *Kukongwakongwa*, meaning a fertile place in Chigogo, a choice of name which now seems particularly ironic.

large reduction in the size of the area being cultivated by the successor Corporation the two districts have been merged and the Kongwa area again forms part of the Mpwapwa District. The District Commissioner is normally assisted by two district officers and representatives of the Agricultural, Education and Medical Departments are normally stationed there. At the time of the last census there were 1,574 Africans, 197 Asians, and 62 Europeans in the Mpwapwa Minor Settlement.

Manyoni [1].—Situated at an altitude of 4,100 feet on the Central Line, 366 miles from Dar es Salaam, Manyoni was formerly the junction of the branch line to Singida and Kinyangiri. This line did not pay its way and was removed in 1950 and the rails used for the branch line to Mpanda. Until recently, Manyoni was a somewhat lonely station and had a rather abandoned air, but with its re-instatement as a separate district—it had been for many years a division of the Dodoma District—it has again begun to thrive. The District Commissioner is assisted by a district officer and representatives of the Veterinary, Agricultural and Game Departments are normally stationed there. At the time of the last census the Manyoni Minor Settlement contained 596 Africans, 82 Asians and 23 Europeans.

Kondoa [2].—Situated at an altitude of 4,500 feet, Kondoa is some two miles off the Great North Road and 100 miles to the north of Dodoma. It is a pleasant station in hilly country built near a remarkable spring which comes bubbling up from the depths and provides a constant supply of clear sweet water. The District Commissioner is assisted by two district officers and representatives of the Veterinary, Agricultural, Medical and Tsetse Survey Departments are normally stationed there. At the time of the last census the Kondoa Minor Settlement contained 5,000 Africans, 335 Asians (including Arabs) and 13 Europeans.

Singida [3].—Singida is pleasantly situated on a hill between two lakes, at an altitude of 4,900 feet. It is the headquarters of a large district which contains the former Mkalama District, and has a population of over 300,000 Africans. The headquarters of the Mkalama District was not well sited, being some distance from the centre of the populated area, and a new site has now been found and headquarters buildings are being built. In the meantime Singida remains the headquarters of both districts. The District Commissioner is assisted by three district officers, one of whom is normally stationed at Kisiriri in the Mkalama division, and there are normally a Resident Magistrate and representatives of the Medical, Veterinary and Agricultural Departments, and of the Police Force, in the District. At the time of the 1952 census Singida township contained 2,269 Africans, 148 Somalis, 117 Arabs, 530 Indians and 37 Europeans.

---

[1]*Manyoni* is the Kinyamwezi word for birds and the name is supposed to have been given to the place by early Nyamwezi travellers. The reason for this choice is not understood as the birds of the area do not, nowadays, seem to be unusually numerous or prominent.

[2]A name supposed to have been given to the place by early Arab traders and Swahilis from the coast who visited the area from Kilosa in search of ivory. In the dialect of the coastal people concerned (possibly Wamakua) *mkondoo*, the name they originally gave to the area, is said to have denoted a road or elephant track.

[3]There are two explanations of the origin of the name *Singida*. One is that it comes from the local vernacular name for a particular type of tree, *msingida*, used for the blocks of wood traditionally inserted in the ears of the people of the area. Another explanation is that the place was named after Singeida, a Barabaig war chief who once lived there. This name, in the Barabaig vernacular, means zebra and is said to have been given to the chief because on the day he was born a zebra was killed to provide particular medicines for his mother.

PLACES OF INTEREST TO THE VISITOR AND SPORTING FACILITIES

The province is not one to which tourists normally make a special visit, but nonetheless there are several places of interest to the visitor and sporting facilities are not lacking.   The Kondoa District is famous for its rock paintings, which have been fully described in a special number of *Tanganyika Notes and Records*. [1] Some of these paintings are to be found only a short distance from the road and are thus easily accessible by car and well worth a visit.

Most varieties of game which occur in the territory are to be found in the province and a traveller on the Great North Road will be unlucky if he does not see several of them in travelling through.   Lion are to be found in all districts, as well as other carnivora, and hyena, wild dog, the commoner kinds of antelope, ostrich and zebra are quite likely to be seen.   Elephant are also to be found in many places and many good tusks have been recorded.   Rhino are so common in parts of the Singida District as to constitute a nuisance to cultivators. [2]

The Veterinary laboratories at Mpwapwa will interest those concerned with research, as will the laboratories of the Department of Geological Survey and the Atomic Energy Authority at Dodoma.

---

[1] See "Tanganyika Rock Paintings" by H. A. Fosbrooke, in *Tanganyika Notes and Records* No. 29 for July 1950.

[2] See also Chapter 13 "Game, The Shooting Grounds".

EASTERN PROVINCE

SITUATION

This province lies in the east central part of the territory, containing much of the land lying between the central plateau and the Indian Ocean and including the large Ulanga District, which forms a sort of appendix extending for some 200 miles to the south-west. The province covers 41,600 square miles—about three-quarters the size of England—and has a population of just under a million. In the north the boundary follows the foothills of the Nguru Mountains and the river Mligasi to the Indian Ocean. In the west it runs through the middle of mountainous country lying to the north and south of the Central Line near Kidete station, then follows the Great Ruaha River where it breaks out of the central plateau, turning south-west at Kidatu to follow the escarpment separating the Kilombero valley from the highlands in the Iringa and Njombe Districts. In the south it goes through a kind of "no man's land" between the Ulanga and Songea Districts and then follows the line of the Mbarangandu, one of the tributaries of the Rufiji river, till it joins the Kilombero and finally the Ruaha. The boundary then swings south-east and passes through the Matumbi Hills, to reach the Indian Ocean again at Mohoro Bay on the southern edge of the delta.

PHYSICAL FEATURES

The physiographical features of the Eastern Province which leap to the eye are three: first, there is the continuous line of hills and tilted escarpments facing east or south-east and running from the Nguru hills astride the Handeni border through the Ukaguru and Usagara mountains in the Kilosa District to the Iringa escarpment, which forms the north-west boundary of the Ulanga District. These hills and scarp faces form part of the much longer chain running from the Usambaras to the mountains near the north end of Lake Nyasa. The great bastion of the Uluguru hills forms, as it were, an advance guard of this spectacular feature.

Second, there are the three notable river systems which rise in or have forced their way through these hills and escarpments to run east to the Indian Ocean: the Wami system in the north of the province, rising in the Ukagurus and draining these mountains and the Mkata plain; the Ruvu system, which takes drainage from the west of the Ulugurus right round both the north and the south of the hill mass (by the Ngerengere and Mgeta rivers respectively) to a point just north of Bagamoyo; and the big Rufiji river system fed by the Ruaha and Kilombero. The total drainage of these three perennial systems is huge and the Eastern Province is, indeed, the "province of the rivers".

Third, there is the breaking of the land through which these rivers flow from the high escarpments to the sea into two distinct parts, by Gillman's[1] "fall line", that almost straight line running south-west from the Pangani Falls to the Ruvuma "over which all our major rivers tumble in falls or cataract stretches." Between this line and the hills to the west lies a foreland of red-soil plateaux, and between it and the present sea coast lie the mixed black and grey soils and sands of the typical coastal strip. In between the river systems this line is marked by visible

---

[1]See "Water Consultant's Report No. 6, 1940", by C.Gillman.

soil and vegetational changes though the altitude difference is usually small. It represents an ancient shore line dating from Jurassic times, the land to the west having been for a much longer time "high and dry" and that to the east having been "the scene of repeated transgressions and regressions of the sea."

The greater part of the Bagamoyo, Uzaramo and Rufiji Districts consists of a coastal plain at an average altitude of less than 500 feet. This plain extends, unbroken, along the whole coastline of the territory from north to south but in the Eastern Province it achieves its greatest penetration inland, extending into the interior for over 100 miles along the valleys of the Great Ruaha and Ruvu rivers. It is undulating in many places and broken by hills rising to 1,300 feet near Maneromango in the Uzaramo District and 1,500 feet in the Matumbi Hills in the Rufiji District. In the Kisarawe District the peculiar step-like formation of the land is most noticeable. The whole of this district lies on the seaward side of the "fall-line" and may be divided into areas each of roughly the same height throughout and separated by a sharp rise of about 20, 35-40, 50, 80 and 100 feet from the next level. This step-like topography is also found in Pemba and Zanzibar, where the same "raised beaches" are found. Another interesting topographical phenomenon in the Kisarawe District is the existence of curiously flat-bottomed, steep-sided creeks or valleys. Their formation and that of the "raised beaches" is due to the fact that, in past ages, there was considerable variation in the level of the sea. With a rise in level, a valley would become filled in by "aggradation" of deposits on its floor, and a new shoreline would be created at the higher level[1].

Further inland lies the great mountain massif of the Ulugurus, rising to a height of 8,858 feet at its highest point; the Ngurus in the north of the same district, rising to 6,928 feet; the Ukaguru mountains in the Kilosa district rising to 7,432 feet; and the Mahenge massif in the Ulanga district, 4,400 feet.

The Rufiji river system drains an area of 68,500 square miles (Wami 18,000 and Ruvu 7,000 square miles), with tributaries as far west as a few miles from Mbeya. The volume of water in the lower reaches varies tremendously and large areas are inundated during the rains. At its mouth it forms a considerable delta, some 40 miles broad, which contains thousands of acres of valuable mangrove forest and other useful timber trees as well.[2] It was in this delta that the episode of the sinking of the German cruiser *Königsberg* took place during the 1914-1918 campaign.

As already stated, the province is thus well watered and the use of its rivers for irrigation purposes has long attracted attention. The possibilities of development, especially in the Kilombero valley and in the Mkata plain, have now been carefully investigated and some account of the findings is given below.

The only lake of any size in the province is Lake Utenge in the Rufiji District.

The Selous Game reserve occupies an area of some 6,000 square miles in the Rufiji basin and is a remote, almost uninhabited area, giving ideal seclusion for game. The total area of the reserve is over 10,000 square miles, the rest being in the Southern Province.

---

[1]See "Physical Features of the Dar es Salaam District" by H. R. Threlfall, in *Tanganyika Notes and Records*, No. 29, for July 1950.

[2]For interesting accounts of the river see "The Delta of the Rufiji River" and "The Rufiji River" by R. de la B. Barker in *Tanganyika Notes and Records*, No. 2, for October 1936, and No. 4, for October 1937.

DISTRICTS

There are eight districts in the Eastern Province; the coastal districts of Bagamoyo, Kisarawe and Rufiji, the Dar es Salaam District which has the same boundaries as the municipality, the island of Mafia and the inland districts of Morogoro, Kilosa and Ulanga. Provincial headquarters was for long at Dar es Salaam but was moved to Morogoro in 1952.

The *Morogoro District* extends from the Great Ruaha River in the south to the Nguru Mountains in the north, a distance of about 150 miles. Within its borders is to be found a great variety of country; "coastal" plain, hot and low-lying flats near the Ruaha, open grassy plains to the north, the great massif of the Ulugurus rising steeply from the plains to heights of almost 9,000 feet in several places, swamps along the Ruvu river, and more mountains in the Ngurus in the north-west corner. The district covers 7,595 square miles and has a population of just over a quarter of a million, of whom about 500 are Europeans, 200 Arabs and nearly 2,000 Indians. 185,000 of the African population live in the Uluguru Mountains, where the density is 375 to the square mile of occupied land.

The *Kilosa District* is divided into two types of country; the plains on the east and the mountain range on the west which separates the central plateau from the coastal belt. The mountain country has fine scenery and runs to peaks over 7,000 feet but contains only a small African population and few roads.

The Mkata plain, with extensions of low and broken country north and south, is also sparsely populated, but recent developments may soon open up this country along the eastern borders of the district.

Historically it is of interest that the Church Missionary Society established a Mission station at Mamboya in the Ukaguru hills in 1879. A small military post had a short time previously been set up there by troops of the Sultan of Zanzibar.

It was in 1884 that the notorious Carl Peters set out from Sadani with three companions and reached Msowero, near Kilosa. He obtained the signature of a headman or minor chief to a "treaty of eternal friendship" which gave his Company the entire rights over the whole of that country. After making eleven more such treaties he returned to Germany and was able to persuade Bismarck to take the territories under "Imperial Protection", although they were claimed by the Sultan of Zanzibar.*

Kilosa Township is situated at a height of 1,600 feet on the central railway, 170 miles from Dar es Salaam by rail and 217 by main road. New main roads pass through the north and the south of the district to the Central and Southern Highlands Provinces respectively and provide rapid communication from the coast to the west of the territory.

The strip of land running north and south between the mountains and the plain is fertile and highly populated. It contains a number of flourishing sisal estates, food farms and African cotton fields, making this one of the richest districts in the province.

The *Ulanga District* was formerly known as the Mahenge District. It covers a large area, 16,094 square miles, and contains about 124,000 people, all Africans except for about 150 Europeans (mostly missionaries) and 280 Asians. The

*See p. 50.

district contains the great valley of the Kilombero river, the highlands near Mahenge, the hilly country to the south and west of these highlands and the uninhabited Selous Game Reserve in the north, east and south.   Communications south of Ifakara on the Kilombero depend upon the state of the river and the pontoon ferry which only operates in the dry season from July to February or March.

The population is sparse throughout the district, a result of decimation after the Maji Maji rebellion in 1905.   The people live in sleeping sickness concentrations, that is, islands of open country kept free of bush and hence of tsetse fly, and most of the district is still uninhabited.

The *Kisarawe District* occupies the country around the capital, Dar es Salaam, which is excluded as a municipality, and lies between the coastal districts of Bagamoyo and Rufiji.   The administrative headquarters is now at Kisarawe in the Pugu Hills twenty miles from Dar es Salaam.

The district covers 4,000 square miles and has a population of nearly 250,000 Africans, 250 Europeans, 300 Asians and over 100 Arabs.   It is a rural area densely occupied round the municipality and up the railway line, where extensive alienations provide work for immigrant labour.   The rest of the district is not very fertile and shows no sign of spectacular development in the immediate future.

The *Bagamoyo District* covers 3,700 square miles and has a population of some 80,000, mostly African but with some 30 Arabs and about the same number of Indians.   Population is sparse outside the coastal strip owing to shortage of permanent water, although the Wami and Ruvu rivers both cross the district and enter the sea north of Bagamoyo Township.   There is an old dhow port at Sadani near the Pangani border.

The district is backward and undeveloped though there are two sisal estates and three salt works on the coast.

The most interesting feature is the influx during the last twenty years of Wakwavi, a cattle-owning tribe related to the Masai, who keep large herds of cattle in areas so far uninhabited and remote from communications.   If water can be provided the establishment of stock will greatly help future development.

The *Rufiji District* contains the Rufiji valley from the junction of the Ruaha and Kilombero rivers a hundred miles from the coast.   The population is 105,000, almost entirely African with a few Arab and Indian traders.   There is little non-native enterprise.   The population mostly lives along the river except for three subchiefdoms to the north near the road to Dar es Salaam.   Like Bagamoyo the district is very backward, but prospects of development by control of the river and large-scale irrigation may transform the situation in the next twenty years.   It is hoped that Africans will take up land and learn to work the irrigated area on the lines of the Gezira Scheme.   Mechanical cultivation by two teams of crawler tractors which plough up rice land in blocks on prepayment by the African cultivators has already become popular and has increased production over the last few years.

Harvest festival dance of the Turu Tribe, Singida.

Photo: V. Eugene Johnson, Singida

Kindiga bowman, Central Province.

Terracing: Uluguru Mountains, Eastern Province.

Test drilling for oil on Mafia Island.

Photo: B-P Shell

The *Mafia District* comprises a group of islands off the Rufiji delta, separated from the mainland by a shallow channel, and formed part of the Rufiji District until 1951. The main island of Mafia is only 152 square miles in area, about the size of the county of Rutland. The population is 12,000 including 400 Arabs and 250 Indians. It has many historical associations and is the "Monfia" of Milton and perhaps also the "Menouthias" mentioned by Ptolemy. In the days before steamers it was an important port of call in the rich trade up the east coast of Africa and there are ancient ruined towns deserving of archaeological investigation. It is now devoted to coconuts and fishing. The coconut plantations were first established by the Arabs from Zanzibar who were able to build up valuable estates when slaves were freely available. The abolition of slavery hit the industry hard and the Arabs have never recovered, but Africans are now building up a more healthy economy.

Fishing is a flourishing industry and the broad Mafia channel, dotted with coral reefs, provides excellent commercial (and also game) fishing. Fish up to 50 and 60 pounds are readily caught on a rod in the channel but the really big ones are found on the continental shelf east of the island.[1]

Recent research by the D'Arcy-Shell Exploration Company, in the hope that oil might be found, has produced disappointing results.

CLIMATE

The climate in the coastal plain is very pleasant in the period June–September, which are the coolest months, when little rain falls and the humidity is not great, but during the rains it can be oppressively hot, largely because of the degree of humidity, which is often 98 per cent on the coast. The thermometer seldom rises above 90°, but, due to the influence of the heated waters of the Indian Ocean, there is often little variation between day and night temperatures near the sea. As one travels away from the coastal plain nights become cooler and in the mountains they are of course often cold, frosts being sometimes experienced in the Ulugurus.

In the coastal areas the annual rainfall averages about 40 inches and the mountainous areas in the Morogoro and Kilosa Districts receive about the same amount, and in places more, but the western parts of the coastal plain are not so well favoured and the distribution is irregular. At Morogoro itself the average is 35 inches and at Utete, the district headquarters of the Rufiji District, about the same.

The island of Mafia and the highlands of the Ulanga District have an exceptionally good rainfall, in both places this averages over 70 inches annually.

Statistics of rainfall at district headquarters are given below:—

District	Altitude in ft.	Average in inches	1950	1951	1952	1953	1954	1955	1956
Bagamoyo ...	30	41·45 (47 years)	56·60	51·21	30·16	42·84	37·32	39·74	35·00
Dar es Salaam ...	47	41·50 (52 years)	38·10	51·87	26·38	53·56	42·64	53·98	38·11
Utete (Rufiji) ...	170	35·02 (31 years)	29·86	42·04	23·33	*	31·87	43·19	31·67
Kilindoni (Mafia)	70	75·10 (20 years)	79·27	60·75	77·17	73·35	83·27	86·76	78·18
Morogoro ...	1,900	34·99 (39 years)	34·24	41·66	29·47	25·10	33·65	33·30	36·09
Kilosa	1,611	39·90 (35 years)	34·74	49·18	38·87	47·23	29·26	30·09	33·91
Mahenge (Ulanga)	3,630	73·16 (45 years)	73·66	78·80	74·41	70·29	61·72	69·05	89·34

*Records incomplete.

[1]See also page 489.

POPULATION

Morogoro District.—Besides some 22,000 Nguu in the north, the Morogoro District contains over 160,000 Luguru living in the Uluguru Mountains, 14,000 Kutu in the lower lands between these mountains and the Great Ruaha river, 5,000 Zigua and 4,000 Kwere. Over 10 per cent of the population are aliens and most of the latter have come to the district to work on estates, some of them having settled permanently.

Kilosa District.—The main tribes are:—

Kaguru	... ...	50,000 (north)
Sagara	... ...	17,000 (centre)
Vidunda	... ...	15,000 (south)
Kwiva	... ...	5,000 (south-west)

The Kwiva have been established in the Ukwiva hills for a considerable time and it is said that the Sagara and Kaguru are descended from them. They live a secluded life and do not seem to be increasing in numbers.

The Kaguru live in the mountains and broken country in the north and west of the district and are increasing rapidly. Their country is, however, still only sparsely populated. They own cattle.

The Sagara occupy the plains and foothills in the centre and appear to be almost static in numbers. They are rather swamped by immigrant tribes who have settled in their fertile country after coming to work on sisal estates.

The Vidunda live in the southern hills but are increasing very rapidly and pushing northwards against the Sagara. They are energetic cultivators and grow rice near Kidodi, also tobacco for exchange with goats from the Central Province. They are related to the Bena in Ulanga.

There are a number of Kwavi in the north-west, where the country changes into Masai steppe, also a colony of Kamba, originally from Kenya.

Ulanga District.—The tribal population is as follows:—

Pogoro ...	... ...	56,000
Ndamba	... ...	20,000
Bena	... ...	15,500
Mbunga ...	... ...	10,500
Ngindo ...	... ...	10,200
Ngoni	... ...	5,500
Hehe	... ...	4,500

The Pogoro live in the hilly parts while the rest of the tribes inhabit the flats, mainly within the Kilombero valley.

Kisarawe District.—The Zaramo constitute 65 per cent of the population and cover most of the district except the south, where the Ndengereko (11 per cent) live between them and the Rufiji. The main tribes are:—

Zaramo	...	150,000
Ndengereko	... ...	27,500
Rufiji ...	... ...	9,500
Luguru	... ...	8,200
Ngindo	... ...	7,000

The total African population is about 250,000, including a great many aliens from all over the territory who have drifted towards the capital and now live or work near it.

The Ndengereko came from the western Rufiji District about 100 years ago and have settled in the south of the Kisarawe District. They are Mohammedans.

Bagamoyo District.—This is one of the few coastal districts with a number of compact independent tribes, perhaps because they were able to hide themselves in the dense and inhospitable bush and so escape the slavers, or perhaps because, paradoxically, they lived so near two of the main slaving headquarters in Tanganyika (Bagamoyo and Sadani) that peace with them was more important than slaving. The tribes are:—

Kwere	... ...	27,000 (1/3)
Zigua	... ...	20,000 (1/4)
Zaramo	... ...	16,000
Doe ...	... ...	6,500
Luguru	... ...	4,000
Ndengereko	... ...	1,200
Others ...	... ...	5,300
Total African Population ...	... ...	80,000

The Zaramo are often indistinguishable from "Swahilis" and many cannot speak Kizaramo.

Rufiji District.—Fifty per cent of the inhabitants are Rufiji and 25 per cent Ndengereko; they are all staunch Mohammedans, as witnessed by the fact that heavy drinking is not one of the local vices.

The Rufiji number 58,000 and the total population of the district is 117,000, including Shirazi[1], Mtumbi and Ngindo (Kilwa District), and Pogoro (Ulanga District).

Mafia District.—The African population of Mafia is 11,500 and tribes are thoroughly mixed, being largely of slave ancestry.

The combined results of the 1948 census, a complete one, and the 1952 census, a partial one only, are given below:—

District	European	Indian	Goan	Arab	Somali	Coloured	Other	Total Non-African	African	Total Population
Bagamoyo ...	85	292	7	310	–	5	11	710	78,979	79,689
Dar es Salaam ...	3,603	19,382	1,595	1,570	10	139	511	26,810	72,330	99,140
Kilosa... ...	296	869	29	327	72	20	25	1,638	123,076	124,714
Kisarawe ...	329	266	35	119	–	2	26	767	187,927	188,694
Morogoro ...	546	1,699	74	194	4	10	43	2,570	230,291	232,861
Rufiji	15	131	2	143	–	1	1	293	104,917	105,210
Mafia	20	220	7	416	1	1	6	671	11,379	12,050
Ulanga ...	132	237	–	6	–	11	2	388	121,328	121,716
	5,026	23,096	1,749	3,085	87	189	615	33,847	930,227	964,074

AGRICULTURAL RESOURCES

The climatic and ecological divisions are as follows:—

The *coastal areas* of the Bagamoyo, Kisarawe and Rufiji Districts and of Mafia Island with moderate rainfall (41 inches or more) and light sandy soils. Population 350,000.

[1]See page 254.

The *riverine areas* of the Rufiji, Ruvu and Kilombero valleys with moderate rainfall (35-60 inches) and fertile alluvial soils. Population 160,000.

The *low-rainfall* areas in the western part of Bagamoyo District and the eastern part of the Morogoro District (33-38 inches). Population 60,000.

The *plains areas* of the Morogoro and Kilosa Districts with light to moderate rainfall (35-41 inches). Population 160,000.

The *mountain areas* of the Morogoro, Kilosa and Ulanga Districts with heavy rainfall (60-80 inches). Population 220,000.

The first three areas are from sea level to 1,000 feet, the fourth about 1,500-2,000 and the fifth from 2,000-7,000 feet.

African Agricultural Production.—The *coastal areas* are characterized by light sandy soils on which coconuts, cassava, dry-land rice, sweet potatoes and pulses are produced. Much of the country is covered with dense thicket in which innumerable pigs, baboons and monkeys find sanctuary. The annual losses of food caused by their depredations must amount to a very considerable tonnage. The most important cash crops are copra, rice and cassava; but a variety of other products are marketed as well, such as charcoal, dried fish, raffia, arrowroot, maize, sorghum and pulses.

In many places the deciduous scrub forest, *vichaka*, has been replaced by a secondary growth, *mashokora*, for which a special system of cultivation has been evolved by the local inhabitants.[1]

The *riverine areas* are characterized by heavy alluvial black cotton soils which are very fertile but are often subject to river flooding during the wet season. Attention has been directed to their development in recent years, particularly to the development of the great potentialities of the Kilombero and Rufiji river valleys: an account of investigations already made is given below (see pages 174–5).

The *low-rainfall areas* suffer from a combination of variable and unreliable rainfall and soils of moderate productivity. Cotton, sorghum and cassava are the most reliable crops, and other crops, such as maize, pulses and rice can only be regarded as catch crops, their failure owing to dry spells being a common occurrence.

The characteristics of the *plains areas* are acacia thorn bush and tall grass on heavy dark alluvial soils of varying fertility. The areas adjacent to the hills are in general very fertile whilst further into the plains much of the soil is black clay, difficult to work. The possibilities of using the Mkata Plain both for increased agricultural production and for ranching have received careful study of recent years and a note on this area is also given below.

The *mountain areas* are characterized by dense cultivation on excessively steep slopes, which were once well wooded but which are now frequently devoid of any forest cover. Grass-fires and sheet erosion have been taking a steady toll

---

[1]See "Mashokora Cultivations on the Coast" by A. V. Hartnoll and N. R. Fuggles-Couchman in *Tanganyika Notes and Records* No. 3, for April 1937.

of the fertility of the land and in many areas the yields are sub-economic and cultivators frequently have to cultivate subsidiary fields of maize and sorghum down on the plains.

A description of development schemes in being or under consideration is given below.

DEVELOPMENT SCHEMES

Uluguru Land Usage Scheme (Morogoro District).—The scheme was initiated in 1950 when funds and staff became available for the purpose of preventing soil erosion, securing sustained or increased agricultural production in the Uluguru area, and maintaining the volume of water in the numerous streams rising in the Uluguru mountains feeding the Ruvu river system and supplying domestic and industrial users between the mountains and the coast.

The importance of these objectives had been recognized for many years but owing to lack of funds the work was confined within the resources of normal departmental activities. The importance of assured water supplies in the Ngere-ngere-Ruvu system high-lighted the urgency of the situation as one of the industries most threatened by an unstable water regime was sisal in the Morogoro district. In all £68,000 was made available and specially trained European and African staff operated throughout the 1,000 square miles of the mountains. The aim was the introduction of sound conservation practices into the traditional pattern of native agriculture, so that these practices would continue to be employed long after the scheme had come to an end. These practices included bench-terraces for annual cropping, protection of river banks, compost manufacture, stall-feeding of livestock, etc.; in a nutshell, the adoption of a system of carefully planned land usage throughout this densely populated and vital catchment area. The scheme reached its peak of achievement in 1954. Opposition had, however, been spreading for some time to the restrictions imposed on traditional methods of agriculture. This led in 1955 to organized opposition to all forms of agricultural practices other than the traditional ones, and widespread defiance of established authority.

Kilosa District.—The lessons learnt in the Ulugurus have been applied to the mountains in the Kilosa District. There is less urgency in Kilosa as the main water catchment summits are already declared forest reserves and the population on the steep slopes is relatively sparse. A forestry scheme of softwood planting in the Ukaguru mountains started in 1956 and will further protect the headwaters of two of the main permanent rivers.

The Veterinary Department has a ranch on the Mkata plains, on which immature cattle are fattened and the cash proceeds devoted to the production of good class bulls which will be used for the improvement of the 'Tanganyika National Herd' (which is almost exclusively in African hands). Tsetse fly has been excluded from the central part and has been pushed back to the broken hilly wooded country where control operations are uneconomic. The scheme is important as it shows that large areas of reputedly useless swamp land in a very strategic position on the central railway line can become of great economic importance to the territory.

The Kilombero Valley.—The great agricultural potentialities of the Kilombero valley have attracted attention for many years. The valley covers an area of approximately 2,000 square miles, and runs in a north-easterly direction from

Utengule in the south-west of the Ulanga District to the junction of the Kilombero and Msolwa rivers in the north-east. In length it is approximately 110 miles and varies in width from seven to thirty-five miles at an average elevation of 800 feet above sea level. The general picture of the valley itself is made up of three distinct parts, the escarpment, the eroded *miombo* foothills and the flats or alluvial fans.

The German authorities carried out a survey in 1909 and 1910 (Rufiji-Nyasa Expedition) seeking a possible railway route through the valley, and a comprehensive survey of the alignment for a rail link from the Central Line of Tanganyika to Manda on Lake Nyasa was subsequently undertaken by the British authorities and a report issued in 1929. In 1928, a detailed reconnaissance of the valley was carried out by A. M. Telford, of the Sudan Plantations Syndicate, in order to assess the prospects of agricultural development.[1] Telford reported that his investigations indicated that there were approximately 250,000 acres of fertile soils suitable for agricultural development. In May, 1952, Sir Alexander Gibb and Partners and Overseas Consultants Inc. submitted their report on the Central African Rail Link Development Survey which deals in part with the Kilombero valley.[2] The rail link survey team, which included agricultural experts, also reported that in their view the valley possessed natural advantages of soil and climate which would permit the cultivation of a wide range of agronomic and horticultural produce on at least a quarter of a million acres. In 1951, R. F. Loxton, assisted by a small team, was appointed by the Government to undertake a land use survey; and a detailed report, covering an area of 300 to 400 square miles between the Lumeno river at Ifakara and the Ruipa river, was produced.[3]

Still more recently the Rufiji Basin Survey team has conducted investigations in the Kilombero valley and an experimental farm has been opened on the Lumemo river near Ifakara to provide more information regarding suitable methods of agricultural irrigation.

The economy of the Ulanga District and the Kilombero valley itself is based entirely on agricultural production. The total cattle population is only some 4,000 to 5,000 head, the fishing industry is still in its early stages, and there are as yet few indications of any substantial mineral potential. The climate, rainfall and the soils of the valley, however, make it possible to grow almost the whole range of agricultural and horticultural crops. Cotton, maize, sugarcane, tobacco, sun-flower, castor and miscellaneous vegetables and fruits are at present successfully grown. Interplanting is frequently practical, the second crop coming to maturity in the moisture remaining in the soil well into the dry season. Paddy is the principal crop of the lower flood plains and production is estimated at approximately 6,000 to 8,000 tons per annum. The output of cotton is not substantial but it is considered that some of the high land lying south-east of the river and with medium texture soils would be suitable for cotton production on a larger scale, and experiments are being undertaken at the Ilonga Cotton Experimental Station to improve the yield and quality of cotton, attention being

---

[1]"Report on the Development of the Kilombero Valley" by A. M. Telford. Government Printer, Dar es Salaam.

[2]Report on Central African Rail Link Development Survey (Overseas Consultants Inc. (New York) and Sir Alexander Gibb and Partners, London.)

[3]Kilombero Valley Land Use Survey: Block A. R. F. Loxton. Government Printer, Dar es Salaam.

directed to variety and strain trials and to pest control measures. Cotton ginneries exist at Malinyi, Kiberege and Mwaya. Ifakara is the commercial and trading centre of the district and the value of goods purchased by Africans at Ifakara has been assessed at over £20,000 per annum.

The Rail Link Survey Team estimated that in the aggregate there are not less than ten million cubic feet of good quality timber in the Kilombero forests.

The valley is, however, subject to tsetse fly infestation. In 1945 a major reorganization of the African population into sleeping sickness settlements was carried out and these have done much to combat the spread of the disease. Reported cases of sleeping sickness are few at the moment but a reappearance of the disease in epidemic proportions is always a possibility demanding constant vigilance.

It seems likely that the valley flats could best be utilized for the production of paddy by means of irrigational works in selected areas rather than for sugar cane cultivation which would require a major drainage and flood control plan, a vast and costly undertaking. The extension of survey work and the formulation of an overall land use plan might open up the possibility of other crops such as cotton and sugar cane.

Rufiji Valley.—The Ruaha and Kilombero rivers combine to form the Rufiji for the last hundred miles to the sea. Much of the population of the Rufiji District lives along its banks and round the delta, cultivating rice and cotton. Prospects for large-scale development are as hopeful here as for the Kilombero. Both are likely to produce very large tonnages of paddy, and perhaps cotton, but the conditions are very different.

The Rufiji river is liable to disastrous floods which sweep away all crops. These occur with increasing frequency as the natural cover in the vast catchment area disappears with growing population and cultivation. It is therefore necessary first to control the flow of the main river by the construction of large dams to restrain the water and to allow irrigation of the flood plain.

The Food and Agriculture Organization has sent experts to assist in planning the future development and Mr. Simansky and his team have already spent some time on the whole Ruaha-Rufiji river system. They report very favourably and have chosen a number of sites for dams and for experimental irrigation on a small scale by pumping. The gauging figures will take some years to compile before large capital expenditure can be put into individual works. Much work has been done on another aspect of the problem, the introduction of mechanical cultivation to a rural native economy. The ploughing scheme started in 1950 is no longer working but the demonstration has resulted in the appreciation by the African cultivators of the advantages of mechanical cultivation over the traditional hand cultivation. There are now ten African-owned tractors working in the valley. Most of their owners are still in some financial difficulty as they have little experience either in working tractors or handling money. They are however very keen and are showing much zeal and initiative.

Mlali Irrigation Scheme (Morogoro District). A small scheme for growing rice and off-season crops by irrigation is being carried out on one of the head-waters of the Ngerengere river in the Morogoro District. This will command some 300 acres of land but it is a pioneer scheme both technically and in land use control. When the proper relationship between the people, the managing committee, the Native Authority and Government has been proved in practice other and larger schemes of the same sort can be started.

Ruvu River (Morogoro, Kisarawe and Bagamoyo Districts).—There have been a number of plans to make the best use of this river and its fertile valley. The most important initial problem is the control of floods with the subsequent provision of irrigation. Little electrical power could be generated by harnessing the river.

A master plan for the valley is being drawn up at the present time. Some land has been given out for dairy farms west of the river at its crossing with the new Morogoro/Dar es Salaam road and also for ranching west of the river and north and south of the road. An area has also been given out for sugar cane farming and manufacture of sugar north of the river downstream of the bridge. A great deal of interest is being shown by potential users in the valley. A small fishing industry exists which is likely to benefit as a result of the implementation of the plans.

Dams in Bagamoyo District.—Apart from the main river systems in this province water is scarce over a wide belt between the mountains and the coastal strip. Much of the Bagamoyo District suffers from this handicap and domestic supplies up country are so unreliable that much good land is not being used. A programme of dam building and the provision of lined wells will, it is hoped, enable this rather backward district to escape the economic vicious circle of poverty and lack of resources and make the best of its natural advantages.

Undeveloped Areas in the Morogoro District.—Reference has been made to the Kilombero, Rufiji and Ruvu rivers and plans to use their fertile valleys; also to the Mkata plain which may have a big future in ranching and breeding of cattle. Parts of Bagamoyo District, where water is to be provided for domestic use and stock, should fill up under increasing African population pressure from the estates and towns along the central railway.

There remain two fairly large areas about which nothing has been said and little is known. These are the plains areas in the north and south of Morogoro District. In the north some work has been done on the prospects of sugar planting, in the south a permanent bridge across the Mgeta river at Kisaki has opened up a good deal of country suitable for increased African settlement and cotton cultivation on the edge of the Selous Game Reserve. As these areas are opened up they will undoubtedly be developed agriculturally, mostly by African settlement.

NON-AFRICAN AGRICULTURAL PRODUCTION

Morogoro and Kilosa are important centres of the sisal-growing industry and travellers on the Central Line will see row after row of these symmetrical but unlovely plants extending on each side of the railway into the dim distance. Production over the past five years has been as follows:—

1952	...	42,000 tons	...	£4,000,000
1953	...	46,000 ,,	...	£3,830,400
1954	...	47,500 ,,	...	£2,870,000
1955	...	42,400 ,,	...	£2,400,000
1956	...	48,000 ,,	...	£2,800,000

Other crops produced by non-Africans are maize (nearly 6,500 tons in 1956, mostly from the Kilosa District), copra, kapok, sugar, sorghum, castor, sunflower, cowpea, gram, rice, papain and rubber. Kapok production is increasing with the continued high prices obtained, having risen from 135 tons in 1951 to 950 tons in 1956, valued at £180,000.

An Indian School of Agriculture, to serve the needs of Indian youths in both Kenya and Tanganyika, was established at Morogoro in 1951, with accommodation for 30 pupils. At no time were more than 27 pupils on the roll and, in view of the fact that the land available near the school proved insufficient for practical farming purposes, the school was closed down in 1954 until a larger unit could be obtained. Two thousand acres have been acquired on the Wami plains 35 miles north of Morogoro and the school restarted there in 1956.

INDUSTRIES

Sisal has been mentioned above, also the production of copra, which are two of the province's most important industries.

Timber is also produced, one of the two large licensees in the Morogoro District providing about 2,500 tons annually, most of which goes to Dar es Salaam. Timber is also produced in the Kisarawe, Kilosa and Ulanga Districts, some 5,000 tons of sawn timber being prepared in the province as a whole. The mangrove concessions in Rufiji District also constitute an important asset and produce about £10,000 annually.

Dairy farming is practised near Dar es Salaam, mainly to provide the capital with milk. The capital's needs are also met from the Kingolwira Prison Farm near Morogoro, which produces some 80,000 gallons of milk a year, most of which is sent to Dar es Salaam. The ranching scheme on the Mkata Plains has been mentioned above.

At Turiani in the foothills of the Nguru Mountains an investigation has been made of the area's suitability for sugar production. This appears promising in limited areas.

There are many rice and flour mills in the province and fourteen cotton ginneries.

MINERALS

The province has long been notable for the production of mica, principally in the Morogoro District, where two mica cutting factories have been established. This mineral has also been found in payable quantities in the Kilosa and Bagamoyo Districts.

Kaolin (china clay) has been mined in a small way from the very extensive deposit of kaolin sandstone which occurs in the Pugu Hills astride the railway and only 17 miles from Dar es Salaam.

Salt is produced in the Dar es Salaam, Bagamoyo and Kisarawe Districts by solar evaporation of sea water, annual production being worth about £56,000.

Graphite is found in the Morogoro, Kilosa and Ulanga Districts. Garnets and phosphatic limestones occur in the Morogoro District, but there has been no commercial production.

The B.P./Shell Petroleum Development Company chose the island of Mafia for the site of their first deep well to test the oil possibilities of the coastal region, followed by a second deep test well in the neighbouring territory of Zanzibar.

13

Both sites were dry but yielded much valuable geological information. Geological, geophysical, seismic and topographical surveys, and core-drilling to ascertain geological structure, have been carried out and are continuing in the coastal region of the Eastern and Southern Provinces.

ADMINISTRATIVE STATIONS[1]

Morogoro.[2] Morogoro[3] is situated on the edge of the plain at the foot of the Uluguru Mountains at an altitude of 1,600 feet above sea level. Its day temperature is often high, but nights are cool. It is a key communications centre and a place of rapidly growing importance. It is 126 miles from Dar es Salaam by rail and slightly less by the new arterial road (opened in 1954). From it another new road has been constructed to the south-west, through Mikumi on the Kilosa-Ifakara road, to connect with the Iringa-Kilosa road at the Ruaha bridge, thus shortening the journey from Iringa to Morogoro by 52 miles and providing a link with the southern part of the territory of vital importance. Morogoro is also the point on the Central Line whence the road departs to connect with the Tanga Line at Korogwe.

In 1952 the Morogoro Township contained 10,064 Africans, 1,210 Asians and 203 Europeans.

The District Commissioner is assisted by two district officers. A Resident Magistrate and representatives of the Agricultural, Forest, Water, Public Works, Medical, Labour, Lands and Surveys, Education, Game, Judicial, Mines, Prisons, E.A.R. & H. and Posts and Telecommunications departments and of the Police Force are normally stationed there. In addition, the headquarters of the Forest Department is situated at Morogoro.

Kilosa.[4]—The township lies at the point where the railway enters the narrow gap, or rift, running right through the mountain chain, providing a perfectly graded line of communication from the coastal belt to the central plateau. It is hot and oppressive to live in, though nights are cool. Sanitation measures have greatly improved the health of the inhabitants and the vagaries of the Mkondoa river, debouching from the mountains into the almost level plains, have been controlled by bunding.

In 1952 there were 2,663 Africans, 405 Asians and 48 Europeans in the town. Besides the three Administrative Officers there are normally a Resident Magistrate and representatives of the Medical, Agricultural, Public Works, Labour, Water Development, Survey, and Veterinary Departments, and of the Police Force in Kilosa.

There are direct communications by main road north to Korogwe and Mpwapwa, south to Mahenge and Iringa, east to Morogoro and Dar es Salaam, but no direct road westwards along the railway route. There is no satisfactory air strip anywhere in the district.

---

[1]For further information see table on p. 542.

[2]For further details of the town see "Tanganyika: A Review of its Resources and their Development", p. 817.

[3]In pre-German times a headman instituted a toll at the crossing of the river now known as the Morogoro River (then the Mwele) at the site of the present town of Morogoro (then a village called Bungodimwe). The toll was paid by travellers in kind with salt, cloth, etc., and apparently without dispute; it did, however, earn the name *Mgogoro* (Swahili for an obstacle or nuisance) for the spot. The Germans subsequently altered the name to Morogoro, finding this variation easier to pronounce.

[4]Derived from the name *Kilosa*, a solitary settler found by the Germans living on the site of the present town.

Mahenge.—Mahenge is the district headquarters of Ulanga.[1] It was at one time the provincial headquarters of a province, now abolished, which comprised the Ulanga and Songea Districts. A company of the King's African Rifles used to be stationed there in those days. It is a very pleasant and quiet hill station with a cool climate, situated at 3,256 feet on the edge of the Mahenge massif looking over the Kilombero plain. It is 168 miles by road from Kilosa and 200 from Morogoro by the new main road from Dar es Salaam to Iringa which crosses the old road to Kilosa at Mikumi. An airstrip has been prepared at Lupiro near the edge of the Kilombero flood plain.

In 1954 the minor settlement contained 500 Africans, 14 Asians and 17 Europeans. The District Commissioner is assisted by one district officer and representatives of the Medical and Agricultural Departments are stationed there.

Kisarawe.[2]—The headquarters station of the district was carved out of thick bush covering a hilltop in 1950, and now forms one of the more attractively laid out stations in the territory. Although only twenty miles from Dar es Salaam,[3] and only 950 feet above sea level, it is appreciably cooler than the capital. It is situated just off the old main road to Morogoro and from it a road goes south-westwards to Maneromango and beyond.

The District Commissioner is assisted by two district officers and representatives of the Agricultural and Forest Departments are normally stationed there.

Bagamoyo.[4]—This township had its origin in the trade between Zanzibar and the mainland in the days of Seyyid Said in the first half of last century. It is a good dhow harbour, that is to say it has a good broad sandy beach uncovered at low tide and suitable for beaching. It lies opposite Zanzibar and was the chief starting point of caravans to the interior.

The German Government built an impressive palace here for the Governor of German East Africa and this is used as the district office and the District Commissioner's quarters.

---

[1]The local (Kipogoro) name for a billhook (a sharp piece of metal fastened to the end of a stick, used for clearing the bush) is *hengo*. Hence *uhenge* means clearing, *mahenge* being the plural. It is thought that the first people who came to the area found it covered in bush, which they cleared, calling the place Mahenge. In the Kipogoro vernacular *lulanga* means a mighty, powerful person. The main river of the district was given this name and it has also been taken for the district, though the first letter has disappeared.

[2]The name *Kisarawe* seems to have been derived from the local vernacular name (*Msarawe*) of a large tree in a valley nearby which was famous for its spring giving abundant pure water.

[3]Part of the present site of Dar es Salaam was originally called Mzizima. It is generally agreed that its present name is a shortened version of *Bandar es Salaam*, meaning harbour or haven of peace, and that this name was given to the place by Sultan Majid of Zanzibar in about 1866, when he established a base there. There are two different explanations as to the reason for the Sultan's choice of name. One is that it was merely because he succeeded in establishing his settlement peacefully, without opposition, and the other is that he regarded the place as a haven of peace in comparison with his own headquarters at Zanzibar, where he felt insecure, probably because of the intrigues of his brothers, Thwain and Barghash. In addition to these explanations it has been suggested, however, that the first part of the name may not have come from the Arabic word *bandar* (harbour) at all but from the word *dar* (Swahili *dari*) meaning a large house or a country. Thus it is suggested that early Arab travellers up-country may have christened the area Dar us Salaam (or Dar-ul Islaam) as being a relatively peaceful place in contrast to the interior which they probably called Dar-ul Harb, denoting a lawless, heathen country.

[4]The name *Bagamoyo* comes, it is said, from *bwaga moyo* (Swahili) meaning the place where we give up hope or lay down the burden of our hearts, a name coined by the slaves who had their last contact with their own country there before the voyage to Zanzibar.

With the abolition of the slave trade and the growth of Dar es Salaam the town has lost nearly all its importance. It has many historical associations; one of the first missions in East Africa was established there in 1868, and Livingstone, Stanley and Emin Pasha are among the many famous men who stayed there and are remembered in local traditions. Scars of the British naval bombardment of 1916 are still to be seen. The original slave markets have gone but there are many relics of the early days, including the blockhouse that guarded the caravan route out of the town to the west.

Both in the town and out in the district at Utondwe, Winde, Kaole and Mbweni, there are archæological remains of early Asian settlement.

The main communication is by road to Dar es Salaam, 44 miles away. The road northward crosses the Ruvu river near the town and then forks for Pangani (92 miles) and Handeni (130 miles). Both roads are passable in the dry season only.

There were 3,300 Africans, 250 Arabs, 192 Indians and 10 Europeans at the time of the census in 1952. The District Commissioner is assisted by one district officer and there is a representative of the Agricultural Department stationed there.

Utete.[1]—Utete lies beside the Rufiji river on its right bank and is built on the only solid rising ground for many miles along the river.

The Germans built a fort there which has been used ever since for office and Government quarters. Two new quarters have, however, recently been built. The fort is of the standard design used in many parts of the territory and remains in remarkably good preservation, like those at Dodoma, Old Shinyanga and Tukuyu.

The station is oppressively hot for much of the year, being some forty miles from the coast and little above sea level, but it now has its own electricity and water supply. It is 120 miles from Dar es Salaam by road but communications depend on the pontoon over the Rufiji river, which can only work in the dry season. During the rains it is usual for the river to flood for many miles beyond its banks.

A dry weather road to the south connects with Kilwa Kivinje (97 miles) and Lindi (200 miles) while district roads give communications up and down the river in the dry season.

In 1952 the Utete Minor Settlement contained 800 Africans, 15 Asians and 7 Europeans. There are three Administrative Officers and a representative of the Agricultural Department is normally stationed there.

Mafia.[2]—The headquarters are at Kilindoni[3], on high land facing north-west towards the mainland. There is a dhow landing beach but the approach is shallow and steamers must anchor well out. There is a small trading centre and an aerodrome suitable for Dakotas which call regularly on the coastal service (E.A. Airways).

---

[1]The name *Utete* comes from the Swahili word *tete* (*matete*) meaning reeds, which were at one time abundant in the area.

[2]It has been suggested that the name of the island itself—Mafia—is a contraction (*Maafya*) of the Swahili *Mahali pa Afya*, a healthy place. Another version of the origin of the name is that it comes from the Arabic *Mafiha hadi* meaning "nobody there"—the story being that when the Arabs launched an attack on the island (at Bweni in the north, near Ras Mkumbi) the local people fled and the Arabs found nobody there. Whatever the derivation, the island was originally known as Chole and the old German Boma as Chole Mjini (spelt "Tshole Mjini" on old German maps).

[3]Swahili for a look-out post—an apt name for a customs post.

The District Commissioner occupies a spacious Arab-type house built by the Zanzibar Government in 1917.

Operations against the Königsberg, the German cruiser lying up in the Rufiji Delta, were carried out by aircraft from Mafia island after it was taken over from the Germans in 1915.

Communications used to be by heliograph to a hill on the mainland about half way to Dar es Salaam, but there is now daily wireless communication with Dar es Salaam post office.

There is constant but irregular dhow traffic between Kilindoni and the mainland and from the Rufiji delta to Dar es Salaam. The Government motor boat is designed for travelling between the islands and across the Mafia channel. There is no regular steamer service, though a lighter calls for copra at intervals.

PLACES OF INTEREST TO THE VISITOR AND SPORTING FACILITIES

The visitor to Dar es Salaam will find much to interest him in and around the capital and will be able to enjoy most forms of sport (except big game shooting!). There is an information kiosk, run by the East African Tourist Travel Association, near the Customs jetty in the harbour and visitors can there obtain copies of a "Guide to Dar es Salaam" and of the "Tanganyika Guide", which will provide them with much useful information about the country and its capital and suggest places to visit during a short stay. Copies of these publications may also be obtained from most bookshops in Dar es Salaam.

As regards places outside Dar es Salaam, the visitor will probably wish to visit Bagamoyo, 44 miles away on a road which has recently been much improved. As indicated above, in this fascinating old Arab town, with its magnificent carved doors, are to be found many relics of the old days. Nearby is the Holy Ghost Mission, the first mission station to be established in the territory.

The visitor who wishes to see something of the sisal industry will find a factory in operation at Msasani, on the outskirts of Dar es Salaam, or, if he has time to see something of the hinterland, near Morogoro, where, in addition, he will be able to see something of the densely inhabited Uluguru Mountains and, if he is a fisherman, enjoy some good trout fishing.

For the sea fisherman sport can be had off Dar es Salaam, and the big game fisherman will find first class fishing in the Mafia Channel.[1]

Most of the game listed on a major game licence is to be found in the province, especially in the Rufiji and Ulanga Districts and in the Mkata plains country of the Kilosa and Morogoro Districts, but some of the larger game animals are found in all districts, and sometimes in unexpected places: lion and leopard have occasionally been seen on the outskirts of Dar es Salaam, a buffalo was shot recently on one of the islands at the entrance to the harbour, and hippo are sometimes seen in the harbour itself.

A game protected area on the new Morogoro-Iringa Road from forty miles out of Morogoro to Mikumi produces a fine display of the larger game animals at most times of the year in the early morning or late afternoon.

---

[1]See also "Sea Fishing" on p. 489.

THE LAKE PROVINCE

SITUATION

The Lake Province covers a large area, 39,000 square miles, (excluding water), in a great arc round that portion of Lake Victoria which is situated in Tanganyika. It may be divided into three parts, with markedly different characteristics. The central part of the province comprises the Sukuma Districts of Mwanza (which is divided into an Urban and a Rural District), Kwimba, Maswa and Shinyanga, to which must now be added the Geita District, which is becoming an overflow area for Usukuma. The eastern division contains the districts of Musoma, North Mara and Ukerewe. On the west are the districts of Bukoba, Biharamulo and Ngara. Provincial headquarters are situated at Mwanza. Of the twelve districts only three, Maswa, Shinyanga and Ngara, do not have a frontage on the lake. The province's boundary with Kenya on the north-east is an artificial one, being part of a straight line drawn from the north of Kilimanjaro to the intersection of the first degree of south latitude with the lake shore, and in North Mara it bisects several of the tribes. Proceeding southwards, the eastern boundary of the Musoma and Maswa Districts goes through the Serengeti Plains and the empty and little-known country near Lake Eyasi. After bisecting the lake it then follows the line of the Sibiti and Manyonga rivers and follows tribal boundaries separating the Nyamwezi areas from those of the Sukuma and Zinza. It then makes a loop to include the Ngara District, which geographically forms part of Ruanda-Urundi, and follows the line of the Kagera River to the Uganda border in the north.

PHYSICAL FEATURES

Generally speaking, the province is flat in the middle, the greater part of Usukuma being situated at an altitude of 3,500–4,000 feet above sea level, gradually rising towards higher land in both east and west. The Serengeti Plains are at a general level of about 5,000 feet, and the highest point in the North Mara District reaches 6,000 feet. Similarly, a large part of the Bukoba District lies above the 5,000-foot contour and most of the Ngara District is also situated above this level. The country in these highland areas wears a very different aspect to that of Usukuma, a difference which is further accentuated by the greater rainfall which these areas receive. In Usukuma the general impression is of a flat rolling country, almost treeless in parts, with granitic outcrops studding the plains. In parts of the Musoma, Geita and Biharamulo Districts there are large areas of wooded grassland and, especially in the Geita-Biharamulo area, of *miombo* bush. Large parts of the Bukoba District have an aspect different from that of most other places in the territory, with rolling, almost downland, country interspersed with outcrops of rock and the banana plantations of the Haya.

The rivers in the province, with the exception of those which drain into Lake Eyasi, flow into Lake Victoria. The more important are the Mori, in the North Mara District; the Mara, which separates that district from the Musoma District to the south; the Grumeti, in the Musoma District; the Mbalangeti, which forms the boundary between the Musoma and Maswa Districts; the Simiyu, which drains a large part of the Maswa and Kwimba Districts; the Ruvuvu, far in the west, which separates the Bugufi and Busubi areas of the Ngara District; and the Kagera, which forms the international boundary between Biharamulo/Bukoba

183

and Ruanda-Urundi. Of these the largest is the Kagera, which is navigable for some 80 miles from its mouth, near the boundary with Uganda. The Bugonzi Falls, 20 miles south of Bukoba, are 530 feet high.

Apart from Lake Victoria itself and a portion of Lake Eyasi, there are no very large lakes in the province. In Bukoba District, however, there are Lakes Ikimba (150 square miles) and Burigi (120 square miles), and a whole string of lakes and swamps along the river Kagera on the inter-territorial boundary. The most attractive of these is Rweru Rwabishonga, christened "Windermere" by Grant when he passed by it in 1862. It is so protected by the surrounding hills that its surface is never rippled by wind. There is also a number of small lakes or ponds—and a considerable number of dams—throughout the province which provide indispensable supplies of water and, incidentally, resting places for an astonishing variety of wild fowl.

CLIMATE

The climate of the lake region generally has already been described in chapter one above; here it will suffice to state that the climate of the province is influenced by three main factors, proximity to the lake, altitude, and situation with respect to the prevailing wind, which is from east to west. Thus the areas closely bordering the lake normally receive a good and sufficient rainfall for the growing of the staple crops, but those to the east and south at some distance from the lake, e.g. parts of the Musoma, Maswa, Shinyanga and Biharamulo Districts, are not nearly so well favoured. The highland areas in the Musoma and North Mara Districts, although lying to the east, nevertheless receive a good rainfall, because of their altitude. To the west, the combination of altitude, proximity to the lake and favourable situation with regard to the prevailing wind results in a rainfall throughout the coastal parts of the Bukoba District of some 80 inches a year.

The rainy season, particularly in the better favoured areas, is not so marked as in other parts of the territory, and in Bukoba, for example, rain is expected every month of the year. Nevertheless, it is generally found that the heaviest rain falls in the period from March to May, and there is often a break in the rains before this period.

Statistics of rainfall over the past seven years are given in the table below:—

Station	Altitude	Average	1950	1951	1952	1953	1954	1955	1956
Shinyanga*	4,000	30·91 (26 years)	30·79	48·88	38·17	24·95	21·12	24·39	38·59
Maswa	4,400	30·79 (29 years)	30·29	46·00	34·69	26·51	27·11	21·51	30·82
Ngudu (Kwimba) ...	4,000	31·08 (27 years)	25·51	50·43	20·30	15·76	18·18	31·55	29·86
Mwanza	3,700	39·17 (31 years)	36·76	58·54	37·03	34·06	38·00	34·30	37·67
Geita†	4,200	37·96 (21 years)	30·97	51·28	35·50	34·37	36·34	30·57	50·16
Nansio (Ukerewe) ...	3,875	44·28 (7 years)	39·14	59·75	36·27	‡	46·62	49·90	35·11
Musoma	3,764	30·29 (35 years)	37·57	37·37	30·77	24·15	39·95	35·17	30·40
Tarime (N. Mara) ...	5,000	52·75 (24 years)	49·07	60·58	47·90	53·79	53·84	44·41	49·14
Bukoba	3,753	80·10 (36 years)	80·21	95·60	75·20	96·26	69·68	77·07	71·07
Biharamulo ...	4,850	38·08 (35 years)	30·51	62·94	31·85	35·62	37·81	35·04	39·69
Ngara	5.900	40·36 (27 years)	47·21	39·57	36·36	46·43	35·30	42·41	37·76

*Recordings made at Old Shinyanga, nearby.
†Recordings made at Geita Gold Mine, nearby.
‡Records incomplete.

POPULATION

The province contains nearly two million people, a quarter of the total population of the territory. The population map on page 283 shows that the most thickly populated areas are Usukuma, Ukerewe, the western part of the Musoma

District, North Mara, the coastal half of the Bukoba District and the Bugufi area of the Ngara District. The unoccupied areas are those bordering on the Serengeti Plains and parts of the Geita, Biharamulo and Bukoba Districts, although there are other small areas, such as in the western part of the Shinyanga District and the eastern part of Busubi, which are also very thinly populated.

By combining the results of the 1948 (complete) census and of the 1952 (partial) census the following results are obtained for the province:—

District	Area in sq. miles	Euro-pean	Indian	Goan	Arab	Somali	Colo-ured	Other	Total non-African	African	Total
Shinyanga	3,580	269	661	26	968	68	12	–	2,004	212,503	214,507
Maswa ...	8,914	57	262	–	216	4	18	1	558	244,968	245,526
Kwimba	1,886	57	451	–	24	–	16	1	549	237,962	238,511
Mwanza	3,820	349	3,027	55	408	–	39	3	3,881	} 438,003	442,902
Geita ...	6,251	195	272	–	95	5	41	26	634		
Ukerewe	1,475	37	233	–	97	–	16	1	384		
Musoma	6,767	153	888	5	10	43	25	8	1,132	141,527	142,659
North Mara	4,257	67	141	–	1	–	6	1	216	115,037	115,253
Bukoba ...	9,685	272	999	16	619	–	42	–	1,948	299,860	301,808
Biharamulo	4,427	29	38	–	8	–	7	–	82	49,849	49,931
Ngara ...	1,093	16	26	–	51	–	28	–	121	104,706	104,827
Totals	*52,155	1,501	6,998	102	2,497	120	250	41	11,509	1,844,415	1,855,924

The European population is largely made up of government officials, missionaries and those engaged in mining or commerce; there are very few settlers in the province. The comparatively large Arab population consists mostly of petty traders, and most of the Indians are small shop-keepers.

In the districts of Shinyanga, Maswa, Kwimba and Mwanza the Sukuma form the overwhelming majority (96½ per cent in Kwimba) of the African population. Similarly in the Bukoba District the Haya represented 86 per cent of the population at the 1948 census. But in the other districts in the province there is not this predominance of one tribe. In the Biharamulo District the Zinza form half the population, the remainder being made up of a number of other tribes with the Ha the next most numerous. In the Ngara District the Hangaza comprise 52 per cent and the Subi 45 per cent. The Musoma District contains an unusual number of different tribes: the Jita 21 per cent, the Kwaya 18 per cent, the Zanaki 16 per cent, the Kuria 11 per cent, the Nguruim 8 per cent, the Ikoma 7 per cent, the Ikizu 6 per cent, the Sukuma (Shashi) 4 per cent and the Luo (Simbiti) 4 per cent. In the North Mara District the Kuria and the Luo are about equally represented (25,000 Kuria and 23,000 Luo at the 1948 census). The population of the Ukerewe District is largely made up of Jita (40 per cent), Kerewe (30 per cent) and Kara (15 per cent); in the Geita District the Zinza comprise about 40 per cent, the Sukuma about 20 per cent and the Subi about 15 per cent.

SUKUMALAND

The area of Sukumaland, containing the six districts of Mwanza Town and Mwanza Rural, Kwimba, Maswa and Shinyanga with, now, the Geita District, covers over 20,000 square miles and has a population of about a million Africans and a stock population of about two million units (five sheep or goats=one head of cattle). The general aspect, as has been stated, is one of wide, rolling, almost

---

*Includes lake areas.

treeless plains, interspersed with rocky outcrops and low ridges of hills, few rising more than 1,000 feet above the general level, which varies between 3,500 and 4,000 feet above the sea.   There are large areas of *mbuga*: sunken areas, usually of black cotton soil, which are liable to flooding during the rains.   The average annual rainfall is in the neighbourhood of 30 inches but, since this often falls in localized storms of great intensity and of uneven distribution, the effect on vegetation is not as great as might be thought.   The whole of Usukuma has been the scene for some years now of one of the more ambitious and extensive development plans in the territory (see page 191 below for details).

The Sukuma.—The Sukuma, who form the northern[1] branch of the largest racial group in Tanganyika (the Sukuma-Nyamwezi and associated tribes) comprise the vast majority of the inhabitants of Sukumaland.   They are a Bantu people of medium height, dark brown in colour.   They are industrious cultivators and stock-owners, until recently very conservative but now moving in the direction of co-operatives and awakening politically.   Unlike such tribes as the Masai, they are not primarily a cattle people and treat the possession of stock as an investment at a very high rate of interest, as it undoubtedly is, particularly since the virtual elimination of rinderpest.   Both the men and women take part in the agricultural work of the household, and men, women and children look after the cattle and small stock.

The earlier inhabitants of Sukumaland seem to have been primarily hunters who also practised agriculture.   As their first requirement was a well-watered country abounding with game, they sought bushland rather than grassland and consequently were not attracted by the dry thorn savanna in the east.   As they settled down to agricultural pursuits they seem to have congregated in groups of about a hundred or more persons under the leadership of *Batemi* (*kutema*=to cut down trees in the bush).   Such settlements had little communication with each other and there seems, similarly, to have been no real conception of tribal unity. It was at this stage that immigrants of Hamitic origin entered the country from the west side of Lake Victoria.   Each of the present Sukumaland chiefdoms has its own traditions which tend to increase the importance of its own *batemi*, and to compete therein with chiefdoms ruled by other branch lines of the same family.   It seems that these Hamitic immigrants were not military conquerors but infiltrated gradually into the area and were accepted as leaders by common consent.   As Cory points out[2] "These immigrants offered many advantages to the latent demand for leadership.   They were ideal judges because they were fully unbiased, belonging to none of the local clans.   For that sole reason they were also the best arbitrators for the just distribution of the spoils of the chase and of clan warfare.   They may also have impressed the indigenous population by superior mental and physical qualities."   In this way the formation of the various chiefdoms came about and the *batemi* of today all trace their descent from some immigrant of Hamitic origin.

D. W. Malcolm describes the traditional (southern) Sukuma village as follows:—

"The Sukuma village was usually situated on high ground if not actually under the shadow of a granite tor.   It was roughly circular in shape and protected by euphorbia (*manyara*) and thorn hedges or even stone ramparts

---

[1]Usukuma means "North" in the Nyamwezi-Sukuma language.

[2]"The Ntemi: Traditional Rights of a Sukuma Chief in Tanganyika", by Hans Cory, Macmillan, 1951.

which are still to be seen amongst the granite outcrops, particularly in the southwest where the name of Mirambo, the Nyamwezi raider, was no myth. Within these fortifications lived the whole village community with their stock, and the present organization of collective labour is a natural result of conditions in which it would have been dangerous to hoe alone. The arable and pasture lands of the village were in its immediate vicinity and were often limited to the area in which the alarm could be heard.

With the advent of the Germans came the practical cessation of tribal warfare and it became safe to settle further from the centre of the village. The German authorities are said to have prohibited the system of land sales between individuals which had been evolved in some places during the period of extreme congestion, and people anxious to obtain good land began to move further afield and cleared new areas such as the present site of Ngudu, the headquarters of the Kwimba District, which was at that time bush country inhabited by buffalo and other game. The spread appears to have been rapid and in a period of about 20 years the occupied area must have been considerably extended."[1]

The Bahi in the Kimali chiefdom of south-east Maswa are thought to be the remnants of an aboriginal people who now number less than 100. The Bahi do not practise agriculture or animal husbandry but live entirely on roots, wild fruits and the spoils of the chase. Malcolm says that "on several occasions the Bahi have been given cows, hoes and maize seed by the chief (to whom they are nominally subject). They keep the cows for a few days but cannot resist the temptation to eat them. They also eat the maize seed and use the hoes for making arrow heads. They prefer their own way of life. They are not taxed."[2]

NORTH MARA

The highlands of North Mara present a general appearance of sweeping downland of red soil, varied by steep hillocks and the usual granite outcrops with considerable vegetative cover in the valleys. Towards the lake the country becomes flatter, sandier and more barren.

The tribes inhabiting the area are the Kuria, Girango or Luo and the Suba.

The Kuria.—The Kuria are described as "Bantu-speaking Hamitic negroids". It seems probable that they came to their present tribal lands from the north, being driven south by encroaching Masai and Luo. Some think that in origin they are Masai and, physically, many of them much resemble the Masai. E. C. Baker[3] thus describes their physical characteristics, pointing out that there are two main types: "The one is tall and cleanly built with splendidly proportioned limbs, though with small feet and hands. The features are often definitely handsome, the face is oval and head long. The other type is often shorter and more thick-set with hands and feet that are often coarser and large in proportion to their larger and somewhat fleshy limbs than are those of the more pleasing type. The head is flatter and the face less refined. One's first inclination is to liken the first type to the Masai whom the Kuria so love to imitate and the second to the Sukuma; but neither type is so clearly defined as it is in these tribes."

---

[1]"Sukumaland: An African People and their Country", by D. W. Malcolm, O.U.P., for International African Institute, 1953.

[2]Malcolm, op. cit.

[3]In an unpublished MS.

The Kuria are intelligent but very highly-strung and temperamental. They crave excitement, finding life tedious without it, and if they cannot allay their restlessness by making war on their neighbours or stealing cattle they must find some other outlet for their energies; these of recent years have often taken the form of litigation in the local courts, but the national sport of cattle stealing still thrives. The Kuria are primarily pastoral, and agriculturists only secondarily. On the lake shore the Simbiti, a sub-tribe of the Kuria, are expert fishermen, using both fish traps and nets.

The Girango.—These people represent every degree of admixture of Kuria and Luo blood, and are the latest arrivals of an immigration which took place in small successive groups. A tendency is now spreading among the tribe to follow Luo and to neglect Kuria customs.

The Suba.—The Suba tribe consists of some 3,500 taxpayers, living mainly in the area between Mori Bay and Mara Bay in the North Mara District. Tribal history traces their descent from one Suba who lived to the north either in Kenya or Uganda. His son Irienyi was the first to reach the North Mara District. Another influx produced Msimbiti, a huntsman, and Muhacha, a fisherman, the founders of the two largest clans in the tribe. There are two other clans, the Busweta and Busurwa. It is impossible to date the arrival of the Suba in the North Mara District. The tribe lost a good deal of ground to the Luo in the course of tribal wars, and the predominant position of the Luo in the area known as Luo Imbo was consolidated with the coming of European administration. It may be that the Suba living just over the border in the Suba/Kuria chiefdom were cut off from their brothers to the south by the later immigration of the Luo.

The German administration divided the tribe into six chiefdoms despite the fact that the indigenous political structure was "segmented". The Suba are now administered by an Area President whose headquarters is at Kinesi.

The tribe grow maize and millet and fish extensively in Lake Victoria. Recently they have experimented with the growing of cotton as a cash crop. There are approximately 36,000 head of cattle in the area.

TRIBES OF THE MUSOMA DISTRICT

At the time of the 1948 census the numbers of the main tribes of the Musoma District were as follows:—

Tribe	Male	Female	Total	Percentage of District Total %
Jita	13,973	15,433	29,406	21
Kwaya	11,763	13,894	25,657	18
Zanaki	10,150	12,586	22,736	16
Kuria	7,094	8,458	15,552	11
Nguruimi	5,130	6,135	11,265	8
Ikoma	4,167	5,320	9,487	7
Ikizu	3,936	5,130	9,066	6
Sukuma	2,990	3,014	6,004	4
Luo	2,911	2,716	5,627	4
All Others	3,213	3,514	6,727	5
Total	65,327	76,200	141,527	100

It will be apparent from this table and from a glance at the Tribal Map on p. 298 that the Musoma District, like the Mbulu and Mbeya Districts, is a meeting place of many tribes, although the differences between some of them are not as marked as those between, say, the Iraqw and the Mbugwe. The Jita and Kwaya come of much the same stock, although their origins are very mixed and both spring from families of Sukuma, Zanaki, Simbiti, Kerewe, Sweta and Girango who filtered into the area in times past and settled down together. The Zanaki are of Taturu origin, allied to the Barabaig or Tatoga of the Mbulu District, with an admixture of Kuria blood from the north and a strong strain of Sukuma blood from the south. The Nguruimi and Ikoma claim to have sprung from the Sonjo of Masailand (see p. 206) but there has been a considerable admixture of Kuria blood, especially in the case of the Nguruimi. (The Kuria are described on p. 187). The Ikizu and Shashi (or Sizaki) are to all intents and purposes the same tribe and are Sukuma in origin, but related to the Ikoma, with whom they inter-marry freely.

OTHER MAIN TRIBES

The Kerewe.—The Kerewe, like so many other tribes in this section of the borderland of Lake Victoria, are of mixed origin. The first immigrants came from Uzinza, but there are now very few people on the island who can trace their origin back to these pioneers. A further wave of immigration is supposed to have come from Buha, via Uzinza and Majita, the immigrants staying a short time in Majita before proceeding to Ukerewe.

After them came people from Ihangiro (Bukoba), and their leader became the founder of the present ruling dynasty. This invasion took place a long time ago; sixteen chiefs have been counted since its arrival.

A good deal later, but still in pre-European times, the Jita, driven by famine in their own land, began to immigrate into Ukerewe in ones and twos, cutting holdings for themselves out of the land. These Jita mixed with the earlier immigrants to the island and all these people of different origins became one tribe, calling themselves the Kerewe.

The Kara.—These people live on Ukara island, about eight miles north of Ukerewe, having immigrated from Bukoba, where the inhabitants of the chiefdom of Maruku are known as Bakara.

Tradition has it that the first immigrants arrived on a floating island, which they successfully defended against foreign visitors, including the Kerewe. However, they say that formerly strangers came only rarely, as Ukara disappeared under the water and only emerged when the undesirables had passed by!

The Kara consider themselves as being ethnologically different from their neighbours, the Kerewe, although it appears that they both have a Jita element in common.

The Haya.—The Haya chiefly clans claim that their origin lies in Bunyoro in Uganda. Little is actually known of these immigrants, but traces of their history may be found in the legends of the indigenous clans. The immigrants seem to have come in family bands under the leadership of one of their members; they entered a sparsely populated country and apparently met with little opposition from the indigenous inhabitants. When they reached a place in which they decided to settle the leader probably became the family or clan head unless some of his family was already settled there, when he placed himself and his band under the existing clan head. In either case there was no further communication with the original home and the new settlers became independent units under their own clan heads. It seems that throughout a long period a continuous stream of newcomers poured into Uhaya but local tradition gives no hint of the reasons which compelled the people to start their migration to the south. (The several wars in Bunyoro which caused extensive depopulation of the country may perhaps have some bearing on it.) That the immigration was not an organized movement seems to be borne out by the fact that local clan heads were independent of each other. The descendants of the original settlement leaders are today the clan heads and not one of them is considered superior to another.

The Zinza.—These people inhabit the Buzinza peninsula, situated between the Emin Pasha Gulf and Smith Sound, but only in the regions adjacent to Lake Victoria. Inland live Rongo or Longo and Subi and an ever-increasing number of Sukuma.

Very little agriculture takes place among the Zinza, except for the perennial banana and large quantities of sweet potatoes, although latterly the planting of cotton has achieved great importance.

It is more than probable that Buzinza was originally inhabited by people of Bantu stock. At the middle or end of the 17th century it became one of the many countries which were more or less peacefully conquered by the Hamitic Hinda family who became the rulers of the country. The people speak a language which is, to all intents and purposes, identical with Kihaya.

The Rongo or Longo are supposed to be the descendants of the aborigines of the country. They were a nomadic tribe, pre-eminently iron-workers and hunters, living in scattered groups of very primitive huts in the forests, and moving from place to place as supplies of iron o e and game animals became difficult to acquire. Recent development shows a tendency to eliminate these characteristic habits of the Rongo, and many of them now live like Zinza or Sukuma, their neighbours.

The Subi.—The rulers of Burundi, Buha and Busubi all belong to the same family, whose homeland is Bunyoro in Uganda.

It is a family of Hamitic stock, and it was a member of its Rundi branch who conquered Busubi, following a decisive battle with a big hunter who had entered Busubi from Karagwe and had established there leadership over the indigenous population—men of Rundi-Bantu stock.

He was not the first man to go hunting in Busubi. The elephant hunters of Karagwe also considered Busubi as their hunting ground. The importance of elephant hunting for the economy of a chiefdom in the olden days was great, and a land with plenty of elephants enticed hunters from all the neighbouring regions. Thus the language and dialect spoken in Busubi show influences from all its neighbours. The situation has been explained as follows: A Munyambo (man from Karagwe) understands Rundi, but cannot answer correctly; a Murundi does not understand and cannot talk Nyambo; a Musubi can understand Rundi and Nyambo, and he will be understood by speakers of both.

The Hangaza.—In the first half of the 19th century the founder of the ruling dynasty in Bugufi begged from the Chief of Urundi dominion over a desolate, outlying portion of his chiefdom. As a sign of authority over the land, he was given the drum *Muhabura*. (This version of history is not accepted by the founder's descendants, however, who state that Bugufi's existence as an independent chiefdom goes back many more years than this.) The founder of the ruling dynasty was a Mtusi (Hamite), and the people who followed him into the new chiefdom were Rundi (Bantu).

The present inhabitants of Bugufi are called Hangaza and are an offshoot of the Rundi ethnic group. Though the Hangaza insist that they are somehow different from the people in Urundi, there exist, to all intents and purposes, no significant differences either in language, customs or law.

The Bugufi highlands of the Ngara District cover an area of about 250 square miles with a population of about 200 to the square mile over most of the area. The rivers Kagera and Ruvuvu form the northern and eastern boundaries and the foot-hills of these are virtually unpopulated, the people being concentrated in large villages on the top and sides of three roughly parallel ranges of undulating hills, 5,500 feet high on the average. The Kagera and Ruvuvu valleys are a thousand feet lower. Climatically the area is humid, with a rainfall of 40 inches a year between the months of September and May. The dew is very heavy and hilltops are frequently covered in cloud for several hours each day. The soil is fertile and conditions are excellent for both pastoral and agricultural activity.

In a dominant position are the pastoral Tusi, the agricultural Hutu being subordinate to them. The country was settled only in the last 200 years. It was originally a wilderness of dense forests, remnants of which still exist. [1]

AGRICULTURAL RESOURCES

Sukumaland Development Scheme.—The Sukumaland Development Scheme was designed to restore fertility to the overpopulated areas in Sukumaland by a natural resources team aided by the local authorities.

The intention has been to rehabilitate central Sukumaland, consisting of about 10,000 square miles, so as to check the deterioration of the land and improve its productive capacity, and to open up about 8,000 square miles of unoccupied land, mainly in the Geita and Maswa Districts. The staff, until the end of 1954, consisted of a team at Malya, under the chairmanship of a co-ordinating officer who was a Deputy Provincial Commissioner, composed of officers of the Agricultural, Veterinary, Forest and Water Development Departments, the executive work being carried out in the districts by district teams under the chairmanship of the District Commissioner. The total cost of the scheme is estimated to be £520,000, of which some £450,000 had been spent by 30th June, 1957.

It has been estimated that the most the soil in the area can support economically is one person to 3½ acres, or 100 persons to the square mile, together with 182 stock units. Fly-infested bush is cleared by hand labour through communal turn-outs of the tribesmen, the cleared areas being then settled under close control. The cost of clearing is merely the cost of feeding the labour involved, as no mechanical methods are used. Soil conservation methods are insisted upon. The Federal Council of Sukumaland has passed land usage

---

[1] See "A Study of Land Tenure in Bugufi" by R. de Z. Hall and H. Cory. *Tanganyika Notes and Records* No. 24, December 1947.

rules which insist on better farming methods for all African land holders and prescribe the necessity for contour ridging, grass leys, hill top and river valley reservation and limitation of stock. Grazing schemes have been planned and carried out in areas where lack of water had previously made ranching of cattle impossible, by the building of dams at strategic points. Dams are surveyed by the Water Development and Irrigation Department. The smaller ones are dug by hand labour provided by communal turn-outs and the bigger ones and those in more remote areas are constructed by the scheme's tractor units under the control of the Agricultural Department. The central stock farm at Malya, where experiments with pasture and stock breeding are undertaken, is controlled by the Veterinary Department, and grade bulls are lent free of charge to selected African farmers for the improvement of their stock.

The basis of the scheme is self-help, the peasantry being approached through their native authorities. The Sukuma are an industrious people who, given new land, are very soon able to bring it into cultivation and settle it. When the peasant starts his move from exhausted land to communally cleared areas, he is responsible for paying his own initial expenses for building and cultivation. There has been little change in the pattern of society, although a tendency has been noted to increase the cultivation of cotton, which is the local enonomic cash crop.

By 1955 the development scheme could be said to have achieved many of its objectives. New areas had been opened up, the five districts were producing more cotton and more food crops than ever before; and the general wealth of the people had increased. Socially the native authorities had realized their obligations to preserve the soil and had passed the necessary rules.

From the 1st July, 1955 the scheme came under the control of the newly formed South-East Lake County Council. The experiment no longer remained a central government concern and became the responsibility of the local authorities, paid for from local revenue. It is intended that the rehabilitation of special areas in all five districts shall continue. The development team, formerly working in Malya, has been disbanded, but the departmental officers in Mwanza are still available to give advice and guidance on the main lines of development. New record cotton crops were achieved in 1956 and 1957.

East Lake Area.—Cotton, groundnuts, rice and sesame are the main crops in the Musoma District, while in North Mara considerable areas are put under maize—the plough being commonly used here—and the surplus crops sold to the mines in the area. Much of the income of the Kuria is derived from pastoral pursuits and, similarly, the people living on the borders of the Serengeti National Park in the Musoma District are pastoralists.

On Ukerewe Island, which is blessed with a good rainfall, cotton and rice do particularly well.

On the island of Ukara, as a result of population pressure on the land, the local people had evolved an unusual and interesting system of agriculture on their own initiative, before the arrival of the European. Crops are grown on a well-planned system of rotation and include species of *Crotalaria* which are dug in as green manure, and fodder crops for stock. Stock—cattle, sheep and goats—are hand-fed in the huts and carefully bedded down, the resulting manure being taken out and placed in heaps for further decomposition. When sufficiently composted it is used on the fields. The number of stock kept is strictly limited

Mwanza Port on Lake Victoria

Photo: E.A. Railways and Harbours

Kuria Elder, North Mara District, Lake Province.

Photo: Mrs. Merrell Dalton

by the amount of fodder and grazing available. They are taken out of the huts for short periods only, for grazing and water, and are muzzled if they have to pass through standing crops.

West Lake Area.—It seems probable that Robusta coffee was introduced into the Bukoba District three or four hundred years ago. It is known that the Galla and other tribes used to take with them on a raid balls made of raw ground coffee berries, as a kind of "iron rations", and that they were well aware of its sustaining power. In fact, amongst those tribes where it was known (including the Haya of the Bukoba District) coffee is regarded as a part of the tribe's armaments and its possession was jealously guarded, only those in positions of authority being permitted to grow it.

Emin Pasha[1], in the brief period of his life when he was in the employment of the German Administration, was resident at Bukoba and one of the last things he did before he died was to lay out a large coffee nursery there and to distribute young plants amongst the local cultivators. This broke down the chiefly monopoly and, with further encouragement from the British Administration, the practice of coffee growing quickly became widespread. From 1905 to 1916 exports ranged from 200 tons to 700 tons a year, but by 1924 had reached 3,500 tons and by 1928, 7,800 tons. In 1956, 9,200 tons valued at £2,740,000 were "passed for export". [2]

Both Arabica (unwashed) and Robusta coffees are the major cash crop of the district. The whole crop is handled by the Co-operative Union. The Union provides the finance for a network of coffee nurseries and is now taking over administrative control of this service. The Coffee Board of Tanganyika provides funds for running a coffee station at Maruku which is staffed by an Agricultural Officer and a Field Officer supplied by central government. Two small sub-stations are in course of development. The work at Maruku also covers pasture and animal husbandry.

The co-operative movement, begun in 1949, has grown rapidly and there are now some 60 primary societies affiliated to the Bukoba Native Co-operative Union. It is estimated that some 90 per cent of the 70,000 African coffee growers have joined the movement and that a similar percentage of the crop is collected by the primary societies and delivered to the zonal agents.

The staple food crop in the Bukoba District is the banana, from which a kind of light beer is also made. This beer is consumed locally much as wine is consumed in France and is an essential ingredient of the diet.

The ease with which food and drink could be produced and money obtained (from coffee) has led to the growth of sociological conditions in the district which for long have given rise to anxiety, not least to the more far-seeing of the Haya themselves. One result has been the unusual number of women who for many years now have left the district, with unfortunate effects on family life. The local authorities are very much alive to the seriousness of this and other problems, and are taking steps to deal with them, but it can be appreciated that no simple or easy solution is possible.

Coffee is also grown in the Ngara District, where, as in the Bukoba District, the banana is the staple crop.

---

[1]See page 65.
[2]1955 figures were 8,500 tons at £2,120,000.

In the Biharamulo District, tsetse-infested and without either the heavy rainfall of Bukoba or the altitude of Ngara, it was essential to find a high-priced economic crop which would do well on the local soils.   Tobacco, which had long been grown in small quantities locally, filled the need and in 1931 the Virginian variety "Heavy Western" was introduced and instruction in fire-curing given.

The following figures are of production for the past five years:—

	Kilos	No. of Growers	Average Cash Receipt per Grower Shs.
1952	76,033	... 2,216	... 38/18
1953	40,970	... 1,530	... 29/94
1954	59,945	... 2,161	... 32/26
1955	31,743	... 1,320	... 38/05
1956	62,635	... 1,740	... 45/89

Tobacco is also of growing importance in the Ngara District.   Production for the past two years was as following:—

1955 ...	...	17,221	... 1,768	...	15/14
1956 ...	...	21,959	... 2,650	...	10/16

MINERALS

The Mwadui Mine of Williamson Diamonds Ltd., near Shinyanga, is not only the most important mineral occurrence in the Province, but potentially one of the richest diamond mines in the world.   The real wealth of the mine only began to be apparent in 1949 when production jumped to over £1,500,000. During the last three years (1954-56) it has averaged close on £3,000,000 per year.   At the smaller neighbouring mine of Alamasi Ltd. exports have been averaging over £100,000 for the last few years.

Geita Mine, the largest gold mine in East Africa, is also situated in the Lake Province and is operated by the Geita Gold Mining Co. Ltd., a subsidiary of Kentan Gold Areas Ltd.   Production in 1956 was valued at just under half a million pounds.   Other gold mines are situated in the Geita, Musoma and North Mara Districts.

The tin mines in the Karagwe area of Bukoba District have been producing small quantities of tin for many years, but production has been declining. Kyerwa Syndicate Limited, the major concern, is now erecting a 1,000-tons-per-day plant which should make a substantial contribution to output in the near future.   Wolfram is also found in this area and is mined by a small concern when prices make this payable.   Instability of the market in recent years has militated somewhat against steady development.

Lake shore sands near Bukoba provide suitable material for glass-making. Diatomite also occurs in this District.

INDUSTRIES

The production of cotton, coffee, tobacco and rice has been mentioned above and these form the main "industries" in the Province.

Cotton.—In 1956 there were thirteen cotton ginneries, which produced some 21,600 tons valued at £5,800,000. [1]

[1]In 1955, 19,300 tons valued at £5,200,000.

Coffee.—Most of the coffee in the west lake areas is hulled by the growers in primitive wooden hand hullers. Quality is often poor because the cherry is harvested at all stages of ripeness and often hulled when inadequately dried. Two processing factories in Bukoba hull the dried cherry and clean the hand-hulled beans. All bags are tested by the Government grader who classifies the coffee as "F.A.Q." or "Undergrade".

Tobacco.—The Nyamirembe Tobacco Board buys tobacco leaf from growers in four grades according to length of leaf. Formerly, all leaf was separated, regraded into seven grades, made into hands, sometimes dried, and baled. This caused heavy labour costs, and also losses by drying, theft and breakage. Now the E.A. Tobacco Company has agreed to accept the four grades as bought from growers.

Rice.—In 1956 there were nine fully equipped rice mills in the Province producing some 2,800 tons valued at £120,000.[1]

In addition, the production of clarified butter is of some importance. In 1956 production amounted to 36,000 tins (of 36 lb.) valued at £168,200. In the cattle-owning districts 132,855 head of cattle were sold in the markets for £762,356, and 32,560 sheep and goats for £40,904, in the same year[2]. The trade in hides and skins is also one of considerable value.

There are four saw mills in the province which produce timber valued at £30,000 annually.

ADMINISTRATIVE STATIONS[3]

Mwanza,[4] provincial headquarters, is situated on Lake Victoria, at the head of Smith Sound, on a narrow stretch of ground just above lake level, and 3,700 feet above sea level. It is sheltered from the prevailing breeze by the hills behind, and is in consequence hot at times. Mwanza[5] is both railhead and port and is of growing importance as a communications centre for the province. Lake steamers call three times a week on their trips round the lake and smaller vessels ply across Smith Sound and to Ukerewe Island. There are weekly air services to Dar es Salaam, Entebbe and Nairobi as well as the local "round-the-lake" service. The East African Medical Survey has a laboratory in the town and the Lake Victoria Fisheries Service has its headquarters there. A large teachers' training centre is sited at Butimba nearby.

In 1952 the population of Mwanza Township comprised 10,668 Africans, 2,718 Asians and 286 Europeans. The Judiciary is represented by a Puisne Judge, a Senior Resident Magistrate and a Magistrate. There is a District Commissioner for Mwanza Town and another for the Mwanza Rural Area. They are assisted by two district officers. At Mwanza are normally stationed representatives of the following departments of Government and of the High Commission: Agriculture, Veterinary, Education, Forest, Water, Medical, Posts and Telecommunications, East African Railways and Harbours, Surveys, Medical Research, Fisheries, and of the Police Force.

---

[1]1955, figures were 3,700 tons of paddy at £100,000.

[2]32,000 tins in 1955, valued at £144,000; 101,535 cattle marketed for £627,066; 32,996 sheep and goats for £27,290.

[3]For further details see "Tanganyika: A Review of its Resources and their Development", p. 820.

[4]For additional information see table on p·542.

[5]Two explanations of the meaning of the name *Mwanza* have been given: one is that it is a corruption of *Ngwa Nyanza*, meaning "to the lake" in Kisukuma, and the other that it comes from *Ng'wanza* meaning a form of friendship. The possible significance of the second explanation is not known.

Ngudu[1] (4,000 feet above sea level), the headquarters of the Kwimba District, is situated between road and railway connecting Mwanza with Tabora, seventeen miles from the road and also seventeen miles from the railway at Malya. It is not on any regular air route. It is in the middle of typically "cultivation steppe" country, in a very thickly populated area.

The District Commissioner is assisted by one district officer and representatives of the Agricultural and Veterinary Departments and of the Police Force are normally stationed there.

Maswa[2] (4,400 feet above sea level), the headquarters of the Maswa District, is situated twenty-three miles from the Tabora–Mwanza branch line at Malampaka, which is sixty-seven miles from Mwanza. It is not on any regular air route. Like Ngudu, it is in typical Sukuma country, but not far away are the Serengeti Plains.

The District Commissioner is assisted by one district officer and representatives of the Agricultural and Veterinary Departments and of the Police Force are normally stationed there.

Shinyanga[3] (3,700 feet above sea level), situated on road and railway, is one hundred and four miles from Mwanza and one hundred and sixteen from Tabora. (The district was at one time included in the Western Province, but, having a majority of Sukuma inhabitants, is now more properly considered as part of Sukumaland.) Nearby is the important Williamson Diamond Mine, at which there is a private aerodrome, but Shinyanga is not on any regular air route. Shinyanga has the largest primary cattle market in the territory.

In 1952 Shinyanga Township contained 1,802 Africans, 646 Asians (including 85 Arabs) and 32 Europeans.

The District Commissioner is assisted by one district officer and representatives of the Agricultural, Veterinary, Medical, Judicial and Public Works Departments and of the Police Force are normally stationed there.

Geita[4] (4,200 feet above sea level) is the headquarters of a district of that name, formed from that part of the former Mwanza District lying to the west of Smith Sound. It is sixty miles from Mwanza and five from the well-known Geita Gold Mine and is in the centre of the area which is absorbing some of the increasing population of the other Sukuma districts. A poor road connects with Biharamulo. It is on the "round-the-lake" air service.

In 1952 the population of Geita (within a three-mile radius of the District Office) was made up of 3,560 Africans, 136 Asians and 136 Europeans. These figures include the population of the Geita Mine.

---

[1]The name *Ngudu* is supposed to refer to a spring which suddenly appeared after an elephant trampled over the spot.

[2]Although for many years known as *Shanwa*, the old name of Maswa, used by the Germans for the district, has now been readopted. The name Maswa was taken from the name of the village in the chiefdom of Ntuzu where the Germans built their boma. The present boma was built 28 years ago at Nyalikungu, a village taking its name from a prominent Nyamwezi hunter of old who camped there and considerably improved the local water hole.

[3]For additional details see "Tanganyika: A Review of its Resources and their Development", p. 821. The name *Shinyanga* is thought to be derived from the Kisukuma *Chalo shi Inyanga*, meaning the district of the *inyanga* trees. These trees, *Jatropha curcas*, Linnaeus, were at one time commonly used in the area for making fences for cattle pens, etc.

[4]The name *Geita* is derived from a Rongo word meaning "to kill" and implies that in the past Africans have considered the area particularly unsuitable for habitation.

The District Commissioner is assisted by two district officers and representatives of the Agricultural, Veterinary and Forest Departments and of the Police Force are normally stationed there.

Musoma[1] (3,800 feet above sea level) is pleasantly situated on a promontory which juts out into Lake Victoria. It is a port of call for lake steamers and is one hundred and forty-three miles by road from Mwanza. It is on the air route Nairobi-Musoma-Mwanza.

In 1952 the Musoma Township contained 4,145 Africans, 736 Asians, and 39 Europeans.

The District Commissioner is assisted by two district officers. A Resident Magistrate and representatives of the Agricultural, Veterinary, Mines and Education Departments and of the Police Force are normally stationed there.

Tarime[2] (5,000 feet above sea level), a most attractive station in the hills bordering on Kenya, is the headquarters of the North Mara District. It is sixty miles from Musoma by road and eighty miles from Kisii in Kenya.

In 1952 the station contained 620 Africans, 30 Asians and 10 Europeans.

The District Commissioner is assisted by one district officer and representatives of the Agricultural and Veterinary Departments and of the Police Force are normally stationed there.

The headquarters of the *Ukerewe* District are situated at Kabingo[3] near Nansio, at a height of 3,900 feet above sea level and 300 feet above the lake. This district, like the Geita District, was until 1951 a part of the Mwanza District. The island is thickly populated, having a density of over 200 persons to the square mile.

The District Commissioner is assisted by one district officer and representatives of the Department of Agriculture and of the Police Force are normally stationed there.

Bukoba[4] receives the cooling effect of the prevailing wind which blows across the lake. It is situated on the shore (3,700 feet above sea level) below the plateau on which live the closely settled Haya tribe. It was at one time provincial headquarters of that part of the present Lake Province which lies to the west of the lake, and is an important port. By all-weather road, it is about 400 miles from Mwanza but only twelve hours by lake steamer. It is 107 miles from Masaka in Uganda. Caspair Airways call there regularly on the "round-the-lake" service.

At the time of the 1952 census Bukoba Township contained 2,799 Africans, 664 Asians and 104 Europeans.

The District Commissioner, who is also Deputy Provincial Commissioner for the East Lake area, is assisted by four district officers, and representatives of the Agricultural, Veterinary, Co-operative, Education, Forest, Public Works Departments and of the Police Force are normally stationed there, together with a Resident Magistrate.

[1] The name *Musoma* comes from the Kikwaya and Kijita name for a headland or promontory—*kumsoma*. Musoma itself is in fact situated at the landward end of a headland jutting northwards into the lake.

[2] The origin of the name *Tarime* is unknown and none of the local inhabitants can explain it. The district takes its name from the Mara River.

[3] *Kabingo* takes its name from a nearby well of great antiquity. The well is surrounded by tall grass of a type known as *mabingo* in Kikerewe.

[4] *Bukoba* takes its name from the Bakoba people who came from the Sesse islands (Uganda) and were the first settlers at the place now known as Bukoba.
For further details of the town see "Tanganyika: A Review of its Resources and their Development". p. 808.

Biharamulo[1] (4,850 feet above sea level) is situated on a small hill in the remote country bordering the south-western corner of Lake Victoria. Because of its altitude it enjoys a better climate than is to be found in other parts of the district. It is 32 miles from the nearest port on the lake, Nyamirembe, 110 miles from Bukoba and 278 miles from Tabora. There is also a road connection with Kibondo, 87 miles away. It is not on any regular air route.

The District Commissioner is assisted by one district officer and representatives of the Agricultural and Tsetse Research Departments are normally stationed there.

Ngara[2] (5,900 feet above sea level) is situated on a ridge in the hilly country bordering Ruanda-Urundi, with magnificent views on all sides and in the midst of lands closely planted by the local Hangaza tribesmen with bananas and coffee. It is 112 miles by road from Biharamulo and 40 miles from Muhinga in Ruanda-Urundi. It is a remote station and not on any regular air route.

The District Commissioner is assisted by one district officer and a representative of the Department of Agriculture.

PLACES OF INTEREST TO THE VISITOR AND SPORTING FACILITIES

Probably the part of the province of greatest interest to the ordinary visitor is that area of the Musoma and Maswa Districts which is included in the Serengeti National Park, although access to it is not very easy and is only possible in the dry season. (An account of the Park is to be found on pp. 465 to 469). The province is not usually visited by big game hunters but in the Bukoba District and in part of the Biharamulo District some good shooting is to be had and the rare sitatunga can be obtained.[3] Bird shooting is to be had in most of the districts, and duck and geese are now to be found, in the season, on most of the dams which have been made in Sukumaland.[4] It should however be noted that some dams are "controlled areas" and may not be shot over without permission.

Those interested in such matters will find the Ukiriguru Agricultural Research Station, 20 miles from Mwanza, well worth a visit. At Old Shinyanga is the tsetse research station where the late C. F. M. Swynnerton did so much of his investigational work and where experiments in control are still being made.

---

[1]The name *Biharamulo* is thought to be a much corrupted derivation of the Kizinza word *kiharu* meaning a very saline type of soil used by cattle as a salt lick. There is supposed to have been such a salt lick at one time not far from the present Station.

[2]*Ngara* took its name from a large tree which used to grow on the spot, the tree being a flat-topped acacia known in Kihangaza as *umunyinya mwingara*. This name was later contracted into Ngara.

[3]See "The Shooting Grounds" on p. 465.

[4]See "Some Notes on the Duck and Geese of Usukuma" by B. J. Dudbridge in *Tanganyika Notes and Records* No. 31, July 1951.

THE NORTHERN PROVINCE

The Northern Province occupies the north centre of the territory. It covers 34,250 square miles and contains over 600,000 people. Its boundary with Kenya is part of the arbitrary line drawn in 1886 when the international boundary between Kenya and German East Africa was demarcated, a line which runs from the intersection of the first degree of south latitude with the eastern shore of Lake Victoria to a point north-east of Mount Kilimanjaro. The arbitrariness of this line is partly mitigated by the fact that, except in the North Mara District at its extreme western end near the lake, it runs through very thinly populated country, favoured by game rather than by man, and by the fact that the main tribe bisected by the boundary, the Masai, pays little heed to it. To the east the boundary is still the inter-territorial boundary, which makes a great sweep round the mountain in the direction of Himo, skirting Lake Jipe, and then it marches with the Tanga Province. On the west are the vast Serengeti plains, lying mostly in the Lake Province, to the south-west the hilly Singida and Kondoa Districts of the Central Province, and to the south and south-east the Mpwapwa and Kilosa Districts.

DISTRICTS

The Northern Province contains only four districts: Moshi, 2,000 square miles, population 264,000[1], the very closely settled area of the slopes of Mount Kilimanjaro; Arusha, 1,000 square miles, population 108,000, the equally closely settled area round Mount Meru; the vast area of Masailand, 23,000 square miles in extent, with a population of 57,000; and the highland country to the west— Mbulu, 6,300 square miles, population 156,000. Provincial headquarters is at Arusha.

PHYSICAL FEATURES AND CLIMATE

With the exception of the central and southern parts of the great Masai appendix the province is largely mountainous and contains, as well as Kilimanjaro (19,340 feet) and Meru (14,979 feet), the peaks of Hanang (11,215 feet) and Oldeani (10,460 feet), situated at the southern and northern ends of the Mbulu District; Monduli[2] (8,722 feet), to the west of Arusha; Essimingor (7,546 feet) still further west; Ketumbeine[2] and Gelai[2] (both 9,653 feet), between Monduli and Lake Natron; and Longido (8,625 feet) due north of Meru. From the plains of central Masailand rise a number of isolated peaks (*inselbergen*), Lolkisale (6,995 feet), Lolbene (6,207 feet) Losogonoi[2] (6,968 feet) and others. Nowhere in the province is one ever out of sight of a peak for long. The greatest concentration of mountains is just north of the Mbulu District, in the area of Masailand which the Germans called the "Winter Highlands", a volcanic region containing the still active volcano of Oldonyo Lengai[3] the majestic Loolmalasin[2] (11,969 feet) and the vast cauldron of Ngorongoro, one of the scenic splendours of Tanganyika. This highland area is quite unlike most of the rest of the territory and has an aspect more temperate than tropical. But this applies only above a certain altitude: as one begins to descend towards the plains the change from temperate to tropical conditions occurs with surprising suddenness. Near the great peaks

---

[1]At time of 1952 census, but now (1957) over 300,000.

[2]See "Some Hints on Climbing Masailand Mountains" by H. F. I. Elliott in *Tanganyika Notes and Records* No. 26; December, 1948.

[3]See "Climbing Oldonyo Lengai" by N. J. Guest, *Tanganyika Notes and Records* No. 31; July, 1951.

of Kilimanjaro and Meru the rapid transition is especially noticeable; here every half-mile makes a difference and one passes with bewildering quickness from the lush greenness of well-watered slopes to the brown aridity of thorn scrub. The contrast can be clearly seen at Arusha, where the country above the town is perennially green and closely cultivated, but, a mile or two below it, an arid plain, grazed by the Masai at certain seasons only.

The great peaks seem to draw the rain clouds to themselves and intercept them on their well-defined courses, as they come from the north-east and the south-east, causing copious precipitation on those sides of the mountains but very little on the opposite slopes or on the plains below. Thus the differences in climate, soil, vegetation and general conditions of life between the comparatively barren north-western and northern slopes of both mountains and their well-watered southern, south-eastern and south-western slopes are most marked. The rainfall at Elandshoek Estate, at a height of 4,000 feet on the eastern side of Meru, averages 28 inches per annum; whereas at Arusha, at a height of 4,500 feet on the southern slopes, it is 48 inches. Still more remarkable, on Kilimanjaro, the average at Kibosho, at 4,850 feet and due south of Kibo, is 104 inches; whereas at Arusha Chini, 20 miles to the south-south-east, at a height of 2,300 feet, it is only 18 inches. Statistics of rainfall at district headquarters are as follows:—

Station	Altitude (feet)	Average rainfall	1950	1951	1952	1953	1954	1955	1956
Arusha...	4,500	47·94 (33 years)	59·54	65·04	38·71	38·23	*	*	26·28
Monduli (Masai) ...	5,200	33·62 (22 years)	28·44	49·97	22·66	22·19	24·10	37·14	21·93
Loliondo (Masai) ...	7,000	31·60 (22 years)	35·87	56·09	26·23	20·09	28·46	35·26	*
Mbulu	5,700	31·16 (38 years)	41·12	55·11	31·14	26·15	24·33	24·01	29·97
Moshi	2,668	33·97 (35 years)	34·13	47·48	21·15	25·85	32·33	36·11	21·18

*Record incomplete.

Much of the rain which does fall on the province finds its way into the Pangani river, one of the few large rivers in the territory and possibly the most important one. Not only is the future development of the lowlands (the natural "over-flow" areas for a rapidly expanding population which can no longer be accommodated on the mountains) dependent on the Pangani, but electrical development depends on it also, for at the Great Pangani Falls is situated a power station which supplies most of the Tanga Province with power and light. The other rivers in the province are comparatively unimportant and most of them drain into one or other of the lakes, Natron, Eyasi or Manyara, which are on or near the line of the great Rift Valley,[1] towards the west. Natron is a soda lake, some 220 square miles in extent, which was investigated by a German geologist in 1912, as suggestions had been made by members of the Reichstag that its deposits should be developed like those of Lake Magadi, not far away in Kenya, and that the Tanga-Moshi railway should be extended to the lake. Samples however when analysed compared unfavourably with Magadi soda, the Natron product being alloyed with common salt, from which the other was free.

The shore of Lake Manyara exhibits the phenomenon of a white crust which disappears as it is approached—the effect of sunlight on its peculiar crystalline formation.[2]

[1]See page 2.

[2]See "Lake Manyara" by J. H. Harris, in *Tanganyika Notes and Records*, No. 30, January, 1951.

The province also contains some delightful crater lakes, perhaps the best-known being Lake Embagai at the top of Elanairobi Mountain in the "Winter Highlands" in Masailand, Lake Chala in the Moshi District and Lake Duluti, a few miles from Arusha on the road to Moshi. The view from the rim of Duluti on a clear evening must be one of the most striking in Africa: the sharp peak of Meru towers above on the left, the smooth waters of the lake lie below, and in front, rising to a stupendous height from the plain, is the snow-clad dome of Kilimanjaro, flood-lit in the rays of the setting sun.

POPULATION

By combining the results of the 1948 (total) and 1952 (partial) censuses we get a total population for the province of 595,651, or 18·5 to the square mile. This total is made up as follows:—

District	Area in Sq. miles	European	Indian	Goan	Arab	Somali	Coloured	Other	Total Non-African	African	Total Population
Arusha	990	1,819	2,702	210	66	393	38	89	5,317	107,904	113,221
Masai	22,974	66	72	4	5	76	21	1	245	57,263	57,508
Mbulu	6,258	313	200	9	2	84	19	–	627	155,546	156,173
Moshi	1,943	1,071	2,793	109	169	261	38	28	4,469	264,280	268,749
	32,165	3,269	5,767	333	242	814	116	118	10,658	584,993	595,651

The map on p. 283 will give some idea of the distribution of population. About half the total is to be found on the slopes of Kilimanjaro, where in one area the density reaches a figure of 800 to the square mile. The Moshi District as a whole is the most densely populated district in Tanganyika, with 138 to the square mile. The Arusha District is also closely populated, with 112 to the square mile and, by contrast, the Mbulu District is sparsely populated with 25 to the square mile and Masailand almost empty with the lowest density of any district, 3 to the square mile. But these figures are misleading. The slopes of Kilimanjaro and Meru are probably as fertile as any land in the territory and are capable of supporting a dense population (although not quite so dense as that which now exists—see page 205), whereas much of the Mbulu District and nearly all of Masailand are of value only to the pastoralist, and then only seasonally. The Masai steppe looks vast on the map—and it is in fact nearly four times as large as Wales—but most of it is semi-arid, with a rainfall of about 25 inches a year.

The Asian population is mostly confined to the towns of Moshi and Arusha.

There are about 100 European settlers (not counting their families) on the slopes of Kilimanjaro and Meru, with a small number (35) at Oldeani and a few elsewhere; the remainder of the European population lives in the two main towns.

THE CHAGGA

The Chagga inhabit the slopes of Mount Kilimanjaro. They numbered 230,000 at the census taken in 1948 and it is estimated that they are increasing at the rate of 2 per cent per annum and thus will double their numbers in 35 years. They are thought to be a mixture of immigrants from neighbouring tribes such as Kamba, Teita, Pare and Sambaa, who have absorbed the aboriginal people (the "Konyingo") whom they found living on the mountain on their arrival. It is possible that there is also a strain of Kikuyu blood, but the Chagga themselves deny this. They are above the average in intelligence and have a passion for education—and for litigation. They live in *vihamba* (sing. *kihamba*), plots of an acre or two (often less), on which are grown the staple crops of bananas and coffee (see p. 212 for further details of the coffee industry). They grow a considerable quantity of maize on the lower slopes of the mountain, and onions, cotton and cassava are also produced.

Eleusine is grown almost entirely for the manufacture of the local kind of beer, and the need of this crop for adequate watering (it is grown in the dry season), has, it is said, led to the construction of the astonishing system of water furrows which are everywhere to be seen on the mountain and which have been there for generations—long before the advent of the European. Dundas thus describes one of the more notable achievements of this unusual tribe:—[1]

"Along the sides of deep valleys which are little less than precipices, the furrows are conducted, one above the other, to the number of five or more, graded so artfully that Europeans have often been inclined to suspect that these Africans have solved the mystery of making water to run uphill; the writer himself, though accustomed to trust to the native's eye for grade, has now and again been deceived into doubting whether the alignment was not faulty, but has always found the Chagga expert to be right. No instruments or contrivances for grading are employed, the alignment is done purely by eye. Here and there the furrow is excavated under a rock, or banked up, sometimes they are six feet deep, while in another place the water is carried over another furrow by a wooden trough. In many places the water is thus conducted 600 feet above the level of the river that flows at the bottom of the ravine. The Mchagga knows the precise point of the river from which to take his furrow, selecting a spot where the flow is least turbulent and the current so directed that it will not eat away the inlet. From the main furrow many branches are led; these are sub-divided, and eventually the field to be irrigated is flooded by innumerable grooves scratched in herring-bone pattern from the sides of the furrow.

"The furrows run for miles; they must be used by many, and most generally the cultivators have the water in turns on specific days. No small degree of regulation is necessitated, and moreover within the course of the furrow ordered conditions must prevail. It is to these circumstances that we may attribute in a great measure the early institution of Chiefship with the consequent development of a stable organization. Thus the cultivation of *mbeke* (eleusine), a much condemned industry, has been responsible not only for a remarkable skill in artificial irrigation, which as time goes on will be of inestimable benefit, but it has directly promoted social development of a relatively high order."

---

[1]"Kilimanjaro and its People", by C. F. Dundas, pp. 261-2.

Kilimanjaro having been such a focus of attention for the early travellers, the Chagga were visited and described long before most of the other inland tribes. Rebmann, von der Decken, New, Thomson, H. H. Johnston, have all left interesting accounts of them.

The first to visit them was Johannes Rebmann, a German in the service of the Church Missionary Society, who caught sight of the gleaming dome of Kilimanjaro on 11th May, 1848, and was ridiculed for years for suggesting that the white substance covering the dome was snow. He thus describes his experience:—

"May 11.—In the midst of a great wilderness, full of wild beasts, such as rhinoceroses, buffaloes and elephants, we slept beneath thorn-bushes, quietly and securely under God's gracious protection. This morning we discerned the mountains of Jagga more distinctly than ever; and, about ten o'clock, I fancied I saw the summit of one of them covered with a dazzlingly white cloud. My guide called the white which I saw merely "Beredi", cold; it was perfectly clear to me, however, that it could be nothing else but snow".[1]

Considered appraisals of the Chagga as a tribe, by men who had lived amongst them for many years, are to be found in Dundas's book and in Gutmann's "Dichten und Denken der Dschagga-Neger" (1909). Dundas[2] writes that he had never found a tribe so responsive to sympathetic study or so ready to discuss frankly their traditions and habits, and indeed his book demonstrates that he had obtained their confidence and trust to an unusual degree. Gutmann describes them as follows:—

"The Wachagga are the most industrious and efficient of the peoples of the region. They distinguish themselves from their neighbours by their more stable political organization. Their special characteristic is a deep feeling for monarchy. Not only the country, but all the inhabitants and their belongings are the personal property of the Chiefs. The latter also act as Chief Justice and Chief Priest and are implicitly obeyed by the masses of the people.

"The Chiefs select their confidential councillors from among the eminent men under them. Each chieftaincy is divided into many small districts to which the Chief appoints a supervisor ("mchili"), usually an influential man who already enjoys a certain esteem. These supervisors pass on the Chief's orders and are helped by a number of assistants. The supervisors have judicial authority and are in charge of the first court hearings and may later present the cases to the Chief.

"This political organization works very smoothly."[3]

In 1923 there were twenty-eight Chiefs, but the number was later reduced to fourteen by amalgamation and the Chiefdoms were grouped into three divisions, Rombo, Vunjo and Hai, with a *Mangi Mwitori* (Superior Chief) in charge of each division. In 1951 a single chief for all the Chagga was elected—T. L. M. Marealle,[4] grandson of the famous Chief Marealle who made himself master of the greater number of the warring sub-tribes in German times.

---

[1]*Travels in East Africa.* Krapf. pp. 235-6.

[2]Dundas, *Op. cit. p.* 95.

[3]Dichten und Denken der Dschagga-Neger. Gutmann—1909.

[4]See also his "The Wachagga of Kilimanjaro" in *Tanganyika Notes and Records* No. 32, for January, 1952.

OTHER TRIBES IN MOSHI DISTRICT

In addition to the Chagga tribe, the Moshi District also contains some 2,000 Kahe (of similar stock to the Chagga but speaking a different language), who live in the south-east corner; a heterogeneous collection from most of the main tribes of the territory, living at Arusha Chini and Boma-la-Ngombe and numbering about 9,000; and a small number of Somalis, Nubians and Abyssinians in the Boma-la-Ngombe area.

The Arusha and Meru.—The Arusha District is inhabited by the Arusha and Meru tribes, numbering 52,000 and 25,000 respectively when the census was taken in 1948.   The Meru (who call themselves the Wa-roh) are an off-shoot of the Chagga and speak an almost identical language but have not developed educationally, politically nor economically in the way the parent tribe has, nor have they been so responsive to missionary influence.   Their tribal system is a mixture of Chagga and Masai customs—a mixture which has not resulted in a satisfactory amalgam.   Like the Chagga, they have an expansion problem (see below).

There are two theories about the origin of the Waarusha.   One states that they belonged to the Gweno group of tribes (an off-shoot of which is to be found in the Pare District) and formerly lived at Arusha Chini at a place which is now in the Moshi District.   They helped the Masai in their wars against another tribe, the Kwavi, and were later attacked by the Kwavi when the latter had recovered from their defeat.   They then fled to the Masai near Arusha and were permitted by them to settle on the wooded slopes of Mount Meru, in which land their protectors had no interest.   Since the Masai have always tolerated in their midst or on their borders certain agricultural tribes who could supply their women and children with grain and other commodities (e.g. the Sonjo[1]) there is nothing inherently improbable in this.   Indeed this version is the one which is favoured by those who have made a special study of the subject.[2]

The other version is that the Waarusha are themselves of Kwavi or Lumbwa origin.   Long ago they and the Masai had frequent fights near Lake Natron (on the Kenya-Tanganyika border).   Eventually the Masai overcame them and drove them south past Ngorongoro to the Kibaya area (now in the extreme south of Masailand).   Some of these fugitives settled down in Kibaya and are now called Kwavi; others settled at Arusha Chini.   The two divisions later became antagonists and, when the Masai again appeared in the area, the Arusha Chini division made friends with them and helped them to defeat the Kwavi.   Then the Kwavi turned the tables on their relatives, with the consequence described above.

As Cory points out, this version has one advantage: it explains the great similarity between the customs of the Masai and those of the Arusha; but it does not explain why the Kwavi at Arusha Chini became agriculturists in their new homes.   As Nilo-Hamites of stock very similar to the Masai, and as friends accepted into the Masai community, it is difficult to understand why they should not have remained with the Masai, being willingly absorbed by them.   The first version, that of their Gweno origin, is, incidentally, that held by the great majority of the Waarusha themselves.

---

[1] See p. 206.

[2] H. Cory's "Tribal Structure of the Arusha Tribe" in MS.

THE EXPANSION PROBLEM

When the Germans alienated land on the slopes of both Kilimanjaro and Meru, for European settlement, it seems that they did not realize that the tribes would increase in numbers so quickly.

As the demand for land for homesteads grew, it became apparent that the result of these alienations was virtually to imprison the tribes within the rings made by the forest boundary on the higher slopes and the non-native farms lower down. Various methods of easing the pressure were tried and several farms were purchased for tribal use. But this of course could not provide a permanent solution. When, therefore, the German farms became available for re-distribution after the 1939-45 war it was decided to take advantage of this opportunity to review the whole land situation on both mountains and the Arusha-Moshi Lands Commission was appointed in June, 1946 to do this and to make recommendations to meet the situation. The report of the commission, (the "Wilson Report") was published in 1947 and contains a full account of the land problems on both mountains and how it came about that they had arisen in such an acute form. Various recommendations were made towards a solution of these problems, the principal ones being the allocation to the tribes of certain key farms (almost all German-owned) at strategic points, the development of the lower and more arid lands by the provision of water and other amenities, and the establishment of a large homogeneous block of alienated land, mostly for ranching, from the western side of Meru (Oldonyo Sambu) right round the north of it (Ngare Nanyuki) to the north-western side of Kilimanjaro (Ngare Nairobi). Most of these recommendations have now been implemented, although not without opposition from both settler and tribesman.

THE MASAI

The Masai are perhaps the best-known, outside Tanganyika, of its inland tribes. They have changed hardly at all since the early travellers described them and the same adjectives can still be applied to them: proud, aristocratic, supercilious, brave, impetuous, scorning agricultural work of any kind, loving their cattle above all else and considering themselves the lords of creation.

The first administrative officer to be stationed amongst them was struck by the fact (which all who meet the Masai will at once notice) that they are fundamentally unlike the peoples who surround them, in appearance, habits and language. "They are quiet and dignified in their bearing, very low voiced, and they use practically no gesticulations. When making a speech, however, a Masai will hold a stick or knobkerry, with which he emphasizes his sentences by raising and letting it fall, quite slowly, with the rise and fall of the periods. This quietness and repose of the Masai is particularly striking, and is one of their most distinguished traits. They have an undoubted gift of oratory, and are greatly affected by it. The similes employed by them are excellent, and they work a speech to a climax in a most masterly manner. Added to natural habits of observation, they possess considerable reasoning faculties, and their sense of justice is particularly strongly developed. They, therefore, have no difficulty in realizing that if they are responsible for personal loss, or theft, it is incumbent upon them to make sure that at least the equivalent is returned. As a race they are intelligent and truthful, and a grown Masai will neither thieve nor lie. He may refuse to answer a question, but, once given, his word can be depended on."[1]

---

[1] "The Last of the Masai" by S. L. and H. Hinde, 1901, pp. 33–4.

The Masai tribal organization is as peculiar to themselves as their physical appearance and way of life and differs fundamentally from that of other tribes. The central feature is the age-grade system, under which every young man passes through the grades of junior warrior, senior warrior and elder. The rights, privileges and liabilities of each grade are closely defined and the transition from one to the other marked by elaborate ceremonies. The system is too elaborate and complicated to describe in a few words—there are right-hand and left-hand divisions in the grades and these are not contemporaneous but overlap by a varying number of years—but it is set out in full by Fosbrooke in his admirable "Administrative Survey of the Masai Social System".[1]

OTHER TRIBES IN MASAILAND

In the north of Masailand live the *Sonjo,* who have been described as "an obscure agricultural-pastoral tribe . . . distinguished as being essentially Bantu in the midst of a Nilo-Hamitic people, and of sufficient personality to have retained their individuality in the midst of the campaigns of rapine, murder and pillage carried on by their more powerful neighbours in the years gone by".[2] They numbered 3,536 at the 1948 census and live in large communal villages which were originally elaborately fortified. They own large numbers of small stock, principally goats, and are great bee-keepers.

The *Dorobo,* of whom eight types have been distinguished,[3] live scattered throughout the area. They are famous as trackers and hunters, their skill in these arts indeed being almost uncanny. It is thus described by one who knew them well: "In hunting, tracking, bush-lore and forest-craft the Mosiroi (one type of Dorobo) is, in my opinion, without equal when in familiar country. He seems to know instinctively what an animal will do in given circumstances, and inability to follow its track will seldom result in the pursuit being abandoned. If the ground is stony or if the passage of other animals has obliterated the trail, the Mosiroi will go quietly forward and will eventually, by a combination of luck, instinct and knowledge of the country and the habits of the quarry, pick up the spoor again. I have seen this happen many times. The Mosiroi knows when extreme caution must be observed and when noise does not matter, he is never at a loss for a vantage-point and, on the whole, is tenacious and plucky in the pursuit of dangerous game." They are expert bowmen and think nothing, it seems, of killing a lion with bow and arrow. The arrows are of course poisoned and the poison used is so effective that death results within a few minutes. Their astonishing ability to live in waterless bush for long periods is thus explained: "If trouble is in the wind, the Mosiroi will always make for the haven he knows best—the bush. There he will live, apparently quite independent of the products of civilization, and in no wise inconvenienced by a total lack of water, for weeks at a stretch, returning (when the trouble has blown over) with a skin bottle or bag bulging with honey. I could not understand the apparent ability of the Mosiroi to live for long periods in country I knew to be waterless until I had been

---

[1] *Tanganyika Notes and Records* No. 26, for December 1948.

[2] Notes on Land Tenure and Land Rights among the Sonjo of Tanganyika Territory." J. E. S. Griffiths. *Tanganyika Notes and Records* No. 9, June 1940. It is, perhaps, equally probable that they retained their individuality because the Masai found them useful.—Ed.

[3] "Il Torobo" by R. A. J. Maguire. *Tanganyika Notes and Records* No. 25, June 1948.

introduced to what they laughingly said was "the dry-season water". This is an enormous tuber with a skin like the domestic potato. Under the skin is a milky, sticky layer about half an inch in thickness. This surrounds the inner core, which is of the appearance and consistency of a raw potato, is slightly fibrous and very moist. When this is chewed (the residue is not generally, but may be, swallowed), it gives great relief to thirst. Squeezing or pounding one of these tubers over a cooking-pot will result in the accumulation of a surprising amount of quite palatable water. A full-grown specimen of this tuber must weigh many pounds, as I have seen them as large as a Rugby football. It is most difficult of detection, having only three or four small oval leaves above ground, but the Mosiroi seem to be able to find it anywhere. It is generally obtained by digging with a sharpened stick under certain bushes".[1]

MASAI DEVELOPMENT PLAN

The days are past when the Masai could be regarded as' 'anachronistic highwaymen", who should be left more or less to their own devices provided that they behaved themselves and did not raid the neighbouring tribes and carry off their cattle. The ordered development of the whole vast area of Masailand has been very carefully considered and a "Masai Development Plan" is being implemented. The objects of the plan are primarily to improve Masailand as a ranching country by the provision of more and better water supplies (the crucial need) and, concurrently, by the improvement of pasturage and pasture management. This will induce a more stable economy, and thus make the provision of improved social services possible. The plan also provides for the clearing of tsetse-infested bush and the provision of "expansion" areas in certain localities for Masai who have to be moved from the peripheral parts of Masailand, for the natural increase in numbers and for those Waarusha who have taken up residence amongst them. The estimated cost of the plan is £333,000, towards which the Masai are contributing by means of a special tax—a local rate varying between Shs. 10/- and Shs. 68/- per taxpayer.

TRIBES OF THE MBULU DISTRICT

The Mbulu District consists of a mountainous plateau, dominated in the south by the 11,000 ft. peak of Mt. Hanang and its smaller neighbour Mt. Ufiome and in the north by the Ngorongoro massif. To the west the land falls away to the arid wastes around Lake Eyasi, and in the east, where the Rift wall is steeper, to the "salt" flats of Lake Manyara and the Great North Road.

Mbulu is the administrative centre for the district of that name. Nearby the country is broken, lying at heights between 5,000 and 8,000 feet above sea level. On the hills to the south of the Boma can be seen the edge of the Nou Forest Reserve.[2] and across a shallow valley to the north-east the 8,000 ft. peak of Guam is within easy walking distance. Both to the north and to the south the country levels out; to provide in the north an ideal ranching country for the pastoral peoples living on it, and in the south a wheat growing area characterized by some European settlement in the neighbourhood of Oldeani.

In the district lives one of the most interesting groups of peoples in the whole of the territory.

---

[1]"Il-Torobo", *Op. cit.*

[2]A second reserve, Marang, lies to the north.

The *Iraqw* or *Mbulu*, living mostly around Mbulu, but dispersing to north and south, have been known as "Hamitic" [1] people, and their language, full of difficult and forbidding sounds, possibly earned for them their alternative name of Wa-Mbulu, "the Babblers", from the Swahili traders who first penetrated into the areas. Tall and light-skinned, some with markedly Semitic features, they appear rather "un-African" to the stranger. They numbered 101,000 in 1948.

It seems likely that they came into the area about two hundred years ago, from the south-west, possibly having travelled there from the area around Lake Victoria. Their neighbours are the Gorowa, from the south-east of the district around Mt. Ufiome and the Alawa (or Wasi) and Burungi from the north and central parts of the Kondoa District of the Central Province. (Some 21,000 in all). While the Iraqw are both cultivators and pastoralists, their fondness for cattle has led in recent years to serious overstocking and impoverishment of the land.

To the south-west of Mbulu lies the *Barabaig* [2] country, open steppes, ideal for the ranching that is carried on by the pastoral Barabaig, a sub-tribe of the Tatoga, who inhabit them. These people were living near Mount Elgon, on the Kenya-Uganda border, about 250 years ago, but whether they were Nandi people who had been separated from the main part of the tribe for centuries, or people of a generic stock common to the Nandi, Kipsigis and Masai, who left the Mount Elgon area after a Nandi invasion, is not certain, although the latter hypothesis is thought to be the more likely. The typical Barabaig male is tall, muscular and well developed. Barabaig women are self-possessed, aggressive and independent and the old women have great influence on clan proceedings. The diet of the Barabaig is notably high in animal protein, being chiefly composed, like that of the Masai, of blood and milk, supplemented by meat from sheep, goats, cattle and game, and, of more recent years, maize. The tribe is organized on patrilineal and patrilocal principles and is made up of clans or "lineages", all the members of which trace descent in the male line from one founding ancestor, but there are, in addition, neighbourhood or community groupings which maintain local control over such matters as grazing and watering, as well as the social activities of its members. The Barabaig number about 18,500.

The *Mbugwe* [3] are a small tribe of Bantu agriculturists and herders of stock living at the base of the Rift Wall in Mbulu District. The 1948 census showed that the tribe totalled only 7,500. Their neighbours in all directions are non-Bantu; the Iraqw to the west, the Barabaig and Gorowa to the south, and the Masai to the east and to the north. All who come into contact with the Mbugwe are unanimous in their surprise that such arid alkaline country should hold any population at all. It is true that one attraction is freedom from tsetse which infests the bush surrounding the Mbugwe flats but the casual observer would think that any reasonable inhabitants would have attempted to ameliorate these conditions by the planting of shade trees, the building of wind breaks, or at least the growing of their high standing *mtama* crops round the houses (like the Rangi's habit of growing castor bushes near the house). As it is, the low mud-roofed houses (*tembe*) of the Mbugwe are scattered over the alkaline flats defenceless

---

[1] As the language remains unclassified it may be incorrect to talk of them as Hamitic.

[2] See "The Tatoga of Tanganyika" by G. M. Wilson, in *Tanganyika Notes and Records*, Nos. 33 and 34 for July 1952 and 1953.

[3] Taken from an article on "Defensive Measures of Certain Tribes" (by H. A. Fosbrooke) published in *Tanganyika Notes and Records*, No. 39 of June 1955.

Masai Warrior.

Photo. Public Relations Department

Masai married woman.

Photo: Mrs. Merrell Dalton

against the scorching sun, drying winds and choking dust-devils. Their situation, however, provided defence against an even more ruthless enemy, namely, man. For the Mbugwe were essentially spearmen and, as such, preferred open country to thick bush or forest. Their proficiency with the spear in an environment in which they were able to practise this art enabled the Mbugwe frequently to repel the Masai. The latter indeed formed such a high opinion of them as enemies that they called them, in common with the Barabaig, by the honorific term *il mangati* (true enemies) rather than the contemptuous *il meek* reserved for the general run of non-Hamitic stock, Chagga, Rangi, Sandawi, etc.

R. F. Gray gives an interesting account of the origin of the tribe[1]. He writes:

"The name "Wambugwe" appears to be a Swahili version of the native name *Vambowe* (sing. *Mombowe*) by which the tribesmen call themselves, the root *mbowe* meaning "partridge". This name comes from the traditional story of their arrival in the country and their origin as a separate tribe. The traditions tell of a parent tribe to the present Mbugwe and Irangi tribes. Some native accounts locate this ancestral group in what is now the Sandawi country in the Central Province, but other informants suggest the Ndareda region, now occupied by the Gorowa tribe, as the homeland. There is general agreement that these ancestors had originally migrated from the west. A time of famine and distress came upon these ancient people and one section of the tribe migrated northwards, drawn by the lure of the plentiful francolin which they trapped and hunted as they do to this day. These people, who were given the soubriquet "Partridge-men" (*Vambowe*) were the forerunners of the Mbugwe tribe."

Gray goes on to say that: "The present Mbugwe possess a distinctive and uniform culture. . . . Two main trends can be discerned: the social organization was marked by a change from a matrilineal to a patrilineal bias; the political system which had been originally based on kinship and lineage was replaced by a territorial system. . . . The present Mbugwe have a mixture of matrilineal and patrilineal elements which comprise their social organization. Clan and lineage membership remains matrilineal. Inheritance customs and rules of residence make up a complex institution which is essentially patrilineal in orientation."

Gray considers that: "It was constant internal wars, together with the threat of outside raiders, that led the Mbugwe to develop the peculiar pattern of settlement —widely separated housing and agricultural land—which is so characteristic. It is largely maintained today by force of habit now that the threat of war has passed and they are united under one Chief. All the houses are sited on the flats to the west of the Great North Road while over 80 per cent of their cultivation is concentrated some four miles away in one area, between the road and Lake Barungi. The soil is fairly sandy and free-draining and is undoubtedly suited to the hardier grain crops such as are grown. It is an impressive sight in the growing season to climb the southernmost of the Pyramid Hills and look over a continuous sheet of *mtama* stretching southward for seven miles or more."

On the other side of the plateau, in the arid country around Lake Eyasi, live a small group of primitive hunters, calling themselves *Hadzapi*, and known to others as Kangeju or Kindiga.[2] The Hadzapi, scarcely more than a few hundreds

---

[1]"The Mbugwe Tribe: Origin and Development" by Robert F. Gray, *Tanganyika Notes and Records* No. 38, March 1955.

[2]Also heard as "Tindiga" probably identical with the group known as Wahi by the Sukuma on the west side of Lake Eyasi.

15

in number, speak a language closely related to the Bushman dialects of South Africa and characterized by "clicking" sounds. [1] A nomadic people without permanent dwellings, the Hadzapi are exclusively hunters and collectors; the men doing the hunting, the women collecting edible roots and wild fruit. The most important item of their equipment is a bow, as much as 6½ ft. in length, and so powerful that an ordinary man is quite unable to bend it. With this they use barbed and poisoned arrows, with unerring skill.[2]

MBULU DEVELOPMENT SCHEME

As in the Moshi and Arusha Districts and in Masailand, there is also a special development plan for the Mbulu District. The local conditions which made such a plan necessary were, briefly, too great a population, both human and animal, on a limited area of land, resulting from a rate of increase above the average and producing soil erosion and loss of fertility to an alarming degree, so that periodic famines occurred. A plan to provide for these needs was accordingly drawn up and in late 1947 the sum of £90,000 was made available from Colonial Development and Welfare Funds for the Mbulu Development Scheme, a five-year programme which began in 1948. Pressure on the land was most acute in the Iraqw tribal area, with an average human density of 120 to the square mile and with 2·5 acres of grazing per head of cattle, with some areas holding 400 persons to the square mile and only 1·4 acres per beast. In Gorowa comparable figures were an average of 105 persons, with local concentrations of 200 to the square mile, and an average acreage for cattle of three acres per head, reduced to two acres in some villages.

The Iraqw and Gorowa are mixed agriculturists with a bias towards stock and their problems are similar except in degree. These tribes in common with the others in the district are hemmed in on all sides by their neighbours and tsetse bush, and since the beginning of the century have lost ground by the advance of fly from all sides, thus adding to the human and stock congestion. Their problems are not peculiar to themselves and the measures taken to deal with them are of general interest.

The simultaneous development of expansion areas and the rehabilitation of the eroded and eroding occupied areas were the primary tasks. Human and stock densities had to be reduced before rehabilitation was possible; but as surplus stock (and it was accepted that they were the primary cause of land deterioration) could not be absorbed sufficiently quickly into the expansion areas, a reduction of their numbers by sale was accepted as essential. It needed a long and carefully planned campaign to convince the cattle-owners of the necessity for culling their stock, but in the end their willing co-operation was obtained, sales were made and the rest of the scheme could then be carried out.

As this is in many respects a model scheme it is of interest to note that the rehabilitation plan involved the improvement of grazing by scrub clearing, the extension of the system of reserves, the licensed use of forest glades seasonally, and the closing of certain eroded hillsides for lengthy periods; the better distribution of people and stock in the occupied area by water development; the

---

[1] See "The Hadzapi or Watindega of Tanganyika Territory", by Dorothea Bleek in *Africa*, Vol. IV, No. 3. July.

[2] "The Kindiga" B. Cooper. *Tanganyika Notes and Records*, June 1949. "The Click Speaking Kindiga of Lake Eyasi". G. Hunter. *Tanganyika Standard*—June 21st, 1951.

improvement of soil fertility on arable lands by sound mixed agriculture and soil and water conservation; increased production by extending swamp cultivation, irrigation schemes and mechanical cultivation; and, finally, afforestation of the denuded highlands.

AFRICAN AGRICULTURE

There is no agriculture worth speaking of in Masailand, so this description will be confined to the districts of Moshi, Arusha and Mbulu. The area covered by the three districts may be divided into four very different ecological regions; the temperate rain forest areas on the southern slopes of Kilimanjaro and Meru, with a rainfall of from forty to as much as a hundred inches; the Acacia-grass savanna comprising the plains to the south of these mountains, with a poor rainfall varying between eighteen and twenty-five inches; the mountain grassland area above the Rift Valley in the Mbulu District and to the west of Arusha, with a rainfall of between thirty and forty inches; and the dry *Miombo* woodland of the Barabaig and Gorowa areas in the south of the Mbulu District, also with a rainfall of between thirty and forty inches.

The rain forest areas on both Kilimanjaro and Meru are now densely covered with banana groves, coffee plots and subsidiary food crops such as sweet potatoes, yams (*Dioscorea*), *Colocasia* and *Dolichos* bean. Some wheat is grown in the lower areas. On Kilimanjaro generally the cattle are stall-fed on banana stems and on grass brought up from the plains by the women—a task involving a laborious trek of several miles daily for many of them. In the Arusha tribal area the cattle are mostly grazed around the homesteads but wherever possible are sent to out-lying parts of the district.

Settlement in the Acacia-grass savanna areas is still largely confined to the more fertile areas where, if a drought occurs, there is also the possibility of producing crops by irrigation. The pressure of population and the provision of water supplies are extending the cultivated area year by year. Maize, beans and cotton are the main products but cassava, sweet-potatoes and onions do well. These areas have hitherto been little exploited by the local population and settlement was formerly confined almost entirely to aliens, the mountain tribes being loth to go into this country on account of the incidence of malaria. The time has come, however, when expansion from the over-populated mountain area into this type of country is imperative and for this expansion large-scale controlled irrigation schemes are necessary and are now being undertaken.

The mountain grassland area comprises the undulating plains of Mbulu and those to the west of Arusha. The problems of this area have been considered above in connection with the Mbulu Development Scheme.

The *Miombo* forest in the Barabaig, Gorowa and Mbugwe areas is sparsely populated. As we have seen, the Barabaig are mainly pastoralists, subsisting on a diet of blood and milk supplemented by a little grain. The Gorowa and Mbugwe grow millets and pulses as their staple foods and also a little maize. Cotton is the main cash crop of the Mbugwe and may be developed in the Gorowa area where onions and sugar (*sukari guru*) are the main sources of income at present.

This gives, very briefly, an account of the different regions and the crops grown in them, but by far the most important African crop produced is coffee and something must be said about the largest African co-operative society in the territory, the Kilimanjaro Native Co-operative Union.

THE KILIMANJARO NATIVE CO-OPERATIVE UNION

Coffee was first grown on Kilimanjaro at the Roman Catholic Mission at Kilema over 50 years ago, and very early in the century a few Chagga began to plant out trees. Others soon saw that coffee brought money, and by 1916 some 14,000 trees were owned by Chagga growers. Little further advance was made during the 1914-18 war, but after it was over Major (later Sir Charles) Dundas, who was in charge of the district for several years, gave every encouragement to the Chagga to plant and the number of trees increased enormously. So popular had coffee-growing become that in 1925 the growers formed the Kilimanjaro Native Coffee Planters Association "to protect and promote the interests of the native coffee growers on the mountain side". In that year the crop totalled 100 tons of parchment and was sold in Moshi for 60 cents a pound (i.e. about 7d.) This association gave place in 1933 to the Kilimanjaro Native Co-operative Union (now widely known simply as the "K.N.C.U."), with some sixteen primary co-operative societies organized on a local basis. The K.N.C.U. has been of the very greatest importance in the development of the Chagga as a tribe and it plays a crucial part in their economic life. It now has 34 societies affiliated to it and a membership of over 35,000 owning about 20,000 acres of coffee. In the year ending 30th June, 1956, it sold coffee to the value of £3,100,000 on behalf of its members.[1] During the 1939-45 war and in the following years all coffee produced was sold to the Ministry of Food, but it is now sold on the open market again. The Union is undertaking the distribution to all growers of specially selected trees, giving a greatly increased yield, which have been grown at the Coffee Research Station at Lyamungu—a task which it will take about twenty years to complete. It is putting up, at Moshi, a community centre costing about £200,000. This is being built in two sections; the first section contains a library, board room, offices, shops, bed-sitting rooms, a roof garden, a canteen, a laundry and a restaurant to seat 250; the second section will contain an assembly hall to seat 750 and an exhibition hall. The first section was opened by the Governor, Sir Edward Twining, G.C.M.G., M.B.E., on 17th March, 1952.

NON-AFRICAN POPULATION

The Province contains a European community numbering about 2,000, and there are some 6,000 Asians, mostly Indians, living in the townships of Moshi (2,900) and Arusha (3,100). There are some 200 Arabs and 450 Somalis.

Nearly all the Europeans live near the two great mountains, but there are about 200 at Oldeani in the Mbulu District. There was also a small settlement at Kiru, near Babati on the Great North Road (also in the Mbulu District), but this had to be evacuated owing to an outbreak of sleeping sickness. In the province are to be found representatives of almost every European state. Before the 1939-45 war about half the European population was German, but there are now very few and nearly all of them, being refugees or of anti-Nazi sentiments, have applied for (or have obtained) British nationality. There are 84 South African Dutch families, most of whom live on the arid "veld" to the north and north-west of Mt. Meru, leading the kind of life which their forefathers led in the Transvaal before they trekked north some fifty years ago. Many of them live in areas of marginal rainfall, on farms which are sub-divided into uneconomc units on the death of the owner, and where mere existence becomes at times precarious.

---

[1] In 1955, £1,925,000.

NON-AFRICAN AGRICULTURE

The great majority of the settlers live on the southern slopes of Mts. Kilimanjaro and Meru, on farms alienated by the Germans in the very early days of their occupation of the country. Most of these are coffee farms and they produce coffee of high quality, which is marketed through the Tanganyika Coffee Growers' Association. When coffee prices soared of recent years these estates did well, but for many years, especially in the Arusha District, they suffered from the results of the uneconomic sub-division which had been made when coffee boomed in the 1920s. In addition to coffee there was a sudden boom in pawpaw growing after the last war when the price of papain rose from Shs. 4/50 in 1939 to Shs. 31/- per lb., and over 123,000 lb. were produced. There are 22 sisal estates, totalling 6,170 acres, in the province, which produce some 6,000 tons of fibre a year. Seed beans are grown on a considerable scale, also wheat and experiments have been made in the growing of plants producing essential oils.

High yields of pyrethrum are obtained (1,000 lb. to the acre) from fields planted on Meru, but the total production of the province is inconsiderable.

INDUSTRIES

The only sugar factory in the territory is situated at Arusha Chini in the Moshi District, where cane is grown under irrigation. The production is between 1,200 and 1,500 tons per annum.

There are saw-mills on both mountain-sides, the output of which in 1956 was 11,475 cubic tons.[1]

MINERALS

The Northern Province contains few mineral occurrences of present importance.

Magnesite has been found near Longido on the Kenya border and soda is available in the Rift Valley Lakes—Natron, Manyara, Balangida and Eyasi—but its commercial exploitation presents difficulties. There is a demand for red ochre, which occurs in the area, by the Masai and the Arusha.

It is estimated that a few thousand tons of sulphur exist in the Kibo crater of Mt. Kilimanjaro and the deposits are slowly increasing, but they have a long way to go before they are likely to give rise to any commercial enthusiasm, situated as they are in a not yet extinct volcanic crater several hundred feet deep on top of the highest mountain in Africa (19,340 feet).

Meerschaum was first discovered close to the Kenya border in the Masai District in 1953. Initially there was some prejudice against the material from a market which relied solely on the best Turkish grades, but a large number of samples were exported in the form of tobacco pipe "blanks", blocks, etc. by the Tanganyika Meerschaum Corporation which is developing the deposits. The industry is now becoming more firmly established and in 1956 the Corporation received a contract for the supply of 30,000 pipes to a continental firm. The factory is in Nairobi.

Aerial prospecting has revealed a number of carbonatites in the Rift area. These are being closely examined for useful minerals.

---

[1] 12,283 cubic tons in 1955.

LABOUR

The province is largely dependent on imported labour for its requirements and the Central Province supplies a considerable proportion of the labourers working on estates. The Chagga, Meru and Arusha do not offer themselves in any numbers for work on the coffee estates on their doorsteps but are themselves in many cases employers of alien labourers.

The Northern Province Labour Utilization Board was established by statute in 1947 in an attempt to rationalize the supply of labour. The Board is now composed of nine representative members nominated by the various employers' associations in the Northern Province; four elected members chosen by ballot of all employers registered with the Board and two ex-officio members appointed by Government to represent African interests and employing departments of Government. The revenue of the Board is derived from charges made for the supply of recruited labourers and from fees paid annually to the Board by all employers who are required to register with it; fees are paid according to a sliding scale which is based on numbers employed. "Registered employers" comprise in the main agricultural concerns with more than twenty employees, though provision exists whereby any other employer may voluntarily become a member.

ADMINISTRATIVE STATIONS[1]

Arusha.[2]—Provincial Headquarters is situated at Arusha[3], 264 miles from Tanga by rail and road and 176 miles from Nairobi on the Great North Road. At the foot of Mt. Meru, in very pleasant surroundings, it is 4,500 feet above the sea. Here also there are normally stationed a District Commissioner and two district officers, a Resident Magistrate, with officers of the Police Force and of the Agricultural, Forest, Labour, Medical, Prisons, Public Works, Tsetse, Veterinary and Water Development Departments. The Soil Conservation Service of the Department of Agriculture, the Headquarters of the Game Preservation Department, the Director of National Parks and a Natural Resources School are situated in the district at Tengeru. There are also local representatives of the Colonial Insecticides Research Unit and of the Customs and the Posts and Telecommunications Departments of the East Africa High Commission.

At the time of the 1952 census the Arusha Township contained 3,571 Africans, 245 Somalis, 59 Arabs, 2,740 Indians and Goans and 974 Europeans (including schoolchildren).

It has a good aerodrome and there are frequent services to other parts of the territory and to Nairobi.

---

[1]For further information see the table on page 542.

[2]Additional particulars are to be found in "Tanganyika: A Review of its Resources and their Development" p. 806.

[3]The origin of the name *Arusha* is by no means certain. It may be the Masai word *arus* denoting a particular cattle colour. It is thought to be more likely, however, that the name came from the root *beresha*, meaning "the despised ones", in Chasu, the Pare language. The Arusha tribe are probably of Bantu stock, perhaps coming from Lambo in the North Pare mountains via Arusha-Chini (see page 204.) It is said that the original movement from the North Pares to Arusha-Chini was not made voluntarily but that the settlement was founded by the exiling of unmarried mothers to this lowland area in the Ruvu valley, where they brought up their offspring. It might be objected that Arusha is too far removed from *beresha* to have come from that root, but the changes which words suffer when adopted from one language by another are considerable.

Moshi.[1]—Moshi,[2] although the centre of the district embracing the highest mountain in Africa, is itself situated at an altitude of only 2,700 feet. It thus tends to be hot at certain seasons of the year, especially before the short rains break in November, but the nights are always cool. The reason why it was not sited higher up the mountain is that it developed as a rail-head town (220 miles from Tanga), on a line which was later extended to Arusha, and there was no need to take it into the foothills, more especially as to do so would have involved bridging the tremendous gorges with which the sides of the mountain are riven.

The District Commissioner has charge of more than a quarter of a million people, and is assisted in his work by four or five district officers. At Moshi are also normally stationed a Resident Magistrate, officers of the Police Force and of most of the Departments of Government. It was formerly the headquarters of the Grain Storage Department, and contains the Police Training Depot. The Coffee Research Station at Lyamungu is twelve miles to the west, in the centre of the Chagga coffee-growing area.

Moshi is 190 miles from Nairobi and is on the regular air service Nairobi-Arusha-Moshi-Mombo-Tanga-Zanzibar-Dar es Salaam.

Monduli.[3]—At Monduli is stationed the District Commissioner, Masailand. It is a pleasant station situated at an altitude of 5,200 feet on the slopes of the Monduli Mountain, 20 miles west of Arusha. The District Commissioner is normally assisted by two or three district officers, one of whom is stationed at Loliondo in the north near the Kenya border, a delightful if somewhat remote station, the highest in the territory (7,000 feet), and in surroundings much more temperate than tropical. At Monduli there are also stationed representatives of the Medical, Veterinary and Water Development Departments. Monduli is not on any regular air route.

Mbulu.[4]—Mbulu is situated in the west of the Province, at an altitude of 5,700 feet (125 miles from Arusha), in open mountainous country through which transport is sometimes difficult at the height of the rains. As the crow flies it is only about 20 miles from the Great North Road, but the most direct route winds through nearly a hundred miles of hill and forest. It is not on any regular air route. At Mbulu the District Commissioner is normally assisted by three district officers and, as we have seen (page 210), the whole of the highland area is the subject of a Development Scheme. Officers of the Departments of Agriculture, Veterinary, Forest, Medical, and of the Police Force, are usually stationed there.

In 1952, at the time of the census, the Mbulu Minor Settlement contained 400 Africans, 50 Asians and 30 Europeans.

---

[1]For additional particulars see "Tanganyika: A Review of its Resources and their Development" p. 818.

[2]The name *Moshi* is said to be derived from the name of a Headman or Chief called Moschi who lived in the area of what is now Old Moshi. Moschi was a leader of some standing and the local village and market were named after him and the people living there called themselves Wamoschi. These people had several skirmishes with the original German colonisers, who established their local headquarters there. Their headquarters were subsequently transferred to the present Moshi, the original site becoming Old Moshi.

[3]The place is named after one Ole Monduli, the first Masai to dig waterholes in the area.

[4]The standard Swahili-English dictionary gives the meaning of *Mbulu* as "a person who says meaningless things because of madness or weak intellect". It is generally believed that this name was bestowed on the area by Swahili travellers and askaris who could make nothing of the difficult, clicking Iraqw tongue (see p. 208.)

PLACES OF INTEREST TO THE VISITOR AND SPORTING FACILITIES[1]

Moshi District.—The Mountain is of course the greatest attraction; information for the intending climber will be found on pages 497-8. For those who do not wish to climb but merely to admire there are good hotels at Marangu, 26 miles from Moshi, in delightful surroundings on the lower slopes. From Marangu there is a mountain road into Moshi—a scenic route of some magnificence—which is open for the greater part of the year. Nearby, not far from the hotels, can be seen an example of the "bolt-holes" or underground caves and tunnels in which the Chagga, with their stock, used to take refuge in the old days on the approach of an enemy.[2]

There is good trout-fishing to be had in the Weru-weru and Kikafu rivers.

For those interested in agriculture, the Coffee Research Station at Lyamungu (12 miles) and the sugar factory at Arusha Chini (13 miles) are well worth a visit.

In Moshi are the imposing new headquarters of the Kilimanjaro Native Co-operative Union, the total cost of which, when complete, will be £200,000.

Further details of the station of Moshi are given on the table on page 548.

Arusha District.—Mount Meru can be climbed, by the energetic, in a day, provided that the start is made from near the forest edge and a guide is taken. The District Commissioner will provide intending climbers with further information.

The mountain can also be easily encircled by road in a day, and the drive through the forest on the eastern side is a memorable experience. From the plains to the north the view of Kilimanjaro is especially impressive.

Game such as waterbuck, impala, hartebeeste, Grant's and Thomson's gazelle, dikdik, duiker, zebra and ostrich, are to be seen on the plains a few miles south of the Arusha-Moshi road; and elephant, buffalo and rhino in the Engurdoto crater fifteen miles from Arusha.

Trout-fishing is to be had in the Temi river, which flows through Arusha Township, and in the Nduruma river, five miles away.

Swimming and riding are also to be had and race meetings are held from time to time.

Lake Duluti is a delightful crater lake just off the Moshi road eight miles from Arusha and well worth a visit.

Further details of the station of Arusha are given on page 547.

Masailand and Mbulu District.—The region near the Rift has great attractions for the hunter, and some record heads (and excellent photographs) have been obtained in the Mto-wa-mbu and Engaruka areas.

The Ngorongoro "crater" in the Serengeti National Park[3] is of course world-famous and has a unique, remote, out-of-this world atmosphere. As the camp is approached, by a mountain road giving wonderful views of the surrounding country, the ordinary world drops away and one enters into another, in which the

---

[1]See also "The Shooting Grounds" on pp. 459–462.

[2]See "Chagga Forts and Bolt Holes" by H. A. Fosbrooke in *Tanganyika Notes and Records*, No. 37 of July 1954.

[3]See pp. 465 to 469.

goblin-like log-cabins at the camp and the lichens festooning the trees seem entirely appropriate, and where the cares of the modern world are easily forgotten in the contemplation of the vast game-filled plain two thousand feet below.

On the way to Ngorongoro one passes Oldeani, where much wheat is grown and where there is an out-lying group of the Northern Province settler community.

Further north is the Olduvai Gorge (see page 20) one of the most productive archæological sites ever found, where the action of an ancient river, cutting through the strata, has exposed to view the geological history of the area in the distant past over an immense period of time.

Further details of the stations of Monduli and Mbulu are given in the table on page 548.

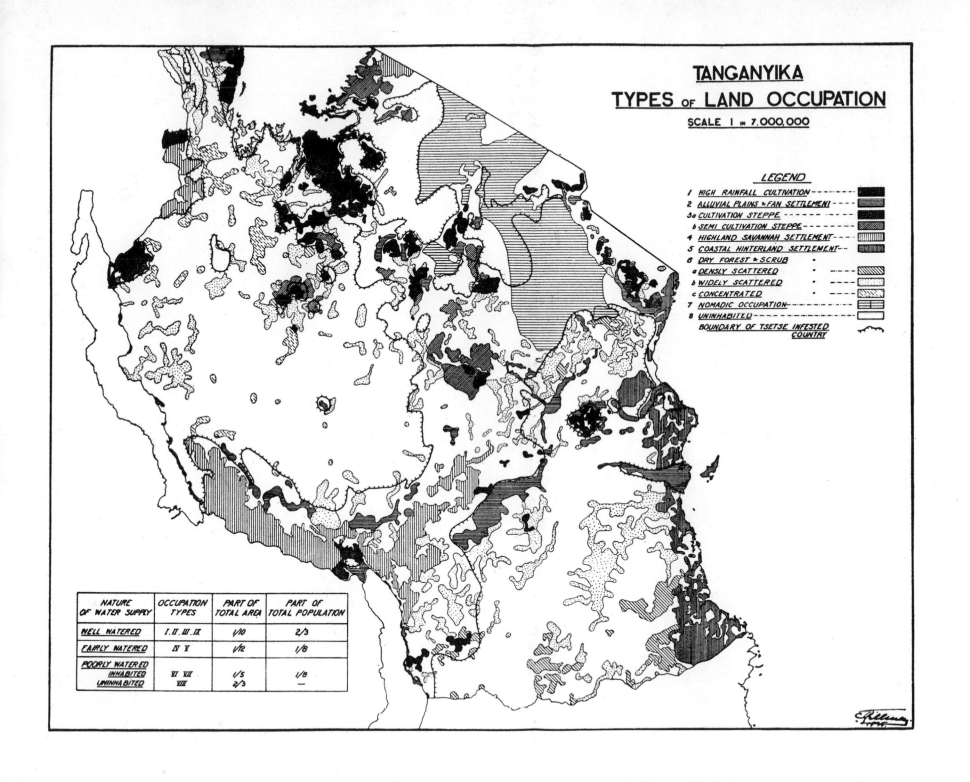

TANGANYIKA

TYPES OF LAND OCCUPATION

SCALE 1 in 7.000.000

LEGEND

1 HIGH RAINFALL CULTIVATION -------
2 ALLUVIAL PLAINS & FAN SETTLEMENT ----
3a CULTIVATION STEPPE --------
b SEMI CULTIVATION STEPPE --------
4 HIGHLAND SAVANNAH SETTLEMENT ---
5 COASTAL HINTERLAND SETTLEMENT--
6 DRY FOREST & SCRUB ·
a DENSLY SCATTERED · ----
b WIDELY SCATTERED · ----
c CONCENTRATED · ----
7 NOMADIC OCCUPATION --------
8 UNINHABITED ----------
BOUNDARY OF TSETSE INFESTED
COUNTRY

NATURE OF WATER SUPPLY	OCCUPATION TYPES	PART OF TOTAL AREA	PART OF TOTAL POPULATION
WELL WATERED	I. II. III. IX	1/10	2/3
FAIRLY WATERED	IV V	1/12	1/8
POORLY WATERED INHABITED	VI VII	1/5	1/8
UNINHABITED	VIII	2/3	—

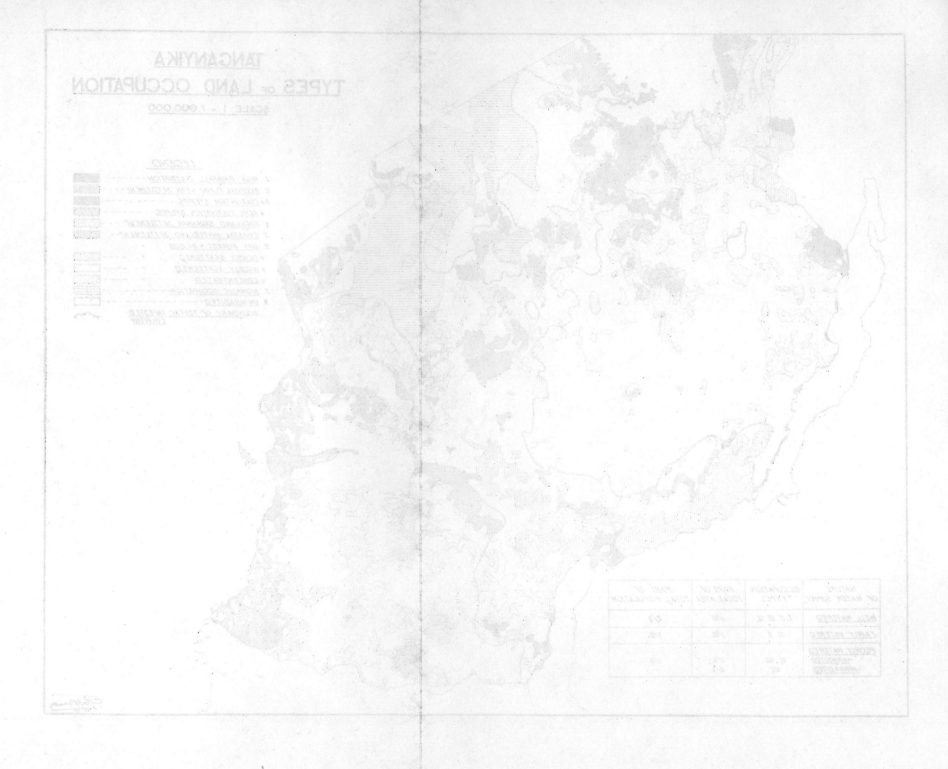

THE SOUTHERN PROVINCE

SITUATION

The Southern Province extends across the whole southern boundary of Tanganyika, lying between Lake Nyasa and the Indian Ocean and between the Eastern Province and Portuguese East Africa. The distance by road from Mtwara on the coast to Mbamba Bay on Lake Nyasa is 550 miles and from the northern to the southern border 250 miles. The province covers an area of 56,000 square miles, (about the size of England and Wales,) and contains nearly a million people. Because of its remoteness and of the somewhat tenuous nature of its communications it was in the past known as the "Cinderella Province", but with the development now taking place and with the tremendous improvement in communications—of which the deep-water berths at Mtwara and the railway line from there to Nachingwea are but two examples—the title is now quite inappropriate.

DISTRICTS

There are eight districts in the province. Along the coast lie the districts of Kilwa, (6,313 square miles, population 94,000), Lindi (4,144 square miles; population 230,000) and Mtwara (1,505 square miles; population 103,000). In the centre of the province, occupying the large area between these coastal districts and the Songea District on Lake Nyasa, lie the districts of Nachingwea (14,400 square miles; population 45,000, formerly known as the Ruponda District and incorporating much of the old Liwale District), Newala (1,763 square miles; population 175,000), Masasi (3,597 square miles; population 127,000) and Tunduru (7,452 square miles; population 66,000). The Songea District in the west covers an area of 16,049 square miles and has a population of 160,000. Provincial headquarters were formerly at Lindi but were moved to Mtwara in 1953.

PHYSICAL FEATURES

The districts of Kilwa, Lindi and Mtwara form part of the coastal plain and present features similar to the districts further north—a sandy or coral shore, with in places mangrove forest, backed by low-lying country, hilly for the most part and well covered by vegetation, which varies from the coconut palms, casuarinas and scrub bush of the coast to the *miombo* woodlands, baobabs and thickets of the hinterland in the west. In the Kilwa District the hills rise to a height of 2,000 feet, and in the west of the Lindi District the land rises to a height of 1,500 feet (2,000 feet on the Rondo Plateau), but most of the land in these three coastal districts lies at an altitude between sea level and 1,000 feet.

The immense block of *miombo* woodland, to which reference was made on p. 5, extends over most of the Masasi, Nachingwea, Tunduru and Songea Districts and this type of vegetation is the distinguishing characteristic of these areas.

The country between Masasi and Tunduru is remarkable for its tall pinnacle peaks and round-topped monstrous boulders of gneiss. (On these there grows a curious bush-like herb which makes excellent tooth-brushes and also a sage-like bush whose tea is much appreciated for medicinal purposes, especially for chest complaints). West of Masasi a mass of these hills forms the Kilimarondo Heights. These gneiss eminences were used by missionaries in the old days to signal to each other by heliograph.[1]

---

[1] See Barker op. cit. on p. 220.

The Makonde plateau occupies most of the Newala District. Rising abruptly from the plains, with an almost sheer drop of 1,300 feet at Newala itself, it forms a compact block of thickly inhabited although naturally almost waterless country, containing a form of dense thicket wherever this has not been cleared by the local Makonde people.

In the Songea District are to be found the greatest variety of physical features. In the east and centre is *miombo* woodland, tsetse-infested, but towards the lake are the Matengo highlands, rising to over 7,000 feet in height and containing some most attractive country. From these highlands the land falls steeply to the lake, where there is a narrow maritime fringe at an altitude of some 1,500 feet, presenting very different features and in places not unlike parts of the coastal districts.

The general impression of the province is one of a land closely covered, the cover varying from *miombo* woodland to light scrub, and the visitor motoring from the coast to Mbamba Bay will be struck by the fact that, judging by its vegetative cover, the land appears to be fertile in most places.

The province contains several rivers of importance,[1] the largest being the Ruvuma, which forms the boundary with Portuguese East Africa for 420 miles. It is navigable by small vessels for a short distance and for much of its length flows through a deep wide gorge. Livingstone was the first to investigate its possibilities for navigation and an account of the expedition is given in Coupland's "Kirk on the Zambesi":[2] The following extracts from Kirk's diary are of interest:—

> "Sept. 16 [1862] "The river gets worse as we advance. . . . Dr. L. still carries on, regardless of his return and of the consequences of a long delay. Sept. 20. We are now not more than 200 miles east of the nearest side of Lake Nyassa and have now explored 100 miles of river in direct line from the mouth. Sept. 25. All afternoon we have come over a wide river-bed, having barely a boat's draught of water and so encumbered with projecting points as to be dangerous even to boats ascending. I cannot believe that this will ever be of use for navigation to any class of vessel. It will not be free from danger to us on the way down. Dr. L. never thinks of getting back. All he cares for is accomplishing his object at any risk whatever. It is useless making any remark to him. . . . He himself now thinks the river unnavigable. Sept. 26. A field of rocks ahead. There is no doubt of this being a check to all navigation at all seasons. Sept. 27. Began our return this morning."

Other rivers flowing into the Indian Ocean are the Matandu, Mavuji and Mbwemkuru in the Kilwa District, the Lukuledi which enters the sea at Lindi, and the Mkundi.

Through the Masasi and Tunduru Districts flow the Mbangala, Lukwika, Lumusule, Muhuwezi and Msinjewe rivers, tributaries of the Ruvuma, together with a large number of feeder streams many of which do not dry up even at the end of the dry season. The area is in fact one of the best watered in the territory.

---

[1] "Rivers of Southern Tanganyika", by R. de la B. Barker, in *Tanganyika Notes and Records*, No. 24 for Dec., 1947.

[2] pp. 242-3.

From the Songea highlands flow the Lumeme and other streams to feed the Ruvuma, and the Ngaka, Kukulasi, Njalila and Lumesi to feed the Ruhuhu, which discharges into Lake Nyasa.

There are no large lakes in the province, but Lake Rutamba in the Lindi District, Lakes Kitere and Chidya in the Mtwara District, Lake Tandahimba in Newala District, Kiurumira in Nachingwea District and Maliwe in Kilwa District are of importance locally.

CLIMATE

Mtwara, being 3 degrees further south of the Equator than Dar es Salaam, tends to be cooler during the hot weather, and the new station at Kilwa Masoko, delightfully situated on a bluff overlooking the harbour and open to the breeze from all sides, is appreciably cooler, but generally speaking the climate at the coast is very similar to that found further north. Inland, in the coastal plain, conditions can be rather oppressive at times, but in the higher parts of the hinterland nights are cool for most of the year. At Newala, at an altitude of only 2,600 feet above sea level, the sudden rise from the plain produces a similar effect to that noticeable in the Usambaras and the climate seems disproportionately cool, fires being required at night for several months in the year. In Songea the effect of altitude is still more noticeable; at district headquarters the temperature sometimes drops as low as 47° and in the mountains frosts are frequent. But on the lake shore during the rains the atmosphere can be very oppressive, with absolute maximum temperatures reaching as high as 102° and with a high rate of humidity.

Rainfall at district headquarters has been recorded as follows over the past seven years:—

Station	Altitude Ft.	Average inches	1950	1951	1952	1953	1954	1955	1956
Kilwa Kivinje	30	38·34 (7 years)	36·25	26·95	20·12	33·31	30·00	35·66	45·19
Lindi ...	133	35·78 (18 years)	34·40	41·18	44·06	33·97	27·23	43·13	*
Mtwara ...	60	46·84 (5 years)	44·66	44·17	40·89	36·39	59·21	*	45·78
Nachingwea	1,200	37·56 (7 years)	43·97	37·72	41·05	23·84	28·89	43·34	44·14
Newala ...	2,600	38·33 (25 years)	37·77	31·83	47·37	32·10	33·94	47·18	62·31
Masasi ...	1,400	33·27 (15 years)	50·89	38·49	35·74	29·05	28·31	35·10	34·52
Tunduru ...	2,300	40·96 (28 years)	40·98	43·22	33·69	36·69	34·04	40·70	65·56
Songea ...	3,783	44·32 (42 years)	48·14	49·22	43·79	41·87	37·41	44·75	*

*Records incomplete.

POPULATION

The combined results of the 1948 census, a complete one, and the 1952 census, a partial one only, are given below:—

District	Area in sq. miles	European	Indian	Goan	Arab	Somali	Coloured	Other	Total non-African	African	Total Population
Kilwa	6,313	24	217	–	95	5	5	–	346	96,552	96,898
Lindi	4,144	311	1,981	100	70	–	28	15	2,505	176,989	179,494
Mtwara	1,505	181	719	15	102	1	9	18	1,045	88,139	89,184
Nachingwea ...	14,400	525	100	9	4	2	1	3	644	44,321	44,965
Newala	1,763	27	286	–	9	–	–	–	322	154,012	154,334
Masasi	3,597	95	169	–	1	–	9	3	277	117,254	117,531
Tunduru	7,452	21	100	–	1	–	–	4	126	65,751	65,877
Songea	16,049	288	198	8	–	–	7	–	501	171,031	171,532
		1,472	3,770	132	282	8	59	43	5,766	914,049	919,815

The Southern Province thus contains nearly a million inhabitants, but since most of these are concentrated in certain areas any calculation of density of population based on the area of 56,000 square miles is quite misleading. The Makonde plateau of the Newala District for instance has a density of about 145 to the square mile, while the figure for Lindi District is only about 47.

Nearly all the Arabs (250) and Indians (3,800) in the province are to be found at the coast in the towns of Lindi, Mtwara, Mikindani and Kilwa.

Of the 1,500 Europeans about one-third are missionaries, one-third are employed in industry or agriculture and one-third are civil servants.

THE TRIBES OF THE PROVINCE

The distribution of the various tribes as shown by the map facing page 298 is approximate only, since there is very considerable intermixture, especially along the southern border, and tribal areas cannot really be distinguished in many parts. The reasons for this somewhat unusual state of affairs (in Tanganyika) are to be found largely in the history of the area. It suffered severely at the hands of the Arab slavers; it was subjected to raids by the Ngoni from the south, who, about the middle of the 19th century, penetrated as far as the Rufiji river in the north; finally, it suffered still more severely at the hands of the Germans after the *Maji Maji* rebellion in 1905-6.[1] A further factor was the lack, among nearly all tribes except the Matengo, of any form of centralized authority. The chief as found amongst the Hehe or Sukuma did not exist and most of the tribes were strongly matrilineal.

Thus, today, members of the Mwera,[2] Makonde,[3] Matambwe, Yao,[4] and Makua groups are to be found in all districts, except possibly in Songea. The Yao predominate in Tunduru, but are numerous in Masasi; the Makonde predominate in Newala and Mtwara but are numerous in Lindi; the Matambwe are mainly found in Newala, but are also found in Mtwara, Masasi and Tunduru; the Mwera predominate in Lindi and Nachingwea but are numerous in Kilwa and are also found in Masasi; the Makua predominate in Masasi, are scattered in Tunduru, but belong largely to Portuguese East Africa, whence all these groups appear to have come.

As a result of many years of Mission work and contact with Europeans these groups have lost many of their earlier customs, but among the Makonde stilt-dancing may still be witnessed and many, among the older generation of women especially, still wear the large wooden lip ring,[5] though there is no tattooing on the face such as characterizes so noticeably the southern section of the tribe, the Maviha, in Portuguese East Africa.

---

[1]See "The Maji Maji Rebellion in the Liwale District" by R. M. Bell, *Tanganyika Notes and Records* No. 28, 1950.

[2]For language, see "A Grammar of Mwera" by Lyndon Harries, Witwatersrand University, 1951.

[3]The Maviha (Mawia) on the plateau south of the Ruvuma in Portuguese territory are an offshoot of the Makonde, indeed they call themselves Makonde, only being known as Maviha by the Tanganyika groups (from the Makonde verb *viha*, to be fierce).

[4]"Some Notes on the Yao", Archdeacon Lamburn. *Tanganyika Notes and Records* No. 29, 1951.

[5]"The lip-ring among the tribes of the Southern Province", D. F. Bowie. *Tanganyika Notes and Records*, No. 27, 1949.

Of the origin of the Ngindo, Magingo, Ndonde, Matumbi and Machinga groups in the Kilwa, Nachingwea, Lindi and Tunduru Districts, very little indeed is known, though the Machinga are probably a Yao offshoot and the Ndonde possibly related to the Ndendeule of Songea—the inhabitants of the area prior to the Ngoni incursion.

Songea District may be divided tribally into three groups. The Nyasa of the lake littoral are a conglomerate, with Pimbwe, Nyasa, Mwera (not to be confused with those of Lindi District) and Pangwa elements. The Matengo[1] of the Matengo highlands seem to have been brought into being by the Ngoni raids, and formerly consisted of a number of disparate groups among the chief components of which were Yao, Kamanga, Pangwa and even Tonga. Linguistically there seems to be much affinity with Pangwa[2]. The Ngoni, descendants of those who made the great journey from South Africa, are divided into two chiefdoms; the Njelu Ngoni under Nkosi Zulu and the Mshope Ngoni under Nkosi Chabuma. Little is known, so far, about the social and political organization of this remnant of the Zulu nation but fairly complete assimilation with the local Ndendeule seems to have taken place.

The Ngoni have had a chequered history in Tanganyika. According to tribal tradition, a number of Ngoni under the leadership of one Izongondaba broke away from Chaka, crossed the Zambezi about the year 1835 and settled near Domira Bay on Lake Nyasa. Thence they went to the area on the western shore of Lake Tanganyika but, finding this area inhospitable and tsetse-ridden, they turned back and settled at Mpimbwe, at the head of the Rukwa valley. Later they penetrated far to the north, settling for a time at Runzewe in the present Kahama District and from there reaching the shores of Lake Victoria before returning to Runzewe.

A second section went through Usafwa, Ukinga and Upangwa (in the present Mbeya and Njombe Districts) to the plains around Songea, where they settled. On arrival, they found at Mbunga, some forty miles north-east of Songea, a third section of Izongondaba's original force, which had broken away after the crossing of the Zambezi. It is this section which is reputed to have harried the coast from Kilwa to Mombasa. War broke out at Mbunga between these two sections and those originally in occupation were forced to flee and went to the Mahenge area, founding the Mbunga tribe there[3].

The remains of a small tribe, the Mawindi, are to be found near Kigonsera, 45 miles west of Songea, and there are some Bena in the north of the district.

AGRICULTURAL RESOURCES

Climatic and Ecological Divisions

The coastal plain with rainfall averaging 36 inches, moderately wooded, comprises a strip varying in width from a few miles to fifty miles, consisting of the eastern halves of the Kilwa and Lindi Districts and the whole of the Mtwara District. The population is nearly 340,000.

---

[1] The word itself means "forest", and the Matengo were originally "the forest people".

[2] But see also "The Classification of Bantu Languages" by M. Guthrie, O.U.P. 1948.

[3] See "The Angoni of Tanganyika Territory" by G. W. Hatchell in *Tanganyika Notes and Records*, No. 25, for June 1948, and "A History of the Songea Ngoni" by P. H. Gulliver in *Tanganyika Notes and Records* No. 41 for Dec. 1955.

The hinterland plain adjoins and frequently intrudes into the coastal strip. It is dotted with baobab trees and is characterized by fairly flat country moderately covered by thorn bush. It comprises the western half of Lindi District, all southern Masasi District, the western half of Kilwa District and most of northern Nachingwea District as well as small scattered sections of Tunduru District. The rainfall is approximately 38 inches and the population is estimated at 250,000.

The Makonde plateau occupies the greater part of the Newala District. It is covered by a type of bush that has become known as "Makonde thicket". It has no rivers and has an average rainfall of 37 inches. The population is approximately 175,000.

The dry miombo woodland occurs over most of Tunduru District and northern Masasi District. The rainfall ranges from 38 to 40 inches and the population is estimated at about 100,000.

The Matengo Highlands of the Songea District, at altitudes between 4,000 and 7,000 feet and receiving a rainfall of some 45 inches a year. Population about 37,000.

The Nyasa lake shore, a strip between the mountains and the lake. Rainfall 66·92 inches a year (at Liuli Mission). Population about 12,500.

Agricultural Conditions

The coastal plain.—Along the strip in the immediate vicinity of the sea the population is dense but becomes sparser as the distance from the sea increases. In Lindi District in the valley of the Lukuledi River, the density of population is greatest, while in the strip that falls in the Kilwa District it is the most sparse. Over the whole coastal plain the staple foods of the people are sorghum and cowpeas with cassava as the principal root crop. Rice, maize, millet, pigeon peas, groundnuts, cashew nuts and coconuts are also grown.

The economic crops are sesame, cotton, castor, cashew nuts and copra. Any food crop surplus is readily sold to local sisal estates or exported to other parts of the territory. The soils vary greatly from grey, sandy, very poor-yielding soils to rich black loams and clays of great agricultural value. Sisal estates employ some 11,000 labourers and many of the local inhabitants rely solely on this employment for their livelihood.

The hinterland plains.—The population is split up around the points of water supply. The supplies in the dry season are mostly from wells of the usual primitive type. The staple foods are sorghums, upland rice, maize, pigeon peas, cowpeas, cassava and groundnuts. The cash income is derived from the sale of the surplus foods, sesame, wild rubber, beeswax, roll tobacco, gums, cotton and cashew nuts. The soils of the plains of the hinterland vary from poor sandy soils to rich valley loams and clays, but the cultivation is often very inefficient, being a mere scratching of the surface soil. In spite of this inefficiency and the natural lethargy of the people, the soil fertility is such that harvests generally are good and affect very favourably the province's exports. The inhabitants of the area earn much of their income by working on estates in the Lindi coastal area. Over roughly half the area sleeping sickness is endemic.

The Makonde plateau.—This area, some 1,200 square miles in extent, is thickly inhabited by the industrious Makonde people and is remarkable in that it contains very few points of water supply. In spite of the fact that great energy has thus to be dissipated by large numbers of the population having to walk as much as twelve hours a day in the dry season to fetch water, the people cultivate large acreages and grow great quantities of food. The staple foods are cassava, upland rice, sorghum, maize and cowpeas, and also swamp rice cultivated in the Ruvuma valley. The principal cash crops grown on the plateau are cassava and cashew nuts. A great effort is being made to develop the Ruvuma valley with a view to supplementing the income gained from cash crops grown on the plateau. On the southern slopes of the plateau, the local inhabitants prepare colombo root and starch as well as wild rubber, all from indigenous shrubs, and beeswax, gum and roll tobacco are also sold for cash. Vast quantities of cassava have been sold to other parts of the territory. The area has no sisal estates but numbers of Makonde go to the coastal estates to earn much of the cash income of the district.

The whole economy of the area is likely to be changed with the implementation of imaginative schemes drawn up for supplying the plateau with water piped up from the plains below. A pilot scheme has already been very successfully carried out and water is pumped up to Newala from the springs 1,300 feet below. This is now being followed up with a much more ambitious, and costly, scheme to pipe water to various points throughout the plateau. The revolution this will cause in the lives of people who now have to walk as much as thirty miles to fetch water can well be imagined. The cost is estimated at £300,000 for the first phase and a unique feature of the scheme is the proposal that the capital be raised by imposing an annual water rate of Shs. 10/- per taxpayer, such rate being regarded as a purchase of a share in the undertaking.

The dry miombo woodland.—The main food crops in the *miombo* areas are maize, sorghum, beans and cassava. Groundnuts and sorghum are also fairly extensively grown (except in the Songea District), while rice is cultivated wherever it will thrive. The cash crops are sesame, roll tobacco, cotton, sunflower, castor seed, and cashew nuts, while surplus groundnuts, rice and beans are sent to the coast for use on sisal estates and for export. An important commodity sold for cash is beeswax. The areas are fairly well watered but the soils generally are poor and sandy, derived from granite and gneiss, except in parts of the Tunduru District where many fertile valleys are to be found. In practically the whole of this *miombo* country, sleeping sickness is endemic.

In the Songea District the foundations of the African fire-cured tobacco industry were laid in 1928 and in the early days the crop was sold on the local market by the Agricultural Department. It is now marketed by the Ngoni-Matengo Co-operative Marketing Union Ltd. which is representative of all growers, about half of the crop being sold to buyers in Liverpool, the remainder being sold in East Africa. All tobacco is conditioned and packed at the factory in Songea, which was built by the Union to handle 2,000 tons of leaf annually.

The Matengo Highlands.—In the past the members of the Matengo tribe took refuge in the mountains from raiders such as the Angoni and there developed a remarkable system of cultivation of their own, called *ngoro*. With the arrival of the *Pax Britannica* and the consequent wider dispersal of the members of the tribe, this system tended to be abandoned but it is still fairly widely practised and is strongly encouraged by all in authority. Briefly, the system consists in the cultivation of a hillside in a series of small pits. Earth from the pits is piled in heaps at the side, and on these heaps the crops (mostly maize) are grown. Weeds and crop residues are thrown into the pits. For the next seasons' crops the heaps are broken down into the pits and fresh pits dug alongside. Hillsides cultivated in this way present an unusual honeycomb-like appearance. The system is most effective both in preventing erosion and in maintaining the fertility of the soil.

In these highlands the Matengo are now growing wheat and coffee on an increasing scale. The coffee is of good quality and fetches high prices at the Moshi auctions. At some of the Mission stations in the higher parts a wide variety of semi-tropical and temperate crops can be cultivated, and apples, pears, peaches and plums are successfully grown.

The Nyasa lake-shore.—This small fringe between the lake and the mountains in the western part of the Songea District differs considerably from the rest of the district, being several thousand feet lower than most of it. The main crops produced are maize, cassava and rice, and fish forms an important element in the diet of the local people. The area is oppressively hot and humid for much of the year and the people (12,500 in all) are somewhat apathetic in consequence.

General.—Two legacies of the Groundnut Scheme—a new and magnificently equipped port with deep-water berths and a railway line, extending inland for 132 miles—should revolutionize agricultural production in the province. As well as the economic crops mentioned above, which are nearly all produced by the local Africans, there are some noteworthy non-African enterprises. Lindi District contains 12 of the province's 15 sisal estates, which in 1956 exported some 15,000 tons of sisal, valued at approximately £900,000. On the Rondo plateau, also in the Lindi District, Messrs. Steel Brothers have been given a concession, in partnership with Government, to exploit the timber in an area of some 1,500 square miles and are producing sawn timber at the rate of approximately 6,000 tons a year. Tobacco farms have already been taken up by immigrant settlers in the Tunduru District and more are available for leasing both in this area and in the Mgwina area of the Songea District.

A cotton ginnery owned by Asian interests has been set up at Tunduru. Its capacity is some 4,000 tons of seed cotton annually but as yet it is producing below capacity.

The Tanganyika Agricultural Corporation's holding in the Nachingwea District totals 150,000 acres but it is not envisaged that more than 20,000 acres will now be cultivated.

The agricultural development planned for the province can perhaps best be seen from the following table, in which the original development plan figures, prepared in 1950, have been revised in the light of progress made since then:—

Product	Tonnages Exported		Estimated Export Tonnages for 1960	
	1947	1952	Original (1950) Estimates	Revised Estimates
Beeswax	52	101	300	220
Cashew-nuts	1,313	9,740	10,000	29,500
Cassava	2,244	16,927	20,000	38,000
Castor seed	–	609	–	1,850
Coffee	–	196	–	750
Colombo root	97	12	300	220
Copra	626	1,070	3,000	2,650
Cotton	31	25	300	555
Groundnuts	991	738	4,000	4,000
Gum Arabic	62	4	200	–
Kapok	–	–	–	90
Maize	1,932	10	2,000	9,150
Mangrove bark	3,548	429	1,000	500
Millet and other grains	783	337	1,000	1,300
Mtama	4,254	15	2,000	9,500
Native Starch	13	–	200	–
Paddy or rice	537	138	3,000	15,900
Pulses	4,976	1,543	6,700	7,450
Sesame...	3,344	1,921	6,000	6,950
Sisal	9,074	11,159	25,000	20,000
Sunflower	–	1,954	3,000	820
Timber...	–	4,540	15,000	15,000
Tobacco:				
(a) fire-cured	126	398	2,000	1,500
(b) flue-cured	–	–	3,500	700
Wheat	–	–	–	300
TOTAL ...	34,003	51,866	108,500	166,905
Add estimated T.A.C. production ...			41,500	6,000
TOTAL ...			150,000	172,905

(All figures are in deadweight tons.)

INDUSTRIES

The main agricultural industries in the province—the production of sisal, tobacco, cassava and cashew nuts—have already been described, and the large timber concession on the Rondo Plateau has been mentioned. There are in addition five other timber concessions in different parts of the province, producing about 5,000 tons of sawn timber annually.

A factory for the extraction of fibre (for paper-making) from the bark of the baobab tree was established at Lindi and production began in 1953.

Another factory for processing cashew nuts—which are normally sent to India for processing—was set up at Mtwara.

MINERALS

The mineral potentialities of this large province are only as yet very approximately known. The immense coal reserves at Ngaka in the Songea District await exploitation. Copper and nickel have been found at Ntaka in the Nachingwea District; graphite both in that district and in Lindi; garnets in the Newala District;

gypsum in the Kilwa District; phosphatic limestone in the Masasi District and beryl in mica pegmatites in the Lindi District. Mica occurs at various places in the province.

Salt is produced in the Mtwara and Lindi Districts by solar evaporation of sea water, annual production being worth about £27,000.

ADMINISTRATIVE STATIONS[1]

Kilwa[2].—There are three Kilwas[3]: Kilwa Kisiwani, "Kilwa on the Island", Milton's "Quiloa", a town of great importance and wealth before the arrival of the Portuguese (see page 27) but now an empty ruin; Kilwa Kivinje, "Kilwa of the Casuarina Trees", seventeen miles to the north on the mainland, which was the administrative centre of the district until 1949; and Kilwa Masoko, the new administrative station, also situated on the mainland but in a much better position—on the southern tip of a peninsula, overlooking the best harbour on the East Coast, immediately opposite Kilwa Kisiwani. Here an entirely new station has been established, with a District Commissioner, one district officer and one district assistant and, normally, representatives of the Public Works and the Agricultural Departments.

Kilwa Masoko is 212 miles from Dar es Salaam by road and 122 miles from Lindi. It is now on a regular air route and 'planes call there once a week in each direction on the route Dar es Salaam-Mtwara.

In 1952, the township of Kilwa Masoko contained 180 Africans, 8 Asians and 7 Europeans, while at Kilwa Kivinje there were 2,164 Africans, 204 Asians and one European.

A new lighter jetty for Kilwa Masoko is now under construction by the East African Railways and Harbours Administration.

Lindi[4].—District headquarters are pleasantly sited overlooking the harbour, and the climate, though very hot at times, is not so oppressive as it often is in the more enclosed coastal stations such as Dar es Salaam. Previously, provincial headquarters were at Lindi[5] but were transferred to Mtwara in 1953. Lindi is 317 miles from Dar es Salaam by road, and from the town a good road runs west to Masasi (96 miles) and thence through Tunduru to Songea. It is a port of some consequence for the export of local produce and steamers call there frequently. It is also well served by planes of the East African Airways Corporation.

---

[1]For additional information see table on p. 542.

[2]For further details see "Tanganyika: A Review of its Resources and their Development", p. 813.

[3]The name *Kilwa* is said to be derived from the Swahili word *kelele* and commemorates the occasion (about the 11th or 12th centuries) when a sea invasion by, probably, Arabs was foiled by a trick. When the invaders' dhows approached, a large number of people hid along the eastern and north-eastern sea shore of Kisiwani and incanted prayers as if they were *walimu* (Mohammedan religious teachers or leaders). This device led the commander of the invading force to believe that the population must be very large to support so many *walimu* and for there to be so many congregations at prayer. He reached the conclusion, it is said, that the population must be so large as to be more than a match for his force and so withdrew, Kilwa Kisiwani thus being saved. *Masoko*, in the name Kilwa Masoko, does not derive, as might be thought, from the Swahili word for markets, but from the verb *kuchokoa*, meaning to dig out crustacea, eels, etc., from holes in the rocks and coral. This was a source of foodstuffs much resorted to during a famine of old and gave the area its name.

[4]For further details see "Tanganyika: A Review of its Resources and their Development", p. 815.

[5]The name *Lindi* seems to have come from *Kilindini*—a place of deep water. According to local legend the marsh on the waterfront to the west of the town at one time used to be a deep pool branching off from the creek and giving rise to the name.

In 1952, the population of Lindi Township was 9,629 Africans, 1,535 Asians and 159 Europeans. The District Commissioner is assisted by two district officers and representatives of all major departments, together with a Resident Magistrate, are normally stationed there.

Mtwara[1].—District headquarters were formerly at Mikindani, a picturesque coastal village, but with the establishment of the new harbour at Mtwara[2] were moved there in 1953. The town has been planned on the most up-to-date town-planning lines, allowing plenty of room for expansion in the future, and is in marked contrast to the old-world Mikindani. It is 72 miles from Lindi by road and from the town a good road runs to Newala (90 miles). From Mtwara also runs the new railway to Nachingwea. Planes of East African Airways Corporation connect Mtwara with Dar es Salaam and other places in the territory. The District Commissioner is assisted by two district officers and a district assistant, and representatives of all the major departments are normally stationed there.

Nachingwea[3].—District headquarters are situated in a town created by the Overseas Food Corporation as part of the Groundnut Scheme. It is 32 miles from Masasi on the Masasi-Ruponda-Liwale road. It has a good bore-hole water supply and electricity. It is also well served by the planes of East African Airways on the route Dar es Salaam-Nachingwea-Mtwara-Lindi-Mafia Island-Dar es Salaam, as well as by the railway line from Mtwara. Nachingwea was created a township on 1st January 1953. Its population in 1954 was approximately 100 Europeans, 50 Asians and 700 Africans.

The District Commissioner is assisted by one district officer and representatives of the Police and the Medical, Agricultural, Veterinary and Tsetse Departments are normally stationed there.

Newala[4].—This is one of the most attractively situated stations in the territory. It is perched on the edge of the Makonde Plateau, near the border with Portuguese East Africa, 1,300 feet above the plains, and 2,600 feet above sea level, with magnificent views over the Ruvuma river towards Portuguese territory. It enjoys a pleasant climate, as already mentioned, and is often quite cold at night during the period June—September. It is 90 miles from Mtwara, 88 miles from Lindi, and 43 miles from Masasi. It is not on any regular air service route. In 1952, the population of Newala Minor Settlement comprised 500 Africans, 100 Asians and 14 Europeans. The District Commissioner is assisted by one district officer and representatives of the Water Development and Agricultural Departments are normally stationed there.

---

[1] For further details see "Tanganyika: a Review of its Resources and their Development", p. 819.

[2] The name *Mtwara* is said to have originated from the Makonde word *litwala*—to carry off another man's wife. On the side of the bay opposite to Mtwara is a small peninsula now known as Msemo. Tradition relates that a man from the peninsula paddled across the bay to what is now known as Mtwara and carried off a woman to his home. This incident and the subsequent negotiations gave the two places their names—*Msemo* (talk or shout) and *Litwala*, later corrupted into Mtwara.

[3] The present township has taken the name of a water-hole which used to exist in what is now the town. The origin of the name is unknown, though it has been suggested that it may possibly have derived from the same root as the Swahili word *kunywea*—to drink at.

[4] As in the case of a number of stations, the name *Newala* is thought to be derived from the name of a prominent early individual settler in the area. It is said that long ago a party of Wamakua including one *Newara* moved to the vicinity of the present Newala station from what is now part of Portuguese East Africa. Newara built his homestead near some springs (about four miles south of the present Boma) and as a result of living in such a prominent position, and, so it is said, of his happy and generous disposition, the area of his home gradually became known by his own name—the "r" being transposed into "l", the two letters commonly being more or less interchangeable in Bantu languages.

Masasi[1].—Masasi was selected in 1875 by Bishop Steere as a place to settle freed slaves.[2]

A new District Office and new quarters for the District Commissioner and others have been built of recent years. Because of its altitude and situation, Masasi tends to be oppressively hot at times, but nights are nearly always cool.

Masasi is 138 miles by road from Mtwara and 96 miles from Lindi. It is not on any regular air route, although a small all-weather air strip is maintained.

The District Commissioner is assisted by one district officer and representatives of the Agricultural and Public Works Departments are normally stationed there. The population of Masasi Minor Settlement in 1954 was approximately 340 Africans, 80 Asians and 13 Europeans.

Tunduru[3].—This is a small station 256 miles from Mtwara and 174 miles from Songea by road. It is built on a hill and commands wide views over undulating woodland country. The altitude is just over 2,000 feet and the climate is comparatively cool for ten months of the year. An airstrip which is normally serviceable (except immediately after heavy rain) is situated some 200 yards from the District Office. The population of Tunduru Minor Settlement in 1954 was made up of approximately 500 Africans, 75 Asians and 12 Europeans.

The District Commissioner is assisted by one district officer and a representative of the Agricultural Department.

Songea[4].—District headquarters are situated in pleasant hilly country at a height of nearly 4,000 feet above sea level. Nights are always cool—sometimes very cold in the dry season. It is a remote station, 450 miles by road from Mtwara by an almost all-weather road and 162 miles from Njombe by a road which is open for about half the year. There is, however, a regular weekly air service connecting the station with Mbeya and Mtwara.

In 1952, the population of the Songea Township[5] comprised 739 Africans, 196 Asians and 48 Europeans.

The District Commissioner is assisted by two district officers and representatives of the Medical, Public Works, Agricultural, Forest and Co-operative Development Departments are normally stationed there.

PLACES OF INTEREST TO THE VISITOR AND SPORTING FACILITIES

Splendid fishing is to be had off the coast, especially in the neighbourhood of Kilwa Kisiwani and Mtwara.

Although the Southern Province is not one of the recognized shooting grounds, in the Kilwa and Nachingwea Districts are to be found all kinds of game listed on a major game licence and the occasional large tusker is still to be had, especially in the Kilwa District.[6]

---

[1]The name *Masasi* is said to have derived from the name of a blacksmith, Akumasasi, who many years ago set up business on the top of what is now known as Masasi Hill.

[2]See "Zanzibar to Masasi in 1876: The Founding of Masasi Mission" by Archdeacon R. Lamburn. *Tanganyika Notes and Records*, No. 31, July 1951.

[3]*Tunduru* takes its name from a small hill a few miles from the Boma. The origin of the name itself is not known.

[4]For further details see "Tanganyika: a Review of its Resources and their Development", p. 822.

[5]The township and district owe their name it is believed to one Songea son of Luafu, who was the leader in the area of the present town when the Germans first arrived there.

[6]See also p. 465.

The fossil beds at Tendaguru have been mentioned on page 17. These are situated approximately 70 miles from Lindi and half an hour's walk from the road.

The rock paintings at Masasi are situated in a cave only a few hundred yards from the District Office, accessible to those wearing tennis shoes, and are worth a visit.

Other rock paintings are to be found at Matekwe in the Nachingwea District.

Construction of quay wall at Mtwara.

Photo: E.A. Railways and Harbours

Bus service. Dodoma-Mbeya.

Photo: E.A. Railways and Harbours

SOUTHERN HIGHLANDS PROVINCE

SITUATION

The Southern Highlands Province—a province of wide vistas and magnificent views—occupies country to the north of Lake Nyasa and between Lake Rukwa in the west and the long valley of the Kilombero River in the east. It covers 45,000 square miles—a little less than the size of England—and has nearly a million inhabitants[1]. It contains most of the "tail" of the great figure 9 described by the territory's mountain system (see page 2). The highlands describe a huge arc running from the borders of the Mpwapwa and Kilosa Districts through the cluster of mountains at the head of Lake Nyasa to link up with the Ufipa Highlands to the east of Lake Tanganyika.

DISTRICTS AND PHYSICAL FEATURES

The province contains five districts: Iringa and Njombe in the east, Mbeya and Rungwe in the centre and south, and Chunya in the north-west. Provincial Headquarters are at Mbeya.

The eastern boundary of the *Iringa District* is formed by the steep escarpment at the foot of which runs the Kilombero river, some 2,000 feet below. Near this escarpment lies some most attractive highland country, including the settled areas of Dabaga and Mufindi and, farther west, Sao Hill. The scarp areas receive an ample rainfall and contain some of the territory's rare rain forests. The north-west corner of the district is comparatively low-lying, adjoining the infertile plains in the south of the Dodoma District, and is thinly populated; much of this area lies in the Rungwa Game Reserve. The Great North Road runs through the middle of the district for some 190 miles, passing over rolling grassland country, ranging in elevation from 5,000 to 6,600 feet and carrying solitary low trees of secondary growth, widely scattered. The district covers 14,000 square miles and contains a population of 184,000, including 800 Europeans and 1,200 Asians.

The lowland country extends into the *Njombe District* to the south and merges into the mountainous region in which are situated the Uwemba block (highest point 7,400 ft.), the Kipengere Range (9,715 ft.) and the Livingstone Mountains (9,600 ft.), the last descending precipitously to the shore of Lake Nyasa. The Njombe District covers 7,970 square miles and has a population of over 200,000, of whom nearly 200 are Europeans and another 200 are Asians.

The small and compact *Rungwe District* occupies a part of the Great Rift Valley, between lakes Nyasa and Rukwa, which has been subjected to great tectonic upheaval and contains, rising in a cone from the floor of the valley, the symmetrical mountain (9,713 ft.) after which the district is named. Near the shore of Lake Nyasa is a well-watered, fertile plain, some 4,000 feet below the average elevation of the highland part of the district. The area of the district is only 1,874 square miles, but it contained 238,000 people at the time of the 1948 census, nearly all Nyakyusa, but including just over a hundred Europeans and about 370 Asians.

---

[1] 855,000 at the time of the 1948 census.

To the north of the Rungwe and Njombe Districts lies the *Mbeya District*, a narrow-waisted area containing the Mbeya Range and Poroto Mountains in the centre, the vast Usangu Plain to the north-east, and the Mbozi highlands and Rukwa plains to the west. It covers an area of 10,900 square miles and contained 186,000 people in 1948, 600 of whom were Europeans and over 1,000 Asians.

The remainder of the province, in the area to the north-east and east of Lake Rukwa, comprises the *Chunya District*, created as a result of the discovery of the Lupa Goldfield between the wars. Only the southern part of the district and a strip along the Chunya-Rungwa road are at all closely populated, the western parts, bordering on the Mpanda District, being very thinly inhabited. The district covers 10,200 square miles and contains only about 42,000 people, including 90 Europeans and 270 Asians[1].

As one would expect in such a mountainous region, the province is unusually well watered. Most of its rivers go to swell the waters which eventually enter the Indian Ocean as the Rufiji. To the west and north of the mountainous area the rivers drain into the Great Ruaha, the more important being the Chimala, Kimani and Mbarali. To the east the Kihanzi, Mpanga, Mnyera, Ruhuji, Pita and Farua (all perennial) and others help to swell the Kilombero, another of the Rufiji's tributaries. Into Lake Nyasa flow a number of small rivers, the Songwe being the most important and forming the territorial boundary with Nyasaland. Another river of the same name flows into Lake Rukwa.

Apart from Lakes Rukwa and Nyasa, which form part of the boundary, the province contains few lakes of any consequence. The crater lakes of Masoko and Wentzel Heckmann in the Rungwe District are however worthy of mention.

The level of Lake Nyasa is subject to an annual variation of about three feet and a periodic variation of as much as eighteen feet. It has now been recommended, however, that the level should be stabilized by means of control at the point where the river Shire leaves the lake. This would reduce the periodic fluctuation to about six feet and leave the annual variation at about three feet.

The Usangu Plain (also known as the Buhoro Flats) covers some 2,000 square miles in the middle of the province. It seems that in fairly recent times the whole of this plain was a great lake, the level of which was about one hundred feet above the present level of the plain[2]. To-day the swamp area to the north covers about 90 square miles and this is surrounded by grassy areas subject to seasonal inundation. The remainder of the plain is not so subject to flooding and contains some excellent alluvial soils.

CLIMATE

The province presents a great variety of climatic conditions, from the steamy heat of some of the low-lying areas along the Great Ruaha river to the frosts common over a great part of the highlands, and from the aridity of the northern plains, with a rainfall of about 20 inches a year, to the verdant greenness of Tukuyu, with its 100 inches or more annually.

---

[1]Includes Somalis, Chinese, etc. Indians alone number 200. Present figures are well below 1952 census figures and are decreasing yearly.

[2]Report on Central African Rail Link Development Survey, Vol. 2, p. 139.

The great wall of mountains which rises steeply to the north-west of the Kilombero valley acts as a precipitating agent on the moisture-laden south-east monsoon and the highlands in the Mufindi and Dabaga areas receive up to 80 inches of rain a year. Further west the rainfall falls off markedly and the average for the downland region along the Great North Road ranges from 25 to 50 inches. The same marked contrast is found further south, where the Uwemba Range and the Livingstone Mountains receive 80–100 inches a year, the Kipengere Range about the same, the Rungwe Mountain area even more; but the Mbeya Range, with the Mbozi area still further to the west, only about 40–50 inches, and the plains near Lake Rukwa as little as 30 inches. In the Usangu Plain the average rainfall is even lower, being only about 15–24 inches a year.

Average temperatures vary as greatly as the rainfall and, as already stated, frosts are common at night in many parts of the highland areas. Strong easterly and south-easterly winds are a feature of the dry season (July–October), especially in the downland country around Sao Hill; and cloudy, misty conditions are not infrequent over the highlands generally. In these areas nights are always cool, even cold during the dry season, when fires are required, and dews are heavy.

Statistics of rainfall at district headquarters are given below:—

Station	Altitude in feet	Average	1950	1951	1952	1953	1954	1955	1956
Iringa	5,380	29·07 (28 years)	23·15	34·19	26·68	24·33	27·64	23·04	32·34
Njombe	6,000	40·17 (6 years)	50·33	*	*	60·40	46·28	34·66	45·21
Tukuyu	5,300	99·07 (39 years)	121·34	79·44	110·90	93·50	78·11	123·43	82·27
Mbeya	5,768	35·73 (29 years)	44·29	38·27	29·81	27·35	22·20	33·70	42·28
Chunya	4,900	30·73 (21 years)	31·26	42·16	27·90	26·30	21·42	33·02	*

*Records incomplete.

POPULATION

Owing to the favourable climatic conditions described above, and the availability of land, parts of the highlands have been found very suitable for settlement by non-Africans, and groups of largely European settlers are now to be found in the neighbourhood of Iringa, at Dabaga, Mufindi and in the Sao Hill area of the Iringa District, at Uwemba and Lupembe in the Njombe District, near Mbeya and at Mbozi in the Mbeya District, and in the tea-growing area of Rungwe District. Their agricultural activities are considered below (see page 243). In 1954 there were 1,856 Europeans in the province, including missionaries and Government employees as well as settlers.

The Asian population numbers about 3,000, most of whom are Indians living in townships as traders and shop-keepers. There is an interesting settlement of some 220 Baluchis in the Usangu Plain. These immigrants have built up a small but thriving farming and trading colony from the inspiration and example of one or two enthusiasts who settled in the area because of their belief in its agricultural possibilities. Accustomed by tradition to irrigation, they have been quick to improvise simple schemes to supplement the meagre rainfall.

The African population was about 850,000 at the time of the 1948 census. The combined results of this census, a complete one, and of the 1952 census of the non-African population, are given in the table below:—

District	Euro-pean	Indi-an	Goan	Arab	Soma-li	Colo-ured	Other	Total Non-Afri-can	Afri-can	Total Popu-lation
Iringa	800	958	33	175	27	51	29	2,073	182,295	184,368
Njombe	184	183	–	1	–	13	1	382	206,953	207,335
Rungwe	113	369	8	1	47	10	1	549	237,099	237,648
Mbeya	596	1,019	39	2	44	38	12	1,750	185,265	187,015
Chunya	163	245	2	15	2	32	23	482	38,383	38,865
	1,856	2,774	82	194	120	144	66	5,236	849,995	855,231

THE MAIN TRIBES

The Hehe.—The main tribe in the Iringa District, and the eighth largest tribe in the territory, is the Hehe, numbering 192,000 at the time of the 1948 census. They are famous in the history of Tanganyika for their fierce resistance to the Germans (see page 60 et seq.). The people nowadays called Hehe[1] are really a political entity of recent growth. Up to the eighteen-fifties, the units now constituting the tribe were a number of small tribes, probably similar in speech and custom, but with no political unity. It is impossible to state exactly how many of these small units there were, but evidence of twenty-nine was collected in the nineteen-thirties, and it is possible that some of these included two or three independent political groups. The pre-existence of these small tribes is still of minor political importance today. All the people of the tribe will, after first announcing that they are Hehe, tell one that their real tribe is so-and-so, naming the original tribe to which they belonged. The term Hehe is applied to the whole group, it is not the name of a tribe that conquered all the rest.

These small tribes were largely welded together by two able men, Muyugumba, the great-grandfather, and Mkwawa, the grandfather of the present chief. Muyu-gumba, of the Va-Muyinga clan, who was a direct descendant of Muyinga, the founder of the clan, was chief of one of these small groups. Shortly after his accession, he seems to have peacefully added to his lands, and this probably made him more powerful than any of the other petty chiefs; so that, whether deliberately or not, he embarked on a career of conquest. By the time of his death, which probably occurred in 1879, he had conquered at least all the peoples now called Hehe, and had waged war with the Sangu and with the more powerful Ngoni. His eldest son, Mkwawa, was initially driven out by a hostile faction when Muyugumba died. After two years, however, he was brought back and established his authority, subsequently following his father's warlike example. The stories of Mkwawa's reign are much the same as those of his father's: reconquest of the Hehe tribes, wars with more powerful enemies, and the general consolidation of the tribe as a whole. His reign and life were terminated by the German conquest[2] (see page 60).

---

[1]This description is taken from "Anthropology in Action", written by G. G. Brown and A. M. B. Hutt and published by the Oxford University Press in 1935.

[2]His skull, which was removed from his body and taken to Germany, was in 1954 returned to the safekeeping of the tribe by the personal intervention of the present Governor.

The Hehe were thus formed into a political unit by conquest, but became a genuinely united tribe by the growth of various sanctions and the development of complex political institutions. But though there was a large group considering itself Hehe, it is almost impossible to determine the exact limits of that group, to decide who became genuine Hehe, who remained mere conquered communities, and who merely acknowledged some sort of hegemony. However, the boundaries of the present Iringa District probably indicate fairly well the area populated by genuine Hehe and it can be said that the people in the central part of the district became Hehe, that is, they considered themselves primarily subjects of the Muyinga rulers. Towards the borders of the district this loyalty lessened, and periodic raids were necessary to reinforce the authority of the tribal rulers, and beyond the borders the superiority of the Hehe was generally allowed but no absorption took place.

The Hehe are classed as of early Bantu stock. They are a patrilineal tribe practising both arable and pastoral farming. The bulk of them live on a plateau at an altitude of between 4,500 and 7,000 feet, while the remainder inhabit the plains in the north and east, at an altitude of about 2,500 feet. Maize is the staple crop, though millet or rice predominates in some of the low-lying areas. They have as subsidiary crops eleusine, beans, potatoes, ground-nuts and marrows. Livestock is a secondary source of wealth, and the large cattle population is increasing as a result of dipping against East Coast Fever. Sheep and goats are also reared.

The Bena, Kinga and Pangwa.—The main tribe in the Njombe District is the Bena, which, numbering 111,000, formed 53½ per cent of the population at the time of the census in 1948. The Kinga, with 42,000, comprised 20 per cent, and the Pangwa, with 27,000, 13 per cent.

Little seems to have been recorded of the earlier history of the Bena. When first the Germans came into contact with them, they were loosely organized under petty chiefs belonging to five or six families. A strong character among these or the need for unity against neighbouring tribes led to a loose unification but no one family achieved a recognized superiority. To this day, the chief is elected from these families, whose members also provide the rulers of the five sub-chiefdoms.

The Kinga are believed to have come from the area south-west of Iringa many generations ago. The chieftainship passes to the eldest son. Ukinga is a deeply dissected mountainous country where the headmen are almost autonomous, obedience to the chief being more religious than political. The Kinga used to dig underground houses in which they hid from their enemies. North of the Rumakarya river the people call themselves Wamagama or Wafungo and have a different language and customs; they somewhat resemble the Wanyakyusa.

The name Pangwa refers more to the area than to the people, who appear to have diverse origins, especially in the warmer south. Upangwa was on the line of the Angoni raiders and suffered accordingly, the population being still scanty and scattered. The ruling families came in from Ukinga.

The Wanji and Kisi.—Two small tribes in the Njombe District are the Wanji, 15,000 (at the 1948 census), who make up 7 per cent of the population of the district, and the Kisi, 3,600, 2 per cent. The former live in the north-west of the district in the mountains between the Elton Plateau and Usangu. They are believed to have come from much the same area as the Kinga, but are in many ways more akin to the Bena.

The Kisi are an interesting community of fishermen and highly skilled potters who live on the shores of Lake Nyasa, from the Songea District to the Nyasaland border of Rungwe District, wherever a break in the precipitous sides of the Livingstone Mountains allows the establishment of a few huts and gardens. They communicate with neighbouring settlements largely by canoe and tend to live very much to themselves. They have contact with the outside world in their pot trade, however, and their weekly pot market at Matema is attended by buyers from almost all over the province and further afield as well, sales amounting to thousands of pots weekly.

The Nyakyusa.—The Nyakyusa numbered just under 192,000 at the time of the 1948 census and form the ninth largest tribe in the territory. They make up 67½ per cent of the population of the Rungwe District, the remainder being made up of Ndali, numbering 50,000 and forming 21 per cent, the small Lambia tribe which is divided by the Songwe river between Tanganyika and Nyasaland, a few Kinga, and others.

The Nyakyusa[1] are a Bantu-speaking people who live on the marshy plain at the head of Lake Nyasa and in the hills that rise steeply to the north and west of it. Across the Songwe river, live the Ngonde (or Nkhonde) and these two groups speak dialects which, though differing somewhat in vocabulary and pronunciation, are easily understood by speakers from both, and their social structure is essentially similar. The area occupied by the Nyakyusa is enclosed by the lake itself, the escarpment of the Livingstone mountains on the north-east, the Poroto mountains to the north-west and the Songwe river and Bundali mountains to the south-west and west.

As in the case of most tribes, the Nyakyusa may be sub-divided into a number of groups: those on the lake-shore plain (Ngonde), those around Masoko, those to the east under the Livingstone mountains Nselya and Saku, and those to the north, viz. the Kukwe and Lugulu. There are also a number of small groups such as the Penja, with old languages and equally distinct cultures of their own, but most of these groups are losing their separate identities and being assimilated into the main tribe.

According to their own traditions the Nyakyusa chiefs came ten generations ago from the Kinga country, on the Livingstone mountains, and found the Rungwe district already occupied by people who had no knowledge of fire, but ate their food raw. The newcomers brought fire with them (and, some say, cattle also) and by virtue of this great benefit were accepted as chiefs.

The Nyakyusa country is fertile, well watered and spectacularly beautiful with its arc of high mountains and sparkling lakes. Agriculture is highly developed and intensive and the people grow a wide variety of crops including bananas (in plantations stretching mile upon mile through the plains and along the crests of the ridges), finger millet, maize, cassava, sweet potatoes, groundnuts and, over the last decade, rice and coffee which have now become the two major

---

[1]This description is taken from "Good Company" by Monica Wilson, published by the Oxford University Press in 1951.

crops of the district. Cultivating is traditionally the work of men and boys but nowadays it is increasingly performed by the women as a result of the exodus, not all of it temporary, of considerable numbers of men to employment outside the district in various parts of Tanganyika but mostly to the mines of the Rhodesias and even to South Africa. Cattle, of a short-horned humped type, are fairly numerous and highly prized.

One of the most interesting features of the Nyakyusa is their village organization, which is quite different from that of most Bantu peoples in that the villages consist of groups of the same age set, not groups of kinsmen. Boys build with contemporaries and remain with them throughout life; and girls join the villages of their husbands at marriage. Thus relatives, other than husband and wife and young children, do not live together. Nevertheless, as in other tribes, kinship ties are important in other spheres and kinsmen are believed to be mystically interdependent in a way in which fellow villagers are not. Another interesting feature is the system of inheritance under which property passes not directly from father to son, but from brother to brother, through each group of full brothers until, when the last full brother is dead, and the son of the eldest is an adult, the family stock comes to him. This custom is, however, now changing at the behest of the Rungwe African District Council.

The social services of the area are comparatively highly developed and there are considerable numbers of schools and dispensaries. The district has been the scene of much activity by missionaries and a considerable proportion of the Nyakyusa are now Christians.

THE TRIBES OF THE MBEYA DISTRICT

A glance at the tribal map facing page 298 will show how diversified tribally is the population of this area. At the time of the 1948 census, the distribution was as follows:—

Safwa	40,751	22%
Nyiha	39,125	21%
Nyakyusa	20,215	11%
Nyamwanga	18,298	10%
Malila	17,426	10%
Sangu	14,981	8%
All other (including 5,741 Wanda)	33,250	18%
Total...	184,046	100%

The Safwa tribe inhabits the highland areas near Mbeya. This tribe is conservative and resistant to improved agricultural practices but has recently evinced interest in the introduction of new crops, e.g. wheat. The tribe is organized into three separate chiefdoms, each with an independent Native Authority (Usafwa, Usongwe and Umbwila).

The Nyiha, who occupy the highlands to the west of Mbeya (the Mbozi area), are the most advanced and industrious of the indigenous tribes of the district. Coffee cultivation, which is expanding rapidly, forms their largest source of income and the industry is organized on a co-operative basis. They are now constructing permanent brick houses and take an intense interest in education.

The Nyakyusa, who are numerically the third largest tribe in the district, have spilled over from the over-crowded Rungwe District during the last 15 to 20 years. They have settled mainly in the Umalila, Unyiha and Usafwa areas.

The Nyamwanga are a tribe who live partly in Northern Rhodesia and partly in the extreme west of the district. They are agriculturists and pastoralists but being remote from markets or developed areas have a very much lower standard of living than their neighbours nearer Mbeya.

The Malila occupy the beautiful highlands south of Mbeya and their main source of wealth is from money brought back by the young men who seek employment in the Rhodesias and on the Rand.

The Sangu are primarily pastoralists, inhabiting the flats north of the Elton Plateau. Following the lead given by the group of Baluchi settlers (see page 235), they are now showing great interest in irrigation and the paddy crop during the last few years has extended enormously. This is a promising feature in a tribe which hitherto has been noted for its resistance to progress.

THE TRIBES OF THE CHUNYA DISTRICT

The tribes in this district are very mixed, the opening up of the goldfield resulting in an influx of members of all the surrounding tribes and of many others besides. At the time of the 1948 census, the African population of the district was made up as follows:—

Bende [1]	...	...	...	...	7,093	...	19%
Safwa	...	...	...	...	4,983	...	13%
Nyasa	...	...	...	...	2,754	...	7½%
Kimbu	...	...	...	...	2,571	...	7%
Fipa	...	...	...	...	2,329	...	6%
Nyika	...	...	...	...	2,249	...	6%
Nyakyusa	...	...	...	...	2,058	...	5½%
Nyamwanga	...	...	...	1,539	...	4%
Konongo	...	...	...	...	1,254	...	3%
Nyamwezi	...	...	...	...	1,166	...	3%
Mbunga	...	...	...	...	1,019	...	3%
All others	...	...	...	...	8,634	...	23%
			Total...		37,649	...	100%

The Kimbu, occupying the northern half of the district, are closely allied to the Nyamwezi of the Western Province. Until concentrated into settlements because of the danger of sleeping sickness, they lived in isolated villages, earning their living from agriculture, hunting and honey gathering. They are still agriculturists and make much money from beeswax gathered from their hives spread throughout the *miombo* bush.

AGRICULTURAL RESOURCES

The Rain Forest Areas comprise the great scarp of the Iringa District, the high mountain masses of the Lukinga and Kipengere ranges in the Njombe and Rungwe Districts, the Livingstone and Rungwe Mountains of the Rungwe and Njombe Districts and the Poroto and Mbeya ranges of the Mbeya District. These high-altitude areas have a rainfall ranging from 50 to 110 inches and are in general (where the vegetation has not been burnt out or otherwise destroyed) covered by dense evergreen forests or bamboo. The population is estimated at nearly 200,000 and the altitude ranges from 6,000 to 9,000 feet.

---

[1]See page 272 for brief description.

Hehe Warrior.

Photo: Public Relations Department

The Miombo Woodland Areas, from 3,500 to 6,000 feet above sea-level, comprise the central Uhehe area of Iringa, the eastern and northern edges and the Upangwa section of Njombe and scattered sections of Mbeya and Chunya, including western Mbeya (Mbozi). The rainfall ranges from 30 inches to 50 inches and the population is estimated at over 500,000.

The Low Rainfall Areas ranging from 2,000 to 4,500 feet consist of most of the Chunya District, the Usangu and the Uwanda sections of Mbeya and the Pawaga, Idodi and Mtandika areas of Iringa. The rainfall is between 20 and 30 inches and the population is estimated at nearly 100,000.

The Shore of Lake Nyasa.—This comprises the high-rainfall, low-altitude strip along the northern and eastern shore of Lake Nyasa in Rungwe and Njombe. It lies at 1,500 feet above sea-level and is open grassland having rainfalls ranging from 80 to 124 inches and an estimated population of over 50,000.

AFRICAN AGRICULTURAL PRODUCTION

The Rain Forest Areas.—These are sparsely populated, and rather low-yielding; maize, eleusine, and peas are the staple food crops. In most parts of these mountain areas European potatoes as well as sweet potatoes are grown as food. In the Njombe area wheat is eaten and the surplus is sold; production has also started in the Mufindi area of Iringa District. Surplus maize and eleusine as well as potatoes and peas are sold to European planters. Many of the Africans living in the mountain areas depend on hiring themselves out as labourers to earn their cash income. The soils are of two types, the more general being a sandy soil of granitic origin and the other a volcanic soil underlain by pumice. The soils are in general covered by varying thicknesses of forest loam. The granitic soils erode easily, and, while initial fertility is high, this does not continue beyond a few years of continuous cultivation. The second type is generally heavier soil of volcanic origin and is of high fertility. Where erosion is prevented and resting periods followed in these latter soils, the high fertility continues for very many years. The latter type is exemplified in the Ukinga area of Njombe. As we have seen, the rain forest areas of the northern part of the Southern Highlands form vast watersheds from which the flow of the Kilombero and the Rufiji rivers commence. Some of the flooding of those distant rivers is caused, initially, by indiscriminate forest destruction in these mountain masses. Much has been done to combat the evil, especially by demarcation of large forest reserves and the movement of the very sparse population from zones of special importance, but much remains to be done.

The Miombo Woodland Areas.—These are more heavily populated than the rain forest areas; mainly, it is believed, because they have a more equable climate and grow more acceptable native food crops. The staple foods are maize, eleusine and beans, with sweet potatoes in some parts, and cassava in others, forming an important part of the diet. In small sections wheat and barley are grown for food. Maize, eleusine and beans form the main economic crops also, and the frequently large surplus over food requirements is sold, for export from the area or for consumption on the mines and on the tea, tobacco, pyrethrum and coffee estates. In Rungwe and Mbeya coffee is being produced by Africans on a steadily increasing scale and is marketed co-operatively; the Rungwe crop now exceeds 600 tons of *Arabica* parchment coffee annually. The soils of the *miombo* "savanna" are generally acid and vary from sandy granitic types to the more clayey red soils originating from gneiss. They are generally shallow, lack organic matter and are deficient in phosphates. The rainfall occurs from December to April leaving the remaining six to seven months quite dry. Conditions for growing crops are exacting in the poor soils, cool climate and very short season. The whole of these sections is subjected to erosion and it is believed that the *miombo* has intruded on what was once a vast rain forest destroyed by repeated burning. Much has been done to combat the evil of indiscriminate grass burning but here also much still remains to be done. Erosion on cultivated land presents an ever present problem, though Native Authority legislation and the continuous efforts of the Agricultural Department have done a great deal to reduce the evils. Shifting cultivation is, however, not as rife in the *miombo* areas as in many of the mountain areas.

The Low Rainfall Areas.—These are largely dry and hot and generally the population is concentrated on the banks of rivers and other scattered points of water supply. The staple foods are maize and sorghum (cassava in the north of the Chunya District). Sweet potatoes, cassava and beans are grown for food also, but to a limited extent. In parts groundnuts, rice and eleusine are produced and also beeswax. Tobacco is now being tried at one place in the centre of the Chunya District. In these areas, as in other sections, work as labourers on mines and estates forms an important source of cash income and the surplus food crops are sold for consumption in the towns, mines and European estates in the province. The soils of the areas generally are of sandy quartzite and granitic origin with intrusions of stiff loams derived from various igneous parent rocks. The large waterless areas of excellent soils are capable of development by opening up irrigation furrows, especially in the Usangu section of Mbeya where a few furrows have demonstrated the great possibilities. In the Pawaga and Mtandika sections of Iringa irrigation has been practised successfully for many years. Desiccation in these areas due to the concentration of stock around the few and very scattered points of water supply is a problem that has engaged the activities of the departments concerned for many years, especially in the Pawaga section of Iringa, but much money and effort is still needed. The needs of the future are the extension of irrigation, the introduction of drought-resistant crops to the peopled areas where irrigation is not possible and the improvement, where possible, of the crops now grown by seed selection and the introduction of new crops to improve the diet.

The Rail Link Survey Report states that the Rukwa–Songwe plain has possibilities for the establishment of a livestock industry, assuming that the tsetse can be controlled and that hazards from disease and wild game can be reduced. It was thought that such valuable cash crops as cotton, rice, sugarcane and certain oil-seed crops should be suited to selected portions of the area, although its remoteness from existing or potential markets suggests that its development should be relegated to the more distant future.

The Usangu Plain offers more promise, indeed those responsible for the Report were obviously very taken with its potentialities and recorded that "the natural resources of the Usangu Plain—its soils, climate and availability of water—offer an outstanding opportunity for large-scale agricultural development, including livestock". They went on to set forth four schemes, three of which depend essentially on large- or small-scale irrigation and one on drainage. A small-scale pilot scheme has been instituted near Rujewa as part of the Rufiji Basin Project.

The Shore of Lake Nyasa.—The main portion of this lies in the Rungwe District and is very densely populated, running to over four hundred people to the square mile. The port on that falls in Njombe is small and unimportant, the main foods being cassava and fish. The surplus cassava is sold to Nyasaland. The main foods of the Rungwe lake-shore area are rice, maize, sweet potatoes, cassava, bananas, millets and beans. This area is one of several in the territory in which milk is a considerable portion of the diet. The largest economic crop is rice, and surplus maize, beans and millets are of steadily lessening importance. The soils are mostly transported soils from the highlands and they are deep and extremely fertile. The high rainfall of up to 124 inches occurs from October to June. The area is capable of great development along the lines of improvement of seed and cultivation methods with all crops grown, and new crops also are being investigated for introduction. The Rungwe lake-shore area probably has as great potentialities as any area of the Southern Highlands Province and was favourably considered in the reports both of the East African Rice Mission and of the Rail Link Survey. In the former[1] report, discussing rice growing in this area, the Mission stated that during their tour of East and Central Africa, they had encountered "no rice cultivation that reproduced so closely conditions obtaining in India and Burma. . . . This area clearly presents great opportunities for developing a sound peasant agriculture". In the latter report, the survey team gave it as their opinion that "the construction of effective drainage systems to prevent flooding due to early heavy rains and a better system of cultivation and land management might well build up an exportable surplus of at least 10,000 tons of paddy"[2].

NON-AFRICAN AGRICULTURAL PRODUCTION

This can perhaps best be considered by reviewing the different crops grown.

Tobacco.—Tobacco is mostly grown in the Iringa area, which has long been a centre of European settlement and has a light-textured sandy soil suitable for this crop. In 1954, 3,269,407 pounds (a record) of flue-cured leaf was produced and it is thought that there is available sufficient suitable land to produce ten million pounds. The present variety grown is "Ehlers", a heavy yielder, but with an increasingly limited demand due to its characteristic "tang" which reduces its value for blending. Experiments with Virginia types have been started.

Tobacco is also grown in the Dabaga area (Iringa District) and at Uhanyana in the north of Njombe.

Tea.—Production is centred at Kibau, in the Mufindi area of the Iringa District, where several former German estates have been brought under unified management, with a modern factory and equipment. The estates lie on the north-westerly slopes of the mountain range and receive an annual rainfall of 70–80 inches. Output in 1956 was some 3,800,000 lb.[3] valued at £460,000. It is estimated that when in full production some four million pounds could be produced annually.

---

[1] East African Rice Mission Report, 1948.
[2] Op. cit. p. 156.
[3] 3,304,000 lb. in 1955.

There are also five tea estates in Rungwe District and three tea factories. Close upon one million pounds of made tea is now being produced annually. Tea has also been started on a small scale at Lupembe in South Uwemba.

Pyrethrum.—This crop is grown principally in the Uwemba mountain region of the Njombe District, some 20 miles south-west of Njombe. It is also grown to a limited extent in the Mufindi and Dabaga areas in the Iringa District. Total production has varied between 200 and 400 tons of recent years; in 1956 it was 261 tons, valued at £65,000, approximately[1].

Coffee.—The main centre for the production of coffee is Mbozi, about 40 miles to the west of Mbeya, an area of rolling country lying at altitudes varying between 5,200 and 5,600 feet, and receiving an annual rainfall of between 40 and 55 inches. This was selected by some German settlers as an area suitable for coffee growing but it was the opinion of those responsible for the Rail Link Survey that it was better suited to livestock production[2]. There are now 40 non-African farmers operating in the area, for whom coffee is the basic crop. In 1956, 310 tons of clean coffee were produced valued at £150,000[3]. The coffee is partially processed locally but is sent to Moshi for further treatment and grading.

Some coffee is also grown in other parts of the Mbeya District, and in Mufindi.

Livestock.—The rolling grassland country in the Sao Hill area of the Iringa District is at first sight eminently suitable for cattle-rearing and meat production, and an enterprising scheme was initiated some years ago by the late Lord Chesham to attract European settlers to the area. Some 200,000 acres were involved in the scheme but in the event it was not as successful as was hoped, largely due to deficiencies in the soil. This area was at one time covered by rain-forest and, with the removal of the forest (before the arrival of the settlers), it lost what fertility it had by over-cultivation and leaching. Only by an intensive and scientific study of pasture improvement in local conditions is it thought that the best use can be made of this attractive region, so suited in other ways for European settlement.

INDUSTRIES

This is primarily an agricultural province and the main agricultural industries have already been mentioned: tobacco, tea, pyrethrum, coffee. The most important industrial undertaking of another kind is undoubtedly the Colonial Development Corporation's wattle scheme in the Njombe District. Here 33,000 acres of wattle trees have already been planted and it is intended to increase this acreage.

In addition, the Bena Native Authority has made a start on a scheme for a further 20,000 acres of wattle under African growers.

The C.D.C. is erecting a factory for extracting tannin, which will be in operation in 1958 and will have a capacity of 7,000 tons of extract per annum.

There are thirty-one Native Authority clarified butter factories in the province, mainly in the Mbeya and Njombe Districts, and production in the year 1956 totalled some 2,780 tins (of 36 lb.), worth approximately £14,000.[4]

---

[1] 235 tons valued at £50,000 in 1955.

[2] See p. 154, Vol. II of Report on Central African Rail Link Survey.

[3] 350 tons of clean coffee valued at £160,000 in 1955.

[4] In 1955, there were 35 factories, which produced 835 tins valued at £5,010.

There is a *Tilapia* fishing industry on Lake Rukwa controlled by a statutory board. Prior to 1950, all fish caught could be sold without difficulty on the Lupa Goldfields and in the Chunya, Mbeya and Tukuyu Districts. In 1949, Lake Rukwa dried up and, when fishing was resumed in 1952, considerable difficulties were experienced in marketing the fish. The local market, considerably reduced by the decline of the Lupa Goldfield, could not absorb the production and the 300-mile road haul to Itigi made Rukwa dried fish more expensive than *dagaa* (from Lake Tanganyika) anywhere on the Central Line. By 1954, an alternative market had been opened in the copper belt of Northern Rhodesia and during that year nearly one million *tilapia*, valued at over £10,000, were sold there. The total catch for the year is estimated at 2½ million *tilapia* and over two hundred tons of other fish, mainly catfish.

On this lake there is also a minor industry in the production of crocodile skins. This at one time averaged 2,000 skins a year, but is now much less.

An innovation which may yield a profitable industry for the rather infertile Sao area in the Iringa District is the establishment of several poultry units on both the battery and the deep litter systems. These are proving successful and the next problem to be solved is to evolve a suitable marketing organization.

The Mafura Soap Mill, in the Rungwe District, manufactures soap from oil extracted from a local wild olive nut (*Trichilia emetica*).

Two Rice Mills operate in the Lake Nyasa plain of Rungwe District and three small mills in the Usangu area of Mbeya District.

MINERALS

The Lupa Goldfield in the Chunya District was discovered in 1922, when a minor "gold rush" occurred. At one time there were over a thousand "diggers" in the field and some remarkable nuggets were found, the largest being 95 ozs. and worth £1,150 at today's prices. Until about 1936 the output was mainly from alluvial workings, but from 1934 onwards reef production increased and became of much greater importance. In 1941 production amounted to 34,368 fine ounces of gold valued at £290,566, but declined thereafter. In 1956 gold production was only 9,937 fine ounces valued at £124,177[1]. Saza Mine, the territory's second largest gold mine, operated by New Saza Mines Ltd., closed down in 1956, due to the exhaustion of its ore reserves, after 18 years' operation.

The Ngaka-Kitewaka coalfields in the Njombe and Songea Districts have been carefully examined by the Colonial Development Corporation. The three coalfields of Mbalawala, Mbuyura and Mchuchuma were reported to contain a total of 216 million tons of proved extractable coal, a further indicated tonnage of 40 million and a possible gross tonnage of over 400 million tons. The coal was found to compare favourably with the best South African and Southern Rhodesian coals and steaming tests carried out on the East African and Nyasaland railways were successful. The ultimate average ash content was found to be from 14·6 to 16·5 per cent. These coalfields are remote from any possible markets and their development would involve a very large initial financial outlay.

---

[1]16,242 fine ounces valued at £203,667 in 1955.

Investigations by the Colonial Development Corporation have been carried out on the Liganga titaniferous iron ore deposits in Njombe District. The deposits are situated about 30 miles north-east of the Ruhuhu coalfields in Njombe and Songea Districts. Here again the possibilities of utilization are largely governed by the lack of communications and the remoteness of the site.

The Colonial Development Corporation has also completed investigations of the Kiwira-Songwe coalfields in Rungwe District. The Rungwe Coal Company has been formed, a mining lease has been applied for, and a sizeable modern coal mine may be developed. In the same field, the small Ilima Colliery has been maintaining a regular production since 1953 and its output, which totalled 1,500 tons in 1956[1], finds a ready market. Coal also occurs at Galula in Mbeya District and there are additional iron occurrences in the Livingstone Mountains.

Salt is produced from the Ivuna Salt Pans near Lake Rukwa, annual production being worth about £3,000. Mica is to be found in the Mbeya District and in the Bundali Mountains of Rungwe District.

A large deposit of pyrochlore-bearing carbonatite has recently been located at Panda Hill, some 26 miles from Mbeya and there is reason to believe that several million tons of ore of a value of 0·3 per cent niobium oxide exist on this site. The metal is in demand for the production of high-temperature-resistant alloys such as those used in the manufacture of jet engines. The Billiton Company have a controlling interest in the Mbeya Exploration Co. Ltd., a company formed to investigate and exploit the deposit. The operation has reached the stage of pilot milling, and mining and treatment methods are being examined. The Colonial Development Corporation is associated with the Billiton Company in this undertaking.

There is an interesting piece of meteoric iron at Mbozi, 40 miles west of Mbeya, which has been fully described by the late F. Oates in *Tanganyika Notes and Records* No. 2 of October 1936.

ADMINISTRATIVE STATIONS[2]

Iringa.[3]—District Headquarters is situated at the top of a lofty escarpment (chosen by the Germans for its defensible possibilities) 5,365 feet above sea level, on the Great North Road, 162 miles from Dodoma on the Central Railway and 247 miles from Mbeya. A first class road, recently constructed, connects the town with Dar es Salaam, via Morogoro, considerably reducing the mileage. It is on the air routes Dar es Salaam-Iringa-Sao Hill-Mbeya-Songea, and Nairobi-Mwanza-Tabora-Mpanda-Mbeya-Iringa-Dar es Salaam, operated by East African Airways twice weekly. It is in the centre of an important farming area, both African and non-African, is the site of the new boys' and girls' secondary school and is of growing importance commercially. It enjoys a pleasant climate.

In 1952 the population of the Iringa township was made up of 6,754 Africans, 990 Asians and 238 Europeans.

---

[1]785 tons in 1955.

[2]For additional information see table on page 542.

[3]The word *Iringa* in Kihehe means a boma in the sense of a hedge or fence surrounding a homestead to protect the cattle from wild beasts.

The District Commissioner is assisted by two district officers; there is a Resident Magistrate, and members of a large number of other Government departments and of the East African Railways and Harbours Administration are normally stationed there[1].

Njombe.[2]—Situated at 6,000 feet above sea level in attractive hilly country, with a perennial river nearby, Njombe is one of the pleasantest stations in the territory. Fires are required at night for most of the year, and, in the cold season, in the offices during the day as well. Njombe is 157 miles from Iringa and 148 miles from Mbeya over all-weather roads, and 168 miles from Songea by a road which is passable in the dry season only. It is not, as yet, on any regular air route.

At the time of the census in 1952, the Njombe Minor Settlement contained 350 Africans, 134 Asians and 10 Europeans.

The District Commissioner is assisted by two district officers and a member of the Agricultural Department is normally stationed there.

Tukuyu[3].—District headquarters are situated at an altitude of 5,300 feet in a region which receives an average annual rainfall of about 100 inches. Tukuyu is thus in marked contrast to stations in the drier parts of the territory, for example, Dodoma. (It is one of the few places where grass greens are a possibility on the local golf course). One of the earliest of its district commissioners was a keen gardener and bequeathed to his successors the largest and most luxuriant station garden in Tanganyika.

Tukuyu is reached by an all-weather road from Mbeya, 48 miles away, and is connected with Mwaya on Lake Nyasa by a road 38 miles long. It enjoys a cool, bracing and healthy climate. In 1952, the Tukuyu Township contained 2,818 Africans, 250 Asians and 42 Europeans.

The District Commissioner is assisted by two district officers and members of the Medical, Agricultural, Forest and Co-operative Departments and of the Police Force are normally stationed there.

Mbeya[4].—Provincial and District Headquarters are situated at the foot of the Mbeya[5] Range, at an altitude of 5,800 feet, with magnificent views over the surrounding countryside, of which the Poroto Mountains form a prominent feature. The climate is pleasant, cool in the dry season, (when however the volcanic dust of the region can be trying), but, as in all the stations in this province, fresh and invigorating for most of the year. The town is a trading centre of growing importance. There are large Government schools serving all communities nearby. Mbeya is 406 miles from the Central Railway at Dodoma and 303 miles from Itigi by the road which passes through Chunya. It is on the same air routes as Iringa (see previous page).

In 1952, the Mbeya Township contained 4,313 Africans, 771 Asians and 447 Europeans.

---

[1]Further details of the town are to be found in "Tanganyika: A Review of its Resources and their Development," pp. 810-11.

[2]The name *Njombe* is believed to come from the local vernacular name, *mnjombe* or *mchombe*, for a tree used for making beehives.

[3]The name *Tukuyu* is the diminutive of the Kinyakyusa word *mkuyu*, meaning a fig tree. The district has taken its name, *Rungwe*, from Mount Rungwe, a mountain covered in a particular type of bamboo forest known as *Lungwe* in Kinyakyusa.

[4]For further details of the town see "Tanganyika: A Review of its Resources and their Development" p. 816.

[5]The town has taken its name from the original Kisafwa name for the mountains, *Mbeye*. The original derivation of the word is not known.

The District Commissioner is assisted by three district officers and a revenue officer. A Resident Magistrate and members of some twenty other departments are normally stationed there.

Chunya[1].—At an altitude of 4,800 feet, Chunya is the lowest of the five stations in the Southern Highlands Province, but it differs little from the others climatically. It was established in 1935 to enable closer administration of the Lupa Goldfield to be effected. It grew into a small township but of recent years its population has been decreasing with the decline in mining activity. At the census in 1952, it had a population of 1,175 Africans, 135 Asians and 45 Europeans. Chunya is 45 miles from provincial headquarters at Mbeya and 258 miles from Itigi on the Central Line. It is not on any regular air service route.

The District Commissioner is usually assisted by one district officer and members of the Mines and Public Works Departments are normally stationed there.

PLACES OF INTEREST TO THE VISITOR AND SPORTING FACILITIES

Scenically, the province has much to offer, and the traveller on the Great North Road will be impelled to stop to admire the view at many points, especially if he makes a detour to visit places such as Mbozi, Mufindi and Dabaga. If he is keen on climbing he will be rewarded with breath-taking views, especially in the cluster of mountains round the head of Lake Nyasa, and if he penetrates as far as the Livingstone range he is not likely soon to forget the prospect of the lake obtained from one of these precipitous peaks. In these mountains too the fisherman can obtain some excellent trout fishing in delightful surroundings.

On the Kiwira River in the Rungwe District there are two self-contained rest camps and there is another on the Lufirio River where the enthusiast can spend the night. These are controlled by the Mbeya Trout Association and permission to use them may be obtained from the Hon. Secretary (address: P.O. Mbeya).

The Hagafiro River, 7 miles from Njombe, has also been stocked and application to fish should be made to the Hon. Secretary of the Njombe Trout Association (address: P.O. Njombe).

Good fishing is also available on the Chimala River in the Mbeya District, near which there is a hotel, but enthusiasts have to walk up a somewhat precipitous escarpment to reach fishable waters.

The province contains some good shooting country, especially in the Usangu Plain.[2]

Those who are not interested in hunting, shooting or fishing will find the remarkable natural rock bridge over the Kiwira River worth a visit. The road from Tukuyu (12 miles) passes over the river half a mile above the rock bridge and nearby is a splendid waterfall.

---

[1]Chunya is the Kiguruka word for "to filter". A particular grass is found along the Chunya stream, the ashes of which, after burning, are said to produce salt when mixed with water and filtered.

[2]See also "The Shooting Grounds" p. 464.

TANGA PROVINCE

SITUATION

This is the smallest province in the territory, the total area being only 13,750 square miles.   It is situated in the north-east corner, between Masailand and the Indian Ocean, bounded on the north by Kenya and extending on the south as far as the Nguru Mountains (north of Morogoro) and thence more or less due east to the sea opposite Zanzibar.   The northern boundary is not a natural one, but an arbitrary line drawn from the mouth of the Umba River in a north-westerly direction towards Kenya, much of it passing through semi-desert country.   On the borders of Masailand the country again becomes arid, but through the centre of the province from near the coast to the border with the Northern Province runs a chain of mountains containing some of the finest country, both agriculturally and scenically, in Tanganyika.   The Usambara Mountains (highest point 7,550 feet) form a compact block nearly 70 miles long and varying between 20 and 40 miles broad, and contain country most un-tropical in appearance, with grassy swards, thick forests, clear streams, mists and, in places, frosts at night. Further to the north-west lie the South Pare Mountains (highest point 8,076 feet) and after a gap the North Pares, both comparable with the Usambaras in size and attractiveness, and forming a link between them and the great mountain masses of Kilimanjaro and Meru.   Just over half a million people live in the province.

DISTRICTS

Provincial headquarters are situated at Tanga, and the province contains five districts, the coastal districts of Tanga and Pangani, the sprawling lowland district of Handeni and the predominantly highland districts of Lushoto (which includes the Korogwe Division) and Pare.

The *Tanga District* comprises a rough quadrilateral of land opposite the island of Pemba, and is one of the smallest districts in the territory (1,833 square miles); nevertheless it contains an African population of 142,000 and Tanga is the second largest town in Tanganyika and the port through which most of the country's vitally important sisal is exported.

The *Pangani District* to the south of it is a still narrower coastal strip containing a population of only 26,000.   Pangani town, which, like Bagamoyo, was once a flourishing centre for the export of slaves, now relies on the copra industry for most of its trade.   Sisal produced on the neighbouring estates is also shipped through the small picturesque port.

The *Handeni District* covers 5,385 square miles and contains a population of 75,000.

The thickly populated *Lushoto Division* (1,756 square miles) of the district of that name contained at the time of the 1948 census about 130,000 people, and the remainder of the district (*Korogwe Division*, 993 square miles) about 90,000.

The *Pare District* covers 3,048 square miles, and again most of its population of 96,000 cling to the highlands.

PHYSICAL FEATURES

The Tanga District presents characteristics common to most of the coastal districts; a gently rising coastal plain, containing much limestone and not infertile (indeed with areas of considerable fertility such as Muheza). Rainfall varies from an average of 87 inches in the Amani Highlands to 20 inches in the northern plains. The Umba and Sigi Rivers contain permanent water, but the former flows through virtually uninhabited country and the latter forms a series of cataracts.

The Pangani District is very similar in general appearance. The Pangani River flows through the district and is navigable for small vessels for about ten miles.

The Handeni District has a backbone of hilly country extending from the Nguru Mountains towards the Usambaras, but leaving a wide gap through which flows the Pangani River, carrying to the sea the waters from the snows of Kilimanjaro and from all the highlands in between.

The Lushoto District contains, as well as the Usambara massif, two blocks of lowland country to the north and to the south-west, thinly populated and inhospitable. Through the district at the foot of the mountains run both road and railway, linking Tanga with Korogwe, Moshi and Arusha. The mountains rise abruptly from the plain and the traveller who drives up into them from the shimmering heat of Mombo enters another world.

The first European to set eyes on it (and leave a record of his visit) was Krapf, the German missionary in the service of the Church Missionary Society. He has given a vivid description of his first visit to "the Kingdom of Usambara" in his book "Travels in East Africa".

On 3rd March, 1852, Krapf reached Utinde, on the summit of what he called one of the loftiest mountains of Bondei, a solid block of granite, rising abruptly like a perpendicular wall and forming an impregnable natural fortress. From this point Krapf could survey almost the whole of Chief Kimweri's dominions and he says that he did not remember having met "a grander prospect in any African country."

Krapf noted that Usambara was much poorer than the Bondei country and the lowlands generally but could not help thinking that they might be so much better off if they knew how to avail themselves of the natural resources of their country. "How many mills and factories might be driven by the numerous streams in this region!"

When Krapf visited "King" Kimweri of Usambara in 1848 and 1852 he found him absolute monarch of a kingdom extending some 60 miles from north to south and some 140 miles from north-west to south-east, and containing, so he estimated, at least half a million people. His dominions extended to the coast between Vanga and Pangani and, since the Sultan of Zanzibar claimed suzerainty over the whole of the East African coast, it is interesting to note the manner in which a conflict of interests was resolved. Tanga and its environs remained under the control of the Sultan's governor, but elsewhere along the coast Kimweri appointed his officers, called Diwans; but their appointment had to be confirmed by the Sultan, who, says Krapf, "makes the candidate a present that he may not lose sight of the Sultan's interests should they run counter to those of the King of Usambara. Thus the Diwan must receive the assent of the sovereign by land as well as of the sovereign by sea."

The Pangani River forms the western boundary of the Pare District and, although not the actual boundary of the Lushoto District also, forms in fact the boundary of its inhabited area.

The highest peak in the Usambaras is Chambolo (7,550 feet) but there are several peaks over 6,500 feet in height, and most of the settlers in the area live at heights between 4,000 and 6,000 feet.

CLIMATE

This small province presents a remarkable range in climatic conditions, from the burning heat of the plains on the borders of Kenya and Masailand to the frosts which occur on the peaks of the Usambaras. Mists are virtually unknown in the coastal regions but common in the hills. The rainfall at Tanga averages over fifty inches a year but at Same is only just over twenty inches.

The presence of the mountain ranges has of course a most pronounced effect on the rainfall and here again it is remarkable how little rain the areas in the "rain shadow" regions receive, also how quickly the rainfall diminishes as one travels from the south-east to the north-west. Thus at Ambangulu in the south-east the rainfall averages nearly ninety inches a year, while at Mkomasi to the north-west it is only about thirteen inches.

The short rains are expected in October and continue until December; the long rains begin in March and peter out in May. From March to July the mountains are enshrouded in mist.

RAINFALL

Figures of rainfall for the last seven years are given below:—

Station	Altitude	Average	1950	1951	1952	1953	1954	1955	1956
Tanga	30	52·17 (28 years)	47·10	77·09	38·73	63·37	40·48	52·25	33·38
Muheza (Substation of Tanga)	600	49·05 (6 years)	44·27	74·27	28·97	58·39	37·50	51·31	41·66
Pangani	30	47·54 (45 years)	42·85	80·56	34·41	47·07	35·90	54·42	46·11
Handeni	2,200	33·44 (29 years)	40·78	45·24	23·19	32·62	25·26	30·58	24·60
Korogwe	960	43·30 (26 years)	38·64	60·25	20·46	49·31	32·78	35·29	31·32
Lushoto	4,580	41·99 (44 years)	38·10	46·12	32·92	38·45	39·09	40·31	32·99
Same (Pare)	2,820	21·26 (22 years)	20·10	35·83	12·40	18·20	16·50	19·29	15·86

POPULATION

The combined results of the 1948 census, a complete one, and the 1952 census, a partial one, are given below:—

District	Area in Sq. Miles	European	Indian	Goan	Arab	Somali	Coloured	Other	Total Non-African	African	Total Population
Tanga ...	1,833	1,114	5,685	607	2,076	71	133	86	9,772	141,606	151,378
Pangani ...	795	103	244	9	562	6	17	7	948	25,377	26,325
Handeni ...	5,385	24	144	–	14	7	30	2	221	75,478	75,699
Lushoto ...	2,749	771	1,020	38	307	76	104	11	2,327	219,152	221,479
Pare ...	3,048	76	169	10	109	28	2	–	394	96,000	96,394
	–	2,088	7,262	664	3,068	188	286	106	13,662	547,212	560,874

THE MAIN TRIBES

The chief tribes in the province are the Digo, Segeju and Bondei in the Tanga District, the Sambaa in the Lushoto District, the Pare in the district to which they give their name, and the Zigua and Nguu in the Handeni District. There is also a small enclave of Mbugu, people of Nilo-Hamitic descent, in the north of the Lushoto District. Along the coast dwell the "Swahili", of mixed descent.

The Digo.—The Digo were driven from their original habitat in Kenya Colony by their neighbours the Galla some ten generations ago and settled on the coastal strip from Mombasa to Tanga, driving out the Bondei who then occupied the coast from Tanga to near the Kenya border. Their tribal organization was a strong gerontocracy which was centred in the *Ngambi* or tribal council. This council was presided over by the *Mchama* or president, and members were admitted on payment of fees which varied in proportion to the importance of the grades to which they gave entry. The old form of the *Ngambi* has practically ceased to exist—one reason for its decline was that the amount of beer consumed by the members during their deliberations would be unseemly now that the tribe has embraced Mohammedanism—but it has been replaced by a council of elders which, under the presidency of the chief, fulfils all the functions of the original organization.

The Segeju, who inhabit the north-eastern corner of the Tanga District, near the Kenya border, migrated from Kenya. The original immigrants consisted of a war party who, cut off from their fellows by the flooding of the Umba River, decided to settle in what was then Digo country. They had no women with them when they arrived, the only female of the party having been killed to avoid the possibility of a dispute as to who should possess her, so they married with the local Digo and Shirazi. Their organization was patriarchal, and though *akidas* were appointed among a certain portion of the tribe, the system never penetrated the northern section, and, according to the elders, was merely a social institution and without political significance.

The Sambaa and Bondei.—The Sambaa, also known on the coast as Shambala, who inhabit the Usambara mountains, have for generations been ruled by the Kilindi, a clan whose ancestor Mbega came from the Nguru mountains of Handeni District. His grandfather is said to have been an Arab, and Mbega, through his astuteness and his prowess as a hunter, established himself as chief of the Sambaa, and appointed his numerous sons as tribal headmen.[1]

The history of the Sambaa is so intermingled with that of the Bondei that the two may be taken together.

The Bondei are concentrated in the undulating country at the foot of the Usambara Hills and extend to the banks of the Pangani River. Their tribal lands were formerly much more extensive than now for they were pushed back from the coast by the Swahili settlers, or were absorbed by them and were also forced back into the present Bondei country by the immigrant Digo. They are a composite tribe, the name signifying the people of the *bonde* or valley, and whether the parent stock was Sambaa or Zigua is a matter of opinion. They never succeeded in achieving any degree of tribal unity, and eventually came under the sway of the Kilindi, who appointed headmen of their own clan throughout the Bondei country.

---

[1]See "The Story of Mbega" by Abdulla Hemedi and Roland Allen, *Tanganyika Notes and Records*, Nos. 1 and 2, March and October, 1936.

In addition to his household officials the chief or *Shebuge* had, in pre-European days, one principal and five subordinate advisers who are said always to have been Sambaa and not Kilindi. He always acted in concert with his council of elders, which also appears to have consisted mainly of Sambaa, and the authority of the Sultan of Zanzibar must have been accepted to some extent, since, on one occasion, permission to exterminate the Kilindi headmen of Bondei was obtained from the Sultan before any action was taken; and it is said that the Sultan or Liwali of Pangani was consulted on all important matters.

A small colony of Taita are settled on the edge of the escarpment above Bwiti and some families of the Mlalo area in the Western Usambaras claim Taita descent, while Segeju inhabit Bwiti, and Digo have been living for many generations at Daluni a few miles away. The dry plains to the north of the Usambaras are inhabited by scattered Kwavi and Kamba.

The Pare.—The Pare, who inhabit the hills from which they take their name, appear to have arrived in the country some two hundred years ago. They are the descendants of three migratory waves from tribes over the Kenya border. The first two waves of immigrants became known as the Bwambo and the Pare; they seem to have had no chiefs and no system of government. The third immigration, the smallest in numbers, were of Taita stock and became known as the Wemjema. They made their headquarters at Bombo in South Pare and established a leadership over the Bwambo and Pare because of their skill in the use of medicines and in rain making. In the three North Pare chiefdoms there was a Zigua dynasty at Same, a Mjema dynasty at Usangi and a Gweno dynasty at Ugweno. There is also an element which comes from the Nguu Hills of Handeni District, and probably also a Chagga strain, since the Chagga of Kilimanjaro were called in to assist the people of Ugweno against those of Usangi, and a portion of the latter area was under Chagga rule for a time.

The Pare form a compact group, only a small alien element having entered the area in order to work on the sisal plantations which lie at the foot of the hills, or to cultivate the rice fields situated in the southern portion of the district. A small number of Pare live in the Usambaras under the suzerainty of the Chief of the Sambaa, the exodus from Upare having taken place on account of famine.

Under the German regime, South Pare was ruled by Sambaa *akidas*, but when indirect rule was established in 1925 Pare chiefs were appointed throughout the tribal area. The chief always acted in concert with a council of elders which investigated cases and brought them before him for judgment. If he disagreed with the opinion of the council the case was discussed and, if necessary, referred back to the elders for reinvestigation. The elders, therefore, had a large say in tribal affairs and without them the chief could not act.

The Zigua and Nguu.—According to German records the Zigua were more warlike than the neighbouring tribes, and individuals who know them well state that they are possessed of greater character than their neighbours, though they may show it in their home life rather than in any superior ability to adapt themselves to modern conditions of life and work. The tribe as a whole is conservative and has in the past shown a marked reluctance to connect itself with modern enterprise.

Though the tribe was never ruled by one chief, individual heads of clans were possessed of considerable personality, which in the case of Bwana Heri was so marked that he attacked and defeated the forces of the Sultan of Zanzibar in

1882. The heads of the clans always acted in collaboration with the elders, without whose co-operation they were powerless; and, though the clans often fought against each other, at times they acted in unison against a common foe. At such times the chiefs of the groups held council and only took such action as was approved by each member of the temporary federation. Usually they seem to have been well disposed towards Arabs, and the heads of clans near the coast, at any rate, referred important matters to the Sultan of Zanzibar.

There is at present only a negligible alien element in Uzigua; the scarcity of water, the lack of markets and the few plantations in the area making it unattractive to alien settlement whether African or non-African. The people have shown an increased interest in the cultivation of cotton which appears to be the most suitable crop for their temperament and environment, but, as indicated above, they are averse to changing their mode of living or to cultivating any crop to which they are unaccustomed.

A group known as the Nguu or Nguru, which inhabits the Nguru Hills, is identical with the Zigua though, as is common, members like to preserve their individual clan and to magnify it into a tribe when it is sufficiently large for them to be able to do so with success.

A branch of the Zigua, the Ruvu, inhabits the islands of the Pangani (or Ruvu) River. They differ but little from the parent stock, but are slightly more sophisticated owing, probably, to greater contact with the neighbouring tribes and with aliens. A small number of Kwavi, an offshoot of the Masai, also live in the district. They are pastoral people, and are controlled by the Zigua chief on whose lands they happen to be living although they have their own head (Ol-Oibon), who is a priest and medicine-man rather than a chief.

The Swahili and Others.—The term "Swahili", which originally signified "a man of the coast", is now used, even by Africans living as far away as Lake Victoria as well as by the coastal population, to denote one who has adopted the Mohammedan religion.

The Shirazi emigrated from Muscat about the tenth centrury A.D., and established themselves at various points on the coast, notably Mtangata and Mkwaja, where they intermarried with the people whom they found in possession of the coast on their arrival. They lived in small communities under a patriarchal organization which merits a brief description.

The head of the community was the *Jumbe*, who had to pay considerable sums in largesse before he could become the *Diwan*, who was the supreme head. The position was kept in the family, that is, in the near circle of relations, but was never inherited in the direct line. Under the *Jumbe* were the *Maakida* (sing.— *Akida*) who controlled the young men, and whose numbers were controlled by the size of the village—a large village might have two Akidas, a small one but one. These Akidas were the heads of the *Ngoma* or dance groups which maintained unity and discipline among the young men, and they also acted as headmen to the parties which journeyed into the interior to trade piece-goods, obtained on credit from the coastal merchants, for ivory or slaves. The *ngoma* danced was the ancient *Goma* which, though monotonous, is dignified and in no way to be confused with the *Beni Ngoma* which was only conceived after the European occupation of the country.

Diwans, Jumbes and Akidas levied toll on every domestic occasion, such as a death or a marriage, and also received other recognised forms of tribute.

There were formerly in the Pangani area five Jumbeates, but with the advent of an industrial era the scale of expenditure necessary for the appointment of Jumbes and Diwans was no longer possible.

The Arabs.—The Arab rule was centred in Pangani, and though the Sultan of Zanzibar appointed a Liwali of Tanga, the Muscat Arabs never became numerous in that area. The Arab administration may never have extended to the interior but there is no doubt that Zigua, Bondei and Kilindi, as well as the inhabitants of the coastal belt, deferred to it to some extent and referred important matters to the local Arab authorities or to the Sultan himself. This was only natural since those up-country relied on the Arabs for their supplies of muzzle-loaders and powder and, so far as the coastal people were concerned, the Arabs represented a civilization which was more refined than their own and so, in their eyes, worthy of imitation.

The Somalis.—A number of Somalis and Comorians made their appearance in the province after European enterprise had opened up the country for trade. The former mix with no one but members of their own tribe, and consider themselves superior to the Africans. All Somali clans were originally classed as natives of Africa but the Ishakia group has now established its right to be classed as "non-native". Since this took place the members of the clan appear to have increased considerably in numbers at the expense of the remaining clans. The Somalis are cattle dealers.

The Comorians.—The Comorians work as personal servants and traders. The majority are indistinguishable from Swahilis, and the language spoken in Great Comoro (Si-angazija) and Johanna Island (Xi-nzuani) are dialects of Swahili. Nevertheless, the people are classed as "non-native" as the Comoro Islands are grouped with Madagascar, the aborigines of which are believed to have been Melanesians and Polynesians and not African negroes, while the Antimerina (Hova) migrated to Madagascar from the East Indian Archipelago about four centuries ago.

Prior to the European occupation, the only *alien* Africans in the area were slaves, who were mostly owned by the coastal population, though slavery was by no means unknown in tribal areas, but European enterprise brought a stream of labourers into the Tanga Province from other parts of the territory and the flow has continued up to the present time. Though the majority of these aliens return to their homes when tired of working on the coast, some have been absorbed by the locals, while others maintain themselves in small groups. Though the members of these groups more or less obey the local native authority many have never entirely relinquished their tribal customs or their intention of ultimately returning to their tribal homes.

The Asian population in the province numbers about 10,000, living mostly in the two major townships of Tanga and Korogwe and engaged in business of one kind or other. The European population amounted to 2,088 in 1952. Many are employed by the large business houses or Government departments in Tanga; the remainder live mostly on sisal or tea estates or have settled in the highlands of the Usambaras.

AGRICULTURAL RESOURCES

Agriculturally, the province divides itself into the following three areas:—

The Coastal Belt, some thirty miles wide, and comprising roughly the Tanga and Pangani Districts. The country is thickly wooded, comparatively well watered and has an annual rainfall of about fifty inches. The population is about 150,000.

The Highlands which, together with the alluvial fan slopes, occupy most of the populated regions of the Pare District, the Lushoto and Korogwe Divisions and part of the Tanga District. The mountain region, as well as the eastern foothills, is characterized by evergreen rain forest, perennial streams and red earth soils which are laterized at altitudes over five thousand feet. The rainfall, except on the north-western slopes, is high, as we have seen, and occasionally exceeds one hundred inches per annum in the east of the Usambaras. The main periods of precipitation are March-May and October-December, with, in certain localities, a third period during July-August. The population is about 300,000.

The Plains comprising the non-mountainous parts of the Pare District and of the Korogwe and Lushoto Divisions and the whole of the Handeni District, with the exception of the area near the Nguru hills in the south-west. Tsetse-infested dry savanna forest covers most of the area in the south and merges into the thorn bush of the Umba steppe north of the Usambara Mountains. Most of the area is poorly watered, and the rainfall, which varies between fifteen and thirty-five inches per annum, is uncertain. The population is about 100,000.

AGRICULTURAL PRODUCTION

The Coastal Belt.—The African population is dense in the immediate coastal strip and in the vicinity of estates, particularly along the railway, but the hinterland of both the north and south is sparsely peopled, the congestion in certain areas giving the impression of a land shortage which, taking the area as a whole cannot really, as yet, be said to exist. This local congestion is exacerbated by the settlement of alien Africans referred to above.

Cassava is the staple food crop of the coastal belt, next in importance being maize, followed by small acreages of sweet potatoes and sorghum. Rice is grown in the vicinity of the Pangani River, and in odd depressions throughout the area, but it is a precarious crop owing to its dependence on rainfall during the growing season. The principal pulses are cowpeas and green gram.

As regards African production, the only important cash crops, as such, are coconuts (for copra) and oranges, whilst bananas and other tropical fruit (and betel nuts) provide a source of income in a few areas. More than half the adult male population are wage earners on estates and in the towns and as a large number of these do not grow their own food there is always a ready market for food surpluses produced by the rest of the population.

Orange growing is centred on Muheza, where the crop varies from 1,000 to 2,000 tons annually. Much of the fruit is used for the manufacture of orange juice at a small canning factory which also processes other fruits and vegetables.

Tanganyika is the world's greatest producer of sisal, and from the Tanga Province comes over half the territory's production. Yet in 1890 there was not a single sisal plant (other than wild varieties of the species *agave*) in the country.

Tanga.

Photo: E.A. Railways and Harbours

Tea pickers on the Ambangulu estate.

Photo: Shell Co.

The history of the introduction of sisal into Tanganyika has indeed an air of romance. It is thus described by the man to whose foresight and perseverance the existence of this great industry is primarily due, Dr. Richard Hindorf:—

"After visiting the Far East, including New Guinea, Java and Sumatra, Australia and India, investigating scientifically the selection and planting of tropical plants, I arrived in Tanga in 1891, where at first I was interested in developing Derema in the Usambara, planting coffee as well as cocoa, tea, pepper and other spices. I was concerned to find a plant suitable to the conditions in the plains from the Usambara to Tanga, where there is neither too little nor too much rain. In the course of my scientific work I kept in touch with the work of Kew, and in the Kew Bulletin No. 62 of February, 1892 I saw an article referring to sisal in Mexico. Against the wish of one of my directors of the Deutschostafrika Gesellschaft, and with the agreement of the others, I followed this matter, but discovered that the import of sisal planting material was prohibited from Mexico. The Kew Bulletin had mentioned that in 1836 the American Consul at Campeche in Mexico had sent sisal plants to Florida. I therefore wrote to Beesoner Bros., plant dealers in Florida, requesting them to send me sisal plants and they sent me 1,000 bulbils to Hamburg. I went from Berlin to Hamburg to examine them and found that 80% had died. I repacked the remaining 200, and they arrived well in Tanga, 62 surviving, which I planted at Kikogwe in the south side of the river at Pangani. Sisal was next planted at Bushiridorf. These plants founded the sisal industry of East Africa."[1]

There are now some 66 estates in the province and in 1956 production amounted to 120,500 tons valued at approximately £7,300,000.

The Highlands.—Except for Eastern Usambara, which consists largely of alienated land, the highlands are the most densely populated of the African agricultural areas. The cattle population is also considerable, and there is an almost equal number of sheep and goats. The staple food is maize, with bananas and sweet potatoes as important supplementaries. Before the advent of Irish blight in 1943, European potatoes were second in importance only to maize in the western Usambaras and since their virtual disappearance food shortages have occurred. Mixed beans are universally grown.

The most important cash crop is rice, which is grown in well watered swamps at the foot of the scarps. Tobacco, fruit, European vegetables, hides, skins and dairy products are other important sources of revenue from the land. Groundnuts have been found to thrive on the alluvial soils at the foot of the mountains. Another crop of importance is coffee. This is grown by both Africans and non-Africans, and production, while not comparable in importance with that of the Northern Province, nevertheless amounted to 440 tons of clean coffee in 1956 valued at £220,000.[2]

Tea was first planted in Tanganyika at Ambangulu in the Usambaras, and the estate concerned is still in production. There are now 11 other estates in the province growing tea (all of which are not yet in production), and output in 1956 amounted to 1,635,210 lb. valued at approximately £200,000[3].

---

[1] Statement made to Sir Eldred Hitchcock by Dr. Hindorf in Berlin in 1947, and quoted in the *Tanganyika Standard* for June 12, 1954.

[2] 330 tons valued at £130,000 in 1955.

[3] 1,176,000 lb. valued at £167,000 in 1955.

A beginning is being made, both by Africans and non-Africans, in planting cocoa. This crop is as yet in the experimental stage, but if it is successful it will compete with coffee in the fertile areas beneath the Eastern Usambaras.

The problems of soil erosion and maintenance of fertility are serious and the stage has already been reached in many areas of the mountains where the available land is simply not capable of supporting the existing population.

The Plains of the Hinterland.—The population of this very large area is for the most part clustered in widely scattered groups round the few existing water-courses and water-holes, which, as often as not, are situated in areas of low soil fertility and remote from the main centres of communication. The population is therefore, on the whole, far from prosperous and subject to recurrent food shortages.

Part of the area is occupied by pastoral tribes (Kwavi and Masai) in particular western Handeni and Pare and northern Lushoto, who between them possess some twenty thousand head of cattle.

Maize is again the staple food crop, closely followed by cassava, with some sorghum here and there, particularly in Handeni. Failure of the maize crop is a frequent occurrence and its partial replacement by sorghums and millets is being encouraged. The principal pulse is the French bean but cowpeas and green gram are also important.

Cotton is the main cash crop and it is well suited to the whole area except western Handeni, where yields are inclined to be low, probably because of low temperatures. Other sources of income are castor and sunflower seed, tobacco, honey and beeswax, and of course a considerable number of people go out to work on estates.

Coffee is being grown increasingly in the Nguru hills and there are now some 50,000 trees in the area.

Pare Scheme.—In the North and South Pares resettlement areas are being developed along the fan slopes of the mountains and, where practicable, on the plains in an attempt to relieve the population pressure. In the mountain areas themselves the people are being taught methods of better land usage and animal husbandry, particularly the stall feeding of cattle.

Usambara Scheme.—As a result of three years of experiments carried out in the Mlalo Basin from between 1946 and 1949, soil conservation measures were introduced into the Western Usambaras, supported by Native Authority legislation in 1951. These include such measures as tie-ridging, removal of steep land from cultivation, control on grazing of cattle and reafforestation. The soil conservation measures have been implemented gradually, but now affect to a greater or lesser degree all inhabitants of the highlands, and have already produced visible improvements on the hillsides.

Side by side with this rehabilitation of the highlands attempts are being made to develop land in the plains as expansion areas for the increasing population. Inadequate rainfall in many parts and soil salinity in others have proved major obstacles, but several projects have been initiated.

AMANI AGRICULTURAL RESEARCH STATION

In 1902 the Germans set up at Amani, fifty miles from Tanga in the Usambara mountains, an agricultural research station which is reputed to have cost £1,000,000 to establish and equip. Here were conducted a whole series of experiments in the production, under local conditions, of a great variety of tropical, sub-tropical and temperate crops: coffee, tea and cocoa; plants of medicinal value such as cinchona; rubber, fibres, spices of various kinds; plants producing oil, tannin, dyes, gums and resins; as well as a variety of fruit trees, timber trees, shrubs and palms. Investigations were made into plant breeding, plant pests and diseases, methods of cultivation and manuring, analysis of soils and the technical study of indigenous plants. Special attention was given to the development of rubber and cinchona and several of the plantations then made still exist and, during the 1939-45 war, were of the greatest value. The Institute was re-established in 1926 as "The East African Agricultural Research Station", financed by the Governments of Tanganyika, Kenya, Uganda, Zanzibar, Nyasaland and Northern Rhodesia, and its research work continued. In 1952 the station closed down and the staff and equipment were transferred to Nairobi. Amani is now the Headquarters of the East Africa Malarial Research Unit and of the staff of the Tanganyika Malarial Unit.

INDUSTRIES

The greatest industry in the province is of course the production of sisal, which has been mentioned above, and a full description of which will be found in "Tanganyika: A Review of its Resources and their Development". Industries other than those of an agricultural nature, such as the production of coffee, tea, copra, fruit juice, rice and cotton are not numerous, but mention must be made of saw-milling and bacon curing. There are fourteen private saw-mills and eleven mills operating in Government concessions, which produced some 18,000 cubic tons of timber in 1954[1].

MINERALS

Mineral occurrences have been found at various places throughout the province, mostly within reasonable reach of the railway. There is a deposit of gypsum at Mkomasi which exports about 5,000 tons a year for use in the Kenya and Uganda cement industries. In Pare District magnesite, kyanite and garnets occur but whether these are deposits capable of commercial exploitation has yet to be proved.

The mining of mica in Pare and Handeni Districts is taking place on a small scale, but it is not anticipated that there will be spectacular development in this field. Salt is produced near Tanga by solar evaporation of sea water.

ADMINISTRATIVE STATIONS[2]

Provincial headquarters are at Tanga[3], an attractive town situated on a good harbour, the possibilities of which, as the natural port for the highlands in the hinterland, the Germans early realised. In the 1914-18 war Tanga was a battle-

[1]12,100 cubic tons in 1955.

[2]For additional information see table on p. 542.

[3]There are several explanations of the possible derivation of the name *Tanga*. One is that it comes from the stem "to shine" (*jua* in many Bantu languages), another that it is an Arabic corruption (there being no "ch" in Arabic) of *Wa Changa*, the name of the tribe living in the vicinity, or possibly of *uchanga*, the Swahili word for sand. Another possibility is that the name of this town comes from the word for mainland in several local vernaculars—the word itself being *Tanga*.

ground and the scene of an unsuccessful attempt to land by the British forces;[1] in the 1939-45 war it was a Royal Naval Air Station. It continues to grow in size and importance and extensions to its berthing accommodation have recently been made.[2]

As well as the railway to Moshi and Arusha, a bituminized road starts at Tanga and goes as far inland as Korogwe (60 miles), whence there is an important road link with the central railway at Morogoro. Tanga is also well served by planes of East African Airways, which connect it with Nairobi, Dar es Salaam and other places by daily services.

The climate can be oppressive in the hot season, but relief may be sought at Amani, in the hills only 45 miles away, where it is always cool at night. In 1952 the Tanga Township contained 14,635 Africans, 1,029 Arabs, 5,779 Indians and Goans and 558 Europeans.

Tanga Township and the adjacent minor settlement of Tanga Nje are administered as a separate district by a District Commissioner (Urban) assisted by one district officer. The district Commissioner (Rural) is assisted by a district officer stationed at Muheza.

At Tanga there are normally stationed a Resident Magistrate and representatives of most of the Departments of Government, of the High Commission, and of the Police Force.

Pangani[3].—Pangani, at the mouth of the river of that name is, like Bagamoyo, a picturesque old town, which gives the impression of living in the past. By some it has been identified as the "Rhapta" mentioned by Ptolemy.[4]

It is 32 miles from Tanga by a good road and 64 miles from Handeni by a road passable in the dry weather only. It is not on any regular air route.

Pangani is the headquarters of one of the smallest districts in the territory, but the district contains a population of over 26,000, of whom nearly 600 are Arabs. In the township, in 1952, there were 1,874 Africans, 287 Arabs, 201 Indians and 7 Europeans.

The District Commissioner is the only administrative officer stationed there but normally there are also representatives of the Medical and Agricultural Departments.

---

[1]See p. 84; also the account in the Official History of the War in East Africa.

[2]A further description of the town will be found on p. 824 of "Tanganyika: A Review of its Resources and their Development".

[3]The commonest explanation of the name *Pangani* is that it is a corruption of the Swahili *pangeni*, with a connotation similar to that of the names Bagamoyo and Dar es Salaam, indicating safety and rest at journey's end, whether from the dangers of the sea or of the interior. A less likely legend is that the name comes from the Arabic word (*pangani*) for a type of sewed boat, now found only at Lamu, but once believed to have been made at Pangani.

[4]For a discussion of this problem see "Pangani, the Trade Centre of Ancient History", by H. C. Baxter, *in Tanganyika Notes and Records* No. 17 for June, 1944.

Handeni.[1]—Handeni (altitude 2,200 feet) is a station "carved out of the bush"—bush which still approaches close to it on some sides. It was an important communications centre in the 1914-18 campaign and is described by Francis Brett Young in "Marching on Tanga." As his description applies, with only a few changes, to other stations with German *Bomas*, it may be of interest to recall it. He writes:—

"In a crude sort of way the *Boma* was impressive, with an air of gloomy solidity. All the hilltop around for a hundred yards or so had been cleared, so that the building dominated the crest. On the further side, where the governor had lived, it was whitewashed and homely, for a deep stoep ran all the length of the house, over which a fine bougainvillaea sprawled, splashing the sunny whiteness with colour; round the drive, in a wide sweep, grew an avenue of the flamboyant tree, whose blood-red blossoms must have been very beautiful in their season. From the windows one might overlook a vast expanse of country, reaching from the cool green of the surrounding plantations to darker sky lines, level and fringed with trees, and beyond all the fantastic shapes of the mountains."

Handeni is on the importout road link between the Central and the Tanga railway lines, 128 miles from the former at Morogoro and 43 miles from the latter at Korogwe. There is also a road from Handeni (dry weather only) to Bagamoyo (122 miles). Handeni is not on any regular air route.

It has grown in size since the days of the 1914-18 campaign but the District Commissioner still uses the original German Boma as both residence and office. He is assisted by one district officer and representatives of the Public Works and Agricultural Departments are normally stationed there.

Lushoto.[2]—Lushoto is one of the most attractively situated of all the stations in the territory. Perched at the head of a narrow valley in the Usambara Mountains, at an altitude of 4,600 feet above sea level, it has a Swiss look about it and is in complete contrast to a station such as Handeni. The climate, disproportionately affected (or so it seems) by the altitude, is more like what one expects to find in Europe than in Africa.[3] It is approached by a well graded road from Mombo, nearly 3,500 feet down in the plains below, where there is a station of the Tanga Line as well as an aerodrome. From Lushoto roads connect with other places in the mountains. Mombo is a regular port of call for planes of East African Airways.

In 1952 the Lushoto Township contained 428 Africans, 45 Asians and 70 Europeans.

[1]There are at least two suggested explanations of the origin of the name *Handeni*. Properly the name itself refers to the hill (3,400 ft.) situated about a mile south-east of the present District Office but it has been extended to cover the whole vicinity—and indeed the whole district as the district name. One of the suggested derivatives of the name is that it comes from the name of a prominent early local settler, one Samhandeni, who set up his home on the hill. Another suggestion is that Handeni is the plural imperative of the Kizigua verb *kuhanda*, meaning to plant—(c.f. *kupanda* is Kiswahili), although why such an order should have been adopted as the name of the place is not known.

[2]The origin of the name *Lushoto* is uncertain but one suggestion is that it comes from the Kisambaa name (*Msote*) for a certain type of tree in the area. There was a large tree of this type near the present Lushoto-Magamba road which gave its name to a village nearby. It is said that when the Germans arrived they took the name of this village for their new town, gradually corrupting the name into Lushoto.

[3]A fuller description of Lushoto is given at p. 815 in " Tanganyika: A Review of its Resources and their Development".

The District Commissioner is assisted by two district officers and one assistant district officer, and representatives of the Agricultural, Forest, Public Works, Medical, and Veterinary Departments are normally stationed there.

Korogwe.[1]—The town of Korogwe (altitude 960 feet) is situated on the Tanga line at the point where the road link with the Central railway line connects with it. It is 60 miles from Tanga over an excellent bituminized road and 51 miles by railway. It has grown up, somewhat haphazardly, as a communications centre, but the old town is very badly sited on the bank of the Pangani river. A new town is being established close by, the hospital having been first built, followed by the new district office and the necessary housing. Because of its low altitude Korogwe is at times very hot, but in the cool season the climate is pleasant and in the hills nearby fires are then necessary at night.[2] It is not as yet on any regular air route.

In 1952 the Korogwe Township contained 2,350 Africans, 66 Arabs, 486 Indians and 36 Europeans.

The District Officer in charge is assisted by two other district officers and representatives of the Police Force and of the Public Works, Labour, Medical, Agriculture (Fisheries), Forest and Veterinary Departments are normally stationed there. (Lushoto is the provincial headquarters of the Forest Department.)

Same.[3] (altitude 2,800 feet) is situated on road and railway line 155 miles from Tanga in the somewhat arid gap between the mountain masses of the South and the North Pares. Like Handeni it can at times be very hot, but at night it is seldom uncomfortably so. It is not on any regular air route. The District Commissioner is assisted by two district officers and representatives of the Social Development, Agriculture, Veterinary, Prisons, and Game Departments are normally stationed there.

PLACES OF INTEREST TO THE VISITOR, AND SPORTING FACILITIES

For many, the attraction will be the Usambara highlands, where, at Lushoto, there are comfortable hotels, and where golf, tennis and riding may be enjoyed in addition to the fishing and delightful walks which this area provides. The Mkussu River was the first river in Tanganyika to be stocked with trout, ova of both rainbow and brown trout having been successfully introduced into it in 1926. Fishing is still good on this river and is controlled by the Mkussu Fly Fishers Association, c/o Magamba Club, Lushoto. Trout have also been introduced into the Saseni and Yangoma Rivers in the South Pare mountains. In neither river are trout plentiful though some big fish await the fisherman who has the necessary patience and skill. On both the Saseni and the Yangoma there are fishing camps which can at present however only be reached by foot. The fishing is controlled by the Game Ranger, Same.

Excellent sea fishing is to be had off Tanga (see also page 489).

---

[1]*Korogwe* is supposed to have taken its name from the name of the first settler in the area of the present town, a Zigua tribesman called Mkorogwe. *Korogwe* in Kizigua is the name of a dish prepared with dried bananas.

[2]A fuller description of Korogwe will be found at p. 814 in "Tanganyika: A Review of its Resources and their Development".

[3]*Same* is a Pare (or more properly, Chasu) word meaning to move or change habitation, its Swahili counterpart being *hama*. It is the original place-name of a pool just below the forest on the west side of Vumari Mountain, overlooking the present Same. Of old, it is said, the water in this natural reservoir was insufficient for the needs of the local people during the height of the dry season. As a result the people would move elsewhere, returning later in the year when the rains had again raised the water level.

The province is not one to which the enthusiast usually comes in pursuit of big game, but in parts of the Tanga, Lushoto and Korogwe Districts most of the usual varieties can nevertheless be found. In the Pare District the early riser who makes a short trip down the "Prince of Wales," road from district head-quarters at Same is likely to be rewarded by the sight of such game animals as elephant, gerenuk, rhino, eland, oryx and buffalo, and indeed by seeing all the usual savanna game except wildebeeste. Lion and cheetah exist but are less frequently seen.

There are sulphur baths at Amboni, 5 miles from Tanga, and unusual "mud volcanoes" can be seen at Moa, 30 miles from Tanga.[1]

The sisal research station at Ngomeni is 18 miles from Tanga and the head-quarters of the E.A. Malarial Research Unit at Amani is situated 45 miles from Tanga.

The Government fish farms at Korogwe are also of interest.

[1]See "The Mud Volcanoes of Moa, near Tanga", by J. J. Richard, in *Tanganyika Notes and Records*, No. 19, for June, 1945.

THE WESTERN PROVINCE

SITUATION AND PHYSICAL FEATURES

The Western Province occupies the large region between the Central Province and Lake Tanganyika, and between Sukumaland and the Southern Highlands Province and Northern Rhodesia. It covers an area nearly as great as the whole of the land area of Uganda, 79,000 square miles, but is estimated to contain only about a million people. These live—as can be seen from the population map on page 283—mostly around the edges of the province, leaving a vast area in the centre practically empty. The northern part of this empty area is made up of a low lying region drained by the Muyovosi river, a tributary of the Malagarasi, which flows through an extensive series of swamps, and the southern part consists of one huge block of *miombo* woodland, some 20,000 square miles in extent. The bulk of the province forms part of the central plateau, but in the west and south-west the country is more broken and contains the Buha, Mpanda and Ufipa highlands. These are isolated mountainous regions and thus, unlike other areas in the territory, their effect on climate and on the general drainage system is local only and of minor importance.

Sixty per cent of the land area of the province is infested with tsetse fly, mostly of the *glossina morsitans* variety, and sleeping sickness is endemic over a wide region.

From the map, the province would appear to be well watered, but in fact there is only one river worthy of the name which never dries up at the end of the dry season—the Malagarasi. This river, some 500 miles long, rises in the mountains to the north of Kigoma and flows north-eastwards to form the boundary with the Belgian Trust Territory of Ruanda-Urundi for about a hundred miles, then it bends to the south-east and, describing a huge arc, flows into Lake Tanganyika less than fifty miles due south of its source. The lower reaches, between the point where the Central Line crosses it and its mouth, are obstructed by rapids, but the middle reaches have been navigated, although with difficulty. This river drains all the area to the north-west of the railway line and, through its tribuatry the Ugalla, much of that to the south as well; but all its southern tributaries become mere strings of pools, and often completely dried up river beds, during the dry season.[1] At this time not a drop of running water is to be found in the whole of Unyamwezi, i.e. in the greater part of the Tabora, Nzega and Kahama Districts. Nevertheless the degree of desiccation is not quite so great as in the Central Province as a rule, since the Western Province generally receives a better rainfall, but if the rains fail the results can well be imagined. In the year 1949, when only 19·49 inches of rain fell at Tabora, water had to be brought by train from the Malagarasi, 150 miles away, at a daily cost of £250.

This, however, was quite exceptional and with normal rains the province wears a pleasing aspect. Indeed Stanley waxed quite lyrical about it and wrote:

"Taken altogether, Unyamwezi may be said to be the finest country in the whole of East and Central Africa. It is one grand rolling table-land, with a gentle western trend towards the Tanganyika (lake), which drains the greater part of it. If one were to take a bird's-eye view of it he would see forests, a

[1]See "The Valley and Swamps of the Malagarasi River", by C. H. B. Grant in *Tanganyika Notes and Records*, No. 23, June, 1947.

purple-coloured carpet of leafage, broken here and there by naked plains and clearings, stretching to all points of the horizon, with now and then dark heaving masses of rocky hill, rising like blunted cones above the gentle undulations, which rise and subside over and beyond the horizon, like the heavy, exhausted waves of an ocean after a storm. Stand upon any coign of vantage you like, on the height of some of those great titanic boulders of syenite which crop up above the crest of the hills and you will behold a scene the like of which you never saw before. There are no grand mountains, or sublime heights; there is no picturesqueness about it—you would call it prosaic, monotonous, perhaps, but there is sublimity in this view of the great, the infinite, apparently endless extent of forests in Unyamwezi."[1]

The border between the Nzega and Shinyanga Districts is formed by the river Manyonga, and although it does not flow for several months during the year it floods quickly during the rains and then disrupts road communications very considerably. The bridging of this troublesome river has been begun as part of the road development programme. The boundary with the Central Province is the Wembere river for much of its length, and here again there is a seasonal flow only, although much of the country through which the river passes is very swampy in the rains. In the south-west nearly all the rivers drain into Lake Rukwa, but there is one which drains into Lake Tanganyika which deserves mention: this is the Kalambo, on the border with Northern Rhodesia, which has a most spectacular waterfall nearly 700 feet in height.

Apart from Lakes Tanganyika and Rukwa the province contains no large lakes of any importance. The area of Lake Rukwa varies very greatly and in 1949 it dried up almost completely. Not only did thousands of hippo and other animals die in the drought but the important tilapia fishing industry received a serious setback, from which it took some time to recover.[2] There are small lakes in nearly all the districts but few are much bigger than large ponds, except perhaps Lake Sagara to the south of the Central Line near Nguruka, Lake Chogu to the north of it and Lakes Katavi and Chada in the Mpanda District.

DISTRICTS

The province is divided into eight districts, with provincial headquarters at Tabora. Three-quarters of the large Nyamwezi tribe, which numbered 363,000 at the time of the 1948 census, live in the Tabora, Kahama and Nzega Districts, where the Nyamwezi make up 60 % of the total population. In Tabora District, with an area of 25,000 square miles, the Nyamwezi numbered 106,000 out of a total population of 158,000; in Nzega District, 5,600 square miles, they numbered 113,000 out of 187,000; and in Kahama District, 7,300 square miles, 47,000 out of 95,000.

The Ha, the third largest tribe in the territory, numbered 286,000 in 1948. They live mostly in the Kibondo and Kasulu Districts, (5,800 and 3,700 square miles respectively) where they form 80 % of the population, and in the Kigoma District (5,300 square miles), where they form 25 %.

The Mpanda District, 17,400 square miles, with 40,000 people, is thinly populated and contains a number of small tribes, the principal being the Konongo (26 %), Pimbwe (15 %), Bende (12 %) and Fipa (10 %).

The Ufipa District, 9,000 square miles, had a population of 108,000 in 1948, 57 % being Fipa.

---

[1]"How I Found Livingstone." pp. 519-520.
[2]See "A History of Lake Rukwa and the Red Locust" by D. L. Gunn in *Tanganyika Notes and Records*, No. 42, for March, 1956

CLIMATE

The province as a whole is not so arid as the neighbouring Central Province. Almost all of it lies in a zone which receives over 30 inches of rain a year and the highland regions of Buha and Mpanda receive from 40 to 50 inches. As so much of it forms a part of the great central plateau, unrelieved by any large and important physical features such as mountains or lakes, there is considerable uniformity throughout this region in climatic conditions, and in the Tabora, Nzega, Kahama and Mpanda Districts it is the presence or absence of tsetse-infested bush which is the really important factor. A noticeable feature of the climate of this area is the wide range in temperature which often occurs during the day. Thus at Tabora a daily range of over 36°F, has been recorded. At the coast the range is seldom over 20°F, but there the nights are often hot whereas in the province the nights are always cool. In the Buha and Ufipa highlands conditions are similar to those obtaining in the other highland regions of the country, except that mists are very seldom experienced and the rainfall rarely exceeds 60 inches per annum. On the shores of Lake Tanganyika at a height of just over 2,500 feet above sea level, the atmosphere can be oppressively hot and humid just before and at times during the rains, but for the greater part of the year the proximity of the lake has a cooling and stabilizing effect and the daily variation in temperature is rarely more than five degrees.

There is normally only one rainy season throughout this region—although a short break in the rains is often experienced—and the rains commence in November/December and continue, intermittently, until mid-May. Statistics of rainfall, in inches, at district headquarters are as follows:—

Station	Altitude	Average	1950	1951	1952	1953	1954	1955	1956
Tabora	4,150	34·45 (48 years)	34·18	51·08	29·76	29·29	28·61	29·01	31·67
Nzega	4,000	31·29 (32 years)	32·84	43·18	25·33	32·71	26·08	26·61	32·52
Kahama	4,000	40·63 (34 years)	55·87	58·82	50·37	62·84	42·19	50·82	*
Kibondo ...	4,980	44·29 (30 years)	43·18	58·82	36·66	39·23	38·93	38·03	41·44
Kasulu	4,530	44·99 (33 years)	47·69	59·92	58·71	52·23	46·75	72·15	42·71
Kigoma	2,550	37·57 (19 years)	44·29	33·43	37·01	40·43	33·50	42·88	34·00
Mpanda	3,600	37·11 (19 years)	28·11	57·44	38·05	31·63	28·55	37·25	37·04
Sumbawanga (Ufipa)	5,650	31·91 (25 years)	24·13	34·57	36·16	*	29·43	*	*

*Records incomplete.

POPULATION

Combining the results of the 1948 (complete) and the 1952 (partial) census, the following results are obtained:—

District	European	Indian	Goan	Arab	Somali	Coloured	Other	Total non-African	African	Total Population
Tabora	389	1,991	60	414	77	54	21	3,006	158,334	162,152
Urambo (Sub-Station)	480	103	7	112	48	26	36	812		187,796
Nzega	81	311	7	598	5	195	4	1,201	186,595	187,796
Kahama	57	258	–	–	297	11	40	663	94,583	95,246
Kigoma	114	682	22	214	1	64	17	1,114	59,538	60,652
Kasulu	54	16	–	28	4	–	–	102	298,803	299,034
Kibondo ...	32	58	–	31	–	8	–	129		
Mpanda	157	93	–	74	4	12	1	341	40,390	40,731
Ufipa	75	26	–	300	–	42	1	444	107,991	108,435
Totals ...	1,439	3,538	96	1,771	436	412	120	7,812	946,234	954,046

This population is very unevenly distributed. Thus nearly two-thirds of the Europeans live in the Tabora and Urambo Districts, those in the latter being at the time of the census mostly employees of the Overseas Food Corporation; the Indians and Goans are mostly concentrated in the towns of Tabora, Kigoma, Nzega, Bukene and Kahama; and there are thousands of square miles of tsetse-infested forest with no inhabitants at all in the southern parts of the province. The 1948 census showed the density per square mile of the African population to be as follows:— Tabora (including Urambo) 7, Nzega 37, Kahama 13, Kigoma 9, Kasulu (with Kibondo) 30, Mpanda 3, Ufipa 12.

A glance at the population map on page 283 will show that the African population is largely concentrated in certain areas: in the comparatively fertile steppe-like country round Tabora and to the north of it, in the Buha highlands of the Kasulu and Kibondo Districts, and in Ufipa. The tsetse-infested *miombo* woodland in the centre and south is empty country. But there are indications that parts of this area are highly mineralized and are therefore unlikely to remain so empty in future.

THE LARGER TRIBES

The Nyamwezi.—The Nyamwezi, "the people of the West" (literally "the people of the Moon"), are the second largest tribe in the territory and are now thought to number close on 400,000. They were well known to the early explorers and provided most of the porters for the caravans between the great lakes and the coast in the early days. They are still great wanderers and are to be found all over East Africa and in the islands of Zanzibar and Pemba. They are Bantu and are primarily agriculturists, but many of them, especially in the Nzega District, keep cattle and it is a poor Nyamwezi who has not got one or two sheep or goats. In language, customs and social organization they are very similar to the Sukuma (see page 186) and both tribes are thought to have a common origin. In the past a Sukuma who left his tribal area to look for work would call himself a Nyamwezi and a member of one tribe can understand without difficulty the language spoken by a member of the other. Much of the following description written of an earlier generation is still true today:—

"The typical Nyamwezi is not bad looking; some would consider him good looking and in youth the members of the tribe show the greatest suppleness and 'style'. Although less slender than the Tusi the Nyamwezi has more noble features than those of many other Africans. Generally speaking, he is not very thick-lipped, the mouth is well proportioned, the teeth good, the nose moderately broad, and in the somewhat large face gleam two bright, lively and intelligent eyes. The skin colour varies from light to dark bronze.

The 'children of the moon' are vain and pay great attention to their personal appearance, taking frequent baths when water is freely available, rubbing themselves with oil and having their hair elaborately coiffured. In vanity the Nyamwezi maidens yield nothing to their European sisters, and although without the same aids to beauty nevertheless are equally successful in their efforts. They often wear a necklace of beads made of copper, strung on a thread made from the long hairs from the tail of a cow, or beads made of glass, of various colours; from the collar is sometimes suspended, hanging down the back, a tassel or fringe of coloured cloth. Against their ebony skins these adornments show up to perfection, and they are worn with an air which the most sophisticated actress might envy. Matrons and maidens alike wear anklets, but these are neither of gold nor of silver but of copper: a large spiral anklet of copper is the heart's desire of any Nyamwezi belle.

Tattooing used to be common, especially amongst the young girls, and is regarded as a work of beauty.

The distinguishing mark of the older Nyamwezi is his filed teeth. Congo natives file to a point all the teeth in the upper jaw, the Nyamwezi merely files a gap between the two incisors. This also is considered a mark of beauty and is (or was) found in men and women alike. They pay considerable attention to the care of the teeth, using as a tooth-brush the teazed-out end of a twig of the *mswaki* tree."[1]

As a tribe they are hard-working, law-abiding and very likeable traditionalists. Although the whole area of Unyamwezi is divided into a large number of chiefdoms, within these chiefdoms the authority of the chief and the sub-chiefs remains strong. Nevertheless it is surprising how democratic these chiefs are and to what extent they have the loyalty and co-operation of their people. The political structure is very similar to that of the Sukuma, which is described on page 186.

Both tribes are notable for the number of societies, secret and semi-secret, which are to be found in their areas. The "Baswezi" are a sect or society which is said to have originated in the lands to the north and to have been introduced along with the Tusi. It is probably now more widespread than it used to be. Its objects were evil and anti-social, and action was taken to suppress it both by government officials and by missionaries for many years, but it is now a reformed "freemasonry" with possibly a wider appeal. On special occasions the Baswezi in full regalia—in which a horned head-dress covered with cowries plays a conspicuous part—are usually to be seen. There are also other societies, including one in which the initiates become extraordinarily skilled in handling snakes, even the most poisonous, and another in which porcupines are sought out in their burrows deep below the ground.

Mirambo, originally the chief of Urambo in what is now the Tabora District, and later the ruler of most of the area extending from Tabora almost to Lake Victoria in the north, Lake Tanganyika in the west and Lake Rukwa in the south, was one of the more remarkable figures in the early history of Tanganyika. From small beginnings, by force of character, ruthlessness and considerable ability as a leader in war, he became what Stanley called "the Napoleon of Central Africa". He subjugated in turn all the neighbouring tribes and attacked others further afield, until be bestrode all the trade routes from Tabora and completely disrupted the Arab trade. The Arabs attacked him, aided by Stanley, but were defeated and Stanley was very nearly captured in his bed. From 1870 until his death in 1884 Mirambo was a power to be reckoned with, and had carved out for himself a small empire in the west which he ruled with considerable ability. Primarily a soldier—and to the last he led his warriors in battle—he also had a shrewd commercial eye and a remarkable gift for organization. He kept a small standing army and saw to it that they were better armed and better trained than any of his enemies, himself superintending their training and going to immense pains to obtain muzzle-loaders, and even breech-loading guns, for them. He had his own secret service. He early realized

[1]Translated from "Les Banyamwezi", by Rev. Fr. P. Bösch, 1930. Published by *Anthropos*, Münster.

that Europeans possessed knowledge and skills which he lacked, and encouraged the Church Missionary Society to establish a mission station near his capital. He sent this message to Sir John Kirk, British Counsul at Zanzibar:—

"Is it expected that if my power is destroyed the petty chiefs of this country would make it easier of access for travellers, more open to traders and more peaceful? ...... I can only say that this country is a hundred times more prosperous, ten-fold more peaceful and a thousand-fold more safe than it ever was before I became chief of it. I wish to open it up, to learn of Europeans, to trade honestly with all and to cultivate peaceful relationship with my neighbours."

After his death the little empire he had built up disintegrated, but his name will never be forgotten in Western Tanganyika.[1]

The Sumbwa.—The Sumbwa are very similar in appearance, language and social organization to the Nyamwezi. Most of them live in the western part of the Kahama District.

The Ha.—The Ha, numbering by now over 300,000 in all, form the third largest tribe in the territory. They are mostly to be found in the districts of Kasulu, Kibondo and Kigoma but have also infiltrated into all the surrounding districts and, like the Nyamwezi, are great wanderers, members of the tribe being found working on sisal and other estates as far afield as Tanga and Dar es Salaam. The visitor's first impression of the Ha may not be very favourable. They are amongst the more primitive tribes in the territory and lack the fineness of feature which distinguishes those with Hamitic blood in their veins from those of Bantu origin. Having lived for so long in a rather remote corner of the territory, they have not been so subjected to civilizing influences as many of the other tribes. Even now, with considerable numbers concentrated in special sleeping sickness settlements, progress and development are slow and the Ha clings stubbornly to his traditional way of life. In this witchcraft plays a very large part, possibly an even larger part than it does in that of most tribes, and the murders which occur can nearly all be traced to its malign influence.

In the southern part of the Buha area, in the highland regions of the Kasulu District, the Ha is usually a cattle-keeping agriculturist and some 70,000 head of cattle are to be found in this area as well as 150,000 sheep and goats. It seems probable that these cattle were introduced by the Tusi, overlords of the Ha, who entered the country perhaps two or three hundred years ago and established themselves in positions of authority by virtue of their superior intelligence and political ability. The chiefly familes in the three Buha Districts are still of Tusi stock and indeed many of the sub-chiefs or *watwale* also claim the same origin.

In the northern part of Buha, that is in the lower-lying areas on both sides of the Malagarasi River, the people are congregated in the specially selected settlements already referred to and in these few cattle can be kept. Only in the Nyaruonga chiefdom, in the extreme north-west of the Kibondo District on the borders of the Biharamulo District, are cattle in any numbers to be found.

[1]See "Mirambo, the Napoleon of Central Africa" by R. J. Harvey, in *Tanganyika Notes and Records* No. 28 for Jan. 1950.

Finding an economic crop for these remote areas has presented difficulties. Coffee was tried in early days without success but a new campaign for its introduction is proving successful. Tobacco also has proved popular and successful and the numbers growing this crop in the Kibondo District increase yearly. It is probably the lack of a suitable high-priced cash crop which has delayed the development of Buha and in part (especially in the north) led to the continued popularity of honey hunting in the surrounding *miombo* woodland. This is a practice which is still followed by thousands of Ha yearly. The length and arduous nature of the journeys they make into the thickly-infested tsetse bush lying to the east seems not to deter them in the least and parties will disappear for weeks at a time to return with this valuable commodity. It is mostly on these trips of course that the sleeping sickness germ is picked up, but the hunters are encouraged to present themselves at the local dispensaries for examination on their return.

OTHER TRIBES IN THE KIGOMA AND MPANDA DISTRICTS

The 1948 census showed that over half of the population of the Kigoma District was made up of members of the Ha (15,000) and Rundi (17,000) tribes. The Rundi, from the Belgian Trust territory of Ruanda-Urundi, are very similar to the Ha in many respects, the languages being almost identical and tribal origins being virtually the same. Similarly, the Jiji (2,000) are more Ha than anything else, although the inhabitants of the large African town of Ujiji are a curiously mixed lot and contain representatives of no less than 50 different tribes in Tanganyika and the Congo. Many of their forefathers arrived with the Arabs or with the early European explorers and missionaries and others are the offspring of former slaves.

This whole area dominated by Mount Mkungwe, which juts into the Lake, seems to have been the meeting place of waves of migration from all points of the compass[1].

The Vinza.—The Vinza inhabit the area on both sides of the railway line in the eastern part of the Kigoma District. The history of their area was formerly one of inter-tribal warfare and of slave trading, the main slave route having passed through it, and there is little doubt that the people suffered considerably from both these causes. In 1878, E. C. Hore of the London Missionary Society, who had established a station on Lake Tanganyika, recorded that Uvinza was then a thriving country and well populated; but in 1883 he records that the many ruined villages speak eloquently of slavery and robbery. The Vinza are similar in many respects to the Ha and their chiefs are said to have come from Ruanda by way of Muhambwe and Mpanda and thus to be related to some of the Ha chiefs. They numbered just over 4,000 at the time of the 1948 census. The importance of Uvinza has always been due to the existence of brine springs at a place formerly called Nyanza on the Malagarasi River. Prior to the European occupation thousands of Africans used to go there annually from all over the surrounding area to win salt, and many and frequent were the quarrels and fights which ensued. The Vinza resisted the Germans but were quickly defeated and the Germans then took over the management of the salt springs and paid an annual tribute to the chiefs. This was paid partly in salt and partly in cash, the sum being fixed originally at about £140 per annum and later increased to £500.

---

[1]See "People living under the Protection of Mt. Mkungwe", by G. W. Hatchell, *Tanganyika Notes and Records*, No. 9, for June, 1940.

The Tongwe.—The Tongwe live to the south of the Vinza. They are not so much a separate tribe as an amalgam of some fourteen small branches of various neighbouring tribes, showing marked traces of Manyema, Ha and Vinza influences. At the time of the 1948 census they numbered 8,500. They claim that when their forefathers entered the country they found it unoccupied. This is probably correct because it must have been tsetse-infested. The area suffered in the early days from the raids by the Angoni and by the Nyamwezi under Mirambo. (See page 269).

The Holoholo.—The Holoholo or Sowa are Congolese in origin, "Holoholo" being a nickname. They inhabit the area along the coast of Lake Tanganyika in the south of the Kigoma District and numbered 4,400 at the time of the 1948 census. The vast majority of those living in "Buholoholo" in Kigoma speak the Tongwe language, and there are few who know more than two or three words of the language of their Congolese forebears.

The Konongo.—The Konongo form the largest tribe in the Mpanda District and numbered just over 20,000 in 1948. They used to be scattered throughout the large expanse of *miombo* country in the east of the district, but are now concentrated in sleeping sickness settlements. They are great travellers and many go to work on sisal estates. They are great honey hunters too, spending up to two or three months in their camps in the bush during the dry season. One man may own up to 500 hives, and beeswax and honey are their main sources of wealth.

The Bende.—The Bende are a small tribe situated between the Holoholo or Sowa and the Konongo. In 1948 they numbered 4,700. They are probably Congolese in origin and are related to the Sowa and Tabwa tribes living on the other side of the lake.

The Pimbwe.—The Pimbwe form the second largest tribe in the Mpanda District, numbering just over 6,000 in 1948.

The Kiko.—Finally, mention must be made of the aboriginal tribe known as the Kiko or Nyahoza, who inhabit the Malagarasi swamps. These people speak a language of their own, which, so far as is known, is different from that of any of the neighbouring tribes. They keep largely to themselves and, until comparatively recently, their relations with their neighbours were confined to the silent exchange of pottery of various kinds for food. They hunt the hippo with spears—beautifully fashioned and balanced weapons with an attachment of dried papyrus stalks so that the spear floats should the marksman miss his aim—and they are also great fishermen. Their women are experts at making pottery and, formerly, the exchange of pots for food was done without the two parties to the transaction meeting: pots were placed at an agreed place during the night and the requisite amount of food in exchange placed ready for collection during the following night. Of recent years, however, the Kiko have been emerging from their seclusion and many of them are to be found trading fish at small settlements along the railway line. Physically, they are very finely developed —a consequence no doubt of their being protein eaters—and they are more at home in a canoe, which they handle superbly, than on dry land.[1]

---

[1] See "Water Gipsies of the Malagarasi" by C. Macquarie, *Tanganyika Notes and Records*, No. 9, June, 1940.

THE FIPA AND OTHER TRIBES IN THE UFIPA DISTRICT

In 1948 the distribution of tribes in the Ufipa District was as follows: Fipa 61,248; Nyika 15,104; Mambwe, 13,311; Rungu 9,617; others 8,711.

Both the Mambwe and Rungu tribes are split in two by the territorial boundary between Tanganyika and Northern Rhodesia, the larger part of each tribe being in Northern Rhodesia.

The whole of the plateau except for a small area along the Rhodesian border is inhabited by Fipa, who have also overflowed on to the eastern shores of Lake Tanganyika and into the Rukwa valley.

The Fipa are of Bantu stock but the chiefs have Hamitic blood in their veins. Tradition has it that two women of Hamitic stock came down from the north. After many wanderings the elder usurped the chiefdom of Fipa. To obtain heirs, they married Nyika husbands but, thereafter, to maintain racial purity, marriage outside the family was forbidden. Be that as it may, the present-day chiefs show distinct traces of Hamitic origin, the men being of much lighter colour than the average Bantu and the women having the slender build and figure of Hamites. Interspersed with the Fipa of the plateau, but not nearly as numerous, are the Nyika. They are supposed to have been forced up from the south by Angoni invasions towards the end of last century. They are primarily a hunting people and have kept to themselves.

The Fipa live in villages on rising ground near streams, most of which never dry up. Eighty per cent of them are now Christians.[1]

The seat of the "aboriginal" chiefs of Ufipa is Itwelele Hill near Sumbawanga; in the villages around this hill live the people who consider themselves pure Fipa—they call themselves Wasukuma and their language Kisukuma.

The Wanyika live scattered all over the district in the more inaccessible places, e.g. the mountain valleys, the plateau and the Rukwa valley plain.

AGRICULTURAL RESOURCES

Ecologically, this large province can be divided into five areas, the Unyamwezi area, the area near the shore of Lake Tanganyika, the Kigoma-Buha bush area, the Buha highlands and the Ufipa highlands.

Unyamwezi.—Population about 400,000. This division comprises the greater part of the Tabora, Nzega and Kahama Districts, an area of moderate and irregular rainfall (30-34 inches). The country bordering on the Shinyanga District of the Lake Province in many instances closely resembles the Sukuma cultivation steppe. Elsewhere the land is covered by an almost uninterrupted stand of *miombo* woodland, except in the Nzega District where large areas exist without any trace of *miombo*. Within this woodland lie swamps, shallow depressions, and inhabited areas, all of which are comparatively free from bush. On the eastern boundaries the *miombo* woodland gives place to the thorn bush and open grassy plains of the Central Province. All of this bush country, which is linked up with that of the Kigoma and Mpanda Districts, is infested with one or other species of tsetse fly, which has compelled the population and their domestic animals to live in closely settled areas where the bush can be kept in check and

---

[1]"Notes on the Fipa" by G. D. Popplewell, in *Tanganyika Notes and Records*, No. 3, April, 1947.

19

the fly excluded. Large numbers of people, formerly living in small scattered communities in the bush, have been brought together and resettled in large settlements specially selected for this purpose and large enough to make effective protective measures possible.

Maize, sorghum and bullrush millet form the staple food crops, but cassava and sweet potatoes are widely planted. Groundnuts are the main cash crop, supplemented by rice and pulses, and, when there is a strong external demand, by maize, millets, sunflower and cassava. The irregular and somewhat scanty rainfall, combined with infertile soils, has on several occasions resulted in acute food shortages. Cotton has been tried but did not prove a success. The areas long free from tsetse contain large numbers of stock both large and small, and stock products are important exports. The soils generally are of low fertility and this is reflected in the crop yields and carrying capacity of the pastures. Attempts to improve both the methods of cultivation and of animal husbandry have so far met with varying success. Erosion is mainly confined to the cultivation steppe. Many of the people accustomed to a bush life, particularly those living in the sleeping sickness settlements, formerly did the minimum of cultivation and gained their living by collecting honey and beeswax, but with better prices and marketing facilities production of agricultural products has increased steadily. Others engage in fishing (in the rivers and swamps before they dry up) and in the utilization of forest produce. It is an almost universal practice in this area to plant crops on ridges, which are constructed by drawing the top few inches of soil over the weeds, grass and other refuse left in the fields. The "tying" of these ridges by means of a short connecting ridge is now a general practice.

At Urambo is one of the three areas opened by the Overseas Food Corporation for groundnut production; 60,000 acres were cleared. For various reasons, including that of heavy incidence of disease in the groundnut crop, the acreage under cultivation has been curtailed, and a quite different pattern of agriculture has developed, in which the production of flue-cured tobacco now plays an important part. The cultivation of groundnuts has been temporarily abandoned, pending the development of a more resistant variety, on which work is now well advanced. A Tenant Farming Scheme for Europeans is being developed, while the African Tenant Farming Scheme, on similar lines to that at Nachingwea is being much expanded.

Lake-shore Areas.—Population about 40,000. These are found at wide intervals along the shores of Lake Tanganyika within the Kigoma, Mpanda, and Ufipa District boundaries. Wherever there is enough land to allow cultivation to take place, but particularly where the rivers flow into the lake, small communities have established themselves, and are engaged in fishing, subsistence agriculture and the growing of rice. The largest of these is found in the vicinity of Ujiji, served by the modern port of Kigoma, the terminus of the Central Railway line. Here are found the rice mills and a steadily increasing population is establishing itself within twenty miles of Ujiji. The climate is a coastal one with a rainfall of from 30 to 40 inches.

Rice is the main crop, but maize, beans and other pulses are widely cultivated, frequently planted immediately after the harvest of the rice crop. On the drier lands maize, sorghums, eleusine, cassava and sweet potatoes are grown as well as oil palms and bananas. The main cash crop is rice, but large quantities are eaten locally. In good years or when the demand exists considerable quantities of beans, maize, dried cassava and pulses are sold. Many of these alluvial soils are of great fertility but much damage is done by flooding. The men are frequently engaged in fishing for *dagaa* (like whitebait), so that trading and most of the agricultural work is performed by the women, aided by paid labourers. Rice cultivation was greatly stimulated by the arrival of the railway at Kigoma just before the outbreak of the war in 1914 and has been an important crop ever since. Dhows and lake steamers have encouraged trade along the shores of the lake, but there has been little evidence as yet of improved agricultural practices. The fisheries are of considerable value and are now being scientifically studied.

Buha-Mpanda Bush Area.—Population about 100,000. This is a vast area stretching from the borders of Urundi and the Lake Province to the Rukwa depression and Ufipa highlands in the south-west—it also links up with the western portions of the Tabora and Kahama Districts and may in fact be regarded as an extension of the Nyamwezi country. It is mainly covered by dense *miombo* woodland infested with tsetse. The Buha portion was formerly sparsely inhabited by people living in the bush and cultivating small patches of crops round their houses. The rapid spread of sleeping sickness from 1930 onwards, however, compelled the taking of drastic measures to move the people into selected areas and over much of this region the people now live in large "sleeping sickness settlements" where, the bush having been cleared and the whole area put under cultivation, the tsetse are excluded. In the area south of the railway line the residents still live in small scattered communities. The rainfall is intermediate between that of the lake shore and of Unyamwezi and averages about 35 inches a year, being most abundant near the hills.

Agricultural conditions vary considerably. The staple crop is sorghum, supplemented by maize, beans and bananas; small areas of eleusine and pigeon pea are also grown. Attempts to introduce groundnuts and simsim have not met with much success. Root crops are grown to a minor extent except in the Malagarasi swamp areas, where sweet potatoes, sorghum and simsim are the staple crops and where, also, there are very considerable potentialities for rice growing. Cattle are practically non-existent, although goats, sheep and poultry are increasing. The former methods of shifting cultivation are still practised, but within the bounds of the settlements there has been a little improvement in the standard of cultivation, which in the past was poor.

South of the railway line agricultural practices follow more closely those of Unyamwezi. The staple crop is maize, but considerable areas of cassava are grown. Beans, rice, eleusine and sorghum are also found but the latter is probably mostly used for brewing. The chief cash crops are rice, maize and beeswax, and small patches of groundnuts are occasionally seen. Stock, apart from goats and poultry, are very scarce.

Buha Highlands.—Population over 300,000. This is a large area of country found mainly in the Kasulu District but with limited areas in Kibondo, mostly at a rather lower altitude. The rainfall varies between 40 and 65 inches a year. Maize, sweet potatoes, bananas and beans are the staple crops—sorghum is planted but is mainly used for brewing. Comparatively little produce is exported, but successful attempts have been made to establish tobacco as a cash crop in the Kibondo District. Formerly these highlands were probably entirely covered by rain forest and bamboo, but the forest has practically disappeared, giving place to open grassland. Stock are fairly plentiful and erosion occurs throughout the areas of red soil. The people are healthier and more prolific than those found in the bush areas and pressure on the land is increasing. Local agricultural practices are generally sound and suited to the soil and climate but the standard of work is low, and mainly done by women. Many men leave the area each year seeking work.

Ufipa Highlands.—Population nearly 100,000. This is a large area lying between the two depressions formed by Lakes Rukwa and Tanganyika. It mostly consists of open grassland and thorn bush. The principal crop in the highland areas is eleusine or finger millet, grown primarily for beer making, but exported in large quantities in recent years. It is cultivated in a way peculiar to Ufipa: in the previous rains the ground is tilled into mounds (*utumba*), which may grow a catch crop of beans, and at the beginning of the planting season these mounds are spread out for the sowing of eleusine.[1] Other crops are maize, beans, cassava (being increasingly planted as a famine reserve), millet, rice on the Lake Tanganyika shore and in the tree belt of the Rukwa plain. Coffee is grown in small amounts by some Africans and sold locally. The highlands offer possibilities for plantation agriculture, especially in view of the growth of mining activities in the adjoining Mpanda District. The soil is, however, of rather low fertility. The rainfall is between 30 and 40 inches a year. Many of the adult males from the hundred thousand or so inhabitants go to work on sisal plantations on the coast and along the Central Railway line.

The province is the largest producer of honey and beeswax in the territory and also produces considerable quantities of gum. Increasing amounts of sisal are being railed from the one or two estates in the area. It is probable that, with the reclamation of the fertile Luiche Swamp near Kigoma, a large increase in food supplies can be obtained. As already noted the growing of fire-cured tobacco is being encouraged in the Kibondo District and the number of growers is increasing rapidly.

INDUSTRIES

In addition to the preparation of beeswax, which can scarcely be called an "industry", red palm oil is produced at Kigoma, which is situated in the only area in the territory where the oil palm is found in any numbers (153,000 were counted in 1949). One of the more important industries is the production of salt from the brine springs at Uvinza. The Government has a controlling interest in this salt works, which has been in operation since German times (see page 271). The production in 1956 was 16,555 metric tons (a record), about a third of which went to the Congo. There is also a considerable trade in smoked fish from the Malagarasi Swamps and Lake Sagara.

Cattle, sheep and goats are of the greatest importance in the economic life of the province. Sales on the markets for the past three years are as follows:—

	1954		1955		1956	
	No.	Value	No.	Value	No.	Value
Cattle	44,479	£204,755	48,152	£221,567	44,495	£220,532
Sheep and Goats	15,534	£11,879	84,679	£13,553	16,982	£14,911

[1] E.A. Agricultural Journal, Vol. XVI, No. 2, October, 1950.

The clarified butter industry produces about 10,000 tins (of 36 lb.) in a good year. In the best year so far 10,294 tins were produced valued at £42,466. The largest pig farm in the territory is situated at Mabama in the Tabora District.

The Western Province is one of the largest producing areas of timber and forest products in Tanganyika. In 1956 production was 7,000 tons of sawn timber and 7,889,983 stacked cubic feet of firewood.

Due to the successful production of flue-cured tobacco by the Overseas Food Corporation, considerable interest in this crop has been aroused among African farmers in Tabora District. An industry is now developing, sponsored by the East African Tobacco Company, in which the Company supplies seedlings to the African growers and purchases green leaf from them for curing in its own barns.

The headquarters of the International Red Locust Control Organization is situated at Abercorn in Northern Rhodesia but much of the field work is done in the Rukwa basin.*

The *dagaa* industry of Lake Tanganyika is the territory's most valuable inland fishery. These small "whitebait" are marketed in a sun-dried form and this product is in great demand by employers of fed labour, particularly in the sisal industry. Over the past few years, the value of exports of dried dagaa from the Lake Tanganyika area has been of the order of £150,000 per annum and approximately one-third of this amount is usually obtained in hard currency from sales to the neighbouring Belgian territories. On the production side the industry is entirely in the hands of Africans and at least 6,000, using upwards of 2,000 canoes, are believed to be engaged in it.

The fishing is conducted at night and only during those nights, or hours of night, when there is no moonlight. The fishing method depends on attracting and concentrating the fish beneath a light on each canoe; when sufficient fish are concentrated beneath the light they are scooped up in a large dip net. For many years the method of illumination used for attracting the fish has been a wood fire carried on a small iron grate fixed forward of the canoe, but with the growing shortage of suitable fuel, paraffin pressure lamps, fitted with reflectors to direct the light on to the water, are now used.

MINERALS

The Mpanda Mine of Uruwira Minerals Limited is situated in the Mpanda District of the province. In 1950 a branch railway was opened to connect the mine with the Central Railway at Kaliua, 131 miles distant. A pilot mill which had been working for a number of years was closed down in 1955 on the bringing into production of a new plant with a capacity of 1,300 metric tons of ore a day. The valuable contents of the ore are lead, copper, silver and gold in that order of importance. In the neighbourhood several very promising occurrences are now being examined and it seems possible that further discoveries will be made.

The Mpanda District is known to contain alluvial gold, mica, graphite, nickel, tungsten, chromite and manganiferous iron in addition to the minerals mentioned. Coal has been located in the Ufipa District to the south; gold occurs in the Kahama and Nzega Districts. Salt has been produced at Uvinza in the Kigoma District since 1902. Production in 1956 was worth about £159,000.[1]

---

[1] £141,074 in 1955.

*See "A History of Lake Rukwa and the Red Locust" by D. L. Gunn in *Tanganyika Notes and Records* for March, 1956, No. 42.

ADMINISTRATIVE STATIONS[1]

Tabora.[2]—Provincial headquarters are situated at Tabora[3], which is also the headquarters of the district of that name. It is situated on the Central Line, 525 miles from Dar es Salaam, at a height of just over 4,000 feet above sea level, and from Tabora goes the branch line to Mwanza, 238 miles away. It is an old town by local standards, having been established by the Arabs about 1840 as a sort of depot at the place where the caravan routes from the great lakes met. From Tabora one route went on to Ujiji on Lake Tanganyika and the Congo and the other to Lake Victoria and to Karagwe and Uganda beyond. The town is dominated by a large German fort built on a hill, whence a good view can be obtained of the surrounding country—which is chiefly remarkable for the immense number of mango trees it carries, a legacy from the Arabs. It is on the air route Nairobi-Mwanza-Tabora-Dodoma-Dar es Salaam.

The Chief of Unyanyembe, the biggest and most important division of Unyamwezi, lives at Itetemia nearby, at a place which has been the chief's "Kwikuru" or "palace" for a hundred years or more. It was near here that Stanley and Livingstone shared a *tembe* (a mud-roofed hut) in 1872 for nearly a month[4].

The population of Tabora at the time of the census in 1952 consisted of 305 Europeans, 2,124 Asians, and 11,555 Africans, figures which establish it as the third largest town in the territory.

The District Commissioner is assisted by four administrative officers and in the station there are normally representatives of the following departments of Government or of the High Commission: Agriculture, Education, Forest, Game, Labour, Lands and Surveys, Medical, Mines, Prisons, Public Works, Town Planning, Tsetse, Veterinary, Water Development, and of the Police Force and the Magistracy, also of the Aviation, Posts and Telecommunications, Railways and Harbours, Meteorological and Customs.

The climate, as stated above, is notable for the great range in temperature which can occur in a day, sometimes more than 36° F., but as the humidity is low at such times the heat experienced at mid-day is not intolerable and the nights are cool; indeed during the months of June to September the nights are cold. Despite its situation in the middle of the vast central plateau, high winds are seldom experienced and climatically the station is a pleasant one.

Tabora is an important educational centre and contains two large Government Secondary School for Africans, one for boys and one for girls. The former was established in 1925 as a school for the sons of chiefs but there are now more commoners than chiefs' sons amongst its 270 pupils. St. Mary's Secondary School for boys, run by the White Fathers' Mission, is also situated in the town

---

[1]For additional information see table on p. 542.

[2]For further details see "Tanganyika: A Review of its Resources and their Development", p. 822.

[3]The name *Tabora* is derived from the Nyamwezi word *Matobolwa*. It seems that in the old days in times of acute food shortage a preparation called *matobolwa* consisting of sweet potatoes which had been cooked, kneaded and dried, was sold as famine food. This was customary throughout Unyamwezi. When Tabora became an important centre on the arrival of the Arabs, it also became the principal selling place for this food, hence it was known by the Arabs as *Matobolwa*. Because of the difficulty experienced in pronouncing this word it was eventually shortened to Tabora.

[4]See "The Tembe at Kwihara, Tabora", by F. Longland. *Tanganyika Notes & Records*, No. 1, p. 84 March, 1936.

and the same Mission has a seminary at Kipalapala, five miles away.   There are, in addition, two Indian schools in the town and a European junior school has recently been opened.   In Tabora are also located the Railway Apprentices' School and the Warders' Training School.

Nzega[1].—The district headquarters of the Nzega District are situated on a good road 75 miles to the north of Tabora and 24 miles from Bukene station on the branch line to Mwanza, in country very similar to that of Sukumaland and at an altitude of 4,000 feet above sea level.   It is not on any regular air route.   The climate is very like that of Tabora, but rather drier.   At the time of the census in 1952, the station contained 29 Europeans, 147 Asians and 351 Africans.

The District Commissioner is assisted by two district officers and there are normally representatives of the Agricultural, Medical, Public Works and Veterinary Departments in the district.

Kahama[2].—The district headquarters of the Kahama District are also situated in country not unlike Sukumaland, at a distance from Nzega of 54 miles by the most direct route and 25 miles from Isaka station, on the branch line to Mwanza. It is not on any regular air route.   The station is also 4,000 feet above sea level, and the climate very similar, but the rainfall is slightly better.

The population of the township at the time of the census in 1952 was 14 Europeans, 281 Asians and 1,187 Africans.

The District Commissioner is assisted by a district officer and a settlement officer and normally there are representatives of the Agricultural, Medical, and Veterinary Departments in the district.

Kibondo[3].—This remote station is pleasantly sited in hilly country, 150 miles from Kigoma and about 12 miles (as the crow flies) from the borders of Ruanda-Urundi, at an altitude of approximately 5,000 feet.   A new District Office and new quarters for the District Commissioner have recently been built. The station is in radio communication with Tabora.   It is not on any regular air route.   The District Commissioner is assisted by a district officer and a district assistant.   A medical officer is also stationed at Kibondo.

The European population of the station was eight at the time of the census in 1952 (five officials and three missionaries), and there were nine Asians.   The station is thus one of the smallest in the territory and the trading settlement at Kakonko, 30 miles to the north, is, comparatively speaking, much bigger, although it had a population of only 12 Asians in 1952.

The climate is very pleasant.   More rain falls than at the other, lower-lying, stations in the province and great extremes of temperature are not experienced. From June to September it is cold enough for fires at night.

---

[1]The name *Nzega* is believed to have been derived from *nzenga nhanya*, meaning in Kinyamwezi a large building, a name given to the place at which one of the original settlers, who moved to the area from Uyogu in Kahama District, built himself a large house.

[2]*Kahama* is thought to come from the Kinyamwezi word for the Borassus palm *mihama* which is found in the area.

[3]The name *Kibondo* comes from the Kiha word *ikibondo*, meaning an infant child.   According to local legend, shortly after the first Ha people moved into the area an infant was found, completely unattended, by the bank of a river in the area.   A few days later the child mysteriously disappeared and it came to be regarded as the spirit who looked after the area.

Kasulu[1].—District headquarters are situated at the end of a ridge of high land which juts out into the plain like the prow of a ship and from which magnificent views of the surrounding country can be obtained.   Scenically this station is one of the most attractive in the territory.   The trading centre, a "minor settlement", lies in the plain a couple of hundred feet below, and the Heru highlands, 750 feet above, form the background.   Kigoma is 58 miles away by road and Uvinza, also on the railway, 48 miles.   It is not on any regular air route.

At the time of the census in 1952, the population of the station consisted of 13 Europeans, 9 Asians and 83 Africans.

The District Commissioner is assisted by a district officer and there are normally representatives of the Agricultural, Forest, Public Works, Tsetse and Veterinary Departments in the district.

The climate is very similar to that of Kibondo, pleasantly "un-tropical" for a great part of the year and quite cold at times.

Kigoma[2].—The district headquarters of the now somewhat truncated Kigoma District[3] (it used to include most of what is now the Mpanda District) are situated on the shores of Lake Tanganyika, at an altitude of only 2,550 feet above sea level and at the end of the Central Line from Dar es Salaam, 772 miles away. It is not on any regular air route.   It has a pleasant little harbour and the residential quarter is situated on the hillside above it.   The climate is more humid than that of the other stations in the province and can be trying just before the rains break in November/December.

The Germans built a fine railway station at the terminus of the line and a good hotel further up the hillside.   The latter has for long been the residence of the District Commissioner.

The township, on the lower ground near the harbour, is steadily growing in size and importance.   There is a Belgian Concession and special arrangements have been made for the Congo transit traffic to pass through in bond.

From the port there are lake steamer services to various other ports on the lake (a round trip on the s.s. *Liemba* of the East African Railways and Harbours Service is a pleasant way of spending local leave).

The population of the station at the time of the census in 1952 comprised 82 Europeans, 605 Asians and 908 Africans.   At Ujiji, five miles to the south, famous as the place where Stanley "found" Livingstone, is the largest African town in Tanganyika, containing a population of nearly 10,000 in 1952.

The District Commissioner is assisted by two district officers and representatives of the Agricultural, Medical, Public Works and Water Development Departments and of the Police Force are normally stationed in the district.

---

[1]The name *Kasulu* comes from the Kiha word *kasulu* or *kasulo*, being the name of a local tree from which bark rope is obtained.

[2]For further details of this town see "Tanganyika: a Review of its Resources and their Development" p. 811.

[3]There are two theories as to the origin of the name *Kigoma*.   One holds that it is a comparatively modern derivation from the Swahili word *Kikomo*, denoting the end of the railway line.   The second explanation is that Kigoma was thus named because it was the place at which the original Goma mmigrants from the Congo landed.

Fishing boats drawn up on the shore of Lake Tanganyika after a night's fishing.

Photo: Shell Co.

Arab.

Photo: V. Eugene Johnson, Singida

Mpanda[1].—The district headquarters of the Mpanda District were established at Kabungu, near to the large silver-lead mine at Mpanda in 1947 and the station buildings are still of a temporary nature[2]. They are situated in the middle of *miombo* woodland and the station is thus not one of the more scenically beautiful in the territory. The climate is not unlike that at Tabora but tends to be rather hotter at times, the place being more enclosed and at a slightly lower altitude.

The population of the station, trading centre and mine at the time of the census in 1952 consisted of approximately 210 Europeans, 170 Asians and 4,250 Africans (Mpanda mine accounting for about 200 Europeans, and 3,000 Africans.) The trading centre is nine miles from the District Office but only two from the mine.

The District Commissioner is assisted by a district officer and representatives of the Agricultural, Forest, and Public Works Departments and of the Police Force are normally stationed in the district.

The railway from the Central Line at Kaliua was completed in 1950. There is an airfield at the Mpanda mine which is served twice weekly by East African Airways, connecting with Nairobi and Dar es Salaam. The opening of the railway to Mpanda has revolutionized the economic outlook of the district. The main line of communication is now via the north-west road which runs through the district from Abercorn to Mpanda and on to Bukoba and Kampala. Subsidiary outlets are via the small ports of Kipili and Kasanga on Lake Tanganyika.

Sumbawanga[3].—The headquarters of the Ufipa District are situated on the plateau, at a height of 5,650 feet above sea level, with a fine view of the forest-clad hills above the Rukwa trough to the east and over the grassy uplands to the west. The climate is delightful, as is to be expected at this altitude, and fires are needed at night for most of the year. Until recently the station was remote and rather inaccessible. It is 361 miles from Tabora by road and the main line of communication is by lake steamer from Kigoma to Kipili and thence by road (97 miles) to Sumbawanga. The station is not on any regular air route.

The population of the station comprised 8 Europeans, 108 Asians and about 2,000 Africans at the time of the census in 1952.

The District Commissioner is assisted by two district officers and representatives of the Agricultural, Medical, Public Works and Veterinary Departments are normally stationed in the district.

PLACES OF INTEREST TO THE VISITOR AND SPORTING FACILITIES[4]

The province abounds in game and the visitor will have no difficulty in seeing most of the commoner varieties. The best shooting grounds are near the Ugalla river in the south-west and the Wembere Steppe in the east. Those who are particularly anxious to see, or shoot, sable antelope will find them most easily in this province. There is also excellent bird-shooting to be had in all districts. The mountainous country near Kigoma is the only part of the territory where chimpanzees are to be found.

---

[1] *Mpanda* takes its name from a nearby river. The origin of the name itself is not known.

[2] It has now been agreed that the temporary district headquarters at Kabungu will be replaced by a permanent administrative station at Mpanda.

[3] The name *Sumbawanga* is said to be derived from the Kifipa *sumba uwanga*, meaning cast aside your witchcraft (when you come here).

[4] See also "The Shooting Grounds" pp. 463-4.

There is no trout-fishing in the province, but good fishing can be had in Lake Tanganyika (see page 490).

A voyage round the lake is a popular and very restful way of spending local leave. And if the visitor has time to motor from the lake port of Kigoma to Nkalinzi in the Kasulu District, a distance of only 20 miles, he will be rewarded with views of some magnificent scenery, with unforgettable vistas across the lake on a clear day.

As all the world knows, Stanley "found" Livingstone at Ujiji, near Kigoma on Lake Tanganyika, and a suitable memorial marks the spot. Here also has recently been set up a small museum containing replicas of Livingstone's letters and other "Livingstoniana" of interest to the visitor. The native-type house or *tembe*, where Livingstone lived and which he shared with Stanley in 1872 has been restored, and an Arab door, similar to the original (now in the Johannesburg Museum) has been specially made for it, to reproduce as far as possible the details of the building in which the greatest of African explorers spent so many months anxiously waiting for porters and supplies before setting off on his last journey.

Chapter 6

THE PEOPLE

AFRICAN

It is usually stated that there are some one hundred and twenty different tribes in Tanganyika. It is not possible to give an exact figure because of the difficulty of defining a "tribe". No universally acceptable definition is available, but for general purposes it may be taken as a group of people sharing a number of common features, political, social, cultural or linguistic, and possessing a sense of unity which causes them to regard non-members of the group as strangers. Thus we get groups from the size of the Sukuma (888,800) to the Sonjo (3,536) regarding themselves as single tribes.[1] Larger than the tribe is what has been termed the "cluster" of tribes, people sharing many features in common and, whilst at times recognizing these common features, none the less lacking that essential feeling of unity which is the basic feature of a tribe. In speaking of "tribes" we must remember that any grouping of humans is a changing, not a static, relationship. We know that some of today's tribes, which display the most ardent group loyalty, have been formed over the last one, two or three centuries from a multiplicity of different elements. In the same way today's cluster may be tomorrow's tribe. The Chagga of Kilimanjaro, now over a quarter of a million strong, are an example of both these processes: some three or four centuries ago small groups of many different stocks settled themselves on the forested lower slopes of Kilimanjaro and in the course of time developed into some twenty-six political units, each under its own chief. But their origins and their development, political, cultural and linguistic, were divergent, so that till recently these numerous tribes could only be regarded as a cluster, not a homogeneous tribe.[2] With the enforced pacification of European rule, easier transport and opportunity for inter-communication, and common economic and political goals, they have recently welded themselves into a unit which now conforms to our definition of a tribe.

Over and above the "cluster" is what might well be called the ethnic group, i.e., people of common origins. We have here in Tanganyika the Bushman group, the Nilotic, the Hamitic, the Nilo-Hamitic and the Bantu, as well as some unidentifiable elements. These groups, described in their Tanganyika occurrences in greater detail below, are mainly defined by physical characteristics, but differences of language, social organization and mode of living also emphasize the distinctions between them. Thus the Bushman group speak a language of which the outstanding characteristic is the use of a variety of clicks in addition to the sounds normally employed in language; they are short-statured, hunting and food-gathering folk, and represent the early inhabitants of Africa, small remnants being scattered from Kenya to the Cape. The Nilotes are a very dark people of negro stock, but distinguished from the true negro by the length

---

[1] All population figures, unless marked with an asterisk, are from the 1948 census. Bantu prefixes to tribal names, Ba-, Wa-, etc., are omitted.

[2] Raum, O. F. (1938) "Some aspects of Indigenous Education among the Chagga"—*J.R.A.I.*, Vol. LXVIII, Jan.-June, 1938.

[2] Raum, O. F. (1940) "Chagga Childhood." London.

of their limbs; their home is in the upper Nile area.   Linguistically the Nilotic languages "have a peculiar pronunciation of their own which at once distinguishes them from most other sorts of languages[1]".

The Nilotic folk have no advanced form of chiefship and may be classified as a segmentary society; they are herdsmen and agriculturists.

The Hamites are brown-skinned, fine-featured, slender people, whose prototype is to be found in the tombs of predynastic Egypt.   With one possible exception, those occurring in Tanganyika have lost their original language and adopted the local Bantu speech.   They brought the art of chiefship to its highest point of development in eastern Africa prior to the advent of the European.

The Nilo-Hamites are, as the name suggests, a blend of the above two groups, though their language is of a structure distinct from both.   Their two dominant characteristics are nomadic pastoralism—though some tribes have settled down to agriculture—and the possession of a social, political and military organization based on the age-set system.

The Bantu, who form 95 per cent of the population of Tanganyika, are more difficult to define.   The term is basically linguistic, but even to define the Bantu languages is difficult; in a recent work[2] it took a skilled linguist over 300 words to work out an adequate definition.   There are, however, two striking characteristics by which most Bantu languages can be recognized.   The first is that, instead of the usual two genders associated with sex, or three genders (masculine, feminine and neuter) in which a distinction between animate and inanimate enters, most Bantu languages have at least five genders or classes, which means that, with differing singulars and plurals, at least ten differently prefixed noun formations exist.   The second feature is the alliterative concord, by which adjective, pronoun and verb have the same prefix as the noun.   Thus in Swahili *Viti vyangu vizuri viwili vimevunjika* means "My two beautiful chairs are broken."

Ethnically speaking, the Bantu are believed to be a mixture between various Hamitic and Negro stocks; the variation in stock and the precise degree of admixture accounts for the great variation which one gets amongst the Bantu.   The Bantu are primarily agricultural people, practising a certain amount of pastoralism; but one finds a range of cultures from the most primitive to the relatively advanced.

From the above brief description it is apparent that from the admixture of the three basic stocks, the aboriginal (yellow), the Hamite (brown), and Negro (black), an infinite variety of tribes has emerged, and it is only seldom that one finds a people conforming to the above broad definitions in physical type and language and culture.

Embarking now on a fuller description of these types as found in Tanganyika, the Bushmen group are a remnant of the original short-statured inhabitants of southern Africa; the best known representatives of these folk are the Bushmen of the Union.   In Tanganyika, we have the Kindiga (calling themselves Hadzabe or Hadzapi and also referred to in literature[3] as Tindiga or Kangeju Bushmen) who live near Lake Eyasi, and the Sandawe of the Kondoa District.   The former still live the life of the nomadic hunter and food gatherer, camping with their families without proper shelter for short periods where game or wild foods are

---

[1]Bryan, M. A. and Tucker, A. N. (1948) "Distribution of the Nilotic and Nilo-Hamitic Languages of Africa", Oxford University Press.

[2]Guthrie, M. (1948).   "The Classification of the Bantu Languages", Oxford University Press.

[3]Cooper, B. (1949) "The Kindiga". *T.N.R.* No. 27, June 1949.

[3]Bleek, D.F. (1931) "The Hadzapi or Watindega of Tanganyika Territory, Africa".

most plentiful. Their distinctive cultural characteristics are their cylindrical stone pipes and their extraordinarily large bows and arrows (see illustration). The Sandawe on the other hand have settled down to agriculture and cattle keeping but possess linguistic, physical and other characteristics which associate them with this group[1]. Both the Kindiga and the Sandawe speak a click language, as defined above. It is well known that the Bushmen of South Africa were responsible for the latest styles of rock-paintings which decorate the kopjies and caves of southern Africa. Tanganyika also is rich in rock-paintings[2] but it is as yet uncertain whether our click-speaking folk were in any way responsible for these, or whether they were the work of some long since extinct types; it may not be entire coincidence that the districts richest in rock-paintings, Kondoa and Singida, are both the habitat of click-speakers.

There are in addition numerous groups of small-statured remnants scattered throughout the territory. In the north-west, they are known as Iru or Twa, this latter name being common for such folk in the Rhodesias. In north-east Tanganyika, nearly every tribe has a tradition of aboriginal inhabitants in the forests, whilst in Masasi District a legend of "fairies" is so akin to the actual traditions of the aboriginal inhabitants of Rhodesia as to leave no doubt about the previous existence of these short-statured folk in southern Tanganyika also.[3]

The legend is also common in northern Tanganyika and, in view of its interest, is recorded hereunder:—

"If you are on a journey and meet one of the "little folk" the first question he will ask is 'Where did you first start seeing me?' Now your answer must be most circumspect; should you say, 'I just saw you a yard or two away on the path'—which is probably correct—you are drawing pointed attention to your questioner's lack of stature. This will anger him and he will most likely shoot you with his bow and poisoned arrow. If on the other hand you diplomatically reply, 'Why, Great Master, I first saw you on yonder hillside'—which you did not—your acquaintance will be duly flattered and will depart on his way pleased and smiling."

The second basic stock in the make-up of the population of southern Africa is the Negroid, of which the only relatively pure example in Tanganyika is the Luo (Jaluo), a tribe of Nilotic origin on the east shore of Lake Victoria.

Hamitic, the name used for our third basic stock, is an ill-defined term covering the tall, light-skinned, fine-featured people characteristic of north-eastern Africa from the pre-dynastic Egyptians to the Abyssinians and Galla of today. In their pure form, they are to be found in western Tanganyika, where they imposed themselves as rulers over the Bantu, probably about the sixteenth century. Their influence is greatest in the countries to the north and west, where dynasties of this stock rule over Ruanda, Urundi and Buganda, political units with large populations, numbering 1,900,000, 1,800,000 and 1,300,000 respectively. In Tanganyika, almost two million of our present population are under the political influence of these Hamitic people, but their own number is difficult to ascertain. Where they have blended they are now enumerated as members of the tribes they

[1]Trevor, J. C. (1947) "The Physical Characteristics of the Sandawe". *J.R.A.I.* Vol. LXXVII Pt. I. London. Werner, A. (1929) "Sandawe", article in *Encyclopaedia Britannica*, 14th Edition, London, and New York. Kimmenade, M. Van de (1936) "Les Sandawe (Territoire du Tanganyika, Afrique)." *Anthropos* Vol. XXXI.

[2]See page 21 et seq.

[3]Clark, J. D. (1950) "A Note on the Pre-Bantu Inhabitants of Northern Rhodesia and Nyasaland". *South African Journal of Science*—Vol. 47, No. 3. Conan-Davies, E. (1944) "Queen Mab in Masasi", *T.N.R.* No. 17.

rule; only when they have penetrated as pastoralists without assuming political power—and in this form they are usually called Tusi—is a count available (see Table on next page). Apart from their physical features and political acumen, the most remarkable characteristics of their culture are the long-horned "Ankole" cattle and the remarkably fine bead-work and basket-work of their womenfolk.

The Nilotic and Hamitic ethnic groups are thought to have blended in the Nile valley so to form another distinct group, the Nilo-Hamitic. Of these, we have two clusters, the Masai and the Tatog. The former consists of the Masai and the Kwavi, with one or two scattered traces such as the Ngassi amongst the Chagga and certain sections of the Dorobo, folk still living as hunters in Masailand[1]. The whole cluster is today about 60,000 in Tanganyika, with a slightly greater number in Kenya. Whilst they suffered heavily in the 1890 famine, they have recovered remarkably since then, both in human and cattle population, so there is no reason to suppose that their past numbers were greatly, if at all, in excess of their present population.

The Tatog cluster is even smaller, comprising the Barabaig (Mangati), Kismajeng and allied tribes of the Mbulu District and the Taturu found in tiny groups in the districts to the west. They represent the southernmost penetration of the Nandi-Kipsigis type in Kenya.

An interesting comparison can be drawn between these two invasions from the north. The Hamites displayed considerable political genius and imposed themselves as rulers on a large indigenous population now nearly ten million strong. The Nilo-Hamites interested themselves solely in their cattle; they occasionally raided their Bantu neighbours, but were not averse to intermarrying with them, or trading foodstuffs in time of shortage. The old concept of the all-conquering Masai lording it over the plains of East Africa whilst the timid Bantu agriculturist led a precarious existence in the forest fastnesses round the mountains cannot be supported in the light of modern knowledge. The truth is that the interests of the pastoralists and of the agriculturists clashed very little. This view is supported by the fact that the latter developed from a few scattered wanderers to flourishing and powerful tribes in the 250 years prior to European rule: this in spite of the presence of their Nilo-Hamitic neighbours.

Transit through the country of the pastoralists was, however, a very different undertaking, as reference to the accounts of the early explorers from the seventeenth century onwards reveals.[2] The Abyssinians in the north did not welcome strangers and the grasslands to the south were inhabited by the Somali, the Galla, the Masai, the Nandi-Kipsigis and the Tatog. It is significant that the northernmost slaving post, Bagamoyo, serving the Tabora–Ujiji route, is due east of the southernmost penetration of the Masai. The Tana, Athi and Pangani Rivers to the north could have given access to the interior just as well as the Ruvu, Rufiji and Ruvuma to the south, but the screen of pastoralists enumerated above was probably the deterrent which did most to save the Lake Victoria region from that ruthless depopulation at the hands of the slavers from which the shores of Lakes Tanganyika and Nyasa suffered.

One very interesting element in the population is the cluster comprising the Iraqw and allied tribes. These were previously regarded as Hamitic, but recent work on their language seems to reveal that it does not fall easily into the Hamitic

[1] Maguire, R. J. A. "Il-Torobo". *Tanganyika Notes and Records* No. 25 pp. 1-28.
[2] Thomson, J. (1885)—*Through Masailand*.
[2] Krapf, J. L. (1860)—*Travels and Missionary Labours in East Africa*.

classification, nor indeed into any other African language group. This fact brings to the fore once more the interesting speculation that these people are perhaps the sole survivors of the neolithic folk who were responsible for the Gumba culture which flourished in Kenya about a thousand years ago. This theory is supported by their peculiar semi-subterranean dwellings, but too much store should not be set by this feature, as housing is a trait that, much more easily than language, can alter as circumstances change. In fact, the Iraqw of one area are known to have changed from subterranean square houses with earth roofs, to above-ground round houses with grass roofs and then to have reverted back to a semi-subterranean type, all in the course of a century or so.

We are now left to deal with the bulk of the inhabitants of Tanganyika, the Bantu. The table below shows that over 7 million of our 7½ million African inhabitants belong to this group. As is usual, it is the exceptions that catch the eye and receive attention disproportionate to their numbers. The position as described so far is as follows:—

Ethnic Group	1948 Census	Percentage of Total Population	Cluster	1948 Census	Tribe	Nos.
Bushmen Type ...	25,000	—	—	—	Sandawe	24,000
					Kindiga	1,000 (estimated)
Nilotic	50,000	—	Nilotic Kavirondo (a)	—	Luo	50,000 (b)
Hamitic	100,000	—	Inter-Lacustrine	100,000	Hima	76,000
					Tusi (c)	24,000
Nilo-Hamitic ...	85,000	—	Masai (d)	60,000	Masai	56,000
					Kwavi	4,000
			Tatog	25,000	Barabaig	15,000
					Kismajeng	5,000
					Taturu	5,000
Unidentified ...	138,000	—	Iraqw	138,000	Iraqw	108,000
					Gorowa	10,000
					Alawa (Wasi)	11,000
			—	—	Burungi	9,000
Total non-Bantu ...	398,000	5				
Bantu	7,003,000 (e)	95				
Total ...	7,410,000					

Notes:—

(a) The majority of this cluster is in Kenya.

(b) Estimated only, as now enumerated with the tribes they rule.

(c) So-called in Western Province, where separately enumerated.

(d) A further 75,000 Masai are in Kenya.

(e) Not yet fully worked out. For broad geographical divisions see Table on p. 288.

In the past, attempts have been made, mainly on linguistic grounds, to classify the Bantu into Elder and Younger, and to ascribe varying proportions of Hamitic blood to the various groups. But the more the protohistory of these regions is studied the more it becomes apparent that the conception of a giant "mixing bowl" in north-east Africa, from which the ethnic groups and tribes of today have emerged, presents only half the picture. The blending has been and is still going on throughout the territory, assisted today by modern transport and the break-down of rigid tribal boundaries.

For example, the Iraqw of Mbulu might at first sight be considered as "pure" a racial stock as might be found anywhere. Physically, they breed to type and the experienced eye stands a very good chance of spotting an Iraqw wherever he is met. Socially they are reasonably exclusive and intermarriage with other tribes is not considerable. Economically, they are self-contained so that the effects of a migrant labour system are not felt. Yet an analysis of their history shows that in the last century or two they have absorbed an unidentified alien element, possibly Nilo-Hamitic, which now forms 10 per cent of the population; the family from which their rainmakers and soothsayers are drawn is an intrusive element from a Bantu area, whilst another of the clan founders came from different Bantu stock from the east.

In the same way, every well-known tribe of today is a blend of recent origin. The Gogo, the Hehe, the Chagga are all tribes about a quarter of a million strong, but all are recent conglomerations of many elements. The Gogo lack a strong sense of tribal unity, but have a common mode of life and common customs and law. The Hehe are a blend of twenty-nine separate tribes or political units,[1] welded into a strong political entity within the last hundred years. Although the Chagga lived in a much more compact area and hence might be expected to have unified earlier, by virtue of the broken nature of their country they maintained their numerous petty political units till very recently and have only now put themselves under a single chief.

In view of this picture of constant flux it is not proposed to present the Bantu tribes classified on a highly conjectural ethnographic basis, but rather to deal with large geographical groupings which make some broad generalizations possible, although of course inaccurate in detail.

The relative size and distribution of these groups can be seen in the following table:—

DISTRIBUTION OF BANTU POPULATION

Group	Main Provinces and Districts	Chief Tribes	Total Population*	Percentage of Territorial Population
I. Hamitic-dominated Lacustrine Bantu	LAKE PROVINCE			
	Bukoba	Haya	270,000	
	Biharamulo	Zinza	57,000	
	Ngara	Hangaza & Subi	100,000	
	Mwanza Maswa Kwimba Shinyanga Geita	Sukuma	888,000	
	Kibondo Kasulu	Ha	287,000	
		(Other tribes)	298,000	
Total ...			1,900,000	29

*The totals of the groups fall short of the total Bantu of the territory owing to the omission of certain of the smaller tribes.

[1]Brown, G. G. and Hutt, A. M. B. (1935) *Anthropology in Action.* International African Institute.

DISTRIBUTION OF BANTU POPULATION—*contd.*

Group	Main Provinces and Districts	Chief Tribes	Total Popu-lation*	Percentage of Territorial Population
II. Northern Hill Bantu	NORTHERN PROVINCE Moshi Arusha TANGA PROVINCE Pare Lushoto CENTRAL PROVINCE Kondoa EASTERN PROVINCE Morogoro	Chagga Arusha Meru Pare Sambaa Rangi Luguru Nguru (Other tribes)	230,000 52,000 26,000 99,000 130,000 95,000 179,000 39,000 68,000	
Total ...			918,000	13
III. Central Plateau Bantu	CENTRAL PROVINCE Dodoma Mpwapwa Manyoni Singida WESTERN PROVINCE Tabora Kahama Nzega	Gogo Nyaturu Iramba, etc. Nyamwezi (Other tribes)	271,000 182,000 171,000 363,000 213,000	
Total ...			1,200,000	18
IV. Southern Hill Bantu	SOUTHERN HIGH-LANDS PROVINCE Rungwe Iringa Mbeya Chunya Njombe WESTERN PROVINCE Ufipa	Nyakyusa Hehe Various Fipa	192,000 192,000 428,000 78,000	
Total ...			890,000	14
V. Lowland and Coastal Bantu† ...	TANGA PROVINCE Tanga Pangani EASTERN PROVINCE Bagamoyo Dar es Salaam Rufiji Kilosa Mahenge SOUTHERN PROVINCE Kilwa Lindi	Various Various Various Various	142,000 25,000 79,000 239,000 116,000 123,000 121,000 113,000 112,000	
Total ...			1,070,000	13

*The totals of the groups fall short of the total Bantu of the territory owing to the omission of certain of the smaller tribes.

†Some of these groups live in hill areas, e.g. around Mahenge, but are included here as being the most convenient category.

20

Distribution of Bantu Population—*contd.*

Group	Main Provinces and Districts	Chief Tribes	Total Population*	Percentage of Territorial Population
VI. Southern Intrusive Bantu ...	SOUTHERN PROVINCE			
	Lindi ⎫	Makonde	281,000	
	Masasi ⎪	Mawia	20,000	
	Mikindani ⎬	Yao	127,000	
	Newala ⎪	Makua	95,000	
	Tunduru ⎭	Nguni	65,000	
		Nyasa	25,000	
Total ...			613,000	8

Note:—

*The totals of the groups fall short of the total Bantu of the territory owing to the omission of certain of the smaller tribes.

When dealing with the Hamites (Hima or Tusi) above, reference has already been made to Group I. The extent of Hamitic domination varies from area to area, consisting till recently of complete feudal overlordship in the case of the Hangaza of Ngara District, through despotic chieftainship—Haya, Zinza and to a lesser extent Ha—to a more benign influence in the Sukuma area. The present standard of living also varies tremendously, but not always in direct correlation with the political set-up. For instance, the Haya, though till recently ruled despotically, enjoyed in the past, and even more so today, a higher standard of living than the rest of the group, not only by virtue of the fact that their climate was more favourable to the banana, ubiquitous through the group, but also because coffee flourished in their area—the Robusta type introduced by the Hima in the sixteenth century. The characteristic dress in pre-German times was bark cloth in the west of the area and hides and skins on the east, though these have been replaced by European clothing except in certain backward areas. Christianity has made headway, more so in some tribes than others, whilst the influence of Islam is small.

Turning now to the Northern Hill Bantu, reference to the tribal map on page 298 will show their position. The Chagga, on the slopes of Kilimanjaro, are in the middle; the Meru, the Arusha and the Rangi on the west; and the Pare, Sambaa, Nguru and Luguru on the east. The favourable climatic environment of these areas has led to a more varied diet and greater possibilities of economic expansion, particularly coffee, with the result that this area is as advanced as any in the territory. All types of political development occur in the area. Though in origin segmentary, based on small independent clans, political development occurred earliest amongst the Sambaa, due to Arab influence. Amongst the Chagga, twenty-six petty chiefdoms had emerged, but the deep gorges cutting the slopes of Kilimanjaro into separate ridges led to local exclusiveness and jealousy and only in the European era, with enforced peace and the development of common economic and political interests, has unification of the Chagga occurred. The Arusha, though largely Bantu in ethnic origin, have so absorbed Masai language and culture that their political set-up is based on the age-grade system. This has also affected the neighbouring Meru and to a lesser extent the Chagga.

Housing still largely consists of round huts, either of the bee-hive or of the conical roof types but stone and cement houses with corrugated iron roofs are making their appearance in the more advanced areas.

Indigenous clothing was made from hides and skins, but these rapidly disappeared from the scene as economic advancement proceeded. Characteristic of the area are indigenous barter markets, which have survived and expanded under present conditions. The riot of colour presented by the women's cotton print dresses and head shawls exhibited at a big market, attended by a thousand or two tribesfolk, is a refutation of the charge that modern conditions have taken all the colour out of tribal life; in this case, the drab hides and skins have been replaced by an infinite variety of material and it is remarkable what a colour sense these women possess.

Whilst Christianity has influenced the whole area, Islam has a considerable hold over the eastern tribes and also, owing to Arab influence, on the Rangi on the extreme west. The Arusha show a greater proportion of paganism than any other tribe in the area.

The Central Plateau Bantu, typified by the Gogo to the east and the Nyamwezi to the west, are agriculturists with a heavier bias towards cattle than either of the previously described groups. As a result of their harsh environment, economic advance has been retarded, and in the case of the Gogo recurrent food shortages necessitate the importation of grain. The existence of large herds of cattle, however, enables the bulk of such relief to be paid for.

The political system of the Gogo was and still is segmentary, whereas the Nyamwezi have to a limited extent developed chieftainship; the units, however, are still small, dividing the tribe into some thirty independent areas. By virtue of Arab penetration, greatly assisted by the Nyamwezi capacity for porterage (at which work they excelled), Islamic religion and culture has a firm hold in the west, whereas the still largely pagan Gogo were little affected.

The Southern Hill Bantu consist of numerous tribes, the largest being the Nyakyusa of Rungwe District, clustered round the base of an extinct volcano at the northern end of Lake Nyasa; and the Fipa, living in plateau country at the southern tip of Lake Tanganyika. Possibly owing to its isolation and to a lesser extent due to the havoc caused by the slave trade the Southern Hill Bantu are less economically advanced than their northern brethren. Missionary work has made considerable progress in the area and the Nyakyusa and Fipa are largely Christian.

The Lowland and Coastal Bantu, as their name implies, stretch from the north to the south of the territory. Some characteristics common to the whole area are listed hereunder; politically they are segmentary and even under the stimulus of indirect rule have failed to develop chieftainship to any marked degree. Possibly owing to a less healthy environment than that of the people further inland the population growth is very small, and some areas would barely hold their own but for immigration from up-country tribes. The whole coastal area suffered heavily from slave-raiding, as did the hinterland from Dar es Salaam southward. In fact, it is largely due to this decimation of population that till recently the Southern Province was known as the Cinderella of the Provinces. The large-scale immigration from the south and west (described under Group VI below) has largely restored the population balance, whilst the economic development which it is hoped will follow the construction of the southern railway should make

the title pointless in the future. A more benign influence than the slave
trade which the Arabs introduced was Islam, which manifests itself not only in its
religious aspect, but in the mode of living of its adherents. Thus the little village
street, lined with square, white-walled and palm-thatched houses is typical of
the whole coastal area; typical men's dress is the white cap and flowing white
kanzu, whilst the women favour the *khanga*—cotton sheets which are sold in
pairs, one to wrap round the body and the second to form a head and shoulder
cover.

The last of our six broad categories consists of those tribes which have
penetrated from the south mainly during the period of European occupation,
filling the vacuum caused by slave-raiding. Three very diverse elements can be
distinguished, the Angoni (Nguni), the Yao and the Makonde-Mawia group.
The Angoni upthrust had its origin in the Zulu ferment in South Africa; the
movement spent itself in what is now Tanganyika, the Nguni settling in the Songea
District—with a small contingent away up in the north-west in Kahama District—
whilst the Mbunga, having harassed the Luguru in the latter half of last century,
settled down in Mahenge District. The Yao likewise spread as the result of an
external influence, in this case the slave trade. More than any other tribe, they
co-operated with the Arabs in their nefarious task, and when issued with muzzle-
loading muskets outdid their masters in the ruthlessness with which they
devastated the south of Tanganyika and the neighbouring territories. They have
now settled down in many of our southern districts.

The third element consists of the Makonde, over a quarter of a million strong,
the Makua, and to a lesser extent the Mawia, the main sections of all of which
tribes dwell further south. The move across the Ruvuma River from Portuguese
to British territory has been going on for some time and continues today. Part
of the movement is motivated by the search for employment; for instance Mawia
families are found on sisal estates as far north as Tanga and Arusha. But in
general the movement represents a search for more favourable economic conditions, and it is more likely that it is a response to physical circumstances, the
natural increase of these tribes moving north to fill the vacuum caused by the
depopulation of the area in the slaving days.

These then are our six broad Bantu groups; further details of the tribes which
go to make these up will be found in the chapter describing the provinces. One
common feature applies to the bulk of our African peasantry, namely, that they
are subsistence peasants, primarengagily ed in feeding and housing themselves
and their families. Only when these basic aims are achieved does the individual
appear as a peasant producer, growing cotton, coffee and other export crops for
the overseas markets, or as a migrant labourer. Another remarkable feature
which distinguishes this area from some other peasant areas is that, almost without
exception, the small family group, either the basic family of father, mother and
children, or the extended family including married sons and grandchildren, lives
on its own plot of land at a distance from its nearest neighbour. In other parts
of the world, e.g. Nigeria, peasant production has not prevented the growth of
indigenous urbanization, with the cultivator leaving his town—in some cases his
walled city—to work on his land and returning in the evening to the shelter and
protection of the city. But in Tanganyika no such cities have emerged, though
there is evidence that in the past, before the establishment of territory-wide law
and order, the dispersal of population over the land was not so great as it is today.

The Masai, however, with their large circular cattle enclosures, round the perimeter of which are spaced their dwelling houses, represent one form of self-defensive community life. Another manifestation is found in the little village streets of whitewashed, palm-thatched houses to be found set in idyllic conditions on the bays and promontories of the coast.

True urbanization exists in the larger towns, Dar es Salaam, Tanga, Tabora, Mwanza, etc., and is increasing. But compared with the overwhelmingly predominant peasant population, the town dwellers do not form a large proportion of the population. Whilst urbanization is increasing, so also is the rural population, so that the proportion of town dwellers is increasing but slowly. Taking the ten largest towns in 1931, these contained 1·2 per cent of the total African population of the territory. Ten years later, the percentage was only 1·6 per cent, whilst in 1951 (the latest year for which figures are available) the proportion was 1·9 per cent—which shows how far Tanganyika remains a rural territory.

The overall density of population is not great; to the north of the Central Railway line, where about two-thirds of the African population live in one-third of the territory's area, the population density is only 31 to the square mile, whilst to the south of the line the figure is 15½. Though to some extent attributable to environment, one of the causes of this uneven distribution is doubtless due to the slave raiding referred to above. Then within these areas one finds great inequalities in the density of population, for instance, taking the Masai District as a whole, the over-all density is about three humans to the square mile, though large areas of land should be deducted from the total to get a true figure, as some tracts are useless because of tsetse fly, lack of rain and poor soil, and others excluded from full human use by Government action (National Parks, Game Reserves, Forest Reserves, etc.). Contrasted with this figure, the overall African population of Arusha and Moshi Districts runs at about 250 to the square mile, when forest reserves and alienated land have been excluded from the district totals. The lower areas are, however, much less favourable than the fan slopes of the volcanoes at 6,000 to 4,000 feet altitude. In these latter areas, densities frequently exceed 500 to the square mile.

It is also in the areas of greatest density that the rate of population increase is greatest. Recent work on the 1948 census figures has revealed very marked divergencies in the rate of increase, thought to be associated with the environment. In the hill areas, the population is doubling itself twice, and possibly three times, in a century. In the steppe land and central plateau area, increase is taking place, but at a lesser rate than in the hills; whilst in the lowland bush and on the coast it is doubtful if the population would hold its own by natural increase alone; immigration from the hinterland, however, is leading to an overall increase.

It will thus be seen that, demographically speaking, Tanganyika's main problems are not those of over-population but rather arise from the uneven distribution of the population. This is, of course, basically due to the fact that the environmental features which attract population—healthy climate, fertile soil, adequate rainfall and permanent water supplies—are not evenly distributed over the land. The population will only redistribute itself when the areas of resettlement are made as attractive as those at present occupied. Much thought, money and energy are being devoted by the Government towards finding a solution to these problems.

Tribes of Tanganyika in Numerical Order

Tribe	1948 Census	Tribe	1948 Census
1. Sukuma	894,298	67. Matambwe	19,665
2. Nyamwezi	362,829	68. Wanji	19,381
3. Ha	286,112	69. Ndamba	19,306
4. Makonde	281,320	70. Manyema	18,670
5. Gogo	278,755	71. Gorowa	17,705
6. Haya	275,586	72. Malila	17,512
7. Chagga	239,215	73. Kutu	17,469
8. Nyakyusa	192,816	74. Suba	17,146
9. Hehe	192,153	75. Mambwe	15,672
10. Turu	181,739	76. Kimbu	14,873
11. Luguru	178,163	77. Machinga	14,499
12. Zaramo	173,518	78. Shirazi	14,049
13. Iramba	171,954	79. Ndone	13,773
14. Bena	158,548	80. Mbunga	13,454
15. Sambaa	151,754	81. Pimbwe	13,137
16. Yao	126,741	82. Mbugu	12,625
17. Zigua	112,113	83. Wasi	12,513
18. Mwera I	109,998	84. Isanzu	12,243
19. Iraqw	102,554	85. Segeju	12,046
20. Pare	98,959	86. Nguruimi	11,973
21. Makua	95,464	87. Rungu	11,144
22. Rangi	95,422	88. Vidunda	10,560
23. Rundi	90,312	89. Burungi	9,716
24. Ngindo	85,189	90. Ikoma	9,711
25. Ngoni	84,694	91. Ikizu	9,303
26. Fipa	78,252	92. Taturu	9,162
27. Subi	74,052	93. Bende	8,836
28. Rufiji	71,531	94. Tongwe	8,513
29. Jita	71,433	95. Wungu	8,291
30. Kuria	67,908	96. Mbugwe	7,913
31. Pogoro	65,042	97. Doe	7,781
32. Nyiha	63,998	98. Wanda	7,677
33. Sumbwa	63,954	99. Lambia	7,467
34. Zinza	62,794	100. Mwera II	6,374
35. Kaguru	62,554	101. Kisii	5,706
36. Luo	61,455	102. Rungwa	5,372
37. Kinga	61,300	103. Kwavi	4,620
38. Masai	60,231	104. Holoholo	4,410
39. Matengo	59,368	105. Vinza	4,029
40. Ndali	57,231	106. Sonjo	3,593
41. Hangaza	54,586	107. Jiji	3,025
42. Ndengereko	54,404	108. Karanga	1,408
43. Arusha	53,888	109. Sizaki	1,255
44. Safwa	49,585	110. Dorobo	890
45. Nguu	45,554	111. Twa	579
46. Matumbi	41,650	112. Bajuni	351
47. Nyasa	36,346	113. Baraguyu	208
48. Kwaya	35,318		
49. Kerewe	34,309	Total in 1948 Census classified by Tribe	7,325,225
50. Kwere	33,494	Africans from outside Tanganyika:—	
51. Digo	32,027	Teita ex Kenya	8,658
52. Regi	31,822	Others ex Kenya	7,340
53. Sangu	29,914	Ex Uganda	12,541
54. Bondei	29,525	Ex Congo	7,064
55. Tusi	29,485	Ex Northern Rhodesia	9,644
56. Sandawe	27,699	Ex Zanzibar	1,753
57. Mawia	27,489	Ex Sudan	1,278
58. Nyamwanga	26,592	Ex Abyssinia	409
59. Pangwa	26,067	Ex Somaliland and Somalia ...	205
60. Meru	25,515	Unclassified, such as Comorians,	
61. Rongo	24,799	South Africans and small numbers	
62. Zanaki	23,237	from many odd tribes in nearby	
63. Sagara	23,091	countries	36,152
64. Barabaig	21,618		
65. Ruanda	20,263	Grand Total ...	7,410,269
66. Konongo	20,044		

TRIBAL NAMES IN TANGANYIKA (1948 CENSUS)

(T. indicates the name of an authentic Tribe)

Tribe	Main Districts of origin	1948 Census	Notes
Alawa	Kondoa-Irangi	—	Classified as Wasi
T. Angoni	Songea-Ulanga	84,694	61,146 Songea: 5,193 Ulanga
T. Arusha	Arusha	53,888	
T. Bajuni	—	351	
T. Barabaig	Mbulu	21,618	Alt: names Tatog, Mangati, Kisa-majeng.
Baraguyu	Dodoma-Iringa	208	To be classified as Kwavi in next Census.
T. Bena	Njombe-Ulanga	158,548	15,376 in Ulanga, including 574 shown as Zanzibar, in 1948 Census.
T. Bende	Mpanda	8,836	Census 1948 included Wungu in the former Bende total. Correct figure now shown.
T. Bondei	Tanga	29,525	
T. Burungi	Kondoa-Irangi	9,716	
T. Chagga	Moshi	239,215	Includes Kahe.
T. Digo	Tanga	32,027	
T. Doe	Bagamoyo	7,781	
T. Dorobo	Masai	890	To include Kindiga in next Census.
Fiome	Mbulu	—	Classified as Gorowa.
T. Fipa	Sumbawanga	78,252	
T. Gogo	Dodoma-Manyoni / Mpwapwa	278,755	Includes 7,501 wrongly classified as Pangwa in 1948 Census.
T. Gorowa	Mbulu	17,705	
Guruka	Chunya	—	Classified as Safwa.
T. Ha	Kasulu-Kibondo	286,112	
T. Hangaza	Ngara	54,586	
T. Haya	Bukoba	275,586	Includes Mwani, Nyambo and Ziba.
T. Hehe	Iringa	192,153	Includes Kosishamba, Zungwa.
T. Holoholo	Kigoma	4,410	
T. Iambi	Singida	—	Classified as Iramba in 1948 Census. Now to be shown separately.
T. Ikizu	Musoma	9,303	
T. Ikoma	Musoma	9,711	Included Issenye and Nata in 1948 Census. Both now to be shown separately.
T. Iramba	Singida	171,954	Includes Irama, error in 1948 Census. See note on Iambi.
Irangi	Kondoa-Irangi	—	Classified as Rangi.
T. Iraqw	Mbulu	102,554	
T. Isanzu	Singida	12,243	
T. Issenye	Musoma	—	Classified as Ikoma in 1948 Census. Now to be separated.
T. Jiji	Kigoma	3,025	
T. Jita	Musoma-Ukerewe	71,433	
T. Kaguru	Kilosa	62,554	Includes Kinongo.
Kahe	Moshi	—	To be classified as Chagga.
Kami	Morogoro	—	Now classified as Luguru.
Kara	Ukerewe	—	Now classified as Regi.
T. Karanga	Kigoma	1,408	
T. Kerewe	Ukerewe	34,309	
Kilindi	Lushoto	—	Classified as Sambaa. 22,288 Kilindi wrongly shown as Nguu in 1948 Census.
T. Kimbu	Chunya-Manyoni	14,873	Includes 2,599 Yanzi from Manyoni shown separately in 1948 Census.
Kindiga	—	—	Sibiti River area. To be classified as Dorobo.
T. Kinga	Njombe	61,300	
Kinongo	Kilosa	—	To be classified as Kaguru.
Kisamajeng	Mbulu	—	To be classified as Barabaig.
T. Kisii	Njombe-Rungwe	5,706	

TRIBAL NAMES IN TANGANYIKA (1948 Census)

(*T. indicates the name of an authentic Tribe*)

Tribe	Main Districts of origin	1948 Census	Notes
T. Konongo	Mpanda	20,044	
Kosishamba	Iringa	—	Classified as Hehe.
Kukwe	Rungwe	—	Classified as Nyakyusa.
T. Kuria	Musoma-N. Mara	67,908	Called Tende in Kenya.
T. Kutu	Morogoro	17,469	
T. Kwavi	{ Bagamoyo-Dodoma Iringa-Handeni Kilosa	4,620	To include Baraguyu, and Lumbwa from Kondoa-Irangi, in next Census.
T. Kwaya	Musoma	35,318	Includes 18,692 classified as Ruri in 1948 Census.
T. Kwere	Bagamoyo	33,494	
T. Lambia	Rungwe	7,467	
T. Luguru	Morogoro	178,163	Includes Kami.
Lumbwa	Kondoa-Irangi	—	Local name for Kwavi.
T. Luo	Musoma-N. Mara	61,455	Includes 2,611 Baluhya.
T. Machinga	Kilwa	14,499	Includes Songo.
T. Makonde	{ Lindi-Mtwara Newala	281,320	
T. Makua	Masasi-Tunduru	95,464	
T. Malila	Mbeya	17,512	
T. Mambwe	Ufipa	15,672	
Mangati	Mbulu	—	Classified as Barabaig.
T. Manyema	—	18,670	Settled from Congo: mainly Tabwa.
T. Masai	Masai	60,231	
Matambwe	See Makonde	19,655	To be classified in next Census as Makonde.
T. Matengo	Songea	59,368	
T. Matumbi	Kilwa	41,650	
Mawanda	Rufiji	—	Classified as Rufiji.
Mawia	—	27,489	Originating from P.E.A.
T. Mbugu	Lushoto	12,625	
T. Mbugwe	Mbulu	7,913	
Mbulu	Mbulu	—	Classified as Iraqw.
T. Mbunga	Ulanga	13,454	
Mbwera	Mafia	—	Classified as Shirazi.
Mbwila	Mbeya	—	Classified as Safwa.
T. Meru	Arusha	25,515	
Mwani	Biharamulo	—	Classified as Haya.
T. I. Mwera	{ Kilwa-Lindi Nachingwea	109,998	
T. II. Mwera	Songea	6,374	
T. Nata	Musoma	—	Shown as Ikoma in 1948 Census. Now to be separated.
T. Ndali	Rungwe	57,231	
T. Ndamba	Ulanga	19,306	
T. Ndendeule	Newala-Songea	—	Now to be separated.
T. Ndengereko	Kiserawe-Rufiji	54,404	
T. Ndonde	Nachingwea	13,773	
T. Ngindo	{ Kilwa-Nachingwea Ulanga	85,189	Includes Ngingo.
Ngingo	—	—	See Ngindo.
Ngoni	—	—	See Angoni.
T. Nguruimi	Musoma	11,973	
T. Nguu	Handeni-Morogoro	45,554	{ After deduction of 22,288 Kilindi. see notes on Kilindi, Sambaa.
Nyagatwa	Kiserawe	—	Classified as Zaramo.
T. Nyakyusa	Rungwe	192,816	Includes Kukwe.
Nyambo	Bukoba-Biharamulo	—	Classified as Haya.
T. Nyamwanga	Mbeya	26,592	
T. Nyamwezi	Kahama-Nzega Tabora	362,829	
Nyanko	Biharamulo	—	Mistake for Nyambo in 1948 Census.

TRIBAL NAMES IN TANGANYIKA (1948 Census)

(T. indicates the name of an authentic Tribe)

Tribe	Main Districts of origin	1948 Census	Notes
T. Nyasa	Songea	36,346	
Nyaturu	Singida	—	Classified as Turu.
T. Nyiha	Mbeya-Ufipa	63,998	Includes 15,104 in Ufipa previously classified as Nyika.
Nyika	Ufipa	—	See Nyiha.
T. Pangwa	Njombe	26,067	
T. Pare	Pare	98,959	
T. Pimbwe	Mpanda	13,137	Includes 1,789 Pimbwe resident in Songea.
T. Pogoro	Ulanga	65,042	
T. Rangi	Kondoa-Irangi	95,422	
T. Regi	Ukerewe	31,822	Formerly known as Kara.
T. Rongo	Geita	24,799	Akin to Sumbwa.
Ruanda	—	20,263	Originating in Ruanda-Urundi.
T. Rufiji	Rufiji	71,531	Includes Mawanda.
Rundi	—	90,312	Originating in Ruanda-Urundi.
T. Rungu	Ufipa	11,144	
T. Rungwa	Mpanda	5,372	
Ruri	Musoma	—	See Kwaya.
T. Safwa	Mbeya-Chunya	49,585	Includes Guruka, Mbwila, Songwe.
T. Sagara	Kilosa	23,091	
T. Sambaa	Lushoto-Tanga	151,754	Includes Kilindi.
T. Sandawe	Kondoa-Irangi	27,699	
T. Sangu	Mbeya	29,914	
T. Segeju	Tanga	12,046	
Shashi	Musoma	—	Classified as Sukuma.
T. Shirazi	Mafia-Tanga	14,049	
T. Sizaki	Musoma	1,255	
Songo	Kilwa	—	Classified as Machinga.
Songwe	Mbeya	—	Classified as Safwa.
T. Sonjo	Masai	3,593	
T. Suba	N. Mara	17,146	
T. Subi	Ngara	74,052	
T. Sukuma	Sukumaland	894,298	Includes Shashi.
T. Sumbwa	{ Geita-Kahama Biharamulo	63,954	
Tatog	Mbulu	—	Classified as Barabaig.
T. Taturu	Manyoni-Musoma	9,162	
Tende	—	—	The Kenya name for Kuria.
T. Tongwe	Kigoma-Mpanda	8,513	
T. Turu	Singida	181,739	The Iambi included in 1948 Census total.
T. Tusi	Nzega-Tabora	29,485	
T. Twa	Kasulu-Kibondo	579	
T. Vidunda	Kilosa	10,560	
T. Vinza	Kigoma	4,029	
T. Wanda	Mbeya	7,677	
T. Wanji	Njombe	19,381	
T. Wasi	Kondoa-Irangi	12,513	
T. Wungu	Chunya	8,291	
Yanzi	Manyoni	—	To be classified as Kimbu.
T. Yao	Masasi-Tunduru	126,741	
T. Zanaki	Musoma	23,237	
T. Zaramo	Bagamoyo-Kisarawe	173,518	
Ziba	—	—	Classified as Haya.
T. Zigua	Bagamoyo-Handeni	112,113	
T. Zinza	Biharamulo-Geita	62,794	
Zungwa	Iringa	—	Classified as Hehe.

112 authentic Tribes originating in Tanganyika.

ASIAN

In the historical section (chapter 3) some account has been given of early connections between Asia and East Africa and it is clear that merchant seamen have sailed from the coastal towns of Arabia, Persia and India to ports on the East African Coast such as Mogadishu, Lamu, Mombasa, Pangani, Tanga and Kilwa for a very long time, almost certainly since pre-Christian times, but for just how long remains to be ascertained. Perhaps the archæological research now being planned at Kilwa will give some indication of when this traffic probably began. Doubtless this was when sailors found that the monsoons were fairly constant and could be relied on to take their vessels to East Africa and, later, to bring them back. For, of course, the direction of the monsoons—north-east at one season and south-west at another—corresponded exactly with the direction taken by vessels sailing between the Asian and African coasts; they had only to set their sails and point their bows towards Africa between November and February to be blown there by the unfailing north-east monsoon; after a stay on the coast of a few months they found that the monsoon had changed and was now behind them and blowing strongly from the south-west as they steered for home.

It is probable that the first Asians to visit the coast were Arabs, but this is mere surmise and they may have been preceded by adventurers from Persia or India. Certainly it was Arab influence which was predominant from the tenth century (and perhaps before) until the appearance of the Portuguese; and, after two hundred years of intermittent struggle, it was the Arabs who triumphed and then, under Seyyid Said bin Sultan at Zanzibar, became undisputed masters of the coast and began to penetrate the interior in search of slaves and ivory. The first alien faces seen by many of the tribes of Tanganyika were undoubtedly Arab and, despite the nefarious trade in which the Arabs engaged, their way of life, with its emphasis on the dignity of men, on courage and on the public worship of Allah, had a great appeal to the African and the religion of Islam became firmly established on the coast and in those centres such as Tabora where the Arabs had settled.

A fuller account of Arab influence is to be found in chapter 3, and even were the historical record to be missing the extent of Arab influence would be immediately apparent from a study of the Swahili language, the lingua franca of East Africa, which owes so much to Arabic.

The Arabs in Tanganyika do not seem ever to have recovered from the setback they received after the rebellion of Bushiri bin Salim had been suppressed by the Germans (see p. 56) and they have not achieved prominence in the public life of Tanganyika as they have done in neighbouring Kenya. Nevertheless they continue to play a not unimportant part in the life of the community.

Some 5,000 out of the total number of 13,025 Arabs recorded at the time of the 1952 census live in townships (1,570 in Dar es Salaam and 1,029 in Tanga). In the provinces they are to be found in the greatest numbers in the districts of Shinyanga (968), Bukoba (619), Nzega (598), Pangani (562), Singida (517), Dodoma (512), Mafia (416) and Mwanza (408).

Indian influence in Tanganyika, while not until the beginning of the nineteenth century comparable with Arab influence, may well be as old and, as Professor Coupland points out, "much of the ocean-shipping was Indian-owned and Indian-manned, and since Arabs in general seem never to have shown much aptitude for the technique of business, it is probable that the Indians were from the earliest days the masters of finance, the bankers and money-changers and money-lenders."[1]

It is possible that early invaders, called "Wadebuli" by the local inhabitants, who established themselves at various places on the coast and on the islands off it, may have come from Dabhol, about 100 miles south of Bombay on the west coast of India.[2]

When Seyyid Said moved his capital from Muscat to Zanzibar in 1840 he encouraged his Indian subjects to go with him and attracted others to settle in the island. His main interest was trade, and he early realized that he could not expect much expert assistance in such matters from his fellow-countrymen. He therefore turned to the Indian merchants and bankers who from time immemorial had been the mainstay of all oversea trade in the Indian Ocean.

"Sa'eed knew that, whatever might be the energy and enterprise of his own born subjects, their commercial transactions would never attain real importance except by the co-operation and under the lead of Indian merchants, and accordingly used every means in his power to allure the Banians of Cutch, Guzerat, and the Concan to Muscat, and by absolute toleration, special immunities, and constant patronage rendered the port a half-Hindoo colony."[3]

Early in the nineteenth century there had been between 300 and 400 "banyans" at Zanzibar and when Said moved his capital there in 1840 he found over a thousand of them already residing there.

Indians were to be found at other places on the coast also, and indeed every coastal town of any size had its Indian traders. There were said to be forty to sixty "constantly resident" in the neighbourhood of Kilwa in 1843. Elton found little groups of them at various places along the coast when he walked from Dar es Salaam to Kilwa in 1873–74. When Kirk arrived at Zanzibar in 1860 he found there were between five and six thousand Indians in the island and in the coastal towns. "Of these about 3,660 came from British India or from Indian states in Kathiawar and Cutch.... The word 'banyan' or trader was often used of the Indians without discrimination; but strictly, of course, the 'banyans' are a Hindu caste, and in 1870 there were only 474 Hindus in Arab East Africa. The great majority of the Indian immigrants were Moslems—2,558 of the Khoja and 588 of the Bohora community".[4]

Said used Indians for the collection of customs dues in his dominions and Customs Masters like Jairam Shivji and Ladha Damji were well known to all the early explorers who outfitted their expeditions in Zanzibar. When the former died in 1866 he left a fortune valued at £650,000.[5] Not all such fortunes were made from the collection of customs; it was the "banyans" of Zanzibar who financed the Arab slave caravans. It should be added, however, that when Great Britain was making determined efforts to stop the slave trade "the more respectable Indian houses" were as anxious as anyone that the trade should be quickly and finally abolished. "They see clearly that, while it is an open question,

---

[1] *East Africa and its Invaders* by Sir Reginald Coupland, p. 27.

[2] *The Wadebuli* by Sir John Gray, *Tanganyika Notes and Records* No. 36, January, 1954.

[3] Quoted by Coupland in *East Africa and its Invaders*, p. 301 from W. G. Palgrave, *Narrative of a Year's Journey Through Central and Eastern Arabia*, London. 1865.

[4] Coupland *The Exploitation of East Africa*, p. 44.

[5] Coupland, *East Africa and Its Invaders*, p. 325.

all other trade must suffer and the full development of the unrivalled commercial capabilities of the coast be indefinitely postponed."[1] And in 1872 the Rao of Cutch informed his subjects in East Africa that they were not to engage in this "inhuman traffic."[2]

Under the Germans Indian settlement on the mainland was not discouraged and Indians were employed as mechanics, artisans and in government service.

In the 1914–18 campaign Indian units formed part of the British forces and took part, amongst other engagements, in the landing at Tanga (see page 84).

After the war, Indians were recruited from India for the civil service and recruitment has gone on ever since.   They formed part of the rapidly growing stream of immigration from India which then began.   Immigration is now strictly controlled but, even so, the number of new permanent immigrants has been in the neighbourhood of 3,000 a year for the last few years.

Indians have played an important part in the history of the country and here it is desired to pay tribute to the part played by the Indian petty trader in the development of the territory.   He has penetrated to every corner of the country and has been largely instrumental in introducing to the local inhabitants a money economy and the advantages of such things as cloth, knives, lamps, matches, shoes, tea, etc.   The typical *duka* in the remoter areas is a small shop made of sun-dried mud bricks (or even of wattle and daub) with corrugated iron roof, in which the Indian trader often lives a life of extreme simplicity, buying the produce brought in by the local inhabitants and supplying their simple wants. These traders have been the pioneers in many areas and they have existed in places and at times when no other traders could have survived.   This should be remembered by those who blame the Indian for the fact that, comparatively speaking, so few African traders are to be found in the country.   It seems that the African in Tanganyika does not take naturally to trade, and there is no tribe whose members are traditionally tradesmen.   In these circumstances the Indian has filled an undoubted need and the petty trader plays a vital part in the economic life of the country.

Indians are now to be found occupying positions of importance in all walks of life, and the results of the 1952 census, showing the occupations of those "gainfully employed", are given at page 303 *et seq*.   The status of the Indian community in Tanganyika is indicated by the composition of the recently-established Legislative Council, on which Indians, Africans and Europeans have equal representation on the unofficial side.

The growth of the Indian population is most clearly seen in the census returns. In 1913 the census showed that there were 8,784 Indians in the territory, as well as 656 Goans and 4,101 Arabs.   By the time of the 1921 census the total number had increased only very slightly, but thereafter there was a rapid increase, as is shown by the following census figures:—

			1921		1931		1948		1952
Indians ...	...	...	9,411	...	23,422	...	44,248	...	56,499
Goans ...	...	...	798	...	1,722	...	2,006	...	3,240
Arabs ...	...	...	4,041	...	7,059	...	11,074	...	13,025
	Totals ...		14,250	...	32,203	...	57,328	...	72,764

[1]Quoted by Coupland in *The Exploitation of East Africa*, p. 202, from Correspondence on Frere Mission.

[2]Coupland, *The Exploitation of East Africa*. p. 203.

The distribution of the Asian population in the territory at the time of the 1952 census is shown in the tables on page 303 et seq. At that time the Indian population represented nearly two-thirds of the total "non-African" population, the Arab population about one-sixth and the European population about one-fifth. In the Eastern Province the Indians formed 69 per cent of the non-African population, and in the Southern Province 65 per cent.

The distribution of the Goan population was rather similar to that of the Indian except that Tanga Province, which had a relatively small percentage of Indians, had a large proportion of Goans.

The Arab population was not evenly scattered throughout the territory. It is interesting to note that in provinces where there was a high proportion of Arabs, the Indian population was comparatively small. The Western and Central Provinces which had the largest Arab population with 27 per cent and 23 per cent respectively of the provinces' total non-African population had the smallest Indian population with 45 per cent and 47 per cent respectively.

The great majority of both Indians and Arabs over 14 years of age who were gainfully employed were engaged in wholesale and retail trading: 50·1 per cent in the case of Indians and 78·1 per cent in the case of Arabs. 14·2 per cent of the Indians were engaged in manufacturing industries and 13 per cent in the public service. The greatest percentage of Goans was to be found in the public service (35·2 per cent), with 19·3 per cent in the manufacturing industries and 17·7 per cent in the wholesale and retail trade.

In 1952 there were 16,667 Indian Shia Ismailia Khojas, 3,543 Indians who returned "Islam" as their religion on their census forms, 10,522 Hindus (so stated), 6,214 Kshatryas, 4,221 Shia Ithnasheri Khojas, 351 Indian followers of the Suni Eschafei sect, 3,221 of the Sunni Hannafi, 63 Shia Ibaadhis, 2,921 Sikhs, 2,841 Brahmins, 2,453 Shia Bohoras, 1,504 Vaishyas and 64 Ahmaddiyas.

With a high birth rate (about 41 per 1,000) and a comparatively low death rate (8–12 per thousand) the Asian population is calculated to be increasing at the rate of about 3 per cent per annum, which means that it will double itself in 24 years.[1]

The various sects have their own organizations, and some, such as the Ismailia Khojas, are very highly organized indeed and have their own arrangements for education, insurance, banking and housing. Mandals, Jamats and similar bodies exist in all towns of any size and a notable feature of the Indian community as a whole is the manner in which they manage their domestic and matrimonial affairs without resort to the courts.

In addition to the Arabs and Indians mention must be made of certain other Asian inhabitants of the territory: the Baluchis, Comorians and Somalis; and a word must be said about the Shirazis.

Baluchis were employed by the Sultans of Zanzibar as soldiers and were well known to the early explorers, who almost always included a few in their entourage, Stanley taking twenty-three of them with him when he went to look for Livingstone. They also fought on the British side in the 1914–18 campaign. Small settlements of Baluchis are to be found in certain parts of the territory; for example, in the Usangi Plain near Mbeya, where they have been responsible

---

[1] See "A Demographic Study of an Immigrant Community; the Indian Population of East Africa" by C. J. Martin, in *Population Studies*, Vol. VI, No. 3, March, 1953.

for a successful irrigation scheme on a small scale. Others have held positions of responsibility in the public service; for instance, the present Liwali of Bagamoyo is a Baluchi. There are about 1,500 of them in Tanganyika.

The Comorians are of Arab descent and, like the Baluchis, have played an honourable (if minor) part in the history of East Africa. They achieved prominence at the Court of the Sultans of Zanzibar and a photograph of Sultan Hamed bin Thwain with his chief ministers, taken in 1893, shows that two of the three were Comorians. There are about 900 of them in Tanganyika.[1]

The Somalis were counted as natives of Africa in the 1948 census, but, having successfully established their claims to be Ishaakias from the other side of the Red Sea, were counted as non-Africans in the 1952 census. At that time they numbered 2,060, most of whom were resident in the Northern Province (814) and Central Province (573) as cattle traders.[2]

Many coastal Africans, when asked to state their tribe, say "Shirazi", claiming descent from Persian ancestors who settled in this country "time out of mind" and intermarried with the local people. There were 14,049 at the time of the 1948 general census who thus called themselves; they are mostly to be found in the Mafia and Tanga Districts.[3]

EUROPEAN

Although the outline of the East African coast was known in classical times, as is evidenced by the account given of it in the "Periplus of the Erythraean Sea", and the existence of the great lakes was known to Ptolemy, nevertheless the country now called Tanganyika remained unexplored, a blank on geographers' maps filled in with drawings of elephants and fanciful pictures of local inhabitants, until towards the end of the nineteenth century.

The Portuguese never looked upon the coast as other than a convenient stopping place on the route to India and to the Far East and seem to have been uninterested in the interior. Although they remained on the coast for over two hundred years (from 1498 until 1727) they did not come as settlers but as soldiers and when they left for good there remained few traces of their occupation apart from one or two fortresses and about a dozen words in the Swahili language.

From the date of their departure until the time when Livingstone and other explorers began to penetrate into the interior very few Europeans were seen and these came only as casual visitors to places like Kilwa or Pangani. The opening up of the continent by exploration and the growth of Germany's interest in colonization on the east coast have been described elsewhere (see pages 40–56). Soon after the proclamation of a Protectorate in 1891 the first German settlers arrived in the territory and took up land near Moshi. Others followed them and settled in the Usambaras, near Tanga, at Morogoro, around Iringa and in remote Rungwe.

In 1913 the census showed a European population of 5,336, mostly Germans.

In 1921 the number had fallen to 2,244, but rose to 8,228 in 1931 and 10,648 in 1948. It should be noted, however, that the increases of recent years are largely due to immigration.

[1]See also page 255 above.
[2]See also page 255 above.
[3]See also page 254 above.

At the time of the 1952 census there were 17,885 Europeans in the territory, distributed throughout the provinces as follows:—

Central	1,234
Eastern	5,026
Lake	1,501
Northern	3,269
Southern	1,472
Southern Highlands ...	1,856
Tanga	2,088
Western	1,439
Total ...	17,885

Of this number, 9,947 were males and 7,938 females. Just under half, 8,860, were resident in townships, 3,603 living in Dar es Salaam. Of those over 14 years of age, some 2,600 were in the public service, about 1,300 were classed as "farmers, fishermen or hunters" and about 1,000 as "craftsmen". There were 1,292 Greeks, 1,071 Italians, 515 Dutch, 499 Germans, 496 Swiss, and 331 Americans. The British formed 69·3 per cent of the European population.

There were 7,795 Anglicans, 4,251 Roman Catholics, 1,607 Greek Orthodox, 1,085 Presbyterians, 488 Dutch Reformed, 320 Lutherans, 268 Methodists and 1,500 other Christians.

Mention must be made of the notable part played in the history of Tanganyika by its second-largest European community, the Greeks. When the Germans embarked on the construction of the Tanga Line in 1892 it was to Greek contractors that the actual construction of the line was entrusted. Greek contractors also built the Central Line, begun in 1905 and finished just before the outbreak of war in 1914. Greeks were pioneers in the planting of coffee in the Northern Province (Mweka Coffee Estate, Moshi, was established in the 1890's), of rubber in the Tanga, Eastern, Central and Western Provinces, of cotton and sisal in many of the places where they are grown now, of tobacco near Tabora and Iringa and, of more recent years, of papain in the Northern Province.

The Greeks now have their own school at Arusha, with accommodation for 250. Their generosity and their support for local charitable causes is a striking characteristic of the community. They have indeed played an indispensable part in the development of the country.

POPULATION OF DISTRICTS

Province and District	Census held February, 1952								Census held August 1948(1)
	Euro-pean	Indian	Goan	Arab	Somali	Colour-ed	Other	Total Non-African	African
Central:—									
Dodoma	386	2,154	59	512	168	23	35	3,337	216,601
Kondoa	81	117	4	254	90	12	7	565	145,366
Kongwa	579	99	6	23	927	7	66	872	42,030
Manyoni	24	149	4	160	9	8	1	353	52,248
Mpwapwa	62	193	10	123	37	10	1	438	58,643
Singida	102	582	—	517	17	31	30	1,439	301,053
Total ...	1,234	3,294	83	1,589	573	91	140	7,004	815,941

POPULATION OF DISTRICTS—*contd.*

Province and District	Census held February, 1952								Census held August 1948(1)
	Euro-pean	Indian	Goan	Arab	Somali	Colour-ed	Other	Total Non-African	African
Eastern:—									
Bagamoyo	85	292	7	310	—	5	11	710	78,979
Dar es Salaam	3,603	19,382	1,595	1,570	10	139	511	26,810	50,765
Kilosa	296	869	29	327	72	20	25	1,638	123,076
Kisarawe	329	266	35	119	—	2	16	767	187,927
Morogoro	546	1,699	74	194	4	10	43	2,570	230,291
Rufiji	15	131	2	143	—	1	1	293	104,917
Mafia	20	220	7	416	1	1	6	671	11,379
Ulanga	132	237	—	6	—	11	2	388	121,328
Total ...	5,026	23,096	1,749	3,085	87	189	615	33,847	908,662
Lake:—				8					
Biharamulo	29	38	—	691	—	7	—	82	49,849
Bukoba	272	999	16	95	—	42	—	1,948	299,860
Geita	195	272	—	2	5	41	26	634	139,028
Kwimba	57	451	—	4	—	16	1	549	237,962
Maswa	57	262	55	216	4	18	1	558	244,968
Mwanza	349	3,027	5	408	—	39	3	3,881	187,646
Musoma	153	888	—	10	43	25	8	1,132	141,527
Ngara	16	26	—	51	—	28	—	121	104,706
North Mara	67	141	—	1	—	6	1	216	115,037
Shinyanga	269	661	26	968	68	12	—	2,004	212,503
Ukerewe	37	233	—	97	—	16	1	384	111,329
Total ...	1,501	6,998	102	2,497	120	250	41	11,509	1,844,415
Northern:—									
Arusha	1,819	2,702	210	66	393	38	89	5,317	107,904
Monduli Division	*57*	*48*	*4*	*5*	*67*	*11*	*1*	*193*	*37,273*
Loliondo Division	*9*	*24*	*—*	*—*	*9*	*10*	*—*	*52*	*19,990*
Masai	66	72	4	5	76	21	1	245	57,263
Mbulu	313	200	9	2	84	19	—	627	155,546
Moshi	1,071	2,793	109	169	261	38	28	4,469	264,280
Total ...	3,267	5,767	332	242	814	116	118	10,658	584,993
Southern:—									
Kilwa	24	217	—	95	5	5	—	346	96,552
Lindi	311	1,981	100	70	—	28	15	2,505	176,989
Masasi	95	169	—	1	—	9	3	277	117,254
Mikindani Division	*55*	*599*	*14*	*88*	*—*	*7*	*14*	*777*	..
Mtwara Division	*126*	*120*	*1*	*14*	*1*	*2*	*4*	*268*	..
Mikindani	181	719	15	102	1	9	18	1,045	88,139
Newala	27	286	—	9	—	—	—	322	154,012
Nachingwea (Ruponda)	525	100	9	4	2	1	3	644	44,321
Songea	288	198	8	—	—	7	—	501	171,031
Tunduru	21	100	—	1	—	—	4	126	65,751
Total ...	1,472	3,770	132	282	8	59	43	5,766	914,049

POPULATION OF DISTRICTS

Province and District	Census held February, 1952								Census held August 1948(1)
	Euro-pean	Indian	Goan	Arab	Somali	Colour-ed	Other	Total Non-African	African
Southern Highlands:—									
Chunya	163	245	2	15	2	32	23	482	37,649
Iringa	800	958	33	175	27	51	29	2,073	180,906
Mbeya	596	1,019	39	2	44	38	12	1,750	184,046
Njombe	184	183	—	1	—	13	1	382	206,732
Rungwe	113	369	8	1	47	10	1	549	236,678
Total ...	1,856	2,774	82	194	120	144	66	5,236	846,011
Tanga:—									
Handeni	24	144	—	14	7	30	2	221	75,478
Lushoto Division ...	*427*	*117*	*14*	*32*	*8*	*48*	*2*	*648*	*104,018*
Korogwe Division ...	*344*	*903*	*24*	*275*	*68*	*56*	*9*	*1,679*	*112,083*
Lushoto	771	1,020	38	307	76	104	11	2,327	216,101
Pangani	103	244	9	562	6	17	7	948	25,377
Pare	76	169	10	109	28	2	—	394	85,599
Tanga	1,114	5,685	607	2,076	71	133	86	9,772	144,657
Total ...	2,088	7,262	664	3,068	188	286	106	13,662	547,212
Western:—									
Kahama	57	258	—	—	297	11	40	663	94,583
Kasulu	54	16	—	28	4	—	—	102	191,310
Kibondo	32	58	—	31	—	8	—	129	107,493
Kigoma	114	682	22	214	1	64	17	1,114	59,538
Mpanda	157	93	—	74	4	12	1	341	40,390
Nzega	81	311	7	598	5	195	4	1,201	186,595
Tabora Division ...	*389*	*1,991*	*60*	*414*	*77*	*54*	*21*	*3,006*	*. .*
Urambo Division ...	*480*	*103*	*7*	*112*	*48*	*26*	*36*	*812*	*. .*
Tabora	869	2,094	67	526	125	80	57	3,818	158,334
Ufipa	75	26	—	300	—	42	1	444	107,991
Total ...	1,439	3,538	96	1,771	436	412	120	7,812	946,234
TERRITORIAL TOTAL ...	17,885	56,499	3,240	12,728	2,346	1,547	1,249	95,494	7,407,517

Source: East African Statistical Department.

(1) Re-grouped, where necessary, to allow for changes in District boundaries after August, 1948.

POPULATION AT THE 1952 CENSUS OF GAZETTED TOWNSHIPS AND CERTAIN OTHER AREAS

	Euro-pean	Indian	Goan	Arab	Somali	Colour-ed	Other	Total Non-African	African	Total of all Races
TOWNSHIPS :—										
Dar es Salaam	3,603	19,382	1,595	1,570	10	139	511	26,810	72,330	99,140
Tanga	558	5,270	509	1,029	50	48	37	7,501	14,635	22,136
Tabora	305	1,833	60	154	77	26	21	2,476	11,555	14,031
Mwanza (1) ...	286	2,594	55	69	—	17	2	3,023	10,668	13,691
Dodoma	360	2,054	59	311	58	10	35	2,887	9,375	12,262
Morogoro ...	203	1,045	39	123	3	7	17	1,437	10,064	11,501
Lindi	159	1,434	60	41	—	5	2	1,701	9,629	11,330
Moshi	459	2,481	82	137	194	20	19	3,392	5,687	9,079
Mtwara	126	120	1	14	1	2	4	268	7,806	8,074
Iringa	238	841	33	115	1	27	4	1,259	6,754	8,013
Arusha	974	2,560	180	59	245	22	87	4,127	3,571	7,698
Mikindani	23	446	14	88	—	7	10	588	5,720	6,308
Mbeya	447	688	38	1	44	28	7	1,253	4,313	5,566
Musoma	39	696	5	3	32	17	—	792	4,145	4,937
Bagamoyo ...	10	185	7	252	—	2	3	459	3,344	3,803
Bukoba	104	638	15	11	—	3	—	771	2,799	3,570
Singida	37	530	—	117	148	9	15	856	2,269	3,125
Kilosa	48	346	11	48	—	—	2	455	2,663	3,118
Tukuyu	42	218	2	—	20	2	—	284	2,818	3,102
Korogwe	36	480	6	66	61	1	1	651	2,350	3,001
Kongwa	482	72	6	23	23	7	66	679	2,000	2,679
Shinyanga ...	32	486	8	85	67	—	—	678	1,802	2,480
Pangani	7	195	6	287	5	7	5	512	1,874	2,386
Kilwa Kivinje ...	1	203	—	1	—	2	—	207	2,164	2,371
Kigoma	82	553	22	30	—	—	6	693	908	1,601
Kahama	14	214	—	56	11	15	—	310	1,187	1,497
Chunya	45	119	2	14	—	5	3	188	1,175	1,363
Kimamba	15	236	8	38	—	—	—	297	895	1,192
Songea	48	188	8	—	—	7	—	251	739	990
Lushoto	70	43	2	—	—	—	—	115	428	543
Kilwa Masoko ...	7	8	—	—	—	—	—	15	180	195
Total ...	8,860	46,158	2,833	4,742	1,050	435	857	64,935	205,847	270,782
OTHER AREAS:—										
Urambo (O.F.C.) ...	480	103	7	112	48	26	36	812	9,415	10,227
Ujiji Minor Settlement ...	17	88	—	79	—	11	—	195	9,542	9,737
Ifakara(2)	32	157	—	—	—	—	2	191	8,342	8,533
Tanga Minor Settlement ...	188	7	18	58	5	—	4	280	6,205	6,485
Nachingwea (O.F.C.)	501	71	8	2	2	—	3	587	4,844	5,431

Source: East African Statistical Department.

(1) Population within the area of the present township, i.e., allowing for the areas incorporated subsequent to the census.

(2) Area within four-mile radius of Post Office, Ifakara.

Chapter 7

THE SYSTEM OF GOVERNMENT

THE CENTRAL GOVERNMENT

The basis of the administration of the territory in international law is the Trusteeship Agreement approved by the General Assembly of the United Nations at New York on 13th December 1946, under which Great Britain is the Administering Power.

The basis of the administration in domestic constitutional law is in Orders in Council under the United Kingdom Foreign Jurisdiction Act, 1890. The constitution of the territory is set out in the Tanganyika Order in Council, 1920, and the Tanganyika (Legislative Council) Order in Council, 1926, (both as amended from time to time).

The territory is administered by the Governor, assisted by an Executive Council consisting of nine official and seven unofficial members. The official members are divided into *ex officio* and nominated members. The *ex officio* members are the Chief Secretary, the Attorney-General and the Financial Secretary (who is also the Minister for Finance and Economics). The nominated official members are the Minister for Constitutional Affairs, the Minister for Natural Resources, the Minister for Local Government and Administration, the Minister for Lands and Mineral Resources, the Minister for Social Services and the Minister for Communications and Works.

The seven unofficial members at present comprise two Europeans, two Asians and three Africans. All the departments of Government are grouped under the official members of Executive Council, while the unofficial members agree to take a special interest in the affairs of certain departments specifically assigned to them. The function of the Executive Council is to advise the Governor on all matters which the law prescribes should be dealt with by the Governor in Council, and on such other matters as he may think fit to refer to the Council. The final decision on all these matters rests, however, with the Governor. He may act in opposition to the advice tendered to him by the Council, but in any such case he is bound to report the circumstances to the Secretary of State, giving the grounds and reasons for his action.

The laws of the territory are normally enacted by the Governor with the advice and consent of the Legislative Council. The Governor has, however, certain reserved powers to enact legislation without such advice and consent. The Legislative Council, as at present constituted, consists of the Speaker and sixty-seven members, thirty-four of whom are on the Government side of the house, and thirty-three (termed Representative Members) on the other side. Of the members on the Government side of the house at present four are *ex officio* and the remainder are termed Nominated Members, a minority of whom are officials of the Government and the remainder, including the seven unofficial members of the Executive Council and six Assistant Ministers, are unofficials who agree to obey the Government Whip when so required. There is no provision in the Order in Council regulating the proportion of *ex officio*, official and unofficial members on the Government side. The Representative Members are appointed by the Governor and consist of eleven Africans, eleven Asians and eleven Europeans, one member of each race to represent each of the ten constituencies, comprising the nine provincial constituencies and Dar es Salaam, and the three remaining members to represent such interests as the Governor may think fit.   The proportion of eleven Africans and eleven Asians and eleven Europeans is laid down in the Order in Council.   Nominated members of the Council hold their seats during Her Majesty's pleasure.   Elections are to be held in five of the constituencies in 1958 and in the remaining five in 1959.   By the end of 1959 therefore all the Representative Members will be elected with the exception of the three members representing general interests.   The seats of both the Nominated and Representative Members become vacant under certain conditions laid down in the Order in Council, the most important of which is the dissolution of the Council provided for at the expiration of not more than five years from the date of the first sitting of the Council after any previous dissolution.

A Bill passed by the Legislative Council does not become law until it has been assented to either by the Governor or Her Majesty.   Ordinances assented to by the Governor may be disallowed wholly or in part by Her Majesty upon the advice of the Secretary of State.

It is possible for Her Majesty to legislate in this territory by Order in Council (although this power has not been exercised except in constitutional matters), and the High Commission has power to legislate for this territory in respect of certain matters laid down in the East Africa (High Commission) Order in Council, 1947.   Subject to these limitations the Legislative Council is a sovereign legislature with full legislative and budgetary competence within the territory.

THE MEMBERSHIP SYSTEM AND THE DEPARTMENTS OF GOVERNMENT

As stated above, the Departments of Government are grouped under the Official Members of the Executive Council, whose responsibilities are set out below:—

The Chief Secretary is the leader for the Government in the Legislative Council.   He is head of the Provincial Administration, responsible for security, the maintenance of public order, establishment matters, external affairs, public relations, printing, and for any other matters which are not the responsibility of one of the other Ministers.   He normally deputizes for the Governor when the latter is absent from the seat of Government.

The Minister for Constitutional Affairs is responsible, in addition to constitutional affairs, for United Nations Organization affairs, defence and immigration. He normally deputizes for the Chief Secretary when the latter is absent from the seat of Government.   He also attends meetings of the Trusteeship Council of the United Nations Organization as the Special Representative from Tanganyika.

The Attorney-General is the Government's legal adviser, responsible for all legal matters, including the drafting of bills and prosecutions.   The Department of the Administrator-General comes under his control and he is responsible for routine liaison between Government and the Judiciary.

The Minister for Finance and Economics is the chief adviser to the Government on these matters and on fiscal and financial policy generally.   Matters relating to customs and excise, industry and commerce, accounting, taxation and statistics, are his concern.

The Minister for Natural Resources is responsible for the Departments of Agriculture (including Fisheries), Veterinary Services, Game, Tsetse Survey and Reclamation, Water Development and Irrigation, Co-operative Development, for the Forest Department, the Government Chemist's Department and the Colonial Pesticides Research Unit.

The Minister for Lands and Mineral Resources is in control of the Departments of Lands and Surveys, Town Planning, Mines, Geological Survey and of the Registrar-General.

The Minister for Social Services is responsible for Education, Labour, Prisons, Antiquities, and Medical matters, and these Departments are under his control. The Commissioner for Social Development is responsible to him for the Probation Service.

The Minister for Local Government and Administration is the chief adviser to the Government on African affairs and is in close touch with the Provincial Administration. Questions affecting Native Authorities, Township Authorities, Municipalities and Local Government generally are his concern. He is also responsible for the system of local courts and for the Social Development Department (except for matters concerning probation).

The Minister for Communications and Works is responsible for communications, buildings, housing schemes, road transport and public works generally. The Department of Public Works and the Fire Services come under his control.

THE DEPARTMENTS

The Accountant-General controls the Treasury and the general accounting system of the territory. He is assisted by a Deputy and a Chief Accountant, also by 47 Treasury Accountants, some of whom are stationed in the larger centres up-country as Revenue Officers. The Treasury is situated in Dar es Salaam and the department comes under the control of the Minister for Finance and Economics.

The Administrator-General, with two assistants, administers the estates of persons who have died in the territory. He is also the Official Receiver in Bankruptcy. His department comes under the control of the Attorney-General.

The Department of Agriculture is one of the largest departments in the territory. The Director is assisted by a Deputy Director and four Assistant Directors. There are, in addition, various specialist officers such as entomologists and botanists, 60 Agricultural Officers and 101 Field Officers (Agriculture). The Director is also responsible for Fisheries. The headquarters of the department is in Dar es Salaam and it comes under the control of the Minister for Natural Resources. A full account of agriculture in Tanganyika and of the activities of the department is given in "Tanganyika: A Review of its Resources and their Development", and briefer descriptions of agriculture in the various provinces are to be found in chapter 5.

A small *Antiquities Department* was set up in 1957 with its headquarters at Bagamoyo. The Antiquities Officer's main task is to arrange for the preservation and protection of antiquities in the territory.

The Audit Department, situated in Dar es Salaam, is a branch of the Colonial Audit Department, which, under a Director of Colonial Audit, has its headquarters in London. Tours of inspection of both Government and Native Treasury accounts in stations up-country are made regularly. The staff of the department consists of a Director, a Deputy Director and seventeen Auditors.

The Colonial Pesticides Research Unit has its headquarters at Arusha. The Entomologist-in-charge is assisted by five Entomologists, six Scientific Officers, a Physicist, a Botanist, three Chemists, a Plant Pathologist and various other technical officers.

The Department of Commerce and Industry, situated in Dar es Salaam, comes under the control of the Minister for Finance and has a Commissioner at its head. He is assisted by an Assistant Commissioner, five Commercial Officers and five Inspectors of Weights and Measures.

The Co-operative Development Department is controlled by a Commissioner who is assisted by a Deputy Commissioner, an Assistant Commissioner and nineteen Co-operative Officers. Its headquarters is in Dar es Salaam, and it comes under the control of the Minister for Natural Resources.

The Education Department is divided into the following branches: Administration and General, African Education, Indian Education, European Education, Technical Training and Natural Resources School. The Director is assisted by a Deputy Director and four Assistant Directors. The headquarters of this very large department is situated in Dar es Salaam. It comes under the control of the Minister for Social Services. A brief description of its activities is given on page 365 et seq.

The Forest Department has its headquarters at Morogoro in the Eastern Province and is in charge of a Chief Conservator, who is assisted by a Deputy Chief Conservator, three Conservators and twenty-seven Assistant Conservators, a Utilization Officer, a Silviculturist, a Beeswax Officer, a Chief Forester, four Senior Foresters, seventeen Foresters and by a number of specialist officers. The department comes under the control of the Minister for Natural Resources.

The Game Department has its headquarters at Tengeru near Arusha in the Northern Province, and is in charge of a Game Warden, who is assisted by a Deputy Game Warden, fourteen Senior Game Rangers and Game Rangers, and by a Biologist. It comes under the control of the Minister for Natural Resources. Its activities are described in chapter 15.

The Geological Survey Department has its headquarters at Dodoma in the Central Province. It is in charge of a Director who is assisted by a Deputy Director, seventeen Geologists and various specialists. It comes under the control of the Minister for Lands and Mineral Resources.

The Government Chemist's laboratory is situated in Dar es Salaam. He is assisted by six Chemists, one of whom is seconded to the Veterinary Department and another to the Department of Agriculture. The department comes under the control of the Minister for Natural Resources.

The Immigration and Passport Department is in charge of a Principal Immigration Officer, with an Assistant Principal Immigration Officer, nine Immigration Officers and a Passport Officer. The headquarters of the department is in Dar es Salaam and it comes under the control of the Chief Secretary.

The *Judiciary* with the Chief Justice at its head, is based on Dar es Salaam, but one of the five puisne Judges is stationed permanently at Mwanza in the Lake Province. There are thirty-two Resident Magistrates.

The *Labour Department* is in charge of a Labour Commissioner, who is assisted by a Deputy Labour Commissioner, an Assistant Labour Commissioner, a Chief Factory Inspector, twenty-six Labour Officers and Assistant Labour Officers and by other technical officers. The headquarters of the department is in Dar es Salaam and it comes under the control of the Minister for Social Services. A brief account of labour matters is given on pages 372 to 375.

The *Department of Lands and Surveys* is in charge of a Director, with a Land Officer, a Chief Surveyor, a Chief Pilot, a Registrar-General, a Chief Valuer and a Hydrographical and Topographical Surveyor in charge of the various divisions. The headquarters is in Dar es Salaam and the department comes under the control of the Minister for Lands and Mineral Resources.

The *Legal Department* is in charge of the Attorney-General, who is assisted by a Solicitor-General, two Legal Draftsmen, an Assistant to the Law Officers, and by ten Crown Counsel. The department is situated in Dar es Salaam.

The *Medical Department* is divided into four divisions: Administration, Stores and Pharmaceutical, Hospital and Health Services, and Specialist Services. The last division comprises Dental, Child Health, Leprosy, Malaria, Mental, Tuberculosis, Sleeping Sickness, Laboratory Services, X-ray, Medical Education and Health Education Services. The headquarters of this large department is in Dar es Salaam and it comes under the control of the Minister for Social Services. Medical and health matters are briefly dealt with in chapter 11.

The *Department of Mines* is in charge of a Commissioner for Mines, who is assisted by an Assistant Commissioner for Mines, nine Inspectors of Mines and four Mining Wardens. The headquarters of the department is in Dar es Salaam and it comes under the control of the Minister for Lands and Mineral Resources. Brief descriptions of mineral occurrences in the territory are to be found in chapter 5.

The *Police Force* is in charge of a Commissioner, with a Deputy Commissioner, three Senior Assistant Commissioners, five Assistant Commissioners, ten Senior Superintendents, twenty-nine Superintendents, one hundred and thirty Assistant Superintendents, and other specialist officers. The headquarters of the Force is in Dar es Salaam and it comes under the control of the Chief Secretary.

The *Printing and Stationery Department* is in charge of a Government Printer, who controls the Government Press, assisted by an Assistant Government Printer, a Press Superintendent and eleven Assistant Press Superintendents. The Press is situated in Dar es Salaam and the department comes under the control of the Chief Secretary.

The *Prisons Department* is in charge of a Commissioner, with a Deputy Commissioner, four Senior Superintendents, eight Superintendents, twenty-five Assistant Superintendents and other technical officers. The headquarters of the department is situated in Dar es Salaam and it comes under the control of the Minister for Social Services.

In the Provincial Administration there are four Senior Provincial Commissioners (Staff Grade A), four Provincial Commissioners (Staff Grade B), twenty Senior District Officers (Class IIA and IIB), 235 District Officers, Cadets and

Women Administrative Assistants (Class III), thirty-nine Assistant District Officers (Class IV), thirty-seven District Assistants, twenty-six District Foremen, and supporting clerical staff. There is a Sociological Research section containing three Sociologists; also a Local Courts Adviser.

The Public Relations Department consists of a Director of Public Relations, a Deputy Director of Public Relations, an Assistant Director of Public Relations, twelve Public Relations Officers, three Education Officers (Broadcasting), and a Superintendent, Photographic Division. It is situated in Dar es Salaam and comes under the control of the Chief Secretary.

The Chairman of the *Public Service Commission* has his headquarters in Dar es Salaam.

The Public Works Department is divided into departmental and stores divisions. The Director has a Deputy and five Assistant Directors and a large staff of Engineers and other specialist officers, including forty-four Executive Engineers and Assistant Engineers. The headquarters of the department and the Government Stores is situated in Dar es Salaam. The department comes under the control of the Minister for Communications and Works.

The Department of Social Development, in charge of a Commissioner, has sections concerned with social development proper and probation. Its headquarters is in Dar es Salaam and it comes under the control of the Minister for Local Government and Administration for social development matters generally, and under the control of the Minister for Social Services for probation. A short account of its work is to be found on page 376.

The Town Planning Department is in charge of a Director of Town Planning, who is assisted by four Town Planning Officers. The headquarters of the department is in Dar es Salaam and it comes under the control of the Minister for Lands and Mineral Resources.

The Township and Aerodromes Fire Services Department consists of a Territorial Fire Officer and one Fire Officer.

The Tsetse Department is in charge of a Director, whose headquarters is in Arusha in the Northern Province. He is assisted by a Survey Entomologist, eight Tsetse Officers and eight Field Officers (Tsetse). The department comes under the control of the Minister for Natural Resources.

The headquarters of the *Veterinary Department* was formerly situated at Mpwapwa in the Central Province but is now in Dar es Salaam. The department is in charge of a Director, who is assisted by a Deputy Director, three Assistant Directors, various specialist officers, thirty-six Veterinary or Livestock Officers, and a large staff of other officers and Veterinary Guards. There are three divisions of the department: Administrative, Laboratory and Research and Field Staff. The department comes under the control of the Minister for Natural Resources.

The Department of Water Development and Irrigation is in charge of a Director, with a deputy Director, an Assistant Director, a Chief Designs and Research Engineer, three Irrigation Engineers, twenty-three Executive Engineers, and various specialist officers, including an Engineering Geologist, three Geologists, and various drilling specialists. Its headquarters is at Dar es Salaam and it comes under the control of the Minister for Natural Resources.

THE STRUCTURE OF GOVERNMENT

```
THE GOVERNOR
```

OFFICIAL MEMBERS OF THE EXECUTIVE COUNCIL

Chief Justice	Chief Secretary	Attorney-General	Minister for Constitutional Affairs	Minister for Finance and Economics	Minister for Social Services	Minister for Local Government and Administration	Minister for Lands and Mineral Resources	Minister for Natural Resources	Minister for Communications and Works

DEPARTMENTS AND SUBJECTS FOR WHICH RESPONSIBLE

Chief Justice	Chief Secretary	Attorney-General	Minister for Constitutional Affairs	Minister for Finance and Economics	Minister for Social Services	Minister for Local Government and Administration	Minister for Lands and Mineral Resources	Minister for Natural Resources	Minister for Communications and Works
Administration of Justice (in other than Local Courts).	Leader for Government in Legislative Council. Security. Internal Administrative Policy. External Affairs. Establishments. Police Force. Public Relations (D).† Printing and Publishing (D).	Legal Dept. Administrator-General (D).	Constitutional Affairs. United Nations Affairs. Defence. Immigration (D).	Accounting (D). Customs and Excise (H.C.).* Economics. Finance. Taxation. Trade Commerce and Industry (D). Statistics (H.C.).	Education and Training (D). Labour (D). Prisons (D). Public Health (D). Probation. Antiquities (D).	Chief Adviser on African Affairs. Local Courts. Municipalities and Township Authorities. Native Administration. Native Taxation. Social Development‡ (D). Sociological Research.	Geological Survey (D). Lands and Surveys (D). Mines (D). Registrar-General (D). Town Planning (D).	Agriculture (D). Colonial Pesticides Research Unit. Co-operative Development (D). Fisheries (D). Forests (D). Game (D). Government Chemist (D). Tsetse Survey and Reclamation (D). Veterinary (D). Water Development and Irrigation (D).	Posts and Telecommunications (H.C.). Public Works (D). Railways and Harbours (H.C.). Urban Housing Schemes. Civil Aviation (H.C.). Fire Services. African Loan Funds. Road Transport. Meteorology (H.C.).

*H.C. indicates an East Africa High Commission service.
†D. Indicates a Department of Government.
‡Except Probation.

THE HIGH COMMISSION

The High Commission is an inter-territorial body, consisting of the Governors of Kenya, Tanganyika and Uganda, which was set up on the 1st January, 1948, to supersede the East African Governors' Conference and to exercise the powers accorded to it by the East Africa (High Commission) Order in Council, 1947, in particular to administer services common to the three territories, for which purpose it may appoint such officers as it considers necessary. To further these purposes and to provide the legislative machinery required, there was also constituted a Central Legislative Assembly. This assembly was established for an initial period of four years but, on the recommendation of the three territorial legislatures, has hitherto been renewed at intervals of four years. The assembly is presided over by a Speaker and has the following membership:

7 official members appointed *ex officio* from the staff of the High Commission services;

5 members appointed and 3 elected from Kenya;

5 members appointed and 3 elected from Uganda;

5 members appointed and 3 elected from Tanganyika;

2 members of the Arab community appointed by the High Commission.

The 8 members from each of the territories are appointed as follows:—

(i) 2 nominated members being territorial officials appointed by the Governor;

(ii) 3 unofficial members appointed by the Governor;

(iii) 3 persons elected from among the members of the Legislative Council by the Representative members of the Council.

The High Commission administers the following inter-territorial services:—

The Department of Economic Co-ordination.
The Desert Locust Survey.
The East African Agriculture & Forestry Research Organization.
The East African Customs & Excise Department.
The East African Directorate of Civil Aviation.
The Lake Victoria Fisheries Service.
The East African Fisheries Research Organization.
The East African Income Tax Department.
The East African Industrial Council.
The East African Industrial Research Organization.
The East African Leprosy Research Centre.
The East African Literature Bureau.
The East African Malaria Institute.
The East African Marine Fisheries Research Organization.
The East African Medical Council.
The East African Medical Survey & Research Institute.
The East African Meteorological Department.
The East African Office in London.
The East African Post & Telecommunications Administration.
The East African Railways & Harbours Administration.
The East African Statistical Department.
The East African Tsetse & Trypanosomiasis Research Organization.
The East African Virus Research Institute.
The Royal East African Navy.

GENERAL SYSTEM OF ADMINISTRATION

For administrative purposes the territory is divided into eight provinces, each in the charge of a Provincial Commissioner, who is responsible to the Governor for the general administration of his province. The provinces are divided into districts in the charge of District Commissioners responsible to the Provincial Commissioner.

The administrative divisions of the territory are as follows:

Province	Districts	Land Area (sq. miles)	Head-quarters of Province
CENTRAL:	Dodoma, Kondoa, Manyoni, Mpwapwa, Singida	35,283	Dodoma
EASTERN:	Bagamoyo, Dar es Salaam, Kilosa, Kisarawe, Mafia, Morogoro, Rufiji, Ulanga	41,604	Morogoro
LAKE:	Biharamulo, Bukoba, Geita, Kwimba, Maswa, Mwanza,* Musoma, Ngara, North Mara, Shinyanga, Ukerewe	38,791	Mwanza
NORTHERN:	Arusha, Masai, Mbulu, Moshi	33,279	Arusha
SOUTHERN	Kilwa, Lindi, Masasi, Mtwara, Nachingwea, Newala, Songea, Tunduru	56,089	Mtwara
SOUTHERN HIGHLANDS:	Chunya, Iringa, Mbeya, Njombe, Rungwe ...	44,950	Mbeya
TANGA	Handeni, Lushoto, Pangani, Pare, Tanga*... ...	14,035	Tanga
WESTERN:	Kahama, Kasulu, Kibondo, Kigoma, Mpanda, Nzega, Tabora, Ufipa	78,675	Tabora

*Now divided into two districts, one Urban, one Rural.

Population figures by provinces are as follows:

Province	Europeans*	Asians*	Africanst	Total
Central	1,234	5,770	815,345	822,349
Eastern	5,026	28,821	899,607	933,454
Lake	1,501	10,008	1,826,022	1,837,531
Northern	3,269	7,389	578,919	589,577
Tanga	2,088	11,574	546,292	559,954
Southern	1,472	4,294	884,679	890,445
Western	1,439	6,373	936,798	944,610
Southern Highlands	1,856	3,380	844,877	850,113
In Transit	—	—	2,752	2,752
	17,885	77,609	7,335,291	7,430,785

*1952 Partial Census. †1948 Census.

It will be seen from this table that the provinces vary considerably in population. For example, over one-third of the Asian population of the territory is in the Eastern Province and one-quarter of the African is in the Lake Province.

Provincial Councils—There are Provincial Advisory Councils in several provinces. They are normally composed of the District Commissioners in the province, together with provincial departmental heads, and approximately the same number of unofficials of all races.

Provincial Advisory Councils are not statutory bodies; their purpose is to bring Government officials and the general public into closer contact with each other and to encourage the leaders of local public opinion to approach problems from a provincial rather than from a parochial point of view.

The councils normally meet twice a year, the procedure taking the form of short reports by departmental heads, followed by questions. Written questions are also sent to the chairman in advance and answered by the appropriate provincial officer.

LOCAL GOVERNMENT

INTRODUCTION

"Local Government Memorandum No. 1" was first issued by Sir Donald Cameron in 1930 as a statement of the aims of native administration in Tanganyika and in support of his institution of "Indirect Rule".[1]

In detail this memorandum is now out of date: the political background has changed and the meaning which is now attached to the term local government has altered from the original conception: but the principles which were set forth remain substantially the same, and there can be no better beginning to the present description than an abbreviated quotation from what was said:—

"The Mandatory Power is under a solemn obligation so to train the natives that they may stand by themselves, at least as part of the whole community in the Territory, and we cannot discharge that obligation if we do not train the people in the art of administration. It must be plain that in any such training we must first teach the people to administer their own affairs, and it seems obvious that in doing the latter, the wise course, if not the only practical course, is to build on the institutions of the people themselves, tribal institutions which have been handed down to them through the centuries. If we set up artificial institutions, those institutions can have no inherent stability and must crumble away at the first shock which they may receive. It is our duty to do everything in our power to develop the native politically on lines suitable to the state of society in which he lives. Our desire is to make him a good African, and we shall not achieve this if we destroy all the institutions, all the traditions, all the habits of the people, superimposing upon them what we consider to be better administrative methods and better principles, but destroying everything that made the administration really in touch with the thoughts and customs of the people.

It may be argued that so far as mere administration is concerned—and this is by no means the same question as the political training of the natives—we can achieve our object by using the chiefs as our mouthpieces through whom the orders of the Government are issued to the people; but with all the disintegrating influences which are at work to impair the authority of the chief over his people that authority will be undermined and completely disappear as certainly as it is disappearing in other parts of tropical Africa, unless we take steps now to prevent its disappearance. As a consequence we should have destroyed the only foundations on which it is possible to build—and train. In place of the alternative of governing directly through Administrative Officers, there is the other method of trying, while we endeavour to purge the native system of its abuses, to graft our higher civilization upon the soundly rooted native stock, stock that has its foundations in the hearts and minds and thoughts of the people and therefore on which we can build more easily, moulding it and establishing it into lines consonant with modern ideas and higher standards, and yet all the time enlisting the real force of the spirit of the people, instead of killing all that out and trying to start afresh. Under this system the native authorities become a living part of the machinery of Government and the political energies and ability of the people are directed to

---

[1]"Principles of Native Administration and their Application." Sir Donald Cameron. Govt. Printer 1930.

the preservation and development of their own institutions. This is a task which will provide in ever increasing measure for those progressive Africans who genuinely desire to serve their own people.

The system adopted by the Tanganyika Government for this purpose is based on the principle known as Indirect Rule, that is the principle of adapting for the purposes of local government the institutions which the native peoples have evolved for themselves, so that they may develop in a constitutional manner from their own past, guided and restrained by the traditions and sanctions which they have inherited (moulded or modified as they may be on the advice of British Officers) and by the general advice and control of those officers. It is an essential feature of this system that the British Government rules through these native institutions which are regarded as an integral part of the machinery of government, with well defined powers and functions recognized by Government and by law, and not dependent on the caprice of an executive officer."

In these terms, a dynamic and evolutionary principle was set forth, which, with adaptations arising out of evolution itself and out of the successful execution of the policy is as applicable to the present day as when it was written. There has been criticism in recent years that the policy of indirect rule was static and ill-fitted to the changing needs of African society, but in truth limitation was imposed by circumstances, particularly the impact of the war of 1939–45.

At the end of the war it was clear that the system of indirect rule had stood the test of the years and that an opportunity was presented to modernize it in the light of current political trends. In particular, it was advisable that the inherently democratic structure of Bantu society should be recognized by the addition, as formal members, of persons other than traditional elders on tribal councils.

At the present time, no less than in the past, the aims of policy are political as well as administrative. They are defined as follows in the report[1] of the 1951 Colonial Office Summer Conference on African Administration:—

(a) to provide efficient representative local government machinery through which the people of a defined area can discuss the needs of that area and provide the services required to meet those needs in so far as such services can appropriately be provided through local government machinery;

(b) to provide machinery through which local representative bodies can assist in carrying out central government policy either as partners or as agents;

(c) to provide a common forum where the problems of all sections of the local community may be resolved, and to provide machinery by means of which common action can be taken in matters of joint local interest;

(d) to foster a sense of civic responsibility and to provide a training ground for fuller participation in central government.

The best approach to the subject will be by a description of the historical background, from which may be seen the nature of the problem to be tackled and the degree of progress which has already been made. This will also show that present policy is not an innovation or a sudden change of emphasis, but merely the next step forward in a continuing process.

[1]African No. 1178, H.M.S.O.

THE HISTORICAL BACKGROUND

Pre-German Tribal Organization.—The difficulties experienced by government in the early twenties in many parts of Tanganyika, in the discovery and restoration of traditional "Chiefs", cannot be properly appreciated without some understanding of the state of African organization before the advent of the Germans. Tanganyika, with its patchwork of soils, and still more of water supplies, intersected with vast areas of bush, was a natural arena for the formation of tribal groups. The internal organization of these groups evolved slowly, as a result of both external and internal stresses. In some areas, a tribe would be welded into unity by wars, with a resultant emergence of leadership in the person of the Chief. In others, wars resulted in a fragmentation into clan or even smaller groups. In yet others, where there were no outside stresses, or internal ones such as a population increase, change, if any, was very slow.

Arab Influence.—The only strong non-African influence was that of the Arabs who, from their settlements on the coast, and their widely-spaced outposts on the well-marked routes leading inland, helped to prevent the evolution of unitary African tribal chiefs. It is Arab influence which accounts in large measure for the lack of traditional tribal chiefs among the coastal tribes of Tanganyika.

Bantu Democracy.—Away from the coast, the land was sparsely occupied even by modern standards, and such tribal histories as are remembered show that when the Germans assumed control the majority of tribes were in the formative stage only. But it is important to remember that African society manages itself on democratic lines, whether the unit be a tribe, or smaller.

Development during the German Regime.—The Germans, with no initial colonial experience, deliberately adopted at first the Arab "akida" system, of local rule by paid minor officials selected for efficiency and not by tradition, consisting commonly of Arabs or detribalized Africans. These *akidas* had both executive and judicial powers, as well as the responsibility for tax collection. The Germans came to recognize the limitations of this system, which was often oppressive and corrupt, and are said to have decided to substitute some form of rule through traditional leaders; but this project came to nothing owing to the outbreak of war in 1914.

The Stabilization of British Government 1917–25.—The British Administration, when it took over in 1917–18, thus found a country organized in a system of local government by aliens, the *akidas*, and grossly disorganized by the war and by a disastrous famine which occurred in 1919. It was thus natural that policy should concentrate first on making order out of chaos, a policy which held the field until the advent of Sir Donald Cameron as Governor in 1924. However, it had from the first been evident to the British Administration that the *akida* system was unsatisfactory, and there was considerable progress in the period 1917–25 in substituting traditional chiefs, where these could be found, for the *akidas*, and in giving them recognized powers of local government, largely by recognition of native courts under their jurisdiction.

The Initiation of Indirect Rule, 1926.—By 1925, the confidence of the people had been secured by just administration, and the advent of a new Governor, who had seen the effectiveness of local administration through the chiefs in Nigeria, gave the opportunity for a transformation in principle and practice. The principles have been quoted at length above. Their application involved ascertaining who were the traditional leaders of the people—whether chiefs of large areas or small, or headmen of village communities; recognizing their authority, both executive and judicial; conferring on them new functions which made them the forerunners of the rapidly developing local government institutions of today; and providing them with the financial resources from which not only the costs of tribal administration but those of nascent social services could be met. There thus emerged what soon became a familiar pattern of Native Authorities, Native Courts and Native Treasuries. Progress was extremely variable and occasionally there were failures and a fresh start was necessary. Among the many tribes of Tanganyika, it was found in a number of cases that the concept of a chief was absent, authority being vested in lesser leaders. Elsewhere, as before stated, wars and jealousies had shattered tribal unity, if it ever existed. Often the chiefs were too petty to head effective administrative units. There followed a period of grouping into councils, of amalgamations and of so-called federations, designed to produce units which could be efficient, in time, and have greater financial strength. The process was almost everywhere carried out by discussion and persuasion, in the face often of deep local jealousies and fears, and evolution from basic tribal institutions was sought everywhere. In the coastal districts it was found, rather later, that the tribal groupings did not produce leadership from the many small headmen, and it was necessary to create chiefs. These still exist, but, subject to control by the central government over appointment and dismissal, they operate in the same way and with the same legal authority as chiefs elsewhere, and are by degrees becoming responsible to the people rather than to the central government.

The Native Authority Ordinance, 1927.—The institutions thus set up functioned partly with and partly without legal sanction. There was at that time no clear theoretical distinction between local and central government. Thus, while developing the theme of seeking out and utilizing indigenous institutions, with their own traditional authority, Sir Donald Cameron spoke at the same time of delegation, not devolution, of the activities of the central government, and of the native authorities being regarded as an integral part of the machinery of government. Their legal basis derived from the Native Authority Ordinance of 1927, the sole contents of which, apart from the establishment of the position of Native Authorities, were an enunciation of the duties of native authorities and natives generally in the maintenance of order and good government, and the conferment of powers to issue legal orders on specified subjects and to make rules, with the assent of the Governor, providing for the peace, good order and welfare of natives. With the exception that fees might be imposed under such rules, the Ordinance was silent on the subject of raising and spending money: there was no provision for the grant of autonomous status, with the result that a native authority could not legally contract, or raise loans; and nothing was said about the services that a native authority might afford. In practice, during the formative phase, the vagueness of the provisions was an advantage, giving flexibility. The list of subjects on which orders might be issued, and liberal interpretation of the phrase "peace, order and good government", as applied to the rule-making power, allowed of the gradual building up of a list of functions which were proper to native authorities, while the provisions for the constitution of authorities were so general as to cover everything from a single powerful chief to a representative council. There was no modification of the law of any significance till 1942, when power to raise rates was conferred, and the major alterations which allowed incorporation and set out financial powers and duties, including audit of accounts, are very recent.

The Period of Consolidation, 1926–45.—An innovation such as the institution of Indirect Rule could not be expected to permit of immediate further evolution, and a period of consolidation was clearly necessary.   In point of fact indirect rule was very quickly subject to the strain of the 1929–32 financial depression, and almost before it had recovered fully from that setback the onset of the 1939–45 war made it necessary to subordinate other considerations to those of efficiency in the prosecution of the war effort.   The indigenous institutions which were recognized in 1926 had to settle down and be made to work, dealing as they were (in addition to the local administration of their area) with unfamiliar matters such as agriculture, health and education services, and the administration of native treasury moneys.   Nor should it be forgotten that the original strength of the system derived chiefly not from the native treasuries as is the case today, but from the native courts which in most areas were novel institutions, in respect of which a considerable degree of support and tuition was, and still is, necessary. The period of consolidation provided a test of the stability and strength of the native authorities, particularly when in the war period demands for increased production of crops, higher sales of cattle, labour for essential production and men for the forces were added to their normal functions.   From these trials the native authorities emerged unscathed and in many cases strengthened in spite of decreased guidance and aid from the attenuated administrative staff during the war period.

Chiefs during Period of Consolidation.—The 1939–45 war accentuated a danger intrinsic in the system of indirect rule as introduced in 1926, in the shape of a tendency for chiefs to be divorced from their democratic traditions.   It had been known from the first that chiefs had their traditional councillors, and until the outbreak of war, it could safely be assumed that the chiefs would not infringe the constitutional safeguards provided by the traditions of their tribes.   But during the war attention was of necessity concentrated on securing efficiency from the chiefs, to the neglect of constitutional safeguards.   Political education had always been concentrated on the chiefs themselves.   Their economic position put them at an advantage over others in securing formal education for those whom they hoped would be their heirs.   It was the chiefs who were in regular contact with officers of the central government, and the process of building up federations of chiefs covering the whole or part of a district, and in one case (involving a single tribe) several districts, often resulted in the discussion of business by the chiefs at a distance from their people.   In brief, although the institution of chiefship was never intrinsically authoritarian, there was an inevitable tendency towards autocracy.

The Development of Local Government, 1945–53.—Even before the end of the 1939–45 war, much thought was being given to the pattern of African local government which would suit modern conditions, and to the changes in the system of indirect rule which would have to be made when possible.   It was commonly believed in East Africa that the return from the war of a large number of African soldiers would result in a widespread demand from them for greater participation in the local government of their tribes.   That this did not eventuate in Tanganyika does not alter the fact that the need for tribal consitutional reform was brought into prominence, and it was commonly agreed that such reform must include not only provision for the appearance of commoners on tribal councils, but also the physical separation in the tribal organization of the executive from the judiciary, owing to the increasing complexity of the former and the impossibility in very

The Boma (District Office) at Mikindani, Southern Province

Photo: Public Relations Department

many cases of combining both as a prerogative of the chief. Instructions were issued to the Provincial Administration throughout Tanganyika that constitutional reform was to be specifically encouraged. At the same time these instructions made it clear that no attempt was to be made to seek a common pattern in the course of adding representative elements to the established native authorities on tribal councils. The wide differences in tribal constitution, the differing degrees of attainment, competence and interest, and, in some parts, difficulties arising from poor communications and scattered population, meant that any such effort would have been unreal. One basic principle was followed, however, that in African local government the system best suited to the conditions of Tanganyika was that of a pyramid, culminating normally in an all-purposes district council, the bulk of the membership of which was derived by selection from the subordinate councils of the district. The disadvantages were recognized that district councils might be slow in action and would undoubtedly be remote from the individual African, and the decision might in some ways be said to negate the principle stated by the Committee on Constitutional Development as follows: "If government is to be good, a quality which demands that it should be humane and personal as well as efficient, it must be exercised executively as near to its subjects as possible, provided that it still remains effective. The nearer decisions can be taken to their places of origin the more consideration are local views and desires likely to receive, the more will local opinion identify itself with the result, and the less will be the inevitable delays and annoyances involved in referring them to the seat of government"[1]. But the idea of the pyramid was familiar: lesser units could not command adequate financial resources or efficient staff: and effective central control and advice could not be applied to more than a basic minimum number of councils.

The Formation of Councils: District Councils.—The similarity in shape of very many of the units of native administration and the regular co-ordination of experience by the Member for Local Government[3] and by the Provincial Commissioners in their conferences, have led to greater uniformity of structure than might have been expected. The situation as it had developed by 1950 was analysed and an account has been published[2]. Since then, the process has been continued by the creation of councils in many of the areas in which they were then absent. Broadly speaking, the same components are to be found in most districts. There are first the chief or chiefs who are the native authorities, sometimes accompanied by their sub-chiefs, and parallel with them in the coastal districts, the appointed executives. Here it should again be emphasized that the office of chief normally contains strong democratic elements: he does not succeed solely by hereditary right, but also by consent of the people. The second component is that of representatives of the village headmen, a body of Africans who in some parts are hereditary or are direct executive appointments by the chief, and in others are selected by, or with the assent of, the village community. Thirdly come the representatives of the people, usually chosen by the divisional council, covering a chiefdom or comparable unit, or by the commoners in it: in some cases, part or all of the commoners are directly elected in the divisions. Finally, there are useful men—junior Government officials, traders, priests and teachers, for example—and occasionally women selected from subordinate councils or co-opted by the council, or nominated by the chief or the District Commissioner.

---

[1]Report of the Committee on Constitutional Development. Govt. Printer, Dar es Salaam.
[2]Development of Local Government in Tanganyika. Colonial No. 277. H.M.S.O.
[3]Now the Minister for Local Government and Administration.

The pattern is by no means universal and there are still districts where the old native authority persists unchanged by time. A similar diversity prevails in the status of the councils. In some districts, particularly where the office of chief is well established, they are solely advisory. In others they have reached a clear status in relation to legislation and finance and the position is best described as that of the Chief- (or Chiefs-) in-Council. In yet others, the chiefs or other executive heads are fully integrated with the council and real executive responsibility is developing.

Divisional Councils.—Much of what has been said above applies to the divisional councils, whence the district councils derive, in respect of constitution, function, and above all, diversity. The usual divisional council consists of the chief (or sub-chief or executive officer), all his village headmen, and commoners chosen by the villages, with occasionally some nominees or co-opted members. In some districts the divisional councils exist but a district council does not, and in other the reverse is the case, since it was necessary to provide councils of chiefs, with advisers as a counterpoise to their authority, without awaiting the creation of a constitutional structure. (This situation has by now become exceptional.) The policy of giving the divisional councils a clear share in local government has been referred to above, and there should be a steady increase in the assignment of specific executive functions to them, such as responsibility for the collection of local revenue and authority to spend money.

Uneven Council Development.—In a detailed study of these institutions, at the point which they have now reached, a feature which stands out most clearly is the considerable degree of unevenness in the rate of progress throughout the territory. This is no new problem, but it is one to which great importance is attached. In a territory where much thought has been given to the question of future constitutional development, the wide variations to be found in the field of African local government may be a weakness and must be a matter for concern. Throughout the territory there are not only wide differences of traditional organization but equally important and sometimes more difficult human factors which call for careful study. While some tribesmen who have a natural liking for "politics" welcome change, and are keen enough on development to take the initiative in seeking it for themselves, others appear to be quite content with the existing system. Some who do not themselves desire changes, offer no resistance to them when made. They need to be told—and indeed want to be told—what to do. They will act upon instructions even if they see no particular merit in them, and appear quite uninterested in the reasons for them. The lagging behind in political development to which reference has been made is particularly marked among certain large tribal groups, the members of which have found no apparent cause for complaint against their traditional tribal authorities. Where there is a well-founded and acceptable system of tribal organization, respected by both chiefs and people alike, the people have often been well content with existing conditions and show no desire for radical changes.

Separation of the Judiciary from the Executive.—Mention has already been made of the desirability of the separation of the judiciary from the executive if the native authority is not to be overwhelmed by volume of work, although it must be remembered that this proposal does not involve such a drastic change as might be thought. In the great majority of districts, the chief admittedly is judge and chief executive, but in his judicial capacity he is assisted by court elders, a different body of men from the subordinate native authorities who help him as chief executive.

Where the chief continues to be the native authority, albeit sitting with his council, a preliminary step in order to avoid offence to tribal prejudices is the appointment, not election, of a judicial deputy who hears the great majority of cases, but still with the assistance of elders. The chief can, however, sit as court holder if he so wishes. From this stage to the appointment of a stipendiary, independent of the native authority, is but a small step, a step which can at once be taken where the native authority is an elected council or an appointed liwali as in the coastal districts.

In courts of first instance, a single stipendiary of a higher standard of education than the clerk is normally desirable, although it may be preferable that the appellate court, particularly where the area of jurisdiction is inhabited by two or more main tribes, should consist of a bench of two or even three stipendiaries. In all cases, however, they would be assisted by elders drawn in rotation from a panel.

The African Chiefs' Ordinance, 1953 and the Local Government Ordinance, 1953.—By 1953 the position had been advanced to the point where it was considered possible to frame a Local Government Ordinance of a comprehensive nature. In case this Ordinance introduced any doubt as to the continuation of the status of chief, the African Chiefs' Ordinance, 1953 was also enacted to make it entirely clear that Government regards the office of chief as a permanency.

It has been noted previously that the Native Authority Ordinance, 1927 was deliberately far from comprehensive. By contrast the Local Government Ordinance, 1953 is deliberately more comprehensive in its definitions and will probably be applicable to any single council established thereunder for many years to come. This is an enabling ordinance, for application only where local demand and necessity arises, and its existence does not vitiate the Native Authority Ordinance, or the Townships Ordinance in respect of those councils which continue to operate thereunder. A council of whatever nature, established under the Local Government Ordinance, will be governed by a formal Instrument, this Instrument containing only such of the provisions in the Ordinance as may be appropriate to the council in question.

AFRICAN LOCAL GOVERNMENT IN A MULTI-RACIAL SOCIETY: GOVERNMENT'S POLICY

Local Government Policy.—The policy of the Tanganyika Government is to establish a working partnership of the three main races. But this is not to say that in the field of local government all councils must *ipso facto* be inter-racial in memberhip, nor is it to insist that a mono-racial council must suffer arbitrary change, to inter-racialism, in its membership. In this matter it is essential to temper theory with practicability and desirability with a sense of the opportune. It will be convenient briefly to examine the situation from both its aspects, the mono-racial obtaining hitherto, and the inter-racial. Government in Tanganyika has hitherto aimed consistently at the formulation, and subsequent improvement, of African local government: and although there is nothing in the Local Government Ordinance to bar non-African membership of a local council, yet it is clear in practice that some, perhaps many local councils, as defined therein, will be in fact purely African councils for years to come. The range of local government activities in which non-Africans are more particularly concerned is at present mainly at district or at higher than district level. An exception to this generalization exists in respect of Townships and Minor Settlements where the non-African already takes his place, side by side with the African, on the local authority.

The Local Government Ordinance.—The Local Government Ordinance, an enabling ordinance, is in effect an enunciation of local government policy in that it defines in general terms the model shape of future County, Local and Town Councils and leaves it to the Instrument establishing each one of these to define the council's precise nature. As an enabling ordinance, it does not attempt to differentiate between African and non-African and expects in fact that each council area, be it a County, a Town, or Local Council area, will have the good sense to formulate its local government body in the best interests and according to the needs of that area.

Financial Autonomy in Local Government.—Here must be mentioned the principle that local government has no solid foundations unless it possesses a significant degree of financial autonomy. It is not sufficient that a local government council should administer funds derived solely from a central government subvention, for in this case a degree of irresponsibility would be inevitable. A local government council must have control over a significant portion of its revenue, which must be derived from local sources. In 1953, the local administrations derived some sixty per cent of their revenue from the share of native taxes returned to them by Government, and the balance from local sources. They used this money to maintain their own organizations, and to provide such æervices to their people as had been delegated to them by central government. It has been publicly reiterated that it is no part of Government's policy to deprive against their wishes local administrations of any of the services with which they may provide their people. It will therefore be clear that, except where councils under the Local Government Ordinance are merely substitutes for existing local authorities, services provided by councils established under the new Ordinance will be a combination of services previously performed by Central Government and now handed over together with such services as the Native Authorities are themselves prepared willingly to surrender. Suitable financial adjustments must, of course, be made.

The Enactment of the Local Government Ordinance.—When the Local Government Ordinance became law there were three types of existing local government councils which could possibly be affected by it, namely, the Native Authority, the Township Authority and the Minor Settlement Authority. Of these the Township Authority and the Minor Settlement Authority were single tier, usually inter-racial, councils. It is visualized that a Township Authority will, where appropriate, constitute a component, with appropriate representation, of a County Council, while the Minor Settlement Authority, unless it develops into a Township Authority, will eventually be a component of a Local Council. The Native Authority by contrast, in its simplest district form, was the apex of a pyramid, based on the informal village meeting with Headman, Sub-Chief and Chiefdom Councils. It is visualized that Local Councils as defined in the Ordinance will eventually replace the Native Authority, either at district or at less than district level, as may be appropriate, these Local Councils being represented on any eventual County Council at district or greater than district level.

In this brief statement of policy it is not possible to discuss every facet, but there are two which must be re-emphasized. The first is that the legal authority behind the many-sided operations of a Native Authority has not hitherto been comprehensive: conversion to the status of local council would, through the Instrument, make it comprehensive. The second is that conversion from Native

Authority to Local Council is not a cloak to obscure the elimination of the chief and his authority. The effect of the development of local government is to convert the chief from an apparent autocrat to a Chief-in-Council. Where the chief is firmly and deservedly established, it will usually follow, in a mono-racial council, that the chief or his nominee will be the president. In a multi-racial Local Council this need not necessarily be so; but the choice of chairman will remain, subject to the approval of Government, with the council itself.

When the Local Government Ordinance became law, there were in Tanganyika few Native Authorities which had reached the stage where it might have been appropriate to convert them by instrument into Local Councils, and there was little expressed local demand for Councils. The Local Government Ordinance was thus, and deliberately so, an enunciation of models for the future, rather than a completion of existing non-comprehensive legislation. The test as to whether the time has come to formulate an Instrument under the Local Government Ordinance for a County, a Town or a Local Council is defined in the phrase coined for native authorities in Nigeria as "cash, competence and consent". The time will have come when any such council can exercise a significant degree of financial autonomy over both revenue and expenditure, when it has the means of operating its budget without an inordinate degree of outside supervision, and when its people have a genuine and general wish which can and should be stimulated for such a step forward.

THE FUNCTIONS OF AFRICAN LOCAL AUTHORITIES

Omission of Functions from N.A. Ordinance.—Local government functions may be divided in two ways, into services to the people represented and controls on their activity in the public interest, or into powers which an authority may exercise if it wishes and duties which are imposed upon it by Central Government. The Native Authority Ordinance was drawn very broadly in respect of such functions. Nothing was said about the services which might be afforded and these were left to develop empirically. Power to impose controls was contained in a list, since much expanded, of subjects on which native authorities might issue orders, and in a general authority to make rules for peace, good order and welfare. Since mention of services was omitted, there was no provision or a duty to afford them; the sole stated duties were those of maintaining order and good government and of preventing crime.

The Duty of Maintaining Law and Order.—The maintenance of good order and the enforcement of law were matters which the native authorities were well fitted to perform, since the traditional essence of their fuctions was to maintain and strengthen the stability and security of the tribal structure. It was a relatively easy transition, therefore, for them to accept the new duties in this respect which came with the unfolding of the native authority system, particularly as they were furnished with judicial means of enforcement through the Native, now the Local Courts. The modernized councils being evolutionary from what went before, it has therefore been both logical and right that they should retain this primary function. Several classes of enforcement officers were at the disposal of the native authority; first his traditional and general functionaries, the sub-chiefs, where they existed, and the village headmen; secondly the staff of messengers, who are a combination of messengers, court officials and policemen; and thirdly the instructorate which has been provided in connection with natural resources and other services. Only the last of these can readily be brought under the direct authority of a council.

Government Departmental Staff.—In addition to the enforcement staff of the local authorities, there is also that of the Central Government, which has the ultimate responsibility for law and order and the execution of policy. It is the aim that the subordinate departmental staff of the Central Government shall be transformed into inspectors rather than instructors, and that enforcement shall rest with the local authorities, but this is not always possible in practice; when it is not, partial or complete secondment to the local authority should be arranged, if possible, and in any event, such staff should operate through the normal machinery of the local authority. It is most improper, for example, that departmental staff should directly prosecute for a breach of an order or by-law. If they have not been seconded, they should report to the appropriate village headman or local authority representative. Here it should be mentioned that it has often been the practice hitherto to insist that court proceedings should be initiated by headmen and not by the departmental staff of the local authority: the purpose of this was to emphasize the responsibility of the headman for all activities in his village, but it will clearly be necessary for this practice to be abandoned, with the increasing range of local government functions.

Police Duties.—With regard to police duties in the prevention of crime and the apprehension of offenders, although there is no intention of whittling away the responsibilities of the African local authorities, there is equally no intention that the messenger staff shall be transformed into a formal local police force. Training and discipline, in which the police can co-operate, are most desirable in the interest of efficiency but apart from any general considerations of policy the African local authorities cannot, and cannot be expected to, finance and control local forces in any way equipped to carry out the multifarious duties of police officers. The position will therefore continue as it is now, that it is the duty of the African local authority to prevent crime and to apprehend offenders so far as it is able, and where it cannot do so rapidly and effectively and in any event in all cases of major crime to report to the nearest police.

Police Posts and Co-operation of Police with Local Authorities.—At one time, it was the policy that detached police posts should not be established in areas under the administration of a native authority. This has ceased to be the case, in view of the requirements of property which needs safeguarding, particularly in trading centres, and of the growth of serious crime. The Commissioner of Police must be the judge of what is needed. In any case his officers at all times maintain close contact with the local authorities, and with the District Commissioners who are primarily responsible for them so that cordial relations may be established and any suspicion or fear of the police which may exist, removed. African local authorities are encouraged to co-opt or invite the presence of responsible police officers for periodical discussion of matters concerning crime and the preservation of order.

General Functions Partly Mandatory, Partly Permissive.—Most of the general functions of African local authorities fall under the general heads of maintenance of the local administrative and judicial structure, health, education, social development, the safeguarding of natural resources and communications. In these, part of the field is that of the Central Government and part local. The division of duties as now laid down is in process of being more clearly stated. A further sub-division will become necessary as inter-racial local government bodies are set up. Within the list, it is not possible to assign precisely what functions it is the definite duty of the local authority to exercise. With the development of the native authority system, there has been a gradual transition from the "may" to the "must" and there is a considerable intermediate range of the "ought". In very broad terms, however, it may be said that provision for local administration and local courts are mandatory, together with the provision of the lowest level of medical services, primary and middle education, the prevention and alleviation of famine and a number of natural resources services and controls.

Trading Activities.—There are two functions to which particular attention is drawn. The first of these is the provision of trading services. It is not the part of local government bodies to supplant normal agencies of trade. They should only step in in cases of emergency, as for instance, the need for organized distribution of hoes during the late war, or where control is needed over sales, as in the case of gunpowder and caps for muzzle-loading guns and of particular types of seed. The African local authorities are, however, primarily the representatives of agricultural producers, and as such have a particular duty towards their constituents. This has been met throughout the territory by the canalizing of the sale of cattle and agricultural produce through markets. This has become a very important duty, and it is one to which constant attention is required in order to ensure that the markets are conducted fairly, efficiently and, from the point of view of the producer, economically: especially, they are not regarded as a means of indirect taxation through the fees charged, though it is legitimate for revenue to be secured which will pay for expansion and improvement of the system. In a number of cases authorities have made themselves the sole purchasers, operating what are familiarly known as No. 2 Accounts. This has been a most successful course in many instances in the stimulation of new products, especially where they need processing before they are finally sold, as in the case of clarified butter, coffee and tobacco. Such activities may legitimately continue, but it is necessary that it should be kept clearly in mind that they are for the benefit of the producer and not of the authority. There should therefore be a conscious aim that when possible the conduct of such activities should devolve on the producers themselves through co-operative societies or, as an intermediate stage, through marketing boards on which the producers are represented. It is a corollary that the profits should be kept separately for the benefit of the producers from whom they are derived and should not be absorbed into general revenue. The same observations apply to the facilities for mechanical cultivation which are now being developed in many areas, though small schemes in the pre-economic stage may be dealt with through the ordinary accounts, provided that these are supplemented by proper costing.

Information Services.—The second particular function to which reference is made is the provision of information services. It is incumbent on an authority to let the Africans over whom it has jurisdiction know what it is doing and why, and in so doing to contribute towards their political education. This has in the past been done by word of mouth, but new techniques using visual aids are becoming available and are adopted whenever opportunity offers. In particular, every effort is made to expand the numbers and circulation of district broadsheets or newspapers, which have been so successfully started in many areas during the past few years. They are important instruments in spreading literacy and knowledge, not only of the actions of the local authority, but also of Government policy and of local affairs generally. Their value is much enhanced where they have space for original contributions, letters and personal items. Authorities are encouraged, once a paper is launched, to employ full-time editors, and not to leave the task to a clerk as a part-time activity.

LOCAL GOVERNMENT: THE POSITION TO-DAY

The existing organs of local government can best be considered as falling under two heads, urban and rural, the first administered through municipal or township authorities and the second through native authorities, local councils and county councils.

URBAN LOCAL GOVERNMENT

There is one Municipal Council, nine Town Councils and twenty-four Township Authorities.

MUNICIPAL COUNCIL

The Municipality of Dar es Salaam came into existence on 1st January, 1949.

The administration of the Municipality is in the hands of appropriate technical officers and staff, who work under the direction of a Municipal Council. The council consists of a maximum of twenty-five members. At present there are seven European, seven Indian, seven African and Arab members and two officials representing Government and the East Africa High Commission.

The head of the Municipality is the Mayor. He is elected from the members of the Council by ballot of the councillors at the first meeting of the Council in each year. The Deputy Mayor is similarly elected.

The work of the council is divided among the following committees:—

1. Town Planning Committee.
2. Traffic, Fire and Lighting Committee.
3. Highways and Works Committee.
4. Public Health Committee
5. Licences Committee.
6. Finance Committee.
7. General Purposes Committee.
8. Parks and Open Spaces Committee.
9. Hotels Committee.

The principal permanent officers of the Municipality are the Town Clerk, Deputy Town Clerk, Municipal Treasurer, Municipal Engineer and Medical Officer of Health.

For the present, certain other matters for which a local authority is normally responsible have not been taken over by the Dar es Salaam Municipality; for example, the Central Government continues to be responsible for the water supply and the Municipality has no powers to dispose of land in the municipal area.

During 1956 the Council received in revenue some £460,000 made up from rates (including Government contributions in lieu of rates) grants and assigned revenues. The latter consist of native tax, trading and other licences, market and other fees. Grants include contributions towards expenditure on public health and maintenance of roads. Rates are levied on property in the municipal area.

TOWN COUNCILS

Town councils, as we have seen, are established under the Local Government Ordinance, 1953, and there are at present nine in existence. The membership of these councils varies, but generally consists of a small number of officials, such as the District Commissioner, the Medical Officer of Health, the P.W.D. Engineer, etc., and a varying number of unofficials appointed by the Minister for Local Government and Administration. An exception is the Tanga Town Council where there is only one official—a district commissioner—and twenty-four unofficials. Unofficial membership of these councils includes persons of all races. The chairman is usually elected from among the councillors but he may be nominated by the Minister for Local Government and Administration. In the latter case he is generally the District Commissioner. The nomination of an official to fill this post is made as an interim measure in order to enable a new council to settle down.

Town councils are semi-autonomous bodies, may (with certain exceptions) appoint or dismiss their own staff, make their own by-laws, and raise and collect their own revenue. Their estimates are subject to the approval of the Central Government.

The duties and functions of town councils include the provision of public health services, sanitary services, maintenance of roads, the enforcement of building rules, etc.

Annual budgets vary from £152,000 in the case of Tanga to £17,000 in the case of Mbeya.

TOWNSHIP AUTHORITIES

The membership of these authorities varies, but usually consists of the District Commissioner as president, a number of officials, including the Medical Officer and the P.W.D. Engineer and a varying number of unofficials nominated by the Provincial Commissioner. The duties of the authorities are generally to ensure that the township is kept in a proper sanitary condition, to maintain the roads and to regulate building. In most townships these duties are carried out by departmental officers but some have full-time executive officers.

Township authorities are advisory bodies only and have no powers to make by-laws or to raise revenue, although most have been given spending powers and twenty now have their own expenditure estimates.

RURAL LOCAL GOVERNMENT

As explained above, the native authorities, except in certain areas, mainly coastal, are the acknowledged rulers of the people under the traditional tribal system, which has been considerably modified in many cases and is gradually being superseded by a system of local councils. There are some 390 gazetted native authorities in the territory, varying from the Chief of Heru in the Kasulu District with over 37,000 taxpayers to the Chief of Chera in the Ulanga District with 330, from the Chief of Kianja in the Bukoba District who receives a salary of £1,348 a year, to the Chief of Ifamba in the Manyoni District who receives £12, from the Iringa District with one authority to the Kahama District with nineteen.

Native authorities have wide powers under the Native Authority Ordinance, the Local Courts Ordinance, and a few other ordinances, covering the whole range of African life in tribal areas. They exercise legislative, judicial, and executive powers. They collect Personal Tax for Government and receive an agency fee.

The legislative powers of native authorities (or local councils where these constitute the native authority) are laid down in the Native Authority Ordinance, Sections 9 and 16. Under Section 9 they are empowered to issue orders controlling many day-to-day activities of the African. Under Section 16 they are empowered to make rules "providing for the peace, good order and welfare" of the African. Rules under Section 16 require the prior consent of the Minister for Local Government and Administration. They also have powers to levy local rates and to impose produce cesses.

Most native authorities either hold or participate in courts of law (local courts) having jurisdiction over Africans to try the great majority of cases arising in their areas.

The Chief, or native authority, is his own executive officer, in the same way as he is often his own magistrate and legislator. The native authority employs its headmen, clerks, messengers, inspectors, instructors, etc., but the Chief is the chief executive, and is paid accordingly. He is the man who is held responsible for the good government of the area. In this respect the system differs fundamentally from, say, the English local government system, where the Mayor or Chairman, although the titular head, bears probably a lighter burden of responsibility than the Town Clerk or Chief Constable.

The need to separate the legislative, judicial, and executive functions of local government is one which is receiving increasing attention as the activities of the local authorities expand.

The 390 native authorities combine for financial purposes into fifty-six native treasuries. These at the beginning of 1956 held balances of £1,565,705, and during 1956 collected revenue totalling over two million pounds and spent about the same amount. Many have, since the war, begun the collection of local rates and produce cesses which have greatly added to their revenues.

To enable the native authorities to keep pace with events considerable efforts have been made since the war to strengthen them and increase their efficiency. These have taken varying forms, e.g., insistence, when possible, on higher standards of education and intelligence in Chiefs, appointment of commoners to native authority councils, establishment of advisory councils of commoners, increased salaries to headmen, clerks, etc., to attract better men.

At the present time the control and direction of the native authorities, subject to overall control of the Central Government, lies in the hands of the provincial commissioners, who delegate much of their responsibility to the district commissioners. The provincial commissioner appoints and removes native authorities, subject to Central Government consent in the case of more important chiefs. He approves the native treasury estimates of revenue and expenditure. He is responsible for the proper functioning of the local courts, and other essential services. He or his district commissioners normally supply most of the initiative on which the legislative action of the native authorities, in so far as it affects development or expansion, is based.

The foundation-stone of the Government of the territory is still the District Office. The district commissioner is responsible for everything that may turn up, and, if there is no one else to handle it, he must handle it himself. This leads to a simplification of administration well suited to African conditions, as the tribal, and indeed the urban African, is in no doubt as to where he should go in any emergency. On the other hand it leads to a concentration of responsibility, power, and work in the hands of the district commissioner, with which, in an expanding economy, he has ever greater difficulty in dealing with proper care.

The provision of more European expert and technical staff, though everywhere urgently demanded, is not, from the point of view of constitutional advance, the answer. It can only tend to make the local authorities less self-reliant, and to raise the machinery of government still higher above the heads of the people. In a country where the drive for development comes not from within but from without the problem of ensuring that political advance keeps pace with social and economic change is thus one of great complexity.

LOCAL COUNCILS

A local council is established under the Local Government Ordinance and replaces the native authority in its area of jurisdiction. There are at present (1954) only two local councils in Tanganyika—those in the Newala and Mafia Districts.

The Newala Local Council consists of the District Commissioner as chairman, the five Liwalis in the district, one Deputy Liwali and thirty-five other nominated members of all races, including twenty-three Africans, six Asians and six Europeans; of these, five Africans, one Asian and one European are women councillors. The Newala Local Council is very similar to a native authority but it has jurisdiction over all races. The Mafia Local Council comprises the District Commissioner as chairman, one Liwali, two Wakili and eleven Jumbes. The unofficial members total nineteen, of whom two are Europeans, four Arabs, one Baluchi, two Asians and ten Africans.

The councils are semi-autonomous, raise their own revenue, prepare their own estimates and make their own by-laws. Their duties and functions correspond to those of a native authority. The position of native law and custom, however, is preserved under a special ordinance and remains in the hands of the chiefs.

COUNTY COUNCILS

The Local Government Ordinance, 1953, authorized the establishment of county councils in Tanganyika over one or more districts. The first such council— the South East Lake County Council—was set up on July 1st, 1955, over eight districts of the Lake Province. Townships are excluded from its jurisdiction.

The council sits under the chairmanship of a deputy provincial commissioner and consists of fifty-four members, thirty-seven of whom are unofficials of all races and include eight native authorities.

The council is a semi-autonomous body with its own staff and with power to raise revenue and to make by-laws. In the first instance, however, its revenue comes from Central Government and other quasi-government bodies in the form of grants, etc. The estimates of the council are subject to the approval of Central Government. The council operates through such functional committees as natural resources, social services, and finance and general purposes, but the day to day work is done by district committees set up in the eight administrative districts comprising the county area.

The duties and functions of the council will include the maintenance of roads, the provision of agricultural and veterinary services, maintenance of public health, and the regulation of buildings in appropriate areas such as trading centres, etc.

THE CIVIL SERVICE

The day-to-day conduct of Government is carried out by a non-racial Civil Service consisting of some 2,800 Europeans, 1,500 Asians, and approximately 23,000 Africans many of whom are in subordinate posts, though every effort is made to fit them for greater responsibility as and when possible.

As far as is possible the Tanganyika Civil Service is staffed from among the indigenous inhabitants, but, where no suitable candidate is available locally, officers are recruited from external sources through the agency of the Secretary of State for the Colonies or the Crown Agents for Oversea Governments and Administrations. The bulk of the clerical staff is recruited locally.

Officers who are newly appointed to pensionable posts are required to serve on probation for two years and are thereafter confirmed in their appointments, if suitable, and if they have satisfied the various pre-requisites for permanent appointment, the most important of which in the case of European officers is the passing of an examination in the Swahili language.

The European officer normally serves a tour of 30 to 36 months' residential service, after which he receives approximately 5 to 6 months' leave on full pay. He travels to and from the United Kingdom either by air or by sea, although he may be required to fly to suit the exigencies of the service.

Owing to the rapid expansion of the service in the past few years, recruitment has outdistanced the building programme for Government houses, nevertheless, while Government does not undertake to house all officers in the Civil Service, an endeavour is made to provide accommodation as far as is possible. Where quarters are provided a deduction from salary is made by way of rental, the amount so deducted depending on the quality and size of the quarters and being normally less than $7\frac{1}{2}\%$ of salary. Separate rent is levied for furniture at rates varying from £6 to £24 per annum according to the scale of furniture supplied.

The normal retiring age for Civil Servants is 50 to 55 years, pensions being computed on the basis of 1/600th of an officer's pensionable emoluments for each month of service.

Asian officers normally do a tour varying from 48 to 60 months. Asians domiciled overseas, and those appointed locally to the permanent establishment before 13th October, 1954, are granted passages to and from their country of origin for vacation leave.

The establishments of the Civil Service departments vary from year to year and are published annually in the Estimates of Revenue and Expenditure for the territory. An abbreviated form giving details of the Civil Service is shown in the Tanganyika Staff List, published annually, and all information regarding conditions of service and details of recruitment is given from time to time in Colonial Office recruitment pamphlets, which are based on the regulations for H.M. Colonial Service and the General Orders currently in force in the territory.

THE JUDICIAL SYSTEM

The supreme judicial organ in the territory is Her Majesty's High Court of Tanganyika, established under the Tanganyika Order-in-Council, 1920. In all districts there are courts subordinate to the High Court and governed by the provisions of the Subordinate Courts Ordinance, 1941, which replaced the Courts Ordinance, 1930. Appeal from the High Court lies to the Court of Appeal for Eastern Africa. Throughout the territory indigenous tribunals, known as Local Courts, have been established under the provisions of the Local Courts Ordinance, 1951, which replaced the Native Courts Ordinance, 1929. This Ordinance prescribes the nature of the constitution of the courts, the extent of their jurisdiction—both civil and criminal—and their procedure. These courts administer the local customary law but may also be empowered by order to administer all or any of the provisions of territorial Ordinances.

Chapter 8
PUBLIC FINANCE

As various areas of the territory were handed over to civil control during the 1914–1918 war, the civil administration assumed financial responsibility for them. In 1919 the civil government assumed full financial responsibility for the whole territory. Its revenues were, however, slender and the budget showed a deficit until 1926.[1] Up to and including 1921 the deficit was met by a grant from the United Kingdom Treasury; thereafter financial assistance towards meeting the deficit took the form of loans, which were eventually remitted in full in 1939.

In the early years the revenue measures in force were largely those previously imposed by the German government; Hut and Poll Tax, import duties and trade taxes were the significant items. Apart from the cost of the "normal" administration the territory's greatest financial liability was the railway, taken over incomplete and badly damaged from the Germans. It was largely because of this liability that the accounts showed a deficit until 1927 when a small surplus was earned by the Railways for the first time. In that year the Railways accounts were separated from the general accounts, the latter showing only the net surplus or deficit (and later, some provision for renewals and works) of the Railways. To complete the picture we may note that on the amalgamation of the Railways with the Kenya and Uganda Railways and Harbours in 1948, as a self-accounting department of the East Africa High Commission, Tanganyika ceased to have any direct financial responsibility for the operation of the Railways, though the territory guarantees, jointly with Kenya and Uganda, loans raised by the department.

Even if Railways finances are set on one side, there is no doubt that during the two decades between the wars the budget was tiny in comparison with the size and needs of the territory (though not in comparison with its resources).

After its initial set-backs the economy of the territory was, by 1927, beginning to flourish and great progress was made in the next few years. Thereafter however the great depression followed by the years of political uncertainty and the recession of 1938 kept a tight rein on revenue and on development. Thus for the period of nearly twenty-one years from April 1919 to December 1939 the total revenues of the territory, exclusive of loans and of the earnings of the Railways, was £33 million and in no year was the revenue as much as £2½ million. Against this background the progress that was achieved in these two decades, recorded elsewhere in this Handbook, is the more impressive.

The two main sources of recurrent revenue during the period were import duties and Native Hut and Poll Tax. Their product was roughly equal and they accounted for over 75% of all revenue in the early years; even in 1938 and 1939 they accounted for over 60% of revenue.

In the early budget over 60% of all ordinary expenditure (excluding, that is, expenditure on capital works and on the Railways) was accounted for by the expenses of the Provincial Administration, and the Police, Public Works and

[1]Until 1932 the financial year ran from April to March. In 1932 a change was made and the financial year ran from January. In 1954 the financial year was changed again to run from July. When years are quoted in the text the reference is to the calendar year in which the financial year began.

Medical Departments. However, with the increase in the public debt and in the civil establishment and in view of the general expansion of government's activities, these departments, though still the heaviest spenders, were, by 1939, accounting for less than 40% of the budget. Indeed in 1939 only the Public Works and Medical Departments were costing significantly more than they had cost in 1923.

The public debt was costing £145,000 a year by 1939; this was exclusive of the cost of loan funds appropriated for Railways expenditures. The total public debt incurred up to that year was £8¾ million, of which £5·6 million was raised on the London market, guaranteed as to principal and interest by the United Kingdom Treasury, while the balance consisted of loans made from United Kingdom Government funds. Approximately £5 million of the total public debt of £8¾ million was on account of the Railways. Thus, taking account of the expenses of issue and discount, the territory's loan expenditure in the two decades, exclusive of expenditure on the Railways, was about £3 million.

Nevertheless this sum of £3 million did not represent all the funds expended on capital development during the period, for in most years provision was found from revenue for a modest programme of Public Works Extraordinary and other capital works. In addition it should be remembered that the United Kingdom Government was making grants as well as loans for colonial development before the introduction of the more well-known Colonial Development and Welfare Acts of 1945 and subsequent years and Tanganyika spent nearly £500,000 of such grants in the years 1931 to 1939.

It was not to be expected that the territory would amass any considerable reserves from its modest resources and by the end of 1939 the reserves, excluding Railways reserves, were only slightly over £¼ million, and the accumulated general revenue balance slightly less than £640,000. What is more important was that the economy of the territory was becoming more buoyant and the finances more stable, while the machinery of Government was functioning efficiently and able to cope without radical overhaul with the complex problems presented during the war years.

During these years the territory's policy was one of self sufficiency in foodstuffs, the production of materials required for the war effort, the restriction of consumption of unessentials and of materials in short supply, the recruitment of manpower and the defence, to a limited extent, of the country. All this caused a substantial alteration in the pattern of the territory's finances, for not only had certain new departments to be created, e.g., for economic control and recruiting, but also the Government intervened extensively in trading activities, buying and selling foodstuffs and raw materials on its own account and on the account of the United Kingdom. At the same time the increased spending power created during the war had to be controlled, and its consequence, higher living costs, compensated for as far as possible. Moreover there was considerable expenditure on the maintenance and repatriation of enemy aliens, and on the reception and maintenance of refugees.

In the event the Budget doubled itself between 1939 and 1945 (overall budgetted expenditure figures were £2,389,000 in 1939 and £4,756,000 in 1945) while "under the line" payments were, in 1945, approximately £16,000,000. Nevertheless development was virtually at a standstill and the increased expenditures of the war years were, in themselves, of moderate value to the

Dar es Salaam Harbour.

The Karimjee Hall, Dar es Salaam.

Photo: Public Relations Department

territory's economy; they represent rather the cost of survival. On the revenue side the chief feature of the war years was an increase in certain taxes and in import and excise duties, and the introduction of Income Tax, which, like the United Kingdom Income Tax of the Napoleonic Wars, was a war-time revenue device which remained as a permanent and essential component of the peace-time tax structure.

There was no significant change in the pattern of public finance in the first two years after the war, for these two years were, naturally enough, mainly a period of stocktaking. Some war-time services came to an end, but as many of the problems of the war years—especially the shortage of materials and men—continued to exist, so did their impact on the public finances continue to be felt. Except that revenue was more buoyant than hitherto the budget in 1946, and the financial procedure underlying it, were still the same as in the budgets in the pre-war years.

Since 1947, however, the pattern changed very considerably and in many respects very rapidly. The extent of the change reflects both the changed economic position and policies of the world as a whole and of the sterling area in particular, and also the growing maturity of the territory; the rapidity of the change pinpoints not only the inherent strength of the finances but also the careful planning which had been carried out.

The pattern is still changing, and will no doubt continue to do so. Nevertheless, it is possible to see how significantly the new pattern differs from the pre-war pattern.

The main features of the changes which have taken place since the war are:—
(a) Inflation and the devaluation of sterling.
(b) The material wealth in the territory and particularly the increase in the size and value of its exports.
(c) The expansion of the Civil Service and of reserves of equipment.
(d) The application of the C.D. and W. Acts of 1945 and subsequent years.
(e) The increase in the territory's financial responsibility.
(f) The transfer of services to the East Africa High Commission.
(g) The devolution of financial responsibility upon local authorities.

The inflation of the post-war years, and the devaluation which occurred, make it difficult to compare the pre-war financial position with the present, except in general terms or minor detail. Nevertheless, if we compare the 1957 budget of £26 million of expenditure with the 1939 budget of £2·4 million the most pessimistic view of the effect of inflation on the true values of these figures cannot disguise the fact that there has been a very considerable increase in the finances of the territory. Two incidental effects of the inflation should be borne in mind. First, it has been necessary to revise Civil Service salaries and certain allowances on three occasions and this will leave a permanent effect on the territory's liability for pensions. Secondly, in order to protect sterling, hard currency purchases have been strictly controlled with, probably, some increase in the last few years in the cost of stores and in delays in obtaining them.

The increase in the territory's wealth has been profound not only in terms of money but also in terms of export tonnages. Moreover, the number of the territory's marketable products has increased and this has lessened the dangers inherent in a one- or two-product economy. The expansion of trade and industry

23

is dealt with in detail elsewhere but the effect of this expansion on the finances of the territory should be mentioned here.   Firstly, the product of taxes, at the old rates, has increased.   Secondly, the territory has been able to meet increases in the rates of taxation.   Thirdly, some of the old forms of taxation have become less relevant to modern conditions and new taxes have been introduced.   Finally, the wider spread of the territory's economy has made revenue collection less sensitive to the fortunes of any one industry, though not, of course, to a general boom or recession.*

The third feature of the post-war period which we have mentioned is the increase in the Civil Service establishment and in the Government reserves of equipment.   Between 1938 and 1947 the establishment increased by nearly 20% and by 1952 had nearly doubled, the peak years for recruitment being 1950 and 1951 when the shortage of expatriate qualified staff, who had been extremely difficult to obtain, was largely overcome.   At the same time equipment, especially for transport and construction, became more easy to obtain and the territory's capital works programme was speeded up, so that in the last few years a considerable number of capital works schemes, of buildings, roads, aerodromes etc., has been completed.   On the score, therefore, of both staff and equipment, expenditure increased rapidly after 1947.

The territory's Development Plan, inaugurated in 1947 under the aegis of the Colonial Development and Welfare Act of 1945, caused considerable changes in the budget.   The plan was based on the financial resources to be found from revenue, from loans and from grants (the latter from Colonial Development and Welfare funds voted by the United Kingdom Parliament).   Its scope and achievements are detailed elsewhere, but some of its financial implications are relevant here.   The territory's allocation of Colonial Development and Welfare grants for the period of the plan was £5¼ million.   In addition Tanganyika had an entitlement to a share of a regional allocation of £3 million made to East Africa as a whole, plus grants for certain research schemes.   The total grants came therefore to approximately £6¼ million up to the end of 1954.   Loan funds totalling just under £9½ million were spent up to the end of 1954, plus nearly £5 million apportioned from general revenue and £2½ million from the Agricultural Development Reserve which had been created out of profits earned on the sale of cotton and coffee during the war.   In addition about £¼ million was spent out of a £1 million loan obtained from funds lying in the reserves of the Lint and Seed Marketing Board.   Finally, mention should be made of the £570,000 granted by the United States Government under the Marshall Plan for meeting half the cost of the construction of the Morogoro/Iringa road. The total of funds from these sources comes therefore to nearly £23½ million, a rough average of £3 million a year (with which may be compared the £2·3 million which was the total expenditure of the country in 1939).

The plan was first budgetted for separately from the ordinary expenditure of the territory but in time portions of it were absorbed into the normal budget as being continuing services properly chargeable direct to it.   By 1954 develop-ment (apart from certain schemes still financed for the Agricultural Development

---

*Nevertheless it must be acknowledged that the economy of the territory is not yet sufficiently buoyant to permit of expansion in government expenditure beyond modest limits; until there has taken place a marked increase in the cash crop sector of the economy in comparison with the subsistence sector, and a greater diversification in the export list, and indeed an increase in industrialization to offset the dangers inherent in dependence upon world primary product prices, the most conservative view will have to be taken of the territory's prospects of economic expansion and viability.

Reserve) had come to mean in effect capital development, the remaining recurrent expenditures having been accepted as a normal annual commitment together with the increased expenditure on maintenance and renewals which follows necessarily upon the provision of capital works. At the same time it should be said that the programme had already begun to affect the revenue of the territory through the increase in productivity which had followed from it, and this too may be expected to have a continuing effect.

A successor plan was drawn up for the period 1955–60, providing for the expenditure of some £26 million and financed as before from loans and grants and from revenue. It was expressly stated to be "a Working Paper . . . to be kept under continuous review" rather than an "inflexible and rigid" formula for development. It was assumed that one-half of the funds required for the fulfilment of the Plan would come from loans—£4¾ million from Colonial Development and Welfare grants and the remainder from revenue and from certain special reserves and local contributions. It was inherent in the flexible framework of the Plan that the particular "sector" plans would be revised to take account of changed conditions since 1945 and 1946 when they were first prepared. This applied especially to the plans for educational and medical services and new plans for these services were drawn up in 1956 and presented to the Legislature. It was apparent, as soon as these plans came to be studied, that the cumulative effect of earlier schemes was going to be severe in terms of the recurrent impact which they would impose on the revenues of the territory. At the same time the Report of the Royal Commission on Land and Population in East Africa, published in 1955, had given rise to inquiry into the optimum needs of the territory in the field of development and particularly of capital development. As no reliable estimate was available of the national income (a deficiency which the Royal Commission attempted to combat for the purpose of its report) it was difficult to estimate the capacity of the territory to meet the increasing cost of the services created or expanded in the first five years of post war development*. Therefore although it was estimated that in the years 1955 to 1965 Tanganyika could spend a total of £96 million in furtherance of the development urged by the Royal Commission, it did not seem practicable to plan for the expenditure of more than £42 million if regard were to be had to the limitations of the capital market and to the absence of any significant source of grants other than those known to be available from Colonial Development and Welfare funds. For it was clear that the territory could not out of its own modest resources hope to satisfy the varied demands made upon it for economic and social development. Indeed the problem had become one of some nicety. On the one hand there was the need to expend more money on furthering the aims of social development (principally education) if the momentum gained in the earlier period of development were not to be lost (and this it must be added against a background of persistent demand for more education). On the other hand there was the realization that without a marked increase in productivity, and hence in production, the territory was not going to be able to afford even to maintain the then level of social services except at the cost of sacrificing some other part of the Government's programme.

---

*An inquiry into the national income was carried out in 1956 and 1957 by Professor A. Peacock and Mr. D. Dosser. They gave an approximate value to the gross domestic product in 1954, which was the year chosen for the start of the inquiry, of £147 million. At the same time they set out the conditions for the compilation of future statistics of the national income.

This realization of the problem caused a reappraisal of the situation. There was a request from the African members of the Legislature that a programme be instituted to increase the productivity of Africans in agriculture and allied fields, as one of the most important possibilities of increasing the wealth of the country and hence its capacity to carry the load of the social services. As a result, partly, of this request an Advisory Committee was set up to review the social service programmes and the economic programmes in order to ensure that the correct balance might be achieved in the light of the finance likely to be available.

Thus at the end of 1957 it may be said that the territory had run through the first ten years of postwar development and had reached the point of stocktaking. In view of the state of the world capital market at that time it was to some extent a period of marking time in any case. The next five years would show whether it would be possible for the territory, without any assistance additional to that which was already known to be available from Colonial Development and Welfare funds (supplemented in 1957 by the grant of a further £¾ million to finance the early stages of the Increased Productivity already mentioned), to keep the needs of social development and economic development in proper balance. One thing was clear at the outset and that was that the danger of annual deficits (against a background of only modest reserves) on the recurrent budget was real, for there were deficits in 1956 and 1957 and the prospect of continuing deficits was the most sobering element in the situation.

The fifth feature which we have noted as being of significant effect on the territory's financial position in the post war period is the increase in local responsibility for the territory's finances.

In 1919 and for some years afterwards, Tanganyika was a "grant-aided" territory; that is to say that the United Kingdom Treasury met the budget deficit. This necessarily meant that the budget was subject to close Treasury control. Indeed the task before the Governor and his Chief Secretary was to prepare the sort of draft budget that the Secretary of State for the Colonies could defend at the Treasury[1].

There was no Legislative Council and practically no opportunity for the public in Tanganyika to comment on the Government's activities.

In 1926 a Legislative Council was inaugurated and it opened with a budget meeting. The Governor made it clear in his opening speech that in submitting proposals to what he called "the tempering influence of a Legislative Council" he did not hope only for an advisory council. Despite the official majority and despite the fact that the final approval of budget proposals and especially of fiscal proposals remained the prerogative of the Governor (who in turn had to take account, in some respect, of the view of the Secretary of State), it was made clear that members of the Council were expected to take their duties seriously. And so they did. The Council went into Committee of Supply on the Supply Bill and referred the draft Estimates to its Finance Committee (on which all unofficial members sat, together with the Chief Secretary and the Treasurer). Despite the newness of the procedure, the discussion on the Estimates and the

---

[1]"Defend", viewed from Tanganyika, was the right word. In 1921 the original draft estimates did not find favour at the Treasury, despite the advocacy of Mr. Secretary Churchill, and it was necessary for revised proposals to be drawn up.

subsequent debate showed that unofficial members were critical, though co-operative, and very much alive to the implications of the budget, and the Government members had to put up a handsome fight for their proposals and for the doings of their departments. This budget debate set a tone which is now traditional and it is in no small measure due to the quality of the early budget debates and discussion that the procedures inaugurated in 1926 operated successfully until the 1950's. In 1955 the committee was reduced to three official members and ten unofficial, thus preserving its unofficial majority. It suffices now to say that in the thirty years that passed since the budget (and the various supplementary estimates) became subject to this control, not once did the Report of the Finance Committee, with its unofficial majority, fail to pass the Legislative Council where the official majority prevails. In 1956 the Finance Committee was dispensed with and now all Estimates and supplementary Estimates are dealt with by the Legislative Council through its Committee (of the full house) of Supply.

Nevertheless, as we have seen, the budget was never large and the finances, because of political uncertainty and trade recession, never really healthy. The Secretary of State continued therefore to take a close interest in the budget and his final consent was required for its provisions up to 1948. In addition his approval was required for certain fiscal proposals, for loan measures and for the writing off of losses.

In 1947 the Secretary of State proposed a substantial measure of devolution of his financial powers, the chief being that the budget would no longer require his approval and audit would become a local responsibility. The benefit obtained from this devolution of power upon the Legislative Council was, apart from its political significance, one of administrative convenience, for no real difficulty had been experienced in obtaining consent to the budget for some years. Nevertheless the increase in the power of the Legislature was much more than a token one, for in addition to having a greater responsibility for the budget the Council assumed final responsibility for the expenditure of funds, and a Public Accounts Committee was set up and began its work with a review of the accounts for 1950. This review was based on the report of the Director of Audit, which had previously been submitted to the Secretary of State but now became a report to the Legislative Council[1].

Ultimate financial responsibility in the territory remains with the Governor as the Standing Rules and Orders of the Legislative Council make clear: "The Council shall not proceed upon any Bill, Amendment, Motion, or Petition which in the opinion of the Speaker would dispose of or charge any public revenue or funds of the Territory or revoke or alter any disposition thereof or charge thereon, or impose, alter or repeal any rate, tax or duty, except with the recommendation or consent of the Governor signified thereto." Subject to this reservation, revenue measures, except where specific ordinances delegate revenue-raising powers (usually in respect of fees chargeable under the ordinances), are dealt with in the Executive Council before going to Legislative Council.[2]

---

[1] It thus became necessary to define the status and functions of the Director of Audit by statute, and this was done in 1956.

[2] Financial measures have however been withdrawn on occasions when the debate has persuaded the Government not to proceed, and on at least one occasion a revenue proposal was defeated because all the Government members abstained from voting.

The two remaining features of the present period are the transfer of services to the East Africa High Commission and the delegation of financial responsibility to local authorities in Tanganyika.

There have always been financial questions or items with a financial implication which have been of joint interest to all the East African Territories. To deal with these matters (and of course with other matters of common interest), a Governors' Conference was established before the 1939–1945 War. During the war, the importance of defence and supplies, on an East African basis, very much enlarged the field of joint action. After the war the old Governors' Conference was replaced by the East Africa High Commission (being the three Governors) with powers laid down by Order in Council. At the same time a Central Legislative Assembly was created, again under an Order in Council, with prescribed law-making powers. A number of services became "High Commission Services" responsible not to the territorial Legislative Councils but to the Central Legislative Assembly. These services fall into two groups. First there are the Railways and Harbours, and Posts and Telecommunications. Then we have the remaining services of the High Commission, chiefly, as far as we are concerned here, the Customs and Excise and Income Tax Departments.

We have seen how the Railways' finances were all along dealt with separately from the ordinary budget of the territory (except that the net loss or profit on the year's working and some provision for renewals and works appeared in the accounts). In 1948 the Tanganyika Railways were amalgamated with the Kenya and Uganda Railways (and in each case are included Harbours) as a self-accounting department of the High Commission, the budget being separate from that of the ordinary High Commission budget. All assets and liabilities of the Tanganyika Railways were taken over by the new department and Tanganyika no longer has direct responsibility for Railways finances.[1]

The Post and Telegraphs department has been similarly amalgamated with the Kenya and Uganda departments into a self-financing department of the High Commission, with the same effect on the territory's finances. In this case, however, the effect on the budget was more direct, for the expenditure and revenue of the department had, until the amalgamation, been part of the "ordinary" budget.

The second group of High Commission departments, (including, as we have said, the Customs and Excise and Income Tax Departments) had also, except where they are new creations, previously been budgetted for in the ordinary budget. These are not self-financing departments, like the Railways and Harbours and Posts and Telecommunications who depend upon the revenue they collect from the public to meet the expenditure they propose. The expenditure of the "non-self-contained" departments is met by contributions from the territorial Governments, according to formulae applicable to each case[2]. Thus, for example, the Tanganyika budget has ceased to provide funds for a Tanganyika Customs and Excise Department and instead contributes its share of the cost

---

[1]Although it joins with Kenya and Uganda in guaranteeing loans raised by the department, and makes special financial arrangement for two railway projects which are in the development stage.

[2]Contributions are also made, to certain services, by other governments interested in them; this applies particularly to Zanzibar. Mention should be made too of the contribution of the United Kingdom to certain services chiefly through Colonial Development and Welfare grants.

of the East African Customs and Excise Department as part of its annual contribution to the budget of the High Commission (the total being over £1 million in
1957). The revenue of the Customs and Excise and Income Tax Departments
continues however to be dealt with on a strictly territorial basis according to
rates prescribed in territorial ordinances.

It is not easy to define precisely where financial responsibility for the "non-
self-contained" departments lies. Their expenditure is provided for in the Central
Legislative Assembly budget but their "revenue" derives almost entirely from
the contributions of the three Governments so that the contributions depend
in the end upon the willingness of the Legislative Councils to vote funds. The
important point, however, is that what is voted is a block contribution
towards the cost of an East Africa department and not a supply vote for a
Tanganyika department.

While financial responsibility has been "delegated" in this way to the East
Africa High Commission and Central Legislative Assembly, Tanganyika has
also, particularly since 1948, been delegating financial responsibility within the
territory.

The separation of the finances of native authorities from those of the central
government was a fundamental feature of the system of indirect administration
adopted after the 1914–1918 war. The Central Government's budgetary concern
for native authorities was limited to the collection of native tax and the payment
to native authorities of agreed rebates on tax collections (although loans were
made to native authorities from time to time for various purposes). Native
authorities were entitled to other, but minor, items of revenue, usually imposed
and collected by themselves. Apart from this and apart from subsidies paid
to missions for medical and educational work, the Central Government until
after 1945 was directly responsible for all "government" services and for
financing them. One or two township authorities had been set up but even
their expenditure was provided for as part of the territory's normal annual
estimates.

Since 1945, and more particularly since 1948, there has been a considerable
delegation of responsibility, and the process is continuing. Under the Municipalities and Local Government Ordinances, local authorities have been, and are
being, created with their own revenues. In addition non-native education
authorities have been set up with statutory financial responsibility and revenues,
while various statutory boards have come into being which have taken over
responsibility for activities which were formerly financed as parts of the annual
estimates. Similarly quasi-Government organizations have been created by
statute, like the Board of Trustees of the National Parks and of the King George
V Memorial Museum, with their own financial responsibilities.

All this has led to some alteration in the pattern of revenue collection and
to a considerable increase in the Central Government commitments for the
payment of grants-in-aid (over £2½ million in the 1957 budget).[1]

At this point it may be useful to set out in tabular form the main details of two
budgets so that we may see how the patterns of revenue and expenditure have
altered, and what the present patterns are:—

---

[1]For example, the government meets in full, at government rates of salary, the cost of the salaries of
approved mission teachers.

Ordinary Revenue								1939 £		1957 £
Import Duties	...	...	...	...	...	...	...	650,000	...	5,700,000
Excise Duties	...	...	...	...	...	...	...	30,000	...	1,950,000
Income Tax	...	...	...	...	...	...	...	—	...	4,250,000
Native Tax	...	...	...	...	...	...	...	650,000	...	
Non-Native Tax	...	...	...	...	...	...	...	50,000	...⎫	1,724,000
Personal Tax	...	...	...	...	...	...	...	—	...⎭	
Vehicle Licences	...	...	...	...	...	...	...	40,000	...	420,000
Fees and Earnings	...	...	...	...	...	...	...	150,000	...	1,313,000
Revenue from Government property		...	...	...	...	...	...	130,000	...	1,401,000
Posts and Telegraphs	...	...	...	...	...	...	...	90,000	...	—
Interest and repaid loans	...	...	...	...	...	...	...	50,000	...	423,000
Other	...	...	...	...	...	...	...	320,000	...	1,846,000
					Total	...		2,160,000	...	19,027,000

Ordinary Expenditure								1939		1957
Public Debt	...	...	...	...	...	...	...	150,000	...	1,019,000
Pensions and Gratuities		...	...	...	...	...	...	110,000	...	861,000
Agriculture	...	...	...	...	...	...	...	70,000	...	684,000
Defence	...	...	...	...	...	...	...	160,000	...	678,000
Education	...	...	...	...	...	...	...	110,000	...	2,472,000
Contribution to Education Authorities			...	...	...	...		—	...	387,000
Medical	...	...	...	...	...	...	...	210,000	...	1,899,000
Police	...	...	...	...	...	...	...	110,000	...	1,266,000
Posts and Telegraphs	...	...	...	...	...	...	...	100,000	...	—
Provincial Administration	...	...	...	...	...	...	...	210,000	...	1,139,000
Public Works	...	...	...	...	...	...	...	150,000	...	2,458,000
Railways (Deficit, Renewals, Works)	...	...	...	...	...	...		70,000	...	—
Colonial Development Fund Schemes		...	...	...	...	...		120,000	...	147,000
East Africa High Commission	...	...	...	...	...	...		—	...	1,037,000
Lands and Surveys	...	...	...	...	...	...	...	50,000	...	328,000
Local Government	...	...	...	...	...	...	...	30,000	...	571,000
Prisons	...	...	...	...	...	...	...	40,000	...	583,000
Transferred Revenue	...	...	...	...	...	...	...	150,000	...	574,000
Veterinary	...	...	...	...	...	...	...	40,000	...	467,000
Water Development	...	...	...	...	...	...	...	—	...	333,000
Other	...	...	...	...	...	...	...	410,000	...	2,787,000
Agricultural Development Reserve Schemes	...		...	...	...			—	...	38,000
					Total	...		2,280,000	...	19,728,000

It will be noted that in each case the ordinary budget shows a deficit. In the case of the 1939 budget, the deficit reflected the correction necessary after the bad budget of 1938 and the fall in agricultural prices. The deficit for 1957 was due in part to the depressed state of the world primary commodity market, but in part, as we have seen, to the dangerous tendency of recurrent commitments, especially for social services, to run ahead of income. In one respect the 1939 budget had a healthier background than the 1957 budget, for the surplus balances and reserves had not in the interim increased proportionately[1].

On the revenue side of the ordinary budget, it will be seen how customs duties have retained their place as the most significant item. The increase in excise duties particularly reflects the increase not only in rates, but also production, duties being levied on locally produced beer, tobacco and sugar. The general rate of import duties is 22 per cent *ad valorem* (against 20 per cent in 1939), a number of luxury items being charged at higher rates and many

---

[1]Surplus balances were £900,000 in 1938, £2,250,000 in 1956.

General reserves were £200,000 in 1938, £2,000,000 in 1956.

semi-necessities at lower rates. There is a considerable free list, covering plant and materials required for agricultural and industrial use. Tobacco, spirits and certain other items are subject to specific duties.

Comparison of the two budgets shows how Income Tax has become the second best revenue producer. It should be noted, however, that the figures in the two budgets are not truly comparable, for Native Tax (and non-Native Poll Tax) disappeared halfway through 1955, to be replaced by Personal Tax. At the same time the rebate payable to Native Authorities (amounting to nearly 45 per cent of the collections as opposed to approximately 25 per cent of collections in 1939) disappears; Native Authorities or Local Authorities, for their part, deriving their main revenue from rates in lieu of the old rebate. Income tax is levied in the normal way on both individuals and companies, the company rate of tax being a flat rate of Shs. 5/- in the pound. The commencing rate of income tax on individuals is Shs. 1/50 in the pound and the maximum rate is Shs. 5/- in the pound. Surtax is chargeable on incomes exceeding £2,000 at the rate of 25 cents per pound rising to a maximum of Shs. 9/-. The commencing rate of income tax for non-residents is Shs. 2/- in the pound (where the chargeable income does not exceed £800).[1]

Native Tax, non-Native Poll Tax and Personal Tax are in effect all forms of income tax but it is necessary to retain them side by side with income tax because there is a great number of persons in the territory living on a peasant economy, whose incomes are insufficiently ascertainable in terms of money to enable income tax, which is highly graduated, to be easily assessed. (Nevertheless it should be noted that a simple form of graduation applies to Personal Tax).

On the expenditure side of the ordinary budget the effect of the deletion of "Railways" and "Posts and Telecommunications" will be seen. On the other hand new items have come into the estimates; for example the contribution to Education Authorities and to the High Commission and the recurrent cost of the Water Development Department. This latter department is a post-war creation and expenditure on it, chiefly on the capital side of the budget, is increasing substantially. Education and public works show the greatest increases in expenditure and there is little doubt that, owing to the shortage of funds, both of these services were inadequately provided for before the war.

Turning to the remainder of the budget, we can see how widely the present-day development expenditure differs from what was possible in 1939.

The capital works shown in the budgets were in 1939 to be financed from surplus balances. In 1957 under the Development Plan, which we have dealt with earlier, nearly £3,500,000 of the expenditure is derived from loan funds, over £1,000,000 from Colonial Development and Welfare grants and the remainder from funds specifically reserved for the plan[2].

---

[1]For some years after its introduction Income Tax came in for criticism mainly on the ground that there were anomalies in the legislation and in the principles underlying that legislation that were restricting economic development. In the end a Commission of Inquiry was appointed, under the chairmanship of Sir Eric Coates, to inquire into the system of income (and profits) taxation, into the ways and means of raising the revenue required by the Governments ("due regard being paid to the points of view of the tax-payer and of the Governments") and into the ruling rates of tax and allowances. The report of the Commission was published in 1957 and is at the time of writing being examined by the Governments and other interested bodies.

[2]Provision for the Tanganyika Agricultural Corporation appeared for the first time in the 1955 Budget. The Corporation was set up in April 1955, to continue the development and experimental work of the Overseas Food Corporation.

So much has been said about the changes that have taken place in the pattern of the territory's finances that it might be thought appropriate to say in conclusion that this is in fact the chief lesson to be drawn from an examination of them. Paradoxically, however, this is not the conclusion to be drawn, but rather that the basic problems have not changed.　"We must" said the Financial Secretary in his 1955 budget speech, "concentrate on developing our economic resources, since if we do not do so we shall be unable to support our programme of social services and it will collapse".　The same theme appears in the first budget debate, in 1926, and in the debates of successive years, and it is fundamental to the country's economy.

Chapter 9

COMMUNICATIONS

By and large, before the 1939–45 war, the problem of communications was not so pressing or important a matter as it is today. The tempo of development of the natural resources of the country was not such as to warrant large capital expenditure on new and costly forms of transportation. In the agricultural sphere, although the emphasis had been on increased production both of foodstuffs and cash crops, there was not that sense of urgency towards economic progress which was imposed during the war years and has been maintained subsequently. The two life-lines of land communications, the Central Railway traversing the territory from Dar es Salaam to Lake Tanganyika with a branch to Lake Victoria, and that from Tanga to the farming areas of Arusha and Moshi, sufficed for the economic transportation of the bulk of the agricultural produce. Most of the sisal estates were situated along these railways or on the coast. Mineral development was in its infancy and industry hardly existed. The population, too, was far more sedentary. The pressure of work both in Government circles and in the field of business and commerce was not so formidable, so that those who had to travel were content to take their time, whether by road or rail. Air transport was developing but as yet played only a small part in the general system.

Thus the development of communications was largely a local problem. There was very little planning on a territorial scale and but small emphasis on inter-territorial co-operation. During the last war all this was changed when the movement of troops and stores became a matter of vital importance. The urgent call for increased supplies of foodstuffs, sisal, rubber and other raw materials, put a severe strain on an unco-ordinated system of communications, and, particularly as regards roads, brought into prominence the weak links and defects in the system. These were dealt with, and the lines of communication kept open, but it was clear that something more than the repair of the existing system was called for, especially in view of the rapidly developing economy of the territory as a whole. After the war, therefore, a detailed ten-year development plan was drawn up, which included proposals for improvements of the communications by road, rail and air, and a good start was made on the implementation of these plans. The advent of the Overseas Food Corporation, the amalgamation of the Kenya and Uganda Railway with the Tanganyika system to form the East African Railways, and the transfer of responsibility for the Posts and Telegraphs to the East Africa High Commission, events which took place between 1947 and 1949, have led to the radical amendment of the original programmes, and indeed intensified development.

No one with any pretensions to knowledge of Tanganyika would be so rash as to maintain that communications of any kind are yet adequate, but equally, no one who knows the difficulties of transport problems in Africa could deny that great steps forward have been made in Tanganyika since the war, as will be recorded in further detail in subsequent sections.

ROADS

The importance of good road communications in Tanganyika, which has a land area six times as great as England and Wales, can hardly be over-stressed. During a phase of rapid economic development, the correct balance of effort both in capacity and in money between communications and other essential needs is never easy to assess. In rough figures £1,000,000 from the annual capital budget of between £5,000,000 and £6,000,000 is now being spent on roads. With about 1,600 miles of railway and 7,000 miles of good and reasonably good roads, the area of 362,688 square miles is still inadequately served. Perhaps £20,000,000 of capital expenditure would raise the principal road links to a satisfactory all-weather standard; but it is clear that a sum of this magnitude cannot be made available rapidly, nor indeed could it be used economically having regard to the general constructional capacity available. A factor which is often disregarded is the recurrent burden of maintenance charges caused by road improvements, which was £775,000 in 1957. It is also seldom realised that bitumen roads are much more expensive to maintain than those with gravel or earth surfaces. The present annual figures per mile are bitumen £330, gravel £210, earth £50–£120.

Against the above restricted background, careful planning and a particularly flexible policy are essential. From 1950 to 1955 building to a high standard on a limited mileage was the policy, and 240 miles of first class road with a stone-base course and an 18-feet wide bituminous surface were built. During this period, a sensational rise in cost per mile to an average of £18,000 led to a radical change in planning. The territory cannot yet afford many roads of that standard, and the present intention is to use stabilized gravel or similar surfaces, while retaining the essentials of good design, such as easy gradients, good lines of sight, sound drainage and adequate bridging. A stretch of 120 miles between Morogoro and Iringa is now complete at this standard at an overall cost of about £10,000 a mile. Other new construction, diversion or improvement is planned at a rather lower standard averaging perhaps £3,000–£5,000 per mile.

Roads are divided into the following categories: territorial main roads (trunk roads), local main roads (the more important feeder roads either to the railway or territorial roads), district roads (less important local links), and township roads (motorable roads within municipalities and major towns). The mileages at the beginning of 1955 under the above categories were as follows:—

Territorial Main Roads	3,517 Miles
Local Main Roads	4,319 Miles
District Roads	11,000 Miles
Dar es Salaam & Townships	490 Miles

In addition, about 8,000 miles of local authority roads were being maintained. These vary from usually passable tracks to quite high standard roads, whose use is largely confined to the inhabitants of a particular area. Of the classified roads, there is an average of one mile of road to every 20 square miles of land.

The intention is to improve and construct, where necessary, territorial main roads in the form of a grid covering the whole country. This grid will consist of four trunk roads from north to south and three from the coastal belt inland to the west. Some sections of these already exist, but other stretches are now either of indifferent standard or requiring a further survey and, in some cases, a complete realignment. It is not intended that these main trunk roads should all be of the same standard throughout, but the general objective is that each stage shall be passable to traffic in all weathers. Many sections will, of course, need a much higher standard, which already exists in a few places. The rate of development of this grid, as well as the location of annual effort, will necessarily depend on factors varying from year to year. A considerable proportion of funds and effort will also have to be applied to the secondary or feeder roads mentioned above. No hard and fast standard can be laid down.

In addition to new construction or realignment, a major effort is being applied to betterment. For many years the work put in on maintenance and improvement to the less important roads was almost all washed away in the annual rains. The policy now is to drain and shape these existing roads, thereby providing permanent improvement while devoting less effort to the actual running surface. The result of this may for a while be less evident to the ordinary motorist, but the long-term results will lead to a generally higher standard.

Maintenance and improvement—and also new construction—have over the past few years been competing with a very rapid rise in traffic. At least ten times as many vehicles use the roads as in 1939; many large lorries are to be seen throughout the country; and the speed of traffic has increased far more than the standard of driving. Heavy vehicles travel at 30 to 40 miles per hour, rapidly developing surface corrugations which, in turn, greatly damage the vehicles increasing their maintenance costs and shortening their working lives.

In general, it can be said that in the race between road development and traffic increase, the road side is at present leading slightly, but no relaxation of progress can be afforded.

RAILWAYS

Central Line

The Central Line runs from Dar es Salaam to Kigoma, a distance of $772\frac{1}{2}$ miles, with a branch line from Tabora to Mwanza, $235\frac{1}{2}$ miles, and a branch line from Kaliuwa to Mpanda, 131 miles.

Construction was commenced in 1905 and the line reached Lake Tanganyika in early 1914. It was metre gauge and well constructed.

The administration of the Tanganyika railway system was taken over from the British Military Authorities by the Tanganyika Government on the 1st April, 1919. Considerable damage had been done to the Central Line when the country was evacuated by the Germans and repair work carried out by the British Military Authorities to enable traffic to resume was necessarily hasty and often in the nature of patchwork. Most of the rolling stock was obsolete by the end of the war and all buildings required renovation. These requirements coincided with a period when money was scarce. For a time traffic was confined to a few stations and revenue was so low that in many cases the receipts were insufficient to pay the wages of the station staff.

The highest point of the line is some 400 miles from Dar es Salaam with an altitude of 4,350 feet above sea level. Kigoma lies at an altitude of 2,500 feet above sea level and is the transhipping point for traffic to and from the Belgian Congo, cargo being transferred to a lake steamer en route for Albertville.

Tabora-Mwanza Branch

The line from Tabora to Mwanza was constructed in the late 1920s and opened to traffic in August, 1928, having taken four years to build. It connects the Central Line with Lake Victoria and the Lake Province and enables the coffee and cotton crops to be evacuated to the coast for shipping from Dar es Salaam. At Mwanza, which is the headquarters of the Lake Province, connection is made with the lake steamers of the Railway Administration which operate on Lake Victoria.

Kaliuwa-Mpanda Branch

The line from Kaliuwa to Mpanda was constructed during the years 1947–1950 to provide an outlet for the mineral deposits worked in the Mpanda area by the Uruwira Minerals Company. Lead is the mineral mined and concentrate is moved from Mpanda on to the Central Line. Since the branch was opened in August, 1950, a considerable quantity of agricultural produce has come out of the area in the immediate vicinity of Mpanda. Throughout its length it traverses dense bush country infested with tsetse fly.

Tanga Line

The Tanga Line, 271½ miles long, connects the port of Tanga with Arusha at the foot of Mt. Meru. It consists of a German-built line from Tanga to Moshi with a length of nearly 218 miles, and a British-built extension from Moshi to Arusha 53½ miles long. The first portion of the line, which links Tanga port with the rich hinterland of Moshi at the foot of Kilimanjaro, was commenced by German private enterprise in 1893. The German Government took over the construction and completed the Tanga/Moshi section in 1911. Although plans for the extension to Arusha were drawn up by the German Authorities the work was not done until 1927 when it was carried out by the Tanganyika Railways Administration and opened to traffic in 1929.

From Moshi there is a direct connection with the Kenya and Uganda Section by way of Kahe and Voi. The Voi/Kahe connection was built by the Military Authorities during the 1914–1918 War to facilitate the advance into German East Africa.

Southern Province Line

The Southern Province Line runs inland from the port of Mtwara to Nachingwea. The line was built between 1947 and 1954 to open up the area around Nachingwea in connection with the activities of the Overseas Food Corporation. It is 131½ miles in length, most of which traverses fertile country. The line runs inland from the new modern port of Mtwara, passing through the coastal fringe which is largely devoted to the growing of sisal. At Ruo (66 miles) it converges on the Lukuledi River whose valley it follows until reaching the terminus at Nachingwea. Since 1952 the object of the line has swung from being complementary to the activities of the Overseas Food Corporation to a general opening up of the Southern Province and its overall potential.

TRAFFIC

The following figures indicate the growth of goods traffic on the railway system of Tanganyika:—

Year	Central Line Tons	Tanga Line Tons	S. Province Line Tons	Combined Tons
1920	30,000 ...	14,000 ...	— ...	44,000
1925	108,000 ...	30,000 ...	— ...	138,000
1930	176,000 ...	73,000 ...	— ...	243,000
1935	157,000 ...	78,000 ...	— ...	235,000
1940	150,000 ...	89,000 ...	— ...	239,000
1945	207,000 ...	148,000 ...	— ...	355,000
1950	406,000 ...	183,000 ...	— ...	589,000
1954	667,000 ...	237,000 ...	55,000* ...	959,000
1955	777,000 ...	354,000 ...	91,000 ...	1,222,000
1956	842,000 ...	408,000 ...	90,000 ...	1,340,000

*From 17th July, 1954 to 31st December, 1954.

On the Tanga and Central Lines sisal is the principal export product and on the Central Line considerable quantities of cattle cake, coffee, oilseeds and cotton are also dealt with.

Typical commodity charges are as follows:—

Commodity	Average Haul miles	Rate per ton Shs. Cts.
Exports—Central Line		
Coffee	780 ...	149 86
Cotton	715 ...	112 45
Cattle Cake	740 ...	53 09
Oilseeds	355 ...	39 42
Sisal	155 ...	42 11
Timber	500 ...	49 95
Exports—Tanga Line		
Sisal	50 ...	20 16

The number of passengers has also increased over the years:—

Year	Central Line	Tanga Line	S. Province Line	Total
1920	76,000 ...	172,000 ...	— ...	248,000
1925	147,000 ...	177,000 ...	— ...	324,000
1930	225,000 ...	314,000 ...	— ...	539,000
1935	209,000 ...	86,000 ...	— ...	295,000
1940	287,000 ...	225,000 ...	— ...	512,000
1945	636,000 ...	888,000 ...	— ...	1,524,000
1950	868,000 ...	1,023,000 ...	— ...	1,891,000
1954	1,157,000 ...	733,000 ...	20,000* ...	1,910,000
1955	1,233,000 ...	627,000 ...	33,000 ...	1,893,000
1956	1,357,000 ...	550,000 ...	42,000 ...	1,949,000

*From 17th July, 1954 to 31st December, 1954.

Since the amalgamation of the Tanganyika Railways and Ports and the Kenya and Uganda Railways and Harbours considerable sums of money have been spent on the acquisition of rolling stock by the E.A.R. & H. Administration for the Tanganyika branch lines. Modern vehicles of all types have been put into service and will undoubtedly raise the standard to that compatible with the interests of the territory and of its traffic potential. The most up-to-date passenger coaches of light aluminium alloy construction have been put into service together with large quantities of goods and livestock vehicles of all types. Out-dated locomotives have been replaced by oil burning engines and the provision of fuelling facilities for this type of locomotive installed.

ROAD SERVICES

The E.A.R. & H. Administration operates extensive road services between the Central Line and the Southern Highlands, two routes being used; one between Dodoma and Mbeya and the other between Itigi and Mbeya. Both passenger and goods vehicles are operated. A service is also provided between Itigi and Singida.

Arusha is served by road from Dodoma and a further connection between the Central and Tanga Lines is provided by a road service between Morogoro and Korogwe.

Lushoto, near the Tanga Line, is served by a lorry service from Mombo, and there is a service for passengers and parcels to Korogwe via Mombo.

The Southern Highlands Road Services connect with buses operating in Northern Rhodesia.

SHIPPING AND STEAMSHIP SERVICES

Tanganyika is well served by shipping lines and the following lines operate services to the territory from the places shown:—

Bank Line	Far East
British India Steam Navigation Co. Ltd	South Africa, India, United Kingdom
Christenson Canadian S.A. Line	Far East
Clan, Hall, Harrison	United Kingdom
Compagnie Maritime Belge	Continent
Deutsch Ost-Afrika Line	Continent
Eastern Shipping Corporation Ltd.	Bombay
Ellerman–City	United States of America
Farrell Line	United States of America
Holland Afrika Lijn	Continent
Indian–African Line	India, Ceylon
L.D. Lines	Gulf and Atlantic Coast
Lloyd Triestino	Continent
Lykes Line	United States of America
Messageries Maritimes	Continent
Nedlloyd Line	United States of America
Oriental African Line	Far East
Robin Line	United States of America
Royal Interocean	Far East
Scandinavian East Africa	Continent
Shaw Saville Line	Australia
Swedish East Africa	Continent
Union Castle Mail Steamship Co. Ltd.	United Kingdom

LIGHTHOUSES

The coast is lighted by lighthouses at Tanga, Dar es Salaam, Ras Kanzi, Mkumbi (Mafia), Fanjove Island and Lindi, the lights of which are all visible for fifteen miles or more.

LAKE SERVICES

The well-equipped steamers of the East African Railways and Harbours Administration maintain a regular weekly service calling at all ports on Lake Victoria and carrying passengers and cargo. A launch service also covers Tanganyika ports at the south end of the lake.

Communications on Lake Tanganyika are maintained by the E.A.R. & H.'s twin-screw steamer *Liemba*, which makes a fortnightly journey down the east side of the lake calling at various ports. This steamer was placed on the lake by the Germans and was known as the *Götzen*. Sunk in Kigoma harbour at the beginning of the 1914–1918 war, she was salvaged in 1924 and reconditioned at a cost of over £20,000. Further extensive reconditioning and alterations were carried out in 1951 and 1952 and she now possesses accommodation for twenty first class passengers and eight second class passengers.

The m.v. *Mwanza* which was reconditioned and powered by diesel engines in 1950 makes a fortnightly journey from Kigoma to Mpulungu at the southern end of the lake and back towing a cargo lighter and carrying a small number of third class passengers; by special arrangement upper class passengers can be carried.

The Grands Lacs Company runs a regular service between Albertville and Kigoma and maintains communications with other lake ports, notably Usumbura, the headquarters of the Belgian Trust territory of Ruanda-Urundi.

On Lake Nyasa there is a steamer service, run by the Federation Railways, connecting Mwaya (Itungi) in the Rungwe District with ports in Nyasaland.

HARBOURS AND WHARVES

In the Port of Dar es Salaam there are three deep water berths with a total length of 1,824 feet, known as the Princess Margaret Quay. There is a minimum depth of water of 30 feet at l.w.o.s.t. alongside. One berth, with an approximate length of 600 feet, was constructed at the expense of the Belgian Government and will be used to handle transit traffic to and from the Belgian Congo and Ruanda-Urundi.

In addition there is a lighterage wharf of 1,929 feet with a minimum of water of 6 feet at all states of the tide. This area is used mainly for exports and coastal steamers are able to moor alongside.

There are no deep water berths at Tanga but a lighterage wharf 1,250 feet long is adequate to handle all cargo.

AIR COMMUNICATIONS

Earlier sections have emphasized the difficulties of surface communication in Tanganyika. The territory is, however, fortunate in the conditions which obtain in the air above it. High winds are exceptional, fog is non-existent, and periods of bad visibility are normally limited to short and intense tropical storms. Such refinements for aircraft as ground controlled approach are unnecessary, although some of the higher aerodromes are difficult to use during certain periods on account of cloud conditions.

24

The rapid advance of civil aviation all over the world has been well matched in Tanganyika, which now has 47 aerodromes and landing strips. The new airport for Dar es Salaam was opened in October 1954 and is of International Class C type. It is designed to take all types of large aircraft which are at all likely to fly through East Africa in the coming years. Provision has also been made for futher expansion if necessary, although it appears that aircraft designers now realise the impracticability of continually demanding longer and stronger runways. The remaining more important aerodromes in the territory are being steadily developed to International Class F Standard, which, in broad terms, provides what is necessary for aircraft of the Dakota type. Additionally, there are a number of landing strips which are suitable for smaller aircraft throughout the year or for larger types during dry conditions. Control of the East African Flight Information Region is exercised by the Directorate of Civil Aviation with Head-quarters in Nairobi and a Regional Representative in Tanganyika. The Directorate operates Air Traffic Control at the three main aerodromes and has flight information services at eight others. The Meteorological Department of the High Commission has observers at the main aerodromes and also makes available continual weather forecasting.

The East African Airways Corporation provides regular and frequent services to all the more important towns in Tanganyika, as well as to Kenya, Uganda and Zanzibar, and a service down the coast to Durban. Weekly tourist services by Canadair aircraft take passengers to London in about 24 hours and to Bombay in about nine hours. Central African Airways operate between Dar es Salaam, Nyasaland and Southern Rhodesia, while Sabena fly to and from the Belgian Congo. Caspair Air Charters also run a regular service around Lake Victoria: the other main charter operator is Messrs. Noon & Pearce.

Some private companies, notably Williamsons Diamonds Ltd., use their own aircraft. The Government has a flight of three Percival Prince machines, whose primary function is air survey; they also, however, are used extensively on transportation work. Additionally, increasing use is being made of aircraft for spraying insecticides, particularly in regard to locust control.

Undoubtedly the most important local organization is the East African Airways Corporation. The figures below demonstrate the growth of this Corporation:—

	1948	1949	1950	1951	1952	1953	1954	1955	1956
Aircraft Mileage ...	1,656,986	1,857,725	2,574,336	2,592,309	2,433,940	2,355,422	2,605,268	2,692,574	3,017,830
Capacity ton-miles offered	859,890	1,620,639	2,554,096	3,364,602	3,839,109	4,395,138	5,643,464	6,702,095	6,930,992
Load ton-miles carried	508,026	844,580	1,338,149	1,885,707	1,869,222	2,198,159	2,880,610	4,057,915	4,052,330
Passengers carried	22,898	36,132	48,699	63,594	65,258	73,062	93,427	98,698	106,162
Cargo (in kilos) ...	209,898	381,081	715,193	937,309	826,547	1,395,797	2,118,337	2,591,000	2,364,000
Mail (in kilos) ...	59,013	76,147	101,942	274,680	190,562	216,674	286,531	357,000	393,000
Gross revenue ...	295,178	473,144	664,450	913,086	959,187	1,069,262	1,176,707	1,357,522	1,524,647

Some of the scheduled routes flown are shown on the map on page 348.

The Corporation now has a fleet of 3 fully pressurized 54 seater Canadairs, 9 D.C.3s and 4 Rapides, and a total staff of over 1,500, and operates to and from 53 stations stretching, as has been shown above, from Durban in the south to London in the north and Bombay in the east. The internal network is very comprehensive; the main stations from Dar es Salaam along the coast to Mombasa have a twice-daily service in each direction. The Southern Province, including the ports of Lindi and Mtwara, have four services a week, while the interior of the territory is also well served.

POSTS AND TELECOMMUNICATIONS

The activities of the Post Office in Tanganyika follow much the same pattern as those of postal and telecommunications administrations in other countries. There is a postal service, a telecommunications service (embracing telegraphs, telephones and radio) and a territorial savings bank. The development of these services over the past twenty-five years has been governed largely by the rate of development and economic position of Tanganyika generally. More recently, however, the expansion of postal and telecommunications services in the territory has gained impetus from the opening up of inland areas due to improvements in other means of communication and also to the vesting of control in a single authority—the East African Posts and Telecommunications Administration—responsible to the territorial Governments through the East Africa High Commission for the administration, co-ordination and development of all P. & T. services in Kenya, Uganda and Tanganyika.

History

When the Government of Tanganyika was constituted under the terms of the Mandate in 1920, a Department of Posts and Telegraphs was set up under a Postmaster-General with headquarters in Dar es Salaam. On the 1st January, 1933, this department was amalgamated with the Department of Posts and Telegraphs, Kenya and Uganda. Control of the new department was vested in a Postmaster-General with headquarters in Nairobi and a Deputy Postmaster-General in charge of Tanganyika. P. & T. headquarters for this territory remained at Dar es Salaam.

The Department of Posts and Telegraphs became an East Africa High Commission Service on the 1st January, 1948. A year later it was made a self-contained service of the East Africa High Commission with its own Capital Account. In 1951 the department was renamed the "East African Posts and Telecommunications Administration".

Post Offices in Tanganyika

There are 91 Departmental Post Offices and 78 Postal Agencies operating in Tanganyika at present. The former provide a full range of services but restricted facilities only are available at Postal Agencies. The growth in the number of offices is clearly shown in the following table:—

Year			Departmental Post Offices		Postal Agencies		Total
1920	...	...	35	...	50	...	85
1925	...	...	44	...	58	...	102
1930	...	...	61	...	65	...	126
1935	...	...	64	...	68	...	132
1940	...	...	58	...	76	...	134
1945			69	...	66	...	135
1950	...	...	72	...	74	...	146
1955	...	...	88	...	76	...	164
1956	...	...	91	...	78	...	169

An alphabetical list of Post Offices with particulars of the business transacted at each is given in the appendix to this chapter on page 359.

Postal Services

A comprehensive range of mail services is provided. Letters, postcards, commercial and printed papers, samples and newspapers are carried and there is also a parcel service for items up to 22 lb. in weight. Facilities are available for registration, cash on delivery, insured and express services for letters and parcels, and for the transmission of money by means of Postal Orders and Money Orders.

Full details of the services available and the rates and charges are given in the "Post Office Guide", a copy of which may be obtained for Shs. 2/50 from any Post Office or by post from the Regional Director, P.O. Box 97, Dar es Salaam, Tanganyika.

Airmail services are available for both letters (first and second class matter) and parcels.

Surface mail is carried by the railways, by the E.A.R. & H. road services and by private bus and transport companies operating under contract with the Post Office. The frequency of despatch of mails depends entirely on the frequency of the transport services available. Mails are despatched to most Post Offices in Tanganyika at least three times a week.

There are daily air mail services between Dar es Salaam, Zanzibar, Tanga and Nairobi and also direct air mail despatches from Dar es Salaam to many up-country offices with a frequency of despatch ranging from once to four times a week. Air mails to the United Kingdom and other foreign countries are despatched daily, either direct or via Nairobi.

Sea mails leave Dar es Salaam at fairly regular intervals of about once every ten days.

Statistics of letters and parcels handled in Tanganyika since 1930 reveal a considerable increase in the amount of correspondence handled over the past seventeen years and provide a reliable indication of the trend of post war development. The increasing literacy of the African population has undoubtedly had a marked bearing on these figures.

Year				Letters		Parcels
1930	...	...	...	5,559,000	...	67,000
1935	...	...	...	4,630,000	...	72,000
1940	...	...	...	3,984,000	...	57,400
1945	...	...	...	13,141,000	...	116,200
1950	...	...	...	16,730,000	...	192,800
1953	...	...	...	21,875,800	...	233,134
1954	...	...	...	20,656,600	...	248,180
1955	...	...	...	21,103,600	...	287,300
1956	...	...	...	25,986,000	...	271,140

The delivery of letters, packets and news items is effected by means of Private Boxes, Private Bags and the *Poste Restante* Service.

A Directory of Private Boxes is published and issued free to box renters. Further copies may be obtained on application to the nearest Post Office or by post from the Regional Director at a cost of Sh. 1/- per copy excluding postage.

Savings Bank

The Savings Bank in Tanganyika is a territorial and not a High Commission service and is managed by the Postmaster-General on behalf of the Tanganyika Government.

The rate of development of the Post Office Savings Bank in Tanganyika over the past 27 years is shown in the following statement:—

Year				Total No. Depositors £		Approximate Totals of Credit Balances £
1930	...	...	...	1,883	...	21,233
1935	...	...	...	5,343	...	73,391
1940	...	...	...	10,130	...	77,657
1945	...	...	...	21,912	...	625,902
1950	...	...	...	59,493	...	1,784,629
1955	...	...	...	86,209	...	2,598,000
1956	...	...	...	94,001	...	2,527,925

Business on these accounts may be conducted at any Cash Account Post Office in East Africa.

E.A. Postage Stamps and Stationery

Postage Stamps are on sale at all Post Offices and Postal Agencies in the following denominations:—

5 cents, 10 cents, 20 cents, 30 cents, 50 cents, 65 cents and Shs. 1/-, 1/30, 2/-, 5/-, 10/- and 20/-.

Stamp booklets are on sale at Sh. 1/- and Shs. 5/- each containing the following stamps:—

	5 cts.		10 cts.		20 cts.		30 cts.		50 cts.
1/- booklet—Contents ...	4	...	8	...	–	...	–	...	–
5/- booklet—Contents ...	4	...	8	...	4	...	4	...	4

Souvenir Stamp Booklets are on sale at Shs. 3/50 and Shs. 42/- each. The 3/50 booklet contains the following denominations of stamps:—

5 cents, 10 cents, 20 cents, 30 cents, 50 cents, 65 cents and Sh. 1/-.

The 42/- booklet contains the following denominations of stamps:—

5 cents, 10 cents, 20 cents, 30 cents, 50 cents, 65 cents and Shs. 1/-, 1/30, 2/-, 5/-, 10/- and 20/-.

Postcards:

Impressed with 10-cent stamp are on sale at 15 cents each.

Impressed with 15-cent stamp are on sale at 20 cents each.

Envelopes:

Embossed with a 20-cent stamp are on sale in two sizes at 25 cents each.

Registered Letter Envelopes:

Embossed with a 40-cent stamp are on sale at 75 cents each.

Unembossed are on sale in two sizes at 20 cents for the smaller and 25 cents for the larger.

Air Letter Forms (Aerogrammes).

Ordinary type forms are on sale at 5 forms for 10 cents.

Forms embossed with a 50 cents stamp are on sale at 50 cents each.

Forms specially printed for Christmas or other similar greetings are sold at 5 cents each.

Stamps and stamped stationery may be purchased at any Post Office. They may be obtained by post from the Postmaster-General, P.O. Box No. 251, Nairobi, Kenya. Applications to this address should be accompanied by a remittance for the full value of the items required plus return postage and registration. Remittances should be made by Bank Draft, Money Order, or Postal Order, made payable to the Postmaster-General, Nairobi.

Telegraph Services

The territory is connected by land lines and radio with Uganda and Kenya to the north and Northern Rhodesia and Nyasaland to the south. Communications with all other countries are available through the Cable and Wireless Company's station in Dar es Salaam. In Tanganyika, telegrams are handled at 197 telegraph offices, including 28 P. & T. radio stations.

Subscribers may rent private telegraph lines to interconnect their offices in certain of the larger towns. A "Printergram" service is also available, under which a subscriber may rent a private telegraph line to the nearest telegraph office.

A ship-to-shore telegraph service is provided at Dar es Salaam and Lindi.

Telephone Services

The Post Office telephone service in Tanganyika covers all the main townships and 51 other centres and has a total of 63 public exchanges capable of serving almost 9,000 subscribers. Of this total 7,026 lines are now in use. The length of wire used in inter-connecting the public exchanges exceeds 10,000 miles. The first automatic exchange in the territory was opened at Dar es Salaam in 1932 and there are now 5 of these exchanges in operation. In addition there are nearly 80 public call offices distributed throughout the territory.

A directory of telephone subscribers is published twice yearly and is issued free to subscribers. Further copies may be obtained by post from the Regional Director, P.O. Box 97, Dar es Salaam, at a cost of Sh. 1/- per copy, excluding postage.

The trunk telephone service has been greatly improved in recent years by the installation, on all the more important routes, of carrier equipment providing for several speech circuits on one pair of wires. The trunk network is continually being extended and the latest addition—a trunk line between Iringa and Mbeya—was brought into service in 1955. Additional speech channels are also being provided on all the more important trunk routes.

An extensive programme of trunk modernization and provision is in progress and several modern automatic exchanges are in course of construction.

A radio telephone service giving connection to most parts of the world is available from any telephone exchange in Tanganyika through the terminal exchange in Nairobi. There is also a ship-to-shore telephone service available to ships within approximately 400 miles of Mombasa.

Miscellaneous Services

In addition to their other services, Post Offices in Tanganyika sell wireless licences (which cost Shs. 10/-) and paludrine.

LIST OF POST OFFICES IN TANGANYIKA

The nature of business transacted at the different classes of Post Offices is shown below. Head and Controlling Post Offices are printed in capital letters.

(A)—indicates a Departmental Post Office which provides a full range of facilities.

(B)—indicates a Departmental Sub-Post Office which provides limited services only, that is, sale of stamps, sale and encashment of postal orders, collection and delivery of ordinary and registered correspondence, including parcels, and the acceptance and delivery of telegrams and cablegrams.

(C)—denotes a Postal Agency which provides the limited services indicated above excluding the acceptance and delivery of telegrams and cablegrams.

(A) Amani	(C) Kirando	(A) Mufindi
(A) ARUSHA†	(C) Kisangiro	(A) Muheza†
(C) Babati	(C) Kiwira	(A) Musoma†
(A) Bagamoyo†	(A) Kondoa-Irangi	(C) Mwadui Mine
(C) Bahi	(A) Kongwa†	(C) Mvumi
(C) Bariadi	(A) Korogwe†	(A) MWANZA†
(C) Berega	(A) Kyela	(A) Nachingwea†
(C) Bereko	(C) Lembeni	(A) Nansio
(A) Biharamulo	(C) "Liemba" (Lake Steamer)	(C) Nassa
(C) Buiko	(A) LINDI†	(C) Ndanda
(A) Bukene	(C) Liuli	(A) Newala
(A) BUKOBA†	(C) Loliondo	(A) Ngara
(C) Bukwimba	(C) Lohumbo	(C) Ngare Nanyuki
(C) Chimala	(A) Lushoto†	(A) Ngerengere
(A) Chunya†	(C) Mabama	(C) Ngombezi
(A) DAR ES SALAAM†	(A) Mafia	(A) Ngomeni
(A) D.S.M. Airport B.O.	(C) Magu	(C) Ngudu
(A) D.S.M. Market place B.O.	(A) Mahenge	(C) Nguruka
(A) D.S.M. Sultan St. B.O.	(C) Makanya	(A) Njombe
(A) DODOMA†	(C) Makuyuni	(A) Nzega†
(C) Fela	(C) Malampaka	(A) Oldeani
(A) Geita	(A) Malangali	(C) Oldonyo Sambu
(C) Gulwe	(C) Malongwe	(A) Pangani
(A) Handeni	(A) Malya	(C) Peramiho
(C) Hedaru	(B) Manda	(C) Pongwe
(C) Himo	(C) Mantare	(C) Pugu
(A) Ifakara	(A) Manyoni	(A) Ruvu
(A) Ifunda	(C) Marangu	(A) Same
(C) Igalula	(A) Masasi	(A) Sanya Juu
(A) IRINGA†	(A) Maswa	(B) Sao Hill
(C) Isaka	(C) Maurui	(C) Saranda
(C) Itigi	(C) Mazinde	(C) Seke
(A) John's Corner	(C) Mbamba Bay	(A) Shinyanga†
(A) Kahama†	(A) MBEYA†	(C) Sikonge
(C) Kahe	(C) Mbinga	(A) Singida
(C) Kaliuwa	(B) Mbosi	(C) Soga
(A) Kamachumu	(A) Mbulu	(A) Songea
(C) Karagwe	(C) Mikese	(A) Soni
(C) Karatu	(A) Mikindani†	(A) Sumbawanga
(C) Karema	(A) Mingoyo†	(A) TABORA†
(C) Karumwa	(C) Missungwi	(C) Tandala
(A) Kasanga	(C) Mkata	(A) TANGA†
(A) Kasulu	(C) Mkomasi	(A) Tanga, Ngamiani B.O.
(A) Kibondo	(C) Mkumbara	(A) Tarime
(C) Kidete	(C) Mlalo	(C) Tengeni
(A) Kidugallo	(A) Mnyusi	(A) Tukuyu†
(A) Kigoma†	(A) Mohoro	(C) Tunduma
(B) Kigombe	(A) Mombo	(A) Tunduru
(C) Kigwe	(A) Monduli	(C) Ugalla River
(C) Kihuhwi	(A) MOROGORO†	(A) Ujiji
(C) Kikombo	(A) MOSHI†	(A) Urambo
(A) Kilosa†	(A) Mpanda	(A) Usa River
(A) Kilwa Kivinje	(A) Mpwapwa†	(C) Usoke
(A) Kilwa Masoko†	(C) Mtotohovu	(A) Utete
(A) Kimamba	(C) Mto-wa-Mbu	(C) Uvinza
(C) Kintinku	(A) Mtwara†	(C) Uwemba

†Denotes an office authorized to conduct Postal Insurance business.

Transporting cut sisal to the factory.

Photo: Public Relations Department

Mining: Sluicing and hand panning cassiterite.

Photo: Public Relations Department

Chapter 10
NATURAL RESOURCES

A full description of the natural resources of the country has been given in "Tanganyika: A Review of its Resources and their Development", the contents table of which is given at pages 531 to 540 to assist those seeking further information and wishing to refer to it. All that is attempted here is a brief statement containing the essential minimum of information to enable the reader to appreciate the nature of the problems now being tackled in Tanganyika and the plans for the future.

First then, the size of the country should be noted. It is commonly forgotten, even by those who live here, that Tanganyika covers such a vast area—232,000,000 acres. It takes two days and two nights to travel by train from Dar es Salaam to Mwanza on Lake Victoria or to Kigoma on Lake Tanganyika. And within its borders are to be found every variety of climate and soil, from the humid heat of the coast to the snow and ice of Kilimanjaro and from the barren scrub lands of parts of Masailand to the rich volcanic soils of the highlands.

Next, the distribution of the population should be noted. This is well shown by the map on page 283. It will be seen that, generally speaking, the areas near the coast are not so thickly populated as the highland areas or as the area around Lake Victoria—where nearly a quarter of the whole population lives. This emphasizes the importance of communications and the necessity for high-priced economic crops if exports from these thickly-populated but remote areas are to reach the coast and still find a market. As regards the very uneven distribution of the population, it should be remembered that the important factors are not solely the availability of fertile land and of an adequate rainfall, but also the distribution of that rainfall—whether well spread over the year or concentrated into a few months—and the presence or absence of the tsetse fly. People naturally tend to be found where living conditions—by local standards—are easiest, and such conditions often exist in places off the main lines of communication, where the cultivation of food crops is easy but the selection of a suitable economic crop presents a problem.

It has been the location of the people on the land that has, to a great extent, dictated the direction of the lines of communication. It is true that the Central Line was pushed through largely uninhabited country in its western half principally for strategic reasons, but the Tanga Line and most of the roads were made to connect centres of population with each other. They are only now being altered to become modern arteries of commerce and here again it is essential to remember the distances they traverse.

Agriculture is the mainstay of the country's economic life, but it is sometimes forgotten that it is not agriculture of the kind common in Europe or North America. There are not four seasons but two, the rainy season and the dry season. When it rains it pours, but during the dry season, *every year*, no rain falls for months on end. These are the "seasonal" aspects of the annual agricultural cycle—a cycle quite different from that which obtains in a temperate climate. Generally speaking the soils are not infertile, indeed it is astonishing to see what apparently barren land can produce when it is properly tilled and the rainfall has been well distributed. Land which has become exhausted by over-cropping will not of course produce food crops even under optimum conditions of rainfall, but for the rest it is the distribution of the rain over the rainy season that matters so vitally. The rainfall in the comparatively arid Ugogo area of the Central Province is just over 20 inches a year, which is marginal, and means that in some years there are food shortages. Yet this is the same rainfall as Kent receives—the garden of England! The difference is in the distribution and in the intensity of the rain when it does come; "the gentle rain from heaven" is comparatively unknown except in the mountain ranges. It is therefore fortunate for the agriculture of the territory that the average rainfall is between 30 and 40 inches annually. This means that self-sufficiency in food supplies can be achieved and that all sorts of economic crops can be grown. The country can indeed be highly productive agriculturally, but it is necessary to appreciate the peculiar local circumstances which condition such productivity.

African farming in these local circumstances has been subsistence agriculture by means of shifting cultivation, the natural form of agriculture where there is no shortage of land and where economic crops are not grown. It is essential to bear in mind that this is the traditional system when one is considering ways and means to improve African farming and to introduce or increase the cultivation of economic crops. Whereas the staple food crops such as millet, sorghum, bananas, cassava and even maize are comparatively hardy and require only a minimum amount of care, greater effort is required to grow economic crops such as cotton, coffee, rice and tobacco successfully. It is sometimes forgotten that the effort required will only be expended if the African himself considers that it is worth while. He often prefers leisure, with just enough to eat, to dull toil and bursting food bins. For many, money has not the attraction the non-African assumes it to have, and once a certain sum to cover immediate needs has been obtained little desire for more is evinced. This attitude may be almost incomprehensible to the western mind but it is not uncommon and where it exists it makes the development of the country agriculturally rather more difficult than it might otherwise be.

The immigrant farmer's problems have been of another kind but, by and large, he has been successful in his efforts to find crops suited to local conditions and in applying scientific knowledge to their production. The outstanding example is of course sisal, a crop eminently suited to withstand the droughts which may be expected in the lowlands where it is grown and which is now showing the results of the years of research which have been spent on it. But much the same can be said of most of the other economic crops grown by non-Africans, and the continued successful production of, for example, coffee, tea, wheat, seed beans, sugar, pyrethrum and papain is a tribute to the ability of these farmers to cope successfully with the vagaries of the two-season year and with the other trials of tropical farming, such as pests and plant diseases.

There are some six million cattle and about the same number of small stock in the country, but these are even more unevenly distributed than the population. The vast majority is African-owned and the immigrant communities have not as yet taken to ranching except in a few instances, although there is considerable scope for ranching in the country. Certain tribes—the Masai, for example—are cattle-owners *tout simple* and cultivate not at all; others, such as the Gogo, combine agriculture with cattle-keeping; still others, such as nearly all the tribes in the Southern Province, do not keep cattle but have sheep and goats. The attitude of the cattle-owners to their beasts varies from the almost mystical attitude of the Masai to the indifference of the Fipa of the Western Province, who have taken to keeping cattle only of comparatively recent years. But all cattle-owners tend to prefer quantity to quality and few realise—although realization is growing—the special value of manure in agriculture. It is against this background that attempts to introduce better methods of farming and animal husbandry must be seen.

It has only to be stated that the closed forests of the country occupy some 4,000 sq. miles out of a total dry land area of 338,325 sq. miles for the paucity of forest cover to be seen. Nevertheless this statement, without further qualification, is misleading, for, as was pointed out on page 5, although the true forests are so small the greater part of the country is wooded, often well wooded. The large areas shown on the population map facing page 306 as virtually unoccupied are the regions to the south of Tabora and to the east of Kilwa. These two huge blocks, which between them cover nearly half the land area of the territory, contain *miombo* woodland for the most part (but are badly watered and infested with tsetse fly). In other parts of the country thickets and savannahs are to be found but there are no true deserts. In one large region—Sukumaland—there is a marked absence of trees, but this scarcity is man-made and is because the Sukuma consider that trees bring birds, which eat their grain crops. They are now being persuaded to grow a certain number of trees for fuel and for building poles, but their attitude dies hard. Generally speaking, the necessity to preserve trees, and the effects of forest cover on water supply, are not appreciated by the indigenous inhabitants, nor is this surprising when it is remembered that the destruction of trees is an essential part of the system of shifting cultivation. Nevertheless plantations are being extended and more forest reserves demarcated every year.

Little attention has until recently been paid to fisheries, but this omission is now being rectified and a three-fold study is being made of the country's fish resources: the coastal fishing, carried on almost entirely by local fishermen from out-rigger canoes, is being investigated, so is the fishing in Lakes Victoria and Tanganyika, and experiments are being made with fish-ponds in certain places inland. Dried fish has always been an article of commerce in the territory and the extension of this trade—as well as the expansion of the trade in fresh fish—will help to supply the local population with much-needed protein. With a coastline of some 500 miles and some 20,000 sq. miles of inland open water it will be appreciated that the potentialities are enormous.

When the vast size of the country is remembered it will not seem strange that its mineral potentialities are only now beginning to be developed. These already are very considerable and the more important mineral occurrences have been noted in the descriptions of the eight provinces. The country contains over eighty million tons of coal and a whole mountain of iron, in addition to its diamonds, lead, gold, tin, mica, silver, tungsten, salt, copper, gypsum, kaolin, magnesite and other minerals of (as yet) lesser importance. The area to the east of Lake Tanganyika is known to be highly mineralized and is now being closely examined. There are many other areas in the country which have not been carefully prospected. With the improvement in communications that is going on steadily over the years, the examination of promising areas and the establishment of an office in Dodoma by the United Kingdom Atomic Energy Authority, considerable development of the mining industry in the territory may be expected.

There are other natural resources also, but it is not necessary to list them all here. What may be essayed instead is some appreciation of the prospects of a successful outcome of the efforts now being made to develop the country. Its size, the vagaries of climate and the conservative attitude of the population towards change have been mentioned. But these obstacles to progress are being overcome. New road links, and better alignments and greatly improved surfaces on the existing roads, new railways, extended air services, are all helping to make communications better, surer and faster. Experience, backed by scientific study and research, is making tropical farming more certain and the farmer more independent of an unpredictable rainfall. Institutions such as the Natural Resources School at Tengeru and the cotton research station at Ukiriguru are spreading knowledge of better farming practices.

There are other assets. Although in some areas congestion of the human and cattle populations is causing concern and special measures have to be taken to deal with the situation, on the whole the habitable part of the country is not over-crowded and there is room for expansion. Rainfall is being conserved, and water being made available, on a territory-wide scale and to an increasing extent. The lessons of successful experiments in the mechanization of African agriculture are being applied. The benefits of co-operative enterprise are now appreciated and the system is spreading. While there are seasonal and local labour shortages these have never reached chronic proportions nor is it likely that the development of the country will be ham-strung for lack of labour. The territory's economy is many-sided, not only are its agricultural products varied but they are supplemented by a growing volume of animal and mineral products. Its industrial possibilities are considerable and the growth of secondary industries has been remarkable of recent years. Finally, and not of least importance, it may be noted that the policy of the Government is to develop simultaneously the country's natural resources, its social services and its political organizations, so that a one-sided economy does not result but rather a natural, vigorous and healthy growth, firmly rooted and recognisably Tanganyikan. The excellent relations which exist between the three main races make it possible to pursue this policy with some hope of success.

Chapter 11

SOCIAL SERVICES

Under the control of the Minister for Social Services come the Education, Medical, Labour and Prisons Departments. He is also responsible for the Probation Service. The Minister for Local Government and Administration is responsible for the Social Development Department.

EDUCATION

History of African Education

Under the German educational system Africans received education both in Government and Mission schools, the number of pupils in attendance at the principal Government schools before the 1914–18 War being about 2,500, while some 3,700 pupils attended the Government elementary schools. There were also about 110,000 African children on the registers of the 1,800 schools conducted by missionary societies. The teaching staff of the German Education Department was composed of 16 European and 159 African teachers.

Education facilities practically came to an end during the 1914–18 war and owing to the dispersal of teachers there were no foundations on which to build the new educational structure when the first Director of Education was appointed in 1920. The Phelps-Stokes Mission to East Africa in 1924 led, amongst other things, to the establishment of the Colonial Office Advisory Committee on Education. It was as a result of the Command Paper of 1925 issued by that Committee that a special conference was held in Dar es Salaam to draft a Bill giving effect to a State scheme of African education with regulations governing a system of grants-in-aid for approved Voluntary Agencies.

As from that date greatly increased financial provision was made and until 1931 the work of the department advanced rapidly. The financial crisis of that year unfortunately brought to an end the era of expansion and very severe reductions in expenditure followed. The educational system had hardly begun to recover during the years 1936–39 when the outbreak of war again brought an end to expansion. By the end of 1945 the department was reduced to a skeleton staff and it was not until the conclusion of hostilities that staff could again be recruited on an appreciable scale.

In 1947 a plan for African Education was formulated to cover the next ten years and was approved by the Legislature, being revised in some of its aspects in 1950.* The purpose of this plan as revised was to provide for three stages in schooling:

Standards I to IV, Primary; Standards V to VIII, Middle;

Standards IX to XII, Secondary.

During the period of this plan the two senior secondary standards were concentrated at Tabora, provincial secondary schools being developed to cover standards VII to X until the number of pupils justified their expansion to full secondary status. The plan also provided for primary education of 36 per cent of children of school age—or some 310,000—and for 200 middle schools for boys and 32 middle schools for girls. At the time of writing the achievement of these targets

---

*A draft five-year plan for African Education 1957–61 was produced in 1956 (available from the Government Printer, Dar es Salaam).

has been surpassed and in the next planning period it is intended to increase the number of middle schools and, where possible, to provide additional primary classes to prevent the use of double sessions, these having been a necessary feature of the rapid expansion undertaken in the 1947–56 period.

Teacher Training

The provision of sufficient teacher training facilities forms the basis of all educational expansion. Teachers are classified as Grade I and Grade II, Grade I having passed the Standard X Territorial Examination and had two years' teacher training, Grade II being Standard VIII with two years' teacher training. There are three teacher training centres for Grade I men, (one Government and two Voluntary Agency), and two for women, (one Government and one Voluntary Agency). The Government Grade I and Grade II teacher training centres are situated at Mpwapwa whither it is intended to move the Grade I women's course and to establish the base for an Institute of Education. In Grade II there are two multi-streamed centres run by Government and twelve by Voluntary Agencies. A feature of the teacher training programme is the running of refresher courses each year and certain selected teachers are sent to the United Kingdom for further training in recognized courses.

Organization and Legislation

While all educational facilities come under the control of the Director of Education, the developments achieved could never have been undertaken without the wholehearted co-operation of the voluntary agencies. Two-thirds of the schools are under their management. The third partner and one which is destined to become of increasing influence and importance is the Native Authorities who at present share with voluntary agencies the provision of primary and middle schools in rural areas, Government accepting special responsibility in urban areas. In certain progressive districts, notably Bukoba, girls' middle schools have been built outside the terms of the Education Plan and are financed wholly from Native Authority revenues.

The legislation covering education is contained in Cap. 71 of the Laws and in subsidiary legislation. All schools and teachers have to be registered by the Director of Education, the register being divided into two parts. The first part is for primary schools and higher standards of education, while schools giving instruction of a lower level than the full primary course, previously known as bush schools, are included in Part II. The latter are not eligible for grants-in-aid but these are paid to Part I schools both for capital and recurrent expenditure under the terms set out in the Grants-in-Aid Rules. These grants have been increased over the years and staff grants for all African teachers now provide the full amount of their salaries which are equivalent to those paid in Government service.

Technical Education

One trade school has been established at Ifunda to provide a three-year training course in the building and engineering trades, the standard of entrance being Standard VIII. This course is followed by two years' "on-training" in industry. A second trade school was opened in 1957 at Moshi in the Northern Province to provide similar training. A multi-racial technical institute is nearing completion in Dar es Salaam which will provide full time courses, evening classes and "sandwich" courses.

Natural Resources School

The Natural Resources School opened at Tengeru near Arusha in 1953 is an interesting experiment in bringing together in one school junior officers of the Natural Resources Departments—veterinary, agriculture and forests—who will be engaged in teaching adults in rural areas the arts of good husbandry, together with trained teachers who require further instruction in agriculture and will, of course, teach African children on return to their teaching duties.

Higher Education

The progress of the Education Plan is shown by the increasing number of students entering the East African University College, Makerere, which in 1957 had 182 Tanganyika students studying arts and science, together with the professional courses of agriculture, veterinary and medicine. In 1956 the Royal Technical College in Nairobi was opened and advanced technological training is now available in East Africa.

In 1957, under a Government scholarship scheme, 47 candidates were selected for training in the United Kingdom. Of this number 33 were Africans, 3 Europeans and 11 Asians. Ten were taking degree courses, the others courses in teacher training, co-operatives or nursing.

A post-secondary bursary scheme was inaugurated in 1953, and under the revised conditions of award published in 1954, provision was made for the annual award from the bursaries fund of one bursary to meet the full cost of a University Degree course, together with the grants of smaller amounts to assist deserving candidates of all races.

European and Indian Education

Before the 1914–18 war there was no provision for the education of Indian children in Tanganyika. It was not until the latter part of the 1920's that the foundation of the present Government and grant-aided school system was laid, Government assuming responsibility in 1929 for the Indian schools in Dar es Salaam and Tanga. From the end of the German regime until 1925 the only schools for European children were three assisted schools in the Arusha District for South African Dutch children and, indeed, up to the outbreak of the 1939–45 war little provision was made for European children's education. On the outbreak of war, however, there was a demand for European children to be educated locally, and this has steadily increased. A school at Mbeya was taken over by Government, while a second school at Lushoto was run as an Assisted School. In 1943 an agreement was reached with the Kenya Government for a number of European children to be admitted to Kenya schools and in 1945 the Church Missionary Society school at Arusha also came under the management of the Education Department, which was responsible for the running of Government schools until 1949.

Reorganization and Legislation

In 1949 new legislation was introduced establishing two Education Authorities, one Indian and one European, with the Director of Education as chairman and the Assistant Director of Education as secretary, with twelve nominated representatives in the case of European education and fourteen for Indian education. At the same time separate Education Funds were established which, subject to the control of the Legislature, are used to finance recurrent education expenditure, revenue being derived from school fees, Non-Native Education Tax and a Government contribution. A special fund was set up for other Non-Native Education, (i.e. for non-natives other than Europeans or Indians) which now includes Goan education, and this is administered by the Director of Education with the assistance of a representative Advisory Committee.

Since that date the educational system for Europeans and Asians has been administered by the Department of Education in accordance with the policy of the European or Indian Education Authority as the case may be. Both systems comprise Government and Assisted Schools, the latter receiving grants-in-aid of the order of two-thirds of capital and recurrent expenditure.

European Education

There are two Government European Primary Boarding schools, one at Arusha and one at Mbeya; at Lushoto and Sao Hill, near Iringa, there are Assisted Schools; while at Soni, near Lushoto, there is an unassisted primary boarding school run by the Rosminian Fathers. A co-educational primary and secondary school is housed temporarily at Kongwa until the two new schools, St. George's for boys and St. Michael's for girls, now being built at Iringa in the Southern Highlands Province, are completed. Each school will provide for 400 secondary pupils in the first instance, with the possibility of extension up to 600. Junior European schools have been established in Dar es Salaam, Dodoma and Moshi, and there are private assisted schools in the majority of provincial centres catering for children up to the age of eight, after which they continue their education at one of the boarding schools. Until full secondary education facilities have been developed parents may receive assistance towards the cost of educating their children in secondary schools outside Tanganyika.

Indian Education

There is a higher proportion of Indian assisted schools than is the case in European education. These comprise Indian Public Schools, Ismaili Schools run by the Aga Khan Schools Administration and a small number managed by other communities. Owing to the wider distribution of schools for Indian children, there are no Indian boarding schools, but hostels are run by the individual communities where there is a demand for such facilities.

There are no post-secondary educational institutions in the territory, but non-natives are eligible to enter Makerere and the Royal Technical College, Nairobi, under the same conditions as African students, and may apply for bursaries.

Other Non-Native Education

In the "Other Non-Native" school system there are no Government schools. St. Joseph's Convent, Dar es Salaam, provides education for non-natives of all races up to School Certificate standard, and receives assistance from the three Education funds. The Goan community has built its own school in the vicinity of Dar es Salaam with the assistance of grants-in-aid, and other schools are run as Assisted Schools.

MEDICAL SERVICES

Departmental Organization. The Medical Department is broadly, responsible for providing, directly or indirectly, a balanced curative and preventive medical service covering the entire country through the medium of a network of

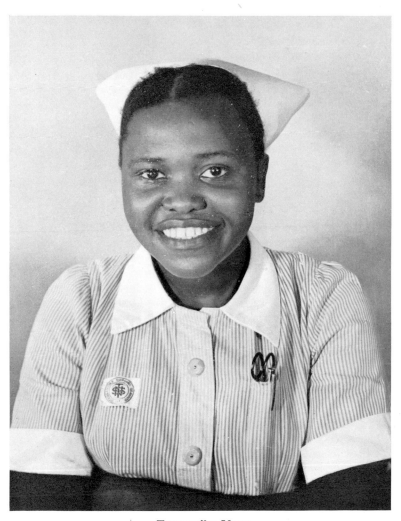

Tanganyika Nurse.

Photo: Public Relations Department

A Hindu teacher.

Photo: Shell Co.

hospitals and dispensaries and public health services in each district. It provides hospitals for special purposes such as for the treatment of leprosy, tuberculosis, infectious disease and for maternity. It provides a laboratory and dental and other ancillary medical services. It undertakes the training of medical, nursing and public health personnel. It subsidizes and co-ordinates much of the medical and medical training work of missionary organizations. It supervises and co-ordinates the medical and public health services provided by local native administrations. Its community health services include rural and urban sanitation, the prevention and control of communicable disease, hygiene of schools, the medical supervision of employed labour (in co-operation with the Labour Department) and health education.

The functions of the staff of the Medical Department may be classified under the following headings:—

    1. Administrative.

    2. General hospital services.

    3. Public health services.

    4. Stores and pharmaceutical services.

    5. Specialist services:

        Tuberculosis, Sleeping Sickness, Leprosy, Malaria, Mental, Child Health, Industrial Health Education, Dental, Laboratory, X-ray, Medical Education.

The Director of Medical Services is the principal medical adviser to the Government, and is responsible for the organization and administration of the Medical Department. His headquarters are in Dar es Salaam.

For administrative purposes the territory is divided into eight provinces, each of which is under the charge of a Regional Assistant Director of Medical Services or a Senior Medical Officer.

Subject to conformity with Government medical policy, the officer in medical charge of each province is responsible to the Director for all medical and public health services provided by the central Government and by local authorities within his province. He also advises the Director of Medical Services in connexion with mission and other non-Government medical agencies in receipt of Government financial assistance and assists in the co-ordination of the services provided by these agencies and those provided by Government. He advises Provincial Commissioners on health affairs and is a member of the provincial team or council.

District medical officers are appointed to local areas, usually administrative districts or groups of districts. They are responsible to the Senior Medical Officer in charge of the province for the organization and supervision of all curative and preventive medical services maintained, sponsored or financed by the central and local Governments within that area. The District Medical Officer is usually responsible for the district hospital or hospitals and their satellite dispensaries and, with the assistance of health inspectors, for all public health work within his area. It is the duty of the District Medical Officer to co-operate with and advise administrative and other departmental officers and also non-Government medical agencies in every aspect of work bearing on health. He is a member of the local district team of which the District Commissioner is chairman.

In the present state of development of the territory a clear distinction cannot be drawn between the curative and preventive medical services. Preventive services can only be built up effectively on a framework of curative medicine, and public confidence and co-operation in preventive medicine can only be secured by the attraction of curative facilities. But most of the diseases for which treatment is sought in this country are essentially preventable. For this reason, the duties of the majority of the members of the medical staff are concerned both with the prevention and the cure of disease. Medical officers of health are appointed specifically to the municipality of Dar es Salaam and the township of Tanga. In other townships district medical officers undertake the functions of medical officers of health. There is also a port health officer in Dar es Salaam. The department provides a staff of health inspectors who, under the direction of district medical officers and medical officers of health, perform public health duties of all kinds in urban and rural areas.

The pharmaceutical section of the department consists of a chief pharmacist, chief storekeeper, five pharmacists and a stores accountant with a staff of stores assistants. The medical stores and pharmaceutical laboratory supply drugs, medical and surgical materials, etc., for all government and native authority medical units, and purchases from the stores may be made by medical missions.

The central Government medical laboratory is located in Dar es Salaam under the control of a senior pathologist who is also responsible for the organization of a laboratory service which extends to the main district hospitals. The functions of the laboratory service include diagnostic pathology, bacteriology and research into clinical and epidemiological problems. It also includes the training of laboratory assistants. The central laboratory is staffed by two pathologists and three laboratory superintendents.

The staff of the dental division includes a senior dental surgeon and five other dental surgeons, a senior and one dental mechanic. Fully equipped dental units are maintained in Dar es Salaam, Tanga, Mwanza and Mbeya. The senior dental surgeon and members of his staff make periodic visits to the main centres of population not yet provided with static dental units, and local arrangements are made whereby persons entitled to dental treatment, free or at reduced rates, can utilize the services of local non-government dental practitioners.

Medical Services Outside Government. There are several missions engaged in medical work in the territory, some of which have been established since before the days of the German occupation. In 1956, missions maintained 34 hospitals with resident qualified doctors and 69 other medical units with accommodation for in-patients, as well as many out-patient dispensaries.

The work of the medical missions is given practical recognition through a system of Government grants-in-aid. These grants, which are based primarily on the numbers of qualified medical and nursing staff employed, have helped the missions to expand and improve their medical services. The amount expended by Government on grants has increased from £8,981 in 1947 to £106,128 paid in hospital and training grants during the financial year 1956/57. In addition, many Native Authorities are now subsidizing mission dispensaries which formerly received grants from the central Government.

A number of mission hospitals train nurses and midwives or ancillary medical staff to the Government syllabus for standard territorial certificates and receive grants-in-aid for this purpose.

In 1957 industrial organizations and estates maintained 21 hospitals with resident doctors and 270 dispensaries or first aid posts of varying sizes.

Charitable dispensaries, nursing homes and maternity centres have been established by several communities for the benefit of their members. Foremost among these are the services provided by the Ismaili community, who employ doctors to serve dispensaries maintained in several of the large towns. A few nursing homes run by private practitioners are maintained in Dar es Salaam and other main centres.

International and Regional Co-operation. The Government of Tanganyika co-operates with neighbouring East African Governments in promoting research into the prevention and control of various communicable diseases, and experts have been appointed on an inter-territorial basis to advise the East African Governments on malaria and leprosy control. The Tanganyika Medical Department provides assistance to the Government of Zanzibar in the supply of drugs and equipment.

Representative Bodies. The British Empire Leprosy Relief Association affords assistance by seconding, at its own expense, European staff amounting to six trained European workers to Government and mission leprosaria in the territory and has provided approximately £10,000 for the construction of a new native authority leprosarium in the Southern Province. The Tanganyika branch of the British Red Cross donated £15,000 towards the erection of a hospital at the Makete Leprosarium in the Southern Highlands Province. But by far the most extensive non-government contributions to the health services of the territory are the numerous hospitals and dispensaries provided and maintained by the various mission organizations to which reference has already been made.

Hospitals. Government hospitals or bedded dispensaries are available to all sections of the community in the towns and rural areas. There are district hospitals in the majority of the administrative districts and a larger hospital at each provincial headquarters. More elaborate hospital facilities including specialist services which are available to patients from all over the territory are provided in Dar es Salaam. Sixty-seven general hospitals and bedded dispensaries are maintained by Government. In all, 6,017 beds are provided in Government hospitals.

Dispensaries. There are 565 dispensaries in the territory maintained by local authorities. It is the aim to develop progressively the rural dispensary system to a higher standard of efficiency, with special emphasis on preventive services, environmental and personal, and to integrate it increasingly closely with the hospital services provided by the central Government. Distances and shortage of medical staff make adequate supervision in many of the rural dispensaries impossible and the mission doctors co-operate wherever possible with Government staff by arranging to make regular visits to rural dispensaries within range of the mission hospitals to which they are posted.

Medical Practice. Before being permitted to practise medicine in the territory medical practitioners must be registered or licensed under the provisions of the Medical Practitioners and Dentists Ordinance, 1952. All persons holding qualifications entitling them to registration by the General Medical Council in the United Kingdom are eligible for registration in Tanganyika, and the Tanganyika Medical Board, appointed under the Ordinance, assesses the standard of qualifications of other applicants. In accordance with the revised Ordinance which became law during 1952, all medical practitioners before they can be registered must satisfy the Board that they have acquired post-graduate experience of such nature, extent and duration as may be prescribed in regulations made by the Governor-in-Council. The registration and licensing of dentists is also controlled under the Medical Practitioners and Dentists Ordinance, and the Tanganyika Medical Board is responsible for assessing for this purpose the standard of qualifications entitling them to registration as dentists in the United Kingdom. At the end of 1957 there were 467 doctors and 33 dentists registered or licensed in Tanganyika. The Medical Practitioners and Dentists (Amendment) Ordinance (No. 17 of 1953) provided for the registration as medical practitioners of graduates of the Makerere College Medical School.

LABOUR

Africans perform unskilled, semi-skilled and skilled work; the more highly skilled craftsmen are usually Europeans and Asians. Approximately 440,000 Africans are in paid employment, the majority of whom (over 200,000) are engaged in agriculture, the most important single branch of which is sisal, employing over 140,000 men, women and children. Over 100,000 are engaged in Government, East Africa High Commission and Local Authority services. Other principal employing groups are mining, timber, transport and manufacturing.

During post-war years the demand for labour—both skilled and unskilled—has increased. Unemployment in the European sense of the term hardly exists in Tanganyika, as only a small proportion of the population is dependent solely upon wage-earning employment for its livelihood. A high proportion of the unskilled labour force is of a migratory character, which often travels long distances to seek employment. Whilst the majority of labour engages itself voluntarily at the place of employment, a proportion is recruited in districts which are generally situated far from the employment areas. Such recruitment is carried out by private employers, organizations of employers or by professional recruiters operating under a system of licences issued by the Labour Commissioner. Recruitment is either prohibited or controlled in certain areas to prevent the spread of disease, particularly sleeping sickness.

Skilled and semi-skilled labour is catered for by employment exchanges which are established at Dar es Salaam, Morogoro, Kilosa, Dodoma, Tabora, Mwanza, Tanga, Korogwe, Moshi, Arusha, Iringa, Mbeya and Lindi, where labour officers are stationed. Sub-Exchanges are also established at Bukoba, and Mtwara. Recently the scope of these exchanges has been extended to include the placing of domestic servants and unskilled labour. They not only cater for African workers but for members of all races, irrespective of occupation. The service is gaining popularity among both employers and workers and a modern central employment exchange to meet the needs of the large urban population in Dar es Salaam was opened in 1953.

The present Government policy regarding the degree of encouragement to be given to the African seeking paid employment is to induce him to contribute either directly or indirectly to the economic wealth of the territory. This will entail his producing, or assisting to produce, something more than the crop of local foodstuffs that he requires for the sustenance of himself and his family at home. This does not mean that he must necessarily produce exportable crops, for not only is industry and mining enterprise assuming greater importance each year, but the need for increasing production of foodstuffs for internal consumption is also increasing. Labourers are encouraged to take their families with them in order that family units may be preserved.

Labour may be employed on various kinds of contract, the most common being

   (i) daily casual rates,

  (ii) monthly contracts,

 (iii) labour cards or "ticket" (*Kipande*) contracts requiring the performance of up to thirty days work within a stipulated period but not exceeding forty-two days,

 (iv) long term contracts up to three years' duration.

In the case of (iv) if the contract is for more than six months it must be in writing. Contracts may be made for more than two years but only if the worker's family accompanies him. The maximum period of service is, in any case, three years. The normal contract is from nine to twelve labour cards of thirty working days.

Where an employee is engaged at a place other than the place of employment the employer is responsible for the transport and welfare of the worker to and from the place of work.

Employers are required to provide housing for their servants in circumstances where they cannot normally return to their homes at night, and minimum standards for housing, sanitary arrangements and the medical care of servants have been laid down. Rations under certain prescribed conditions must be issued at the expense of the employer and must be on the scale prescribed, the cost of which averages between Shs. 25/- and Shs. 30/- a month.

The Labour Department has been established with the object, among other things, of advising both employers and workers on all matters concerning employment; of supervising the operation of labour legislation; inspecting places of employment; of offering advice and assistance in the formation of responsible trade unions; of assisting the free movement of labour and of fostering good relations between employers and employees in industry and commerce. Trade unionism in Tanganyika is still in its infancy, and there are at present only seventeen registered trade unions in the territory. In the absence of an effective trade union movement encouragement is being given to the creation of simple consultative machinery in individual undertakings.

Advice concerning rates of wages, conditions of employment and any other labour matters may be sought from the headquarters of the Department of Labour, P.O. Box 178, Dar es Salaam, or from any Labour Office.

Wage Rates of Manual Labour:

Supervisors and skilled artisans: £80 a month.

Semi-skilled artisans: £20–£70 a month.

Agricultural labour: from Shs. 15/- to Shs. 39/- a labour card of 30 daily tasks, plus rations on approved scale. Government unskilled labour averages from Sh. 1/- a day (rural areas) to Shs. 2/40 (urban areas), Dar es Salaam from Shs. 3/40 a day. Artisans—Shs. 100/- to Shs. 400/- a month.

Wage Rates of Clerical Workers:

Shorthand-typists: £40–£70 a month.

Copy typists: £30–£42 a month.

Clerks: £9–£46 a month according to educational standard, experience and ability.

Legislation:

The principal legislation affecting labour is as follows:—

The Employment Ordinance, 1955 (Cap. 366 of the Laws).

This comprehensive measure together with its related subsidiary legislation consolidated and replaced previous labour legislation. The Ordinance is non-racial in character and its provisions relate to the powers and duties of officers, contracts of service, the protection of wages, the employment of women, children and young persons, care and welfare of employees, recruitment and forced labour.

The Regulation of Wages and Terms of Employment Ordinance (Cap. 300 of the Laws).

This Ordinance provides for the establishment of Minimum Wage Boards and Wages Councils.

The Workmen's Compensation Ordinance (Cap. 263 of the Laws)

This Ordinance provides for the payment of compensation for death or incapacity suffered by a workman as a result of an accident arising out of and in the course of his employment. Compensation is also payable in cases of certain prescribed occupational diseases.

The Factories Ordinance (Cap. 297 of the Laws).

This Ordinance, which is based on the Factory Acts of the United Kingdom, deals with all aspects of safety, health and welfare in factories.

The Trade Unions Ordinance (No. 48 of 1956).

This measure provides for the registration of trade unions and the regulation of combinations whether temporary or permanent, the principal purposes of which are the regulation of relations between employees and employers, employees and employees or between employers and employers. It also covers the law of conspiracy in trade disputes, intimidation and peaceful picketing, and tortious liability in trade disputes.

The Trade Disputes (*Arbitration and Settlement*) Ordinance (No. 43 of 1950)

This Ordinance makes provision for settlement of or enquiry into trade disputes, if need be, by reference to an Arbitration Tribunal or a Board of Enquiry, in cases where settlement cannot be effected by existing machinery in the industry or concern in which the dispute has arisen. Special provisions are made relating to trade disputes in certain essential services.

PRISONS

Prisons are divided into three classes; first class prisons for all types of offenders, second class for prisoners serving sentences of not more than three years, and third class for prisoners serving six months or less. Offenders serving a sentence of less than six months or who are unable to pay fines of up to Shs. 100/- may be released from prison for employment on public work outside, when they live either at home or in camps, receiving daily rations or an allowance therefor, but no other payment.

Each province has a major first class prison, built since the 1939–45 war, where training is given in various trades. Prisoners are employed on works of public utility, such as quarrying, road construction, land reclamation, anti-malarial work, tsetse clearance, animal husbandry and bricklaying. Prison camps have been established in several places where development is being undertaken and prison labour could not otherwise be supplied.

A feature of the Tanganyika Prisons Service is Kingolwira Prison Farm, accommodating 1,000 prisoners under conditions of minimum security, where prisoners are trained mainly in agriculture. All inmates are first offenders. The number of attempted escapes has been few, and this institution, which developed from an agricultural experiment, has fully justified the decision to establish an "open" prison.

A new institution for juvenile delinquents has been built at Malindi, on the coast twenty miles north of Dar es Salaam, where the segregation of young offenders from older boys who have committed serious crimes is more practicable than it was in the former Approved School at Kingolwira.

Criminal lunatics are confined in the Broadmoor Institution at Dodoma, where occupational therapy has proved its value in stabilizing the mentally deranged. The institution is in the care of a trained male mental nurse and shares with the Mirembe Mental Hospital nearby the services of a psychiatrist.

THE PROBATION SERVICE

It is only comparatively recently (1951) that the Probation Service has been introduced into Tanganyika but its value has been recognized by all those who have come into contact with it. The Probation Service is at present very small but it is growing as quickly as staff can be trained. At first the service was only available in the High Court and the other courts directly subordinate to it, but a way has been worked out of applying the same system in the courts presided over by the traditional native authorities, and a special ordinance has been passed for the purpose.

SOCIAL DEVELOPMENT

Community development and welfare matters are the concern of the Department of Social Development, a small department whose officers act as specialist assistants to the Provincial Administration, helping, in rural areas, to implement the district development plans by securing the willing co-operation of the people and, in urban areas, helping the District Commissioner to keep in closer touch with the people and assisting the people to adjust themselves to the changes going on around them. In their work they make full use of audio-visual aids and in particular of the film, especially of locally made films with a sound track in the vernacular. In towns they help (amongst their other activities) in making the former "welfare" centres into genuine community centres. In rural areas they encourage and initiate self-help schemes, for which a special allocation of funds is made every year, for such projects as roads, the protection of wells, adult literacy, the levelling of football grounds and many other works on which the local people are prepared to labour provided that they can receive assistance to purchase such things as cement, tools, blasting materials, etc.

The department has a small fleet of mobile cinema vans, runs a film library for the hire of 16 mm. films (both educational and for entertainment), and has a specialist visual aids officer.

Work amongst women is being extended, more women social development officers are being recruited and a training centre for women club supervisors has been set up.

Chapter 12

MISSIONS

Except for an attempt by the Franciscans to establish a mission at Kilwa Kisiwani during the brief Portuguese occupation of that place (1505–1513) there is no record of any missionary enterprise in Tanganyika until the latter half of the nineteenth century.

In August, 1863, Antoine Horner, who had arrived only two months before in Zanzibar as Superior of the Fathers of the Holy Ghost, crossed over to Bagamoyo with letters of recommendation from the Sultan of Zanzibar and began to erect a mission station there, which was primarily designed as an orphanage for children whom the Fathers had redeemed from captivity in the Zanzibar slave market. The Sultan of Zanzibar, Seyyid Barghash, granted the mission a concession of first class agricultural land for the training of the boys of the orphanage. By the beginning of 1872 the station in addition to its agricultural projects boasted workshops, elementary schools, a nursery and a novitiate for African sisters. In April of that year they suffered a serious set-back as the result of a cyclone which laid practically the whole of the establishment level with the ground. Despite this disaster and despite the depletion of their resources owing to the French disaster in Europe two years previously, the Fathers set to work to build again what had been cast down. When Sir Bartle Frere visited the mission a year later, he wrote, "I would recommend it as a model to be followed in any attempt to civilise and evangelize Africa". A few months later a party of Africans deposited at the feet of the Father Superior a very precious burden. It contained the mortal remains of David Livingstone, which rested in the Mission Church until they were conveyed by the crew of H.M.S. *Vulture* to Zanzibar. For many years afterwards the British Navy handed over to the Mission numbers of the captives whom they had rescued from slave dhows.

Father Horner did not confine his labours to the coast. He was indefatigable in his efforts to discover suitable out-stations farther inland. In 1877 he reached the Uluguru Mountains and established a mission station there at Mhonda near Morogoro. After sixteeen years of devoted service ill health compelled him to retire to France, where he died in 1880.

In Great Britain interest in the evangelization of the peoples of East Africa was first aroused by David Livingstone's appeal to the members of Cambridge University to help to make Africa "free, civilised and Christian". This appeal led to the formation of the Universities Mission to Central Africa. The original goal of this mission was Lake Nyasa. In 1861 Livingstone advised the members of the Mission to approach this goal by way of the River Ruvuma, but it was found that cataracts obstructed navigation some 150 miles upstream. Accordingly the mission party withdrew and proceeded to make their approach by way of the Zambezi and Shire Rivers, but here again overwhelming difficulties were encountered and in 1864 the mission was temporarily withdrawn. At the end of that year Bishop Tozer moved his headquarters to Zanzibar with the object of using it as a base for the renewal of operations on the mainland.

In 1867 C. A. Alington made the first contact with the mainland, when he visited Kimweri, paramount chief in Usambara. Though Kimweri would not allow the mission to establish itself at his headquarters, he gave permission in 1868 for the establishment of a mission station nearer to the coast. A station was accordingly selected at Magila in the Usambara country. Owing to shortage of staff, climate and disease it could at first only be supplied intermittently. More than once it had to be temporarily closed down owing to the death or invaliding of the missionary in charge. From 1873, however, when the Rev. J. P. Farler took charge, the work was carried on without interruption. Offshoots were planted by him at Pambili in 1876 and at Umba in 1877.

In 1873 Bishop Tozer resigned the bishopric and was succeeded by Bishop Steere, who had been a member of the second U.M.C.A. party which attempted to found a station on Lake Nyasa in 1863. In 1875 Steere decided to renew the attempt. He set out from Lindi, with Livingstone's servant, Chuma, as headman of his porters, and eventually reached the headquarters of a chief named Mataka within seventy miles of the lake. Mataka refused to allow him to establish a mission station at or near his own village, but did not oppose such an establishment elsewhere in his dominions. In 1876 Steere returned and eventually selected as a station Masasi, lying to the north of the Ruvuma and about 100 miles west of Cape Delgado, where he settled a number of freed slaves who had been entrusted to the care of his Mission by the British Consul at Zanzibar. In 1878 an offshoot was planted at Newala, a little to the south-east of Masasi.

When Henry Morton Stanley was in Uganda in 1875, he sent to the *Daily Telegraph* an appeal for Christian missionaries to work in the land of Mutesa, Kabaka of Buganda. In response to this appeal three missionary societies came into the field. The members of the first missionary party belonged to the Church Missionary Society and reached Zanzibar in 1876. It was decided to approach Uganda by the recognized Arab trade route, namely, that from Bagamoyo to Tabora and thence northwards to the southern shores of Lake Victoria. The first party decided to make for the proposed field of their labours as soon as possible and so pushed on straight for Lake Victoria and Buganda, where two of their number arrived in 1877. But it became obvious that intermediate stations must be set up along the lines of communication between the coast and the lake. Accordingly Mpwapwa was occupied by a lay agent in 1876, but had to be abandoned when his health broke down. It was, however reoccupied in 1878, when four missionaries were assigned to it, including a doctor. A year later other stations were founded at Mamboya, near Mpwapwa, and Uyuwi, near Tabora. In 1883 another station was established at Msalala, near the shore of Smith's Sound, one of the southern inlets of Lake Victoria. In 1887 other stations were established close to the southern shore of Lake Victoria, at Nassa and Usambiro.

Livingstone's old society, the London Missionary Society, also took up Stanley's challenge, In 1876 Roger Price, who had many years' experience in the mission field in South Africa, experimented with ox transport with apparent success as far as Mpwapwa. In 1877 he led another party which included five European companions. This time the oxen were soon attacked by tsetse and died *en route*. Price then departed to visit England to consult the Directors of the Society. Three members of the party pushed on and reached Ujiji at the end of August, 1877, where they were joined by a fourth, A. W. Dodgshun, in the following March. But misfortune still dogged their footsteps. One of their number, J. B. Thomson, had died in the previous September and Dodgshun died within a week of his arrival at Ujiji. During the next fifteen years six other missionaries died and fourteen had to be invalided home. Others struggled on to keep the station at Ujiji open and also opened another station at Urambo between Ujiji and Tabora.

In 1884 the station at Ujiji was abandoned for one on the island of Kassala off the western shore of the lake. In 1898 the sole remaining station at Urambo was handed over to the Moravians. Thereafter the activities of the London Missionary Society were transferred to the southern end of the lake in what is now Northern Rhodesia.

An outstanding figure amongst the members of the London Missionary Society was Edward Coode Hore, a master mariner formerly in the service of the P. & O. line, who was responsible for the launching of the first steamer, the *Good News*, on Lake Tanganyika. Until his retirement in 1888 he displayed remarkable ability for tactful handling not only of the local inhabitants, but also of the very miscellaneous assortment of persons of all nationalities and creeds who passed through Ujiji during the "Scramble for Africa".

On 24th February, 1878, Pope Leo XII signed the brief by which he entrusted the evangelization of the regions of the Central African Lakes to the society which is now so widely known as the White Fathers and which had been founded five years previously by Cardinal Lavigerie. The first missionary party reached Africa two months after the papal brief was signed. Its members set out from Bagamoyo, in the words of one of the Society's earliest leaflets, *à l'assaut des pays nègres*. Their two main objectives were Lake Tanganyika and Lake Victoria. At Tabora the party divided into two. One party proceeded to the court of Mutesa, ruler of Buganda. The other reached Ujiji in the early days of 1879, where they established a station at Kibanga (Lavigerieville) on the peninsula opposite to Ujiji. Later it was decided to establish a nodal point of communication between the coast and the two lakes. Tabora was the obvious place to select for this purpose. It so chanced that the African International Association, which had been formed in 1876 to promote the exploration and civilization of Central Africa, had decided to close down its base at Tabora[1] and the officer in charge offered Father Guillet the option to purchase it. Father Guillet readily accepted the offer and in 1882 established there an orphanage for redeemed slave children. In the same year the Mission Station of Our Lady of Kamoga was planted at Bukumbi at the southern end of Lake Victoria by White Fathers, who had been instructed by Cardinal Lavigerie to withdraw temporarily from Buganda owing to the disturbed state of that country and the murder of Father Deniaud in Urundi. In 1885 another station was formed at Karema on the shores of Lake Tanganyika. In 1887 Jean-Baptiste Charbonnier was consecrated titular Bishop of Utica and Vicar Apostolic of Tanganyika. He died little more than six months later and was succeeded by Bishop Bridoux.

The foregoing is nothing more than a bare narrative of the progress made by English and French missionaries in the country which was to become Tanganyika. It says nothing about the obstacles which had to be overcome or the trials which had to be undergone. The casualty lists were heavy. Many succumbed to the climate and others had to be invalided home. Moreover,

[1]See page 49.

although there was no rash courting of the martyr's crown, some were the victims of attacks by hostile natives. There were never at this period, however, any widespread or concerted attacks on missionaries on account of their Christian propaganda. In 1877 Shergold Smith and O'Neill, two of the first C.M.S. party to Uganda, were murdered on Ukerewe Island in Lake Victoria because they were involved in a dispute between the local chief, Lakonge, and an Arab who had sold them a dhow constructed with timber purchased from the chief and not paid for. In 1878 members of a caravan of a certain Abbe Debaize, who despite his title was not a missionary but a none too competent explorer, had seized and killed two natives on their way to Tabora. The local chief, Jiwe la Singa, gave orders that revenge should be taken on the next European caravan, which happened to be that of C. Penrose, another C.M.S. missionary, who was massacred with all his men. With the death of Mirambo[1], chief of Unyanyembe, in 1884, his dominions broke up and the whole region was thrown into a state of disorder. In 1887 the mission station at Kibanga on Lake Tanganyika was attacked and later the missionaries had, temporarily, to abandon Tabora.

Nearer to the coast the U.M.C.A. had been experiencing trouble in two different quarters. In 1881 the Bondei objected to a church being built at Magila, apparently on the ground that they believed it to be a fortress intended to dominate the whole country, and threatened to pull down the partly constructed building. In the circumstances Archdeacon Farler decided temporarily to suspend building operations. In the following year the U.M.C.A. station at Masasi was attacked by a band of Mangangwara, when some of the converts and their children were killed and others enslaved. These last were later redeemed by the European missionaries in charge. As the raiders continued to dominate the district, it was decided that Masasi must be temporarily evacuated.

It will thus be seen that at the time when the "Scramble for Africa" set in five missionary societies were at work in what is now Tanganyika, two Anglican and one Non-Conformist (U.M.C.A., C.M.S. and L.M.S.) and two Roman Catholic societies (the White Fathers and the Fathers of the Holy Ghost). The three former societies were English and the two Roman Catholic were French. So far no German society was at work. Within a few years of the occupation of the country by Germany five German missionary societies were established in the new territory.

In 1886 a society was formed specifically for service in German East Africa. This was the Berlin Evangelical Missionary Society for East Africa—commonly known as Berlin III to distinguish it from two earlier societies bearing somewhat similar names. In its early days this society had a somewhat chequered career. In 1889 Pastor Greiner erected an imposing headquarters at Immanuelskap at the entrance to the harbour of Dar es Salaam, which was originally used as a hospital staffed by members of the Mission. At this stage much of the energies of the missionaries was diverted from evangelical work to other spheres of labour. In 1890 the direction of the Society passed into the more competent hands of Pastor von Bodelschwingh, who a year later started a missionary training centre at Bethel-bei-Bielefold, which eventually became the Society's headquarters.

In 1892 work was begun at Kisarawe, about eighteen miles south-west of Dar es Salaam. In 1895 another station was opened thirty miles to the southwest of Kisarawe at Maneromango. In 1903 the work in Dar es Salaam and at

[1]See page 269.

these two stations was taken over by the Berlin Missionary Society (commonly known as Berlin I), thus enabling Berlin III to devote its attention to Usambara. Kraemer, a member of Berlin III, had started work in 1890 which was gradually extended into the Usambara country, where a station was eventually established at Vuga, the headquarters of the paramount chief Kimweri. In 1903 the Usambara stations passed entirely into Pastor von Bodelschwingh's capable direction and the mission become designated the Bethel Mission.

The first German Roman Catholic missionaries to work in Tanganyika were Benedictines of the Congregation of St. Ottilien, who started work at Pugu, twelve miles to the west of Dar es Salaam, in 1888, and built a church on the shores of the neighbouring Kurasini Creek. Within little more than a year tragedy overtook them. During the Arab rising, on 13th January, 1889, their station at Pugu was attacked.[1] Two brothers and a sister were savagely done to death; two brothers managed to make their escape, and three other brothers and a sister were made prisoners. Eventually these last were ransomed by the Fathers of the Holy Ghost at Bagamoyo.

In 1891 the Berlin Missionary Society (Berlin I) and the Moravians entered the southern portion of the German protectorate simultaneously. By a friendly agreement the two societies apportioned the territory north of Lake Nyasa between them.

The Berliners, led by Alexander Marensky, approached their mission field by way of the Zambezi and Shire Rivers and Lake Nyasa. Their first station was at Pipagika to the north-east of that lake. In the course of the next three years stations were established amongst the Konde and Kinga at Mano, Mwakeleli, Ikombe, Bulongwa and Tandala.

The Moravians approached their field by the same route as had the Berliners, and travelling northwards reached the Rungwa River to the north of Lake Rukwa, where they met with a friendly reception from Chief Makapalile. They made their first station on the banks of the Rungwa. Later other stations were planted at Rutenganio, Ipiyana and Utengule. When in 1893 Baron von Eltz, Wissmann's second-in-command, captured a slave caravan just north of Lake Nyasa, he confided the women and children, to the number of over one hundred, to the Moravians and the Berliners.

In July, 1885, the English Church Missionary Society had opened a station at Moshi in response to a request made seven years previously by Mandara, the paramount chief of the Chagga. Mandara died in 1891 and the Germans appointed his son, Meli, as his successor. Meli's relations with the Germans became strained[2] and in 1892 a collision took place in which Baron von Bulow, the acting Commissioner, and another officer were killed. The Rev. A. R. Steggall, the English missionary in charge at Moshi, had been asked by the German Governor von Soden to try to procure Meli's submission and had done everything which could be done in a highly delicate situation to try to keep the peace but, in the words of Bishop Tucker, "this position of mediator was galling to the German authorities. His very safety was a reflection upon themselves. No German, unarmed or unattended by soldiers, dared venture one hundred yards from the Fort whereas Mr. Steggall was free to travel anywhere in perfect

---

[1]See page 58. [2]See page 65.

safety. The prestige of Germany was suffering. The Mission must go.". So Tucker agreed to withdraw it, under protest. For a year the mission station at Moshi was unoccupied. Then, in 1893, it was taken over by the Leipzig Evangelical Lutheran Mission. Shortly afterwards the newcomers planted two offshoots on the slopes of Mount Kilimanjaro at Machame and Mamba.

With this exception, which was due to fear that an extraneous loyalty might be damaging to national prestige, the attitude of the German officials to English Missions would appear to have been far from unfriendly, although, not unnaturally, German missionaries were preferred and encouraged. In so far as the missionaries of the two countries were concerned, all parties usually came to a friendly *modus vivendi*, whereby no individual society encroached upon another society's sphere of influence.

Roman Catholic missions presented a somewhat different problem, which was eventually solved by the setting up in Germany of seminaries for the training of German nationals as Catholic missionaries. Thus the Fathers of the Holy Ghost established a seminary at Cologne and the White Fathers one at Trier.

As has been shown[1], the advent of German rule was not tamely accepted by the Arabs and coast dwellers. The subsequent rising under the leadership of Bushiri bin Salim el Harthi caused a serious set-back to missionary enterprise in many parts of the country. The U.M.C.A. station at Magila was the first to be involved in this rising. Bishop Smythies decided that the path of duty led him there. He accordingly proceeded there in company with Livingstone's former servant, Susi. His ship was fired on when he arrived at Pangani. He nevertheless landed and was surrounded by a hostile mob. He owed his life at this point to the personal courage and protection of Bushiri himself and was allowed to proceed under an Arab escort to Mkuzi, where he found the European ladies of the mission. These he sent under the escort of three of the male members to Zanzibar for safety. To the rest the Bishop gave the choice to go or to stay. They all remained and he remained with them until the danger had passed.

As his relations with Bishop Smythies show, in the early stage of the rising Bushiri showed some measure of chivalry in warfare, but this disappeared when von Wissmann denounced the armistice which had been concluded before his arrival. As already recounted, the Bendictines at Pugu were attacked, two brothers and a sister were done to death and three brothers and a sister taken prisoner. Arthur Brookes of the L.M.S. was murdered on his way down to the coast. Mr. and Mrs. Roscoe and Mr. Douglas Hooper of the C.M.S. were made prisoners but were eventually ransomed through the mediation of the Fathers of the Holy Ghost at Bagamoyo, who were themselves in a position of no little danger but who also managed to ransom the Benedictines taken prisoner at Pugu. Up country, Bishop Bridoux and a party of White Fathers were made prisoners at Tabora, but were saved from massacre by Tippu Tib's trading partner, Rumaliza, who however charged a large fee for his services. A party of L.M.S. missionaries under the leadership of A. J. Swann also owed their lives to Rumaliza who saw to it that they were safely conducted from Ujiji to the southern end of Lake Tanganyika. The White Fathers had temporarily to abandon their station at Kipalapala near Tabora.

---

[1]See chapter 3.

The sixteen years which followed the suppression of Bushiri's revolt were spent by missionary societies in recovering lost ground and expanding their efforts, only to be met in 1905 with another serious set-back in the Maji Maji rebellion. As recounted elsewhere[1], the rising owed its inception and its early measure of success to faith in the magico-religious medicine which was believed to turn the bullets of the European rifles into water. European missionaries in the areas particularly involved by the rising were regarded as special objects for attack. The area involved in the rebellion was the stretch of country to the south of a line drawn from Dar es Salaam to Lake Nyasa through Kilosa—and more especially the coast and immediate hinterland between Kilwa Kivinje and Lindi. Naturally therefore the missionary societies in that area were the greatest sufferers. For the second time Benedictines of St. Ottilien had to bear the most grievous loss. Bishop Cassian Spiess with two brothers—Andreas Scholzen and Gabriel Sonntag—and two sisters—Felicitas Hiltner and Kordula Ebert—had set out from Kilwa Kivinje to visit the mission station at Peramiho[2]. On the way they were deserted by their Angoni porters, who were forced to drink the magic "medicine". The missionaries themselves were surrounded at Mikikuyumbu, about seventy miles south-west of Kilwa, where they were shot down and killed. Their remains were afterwards discovered and buried at the scene of their murder, but were later exhumed and laid to rest beneath the altar of St. Joseph's Cathedral, Dar es Salaam.

The rebels also attacked the Benedictine convent at Nyangao about thirty-five miles south-west of Lindi[2]. Here there was a Father Superior, a brother and three sisters. There was no possibility of resistance and after both Father Leo and Brother Cyprean had been wounded the sisters made ready for immediate death. Father Leo gave them absolution, making the sign of the Cross. Believing that they had seen some act of omnipotent witchcraft, the rebels incontinently fled and the missionaries were able to make their escape to Lindi. One sister became separated from the party on the way and was not heard of again.

Two Benedictine Fathers at Lukuledi, who had learnt of the tragedy at Mikikuyumbu, fled to the U.M.C.A. station at Masasi and were thus able to give the missionaries there warning that the rebels were advancing their way. It was realized that the war was being waged against the Europeans and not against Christianity. For the five men and two women to have stayed on there might have been deemed heroic, but it would most certainly have been useless and would have involved their followers in the same disaster as would have befallen themselves. Archdeacon Carnon therefore decided that they must leave and they eventually reached Lindi in safety, as has already been recounted[2].

In the south-west corner of the territory the Berlin missionaries had no hope of any immediate assistance from German troops. On 19th September, 1905, two thousand rebels attacked their station at Jakobi, but the missionaries Groschel and Hann gave so good an account of themselves that the enemy withdrew[3]. It was clear, however, that neither that station nor Milo could be held for any length of time. Accordingly both missionaries withdrew into Nyasaland.

When the trouble began to spread northwards into Usagara, the Church Missionary Society withdrew all its missionaries from their outstations to Kiboriani, near Mpwapwa, where German protection was available.

Though the main revolt was quickly suppressed, the smouldering embers were not finally extinguished until early 1907 and then only after the wholesale destruction of crops and villages in the insurgent districts, which brought about famine and increased the death roll to some 120,000 souls. As may be surmised, these hostilities once more set back considerably the work of many missionary societies. Despite these and many other set-backs, however, missionary efforts made remarkable advances during the brief respite between the end of the Maji Maji rebellion and the outbreak of the First World War.

Notwithstanding two great tragedies the Benedictines of St. Ottillien had been able to extend their field of labour considerably. A mission house and sisters' convent had been founded at Dar es Salaam in 1890, and the Kurasini Mission in 1894. In 1894 they also established another station at Madibira in the Southern Highlands. Next year they founded mission stations at Nyangao, and also at Lukuledi, a few miles to the north of Masasi, the latter being destroyed during the Maji Maji rebellion and afterwards moved to Ndanda. Peramiho had been founded by Bishop Spiess in the south-west corner of the territory in 1898. From each of these centres small out-stations were gradually planted out in the surrounding districts.

In 1886 the Vicariate of Tanganyika was divided into two one retaining the old name and the other being called the Vicariate of the Upper Congo. In the following year there was a further subdivision of the older Vicariate by the creation of the Vicariate of Unyanyembe, with headquarters at Kipalapala, near Tabora. The older Vicariate was thereby momentarily reduced to a single station at Karema, but the White Fathers soon found pastures new, spreading southwards along the lake shore. After establishing new stations at Kala in 1892 and Kiranda two years later they proceeded across the Fipa plateau to Lake Rukwa.

After the establishment of the Uganda Protectorate in 1894, the old Nyanza Vicariate was divided. That portion of the old Vicariate which lay in German territory was so great that in 1912 this Vicariate was itself subdivided by the creation of the Kivu Vicariate in what is now the Trust Territory of Ruanda.

The Fathers of the Holy Ghost remained for many years under the superintendence of the Vicar Apostolic of Zanzibar. In 1906 the Bagamoyo Vicariate was created, but the work therein grew so rapidly that it was subdivided four years later by the creation of the Kilimanjaro Vicariate.

Both the Berlin and Moravian Missions likewise made rapid progress. The Berlin Mission's principal extension of labour was in what was formerly the Iringa Province and amongst the tribes of the Southern Highlands. In 1898 after the final subjugation of the Hehe the German Government invited the Mission to enter the Uhehe country as peacemakers. The Bena, who had constantly been at war with the Hehe, also sought the members of the Mission as friends and protectors. By 1914 the Society's mission field extended from the Livingstone plateau up to Uzaramu.

The Moravians had made equal progress. As shown, they had in 1898 taken over the last surviving station of the L.M.S. at Urambo in Unyamwezi. Their work rapidly expanded there as well as in their older sphere. By 1914 they were maintaining nine stations in the Konde country and six in Unyamwezi.

Dar es Salaam Commercial area.

Photo: Air Survey Division

Market scene.

Photo: V. Eugene Johnson, Singida

As already mentioned, the Leipzig Mission had stepped into the shoes of the C.M.S. at Moshi. Operating thence, they had planted offshoots westwards in the foothills of Mount Meru, south-eastwards in the Pare Range and south-westwards into the Iramba country.

The Bethel Society was at work nearby in the Usambara country, where by 1914 they had half a dozen central stations.

As Dr. Oliver has said, "for the Anglican missions working in German East Africa the period from 1884 to 1914 was a time of holding and developing ground previously gained." Though relations with the Germans were on the whole quite amicable, it was very understandable that the German administration preferred to see their own nationals breaking the soil in new mission fields. It was also equally understandable that recruits to the two missionary societies preferred to work under the British flag rather than an alien one. The C.M.S. continued to maintain their stations at Mpwapwa and in its vicinity, but in 1909 handed over that at Nassa, at the southern end of Lake Victoria, to the Africa Inland Mission. The U.M.C.A. continued to hold their outposts in and near Masasi in the south-east and Magila in the north-east. So far from allowing their work in German territories to stagnate both societies maintained a healthy life in their spheres of labour.

For British missionaries in East Africa the outbreak of the First World War was as much a bolt from the blue as the Maji Maji rising. During the next four and half years there was hardly a square yard of land which did not at one time or other become a theatre of war. The result inevitably was once more a complete disruption and disorganization of the labours of all missions, British and German alike.

The immediate consequence of the outbreak of war was the internment of all British missionaries, who remained in captivity until the Belgian forces reached Tabora in September, 1916. The treatment of these missionaries left a great deal to be desired, but worse still was the treatment meted out to the African clergy and teachers, many of whom were thrown into chains and subjected to the greatest possible indignities. Some were beaten without provocation and others left to die by the roadside. Places of worship were given over to purely secular uses, as offices and stores. When General Smuts drove the Germans southwards, British missionaries were able to return to their societies' former stations.

With the turn of the tide it inevitably followed that German missionaries had for the most part to be interned, with the result that, more particularly in the Protestant missions, a great deal of missionary work had to be curtailed. Even before the end of the East African Campaign, attempts were made to fill the gaps. Thus German Benedictines were replaced by French and Swiss members of that Order and the Berlin Missions were taken over temporarily by the Church of Scotland Missionary Society. First of all the C.M.S. and later the Methodist Missionary Society took over the work of the Bethel Mission on the western shores of Lake Victoria. In accordance with the Treaty of Versailles all ex-enemy missions were directed to be handed over to missions of the same denomination of allied or neutral origin. Eventually, however, the Government of Tanganyika agreed to the return of all ex-enemy missionaries and to the handing over to them of all their former properties.

26

During the years which immediately followed the First World War there was a fairly considerable extension of the work of the English Missions. Thus the Universities' Mission opened up a number of stations in the hinterland behind Dar es Salaam, where in 1925 a Teachers' Training Centre was opened at Minaki. The work radiating from their other two centres at Masasi and Magila was likewise expanded.

The Church Missionary Society, with recruits to its ranks from Australia and also increasing encouragement and support from that continent, was not only able to extend its work in the region of Dodoma, but also to open a new field in the region bordering on the Belgian mandated territory of Urundi. Until 1923 the Mission was included in the diocese of Mombasa. In that year a new Bishopric was created, with its See at Dodoma.

After their return the Benedictines of St. Ottilien left it to Swiss Capuchins from the Seychelles and Italian Consolata Fathers from Kenya to carry on their work to the south-west of Dar es Salaam and in the Southern Highlands, whilst they concentrated in their former sphere south-west of Lindi in the regions of Peramiho and Ndanda.

The White Fathers, who had for many years laboured in Ruanda and Urundi, opened up a new field on the borders of the latter territory.

In 1926 the Augustana Synod, American Lutherans of Scandinavian origin, began to work in virgin soil to the north of the Central Railway, devoting their attention to the Iramba and Turu tribes.

Other fresh entrants into the mission field were the Pallottine Fathers and the Passionists. The first of these came from the Pious Society of Missions, founded in 1835 by Vincent Mary Pallotti. They started work in the region of Dodoma, which was created a Prefecture Apostolic in 1935. Like the Pallottines, the Passionists belonged to an order of Italian origin, founded in 1720 by St. Paul of the Cross as a barefooted order. They opened up a new field to the north of the Pallottines in Mbulu District, which was created a Prefecture Apostolic in 1943.

The outbreak of the Second World War once again caused a temporary set-back in more than one mission field. This had to some extent already begun with the Nazi accession to power in Germany. The economic policy which was introduced by that party compelled the Lutheran missions to live at a mere subsistance level and resulted in an appreciable decline in their efficiency and the disappearance of their reserve funds. To a lesser extent this policy also affected those Roman Catholic missions which in any large degree depended on German sources for their income. The outbreak of the war led to the withdrawal and eventual expulsion of all German missionaries from the Lutheran missions working in the Moshi, Pare, Usambara, Bukoba and Dar es Salaam areas. At Dar es Salaam itself it was found that, in one of the rooms of the mission house, an ardent Nazi pastor had placed an altar beneath an effigy of Hitler painted on the wall by a compatriot of the same political complexion. The withdrawal of these missionaries was a very necessary measure for security reasons, but it left a gap which could not easily or quickly be filled. Roman Catholic missions were also hit by the outbreak of the war—more especially when the Germans overran the countries upon which they had been mainly dependent for their income. In their case, however there was not the necessity for the same withdrawal and removal of personnel. In the case of the Lutheran missions the Augustana Synod eventually stepped into the gap and took over the work in the Bukoba, Singida, Pare, Usambara, Uzaramo, Ubena and Konde Districts, whilst Danish Moravians supplied the gap in the region of Lake Rukwa.

There are at present four Anglican dioceses in Tanganyika, namely;

Zanzibar (which includes Usambara and Uzaramo and the region in between).

Masasi.

South-west Tanganyika.

Central Tanganyika.

Of these, the last is served by members of the C.M.S., the remainder being served by the U.M.C.A.

The following are the Apostolic Vicariates or Prefectures of the Roman Catholic missions:—

White Fathers—Bukoba, Mwanza, Musoma-Maswa, Kigoma, Tabora, Karema, Tukuyu.

Holy Ghost Fathers—Kilimanjaro, Bagamoyo.

Pallottine Fathers—Mbulu.

Passionists—Dodoma.

Benedictines of St. Ottilien—Peramiho, Ndanda.

Capuchins—Dar es Salaam.

Consolata Fathers—Iringa.

No attempt has been made here to describe the activities of all the many missionary societies operating in Tanganyika, still less to appraise their contribution to the welfare of the people. Others will be able to assess properly the value of their spiritual labours, but even the sternest critic of missions cannot in fairness deny that they have contributed to the moral and social uplift of many formerly pagan tribes. In purely secular matters such as education and public health some missions were at work before any European government took over the administration of the country. After the assumption of control the Administration was for many years largely dependent on missionary societies for their assistance. That help is, fortunately, still forthcoming. The labours of many of the pioneer missionaries took them in journeyings, often in perils of many kinds, and in weariness and painfulness, which it is difficult for a later generation to appreciate and for which no praise can be too high.

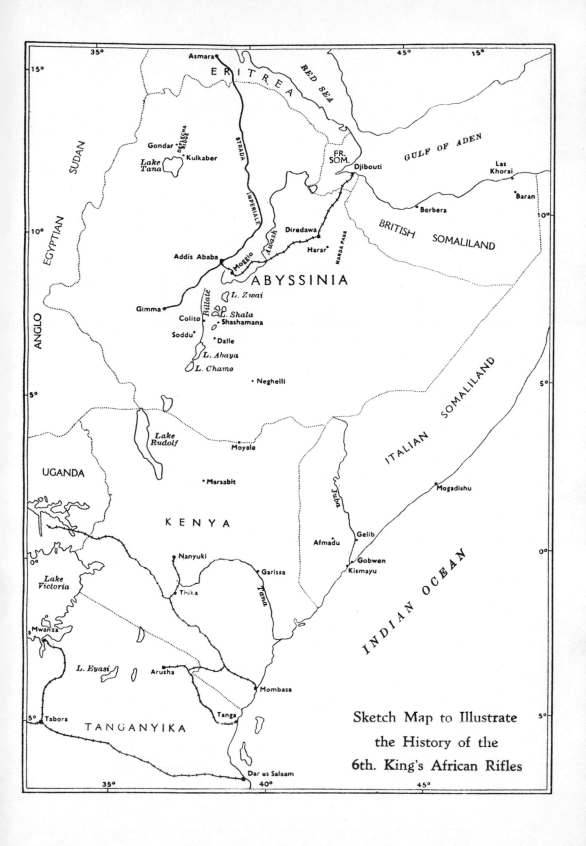

Sketch Map to Illustrate
the History of the
6th. King's African Rifles

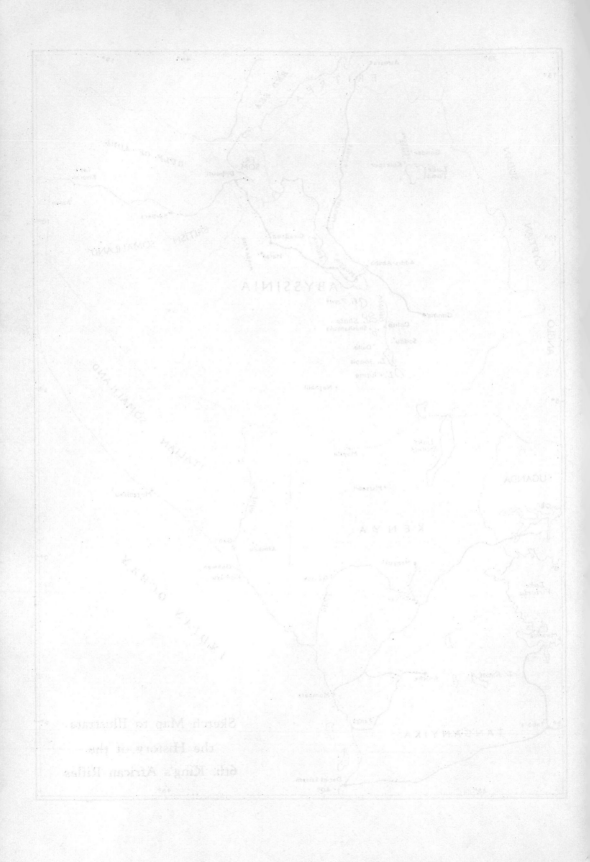

Chapter 13

THE KING'S AFRICAN RIFLES

HISTORY OF 6TH BATTALION KING'S AFRICAN RIFLES

The permanent military forces of the East African dependencies are comprised of units of the King's African Rifles, a regiment of African troops with British officers and N.C.O.s seconded from the Regular Army. The regiment came into being under its present title on 1st January, 1902, when its battalions were formed from the troops of three earlier regiments, the Central Africa Regiment (formerly designated Rifles) the East Africa Rifles and the Uganda Rifles, and also from certain levies in British Somaliland. From the start, therefore, the regiment has possessed strong territorial connections, and care has been taken to cherish and maintain them. A long history of military service in peace and war now lies behind the King's African Rifles, but it is only intended here to give a brief account of those battalions that have had particular connections with Tanganyika.

THE 2ND BATTALION

Mauritius.—The first attempts at administration in British Central Africa (now Nyasaland) evoked the hostility of the Arab and Swahili slave traders operating in the area, and the result was a spasmodic "war" that lasted for some five or six years. Although Sikh volunteers from the Indian Army were the mainstay of the forces employed, native levies were enrolled in increasing numbers as time went on, and in 1896 were formed into the Central Africa Rifles. In 1899, when Britain was in difficulties over garrisoning foreign stations on account of the demands made by the South African War, a second battalion was raised in Central Africa for service abroad under the War Office. In June of that year, after very little training and with no proper uniforms or equipment, the 2nd Battalion was posted to Mauritius. The inhabitants of the island made no attempt to disguise their resentment at the presence of an African garrison, and despite all attempts to prevent trouble an unfortunate incident occurred in December, when some of the troops retaliated on the ringleaders of the Creoles. This led to the withdrawal of the battalion, which was ordered in February, 1900, to British Somaliland, where the first of a long series of campaigns against the "Mad Mullah" was being planned.

West Africa.—The battalion was destined, however, to see active service for the first time in West Africa. In April, 1900, the Ashanti chiefs rose in rebellion and for a time the Governor of the Gold Coast was imprisoned at Kumasi. An expedition was raised under the Commandant of the West Africa Frontier Force, who relieved Kumasi in July, but much remained to be done in destroying the Ashanti power and in pacifying the country generally. Reinforcements were requested, and among other units half the 2nd Battalion C.A.R. was withdrawn from Somaliland. In a difficult campaign, in thickly-forested country at the height of the rains, the troops took part in a number of operations against the strong stockades built by the Ashantis across the narrow forest tracks, notably at the engagements of Jachi and Ejisu and the final pitched battle at Obassa. In December, 1900, the remainder of the battalion was despatched to the Gambia River to take part in a punitive expedition against the murderers of two travelling commissioners in the previous June.   This task was successfully accomplished and was followed by minor operations against a native slaving chief, in co-operation with the French.   In April, 1901, the 2nd Battalion was reunited on the Gold Coast, and returned to Central Africa in July.   By that time it had earned a considerable reputation for the African askari as a fighting soldier, and when the reorganization was planned that resulted in 2nd C.A.R. becoming 2nd K.A.R., the unit was chosen as the Reserve Battalion, to be held in readiness for service in any protectorate where need arose.

Somaliland.—It was not long before the newly-recruited 2nd Battalion K.A.R. was again abroad.   In July, 1902, three companies and two maxim gun sections left for Somaliland, where another expedition was preparing against the Mad Mullah.   On 6th October an action took place in thick bush at Erego, a day's march north of the Mudug Oasis.   When the dervishes attacked the square, some of the newly-raised local levies fell back in panic, but were rallied by the steadiness of the Yaos, who formed the right of the formation.   Operations were resumed on a greatly increased scale in 1903, when the remaining companies of 2nd K.A.R. and other K.A.R. and Indian units were sent to Somaliland. A serious disaster was experienced near Gumburu on 17th April.   "C" Company 2nd K.A.R. under Captain H. E. Olivey had been sent out on reconnaissance from a column seeking a route to the water holes at Wardair, and on its way back to camp was attacked by some thousands of dervishes on horse and foot. Major A. W. V. Plunkett went to its relief with "A" Company and some men of the 2nd Sikhs.   The two parties joined forces, but were then attacked and completely overwhelmed by the dervishes, who killed all nine British officers (seven of whom belonged to 2nd K.A.R.), two Indian officers and 185 rank and file.   Early in 1904, three companies of the battalion again took part in a major action at Jidbali, though on this occasion the dervish attack was so quickly beaten off that the troops of 2nd K.A.R., who were stationed on the rear face of the formation, were scarcely engaged.   In July, 1904, the battalion embarked for East Africa, where three months were spent in the unfamiliar climate of Nairobi before returning home.

It had now been decided that the 1st and 2nd Battalions were to become home and foreign service battalions alternately.   The 2nd Battalion was therefore due for a period in Central Africa.   In 1908 it was again abroad on garrison duty, with some of its companies stationed in East Africa and some at Zanzibar. At this time the authorities were anxious to reduce military expenditure and to develop their police forces to meet the needs of internal security, and in 1911 the decision was taken to disband 2nd K.A.R.   Most of the officers were absorbed by other battalions, but unfortunately many of the askaris crossed the frontier and took service in the forces of German East Africa.

The War of 1914-18[1].—Even before the outbreak of war in 1914 it was realised that the reductions in the K.A.R. had been excessive, and some increase in the strength of battalions had been effected.   For the first few months of the war only the K.A.R. was available to defend the frontiers of British territory, and to protect the railway to Uganda.   Gradually a considerable force of Indian, Rhodesian, South African and British troops was built up, and the regular battalions of the K.A.R. formed a part of this army during the invasion of German East Africa from the north that resulted in the occupation of the Central Railway. After the end of 1916, however, most of the other troops were withdrawn, and

---

[1]See also pp. 82 to 87.

the task of driving von Lettow from German territory and hunting him through Portuguese East Africa was entrusted to the K.A.R. The strength of the regiment rose to twenty-two battalions, and the first of the new ones to be raised was a reconstituted 2nd K.A.R., formed at Nairobi in April, 1916, with a nucleus of four companies of 1st K.A.R. and some 1,100 recruits and reservists from Nyasaland. Like most of the other battalions, the 2nd became a regiment that expanded before the end of the war to three service battalions and one training battalion. 1st/2nd K.A.R. and 2nd/2nd K.A.R. were the first of the new units to take the field, in August and September, 1916, respectively.

The fortunes of the service battalions of 2nd K.A.R. during the years 1916-18 cannot be described here in detail. 1st/2nd K.A.R. first went into action at Kimbarambara on 11th October, 1916, and a few weeks later took part in the defence of Kibata against a prolonged series of determined attacks by von Lettow's forces, the only action of the whole campaign that could properly be described as trench warfare. Later on the battalion formed part of a column advancing from Lindi, and after a number of engagements took part in the pitched battle at Mahiwa on 17th-18th October, 1917, the result of which was the virtual destruction of von Lettow's offensive power. 2nd/2nd K.A.R. also took part in the Kibata operations, and afterwards formed part of a column in the Kilwa area. This battalion bore the brunt of the attack against the German defences at Narungombe on 19th July, 1917, and took part in several other actions designed to drive a wedge between the enemy's forces at Mahenge and those in the Lindi area. 3rd/2nd K.A.R. also took part in the advance from Lindi. So heavy were the casualties suffered at Mahiwa that for a time 1st/2nd and 3rd/2nd K.A.R. were combined for tactical purposes as a single unit. At the end of 1917 the three battalions of 2nd K.A.R. were formed into the 1st Brigade, which a few months later was reorganized as Kartucol (the 2nd K.A.R. column). Von Lettow crossed into Portuguese territory, where he replenished his stock of arms and ammunition, and an exhausting pursuit under the worst possible conditions began, in which the initiative lay with the enemy. It was not easy to bring the German forces to action, but engagements were fought at Lioma on 31st August, 1918 and at Pere six days later. Soon afterwards the pursuit was taken up by other forces and the service battalions of 2nd K.A.R. were withdrawn to quieter regions. Altogether 5,609 African ranks served with these battalions during the war, and the total casualties numbered 2,374.

Early in 1919, 1st/2nd K.A.R. was officially disbanded and such men of 2nd/2nd and 3rd/2nd K.A.R. as were not due for discharge were combined to form a new 2nd Battalion. In March, 1919, this battalion was stationed at Tabora, where it remained until 1933. It then returned to Nyasaland following the reorganization that brought the Southern Brigade into being, and the long association of this unit with Tanganyika, both during and after the first world war, came to an end.

THE 6TH BATTALION

Formation.—The title 6th K.A.R., now held by the battalion territorially connected with Tanganyika, was first borne by the battalion planned for British Somaliland under the reorganization scheme of 1902, but which owing to the operations against the Mullah was not actually formed until 1904. The life of this battalion was short, for in March, 1910, British administration was withdrawn to the coastal areas of Somaliland and the battalion was disbanded in favour of a Camel Constabulary. When in 1917 it was decided to raise another regiment of the K.A.R. instead of adding yet more battalions to the existing regiments, as originally intended, the designation 6th K.A.R. was revived. The recruits drafted to the new regiment came from Uganda and East Africa as well as from Tanganyika, but contained a fair proportion of ex-German askaris. For this and other reasons the regiment was not actively employed against von Lettow's forces. The 1st/6th K.A.R., formed on 1st June, 1917, was drafted to general reserve in July, and early in 1918 moved to the Abyssinian frontier. 2nd/6th K.A.R., formed on 1st August, 1917, was employed on garrison duty in Tanganyika. A third battalion came into existence at Mbagathi before the end of the war. Early in 1919 a new 6th (Tanganyika) Battalion K.A.R. was constituted. No. 1 Company was formed from coastal tribes serving in 7th K.A.R., one of the battalions due for disbandment. Nos. 2 and 3 Companies were formed from the service battalions of 4th K.A.R., and No. 4 Company later in the year from 2nd/6th K.A.R. There was therefore a mixture of tribes, not all being drawn from Tanganyika at that time. Headquarters were established at Dar es Salaam.

Somaliland.—The establishment of the K.A.R. as a whole was to have been reduced to six battalions as from 1st April, 1919. For a time unrest in different parts of the continent prevented this policy from being carried out. A new campaign was planned against the Mad Mullah and his followers, and before the end of the year two companies of 6th K.A.R. had left Tanganyika for Somaliland, to be joined later by a third company of 6th K.A.R. and a company of 2nd K.A.R. This composite battalion disembarked at Las Khorai and was charged with the task of attacking the Mullah's fortress at Baran and preventing his escape eastward into Mijertein, while the Camel Corps, Indian troops and Somali levies approached from the west. On 23rd-25th January, 1920, the stone fort at Baran was besieged and finally stormed just as the defenders were attempting to escape. The Mullah was not present at Baran, and while the Camel Corps and a flight of K.A.R. bombers were chasing him from British territory the composite battalion continued to round up his followers and stock. The troops returned to Dar es Salaam in the following May.

Inter-War Reorganization.—In 1923 the K.A.R. was honoured by a grant of colours to all battalions, bearing the battle honours of the regiment as a whole. Colours for 6th K.A.R. were presented by H.E. the Governor on Empire Day. In 1925 the regiment was further honoured when H.M. the King consented to become Colonel-in-Chief.

The establishment authorized for Tanganyika after the 1914-18 war consisted in all of 2,000 combatant native ranks, with 72 British officers and N.C.O.s. This included a portion of the 2nd/1st (Nyasaland) Battalion, which was stationed for a time in the south of the territory. On the disbandment of this battalion in 1923 a reduction was effected to 65 officers and N.C.O.s and about 1,700 men. After the completion of the Tabora-Mwanza Railway in 1928 a detachment of the 2nd Battalion, which had been stationed at Mwanza, was also disbanded, thus further reducing the total establishment by three officers and nearly 300 men.

A major reorganization of the K.A.R. took place during the years 1929-1931. Battalion establishments were reduced to majors' commands, consisting of two rifle companies and a machine-gun company. In the case of 6th K.A.R. the

problem of premature discharge of askaris was solved by the creation of a 6th
K.A.R. Reserve of 100 men, administered through district officers and involving
the obligation of a month's training per annum. The K.A.R. Reserve of Officers
also came into being as a voluntary organization. The battalions of the regiment
were formed into two brigades, the northern comprising the troops in Kenya
and Uganda, and the southern those in Tanganyika and Nyasaland. Headquarters of the Southern Brigade were established at Dar es Salaam, and the
first distribution of troops was as follows:—

> 1st K.A.R.: headquarters Zomba, with detachments at Masoko and Songea.
>
> 2nd K.A.R.: headquarters Tabora, held as a reserve.
>
> 6th K.A.R.: headquarters at Dar es Salaam, with detachments at Mahenge
>   and Arusha.
>
> Brigade Signal Section   ⎫
> Brigade Supply and Transport Corps ⎬ Dar es Salaam.

In 1932 further reductions were made in establishment. The 6th K.A.R.
Band was abolished and not reformed until 1937, and the machine-gun company
was reduced to a platoon forming part of a new headquarter wing. The strength
of 6th K.A.R. then stood at 12 officers, 1 British warrant officer, and 385 African
ranks. In addition to their military training this small body of troops was also
employed on locust control and pioneering work such as road construction.
It was not until the approach of war in 1939 that the establishment was increased
once more with the restoration of the two rifle companies, one in April, 1939
and the other in August, formed partly by mobilization of the Reserve and
partly by recruitment.

The War of 1939-45.—Throughout most of their history, the forces of the
East and Central African dependencies had been under the control of the Foreign
Office or the Colonial Office. In 1939 the exigencies of the situation made it
imperative for the War Office to take over, and the K.A.R. has remained under
War Office control until 1957, when the East African Land Forces Organization
came into being.

It is not possible within the scope of this short account to give a detailed
review of the service performed during the last war by all those troops who had
been stationed—or in due course were raised—in Tanganyika, but a brief account
of the operations in which 6th K.A.R. participated must be recorded.

Three battalions of 6th K.A.R. took part in the campaign in East Africa.
Soon after the outbreak of war 1st/6th K.A.R. left Tanganyika to join the newly-
formed 22nd (E.A.) Brigade in Kenya. For some months the battalion was
stationed in the Northern Frontier District, engaged on frontier patrols. In
June, 1940, Italy entered the war on the side of Germany, and Italian East Africa
became hostile territory. Soon afterwards the battalion was called upon to
support the K.A.R. garrison on its withdrawal from the frontier fort at Moyale.
When the British offensive was planned in Cairo that year, General Wavell's
intention was to forestall any further offensive by recapturing the frontier posts
occupied by the Italians in Kenya and the Sudan, and to follow this with a limited
advance from Kenya as far as the River Juba, occupying Kismayu *en route* as a
supply port. As many troops as possible were then to be withdrawn from the
Sudan and East Africa to strengthen the main effort against Cyrenaica. Events
turned out very differently, for out of these small intentions was born the swiftest
fighting advance in military history and the first complete land victory of the war.

Two routes were feasible for an advance across the Northern Frontier District: from railhead at Nanyuki through Marsabit to Moyale: or from railhead at Thika to Garissa on the River Tana, and thence across the frontier to Afmadu and Kismayu. The latter route was chosen; in great secrecy the concentration of troops was completed by January, 1941, and early in February the advance began, with 22nd (E.A.) Brigade in the lead. 1st/6th K.A.R. took part in the action for the first objective, the wells at Afmadu. Kismayu and Gobwen were taken soon afterwards, and the attack came up against the main Italian defence line along the River Juba. The crossing of the river had to be effected in the face of greatly superior forces, and was strongly contested. While the frontal attack was pressed along the lower reaches, 1st/6th K.A.R. took part with the rest of 22nd Brigade in an outflanking attack that forced a way through dense, trackless bush to cross the river near Gelib and cut the Italian main line of retreat to Mogadishu. The defence of the Juba collapsed, and with it went the whole of Italian Somaliland, for the Italians had made no defensive preparations in rear of the Juba position. The Brigade led the pursuit to Mogadishu and then came into reserve for a time while the advance continued northward into Abyssinia, pressing in the Italian rearguard at the Marda and Fiumbiro Passes, occupying Harrar and Diredawa, and continuing along the road and railway to the next line of enemy defence, where the River Awash flows through a deep gorge cut in the depression of the Rift Valley. Here again 1st/6th K.A.R. and the rest of 22nd Brigade came into the lead, forced the crossing of the river in the face of the enemy and so reached Addis Ababa, which was formally entered on 6th April, 1941.

The Italian armies were now irretrievably split, and had scattered north along the route to Asmara, west towards Gimma and the Sudan, and south into the area of the lakes. 1st/6th K.A.R. was employed in the last-named area, where the battalion fought one of its most important actions. While the 12th Division moved inland from Somalia and began to penetrate the lakes from the direction of Neghelli, 22nd Brigade forestalled a threat to the Diredawa-Addis Ababa line of communication by advancing south from Moggio, forcing the crossing of the Little Dababa River by a double outflanking movement, and entering Shashamana and Dalle, which were abandoned without a fight. By this time the rains had broken and the dirt tracks had been churned into a sea of mud, but the Italians were trapped between two opposing forces with an escape route only to the west, which it was essential to close. The task fell to 22nd Brigade, which streamed into the gap, advancing from both sides of Lake Shala to converge on Colito, where the Italians had taken up their position defending the River Billate. The brunt of the ensuing battle, which was fought on 19th May, 1941, fell upon 1st/6th K.A.R. Supported by artillery, the battalion assaulted the position and two companies succeeded in crossing the river and establishing a bridgehead. At that moment the Italians counter-attacked with light and medium tanks. The troops had no anti-tank weapons with which to meet the assault, but Sgt. Nigel Leakey of 1st/6th K.A.R. leapt upon one of the tanks, wrenched open the turret and shot the commander and all the crew except the driver. With an African C.S.M. and two askaris he began to stalk the others, mounted one of them, and was apparently shot down. His courage was an inspiration to all the troops who witnessed it, and in spite of the odds that faced them they succeeded in holding the position. In 1945 a posthumous award of the Victoria Cross was made for this act of gallantry.

As a result of the battle of Colito the key position of Soddu was abandoned by the Italians without resistance, and two generals, nearly 5,000 troops and a number of guns fell into British hands. By this time the roads in the lakes area were in imminent danger of collapse. 22nd Brigade was transferred across country to a point on the Gimma-Addis Ababa road, and took part in the final round-up of the Italian armies in the west, which were forced to retreat into the arms of the troops who had meanwhile approached from the Sudan to seal the frontier. 1st/6th K.A.R. was then for a time stationed on the Strada Imperiale, the great highway connecting Addis Ababa with Asmara.

2nd/6th K.A.R. also took part in the concluding stages of these operations. In October, 1940, the battalion had left Kenya for the Sudan, where it joined the Sudan Defence Force in operations along the frontier, culminating in the final surrender of the western Italian armies. 2nd/6th K.A.R. was then employed in evacuating prisoners of war, which was carried out by sea from Berbera, where the battalion again concentrated in September, 1941. By that time 3rd/6th K.A.R., which had been serving on the Juba as part of the 12th Division while the main advance on Addis Ababa was taking place, was also in Somaliland.

Sealed off for a time by the coming of the rains, the final remnant of the Italian armies in Abyssinia, numbering some 30,000 men all told, remained secure on the high and fertile plateau around Gondar until November, 1941. As soon as the roads became passable a converging attack was mounted on the position by 25th (E.A.) Brigade, 26th (E.A.) Brigade, a composite body known as South Force, and a battalion of the new Abyssinian army. On 13th November 1st/6th K.A.R. delivered an attack on Kulkaber which was only partly successful. A second attack on 21st November, in which 25th Brigade also participated, stormed the Kulkaber position. Afterwards 1st/6th and 3rd/6th K.A.R. took part in the general assault from the east against Deflecha Ridge. The attack was pressed simultaneously from all sides, and General Nasi, the Italian commander, surrendered on 27th November, well pleased with himself for having prolonged resistance so long.

With the Italian threat finally removed, the position of the East African territories now appeared secure, but the situation was entirely altered by the entry of Japan into the war in December, 1941, and the conquest of Burma and Malaya that so rapidly followed. In the words of the Commander-in-Chief, East Africa now had to face east instead of north. For a time there was some danger that the Japanese Navy might dominate the Indian Ocean, as her submarines were known to be operating in African waters. 2nd/6th K.A.R., which had returned to Kenya early in 1942, was brought up to strength and sent to Mombasa to form part of the defence of the port. The attitude of the Vichy French Government in Madagascar could not be trusted, so to prevent the use of Diego Suarez harbour by the enemy, a force from the United Kingdom landed in May and occupied the town. In June 1st/6th K.A.R., as part of 22nd (E.A.) Brigade Group, reached Diego Suarez as part of the garrison.

It soon became apparent that to share Madagascar with the Vichy French was merely to perpetuate a dangerous situation. The first step necessary was the occupation of the island of Mayotte to secure a seaplane base near the Mozambique Channel. 1st/6th K.A.R took part in this, the first combined operation to include African troops. In great secrecy plans were then matured to complete the conquest of Madagascar. On the night of 9th-10th September, 1942, a convoy of 49 ships, with 29th Independent Brigade from Mombasa and 22nd (E.A.) Brigade from Diego Suarez anchored off Majunga. The town was taken by 29th Brigade after slight resistance, and 22nd Brigade was landed, to advance with all possible speed to capture the two main bridges on the road to Tananarive. The advance was led by 1st/1st K.A.R., and although the most important bridge at Betsiboka had been blown, it was found possible to get across it. The Brigade continued against a series of road blocks. More serious opposition was offered at Mahitais, but Tananarive was entered on 23rd September. Meanwhile other landings were in progress at Tamatave and elsewhere on the coast.

On withdrawing from Tananarive the French went south towards Antsirabe, with Ambositra and Fianarantsoa beyond. After a pause the pursuit was resumed against stiffening opposition, with 1st/6th K.A.R. and the armoured cars in the lead. The old task of clearing road blocks was resumed, and Antsirabe was reached on 2nd October. Soon afterwards 5th K.A.R. became the advance guard. Ambositra was entered on 13th October, and five days later an enemy position of some strength was encountered at Andriamanalina. A combined attack was planned, to be carried out by 1st/6th K.A.R. and 5th K.A.R., supported by artillery. This necessitated a twenty-four hour march by the former to outflank the enemy and reach his rear, which was executed so successfully that the attack, simultaneously mounted at dawn on 19th October by both battalions, carried the position and captured 700 prisoners and a number of guns. Fianarantsoa was occupied on 29th October and a few days later the French sought an armistice. 22nd (E.A.) Brigade subsequently returned to Kenya, where it was used to reinforce other brigades, and 1st/6th K.A.R. was called upon to train reinforcements for the units serving in Burma. Had not peace with Japan come sooner than expected, the battalion would have seen service there also, during the final campaign that was planned for the latter part of 1945.

On the extension of the war to South-East Asia, 11th (E.A.) Division had been re-formed, as it was intended to use the K.A.R. for the first time on active operations outside the continent of Africa and its adjacent islands. 2nd/6th K.A.R. and 3rd/6th K.A.R. both served as part of this division, which left East Africa in June, 1943, and continued its training in jungle warfare for another year in Ceylon. By the time the Division arrived in Burma the Japanese attempt to invade Assam had resulted in a costly failure and the British offensive was about to begin. The first objective was the establishment of a bridgehead across the Chindwin River, so that the enemy could be brought to battle on the plains of Central Burma, where superiority in armoured vehicles could be fully exploited.

To reach the Chindwin two difficult routes, via Tiddim and via Tamu, had to be followed from Imphal to Kalemyo, continuing thence down the valley of the River Myittha to Kalewa, where the crossing of the Chindwin was to be made. The Tiddim route was allotted to 5th (Indian) Division, and the Tamu route to 11th (E.A.) Division, which took the lead after the capture of Tamu on 4th August, 1944, for the terrible advance down the Kabaw Valley, or "Valley of Death". The Japanese fought rearguard actions all the way; appalling weather converted the tracks to a mass of mud from six to eighteen inches deep, and the area was malarial and unhealthy. While part of the division advanced east to occupy Sittaung, the nearest point on the Chindwin, the remainder, which included

2nd/6th and 3rd/6th K.A.R., continued throughout September to make steady progress down the valley. On 4th October Yazagyo was captured. Soon afterwards the monsoon ceased and quicker progress was possible. On 13th November a junction was made with 5th (Indian) Division, and two days later the combined force entered Kalemyo, which was found to be deserted. The attack now turned east down the Myittha gorge towards the Chindwin. 3rd/6th K.A.R. became the divisional headquarters battalion, but for the last five days 2nd/6th K.A.R. was in the lead and was first to enter Kalewa on 2nd December, 1944. The Japanese had been relentlessly pursued since the previous July, and their losses were considerable. While the British forces streamed across the Kalewa bridgehead into Central Burma, 11th (E.A.) Division was withdrawn to a quieter area. It had carried out successfully one of the most difficult operations of the whole campaign, in which 2nd/6th and 3rd/6th K.A.R. had taken full part.

Post-War Reorganization.—The five battalions to which 6th K.A.R. had expanded during the course of the war were reduced to a single battalion in July 1946, when the troops who had served in Burma returned home. The battalion was stationed at Dar es Salaam with two companies (later reduced to one) at Moshi. A detachment from the battalion took part in the Victory Parade in London that year.

A great deal of reorganization had to be carried out in the early post-war period. Administration began once more on a peace footing; cross-postings of askaris took place to adjust the territorial representation of the unit: guard mounting was taken over from the police at Government House, and the general peace-time routine of recruitment, training and battalion camps was resumed. In 1948 the Band returned on permanent duty after an absence of eight years.

In February, 1950, 6th K.A.R. left Dar es Salaam for Mauritius, where the whole battalion was able to serve together for the first time on garrison duty in peace. On 19th May that year the practice was inaugurated of commemorating "Colito Day" in honour of the battle and the heroism of Sgt. Leakey, V.C.

In 1951 it was decided to raise two new battalions of the K.A.R. One of them, 26th K.A.R., was formed on 18th July from certain officers, N.C.O.s and specialists of 6th K.A.R., together with "C" and "D" Companies, which were transferred complete. These troops left Mauritius for Dar es Salaam and recruiting then began to bring up to strength both the battalions that are now raised and recruited in Tanganyika.

The remainder of 6th Battalion K.A.R. returned from Mauritius in November, 1952.

In spite of a large backlog of leave to be made up, half the battalion went straight to Kenya, where the Mau Mau emergency was just starting, most of the remainder moved into the old 6th Battalion barracks at Kilwa Road, Dar es Salaam, but one company was stationed at Moshi.

At this time the new barracks, now known as Colito Barracks, were taking shape at Observation Hill, while the old Officers' Mess at Dar es Salaam was being bulldozed into the sea to make way for deep-water berths and railway sidings, and buildings were springing up all over the former barrack area.

In July and August, 1953, the new barracks were taken over and the move to Observation Hill took place.

For the remainder of 1953 and 1954 Dar es Salaam became the base and rest station, Rifle Companies spending periods of three months out of the line.

In January, 1953, the Moshi cantonment was closed down completely and Headquarters Southern Area moved to Colito Barracks, where it remained until the Federation of Rhodesia and Nyasaland finally claimed 1st Battalion Northern Rhodesia Regiment, 1st Battalion K.A.R. and 2nd Battalion K.A.R. at the beginning of July, 1954. Southern Area then ceased to exist and 6th Battalion came directly under East Africa Command for administration.

In June, 1954, a second company of 6th Battalion was sent to Dar es Salaam in order to prepare a strong company of 185 rank and file to relieve 26th Battalion K.A.R. in Mauritius in December. This virtually swallowed up "A" and "D" Companies complete.

To return to the half battalion which had gone to Kenya. These two companies nearly always had companies from other battalions under command to compensate for the missing companies in Tanganyika; invariably one or two companies of 26th Battalion K.A.R. and on occasion companies of 4th Battalion, 3rd Battalion, 7th Battalion, 23rd Battalion, 156th Battery East African Artillery and the East African Armoured Car Squadron, 1st Devons, 1st Buffs, 1st R.M.F. and 1st Black Watch.

In South Nyeri at the start of the emergency the force was split up into small platoon detachments all over the reserve, apart from a small "I" force at Nyeri. Approximately sixteen Kenya Regiment officers and sergeants were posted to the battalion to bring it up to strength, as missing detachments in Dar es Salaam, Moshi and elsewhere in Kenya made it very short of British personnel and it was considered essential to have British ranks with each platoon or detachment.

To start with, only minor incidents took place, but as time went on the terrorists became organized into gangs and were set on exterminating the Kikuyu Guard, then in its infancy, before it could become effective. This called for small platoon posts within call of the Kikuyu Guard posts, especially near the forest edge, and for well planned counter-offensive measures immediately an attack occurred.

In early May there were several actions round Othaya Division, where "C" Company was spread out in platoon posts endeavouring to protect an area which was later the responsibility of a complete British battalion. After a series of attacks on Kikuyu Guard posts, Othaya Police Post itself was attacked by a gang of 180 on 8th May, 1953. Unluckily for the gang they chose the corner of the post held by Major Crombie, R.M., O.C. "C" Company, C.S.M. Rushworth, African C.S.M. Eleuteri and eight African ranks of "C" Company Headquarters, the remainder of the post being held by raw police askaris. It is thought that the gang had dosed themselves with bhang as they paid little heed to the grenades hurled at them or to the rifle and automatic fire. Three determined attacks were made between 0145 hours and 0430 hours.

At first light fourteen bodies, a bren gun (previously captured from an ambushed Kenya Regiment patrol) and two rifles were lying outside the wire, five wounded were rounded up and thirteen further bodies were pulled out of the River Ziti nearby. Later it was discovered from intelligence sources that the total enemy casualties were approximately eighty killed.

A series of attacks and counter-attacks and forest engagements took place throughout May and then with the arrival of 39th Infantry Brigade and the additional troops available the situation improved. The battalion continued to operate in South Nyeri, mainly in the Reserve and at times in Fort Hall. Sometimes it was under the command of 70th East African Brigade, sometimes under 39th Infantry Brigade; sometimes operating in or opposite the Aberdares, at other times on the Mount Kenya side.

In September, 1953 the battalion moved to Kiambu to replace 23rd Battalion K.A.R. Here one company was permanently engaged in guard duties at Government House and the Commander-in-Chief's House and the other two were available for operations.

At this time the Kiambu settled areas and reserve were quiet and activities were mainly concentrated on the bamboo forest.

Later the situation deteriorated in the Thika settled area and to combat this in the new year "N" Force was formed under the Officer Commanding 6th Battalion K.A.R. This consisted of two companies of 6th Battalion, 156th Battery East African Artillery, one company of the Buffs and one company of the Black Watch, and was responsible for Kiambu, Nairobi and Thika Districts, holding the fort while the three brigades finished cleaning up Nyeri, Nanyuki and Fort Hall.

By the end of February, 1954, planning for operation "Anvil" and the post-Anvil period was well under way and in mid-March "N" Force was absorbed into 49th Independent Infantry Brigade. During operation "Anvil" 6th Battalion was mainly responsible for the outlying posts of Nairobi and the Kiambu-Nairobi Border.

This operation produced a considerable improvement in the city but the situation at once deteriorated in Kiambu and Thika Districts.

6th Battalion now came under command of 39th Infantry Brigade once again for operation "Pugilist" which was intended to eliminate terrorist gangs which had moved out of Nairobi into Kiambu and Thika and to build up and train the Kikuyu Guard and Farm Guards in the two districts into an effective force.

At the end of May a terrorist gang infiltrated into the Mount Meru-Kilimanjaro area of Tanganyika. "D" Company was sent hot-foot from Dar es Salaam to Arusha to deal with the situation. They patrolled the Longido and Loliondo areas for approximately a month and then returned to Dar es Salaam. Also during May "C" Company 6th Battalion moved to Manyani and Mackinnon Road in case of trouble at the internee camps. They were relieved by "B" Company 26th Battalion in July.

In August 39th Infantry Brigade moved north to Mount Kenya and the battalion once more assumed responsibility for the whole of Kiambu.

In early September it became clear that the Mau Mau were making a determined attack on the Limuru and Kiambu settled areas. The situation in Nairobi and in the reserves was now under control, except for Dagoretti and Kabete, and the terrorists were forced into thick cover.

Many incidents occurred and the battalion was successful in capturing numerous arms and a quantity of ammunition and obtained a higher number of successes in the course of the month than any one brigade. It was then reinforced by the East African Armoured Car Squadron, and "I" Company Kenya Regiment and two companies of 4th Battalion came back under command. With this more formidable force the battalion set about cleaning up the settled area in conjunction with the Administration and a drive was started to clear unnecessary bush, concentrate the labour and get the Farm Guard better organized. From October onwards planning was going on for the battalion's move to Dar es Salaam and the relief of 26th Battalion in Mauritius.

On 2nd December, 1954, the battalion entrained for Mombasa, embarking on the *Cheshire* for Dar es Salaam. The day they arrived "D" Company embarked on the same ship for Mauritius.

When the battalion reached Dar es Salaam it marched through the town with bayonets fixed and colours flying, His Excellency the Governor and the Mayor taking the salute.

Chapter 14

NATURAL HISTORY

VEGETATION AND FLORA

Tanganyika with an area of some 365,000 square miles has an altitudinal range from sea level to 19,340 ft. (Mt. Kilimanjaro) and is bounded by Lakes Victoria (3,717 ft. alt., 26,000 square miles) Lake Tanganyika (2,515 ft. alt., 12,700 square miles) and Lake Nyasa (1,645 ft. alt., 14,200 square miles). Other lakes are Lake Rukwa, Lake Eyasi, Lake Manyara and Lake Natron, all of which are brackish.

Its most important rivers are the Umba, Pangani, Wami, Kingani, Rufiji, Matundu, Mbemkuru, Lukuledi and Ruvuma, all flowing into the Indian Ocean. Those which flow into Lakes Victoria, Tanganyika, Rukwa and Nyasa are the Mori, Mara, Kagera, Malagarasi, Songwe or Rukwa, Saisi, Songwe and Ruhuhu Rivers.

With a range of altitude from sea level to over 19,000 ft. and comparatively well watered, the rainfall of the territory varies greatly as the following figures for three of the wettest and three of the driest stations will show:—

Wettest Stations (period 1940-1949)[1]

Tukuyu, 5,069 ft. alt., Rungwe District, Southern Highlands Province; 96·52 in. annual average; maximum 130·77 in. in 153 days, minimum 71·22 in. in 133 days.

Bukoba, 3,709 ft. alt., Bukoba District, Lake Province; 81·08 in. annual average; maximum 105·38 in. in 190 days, minimum 64·53 in. in 138 days.

Amani, 3,001 ft. alt., Tanga District, Tanga Province; 74·10 in. annual average; maximum 83·71 in. in 174 days, minimum 61·55 in. in 181 days.

Driest Stations (period 1940-1949)

Mkomazi, 1,520 ft. alt., Lushoto District, Tanga Province; 13·59 in. annual average; maximum 26·70 in. in 55 days, minimum 4·45 in. in 15 days.

Kisangiro, 2,903 ft. alt., Pare District, Tanga Province; 14·34 in. annual average; maximum 25·73 in. in 35 days, minimum 8·39 in. in 16 days.

Kidete (1937-1946) 2,230 ft. alt., Kilosa District, Eastern Province; 17·60 in. annual average; maximum 27·24 in. in 34 days, minimum 5·05 in. in 48 days.

At Bismarck Hut at about 8,000 ft. alt. on the eastern slopes of Kilimanjaro a recording rain gauge gave the following rainfall data:—

1945	...	73·06 in.
1946	...	62·37 in.
1947	...	71·23 in.
1948	...	101·98 in.

an average of 77·16 in. for the four years

In spite of the territory being comparatively well-watered, the vegetation of the country as a whole is of a dry type and the great extremes of rainfall are reflected in the vegetative types of the localities for which rainfall figures have been quoted.

---

[1] I am indebted to the Director, E.A. Meteorological Department, Nairobi, Kenya, for supplying me with these rainfall figures.

There are eight main physiognomic vegetation types represented in Tanganyika. They are:—

1 Forest, 2 Woodland, 3 Bushland and Thicket, 4 Wooded Grassland, 5 Grassland, 6 Permanent Swamp Vegetation, 7 Desert and Semi-Desert and 8 Vegetation actively induced by man.

These types can be further divided into sub-types.

Forest

For a land area of some 365,000 square miles the area covered by forest is pitifully small and very scattered throughout the territory. The type forest can best be described as vegetation composed of a continuous stand of trees, which may attain a height of 150 ft. or more, with crowns touching or inter-mingling and often freely interlaced with lianes. The canopy may be of great thickness and usually consists of several distinct layers or stories. Epiphytic plants, including orchids, ferns and giant mosses are characteristic, especially in the wetter types. Various lichens, especially Old Man's Beard (*Usnea*), are often a conspicuous feature, especially in the Upland types. The trees have simple or buttressed boles and in most types the majority of them are in full leaf all the year round. In a few types deciduous species predominate. The forest floor may, where the light permits, be covered with herbs and shrubs from a few inches to several feet high and interspersed with perennial climbers. If the tree canopy is particularly dense, excluding light, the ground is bare of herbs, but may be covered with mosses; but this type is rare in Tanganyika. Grasses, if present, are highly specialized, comparatively localized and inconspicuous.

The following types and sub-types of forest are represented in the territory:—

Lowland Rain Forest, Upland Rain Forest; Lowland Dry Evergreen Forest; Upland Dry Evergreen Forest; Deciduous Forest; Ground-water Forest and its sub-types Riverine Forest and Swamp Forest, e.g. Fresh-water Swamp Forest; Saline-water Swamp (Mangrove) Forest.

Rain Forest:—Good examples can be seen in parts of the East and West Usambaras, North and South Pare, the southern slopes of Kilimanjaro, Nguru and Uluguru Mountains and other mountain masses from about 3,000 to 8,000 ft. altitude.

Lowland and Upland Dry or Mist Forest:—The Lowland in scattered patches in the coastal belt is composed of a diversity of species. The Upland on most of the mountain masses is dominated for the most part by Cedar, *Juniperus procera* Hochst, ex A. Rich., Olives, *Olea* spp., *Rapanea* spp., Pillar woods, *Cassipourea*, East African Camphor, *Ocotea*, *Myrica*, *Agaurea* and other *Erica-ceae*. Examples are to be seen on the northern end of the West Usambaras, parts of the Pare Mountains, northern slopes of Kilimanjaro, Meru, the Crater Highlands, Mporoto and Livingstone Mountains.

Deciduous forest:—Extremely rare.

Ground-water and Riverine Fringing Forest:—Good examples are to be seen in the foot-hills of the eastern Usambaras, parts of the eastern side of the Pare Mountains, the Rau Forest at the south-eastern foot of Kilimanjaro, on the eastern side of the Nguru Mountains and on the banks of the major rivers.

Swamp Forest.—This again can be divided into two sub-types, Fresh-water or Saline. The former can be observed in the Bukoba District, particularly

on the Tanganyika–Uganda border.   The latter, Mangrove Forest, is found
in broken patches from the mouth of the Ruvuma river in the south to the
Kenya–Tanganyika border in the north, the finest examples are to be seen in the
Rufiji delta, limited patches on Mafia island, in the mouth of the Pangani river
and it is well developed in the numerous creeks and bays north of Tanga.   The
dominant genera, all of economic importance, are in order of frequency, *Avicen-
nia marina* (Forsk.) Vierh., *Rhizophora mucronata* Lam., *Bruguiera gymnorrhiza*
(L.) Lam., *Ceriops tagal* (Perr.) C. B. Robinson, *Xylocarpus*, *Lumnitzera racemosa*
Willd., and *Sonneratia*.

Woodland

About three quarters of the territory is covered by woodland,   which
floristically is very varied owing to differing combinations of climatic and edaphic
factors.   It can only be subdivided by its dominant genera such as *Brachystegia*,
Isoberlinia, *Pseudoberlinia*, *Acacia*, *Combretum* and *Uapaca* woodlands.   Woodland is land carrying an open cover of trees whose crowns do not form a thickly
interlaced canopy and which, as a rule, are leafless for some period of the year.
Scattered evergreen shrubs may be present but are not conspicuous, whilst
grasses and herbs form the dominant ground cover; epiphytic plants are rare,
though there may be lichens.   It can pass into a Bushland and Thicket type,
or with a stand of trees and bushes covering less than 50 per cent of the ground
when it would be classed as Wooded Grassland.

Bushland and Thicket

This is land carrying a more than 50 per cent cover of densely growing shrubs
or small trees; the trees and bushes may be evergreen or deciduous, spiny or
non-spiny.   The bushes have no clearly defined boles and may be from one to
thirty feet high.   Tall trees may be present, either in clumps or as widely scattered
individuals, but do not of themselves form a continuous canopy over the main
bush cover; climbers are common.   In the evergreen sub-types epiphytics are
present.   Herbs both ephemeral and succulent, and dwarf grasses, may form part
of the ground cover in deciduous bushland.   Thickets are close assemblages of
coppicing virgate bushes.

Bushland and thicket are well represented in the Umba Steppe north of the
western Usambaras and in the coastal belt.   The so-called Itigi Thicket on the
Central Railway centred at Itigi is a good example.   Another is the Msua
Thicket also on the Central Railway in the coastal sector west of the Ruvu valley,
which is composed of semi-thicket and low trees, containing many tree species,
numerous succulent or spiny shrubs and creepers, in places lichen-covered,
maintained probably by the mists that penetrate from the sea through the wide
depression of the Ruvu valley.

Wooded Grassland

This is land covered with grasses and other herbs, generally perennial, with
trees and bushes, either evergreens or deciduous, grouped or scattered, occupying
less than 50 per cent of the ground.   The grasses dominate the aspect but the
woody species are always conspicuous.   This type contains a great variety
and mixture of sub-types including *Acacia-Commiphora* and the woody forms
growing more or less exclusively on termite mounds and Palm Stands Grasslands
(*Borassus* or *Hyphaene* palms).   Examples are to be met with on the Ardai
plains, parts of the Serengeti plains, the Wami plains and the Bohora flats.

Grassland

This is land covered with grasses and other herbs, sometimes with evergreen or deciduous trees or shrubs widely scattered or in small isolated groups, and occupying not more than 10 per cent of the ground. Grassland can be divided into Flood Plain, Pan and Valley Grasslands, Seasonal Swamp Grasslands and Upland Grasslands, the latter with a sub-type Moor Grasslands. The best example of the latter is to be seen on Mt. Kilimanjaro between Bismarck Hut and Peter's Hut after passing through an Upland Rain Forest zone and before entering the sub-type Upland Moor of a Bushland, Thicket, Scrub type; others are the Elton and Lukwangule plateaux.

Flood Plain, Pan and Valley Grasslands are to be observed in the Rukwa trough, north of Lake Nyasa, the Wembere steppe, the Weda and Huru Huru *mbugas*, the Masai steppe *mbugas* and the Yaida, and along the banks of the more important river systems where not occupied by Riverine or Swamp Forest.

Seasonal Swamp Grasslands are found along with Flood Plain, Pan and Valley Grasslands on plains, usually with a black cotton soil which during the rains become water-logged and may even be flooded to a depth of several feet for some months of the year. A good example is between Magunga and Korogwe on the old Tanga–Korogwe road and others between Mkomazi and Lembeni on the road to Moshi.

Upland Grasslands are to be observed on the Ardai and Serengeti plains; at Mufindi, Dabaga and Sao Hill; in the Njombe District, which has some very fine examples; in parts of Mbeya (near the Tukuyu turn-off at Njiapanda) and on the Mbeya range.

Permanent Swamp Vegetation

This consists of grasses, reeds (mostly papyrus) and rushes, sometimes ferns, the components of this type of vegetation with their stems arising out of the free water accumulated on the surface either from perennial flooding or from an outcropping ground water table. When covered with trees or shrubs it is classed as Swamp or Ground Water Forest.

This type can be subdivided into four sub-types, Grass Swamps, Reed (Papyrus) Swamps, Rush Swamps and Fern Swamps, all or most of them around the shores of Lakes Victoria, Tanganyika, Rukwa and Nyasa, and along the banks of the more important rivers.

Desert and Semi-Desert Vegetation

No true desert is found in Tanganyika unless one classes as desert the almost bare and boulder-scattered saddle between Kibo and Mawenzi on Kilimanjaro, the upper flanks on the western side of Kibo, and the rocky pinnacles of Mawenzi, also the upper slopes, particularly on the north and west of Mt. Meru.

Semi-desert vegetation consists of low bushes and stunted trees, mostly spiny or thorny, either deciduous or evergreen, sometimes with succulent climbers, thinly scattered tufted perennial or ephemeral grasses, succulent plants and other herbs mostly bulbous or tuberous rooted, which fluctuate according to the season. The important characteristic of semi-desert is that at all seasons of the year more than half the surface of the ground is bare of vegetation, so that the general aspect is dominated by the colour and character of the soil rather than that of the plants. The surface soil can be very hard and compacted, stony or rocky, or loose and very sandy.

Semi-Desert vegetation can be divided into Semi-Desert Scrub and Semi-Desert Grassland. In Semi-Desert Scrub the woody vegetation is prominent, dwarf Euphorbias and *Sansevieria* are sometimes conspicuous and perennial grasses absent, but after rain ephemeral grasses together with bulbous and tuberous rooted herbs may be conspicuous.

Semi-Desert Grassland is an open cover of perennial tussock grasses, such as *Chloris myriostachya* Hochet. or *Chrysopogon aucheri* (Boiss.) Stapf var. *quinqueplumis* Stapf, with widely spaced or very scattered spiny or unarmed bushes, shrub-like perennial herbs and an occasional solitary stunted or dwarfed tree. The chief characteristics of this type are the widely spaced tussock grasses, and sometimes a scattered woody herbage.

Examples of both types are to be seen between the southern Pares and the northern end of the West Usambaras, the Umba Steppe, the north-western side of the northern Pares and in that sector of the Northern Province through which the Great North Road passes north of Mt. Meru to Longido, westwards to the Rift and eastwards to the north-western foot of Kilimanjaro.

Vegetation Actively Induced by Man

This covers crops grown by all races and vegetation types induced by grazing stock. Crops can be divided into two groups, perennial and annual.

Perennial crops.

Tree and bush crops—such as coconut and oil palms and mangoes, mainly in the coastal belt, wattle, eucalyptus, coniferous and quinine upland plantations of the Forest Department and of planters, mainly in the areas; tea plantations in the East and West Usambaras and Southern Highlands Province, mostly around Mufindi and Tukuyu; coffee, mostly centred on the slopes of Kilimanjaro, Meru and in the Bukoba District, the bulk grown by Africans; fruits, such as citrus, apples, pears, plums, peaches, grapes, pawpaws for papain, in limited areas.

Herbaceous perennial crops.

Sisal, well represented in the coastal belt but also grown elsewhere; bananas in most areas with a high rainfall or a high ground-water table, the largest concentrations being around Kilimanjaro, Meru, Bukoba and Tukuyu; pineapples, planted and wild in the coastal belt, but not grown commercially; sugar-cane, only one commercial plantation at Arusha Chini, but extensively grown by Africans in areas suited to it; cassava, grown mainly by Africans and mostly concentrated in the coastal belt.

Annual crops.

Cotton grown by all races, mostly in the Eastern and Lake Provinces.

Grains.

Rice, grown by Africans mainly concentrated in the coastal belt and Lake and Southern Highlands Provinces; wheat and rye, grown by Europeans and Africans in the upland areas; maize, grown by all races generally throughout the territory; kaffir corn (sorghums) and millets (Bulrush and Finger), grown by Africans generally throughout the territory in localities suited to the different kinds.

Oil seeds.

Sim-sim, grown in the coastal belt by Africans, mostly on soil containing calcium in one form or another; ground-nuts, grown by Europeans and Africans in the Southern, Eastern, Central, Western and Lake Provinces. Pulses, beans, peas and grams, grown by all races everywhere with certain areas restricted to individual kinds, for example, cow peas in the coastal belt, peas in upland areas, kidney or french beans generally, but more favourably in upland areas, lentils in the Lake Province, and pigeon peas mostly in lowland areas.

European vegetables are mostly grown by Europeans and Africans everywhere in localities suited to the different kinds, but commercially in the West Usambaras, Ulugurus, Kilimanjaro, Meru and the Rungwe and Mbeya Districts. The European potato, although perennial, is included in this group for convenience of classification.

The Flora

With the altitudinal range already mentioned—from sea level to over 19,000 ft. and a known rainfall varying from 4·45 in. in 15 days (Mkomazi) to 130·77 in. in 153 days (Tukuyu) in any one year, the flora is as rich and varied as one would expect.

The marine flora is very poor in comparison to that of the northern temperate regions and central American waters and a study of our East African sea weeds and marine plants has yet to be made; our knowledge of this very specialized flora is greatly lacking.

Representatives of most of the African floral regions meet and frequently overlap in the territory and much has still to be learned about the distribution of the genera. There are too representatives of a European flora, such as Cuckoo-flower, *Cardamine*, Rockcress, *Arabis* in the Cruciferae and certain grasses such as *Poa annua* L. Are these relics of a past temperate region flora or have they been pushed down from Europe by an advancing ice cap from the north and left stranded on the various high mountain blocks by the recession of the last ice age?

With higher rainfall and temperatures did the type Rain Forest extend across tropical Africa from the west to the east coast of Africa? This question is posed because representatives of the West African flora are found in the Bukoba District as one would expect. There is then a discontinuous distribution of certain West African genera, and even species, to Kasulu in the west, with a great gap until we reach a narrow strip on the eastern side of the Western Usambaras, and the whole of the Eastern Usambaras. Further discontinuous distribution of the West African flora is again met with on the gneiss massifs of the Nguru and Uluguru Mountains, its most south-eastern known extension, although one or two occurrences have very recently been recorded from the Makonde Plateau where *Gardenia abbeokutae* Hiern, originally described from Abeokuta, West Africa, in 1877, has been discovered.

Species of an Ethiopian flora are found on most of the high mountain blocks, Khat, *Catha edulis* Forsk. for example, extends right down to the Cape. Khossus, *Hagenia abyssinica* (Bruce) J. F. Gmel., is found on all the high mountain massifs, especially those of volcanic origin, as far south as Mt. Rungwe. *Oxytenanthera abyssinica* (A. Rich.) Munro, as it name implies, from Ethiopia, extends into Uganda, missing Kenya, then with a broken distribution into the Western, Eastern and Southern Provinces. In the reverse direction Pear Wood, *Apodytes dimidiata* E. Mey. extends from the Cape up to Ethiopia. The Cape Chestnut *Calodendrum capense* Thumb. is similar.

Species of the Angolan flora are found in the Western Province as one would expect and they extend by way of the Southern Highlands Province into the Southern Province. A Nyasaland–Northern Rhodesian flora extends into the Southern and Southern Highlands Province and since these two provinces are contiguous to these countries, this is not surprising, but *Stophanthus kombe* Oliv., of economic importance to Nyasaland and found in Portuguese East Africa, appears again in the Dar es Salaam District, in Tanga Province, and in the Kenya coastal belt. On Mt. Hanang, Northern Province, a *Polygonum* has been found that has hitherto only been known from the Aberdares in Kenya; there are also several species on Mt. Hanang which until now have only been known from Nyasaland. Representatives of a Somaliland flora extend from Somalia by way of the Northern Frontier Province of Kenya down through the coastal hinterland of Kenya across the Umba Steppe as far south as Mkomazi, the northern limits of the Tanga Province. Since very little botanical collecting has been done on the eastern side of Masailand one does not know how far this Somaliland flora extends to the west of the Pangani River drainage basin or how far south to Kibaya on the old slave route from Pangani via Kondoa Irangi to Lake Victoria.

The grass flora of the territory is very rich and varied; there are certain genera only found on the high mountain blocks above 8,000 ft. and there are other genera which are only found in rain forest and in no other habitat. The most widespread in the grassland areas are Red-oat Grass, *Themeda triandra* Forsk., *Andropogon, Digitaria, Pennisetum, Panicum, Brachiaria, Setaria, Hyparrhenia* and *Cymbopogon*. Weeds of cultivated ground are *Eragrostis ciliaris* R. Br., *E. chalcantha* Trin., *Dactyloctenium aegyptium* Beauv., *Rhynchelytrum repens* C. E. Hubbard, Natal Red Top, *Imperata cylindrica* Beauv., Cotton Grass, *Digitaria scalarum* (Schweinf.) Chiov., and *Panicum trichocladum* Hack. ex Engl.

The familes Euphorbiaceae, Leguminosae, Burseraceae, Rubiaceae, Compositae, Acanthaceae and Orchidaceae, besides the Gramineae, are the most dominant in the flora. The Combretaceae though not large contain many species of *Combretum* which range from herb-like shrubs a few inches high to tall trees, quite a number with very showy flowers in shades of red to pale pink and white and well worth a place in the garden.

In Euphorbiaceae the genus *Euphorbia* is the richest, ranging from annual herbs a few inches high, often weeds of lawns, to succulent trees over 60 ft. tall, species of which can be observed in Rain Forest and others which sometimes dominate the scene in parts of the most arid areas of the territory.

The Leguminosae can be separated into three sub-families:—

1. The Caesalpinieae contains amongst many genera the Cassias with their attractive yellow flowers, varying from herbs and shrubs to trees; the Camel-foot, Bauhinias, species with white or yellow flowers in varying shades; *Brachystegia*, the dominant genus of the Woodlands of the southern parts of the territory, but found also to a lesser extent in the Eastern, Tanga, Central and Lake Provinces.

2. Mimoseae, the dominant genus in this family being *Acacia* of which fifty species have been recorded. The species range from insignificant shrubs to magnificent trees about 60 ft. tall, such as the Apple-ring Acacia, *A. albida* Delile or the very beautiful Umbrella Acacia, *A. tortilis* (Forsk.) Hayne. Another species *Acacia pennata* Willd. behaves in Semi-desert as a scruffy shrub 4 to 6 ft. tall, whilst it appears in Rain Forest as a liane clambering over trees 120 ft. tall.

3. The Papilioneae contains many genera mostly with very ornamental flowers ranging in colour from white through pink, red, mauve and blue to yellow; this last colour being most dominant. The family contains many species of economic importance as foods such as beans, peas, grams and pulses, and also some important timbers. The genus *Crotalaria* has the largest number of species, ranging from small herbs through shrubs to trees up to about 25 ft. tall. *Indigofera* with pink to red flowers, mostly herbs with a few shrub species, runs *Crotalaria* pretty close. There are clovers, *Trifolium*, found above 4,000 ft. altitude in Grasslands, *T. usambarensis* Taub. being the most widely distributed, extending from the northern parts of the territory as far south as the Rungwe District. The Kaffir-boom *Erythrina abyssinica* Lam. with its spikes of coral-red flowers normally produced when the tree is quite leafless has a great range of altitude, from about 500 ft. to 8,000 ft. It normally occurs as scattered, often solitary, individuals in Wooded Grassland and open Woodland and is a conspicuous feature of the landscape above the Rift Wall on its western side in the Oldeani District, in the Uluguru, in the Bunduki Valley, and quite a number of miles of country are occupied by it between Sao Hill and Njombe in the Southern Highlands Province. *Pterocarpus*, a genus of trees of Woodland, Bushland and Forest, has several species of economic importance for their timbers, the chief being Mninga, *P. angolensis* DC. It is found in Woodland and Bushland in the Tanga and Eastern Provinces but its greatest concentrations, usually in *Brachystegia* Woodland, are in the Western and Southern Provinces. Another species of economic importance is *P. zimmermannii* Harms found in Forest in the Usambaras, and particularly Riverine Forest in the Ngurus and Ulugurus, then reappearing in the Songea and Rungwe Districts of the Southern and Southern Highlands Provinces. Unfortunately the species is by no means common so its timber is rare.

Burseraceae is a small family in regard to the number of Tanganyika genera it contains, but one genus *Commiphora* has about fifty-four species which are a conspicuous feature with Acacias in Bushland and Semi-Desert. It is well represented in the more arid portions of the Tanga, Northern and Eastern Provinces, and its greatest concentrations are to be seen in the Central and Southern Highlands Provinces between Dodoma and Iringa, then again south of Sao Hill to the northern foot-slopes of the Mporoto Mountains on the southeastern side of the Bohora Flats. There are also one or two representatives in Rain Forest.

Rubiaceous genera range from small herbs to large trees and their habitats are very varied. Mention can only be made of a few. The genus *Canthium* which consists of shrubs, lianes and trees has insignificant flowers. *Mussaenda*, lianes of forest and forest margins has very colourful flowers usually with large calyx lobes in shades of red, orange and yellow, *M. arcuata* Poir., a West African species being the most widely distributed and remaining as a relic of previously existing forest in the Njombe grasslands. European representatives are Bedstraw

Logging on the Rondo Plateau, Southern Province.

Photo: Public Relations Department

A Spectacled Elephant Shrew.

An Aardvark feeding at a termitarium.

Reticulated Giraffe.

Photo: Public Relations Department

and Madders, *Galium* and *Rubia*, with pale green or yellow flowers, to be seen mostly in Grassland but also on the margins of Forest. The roots of *Rubia* are the source of Madder used by the Masai for dyeing the scabbards of their short swords a bright red. *Vangueria*, a genus of shrubs and small trees, has fruits not unlike a medlar in flavour, which are eaten by Africans, and the roots of some species are used as an anthelmintic. *Coffea* is the most important genus economically as it contains Robusta coffee, *C. canephora* Pierre and Arabian coffee, *C. arabica* L., both of which are cultivated, but wild species are found in Forest and Bushland. The genus *Cinchona*, Quinine, is also a member of the Rubiaceae, an introduction from South America; its economic importance to the territory is now receding with the advent of synthetic drugs for the treatment and cure of malaria.

The family Compositae containing many genera is richly represented in the flora of the territory. They range from small herbs through shrubs to large trees, e.g., False sandal-wood, *Brachylaena hutchensii* Hutch., and their habitat is equally varied, but they are mainly inhabitants of Grassland and Bushland though some are found in Forest. Compositae contains many weeds, such as Black Jack, *Bidens pilosa* L. and exotics such as Khaki weed, *Tagetes minuta* L., and Macdonaldii, *Galinsoga parvifolia* Cav. a weed of coffee plantations, both from America, have now become part of the territory's flora, not to mention *Tridax procumbens* L., a weed of lawns and native gardens in the coastal belt. The genus *Vernonia* is represented by many species in the territory, ranging from small herbs with very colourful flowers in Grassland, weeds in native gardens, shrubs in Woodland, Bushland and on Forest margins, to small bushy trees in all types of habitat, and lianes in Rain Forest. The Everlasting flowers, *Helichrysum* is another genus occurring in very varied habitats, and those with the most conspicuous flowers in shades of yellow, red, pink and white are to be seen on most of the mountain masses, particularly about 7,000 ft. altitude on Kilimanjaro, Meru, Hanang and Rungwe Mountains. The family also contain the groundsels, of which there are many herbaceous and some shrubby species, as well as the four Giant Groundsels. Three of the latter are confined to Mt. Kilimanjaro: *S. johnstonii* Oliv., in Forest between 8-10,000 ft., *S. kilimanjari* Mildbr., from 9-13,000 ft., and *S. cottonii* Hutch. & Taylor, 12-15,000 ft. These last two in Moorland. The fourth is restricted to Mt. Meru from 9,000 ft. alt. upwards. All four species are confined to seepage zones and bogs on these two mountains.

Whilst on the subject of giants in the Tanganyika flora, mention must be made of the Giant Lobelias of the Lobeliaceae; eight species of which have been recorded. All these, with the exceptions of *Lobelia gibberoa* Hems/., and *L. burtii* E.A. Bruce, are, like the Giant Groundsels, restricted to their individual mountain mass.

The family Acanthaceae, consisting mostly of herbs and shrubs, many with conspicuous flowers, is found in all sorts of habitats and both herbs and shrub members are very often a conspicuous feature of the ground flora of Rain Forest. To pass to an extreme, Semi-Desert vegetation is often composed of dwarf, bushy, frequently armed, members of the family, especially the genera *Blepharis* and *Barleria* and a widely distributed and well known member is the Black-eyed Susan, *Thunbergia alata* Bojer, with its trailing and procumbent stems and flowers in varying shades of yellow and orange.

The orchid family, Orchidaceae, is very richly represented, both by epiphytic and terrestrial species. The Leopard Orchid, *Ansellia africana* Lindl., belonging to the first group, is frequently cultivated. *Eulophia* is the largest genus, with flowers ranging in colour from green through white, yellow, pink, mauve to purple. There are several wild Vanillas and quite a number of genera represented by a single species only. In comparison to Asiatic and American orchids, most of the East African orchids are dull from a horticultural point of view, but they are of great interest to botanists, as they pose many problems in distribution and in the structure of their flowers.

MAMMALS

In a Handbook such as this, limited space precludes detailed descriptions of the numerous and smaller animals found within the territory's borders, and this account of the mammal fauna must of necessity be very general.

Somewhere in the region of 430 species and subspecies of mammals, representing twelve orders, have been recorded in Tanganyika. The fauna is now fairly well known and it is unlikely that any striking discoveries remain to be made. In fact, with further collecting, it is probable that certain forms now considered distinct, will be found to be similar to other described forms and the list will tend to shrink rather than to expand.

The various forms of mammals are dealt with in systematic order. In the section of the bibliography (at the end of the book) dealing with zoology will be found a list of works to which readers may refer for further information.

Order Insectivora: Insectivores

The first order to be considered is the Insectivora which contains the smallest of all living mammals. All are small, long-snouted animals, with numerous small sharp teeth for catching, holding and eating up insects. The fur is usually soft, sometimes with spines intermixed, or the body may be completely covered with spines.

Four families of insectivores have been recorded in Tanganyika. The Elephant-Shrews, Macroscelididae, with long hind legs and a jumping gait, are outwardly not unlike Jerboas. In size they resemble a large rat, and have prominent eyes and ears, and a very pronounced snout. The fur is fawn or brown, or brown and black, and the tail is long and sparsely haired. Three types are found in Tanganyika: the Spectacled Elephant Shrews, *Elephantulus (Nasilio) brachyrhynchus* (A. Smith), *E. (Elephantomys) intufi* (A. Smith), and *E. (Elephantulus) rozeti* (Duvernoy), from southern, central and western Tanganyika; the four-toed Elephant Shrews, *Petrodromus tetradactylus* Peters, *P. sultan* Thomas, and *P. rovumae* Thomas, from eastern, southern and central Tanganyika; the Chequered Elephant-Shrew and the Black-and-red Elephant-Shrew, *Rhynchocyon (Rhynchocyon) cirnei* Peters and *R. (Rhinonax) petersi* Bocage, from eastern and southern Tanganyika.

Hedgehogs (Erinaceidae) are widespread and, with the whole of the dorsal region of the body covered with stiff spines, closely resemble the English Hedgehog. The feet have simple claws unmodified for digging or burrowing and the tail is short, generally less than an inch in length. They are largely nocturnal but may occasionally be found abroad by day. One species, *Erinaceus (Atelerix) albiventris* Wagner, has been recorded.

The true Shrews (Soricidae) are represented by two genera and a large number of species and subspecies. Outwardly they are very uniform in size and shape, mostly of the size of a small mouse, with sharply pointed muzzles, short legs, moderately long tails, close fur, small eyes, and with the short ears often partly or entirely hidden in the fur; there is a gland for secreting a defensive musky-smelling fluid at the base of each forelimb. The most obvious distinction between the two local genera lies in the number of teeth, all species of *Crocidura* having 28 teeth, while those of *Suncus* have 30 (rarely 32) teeth. They are widespread in most areas. They are often seen dead on paths and this has given rise to the Swahili name *Kirukanjia*, the idea being that when they try to cross a path they die.

The Golden Moles, (Chrysochloridae) are, like the true moles, wholly subterranean and, possibly on this account, are uncommon in collections. Eyes and ears are rudimentary, there is no tail, the middle toe of each forefoot has a very large and strong digging claw, and the light-coloured fur has an iridescent sheen. Two species, *Chrysochloris stuhlmanni* Matschie and *Amblysomus tropicalis* (Allen & Loveridge) are known to occur in Tanganyika.

Order Chiroptera: Bats

This order contains the bats which are remarkable for the fact that they are the only mammals capable of true flight, as opposed to the gliding flight of certain squirrels. The order is divided into two distinct suborders, the Fruit-Bats and the Insect-eating Bats. The former (Megachiroptera) are large animals with a wingspan of up to five feet, though others are smaller. They are characterized by the presence of a claw on the index finger as well as on the thumb, and by the margin of the ear forming a ring. They are migratory in habit, roosting in colonies in trees and moving from one area to another according to the ripening of the various fruits which form their main food. Among the Fruit-Bats are the Flying Foxes, *Pteropus* spp.—so-called because of their russet heads and shoulders and pointed faces—which just reach our eastern seaboard, the Yellow Fruit-Bats, *Eidolon helvum* (Kerr), the Epauletted Fruit-Bats of the genera *Epomophorus* and *Micropteropus*, and the Dog-Bats of the genus *Rousettus*.

The Insect-eating Bats (Microchiroptera) are smaller than the Fruit-Bats, they lack the claw on the index finger and the margin of the ear does not form a ring. They subsist on a diet of insects caught on the wing. To assist them in avoiding obstacles at night and in catching their prey, they make use of an echo-sounding device, high-pitched sound waves being emitted which are reflected back off objects in their path and picked up in time to enable them to avoid any obstacle. It is, perhaps, in conjunction with this echo-sounding device that a number of forms have queer fleshy growths on their faces, the so-called nose-leaves.

The Emballonuridae, or Sheath-tailed Bats, comprise a group of free-tailed bats, but with shorter tails than the Molossidae, the end of the tail perforating the upper surface of the interfemoral membrane; legs slender; tragus, or earlet, small, often broad, ears large, often united.

The Nycteridae, or Hollow-faced Bats, contain a number of large-eared species which possess a deep frontal groove margined by pointed nose-leaves. All are included in the single genus *Nycteris*. They have the tail of considerable length and entirely enclosed within the tail membrane, and a well-developed tragus.

The Megadermatidae, or Big-eared Bats, contains a number of large-eared species which possess long erect and pointed nose-leaves. They are distinguished by the absence of upper incisor teeth and the extreme shortness of the tail; the fur is long and woolly in African forms and the tragus is bifid.

The Rhinolophidae, or Horseshoe Bats, are remarkable for their complicated nose-leaves and large ears. There is no tragus, and the upper incisors are rudimentary. They are mostly small or medium-sized bats confined to the temperate and tropical parts of the Old World.

The Molossidae, or Free-tailed Bats, are easily recognized by the fact that the tail extends fully half its length, or even more, beyond the reduced inter-femoral membrane. The wings are long and narrow, thick and leathery: legs short and stout; nostrils usually have protuberances on them; no tragus is present, the ears are approximated or united above the eyes.

The Vespertilionidae is the common family of bats and contains such well-known forms as the Pipistrelles, Serotines, Mouse-eared Bats, Painted Bats, and Long-winged Bats. The bats of this family are rather small, have big ears with a prominent tragus; the tail is long, but enclosed completely or nearly so in the interfemoral membrane; the muzzle is without nose-leaves; the legs are long and slender.

Order Primates

This order contains the great apes, monkeys, baboons, bush-babies and, though some of us may not like to be reminded of the fact, man. They are widespread in distribution, occurring from the coastal belt to the upper limits of tree growth. Some are rare and in need of special protection; others are common and, because of the damage they do to crops, are classified as vermin.

Smallest of the Primates are the Lorisidae or Bush-babies, of which three species are found in Tanganyika, the Greater Galago, *Galago crassicaudatus* (E. Geoffroy), about the size of a cat, with a long bushy tail, the Bush-baby proper, *Galago senegalensis* (E. Geoffroy), a smaller version of the Greater Galago, and the Least Bush-baby, *Galago demidovii* Fischer, a species rarely recorded in Tanganyika. Unlike the other Primates, Bush-babies are largely nocturnal, and their harsh call may be heard at night in most areas including towns.

The largest family, the Cercopithecidae, is represented by 23 forms in Tanganyika. One of the rarest is the Black Mangabey, *Cercocebus albigena* (Gray), a Congo form which has been recorded from Bukoba District. It is a forest dweller. Two species of Baboon occur, the Yellow Baboon, *Papio cynocephalus* (Linnaeus), from eastern Tanganyika, and the Olive Baboon, *Papio ursinus* (Kerr), from the west. Both are a menace to cultivation but are rarely shot by farmers since their meat is normally considered unpalatable. The Guenons or Vervets, *Cereopithecus aethiops* (Linnaeus) are common in most areas of deciduous woodland. Known locally as *tumbili* they are easily recognizable by their black faces and greenish-grey fur. Slightly larger, and darker in colour, are the Blue or Sykes Monkeys, *Ceropithecus mitis* (Wolf)—the *kima* of the Africans—which show a preference for evergreen forest. Two comparative rarities are the Putty-nosed Monkey, *Cercopithecus nictitans* (Linnaeus), another Congo species which just enters western Tanganyika, and the Patas or Hussar Monkey, *Erythrocebus patas* (Schreber), which is found along our northern border. Reddish in colour, it would appear to choose dry thornbush country to live in.

Most handsome of the Cereopithecid monkeys are the Black-and-White Colobus, or Guereza, *Colobus polykomos* (Zimmermann), which are found in evergreen forest in many parts of the territory from sea-level to over 9,000 feet. A more localized form of this monkey, the Red Colobus, *Colobus badius* (Kerr), is found in Iringa District, and in our Western and Lake Provinces.

Finally among the Primates is the Chimpanzee, *Pan troglodytes* (Blumenbach), another West African animal whose range just reaches Tanganyika. They may be found in fair numbers in the hills bordering on Lake Tanganyika, north from the Mahari Mountains to the Urundi border. They feed by day and at night sleep on platforms made by bending the topmost branches of trees inwards.[1]

Order Pholidota

The Ground Pangolin or Scaly Anteater, *Manis temminckii* (Smuts), is generally distributed throughout the country, other than in evergreen forest and on the higher mountains but, on account of its nocturnal habits, is rarely seen. It feeds largely on ants and termites. Its flesh is considered a delicacy by the natives and its scales are often used to ward off evil spirits. The upper parts of the body and legs are covered with horny plates overlapping one another like scale armour; the jaws are devoid of teeth; the tongue is long, the mouth small; the limbs are short, the forefeet with long digging claws.

Order Lagomorpha

Formerly Rabbits and Hares were grouped with the other rodents in the order Rodentia, but recent practice is to separate them as a separate order on account of the four upper incisors, as opposed to two in the Rodentia.

Three species of Hare have been recorded from Tanganyika, namely the Cape Hare, *Lepus capensis* (Linnaeus), the East African forms of the European hare, *L. europaeus* (Pallas), and Whytc's Hare, *Lepus whytei* (Thomas). They are largely nocturnal and may be seen on the roads at night in the headlights of motor cars. They are often seen close to habitation.

Order Rodentia

The Rodents are well represented with a variety of forms, of which 136 have been recorded from Tanganyika.

Two groups, resembling moles in their burrowing habits and external form, contain the Molerats and Blesmols (*Heliophobius, Cryptomys* and *Tachyoryctes*). They tunnel underground, raise mole hills and are frequently referred to as Moles. But they may be distinguished from the true Moles, which belong to the order Insectivora, by a glance at their front teeth, which are large and rat-like. Their eyes and ears are rudimentary.

Among the largest of the rodents found in Tanganyika are the Canerats (Echimyidae, Swahili, *ndezi*) of which two species occur, the Lesser Canerat, *Thryonomys gregorianus* (Thomas), and the Larger Canerat, *T. swinderianus* (Temminck), with head and body about 20 inches in length, tail about 7 inches long. They are commonly found in reed beds bordering rivers and lakes and are much prized by Africans for their meat. Their fur is harsh, almost spiny in texture. They do a considerable amount of damage to sugar cane plantations.

---

[1]See "The Distribution of the Chimpanzee in Tanganyika", in *Tanganyika Notes and Records* No. 14, p. 52; also further notes on distribution in No. 16, p. 101 and No. 19, p. 68.

Two species of Porcupines (Hystricidae, Swahili, *nungu*) occur, *Hystrix africaeaustralis* (Peters), and *H. galeata* (Thomas). They are easily recognizable by their heavy bodies covered by long, backwardly directed quills; the tail is short and bears a dense mass of quills; the legs are short and the feet broad. By day they live in deep burrows and venture out at night, often to feed on standing crops. They are hunted by certain tribes, who follow them into their burrows and spear them.

Squirrels (Sciuridae) are common in most parts of the country except open grassland. Some species of Forest Squirrels (*Heliosciurus*) are brightly coloured, while the Bush Squirrels (*Paraxerus*) and Ground Squirrels (*Xerus*) are generally of more sombre hues. They closely resemble English Squirrels in form and habit, with more or less bushy tails. The Ground Squirrels alone, as their name suggests, live on the ground and take refuge in holes underground.

One species of Flying Squirrels, *Anomalurus derbianus* (Gray), is found in eastern and southern Tanganyika. The body is covered with soft fur and from the side of the body, between the fore and hind legs, is stretched a membrane which enables them to glide from tree to tree but not to indulge in true flight. The tail is long, moderately haired and covered with scales on the under surface.

Spring Hares, *Pedetes capensis* (Forster), are widespread and sole representatives of the family Pedetidae. They are Jerboa-like in form and progress by leaps on their hind legs, the forelegs being of normal proportions, but with well developed claws to assist in digging. The hind toes are provided with hoof-like nails. The fur is long and silky and the tail is long with a tassel of black hairs on the end. They do a great deal of damage to crops.

Dormice (Muscardinidae), are mostly arboreal animals with habits and aspect somewhat intermediate between mice and squirrels. One genus, *Graphiurus*, occurs in Tanganyika, small grey animals with bushy tails, large ears and eyes and short forelimbs.

The cosmopolitan family Muridae is more abundantly represented in genera, species and individuals than any other similar group of mammals and among its members contains forms specialized for life in forests, swamps, grassland, sand dunes and so on. About 93 forms have been recorded from Tanganyika. The family is divided into a number of subfamilies of which five occur in Tanganyika. The subfamily Murinae contains the typical rats and mice.

The genus *Grammomys*, containing the Forest Mouse, *Grammomys dolichurus* (Smuts), is characterized by its long and well bristled tail, the feet with short, curved claws characteristic of climbing mice, and the underparts of the body are pure white. It inhabits evergreen forest.

Arvicanthis contains the unstriped grass rats, *Arvicanthis abyssinicus* (Rüppell), which are medium sized diurnal rats, with the tail shorter than the body and the fur grizzled grey dorsally. They are common in most areas.

The genus *Rattus*, is the most widely distributed and abundantly represented group in the subfamily Muridae. Besides the two forms of house rat, the Black Rat, *Rattus rattus* (Linnaeus), and the Norway or Brown Rat, *Rattus norvegicus* (Berkenhout), which are both now well established in most of the larger towns and villages, the genus contains a number of closely allied feral forms, grouped in three subgenera. Of these, the largest are the rats of the subgenus *Aethomys*, having the head and body length 130 mm. and more, with the tail generally longer than the head and body, though in one or two forms it may be shorter. Females have 4 or 6 or 8 mammae. The Black-tailed Tree Rat, *Rattus (Aethomys) paedulcus* (Sundevall), is an arboreal form occurring in the dry acacia woodlands, characterized by having the tail and the fifth toe relatively long. The fur is long and coarse on the back. The other forms are all terrestrial, with a relatively short fifth toe. In the Kaiser's Rat, *Rattus (Aethomys) kaiseri* (Noack) the tail is equal to or less than the length of the head and body, and the skull is relatively narrow. The Nyika Rat, *Rattus (Aethomys) nyikae* (Thomas), resembles the Kaiser's Rat in regard to the length of the tail but has a relatively broader skull. The Red Veld Rat, *Rattus (Aethomys) chrysophilus* (de Winton), on the other hand, has the tail noticeably longer than the head and body; the fur is bright reddish fawn above, white below.

The subgenus *Mastomys*, containing the Multimammate Rats, *Rattus (Mastomys) natalensis* (A. Smith), is distinguished by its smaller size, relatively short tail (only rarely as long as or a little longer than the head and body), and by the unbroken line of mammae from the pectoral to the inguinal region, numbering more than 10 pairs.

The subgenus *Praomys*, represented in Tanganyika by the Soft-furred Rat, *Rattus (Praomys) morio* (Trouessart), is another small species with the tail considerably longer than the head and body, and mammae 4, 6, 8 or 10 (6 in Tanganyika specimens).

The subgenus *Hylomyscus* contains another species of arboreal rat found in Tanganyika, the Climbing Wood Mouse, *Rattus (Hylomyscus) carillus* (Thomas), a small, long-tailed, apparently rare animal.

Members of the genus *Rhabdomys* may be recognized by the four black stripes running down the back with three light coloured stripes between them. The Four-striped Rat, *R. pumilio* (Sparrman), is a medium-sized, diurnal rat with a much reduced fifth toe on the hindfoot.

Two species of the genus *Lophuromys* are found in Tanganyika, the Harsh-furred Rat, *L. sikapusi* (Temminck) in which the fur is dark but not speckled, and *L. flavopunctatus* (Thomas) in which the fur is dark and finely speckled. Both are short-tailed, nocturnal forms, with a very soft skin.

The genus *Mus* contains, besides the House Mouse, *Mus musculus* (Linnaeus), a number of feral forms of small mice, formerly referred to the genus *Leggada* but now classified with the house mice. All are small, some minute, the smallest, *M. minutoides* (A. Smith), being fawn above, white below, others, such as *M. triton* (Thomas) being grizzled above, grey below.

The genus *Dasymys* includes the African Water Rat, *D. incomtus* (Sundevall), a long haired animal, partially aquatic in habits, with broad feet and short toes; the tail is shorter than the head and body, nearly naked and well scaled; the ears are rather small and rounded. It frequents streams and river banks, marshes and reed beds.

Pelomys is another swamp rat, *P. fallax* (Peters) occurring in coarse vegetation along streams and rivers. It is characterized by having the upper incisors grooved, a unique condition in Murine rodents. As in *Lemniscomys*, the fifth finger is so reduced that the forefoot has only three functional digits. The fur on the back is coarse, grizzled, with an indistinct darker dorsal line.

Lemniscomys contains the multi- and single-striped grass rats, coarse haired, diurnal, terrestrial rats that are characterized by having a single dorsal stripe, or with the entire dorsal surface striped or spotted, and, like *Pelomys*, have a much reduced fifth digit on the forefeet, thereby differing from *Rhabdomys*, which has four dorsal stripes and a normal fifth digit on the forefeet. The single-striped Grass Rat *L. griselda* (Thomas) is not unlike a *Pelomys* but may be distinguished by the ungrooved upper incisors. The Multi-striped Grass Rat, *L. barbarus* (Linnaeus), has the whole dorsal area covered with longitudinal stripes, thereby differing from the Spotted Grass Rat. *L. striatus* (Linnaeus), which has a single mid-dorsal stripe on either side of which are several rows of spots.

Acomys contains the Spiny Mice of which two or three species occur in Tanganyika. They are small mice characterized by having the dorsal hair harsh and spiny, and a very thin skin. They are generally found among rocks and are very locally distributed.

Two genera of rats found in Tanganyika have cheek pouches in which food is stored. The smaller one, *Saccostomus*, with a single species, *S. campestris* (Peters), is a medium sized, robust rat with short strong legs and toes, a short tail tapering from a thick base, and short rounded ears. The larger genus, *Cricetomys*, representing one of the largest of the African rats, with the head and body some 13 to 15 inches in length and tail 15 to 17 inches, is a shy, nocturnal animal which can be easily handled without fear of being bitten.

The subfamily *Dendromurinae* contains a number of small sized rodents with scaly, sparsely haired tails. In all Tanganyika forms, the upper incisors are grooved.

The genus *Dendromus* contains arboreal species characterized by having only three functional digits in the forefeet, no claw on the hallux, the tail longer than the head and body and, at least in some specimens, a mid-dorsal stripe. The ears are rather large and hairy and the claws long. The Chestnut Tree Mouse, *D. mesomelas* (Brants), is generally brown, the hairs of the underparts white, slightly tinged with rufous usually slaty at the base, the fifth hindtoe with a claw, averaging larger than the next species, the Lesser Climbing Mouse, *D. mystacalis* (Heuglin), which has the hairs of the underparts either white to the base or tinged with orchraceous. The Grey Pigmy Tree Mouse, *D. melanotis* (A. Smith), is another small species, generally coloured grey, with a nail, not a claw, on the fifth hindtoe.

The genus *Steatomys* contains the Fat Mice, and is represented by one species, *S. pratensis* (Peters), in Tanganyika. The tail is short, at most 60 per cent of the head and body length, the forefeet have four functional digits, the hallux is clawed and there is no indication of a mid-dorsal stripe. The Fat Mice are so called because of their plump appearance, due to a layer of fat under the skin. They are terrestrial in habit living in grassland, bush country and in cultivation.

The subfamily *Otomyinae* contains the Vlei or Groove-toothed Rats, robust, rat-like animals, the fur grizzled ochre-brown and black, nose short, tail about half the length of head and body, ears usually large, hind-feet short, upper incisors generally grooved. A number of species of the genus *Otomys* have been recorded from Tanganyika.

The subfamily *Cricetinae* contains only a single species in Tanganyika, *Mystromys longicaudatus* (Noack), known only from the type-locality south of Tabora. It has soft, rather woolly, fur and large broad ears, short tail, ungrooved incisors, cheek pouches, and is nocturnal and terrestrial in habit.

Thomson's Gazelle.

Photo: B. Cooper, Game Ranger

Defassa Waterbuck, near Banagi Hill

Photo: B. Cooper

The subfamily *Gerbillinae* contains the Gerbils, with short forelegs and elongated back legs which enable them to progress by leaps, large eyes, upper incisors grooved, the body externally modified for life in plains and deserts. The pigmy Gerbils, of the genus *Gerbillus*, are small animals, head and body about 4 inches in length, fawn above, white below. Gerbils of the genus *Tatera* are larger, head and body 5 inches or more in length.

Order Carnivora

The Carnivores are well represented both in point of numbers and of varieties, fifty-three forms being recorded. Most are carnivorous in habits and are immediately recognizable by the presence of a specially modified flesh-tooth, or carnassial, in each jaw.

The family Canidae includes the domestic Dogs, true Wolves, Jackals, Wild Dogs and Foxes the last three of which are represented in Tanganyika by five species. The form is rather light, the legs long and there are never more than four toes on the hindfeet, four or five on the forefeet.

Three species of Jackal occur; the Golden Jackal, *Canis aureus* (Linnaeus), a misnomer because it is a scruffy animal with little of gold about it; the upper parts are buffy cinnamon, clouded by black hair tips along the dorsal region, nearly clear on the sides, and becoming clear bright cinnamon on the outer surface of the legs; the side-striped Jackal, *Canis adustus* (Sundevall), which is easily distinguished because of the faint stripe along the flanks between shoulder and hips, and by the white tip to the tail; and the Black-backed Jackal, *Canis mesomelas* (Schreber), the most common species, with a silver-flecked black back and reddish flanks.

Wild Dogs, *Lycaon pictus* (Temminck), are frequently seen, though perhaps they are not so common as generally believed since each pack has a very wide hunting range. They are distinguished by their dog-like appearance, mottled colouring, large ears and the white tail-tip. They hunt in packs and their mere presence will drive game from an area.

The Bat-eared Fox, *Otocyon megalotis* (Desmarest), is a charming little animal which spends much of the day underground. It is characterized by its small size, very large ears and by its white eyebrows and bushy tail.

Five species of Mustelidae have been recorded. The form is usually slender, the legs always short, the size is moderate or small (including the smallest of known carnivores), and there are five toes on fore and hind feet. The Polecat, *Ictonyx striatus* (Perry), is an apparently uncommon animal, marked black and white; the Striped Weasel, *Poecilogale albinucha* (Gray), is much like the former, but with a white nape; the Honey Badger, *Mellivora capensis* (Schreber), is one of the toughest of all African animals, dirty white above, black below, which will attack anything from a beehive to a buffalo, as well as domestic poultry; the Spotted-necked Otter, *Lutra maculicollis* (Lichtenstein), and the Clawless Otter, *Aonyxca pensis* (Schinz) are both widespread but rare in collections. Their occurrence is more often noted by the presence of crab shells on river banks than by a sight of the animals themselves. Both species of otter have the fur very dense, the legs unusually short, the toes webbed, the claws short or absent and the tail long and highly muscular.

28

The Civets, Genets and Mongooses (Fam. Viverridae) are slender-muzzled, moderate sized animals with long tails, long, low-slung, rather slender bodies, the legs moderately short, often well-developed anal scent glands. Many are striped or spotted. The majority are terrestrial, but the Tree Civet, Genets and Lesser Mongooses are also arboreal in habits.

Genets are small, short-legged, cat-like animals with the body boldly marked with brown or black spots on a light ground and the tail ringed with alternate light and dark rings, the ear narrow and high, the soles and palms densely furred, except on the pads; the claws are short and retractable. Two species, *Genetta genetta* (Linnaeus) and *G. tigrina* (Schreber), have a wide distribution in Tanganyika. They are largely nocturnal, agile tree climbers and feed on a variety of small birds, rats and mice, as well as insects and eggs.

The Civet, *Viverra (Civettictis) civetta* (Schreber), is a larger animal, coarse haired, grey with black spots and stripes. It is nocturnal and feeds on much the same food as do genets. It also eats the seeds of certain plants. It has the curious habit of returning to the same place nightly to defecate so that in time considerable mounds of droppings are formed. One such place was on a gravestone in the Manyoni graveyard. Civets were at one time much sought after for the valuable musk of their scent glands which was used in the preparation of cosmetics.

Smaller than the Civet, and with less conspicuous markings, is the Tree Civet, *Nandinia binotata* (Gray). It is rare in collections, and has been recorded in Tanganyika only from the forested mountains of the north-east and south-west. It feeds on fruits, but is also carnivorous.

A great variety of Mongooses occurs in Africa and some twenty-two species and subspecies have been recorded in Tanganyika. For the most part they are small, long-tailed, short-legged, ferret-like animals, with coarse, unstriped hair, the ears low and narrow, the soles and palms naked, the claws short, non-retractable. Some are nocturnal in habit, others diurnal, some solitary, others colonial. All feed on small birds, mammals, eggs, insects and carrion. The best known forms are: the Greater Grey Mongoose *Herpestes (Herpestes) ichneumon* (Linnaeus), with a long, thin, tassel-tipped tail; the Lesser Mongoose, *H. (Galerella) sanguineus* (Rüppell), smaller than the former but with the same general build, without a tassel at the end of the tail; the Dwarf Mongoose, *Helogale parvula* (Sundevall) and *H. victorina* (Thomas), small, red or brown weasel-like animals, gregarious and diurnal; the Marsh Mongoose, *Atilax paludinosus* (G. Cuvier), a large reddish brown form which, as its name implies, favours swamps and other well-watered areas; the Banded Mongoose, *Mungos mungo* (Gmelin), a medium sized colonial form having the back marked with a number of transverse dark bands; the White-tailed Mongoose, *Ichneumia albicauda* (G. Cuvier), a large grey animal with a white bushy tail, which feeds on small mammals as well as mollucs, berries and wild fruit; Meller's Mongoose, *Rhynchogale melleri* (Gray), which in size and form resembles *H. ichneumon* (Linnaeus), but has the tail bushy as in *I. albicauda* (G. Cuvier) except that it darkens to black towards the tip; and the Four-toed Mongoose, *Bdeogale crassicauda* (Peters), with a long bushy black-tipped tail, distinguished by the presence of a median naked groove from the nose to the upper lip and by the absence of the inner toe on each foot.

The Hyaenidae, comprising the Hyaenas, is a small family confined to Africa and southern Asia. They have massive heads, short hindlegs and tail, with the skull, jaws and teeth extremely powerful. The body slopes downwards from the high shoulders to the low hind quarters. All are carrion feeders, feasting on dead bodies and bones, though they will occasionally kill small animals. They lie up by day in holes in the ground, or in rocky kopjes, often a dozen or more sharing the same burrow. At night they wander forth to feed and render the night hideous by their fantastic cries. The Striped Hyaena, *Hyaena hyaena* (Linnaeus), about five feet long, has blackish stripes on a grey body; it appears to be rare in Tanganyika. The Spotted Hyaena, *Crocuta crocuta* (Erxleben), is a spotted animal with short hair, widespread in distribution.

Very similar to, but smaller than, the Striped Hyaena, is the Aardwolf, *Proteles cristatus* (Sparrman); its jaws are extremely weak and its teeth are small and degenerate. It is rarely encountered, though widely distributed throughout northern and central Tanganyika, by day it lies up in burrows made by the Antbear and emerges at night to feed on termites.

The Felidae, or Cat family, is the most highly specialized of the land Carnivora. Characteristics of the Cats are the completely retractile claws on fore and hind feet, the contracting pupil of the eye and the shortened muzzle. The form is usually slender, the legs moderately long; size moderate to large; five toes on the forefeet, four on the hindfeet. In many areas the Domestic Cat, *Felis catus* (Linnaeus), has gone feral and interbred with the local Wild Cats, *Felis silvestris* (Schreber).[1] The latter are larger than the domestic tabby, with more or less defined spots on the body. They are common in most localities.

The Caracal, *Felis* (*Caracal*) *caracal* (Schreber), is larger than the Wild Cat, heavier and less typically feline, of a uniform reddish colour with some spotting on the undersurface and on the legs. The ears end in a "pencil" of long hairs. They are widespread but rarely seen.

The Serval Cat, *Felis* (*Leptailurus*) *serval* (Schreber), is about the same size as or slightly smaller than a Caracal, but easily distinguished from the latter by having the body completely covered by black stripes on the middle of the back and black spots elsewhere. Being nocturnal it is generally considered rare, though it is widespread in the drier areas.

There remain the three large cats, the Leopard, the Lion and the Cheetah. The first two are so well known as not to require any description. Leopards, *Panthera* (*Panthera*) *pardus* (Linnaeus), are largely nocturnal in areas where they are hunted, but in remote areas they may be seen in the open by day. When they have made a kill it is their custom to carry it to the topmost branches of a tree where they may eat in peace. They are equally at home in evergreen forest, deciduous woodland and thorn bush country. There is said to be the body of a leopard high up on Kilimanjaro, though it is more likely that it is a large Serval Cat, which are frequently recorded from the moorland.

Lions, *Panthera* (*Leo*) *leo* (Linnaeus), appear to be equally in evidence by day as by night. They are not agile climbers and feed on the ground. They show a preference for open grassland or open wooded grassland and are rarely seen in evergreen forest.

---

[1]The East African Wild Cats are normally called *Felis libyca* (Forster), but the present author agrees with Haltenorth (1953) that *F. libyca* is conspecific with the European Wild Cat, *F. silvestris* (Schreber).

The Cheetah, *Acinonyx jubatus* (Schreber), is reckoned to be the fastest of all land mammals over a short distance, having been paced at 70 miles an hour. It has long legs and only partially retractile claws. At first glance its body markings resemble those of a Leopard but on closer examination it will be seen that while the black spots on a leopard are arranged in definite rosettes, those on a cheetah form no definite pattern. Another distinction is the presence of a black stripe on the face of the cheetah, extending from the inner corner of the eye to the outer corner of the mouth. Cheetahs favour open grassy plains and open wooded grassland.

Order *Tubulidentata*

This order comprises the single family Orycteropodidae, or Aardvarks. Only one species, *Orycteropus afer* (Pallas), has been described. Aardvarks, or Antbears, are characterized by their six-foot long bodies, their long, narrow heads with pig-like snout, long, slender, erect ears, grey body so thinly haired as to appear naked, and long tail tapering from a thick root. The tongue is long and slender to enable the animal to extract termites from their homes, and the cheek-teeth—the only teeth in the weak jaws—are few in number, peg-like in structure and lack enamel. By day they lie up in burrows of their own digging, venturing forth at night to seek their food.

Order *Proboscidea*

The Elephant, *Loxodonta africana* (Blumenbach), sole representative of this order, requires no description. With its massive, ten-feet tall, four-ton body, pillar-like legs and prominent tusks, it is probably the best known of all our fauna. Widespread from sea-level to the moorland on Kilimanjaro—there is the skeleton of an elephant at about 14,000 feet—wherever water is available. With new areas now being opened up for man's use, generally around existing water supplies, the country and water available to the ever-increasing elephant population diminishes yearly.

Order *Hyracoidea*

Distantly related to the Elephant are the Hyraxes, or Dassies—the Coney of the scriptures—which are small, tailless animals living on rocky hills or in evergreen forest trees, with blunt heads, short ears and short legs. There are blunt, hoof-like nails on the four toes of the forefeet and on two of the hind toes, the third bearing a curved claw. The short soft fur is generally greyish brown, and a patch of black or whitish fur on the middle of the back outlines a naked glandular area. Rock Rabbits, *Procavia capensis* (Pallas) and *Dendrohyrax (Heterohyrax) brucei* (Gray), live in holes in rocks, while Tree Hyraxes, *Dendrohyrax (Dendrohyrax) arboreus* (A. Smith), as their name implies, live in holes in tall forest trees. All are herbivorous and the way the naked soles of their clawless feet enable them to climb steep rock faces and trees is remarkable.

Order *Perissodactyla*

This order is characterized by having an odd number of functional toes on each foot, one in the Zebras, three in Rhinoceroses. The Zebra, *Equus burchellii* (Gray), close relative of horses and asses, is distinguished by its striped body and the single hoof on each foot. It is found in large herds in open grassy plains and wooded grassland.

The Rhinoceros, *Diceros bicornis* (Linneaus), has two horns on top of the nose, placed one behind the other and composed of dense fibrous tissue unconnected with the skull. This horn is highly prized as medicine in the East and fetches a high price on the local market. Rhinoceroses are browsers and are found in bush country and forest bordering on grassland.

Order Artiodactyla

This order contains all the even-toed, herbivorous, terrestrial animals with paired toes, normally hoofed, either two or four in number. The outer pair, when present, are reduced or rudimentary.

There are two suborders in Tanganyika, the non-ruminants or Suiformes, with four-toed feet and simple stomachs (Pigs and Hippopotami); and the Ruminantia, with hoofed feet having two or four toes, complex stomachs, and, usually, horns or antlers in at least one sex (Cattle, Sheep, Giraffe, Antelope, Deer).

Three species of Pig occur: the Bushpig, *Potamochoerus porcus* (Linneaus), which is strictly nocturnal, lying up by day in thick bush or forest; the grotesque Warthog, *Phacochoerus aethiopicus* (Pallas), with prominent wart-like outgrowths on the face, a dweller in open or wooded grassland, and diurnal in habits; and the Giant Forest Hog, *Hylochoerus meinertzhageni* (Thomas), a dweller in mountain forest and bamboo.

The Hippopotamus, *Hippopotamus amphibius* (Linneaus), is found in most permanent rivers and lakes, lying up by day in the water and feeding on land at night. They occur on Mafia Island, having crossed the short stretches of sea dividing the Rufiji Delta from the neighbouring islets.

There are two families of Ruminantia in Tanganyika, the Giraffidae and the Bovidae. The former contains only the Giraffe, *Giraffa camelopardalis* (Linnaeus), characterized by its greatly elongated neck and legs and dappled colouring. It is an interesting fact that the neck of the giraffe, though much longer than that of any other land mammal, has no more than the seven cervical vertebrae common to most mammals.

The Bovidae, besides containing the Cattle, Sheep and Goats, contains the vast concourse of Antelopes which constitutes the greater part of the game fauna of Tanganyika. Many species are gregarious in habit, others are solitary or live in small family parties; some prefer open plains, others forests or swamps; all have horns in the males, some have horns in the females as well, and in others again the females are hornless; some browse off trees and bushes, others graze; some are not much bigger than a rabbit, others again are among the largest of land mammals.

Among the smaller antelopes are the Duikers, of which four species occur. The largest, with shoulder height about 24 inches, is the Abbott's Duiker, *Cephalophus* (*Cephalophus*) *spadix* (True), recorded from a number of mountain forest areas in Tanganyika. It is very dark brown, almost black in some specimens, with diminutive horns, in size about equal to the Yellow-backed Duiker of West Africa and the Congo. Smaller than Abbott's Duiker, but larger than the next two species, is the Common Duiker, or Duikerbok, *Sylvicapra grimmia* (Linnaeus), which is widespread in most areas, except possibly south-east Tanganyika. It is grizzled fawn in colour. Two species of small forest Duikers occur, the Red Forest Duiker, *Cephalophus* (*Cephalophus*) *natalensis* (A. Smith), and the Blue Forest Duiker, *C. (Philantomba) monticola* (Thunberg). The former is reddish brown in colour and about 18 inches high at the shoulder, the latter slaty grey, and standing about 13 inches only. All duikers are characterized by the presence of prominent facial glands opening in a long slit down each side of the face in front of the eyes, and by having the rump higher than the withers. The horns are short and spike-like, rarely longer than the tuft of hairs on the top of the head.

Another small antelope is the Steenbok, standing about 22 inches at the shoulder, of which two species are known to occur in Tanganyika. The Steenbok proper, *Raphicerus campestris* (Thunberg), has a coat of a uniform reddish colour above, white below and on the top of the head there is a more or less distinct dark horseshoe mark. There is no tuft of long hairs on top of the head such as is found in the Duikers. Sharpe's Grysbok, *Raphicerus sharpei* (Thomas), is very similar to the Steenbok but it has the reddish coat speckled with numerous brittle, white hairs interspersed amongst the reddish ones. These white hairs are easily shed and their presence on the ground indicates the place where a Grysbok has been lying up. Both species have short horns and are found in wooded grassland, the former favouring more open country than the latter.

The Oribi, *Ourebia ourebi* (Zimmermann), is larger than the Steenbok, with a shoulder height of 24 inches. It has a uniform fawn-coloured coat and is distinguished by the presence of a bare glandular patch on the sides of the face below each ear, and by having dark-coloured "knee" tufts. The Oribi may be found in open wooded grassland and, when alarmed, will emit a whistling call.

The smallest of all the Tanganyika antelopes is the Suni, or Pigmy Antelope, *Nesotragus moschatus* (von Dueben), another forest and thick-bush dweller. It stands about thirteen inches at the shoulder and its horns, which are found in the male only, are very heavily ringed. It is found only in the eastern districts.

The Klipspringer, *Oreotragus oreotragus* (Zimmermann), is a small rock-jumping species with tiny cylindrical hoofs and a peculiar coarse coat made up of pithy hairs. It stands about 22 inches at the shoulder and is widespread in suitable localities.

The last of the small antelopes, standing about 14 inches at the shoulder, are the Dikdiks, *Madoqua (Rhynchotragus) kirkii* (Günther), which are found in the dry thorn bush country of northern and central Tanganyika. They have tufted crowns, mobile elongated snouts, short, straight horns and grizzled coats of grey and russet. They have a conspicuous round glandular opening in front of the eyes.

Three species of Reedbuck are found in Tanganyika; the Mountain Reedbuck, *Redunca fulvorufula* (Afzelius), is the smallest of the three, standing about 30 inches at the shoulder, with short horns placed close together and bent sharply forward towards the tips, greyish fawn in colour, occurring on the grassy tops of hills in suitable localities in northern Tanganyika; the Bohor Reedbuck, *Redunca redunca* (Pallas), is slightly larger, standing 31 inches at the shoulder, with more open horns ending in a less sharp curve, body colour redder; and the Southern Reedbuck, *Redunca arundinum* (Boddaert), which stands 36 inches at the shoulder, with widely diverging horns which are longer and less curved than in the two preceding species. The two latter species prefer grass and swamp country near watercourses and lakes. The Bohor Reedbuck is a northern species which meets and overlaps the range of the Southern Reedbuck in Tanganyika. All

Reedbucks are characterized by a short bushy tail, a bare glandular patch below the ear, and a whistling call (compare the Oribi, which is smaller and has a short-haired tail).

Two species of Waterbuck occur, distinguished by the distribution of white on the rump. The Defassa Waterbuck, *Kobus defassa* (Rüppell), is a western species characterized by having a white patch on the rump, while the eastern Common Waterbuck, *Kobus ellipsiprymnus* (Ogilby), has a white elliptical band encircling the rump. Their ranges meet in the area of the Great Rift Wall. Both are large animals, standing 48 inches at the shoulder, with shaggy grizzled coats and long horns curving forwards. They are found near water, though they will often move on to surrounding hills by day.

A related but smaller species is the Puku, *Kobus* (*Adenota*) *vardonii* (Livingstone), with a less shaggy coat and short, lyrate horns. Its shoulder height is about 38 inches. It occurs in very large herds in the grasslands of the Rukwa and Kilombero valleys.

An animal which at first sight resembles the Puku is the Impala, *Aepyceros melampus* (Lichtenstein), but which on close examination is seen to be less stocky, with longer more slender horns, with a vertical black streak on each rump and a glandular patch covered with black hairs in place of the lateral hoofs on each hind leg. Impala are medium sized antelopes, standing about 36 inches at the shoulder and occurring in large herds in wooded grassland.

Three species of Gazelle occur, the smaller Thomson's Gazelle, *Gazella thomsonii* (Günther), 26 inches at the shoulder, with reddish upper parts and white belly, the flanks being marked with a bold longitudinal black band; the larger Grant's Gazelle, *Gazella granti* (Brooke), fawn coloured above and white below with a less pronounced lateral band, with shoulder height 33 inches. Both the above occur on the grassy plains of northern Tanganyika, south to about the Ruaha River. The third species is the Gerenuk, or Waller's Gazelle, *Litocranius walleri* (Brooke); it is a species of the arid country of Somaliland and reaches the southern limits of its range in southern Masailand. It is a reddish animal characterized by the elongated neck and long legs, standing about 39 inches at the shoulder.

Another northern species which reaches its southern limits in Tanganyika is the Oryx, *Oryx besia* (Rüppell), a large grey antelope the size of a donkey with long straight horns in both sexes. It stands 48 inches at the shoulder. The Tanganyika form differs from the forms to the north by the presence of some long hairs on the tips of the ears—hence the name "Fringe-eared" Oryx.

The Roan Antelope, *Hippotragus equinus* (Desmarest), is widespread in suitable localities. It is distinguished from the Sable by its large body size (57 inches at the shoulder), shorter horns and pale brown colouring. The horns are swept back in a single curve. The Sable Antelope, *Hippotragus niger* (Harris), though smaller than the Roan, standing only 54 inches at the shoulder, nonetheless is a much more handsome animal with its black colouring in mature males (chestnut in females and immature males) and its long backward sweeping horns. It is found in most parts of Tanganyika where miombo woodland occurs.

The Topi, *Damaliscus korrigum* (Ogilby), is probably a northern race of the Sassaby. It is found in suitable localities in western Tanganyika east as far as the Serengeti Plains and the Usangu. As with its near relatives the Wildebeest

and the Hartebeest, the body slopes downwards from the withers to the hips*
Shoulder height is about 50 inches.   The body is light chocolate in colour*
darker above, lighter on the flanks, with large patches of liver colouring on the
shoulders and thighs.   Topi are found in large herds on open grassy plains.

Two species of Hartebeest, *Alcelaphus buselaphus* (Pallas), and *A. lichtensteinii* (Peters), occur, distinguished by the shape of the horns.   Both are reddish
in colour and stand about 48 to 49 inches at the shoulder.   The local representative of the former, Coke's Hartebeest, is found on the open plains of northern
Tanganyika; its horns are bracket shaped, extending outwards from the top
of the head, then upwards.   Lichtenstein's Hartebeest occurs in the miombo
country of southern and western Tanganyika; its horns extend outwards, upwards,
inwards, and finally backwards.   Both species are gregarious.

Two very distinct forms of Wildebeest occur.   The White-bearded Wildebeest,
Connochaetes (*Gorgon*) *taurinus albojubatus* (Thomas), of the open plains of
northern Tanganyika, and the Nyasa Blue Wildebeest, *C.* (*Gorgon*) *t. johnstoni*
(Sclater), of southern Tanganyika.   Both are dark coloured, with manes on their
necks and on their throats, and with long tails.   They stand about 52 inches at
the shoulder.   The horns extend out sideways from small bosses, then curve
upwards and inwards, reminiscent on a very reduced scale of the horns of buffalo.
The main distinction between these two gregarious animals is the white beard
in the former and the black beard in the latter.

The next group contains the spiral-horned antelopes.   All members have
spiral-horns, and the body marked with white patches, stripes or spots.   First
of these is the Bushbuck, *Tragelaphus* (*Tragelaphus*) *scriptus* (Pallas), a medium
sized animal (about 33 inches at the shoulder) with large ears.   Old males are
dark brown in colour, females and young males reddish.   They are widespread
in suitable localities, i.e. thick bush and forest, and may even lie up by day in
and around cultivation.   Closely related is the Sitatunga, *T.* (*Tragelaphus*)
spekii (Sclater), a marsh-haunting form in which the hoofs have become greatly
elongated as a result of the soft ground on which the animal walks.   This assists
the Sitatunga to live on swampy ground which would not be possible had the
animal normal-shaped hoofs.   They are larger than the bushbucks, standing
about 40 inches at the shoulder.

Two species of Kudu occur.   The Greater Kudu, *Tragelaphus* (*Strepsiceros*)
strepsiceros (Pallas), is a magnificent animal with widespread open spiral horns
in the males.   The body is greyish and the flanks are marked with seven to
nine white stripes.   Males have a small mane on the hind neck and shoulders
and a fringe of hair on the throat.   Shoulder height is 58-60 inches.   They are
widespread in suitable localities.

The Lesser Kudu, *T.* (*Strepsiceros*) *imberbis* (Blyth), is a smaller version of
the Greater Kudu, with shorter, less widely spread horns and more stripes on the
side of the body.   It is an animal of the arid thornbush country and ranges
south to about the Ruaha River.   Shoulder height is about 41 inches.

The Eland, *Taurotragus oryx* (Pallas), is the largest of all the antelopes,
standing six feet at the shoulder, massive in bulk, with a dewlap, and horns,
in both sexes, forming a close spiral.   Adult males weigh up to 1,500 pounds.
They are widespread in all areas, except evergreen forest, from sea level up to
14,000 feet.

And finally there is the Cape or Black Buffalo, *Syncerus caffer* (Sparrman), a massive ox-like beast with large horns spreading sideways from a flattened boss. Shoulder height is about 60 inches. Buffalo are gregarious and, where disturbed, retiring, spending the day in long-grass swamps and forests. Where they are not disturbed, they often remain in the open all day. They are common from sea-level to the upper limits of forest at about 10,000 feet.

Of the marine mammals found off the shores of Tanganyika mention may be made of the Dugong, *Dugon dugon* (Müller)—the "mermaid" of mariners—which may be seen along the coast. It is occasionally caught in fishermen's nets and is considered a delicacy by those who eat it. Adult specimens reach a length of nine feet; the tail is abruptly notched in the midline and the flippers bear no signs of nails. In the adult male the incisors grow into large, rootless tusks, while in the female these teeth, though present, remain small.

REPTILES AND AMPHIBIANS

Reptiles (Class Reptilia)

Tanganyika, principally by reason of its larger area but in part due to the diversity of its topography, possesses a considerably richer reptile fauna than either of its northern neighbours. Uganda, for example, has only 102 species or races; 177 have been recorded from Kenya, while the actual figures for Tanganyika are 257, an increase of 27 during the past twenty-seven years. All the principal orders and suborders of living reptiles[1] are adequately represented in the territory, the various groups being composed as follows:—

Crocodiles (Order *Crocodylia*)	2
Turtles, Terrapins and Tortoises (Order *Testudinata*)	12
Lizards and Chameleons (Order *Squamata*, Suborder *Sauria*)	129
Snakes (Order *Squamata*, Suborder *Serpentes*)	114

Crocodiles.—The common crocodile of the Territory is the wide-ranging species usually known as the Nilotic Crocodile (*Crocodylus niloticus*) which, in all probability, is annually responsible for more fatalities than the rest of the reptiles put together. In some areas Africans intelligently prevent a heavy mortality by providing their women with bailers consisting of gourds with long bamboo handles attached, thus making it unnecessary to approach the water within swishing distance of the crocodile's tail. In a few places, such as Mwaya on Lake Nyasa, the locals apparently regard a monthly mortality of half a dozen women with complete indifference, the women-folk walking into the rivers to submerge their water-gourds. Visiting officials or sportsmen may be importuned to shoot the basking crocodiles, yet the people themselves make no attempt to reduce the numbers of these reptiles by destroying their eggs.

In the early days of the British Administration, the Government, following the example of its predecessor, offered a reward of a cent apiece for crocodiles' eggs. So easy were these to get during certain months around Lake Victoria that the local authorities became embarrassed by the daily procession of natives bearing baskets of eggs which had to be counted, destroyed, and decently interred.

For many years the inclusion of a second species of crocodile in the Tanganyika list, was based on a single German record of the occurrence near Ujiji of the West African Sharp-snouted Crocodile (*Crocodylus cataphractus*). More

---

[1] i.e. excluding the Tuatara (Order *Rhynchocephalia*) of New Zealand.

recently at least two others have been shot in the vicinity of Kigoma by British residents. As this species occurs in the Lukuga River near Albertville, it is probable that occasional individuals leave the Congo coast and cross Lake Tanganyika.

Turtles.—Of the twelve testudinates three are marine, and include the well-known herbivorous Green Turtle (*Chelonia mydas*) which furnishes the turtle soup for aldermanic dinners, and the inedible, carnivorous Hawksbill Turtle (*Eretmochelys imbricata*) that provides the "tortoise-shell" of commerce.

Four other species are aquatic but inhabit freshwater. One of these, the Zambezi Mud Turtle (*Cycloderma frenatum*) is distinguished from all others in the Territory by the leathery integument bordering its shell; shell and integument together measure nearly two feet in length. Such a reptile may weigh as much as thirty pounds. These big turtles subsist chiefly on the molluscs to be found in Lake Nyasa and the larger southern rivers.

Tortoises.—The remaining semi-aquatic species, frequently called terrapin or side-necked water tortoises, may occasionally be seen basking on the banks of rivers or pools in whose mud they remain buried during periods of drought. When liberated by the monsoon rains, terrapin roam about in search of more congenial quarters; at such times they are sometimes encountered crossing roads or paths.

The Southern Marsh Terrapin (*Pelomedusa s. subrufa*) is readily distinguishable from Smith's Terrapin (*Pelusios sinuatus*) and the Black Terrapin (*Pelusios subniger*) by the immobility of its lower shell (plastron), the anterior portion of which is movable in both the others. The other two withdraw the head and forelimbs within the shell when danger threatens, then raise the lower portion like a drawbridge, which completely protects the head and forelimbs from attack.

In this connection it is interesting to observe that one of the entirely terrestrial tortoises in the territory also has developed a hinge. But this is on the posterior portion of the upper shell (carapace), enabling Bell's Tortoise (*Kinixys b. belliana*) to close the rear end down and thus protect the tail and hind limbs. In the young this leathery hinge is absent, and somewhat obscure in the adults, but serves to distinguish a mature Bell's tortoise from all others in the territory.

The Soft-shelled Land Tortoise (*Malacochersus tornieri*), though rarely seen except by those who make a special search, is unusually interesting on account of its having undergone shell-reduction. The bony carapace is now but little thicker than paper, while the central part of the plastron has entirely disappeared, leaving a diamond-shaped fenestration. This species, known chiefly from the Central Province, occurs also at Tabora and near Lindi. Its shell-reduction and pancake-like shape are correlated with unusual habits, for it seeks protection beneath the boulders and rocks of the kopjes on which it dwells. If one attempts to remove a soft-shelled tortoise from its retreat, the reptile inflates its lungs to exert pressure against boulder and ground, braces its legs as struts, and then tenaciously resists all efforts to withdraw it from its place of refuge.

More commonly met with is the Eastern Leopard Tortoise (*Testudo pardalis babcocki*). This handsomely-marked reptile attains a size far surpassing that of an ordinary sun-helmet, but such large examples are becoming increasingly scarce. They are much sought after for food by such tribes as the Hehe and Taturu. Like other testudinates the female leopard tortoise excavates a hole with her hind feet in which to drop her numerous, white, hard-shelled eggs that bear a striking resemblance to ping-pong balls. Without ever turning to inspect her progeny, the parent proceeds to fill in the excavation and, after tamping down the earth with her flat plastron, abandons them for ever.

Lizards.—Probably the first of Tanganyika's 129 species of lizards to be observed by a new arrival in the territory, will be the House Gecko (*Hemidactylus mabouia*). Its pallid form, with bright beady black eyes, is to be seen in most hotels as it glides down a white-washed wall shortly after the lights are switched on. Notwithstanding native statements to the contrary, there is no poisonous lizard in the entire African continent. For that matter, if one excludes the big monitors, which are harmless enough unless cornered, there is not a single species which might be termed dangerous. In the forests and upon the kopjes will be found nearly thirty relatives of the house gecko. One of the most familiar is the Yellow-headed Gecko (*Lygodactylus p. picturatus*), numerous on the tree-trunks in the avenues of Dar es Salaam, Tanga, Morogoro and elsewhere. They deposit a pair of hard-shelled, pill-like, white eggs in the interstices of the bark.

Another tree-dweller is the handsome Black-necked Agama (*Agama cyanogaster*), a rough-scaled, foot-long species whose males have blue or bluish-green heads, the females being more apt to be brown like the young ones. Most of the territory's agamas, however, frequent rocks where from the summit of some boulder they bob their red or yellow heads at passers-by. This habit is said to give offence to some Moslems who suppose their actions at prayer are being ridiculed. In reality the lizard's nervous behaviour is associated with sexual display in which the male exhibits his throat; differently coloured in each of the several local races. Though partly herbivorous, most agamas subsist on ants, and the numbers which one lizard manages to consume during the course of a day is prodigious.

Recent anatomical researches have revealed that the agamas are closely related to chameleons and the latter can no longer be assigned to a separate suborder (Rhiptoglossa). The chief reason for separation was the peculiar extensile tongue whose sticky tip is projected with lightning-like rapidity at some hapless insect. Faulty observation of this action has resulted in natives asserting that chameleons spit poison, and in some regions like the Ubena highlands it is quite usual to find chameleons, that have been killed by the Bena, lying dead along the paths.

An examination of many scores of chameleon stomachs revealed that their diet consists largely of beetles, grasshoppers and caterpillars. Certain species appear to specialize or show preference for one or other of these groups. An enlightened planter in the Usambara Mountains used to encourage Africans to bring and release chameleons upon his coffee trees. Undoubtedly the presence of chameleons is an asset to any plantation, and Europeans should lose no opportunity of dispelling the groundless fears natives entertain with regard to chameleons. No chameleon is poisonous, and the bite of all but the largest is unable to break the human skin, the reptile's blunt-crowned teeth being adapted for crushing insects.

In size chameleons range from the two-inch Pigmy Chameleon (*Brookesia ionidesi*) to the two-foot Giant Chameleon (*Chamaeleo melleri*) on whose snout is a single short horn. Other species bear two or three horns, used by the males for fighting among themselves. In most forms the females are hornless, as is the case with both sexes of the majority of the twenty-eight kinds of chameleons to be found in Tanganyika. All members of the genus *Chamaeleo* possess prehensile tails and simulate the green tints of the foliage among which they dwell. *Brookesia*, on the other hand, is characterized by a short, non-prehensile tail, and pigmy chameleons can only assume the dark shades of the dead leaves which they resemble.

Mention has been made of the monitors, often miscalled "iguanas" by the misinformed. The Nile Monitor (*Varanus n. niloticus*) is inclined to a semi-aquatic life, and the unusually fine examples found around the great lakes may measure as much as five feet in length. They dig up and devour many crocodile eggs, but when a monitor takes to robbing hen roosts it is best destroyed. The activities of most monitors, however, are distinctly beneficial for they destroy large numbers of slugs, snails, caterpillars and crabs. The Savannah Monitor (*Varanus exanthematicus microstictus*), as its name suggests, inhabits dry bush country where, when disturbed, its sudden rush to hide may startle the traveller. In conformity with its habitat, the savannah monitor is a sandy buff, browner when young, but it is not nearly as common as the dark olive Nile monitor.

The dominant lizard family in the territory is that of the skinks, of which there are thirty species known from Tanganyika. Everyone will be familiar with the glossy-scaled, brownish, Two-striped Skink (*Mabuya s. striata*), the "mjusi islam" of the Swahili, so named perhaps because it dwells in peace with the owners of the huts on whose posts it basks, or in whose thatch it spends the night. Only slightly less abundant is the Variable Skink (*Mabuya v. varia*) in which the white stripe is on the flank, instead of the back, which may be flecked or variegated with white and black.

Along the coast, where coral rag occurs, the Marine Skink (*Ablepharus boutonii africanus*) seeks a livelihood, pursuing shrimps and slaters at the very edge of the waves, from whose incoming boisterousness it flees to seek shelter in the numerous crevices provided by the rocks. Other skinks have had their limbs reduced in size or lost them altogether, an adaptation to a subterranean life. One of these limbless lizards (*Scolecoseps acontias*), a glossy black or brown skink of three inches in length, dwells among the roots of shrubs growing in sandy soil near the coast. It was described in 1913 as coming from Dar es Salaam, but has never been seen there since.

The Cordylidae are represented by ten rough-scaled species, three of which wriggle like snakes, for which they are usually mistaken. In the Northern Snake-lizard (*Chamaesaura anguina tenuior*) the inconspicuous limbs are reduced to one- or two-toed vestigial flaps. This form lives in the grassy uplands of the northern highlands. In the southern highlands occurs a species (*Chamaesaura miopropus*) with minute forelimbs but no trace of hind limbs. While these two lizards average about two feet in length, the remaining two are usually less than six inches. Both have well-developed, five-toed limbs, and can be readily recognized by the whorls of spines encasing their tails. The Eastern Girdle-tail (*Cordylus c. tropidosternum*) is coastal belt in habitat, the Dwarf Girdle-tail (*C. ukingensis*) appears to be restricted to the southern highlands.

The only other spiny-tailed lizards in the territory are three forms of the Great Plated Lizard (*Gerrhosaurus major*) which live in abandoned termitaria or among rocks, especially the kopjes of the Central Province. Better known are two smaller species rarely attaining more than eighteen inches in length. Both are handsomely striped in red, yellow and black. Though ubiquitous they are more often heard, rustling rapidly through dry grass, than seen. All six Tanganyika members of the "Gerrhosauridae" have recently been merged in the Cordylidae.

The typical lizards (Lacertidae), tropical relatives of the sand and viviparous lizards of Britain, have fourteen representatives in the territory. Many are handsomely coloured but relatively small, except the Long-tailed Lizard (*Latastia longicaudata revoili*) which may exceed a foot in length, two-thirds of this being "tail". These are the active little creatures that dart across or along footpaths in many parts of the country. While most of the species are terrestrial, several are arboreal, and visitors to Amani or Liwale should be on the look out for the beautiful blue-striped *Holaspis guentheri laevis* that occurs there.

The most un-lizard-like members of the entire order are the limbless worm-lizards (Amphisbaenidae), represented in Tanganyika by nine species, three having been discovered since the first edition of this Handbook was published in 1930. In appearance all resemble semi-transparent, pinkish worms, their colour being due to the blood vessels showing through the skin. The scales have degenerated into rectangular grooves. Amphisbaenids subsist on termites and rarely come to the surface except when driven out by rain or the attacks of driver ants (*siafu*).

Snakes.—Of all reptiles it is the snakes which most frequently form the subject of enquiry from newcomers, since to many minds the words "Tropical Africa" conjure up visions of deadly serpents in considerable profusion. As a matter of fact, of the hundred and fourteen kinds of snakes occurring in Tanganyika, not more than twenty-two could be classed as dangerous to man, while cases of snakebite are distinctly uncommon.

Quite twenty are popularly known as "blindworms," a name more properly belonging to the English Slowworm (*Anguis fragilis*) which, like most limbless lizards, has a movable eyelid. In all snakes the eyelid is immovable and transparent, covering the eye like a watch-glass. Neither the blind snakes (*Typhlops*) nor the three worm-snakes (*Leptotyphlops*) can open their mouths wide enough to bite. If they could it would be seen that the former had teeth only in the upper jaw, the worm-snakes only in the lower. Just enough to restrain the termites, slugs and caterpillars upon which these burrowers feed.

The largest snake is the widespread African Python (*Python sebae*), usually found in the vicinity of the larger rivers. Freshly removed skins measure up to thirty feet in length. However, that only means a snake of twenty-two-and-a-half feet, for a skin is at least 25 per cent longer than when on the snake. The only boa in East Africa is usually less than two feet in length. This Sand Boa (*Eryx colubrinus loveridgei*) occurs only around Kahe and is adapted to a burrowing life. It is a handsomely-coloured snake, being salmon-pink heavily blotched with chocolate-brown. It feeds upon mice and small birds which it constricts in true boa fashion before swallowing.

The commonest snake in East Africa is the Brown House Snake (*Boaedon l. lineatus*) which, despite the presence of one or two light lines along the side of the head, is, in its black phase, frequently mistaken for a young "black mamba." Though harmless, house snakes will bite readily if molested. It is in search of mice that they prowl about buildings, but they are even more frequently to be found beneath rubbish. Many other South African snakes are common to Tanganyika; among them one might mention the Cape File Snake, Wolf Snake and Olive Grass Snake.

The slender and graceful green snakes (*Philothamnus*) are specially well represented in the territory by six species. They are often to be seen sunning themselves upon bushes and, though ready enough to bite when first seized, soon tame and do well in captivity if fed on frogs. Care should be taken, however, not to confuse them with young green mambas which are superficially very similar, both species having a round pupil. The green snakes, of course, lack the long front fangs of the mamba.

The ill-informed attitude of killing every snake on sight is much to be deplored in view of the fact that the great majority of species are non-venomous, further, many species are highly beneficial from the agriculturist's point of view. In the Iringa highlands is an olive-brown snake (*Duberria lutrix shirana*) which subsists almost entirely upon slugs. This little reptile is of the thickness of a pencil and usually about nine inches in length; it never attempts to bite when picked up.

Another beneficent group, collectively known as black-headed snakes (*Aparallactus*), feeds exclusively on centipedes. They occur chiefly in the coastal belt but are also found in arid inland areas wherever centipedes are abundant. Slender and under a foot in length, their body colour may range from olive, in forest-fringe forms, to the sandy-brown of dwellers in dry bush, some becoming entirely black when full grown.

The Egg-eater (*Dasypeltis scabra*), with three very distinctively coloured races in Tanganyika, has undergone tooth-reduction; teeth being incompatible with the swallowing of small birds' eggs intact. Once the eggs are safely in the snake's gullet, the reptile cracks them by means of its vertebral processes; in this way none of the contents is lost. The crumpled shells are subsequently ejected.

Tanganyika has many back-fanged representatives of the Colubridae. In these snakes the hindmost maxillary teeth are grooved to convey venom that administers a quietus to struggling prey. When a man is bitten the venom teeth do not normally come into play, being set too far back in the jaw. The solitary exception is a large Boomslang (*Dispholidus typus*), for apparently examples of six feet or over can gape widely enough to do damage. This arboreal reptile presents a bewildering variety of colouring, for wholly black, brown, fawn, red and green examples occur, besides intermediate variations. Like its near relative the Vine Snake, also common in Tanganyika, the boomslang feeds chiefly on chameleons, but also on birds.

Though it has never been recorded from Tanganyika, the Black-and-yellow Sea Snake (*Pelamis bicolor*) probably occurs along the coast as a rare visitor. When cast upon the shore by a high tide this reptile is helpless as it lacks the broad belly scales by means of which terrestrial snakes progress. Its numerous small body scales immediately distinguish it from the smooth-skinned and venomous muraenid eels. The sea snake has short immovable poison fangs, valvular nostrils, and a strongly compressed tail with which it propels itself through the water in pursuit of the fish on which it preys.

The most dangerous of all African snakes belong to the Elapidae and resemble the sea snake in having a fixed poison fang on either side of the front of the mouth. In Tanganyika there are two distinct mambas, though long regarded as but colour phases of one species as they occur together. The Green Mamba (*Dendroaspis angusticeps*), which reaches a length of eight feet, appears to be less aggressive than the so-called "Black" Mamba (*D. polylepis*) which has been known wantonly to attack both Europeans and Africans. The latter is a dull green when young, olive to buffy-brown when adult, and attains a length of at least twelve feet. The differences may be tabulated as follows:

Common or Green Mamba	*"Black" (green or brown) Mamba*
Inside of mouth white to bluish white	Inside of mouth bluish grey to black.
Scales around middle 17 to 21	Scales around middle 21 to 25.
Shields from throat to anus 201 to 232	Shields from throat to anus 242 to 282.
Paired shields on underside of tail 99 to 126	Paired shields on underside of tail 105 to 127.

A truly black snake, though occasionally brown, which is often mistaken for a "black" mamba, is the Black-and-white Cobra (*Naja melanoleuca*). The commonest form is uniformly glossy black above, white with black crossbars on the throat, and black posteriorly. Its most distinctive features are the alternate black and white barred lip shields. Primarily a forest species, it occurs in extreme western Tanganyika and again as a rare survivor along the coast, where a seven-and-a-half-foot specimen has been taken at Mikindani.

Of similar dimensions, but still rarer, is the Egyptian Cobra (*Naja h. haje*) known from the Kilosa and Shinyanga Districts. It is uniformly olive above and differs from other Tanganyika cobras in having small scales interposed between the eye and lip shields. Neither of these snakes ejects venom. This is done by the "spitting snake" or Black-necked Cobra (*Naja n. nigricollis*), abundant throughout the territory and not to be confused with the Ringhals (*Hemachatus haemachates*) which is unknown from north of the Zambezi. When the venom strikes the eyes, which it may do from a distance of six feet or more, it causes instantaneous agony and should be immediately washed out with milk, water, or a boric solution if the sight is not to be permanently impaired. When the venom falls on bare skin, provided there is no abrasion or scratch, it does no harm but should be sponged away at the earliest opportunity. The spitting cobra is a highly variable species, perhaps the commonest form is a slightly iridescent, plumbeous black, others are brown, olive, and around Mt. Longido a distinctive salmon-pink race is to be found.

The Eastern Aquatic Cobra (*Boulengerina annulata stormsi*) is found only in Lake Tanganyika,. There it hunts fish by day, emerging towards sunset to bask among the rocks where it spends the night. When molested, the aquatic cobra spreads a hood that is possibly not so well developed as those of the other three cobras mentioned above. The only other members of the Elapidae in Tanganyika are the garter snakes (not to be confused with the innocuous North American reptiles of that name). The African garter snakes are the Old World counter-parts of the coral snakes of the Americas. Like them they prey on other snakes and, though highly venomous, are not aggressive. The name is derived from the numerous white cross bands of the young garter snakes, but these tend to disappear with growth so that the adults of at least one race (*Elapsoidea guntherii nigra*), very plentiful at Amani, are entirely black.

The vipers (Viperidae) are distinguished by the possession of a pair of long, tubular, poison fangs that *fold* back along the palate when not in use. In the burrowing adders (*Atractaspis*), of which there are three species in Tanganyika, the fangs are so large that they have to come down on either side of the lower jaw when erected. The heads of these burrowers are no broader than their bodies, so that even herpetologists have occassionally mistaken them for harmless colubrines. All three species are glossy iridescent black and their venom is very potent. Secreted in a gland posterior to the eye, it passes along a duct to the base of the tooth and is discharged from an aperture near its point.

Three species of night adders (*Causus*) occur in the territory. They are not only vicious, but are capable of injecting very large doses of venom from poison glands that extend backwards from the head along either side of the backbone for quite a distance. In districts where they occur, night adders are usually met with towards evening when they are setting out in search of the toads which form their staple article of diet. Night adders, like burrowing adders, lay eggs.

The tree vipers (*Atheris*), again with three species in Tanganyika, are truly viviparous. As they prey on tree or sedge frogs these snakes are usually associated with rain forest at high altitudes (Usambara, Uzungwe and Rungwe Mountains), or upland swamps. A tree viper is most readily recognized by its very short, strongly curved, prehensile tail. In colour the species range from vivid light green to olive, flecked with yellow or mottled with brown; some possess a zigzag vertebral band. Some those of which have been caught appeared reluctant to strike and it is probable that their venom is not very toxic.

Best known of all African vipers is the heavy-bodied Puff Adder (*Bitis arietans*) widely distributed at altitudes below 5,000 feet. The chief danger from this reptile lies in its unwillingness to move out of the way, while its variegated colouring often blends with the littered ground on which it may be basking. There is no truth in the oft-repeated statement that a puff adder strikes backwards. In the Usambara Mountains and south-east near Kilwa a near relative, the Gaboon Viper (*Bitis gabonica*), is present. Both species subsist chiefly on rodents, though the puff adder, particularly when young, is partial to toads.

Amphibians (*Class Amphibia*)

The amphibians of Tanganyika have until recently received less attention than the reptiles, consequently every fresh expedition results in some slight increase in the number of recorded species. Owing to the uncertainties as to what constitutes a species among sedge frogs (*Hyperolius*) it is best to say that the total number of amphibia in the territory is about 121, with approximately 68 in Kenya and 44 in Uganda.

Caecilians.—Not all amphibians have limbs, and except for their moist and scaleless skins the worm-like caecilians might well be mistaken for snakes. Six of the seven species dwell in the damp leaf-mould of the rain-forests of the Usambara, Nguru and Uluguru Mountains and the southern highlands. Members of the genus *Boulengerula* are less than a foot in length and of a grey or purplish pink hue; those of *Scolecomorphus* are somewhat larger and glossy black with, or without, a brown dorsal stripe. All feed on termites, possibly varying this diet with ants. At least three produce living young which resemble their parents.

Otter.

Insects.

1. *Eligma laetipicta* Ob.
2. *Charaxes protoclea azota* Hew. (female)
3. *Hypolimnas antevorta* Dist.
4. *Chrysiridia croesus* Gerst.
5. *Hadrothemis scabrifrons* Ris.
6. *Pseudocreobotra wahlbergi* Stal.
7. *Xylocopa nigrita* F.
8. *Hyperechia* sp.
9. *Rhina afzelli* Fhs.
10. *Ityraea gregorii* Dist.
11. *Cymothales eccentros* Walk.

ALL FIGURES HALF NATURAL SIZE

Photo: Pegas Studio, Nairobi

Frogs and Toads.—Of the many kinds of toads and frogs in Africa only three (*Nectophrynoides*) give birth to live young. One was recently discovered on Mount Nimba on the Ivory Coast, the other two (*N. vivipara* and *N. tornieri*) have long been known from the Usambara and Uluguru Mountains. During September females will be found distended with ova, in October these have turned to tadpoles, and in November to perfectly formed toads no larger than bluebottle flies. Both species may be found hopping about on the wet, leaf-strewn ground in the montane forests, but while the tiny *tornieri* hides high up in the wild bananas (*Musa uluguruensis*), the larger *vivipara* shows a preference for hiding in the hollow centres of broken bamboos.

In these same mountains occur most of Tanganyika's ten pug-faced toads (Microhylidae). Those of the genera *Hoplophryne* and *Parhoplophryne* live in bamboos or between the outer leaf-stalk and main stem of the wild bananas. It is on the smooth stem they deposit their eggs. Irrigated by the moisture constantly seeping over them, the eggs eventually give rise to tadpoles which, aided by their exceptionally long tails, go slithering down the stem into the select bathing pool provided by the water retained at the base of every leaf stalk. The resulting toads are of small size and present some unusual features. For example the male of one species retains only the basal portion of a "thumb" from which protrudes the needle-like bone.

Some larger toads (*Probreviceps*) of the same family, as well as *Arthroleptis stenodactylus whytii*, a webless member of the Ranidae, are provided with shovel-shaped tubercles on their heels. With the help of these primitive tools the females dig burrows in which they deposit their large round eggs and guard them until, having passed through the tadpole stage within the egg, the frog or toad emerges as a miniature of its parent. As all these unusual adaptations occur in the mountains, it is assumed they have been developed to eliminate the risk of spawn or tadpoles being swept away during a heavy rainstorm.

Another member of the Ranidae, the Sharp-snouted Frog (*Hemisus m. marmoratum*) which rather resembles a little rubber ball, has somewhat similar habits. As it lives on the sandy coastal plain, however, the purpose would appear to be to tide the tadpoles over the interval between the first downpours of the monsoon rains and the rise of the water table through the sand. At Bagamoyo and elsewhere have been found sharp-snouted frogs crouching over their eggs in damp sandy soil at the base of domestic bananas. In some instances the eggs had already hatched and a seething mass of tadpoles was wriggling in the jelly that formerly surrounded the eggs. On this they subsist until liberated by the rising water flooding the area.

Of less obvious advantage is that practised by Peter's Tree Frog (*Chiromantts petersi*) of the Central Province. This putty-coloured frog deposits albumen with her eggs at the edge of a pool, or on grass if there happens to be any. Then the parent, by treading motions of her hind legs, works the albumen into a frothy mass many times her own size. The eggs, concealed within, undergo development, and the active wriggling of the tadpoles as they feed on the albumen resolves the central portion of this strange "nest" to fluid which, breaking out, carries the tadpoles with it as it flows into the pool. As often as not, however, one sees many stranded tadpoles—provided their nest has escaped the hooves of cattle or game that so often trample them into the mud. Obviously better

29

is the procedure of a related species (*C. xerampelina*) inhabiting the dry coastal savannah. The meringue-like nest is attached to a branch or leaves of a tree overhanging a pool of water, into which the tadpoles fall to complete their metamorphosis.

These two tree frogs belong to the Rhacophoridae, which includes the multicoloured little frogs (*Hyperolius*) one sometimes finds squatting on window sills, verandah posts or rose bushes, though their natural habitat is banana stands or sedges. In the latter situation it is frequently necessary to pull apart the sedge to reveal the frog concealed within.

Where plantations of bananas are extensive a shiny black frog (*Phrynomerus b. bifasciatus*) with scarlet markings is frequently to be found. When handled this frog exudes a milky-white secretion from its dorsal glands. If rubbed on the hand, or the frog held by a hand that has been immersed in water, swelling and irritation follows and may even be felt in the arm. It has long been known that toads (*Bufo*) protect themselves from dogs or other carnivores by secretions of the parotid glands. Apart from this no East African amphibian possesses any means of defence. It has never been known to bite and none is provided with venom should it do so.

Of the dozen species of toad (*Bufo*) in the territory, the Square-marked Toad (*B. r. regularis*) is by far the most abundant. If, at the commencement of the rains, a pool should form near a European's residence the sonorous sawing calls of the male toads are likely to make sleep impossible. This toad, like its European counterpart, and over a dozen local representatives of the genus *Rana*, to which belongs the common frog of Europe, follow the usual practice of spawning in water.

The smooth clawed frogs (*Xenopus*) of the family Pipidae may be recognized by the presence of conical black claws on their fully-webbed feet. So entirely aquatic are the four forms found in Tanganyika that they are rarely to be met with out of the muddy ponds, lakes or sluggish streams which form their chosen habitat. The eggs are deposited singly on submerged vegetation, and the tadpoles, provided with a pair of trailing barbels, resemble tiny catfish. The species are self-sufficient to a remarkable degree, for not only are the emerging froglets so voracious that they eat each other but the adults prey on both tadpoles and young frogs.

ANNOTATED TITLES OF VARIOUS DEGREES OF USEFULNESS TO ANYONE STARTING WORK ON THE HERPETOLOGY OF TANGANYIKA*

N.B. It is difficult for beginners in this field to realise that almost everything written over twenty years ago that involves nomenclature is today as obsolete as would be a 1930 treatise on aviation. The mis-statements, mis-identifications and misleading locality records of pioneers in this field are the subject of criticism and correction in a constant stream of articles in the various zoological publications.

BOULENGER, G. A.

1915.—"A List of the Snakes of East Africa, north of the Zambesi and south of the Soudan and Somaliland, and of Nyassaland." *Proc. Zool. Soc.* London, pp. 611-640, figs. 1-3. (Still the handiest aid to an approximate identification of the snakes, though the nomenclature is even more obsolete than the spelling of Zambezi, Sudan and Nyasaland).

*See also Bibliography.

LOVERIDGE, A.

1916 to 1956.—Approximately 100 contributions to the herpetology of East, as distinct from West, Africa, including reports published by the Museum of Comparative Zoology in 1928, 1933, 1935, 1937, 1942 and 1952, on the herpetological results of five expeditions. Revisions of snake genera (1939, 1940, 1944), the Pelomedusidae (1941), and sundry lizard families (Amphisbaenidae: 1941; Gerrhosauridae: 1942; Cordylidae: 1942; and— with Dr. E. E. Williams—a monograph of all African families of Cryptodira: 1956).[1]

1923.—"A List of the Lizards of British Territories in East Africa . . . with Keys for the Diagnosis of the Species." *Proc. Zool. Soc.* London, pp. 841-863 (Moderately serviceable; should be used in conjunction with family revisions listed above).

1930.—"A List of the Amphibia of the British Territories in East Africa . . . together with Keys for the Diagnosis of the Species". *Proc. Zool. Soc.* London, pp. 7-32. (Rather useless as almost fifty species have been added, and some removed, since 1930).

1947.—"Revision of the African Lizards of the Family Gekkonidae." *Bull. Mus. Comp. Zool.*, 98, pp. 1-469, pls. i-vii. (Includes 29 of the 30 Tanganyika species and a synopsis of all that is known of the life history, enemies, parasites, etc. of each).

NIEDEN, FRITZ.

1907 to 1926.—During this period a dozen contributions (in German) by this author were published, mostly by the Berlin Museum. The two most important were:

1913.—"Neues Verzeichnis der Kriechtiere (ausser den Schlangen) von Deutsch-Ostafrika. I. Reptilia." *Mitt. Zool. Mus.* Berlin, 7, pp. 51-100.

1915.—"Neues Verzeichnis der Kriechtiere (ausser den Schlangen) von Deutsch-Ostafrika. II. Amphibia." *Mitt. Zool. Mus.* Berlin, 7, pp. 345-390.

PITMAN, C. R. S.

1938.—"A Guide to the Snakes of Uganda." (Kampala), pp. xxi + 362, pls. i-xxviii, col. pls. A-Q, diagrams I-II, maps. (Though extralimital, probably three-quarters of the species dealt with are common to Tanganyika and not more than a quarter peculiar to Tanganyika missing. The excellent figures and coloured plates make this work invaluable to beginners. A new and revised edition is in course of preparation).

STERNFELD, ROBERT.

1908 to 1917.—During this period ten papers (in German) by this author appeared, most being published by the Berlin Museum. A useful one, though a most uncritical compilation in which the author merely translates measurements and descriptions from Boulenger into German, then adds localities of material in the Berlin Museum, is:

1910.—"Die Schlangen Deutsch-Ostafrikas." in "Die Fauna der deutschen Kolonien." (Berlin), Ser. 3, pt. 2, pp. iv + 47, figs. 1-54, map.

---

[1]In 1957 a comprehensive, annotated "Check List of the Reptiles and Amphibians of East Africa (Uganda; Kenya; Tanganyika; Zanzibar)," furnishing full synonymies of all genera and species, together with their distributional ranges in considerable detail, is to be published in the Bulletin of the Museum of Comparative Zoology, Cambridge, Massachusetts, U.S.A.

TORNIER, GUSTAV.

 1896 to 1912.—About fourteen papers (in German) were published which dealt wholly or in part with Tanganyika. The first, though hopelessly erroneous today, is important as being the first attempt at a herpetology of German East Africa. Many localities are included which are in neighbouring countries.

 1896.—"Die Kriechthiere Deutsch-Ost-Afrikas. Beiträge zur Systematik und Descendenzlehre." (Berlin: reprinted 1897), pp. xiii + 164, figs. 1-11, pls. i-v.

BIRDS

 A study of the physical map of Africa correctly suggests that Tanganyika is as likely as any part of the continent to be endowed with a rich and varied avifauna. Besides possessing the highest mountain and a lion's share of the greatest lakes, the territory has several fine rivers, a long and by no means featureless coastline, considerable areas of forest, swamp and highland, and vast tracts of the scattered-tree grasslands characteristic of so much of Africa— in fact a wide variety of climatic and vegetational conditions likely to suit the requirements of an equal variety of birds. No complete and authoritative check-list of the birds known to occur in the territory yet exists, but it is safe to say that records from within its borders must now include at least a quarter of the five thousand or so species and races credited to the Ethiopian Region. That this is a high proportion can be appreciated when it is remembered that in the "Ethiopian Region" is customarily included not only all of Africa and Arabia south of the Tropic of Cancer, but also the off-lying islands, great and small, ranging from Madagascar to far away Tristan da Cunha. Oceanic and desert-dwelling genera are among the few that are comparatively poorly repre- sented in Tanganyikan records, but even of these quite a number penetrate within the territorial limits by way of the Mozambique Channel and the arid "Mkomasi Gap" (between the Pare and Usambara mountains), respectively.

 As long ago as 1894, when only about 15 years of exploration had followed, after a considerable interval, the pioneer collecting done by Speke and Grant, Dr. Anton Reichenow was able in his "Birds of German East Africa" to list no less than 728 species. But up to the first world war ornithologists, though mainly concerned with the description and distribution of birds, had curiously neglected many of the most interesting parts of the country, recent exploration of which has added numerous records to the territorial list. None the less the names of many of our most familiar birds commemorate the explorer-scientists of that era: for example *Agapornis fischeri*, the little love-bird of the country south and east of Lake Victoria; *Aerops boehmi*, one of the many colourful species of bee-eaters; *Nectarinia johnstoni*, the sunbird of highest altitudes appropriately first collected on Kilimanjaro; Reichenow's and Stuhlmann's Weavers first discovered at Arusha and Bukoba respectively; *Eminia lepida*, the warbler whose splendid song bursts from the thickets around Lake Victoria and is also to be heard in the highland forests of Masailand; and, another prettily named tribute to Emin, *Sorella eminibey*, the Chestnut Sparrow of the Masai steppe.

 The results of the initial period of discovery long remained rather inaccessible and, as recently as 1930, it was not at all easy to identify even quite common species to be met with in Tanganyika. At about that date, however, handbooks on the birds of many parts of Africa began to appear in abundance and, in particular, W. L. Sclater's great check-list for the whole Ethiopian region was published. Now with the completion of Mackworth-Praed and Grant's "Birds of Eastern and North Eastern Africa", the ornithologist in Tanganyika is really very well equipped with all that is necessary for basic reference and, what is most important, with a clear indication of how much—or often how little—is known of each species. Apart from this it was also in the early 'thirties that R. E. Moreau, then Secretary to the E.A. Agricultural Research Institute at Amani, began his enthusiastic and far-reaching investigations. It is not too much to say that his work and that of the African collectors and observers trained by him, together with the inspiration and assistance given to so many others, revolutionized the aspect and status of ornithology in Tanganyika. One may mention especially the studies of individual species which have brought our knowledge of them to the level of many long familiar European birds—an outstanding example being E. G. Rowe's life history of Verreaux's Eagle. This, one of the most magnificent of all eagles with its black plumage off-set by a white patch on the back and a golden beak, had hardly been recorded anywhere between Abyssinia and the Cape when Rowe found it nesting near Mbulu. It has since proved to be a characteristic bird of the Tanganyika section of the Great Rift Valley.

In spite of all the progress of recent years there is a wide field for discovery left open, and the bird lover of today has the inestimable advantage of an ample literature to help him to turn the most limited opportunities for observation into fruitful as well as pleasurable channels. There is certainly material enough in the territory to suit every taste and interest, as a brief consideration of some of the salient features of the bird life may perhaps show. One of the most immediately striking of these features is the prevalence of birds in almost all types of country and the fact that such a high proportion are of brilliant plumage or remarkably intriguing form or habits. Only the more extensive plantations seem comparatively birdless though even a sisal estate is often well supplied with bee-eaters and sunbirds. Nor is there any sharp distinction here between town and country. The very entrance to Dar es Salaam port, for example, is a notable assembly point for waterfowl and waders and a short walk from the docks will enable such species as the Marsh and Terek Sandpipers to be inspected at close range. The most casual observer will notice the Coucals or "Water-bottle" birds in the garden hedges of the town or, between November and March, the lovely Carmine Bee-eaters hawking from the telephone wires in the open spaces.

Although the hinterland of Tanganyika coastal towns tends to be dreary, its birds offer much in the way of refreshment. A short drive is likely to be rewarded by the sight of such species as the Whydahs of extraordinary tail development, by golden and scarlet weavers and bishop birds, the blue flash of one of the bush-haunting kingfishers, or a lazily circling Harrier-Eagle (for this is one of the few countries where birds of prey have so far escaped being sense-lessly classified as "vermin"). Anyone who can spare the time to stroll just off the roads into the thick but not really impenetrable coastal forests stands a good chance of seeing some of the most colourful birds of Africa, such as the Louries, Trogons and Four-coloured Bush-shrikes, or of adding to our scanty knowledge of such a charming but secretive species as the robin-like Akalat. Indeed in the country as a whole it is an interesting and consoling fact that the more dull and unattractive the type of bush, the more immediately noticeable are the beauty, visibility and variety of its birds. Thus the thorn scrub of Masailand and the Central Province or the woody wastes south of Tabora and of the Southern Province abound in species ranging in size from the Ostrich to the tiny but skilful "Cappoc-vogel", in colour from the gaudy Pitta, Barbets and Waxbills to the numerous Grass-Warblers which can barely be distinguished except by voice, and include creatures of such remarkable habits as the Hornbills, Wattled Starlings and Helmet Shrikes. It is true that in the *miombo* or deciduous woodland which occupies so much of the country one can sometimes walk many miles without seeing a bird, but round the next corner one may encounter gems like the Racket-tailed Roller or Fork-tailed Bee-eater, a real rarity such as the African Tree-creeper, or a mixed foraging party of up to a dozen species at once, and when darkness falls the woods will be full of the voices of owls and nightjars.

It is commonly believed that the birds of a tropical country are deficient in calls and song. No doubt the more conspicuous species, especially of urban or cultivated localities from which thicket and other dense cover have been cleared, generally tend to have raucous or negligible voices. The same after all applies in Britain in the case of Rooks, Magpies, Sparrows and the like, but is less noticeable in a country where hedgerows and bosky gardens everywhere shelter the best-known songsters. Another factor in the situation is that in the tropics the quicker onset and intensity of midday heat often completely subdues bird-song at quite an early hour. Nevertheless the song of birds and the amazing variety of their calls are certainly a pleasing feature of Tanganyika, as would be acknowledged by anyone who listens to the Morning-Warbler in full voice on a garden lawn before the dew is dry, the sweet trilling of the sunbirds at the cloud levels of any of the mountains, the imitative repertoire of the Robin-Chats, or the stupendous burst of whistles, warbles, coos and squawks which greets the dawn in highland and lowland forest alike, often to be entirely extinguished as soon as the sun rises. It is delightful too to learn the calls of so large a number of cuckoos and owls, all quite distinctive and for the most part very melodious.

The brilliant coloration of many Tanganyikan birds has already been mentioned. Eyes accustomed to the blacks, browns, whites and generally concealing hues of northern birds may find the preponderance of reds, greens, golden-yellow, blue and violet a trifle reminiscent of a zoo aviary. But it is at the same time no uncommon thing to meet with species of a more homely category. The territory's list includes just about a hundred palaearctic migrants, though some of these may belong to breeding populations not necessarily very remote and others may seldom be seen except on brief passage. Many however appear in October or November and stay till March or April, so that the arrival of the first Swallows, Spotted Flycatchers, Tree Pipits, Willow Wrens, Red-backed Shrikes, Hobbies and other winter visitors can give almost the same lively pleasure as their springtime appearance in England.

To those whose interests centre on opportunities for sport, Tanganyika still offers exceptional advantages. The territory seems to have escaped the worst effects of the era when the size of the bag was the sole criterion of a successful day and measures for conservation were unknown—a state of affairs which, combined with excessive snaring and trapping, has elsewhere in Africa obliterated many a wildfowl paradise and made rarities of such species as bustards and guineafowl. There are few parts of Tanganyika where some gamebird or other is not plentiful, whether Duck, Geese, Francolin (the "partridge" of so many kinds and voices), Guineafowl, Quail, Pigeon, Bustard or Snipe. Some of the best shooting is to be found in the vicinity of certain dams and small lakes where each of several sorts of Sandgrouse has its favoured time for coming in to water and where a great influx of Garganey, Shoveller, Pintail and other European duck joins the more sedentary (and usually slower flying) species during the months of the northern winter. In the comparatively impoverished coastal areas Green Pigeon fill the gap and are a real test of skill as they come rocketing from some heavy-foliaged tree.

Some mention may be made in conclusion of the nesting habits of Tanganyikan birds, for to many the finding of a nest and, nowadays, the recording of observations on incubation, fledging and other details of breeding biology rather than the mere accumulation of egg-shells, are the most fascinating aspect of ornithology. Bird-nesting admittedly needs considerable patience and perseverance in a country where barriers of thorns or giant nettles may hamper search and the possibility of an associated wasps' nest or lurking snake has to be remembered. The incidence of desertion or destruction of nests also seems to be higher than in more temperate regions. On the other hand there is the compensation that nests are to be found in every month of the year. This does not of course mean that individual species are breeding perenially. Indeed as our knowledge of tropical breeding seasons improves, it is becoming clear that with few exceptions each species in each locality has its regular and narrowly defined time for laying. But whereas, for example, most birds of prey begin nesting in the dry season, other species choose the onset, middle or end of the short or long rains as the case may be, and between them all there is no time of year when occupied nests cannot be discovered. In this as in all other respects, Tanganyika is well favoured from the point of view of the bird-lover, sportsman and ardent ornithologist alike.

INSECTS

Insects of any tropical or subtropical country are so vast in number of species that it is almost impossible to record all the known ones in any territory. Tanganyika is certainly no exception to this and even the butterflies, which form the smaller section of the order Lepidoptera, show an imposing number, well over six hundred species in fact, without including the great number of varieties of intra-specific value. Even so, comparatively little is really known yet about the butterflies, their distribution and habits. There are great tracts of the territory only sparsely collected and certain areas are quite unrecorded. Moths, which form by far the greater part of the Lepidoptera, and other insect orders are less known than the butterflies. The total number of species of insects in Tanganyika is probably little short of 60,000.[1] Consequently for the purpose of this article it will be impossible to mention more than just a few of the more striking insects of the country. As butterflies enjoy more popular appeal than other insects they will be discussed first and at greater length.

Lepidoptera (*Butterflies and Moths*)

As stated above, well over six hundred species of butterflies, not counting varieties, and a far larger number of moths, are known from Tanganyika.

---

[1]These remarks do not take into consideration spiders, ticks, scorpions, etc. which are *not* insects.

Butterflies.—In Africa there are certain groups (genera), as well as isolated species, which are more or less peculiar to that part of the continent south of the Sahara. These include the large genera *Charaxes*, represented elsewhere only by two or three species in India and one in Europe; *Acraea*, replaced in India by the related genus, *Telchinia*, and equivalent in habits and form to the quite distinct tropical American family, *Heliconiidae;* some Lycaenid genera such as *Lepidochrysops;* and *Colotis*, of which there are fewer species in India. Certain other genera are shared more equally with other continents, such as *Hypolimnas*, while others again, *Cyrestis* and *Argynnis* in particular, are better known in the Palaearctic Region. A few species themselves are widespread outside Africa, for instance, *Phalantha phalantha* (Leopard Butterfly), *Danaus chrysippus*, *Vanessa cardui* (Painted Lady) and *Lampides boeticus*. These remarks all apply to Tanganyika as much as to other regions of Africa.

There is, of course, a limited number of species of butterflies and other insects which are only known from Tanganyika, and others which are rare beyond her borders, but as more and more information is accumulated and areas of Africa are better collected the distribution of species thought to be severely local is found to be more general. In the case of subspecies (i.e. geographical races of a species) local conditions and isolation can produce and stabilize such forms in comparatively small areas. Probably less is known about Tanganyika species than about those in the adjoining East African territories, for example the enormously rich Uganda Protectorate, enclosing as it does a wealth of species from West Africa and disclosing new species or new records nearly every year. This is because of the paucity of collectors in Tanganyika on the one hand and the energy displayed by certain collectors now and in the past in Kenya and Uganda on the other. In emphasizing the need for more collectors, as well as for more knowledge of the habits and life cycles of the insects, it would be as well to point out that the gradual clearing of land for agriculture, mining and so on will tend to thin out the populations of animals and although this may be welcome in the case of tsetse and other injurious insects it is to be hoped that more collectors and naturalists will start to gather information in the next few years while there is still some virgin forest intact.

Two of the most interesting phenomena in African butterflies are the closely connected subjects, Mimicry and Polymorphism. The species of families Danaidae and Acraeidae are distasteful to their vertebrate enemies, chiefly birds and reptiles, although amphibia probably also take their toll of butterflies. Many species of other families, although not themselves distasteful, have colours and patterns so closely imitating the Danaid and Acraeid models that it is difficult to tell them apart, particularly in flight. Birds and some lizards are known to avoid tackling butterflies with these patterns, mindful of having sampled the wrong ones on some previous, dire, occasion. Two of the most remarkable mimics are the polymorphic species, *Pseudacraea eurytus* (Nymphalidae) and *Papilio dardanus* (Papilionidae), the former species exhibiting various forms each almost peculiar to localities frequented by different species of *Acraea*, the local models; the latter showing (in the female sex only) patterns equivalent to the Danaids of their habitat. The mimetic resemblances to the two distasteful families are extended into some of the day-flying moths. Other butterflies derive protection by the cryptic coloration of the underside of the wings which, at rest with the wings closed, resemble dead leaves. Many Nymphalids, such as *Precis tugela*, *Charaxes varanes* and the Satyrid, *Melanitis leda africana*, show variable underside colours of dead-leaf patterns.

We may mention a few butterflies in their respective families. In brackets after each family name is the number of species (disregarding varieties, subspecies) of that family known in Tanganyika.

DANAIDAE (10). This small family includes the "Monarchs", of which the most familiar, as well as one of the commonest butterflies in Africa and India, is *Danaus chrysippus*, a large, reddish-brown, slow-flying species with black margins, usually with a row of white spots across the black tips of the wings. Other species are more confined to forests and include a large black and white species, *Amauris niavius dominicanus*, often abundant at the coast. All of them are easily confused with their mimics. Their caterpillars are characterized by pairs of fleshy prominences on some of the segments.

ACRAEIDAE (about 60). These are narrow-winged, slow-flying insects, mostly coloured black and reddish or yellowish-brown, sometimes with white bands or spots, and always with black dots on the hindwing, particularly near the base, sometimes also on the forewing. Many of the *Acraea* have the wings very thinly scaled and the outer half of the forewing is often devoid of colour. In one species, *Acraea chilo*, the male is red with several black spots on both wings, but the female is almost entirely without colour, merely showing a few dots on the hindwing and presenting a very washed-out appearance. *Acraea damii cuva*, which occurs in the coastal strip, is red in the male with half the forewing and the margin of the hindwing colourless, the hindwing having a row of largish round spots. In the Amani forest there is a fine large transparent species, *A. pentapolis epidica*, with two black smears on the forewing but the only coloured area being a pale yellow patch on the hindwing. As an example of a "fully clothed" species there is *A. oreas*, whose upperside is black, the forewing with six yellow spots in two rows of three, the hindwing with a yellow rectangle.

NYMPHALIDAE (at least 125). One of the finest of the forest butterflies is *Euxanthe tiberius*, found in such places as Amani, Turiani and the Uluguru Mountains. This is a large species, about four inches across in the male, blackish-brown with white marginal spots; on the forewing with two rows of yellow spots and a red patch at the base. The female is still larger, with the forewing spots white and with a white patch on the hindwing. This and the *Charaxes*, of which there are about thirty-four species in the territory, are frequently caught at bait such as rotting fruit or animal droppings. They are all robust species, mostly large and usually with tails on the hindwing. *Charaxes protoclea azota*, is a handsome species, the male black with broad red marginal band, in the female with a very wide central white band (Fig. 2). Another beautiful species of these forests as well as of bush country is *C. bohemani*, light blue at the base of the wings, the rest black except a few white apical spots; the female with a broad white bar on the forewing. Other striking forest species include the "Mother of Pearl", *Salamis parhassus aethiops*, widespread and common, and its rather scarcer relative *S. cacta amaniensis*, a "leaf butterfly", the upperside glinting with purple, margined with black. *Euphaedra neophron* is a purplish—or greenish-blue—species with black apex traversed by an orange bar. It flies low over the ground in forest glades in many localities, but a more restricted relative, the beautiful *Euphaedra zaddachi elephantina*, is found in certain of the more western forests. The forewing is black with a green sheen, crossed by two yellow stripes, the hindwing red with a black border. There are too many striking Nymphalids to mention here, but this introduction would be inadequate without referring to one of the largest Tanganyika butterflies, *Hypolimnas antevorta*, a rather rare species found at Amani. It is nearly five inches across, black, with white submarginal flecks, a white subapical stripe, and each wing with a blue band across the middle.

SATYRIDAE (over 40). As in other countries most of these are brown butterflies with "eyespots". *Melanitis leda africana*, related to the Indian "Rice butterfly", is familiar in nearly all shaded spots, but a much rarer species, *M. libya*, is found in forests such as Amani. Several species of the larger genera, *Monotrichtis* and *Neocoenyra*, are only known from Tanganyika.

LIBYTHEIDAE (2). The "Snout butterfly", *Libythea labdaca laius*, is a common migrant at the lower altitudes. Its only relative here is the tailed white and brown species, *Abisara delicata*, again an Amani species.

LYCAENIDAE (over 150). There are many genera of "Blues" with tails on the hindwing, *Deudorix*, *Hypolycaena*, *Iolaus*, *Aphnaeus*, *Spindasis*, and so on, many of them brilliantly coloured, particularly the *Iolaus* group. One of the finest is *Myrina silenus ficedula*, the "Fig-tree blue", a brilliant blue butterfly with reddish terminal band on the forewing and long brown tails on the hindwing. Another common but striking species is *Hypolycaena ceres coeculus*, violet-blue with black borders, the hindwing with two slender tails, and the underside grey or white crossed by red lines. *Spindasis* have orange stripes, usually, on the forewing, and the underside of both wings shows broken reddish or silvery bars. Of the large genus *Lepidochrysops*, the finest species is *stormsi* found in southern Tanganyika near the lake. A commoner species, also fairly large, is the greyish *L. peculiaris*, found near the coast. In the highlands there is a small relative of the European "Copper" butterflies, *Lycaena phlaeas abbotti*. In forests, particularly near the coast, there are several species of Pentilinae, some of them resembling Acraeidae and quite unlike Lycaenids in appearance.

PIERIDAE (about 70). The chief genera of the "Whites" are *Mylothris*, which have marginal dots on the wings and a coloured basal spot, more distinct on the underside; the rather similar *Appias* and *Dixeia;* the common whites of the genus *Belenois;* and the large genus *Colotis*, which have coloured tips to the forewings in most species. One of the finest of the latter is *Colotis regina*, the male with a broad purple tip. Most of them are extremely fast fliers and one of the hardest to catch is *C. protomedia*, of coast and low altitude thorn bush country, a black and yellow species.

PAPILIONIDAE (about 28). One of the largest "Swallowtails" in the territory is *Papilio pelodorus*, a black species with pale yellow band and spots, occurring in forests of the Usambaras and Ulugurus. *P. dardanus*, the common yellow species with black borders, has a number of different tailless female forms, which, unlike the tailed yellow male, mimic various Danaids. There are several black species with green bands and some white and black tailless species. Of the "Swordtails" the finest is the coastal species, *P. colonna*, a deep black species with the green restricted on the hindwing to the base and margin.

HESPERIIDAE (over 140). One of the most striking "Skippers", *Coeliades chalybe*, a black species shot with blue at the base, occurs at Amani, and probably elsewhere in the territory. Another large Tanganyika species is *Celaenorhinus kimboza*, a black species with white bar on the forewing. Some of the bigger Skippers, *Zophopetes* and *Artitropa*, fly at dusk.

Moths.—We can only touch briefly on some of the innumerable families of other insects.

URANIIDAE. By far the most resplendent moth is the coastal *Chrysiridia croesus* a black insect with streaks of iridescent green, the hindwing ornamented with a purplish patch and edged with white-fringed tails. At certain times of year it can be seen in numbers at Tanga, Dar es Salaam and Morogoro.

GEOMETRIDAE. One of the finest of this large family is *Victoria fuscithorax*, a white species with toothed margins and ornamented with green streaks. Some of the largest Geometers (*Cartaletis* and related genera) have a pattern mimetic of *Danaus chrysippus*.

AGARISTIDAE. These are mostly day-flying "Tiger moths", only distantly related to the European "Tigers". One of the commonest is *Heraclia superba*, the forewing black and blue with orange spots, the hindwing crimson with black border.

NOCTUIDAE. The largest species of this enormous family is the common *Nyctipao walkeri*, five inches across, brown with wavy lines and a bluish eyespot on the forewing. It frequently takes refuge in dark corners of houses. Related to this is a smaller species, *Cyligramma latona*, characterized by a creamy-yellow transverse stripe. A common day-flier at the coast is *Egybolis vaillantina*, a dark steely-blue or greenish species with vivid orange spots on the forewing. Most striking of the family is the forest species, *Miniodes discolor*, of about three and a half inch wing-span, which at rest appears orange mottled with brown, and ornamented with two or three central pearl spots. When disturbed the entirely scarlet hindwings are displayed.

AMATIDAE. The greater part of this family consists of small day-flying moths, blackish, with the wings marked with transparent "windows". The genus *Euchromia*, however, are very wasp-like, with gaudily striped bodies and narrow wings marked with yellow or orange.

ARCTIIDAE. There are many species of "Footmen moths" (*Eilema*, etc.) and "Ermines" (*Spilosoma*, *Estigmene*) but true Tiger moths are absent, although there are species of somewhat similar appearance, and marked more like the carnivore itself, such as *Amphicallia tigris*, an orange species with blue-black stripes. A very common species is *Teracatona euprepia*, variable in markings, the hindwing scarlet, the forewing pale fawn with darkened veins and other markings. A few of the Hypsids repeat the *Danaus chrysippus* pattern. The Nycteolids include the day-flying forest genus, *Eligma*, such as *E. laetipicta*, the forewing greenish-black with sulphur spots, the hindwing orange with black border.

LYMANTRIIDAE. There are not many striking members of this family. The majority are white or yellow, some are semi-transparent or entirely so. A few, like *Aroa discalis*, fly by day. In one or two species, such as *Aroa melanoleuca* and the genera *Orgyia* and *Bracharoa*, the females are wingless.

NOTODONTIDAE. *Phalera imitata*, like a small piece of wood when the wings are folded round the body, is extremely similar to the European "Buff-tip". The finest of the "Prominents" is *Amyops ingens*, the female over three inches across, pinkish-white on the forewing, streaked with blackish, the hindwing white with a black border.

EUPTEROTIDAE. The "Processionary moths" of the genera *Thaumetopeia*, *Anaphe* and *Epanaphe* make communal nests of hundreds of individuals, often enclosed in a leathery bag. The largest members of the family belong to the genus *Jana*, brown or reddish, broad-winged moths with black transverse bands, the wing-span up to nearly six inches.

BRAHMAEIDAE. The only genus here is *Dactyloceras*, large brown moths with the outer half of the wings traversed by a number of continuous wavy lines followed by a submarginal row of eyespots.

SATURNIIDAE. The "Emperor" moths are well represented. One of the finest is the long-tailed green *Argema mimosae*, of "Lunar moth" pattern. The wing-expanse is five and a half to six inches and the hindwing, with tail, four to four and a half inches. It is fairly common in thorn bush country. The largest genus is *Nudaurelia*, large red or yellow moths with a coloured eyespot in the centre of the hindwing and sometimes in the forewing. Closely related are the *Lobobunaea*, of which *ammon* and *tanganicae* have wing-expanses of eight inches, while *Imbrasia deyrollei*, with short tails on the hindwings, is rather larger, about eight and a half inches. It is perhaps the largest known African insect in wing-area and occurs at Amani. Similar in shape to this is a magnificent species, *Athletes semialba*, about seven and a half inches across. The wings are rich chocolate brown, the forewing having the basal half powdered with white, the eyespot of the hindwing ringed with red.

SPHINGIDAE. The "Hawk" moths include several European species, such as the "Death's Head" (*Acherontia atropos*), "Convolvulus Hawk" (*Herse convolvuli*), "Oleander Hawk" (*Deilephila nerii*), "Striped Hawk" (*Celerio livorniea*) and "Silver Striped Hawk" (*Hippotion celerio*). Larger genera are *Polyptichus*, *Temnora* and *Nephele*. Rarities of the last genus which occur at Amani include *Nephele rosae illustris* and *N. oenopion continentis*, which, like the much commoner *N. argentifera*, are green with white bands on the forewing. The largest is the "Arrow Hawk", *Lophostethus demolini*, a brown species up to six inches across, easily recognizable by the white arrow-head and dot on the forewing. The most striking species is *Euchloron megaera* (up to five inches), with a vivid green forewing and yellow and brown hindwing.

LASIOCAMPIDAE. This is a large family with most of the species impossible to describe in the brief remarks required for this section. Two of the biggest genera are *Gonometa* and *Pachypasa* and in both of these there is such strong sexual dimorphism that it is difficult to correlate the sexes in a collection and a great deal remains to be found out by breeding. The caterpillars are generally very hairy and many of them part only too readily with short black stinging hairs if they are handled. Female moths of the genus *Catalebeda* may be over five inches, and as the bodies are proportionately large the caterpillars are also enormous.

ZYGAENIDAE. The "Burnets" in Tanganyika are largely metallic green, often with transparent spots, but usually of the normal shape, narrow winged. There are a few species with red or yellow markings such as the genera *Netrocera* and *Arniocera*, while one of the commonest is *Zutulba zelleri*, the forewing black with white spots, the hindwing red with a black border. The most remarkable are the *Himantopterinae*, in which the wings are thinly scaled, yellowish and brown, with the hindwing drawn out into a long tail.

PYRALIDAE. Of this huge family mention will only be made of one of the largest species, *Glyphodes sericea*, two to two and a half inches, thinly scaled, light green in colour, common in most parts of the territory.

LIMACODIDAE. These small moths are well represented, many of them as in *Parasa*, marked with bright green, a few, such as *Micraphe lateritia*, are pink and others again are white, yellow or brown.

SESSIIDAE. The wood-boring "Clearwings" are very poorly known but there are certainly a lot of species. Some of the larger species, with very bristly hindlegs are in the genus *Melittia*, for instance *M. occidentalis*, occurring at Amani and looking and sounding like a "Bumble bee" in flight.

COSSIDAE. Having similar habits to the last family the "Goat moths" are also very inadequately known although there are plenty of species. One of the largest is *Xyleutes crassus vosseleri*, in which the female attains a width of seven inches and a body length of three or more inches.

Omitting the rest of the moth families let us pass on to the beetles.

Coleoptera (Beetles)

This is an even larger group than the Lepidoptera and there is only space to mention examples from just a few of the many families.

SCARABAEIDAE. The "Fruit Chafers" (*Cetoniinae*) include a wide selection of brilliantly coloured species as well as some of sombre hues, but the one that takes first place is the "Goliath" (*Goliathus goliathus*), up to three and a half inches overall length, the head and thorax white with black stripes, the wing-cases maroon, usually marked with white to a greater or lesser extent. It occurs in forests from south-west to north-west. *Smaragdesthes africana* is a much smaller insect, barely three-quarters of an inch, which varies in colour from bright metallic green to deep blue or purple. Of the "Dung-beetles" (*Coprinae*, including many "Scarabs", *Scarabaeus*), the largest belong to the genus *Heliocopris*, *H. colossus* being two and a half inches long and broad in proportion. They are frequent visitors to artificial lights, but probably as unintentional as they are unwelcome. There are two common species of "Rhinoceros beetles" (*Oryctes*) and a number of small species with similar "horns" on their heads, but the "Giant Rhino beetle" (*Oryctes gigas*), nearly three inches long, is evidently scarce.

LUCANIDAE. A few species of "Stag beetles" occur in the forests, both at the coast and inland. Those of the genus *Metopodontus* have reddish wing-cases marked with black.

CURCULIONIDAE. One of the largest species of this enormous family is the "Palm weevil", (*Rhynchophorus phoenicis*), found along the coastal belt, a black species with dark red stripes. Other large Weevils of the genus *Brachycerus* infest bulbs, such as *amaryllis*. One of the biggest, with a round, bloated body, unlike the lumpy, tubercular body of some of its relatives, is *B. ornatus*, a black species with bright red spots. Another coastal species, *Rhina afzelli* might be called the "Bearded Snout" because of the ginger hair protruding from its long snout.

CERAMBYCIDAE. Some of the "Longicorns" are strikingly coloured, for instance the genus *Philematium*, in which the species are metallic blue or green with red legs. Then there are the *Sternotomis*, black with red spots or shades of green or purple with yellow spots.   *Ceroplesis* are black with red bands or streaks. *Acanthophorus* are more noticeable for their great size, up to three and a half inches long, as they are brown sprinkled with patches of short yellowish hair. *Nitocris* and a few other genera, with their slender abdomens banded with yellow or silvery white and their narrow black wing-cases, only relieved by orange at the base, look very wasp-like in flight, a distinct case of mimicry.   Certain *Nitocris*, and *Anthores leuconotus*, a brown and white species, are notorious as borers in coffee trees.

It is necessary to pass by the great families Chrysomelidae, many of them like brilliant little gems or beads as they cluster on the foliage of a plant (sometimes to the detriment of some crop or garden "special"), and Tenebrionidae, some of them fantastically shaped, since it is not easy to select examples for special notice. There must also be omitted a host of other families owing to lack of space.

MELOIDAE.   The "Oil beetles" are worth mentioning because of the familiar group *Mylabris*, black species with red or yellow spots or bands and often yellow antennae, which sit feasting on the petals of flowers.   The larvae in this family are parasitive on certain bees.

BUPRESTIDAE.   The large, rather bullet-shaped beetles of the genus *Sternocera* are reddish-brown, black or metallic green or blue, in some species adorned with sulphur spots or tufts of hair.   *Steraspis* are also large, but a little more flattened, scintillating with iridescent green or copper.

ELATERIDAE.   The large black "Click" beetles of the genus *Tetralobus* are interesting in that their very hairy larvae live in termite nests.

LYMEXYLONIDAE.   *Atractocerus* are queer beetles with extremely short wing-cases, hardly noticeable, so that their hindwings are entirely exposed, and this feature combined with their elongated abdomen causes them to be confused by the uninitiated with the so-called "Sausage flies", which are really ants.   *Atractocerus brevicornis* is largely coastal, associated with palm trees.

CANTHARIDAE.   The most familiar of these are the *Lycinae*, somewhat flattened and crinkly, often more or less circular, orange-brown with black markings.   They frequently rest on grass-stems and take lazily to flight.

COCCINELLIDAE.   There are, of course, a great many Tanganyika "Lady Birds" which deal effectively, as in other countries, with the plant-sucking bugs, "Green-fly" (*Aphididae*) and "Scale insects" (*Coccidae*).   There are also numerous species, however, which have quite other interests as they eat the leaves of potato and some other plants.   These are the *Epilachna* and probably do not warrant the same popular name.

STAPHYLINIDAE.   The numerous beetles of this family are most easily described as being something like "Earwigs".   Of special note is the genus *Paederus* as one or two species, small red ones with metallic blue-black head, wing-cases and tip of abdomen, are the cause of the dermatitis known as "Nairobi Eye".

CARABIDAE.   Largest of the "Ground beetles" are the *Anthia*, black, usually with white spots or lines.

CICINDELIDAE.   All the "Tiger beetles" are dwarfed by the southern African giants of the genus *Mantichora*, bulky black species with large jaws.   They extend northwards into southern Tanganyika.

Hymenoptera (Bees, Wasps, Ants).

APIDAE. Largest of the Bees are the "Carpenters", *Xylocopa*, which make their nests in timber. They do not have things all their own way as they are parasitized by *Hyperechia* flies (*Asilidae*) which mimic and in fact resemble them in size, hairiness and colour, whether entirely black or banded with white or yellow, a good example of Muellerian mimicry. *Crocisa* are pretty little bees with white or pale blue broken bands on the abdomen. *Anthophora cincta*, unlike most of its brown relatives, has its abdomen banded with metallic blue. The "Leaf Cutters" (*Megachile*) are familiar in houses where they insert their leaf-nests into any available holes or crevices. *Melipona* are tiny bees which make little wax funnel entrances to their minute hives in logs or verandah posts.

MUTILLIDAE. These are ant-like wasps, often wingless, which run swiftly over the ground. The thorax is red or black, the abdomen black with white spots. There are beetles which mimic them.

VESPIDAE. Very well known are the *Belanogaster*, long-waisted, brown and reddish wasps which make semi-colonial papery nests hanging from ceilings or beams. Equally familiar are the large black "Mason" wasps, *Synagris* (and some *Odynerus*), with orange tips to their abdomens, which fix their mud nests to similar supports or walls.

SPHEGIDAE. Best known of these are some species of *Sceliphron*, black wasps with long yellow waists and yellow spotted legs, which also fly into dwellings and house their families in mud nests. *Ampulex* include slender, brilliant metallic green wasps with red legs, probably mimicked by the *Philematium* beetles (*Cerambycidae*) mentioned above. *Bembex* are yellow-banded solitary wasps, making their nests in the soil and looking superficially like the European "Social wasps" which are all too familiar overseas.

POMPILIDAE. These include giant species of the genus *Hemipepsis*, black with long legs, steel blue wings and curly antennae, which prey on spiders.

CHRYSIDIDAE. These are parasitic wasps with bodies of metallic blue or green. They often enter houses looking for their larval prey.

FORMICIDAE. The only ants which we can mention here are the so-called "Sausage flies" which are really the winged males of an ant (*Dorylus*), the queens of which are rarely seen.

The vast assembly of parasitic wasps of the groups *Ichneumonoidea* and *Chalcidoidea* must be omitted here.

Diptera (Flies).

Only a very sketchy reference to this large order can be given as flies can scarcely, in any sense, be considered popular. Tanganyika is, of course, rich in the so-called "Biting flies", with their piercing stylets: Mosquitoes (*Culicidae*); *Tabanids* or "Horse flies", of which *Pangonia* and their relatives with very long probosces, singularly painful, are outstanding examples; "Stable flies "(*Stomoxys*) and "Tsetse" (*Glossininae*). Then there are the "Nuisance" flies and "germ" carriers; and crop pests such as the "Fruit flies" (*Trypetidae*, etc). Again, there are some "Beneficial flies", such as the *Tachinids*, etc., which parasitize caterpillars, and the *Bombyliidae* or "Bee flies" of similar habits, for instance the rather elegant *Hyperalonia venus*, with long, brown-spotted wings and a golden banded abdomen; and the "Robber flies" (*Asilidae*) which attack other insects and suck their juices with their sharp "beaks": Such as the large hairy *Hyperechia* (Fig. 8) which mimic their prey, the Carpenter bees, as mentioned above. The "Lake flies" (*Chironomidae*) which rise out of Lake Victoria in their myriads are adults of vermiform maggots in the lake which form a large portion of the diet of the fish. While of interest rather than of real economic importance are the "Tick flies" (*Hippoboscidae*), highly specialized, flattened parasites of game animals and birds; the even more specialized *Nycteribiidae* and related families, wingless, hairy and spider-like, which are parasites of bats or live in the refuse and guano of bat caves; the *Diopsidae*, with eyes and antennae periscoped on long slender stalks, living in thousands in swampy places; and lastly the *Otitidae*, favouring odorous flowers and rotting fruit, of which a common species is *Bromophila caffra*, with blue-black body, brown wings and a large bright red head and small beady eyes.

Hemitera (*Bugs*).

PENTATOMIDAE (Shield bugs). Of this very large family there are several brilliantly coloured species such as those of the genus *Callidea*, rather narrow bugs, in metallic green, blue or red with black spots. *Stenozygum* and certain of the *Antestia* (including the coffee cherry pests) are black Shield bugs with reddish dots. *Plataspis* are highly convex and polished brown bugs, finely speckled with yellow.

COREIDAE. One of the largest of these "Stink bugs" is *Petascelis remipes*, dark purplish brown, with dark red thorax and flattened foliate legs.

PYRRHOCORIDAE. The *Dysdercus* are the best known of these as they are the chief "Cotton Stainers", attacking cotton, mallows and other *Malvaceae* as well as baobabs and *Sterculia*. They are red or yellowish with a black bar across the wings. The abdomen underneath is yellow with red bands.

HYDROMETRIDAE. Of the "Water Measurers" the most interesting are the *Halobates*, one of the very few genera of marine insects. They have a small rounded body, covered with a whitish bloom, and spindly legs, and can be seen darting about on the surface of the sea, especially near the reefs.

REDUVIIDAE. Largest of the "Assassin bugs" are the *Platymeris*, black with two red spots on the "back" and red-banded legs. Of particular interest are *Phonoctonus* which mimic and prey on the Stainers of the *Dysdercus* genus.

BELOSTOMATIDAE. The "Giant Water bug" which is often attracted to light belongs to the genus *Lethocerus*.

There are various other aquatic bugs which we cannot deal with here "Water Scorpions", "Boatmen", etc. All too familiar is the "Bed bug", genus *Cimex*. Then there are the *Cicadidae*, so-called "Christmas Bees", with their shrill, monotonous "song" in the trees.

FULGORIDAE. The grotesque "Lantern flies" include the genus *Pyrops*, reddish or grey species with a long snout on the head.

FLATTIDAE. Interesting among these "Hoppers", which close their short, broad wings down below the body so that they appear flattened, is *Ityraes gregorii* the forewing either green or orange, edged with red. They cluster on stems, segregated into their colours, to simulate a maturing, racemose inflorescence.

CERCOPIDAE. Common among the "Frog-hopper bugs" are the *Locris*, gaily coloured red or orange and black bugs which congregate on grass. The dripping of the "Rain-trees" is due to the exudations of myriads of *Ptyelus*, sucking energetically at the rising sap. The adults are yellow with black dots or black with white spots, while the young nymphs are covered with an amorphous white excretion and look like animated bits of cotton wool.

Finally we will mention the *Membracidae*, small blackish monstrosities with the thorax contorted into spinular projections at various angles.

Neuroptera

MYRMELEONIDAE. The most conspicuous of the *Neuroptera* are the "Ant-lions" although it is not so generally known that the huge winged insects, banded or spotted with brown, which flop along in a rather clumsy flight, eager to settle again as soon as possible, are the adults of the squat grubs with long, curved jaws which live in the small pits in the sand. Some of the *Palpares* may be six or more inches across. A much smaller species is the pretty *Tomatares lemonias*, with pale yellow wings marked with purplish ramifying streaks. *Cymothales eccentros* (Fig. 11) is a very delicate slender-bodied species with sharply pointed wings ornamented with small brown blotches. Most of the species are however unmarked on the wings, by far the commonest being the communal *Hagenomyia tristis*, which sometimes flutter up in small shimmering clouds from long damp grass under trees.

ASCALAPHIDAE. These Ant-lions have very long knobbed antennae and petiolate wings and have a rather stronger, but jerky flight. *Tmesebasis* have the wings marked with an irregular brown border pattern and, in at least one species, with the centre of the wing clouded with brown.

Relatives of these are the extraordinary *Nemopteridae*, the head drawn out as a snout, the hindwing formed into a long narrow ribbon-like tail. Then there are the various "Lacewing" families, and a peculiar group, the *Mantispidae*, with the forelegs bent into the "praying" attitude adopted by the true Mantids (see later).

Odonata (Dragonflies)

This is a comparatively small insect order, including about one hundred and fifty species in Tanganyika. The more delicate, thin-bodied species fall into a distinct sub-order, the *Zygoptera*, having their four wings all of the same shape. Outstanding among these in Tanganyika is the great long-bodied species, *Coryphagrion grandis*, with a body nearly four and a half inches long and a wing-span of four and a quarter. It is found in rain forests near Tanga and Morogoro. A smaller species, *Umma declivium*, two and a quarter by under three inches, is a rarity occurring in dense forest at Amani. The body is jet black with vivid green bands on the sides of the thorax. The wings, as in most of the *Zygoptera*, are quite clear but in certain lights, such as the filtered jets of its sylvian haunts, they shimmer with iridescent purple. A similar effect is produced with a slightly larger relative, less striking and very much commoner, *Phaon iridipennis*. One of the most interesting species is the elegant *Platycypha caligata*, with sky-blue abdomen smeared with red near the base and recognizable by bright red, flattened legs, short, rather stumpy body and a blunt snout. Largest of the genera is *Pseudagrion*, but not separable from several related genera by any simple diagnosis.

30

The robust dragonflies fall into the sub-order *Anisoptera*, with the hindwing wider at the base than the forewing. Largest of African Dragonflies is the great Aeshnid, *Anax tristis*, the male having a body four and a half inches and a wing expanse of five inches. The body is black with yellow spots. It ranges with powerful flight over tropical and subtropical Africa, usually to be seen on its own.

LIBELLULIDAE. This is the largest family. A characteristic species of the territory is *Hadrothemis scabrifrons*, nearly four inches across, with a thick bright red body and broad reddish tips to the wings. It is a denizen of the thicker forests such as Amani, Turiani and Ulugurus. More familiar is the small *Palpopleura lucia*, with the wings partly or mainly black and the body short, stout and, in the male, coated with light blue. This, and a black-bodied species, *Brachythemis leucosticta*, having a black bar across the wings, are among the commonest and most widespread species, especially at quiet pools and swamps. There are a mumber of strong-flying migrants, especially along the coast, such as *Trapezostigma limbata* and *T. basilaris*, both known in Asia.

Orthoptera

BLATTOIDEA. The Cockroach families are familiar residents, the largest species being *Rhyparobia grandis*, with a five inch wing-span, fawn coloured with black dots. A specialized group, the *Derocalymna*, are wingless and look like large "Wood-lice". They live under bark and debris.

MANTOIDEA. There is a wide selection of the "Praying Mantids", one of the most striking and common is *Pseudocreobotra wahlbergi* characterized by a black and yellow spiral (suggesting an aircraft emblem) on a green patch on each forewing. The general colouring is pale green, usually suffused with pink, especially in the immature individuals. *Idolum diabolicum* is a huge species in mottled shades of green, broad in proportion and adorned with wide leafy expansions on thorax and legs. Although a striking insect it hardly deserves its specific name.

PHASMIDA. Of the "Stick insect" groups the finest species is the giant *Palophus reyi*, with a body about nine inches long, decorated with thorns for camouflage in thorn trees. It has short, round hindwings for display and to scare off enemies.

TETTIGONIIDAE. The "Long-horn grasshoppers" are a large family, very incompletely known. *Clonia wahlbergi*, of southern Tanganyika, is green, with narrow forewings and long spiny legs. *Zabalius* and *Mustius* include large species with broad wings, leaf-shaped and "veined". The *Heterodininae* are wingless, brown, with bloated abdomens and very spiny thoraxes. Somewhat similar to these are the forest *Gryllacridae* but without the thoracic armature.

GRYLLIDAE. Largest of the crickets is the brown and yellow "Sand cricket", *Brachytrypes membranaceus*. *Homogryllus*, often coming into houses, have short wings and very long spotted legs. *Gryllotalpa*, the "Mole crickets", with their greatly developed front legs for digging, frequently come to lights.

PNEUMORIDAE. This peculiar South African family extends its range with a giant species of *Cystocoelia* into Liwale District, a noisy nocturnal visitor. The body, up to four inches long, is like a green balloon, the abdominal cavity increasing its volume of sound like the bag of some musical instrument.

ACRIDIDAE. The "Short-horn grasshoppers" form the largest and best known family. Truxalis and their relatives are large, but slender green or brown species with very elongated heads, curved upwards, flat antennae and often with red or blue hindwings chequered with brown. In flight they make a noise something like the hand-rattles used by enthusiasts in a cheerful crowd to increase the din. Some species of *Gastrimargus* and *Oedaleus* have yellow hindwings crossed by a curved black band. More spectacular is the common large green *Phymateus viridipes*, with knobbly thorax and the hindwing blue and red with black spots. The nymphs of this large, gaudy species are black with red and yellow dots, gregarious in habit, unlike their parents. The *Lamarckiana* are large brown, sluggish grasshoppers, with a highly curved thoracic crest; the male winged, the female wingless. *Acanthoxia gladiator* is named from the blade-like prominence from the front of its head. Locusts are, of course, merely certain species of grasshoppers which have acquired a migratory phase in community and have achieved notoriety by their advances on civilization. Three well-known species immigrate into the territory at times, the "Migratory locust", (*Locusta migratoria migratorioides*), the "Desert locust", (*Schistocerca gregaria*) (much yellower than the others when in its swarm phase), and the "Red locust", (*Nomadacris septemfasciata*.) Rather similar to the last, but larger and with a much more prominent thoracic crest is a grasshopper, *Ornithacris cyanea*, the female over five inches in wing-span. The hindwings at the base are a beautiful crimson or purple. In the forests a common species is the green *Abisares viridipennis* with blue hindwings.

There are several other smaller insect orders which we can only just indicate.

Aphaniptera

Fleas are notorious. Apart from the familiar ones on cats, dogs and other household species there is a wide selection on wild animals, while in sandy districts there are the "Jiggers", (*Tunga penetrans*), which make their presence known by working into the toes.

Mallophaga and Anoplura (Lice)

Birds and, to a lesser extent, mammals are quite often heavily infested with small lice, *Mallophaga* (Biting Lice) chiefly on birds, *Anoplura* (Sucking Lice) prefering mammals and ourselves.

Ephemeroptera (Mayflies). Mayflies, breeding in streams and pools, and Stoneflies (*Plecoptera*), in rocky torrents and waterfalls, are well-known to anglers. It appears probable, however, that there is only a single species of Stonefly in Tanganyika, (*Neoperla spio*), but there are numerous Mayfly species.

Mecoptera (Scorpion Flies), some of them looking rather like Craneflies (*Tipulidae*), but four-winged; *Trichoptera* (Caddis Flies), their larvae making small cases of sand or debris in streams; *Psocoptera* (Book-Lice); *Embioptera*, very primitive tropical insects; *Strepsiptera* (Stylops), parasitic on some Hemiptera and Hymenoptera; *Thysanoptera* (Thrips), very small, feathery-winged insects which infest plants and sometimes carry virus diseases to them. *Dermaptera* (Earwigs), familiar to most people; *Collembola* (Springtails), minute insects living in myriads in soil or under bark or as black specks sometimes covering the surface of water in a tank; and the very primitive *Thysanura*

(Bristle-tails), mostly retiring insects living among rocks or on bark, but including the domesticated "Silver Fish" (even less accurately termed a "Fish Moth"), *Lepisma saccharina:* All these are represented in the territory.

Isoptera

Termites, often undermining structures of civilization in the tropics, are the erroneously called "White Ants". Apart from the social status they have attained they have practically nothing in common with the true ants, being much more primitive in structure and development. The large mounds or tall chimneys made by some of the species are familiar sights on the landscape, but there are some species such as the "Harvesters" (*Hodotermitidae*) which have completely subterranean nests. In the rainy seasons the winged "Kings" and "Queens" are to be seen fluttering up in thousands, eventually to alight, cast off their wings and look for a suitable nesting sight. In the termite colony there are the "Worker" and "Soldier" castes, as well as a number of "Camp Followers" (Inquilines), such as certain beetles, bugs, etc., some of them predatory or parasitic, others scavengers. On a foraging safari the workers are staunchly protected by the soldiers, which often make a very audible rattling noise with their heads and jaws as one approaches.

In concluding this brief survey of the insects of Tanganyika it may be as well to mention certain other groups often popularly classed with insects but scientifically considered quite separate:—

ARACHNIDA. This enormous animal class includes the Spiders (*Araneae*), Whip Scorpions (*Pedipalpi*), *Pseudoscorpionida, Solifugae*, Scorpions (*Scorpionida*), *Acarina* (ticks and mites) and others.

Distinct again from *Arachnida* and *Insecta* are the CRUSTACEA (crabsl lobsters, woodlice, etc.), the MYRIAPODA (millipedes and centipedes), and stil, other major groups, or classes. All these classes are included in the vast Phylum ARTHROPODA.

Literature on insects of Tanganyika is sparse. There are many papers, for instance, the Reports of the Swedish Expedition to Kilimanjaro near the start of the century, dealing with species of various groups, but the only comprehensive work is Seitz' "Macrolepidoptera of the World" which, in the African volumes, deals with the butterflies and the larger moths. These books are now becoming out-of-date with the discoveries of new records and the changes in nomenclature. It is therefore suggested that anyone really interested in collecting insects or some information on them should approach the Coryndon Museum in Nairobi. Two large collections from the territory are in the Coryndon Museum, one from the Amani Biological Research Station and the other built up by the late Father Conradt who was for many years on Ukerewe Island in Lake Victoria. Yet neither of these collections, large as they are, is anything like complete in any insect group, even for the areas they represent.

Chapter 15

SPORT

GAME

The Preservation of Game

The picture has changed since the previous edition of the Tanganyika Handbook was published, but the old controversy of game versus man remains as strongly disputed as ever. Within recent years public opinion both in the territory and at home has swung round in favour of the preservationist's viewpoint with the gathering realization that if some adequate measures are not promptly taken there will within a short time be little or no wild life left in the territory except in National Parks and other sanctuaries.

It is now essential to take a broader view of the problem. Formerly, when game was plentiful, the attitude towards it was that where game was detrimental to the interests of agriculture then it must go. The result is that, owing to the rapid spread of development, the game areas are becoming few and far between.

It is appreciated that game has an economic value as well as an ethical one. The wild animals bring in a very considerable revenue to the territory, not only from the sale of game licences and Government trophies but also as an attraction to tourists, many of whom these days cross the Atlantic to enjoy the sporting facilities of the country. Thus the fauna of the territory plays its modest part in helping to close the dollar gap.

There is also another problem in this connection and one to which a complete answer is not possible. The balance of nature is efficient. Man and man only is able to upset it and when he does this drastically no one can say what unpredictable results may occur. A minor case may be quoted here to illustrate this. In a certain colony where large-scale destruction of game had taken place in order to combat trypanosomiasis in cattle the results were both unexpected and undesirable; the incidence of trypanosomiasis increased, as the tsetse flies, deprived of their normal hosts as a source of food, were forced to concentrate their attentions on domestic stock.

To afford additional protection to the fauna, the game laws have recently been entirely re-written. The new Fauna Conservation Ordinance is, without doubt, the most important and constructive step that has been taken in recent times to safeguard the animals of the territory and there can be no doubt that it will be welcomed by all concerned as a fair-minded and genuine attempt to solve all aspects of game problems.

The average African regards game from a purely realistic point of view. In his opinion it is something which invades his plantations, kills his stock (and occasionally himself), which was created to be eaten, and, latterly, which is a certain source of income.

There is no doubt that up to a point he is correct, and no right-minded individual would grudge him protection against plantation and stock raiders. Similarly no one would grudge him a reasonable amount of game meat with which to augment his protein-deficient diet. Indeed, it is the duty of the Game Department to see that he has these benefits. The trouble is, however, that the majority of native hunters do not know when to stop, and under their auspices a hunt is likely to degenerate into a massacre. Also the "black marketing" of game trophies is very much more prevalent than is generally realised. An illegal trade in elephant tusks and rhinoceros horns is carried on and it is here that the African plays the major role, for in nine cases out of ten it is he who provides the trophy in the first place. Leopards (valuable assistants in the control of vermin) are trapped for their skins, giraffe and wildebeeste are still killed, the latter in large numbers, purely for the sake of their tails which are made up into fly whisks and sold at a good profit. Certain tribes still hunt and kill lions in order to obtain their manes which are much coveted as headdresses on ceremonial occasions. The illicit trade in the sale of game meat is not inconsiderable.

The problem is thus not a simple one. As was pointed out at a recent fauna conference, the wild game form a valuable reserve of food for the African in the event of famine, and it is therefore important to preserve this stock. It is comparatively easy to make just provision for native hunting, but it is virtually impossible to prevent these provisions from being grossly abused. The Fauna Conservation Ordinance goes a long way towards tackling this problem, by balancing the interests of the African and the preservation of game with admirable fairness.

One of the most pressing problems is the role that wild animals play in the transmission of disease to domestic stock, and this is still little known. Some facts are established but there are many theories as yet unproved.

The development of the trade in crocodile skins has lately brought this reptile much into prominence. They are now being slaughtered in great quantities and it is yet too early to tell if this will have any far-reaching effect. It is anticipated that the *Tilapia* fisheries may suffer as a direct result, since the decrease in the numbers of crocodiles may lead to an increase in the species of fish which prey on the *Tilapia*, but this is pure surmise. Another result of the wholesale destruction of crocodiles may be an increase in malaria, as the newly hatched reptiles are insectivorous and it is believed that they eat quantities of mosquito larvae.

Whatever the outcome no one has much sympathy with the crocodile and the development of the industry should produce a welcome addition to the revenue of the territory.

Details of animals which may be shot on licences, the fees for licences, boundary definitions of game reserves, controlled areas and partial game reserves may be found in the Schedules to the Fauna Conservation Ordinance.

The Game Laws

It is essential that any visitor or resident wishing to shoot or photograph game in Tanganyika should be acquainted with the Game Laws. These are contained in the Fauna Conservation Ordinance (No. 17 of 1951), the main provisions of which are given below. The schedule of animals which may be shot, together with the fees payable, are given at page 457.

Game Reserves

The accompanying map shows the areas which have been gazetted as total reserves, entry into which is prohibited without a permit issued by the Game Warden. There are a few exceptions to this prohibition of entry, namely, persons travelling through a reserve along a road, persons who normally reside therein or public servants on duty. Firearms may not be carried nor may any vegetation be cut or burned.

It goes without saying that any form of hunting within a reserve (which may be defined as a sanctuary for breeding and a reservoir against human depredations) is forbidden; although permits are occasionally issued for purposes of scientific research, for control measures, or for photographic purposes.

Controlled Areas and Partial Reserves

There is no bar on entry into the areas, which have been set aside so as to ensure hunting for the true sportsman in future years; but certain or all animals are protected (see map). Sportsmen wishing to obtain a particular trophy in any of these areas should apply to the Game Warden who may, if the circumstances warrant it, issue permits.

Hunting of Animals

No one may hunt any animal or bird, apart from vermin, without first obtaining the appropriate licence or permit. Vermin includes baboons, vervet monkeys, porcupines, hunting or wild dogs, spotted hyenas, bush pigs, seed-eating birds, and pied crows; in addition, in certain areas only, the hippopotamus and zebra.

Licences, except for professional hunters and trophy dealers (which can only be obtained from the Game Warden) are issued by Revenue Officers or Sub-accountants at all district headquarters and are valid for one year, with the proviso that a supplementary licence is only valid during the currency of the general licence.

Prior to 1951, Africans were able to hunt most of the commoner varieties of game animal without any licence for the sake of providing food for themselves and their dependants. This concession was much abused, causing tremendous inroads into the game population. The new ordinance provides for a local (African) game licence, issued by Native Authorities.

A person applying for a licence must be in possession of a suitable weapon; it has been laid down, for instance, that an elephant hunter may not use a rifle of a calibre smaller than a ·375 magnum. Detailed information can be obtained from the Game Warden, Tengeru, Arusha.

For scientific, educational or complimentary purposes, or for the supply of food in emergencies, the Governor may issue a special licence (called a Governor's Licence); the conditions under which such a licence is issued are entered thereon.

A permit, issued by the Game Warden, is necessary in order to hunt any animal not shown on any Schedule to the Ordinance, or to capture any animal for zoological gardens or similar institutions. Crocodiles are included in the list of unscheduled game.

Certain animals, including the chimpanzee, giraffe, and ant-bear, and birds such as vultures, hawks and flamingos, are classified as royal game and may not be hunted except by the holder of a Governor's Licence issued for that purpose.

Before hunting any dangerous game—which includes elephant, rhinoceros, lion, leopard, buffalo and hippopotamus—the licence holder must inform the administrative officer in charge of the district concerned of his intentions; and should he wound a dangerous animal a report must be lodged without delay with the nearest Game Ranger or Administrative Officer.

A Government Trophy is:—

"1. Any game animal killed or captured without a licence and the trophy thereof (a 'trophy' means any durable portion of an animal; 'animal' includes birds and fish).

2. Any game animal, or the trophy thereof, found dead.

3. Any animal killed or captured in contravention of the provisions of the Ordinance, including the trophy of any such animal.

4. Any animal or trophy believed to have been stolen or otherwise unlawfully obtained.

5. The tusks of an elephant weighing less than 11 lb. each (or 22 lb. the pair)."

To enforce the provisions of the Ordinance, the Game Department employs a staff of Game Rangers and Game Scouts, who are empowered to search, detain or arrest persons suspected of committing or having committed any breach of the Ordinance.

In the past, and particularly during the last war, game suffered severely; human requirements had necessarily to take priority, which resulted in animals being slaughtered not only to provide a source of food, particularly in famine areas, but also to drive them away from ever-increasing areas of cultivation. Although it is still a primary duty of the Game Department both to protect crops and to ensure an adequate reservoir of meat for times of emergency, as well as to preserve game for posterity, it is hoped that the provisions of the new Ordinance will strike a happy mean and that man and game will thereby be able to live in proximity without either the ruin of man's property or the decimation of the game.

Licence Fees

	Shs.
General Game Licence	100 (Resident)
	1,000 (Visitor)
Bird Licence	20
Professional Hunter's Licence ..	500
Trophy Dealer's Licence	200

Game Animals (*Licences*)

Except where otherwise provided for in the Ordinance, the animals specified in this Schedule may only be hunted on such game licences, in such numbers and upon payment of such fees as are set out opposite:—

A.—General and Supplementary Game Licences

1	2	3	4	
	General Game Licence.	Supplementary Game Licence		
Species	Maximum numbers of animals	Maximum numbers of animals	Fee per animal payable by the holder of a Resident's Licence Shs.	Fee per animal payable by the holder of a Visitor's Licence Shs.
Buffalo, *Syncerus caffer* (Sparrman)	1	1	50	100
Bushbuck, *Tragelaphus scriptus* (Pallas), males only ...	2	3	10	20
Caracal (Lynx), *Caracal caracal* (Schreber)	—	1	15	30
Dikdik, *Rhynchotragus kirkii* (Günther)	2	2	5	10
Duiker:				
Abbott's, *Cephalophus spadix* (True)	—	1	25	50
Blue, *Guevei caerulus* (H. Smith)...	2	1	10	20
Common, *Sylvicapra grimmia* (Linnaeus)	2	3	10	20
Red, *Cephalophus harveyi* (Thomas) and *C. natalensis* (A. Smith)	2	1	10	20
Eland, *Taurotragus oryx* (Pallas), males only	1	1	100	200
Elephant, *Loxodonta africana* (Blumenbach)*	—	3	600	2,000
Gazelle:				
Grant's *Gazella granti* (Brooke), males only	2	1	10	20
Thomson's, *Gazella thomsonii* (Günther), males only ...	3	2	10	20
Gerenuk, *Litocranius walleri* (Brooke), males only ...	—	1	100	200
Giant Forest Hog, *Hylochoerus meinertzhageni* (Thomas)	—	1	50	100
Hare, *Lepus capensis* (Linnaeus,) *L. victoriae* (Thomas), and *L. whytei* (Thomas)	10	—	—	—
Hartebeest:				
Coke's, *Alcelaphus buselaphus cokii* (Günther)	2	1	20	40
Lichtenstein's, *Alcelaphus lichtensteinii* (Peters) ...	2	1	30	60
Hippopotamus, *Hippopotamus amphibius* (Linnaeus) ...	2	2	50	100
Impala, *Aepyceros melampus* (Lichtenstein), males only ...	2	1	10	20
Klipspringer, *Oreotragus oreotragus* (Zimmerman) ...	—	1	20	40
Kudu:				
Greater, *Strepsiceros strepsiceros* (Pallas), males only...	—	1	100	200
Lesser, *Strepsiceros imberbis* (Blyth), males only ...	—	1	100	200
Leopard, *Panthera pardus* (Linnaeus)	—	1	250	500
Lion, *Panthera leo* (Linnaeus) males only	—	1	200	500
Monkey:				
Black-and-white Colobus, *Colobus abyssinicus* (Oken) and *C. angolensis* (P. L. Sclater)	—	2	20	40
Blue (Sykes'), *Cercopithecus mitis* (Wolf)	—	2	20	40
Oribi, *Ourebia ourebi* (Zimmerman)	1	1	10	20
Oryx, *Oryx beisa callotis* (Thomas)	—	1	100	200
Ostrich, *Struthio caemlus massaicus* (Neumann)	—	1	100	200
Otter, *Lutra maculicollis* (Lichtenstein), and *Aonyx capensis* (Schinz)	1	—	—	—
Pigmy Antelope (Suni) *Nesotragusm oschatus* (von Duzeben)	2	1	5	10
Puku, *Adenota vardonii* (Livingstone), males only ...	1	1	20	40
Reedbuck:				
Bohor, *Redunca redunca* (Pallas), males only	1	1	10	20
Mountain, *Redunca fulvorufula* (W. Rothschild), males only	—	1	20	40
Southern, *Redunca arundinum* (Boddaert), males only	1	1	10	20
Rhinoceros, *Diceros bicornis* (Linnaeus)	—	1	300	800
Roan Antelope, *Hippotragus equinus* (Desmarest) ...	1	1	30	60

*Only elephants with tusks weighing twenty-two pounds the pair or more, or eleven pounds or more in the case of an elephant having only a single tusk, may be shot (*vide* Section 24 (3) and the First Schedule and Section 47 (f) of the Ordinance).

A.—General and Supplementary Game Licences.

1	General Game Licence	Supplementary Game Licence	
	Maximum numbers of animals	Maximum numbers of animals	Fee per animal payable by the holder of a Resident's Licence Shs.	Fee per animal payable by the holder of a Visitor's Licence Shs.

1	2	3	4	
Rock Rabbit, *Heterohyrax syriacus* (Schreber) and *Procavia johnstoni* (Thomas)	—	2	5	10
Sable Antelope, *Hippotragus niger* (Harris), males only ...	—	1	100	200
Serval Cat, *Leptailurus serval* (Schreber)	—	1	10	20
Sharpe's Grysbok, *Raphicerus sharpei* (Thomas)	—	1	10	20
Sitatunga, *Limnotragus spekii* (P. L. Sclater), males only	—	1	50	100
Steinbuck, *Raphicerus campestris* (Thunberg)	2	1	10	20
Topi, *Damaliscus korrigum* (Ogilby)	2	1	30	60
Tree Hyrax, *Dendrohyrax* spp.	—	2	10	20
Warthog, *Phacochoerus aethiopicus* (Pallas)	3	3	5	10
Waterbuck:				
Common, *Kobus ellipsiprymnus* (Ogilby), males only ...	2	1	30	60
Defassa, *Kobus defassa* (Ruppell), males only	1	1	30	60
Wildebeest:				
Nyasa, *Gorgon taurinus johnstoni* (P. L. Sclater) ...	1	1	30	60
White-bearded, *Gorgon taurinus hecki* (Neumann) and *G. t. albojubatus* (Thomas)	2	2	30	60
Zebra, *Equus burchellii* (Matschie)	3	1	30	60

B.—Bird Licences

The following birds are classified as game birds:—

Species	Number that may be hunted	
1. Ducks and Teal, including the genera *Erismatura, Thalassornis, Nyroca, Spatula, Anas, Dafila* and *Dendrocygna*	All species	Unlimited
2. Geese, including the genera *Nettapus, Sarkidiornis Alopochen* and *Plectropterus*	do.	do.
3. Button-Quails, *Turnix* spp.	do.	do.
4. Francolin (including Spur-fowl), "Partridges" and "Pheasants", including the genera *Francolinus* and *Pternistis*	do.	do.
5. Quail, including the genera *Coturnix* and *Excalfactoria*	do.	do.
6. Guinea-fowl, including the genera *Numida, Guttera* and *Acryllium* ..	do.	do.
7. Lesser Bustards, including the genera *Eupodotis, Lissotis* and *Lophotis*	do.	do.
8. Snipe, including the genera *Capella* and *Rostratula*	do.	do.
9. Sand-grouse, *Pterocles* spp.	do.	do.
10. Pigeons (including Green Pigeons and Rock Doves), including the genera *Columba* and *Vinago*	do.	do.

The Shooting Grounds

Serengeti Plains

The area known as the Tanganyika Serengeti is bounded on the north by the Kenya–Tanganyika boundary, extends southwards to Lake Eyasi, includes part of the Musoma District and the south-eastern portion of the Maswa District, and on the east is bounded by the Rift Wall. The area is to be distinguished from the Kenya Serengeti, which lies between Moshi and Voi.

A large portion of this area now lies within the Serengeti National Park which extends from the Crater Highlands on the east to Lake Victoria on the west. In addition, most of the country lying to the north and west of the Park has been declared a Partial Reserve. In the Park shooting is prohibited; in the Reserve certain species only may be shot. Entry into the Park to watch or photograph game may be obtained from the Park Warden, who lives at Ngorongoro Crater. Accommodation, comprising furnished log cabins, is available at Ngorongoro.[1]

The plains consist of undulating country with open spaces or acacia wooding. They are mostly free from the presence of cultivating Africans, but are grazed in part by herds of Masai cattle. The area is notable for the amount of plains game which it contains: Coke's hartebeest, wildebeest, Grant's and Thomson's gazelle, zebra, ostrich, giraffe, eland, impala and oribi in parts, roan antelope, topi and rhinoceros. There are a number of lion. As a rule the early rains are light in the Serengeti, and roads are usually passable from July until towards the end of the following February.

The best shooting now lies to the south-west of the Park in the vicinity of the Simiyu and Duma Rivers. Another good area outside the Park is found on the north bank of the Grumeti River.

The Northern Province

Although parts of it are now much settled and considerable shooting out of game has taken place in localities in which it formerly abounded, the Northern Province still affords some of the great game shoots of the territory.

The diverse nature of the country, with its open volcanic plains, its stretches of thorn-bush, its lofty mountains and scarps covered or chequered with rain forest, and its stretches of nearly impenetrable secondary thicket, assures a great variety of game animals. The province contains the heavy game to be found in the thick-bushed areas such as Magenge, but, in contrast to these, it is also, in the highest degree, a "plains game" area.

A number of its finer localities will here be taken seriatim, but as the province is a favourite centre for shooting parties, and as settlement is developing, there can be no guarantee that what was a good locality yesterday will still remain so tomorrow.

Moshi may be regarded as the centre for the following shoots:—

Lake Jipe.—This lake, lying on the border of Kenya Colony and Tanganyika, is the centre of good shooting country. Rhinoceros and lesser kudu abound in the thick bush of the slopes of the northern Pare Mountains; buffalo are present; greater kudu have been reported, and, between the hills and the lake, where much of the country is more open and where permanent waters are scattered, are numbers of eland and all the usual plains game. To the south-east lies the Mkomazi Game Reserve.

Arusha-Chini is on the Moshi–Kibaya road. It is situated in rough, thick bush country which does not afford easy shooting, but the area offers an abundance of a few species of game, such as elephant, rhinoceros, buffalo, lesser kudu, waterbuck and impala. The Ruvu River Controlled Area lies further to the south.

The two small salt lakes in a straight line between Ngeraragwa and Ngare-Nanyuki often afford good duck shooting, as does the Masai furrow on the Ngaserai plain.

---

[1] For further details see pages 216-7.

[1]Arusha is a good centre for the following localities:—

Monduli Mountain, about sixteen miles from Arusha. In the dense forest on the hill are rhinoceros and buffalo and also the great forest hog. Elephant, from Mount Meru, are very occasionally present. Eland are sometimes plentiful and round the mountain are the ordinary plains game. At Feregi, on the northern side, the rhinoceros lie up in the bushy ravines that traverse the more open country. The rhinoceros of Monduli Mountain have shared with those of Ngorongoro, Bukoba and Sonyo the reputation of having perhaps the best horns in the territory. There are permanent waters round Monduli Mountain.

To the east lies the Mount Meru Game Reserve, the boundaries of which lie on the edge of the dense rain forest surrounding the mountain; Engurdoto Crater is included in this area.

From the Great North Road the following areas are accessible—

Eighty miles from Arusha the traveller reaches Mbugwe, an open and closely settled plain with a trading centre at Madukani. It may be taken as the centre for the following shoots:—

Kwa-kuchinja, about eighteen miles back from Mbugwe on the Arusha road. All the plains game, oryx and plenty of lion may be obtained. There is a small Nyamwezi settlement on the road, and permanent water.

The Tarangire River, which runs from Kwa-kuchinja in a southerly direction past Mount Ufiume. It is a permanent stream and swamp, and elephant, buffalo in plenty, hippopotamus, lesser kudu, oryx, eland and the usual plains game are found. Lion are plentiful. There is a good camping site and excellent water at the south end of the swamp. That in the swamp itself is brackish.

Mount Essimingor and Mto-wa-Mbu.—In the forest on the mountain may be found good rhinoceros and buffalo. Below, and across to Mto-wa-Mbu on the north of the Mbugwe swamp, is good country for buffalo, hippopotamus and elephant, while in the more open country oryx and the other plains game are obtainable. Between Kwa-kuchinja and Essimingor Mountain there have at times been a number of cheetah. There are good waters round the mountain, but a more usual camp is Mto-wa-Mbu, where also are plenty of lion. Here is the headquarters of a Game Ranger.

A little south of Mto-wa-Mbu is another good camp site, Maji-ya-Moto, with elephant, rhinoceros, buffalo, hippopotamus, eland and lion.

Engaruka (Kitete), fifteen miles north-east of Mto-wa-Mbu. This is an alien native settlement on rich soil at the south-west corner of Lake Natron Game Reserve. The village lies under the Great Rift Wall and ruins of stone houses belonging to prehistoric inhabitants are of interest.[2]

It is an excellent camp for a shoot. Elephant are sometimes present and buffalo always. It is a good spot for oryx, eland and lesser kudu, while gerenuk can also be shot. There are plenty of lion in the vicinity. Nearly in the Reserve and overlooking Lake Natron is the active volcano Ol'Donyo Lengai.[3]

---

[1]The Headquarters of the Game Department are situated at Tengeru, 10 miles east of Arusha off the main road to Moshi.

[2]See "Preliminary Report on an Examination of the Engaruka Ruins" By L. S. B. Leakey, *Tanganyika Notes and Records* No. 1, p. 57.

[3]See page 199.

Between Mbugwe and Babati, in a tsetse-fly belt, are plenty of impala, eland and zebra, and some hartebeest; while near the Rift Wall to the west are elephant and buffalo, waterbuck and a few rhinoceros.

From Mbugwe to Mto-wa-Mbu.—From Mbugwe to the scarp and from there to Mto-wa-Mbu, between Lake Manyara and the Rift Wall, is a strip of excellent country for a few species only, namely, elephant, buffalo in plenty, rhinoceros, impala and lion.

The Babati area, in which is an excellent roadside camp with a charming lake and an aerodrome on the Great North Road, is some twenty-five miles south of Mbugwe. Not much game is found at Babati itself except reedbuck and impala, with duck and a few hippopotamus in the lake. The hunting of hippopotamus on the lake (as well as on Lakes Basuto and Basodesh) is prohibited.

Ufiume Mountain.—On the mountain are elephant, buffalo and greater kudu. Between Ufiume Mountain and the Tarangire elephant pass to and fro, and there are rhinoceros in numbers, greater kudu, lesser kudu, impala and eland, and the usual plains game and lion. At times there are plenty of oryx and roan. From Pienaar's Heights, south of Mount Ufiume, a road branches off east to the Galapo Mission and thence southwards skirting the bottom of the escarpment before joining the Great North Road again south of Kondoa. This traverses useful game country and a large open wet-weather swamp.

Dareda to Mount Hanang or Guruwe.—A motor road serving a group of farms runs from Babati to Dareda, under the Rift Wall and near the source of the Bubu River. From here two roads pass close to Mount Hanang, a conspicuous extinct volcano that stands in the Great Rift Valley; the northerly route goes on to Mbulu and thence south to Lake Basuto where it joins the other road which skirts the south of Hanang. This road then winds away to the west until it reaches Singida. There are hippopotamus in the Bubu river, and between that point and the mountain are traversed some open plains, the country of the Barabaig tribe, with numbers of animals of the usual plains species. Parts of Mbulu are excellent country containing plenty of rhinoceros. The following localities deserve mention:—

North Mbulu.—This area lies between the Serengeti National Park to the north, Lake Eyasi to the north-west and Lake Manyara to the north-east, and contains elephant (though no very large tuskers have been obtained recently), rhinoceros and buffalo, as well as some fair mixed shooting.

The Yaida Valley and Swamp and the surrounding area are particularly excellent country for rhinoceros, both as regards numbers and size of horn. Buffalo are present and elephant pass. The general shooting is good.

Southern Masailand.—Some of the finest shooting in the territory occurs in the region known as Southern Masailand (or the Masai Steppe), lying to the south of Arusha and bounded roughly on the west by the Great North Road, on the east by the Ruvu River and on the south by the Kondoa–Handeni road which passes through Kibaya. The country consists of thorn-bush, extensive dense thicket and occasional large open plains, while here and there appear isolated hills such as Lolkisale.

Most of the plains game, including oryx, Grant's gazelle, wildebeest, zebra and hartebeest are found here, and elephant are numerous. Some very large tuskers have been killed in recent years, especially in the vicinity of Kibaya; in the same area are found buffalo and greater kudu.

The main route through this country branches off the Great North Road about twenty miles south of Arusha, passing through Lolkisale, Loiborsoit and Naberera and thence southwards until it joins the Kondoa–Handeni road at Kibaya.

Further east near Kiberashi, just over the Handeni border, the general shooting is good, and elephant, including some with heavy ivory, are found to the north. Hunting in this area is difficult, the bush being very dense.

At Kilima-cha-Mbogo, opposite the well known Kisima-cha-Mungu on the road to Kibaya, are buffalo, elephant and rhinoceros, with greater kudu on the top of the hill, whilst on the flats is a mixed assembly of game.

During the dry season water is very scarce; game congregates near the scattered water holes and hunting is comparatively easy.

Singida and the Neighbouring Districts

The south and south-west of Singida District is good for elephant and magnificent tusks have come out of it, though these are now hard to get. Rhinoceros are plentiful, particularly in the thicket country at Samumba, in the east of the district. Greater kudu are present and move back and forth from ten miles south-west of Singida to about forty miles farther away.

Lion and leopard are numerous on the rocky bush-clad hills. On the road to Mbulu are open plains with the usual plains game, the hartebeest still being *Cokei*. Near Basuto Lake, which is a hippopotamus reserve, there are very fine impala, also eland, Grant's and Thomson's gazelle, giraffe, leopard and lion, while great numbers of guinea-fowl may be shot here.

Along the Mponde River elephant, rhinoceros and buffalo are common.

Kondoa Irangi, noted for greater kudu, is a passage-way for elephant between Kibaya and Singida. Some big tuskers have been shot in the east of the district, bordering Masailand.

A party passing between Kibaya and Singida might obtain some fair incidental shooting south of the area but much of the country is covered with thick bush, making hunting difficult. Roan antelope, greater and lesser kudu, eland, zebra, giraffe, buffalo and rhinoceros are present, the last-mentioned in fair numbers sometimes near Samba and Handa. The second of these two places offers fairly easy conditions for rhinoceros shooting, but large horns cannot be expected.

Manyoni.—A great thicket area extends from Matalele in east Singida, south of the Wembere Steppe, south-eastwards through Itigi and across the Central Railway to a point twenty or thirty miles south of the latter. It appears to act as a barrier to the advance of tsetse fly from the Western Province and the south and is also fairly exclusive of most species of game, although a good many rhinoceros and lion inhabit it, while, in parts, there are greater kudu on its margin and elephant use it much. Very big elephant are reported in the southern parts of this thicket, tusks of 100 pounds a side being not uncommon in the Kisigo River area. Greater kudu, impala and lion are plentiful in parts of Manyoni, especially in the south, bordering on the Rungwa River Game Reserve.

The Wembere Steppe, Lake Kitangiri and Mkalama

The Wembere Steppe may be approached from Manyoni via Singida by motor road to Mkalama; from Tabora by motor road to Asmani's village (one hundred and six miles) or Sekenke; or from Nzega or Shinyanga by motor road to Sekenke, a former gold mine on the edge of the steppe. Much of the area is, however, under water during the rains, and it is seldom possible to cross over before September.

The Wembere Plain is nearly a hundred miles long and up to twenty in breadth. It empties when full into Lake Eyasi through the channel of the Sibiti and Manonga Rivers.

Like many such steppes it has its periods of much game and of little. The animals are flooded out of it in the heavy rains, but return fairly early in the dry season. They tend, however, to leave its southern portions again at the end of July.

The following animals may be found on the open steppe during the drier periods or in the more bushy country to the south and on the north along the Manonga River:—buffalo, (especially in the south); white-bearded wildebeest (abundant on the plain); roan antelope (in the light bush near the plain); Coke's hartebeest (on the plains); Lichtenstein's hartebeest in small numbers (in the bush on the edge of the plain); eland (sometimes on the plain); impala and greater kudu; a few lesser kudu (in the thick bush on the west); giraffe; ostrich and zebra, which are both very numerous in the open; a few rhinoceros in the direction of Singida and a fair number of lion. During the rains, elephant are common on the higher ground on the west and east, though big tuskers are seldom seen. During the dry weather large herds congregate in the dense tree-grass country around Lake Kitangiri where they live in company with buffalo. The Wembere is a paradise for duck and geese; in addition are found the large Imperial and smaller Pintail sandgrouse, which are extremely abundant; greater and lesser bustard; the spur-fowl and the helmeted guinea-fowl.

Mkalama.—The country in the region of the Dulumo River just north of Mkalama and thence near the motor road round to Sekenke is often full of game such as rhinoceros and elephant (though there are no good tuskers), eland, impala, Coke's hartebeest, zebra, etc.

The Western Province (with its headquarters at Tabora)

Game is moderately well distributed in the enormous open *miombo* forest which fills the bulk of the Western Province, but much of it is invisible due to the nature of the country.

The finest shooting lies along the Ugalla River system which is crossed by the Mpanda Railway line. Here may be found sable antelope, roan, buffalo, lion, leopard, waterbuck (Defassa), eland, hartebeest, zebra, giraffe, reedbuck, oribi, klipspringer, impala and greater kudu. Sable are particularly common. Sharpe's steinbuck as well as the common steinbuck are present.

The Muyowozi river area draining into the Malagarasi north of the railway line contains many herds of buffalo and topi, whilst sitatunga are found in the swamps.

Elephant are fairly numerous on the Malagarasi and Ugalla Rivers, tusks of between 80 and 100 pounds a piece being not uncommon.

On the shores of Lake Tanganyika about twenty miles north of Kigoma there is a chimpanzee reserve. The only other locality in the country where chimpanzees are found is the inaccessible region around Mkungwe Mountain, a hundred miles to the south.

Rhinoceros are few, and are confined largely to the slopes of the Wembere basin and the Mwala, Nyahua and Nkululu Rivers.

Francolin breed from February to April and are fit to shoot by August.

Duck do not appear to breed, as they are always in flocks and depart in April, presumably for their breeding grounds, but spur-winged geese breed in the reed-beds along the Ugalla. There is good snipe shooting in parts of the province, notably at Tabora.

The Rukwa Valley

Lying to the south of the Katavi Game Reserve (which itself covers the southern portion of Mpanda District in the Western Province) is a long depression filled by the waters of Lake Rukwa. Shooting is controlled within five miles of the lake. Most of the game already mentioned as being found in the Western Province occurs here also, a notable addition being the puku.

Big elephant have been shot in the country to the north and east of the Rukwa and particularly on the Rungwa River. Buffalo are plentiful in this area; they may also be found in the valleys lying between Namanyere and Lake Tanganyika.

Lake Rukwa is the home of thousands of hippopotami. During the drought of 1950 the water disappeared (apart from a few muddy holes) and the death-roll was extremely heavy. Recovery was, however, remarkably rapid; within two years the hippo population appeared to be as great as ever.

Bird-life on the lake shore is varied and prolific.

The Bohoro Flats and the Upper Ruaha

Round about the Ruiwa River on the way to the Bohoro flats from Mbeya are oribi, and from the swamps on the north of the road at the west end of the Bohoro flats, below the Usangi escarpment, sitatunga have been reported. On the Bohoro flats themselves is an abundance of game of certain species: Lichtenstein's hartebeest, eland, topi, impala, reedbuck, giraffe, zebra, buffalo and elephant.

The southern bank of the Ruaha River, followed thence in a north-easterly direction, provides good shooting, there being present impala, eland, greater kudu, waterbuck and other species, as well as plenty of elephant. In 1950 a bull with tusks weighing 150 pounds each was shot near Rujewa.

In the rains, elephant leave the swamps and riverine belts, moving into the higher ground to the south. During the dry season, large herds congregate in the swamps, seldom leaving the water. As a result, their feet become remarkably soft.

There is a connection between the elephant of Rukwa and Katavi by way of the dense Tantatamali forest.

The area to the north of the Ruaha River, as far as its junction with the Little Ruaha, lies within the Rungwa Game Reserve; the country to the east of the junction and south of the Ruaha falls within the Iringa Controlled Area.

Ngorongoro Camp.

Photo: P. J. Molloy

Kilosa and Mahenge

Much of the country lying to the south-east of Kilosa is now a reserve. However, there is good shooting to the south and west; buffalo, sable, Lichtenstein's hartebeest, wildebeest, eland and impala being fairly numerous. Further west, towards Kongwa and Mpwapwa, rhinoceros as well as greater kudu are common.

The Mahenge shooting area includes parts of the Kilosa and Rufiji Districts, and the Kilombero valley, outside the Selous Game Reserve. Elephant are very numerous but there are no big tuskers. The Kilombero valley in particular holds a heavy game population, including sable, eland, impala, Lichtenstein's hartebeest, greater kudu, puku, rhinoceros, buffalo and lion. This area however, is difficult of access except during the height of the dry season (August to November).

Kilwa, Lindi and Songea

In many parts of these areas there is a fair abundance of game, and elephant are present in all, though there are few good tuskers today; the general remarks made of the Western Province hold good here. A sportsman going to these areas may get good shooting, particularly on the Ruvuma River, but there are other areas which provide better sport.

Communications within this area, much of which now lies within the Selous Game Reserve, are difficult.

Bukoba

The Kagera country, in the east of the Bukoba District (Lake Province), is a fine game area. Elephant are present and buffalo and rhinoceros are abundant, particularly the latter, which often possess good horns. Defassa waterbuck, reedbuck, oribi, roan, topi, impala and eland are all found in considerable numbers. Hippopotamus are present in the Kagera River and Lake Victoria. Sitatunga are found in the lake-shore swamps.

Part of this area lies within the Nyamirembe Game Controlled Area in the Biharamulo District, and a permit is necessary to shoot there. The rest of the Biharamulo District is not particularly good game country.

National Parks

The Serengeti National Park

The Park is remarkable for the variety and number of species of game it contains and unique as regards concentration of game. Habitats vary from dense cedar and bamboo forests as high as 12,000 feet, to almost flat, featureless, grassy plains, or acacia bush country infested with tsetse fly.

The forested Crater Highlands are the home of the larger species—elephant, black rhino and buffalo—and these can frequently be seen from the road along the rim of the crater, grazing peacefully in full view in the glades bordering the forest. Waterbuck (Defassa) and bushbuck can also be seen and an occasional glimpse of Abbott's or red duiker. Positive identification has been made of the giant forest hog, and speculation continues as to whether there are bongo in the Oldeani Mountain bamboo forest. Of the carnivores, leopard abound and lion are frequently heard at night.

The floor of the Ngorongoro Crater contains most of the species found on the Serengeti Plains, wildebeeste predominating with zebra and Thomson's gazelle scarcely less numerous. Eland, hartebeest, Grant's gazelle, warthog and ostrich are in lesser numbers. Of the carnivores there is usually at least one pride of lion and many more during the wildebeeste calving season from January to April. Cheetah are frequently seen. Spotted hyena are all too abundant and hunt in packs, attended by jackals. Wild dog occasionally visit the Crater floor.

Elephant are sometimes to be seen drinking in the early morning or evening, but are making less and less use of this area, as the once forested slopes are progressively destroyed by annual grass fires. One or two black rhino can usually be found in the open a mile or two from cover, grazing among the antelope, while the majority still prefer the shelter of the Lerai Forest below the Ngorongoro Camp. In the area of swamp formed by three streams and a series of springs there lives a herd of rather less than twenty hippo, which has suffered severely in the last ten years at the hands of the cultivators. Since these latter have now been moved it is hoped the numbers of hippo will increase in the course of time.

Westward of the Crater Highlands lie the famous Serengeti Plains—an expanse of undulating grassland and scattered thorn-scrub, stretching for sixty miles to the Itonjo Hills in the Lake Province. These plains, from which the park takes its name, hold a fabulous concentration of game, attended by carnivores. Wildebeeste and zebra can be seen in tens of thousands and Thomson's and Grant's gazelle dot the plain as far as the eye can see. Herds of eland, hartebeeste and topi are common. Giraffe are distributed throughout the areas of acacia bush, where the odd black rhino also is found. During the 1930's this area became world famous for its lion which, though in sadly reduced numbers, still provide a great attraction today.

The line running roughly north and south through Banagi and the Itonjo Hills marks the edge of the flybush, which continues westward for sixty miles to the shore of Lake Victoria. Though many of the species of the plains are also found here, such as giraffe, rhino, hartebeeste, topi and the gazelles, the area holds additional species such as buffalo, roan antelope, impala and bushbuck. Klipspringer, which occur elsewhere in the park only in the Olduwai Gorge, are found on most of the hills.

Access to the Serengeti National Park

The main park entrance at Lodoro is 110 miles from Arusha by public highway, which continues through the park to Loliondo in the north, with a branch to Endulen on the south-west. This highway is maintained by the Public Works Department for a total distance of 30 miles over the hump of the Crater Highlands to the plain of Ol Balbal. From here a district road continues to Loliondo, and a Park track runs across the Serengeti Plains to the western Park entrance at Banagi.

In 1954 the park authorities took over from the Administration the road from Ngorongoro to Nainokanoka along the eastern rim of the crater, and graded it. At the same time a road was made around the western rim. Another park road has been started to make a circuit through the forested slopes of Oldeani mountain, south-west of the Ngorongoro Safari Lodge.

But the major road-making project in the park is the road descending the southern wall of the crater almost below the Safari Lodge. This was commenced early in 1954 and is making good headway against great difficulties, mainly falls of loose lava rock, and it is hoped the road will be completed soon.

This road, besides providing a drive of great scenic beauty, will put the floor of the crater within twenty minutes' motoring of the Safari Lodge, instead of nearly two hours by the Nainokanoka road as at present.

Accommodation Available

The accommodation for visitors (as at 30th June, 1957) consists of:—

Ngorongoro Safari Lodge	...	40 persons
Seronera Safari Lodge ...	...	12 persons
Lerai Camp	...	4 persons

Bookings for park accommodation should be made only with the Secretary to the Park, in the Directorate office at Arusha. A booking fee of Shs. 10/- per person is collected, which is refundable on the bill. Visitors arriving unbooked at a camp may be allotted accommodation unclaimed by 6 p.m.

Ngorongoro Safari Lodge

This consists of sixteen cabins for from two to eight persons, ten bathrooms and ten kitchens, accommodating a total of forty persons. The original cabins were built as a Rest Camp in 1936 on a Swedish log-cabin design which, for lack of suitable timber, it has not been possible to copy in the later additions. There is a camp shop, where tinned foodstuffs can be bought, and a large central clubroom with a bar.

Four of the cabins are self-contained; i.e. complete for up to four persons with bedding, crockery, cutlery, table linen, cooking utensils and lamps, and include the services of a cook-houseboy. The charge for the two cabins with three rooms is Shs. 65/- per night, and the two with two rooms Shs. 50/- per night. The remaining cabins are provided with basic furniture; i.e. beds or bunks, mattresses and pillows, table, chairs and washstand, and cost from Shs. 10/- single and Shs. 15/- double occupancy to Shs. 80/- per night according to capacity.

From the camp store can be hired bedding, crockery, cutlery, table linen, cooking utensils and lamps, and the services of a camp cook (if not already engaged).

The altitude is 8,000 feet and a fire is welcome at night throughout the year. Firewood is provided free to all cabins.

Petrol and oil is on sale, and two or three safari-type vehicles are available for hire to visitors wishing to descend to the floor of the crater or to cross to Seronera. Both of these trips have been done in saloon cars, but this is inadvisable owing to the rough going.

This Lodge is the base for trips in the highlands, to the floor of the Ngorongoro Crater and to the archaeological sites in the Olduwai Gorge.

Seronera Safari Lodge

Accommodation is provided for twelve persons in six large, grass-roofed rondavels, arranged in pairs, each with kitchen and bathroom adjacent. There is also a central mess hut. The rondavels are provided with basic furniture, and crockery, cutlery, table linen, cooking utensils and lamps can be hired. The services of the camp cook can be hired if not already engaged. The charges are Shs. 10/- for single and Shs. 15/- per night for double occupancy.

This safari lodge has no shop or bar as at Ngorongoro, and all provisions must be brought by visitors. Petrol and oil are on sale, and arrangements can be made for the hire of a safari vehicle if notice is given in advance.

This lodge is at 5,000 feet and a fire is not required at night though a jersey is welcome.

Seronera is the base for a visit to the Western Serengeti—and the area which is world-famous for its vast herds of plains game and its lions. To the south lie the Moru Kopjes, an area of great scenic beauty, and westwards is a "corridor" of bush country running for sixty miles almost to the shore of Lake Victoria. Roads are as yet very few at this end of the park, and a safari vehicle is definitely necessary to explore the country and see the best of the game.

Lerai Camp

This consists at present only of a two-roomed cabin, bathroom and kitchen, located by a stream at the foot of the crater wall beneath the Ngorongoro Safari Lodge. Access is by a footpath down the crater wall, or alternatively by motoring round by the Nainokanoka road—a distance of some forty miles. When the new motor road to the floor of the crater is completed the accommodation at this camp will be increased to anticipate its greatly enhanced popularity.

The cabin at present has basic furniture only and all additional equipment and provisions must be taken by visitors. The nightly charge is Shs. 10/- single and Shs. 15/- double.

Observation Cabin No. 1

This cabin was built as an experiment overlooking a pool in thick forest on the crater rim. Although it undoubtedly offers great opportunities to the patient observer and photographer, little use has been made of it by visitors to date, partly perhaps because the park offers so much to see which demands so much time that the average visitor cannot spare a day sitting in one place.

Control of National Parks

Control of the National Parks is vested in a Board of Trustees, appointed by the Governor, the object being to place the National Parks as far as possible outside the varying policies of Government as regards provision of finance, land usage, etc. Park legislation can only be altered by consent of the Legislature, thus ensuring the maximum degree of security and permanence.

The existing legislation provides for the appointment by the Governor of Trustees as under:—

> Three Ex-officio members: Member for Local Government, Conservator of Forests, Game Warden.
>
> Three persons nominated by the Unofficial Members of the Legislative Council.
>
> One person nominated by the Dar es Salaam Chamber of Commerce.
>
> One person nominated by the Tanga Chamber of Commerce.
>
> Six persons appointed by the Governor on his own nomination.

To date only the Serengeti National Park has been established but additional parks are under consideration. The Serengeti National Park is, however, likely to remain by far the most important.

The address of the Director of National Parks is Barclays Bank Building, Arusha.

The Game Animals[1]

In Tanganyika "game" includes elephant, buffalo, antelope, giraffe, hippopotamus, zebra, rhinoceros, the larger carnivora and a few other mammals of the chase, as well as such birds as guinea fowl, francolin, bustard, duck, geese and so on.

Game can only be killed (with few exceptions) by persons holding game licences (see pp. 455 to 458 describing the Game Laws).

The following notes on game deal only with the more conspicuous forms.

Family: Elephantidae

The East African Elephant (*Loxodonta africana knochenhaueri* (Matschie)).

Kiswahili: *Ndovu* and *Tembo.*

Elephant need no description, particularly to residents of Tanganyika, who have many opportunities of seeing them. They are almost ubiquitous, occurring from sea-level to over 14,000 feet—there is a skeleton of one at the foot of Mawenzi Peak on Kilimanjaro. As might be expected with an animal which has only one real enemy, they favour a variety of habitats, being found in forest, wooded savannah plain and swamp. However, as a result of continuous hunting, they tend to seek out thick impenetrable bush during the daytime. In areas where they are undisturbed they may often be seen in more open country throughout the day. They rely entirely on vegetable matter for their food and thrive on a diet of maize or millet as much as they do on wild fruits and leaves. They drink daily.

Elephant, perhaps more than any other game animal, undertake marked seasonal migrations, moving largely by night. During the rains they tend to leave the thick forests and take to more open country. The reason for this may be that they object to the drips from the trees, but they can also be driven out by the *siafu* ants that are active at that time.

Successful hunting of elephants requires a close approach and there should be no excuse for shooting elephants at more than thirty yards' range. Most experienced hunters prefer to close to under twenty yards. Shooting from a distance cannot be condemned too strongly as it can only result in the wholesale wounding of animals and the creation of rogues. The practice of "still" hunting, i.e. lying concealed at water holes and waiting for the victim to approach, is prohibited.

The novice should take the heart shot, as the heart and its arteries present a large mark, whereas the brain is a very small one, requires experience to locate, and is surrounded by huge bony structures. He should also use the heaviest rifle he can handle effectively and leave the small-bore rifle to very old hands.

The holder of a Resident's or Visitor's General Game Licence may take out supplementary licences for two elephant at a cost of £30 each. Tusks of eleven pounds or under must be handed over to Government. Other tusks must be registered with the nearest licensing authority within one month after shooting.

---

[1] "Game" is the term applied to wild animals which are protected by the game laws.

The likeliest areas now in which to obtain fair tuskers are perhaps southern Masailand, where elephant are fairly numerous, the Central Province (in particular Dodoma and Manyoni Districts) and parts of the Iringa and Mbeya Districts. It is by no means uncommon for tusks weighing over 100 pounds to be obtained.

Family: Rhinocerotidae

Cape Black Rhino (*Diceros bicornis bicornis* (Linnaeus)).

Kiswahili: *Faru.*

Rhinoceros are present in most parts of the territory other than the extreme south and south-west. They are particularly common in Bukoba, Masailand and Mbulu.

They have a reputation for stupidity which they live up to; their reaction to the presence of humans being often a stupid rush, occasionally in the direction of their disturbers; still more occasionally this may develop into a purposeful charge. This very stupidity, combined with a blind ferocity, makes them potentially dangerous, particularly when one is accompanied by porters who are hindered from free movement by their loads. They are not, however, to be compared with the purposefully charging, deliberately waiting buffalo. They are very blind and it is possibly this that makes them "charge" towards an intruder with much blustering, snorting and breaking of wind, as though they did not know what was there but did not want it to be thought that they were frightened. They will often charge right up to a human being but rarely do they drive home their charge. They generally stop when a few feet distant, turn round and make off in the opposite direction, or change course a few degrees and rush past. Even if they do continue in a straight line it is not a difficult matter to avoid them by stepping aside at the last moment. However, many rhinos have been shot because of their stupid habit of blustering towards an intruder.

The novice is advised to take the heart shot. The mark is large and, should the heart be missed, even a lung shot is apt to be more rapidly effective than with elephant.

They are partial in their diet to succulents and are particularly fond of the spike-shaped leaves of *Sansevieria.* They are more often found in thorn-bush country than in other habitats, but where they are undisturbed they may occasionally be seen on open plains away from all cover.

Twelve-inch horns are common, an eighteen-inch horn is good and horns more than double this length have been recorded. Good horns have been obtained in Bukoba, Sonjo (North Masailand), and Arusha, but the biggest come from the region of the Crater Highlands in the Northern Province.

Not more than two rhinoceros may be shot in one year by holders of supplementary licences, at a cost of £10 each. As in the case of elephant tusks, the horns of any rhinoceros shot must, within one month of the killing, be produced to the nearest licensing authority for registration.

Family: Felidae—*Sub-Family:* Pantherinae

Lion (*panthera leo massaica*).

Kiswahili: *Simba.*

There is hardly a part of the territory in which lion are not found. They have visited Dar es Salaam and been seen more than once in the streets of Tabora. There are the plains lion, abundant on the Serengeti and other game plains of the territory, that live on various antelope and warthog, zebra and an occasional giraffe. There are also the bush lions, especially of parts of the southern half of the territory, often dark in colour, which spend much of their time hunting bush-pig. Occasionally, in March, when the grass and the crops are high overhead, one or more of these lions will take to perambulating the paths from village to village, no longer looking for pigs but for humans.

Lions are popularly believed to eat locusts and the local Africans assert that they eat certain fruits, the *masuku* of the south of the territory being regarded as a favourite. Lions are also cannibals and a case is known in which a lion and lioness, after vainly laying siege to a village for four days, ultimately ate their own cub before the inhabitants were finally starved into showing themselves. Although lions will often go some days without food, these were obviously suffering from exceptional famine. Lion are specially fond of pig, though zebra, donkey, kudu and eland rank high in their esteem; kudu skulls are frequently found with only the nose eaten off—the mark of the lion.

The common belief that lions fear fire is certainly erroneous, for lions hunt regularly in front of grass-fires, dashing close up to or through them, and in many cases they have come into camps where fires were burning. In one case in the Game Department's experience a large party of lions took four Africans in turn from beside the fire, which, with each casualty, was piled higher, and left but one survivor. Selous records an exactly similar case. In another case, a lion stood with his feet in the ashes at the side of the fire.

East African Leopard (*panthera pardus fusca*)

Kiswahili: *Chui.*

The leopard was formally very abundant in the territory, but in recent years, with the high price fetched by the sale of its skin, illegal trapping has caused a considerable decrease in many localities. In certain areas, particularly in hilly bush country, it is still common.

Being mainly nocturnal, and with secretive habits and protective colouring, it is seldom seen except, perhaps, in the head-lights of a motor car. The average leopard will weigh little more than 100 lb., or one-fifth of the weight of a lion. A previous Game Warden once shot one of 130 lb. and saw a magnificent skin of one that weighed 150 lb.

Cases of unprovoked attack by leopards on man are uncommon, but near Morogoro it was ascertained that a leopard which ran amok killed and wounded no less than eleven people. In a similar instance which occurred recently, the leopard was found to be suffering from rabies. In one or two cases, a leopard has dropped from a branch on to an African passing below, while at times a leopard has broken through the thatch of a hut (a commoner feat on the part of a lion) and taken young children.

Goats and fowls are frequently seized and dogs are a favourite food. A leopard is specially wanton and every goat in a hut or kraal will sometimes be killed, though only one or two may be taken. On one occasion, one leopard killed no less than eighty goats in one attack.

In general the leopard is beneficial to man in that its main diet consists of baboon and pig. These two species of vermin are responsible for more damage to crops than all the rest of the game animals put together; and where leopards have been almost exterminated crops have suffered heavily. For this reason leopards are now protected; the sportsman wishing to obtain a trophy has to pay five hundred shillings for his licence.

Sub-Family: Acinonychinae

Cheetah (*Acinonyx jutatus*)

Kiswahili: *Duma.*

Standing high on its legs, more dog-like in its movements and with claw-marks showing in its spoor, the cheetah is a complete contrast to the leopard. It differs in markings by possessing small, solid, round spots instead of the hollow, broken rosettes of the leopard. The young is a ball of wool, with a general colouring that faintly recalls the acryptic colouring of the skunk and the honey-badger, being whitish above and black below.

The cheetah is found in small numbers almost throughout the territory. In Kibaya in Masailand, the Serengeti plains and a few other northern localities it is common, and a family party may occasionally be seen, some lying with head erect, others sitting high on their haunches like dogs.

Stock is taken occasionally, but on the whole the cheetah does little damage, living on small antelopes which it secures by its speed. Nevertheless it can be run down by a horse in the end and then lies down and awaits its fate.

Sub-Family: Felinae

Serval Cat (*Leptailurus serval hindei*).

Kiswahili: *Mondo.*

The serval cat, also with leopard-like colouring, is fairly abundant. It kills small antelopes, birds and rats and does not refuse large insects. Serval cats sometimes make good pets but are apt, if two are together, to become independent and fierce.

Ankole Wild Cat.

Kiswahili: *Kimburu, paka pori.*

This little cat is very similar to the domestic cat, and there is no doubt that the two interbreed. Its average weight is between 6½ and 8½ lb. and the height at the shoulder about 7 to 8 inches. Its colour is normally grey and tabbies do occur. There is an erectile ruff on the neck.

It is represented in Tanganyika by the species *F. ocreata ugandae*, and rarely *F. ocreata taitae* of which only one authentic record exists in the territory.

Its main diet consists of birds, rodents, moles, lizards, insects, hares, etc.

Caracal.

Kiswahili: *Simba-mangu.*

This animal is sometimes known as the African lynx and is represented in Tanganyika by a single species *C. caracal nubicus*. It weighs about 40 lb., the height to the shoulder being 18 to 20 inches, and its length 30 inches excluding the tail of 10 inches. The general colour is tawny fawn to almost chestnut with a lighter belly. The ears are white on the inside, black on their backs and have long black tufts. The tail is short and usually has a black tag.

The caracal is essentially carnivorous, living on small antelope, game birds, poultry and snakes. It sometimes kills domestic stock such as sheep and goats. It normally lives in forested or thickly-bushed country and is a shy and nocturnal animal. Its distribution is widespread in suitable localities, various races of it occurring in Africa, from the Cape to Egypt and Algeria, and in Asia from the Middle East to India.

Family: Equidae

East African Burchell's Zebra (*Equusquagga böhmi*).

Kiswahili: *Punda-milia.*

Zebra are found almost throughout the territory, frequently in very large numbers, particularly in the more open country of the north. Zebra always appear sleek and bursting with fat, and herds of this beautiful animal will probably continue to please the eye for many years to come, particularly away from cultivation. They are a menace to wheat and other crops.

There is no sport in shooting the zebra itself, though it is much sought after for feeding labour and porters. The hide fetches a considerable price and is used for making into suitcases and small bags.

Attempts to domesticate this species have resulted chiefly in proving it to have little heart and much vice. It is possible that selective breeding over a period of years might produce something good, but the cost would probably be high.

Family: Giraffidae

Giraffe (*Giraffa camelopardalis tippelskirschi*).

Kiswahili: *Twiga.*

A giraffe's head is the crest of the territory, and if abundance is a qualification for that honour the giraffe is well entitled to it.

A certain number of giraffe are killed by Africans, both for the meat and hide as well as for their tails, which are either used as fly-whisks or made up into bracelets for their women-folk. The giraffe is also a favourite form of diet with the lion. Apart from casualties suffered as a result of these malpractices, the giraffe is seldom molested, the true sportsman having no wish to kill such a harmless and attractive animal. The delightful result is that the species in Tanganyika is not merely plentiful but also exceedingly tame. In the Arusha District especially, giraffe are frequently seen quite close to the roads, and no one should have any difficulty in getting an extremely fine series of photographs of this mild, spectacular animal.

In the eastern half of the territory the distribution of giraffe comes to a stop, southward, with the Kissaki country. The south-eastern area, namely, the Southern Province and the Rufiji and Mahenge Districts of the Eastern Province, appear to be devoid of giraffe, while on the west the species is found as far as Lake Rukwa, the dividing line being, very roughly, the Iringa Highlands and the Rufiji River. A good many giraffe have been captured in Tanganyika for zoological gardens, but the greatest care and experience is essential as any over-strain during capture results in the death of the animal in a short time.

The future of the giraffe has been safeguarded under the provisions of the latest game ordinance, in which they have been declared Royal Game.

Family: Hippopotamidae
Hippopotamus (*Hippopotamus amphibius amphibius*).
Kiswahili: *Kiboko.*

Hippopotami are found in each of the great lakes, in all the large rivers and in a large proportion of the small ones. Trekking across the land, they also find their way to the smallest and most isolated of crater lakes; that of Ngorongoro, for instance, and those near Arusha, and even to mere wet-season pans and swamps.

Hippopotami add immensely to the interest of a journey on some of the larger rivers, and occasionally, where they have been much shot in order to check their garden-raiding habits, to its excitement, for canoes are not infrequently attacked by a wounded animal or a cow with calf. Great numbers have had to be killed in the Rufiji river and elsewhere, for the protection of native gardens of which they are inveterate raiders, but the animal remains abundant.

The shooting of hippopotami in water is the reverse of sport, but a supply of excellent fat may be obtained for the safari should one be shot. Near small waters they spend much of their time on land, even lying about in the bush. When found on land the animal is apt to be dangerous if met on its path back to water. They are full of curiosity, and, where they have not been much shot at, may be attracted nearer and nearer to the bank by noises and waving of cloths.

When shot in the water, the body of a hippopotamus sinks and may take nearly a day to rise, although in particularly hot weather the corpse may come to the surface in an hour or two.

Family: Suidae
Warthog (*Phacochaerus aethiopicus aeliani*).
Kiswahili: *Ngiri.*

This pig is more or less common throughout the savannah country, where it lives largely on grass roots. Warthog do some damage to crops and at times a great deal to mealies, but are very much less destructive in this respect than bush-pigs. When running or trotting away it presents a comical picture of self importance with its ugly face and erect tail. A warthog, as is well known, goes into his burrow backwards and if disturbed shoots out like a jack-in-the-box, ready to sell his life dearly.

Bush-pig (*Porcus daemonis*).
Kiswahili: *Nguruwe.*

The young of this pig are red, with a conspicuous pattern of white spots and stripes, but the older animals vary greatly. The bush-pig of Kilimanjaro is pitch black, with a white face and unusually long hair.

The damage done to crops by this species is enormous. As its habits are nocturnal it is hard to guard against its depredations. It is classified as vermin throughout the territory.

Family: Bovidae
East African Buffalo (*syncerus caffer caffer*).
Kiswahili: *Nyati, Mbogo.*

While parts of the territory are devoid of buffalo, this animal is, on the whole, widely distributed, from sea-level up to 14,000 feet, on Kilimanjaro. It is found throughout the western districts from Bukoba to Rukwa, thence up the Ruaha and through the Rungwa Game Reserve to Singida, also in Kondoa and Kibaya, on the Wembere Steppe, in Mkalama, south-east Shinyanga, south Mwanza, at Mbulu and Mbugwe in the Northern Province and at points farther north on the Rift Wall. It is prevalent at Lake Manyara, south-east of Arusha, and in the mountain forests of the whole north of the territory from Arusha to Tanga, and thence southwards through the various coastal districts and extending back to the Iringa border, but becoming, perhaps, most abundant in the Kilosa and Mahenge Districts.

Despite considerable losses at times from rinderpest, buffalo are on the increase, especially from Kilosa southwards.

The buffalo is generally regarded as the most dangerous of African game. To the real sportsman, who is also an accurate, quick and confident shot, buffalo hunting in difficult country is nowhere to be surpassed. A locality like Mbugwe or Kilosa, where the buffalo come out of their thickets to feed in the open glades or clean-stemmed savannah country, is ideal, but the utmost caution must be observed in following a wounded animal through thicket or high grass. Wounded animals will not infrequently return on their tracks and await their pursuers in or behind dense bush. A heavy rifle, and one in reserve, is advised for any such work. A novice should not attempt to hunt buffalo unless accompanied by an experienced companion.

In horn-measurement the local buffalo are second to none, and very fine heads have been obtained at Lake Manyara, Monduli Mountain, near Arusha, at Mbugwe and at various points in the south. There is great variation in the shape of the horns, even within a herd, and several "sub-species" previously described as such are certainly merely individual variations.

Tanganyika Greater Kudu (*Strepsiceros strepsiceros frommi*).
Kiswahili: *Tandala mkubwa*.

For abundance of greater kudu, the handsomest of the larger antelopes, it is probable that no country approaches Tanganyika. Greater kudu are found in small, separated herds in most parts of the *miombo* woods which cover two-thirds of the territory, and in very considerable numbers almost throughout the dry Central Province and in north Iringa. Good heads of 54 inches or thereabouts may be obtained in most of these localities.

The colouring, which is very protective, is grey with distinctive vertical white stripes running from the back to the belly. The heavy ruff is also grey. The horns are spiral and have "tips".

Kudus are browsers. They are not easy to get, and their hunting provides excellent sport. They are particularly wary, and their senses are extraordinarily acute; they are addicted to dense, or fairly dense, bush and are expert in travelling through it with their horns laid back on their withers or slanted to this side or that so as to pass through narrow openings. They tend to live in broken country, and fairly hard walking may be necessary for the sportsman who wishes to obtain this king of antelope trophies. The great-eared females are hornless, and are much smaller than the bulls.

Southern Lesser Kudu (*Strepsiceros imberbis australis*).

Kiswahili: *Tandala mdogo*.

While, owing to retiring habits and protective colouring, the lesser kudu is relatively seldom seen, it is by no means uncommon, and it is well distributed throughout Masailand east of the Rift Wall—a region characterized by acacia and thicket as opposed to *miombo*. Its range comprises nearly the whole of the Northern and Central Provinces and north Iringa.

The colouring is very similar to that of the Greater Kudu; in body it is considerably smaller.

The very beautiful horns differ from the much larger horns of the greater kudu in that they seldom run to a great space between the tips, while their spiral is closer. South Mpwapwa, parts of the road between Dodoma and Iringa, parts of Kibaya, and Engaruka, Mbuguni and Ngare-Nanyuki in the Arusha District are only a few of the many spots where this handsome antelope is found.

Bushbuck (*Tragelaphus scriptus*).

Kiswahili: *Mbawala, pongo*.

Bushbuck, of which there are several varieties, are scattered fairly generally throughout Tanganyika. The call is a single hoarse bark, which is used as an alarm note, and frequently indicates the detection of a carnivore or follows the grunt of a leopard.

The bushbuck is quite the most sporting of the smaller antelopes. Many a dog has been killed by it, and many men on going up to a wounded ram have been pierced by the sharp twisted horns, for the bushbuck is not only plucky, but remarkably quick. The female is hornless.

Sitatunga (*Limnotragus spekii*).

Kiswahili: *Nzohe*.

Sitatunga are present in very fair numbers in the swamps and rivers of the Malagarasi system, including the Ugalla waters which empty into Lake Tanganyika, and in the swamps round the margins of Lake Victoria. The Northern Rhodesia species occurs in the vicinity of Lakes Rukwa and Chada, and in scattered localities in Ufipa.

They spend most of their time in the swamps, and their curiously elongated hooves splay out and keep them from sinking. They are excessively hard, indeed almost impossible, to see in the tall, dense papyrus, but they feed outside it at night, and may be seen before they return to it in the early morning.

Eland (*Taurotragus oryx*).

Kiswahili: *Pofu, mbunju*.

The eland is the largest of the antelopes, and a full-grown bull is heavier than a large ox, weighing up to 1,500 or 1,600 lb. Elands are strong and of good shape, and an occasional animal has been trained to pull in the yoke. They are placid and docile, and even full-grown animals have been readily tamed after capture.

Eland are susceptible to rinderpest and are also highly prized for their meat. As a result, their population has been steadily declining over the years—though in certain localities they are still fairly abundant. They often run in quite large herds, occasionally containing as many as two or three hundred individuals.

Thirty-inch horns are of not too infrequent occurrence, particularly in the cows, the horns of which are much thinner than those of the bulls. In old bulls the horns are often greatly worn down.

The East African Eland (*T. o. pattersonianus*) is the most widespread of the species in Tanganyika; it has been seen on Kilimanjaro up to 16,000 feet.

The other two species are Livingstone's Eland (*T. o. livingstonii*) found in south-western Mbeya, Rungwe and southern Ufipa Districts, and the Iringa Eland (*T. o. billingae*) recorded only from Ulete in Iringa District.

Sub-Family : Cephalophinae

Abbott's Duiker (*Cephalophus spadix*).

Kiswahili: *Minde.*

This stocky, thick-set animal is as heavy as a bushbuck and is a species which no one acquainted only with the common type would recognize as a duiker. The horns are thick and average 4½ inches in length, the colour is a dark chestnut and the coat is glossy. It inhabits dense rain forests in the Usambara Mountains, on Kilimanjaro, whence it was described, and in the Uluguru hills in Morogoro. It is very difficult to find and the glimpse is apt to be momentary.

Harvey's Red Duiker (*Cephalophus harveyi harveyi*).

Kiswahili: *Funo.*

This bright chestnut-red duiker, with glossy coat, rather thick-set body and thick-based horns, is found in localities as far apart as Lindi, Kilosa, Kilimanjaro and the Usambara Mountains, so that it is possible that it is fairly generally, if sparsely, distributed throughout the thickets of the territory. Though bright in colour it is a skulker in thick bush and can easily be overlooked.

Blue Forest Duiker (*Guevei caerulus*).

Kiswahili: *Paa.*

This genus, described from Usangu, represents a somewhat larger race than the southern blue duiker. This, or another race, occurs also in the rain forests of Bukoba. It is a very attractive, diminutive, neatly formed antelope of the height of an English hare, dark slaty-brown in colour. Scurrying about in dense forest, it feeds largely on fallen leaves. Native poachers make low fences of small sticks across hundreds of yards of forest and, setting snares in openings every few yards take considerable numbers of this buck.

Common Duiker (*Sylvicapra sylvicapra grimmia*).

Kiswahili: *Nsya.*

Bush duikers are common throughout Tanganyika, except, apparently, in the south-eastern coast area.

Sub-Family: Hippotraginae

Water buck.

Kiswahili: *Kuro.*

Both species of waterbuck are present in Tanganyika—*Kobus ellipsiprymnus*, or the common waterbuck, in the east, north and centre, and the *Kobus defassa* (Defassa waterbuck or "Sing-sing") west of the Rift Wall and south-west as far as the Rhodesian border.

The common waterbuck is distinguished from the Defassa by the white circle round its rump, which makes it readily recognizable at a distance. The Defassa species has the better horns. Each, with its shaggy hair and splendid carriage, is a fine-looking animal.

Neither species is found far from water or the hills and bush that border it. Each tends to run in herds, usually of several females and one or two males. Small parties of bulls may be found separately. Each, where it occurs, is fairly abundant.

Waterbuck meat is commonly rank in flavour. In areas where the two species meet, inter-breeding takes place.

Northern Puku (*Adenota vardonii senganus*).

Puku are very localized, but are very abundant where they occur.

They are distributed in south-west Tanganyika around the north shore of Lake Nyasa; the south and west shores of Lake Rukwa between Ngomba and Ntakasangwa; the upper Ulanga Valley from the Ifakara ferry in the east to within fifteen miles of Utengule in the west, and from the base of the Uzungwa Mountains in the north to the Lupiro–Malinyi district motor road in the south.

Reedbuck (*Redunca*).

Kiswahili: *Tohe*.

Three main species are found in Tanganyika:

Southern Reedbuck (*Redunca arundinum occidentalis*).

The very fine reedbuck of South Africa and the Rhodesias extends well into the territory. The shoulder-height of a ram is about 36 inches. The hair has a strong fulvous fringe; the horns (which are sometimes very long) bend well forward.

This reedbuck, though found near reed-beds, as its name implies, is particularly fond of open uplands grass-country. Usually roaming in pairs or threes, as many as six, eight or ten may sometimes be found together.

The call is a whistle, which some have suggested, incorrectly, is made by the driving of wind from the inside of the thighs, as these are sometimes drawn in when the sound is made.

The Bohor Reedbuck (*Redunca redunca*).

The coat is yellower and less grizzled than in the southern reedbuck and the tail less bushy. The shoulder is 27 or 28 inches in height. The horns are shorter and relatively stouter than those of the southern reedbuck. They have a length up to about 15 inches and, as a rule, are abruptly hooked at the tips.

The Bohor reedbuck is well distributed throughout the north of the territory, and is found at least as far south as the Ugalla River.

Chandler's Mountain Reedbuck (*Redunca fulvorufula chandleri*).

Chandler's reedbuck, like the Bohor, is fairly widely distributed, particularly on high ground in the Northern Province, and is often found in the same localities as the other.

It is a small reedbuck with a rufous coloration, and a broad skull, with horns slightly hooked at the tip.

East African Roan Antelope (*Hippotragus equinus langheldi*).

Kiswahili: *Korongo.*

The roan is the largest of antelopes after the eland, though its weight cannot be much more than half that of an eland, while its horns are dwarfed by those of its relative, the sable antelope.

In Tanganyika the species is distributed in small herds throughout the west of the territory from Ufipa, including Rukwa, up through Tabora and Shinyanga into Bukoba. It is also found across much of the north, in the whole of east Mwanza and Masailand nearly to Lolkisale, in Kondoa Irangi and in Kibaya. A curiously isolated locality, connected perhaps through Handeni and Kibaya, is the district of Bagamoyo. The roan is found in the *miombo* forest, in which, in the late dry season and early rains, it is often seen out in the open clearings, and in the far drier *acacia-commiphora* country which covers much of the north; and it even overlaps with the oryx, inhabitant of semi-desert.

Areas in which the roan is common enough to be worth hunting by a visitor to the territory are the Namanyere area in Ufipa, south-west Tabora generally, north-west Bukoba, the Balangeti area of east Mwanza for a few months from August on, and, later in the year, the country further east. Between Ufiome and the Tarangire the species is sometimes found in fair numbers.

The roan is one of the most dangerous of antelopes if it is approached when wounded. It is not always easy to tell the bulls from the cows, and mistakes are sometimes made.

Northern Sable Antelope (*Hippotragus niger rooselvelti*).

Kiswahili: *Palahala, Mbarapi.*

The handsomest of the larger buck after the greater kudu, the sable occurs in small herds throughout nearly two-thirds of the territory. It is closely associated with *miombo* woodland though it may be found outside it in areas in which *Berlinia* occurs on the hills.

There are few more pleasing sights than a herd of this splendid antelope, with its coal-black, white-bellied old bull and its fox-coloured heifers and calves in the tall clean-stemmed *miombo* which they love. Old solitary bulls are also frequently found. As a species it sometimes tends to join other animals, and sable, on a few occasions, have even been known to graze with cattle.

The sable antelope is one of the species which a hunter must not approach too closely when it is wounded. In several instances men have been treed by them, and the ease with which a sable at bay can ward off spears thrown by natives, catching them on its horns and throwing them aside, broken, has been recorded.

The sable is not highly abundant although it is widespread throughout most of the Southern Province. As a general rule, the further south the sportsman travels, the better will be the head; the record horn measurement is 47 inches, from the Ugalla River in Tabora District.

In the Rhodesias and Portuguese Territories horns up to 54 inches have been recorded, whilst in Angola the Giant Sable's horns go up to 64 inches.

The northernmost point reached by the species is recorded as slightly north of Biharamulo, to the south-west of Lake Victoria.

Kilimanjaro Fringe-eared Oryx (*Oryx beisa callotis*).

Kiswahili: *Choroa*.

This oryx occurs only in Tanganyika and in southern Kenya.

In Tanganyika it is found mainly in the Northern Province, particularly in the Longido country; it is widespread in Masailand east of the Rift Wall. There are a few herds west of the Rift Wall on the Sanjan Plains. Its southernmost limit is in the region of Kibaya.

It inhabits the driest of country, namely, open plain and thorn and *nyika* scrub.

The fringe-eared oryx is a very wary and unapproachable species where it has been much hunted. As in the case of the other species of oryx, instances have been recorded of successful encounters with lion on the part of this antelope. It is possessed of considerable vitality, and like the sable and roan, it should be approached warily when wounded.

Topi (*Damaliscus korrigum jimela*).

Kiswahili: *Nyamera*.

The topi extends from Jubaland to the south of Lake Tanganyika. It is found in small herds over a great part of the western area from Lake Rukwa up to the Kagera River, and in the north across into the Serengeti. In most parts of its range it is accompanied by the roan antelope. Wherever it is present at all it is very abundant, and it seems to be at home in all types of bush and plain, avoiding only thicket.

With its rich red-brown colour, purple-black thighs and shoulders and marvellous satiny sheen, the topi is an attractive animal, as befits the relative of the now nearly extinct bonte-buck of the Cape.

Coke's Hartebeeste (*Alcelaphus buselaphus cokii*).

Kiswahili: *Kongoni*.

Coke's hartebeeste, with its wide bracket-shaped horns, occurs from Mpwapwa and Handeni northward to and beyond the Kenya border. The hartebeeste is in the main a plains species. Moving with a gait that is reminiscent of a bouncing ball, it is speedy enough to outrun a fast horse. It is a wary animal where hunted and it is usual for a look-out to be kept on an anthill by one of the party. It occurs mostly in herds of a dozen or two, though sometimes considerably more are found together. It is common in much of the north of Tanganyika.

Lichtenstein's Hartebeeste (*Alcelaphus lichtensteinii*).

Described first from Tete, on the Zambezi River, this handsome red hartebeeste, with its saddle-like marking and typical hartebeeste shape and action, is found in Portuguese East Africa from the latitude of the Sabi northwards, and in Southern and Northern Rhodesia, Nyasaland and Tanganyika. It occupies, in small herds, the whole south of the territory, and extends north to the Handeni District on the east, and to Uzinza on Lake Victoria on the west. The horn pedicle forms a flat, broad palm, the horns curving inwards and then backwards.

Like the sable antelope, and unlike Coke's hartebeeste, it dwells mainly in the wooded *miombo* forests such as occur in the Western Province, though it may be seen in open spaces, particularly during cool weather.

Kole Kole, 60 lb., caught off Dar es Salaam.

Photo: Public Relations Department

The Blue Wildebeeste or Brindled Gnu (*Gorgon taurinius*).

There are two distinct races, in one of which occur two varieties:

Nyasa Blue Wildebeeste (*Gorgon taurinius johnstoni*).

The Nyasa gnu, distinguished by a white frontal chevron, is found in Mahenge and elsewhere in the south and south-east of the territory. Its distribution, like that of the sable antelope and Lichtenstein hartebeeste, does not appear to be coterminous with a particular type of woodland; and the boundary between it and the next sub-species, which is seldom found south of the Central Railway but becomes commoner as one goes north into Kenya, has not been determined.

White-bearded Gnu (*Gorgon taurinius albojubatus*).

This race of the blue wildebeeste or its variety, *G. t. hecki*, occurs throughout the north of the territory. *G. t. hecki* has been described from Kibaya in southern Masailand. It has black hairs in the throat-fringe and a face varying from greyish-white to rufous.

The wildebeeste, with its bison-like appearance and extraordinary antics, may be found on most open uninhabited plains or in the bush which often, in the north, contains great herds.

The Mkata plains near Kilosa, the plains of the Northern Province and the Serengeti country are amongst the best areas. Wildebeeste when hunted tend to keep to the open, even circling round a limited open space, for their defence is, essentially, wariness and keeping to ground on which an enemy's approach can hardly pass undetected.

The hairs of the wildebeeste tails are in great demand amongst Africans, being used as the pliable cores of a form of thin wire bracelet. The tail itself is often used as a fly-whisk.

Sub-Family: Antilopinae

Klipspringer (*Oreotragus oreotragus schillingsi*).

Kiswahili: *Mbuzi mawe, Nguru-nguru*.

Schilling's race is the klipspringer of the north of the territory. It is distinguished by the fact that the thighs, which are clear grey or rufous, differ markedly from the body in colour, by the dark middle line of the back and by the fact that horns are commonly present in the female.

The klipspringer occurs on most rocky kopjes and hills of any size in the territory, and its hunting may entail fairly hard work. It leaps from rock to rock like a chamois; it stands and walks on the tips of its hooves, and its hair is extraordinarily coarse, like thin hedgehog quills.

The two other races which occur only in the extreme south of the territory are the Northern Rhodesia Klipspringer (*O. o. centralis*) and Noack's Klipspringer (*O. o. aceratos*).

Oribi (*Ourebia ourebi*).

Kiswahili: *Taya*.

Powel-Cotton's Oribi (*O. o. cottoni*) is found in the west of Tanganyika between Lakes Basuto and Rukwa. Other races which have been recorded are the South African Oribi (*O. o. ourebi*) in the south-west, Peter's Oribi (*O. o. hastata*) in the south-east, and the Uganda Oribi (*O. o. ugandae*) in the north-west.

32

It is a particularly graceful little buck with its pleasing red-fawn colour, high, slender legs and light bounding run. It is usually found in pairs on open plains or down-like hills. It is not common in the territory generally, except perhaps on the Ugalla River and in Musoma District.

Tanganyika Steinbuck (*Raphicerus campestris neumanni*).

Kiswahili: *Dondoro.*

This race occurs in most of the north, central and south-west parts of the territory. It differs from the typical South African steinbuck in lacking, in the male, that animal's dark crescentic mark on the head, its generally paler colour and the greater development of white facial markings.

The steinbuck is an abundant little buck, which takes refuge like the dikdiks in the thickets of the *commiphora* savannah.

Sharpe's Grysbok (*Raphicerus sharpei sharpei*).

This species is sparsely distributed in the south; it has also been recorded in scattered localities in the west and north-west. It is much redder in colour than the common steinbok and has hairs intermingled. Only the male has horns.

East African Suni (*Nesotragus*).

Kiswahili: *Paa.*

The species is divided into races. The following key is from Swynnerton's Checklist of Land Mammals:

1. Zanzibar Suni (*Nesotragus moschatus moschatus*). Found on Zanzibar Island and two small neighbouring islets.

2. Mount Meru Suni (*N. m. kirchenpaueri*). Habitat: Northern and Eastern Tanganyika as far as the Rufiji Delta and including Mafia Island.

3. Livingstone's Suni (*N. m. livingstonianus*). Recorded from the thick forests of the Southern Province.

The suni or pygmy antelope, the smallest of all, is abundant in dense wooding. In colour it varies from red to fawn.

Long-snouted Dikdiks (*Rhynchotragus*).

Kiswahili: *Dikidiki, suguya.*

There are two races which occur in the territory:

1. Taita Dikdik (*R. kirkii nyikae*). Generally distributed in suitable localities in Lushoto and Pare Districts.

The back is ochre-tawny, passing into buff on the flanks and to white beneath. A pepper-and-salt effect is caused on the back by the dusty rings on the hairs. The general colour is dull yellowish grey, while the limbs are rufous.

2. Ugogo Dikdik (*R. kirkii thomasi*). Widely distributed throughout most of the territory.

It resembles the Taita dikdik, but is distinguished by the more uniformly rufous-tawny colour of the whole of the upper parts, only the middle of the line of the back being dark rufous in the latter, while the sides are olive or fulvous.

The diminutive dikdiks are to be found almost everywhere and throughout the north are particularly abundant. They live in the thickets and are even found hiding in the planted Euphorbia hedges in the cultivated steppe of Shinyanga.

Impala (*Aepyceros melampus*).

Kiswahili: *Swala-pala.*

As Grant's gazelle is the paragon of the nearly waterless areas, so the impala, graceful in form and carriage, with beautiful, ringed, lyrate horns, is the loveliest of the middle-sized buck elsewhere.

Large herds of the hornless females (thirty or forty) may often be seen with no ram at all, and small herds of rams will be found elsewhere. Sometimes up to a hundred animals may be found in one herd. They favour the more open spaces of park-like country or scattered thorn bush where water is not too far distant.

As the eland is the most widely distributed of the greater antelopes, so is the impala of the smaller.

Gazelles (*Gazella*).

Grant's Gazelle (*Gazella granti*).

Kiswahili: *Swala granti.*

This gazelle, found in small herds consisting of a ram or two to several females, is more or less abundant across the north of Tanganyika from Moshi to the Serengeti, and extends southwards to various points. The Wembere Plain is perhaps the western limit of the species, but, through Kibaya, it runs right down to Mpwapwa and finds its southernmost points in the southern end of the district, and, further west, in the angle formed by the Kisigo and Ruaha Rivers.

It is a particularly delightful animal with its graceful form, handsome colouring and splendid horns, which are huge for the size of the bearer. The brown flank-stripe of the males is, in the young and in some of the females, replaced by a black side-stripe like that of Thomson's gazelle, from which it is distinguished by the broad white rump and (in the older males) by the absence of the dark stripe.

This species and Thomson's gazelle are found in the driest country, and seem to subsist for long periods without water. The stomach in these cases is often filled with juicy fruits, notably the large fruits of a solanum that grows on old Masai grazing grounds.

Thomson's Gazelle (*Gazella thomsonii*).

Kiswahili: *Swala, tomi, lala.*

Thomson's gazelle is more abundant even than Grant's and is often extremely tame. It extends, to the westward at least, as far as Grant's Gazelle is found.

Both gazelles are found in great numbers on the Serengeti, to which wholesale migrations of thousands of animals take place, reminiscent of the springbok migrations in South Africa years ago.

Gerenuk or Waller's Gazelle (*Litocranius walleri walleri*).

Kiswahili: *Swala-twiga.*

The Generuk is widespread and comparatively common in certain parts of the eastern Masai districts and in Pare; it is also found in dry country north of Mount Meru and on the Umba Steppe.

It lives in dry, fairly thick scrub and is therefore not always easy to find, despite its red colouring and the extraordinarily elongated neck which has given it the name of the giraffe gazelle. Its horns are thick, lyrate and strongly ringed.

Family: Canifae—*Sub-Family: Simocyoninae*

Hunting Dog (*Lycaon pictus lupinus*).

Kiswahili: *Mbwa-mwitu.*

Packs, large or small, of wild dogs range most parts of the country and their melodious signal call, a long drawn "hoo" can often be heard. They hunt at night, but a great deal also by daylight.

Wild dogs sometimes take to killing stock, but only very rare cases have been recorded of attempted attacks on man. They commonly show no fear whatsoever but, after gazing and braking, it may be from ten yards away, move quietly off.

They are a veritable scourge to game, never ceasing to harry it and attacking even the larger species of antelope. They have often been reported as driving lions from their kills.

The colour is a medley of fawn, black and white; in stature they are fairly tall; the head is rather hyena-like and they smell abominably. Sometimes the dogs are mangy, sometimes in excellent coat. They are fairly easily tamed and make amusing pets.

The hunting dog is now classified as vermin.

Family: Hyaenidae—*Sub-Family: Hyaeninae*

Spotted Hyena (*Crocuta crocuta*).

Kiswahili: *Fisi.*

Hyenas are fairly abundant in the territory and to some tribes they are sacred. The Mmbulu, Fiome and Masai especially, who leave their dead to be eaten by hyenas, resent the killing of these animals.

Hyenas in game areas live largely on what the lions leave, but in many parts they are a nuisance, sneaking round villages and camps for what they may seize and run off with, removing, very occasionally, a piece of flesh, a cheek or buttock of a sleeping African, or killing cattle by tearing out udder or entrails. Man-eating hyenas have on rare occasions been reported and one killed in Rufiji District was credited by the natives with something like thirty deaths.

Skins and hides should not be left at night within reach of hyenas. The spotted hyena has been declared vermin throughout the territory.

Striped Hyena.

This is the common hyena of the Middle East although it occurs in North Africa and reaches as far south as Tanganyika. It is smaller than its cousin the spotted hyena and tends to inhabit semi-desert areas.

The striped hyena is a dirty grey colour with black transverse stripes down each flank, and black horizontal stripes on the upper legs. There is a longish mane on the neck and back. The muzzle is more pointed than that of the spotted hyena and the tail longer and bushier. Its main diet is carrion, but it will on occasion kill animals up to the size of goats and sheep. The Arabs in the Sinai and Akaba areas make a considerable fuss about this animal, crediting it will all sorts of occult powers and man-killing activities.

This hyena is a much more solitary and nocturnal animal than the spotted variety.

Sub-Family: Protelinae

Aardwolf.

Kiswahili: *Fisi mdogo, fisi wamkole.*

This seldom-seen animal is represented in Tanganyika by the species *P. cristatus termes.* It is completely protected throughout the territory.

The aardwolf has been classified as belonging to the hyena family as he resembles the other hyenas in many respects.

Its length is 34 inches, excluding the tail of 12 inches, and its height at the shoulder is 28 inches. The coat is long and soft and pale grey in colour. There are black vertical stripes down each flank and horizontal black bars on the legs. The ears are long, the muzzle pointed, and the tail bushy. The teeth are very small and weak, and are only 16 to 20 in number. The forelegs are longer than the hind. There is a crest of erectile hair extending from the back of the head along the spine to the root of the tail. The front feet have five toes and the hind four, whereas all other hyenas have four toes on all feet.

In its habits it is strictly nocturnal and lives and hunts on plains, retiring into burrows during the day.

Its main food consists of termites, but it will eat carrion. It makes a whistling noise.

Family: Viverridae—*Sub-Family: Viverrinae*

Genets.

Kiswahili: *Kanu.*

These little cat-like animals are represented by two species and several sub-species in Tanganyika.

Genetta tigrina. The large spotted genet, three sub-species of which occur in the territory.

G. g. neumanni. These little animals have long bodies and tails, short legs, and pointed rather fox-like masks. The average weight is 2 to 3 lb. and the body length 8 inches excluding the tail which is about the same length. The colouration varies with the different races and also with different individuals. In general the ground colour is a grey or greyish yellow on which there are a number of solid black spots. The tail is heavily ringed with black. Melanism is fairly common. The claws are semi-retractable.

In their habits they are nocturnal and mainly solitary, although they are sometimes encountered in pairs. They are very arboreal and often live in hollow trees. Genets are carnivorous but their taste is catholic. They live on birds (including poultry), rodents, insects such as crickets, locusts, and beetles, also crabs, lizards and snakes.

If caught young they are easily tamed and make pleasant pets; captured when adults they are fierce and intractable.

When angry or alarmed they utter a sort of coughing spit, and also a low growl.

Civets.

Kiswahili: *Fungo.*

This is one of the largest of the *viverridae*, being approximately 14 inches in height at the shoulder, 32 inches in length excluding the tail of 18 inches, and have a weight of about 20 lb. Their body colour is ashy grey, closely spotted and blotched with black. There is an erectile mane of dark hairs on the back. The longish tail is yellow-grey in colour, being ringed with black and having a black tip. The anal glands give off a musk-like secretion which is used in the preparation of many scents.

The civet is solitary and nocturnal. It lives in thick bush or forests, eating birds, eggs, rodents, snakes, and also certain fruit and plants.

Sub-Family: Herpestinae

Mongooses.

Kiswahili: *Nguchiro*.

As there are many genera and many races of mongooses in the territory it is not proposed to go into any detail here.

The commoner species seen in Tanganyika are as follows:—

1. The great grey mongoose. This animal is about 24 inches long excluding the tail of 18 inches, which is tapering and has a well defined black tag. The ground colour is grey (individual hairs being annulated black and white). The weight of the male is approximately 5½ lb. The nose is black, and the legs and feet very dark.

It is largely nocturnal and solitary, feeding on small animals, reptiles, birds' eggs, also fruit and roots. There are three sub-species recorded in Tanganyika.

2. The slender mongoose. Much smaller than the above species (no measurements available). Each hair is annulated black and brown or else black and grey, giving a ground colour of grey-brown. It is solitary and mainly diurnal. There are ten distinct sub-species occurring in Tanganyika.

3. The water mongoose, sometimes called the marsh mongoose. This is a large mongoose having a length of 24 inches, excluding the tail of 12 inches. The body is stocky and dark brown in colour, with a tapering tail and darker legs. It is solitary and essentially nocturnal, living mainly on frogs, crabs, water-snakes, and sometimes rats and birds. It is a good swimmer and diver. There are two sub-species in the territory.

4. The banded mongoose. This is a much smaller mongoose, its length being about 16 inches excluding the tail of 8 inches. It is easily recognised by the alternate light and dark bands which transverse the rear half of its body. There are five toes on each foot. These little mongooses are diurnal and go about in small parties making their homes in disused anthills. Their food consists of insects, eggs, roots, berries, etc.

5. The dwarf mongoose. Four races occur in Tanganyika. The colouration varies greatly with the race. They are either black, black-flecked with white, or else rufous. In their habits they resemble the banded mongoose as they are diurnal and go about in small packs.

6. The white-tailed mongoose. This is a very large mongoose weighing up to 8½ lb. and having a length of 24 inches excluding the tail of 18 inches. The ground colour is dark grey; the tail is long and bushy, the rear half of which is white.

It is very nocturnal and solitary, feeding on small animals, birds, lizards, insects and eggs.

Sub-Family: Caninae
Jackals.
Kiswahili: *Mbweha.*

Jackals are too common to need any description here. It will be sufficient to say that there are three races in Tanganyika; the black-backed jackal, the side-striped jackal, and the golden jackal.

Sub-Family: Otocyoninae
Bat-eared Foxes.

These quaint and attractive little animals are localized in their distribution, and it is only in certain parts of Tanganyika that they can be seen. Rather like the jackal in appearance, they can easily be distinguished by their "foxy" masks, very large pricked ears, woolly grey coats and bushy tails with distinctive black tags. They are slightly smaller than the jackals, being 24 inches in length (excluding the tail), 14 to 16 inches in height at the shoulder and weigh between 7 and 8 lb.

This little fox is diurnal in its habits, and is usually seen in pairs or small packs. When alarmed it often arches its back and snarls at its adversary, before diving into ground in the shallow burrows which form its home.

Its main food consists of insects, mainly white ants; but it will eat small birds, lizards, and rodents when available.

These foxes are widely distributed throughout Africa except in the north where they are replaced by the fennec.

Family: Mustelidae—*Sub-Family: Lutrinae*
Otters.
Kiswahili: *Fisi maji.*

There are two genera of otters represented in Tanganyika:

1. *Aonyx*, the clawless otter.
2. *Lutra*, the spotted-necked otter.

The clawless *Aonyx capensis helios* is by far the commonest of these two. It is bigger than its cousin, weighing 40 to 50 lb., and attaining a length of 36 inches excluding the tail of 12 to 14 inches. (There is a record of a 62½ lb. clawless otter). The feet are not webbed, and as the name implies, the claws are greatly reduced. The body colour is dark brown with light underparts.

The clawless otter lives on a mixed diet of fish, frogs, crabs, mussels, monitor lizards, birds and their eggs. It hunts mainly at dusk and by night.

The spotted-necked otter (*Lutra maculicollis*) weighs about 20 lb. and has a length of 24 inches. Its feet are strongly webbed and the claws well pronounced. White or yellowish spots on the throat and chest may or may not be present.

This species is not often encountered in Tanganyika, but it does occur. There is at present a tame one at Musoma and a most attractive pet it is.

The food of the spotted-necked variety is much the same as that of the clawless variety, but it is more aquatic in its habits.

Game Birds

Game birds are to be found in varying numbers almost everywhere. The number of species is large and slight local variations make the number of sub-species larger still. Bags never have approached those of Europe, India or America, but good sport can be obtained almost everywhere except in coastal bush.

The best-known shooting grounds are around Arusha, Shinyanga and in the Rukwa valley (now a game sanctuary). Variety is the most noticeable asset of the bird shooting. There occur twenty species of duck and geese, about thirty species of francolin (partridge), four of guinea fowl, three of quail, five of sand grouse, five of snipe, and half a dozen of pigeon and bustard.

Duck and Geese. The largest of these birds is the spur-wing goose, which weighs about 14 lb.; the smallest, the pigmy goose and the Hottentot teal, weighing less than a pound each.

Duck and geese are common on almost all open water except on the great lakes. It is remarkable that they are rare on these lake shores and do not occur on the sea coast at all. They appear on rain ponds as soon as water begins to lie. To obtain good sport with duck several guns in hides are usually required, and lines of flight may be found between stubble fields and water, when very good shooting can be obtained. The best-known duck areas are at Singida, and around Shinyanga, Tabora and Arusha.

Francolin ("*Partridges*"). There are numerous species to be found in the territory. The true francolins with feathered throats are often great skulkers, affording little sport, though some of the red-winged species of open grasslands behave and fly very like the European partridge. Of the bare-throated "spurfowl" those with red legs prefer to run rather than fly, but the black-legged yellow-throated variety, sometimes in coveys of up to ten, gives good sport even to a lone gun.

Guinea-fowl. These are the most frequently shot game birds and sometimes occur in flocks up to several hundred. They run fast and far and do not often give sporting shots unless treed by a dog and then put over the gun. The vulturine guinea-fowl with the brilliant blue breast, inhabiting desert country, and the crested forest guinea-fowl, are both localized species and not often seen.

Quail. These are widespread and commonest during the rains, when they pass through on migration. Some species breed here in large numbers.

Snipe. These are restricted by their feeding habits to special areas, and are commonest in the months of November and December and in April and May.

Sandgrouse. These occur in the short grass areas and afford good shooting when dropping into rivers or pools to drink; good bags may be had in a short time if the right pool is found. One of the best shoots is at the Meserani Dam, near Arusha.

Bustard. The greater bustard weighs as much as 20 lb. but is now protected. The lesser bustards (*Floricans* and *Korhaans*) are widespread, but nowhere common, and can generally be located in the evening by their raucous call.

Pigeons. Several species of green pigeon occur, and give very sporting shooting if the fig tree in which they happen to be feeding is located, and a good tactical stand chosen.

The olive pigeon gives very difficult shooting as it swings through the tree tops on its way to or from some olive or cedar in full fruit.

No particular equipment or gun is required, but a good pair of legs is an asset.

Useful books are:—*Game Birds of Kenya and Uganda*, by Sir Frederick Jackson (Williams and Norgate, London), *The Birds of South Africa*, by Dr. Austin Roberts (H. F. and G. Witherby, London), and *A First Guide to the Birds of South Africa*, by Gill (Maskew Miller, Cape Town). These give descriptions of most of the Tanganyika species.

FISHING

Sea Fishing[1]

The seas off the east coast of Africa almost certainly contain as big fish—and as great a variety of fish—as are to be found in the better known game fishing waters of the world. They are as yet very largely untried, largely because suitable craft for big game fishing have not been available. The few who have fished in these waters, especially those who have tried the Mafia Channel, have reported some astonishing catches. Thus the world's record Dolphin (75 lbs.) was obtained by Mr. A. Conan Doyle in 1950, horse mackerel weighing 80 lbs. have been taken, king-fish of over 50 lbs., American jack and marlin of 60 lbs. sail fish over 100 lbs., and a rock cod of no less than 500 lbs. For those who are not interested in the bigger game fish there is much pleasant sport to be had in the waters off ports such as Dar es Salaam, Tanga, Lindi or Mtwara, where the sportsman will be unlucky if in a day's fishing he does not land a king-fish, "Kolekole" (caranx), barracuda or rock cod of sizeable proportions—often he will come back with several of each, and also, in the season, with tunny, queen fish, five-fingered jack or dolphin. Even if he is unable to find a suitable boat he can still obtain good sport by fishing from the shore for garfish, which is an art easily learned and often more rewarding than trolling from a motor-boat.

The type of fish likely to be caught depends on the direction of the monsoon, the time of day and the state of the tide. With the north-east monsoon, between December and March, come the big migratory fish, the sail fish and sword fish. The yellow-finned tunny will also frequent the coast at this season. During the south-east monsoon, from May to October, the bigger varieties of the local fish are met with. Trolling is the usual method of fishing and the best times are on an incoming tide from daybreak to 10 a.m., from 4.30 p.m. to dusk, and during a full moon between 9 p.m. and 2 a.m.

Visiting anglers can always be assured of plenty of sport with big fighting fish around Pemba Island, in the vicinity of Mafia Island, off Ras Kankadya and Bongoyo Island, and in Lindi Bay.

Good tackle is essential. The safest to use is a stout, one-piece rod, a reel with a capacity of 500 yards of line and capstan brake, a 24-thread line and heavy piano-wire traces with three to four swivels at intervals. Some use, in addition, a non-kinking lead, fixed at the point between line and first trace swivel.

The favourite artificial bait is the spoon and the usual size about six inches.

Lake Fishing

Lake Tanganyika is the only large lake of any real interest from the point of view of fishing for sport. It is the second deepest lake in the world and, in places, the bottom is several thousand feet below sea level. Severe storms with high seas can arise without much warning and no one should venture far from shore in small boats without expert guidance.

[1]Interesting and informative accounts of "Sea-fishing on the Tanganyika Coast" and of "Spoon-fishing in the Mafia Group" are to be found in *Tanganyika Notes and Records*, No. 37, reprinted as a booklet (Price Shs. 2/50) and obtainable from the Secretary, The Tanganyika Society, P.O. Box No. 511 Dar es Salaam.

In the case of Lake Nyasa the territorial boundary is the eastern shore line and all the waters of the lake belong to Nyasaland. Most of the Tanganyika shore is inaccessible owing to the precipitous slopes of the coastal mountains and there is little scope for sport fishing from Tanganyika. There is, however, an excellent account of the sport available from Nyasaland's shores in the tourist handbook issued by the Nyasaland Government.

All the species of predatory fish, e.g. Nile perch and tiger fish, which provide sport on other East African lakes, are missing from Lake Victoria, and the best the fisherman can hope for there is some unadventurous bottom fishing in the hope of landing one of the larger catfish.

Anyone prepared to leave the beaten track and to experiment can often obtain fair sport in many of the lesser-known waters of the territory. Several of the larger river systems (e.g. Rufiji and Malagarasi) contain tiger fish which can be caught by trolling or by spinning from the bank. Most perennial rivers, small lakes and dams contain a variety of fish which can be caught by float or bottom fishing methods.

For general safari purposes the best equipment is probably a pike spinning rod which can be adapted for bottom fishing. Several of the indigenous freshwater fishes such as the tilapias (which are excellent eating) have been known to take a fly, and a cast with a trout rod is worth a trial on some waters, particularly in the evening if fish are seen rising. With the exception of trout, no licences are required for sport fishing anywhere in the territory.

Fishing in Lake Tanganyika.—Lake Tanganyika provides excellent fishing, containing over two hundred known varieties of fish in all weights up to a hundred pounds or more, furnishing both food and sport. The heavier fish are comparatively rare in sport but many are taken by local fishermen in nets and traps. The comparative inaccessibility of the lake, coupled with the lack of facilities available to the angler in the shape of suitable craft, are handicaps, but it is sometimes possible to fish from the *Liemba*, the East African Railways and Harbours steamer operating on the lake, and a limited number of other craft are available. There is as yet little danger of over-fishing of the lake, although there is a considerable local native fishing industry which exports dried fish to the Congo and to various parts of Tanganyika, as well as meeting local requirements of fresh fish.

Trolling is the method mainly used for sport on Lake Tanganyika, although sport may be obtained also, (at Kigoma for instance), from piers, wharves and rocky promontories for the smaller varieties of fish. Fly fishing near the river mouths and other sheltered places has been little tried.

The common procedure for fishing is to keep as close in-shore as is safe, choosing a rocky shore where possible, and therefore, as the boat will generally be in comparatively shallow water or over a rocky bottom, the use of a weighted trace is not recommended. To any one who had the time, it would be very interesting to use a weight further out from the shore to test a theory that one might then encounter rarer or at least heavier fish. When fishing from a motor boat it is usual to have two rods out, or one rod and a handline, and on a few occasions handlines only. When using the latter, it is advisable to wear a glove to avoid cut fingers from the rush of a tiger fish or the heavy pull of a Nile perch.

Opinions differ as to methods of trolling, type of gear to be employed and bait to be used in order to produce the best results. Probably, nowadays, it would be universally agreed that trolling at slow speed (two and a half to three knots) from a motor boat is best, but this does not rule out the possibilities of enjoying sport from a rowing boat or even a canoe. Gear and bait are items more for individual preference and experience, but it may be safely said that where fish are taking freely almost any kind of line and small lure will be successful, and some odd gear has been contrived before now in the days when fishing tackle was difficult to obtain. For good sport most people prefer a light to medium sea-rod with a fair sized reel (four-and-a-half inches is somewhat small), two hundred yards of eighteen-thread line and a piano-wire trace. As to size and type of spoons and hooks, much depends on the conditions of the moment and the species of fish likely to be taken in the particular neighbourhood at that time of year. Spoons are most commonly used although other lures including dead bait have also been successful. For general purposes it is suggested that a supply of medium-sized spoons, copper and red-painted, and medium-sized triple hooks be taken. A good supply of both traces and lures is essential as they are frequently lost, the greatest offender being the tiger fish who readily bites through traces and even hooks as though he liked them. A gaff should be included in the equipment.

Generally speaking the best time for fishing is in the early morning from sunrise, or in the evening until sunset, although good "baskets" have been secured at midday. There is never much sport when there is no sun or when it is very bright. Fishing by moonlight has been tried but with no success. It has been observed that fishing is poor when the following conditions prevail:—

1. During rain, and also when the lake is rough.
2. During the height of the *dagaa*[1] season. At this time Nile perch, yellow belly and tiger fish all feed on the *dagaa*.
3. When shoals of *ngege* are seen around the surface. (The reason for this is not known).
4. When quantities of jelly fish are seen.
5. When scum is common. This scum, yellow-green in colour, somewhat resembles the oil discharge from ships' bilges.

There are no tides in the lake, but wind affects the surface very quickly. As to the effects of the prevailing winds, statistics show that the best fishing months more or less correspond to the change in the monsoon as experienced on the lake.

The commoner fishes to be found are:—

Centropomidae (Nile Perch Family).

Lates microlepis, L. augustifrons and *L. Mariae.*

Three closely-related species known collectively as "Nile Perch" and by various vernacular names of which the commonest is *Sangala* (also *Pamba* and *Nonzi*). These species are peculiar to Lake Tanganyika and are not known to attain the size of the true Nile Perch (*Lates niloticus*).

All three may be caught by trolling and give good sport. The heaviest recorded specimen (species unknown) weighed 110 lb.[2] but the average landed rarely exceeds 30 lb.

---

[1] A small fish like whitebait.

[2] But see "Giant Fish in Lake Tanganyika" By G. W. Hatchell, *Tanganyika Notes and Records*, No. 36, January, 1954.

A much smaller, related species, *Luciolates minor* (*Mgebuka*) rarely exceeding 1 lb. in weight, also occurs in the lake but it keeps to the open waters and is unlikely to be encountered when trolling.

Nile perch makes good eating although the flesh of larger specimens is rather coarse.

Characindae (Tiger Fish Family).

Hydrocyon lineatus (*Kibebe*).

Commonly caught, up to 10 lb. or so.   Gives a good fight; is edible but bony.

Alestes macrophthalmus (*Manzi*).

Caught frequently in varying weights up to 5 lb.   Not much of a fighter. Edible but bony.

Cichlidae.

Boulengerochromis microlepis—The Yellow Belly (*Kuhe*).

This species of cichlid, known only from Lake Tanganyika, is the most prized fish of the lake from the edible point of view and forms the largest proportion of troll catches.   The yellow belly rarely exceeds 6 lb. in weight and opinions on its fighting qualities vary.   Light tackle is essential for good sport.

Tilapia spp. (*Ngege*).

There are four species of *Tilapia* known from Lake Tanganyika, the commonest being *T. tanganicae*.   All are excellent eating but cannot be caught by trolling.   *Ngege* take worm baits, etc. and have occasionally been caught on a fly.

Among other fish are the lungfish, various species of catfish, spiny eels and characins and many small species of cichlids.   In point of numbers, by far the commonest fish in the lake is the small sardine-like *Dagaa* (*Stolothrissa tanganicae*) which occurs in untold millions and is the staple product of the very valuable native fisheries as well as the natural prey of the Nile perch and other predators.

Trout Fishing

Before the war trout fishing in Tanganyika was in its infancy but was improving every year.   In the war years some streams suffered perforce from lack of adequate supervision while others were undoubtedly overfished.   Since the war there has been a marked revival of interest in all districts, which should rapidly bring the local fly-fishing back to its former high standards.

Cold streams abound in the highlands of West Usambara, Upare, Kilimanjaro and Arusha, as well as in the Livingstone and Poroto Mountains in the south-west and in the Uluguru Mountains at Bunduki, near Morogoro.   Private enthusiasts and the Government have been co-operating with a view to stocking all potential trout waters, and fair success has rewarded their efforts.   The prolific and hard-fighting rainbow trout is generally more suited to the type of water commonly found in the mountains of this country, where deep, rather still reaches prevail and temperatures range between 58° F. and 65° F.

But there are also a few colder, more rapid brooks, eminently suited to the brown variety, which have been stocked with this species.

Stocking has been done by means of eyed ova imported from England, South Africa and Scandinavia, and conveyed to small temporary hatcheries conveniently sited in the more accessible highland districts.   When the trout become established in one stream and are breeding freely they form a nucleus from which fingerlings are transferred in containers by rail, car and porter's head to other and more remote places. Often such transfers have been fraught with great difficulty but the majority of them have been successful.

For residents, fishing licences cost Shs. 25/- a year, Shs. 10/- a fortnight, or Shs. 3/- a day. The cost of both Resident's and Visitor's Fishing Licences is the same. A Resident's Licence expires on 31st December each year irrespective of the date of issue whereas a Visitor's Licence expires one year from the date of issue. Licences are issued by Revenue Officers, and by officers of the Game and Forest Departments.

The most suitable outfit is a seven or eight-foot split cane rod, stout casts and medium-sized brightish flies. Flies are usually fished wet, down-stream, but even the dry-fly purist, using the most delicate tackle, will enjoy himself on the many quiet reaches.

Details of the fishing available in the provinces is given below.

Tanga Province

Mkussu River and tributaries (about 25 miles) Lushoto District.—There are two clubs, Magamba Hotel and Country Club, and the Mkussu Flyfishers Club, and about a dozen stretches of private water in addition to public waters. Government limits size to 8 inches. Magamba Club limits size to 9 inches. Mkussu Flyfishers Club limits size to 10 inches and number to 10 a week. There is at present no close season. The fishing can be reached by car or on foot. The distance of public water from Lushoto is 8 miles. Magamba Hotel has several miles of well stocked water running through the estate. There is excellent accommodation both at Magamba Hotel and the Lawns Hotel, Lushoto. Golf and tennis are obtainable and there is beautiful country all round. The nearest stores are at Lushoto, petrol supplies at Lushoto and Magamba. Licences and tackle can be obtained at Magamba Hotel and Country Club together with information regarding the Mkussu Flyfishers Club. Some of the streams run through forest but all are cleared. Rainbow trout are plentiful and fish have been caught weighing up to three pounds.

Yangoma River, Pare District.—Close season 16th August–15th December. The river is best reached by 1½ hours stiff climb on foot from Gonja (half-way between Same and Mkomazi on the Tanga–Moshi motor road). There is no hotel accommodation, but at the Yangoma is an unfurnished two-roomed Government rest camp. The country round is beautiful. There are small Indian shops at Ndungu, Kihurio and Same on the main motor road. Petrol is obtainable at Kihurio and Same. The river runs to a large extent through uncleared forest country. Waders will be found useful. Rainbow trout up to 4½ pounds have been taken. Size limit 10 inches. Number limit: 5 a day, 20 a week.

Sasseni River, Pare District.—No close season. No limit to size or numbers. The Sasseni is best reached by a six-hours' stiff climb on foot from Gonja or Makanya Railway Station. There is a large and comfortable, though unfurnished, fishing camp at the river, which is kept partially clear. Rainbow trout of a similar size to those in the Yangoma are obtainable. Stout casts are recommended as there are many snags in the stream.

The upper reaches on Shengena moorland are now very over-fished. Good sport can be had at Mamba down stream in the Pare shambas. The ten miles of forest reaches between moor and shambas represent virgin water and would doubtless repay the hardy explorer.

Eastern Province

Mgeta River, Morogoro District.—The trout fishing is reserved to the Uluguru Fly Fishing Association and extends from the boundary of the Mgeta Mission to half a mile or so beyond the top of the Hululu Falls, a distance of somewhat over six miles. The trout are all rainbow. For information as to membership of the Association or permission to fish, fees, licences, reservation of fishing camp accommodation, application should be made to the Honorary Secretary, Uluguru Fly Fishing Association, c/o Forest Department, Morogoro.

From 1946 to 1949 the average annual recorded number of trout taken was three hundred and eighty. This included quite a number of one- and two-pounders, occasionally some of three pounds. The largest landed since the war weighed five pounds, one ounce. Fish under 10 inches in length must be returned to the water.

Morogoro is one hundred and twenty-five miles from the coast and can be reached by rail and road (three hours). There are three hotels there. The fishing is reached by road from Morogoro (thirty miles). At present there is no close season; heavy rain affecting river and road from the middle of March to the middle of June practically puts a stop to fishing and during this period it is not recommended.

For the remainder of the year (subject, as on all streams, to favourable weather conditions) sport can be enjoyed.

Northern Province

Rainbow trout have been established in the following streams in the Northern Province:—

Arusha: The *Temi* and the *Nduruma*.

Moshi: The *Ngare Nairobi* (*North*), the *Ngare Nairobi* (*South*), the *Ngararagua*, the *Kikafu*, the *Semira*, the *Weru-weru*, the *Mue* and the *Himo*. The two last named have not yet been declared open to fishing.

Brown trout have been established in the Upper Kikafu and the Wona, a tributary of the Himo, but these stretches have not yet been opened to fishing.

Rainbow trout run very little above 1½ pounds in either Moshi or Arusha, though larger fish have been seen in the Ngare (North) well into the forest. Nevertheless they fight well and provide excellent sport. Fine tackle (3x) is recommended, and one should fish slow and deep and preferably up-stream, to catch the larger fish. Dry fly is not much used as streams are too fast.

The Moshi streams can be fished from Moshi as all are readily reached by car. Alternatively one can stay at either the Kibo or Marangu Hotels, from which the Wona, Himo and Mue rivers are easily reached. The Ngare Nairobi streams are 38 miles from Moshi but the Ngararagua Country Club is no longer open.

Trout fishing in the Arusha District is controlled by the Arusha Trout Fishing Association, which has the trout fishing rights over the Temi and Nduruma rivers. The Ngare Ol Motonyi (North) river is closed to fishing. The Temi flows through the township, and the Nduruma is some six miles from Arusha. Both are accessible by motorable roads throughout the year.

Arusha is situated on the Great North Road from Kenya to Northern Rhodesia and is connected by road, rail and air with most parts of East Africa.

The township has several good hotels, garages, shops and other amenities. Fishing tackle and ammunition can be bought. (There is some rough bird and buck shooting in the neighbourhood.)

For further particulars about fishing in the province apply to the Honorary Secretary, Kilimanjaro Fishing Club, Moshi, or the Honorary Secretary, Arusha Trout Fishing Association, Arusha.

Southern Highlands Province

The best fishing months are May to November, during the rest of the year the rivers, being in spate, are impossible to fish.

Here it has been the experience that brown trout do not thrive, rainbow thrive very well in a number of rivers and are exceedingly lively when hooked. Loch flies are recommended.

As in other tropical areas, rivers stocked with rainbow yielded some spectacularly large fish while acclimatization was taking place, and though the Southern Highlands' record is still held by a 6 pound 15 ounce brown trout taken in the late '30s, more than one 6-pound rainbow was caught in the early '40s, before the rivers settled down to smaller averages. Rainbow are now breeding freely wherever the temperature is not excessive, i.e. roughly down to 5,600 feet.

The tendency in this province is to entrust the control of trout and their taking to local associations whose members, living near at hand, are personally interested in the provision of amenities and the prevention of abuses. There is, however, one well-stocked river under public control, the Chimala, reached by a mountainous road, passable in the dry season only, from the Chimala River Hotel via the Elton Plateau to Matambo village. It is from this river that efforts are being made to stock both the Hagafiro and Ruhuji rivers near Njombe, with promising results in the former.

The best fishing in the province is in the waters of the two associations (both of which welcome strangers subject to compliance with their by-laws). The Mbeya Trout Association controls the Kiwira river and its tributaries down to its confluence with the Chipoke, and the Lufirio river, with its tributaries, of which the best known is the Mwatesi, down to a point four miles below their confluence. The Kiwira system gives many open and wooded stretches of water between 26 and 35 miles of Mbeya and the association maintains three camps where accommodation and all necessities save food are obtainable at a reasonable fee. It also maintains one similar camp on the Lufirio but this river system is less accessible than the Kiwira and in periods of heavy rainfall is difficult to approach. The Lufirio camp is about 23 miles from Tukuyu and 43 or 66 from Mbeya according to the road chosen. Either road is very mountainous, and the scenery at the foot of the Livingstone Mountain range is magnificent.

There is a fishing limit on the Kiwira and baskets of up to one pound average can be had on its lower reaches; all fish caught must be kept. The Lufirio average can be rather higher but a limit is imposed on this water of eight fish a day or thirty fish a week. The association does not allow fishermen to use any one of its camps for more than a week in any period of 35 days. It employs a corps of fish guards and clears many miles of riverside paths each year. Lack of bridges however makes wading essential for satisfactory fishing.

The Mufindi Trout Association is a young association which controls the various stocked streams and dams in the vicinity of the Kigogo Forest reserve in the Iringa District. Here the rivers are very much smaller than those of the Mbeya Association though they yield nice fish of limited numbers. The area is some 30 miles from the Highlands Hotel and the rivers are generally heavily wooded.

YACHTING

The environs of Dar es Salaam must immediately strike the newcomer as ideal for sailing small craft. The town lies on the northern shore of the harbour, which is seen to be a large L-shaped expanse of water whose longer limb runs southwards. Here is absolute shelter where one can sail for three miles or more up the creek in a fresh breeze, which is often stronger than that out to sea. The safety of this inner harbour suits the less experienced and in the hot season it provides a perfect playground for those who like to sail for an hour or so after work. The narrow entrance to the harbour with its strong tides of up to four knots provides great scope for the cunning yachtsman, especially in races when the proper use of back eddies and pockets of wind between the trees make all the difference in gaining the open sea beyond. The outer channel is also narrow but is wide enough for beating and is sheltered by its shallow bounding reefs and by the Mwakatumbe Islands. A favourite afternoon sail is out to one of these islands for a bathe from the sand spits running out from the rocky coral shores.

The larger boats often go out for day cruises up or down the coast to other islands where there are especially good coral sand beaches running down to the clear deep water of the Indian Ocean. These cruises are as safe as cruising anywhere, the monsoon can be relied upon and the ocean swell is long and comfortable. Occasionally the yacht club pays a visit to Zanzibar, about forty-five miles away, and even some of the smaller craft are ambitious enough to take part with conspicuous success. The visit is usually made on August Bank Holiday, so that each boat has three days in which to complete the trip. This part of the African coast seems to be singularly free from dangerous sharks and people bathe freely from any beach. The only exception is the harbour of Dar es Salaam, where sharks are sometimes seen, having followed the ships in, and visitors should not bathe in the vicinity of the anchorages.

The present *Dar es Salaam Yacht Club* was founded in 1933, although there is evidence that a yacht club existed in 1922 but apparently failed for lack of boats and people keen enough to race regularly.

Early in its history the club decided to adopt "Snipes" as a class and three were built. These, however, did not prove a popular class and since the last war the club has adopted a 19-foot O.D. class which has proved very popular and successful.

The club, just prior to the last war, was granted the privilege of wearing the Blue Ensign defaced, but owing to lack of sufficient boats large enough to be registered the club was not able to retain the privilege.

The yacht club premises are well situated on the shore in front of the Dar es Salaam Club and there is comfortable anchorage for a number of craft. There is a shelving beach of hard sand where boats may be drawn up for cleaning and repairs and a shelter ashore with storage room for gear. A yearly programme of racing and cruising is arranged and non-owners have opportunities to crew, so that anyone who is keen can arrange a sail and fresh blood is always welcome.

Kilimanjaro.

Kibo from Mawenzi.

Photo: G. L. Boedecker

The sailing season is from the latter end of May until December but sails can be enjoyed during the other months when the wind is suitable. There is a race about once a fortnight in the season and courses are run both inside and outside the harbour according to the tides. They are designed to suit both large and small craft, which race together on handicap based on previous performances, and the events are closely contested. Several cups are competed for annually and with the constant change in owners and even in boats over a period of years the results are very open and give every opportunity to the "dark horse". Visiting boats from other ports are always welcome. No yachts are as yet available for hire, all craft being privately owned.

During the season the south-east trade winds blow steadily and conditions can be predicted in advance, so that plans can be made ahead and good races relied upon with certainty. The direction of the wind is constant between south and south-east, except at the change of the monsoons in December and May, so that the tides in the channel are the chief factors to be allowed for in planning cruises and races. Between December and March–April the north-east monsoon blows and the rains are on, so that sailing is more uncertain but there are many good days when the tide will help one out and a bright sun and clear air belie the time of year.

The Tanga Yacht Club, situated at Ras Kazone, was started as an anchorage for yachts in 1932 and officially founded in 1944. The club is restricted in membership but has a roll of rather more than 100, of whom almost half are boat owners.

The racing season extends from April to November, and there are races at least fortnightly for either a trophy donated by present or past members or mugs presented by the club. Although there is no established class of boat the races are made interesting by means of a handicap system. Races are held both inside and outside the harbour and a large variation in courses is possible. Several cups are presented to encourage coastal cruising and racing. The club is affiliated to the Royal Yachting Association.

There is also a Yacht Club at Mwanza.

MOUNTAIN CLIMBING

Tanganyika possesses many mountains that appeal to the mountain climber, with steep precipitous cliffs and rocky pinnacles. These mountains are scattered over the territory and generally speaking are not readily accessible to visitors.

The main mountain mass, Kilimanjaro, the highest mountain in Africa, is, however, easily accessible from Mombasa or Tanga by train. The ice-covered dome is an attraction both to the mountaineer and to the more modest climber.

The climb of Kibo, (the main peak, 19,340 ft.) although strenuous, is neither difficult nor dangerous and provided the advice of the local secretary of the Mountain Club of East Africa is followed, can be undertaken by anyone sound in wind and limb.

The territory offers plenty of scope for the more adventurous mountaineer who has both the time and the inclination to go farther afield and to attack some of the less well-known peaks, where there are no huts or rest camps, but for the majority Kilimanjaro will be the main centre of interest.[1]

---

[1]Further details of the climb can be found in the "Tanganyika Guide".

Kibo is the most recent of the three extinct volcanoes to which the mountain owes its origin. Shira (13,140 ft.), which lies to the north-west, is the oldest and has eroded away leaving a jagged and ill-defined crater rim, as yet unexplored by rock climbers. Climbing on the second peak, Mawenzi (17,564 ft.) is interesting and difficult, and very few climbers indeed have succeeded in reaching the summit. The mountain has yet to be climbed from the south, and the approach from the west by way of the Shira ridge and the western glaciers is still practically unexplored.

Marangu is the usual starting point for the ascent of Kilimanjaro. Two hotels at this centre cater for mountain expeditions; guides, porters, food, bedding, and suitable clothing are provided, and the climb takes five days under normal conditions. Mountain Club huts situated at 9,000, 12,000 and 16,000 feet are open to allcomers at a small charge, and for the ascent of Mawenzi there is a small but adequate shelter situated directly below the peak at 15,200 feet.

Mount Meru (14,978 ft.) is a tough and exceedingly interesting scramble. The ascent can be achieved comfortably in two days. It is usual to spend the first night just above the forest, and to make the summit and the return trip the next day. As on Kilimanjaro, temperatures on Meru are low and snow is not unusual. Arrangements for this ascent should be made by the climbers themselves. The peak is best approached from the west, and as a rule it is possible to obtain a guide and a few porters from one of the high pyrethrum farms, but the forest is a maze of game tracks, and provided the climber is prepared to be on the lookout to avoid rhino and elephant it is possible to find a route through the forest to the higher levels, where all vegetation ceases.

Light woollen underwear and windproof outer garments are essential at the high altitudes on Kilimanjaro and Meru, and, for the nights, quilted down-filled arctic-type sleeping bags are warmer and easier to transport than blankets. Snow glasses should be worn on the snow and glaciers of Kibo, and in view of the brilliant light and the scorching effect of the sun and wind a good felt hat or topee is recommended above 14,000 ft.

SWIMMING

The palm-fringed sand and coral cliffs that fill the imagination when the words "tropic beaches" are mentioned are solid realities along practically the whole of Tanganyika's coastline. One of the most delightful experiences is to fly fairly low along the coast—as can be done very easily on one of the local air services—and watch the jewel-bright colours where the Indian Ocean creams into long lines of curving breakers on sand of the palest gold—beaches ideal for swimming and sunbathing.

Indeed, an early film of Stacpoole's novel "The Blue Lagoon"—which did more than any other story to establish the idea of the halcyon beauty of the tropic beach—was made in a Tanganyika bay. And the water is just as blue now as when it attracted the film-makers.

The beaches in and near Dar es Salaam, the capital, are typical. There are about 15 miles of coast-line—lagoon, harbour, headland, bay, cove and open sea—within the municipal area. Most of the beaches are of sands which provide excellent bathing and are easily accessible, for a first class motor road follows the shore-line. At high tide one can in many places be into swimming depth within a dozen strides of the road.

There is no danger—although one or two places have powerful currents when the tide is running strongly—and no formality.   There is plenty of room to change on the beaches, and no more than reasonable discretion is required.

There are two modern swimming clubs at the harbour entrance, within a mile of the centre of the town.   They cater for visitors and provide changing rooms, showers and other amenities.

Tanga also has its swimming club.

There are one or two things to remember.   By definition, the tropic sun is hot, so sunbathe with care.   And coral rock is sharp, so explore with caution and wear shoes.   Dangerous fish exist in all tropic seas, but encounters with them are so rare as to be almost unknown in Tanganyika.   If, however, you swim out into the deep-water channels where the big ships go, you may find the occasional shark following the ships.   And if you hunt long enough among the rocks uncovered at the lowest tides, you may come across the poisonous stonefish.   But for all ordinary bathing the shores of Tanganyika are as safe as anywhere in the world. In one respect they are a great deal safer than those of "temperate" climates: there is absolutely no risk of shock or cramp through chill.   On the contrary, the bather in the Tanganyika seas can relax in caressing luxury, or spend as long as he likes without a shiver in the sport of "goggle-fishing", for which Tanganyika's clear, warm waters, lovely corals and spectacular fish make the ideal playground.

GAMES

Association football may be described as Tanganyika's national game and is by far the most popular sport among the African inhabitants.   It is widely played throughout the territory and the annual inter-provincial knock-out competition for the Sunlight Cup and inter-territorial games between Kenya, Uganda, Zanzibar and Tanganyika for the Gossage Cup arouse intense enthusiasm.   The African teams play barefooted and are remarkably fast.   The Tanganyika Football Association (P.O. Box 1574, Dar es Salaam) is the governing body for football in the territory.

A Tanganyika Amateur Athletic Association (c/o Social Development Department, Private Bag, Dar es Salaam) was formed in 1954 to encourage athletics and held its first championships in the same year.   The territory competed with Kenya and Uganda in the annual inter-territorial competition from 1955 onwards, and athletics are gaining in popularity.

Golf and tennis are probably the most popular sports with Europeans and the latter is also widely played by Asians.   Almost every station, however small, has a tennis court or two: they are usually made of *murram*, which compares favourably as a surface with that of ordinary hard courts in England.   Many stations also possess golf courses and in some cases natural conditions (including, in one or two places, such hazards as wandering hippo) add greatly to their interest.   A nine-hole course is the most usual, but some of the larger places provide the full eighteen holes.   The newcomer will find the absence of grass greens disconcerting, but the "browns" are kept as true as possible and are preferable to "greens" of indifferent quality.

The standard of hockey in the territory is probably higher than that of any other sport.   It is widely played by Europeans and Asians and many members of the Sikh and Goan communities are specially proficient at the game, their teams in the larger centres such as Dar es Salaam and Tanga reaching very high standards.

Cricket, again, is popular with Europeans and Asians and is played in most of the larger centres. Of recent years "Test" matches against the neighbouring territories have been held. There have also been inter-territorial fixtures at rugby football, a game which is played—as yet—almost exclusively by Europeans. In view of the necessity for a reasonably soft ground, rugger is restricted to a rather short season and is played in a limited number of centres—Dar es Salaam, Tanga, the Northern Province and, rather unexpectedly in view of its very dry climate, Dodoma. Matches on the coast against teams from visiting naval ships provide a highlight in this sport—as they do in the case of soccer, hockey and cricket as well.

Volleyball is played to a considerable extent by Asians, and squash and badminton are to be found in a limited number of places. There is a small but enthusiastic Tanganyika Rifle Association (Private Bag, P.O., Dar es Salaam) which organizes shooting, mainly in the capital and the Northern Province. Two sports new to the territory—boxing and cycle racing—have lately become established in Dar es Salaam and are likely to spread and gain rapidly in popularity—particularly with the African community—in the years ahead.

While there is no full scale motor racing in the territory there is a Tanganyika Motor Sports Club and various hill climbing and other tests and rallies are held at Dar es Salaam and one or two of the other larger towns of the territory. In addition there is an East African regional event, the "Coronation Safari", instituted in 1953 and organized by the *East African Standard*, which is held annually over a long and gruelling circuit, providing one of the stiffest tests of men and machines of its kind in the world. It is restricted to standard production cars, divided into classes on the basis of price.

Of less arduous games, snooker, billiards and darts are played in most clubs and many hotels, and table tennis is popular.

Owing to the unsuitable climate and the prevalence of tsetse fly there are few places where horses or ponies can be kept and thus riding is restricted and polo is not played at all. Lushoto is one of the few places where a mount can be obtained.

Golf clubs, tennis racquets and sports equipment generally can be bought in the larger towns but there is nothing like the same range of choice as is available in the United Kingdom.

Hunting, fishing, yachting, swimming, and flying are dealt with elsewhere in this chapter.

PHOTOGRAPHY

The keen photographer motoring along the dusty roads may be disappointed at the apparent lack of subject matter, but Tanganyika can provide a very varied range of subjects for the camera. For example there is the impressive mountain scenery around Kilimanjaro for which the readily accessible Peters Hut makes an ideal centre, there are delightful scenes on the streams and water falls around Marangu in the Lushoto District, impressive herds of game on the plains near Arusha, places of great historic and architectural interest such as Bagamoyo and Kilwa, the fishermen's villages and fishing boats on the coast and islands and the never ending variety of African tribal village life and customs.

The exposure varies little from that required during the height of summer in Europe, except that photography between 11 a.m. and 1.30 p.m. should generally be avoided due to the unsatisfactory lighting caused by the sun being almost vertically overhead, and it must be remembered that night falls at about 7 p.m. all the year round.

Most well-known makes and types of film are usually obtainable, but the bright light makes the use of the very fast panchromatic film unnecessary and inadvisable since its great sensitivity makes it more likely to be spoiled under adverse conditions.   For the same reason the use of a hood and suitable filter is a necessity in most cases.

Colour photography can be most successful, in particular on the coast of Tanganyika, provided that the manufacturers' exposure guides or an exposure meter is carefully followed, and the use of a tripod will ensure that no movement occurs with the lower exposures required.

Great care should be taken to keep the camera free from dust and when travelling the popular ever-ready type of case may be inadequate and the use of a box or zip-fastener case is advisable.

The great heat and the humidity on the coast cause rapid deterioration of film and it should be exposed and developed as quickly as possible and not allowed to remain for long in the camera.   Care should be taken to keep the camera and film away from the sun and heat and to wrap the exposed film in the original wrapping immediately it is removed from the camera.

Advice should be sought to ascertain which firms can be relied upon to develop and print the film satisfactorily since not every firm has the necessary equipment and experience to cope with the processing of film at high temperatures.

Users of miniature film are advised to execute the developing themselves, since few firms specialize in fine grain development.   Development at high temperatures may not cause harm, but the transfer of the film between solutions varying greatly in temperature may ruin it.   Useful booklets on processing in the tropics may be obtained from the manufacturers' agents.

FLYING

Owing to the nature of the roads and the absence of a railway line running from north to south, perhaps the easiest way—certainly the quickest and most comfortable way to travel in Tanganyika—is to go by air.   All the towns of any size, and many places that barely qualify for the name, boast their aerodromes or landing grounds.   Quite a few farms and sisal estates also have their private aerodromes.   There are, in fact, rather more than fifty airfields throughout the territory and, incidentally, Kenya and Uganda are equally well covered.

An Air Traffic Control Service is responsible for the safe movement of all aircraft, for providing advice and information on aeronautical matters and, if necessary, for the alerting of the search and rescue organization.

To avoid incurring the wrath of the East African Directorate of Civil Aviation, and indeed for his own safety, the pilot must submit a flight plan on the appropriate form and obtain clearance for an intended flight.   Should he be in one of the remoter districts where there is neither an aerodrome controller nor his representative, he must send a notice of arrival and departure through the District Commissioner or the Police by means of a telephone call or telegram, a service which is provided free if the prefix "Air Navigation" is used.

International air rules as laid down by I.C.A.O. are in force, and copies of local rules and regulations and "Notices to Airmen" may be had on application from the Directorate of Civil Aviation, Nairobi, the overall aviation administrative body for East Africa.

Maps giving aeronautical information and in various scales may be had from the Lands and Surveys Department, Dar es Salaam.

Weather reports and route forecasts are available through the Meteorological Office at moderately short notice.

A refuelling service, provided by the Shell Company of East Africa, is available at almost all the licensed airfields throughout the territory. In addition the Standard Vacuum Oil Company operate refuelling services at the bigger airports.

The migrant aeronaut may obtain customs clearance from any of the listed aerodromes on the borders of the territory.

Maintenance and repair work is normally carried out only in Dar es Salaam; the aviator is therefore strongly urged to do his servicing before leaving the capital.

In the main Tanganyika has good flying weather; cloud is as a rule broken and the ground very seldom totally obscured, though in the dry season the air can be bumpy due to thermal activity and sometimes quite hazy due to bush fires.

Navigation from a map-reading point of view is comparatively easy owing to the large number of unmistakable natural features, particularly in the shape of mountains and lakes, and the artificial features such as roads and railways are few enough to leave no doubt as to their identity.

A flying club was formed in Dar es Salaam a few years ago but no longer functions and the only club at present in existence is that at Williamson's Diamond Mine near Shinyanga in the Lake Province.

Chapter 16
MISCELLANEOUS INFORMATION

BANKS

The location of banks in the territory is as follows:—

Town	Province	Bank
Arusha	Northern	Barclays Bank (D.C.O.) Standard Bank of South Africa.
Bukoba	Lake	National Bank of India. Standard Bank of South Africa.
Dar es Salaam	Eastern	Barclays Bank D.C.O. National Bank of India. Nederlandsche Handel Maatschappij, N.V. Standard Bank of South Africa.
Dodoma	Central	Barclays Bank D.C.O.
Iringa	Southern Highlands	Barclays Bank D.C.O.
Lindi	Southern	Barclays Bank D.C.O. National Bank of India. Standard Bank of South Africa.
Mbeya	Southern Highlands	Barclays Bank D.C.O.
Mikindani	Southern	National Bank of India.
Morogoro	Eastern	Barclays Bank D.C.O.
Moshi	Northern	Barclays Bank D.C.O. National Bank of India. Standard Bank of South Africa.
Mtwara	Southern	National Bank of India. Standard Bank of South Africa.
Musoma	Lake	Barclays Bank D.C.O.
Mwanza	Lake	Barclays Bank D.C.O. National Bank of India. Standard Bank of South Africa.
Tabora	Western	Standard Bank of South Africa.
Tanga	Tanga	Barclays Bank D.C.O. National Bank of India. Standard Bank of South Africa.
Tukuyu	Southern Highlands	Barclays Bank D.C.O. (agency).

CINEMAS

There are commercial cinemas in the following towns: Arusha, Bukoba, Dar es Salaam, Dodoma, Iringa, Korogwe, Lindi, Mbeya, Morogoro, Moshi, Musoma, Mwanza, Singida, Shinyanga, Tabora, Tanga and Ujiji (Kigoma).

CLOTHES (OUTFIT)

A light felt hat or panama is normally suitable for persons who are only exposed to the sun for short periods, e.g., indoor workers, but a more adequate protection such as a well-ventilated double felt hat or pith helmet, as a filter and reflector of radiant heat, is recommended for field workers or those who by standing or walking more than a short distance expose themselves to the direct rays of the sun during the hot part of the day.

Glare, direct or reflected, has adverse effects on the eyes. Sunglasses, as recommended by competent oculists, prevent the complications arising from this form of exposure.

Men's Clothing

Tropical clothes are needed for the coast and lower-lying districts; clothes of ordinary thickness for the cold nights and mornings of the highlands.

Light-coloured or white tropical suits of palm beach, tussore, white drill, etc., are usually worn at the coast. Such suits can be made locally. Prices range from about Shs. 80/- to about Shs. 250/- according to the material used. "Aertex" or other thin shirts with short sleeves are the most comfortable. In the cool season ordinary evening wear can be worn without discomfort, but for the hotter months most people wear mess jackets or white dinner jackets. In the highlands warmer apparel is necessary, and tweeds and flannels are normally worn.

Good strong shorts and bush shirts for safari can be made both well and cheaply in the territory. All kinds of clothing can be bought in Dar es Salaam and some of the larger towns such as Tanga and Arusha.

Women's Clothing

Since on the coast and in the low-lying parts of Tanganyika the temperature is high for most of the year only very light underclothes are necessary. They are best made of strong silk or some other material (such as nylon) that will stand continual washing without showing signs of wear.

Dresses should also be made of washing material of fast colours, as the sun is strong and fades clothes badly. Linen is good if not too thick, and "Tobralco" excellent. It wears well, is light in weight, and does not fade. It is wise to bring with one clothes well cut for copying in other materials by local tailors. As the temperature falls a little in the evening it is good to guard against a chill by having a light-weight tennis coat or thickish jumper to put on after games, which are usually played between 4.30 and sunset at about 6.30 p.m.

At higher altitudes the same kinds of clothes may be worn with the addition of something heavier for the cold of the evening and early morning. A few evening dresses should be brought out, but they can also be made locally. They should be of washing material if possible. Evening cloaks are useful in the cool season and in the highlands for those who feel the cold.

On safari the most comfortable things to wear are aertex-type shirts and slacks or shorts or a short skirt of unbleached linen or light flannel. Mosquito boots and a jumper are needed for the evenings. Woollen non-shrinkable golf socks are useful but men's stockings are better for those who are not wearing slacks or who sun burn easily. Strong walking shoes and a good sun helmet are essential and a mackintosh and umbrella are useful.

Further details about clothing, etc., will be found in a booklet compiled by the Women's Service League, called "Notes for Newcomers to Tanganyika" which is obtainable from the Women's Service League, P.O. Box 344, Dar es Salaam or, in London, from the East Africa Office, Trafalgar Square.

CONSULAR REPRESENTATIVES

The following is a list of the Commonwealth Commissions and Foreign Consulates for Tanganyika. In a number of cases the representatives are based at Nairobi but are responsible for Tanganyika in addition to Kenya.

Belgium … … … … … *Office title:* Consulate of Belgium.
Postal address: c/o Belbase, P.O. Box 332, Dar es Salaam
Telephone: Dar es Salaam 2329.
Telegrams: Belsulat, Dar es Salaam.
(L. VAN GORP, Honorary Consul.)
There is also an office at Kigoma.

Denmark … … … … … *Office title:* Royal Danish Consulate General.
Postal address: P.O. Box 412, Nairobi.

France … … … … … … *Office title:* Consulate General de France.
Postal address: P.O. Box 1784, Nairobi.

Germany … … … … … *Office title:* Consulate General of the Federal Republic of
Germany.
Postal address: P.O. Box 3480, Nairobi.

Greece … … … … … *Office title:* Royal Consulate of Greece.
Postal address: P.O. Box 766, Dar es Salaam.
Telephone: Dar es Salaam 2070.
(G. N. ARNAUTOGLU, C.B.E., Honorary Consul.)

India … … … … … … *Office title:* Office of the Commissioner for the Government
of India.
Postal address: P.O. Box 2274, Nairobi.

Israel … … … … … … *Office title:* Consulate of Israel.
Postal address: P.O. Box 1334, Nairobi.

Italy … … … … … … *Office title:* Italian Vice Consulate.
Postal address: P.O. Box 599, Dar es Salaam.
Telephone: Dar es Salaam 2661.
(RENATO TARANTINO, Hon. Vice Consul.)

Japan … … … … … … *Office title:* Japanese Consulate;
Postal address: P.O. Box 6717, Nairobi.

Netherlands … … … … … *Office title:* Consulate of the Netherlands.
Postal address: P.O. Box 1174, Dar es Salaam.
Telephone: Dar es Salaam 3105.
Telegrams: Hollandia, Dar es Salaam.
(E. H. VAN EEGHEN, Honorary Consul.)

Norway … … … … … *Office title:* Royal Norwegian Consulate.
Postal address: P.O. Box 6363, Nairobi.

Pakistan … … … … … *Office title:* The Commissioner for Pakistan in British East
Africa.
Postal address: P.O. Box 5555, Nairobi.

Portugal … … … … … *Office title:* Portuguese Consulate.
Postal address: P.O. Box 464, Dar es Salaam.
Telephone: Dar es Salaam 2495.
(CAETANO MARTINS, Honorary Consul.)

Federation of Rhodesia and Nyasaland … *Office title:* Commissioner for the Federation of Rhodesia
and Nyasaland.
Postal address: P.O. Box 1612, Nairobi.

Sweden … … … … … *Office title:* Royal Swedish Consulate.
Postal address: P.O. Box 432, Nairobi.

Switzerland … … … … … *Office title:* Consulate of Switzerland.
Postal address: P.O. Box 102, Tanga.
Telephone: Tanga 246.
Telegrams: Swiss Consulate, Tanga.
(M. E. BELART, Honorary Consul.)

Union of South Africa … … … *Office title:* Commissioner for the Union of South Africa.
Postal address: P.O. Box 731, Nairobi.

United Kingdom (Trade Commissioner and
representative of Commonwealth countries
not themselves represented) … … *Office title:* United Kingdom Trade Commissioner in
East Africa.
Postal address: P.O. Box 220, Nairobi.

United States of America … … … *Office title:* American Consulate.
Postal address: P.O. Box 123, Dar es Salaam.
Telephone: Dar es Salaam 3778.
Telegrams: Amconsul, Dar es Salaam.
(ROBERT E. WARE, Vice Consul.)

COST OF LIVING

In common with most other parts of the world there has been a steady increase in the cost of living in Tanganyika since the war, and the official cost of living index (assessed by the East African Statistical Department) for Dar es Salaam (excluding rents) stood at 139 on 30th June, 1957, the base of 100 being at 31st December, 1950, and the figure for 31st December, 1947, having been 83. The cost of living varies, of course, from place to place but tends to be appreciably higher—particularly in respect of rents and fresh foodstuffs—in the larger towns and on the coast.

The average retail prices of some common consumer goods in October, 1957 at Dar es Salaam were as follows:—

Article	Unit	Price Shs. Cts.
Beef, Sirloin (Top Grade, Kenya)	... 1lb.	3　75
Beer, East African, excluding bottle	... 1 bottle	1　50
Bread, White	... 1 lb. loaf ...	0　72
Butter	... 1 lb. ...	4　10
Cabbages	... 1 lb.	0　60
Cigarettes, East African, "Clipper"	... pkt. of 50 ...	4　15
Coffee, "Aroma"	... 1 lb. pkt. ...	7　70
Dress Materials, "Tobralco"	... 1 yard ...	8　50
Eggs, European Farms	... 1 doz. ...	5　50
Handkerchiefs, Gents', "Pyramid"	... 1 doz. ...	42　00
Khaki Drill, "Stockport"	... 1 yard ...	6　00
Maize Meal (Posho)	... ½ kg. ...	0　30
Milk, Fresh	... 1 pint ...	0　90
Mutton, Leg (Local)	... 1 lb. ...	2　80
Paraffin	... 4 1/6 gal. tin ...	12　00
Petrol	... 1 gal. ...	2　80
Potatoes	... 1 lb. ...	0　50
Sugar	... 1 lb. ...	0　70
Tea, "Booke Bond", Green Label	... 1 lb. pkt. ...	5　90

CURRENCY

The standard coin in East Africa (Tanganyika, Kenya, Uganda and Zanzibar) is the East African shilling, equal to one-twentieth part of a pound sterling. It is divided into 100 cents, and equivalent values are therefore:—

£1 sterling	= 20 shillings East African
1 shilling sterling {	= 1 shilling East African
	= 100 cents East African
6d. sterling	= 50 cents East African
3d. sterling	= 25 cents East African

East African currency notes in common use are in denominations ranging from 5 shillings to 100 shillings. The one-cent, five-cent and ten-cent coins are of copper, and the fifty-cent and one-shilling coins, formerly of silver, are being replaced by cupro-nickel coins. (There are no 25-cent (3d.) coins.)

The following is a brief history of the coinage of the territory.

Pre-war coinage

The coins minted in Germany before the 1914–18 war consisted of: —

Deutsche Ostafrikanische Gesellschaft (the Company).	Deutsche Ostafrika (the Government).
Zwei Rupien.	1 Rupie.
Eine Rupie.	½ Rupie.
½ Rupie.	¼ Rupie.
¼ Rupie.	10 Heller (nickel).
Pesa.	5 Heller (nickel).
	5 Heller (copper).
	1 Heller (copper).
	½ Heller (copper).

Arising out of the transfer to the German Imperial Government of the sovereign rights of the Sultan of Zanzibar over the territory, a contract was made in 1890 between the German Imperial Government and the Deutsche Ostafrikanische Gesellschaft (D.O.A.G.), under which certain prerogatives were retained by the company, one of which was to coin and issue copper and silver coinage which was to be accepted as legal tender in the public offices of the Government.

The Deutsche Ostafrikanische Gesellschaft minted four silver coins, namely: two rupees, one rupee, a half rupee and a quarter rupee, and one copper coin known as the "pesa"*. The large two-rupee coin was issued to replace the Maria Theresa dollar, the latter being withdrawn from circulation by an ordinance of the German Governor dated 1896. The other coins were similar to the Indian coinage, as it was decided that the coinage for German East Africa should, as far as possible, correspond to the Indian coin current in East Africa. The copper "pesa" was withdrawn from circulation early in 1910.

In a contract dated November, 1902, between the German Imperial Government and the Deutsche Ostafrikanishche Gesellschaft, the latter renounced the right of mintage and issue of coinage reserved to them under the contract of 1890.

With regard to the German Government coinage, ordinances were passed providing for four silver coins, one nickel coin, and three copper coins. The silver coins were two rupees, one rupee, a half rupee and a quarter rupee; the nickel coin was a ten-heller piece; and the three copper coins were five, one and one-half hellers. A subsequent ordinance in 1912 introduced another nickel coin, a five-heller piece.

With regard to the two-rupee coin, it is interesting to note that the Deutsche Ostafrikanische Gesellschaft minted this coin, but although the German Government ordinance provided for the coin, it was never minted by the Government. The history of the matter appears to be as follows:—

At the time the Company became established, the Maria Theresa taler (dollar or real) had been in circulation for over a century. This coin was preferred in certain districts to the Indian rupee, the latter being mostly used by the Indian and Arab traders on the coast. An ordinance dated 1893 prohibited the import of the Maria Theresa dollar and other dollars, and by an ordinance of 1896 the Maria Theresa dollar was withdrawn from circulation. To replace this coin the Company introduced a silver two-rupee coin which was about the same size as the Maria Theresa dollar, and was made receivable at public treasuries. Two-rupee coins to the value of Rs. 7,008 in 1893, and in 1894 to the value of Rs. 94,700, were minted by the Company. As the one-rupee came into general use the demand for the two-rupee coin became less. When the German Government took over coinage in the territory the coin values of the Company were continued, with the exception of the copper pesa. Hence, although the two-rupee coin was authorized as one of the coins of the territory in accordance with the Currency Ordinance of 1904, it was never minted under that ordinance, the quantity of the Company's two-rupee coins in currency being sufficient for the demand. It appears that this two-rupee coin minted by the Company was never withdrawn from circulation.

*64 pesa = 1 rupee.

Locally Minted War Coinage

A certain number of coins were minted locally by the Germans during the 1914–18 war, but none of these coins was recognized by the British Government. They were as follows:—

> Twenty heller (copper).
> Twenty heller (brass).
> Five heller (brass).

There was also minted at Tabora a gold sovereign, worth fifteen rupees, from gold obtained from the Sekenke mine. At one time there was a demand for these sovereigns as curios, and they fetched much above their face value.

Until the scarcity of small coinage was relieved, some of the plantations and other employers of labour had issued private tokens called "marken". One such, stamped from brass, was issued by the Afrikanische Plantagen Georg Hirsch, Morogoro. It bears on one side a pair of antlers over the letter "H" enclosing a heart, on the other side the value, the numeral "15" in large figures over the word "Heller".

German Pre-War Notes

The prerogative to issue a paper currency was first conferred on the Deutsche Ostafrikanische Gesellschaft by the Sultan of Zanzibar in 1888, and was subsequently confirmed by the agreement of 1890 between the Company and the German Government. The Company restricted its currency efforts from 1890 to 1901 to the mintage of metal coins, and, by the later agreement with the German Government of 1902 referred to above, waived claims to the right of circulating notes as well as coinage. About this time, however, economic developments indicated the necessity for the circulation of a paper currency. Chiefly in order to supply this need, a syndicate of German banks, in conjunction with two local firms (the Deutsche Ostafrikanische Gesellschaft and Hansing & Company), succeeded in creating the Deutsche Ostafrikanische Bank, with its head office at Berlin, on 6th January, 1905.

In order to regulate the issue of notes in the Protectorate, an Imperial Ordinance was introduced in 1904, which authorized the issue of paper currency in the Protectorate, which privilege could only be acquired through a concession conferred by the German Imperial Chancellor. A concession was duly granted to the Deutsche Ostafrikanische Bank in 1905.

The first issue of notes by the Deutsche Ostafrikanische Bank at a face value of Rs. 5 was advertised on 1st December, 1905. In February, 1906, the Bank extended their issue to Rs. 50 notes. In May, 1906, the Deutsche Ostafrikanische Bank reported their first issue of Rs. 10 notes, and in August, 1907, the first issue of Rs. 100 notes. In 1912 the Deutsche Ostafrikanische Bank, encouraged by the favourable economic conditions then existing in the Protectorate, applied for and obtained Imperial sanction to issue Rs. 500 notes. The Deutsche Ostafrika- nische Bank reported in March, 1915, that up to 28th February, 1915, the total issue, after deduction of damaged notes withdrawn from circulation, amounted to Rs. 4,387,350, of pre-war notes whereas according to the Concession it was entitled to issue three times the amount of fully paid up capital (in 1911 Mks. 2,000,000 or Rs. 1,500,000), or an aggregate amount of Rs. 4,500,000, leaving a concessionary balance of Rs. 112,450, which the Bank was at the above date, 12th March, 1915, still entitled to issue.

German War or Interim Notes

In March, 1915, the Bank supply of pre-war notes had dwindled down to Rs. 50,000. Owing to this scarcity of notes, the Bank asked the German East African Government for authority to issue Interim Notes. Authority was given to the Bank to print and issue Interim Notes as a measure of expediency for the duration of the war, with the stipulation, at first, that they would be withdrawn after the war and replaced by notes printed in Germany.

The Interim notes were of the following values:—

Rs. 1, 5, 10, 20, 100, 200 and 500.

It will be seen that values of Rs. 1, 20 and 200 were issued in Interim Notes, although these values were not included in the pre-war notes.

The New East African Currency

The rise in exchange value of the Indian rupee towards the middle and end of 1919 from 1s. 4d., which had been practically constant for a great number of years, to 2s., and at the beginning of 1920 to 2s. 8d., had placed a serious handicap on the inflow of British capital into East Africa, and with a view to counteracting these adverse conditions the rate of exchange was reduced and stablilized at 2s. early in 1920. Shortly after the stabilization of the rupee, however, the exchange value of the rupee in India fell below this figure, with the result that Indian rupees and notes were smuggled into Kenya and Tanganyika, where automatically they became worth two shillings. It was decided to replace the Indian rupee and its subsidiary coinage by an East African shilling, and a Currency Board was constituted in London to control a new coinage for East Africa. The new coinage was introduced into Kenya, Uganda and Tanganyika, and consisted of a silver shilling as the standard, with a silver fifty-cents coin (half-shilling), and subsidiary copper coinage of ten, five and one-cent pieces. Redemption of the Indian silver coinage was effected at the rate of two shillings to the rupee, and ceased to be legal tender in the territory as from the 23rd July, 1921. In 1948 cupro-nickel coinage was introduced to replace the silver coinage which is being gradually withdrawn. There is a note issue[1] consisting of notes in the following denominations:

Shs. 1,000[2]
200[2]
100
20
10
5

As already indicated, the East African Currency area covers Tanganyika, Kenya, Uganda and Zanzibar, and there is free movement of currency between these territories.[3] No other currency circulates in Tanganyika.

CUSTOMS

There is a uniform Customs tariff for the three East African territories, the basic rate of duty being 22 per cent *ad valorem*, with the duty on certain luxury goods and toilet preparations being as much as 60 per cent *ad valorem*.

---

[1] During the 1939-45 war one-shilling notes (which were very unpopular with Africans) were issued.

[2] These notes have been withdrawn from free circulation.

[3] E.A. currency is also legal tender in Aden.

Bona fide baggage accompanying a passenger or landed within two months of the arrival of a passenger, or such further period as the Commissioner may allow, may be imported free of import duty and may include the following in such quantities as the Commissioner may consider appropriate to the passenger:

(a) Wearing apparel and personal effects;

(b) Binoculars, cameras, sports requisites, portable typewriters, toys and articles for household use (such as sewing machines, perambulators, furniture, carpets, pictures, glassware, linen, cutlery, crockery and plate) which the Commissioner is satisfied have been in the personal or household use of the passenger;

(c) Photographic films and plates;

(d) Instruments and tools for the personal use of the passenger in his profession or trade.

The following are not admitted free as baggage:—

Arms, ammunition, bicycles, motor vehicles, cine-projectors, sound recording machines, wireless apparatus, gramophones, gramophone records, musical instruments (unless elsewhere provided for), piece goods, provisions, stationery, potable spirits, perfumed spirits, cigars, cheroots, cigarettes, cigarillos, snuff or tobacco, wines, saddlery or any trade goods; provided that, at the discretion of the Commissioner of Customs, import duty may not be charged on alcoholic liquors or perfumed spirits not exceeding one pint or on cigars, cheroots, cigarettes or tobacco not exceeding in all one-half pound in weight. Any excess of the above amounts renders the whole quantity in the possession of any passenger liable to duty.

Goods may be freely transferred between the three East African territories after importation without the payment of duty provided transfer forms, which can be obtained at any Custom House or Railway Station, are completed.

In addition to the concessions granted to a passenger, a bona fide tourist visiting East Africa for a period not exceeding six months may import free of duty reasonable quantities of foodstuffs and non-alcoholic beverages appropriate to his personal requirements.

Provision has also been made under the Customs Management Act, 1952, for the temporary importation of goods, except cinematograph films over 16mm. in width and 500 metres in length, intended for the use, convenience or comfort of a tourist during his stay in the territories, on the deposit of a sum equal to the duty payable on the goods, which is refunded if the goods are exported within six months from the date of importation or such further period as the Commissioner may allow.

Except at Mtwara, and in the near future Dar es Salaam, all ships entering Tanganyika ports lie at anchor and disembark passengers by launch. Passengers are therefore advised that only hand luggage should accompany them ashore. All heavy packages are discharged into lighters and landed at a wharf or jetty where they must be claimed and will be examined by Customs.

The importation of certain goods is restricted or prohibited and includes the following:—

Live animals, arms and ammunition, guns, toy pistols, birds and bird's eggs, dangerous drugs, plants, seeds, seedlings, bulbs, rat virus, and trophies, including ivory, rhino horn and hippo teeth. Passengers should be particularly careful to declare any such articles in their possession.

ELECTRICITY

Public electricity supplies are available in fourteen towns in Tanganyika. In every case distribution is at 400/230 volts, 50 cycle alternating current on the 3-phase 4-wire system. The electricity supply systems are, of course, constantly being expanded but particulars as at 1st September, 1957, are given in the table below:—

TOWNSHIP	INSTALLED CAPACITY IN KILOWATTS			TOTAL CAPACITY KILOWATTS
	Diesel	Steam	HYDRAULIC	
Dar es Salaam	11,710	—	—	11,710
Morogoro	883	—	—	883
Tanga Province	—	—	17,500	17,500
Moshi	299	—	1,160	1,459
Tabora	640	210	—	850
Arusha	2,020	—	—	2,020
Mwanza	1,660	—	—	1,660
Dodoma	470	300	—	770
Lindi	480	—	—	480
Iringa	327	—	260	587
Mbeya	320	—	160	480
Kigoma	143	50	—	193
Mtwara	540	—	—	540
Nachingwea	250	—	—	250

HOTELS

The following is a list of the principal hotels in the territory. Rates vary from about Shs. 25/- to Shs. 50/- per day (including meals) with reductions for long stays.

Town	Province	Hotel
Arusha	Northern	Athenaeum Hotel.
		Hunter's Lodge.
		King's Hotel.
		Meru Hotel.
		New Arusha Hotel.
		Safari House.
Bagamoyo	Eastern	Bagamoyo Country Club.
Bukoba	Lake	Lake Hotel.
Chimala	Southern Highlands	Chimala Hotel.
Dar es Salaam	Eastern	Etienne's.
		Inn by the Sea.
		Metropole Hotel.
		New Africa Hotel.
		New Palace Hotel.
		Palm Beach Hotel.
		Rex Hotel.
		Splendid Hotel.

Town	Province	Hotel
Dodoma	Central	Railway Hotel.
Iringa	Southern Highlands	Iringa Hotel.
		White Horse Inn.
Kigoma	Western	Stanley Hotel.
Kilosa	Eastern	New Kilosa Hotel.
		Parthenon Hotel.
Kimamba	Eastern	New Planters Hotel.
Korogwe	Tanga	Korogwe Hotel.
Lindi	Southern	Beach Hotel.
Lushoto	Tanga	Jagertal Hotel.
		Lawns Hotel.
		Soni Falls Hotel
		Magamba Hotel and Country Club.
Mbeya	Southern Highlands	Mayfair Hotel.
		Mbeya Hotel.
Morogoro	Eastern	Acropol Hotel.
		Savoy Hotel.
Moshi	Northern	Kilimanjaro Hotel.
		Livingstone Hotel.
		Ridgeway Hotel.
		Piccadilly Hotel.
		Kibo Hotel.
,, (Marangu)		Marangu Hotel. (25 miles from Moshi on slopes of Kilimanjaro.)
Musoma	Lake	Musoma Hotel.
Mwanza	Lake	Mwanza Hotel.
Njombe	Southern Highlands	Njombe Hotel.
Sao Hill	Southern Highlands	Highlands Hotel.
Shinyanga	Lake	Diamond Fields Hotel.
Singida	Central	Central Hotel.
Songea	Southern	Angoni Arms Country Club.
Tabora	Western	Railway Hotel.
Tanga	Tanga	Africa Hotel.
		New Hotel.
		Palm Court.
		Park Hotel.
		Sea View Hotel.

HOURS OF BUSINESS AND LICENSING HOURS

The official hours of business of Government offices at Dar es Salaam and at most stations on the coast are 7.30 a.m.–12 noon and 1.30 p.m.–4 p.m. (mornings only on Saturdays). Up-country there are variations between stations but the most common arrangement is 8 a.m.–12.30 p.m. and 2 p.m.–4.30 p.m. Most shops, offices and garages are open from between 8 and 9 a.m. until noon and from 2 p.m. until anything between 4.30 and 6.30 p.m. Most European firms in Dar es Salaam and Tanga close at 4.30 p.m. Banks are usually open from 9 a.m. until noon (11 a.m. on Saturdays) and most Government Revenue Offices and Sub-Accountancies maintain similar hours for receiving and making payment.

The licensing hours for bars are 10 a.m. to midnight on ordinary days and 11 a.m. to 2 p.m. and 6 p.m. to 10 p.m. on Sundays, Christmas Day and Good Friday. Extensions of hours are granted in special circumstances. Licensed restaurants can serve liquor to persons taking meals between twelve noon and 2 p.m. and from 6 p.m. to midnight. Retailers with off-licences can normally sell from 8 a.m. to 7 p.m. while hotels may serve residents with liquor at any time.

A typical village between Songea and Lake Nyasa.

Photo: Shell Co.

Preparing Beeswax, Tabora District, Western Province.

Photo: F. G. Smith

Africans playing traditional game—Bao.

Photo: V. Eugene Johnson, Singida

IMMIGRATION

Passports

British Subjects and British Protected Persons, as well as aliens, must be in possession of valid passports and must conform with the immigration requirements given below.

Visas

Visas are required except for:—

(a) Nationals of the following countries:—

Denmark	Luxembourg	San Marino
Iceland	Netherlands	Sweden
Italy	Norway and Colonies	Switzerland
Liechtenstein		

(b) passengers entering the territory in the course of a continuous and unbroken journey and leaving by the same ship or aircraft;

(c) resident aliens of one of the British African territories holding valid Immigration Inter-Territorial Passes issued by the Government of Kenya, Tanganyika, Uganda or Zanzibar;

(d) aliens in whose passports are stamped valid immigration Re-Entry Passes or Certificates of Permanent Residence granted by the Government of Tanganyika;

(e) members of an African tribe indigenous to the territory, of Portuguese East Africa or of Ruanda-Urundi.

Ordinary and Single Journey Visas—Subject to special instructions relating to Colonies, Protectorates, Mandated Territories and Trust Territories, in force from time to time as regards particular classes of aliens, a visa may be granted without reference except in the following cases:—

(a) Nationals of Albania, Bulgaria, China, Czechoslovakia, Estonia, Germany, Hungary, Japan, Latvia, Lithuania, North Korea, Poland, Roumania, Soviet Russia and Yugoslavia.

(b) Applicants against whom there is some local personal objection or doubt.

(c) Immigrants. (See Immigration Requirements below.)

(d) Prohibited Immigrants. (See below.)

(e) Stateless persons.

(f) When a visit is expected to exceed six months.

Transit Visas—A transit visa may be granted when the period required to complete the journey through the territory is not expected to exceed one month, provided that the applicant produces evidence that he will be accepted in the country of his final destination, has made arrangements for the continuation of his journey and has sufficient funds for the purpose.

Comprehensive Visa—(*Tanganyika, Kenya, Uganda, Zanzibar*)—Subject to the requirements of the other three East African territories and the provisions above, a comprehensive ordinary or single journey visa, according to nationality, may be granted, for which a single fee may be charged, valid for two or more of the above territories.

34

Immigration Control

Immigration is controlled by a system of Entry Permits and Passes; Entry Permits for those who desire to settle permanently, and Temporary Employment Passes for employees who may be required to leave the territory on the expiration of their immigration passes. The interest of the population, the requirements of industry, and the availability in the territory of manpower, sufficiently skilled to meet the demands of a developing community, are always taken into consideration before an Entry Permit is approved. The issue of any immigration pass is in the absolute discretion of the Principal Immigration Officer.

Entry Permits for those who desire to remain permanently or for an indefinite period in the territory are classified into categories designated in alphabetical sequence "A" to "H". Class "A" are granted to permanent residents of the East African territories, those in the Government or East Africa High Commission services, and to missionaries in the service of an approved missionary society. All applications in Classes "B" to "G" from those who desire to engage in agriculture, mining, prospecting, business, manufacture, to practise a profession, or to accept permanent employment, are subject to examination and approval by the Immigration Control Board, before an Entry Permit may be issued. Those with an assured annual income may be granted an Entry Permit Class "H".

Immigration Requirements

Exemptions—An immigration pass or permit is required by all persons (including British subjects) entering the territory, with the following exceptions:—

(a) a serving member of Her Majesty's Forces, a civilian employee of any of Her Majesty's Departments of State, and the wife and children of any such persons;

(b) an accredited representative in the territory of the Government of any country within the British Commonwealth and the members of such person's staff and household;

(c) a person duly accredited as a Diplomatic or Consular representative to the territory and the members of such person's staff and household;

(d) a member of an African tribe indigenous to Tanganyika, Kenya, Uganda, or Zanzibar.

Residents—A resident intending to return within two years should obtain a Re-Entry Pass before departure from Tanganyika or from the East African Commissioner, East African Office, Grand Buildings, Trafalgar Square, London, W.C.2.

Visitors—A visitor may obtain a Visitor's Pass, valid for a period not exceeding six months, in the first instance, from the Principal Immigration Officer, Dar es Salaam, the East African Office, London, or on arrival at the port of entry. A visitor may be called upon by the Immigration Officer at the port of entry to Tanganyika (air or sea) to provide security by bond or cash deposit up to a maximum sum per adult of £150, depending on the place of domicile.

Where an Immigration Officer is satisfied that a visitor desires to enter the territory for the purpose of passing through the territory to a destination outside the territory, and that the visitor is in possession of the necessary documents to permit him or her to enter the country of destination, an In-Transit Pass may be issued in lieu of a Visitor's Pass, entitling the holder to enter the territory and remain therein for such period, *not exceeding one month*, as may be stated in the Pass.

Immigrants—An intending immigrant, which includes a person coming for temporary employment, should apply in advance for an Entry Permit or Temporary Employment Pass to the Principal Immigration Officer, P.O. Box 512, Dar es Salaam, Tanganyika. Telegraphic address: "Princim", Dar es Salaam.

Prohibited Immigrants—Unless they are exempted from immigration requirements, the following persons are prohibited immigrants and may be refused permission to enter the territory:—

    (a)   destitute persons;

    (b)   persons suffering from mental disorder;

    (c)   persons with criminal records;

    (d)   prostitutes;

    (e)   persons deemed to be undesirable immigrants;

    (f)   persons who are not in possession of valid passports.

Fees

No fee is charged for a Visitor's Pass, In-Transit Pass or any Pass issued under the Immigration (Control) (Exemption) Regulations.

Fees payable in respect of Certificates, Permits and Passes under Regulation 41 of the Immigration (Control) Regulations, Chapter 251 of the Laws of Tanganyika, are as follows:—

	Shs.
Entry Permit	40/-
Temporary Employment Pass	20/-
Inter-Territorial Pass	20/-
Renewal of Inter-Territorial Pass	10/-
Dependant's Pass	20/-
Special Pass	40/-
Permit for Prohibited Immigrant to enter	40/-
Certificate of Permanent Residence (not being a renewal or a re-endorsement)	20/-
Duplicate of lost Certificate, Permit or Pass	10/-

Temporary Employment Passes

A Temporary Employment Pass may be issued by the Principal Immigration Officer upon application being made to him by any person if the Principal Immigration Officer is satisfied, after consultation with the Labour Commissioner:

    (a)   that such person is qualified to undertake employment in the trade, business, or calling in respect of which the application is made;

    (b)   that there is not already unemployment of persons skilled in that class of trade, business or calling; and

    (c)   that the taking of such employment will not be to the prejudice generally of the inhabitants of the territory.

A Temporary Employment Pass entitles the holder to enter the territory within the period stated in the pass and to remain in the territory for the purpose of engaging in the employment specified in the pass for such period *not* exceeding four years as is stated in the pass.

Before a Temporary Employment Pass is issued security by bond or a cash deposit up to a maximum sum of £150 may be required.

Enquiries

Enquiries should be addressed to:—

The Principal Immigration Officer,
P.O. Box 512,
Dar es Salaam,
Tanganyika.

Telegraphic address:—

"Princim"—Dar es Salaam.

INSURANCE

The following insurance companies are among those represented in Tanganyika:—

Company	Branch or Principal Agents
ATLAS INSURANCE CO. LTD.	Smith, Mackenzie & Co., Ltd., P.O. Box 479 Dar es Salaam.
BRITISH INDIA GENERAL INSURANCE CO., LTD. ..	P.O. Box 795, Dar es Salaam.
BRITISH OAK INSURANCE CO., LTD.	Mr. Z. G. Michaelides, P.O. Box 832, Dar es Salaam.
BRITISH TRADERS' INSURANCE CO., LTD. ...	Mr. Baldev N. Varma, P.O. Box 661, Dar es Salaam.
CAR & GENERAL INSURANCE CORP. LTD. ...	Griffith & Co., P.O. Box 30, Arusha
CENTRAL INSURANCE CO., LTD.	Liverpool & E.A. (Agencies) Ltd., P.O. Box 357, Dar es Salaam.
COLIN HOOD INSURANCES LTD. (Insurance Brokers)	P.O. Box 1615, Dar es Salaam.
CORNHILL INSURANCE CO., LTD.	A.W. Black & Co., Ltd., P.O. Box 388, Dar es Salaam.
DOMINION INSURANCE CO., LTD.	Col. E. H. Tapson, P.O. Box 280, Moshi.
ESSEX & SUFFOLK EQUITABLE INSURANCE SOCIETY, LTD.	Smith, Mackenzie & Co., Ltd., P.O. Box 479, Dar es Salaam.
GAILEY & ROBERTS (INSURANCES) LTD. (Insurance Brokers)	P.O. Box 296, Dar es Salaam.
GENERAL ACCIDENT, FIRE & LIFE ASSURANCE CORP., LTD.	Cooper Brothers & Co., P.O. Box 45, Dar es Salaam.
GUARDIAN ASSURANCE CO., LTD.	British East Africa Corp., Ltd., P.O. Box 330, Dar es Salaam.
JUBILEE INSURANCE CO., LTD.	A. G. Abdulhussein & Co., Ltd., P.O. Box 84, Dar es Salaam.
LIVERPOOL & LONDON & GLOBE INSURANCE CO., LTD.	Tanganyika Cotton Co., Ltd., P.O. Box 655, Dar es Salaam.
LLOYDS UNDERWRITERS	Smith, Mackenzie & Co., Ltd., P.O. Box 479, Dar es Salaam.
LONDON & LANCASHIRE INSURANCE CO., LTD. ...	United Africa Co. (Tanganyika) Ltd., P.O. Box 555, Dar es Salaam.
MARINE & GENERAL MUTUAL LIFE ASSURANCE SOCIETY LTD.	Smith, Mackenzie & Co., Ltd., P.O. Box 479, Dar es Salaam.
MARINE INSURANCE CO., LTD.	Smith, Mackenzie & Co., Ltd., P.O. Box 479, Dar es Salaam.
MERCHANTS MARINE INSURANCE CO., LTD. ...	Smith, Mackenzie & Co., Ltd., P.O. Box 479, Dar es Salaam.
MOTOR UNION INSURANCE CO., LTD. ...	Mr. Baldev N. Varma, P.O. Box 661, Dar es Salaam.
NATIONAL EMPLOYERS' MUTUAL GENERAL INSURANCE ASSOCIATION LTD.	East African Engineering & Trading Co., Ltd., P.O. Box 410, Dar es Salaam.
NEW GREAT INSURANCE CO. OF INDIA LTD. ...	Bharat Agencies Ltd., P.O. Box 202, Tanga.
NEW INDIA ASSURANCE CO., LTD.	Karimjee Jivanjee & Co., Ltd., P.O. Box 51, Dar es Salaam.
OCEAN ACCIDENT & GUARANTEE CORPORATION LTD.	Kettles-Roy & Tysons Ltd., P.O. Box 171, Dar es Salaam.
ORIENTAL FIRE AND GENERAL INSURANCE CO., LTD.	P.O. Box 795, Dar es Salaam.
ORION INSURANCE CO., LTD.	British East Africa Corp., Ltd., P.O. Box 336, Dar es Salaam.

Company				*Branch or Principal Agents*
PHOENIX ASSURANCE CO., LTD.	...	...	...	Wigglesworth & Co. (Africa) Ltd., P.O. Box 416, Dar es Salaam.
PROVINCIAL INSURANCE CO., LTD.	...	...	...	Mr. A. J. R. MacEwan, P.O. Box 180, Arusha.
ROYAL EXCHANGE ASSURANCE	...	...	...	Griffith & Co., P.O. Box 30, Arusha.
ROYAL INSURANCE CO., LTD.	...	...	...	Branch Office, Holland House, P.O. Box 1878, Dar es Salaam.
SCOTTISH UNION & NATIONAL INSURANCE CO.		...		P. P. Sondhi & Co., P.O. Box 327, Dar es Salaam.
SOUTH AFRICAN MUTUAL LIFE ASSURANCE SOCIETY LTD. ...	... ...	...	...	Smith, Mackenzie & Co., Ltd., P.O. Box 479, Dar es Salaam.
SUN INSURANCE OFFICE LTD....	...	...	...	Gibson & Co., Ltd., P.O. Box 466, Dar es Salaam.
UNITED BRITISH INSURANCE CO., LTD.		...	...	Mr. Baldev N. Varma, P.O. Box 661, Dar es Salaam.

NEWSPAPERS

The following are the principal newspapers and periodicals published in the territory:—

Tanganyika Standard, P.O. Box 33, Dar es Salaam. Daily. English.

Tanganyika Opinion, P.O. Box 455, Dar es Salaam. Daily. English and Gujerati.

Sunday News, P.O. Box 33, Dar es Salaam. Weekly. English.

Young Africa, P.O. Box 908, Dar es Salaam. Weekly. (Fridays). Gujerati.

Mnyima, P.O. Box 365, Arusha. Monthly. Greek.

Tanganyika Notes and Records, P.O. Box 511, Dar es Salaam. The quarterly journal of the Tanganyika Society. English.

In addition there are the official *Gazette* (weekly, on Fridays, with other special editions from time to time) published by the Government Press, Dar es Salaam, and the Swahili publications of the Public Relations Department, *Mambo Leo*, *Baragumu* and *Mwangaza*. There are also some thirty other publications in Swahili and tribal vernaculars including two private African-owned newspapers (*Bukya na Gandi* and *Zuhra*) and seven monthlies published by missions. The balance is made up of local district newspapers, mainly monthlies published under Government or Local Government auspices.

There are a number of English, Gujerati and Swahili newspapers and magazines published in Nairobi, Kenya, which deal with East Africa on a regional basis. The best known of these is the *East African Standard* (P.O. Box 280, Nairobi), an English daily. The weekly *East Africa and Rhodesia*, published in London (66 Great Russell Street, W.C.I.), is also widely read in the territory.

Shops in the larger towns stock copies of several popular United Kingdom newspapers as well as a good range of illustrated periodicals from overseas.

POSTAGE STAMPS

In 1893 the first issue of postage stamps was made for use in the newly acquired colony of German East Africa, though occasionally envelopes are found posted from the colony to Europe bearing stamps of the issue then used in Germany. As in the case of German South West Africa and other German colonies, this first issue consisted of certain values of the 1889 German stamps adapted for colonial use.

At the time, the colony's currency was the rupee, which was divided into 64 pesa. Thus this first issue consisted of:—

	3 Pfennig surcharged as		2 Pesa
5	,,	,,	,, 3 ,,
10	,,	,,	,, 5 ,,
20	,,	,,	,, 10 ,,
50	,,	,,	,, 25 ,,

The surcharged value was added in a horizontal line at the foot of each stamp.

Three years later the above surcharge was changed to a diagonal one on the then German stamps. The values surcharged were as above, and the words "Deutsch-Ostafrika" were included in the inscription.

In 1900 the standard designs for German Colonial stamps, which embodied a picture of the Kaiser's yacht *Hohenzollern* were adopted. The values issued were: 2p, 3p, 5p, 10p, 15p, 20p, 25p, 40p and 1, 2 and 3 rupee.

To meet the change in currency from pesas to hellers, a new issue was made in 1905, the same key type of design being used, but the lower values being changed to 2½h, 4h, 7½h, 15h, 20h, 30h, 45h, and 60h. A fresh issue was printed the following year of all the above heller and rupee values, but this time paper watermarked with a diamond pattern was used. Of this issue the one rupee and two rupee values were not actually brought into use.

As might be expected, the effective allied blockade led, early in the war, to a shortage of postage stamps within the colony. This was first met by franking correspondence with rubber stamps. Persons sending letters handed them with the required amount to the postal clerks, who affixed the seal to the envelope and returned it to the sender for posting. It was permissible to have envelopes franked thus in advance.

The rubber seals used were two, one oblong:

FRANKIERT

MIT. 7½H

the other circular, of which the design included the Imperial Eagle, with the words

KAISERL POSTDIREKTOR

DEUTSCH OST AFRIKA

round the circumference.

True to their policy of improvization, however, the postal authorities had an issue printed locally in 1916. These were printed at Vuga mission, near Lushoto, on paper manufactured in the colony, which proved to be very brittle. The values printed were 2½ and 7½ hellers and 1 rupee, the designs of necessity being very crude. In the absence of the necessary machinery, these stamps were rouletted, not perforated and were not gummed. But in March 1916 the German blockade runner s.s. *Marie* succeeded in reaching Sudi bay, between Lindi and Mikindani, bringing, with other much needed supplies, a stock of postage stamps of the pre-war design. In consequence, the above locally printed stamps, of which 100,000 of the 2½h, 300,000 of the 7½ and 16,000 of the 1 rupee values had been printed, were buried at Morogoro, to escape capture by the British forces, or for future use if necessary. In 1921 they were recovered under the supervision of the then Keeper of German records, the late R. W. Gordon, O.B.E., but many had disintegrated owing to the dampness of the soil.

The withdrawal of the German forces led to the issue of provisional stamps by the Military Administration of Mafia, the island having been captured in January 1915 by troops landed from H.M.S. *Kinfauns Castle,* and by the Nyasa-Rhodesian Force.

There also came into use Indian postage stamps overprinted "I.E.F." for use by members of the Indian Expeditionary Force. Stamps have been found of the former German issue overprinted G.R. These are bogus.

When Mafia was occupied and used, incidentally, as a base for operations against the German light cruiser *Königsberg* which had retreated into the Rufiji delta, a small quantity of the above German East Africa Ship type, and a very few current Zanzibar stamps, were found. With a child's rubber printing set these were overprinted G.R. MAFIA, or in some cases initialled by Colonel J. D. Mackay, who was in command of the island. This overprinting soon proved unsatisfactory, however, and a die was obtained from Zanzibar which read

GR

Post

6 Cents

Mafia

and was used on all values of the German East African stamps, which were sold at the above flat rate. But by the end of July the supply of stamps was exhausted, and recourse was had to using a supply of German Fiscal stamps which had come to light in Chole Customs house. These were overprinted with a circular die "O.H.B.M.S. Mafia". A supply of the above-mentioned Indian Expeditionary Force stamps now arrived and to these was added the overprint "GR-Post Mafia".

In September 1916, Lt.-Commander Clarke, R.N., later a Provincial Commissioner in Tanganyika, assumed charge of the island, which was now under the Zanzibar Government's administration. A fresh supply of I.E.F. stamps was obtained and overprinted as above, the lettering of the overprint being in italics. In August, 1918, Mafia Island was transferred to Tanganyika Territory. The above improvized adaptation led necessarily to many varieties and, incidentally, to many forgeries. Closer study of these issues may be made by reference to the books listed below.

In 1916 five values of the current Nyasaland stamps, the ½d., 1d., 4d. and 1/-, were overprinted N.F. and used by the Nyasaland and Rhodesian Forces.

The Belgian forces had by now occupied the north-west of the territory and hence Belgian Congo stamps may be found bearing the postmark of Kigoma and other stations occupied by them.

Particulars of the various Army Post Offices in existence during the campaign may be found in Robson Lowe's Encyclopaedia of British Empire Postage stamps.

In November, 1917, the German forces having retreated to the extreme south of the territory, and a Civil Administration having been established, the first official issue of stamps was made. Seventeen values of the current British East African Stamps were overprinted "G.E.A." and issued. These were the 1 ct., 3 cts., 6 cts., 10 cts., 12 cts., 15 cts., 25 cts., 50 cts., 75 cts., and 1 r, 2 r, 3 r, 4 r, 5 r, 10 r, 20 r, and 50 r. The higher values were seldom used, save for fiscal purposes. This issue continued in use until 1922, although, in 1921, a change of watermark was made in six of the values. During 1922, owing to a change in postage rates accepted by the Postal Union Congress of 1920, and the non-arrival of fresh supplies of stamps, the supply of one-cent and ten-cent stamps was nearly exhausted. Permission was therefore granted for the Government Printer, Dar es Salaam, to overprint supplies of these stamps, obtained direct from Nairobi. In all 48,000 stamps of each value were thus overprinted. The results were examined closely by officials duly appointed, and any varieties found with double or inverted overprints are definitely forgeries.

The above issue continued in use until July, 1922, when it was superseded by an issue printed by Messrs. Bradbury Wilkinson & Co. To meet the change in currency, the denominations of these are shillings and cents viz: 5 cts., 10 cts., 15 cts., 20 cts., 25 cts., 30 cts., 40 cts., 50 cts., 75 cts., Sh. 1/-, Shs. 2/-, Shs. 3/-, Shs. 5/-, Shs. 10/- and Shs. 20. The design is a giraffe's head and the inscription "TANGANYIKA".

To comply with the decisions of the 1924 Postal Union Congress, the colours of the 5 cts., 10 cts., 25 cts., and 30 cts. were changed in the following year.

In 1927 a further issue appeared bearing the inscription "MANDATED TERRITORY OF TANGANYIKA" and a portrait of His Majesty King George V. The denominations were those of the preceding issue, save that the 30 cts. value did not appear until 1931.

The above three issues were used for fiscal as well as postal purposes, hence specimens may be found, particularly of the giraffe head issue, which have been removed from documents, cleaned and faked by the addition of a postmark.

On 1st May, 1935, a postal union having been formed with Kenya and Uganda, the territory's first pictorial stamps appeared. The issue comprised the following values: 1 ct., 5 cts., 10 cts., 15 cts., 20 cts., 30 cts., 50 cts., 65 cts., Sh. 1/-, Shs. 2/-, Shs. 3/-, Shs. 5/-, Shs. 10/- and £1. From the many designs submitted, the following were selected:

Crowned Cranes	...	...	... 1 ct., 20 cts., Shs. 10/-
View of Lake Victoria	...	...	... 5 cts., 50 cts.
East African Lion	...		... 10 cts., £1.
Jinja Bridge	...	...	... 30 cts., Shs. 5/-
Mount Kilimanjaro	...	...	... 15 cts., Shs. 2/-
Mount Kenya	...	...	... 65 cts.
View of Lake Naivasha	...	...	... Sh. 1/-, Shs. 3/-

The King's head was shown on each stamp.

The above were printed by Messrs. De La Rue & Co.

A minor alteration, made subsequently to the design of the 5 cts. value, is much sought after by collectors; as is a rare variety of perforation of the one shilling value.

At this time the airmail postage rate to the United Kingdom was sixty-five cents a half ounce, hence this value was included in the issue. The design shows an aeroplane flying over Mount Kenya.

In May, 1935, there was a further departure in the territory's postal history, when the first commemorative stamps appeared.

On the occasion of the Silver Jubilee of His Majesty King George V a set of four values, 20 cts., 30 cts., 65 cts. and Sh. 1/- were issued. The design was that used for all Crown Colonies, bearing the King's head with a view of Windsor Castle. The issue was withdrawn in January, 1936.

In May, 1937, another commemorative issue appeared on the occasion of the coronation of His Majesty King George VI. It comprised three values, 5 cts., 20 cts. and 30 cts., the design being that used for all Crown Colonies and showing portraits of the King and Queen.

By this time stamp collectors had developed a demand for stamps postmarked on the first day of their issue, and on Coronation Day Post Offices were accordingly besieged, for the one hour during which they were open, by persons wishing to obtain these First Day Covers.

In April, 1938, occurred the new issue of King George VI stamps, again printed by Messrs. De La Rue, who had printed the above two commemorative issues. The designs used were those of the 1935 issue, with the new King's head, but the 65 cts. value was omitted. The charge for airmail postage to the United Kingdom had been reduced to 20 cts. a half ounce, so the necessity for issuing this value had disappeared. This issue continued on sale until the end of May, 1954, and the intervening sixteen years saw the appearance of two values, the 25 cts. and 40 cts., the demand for which was remarkably small. In this period there were also changes of colour in the 5 cts. and 10 cts. values to comply with the Universal Postal Union's requirements.

Thus, in all, fifteen values of this issue appeared with the following designs:

Crowned Cranes ...	...	...	1 ct., 20 cts., 40 cts., Shs. 10/-
View of Lake Victoria	...	...	5 cts., 25 cts., 50 cts.
East African Lion ...	...	...	£1.
Jinja Bridge ...	...	...	30 cts., Shs. 2/-
View of Lake Naivasha	...	...	10 cts., Shs. 1/-, Shs. 3/-
Mount Kilimanjaro	...	...	15 cts., Shs. 2/-

Comparison with the above table for 1935 shows that, though no new designs appeared, a different design was used for the 10 cts. value. Again, a much sought-after variety appeared: in some early copies of the 50 cts. value, the sheet attached to the sail of the dhow in the foreground appears as a broken line.

With the declaration of war, the rate of air mail postage to the United Kingdom was raised abruptly to Shs. 1/60 a half ounce, and before the end of the war airgraphs and airmail letter cards were in regular use for this correspondence. In the case of airgraphs, the sender wrote on a special form which was handed in at the Post Office, photographed, and the negative itself, about the size of a postage stamp, was flown to England, where an enlarged print of it was made and delivered to the addressee. For this service the charge was seventy cents.

The airmail letter card, which was really a re-appearance of the letteret of Victorian days, is still in general use at present. Postage was, as now, 50 cents.

In England, the heavy enemy air raids of December, 1940, caused extensive damage to the stamp printers' machinery. This led to several changes in the perforation of East African stamps, some of which have become very popular with collectors, particularly the first printing of the £1 stamp. Shortage of stamps through enemy action led to the appearance, in July 1941, of the only provisional issue used in East Africa during the war. Stamps from the Union of South Africa, printed alternately in English and Afrikaans, were imported and overprinted, by force of circumstances rather crudely, for use in the East African territories. Their original values were also surcharged to meet local requirements, viz: the penny stamp was surcharged 5 cts., the threepenny 10 cts., the sixpenny 20 cts., and the one shilling 70 cts. These provisionals remained on issue until the following year.

On 11th November, 1946, two stamps were issued to commemorate the allied victory, the design being that used by all Crown Colonies, showing the River Thames and Houses of Parliament and bearing the King's head. There were two values, 20 cts. and 30 cts.

In the six years 1948 to 1954 there were five commemorative issues of East African stamps. In December, 1948 were issued two stamps, the 20 cts. and £1 to commemorate Their Majesties' Silver Wedding, the design being that used in all Crown Colonies. In October, 1949, four values, the 20 cts., 30 cts., 50 cts. and Sh. 1/-, were issued on the occasion of the seventy-fifth anniversary of the Universal Postal Union. In February, 1952, Her Royal Highness Princess Elizabeth and the Duke of Edinburgh visited Kenya. To mark the event, a special issue of two values was made, comprising the then current 10 cts. and Sh. 1/- stamps, but bearing the added inscription "ROYAL VISIT 1952". This issue was to continue only for the period of the visit, but was withdrawn prematurely when Her Royal Highness had to return home suddenly on account of the death of His Majesty King George VI, thus these stamps are now uncommon. On 2nd June, 1953, on the occasion of Her Majesty's Coronation, there was issued a twenty-cent stamp showing a medallion containing the Queen's head, inscribed "Coronation" and the date of that event, with "Kenya, Uganda, Tanganyika" at the foot. The number sold of this issue is stated to have been over eleven million, though allowance must be made for those purchased by stamp collectors.

In April, 1954, there was a second Royal Visit and the opening of the Owen Falls Dam. To commemorate the event there was issued a 30 cts. stamp bearing Her Majesty's head, with a view of the dam, and inscribed "Royal Visit 1954".

This brings us to the current issue of East African stamps, the designs of which depart entirely from the pre-war issues and are:

Owen Falls Dam	5 cts., 30 cts.
Giraffe	10 cts., 50 cts.
East African Lion	20 cts., Sh. 1/-
View of Mount Kilimanjaro ...	Shs. 2/-
Elephants	Shs. 5/-
Her Majesty's Lodge at Sagana ...	Shs. 10/-
Portrait of Her Majesty	£1.

Not until the Postal Union of 1935 were Postage Due labels used in Tanganyika, when six values, 5 cts., 10 cts., 20 cts., 30 cts., 40 cts. and Sh. 1/-, were issued.

The foregoing is only an outline history of the stamps of Tanganyika. Detailed references to minor varieties, watermarks, changes of perforation, retouches, shade variations and postal stationery have been omitted. A closer study of these may be made by reference to the catalogues of Messrs. Stanley Gibbons, Whitfield King and the Commonwealth Stamp Co. Other useful books are:

Robson Lowe	The Encyclopaedia of British Empire Stamps.
C. H. Greenufod	The Provisional Issues and Postage Stamps of Mafia.
R. D. Berrington	A Handbook on King George VI issues of Kenya, Uganda and Tanganyika.
W. J. W. Potter	The Printings of George VI Colonial Stamps.
Stamp Collecting	26th March, 1927 and 27th July, 1946.

PUBLIC AND SEMI-PUBLIC BOARDS, CORPORATIONS, ETC.

The major public and semi-public boards, corporations, councils, committees, etc. (excluding Local Government Authorities), are listed below. In most cases their general functions are made clear by their titles. The address of most of these bodies is c/o the Office of the Chief Secretary, Private Bag, P.O., Dar es Salaam, and in any event all addresses may be obtained from the Ministerial Secretary.

Advisory Committee on African Education.
Advisory Committee on other Non-Native (including Goan) Education.
Advisory Committee on Technical Training.
Aerodromes Advisory Committee.
African Loans Fund Committee.
Assayers Licensing. Board.
Board of Control of Land Surveyors.
Board of Management, Government Employees' Provident Fund.
Board of Registration of Architects and Quantity Surveyors.
Board of Trustees, National Parks.
Central Board, Provident Fund.
Central Court of Appeal (Local Courts.)
Central Tender Board.
Coffee Board.
Cotton Board.
East African Currency Board.
Electricity Board.
European Education Authority.
Immigration Control Board.
Indian Education Authority.
King George V Memorial Museum Board of Trustees.
Languages Board.
(Cotton) Lint and Seed Marketing Board.
Local Councils Board.
Makerere College Council.
Makonde Water Corporation.
Military Pensions Appeals Tribunal.
Mining Loans Board.
Newspapers Advisory Board.
Nurses and Midwives Council.
Pharmacy and Poisons Board.
Public Service Commission.
Public Trustee Investment Board.
Pyrethrum Board.
Rent Restriction Board.
Royal Technical College of East Africa Council.
Seeds Board.
Southern Highlands Province Non-Native Tobacco Board.
Standing Committee on Training.
Tanganyika Agricultural Corporation.
Tanganyika Broadcasting Corporation.
Tanganyika Civil Service Advisory Board.

Tanganyika Medical Board.
Tanganyika Sisal Board.
Tanganyika Travel Committee.
Tea Board.

In most of the large towns are to be found Cinematograph Censorship Boards, Hotel Boards, Housing Committees, Rent Restriction Boards and Siting Boards.

The Overseas Food Corporation, which managed the Groundnut Scheme from 1948, handed over responsibility for the remaining experimental work on 1st April, 1955, to the Tanganyika Agricultural Corporation. Most of the Overseas Food Corporation's surplus assets in the territory had been disposed of by the end of 1954 and their remaining assets and staff (down to little over 4,000 all told against a figure in excess of 20,000 three years before) in Tanganyika were taken over by the new corporation which is controlled by the Tanganyika Government.

PUBLIC HOLIDAYS

The following days are observed as Public Holidays:—

New Year's Day.
Good Friday.
Easter Monday.
The first Monday in August.
Queen's Day (the second Monday in October).
Christmas Day.
Boxing Day.
Id-el-Fitr (two days).

Where a public holiday falls on a Sunday the following day is usually declared a public holiday. The official Queen's Birthday and Remembrance Day (second Sunday in November) are usually marked by parades but are not official public holidays. A number of additional religious festivals are observed by different communities while not being official holidays and leave of absence is usually granted to employees by their employers on such days.

RESIDENTIAL AND BUSINESS ACCOMMODATION

A very considerable amount of building of both residential and business premises has been undertaken since the war and the position with regard to business accommodation in most towns is now comparatively easy. Residential accommodation, however, has still not quite caught up with the demand created by the tremendous expansion of the country's economy in the post-war years.

The boom in building probably reached its peak in quantity and costs about 1951/52 and both the amount of construction being undertaken and the costs have been coming down fairly steadily since. It is doubtful, however, whether building costs, which are now down to about Shs. 25/- to Shs. 35/- per square foot for the better type of residential bungalow, will decline much further. Government has built a large number of houses since the war, both for Civil Servants and for renting to Africans in Dar es Salaam and other towns.

Until the 1st January, 1957, rent control on business premises was maintained (under the Rent Restriction Ordinance, No. 16 of 1951, as amended by Ordinance No. 10 of 1954) on residential premises and on business premises completed before 1st January, 1955, where the "standard rent", as defined in the Ordinance, did not exceed £500 per annum. The standard rent, in respect of post-war buildings, represented the maximum rent which might be charged and was calculated of the basis of 11 per cent on the market cost of construction of the premises, plus the rates actually paid, plus an annual equivalent of 5 per cent on the land as valued for rating purposes in the case of free-hold property, or the right of occupancy rent in the case of leasehold property. It is thus very difficult to give an indication of the general level of rents since so much depends on the standard of construction of the building and the date at which it was built. However, typical two- or three-bedroomed bungalows may be obtained at a rent of Shs. 500/- to Shs. 600/- per month (unfurnished) in Dar es Salaam, while flats cost somewhat less—small two-roomed flats being procurable at as little as Shs. 120/-. The maximum rents payable in respect of older buildings are fixed at the rates as at 3rd September, 1939, plus 50 per cent.

The Rent Restriction Ordinance is applied to most towns in Tanganyika and is administered by Rent Restriction Boards. Rents up-country tend, generally speaking, to be a little lower than in Dar es Salaam.

There are two building societies operating in Tanganyika: they are the First Permanent Building Society, P.O. Box 1723, Dar es Salaam, and the Savings and Loan Society Ltd., P.O. Box 45, Dar es Salaam.

TIDES

In common with all other coasts, the highest tides occur at the full and change of the moon. Tide heights at Dar es Salaam are as follows:—

High water means	Springs	10·3 ft.
	Neaps	6·8 ft.
Low water means	Springs	0·3 ft.
	Neaps	3·1 ft.

These tide heights generally hold good for the whole of the Tanganyika coast but there are slight variations in the times of the tides at some places. Tides are thus 12 minutes ahead of Dar es Salaam at Kilwa Kivinje and 27 minutes ahead at Kilwa Kisiwani. The times at Tanga and Mtwara, however, are the same as those at Dar es Salaam. Further information on tides may be obtained from *The Tide Tables for East African Ports* (available from the Port Offices at Mombasa and Dar es Salaam) and from the Admiralty charts of the area.

TIME

East African Standard Time is three hours ahead of Greenwich Mean Time There are two marked differences between the relationship of the hours of daylight and darkness in Tanganyika and the United Kingdom. One is the comparatively short periods of twilight at dawn and dusk in Tanganyika (and, of course, in other places of similar latitude) as compared with those experienced in Europe (and, again, in other parts of the world similarly distant from the equator). The second difference is the very small variation in the hours of daylight during the different seasons of the year: in countries, such as Tanganyika, situated near the equator, there is no variation to compare with the short winter days and the contrasting long hours of daylight in summer in Britain. Thus, in Dar es Salaam, the earliest sunrises are in late November (05.55 hours E.A.S.T.) and the latest during the second half of July (06.37 hours), a difference of only 42 minutes. The earliest times of sunset (18.11 hours) occur at the end of May while the latest, at the end of January, are at 18.47 hours—a difference of a mere 36 minutes. There is thus, very roughly, twelve hours daylight and twelve hours of darkness per day throughout the year. The extent of the territory makes a considerable difference to the times of sunrise and sunset between places in the extreme east and west. Thus in Tabora, headquarters of the Western Province, these are nearly half-an-hour later than in Dar es Salaam, while Kigoma, on Lake Tanganyika, is even further behind the east coast. At noon, the sun is almost exactly overhead in Tanganyika and at certain times of the year is, in fact, precisely so.

WEIGHTS AND MEASURES

Imperial and metric weights and measures are both in use in the territory, but nowadays there is a trend for traders to favour the Imperial system. From 1st January, 1953, the East African Railways and Harbours converted all their weighings from the metric to the Imperial system and the process of converting all their weighing machines is still going on. It has been found that the majority of local industries are using the Imperial system for their produce, and all petrol and oil is sold by Imperial units of measure.

In certain more remote areas of the territory, however, such as parts of the Western and Southern Provinces, there is still a preference among the shopkeepers to use the metric system, and any attempt to bring in legislation to provide for only one system would be liable to meet considerable opposition.

The Weights and Measures Ordinance (Cap. 221 of the Laws) came into force on 15th July, 1931, and regulations and amendments have since been made. The territory's standards of weights and measures are kept in a strong room at the Treasury, Dar es Salaam, and are only brought out once each year in order to carry out comparison with the secondary standards which are in daily use. The territory's standards are sent to the United Kingdom once in ten years for examination by the Board of Trade.

All weights and measures in trade use in the territory including those used by Government departments are liable to verification and inspection, and a small staff of qualified Inspectors is employed by Government to administer the law.

Prior to the introduction of the metric system by the German Government in 1910, Arabic units of weights and measures were in general use in German East Africa. Due to the continued use of certain of these denominations by traders and Africans to denote the metric measures introduced by the Germans, although the metric measures were larger than the actual native measures, the law still provides for their continued use provided they are of the capacity of the metric or Imperial equivalent laid down (*vide* the Weights and Measures (Customary Weights and Measures) Regulations, 1953).

The following is a list of such weights and measures permitted:—

Measures of capacity:

Robo Kibaba	...	...	...	0·25 litre
Nusu Kibaba	...	...	...	0·5 litre
Kibaba	...	...	...	1 litre
Pishi ...	...	...	...	4 litres.

Denominations of weight:

Ratili...	...	...	...	1 pound avoirdupois
Frasila	...	...	...	36 pounds

Linear measure:

Mkono	...	...	...	18 inches

GLOSSARY OF WORDS IN COMMON USE

AKIDA. An official or agent, usually of Arab or Swahili extraction, through whom the African administration was formerly conducted. The term was originally applied to a leader or commander of soldiers.

AMERIKANI. Cotton cloth, manufactured and first imported from America, from which it derives its name. The cloth is used for clothing and was the staple article among trade goods over Central Africa.

ASKARI. A soldier. Used of the rank and file of the King's African Rifles and Police.

AYAH. An African nurse.

BABU. The name generally applied by the African to Indian clerks or Asiatic subordinate officials.

BANDA. A temporary or semi-permanent house, generally constructed of mud and poles, or a grass shelter.

BANYANI. The usual African name for the Indian trader.

BARAZA. An Arabic word meaning seat or bench, where the house-owner usually sat to receive his friends. Now commonly used to denote a public meeting or an assembly of elders, a court-house, or a verandah.

BIBI. An African woman. A polite form of address to a woman.

BIN; BINTI. Son; daughter of; e.g. Abdallah bin Hamisi, Abdallah, son of Hamisi.

BOMA. Originally a palisade or stockade serving as a fortification for towns or villages. The majority of Government stations were, in the early days, protected by some form of stockade, and the term has thus come to denote a Government station.

BORITI. Thick poles laid across from one wall to another in African houses to support the roof. The poles are often cut from mangroves which are hard and termite resistant.

BUNI. Coffee berries (cherries) or raw coffee, as apart from the prepared bean.

BWANA. Master or Mister. The title by which a man is usually addressed. It is prefixed to words descriptive of an occupation or profession; e.g. Bwana Shauri, an administrative officer, Bwana Shamba, a planter, Bwana Miti, a forest officer, and so on.

DEBE. A four-gallon kerosene tin, used as a convenient receptacle, e.g. for the conveyance of grain to market. It has thus come to be used as a rough measure of weight.

DHOW. The lateen-rigged vessel of Arabia. The dhow formerly played a notorious part in the slave trade between the East African coast and Arabia.

DUKA. A shop.

FRASILA. A measure of weight equal to about 36 lb.

FUNDI. A skilled workman.

HABARI. News or information.

HELLER.   One of the units of the German currency, still occasionally used by the older generation of Africans as the equivalent of two cents.

HODI.   A cry made by a visitor inquiring, outside the door of the house, whether the occupant is at home.   In East Africa, where few houses have bells, the term is used by Africans and non-Africans alike before entering a house.

JAMBO.   The usual Swahili salutation, meaning "How do you do?"

JAMVI.   A large mat of coarsely plaited palm leaves.

JUMBE.   A headman.

KANZU.   A long garment, resembling a night-dress and reaching to the feet, worn by most coast Africans and generally by all personal servants.

KARANI.   A clerk.

KARIBU.   To approach.   "Karibu" is the reply to "Hodi" (see above) and is an invitation to the visitor to enter the house.

KADHI.   The presiding official (usually Arab or Swahili) over a Mohammedan court.

KIBABA.   A measure used by Africans, equal to about 1 pint or 1½ lb.

KIONGOZI.   A leader of a caravan or guide.

KODI.   A tax.   The name usually applied to the house and poll tax.

KORJA.   A commercial expression, possibly of Indian origin, denoting a score or bale.

LIWALI.   An Arab or Swahili judge of a Mohammedan court, who sometimes also exercises executive functions over a township.   He is superior in status to a Kadhi.

MAMBO.   Affairs or news.   *Mambo Leo* or "News of To-day" is a newspaper published in Swahili.

MARIDADI.   Smart, decorative.

MIOMBO.   *Brachystegia-Isoberlinia* woodland.

MPAGAZI.   A porter.

MZUNGU.   A European.

NGALAWA.   A small canoe with outriggers, used by fishermen on the coast. The boat is hollowed out from the trunk of a tree.

NGOMA.   A drum, but more generally used of a dance at which the drum or tom-tom supplies the music.

PESA.   A small copper coin introduced into Zanzibar from India about 1845. Still used to denote nickel or copper coinage generally.

POMBE.   African "beer", usually made from fermented grain.

POSHO.   The daily food ration of an African labourer.

RATILI.   A weight equivalent to 1 lb.

RUPIA.   The Indian or German rupee, now no longer current.

SAFARI.   A voyage or journey.   A hunting expedition is called a "safari".

SERIKALI.   The Government.   "Mtu wa Serikali" means a government official.

SHAMBA.   A garden, or piece of cultivated land.   Applicable to the compounds of European houses and also to farms and plantations.

SHAURI. Advice, plan or agreement. One of the commonest words in the language, used in every conceivable connexion by Africans and non-Africans to denote an affair or business of any nature.

SHENZI. Uncivilized, uncouth.

SHIBIRI. The span between the thumb and little finger extended: used for measurement and equivalent to about nine inches.

SOKO. A market. Used to denote the Indian bazaar or the collection of shops that exists in even the smallest townships.

SULTANI. A chief. The word "mtemi" or "mwami" is generally used of chiefs in the west of the territory.

TEMBO. Fermented palm-wine from the coconut tree. Used, generally, to denote any form of intoxicating liquor.

THUMUNI. Formerly an eighth part of a dollar; and, later, the quarter rupee, and now used of a 50-cent piece.

WALI. An Arab ruler or governor.

WARI. A measure of length equivalent to one yard.

FOOTNOTE

In Swahili, and in many other of the languages spoken in Tanganyika, changes in number are indicated by prefixes; thus, *m*pagazi, a porter; *wa*pagazi, porters; *M*pare, (pronounced mpahray, the *m* sounded with the lips closed), a Pare, a member of the Pare tribe, *Wa*pare, members of the Pare tribe; *Ki*pare, the Pare language. It is now accepted practice however—and prevents confusion—to omit all prefixes in referring to members of tribes; it is better to talk of a Pare, the Pare, a Nyamwezi, the Nyamwezi, and thus avoid the common errors which are found when prefixes are used; for example, "a Wanyamwezi" (which is the equivalent of saying "an Englishmen"), "Wanyamwezis" (comparable to "Englishmens"), "the Wanyamwezi tribe" (the Englishs).

APPENDIX A

CONTENTS TABLE OF COMPANION VOLUME
TANGANYIKA: A REVIEW OF ITS RESOURCES AND THEIR DEVELOPMENT

PART ONE

THE COUNTRY AND THE PEOPLE

PART SIX

PRODUCTION: ECONOMIC RESOURCES OF THE TERRITORY

MAPS

TABLES

TABLES—*contd.*

TABLES—*contd.*

CHARTS

Appendix B

List of Governors and Commanders-in-Chief

1916—1924.   Sir Horace Archer Byatt, K.C.M.G. (1916-1920 with title of "Administrator").

1925—1931.   Sir Donald Charles Cameron, K.C.M.G., K.B.E.

1931—1933.   Lt.-Col. Sir George Stewart Symes, K.C.M.G., K.B.E., D.S.O.

1934—1938.   Sir Harold MacMichael, K.C.M.G., D.S.O.

1938—1942.   Sir Mark Aitchison Young, K.C.M.G.

1942—1945.   Sir Wilfred Edward Francis Jackson, G.C.M.G.

1945—1948.   Sir William Denis Battershill, K.C.M.G.

1949—1958.   Sir Edward Francis Twining, G.C.M.G., M.B.E.

List of Chief Justices

1920—1924.   Sir W. M. Carter, C.B.E.

1924—1929.   Sir W. A. Russell, K.C.

1929—1934.   Sir J. Sheridan.

1934—1936.   Sir S. S. Abrahams, K.C.

1936—1939.   Sir L. C. Dalton.

1939—1945.   Sir A. H. Webb, K.C.

1945—1952.   Sir G. Graham-Paul.

1952—1955.   Sir H. Cox, K.C.

1956—   E. J. Davies, Q.C.

List of Chief Secretaries

1919—1924.   A. C. Hollis, C.M.G., C.B.E.

1924—1928.   J. Scott, C.M.G.

1929—1934.   D. J. Jardine, C.M.G., O.B.E.

1934—1935.   P. E. Mitchell, C.M.G., M.C.

1935—1939.   H. C. D. C. Mackenzie-Kennedy, C.M.G.

1939—1944.   L. B. Freeston, C.M.G., O.B.E.

1944—1946.   G. R. Sandford, C.M.G., O.B.E.

1946—1951.   Sir E. R. E. Surridge, C.M.G.

1951—1954.   A. M. B. Hutt, C.M.G., O.B.E.

1954—1956.   R. de S. Stapledon, C.M.G., C.B.E.

1956—   A. J. Grattan-Bellew, C.M.G., Q.C.

DISTRICT HEADQUARTERS STATIONS IN TANGANYIKA

Abbreviations and symbols used:—

A...	...	Aerodrome.
B.B.	...	Barclays Bank (D.C.O.).
C. of E.	...	Church of England (i.e. Church Missionary Society and Universities Mission to Central Africa).
E...	...	Electricity.
Hq.	...	Provincial Headquarters.
N.B.I.	...	National Bank of India.
P.	... ...	Protestant, (e.g. Lutheran, Mennonite, Moravian, Swedish Free Mission, Adventist, Salvation Army, etc.).
R.C.	...	Roman Catholic.
S.B.S.A.	...	Standard Bank of South Africa.
Tg...	...	Telegraph.
Tp...	...	Telephone.
Wt.	...	Wireless Station.
W....	...	Piped Water Supply.

Station	Altitude in feet	*Average annual rainfall ins.	Mean annual temp. deg.	Normal senior Government staff	†Medical Facilities (showing number of beds in hospitals)	Hotels (No. of beds and minimum single daily tariff)	‡Rest Houses	Garages	Shops	Banks	Churches	Sports	Remarks
Central Province													
Dodoma Hq. A. E. Tg. Tp. Wt. W.	3,675	23	73	114	Hospital 148	Railway Hotel 43 Shs. 35/-	—	Good	Good	B.B.	C. of E. R.C.	Cricket Football Golf Hockey Rugby Tennis	Grade I aerodrome. Important communications centre. Cinemas.
Kondoa A. Wt.	4,550	25	70	8	Hospital 46	—	Two	—	Poor		P. R.C.	Football Shooting Squash Tennis	Grade III landing strip. Centre for rock paintings of great interest.
Manyoni Tg. Tp. W.	4,000	25	70	5	Dispensary 22 Mission Hospital 60	Railway Dak Bungalow at Itigi (24 miles). (Food provided)	One	None (Except Railways Itigi)	Poor		C. of E. R.C.	Big game shooting Football	Grade III landing strip.
Mpwapwa A. Tg. Tp. W.	3,700	25	71	29	Hospital 26 Kongwa Hospital (25 miles) 75		One	—	Fair		C. of E. R.C.	Football Golf Swimming Tennis	Grade III landing strip. Grade I aerodrome at Kongwa. Important Veterinary centre.

Station	Alt.				Medical	Hotels				Banks	Churches	Sports	Remarks
Singida A. Tg. Tp.	4,900	25	70	17	Hospital 44	Central Hotel 9 Shs. 25/-	Two	Poor	Fair	B.B.	P. R.C.	Football Game and bird shooting Tennis	Grade III landing strip. Electricity and piped water supplies planned. Cinema.
Eastern Province Bagamoyo E. Tg. Tp. W.	—	41	78	5	Hospital 40	Country Club 15. Shs. 30/- (Plus Membership Fees)	One	—	Poor	—	R.C.	Football Tennis	Important centre of old Slave Trade: of great historic interest.
Dar es Salaam A. E. Tg. Tp. Wt. W.	—	42	78	Large	Hospitals 538 Several Nursing Homes and Clinics	Numerous	—	Good	Good	B.B. N.B.I. SBSA Netherlands Trading Society Bank of Baroda Ltd Bank of India Ltd.	C. of E. P. R.C.	Athletics Boxing Cricket Fishing Football Rugby Swimming Tennis Yachting, etc.	Grade I aerodrome (approx. 8 miles), Capital of Territory and main port with cosmopolitan population of over 100,000. Cinemas.

*Rainy seasons, in most places, are November–December and February–May, when it is hot. Cool in dry season, June–September, cold at night at stations over 4,000 feet.

†"Hospital" implies that a registered medical practitioner is in charge, "dispensary" that a licensed practitioner or Medical Assistant is in charge and that in-patients may or may not be catered for.

‡Except where otherwise indicated it may be expected to find Rest Houses furnished with basic heavy furniture but not equipped with linen, cutlery, utensils, etc.

DISTRICT HEADQUARTERS STATIONS IN TANGANYIKA

Abbreviations and symbols used:—

A.... :: Aerodrome.
B.B. :: Barclays Bank (D.C.O.).
C. of E. :: Church of England (i.e. Church Missionary Society and Universities Mission to Central Africa).
E.... :: Electricity.
Hq. :: Provincial Headquarters.
N.B.I. :: National Bank of India.

P. ... :: Protestant, (e.g. Lutheran, Mennonite, Moravian, Swedish Free Mission, Adventist, Salvation Army, etc.).
R.C. :: Roman Catholic.
S.B.S.A. :: Standard Bank of South Africa.
Tg.... :: Telegraph.
Tp.... :: Telephone.
Wt. :: Wireless Station.
W. :: Piped Water Supply.

Station	Altitude in feet	*Average annual rainfall ins.	Mean annual temp. deg.	Normal senior Government staff	†Medical Facilities (showing number of beds in hospitals)	Hotels (No. of beds and minimum single daily tariff)	‡Rest Houses	Garages	Shops	Banks	Churches	Sports	Remarks
Eastern Province													
Kilosa A. Tg. Tp. W.	1,600	40	76	13	Hospital 90	New Kilosa Hotel 8 Shs. 25/- Parthenon 15 Shs. 20/- New Planters' Hotel, Kimamba (11 miles) 30 Shs. 30/-	Two	Fair	Fair	—	C. of E.	Football Golf Shooting Tennis	Grade II aerodrome. Important sisal growing centre.
Kisarawe Tg. Tp. W.	900	46	77	6	Mission Hospital Minaki (2½ miles)	—	One (un-furnished)	—	Poor	—	C. of E. (2½ miles) R.C. (5 miles)	Football Tennis	Important African Secondary Schools at Minaki and Pugu. Nearest rural District Headquarters to Dar es Salaam.
Mafia A. Wt. W.	—	72	78	1	Hospital	Deep-sea Fishing Camp at Utende Shs. 30/-	One	—	Poor	—	R.C.	Fishing Swimming Tennis	Grade I aerodrome. Headquarters of an island district. First class big game fishing.

Station	Altitude (feet)				Medical	Hotel	Accommodation		Water	Bank	Church	Sport	Remarks
Mahenge (Ulanga) Wt.	3,500	73	73	7	Hospital 78	—	One	—	Poor	—	P. R.C.	Football Tennis	Landing strip at Lupiro (25 miles).
Morogoro Hq. A. E. Tg. Tp. Wt. W.	1,900	76	35	60	Hospital 190	Acropol 25 Savoy Shs. 28/-	—	Fair	Good	B.B. SBSA	C. of E. R.C.	Cricket Football Golf Squash Tennis	Grade II aerodrome. Also landing strip at Kingolwira. Important communications and sisal centre at foot of Uluguru mountains. Cinema.
Utete (Rufiji) A. E. Tg. Tp. W.	100	81	35	6	Hospital 44	—	One	—	Poor	—	—	Football Tennis	Grade III landing strip. Hot and humid. Parts of district liable to flooding during rains.
Lake Province Biharamulo A. Tg. W.	4,850	70	38	3	Dispensary 41	—	One	—	Poor	—	C. of E. R.C. (6 miles)	Bird and Big Game shooting Football Tennis	Landing strip of Grade III size (dry weather only). Vast but sparsely populated district; heavily infested with tsetse flies.
Bukoba A. Tg. Tp. Wt. W.	3,750	70	80	38	Hospital 137	Lake Hotel 28 Shs. 32/50	Judge's Lodgings available by arrangement with the Judiciary, Mwanza	Fair	Good	N.B.I. SBSA	C. of E. P. R.C.	Cricket Football Golf Swimming Tennis	Grade II aerodrome. Centre of prosperous and progressive coffee growing district. A Lake Victoria port. Cinema.

*Rainy seasons, in most places, are November–December and February–May, when it is hot. Cool in dry season, June–September, cold at night at stations over 4,000 feet.

†"Hospital" implies that a registered medical practitioner is in charge, "dispensary" that a licensed practitioner or Medical Assistant is in charge and that in-patients may or may not be catered for.

‡Except where otherwise indicated it may be expected to find Rest Houses furnished with basic heavy furniture but not equipped with linen, cutlery, utensils, etc.

Appendix C

DISTRICT HEADQUARTERS STATIONS IN TANGANYIKA

Abbreviations and symbols used:—

A.	...	Aerodrome.
B.B.	...	Barclays Bank (D.C.O.).
C. of E.	...	Church of England (i.e. Church Missionary Society and Universities Mission to Central Africa).
E.	...	Electricity.
Hq.	...	Provincial Headquarters.
N.B.I.	...	National Bank of India.

P.	...	Protestant, other (e.g. Lutheran, Mennonite, Moravian, Swedish Free Mission, Adventist, Salvation Army, etc.).
R.C.	...	Roman Catholic.
S.B.S.A.	...	Standard Bank of South Africa.
Tg.	...	Telegraph.
Tp.	...	Telephone.
Wt.	...	Wireless Station.
W.	...	Piped Water Supply.

Station	Altitude in feet	*Average annual rainfall ins.	Mean annual temp. deg.	Normal senior Government staff	†Medical Facilities (showing number of beds in hospitals)	Hotels (No. of beds and minimum single daily tariff)	†Rest Houses	Garages	Shops	Banks	Churches	Sports	Remarks
Lake Province													
Geita A. Tg. Wt. W.	4,200	38	72	12	Geita Mine Hospital 50	—	One	One	Fair	—	C. of E.	Cricket Football Golf Tennis	Grade II, private licensed aerodrome. Near Territory's largest gold mine. Centre of a rapidly developing district.
Nyalikungu (Maswa) W.	4,400	31	72	9	Hospital 30	—	One (unfurnished)	—	Poor	—	—	Football Tennis	Grade III landing strip. With Geita, Kwimba, Mwanza and Shinyanga, one of the five districts forming Sukumaland.
Musoma A. Tg. Wt. W.	3,730	30	74	20	Hospital 135	Musoma Hotel 16 Shs. 30/-	Judges' Lodgings available by arrangement with the Judiciary, Mwanza	Fair	Good	B.B.	P. R.C.	Cricket Football Swimming Tennis	Grade II aerodrome. Lake port. Cinema.

Station					Medical†	Hotels	Houses			Churches	Banks	Sports	Remarks
Mwanza Hq. E.A. Tg. Tp. Wt. W.	3,700	59	74	82	Hospitals 182 Hq. E.A. Med. Research Unit	Mwanza Hotel 53 Shs. 35/-	One (unfurnished)	Good	Good	C. of E. P. R.C.	B.B. SBSA. N.B.I.	Athletics Cricket Football Golf Swimming Tennis Yachting	Grade I aerodrome. Population of approx. 13,700 in 1952 census. Important lake port and centre of Territory's biggest Province. Cinemas.
Nansio (Ukerewe) W. Wt.	3,800	50	72	3	Hospital 56	—	One	—	Poor	P. R.C.	—	Football Tennis	Grade III Landing strip. On an island in the lake.
Ngara W. Wt.	5,900	40	68	3	Dispensary 24	—	One (unfurnished)	—	Poor	C. of E. R.C.	—	Football Tennis Some shooting	Grade II aerodrome. Remotely situated near Ruanda-Urundi border. Temperate climate. Fine scenery.
Ngudu (Kwimba) Tp. W.	4,000	32	75	9	Dispensary 16 Sumve Mission Hospital 120	—	One (unfurnished)	—	Fair	—	—	Shooting Tennis	Grade III Landing strip. Important cotton growing area.
Shinyanga A. Tg. Tp.	3,700	30	74	13	Hospital 80	Diamond Fields Hotel 12 Shs. 25/-	—	Fair	Fair	P. (9 miles) R.C. (3 miles)	S.B. S.A.	Football Shooting Tennis	Landing strip (7 miles). Grade II aerodrome at Mwadui (centre of the Territory's diamond mining industry). Cinema. Mild climate and attractive scenery.
Tarime (North Mara) Wt.	4,700	53	68	7	Dispensary 8	—	One (unfurnished)	—	Fair	P.	—	Football Tennis	
Northern Province Arusha Hq. A. E. Tp. Tg. Wt. W.	4,500	48	67	80	Hospitals 164	King's Hotel 9 Shs. 25/- Meru Hotel 38 Shs. 20/- New Arusha Hotel 72 Shs. 32/- Safari House 56 Shs. 32/50	—	Good	Good	C. of E. P. R.C.	B.B. SBSA.	Athletics Boxing Cricket Football Golf Riding Rugby Tennis	Grade I aerodrome. Centre of European farming area. Usual base for safaris to see or hunt big game. Cinemas.

*Rainy seasons, in most places, are November–December and February–May, when it is hot. Cool in dry season, June–September, cold at night at stations over 4,000 feet.

†"Hospital" implies that a registered medical practitioner is in charge, "dispensary" that a licensed practitioner or Medical Assistant is in charge and that in-patients may or may not be catered for.

‡Except where otherwise indicated it may be expected to find Rest Houses furnished with basic heavy furniture but not equipped with linen, cutlery utensils, etc.

DISTRICT HEADQUARTERS STATIONS IN TANGANYIKA

Abbreviations and symbols used:—

A.	...	Aerodrome.
B.B.	...	Barclays Bank (D.C.O.).
C. of E.	...	Church of England (i.e. Church Missionary Society and Universities Mission to Central Africa).
E.	...	Electricity.
Hq.	...	Provincial Headquarters.
N.B.I.	...	National Bank of India.
P.	...	Protestant, other (e.g. Lutheran, Mennonite, Moravian, Swedish Free Mission, Adventist, Salvation Army, etc.).
R.C.	...	Roman Catholic.
S.B.S.A.	...	Standard Bank of South Africa.
Tg.	...	Telegraph.
Tp.	...	Telephone.
Wt.	...	Wireless Station.
W.	...	Piped Water Supply.

Station	Altitude in feet	*Average annual rainfall ins.	Mean annual temp. deg.	Normal senior Government staff	†Medical Facilities (showing number of beds in hospitals)	Hotels (No. of beds and minimum single daily tariff)	‡Rest Houses	Garages	Shops	Banks	Churches	Sports	Remarks
Northern Province Mbulu W. Wt.	5,700	31	65	14	Hospital 97	—	One	—	Poor	—	P. R.C.	Football Squash Tennis	Spectacular scenery.
Monduli (Masai) Wt. W.	5,200	36	66	8	Hospital 34	—	One	—	Poor	—	P. R.C.	Football Shooting Squash Tennis	24 miles from Arusha. Headquarters of the Masai district.
Moshi A. E. Tg. Tp. Wt. W.	2,700	40	74	60	Hospitals 182	Kilimanjaro Hotel 32 Shs. 25/-; Piccadilly Hotel 20 Shs. 25/-; Coffee Tree Hostelry 30 single 9 double Shs. 5/- per night	—	Good	Good	B.B. N.B.I. SBSA.	C. of E. P. R.C.	Athletics Cricket Football Golf Mountaineering Rugby Tennis	Grade I aerodrome. At foot of Kilimanjaro, Africa's highest peak, and centre of prosperous and progressive coffee growing district. Cinemas.

| Kilwa Tg. Tp. W. | — | 36 | 78 | 4 | Hospital 36 | — | One | — | Poor | — | C. of E. | Fishing Football Swimming Tennis | Grade I aerodrome. Historical remains of great interest. |

A la carte dishes from 1/50 to 4/50 Marangu Hotel 40 Shs. 22/50 Kibo Hotel Kilimanjaro 55 Shs. 20/- plus 5 per cent service Ridgeway Hotel 28 Shs. 27/50 Livingstone Hotel 100 (14 bathrooms) Shs. 28/- Simba Coronation Hotel 6 Shs. 16/- per night

*Rainy seasons, in most places, are November–December and February–May, when it is hot. Cool in dry season, June–September, cold at night at stations over 4,000 feet.

†"Hospital" implies that a registered medical practitioner is in charge, "dispensary" that a licensed practitioner or Medical Assistant is in charge and that in-patients may or may not be catered for.

‡Except where otherwise indicated it may be expected to find Rest Houses furnished with basic heavy furniture but not equipped with linen, cutlery utensils, etc.

Abbreviations and symbols used:—

A... ... Aerodrome.
B.B. ... Barclays Bank (D.C.O.).
C. of E. ... Church of England (i.e. Church Missionary Society and Universities Mission to Central Africa).
E... ... Electricity.
Hq. ... Provincial Headquarters.
N.B.I. ... National Bank of India.

P. ... ... Protestant, other (e.g. Lutheran, Mennonite, Moravian, Swedish Free Mission, Adventist, Salvation Army, etc.).
R.C. ... Roman Catholic.
S.B.S.A. ... Standard Bank of South Africa.
Tg.... ... Telegraph.
Tp.... ... Telephone.
Wt.... ... Wireless Station.
W.... ... Piped Water Supply.

DISTRICT HEADQUARTERS STATIONS IN TANGANYIKA

Station	Altitude in feet	*Average annual rainfall ins.	Mean annual temp. deg.	Normal senior Government staff	†Medical Facilities (showing number of beds in hospitals)	Hotels (No. of beds and minimum single daily tariff)	‡Rest Houses	Garages	Shops	Banks	Churches	Sports	Remarks
Southern Province													
Lindi A. E. Tg. Tp. Wt. W.	—	35	79	30	Hospital 88	Beach Hotel 30 Shs. 22/50 Ras Bura Hotel 12 Shs. 23/50	—	Fair	Fair	B.B. N.B.I. SBSA.	C. of E. R.C.	Deep-sea fishing Football Golf Swimming Tennis	Grade I aerodrome at Kikwetu. Grade III landing strip on Rondo Plateau. m.v. *Mombasa* calls fortnightly on coastal service. Cinema.
Masasi A. Tg. Tp. W.	1,400	34	76	5	Mission Hospital	—	One	—	Poor	—	C. of E. R.C.	Football Tennis	Grade II aerodrome.
Mtwara Hq. A. E. Tg. Tp. W.	—	32	78	30	Hospital 63	Fishing Camp and Club 7 Shs. 25/- Marine Hotel 24 Shs. 25/-	One	Fair	Fair	N.B.I. SBSA.	C. of E. R.C.	Cricket Deep-sea fishing Football Swimming Tennis	Grade I aerodrome. Fine harbour with 2 deep-water berths. Ambitious town plan provides for large scale future development.
Nachingwea A. E. Tg. Tp. W.	1,200	35	74	9	Hospital 81	—	One (unfurnished)	—	Fair	—	C. of E. R.C.	Football Swimming Tennis	Grade I aerodrome. Ex-Headquarters of Southern Province Groundnut Scheme areas, now scene of Tanganyika Agricultural Corporation activities. Terminus of Southern Province Railway.

Station	Alt.				Medical†	Hotel‡				Bank	Church	Sports	Remarks
Newala A. W.	2,600	36	72	6	Mission Hospital	—	One	One	Fair	—	C. of E. R.C.	Football Golf Hockey Tennis	Grade III landing strip. Uniquely situated on edge of 1,000 foot escarpment with magnificent view over Ruvuma River.
Songea A. Tg. Wt. W.	3,800	44	70	15	Hospital 54	Angoni Arms Country Club 8 Shs. 25/-	One	One	Fair	SBSA.	C. of E. R.C.	Football Golf Hockey Tennis	Grade I aerodrome. Remote but fertile and productive district with valuable tobacco industry and coalfields as yet undeveloped.
Tunduru Tg. Wt. W.	2,300	40	74	4	Dispensary 25	—	One	Poor	Poor	—	C. of E.	Football Tennis	Grade III landing strip. Tanganyika's most southerly station.
Southern Highlands Province													
Chunya A. Tg. W.	4,800	31	70	3	Dispensary 41	Chunya Hotel 10 Shs. 22/-	One	—	Fair	—	C. of E. P. R.C.	Football	Grade II aerodrome. Centre of declining Lupa (alluvial) goldfield.
Iringa A. E. Tg. Tp. W.	5,400	30	66	40	Hospital 106	Iringa Hotel 40 Shs. 25/- White Horse Inn 24 Shs. 20/-	—	Good	Good	B.B. SBSA.	P. R.C.	Cricket Football Golf Rugby Shooting Tennis	Grade I aerodromes at Iringa and Southern Highlands Club. Commercial centre of important settlement area. Cinema.
Mbeya Hq. A. E. Tg. Wt. W.	5,800	34	70	50	Hospitals 109	Mbeya Hotel 53 Shs. 25/- Queen's Hotel 27 Shs. 24/-	—	Good	Good	B.B.	C. of E. R.C.	Football Golf Rugby Squash Tennis	Grade I aerodrome. Small but attractive communications and marketing centre with temperate climate. Cinema.

*Rainy seasons, in most places, are November–December and Febuary–May, when it is hot. Cool in dry season, June–September, cold at night at stations over 4,000 feet.

†"Hospital" implies that a registered medical practitioner is in charge, "dispensary" that a licensed practitioner or Medical Assistant is in charge and that in-patients may or may not be catered for.

‡Except where otherwise indicated it may be expected to find Rest Houses furnished with basic heavy furniture but not equipped with linen, cutlery, utensils, etc.

DISTRICT HEADQUARTERS STATIONS IN TANGANYIKA

Abbreviations and symbols used:—

A.... :: Aerodrome.
B.B. :: Barclays Bank (D.C.O.).
C. of E. :: Church of England (i.e. Church Missionary Society and Universities Mission to Central Africa).
E.... :: Electricity.
Hq. :: Provincial Headquarters.
N.B.I. :: National Bank of India.

P. ... :: Protestant, other (e.g. Lutheran, Mennonite, Moravian, Swedish Free Mission, Adventist, Salvation Army, etc.).
R.C. :: Roman Catholic.
S.B.S.A. :: Standard Bank of South Africa.
Tg.... :: Telegraph.
Tp.... :: Telephone.
Wt. :: Wireless Station.
W. .... :: Piped Water Supply.

Station	Altitude in feet	*Average annual rainfall ins.	Mean annual temp. deg.	Normal senior Government staff	†Medical Facilities (showing number of beds in hospitals)	Hotels (No. of beds and minimum single daily tariff)	‡Rest Houses	Garages	Shops	Banks	Churches	Sports	Remarks
Southern Highlands Province													
Njombe A. Tg. W.	6,100	41	61	3	Hospital 30	Njombe Hotel 11 Shs. 25/-	One	One	Fair	—	C. of E. P. R.C.	Football Riding Shooting Tennis	Grade I aerodrome. Centre of important Colonial Development Corporation Wattle Scheme.
Tukuyu (Rungwe) Tg. W.	5,300	99	62	15	Hospital 81	—	One (unfurnished)	—	Good	B.B.	Two	Football Golf Tennis Trout fishing	Headquarters of progressive and densely populated district. High rainfall.
Tanga Province													
Handeni Tg. Tp.	2,200	34	—	5	Dispensary 24 Mission Hospital at Kideleko (5 miles)	—	One (fully furnished)	—	Poor	—	C. of E. R.C.	Football Squash Tennis	Has good example of old German "Boma" building.
Korogwe E. Tg. Tp.	1,000	45	76	15	Hospital 69	Korogwe Hotel 22 Shs. 25/-	—	—	Fair	B.B. SBSA.	C. of E. R.C.	Football Game and bird shooting Tennis	Important centre of sisal industry. Cinema.

Station	Alt.				Medical	Hotels				Banks	Churches	Sports	Remarks
Lushoto E. Tg. Tp. W.	4,600	43	64	19	Hospital 50	Jaegertal 20 Shs. 20/- Lawns Hotel 31 Shs. 27/50 Magamba Country Club (5 miles) 41 Shs. 27/50 Soni Falls Hotel (10 miles) 25 Shs. 25/-	—	Fair	Good	—	C. of E. P. R.C.	Fishing Football Golf Riding Tennis	Grade I aerodrome at Mombo (20 miles). Attractive small town in European settled Usambara Mountains.
Pangani E. Tg. Tp.	—	47	78	3	Hospital 22	One	—	—	Poor	—	—	Fishing Football Swimming	Quiet coastal town with historical associations. Falls on Pangani River, 40 miles inland, an important source of hydroelectric power.
Same (Pare) A. Tg. Tp. W.	2,800	22	72	7	Dispensary 30	One	—	—	Poor	—	P.	Football Shooting Tennis	Grade II aerodrome. Small centre at foot of Pare Range, the mountains being thickly inhabited by progressive Pare tribe.
Tanga Hq. A. E. Tg. Tp. Wt. W.	—	53	79	80	Hospitals 313	New Hotel 12 Shs. 20/- Palm Court Hotel 16 Shs. 30/- Park Hotel 25 Shs. 26/- Sea View Hotel 22 Shs. 25/- Splendid Hotel 13 Shs. 20/-	—	Good	Good	B.B. N.B.I. SBSA.	C. of E. R.C.	Cricket Football Golf Swimming Tennis Yachting	Grade I aerodrome. Tanganyika's second town and port with a population well over 20,000. Centre and port for Territory's main sisal growing area. Cinemas.

*Rainy seasons, in most places, are November–December and February–May, when it is hot. Cool in dry season, June–September, cold at night at stations over 4,000 feet.

†"Hospital" implies that a registered medical practitioner is in charge, "dispensary" that a licensed practitioner or Medical Assistant is in charge and that in-patients may or may not be catered for.

‡Except where otherwise indicated it may be expected to find Rest Houses furnished with basic heavy furniture but not equipped with linen, cutlery, utensils, etc.

Appendix C

DISTRICT HEADQUARTERS STATIONS IN TANGANYIKA

Abbreviations and symbols used:—

A. ... ... Aerodrome.
B.B. ... Barclays Bank (D.C.O.).
C. of E. ... Church of England (i.e. Church Missionary Society and Universities Mission to Central Africa).
E. ... Electricity.
Hq. ... Provincial Headquarters.
N.B.I. ... National Bank of India.

P. ... ... Protestant, other (e.g. Lutheran, Mennonite, Moravian, Swedish Free Mission, Adventist, Salvation Army, etc.).
R.C. ... Roman Catholic.
S.B.S.A. ... Standard Bank of South Africa.
Tg. ... Telegraph.
Tp. ... Telephone.
Wt. ... Wireless Station.
W. ... Piped Water Supply.

Station	Altitude in feet	*Average annual rainfall ins.	Mean annual temp. deg.	Normal senior Government staff	†Medical Facilities (showing number of beds in hospitals)	Hotels (No. of beds and minimum single daily tariff)	‡Rest Houses	Garages	Shops	Banks	Churches	Sports	Remarks
Western Province													
Kahama Tg. Tp. W.	4,000	38	74	6	Hospital 61	—	One	—	Fair	—	P. R.C.	Football Tennis	With Nzega and Tabora one of the three Nyamwezi Districts.
Kasulu W.	4,500	43	71	7	Hospital 17 Mission Hospital (4 miles)	—	One	—	Poor	—	C. of E. R.C.	Football Golf Shooting Tennis	Grade III landing strip. With Kibondo, a centre of a remote but developing highland area bordering Ruanda-Urundi.
Kibondo Wt. W.	5,000	45	70	7	Hospital 31	—	One (unfurnished)	—	Poor	—	C. of E.	Football Golf Tennis	Grade III Landing strip. Mild climate and attractive scenery.
Kigoma A. E. Tg. Tp. W.	2,550	37	74	19	Hospital 64	Stanley Hotel 28 Shs. 25/-	One (equipped)	Poor	Fair	—	C. of E. R.C.	Boating Football Golf Swimming Tennis	Grade I aerodrome. Grade III landing strip at Uvinza. Five miles from Ujiji, historic meeting place of Stanley and Livingstone Western terminus of Central Railway and a beautifully situated Lake Tanganyika port. Cinema.

Station					Hospital/Medical	Hotel	Rest Houses		Water	Bank	Religion	Sports	Remarks
Mpanda A. Wt. W.	3,600	37	73	4	Uruwira Mine Hospital	Mpanda Hotel 7 Shs. 25/-	One	—	Fair	—	P. R.C.	Football Tennis	Licensed Grade I aerodrome at mine. Terminus of branch line from Central Railway serving Uruwira Minerals Ltd., a developing mine producing lead, copper, etc.
Nzega Tg. Tp. W.	4,000	31	73	9	Hospital 40	—	One	—	Fair	—	P. R.C.	Football Shooting Swimming	Small local marketing centre on Nyamwezi steppe.
Sumbawanga (Ufipa) A. Tg. Wt. W.	5,650	32	66	5	Hospital 24	—	One	—	Poor	—	—	Football Squash Tennis	Grade II aerodrome. Small centre of remote but healthy and fertile district with development potential.
Tabora Hq. A. E. Tg. Tp. Wt. W.	4,100	35	73	105	Hospitals 200	Railway Hotel 42 Shs. 25/-	None	Fair	Fair	SBSA.	C. of E. P. R.C.	Athletics Cricket Football Golf Squash Tennis	Grade I aerodrome. Historic associations as *entrepot* on old slave and ivory caravan route, and for stay of Livingstone and Stanley in 1872. Important railway centre. 1952 population approx. 14,000. Cinema.

*Rainy seasons, in most places, are November–December and February–May, when it is hot. Cool in dry season, June–September, cold at night at stations over 4,000 feet.

†"Hospital" implies that a registered medical practitioner is in charge, "dispensary" that a licensed practitioner or Medical Assistant is in charge and that in-patients may or may not be catered for.

‡Except where otherwise indicated it may be expected to find Rest Houses furnished with basic heavy furniture but not equipped with linen, cutlery, utensils, etc.

APPENDIX D
CHIEF EVENTS OF THE YEARS 1955 TO 1957

When the main events of these three years, which it is the purpose of this appendix to record, come to be written for a further edition of this Handbook, it may be that economic or social developments will be found to provide the most significant features of the period; without the benefit of historical perspective, however, the rapid constitutional reforms, both in central and local government, claim first attention.

LEGISLATIVE COUNCIL

As we have seen (pp. 135–6), the committee appointed in 1949 under the chairmanship of the Attorney-General, now Sir Charles Mathew, recommended the introduction of parity of the three main races on the representative side of the legislature. A new constitution was accordingly laid before Parliament on 22nd March, 1955 and brought into operation in Tanganyika on the following day. It provided for a Council with a Speaker, an appointment which was first made in 1953*. The Government side comprised thirty-one members, eight *ex officio*, being the officers of Government responsible for groups of departments under the Membership System, and twenty-three nominated members, fourteen of whom were unofficials (including the six unofficial members of Executive Council) and nine government officials appointed in a personal capacity. No provision was made in the constitution as to the proportion of unofficial to official nominated members and their numbers have varied from meeting to meeting, the practice being to appoint, often as a temporary nominated member, a head of department having an important piece of legislation coming before Council at that meeting. On the opposite side of the House there were thirty representative members—ten Africans, ten Asians and ten Europeans—one of each race representing the nine constituencies which are the eight provinces of Tanganyika, and Dar es Salaam, the remaining three being appointed to represent the general interests of the territory.

The reconstituted council opened its first meeting on 19th April, 1955 and a graceful tribute was paid by the unofficial members of the former council by their invitation to Sir Charles Mathew to attend the ceremonial opening of the new legislature which his chairmanship of the Constitutional Committee six years before had done so much to promote.

On the Government side of the Council the nominated unofficials have on occasion taken a liberal view of their right to criticize Government on points of detail while pledged to follow the Government lead on principle and policy; the *ex officio* members and the departments for which they answer have responded to the stimulus of questions and criticism from the other side of the House. The representative members have been temperate in opposing government measures and have brought wise counsel to debate. It has been exceptional for members to divide on a racial basis and the tendency has been for all the representatives from a particular constituency or constituencies to press for measures in which they have a common interest; while members have not hesitated to present a united opposition when they have seen fit. Although equipped with a majority of one vote which enabled it to carry its policies into law, the Government on its part has deferred to the views of the representative members and many proposals have been modified as a result.

While it is early to assess the value of this revision of the constitution, it is likely that its most notable achievement will be judged to be representation on a constituency basis,† which has promoted a non-racial approach to common problems, rather than the introduction of the parity principle, which, though expedient in the present stage of the territory's development, is recognized as likely to perpetuate a racial outlook.

---

*Legislative Council formerly met with the Governor as President.

†At the end of 1957 the Lake Province was divided into two constituencies, the number of representative members being increased from thirty to thirty-three. A corresponding increase was made on the Government side, which now has thirty-four members (the Chief Secretary, Attorney-General, seven Ministers and twenty-five nominated members.)

ELECTIONS TO LEGISLATIVE COUNCIL

The importance attached to constitutional matters was marked by the creation in 1956 of the new office of Member for Constitutional Affairs. In May, 1956, a committee was appointed by the Governor under the Chairmanship of the Chief Secretary, with six unofficial Members of Legislative Council selected in consultation with the Tanganyika Unofficial Members' Organization, and three unofficials, to consider Government's proposals for elections to Legislative Council and any other proposals which might be presented to it by the public. The Committee made a unanimous report in October, 1956, in which it recommended a broadening of the original franchise proposals. Its recommendations regarding the qualifications required by voters were accepted in full by the Secretary of State for the Colonies on the recommendation of the Governor; those for candidates however with two reservations, since Government wished to adhere to the higher income and education qualifications in its original proposals.*

The Bill providing for elections to Legislative Council was passed in June, 1956, and establishes a common electoral roll based on a qualitative franchise and the election by voters of one African, one Asian and one European candidate from each constituency. Elections will be held throughout the territory during the two years 1958–1959 and, as the life of the Council has been extended from three to five years (being dissolved in 1957) the elected representative members will hold their seats for at least three years before the next dissolution. The Northern, Tanga, Eastern, Western and Southern Highlands Provinces constituencies have been chosen for elections in the first year; the size of the Lake Province, which has had to be subdivided into two constituencies, and the administrative difficulty of holding elections simultaneously in all constituencies, having necessitated the postponement of elections in these important areas until 1959. Thereafter elections will be held at the same time throughout the territory.

In order to register for a vote three conditions must be fulfilled, of which two are obligatory: a man (or woman) must be twenty-one and must have lived in Tanganyika for three out of the last five years. The third condition may be any of the following: education up to Standard VIII or its equivalent; or an income of not less than £150 a year; or tenure of one of the offices listed in s. 9 of the Legislative Councils Elections Ordinance—which includes membership of Legislative Council, a Municipal Council, Local Government or Township Authority and numerous other consultative bodies at provincial and district levels; or an appointment as chief or other responsible position in a Native Authority; or the holding of a position as head of a clan or kindred group described by the Swahili word *ukoo*.

The qualifications for candidates are higher, the minimum age being twenty-five and residential qualification either a Certificate of Permanent Residence or residence in Tanganyika for four out of the past six years. A candidate must be literate in English (in order to understand Legislative Council documents) and speak either English or Swahili fluently. A necessary alternative condition is either education up to Standard XII or an income of £200 a year or former membership of Legislative Council. Further conditions are nomination by at least twenty-five registered voters (of whom ten must be of the candidate's own race), payment of a deposit of £25 and freedom and consent to take the Oath of Allegiance.

THE MINISTERIAL SYSTEM

As a corollary to the enlargement of Legislative Council and the great increase in public business which has resulted, central government has been reorganized; the former *ex officio* members of Legislative Council have been appointed Ministers and six new appointments of Assistant Minister created. The latter posts have been filled in the first instance by unofficials, of whom four are African, one Asian and one European. Each Ministry has had appointed to it a senior civil servant as Ministerial Secretary. This as yet embryonic

---

*Government Paper No. 1 of 1957: Report of the Committee appointed to Study Government's proposals regarding the Qualifications for Voters and Candidates for Elections to Legislative Council together with copies of despatches exchanged between H.E. the Governor and the Secretary of State for the Colonies.

Ministerial system has what are and should be the essential features of such a system, namely: a Minister who is freed to devote himself to the formulation of balanced policies (he will, for example, no longer be called upon to serve on statutory Boards or Committees); an Assistant Minister who besides being vested with executive powers and responsibilities will have the duty of adjusting the direction of policy to practical considerations and the needs of the people; and permanent officials whose duty it is to see that the policy is founded on complete data and technical advice and, when put into practice, is equipped with the best organization and machinery that can be devised.

LOCAL GOVERNMENT

The Local Government Ordinance, an enabling Ordinance which was introduced in 1953 and provided for three types of local government council, county councils, town councils and local councils, has already been described (p. 137). The Ordinance had three essential features: each council was required to be established under an individual and separate instrument requiring the approval of the Legislative Council, no council might be set up without the consent of the people affected, and membership was not confined to any one race.

RURAL LOCAL GOVERNMENT

The three years under review have been a period of experiment to find the most efficient unit which the new county and local councils might serve. The Lake Province was selected for the first County Council as it already had a Provincial Council which, though mainly advisory, controlled a budget and was known to and accepted by the Native Authorities. To avoid misunderstanding by the latter the South East Lake County Council was extended to cover Ukerewe, Musoma and North Mara as well as the five Sukumaland districts, and after running for twelve months as a shadow organization to gain experience was established by Instrument in May, 1955. Townships within the County area were excluded from it. The Council comprised fifty-four members appointed by the Member for Local Government (now Minister for Local Government and Administration) under the initial chairmanship of the Deputy Provincial Commissioner of the Lake Province. The Member was required by statute to appoint the eight District Commissioners of the administrative districts included in the county, eight Lake Province chiefs and the provincial representatives of the Natural Resources and Social Services departments, together with the Divisional Engineer and Revenue Officer. The Council's functions were permissive rather than mandatory, covering natural resources extension work, social and public health services, and general services including the making of roads. It had three main committees: Finance and General Purposes, Natural Resources, and Social Services; with District Committees under the chairmanship of each District Commissioner, which were in fact the main executive bodies of the Council. The constitution of the District Committees has been increased to give additional representation to Native Authorities; four African members of the Native Authority District Councils now being included. The tendency is for these District Committees to assume greater powers and become increasingly independent of the parent council.

Experience and a close examination of the working of this council has shown its area of jurisdiction to be too large to arouse and sustain public interest and confusion has arisen between the proper functions of central and local government.

In contrast to the County Council, the two Local Councils set up in the Mafia and Newala Districts have attained no small measure of success. Both have evolved from Native Authorities at the district level (to which non-officials had already been co-opted) and, as required by law, were established under individual instruments. The Newala Council has the District Commissioner as chairman, five liwalis, one assistant liwali and thirty-five other members nominated by the Provincial Commissioner. The main work is done through committees, of which the Finance Committee is the most important. An interesting comment on this development was made by an African representative member of Legislative Council, who was also a liwali on the Newala Local Council:

"In Newala we have got three races living side by side, Asian, European and African. Before we had our Local Council we had an African Advisory District Council. Sometimes a member brought up a subject which concerned other races—and there was nobody to represent them. What we used to do was to complain and the minutes were sent to the District Commissioner, who did whatever he saw fit; whether he informed those people or not we did not know. Then finally we thought that as we knew that Europeans—I speak particularly of the missionaries who have done a great deal in the development of the Southern Province—would remain there, and Asians would remain there, how could we live side by side with these people if we did not meet them? How were they going to understand us? . . . So we thought that the only way we could get together was by having a meeting where we could discuss the common problems. . . ."

The conclusion drawn from these experiments with county and local councils is that the efficient unit for local government must in the meantime remain the administrative district. The future of the South East Lake County Council has yet to be determined but it is apparent that the county pattern, incorporating several districts, will not necessarily be repeated. The current proposal which is being considered by the Legislative Council in the form of an amending bill to the Local Government Ordinance provides enabling legislation to establish a District Council to serve a whole district. Unlike the Local Council, however, the District Council, aided by central government funds, would take over certain services previously performed by government, in addition to carrying out the services hitherto the responsibility of the Native Authority at district level. There is a fair possibility of a demand for this type of council since in thirty of the fifty-seven administrative districts non-Africans have by invitation been informally associated with Native Authorities with considerable success.

ELECTIONS IN URBAN AREAS

In 1956 the Local Government Elections Bill was passed. This is another enabling measure providing for elections to be held in all town council areas and in the municipality of Dar es Salaam. Each area will have to initiate the holding of elections by seeking an amendment to its statutory instrument, thus ensuring that this step is taken at the will of the people affected. The Ordinance provides for candidates for local government elections to be twenty-five years of age and confers a vote on all adult ratepayers, both men and women. The municipality of Dar es Salaam and two of the existing nine town councils, Arusha and Morogoro, will hold elections in 1958.

LOCAL GOVERNMENT TRAINING

The greater responsibility which has devolved on the local government authorities at all levels has called for executive and clerical officers of better education and training than was required before the war. The Local Government School at Mzumbe in the Eastern Province was started in 1953 to meet this need. Students who attend are generally chiefs, and clerks selected by the Native Authorities. The main subjects taught are court work, accountancy and the principles of local government finance and administration. The school has recently been enlarged to take one hundred students at a time, of which eighty will study local government subjects and twenty attend a course on co-operation run by the department of Co-operative Development.*

SEPARATION OF JUDICIAL AND EXECUTIVE FUNCTIONS

In Dodoma a permanent African magistrate has been appointed in place of what used to be the Dodoma Chiefs' Council Court, but progress in this separation is variable from area to area. In the Lake Province, for instance, the Sukuma chiefs cling to their judicial powers, while at Bukoba, across the lake, the Court of Appeal is now staffed by professional court-holders and appeals at chiefdom level are heard by the same court-holders acting as itinerant justices.

---

*A detailed description of Local Government authorities and organization is given on pages 316 ff.

THE HIGH COMMISSION AND CENTRAL LEGISLATIVE ASSEMBLY

Resolutions were passed by the legislatures of the three East African Governments extending the life of the East Africa High Commission and Central Legislative Assembly for a further four years from 1956. A suggestion made in debate by an African representative member of the Tanganyika Legislative Council led to an increase in the number of unofficial members from each territory in the Assembly. Of the eight members who represent Tanganyika, only one of the two nominated members appointed by the Governor is required to be an official; three unofficial members are appointed by the Governor and three further unofficial members are elected by the representative members of Legislative Council from amongst the unofficial members of that Council. There is thus far closer association of unofficials with the working of the East Africa High Commission than was possible under the former constitution of the Assembly, which had only three unofficial members appointed by each of the Governors of the three territories.

POLITICAL ORGANIZATIONS

During the three years under review two major political associations which are territorial in scope have emerged: the Tanganyika African National Union which was formed as a result of a territorial conference called in June, 1954, by the former Tanganyika African Association which it superseded, and the United Tanganyika Party formed a year later with the support of the majority of the unofficial Members of Legislative Council of all races. The Tanganyika African National Union, whose membership is restricted to Africans, has as its principal aims "to prepare the people of Tanganyika for self-government and independence", and "to work relentlessly for the establishment of a democratic form of government". The United Tanganyika Party, which claims membership in the ratio of 60 per cent African, 30 per cent Asian and 10 per cent European, is pledged to a policy of multi-racialism with the ultimate objective of self-government within the Commonwealth.

THE REPORT OF THE ROYAL COMMISSION ON EAST AFRICA

The Times hailed the report of the Royal Commission on Land and Population in East Africa with the comment: "The Report has about it an intellectual incisiveness and doctrinal clarity characteristic of some of the great commissions of the past. Its conclusions lead one to suppose that besides the economic problem the political one is less radical and will more easily be solved once the economy is sound". The Commission's terms of reference were wide but the most important was an examination of the measures necessary to achieve an improved standard of living. Its members were impressed by the poverty of the East African region as a whole and the extent to which this poverty was conditioned by physical factors, low rainfall, poor soil and disease. It deplored the failure to utilize on a regional basis the resources which were available, finding these resources divided not only between territories and communities, but even between one tribe and another. It recognized that a society having a paucity of mineral wealth and industrial techniques must for long be dependent on an agricultural economy. The first need was thus to revolutionize the present subsistence level of agricultural production and enable the African cultivator to enter and play an increasing part in a modern exchange economy. The proper use of land (as distinct from bringing more areas of land into marginal production) was essential. It followed that until agricultural productivity could be increased a limit was set to the expansion of the domestic market, hence industrial development should not be regarded as a means of relief from the pressure of over-population, where this occurred, but as a complement to agricultural improvement. The establishment of a modern exchange economy called for improved communications, freedom of trade from the complex of restrictions intended to protect the African producer, and urban development designed to integrate the way of life of industrial workers with that of the immigrant communities living in the towns.

The Commission's advocacy of individualization of land ownership with a degree of mobility in the transfer and disposition of land which, without ignoring existing property rights, will enable access to land for economic use, is probably the most important recommendation of the Report; on the one hand it is regarded as a fundamental step towards the evolution of a modern exchange economy and on the other as cutting across the deep-rooted tradition of customary tribal land tenure.   The Tanganyika Government has accepted the need to revise the Land Ordinance to provide for a system of individual tenure with suitable safeguards regarding fragmentation and the transfer of lands between Africans and non-Africans.   It stresses however that the adoption of a novel system of individual tenure must be gradual, and progress will vary widely throughout the territory.   Registration for registration's sake can have no appeal to an African peasant and the prospect of increased productivity of the land will require demonstration; hence the first areas to be selected for adjudication and registration of existing rights should be those where a system of individual tenure has already evolved and is understood.

The practical implementation of all the recommendations made by the Commission and acceptable to the Governments is hampered by shortage of funds to give effect to them; the Governor of Tanganyika's dispatch to the Secretary of State setting out the measure of his Government's agreement with the Report gives an analysis of the amount of money required compared with that available and estimated to be available over the ten-year period 1955–1964.   This shows a shortage of some £48 million over the ten years and, while the Royal Commission Report will form the basis of policy for many years to come and much can be done without great capital expenditure, progress is unlikely to be spectacular without the larger capital sums required.

THE ROYAL TOUR

The visit of Her Royal Highness the Princess Margaret to Tanganyika for eleven days in October 1956 made that year "the year of the Princess".   Written accounts of royal tours tend to depict an endless number of formal functions succeeding each other in the right places and always attended by the right people; too often they suggest that both the royal personage and the spectators may have suffered a surfeit of standing in too hot a sun. So let it be said for the benefit of posterity that the visit of Her Royal Highness was, for the populace, great fun and that the charm and grace of the Royal visitor made them feel that she, too, had enjoyed it.   Thousands of people of all races had during the weeks and months preceding the visit divided their time between their normal avocations and working for the success of the tour—and were happy to do so.

Her Royal Highness arrived at Dar es Salaam in the Royal Yacht *Britannia* early on Monday, 8th October, a public holiday, and was greeted by cheering schoolchildren massed at the harbour entrance.   Her first function was to open the new deep-water berths on which some £4 million has been spent, a quarter of this sum being contributed by the Belgian Congo for one of the berths which is used for Congo traffic.   Later she opened the new Group Hospital in Dar es Salaam, which will be the centre for medical training in Tanganyika. At the *Baraza* held at the airport the Princess delighted spectators by mingling with the crowds to watch displays of African dancing.

In the provinces Her Royal Highness attended *barazas* in Tanga, Tabora, Iringa, Mwanza and Arusha and, as in Dar es Salaam, had presented to her the District Commissioner and leading Africans from each district.   The provinces vied with each other in the magnificence of their displays of traditional dancing in the confidence that the royal visitor's knowledge and interest in music and dancing assured them of an appreciative audience.   At Ngurdoto Crater near Arusha she had a glimpse of wild life and at the Moshi Trade and Agricultural Show an indication of what Tanganyika can grow.   At Mwadui she saw the late Dr. Williamson's diamond mine although he himself was absent through illness and unable to present the fine diamond brooch which he has since given her.

THE SERENGETI NATIONAL PARK

Much public interest had been taken in the Serengeti plains and their wild life had had some measure of protection for twenty years before the plains were formally included in a national park administered by trustees under an Ordinance introduced in 1951.   The Park extended over some 4,800 square miles, from the eastern side of the Ngorongoro Crater in the Northern Province to Baridi Hill in the Lake Province, providing sanctuary for herds of grazing animals and their attendant carnivora on a scale unequalled elsewhere in Africa, or indeed anywhere in the world. When the park was set up the Masai then living in the area where not disturbed, since it was then thought that the exercise of their existing rights would in no way conflict with the purposes of the Park. Unfortunately the Park was established during a cycle of low rainfall which particularly affected grazing in Masailand, while water supplies, which had been intended as an inducement to Masai living in the Park to move out of it, failed. The Masai, so far from moving out, moved into the Park in greater numbers, and a clash between the interests of a people who had for centuries roved the plains at will and of the wild life, which it was the purpose of the Park to preserve, was inevitable.

In 1956 the Trustees were forced to the conclusion that the continued presence of the Masai and their domestic livestock within a National Park was irreconcilable with its purposes; they therefore proposed the establishment of a new Park freed from human habitation in a limited area within the old Park boundaries, the remainder being accessible to the Masai, subject only to close control of hunting. This suggestion formed the basis of the proposals laid before the Legislature in a White Paper* which led to protests from wild life societies in all parts of the world. The Fauna Preservation Society commissioned Professor Pearsall to visit the Serengeti during the dry season of November and December 1956 and his report was published in April, 1957. This Report, commended for the excellence of its data and inferences, divided the Park into Eastern and Western Regions with different conservation problems: the east being concerned with water supplies, forests and pasture and the west with the preservation of the vast herds of plains animals migrating there each year during the breeding season. Its conclusions have been largely accepted by the Committee of Inquiry appointed by the Governor in 1957 under the Chairmanship of Sir Barclay Nihil (until recently President of the East African Court of Appeal), as the basis for its recommendations. The Report of the Serengeti Committee of Inquiry, 1957, has been published and the Government's decisions upon it is awaited. The Report states firmly as a principle "that a National Park established for the preservation of wild animal life in Africa is not likely to succeed as a long-term project unless human rights are excluded from the area so designated," but has endeavoured to set its proposals on what is feasible of attainment both in terms of finance and existing human interest.

DISCRIMINATORY LEGISLATION

One of the chapters of the Laws of Tanganyika which was formerly cited as discriminatory concerned the restriction on the sale of spirituous liquors to Africans, who were permitted to buy only beer or "native liquors". A committee had been set up in 1953 to look into the matter and its recommendations led to the passage of the Intoxicating Liquors Bill in 1955, which removed any discrimination by race in the sale of strong drink. The measure was warmly supported in the Legislature by all the African members who, by contrast, were not happy about a further item of legislation destined to remove discrimination of this kind. The Credit to Natives (Restriction) Ordinance has been referred to on page 95 and the passage of a Bill repealing this Ordinance, introduced into Legislative Council in 1957, has been deferred pending further consultation with Native Authorities and Chiefs concerning the wisdom of removing this law from the statute book.

1957 CENSUS

A territorial census was held in 1957, non-Africans being counted separately in February, Africans in August. The results of the non-African census are now complete and show a total of 123,747, compared with the earlier figure in 1952 of 95,494. Numbers by race are as follows:

Indians and Pakistanis	...	72,167		Goans	...	...	...	4,788
Europeans ...	...	...	20,619		Somalis	...	...	...	3,152
Arabs	...	...	...	19,175		Others	...	...	...	3,846

123,747

The provisional figure for the total African population has been given as 8,654,000, but this remains to be checked by further analysis by districts.

*Sessional Paper No. 1 of 1956. The Serengeti National Park.

ECONOMIC CONDITIONS

Statistics for the year 1957 are not yet available, but the main figures for 1955 and 1956 may be mentioned. The year 1956 was a good one for the production of the major crops, although prices, except in the case of coffee, were slightly lower than in 1955; but the value of total production was higher than in recent years.

Exports (including exports to Kenya and Uganda) were valued at £46·8 million compared with £37·9 million in 1955. Imports (including imports from Kenya and Uganda) were valued at approximately £40 million compared with £48 million in 1955. Thus, compared with an overall trade deficit of £10 million in 1955, a surplus of over £6 million was achieved in 1956. The decline in imports was due in part to overstocking which had taken place in 1955 and in part to the effects of credit restriction in the United Kingdom.

There was a decline in capital investment compared with 1955. The import of producer capital goods was £8·3 million compared with £9·2 million in 1955 and other producer materials imported were valued at £10·7 million compared with £13·6 million in 1955. The decline in urban building activity which started in 1955 continued in 1956. External trade in cement fell by 55,000 tons, although inter-territorial trade rose by 10,000 tons. Capital expenditure on industrial and agricultural machinery remained roughly unchanged but the value of transport equipment imported fell by 20 per cent, due mainly to a decrease in purchases of railway stock.

Consumer prices were relatively stable during the year, the Dar es Salaam cost of living index increasing by only 2 per cent over the year; while prices of some goods consumed mainly by Africans fell during the year.

THE DEVELOPMENT PLAN

As already stated, the original Ten-Year Development and Welfare Plan for Tanganyika drawn up in 1946 was replaced by a revised plan covering the years 1950 to 1956, the latter plan in turn being replaced by another for 1955–60, mainly on account of the general trend of economic and social development whereby priorities have had to be altered and of the necessity to re-estimate costs which have risen considerably over the last few years. The revised plan involves an expenditure of approximately £26 million comprising the following:

	£
Development of Natural Resources	4,950,000
Communications	7,470,000
Urban Development	3,215,000
Electricity	2,000,000
Social Services:	
Medical	1,400,000
Education	3,793,667
Broadcasting and Films	100,000
Public Buildings	1,950,000
African Urban Housing	970,000

THE SOCIAL SERVICES PLANS

As both the Education and Medical Plans 1956/61 end a year after the main territorial development plan, they merit some mention, particularly as both were introduced into the Legislature on motions seeking their approval as statements of departmental planning policy to be implemented as and when the necessary funds became available. The Revised Ten-Year Plan for African Education (described on page 140) was successfully concluded at the end of 1956 and had exceeded its objective in enrolling one-third of all children of school age in primary schools, a fact which was taken into account in preparing the current plan. A notable achievement in the last years of the plan was the development of technical education, two trade schools being established at Ifunda and Moshi during that time to give training in a wide variety of trades, while a technical institute to provide the intermediate level of technical education was built in Dar es Salaam with the assistance of Colonial Development and Welfare funds. Instruction at the advanced level will be available at the Royal Technical College, Nairobi, to which this territory contributes. The current education plan provides for a doubling of secondary schools by the end of the five-year period and for Higher School Certificate classes to be established at three schools by 1959. The number of middle schools will also be doubled and development of primary education will be concentrated on the abolition of double sessions (a feature of the first plan which has been severely criticized) by building additional classrooms at existing primary schools, and on the introduction of English in Standard III.

The Medical Plan covering the five years 1956/61 provides in fact for another instalment, as it were, in the implementation of the report by Dr. E. D. Pridie (now Sir Eric Pridie), Chief Medical Officer at the Colonial Office, which he made in 1949 and which was accepted by the Legislature in 1950 as the basis for medical development. The Pridie Report comprised, briefly, a plan of balanced development of preventive and curative services with the objective of supplying one hospital bed per thousand of the population. As it is surmised that the African population in its present stage of development can only be expected to accept preventive medicine through knowledge of the curative services, the greater part of the capital expenditure under the plan is designed to expand hospital services, coupled with an intensive staff training programme.

TRUSTS AND CORPORATIONS

It has been seen that as far back as 1951 the Serengeti National Park had been put under the care of a Board of Trustees, and since then there has been a marked trend towards this type of management for important projects in which there is a clear advantage in having members of the public associated from the outset, particularly when those concerned can bring long experience or highly specialized knowledge to their task.

An example is the Tanganyika Agricultural Corporation, set up by a special Ordinance in 1954, to which was transferred in March, 1955, the undertaking (the outcome of the Groundnut Scheme) with which the Overseas Food Corporation had been charged: "a scheme of large-scale experimental development to establish the economics of clearing and mechanized, or partly mechanized, agriculture, in tropical conditions."* The Corporation has not only continued the experimental work which was proceeding at Kongwa, Urambo and Nachingwea, and consolidated them into permanent viable undertakings, but has expanded its scope far beyond that anticipated by its predecessor. At Nachingwea, the best agricultural region of the three former O.F.C. areas, in addition to the Corporation's own production schemes, an African tenant farmer scheme has been established with some success; at Urambo the promising results obtained from growing flue-cured tobacco suggested its consolidation into an economic communal enterprise, with other crops and possibly stock playing their part in future development. The Corporation remains the landlord and acts as an administrator and advisory body to the tenants, who thus have available to them the experience gained from former experiments in the area. At Kongwa the hazardous rainfall added doubts as to the success of large-scale mechanized agriculture in that area, and the cattle ranching project, started in 1950, has been expanded to cover the whole acreage of cleared land. The farmers on the African tenant scheme in this area enjoyed in 1956 a particularly successful year.

In addition to the "transferred" undertakings described, the Corporation has by separate agreement with the Tanganyika Government undertaken a scheme to investigate, with the help of experts provided by the Food and Agriculture Organization and a substantial grant from Her Majesty's Government, the potentialities of the Rufiji Basin as an area for extensive agricultural production. A second project is the Ruvu Ranching Scheme in an area of some 78,000 acres fifty miles west of Dar es Salaam: a small herd of cattle was introduced in 1956 to assess the incidence of tsetse and, when fully stocked, this ranch is intended to hold some 8,000 head.

---

*Cmd. 8125.

The Royal Commission in its Report* commended the Tanganyika Agricultural Corporation's work, which it described as the application of managerial and technical knowledge and of capital to modernize the indigenous economy so that the people are finally left with both the trained ability and experience with which to create their own capital for their own future development.

The Makonde Water Corporation came into being on the 1st January, 1955, and was also the subject of a special Ordinance, passed in 1954. Its purpose is to convey water to the Makonde plateau, a populous and fertile area, whose inhabitants have however been accustomed in the dry season to travel many miles for water, a journey which involved a descent of a thousand feet into the Ruvuma Valley. The shortage of water had led to the over-crowding of the areas nearest to supplies, with consequent reduction in soil fertility. Investigations showed that water could only be pumped to the area at high capital cost, and it was thereupon decided that this major engineering operation should be administered by a corporation consisting of all the tax-payers of the Newala District. The necessary capital has been borrowed from a local bank and the scheme underwritten by the Tanganyika Government up to the sum of £600,000. A special annual water rate of Shs. 10/- has been levied and water is sold from distribution points at ten cents for three gallons. Sales have increased steadily as water supplies have been extended and the Corporation is confident of its ability to meet its commitments as they fall due.

The Board of Trustees of the Tanganyika Higher Education Trust Fund was established in 1956, again under a special Ordinance; it has not less than six members, three of whom must be unofficials, and its purpose is to husband and increase the Fund set up under the Ordinance with, as its first gift, £711,111 derived from Custodian of Enemy Property moneys. The Fund is intended for the development of institutions of higher education in Tanganyika, and the provision of an endowment fund for scholarships and bursaries. The Board of Trustees may accept gifts to the Fund, including land, and is required to produce schemes for increasing the money accruing to it.

Another educational trust (under another ordinance) has been created for the management of St. Michael's and St. George's Schools, which are secondary schools intended initially for European boys and girls. The schools have been built from the portion of Custodian of Enemy Property money allotted to European education and are situated at Iringa in the Southern Highlands Province.

Broadcasting has grown from a small experimental service started with an old Army transmitter in July, 1951, into a service capable of broadcasting to all parts of the territory. New studios have been built and new and powerful transmitters installed, largely from Colonial Development and Welfare funds. Under Ordinance No. 4 of 1956 the Tanganyika Broadcasting Corporation was set up, with the object of giving the broadcasting service a more independent character. The Corporation consists of a chairman and a board of not more than seven members, half of whom must be unofficials. The Corporation is responsible for maintaining, through its employees, a broadcasting service "for the information, education and entertainment of the public"; it derives its funds from government in the form of grants, and from revenue earned by licences and advertising; it must submit an annual report and audited accounts to the Chief Secretary.

As will be seen from this brief description of them, the range of functions entrusted to the corporations and trusts is very wide; they cover aspects of development vital to the territory in the fields of agriculture and education, while the most important of all information services, judged from the results of listener research in more developed parts of the world, broadcasting, has also been put in the hands of a small board which enjoys considerable freedom of action. Each of these bodies has a number of Africans amongst its members, who have thus the opportunity of studying methods of management which are new to them, while at the same time taking part in responsibility for the expenditure of large sums of public money, an experience which should prove valuable in years to come.

*Chapter 22, paragraphs 84 and 85.

BIBLIOGRAPHY

This bibliography is neither exhaustive nor definitive: even if it were possible to compile such a bibliography it could not be done within the span of a book of this size—it would require a volume to itself. What has been gathered together, by many hands, is a list of works which it is thought will be of value or interest to the searcher after further knowledge. Many sources have been tapped and a considerable number of existing bibliographies have been consulted, especially the following:—

Bibliography of the Negro in Africa and America, by M. N. Work. New York, 1928.

Bibliography of Published Sources relating to African Land Tenure. Col. No. 258, 1950. H.M.S.O.

Bibliography of Ethnographical Literature for Tanganyika Territory, by R. de Z. Hall, in *Tanganyika Notes and Records*, No. 7, June, 1939.

Select Annotated Bibliography of Tropical Africa, by Daryll Forde. London: International African Institute for Twentieth Century Fund, New York. 1956.

In addition, the lists given in *African Abstracts, Africa, African Affairs, African Studies, Man, The Colonial Review, The Journal of African Administration, Corona, The Journal of the Royal Anthropological Institute, Anthropos*, and other periodicals concerned with East Africa have been found useful.

Further information about various aspects of life in the territory will be found in the reports, periodicals and other publications listed in the Preface to this Handbook.

The Tanganyika Atlas (price Shs. 60/-) contains maps, charts and statistics about most aspects of the country's economy and has become justly famous as a model of its kind. A list of other maps available can be obtained from the Department of Lands and Surveys.

To make it easier to consult the bibliography the references have been arranged under subject headings and in each case books, reports, pamphlets, etc. have been shown separately from articles in periodicals. In some cases the same book has been included under more than one heading, for example, under "History" as well as under "Geography". When a book sought under one heading cannot be found there the enquirer is advised to look under another heading for it—the compiler's opinion of its classification may not be the same as the enquirer's.

A special list of abbreviations used precedes the bibliography, since in several instances the abbreviations used by the compilers do not conform to those shown in the World List of Scientific Periodicals.

List of Abbreviations Used

A.A. (J.R.A.S.)	African Affairs (Journal of the Royal African Society).
A.f.A.	Archiv für Anthropologie.
A.f.R.	Archiv für Religion.
Anth.	Anthropos.
A.S.	African Studies.
B.A.	Baessler-Archiv.
B.A.Z.	Beitrage zur Allgemeinen Zeitung, München.
B.f.K.	Beitrage für Kolonialpolitik.
B.J.P.	British Journal of Psychology.
B.K.u.K.	Beitrage zur Kolonialpolitik und Kolonial-Wirtschaft, Berlin.
B.L.u.F.	Berichte über Land und Forstwirtschaft in Deutsch-Ostafrika, Heidelberg.
B.S.	Bantu Studies.
C.	Corona.
C.R.	Colonial Review.
D.K.B.	Deutsches Kolonialblatt.
D.K.Z.	Deutsche Koloniale Zeitung.
E.A.A.J.	East African Agricultural Journal.
Emp.For.J.	Empire Forestry Journal.
E.N.	Ethnologisches Notizblatt.
Gl.	Globus.
G.J.	Geographical Journal.
G.P.D.	Government Printer, Dar es Salaam.
G.Rev.	Geographical Review.
H.M.S.O.	Her Majesty's Stationery Office.
Int.Rev.Miss.	International Review of Missions.
J.E.A. and U.N.H.S. ...	Journal of the East African and Uganda Natural History Society.
J.Ecol.	Journal of Ecology.
J.R.A.I.	Journal of the Royal Anthropological Institute.
K.R.	Kolonial Rundschau, Berlin.
M.a.d.S.	Mitteilungen aus den Deutschen Schutzgebieten.
M.A.G.	Mitteilungen der Afrikanischen Gesellschaft in Deutschland.
M.d.G.G.	Mitteilungen der Geographischen Gesellschaft in Hamburg.
M.S.O.S.	Mitteilungen des Seminars für Orientalische Sprachen zu Berlin.
M.Z.	Meteorologische Zeitschrift, Berlin.
P.G.S.	Proceedings of the Geographical Society.
P.M.	A. Petermann's Mitteilungen.
S.M.	Smarre Meddelingen.
S.P.C.K.	Society for the Promotion of Christian Knowledge.
T.N.R.	Tanganyika Notes and Records.
V.G.E.B.	Verhandlungen der Gesellschaft für Erdkunde zu Berlin.
Z.E.	Zeitschrift für Ethnologie, Berlin.
Z.f.E.	Zeitschrift für Ethnographie.
Z.f.K.	Zeitschrift für Kolonialpolitik, Kolonialrecht und Kolonialwirtschaft, Berlin.

INDEX

GENERAL, including Administration and Political.

Books, Reports, Pamphlets

African Population of Tanganyika Territory (Geographical and Tribal Studies), 1950. E.A. Statistical Office, Nairobi.

ALEXANDER, G.	Tanganyika Memories. London, 1936.
ANDERSON, J. N. D.	Islamic Law in Africa. Col. Research Publications. London, 1954.
ARNING, W.	Deutsch-Ostafrika gestern und heute. Dietrich Reimer, Berlin, 1936.
Atlas of Tanganyika	Department of Lands and Surveys, Dar es Salaam.
BAKER, E. C.	Report on Social and Economic conditions in the Tanga Province. G.P.D., 1934.

Barclays Bank, D.C.O. Tanganyika an economic survey. London (Barclays Bank), 1955.

British East Africa: Economic and commercial conditions in British East Africa (Kenya, Uganda, Tanganyika and Zanzibar), by G. T. Dow-Smith. London: H.M.S.O., 1953. (Overseas Economic Surveys).

The British Territories in East and Central Africa, 1945-50. London: H.M.S.O., 1950. (Cmd. 7987).

Bibliography of Published Sources relating to African Land Tenure. Col. No. 258, 1950. H.M.S.O.

BROWNE, G. ST. J. Orde- ...	Labour in Tanganyika Territory. H.M.S.O. Col. No. 19. 1936.
Blue Book, Tanganyika ...	Govt. Printer, Dar es Salaam (up to 1948).
BUELL, R. L.	The Native Problem in Africa. New York, 1928.
CAMERON, Sir DONALD ...	My Tanganyika Service and some Nigeria. Allen and Unwin Ltd. London, 1939.
CHARRON, K. C.	The Welfare of the African Labourer in Tanganyika. G.P.D. 1944.
CHURCH, A.	East Africa: a New Dominion. H. F. and G. Witherby, London, 1928.

Closer Union. Report of the Commission on (Sir E. Hilton Young, Chairman) Cmd. 3234. London: H.M.S.O., 1929.

Colonial Problem, The... ...	The Royal Institute of International Affairs. O.U.P. 1937.

Commerce and Industry in Tanganyika. 1957. 104 pp. Dept. of Commerce and Industry, P.O. Box 234, Dar es Salaam.

CORY, H., AND HARTNOLL, M. M. Customary Law of the Haya Tribe. International African Institute. 1945.

Development of African Local Government in Tanganyika. (Containing two despatches from the Governor and a memorandum by Mr. Hall, the Member for Local Government). London: H.M.S.O., 1951.

G. T. Dow-Smith ... ... British East Africa, London: H.M.S.O., 1953. (Overseas Economic Surveys).

Culwick, A. T. and G. M. ... Ubena of the Rivers. London, 1935.

Development Plan Reports. 1947, 1948. G.P.D.

Dalton, A. K. ... ... Tanganyika: A government in a plural society. Leiden, 1955.

Davis, J. Merle ... ... Modern industry and the African. London: 1933.

Development of African Local Government in Tanganyika. Cmd. 277, H.M.S.O. 1951.

Dundas, Sir C. ... ... African Crossroads. London, 1955.

East African Royal Commission Report. Cmd. 9475. London: H.M.S.O., 1955.

East African Economic and Statistical Bulletin. Published quarterly by the E.A. Statistical Department. G.P. Nairobi.

East African Statistical Department. African Population, Tanganyika Territory. Nairobi: 1950. (Geographical and tribal studies).

East Africa High Commission: Report of the (Hon. W. Ormsby-Gore, Chairman). Cmd. 2387. London: H.M.S.O., 1925.

East African Territories: An Economic Survey, Vol. II London: H.M.S.O., 1954.

East African Railways and Harbours. Report on an engineering survey of a rail link between the East African and Rhodesian railway systems. Nairobi: Railway Headquarters. 1952.

An economic survey of the colonial territories, 1951. Vol. II: The East African territories—Kenya, Tanganyika, Uganda, Zanzibar and the Somaliland Protectorate, with Aden, Mauritius and Seychelles. London: H.M.S.O., 1954. (Colonial No. 281(a)).

Economy of East Africa—A Study of Trends. E.A. Railways and Harbours, Nairobi, 1955.

Education, Higher, in East Africa—Report of the Commission. Col. 142. London: H.M.S.O., 1947.

Farquharson, J. R. ... ... Tanganyika Transport: A Review. Dar es Salaam, 1945.

Financial Mission to Tanganyika, Report on, by Sir S. Armitage-Smith. Cmd. 4182. London: H.M.S.O. 1932.

Fortes M. and Evans-
Pritchard, E. E. ... ... African Political Systems. O.U.P., for International African Institute. London, 1940.

Ford, V. C. R. ... ... The trade of Lake Victoria: A geographical study. Kampala (E.A. Institute of Social Research), 1955.

Gibb, Sir A. and partners. Report of the Central African rail link development survey. London: Colonial Office. 1952.

GIBB, ROGER ... ... Railway Rates in Kenya, Uganda and Tanganyika Territory. Cmd. 4235. H.M.S.O. 1933.

GORDON-BROWNE, G. AND
A. McD. BRUCE HUTT ... Anthropology in Action. Oxford, 1935.

GUTMANN, B. ... ... Das Recht der Dschagga. München, 1926.

GUNTHER, J. ... ... Inside Africa. London (Hamilton), 1955.

GULLIVER, P. H. ... ... Labour Migration in a Rural Economy. E.A. Inst. for Social Research, Uganda, 1956.

HAILEY, LORD ... ... An African Survey. London, 1957.

HAMMOND, F. D. ... ... Report on the Railway Systems of Kenya, Uganda and Tanganyika. Parts I and II. Crown Agents, London. 1921.

Report on the Railway Systems of Tanganyika Territory. Crown Agents, London, 1930.

Higher education in East Africa: Report of the commission appointed by the Secretary of State for the Colonies, September, 1937. (Earl de la Warr, Chairman) London: H.M.S.O., 1937. (Colonial No. 142).

HILL, J. F. R. AND
MOFFETT, J. P. ... ... Tanganyika: A Review of its Resources and their Development. London (Crown Agents), G.P.D., 1955.

HOLMES, SIR M. ... ... Report of the Commission on the Civil Services of Kenya, Tanganyika, Uganda and Zanzibar, 1947-48. Col. 223. London: H.M.S.O. 1948.

JEX-BLAKE, A. J. ... ... Gardening in East Africa. London, 1934.

JOHNSTON, H. H. ... ... The Colonization of Africa by Alien Races. London, 2nd edition, 1912.

Joint Committee on Closer Union in East Africa. H.C. No. 156. London: H.M.S.O. 1929.

Justice—Report of a Commission of Enquiry into the administration of justice in Kenya, Uganda and Tanganyika in criminal matters. Cmd. 4623, H.M.S.O. 1934.

KÖBNER, O. ... ... Einführung in die Kolonialpolitik. Jena, 1908.

KUCZYNSKI, R. R. ... ... A Demographic Survey of the British Colonial Empire. Vol. II, O.U.P., 1949.

Land Development Survey, First Report, 1928/29: Iringa Province, by Bagshawe, F. J.; Wolfe, H; McGregor, C. J.; Bell, M. F. Crown Agents for the Colonies 1929.

Land Development Survey, Second Report, 1930: Iringa Province, by Bagshawe, F. J., and Hill, W. J. Dar es Salaam, 1930.

Land Development Survey, Third Report, 1929/30: Uluguru Mountains, Eastern Province by Bagshawe, F. J., and Hill, W. J. Dar es Salaam, 1931.

Land Development Survey, Fourth Report, 1930: Mbulu District, by Bagshawe, F. J. Dar es Salaam, 1931.

Land Development Survey, Fifth Report: Eastern Province, by Bagshawe, F. J. Dar es Salaam, 1932. ..

Law Reports; Her Majesty's High Court of Tanganyika. Published periodically as supplements to *Tanganyika Gazette* by G.P.D.

Laws of Tanganyika, 1947-50. 10 volumes. G.P.D. or Crown Agents for the Colonies.

Legislative and administrative system. G.P.D., 1950.

LEUBUSCHER, C. ... ... Tanganyika Territory: A Study of Economic Policy under the Mandate. London, 1944.

LIDBURY, SIR DAVID ... ... Report of the Commission on the Civil Services of the East African Territories and the East Africa High Commission. Crown Agents. London. 1954.

Local Government Memoranda: No. 1, African Local Government G.P.D., 1954.

Local Government in Tanganyika—The development of African, 1955, pp. 68. G.P.D.

LUCAS, C. ... ... The Partition and Colonization of Africa. The Clarendon Press, Oxford, 1922.

LUGARD, SIR F. D. ... ... The Dual Mandate in British Tropical Africa. Edinburgh, 1929.

MACKENZIE, W. J. M. ... ... Constitutional Development Commission: Report of the Special Commissioner appointed to examine Matters arising out of the Committee on Constitutional Development (Tanganyika). G.P.D., 1953.

MACMILLAN, M.... ... ... Introducing East Africa. Faber, London, 1952.

MAIR, L. ... ... Native Policies in Africa. George Routledge & Sons, London, 1936.

A preparatory investigation of the manpower position 1951. G.P.D., 1951. See also: Tanganyika—Report of the committee on manpower. G.P.D., 1951.

MATHEW, C. ... ... Report of the Committee on Constitutional Development. G.P.D., 1951.

MAYER, A. ... ... Das Buch der deutschen Kolonie. Potsdamn Leipzig, 1933.

MEYER, M. ... ... Das Deutsch Kolonial Reich. Leipzig, 1909.

MEEK, C. K. ... ... Land Law and Custom in the Colonies. London, 1946.

Memorandum on Closing of Land in Tanganyika Territory to Alienation. G.P.D., 1937.

Memorandum on Native Policy in East Africa, Cmd. 3573. London, 1930.

Memorandum on the Recruitment, Care and Employment of Government Labour. G.P.D., 1933.

MITCHELL, SIR P. ... ... African Afterthoughts. London (Hutchinson), 1954.

MURRAY, A. V. ... ... The School in the Bush. Longmans, Green & Co., London, 1929.

Native courts. Part I. Introduction to the local court system. Part II. Section-by-section commentary on the Local Courts Ordinance. Part III. Handbook for courtholders and their clerks. G.P.D., 1953. (Local government memoranda No. 2. This supersedes Native administration memorandum No. 2, 2nd ed. pub. 1930).

Native treasuries. Part I. Finance (Native treasuries). Part II. Accounting rules. G.P.D., 1949-50. (Local Government Memoranda No. 3. This supersedes Native Administration Memorandum No. 3 published in 1926).

NEWLYN, W. T. AND
ROWEN, D. C. ... ... Money and Banking in British Colonial Africa. London, 1954.

NORTHCOTE, R. C. ... ... A Memorandum on Native Land Tenure. G.P.D. 1945.

OSBORNE-RANCE, BRIG.-GEN.
SIR H. ... ... Report on Co-ordination of Transport in Kenya, Uganda and Tanganyika Territory, 1937.

Observations of the Administering Authority on the Report of the United Nations Visiting Mission to Tanganyika, 1954. G.P.D. 1955.

ORDE-BROWNE, MAJOR G. ST. J. Labour in Tanganyika Territory. 1936. H.M.S.O. Col. No. 19.

Labour Conditions in East Africa. 1946. H.M.S.O. Col. No. 193.

PIM, SIR A. ... ... The Financial and Economic History of the African Tropical Territories. 1940. Clarendon Press, Oxford.

Principles of Native Administration and their application. 2nd ed. G.P.D., 1930. (Native Administration Memoranda; No. 1).

Provincial Commissioners' Annual Reports. G.P.D.

READ, M. H. ... ... Education and Social Charge in tropical areas. London (Nelson). 1955.

Report of the Arusha—Moshi Lands Commission (Wilson Report), 1947, by Mr. Justice Mark Wilson. G.P.D.

Report of the Central Development Committee (G. R. Sandford, Chairman), 1940, pp. 242. G.P.D.

Report of the Central Education Committee. G.P.D. 1943.

Report on the Census of the Non-native Population taken on the night of 25th February, 1948. G.P.D., 1953.

Report of the Committee on Constitutional Development (and despatches between the Governor and Secretary of State). Charles Mathew (Chairman). G.P.D., 1951.

Report of the Special Commission appointed to examine matters arising out of the Report of the Committee on Constitutional Development. G.P.D. 1953.

Report by the Development Commission: A Ten-Year Development and Welfare Plan for Tanganyika. G.P.D. 1946.

Report of the Special Committee on European Education, 1951. G.P.D.

Report of the Special Committee on Indian Education, 1951. G.P.D.

Report and recommendations regarding Industrial Development. (East African Industrial Council), Nairobi: Govt. Printer. 1945.

Report of a Committee appointed by His Excellency the Governor to submit proposals in connection with Land Development and the provision of Financial Assistance to Settlers and Planters (R. W. Taylor, Chairman). Sess. Paper No. 3 of 1930. pp. 21. G.P.D.

Report of Special Committee on Non-Native Education, 1948. G.P.D.

Report of the Tanganyika Railways Commission. Crown Agents. London, 1930.

Report of the Committee on rising costs. G.P.D., 1951.

Report to the Government of Tanganyika by the Committee on Social Welfare. (Sessional Paper No. 1 of 1949). G.P.D.

Report on Tanganyika Territory covering the period from the conclusion of the Armistice to the end of 1950. Cmd. 1428. 1921.

Report by H.M. Government to the General Assembly of the United Nations on the Administration of Tanganyika (annual since 1946.) London: H.M.S.O.

Report of the Visiting Mission to the trust territory of Tanganyika under British administration. United Nations: New York: 1948. (T/218: T/218/Add. 1).

United Nations Visiting Mission to trust territories in East Africa. 1951: Report on Tanganyika together with related documents. (Enrique de Marchena, Chairman). United Nations: Trusteeship Council. New York: 1952. (T/1032).

RICHTER, J. ... ... Tanganyika and its Future. World Dominion Press.

ROBERTS, C. C. ... ... Tangled Justice. Some Reasons for a change of Policy in Africa. Macmillan, London, 1937.

ROBERTSON, SIR BENJAMIN ... Report (dated 4th August, 1920) regarding the proposed Settlement of Indian Agriculturists in Tanganyika Territory and letter from the Government of India to the Secretary of State for India dated 10th February, 1921. Cmd. 1312. 1921.

Roux, L. ... ... L'Est Africain Britannique: Kenya, Tanganyika, Uganda et Zanzibar. Société d' Editions Géographiques, Maritimes et Coloniales. Paris. 1950.

Royal Commission Report. Despatches from the Governors of Kenya, Uganda and Tanganyika and from the Administrator, East Africa High Commission, commenting on the East Africa Royal Commission 1953-1955 report. Pp. 196. London: H.M. Stationery Office (Cmd. 9801). Commentary on the above. Pp. 6 Cmd. 9804. 1956.

Russell, A. ... ... Handbook for Magistrates. G.P.D.

Schultz-Ewerth, E., and
Adam, L. ... ... (Editors), Das Eingeborenrecht. Vol. 1, Ankemann, B., Ostafrika.

Steer, G. L. ... ... Judgment on German Africa. Hodder & Stoughton Ltd., London, 1939.

Symes, Sir Stewart ... ... Tour of Duty. Collins, London, 1946.

Taeuber, I. B. ... ... The population of Tanganyika. United Nations Dept., of Social Affairs, Population Division (Reports on the Population of Trust Territories, No. 2). Lake Success, New York. 1949.

The Tanganyika Guide. Public Relations Office, Dar es Salaam.

Tanganyika Notes and Records, published half-yearly by the Tanganyika Society, P.O. Box 511, Dar es Salaam.

The Tanganyika (Legislative Council) Order in Council, 1926. London: H.M.S.O. (Statutory rules and orders, 1926, No. 991).

The Tanganyika (Legislative Council) (Amendment) Order in Council, 1945. London: H.M.S.O. (Statutory rules and orders, 1945, No. 1371).

The Tanganyika (Legislative Council) (Amendment) Order in Council, 1948. London: H.M.S.O. (Statutory instruments, 1948, No. 105).

Tanganyika Territory. The Tanganyika (Legislative Council) (Amendment) Order in Council, 1943. London: H.M.S.O. (Statutory instruments, 1953, No. 1208).

Tanganyika: Development Commission. A ten-year development and welfare plan for Tanganyika Territory. G.P.D., 1946.

Ten-Year Plan for the Development of African Education, 1947. G.P.D.

Ten-Year Plan for African Education (Scheme for Revision, 1950). G.P.D.

Territorial Annual Reports to the United Nations Organization. H.M.S.O.

Telford, A. M. ... ... Report on the Development of the Rufiji and Kilombero Valleys. Crown Agents for the Colonies, 1929.

Trade Reports. G.P. Nairobi.

Trusteeship Agreement, Text of, as agreed by General Assembly of United Nations Organization. Cmd. 7081. London: H.M.S.O. 1946.

WILSON, SIR SAMUEL ... ... Report on his visit to East Africa, 1929. Cmd. 3378. H.M.S.O.

WOODS, SIR W. ... ... Report on a fiscal survey of Kenya, Uganda and Tanganyika. Conference of East African Governors. Nairobi, 1946.

WORTHINGTON, E. B. ... ... Science in Africa: a review of scientific research relating to Tropical and Southern Africa. London: O.U.P., for Committee of the African Research Survey. 1938.

A survey of research and scientific services in East Africa, 1947-50. Nairobi: East Africa High Commission. 1952.

WRIGHT, F. C. ... ... African Consumers in Nyasaland and Tanganyika. (Colonial Research Studies No. 17). London: H.M.S.O., 1955.

The Year-book and Guide to East Africa, ed. by A. Gordon Brown   London: Hale.

GENERAL, including Administration and Political.
Articles in Periodicals

BROOKE, N. J. ... ... The changing character of customary courts. *J.Afr.Admin.* 6, 2, 67-73, April, 1954.

BULMAN, W. E. AND
FARQUHARSON, J. R. ... The climate and welfare of Tanganyika. *T.N.R.* 20, 1945, p. 24.

CORY, H.... ... ... The people of the Lake Province Region. *T.N.R.* 33, 22-9, July, 1952.

Land Tenure in Bukuria. *T.N.R.* No. 23, pp. 70-79. 1947.

The necessity of co-ordination of economic and political development. *T.N.R.* 30, 1951, p. 78.

CULWICK, A. T. AND G. M. ... A study of factors governing food supply in Ulanga, Tanganyika Territory. *E.A. Med.J.* Vol. XVI, No. 2.

DE MESTRAL, C. ... ... Christian Literature for Africa. *Int.Rev. Missions*, 43, 172, 436-42, October, 1954.

DOBSON, E. B. ... ... Comparative land tenure of ten Tanganyika tribes. *J.Afr.Admin.*, 6, 2, 80-91, April, 1954.

Land tenure of the Wasambaa. *T.N.R.* No. 10. pp. 1-27, 1940.

DUDBRIDGE, B. J. AND
GRIFFITHS, J. E. S. ... ... The Development of Local Government in Sukumaland. *J.Afr.Admin.*, 3, 141-6, July, 1951.

FOSBROOKE, H. A. ... ... Government Sociologists in Tanganyika. A Sociological View. *J.Afr.Admin.*, Vol. IV. No. 3, July, 1952.

A brief record of archaeological remains in Tanganyika. *T.N.R.*, 33, 60-6, July, 1952.

FOSBROOKE, H. A. AND
MAREALLE, CHIEF PETRO I ... The engraved rocks of Kilimanjaro. *Man.* 52, 244, 161-2, 263, 179-81, November— December, 1952.

GOWER, R. H. ... ... An experiment in District training. *J.Afr. Admin.*, 4, 1, 6-9 January, 1952.

HAMLYN, O. T. ... ... Provocation in the Law of Tanganyika. *Journal of Comparative Legislation and International Law*. London. 3rd ser. 29, November, 1947.

HALL, R. DE Z. ... ... *Bao. T.N.R.* 34, 57-61, January, 1953.

HUNTER, G. ... ... Hidden drums in Singida District. *T.N.R.* 34, 28-32, January, 1953.

IONIDES, C. J. P. ... ... Stories of the Wangindo. *T.N.R.* 31, 81-2 July, 1951.

IRVINE, F. R. ... ... Health and agriculture in Africa. *Afr. Affairs* 53, 211, 132-42, April, 1954.

JANISCH, M. ... ... The purpose of the education of the African child. *E.Afr.Med.J.*, 31, 3, 169-74, April, 1954.

JEFFREYS, M. D. S. ... ... The history of maize in Africa. *S.Afr.J.Sec.*, 50, 8, 197-200, March, 1954.

JOHNSTON, P. H. ... ... Land tenure on Kilimanjaro and the Vihamba of the Wachagga. *T.N.R.* No. 21, pp. 1-20. 1946.

Chagga constitutional development. *J.Afr.Admin.*, 5, 3, 134-40, July, 1953.

JOHNSON, V. Eugene ... ... African harvest dance. *T.N.R.* 37, 138-42, July, 1954.

JONES, A. M. ... ... African rhythm. *Africa*, 24, 1, 26-47, January, 1954.

KINGDOM, Z. E. ... ... The initiation of a system of local government by African Rural Councils in the Rungwe District of Tanganyika. *J.Afr.Admin.* Vol. III, No. 4, October, 1951.

KING, R. S. ... ... Town houses for Tanganyika Africans. *Corona*, 5, 11, 411-5, November, 1953.

KINGDOM-HOCKINGS, D. ... Race relations and social structure in Tanganyika. *Overseas Educ.* 24, 3, 12-14, October, 1952.

KOENIG, O. ... ... The ancient wells of Ngassumat in South Masailand. *T.N.R.* 31, 53-4, July, 1951.

LIEBENOW, J. GUS. ... ... Some problems in introducing local government reform in Tanganyika. *J.Afr. Admin.*, 8, 3, 132-9, July 1956.

MASON, H. ... ... Progress in Pare. *Corona*, June, 1952, p. 212.

MCGAIRL, J. L. ... ... Urban community development through adult literacy. *Community Dev. Bull.*, 4, 71-7, September, 1953.

MNTAMBO, P. C. ... ... The African and how to promote his welfare. *T.N.R.* 18, 1944, p. 1.

MOFFETT, J. P. ... ... One hundred years ago in Tanganyika. *T.N.R.* 33, 83-90, July, 1952.

MORRIS, STEPHEN ... ... Indians in East Africa: a study in a plural society. *Brit.J.Sociol.*, 7, 3, Sept. 1956, 194-211.

MTAWALI, C. V. A. ... ... A health campaign in Tanganyika Territory. *Com.Dev.Bull.*, 2, 3, 54-6, June, 1951.

NORTON, I. H. ... ... An inter-racial local council in Tanganyika. *J.Afr.Admin.* 8, 1, 26-32, Jan. 1956.

PERHAM, M. F. ... ... The system of native administration in Tanganyika. *Africa*. Vol. IV, No. 3.

Tanganyika Trade Bulletin, published quarterly by the Dept. of Commerce and Industry, P.O. Box 234, Dar es Salaam.

TWINING, SIR EDWARD ... A chief's skull returned to his people (Hehe of Tanganyika). *Times. Brit. Colon. Rev.*, 15, 11-12, Autumn, 1954.

The situation in Tanganyika. *A.A. (J.R.A.S.)* October, 1951, p. 297.

WINNINGTON-INGRAM, C. ... Reforming local government in a Tanganyika district. *J.Afr.Admin.*, Vol. II, No. 2.

WRIGHT, A. C. ... ... Sociology in Sukumaland. *Corona*. 5, 3, 100-3, March, 1953.

YOUNG, CULLEN, AND
   MALEKEBU, BENNETT E. ... African Playtime. *Nyasaland J.*, 6, 1. 34-44 January, 1953.

HISTORY AND PREHISTORY
Books, Reports, Pamphlets

ABOUFLEDA ... ... Geographie. French translation by Reinaud, Paris, 1848.

Admiralty and War Office—Handbook of German East Africa, 1916.

ADOLPHI, H. AND SCHANZ ... Am Fusse der Bergriesen Ostafrikas. Geschichte der Leipziger Mission am Kilimandjaro und in den Nachbargebirgen. Leipzig, 1912.

Africa Pilot—Vol. III—South and East Coasts of Africa. London, 1929.

AFRICANUS, LEO ... ... The History and Description of Africa done into English in the year 1600 by John Pory. Hakluyt Society—3 vols—1896.

AICHISON, C. U.... ... ... A Collection of Treaties, Engagements and Sunnads. Calcutta, 1876.

ALBUQUERQUE, AFONSO... ... Cartas de seguidos do documentos que es elucidam, Vols. I to VII, Lisbon, 1884-1935.

AMERY, L. H. ... ... The German Colonial Claim. London, 1939.

ANKERMANN, B. ... ... Das Eingeborenrecht—Ostafrika. Stuttgart, 1929.

ARNING, W. ... ... Vier Jahre Weltrieg in Deutsch-Ostafrika. Gebruder Janecke, Druck und Verlagshaus, Hanover (Undated).

AXELSON, E. ... ... South East Africa, 1488—1530. London, 1940.

BADGER, G. P. ... ... History of the Imams and Seyyids of Oman. Hakluyt Society, 1871.

BALL, N. ... ... Zanzibar Treaties. London, 1910.

BANNING, E. (trans. PFUNGST, A.) ... ... Die Politische Theilung Afrika's nach den neuesten internationalen Verein-barungen (1885 bis 1889) Berlin, 1890.

BARBOSA, DUARTE ... ... A Description of the Coasts of East Africa and Malabar in the Beginning of the Sixteenth Century. Transl. by E. J. Stanley for Hakluyt Society, 1866. O livro de (1554). Translated into English by M. L. Dames for Hakluyt Society, 1918—20.

BARROS, J. DE ... ... Asia, dos factos que os Portuguezes fozerom no descobrimeto et conquista dos mares et terras do Oriente. Lisbon, 1553. Transl. by E. G. Ravenstein for the Hakluyt Society.

BARROS, J. DE	Decadas da India, Vols. I to VII. Lisbon, 1777-8.
	Da Asia (Lisbon 1777-78)—extracts translated into English by Theal (q.v.).
BARTLETT, LT.-COL. H. MOYSE-	The King's African Rifles: a study in the military history of East and Central Africa, 1890-1945. Aldershot (Gale & Polden) 1956. Pp. xix. 727. ill. maps.
BATUTA, IBN	The Travels of—Extracts translated into English by S. Lee (London, 1829) and H. A. Gibb (London, 1929) and in fuller detail into French by Guillain (q.v.) and Defrémery, C and Sanguinetti, P. (Paris, 1853-58).
BAUMANN, O.	Durch Masailand zur Nilquelle. Berlin, 1894.
BAUR AND LE ROY, PP. ...	A travers le Zanguebar. Tours, 1886.
BECKER, J.	La vie en Afrique. Paris, 1887.
BERJEAU, J. PH.	Le Second Voyage de Vasco da Gama à Calicut—Relation Flamande editée vers MDIV. Paris, 1881.
BEHR, H. F. VON	Kriegsbilder aus dem Araberaufstand in Deutsch Ostafrika. Leipzig, 1891.
BERLIOUX, E. F.	La Traite Orientale—Histoire des chasses a l'homme organisées en Afrique depuis quinze ans. Paris, 1870.
	The Slave Trade in Africa in 1872. London, 1872.
BOCARRO, A.	Decada 13 da Historia da India. Lisbon, 1876.
BOEHM, DR. R.	Von Sansibar zum Tanganjika: Briefe aus Ostafrika, map and portrait, Leipzig, 1888.
BOTELER, T.	Narrative of a Voyage of Discovery to Africa and Arabia. London, 1835.
BOTELHO, GENERAL J. J. T. ...	Historia Militar e Politico dos Portuguezes em Mocambique de descoberta a 1833. Lisbon, 1936.
BOTELHO, S. X.	Memoria Estatica sobre os dominios Portuguezes na Africa Oriental—Vols. I and II. Lisbon, 1832 and 1835.
BRADY, C. T.	Commerce and Conquest in East Africa. Salem, 1950.
BRIGGS, J. H.	In the East African War Zone. London, 1918.

BRODALO, M. F. AND LIMA, J.... Ensaios sobre a estatistica das possessoes Portuguezas na Africa Oriental. Lisbon, 1859.

BRODE, H. ... ... Tippu Tip. Wilhelm Baensch. Berlin, 1905.

Tippoo Tib. Edward Arnold, London, 1907.

British and German East Africa. Edward Arnold. London, 1911.

BUCHANAN, A. ... ... Three years of war in East Africa. John Murray, London, 1920.

BURTON, ISABEL ... ... The life of Captain Sir Richard F. Burton. London, 1893.

BURTON, R. F. ... ... The Lake Regions of Central Africa. London, 1860.

Zanzibar—City, Island and Coast. London, 1872.

BUXTON, T. F. ... ... The African Slave Trade and its Remedy. London, 1839.

CABRAL, P. A. ... ... The Voyage of—English translation of Portuguese records by W. B. Greenlee for Hakluyt Society, 1938.

CALCOEN, V. DE ... ... Tweede Reis van Vasco da Gama naar India. Antwerp, 1903.

CALVERT, A. F. ... ... The German African Empire. London, 1916. German East Africa. London, 1917.

Cambridge History of the British Empire—Vol. VIII—South Africa. London, 1936.

CAMERON, D. ... ... My Tanganyika service and some Nigeria. George Allen and Unwin Ltd. London, 1939.

CAMERON, V. L. ... ... Across Africa. London, 1877.

CASATI, G. ... ... Ten years in Equatoria and the return with Emin Pasha. Frederick Warne & Co. (2 vols.). London, 1891.

CHAMBERLAIN, D. ... ... Some letters from Livingstone. 1840-72. Oxford, 1940.

CHARLEWOOD, C. J. ... ... Channels, Cloves and Coconuts. Westward Ho, 1955.

CHATTERTON, E. KEBLE ... The Koenigsberg Adventure. London, 1952. Severn's Saga. London, 1938.

CLIFFORD, HUGH ... ... The Gold Coast Regiment in the East African Campaign. London, 1920.

COLE, S. ... ... The Prehistory of East Africa. London, 1954 (Penguin books).

COLOMB, P. ... ... Slave Catching in the Indian Ocean. London, 1873.

COLVILLE, F. N. ... ... The War In German East Africa, in "The British Empire at War". Vol. IV, 1924.

COOTE, C. H. ... ... The Voyage from Lisbon to India 1505-6, being an Account and Journal by Albericus Vespuccio. London, 1894.

CORREA, GASPAR ... ... Lendas da India—Vols. I to IV. Lisbon, 1858-66.

CORTEZAO, J. ... ... A expedicio de Pedro Alvares Cabral. Lisbon, 1922.

CORVO, J. DE ANDRADE ... Estudos sobre as Provinciales Ultramarinas— Vols. I to IV. Lisbon, 1883-1887.

COSTA QUINTELLA, VICE-
ADMIRAL I. ... ... Annaes da Marinha Portugueza, Vols. I and II. Lisbon, 1839-40.

COUPLAND, SIR R. ... ... Kirk on the Zambesi. Oxford, 1928.

The British Anti-Slavery Movement. London, 1933.

East Africa and Its Invaders. Oxford, 1938, reprinted 1956.

The Exploitation of East Africa, 1856-1890. London, 1939.

Livingstone's Last Journey. London, 1945.

COUTO, D. DE ... ... Da Asia (Lisbon, 1778)—extracts translated into English by G. M. Theal (q.v.).

Decades da India (continuation of Barros, Joao de, *vide supra*).

CROFTON, R. H. ... ... The Old Consulate at Zanzibar. O.U.P. 1935.

Zanzibar Affairs, 1914-1933. London, 1953.

CROW, J. H. V. ... ... General Smuts's Campaigns in East Africa. London, 1918.

CUMPSTON, I. M. ... ... Indians Overseas in British Territory, 1834-1954. London, 1954, O.U.P.

DECKEN, BARON C. C. VON DER Reisen in Ost-Afrika. Leipzig and Heidelberg, 1869.

DECLE, L. ... ... Three Years in Savage Africa. London, 1898.

DEHERAIN, HENRI ... ... Etudes sur l'Afrique. Paris, 1904.

DE L'EPRENIER ... ... Mére Marie Clare. Paris, 1927.

DEPPE, L. ... ... Mit Lettow Vorbeck durch Afrika. Verlag August Scherl. G.M.B.H. Berlin.

Deutsches Kolonial Blatt, Vols. I to XXV, 1890-1914.

DOWNES, W. D. ... ... With the Nigerians in German East Africa. Methuen & Co., Ltd., London, 1919.

DUNDAS, SIR CHARLES ... ... African Crossroads. London, 1955.

DUYVENDAK, J. J. L. ... ... China's Discovery of Africa. London, 1949.

ELTON, J. F. ... ... Travels and Researches among the Lakes and Mountains of Eastern and Central Africa. London, 1879.

EVANS, I. L. ... ... The British in Tropical Africa. Cambridge University Press, 1929.

FENDALL, C. P. ... ... The East African Force, 1915-1919. London, 1924.

FISCHER, G. A. ... ... Mehr Licht im dunkeln Weldteil. Hamburg, 1885.

FONCK, H. ... ... Deutsch-Ost-Afrika. Vossische Buchhand-luhg. Berlin, 1907.

FROBEVIUS, L. ... ... Kulturgeschicte Afrikas. Phaidon-Verlag. 1933.

GAMA, VASCO DA ... ... Diario da Viagem de, Lisbon, 1945.

The three Voyages of, Hakluyt Society, 1869.

GOTZEN, COUNT VON ... ... Deutsch Ost-Afrika in Aufstand. Berlin, 1909.

GRANT, J. A. ... ... A Walk across Africa. London, 1864.

GUENTHER, K. ... ... Gerhard Rohlfs. Lebensbild eines Afrika forschers. Freiburg, 1912.

GUILLAIN ... ... Documents sur l'histoire, la géographie et le commerce de l'Afrique Orientale, Paris, 1856.

HAGEN, M. VON ... ... Bismarck's Kolonial Politik. Berlin, 1923.

HAILEY, LORD ... ... An African Survey. O.U.P., 1957.

Native Administration in British African Territories. 4 vols. H.M.S.O. 1950.

HAMERTON, A. ... ... A Report on the Affairs of the Imam of Muscat, 1844 (Selections from the records of the Bombay Government, 1856).

Brief Notes on various points connected with His Highness the Imam of Muscat (ibid).

HAMILTON, G. ... ... In the Wake of da Gama. Skeffington and Son, Ltd., London, 1951.

HERTSLET, E. ... ... The Map of Africa by Treaty. Harrison & Sons, London, 1896.

HOEEMANN, W. ... ... With Stanley in Africa. Cassell, London, 1938.

HOLLINGSWORTH, L. W. ...	A short history of the East Coast of Africa. Macmillan, London, 1929.
	Zanzibar under the Foreign Office. London, 1948.
HORDEM, CHARLES	Military Operations East Africa. Vol. I. London, 1941.
HORE, MRS. A. B.	To Lake Tanganyika in a Bath Chair. London, 1889.
HORE, E. C.	Tanganyika: Eleven years in Central Africa. London, 1892.
HOURANI, G. F.	Arab Seafarers in the Indian Ocean. Princeton Univ. Press, 1952.
HUNTINGFORD, G. W. B. and BELL, C. R. V.	East African Background. London, 1945.
HUTCHINSON, E....	The Slave Trade of East Africa. London, 1874.
HUXLEY, E.	White Man's Country. 2 Vols. London, 1935 (reprinted 1953).
HUXLEY, J.	Africa View. London, 1931.
HVID, FRANK	H. M. Stanley. The Authoritative Life. London, 1935.
IDRISI, MUHAMMAD IBN MUHAMMAD AL	Géographie—French translation by P. A. Jaubert. Paris, 1836.
INGRAMS, W. H....	Zanzibar. London, 1931.
JACKSON, F.	Early Days in East Africa. London, Edward Arnold & Co. 1930.
JACKSON, M. V.	European Powers and South East Africa, 1796-1856. London, 1942.
JACOB, E. G.	Deutsche Kolonialpolitik in Dokumenten. Dieterich'schen verlagsbuchhandlung, Leipzig, 1938.
JANTZEN, GUNTHER	Ostafrika in der deutsch-englischen Politik, 1884-1890. Hamburg, 1934.
JAYNE, K. G.	Vasco da Gama and his successors. London, 1910.
JOHNSON, W. P.	My African reminiscences, 1875-1895. Universities Mission to Central Africa. London.
JOHNSTON, SIR H. H.	The Kilima-Njaro Expedition. London, 1887.
	British Central Africa. London, 1897.
	The Nile Quest. London, 1903.
	The Opening up of Africa. London, 1911.

JOHNSTON, SIR H. H. ... ... The Colonization of Africa by alien races. Cambridge, 1913.

A Comparative Study of Bantu Languages. 1919.

The Story of my Life. London, 1923.

JUNKER, W. ... ... Travels in Central Africa, 1882-1886. London, 1892.

JUNKERS, DR. ... ... Peterman's Mitteilungen, 1886.

KALKHOF, R. ... ... Parlamentarische Studienreise nach Deutsch-Ostafrika. Berlin, 1907.

KANDT, R. ... ... Caput Nili. Berlin, 1925.

KASSNER, T. ... ... My journey from Rhodesia to Egypt. London 1911.

KELTIE, J. S. ... ... The partition of Africa. Edward Stanford, London, 1895.

KERSTEN, O. ... ... Baron Carl Claus von der Decken's *Reisen in Ost-Afrika*. Leipzig, 1869.

Tabellarische Uebersicht der Geschichte Ost-Afrikas. Leipzig, 1879.

KOHL-LARSEN, L. and M. ... Felsmalereien in Inner Afrika. Stuttgart, 1938.

KOLLMAN, P. ... ... Auf deutschen Boden in Afrika. Berlin, 1900.
The Victoria Nyanza. London, 1899.

KOSCHITZKIFS, M. ... ... Deutsche Kolonial Geschichte. Leipzig, 1888.

KRAPF, J. L. ... ... Travels, Researches and Missionary Labours in Eastern Africa. London, 1860.

LAFITAU, P. ... ... Historia des Descobertas e Conquistas dos Portugueses em Africa, Asia e America Lisbon, 1843.

LANGHELD, W. ... ... Zwanzig Jahre in Deutschen Kolonien.

LEAKEY, L. S. B. ... ... Proceedings of the first Pan-African Congress on Prehistory, 1947. Oxford, 1952.

Stone Age Africa. London, 1936.

LETTOW-VORBECK VON ... ... Meine Erinnerungen aus Ostafrika. K. F. Koehler, Leipzig, 1921.

My reminiscences of East Africa. Hurst and Blackett. London, (undated).

LEUBUSCHER, C. ... ... Tanganyika Territory. O.U.P., London, 1944.

LEUE, A. ... ... Dar es Salaam. Berlin, 1903.

LEWIN, E. ... ... The Germans and Africa. Cassell. London, 1915.

LIEBERT, GENERAL-MAJOR ... Neunzig Tage im Zelt: meine Reise, nach
(Governor of German East Uhehe, June-September, 1897, sketch-map,
Africa) Berlin, 1898.

LIMA, J. J. L. DA ... ... Ensaios sobre Estatisca des Possessoes Portuguezes. Lisbon, 1859.

LIVINGSTONE, D. and C. ... Narrative of an Expedition to the Zambezi
and its Tributaries. London, 1865.

(Livingstone) The Way to Ilala. F. Debenham. London, 1955.

Livingstone's Last Journals. Ed. by H. Waller. London, 1874.

Livingstone's Travels. From his own diaries. Edited by Rev. J. I. Macnair.
London, 1954.

LLOYD, C. ... ... The Navy and the Slave Trade. London,
1949.

LLOYD-JONES, W. ... ... K.A.R. London, 1926.

LORIOT, FLORENTIN ... ... Explorations et Missions dans l'Afrique
Equatoriale. Paris, 1890.

LUCAS, SIR C. P. ... ... The Empire at War. Vols. IV and V. Oxford,
1924-1926.

LUGARD, F. D. ... ... The Rise of our East African Empire.
London, 1893.

LUTTEROTH, A. R. ... ... Tunakwenda. Auf Kriegssafari in Deutsch-
Ostafrika. Hamburg, 1938.

LYNE, R. N. ... ... An Apostle of Empire (Life of General
Mathews of Zanzibar). George Allen and
Unwin Ltd. London, 1936.

Zanzibar in Contemporary Times. London,
1905.

MADER, F. W. ... ... Am Kilimandjaro. Union Deutsche Verlags-
gesellschaft, Berlin.

MacGRINDLE, J. W. ... ... The Commerce and Navigation of the
Erythraean Sea. London. 1879.

MACLEOD, LYONS ... ... Travels in Eastern Africa. London, 1860.

MACMILLAN, M. ... ... Introducing East Africa. London, 1952.

MACMILLAN, W. M. ... ... Africa Emergent. London, 1938.

MADAN, A. C. ... ... Kiungani—Story and History from Central
Africa. London, 1887.

MARSH, Z. AND
KINGSNORTH, G. W. ... ... An introduction to the history of East Africa.
London (C.U.P.) 1957.

MATHIESON, W. L. ... ... British Slavery and its Abolition (1823-1838)
Longmans, Green and Co. Ltd. London,
1926.

MATHIESON, W. L. ... ... Great Britain and the Slave Trade. (1839-1865) Longmans, Green and Co. London, 1929.

MECKLENBURG, DUKE ADOLPHUS
FREDERICK OF ... ... In the Heart of Africa. London, 1910.

MELLAND, F. J. and
CHOLMELEY, E. H. ... ... Through the Heart of Africa. London, 1912.

MERENSKY, A. ... ... Deutsche Arbeit am Nyassa, Deutsch-Ostafrika. Berlin, 1894.

MEYER, HANS ... ... Across East African Glaciers. London, 1891.

MITCHELL, SIR PHILIP ... ... African Afterthoughts. London, 1954.

MOLONEY, J. A. ... ... With Captain Stairs to Katanga. London, 1893.

MONGARDI, A. ... ... Thirty Years in Africa. Rome, 1950.

MOORE, J. E. S. ... ... The Tanganyika Problem, London, 1903.

MOIR, F. L. M. ... ... After Livingstone. An African Trade Romance. Hodder and Stoughton Ltd. London, undated.

MOULAERT, G. ... ... La campagne du Tanganyika. L'édition universelle S. A. Brussels, 1934.

NEW, C. ... ... Life, Wanderings and Labours in Eastern Africa. London, 1873.

"One of them" Uganda volunteers and the War. Kampala, 1917.

O'NEILL, H. E. ... ... Sketches of African Scenery from Zanzibar to Victoria Nyanza. C.M.S. 1878.

O'SWALD... ... ... The Story of the House of, Hamburg, 1931.

OWEN, W. F. W. ... ... Narrative of Voyages to explore the Shores of Africa, Arabia and Madagascar. London, 1833.

PARKE, T. H. ... ... Experiences in Equatorial Africa. London, 1891.

PASSARGE, E. AND OTHERS ... Das Deutsch Kolonialreich. Leipzig, 1909.

PAULITSCHKE, P. ... ... Die Afrika-Literatur in den Zeit von 1500 bis 1750. N.Ch. Vienna, 1882.

PEARCE, F. B. ... ... Zanzibar, Island Metropolis of Eastern Africa. London, 1920.

PERBANDT, C. VON, and others Hermann von Wissman—Deutschlands grosster Afrikaner. Alfred Schall, Berlin, 1906.

PETERS, C. ... ... New Light on Dark Africa. Ward, Lock & Co., London, 1891.

Die Gründung von Deutsch-Ostafrika. C. A. Schwetschke & Sohn, Berlin, 1906.

PETERS, C. ... ... Wie Deutsch-Ostafrika entstand. R. Voigtländers Verlag, Leipzig.

Die Deutsch Emin Pascha Expedition Hamburg, 1907.

PFEIL, J. VON ... ... Zur Erwerbung von Deutsch-Ostafrika. Karl Curtius, Berlin, 1907.

PIM, A. ... ... The financial and economic history of the African tropical territories. The Clarendon Press, Oxford, 1940.

PRINCE, M. ... ... Eine deutsche Frau im Innern Deutsch-Ostafrika. E.S. Mittle & Sohn, Berlin, 1905.

PRINS, A. H. J. ... ... The Coastal Tribes of the North Eastern Bantu. London, 1952.

PRIOR, J. ... ... Voyage along the Eastern Coast of Africa in the *Nisus* Frigate. London, 1819.

Narrative of a Voyage in the Indian Seas in the *Nisus* Frigate during the years 1810 and 1811 (London, 1820).

PRUSSE, A. ... ... Zwanzig Jahre Ansiedler in Deutsch-Ostafrika Schrecker & Schroder, Stuttgart, 1929.

RABAUD, A. ... ... L'Abbe Debaize et sa mission geographique et Scientifique dans l'Afrique Centrale. Marseille, 1883.

La Côte Orientale d'Afrique et l'Afrique Orientale. Marseille, 1881.

RAVENSTEIN, E. G. (ED.) ... A Journal of the first voyage of Vasco da Gama. 1497-1499. The Hakluyt Society, London, 1898.

RECK, H.... ... ... Oldoway. Die Schlucht das Urmenschen. Leipzig, 1933.

REHSE, H. ... ... Kiziba: Land und Leute. Stuttgart, 1910.

REICHARD, P. ... ... Deutsch-Ostafrika. Otto Spanner, Leipzig, 1892.

REUSCH, RICHARD ... ... Der Islam in Ost-Afrika. Leipzig, 1937.

History of East Africa. Stuttgart, 1954.

RITCHIE, E. MOORE ... ... The Unfinished War. London, 1940.

RITCHIE, J. E. ... ... The life and discoveries of David Livingstone. James Sangster & Co., London.

ROSCOE, J. ... ... Twenty-five years in East Africa. Cambridge, 1921.

RUETE, S. R. ... ... Said bin Sultan (1791-1856). Alexander-Ouseley, Ltd. Windsor House St., Westminster, London, 1929.

RUSSELL, MRS. C. E. B. ... ... General Rigby, Zanzibar and the Slave, Trade London, 1935.

SANDFORD, G. R. ... ... An Administrative and Political History of the Masai Reserve. London, 1919.

SAMASSA, P. ... ... Die Besiedlung Deutsch-Ostafrikas. Berlin, 1909.

SANTOS, J. DOS ... ... Ethiopia Oriental (Lisbon 1891)—extracts translated into English by G. M. Theal.

SCHNEE, DR. H. ... ... German Colonization, Past and Future. London, 1926.

SCHNEE, A. ... ... Meine Erlebnisse wahrend der Kriegszeit in Deutsch-Ostafrika. Verlag Luelle & Meyer, Leipzig, 1918.

SCHOFF, W. H. ... ... The Periplus of the Erythraean Sea. London, and New York, 1921.

SCHONFIELD, H. J. ... ... Richard Burton: explorer. Herbert Joseph, London, 1936.

SCHWEINFURT, G. A. ... ... The Heart of Africa. 2 vols. New York, 1874.

SCHWEITZER, G. ... ... Emin Pasha, his life and work. Archibald Constable & Co., London, 1898.

SCOTT-ELLIOTT, G. F. ... ... A Naturalist in Mid-Africa. London, 1896.

SELIGMAN, C. G. ... ... The Races of Central Africa. London, 1930.

SHARPE, SIR ALFRED ... ... The Backbone of Africa, London, 1921.

SHELDON, MRS. FRENCH ... From Sultan to Sultan. London, 1892.

SIMMONS, J. ... ... Livingstone and Africa. London, O.U.P., 1955.

SMYTH, W. H. ... ... The Life and Services of Captain Philip Beaver. London, 1829.

SPEKE, J. H. ... ... Journal of the Discovery of the Source of the Nile. London, 1863.

What led to the Discovery of the Source of the Nile. London, 1864.

STANLEY, D. (ED) ... ... Autobiography of Henry M. Stanley. Sampson Low, Marston, Searle & Rivington, London, 1909.

STANLEY, HON. E. J. ... ... The Three Voyages of Vasco da Gama. Hakluyt Society, 1865.

A description of the Coasts of East Africa and Zanzibar. Hakluyt Society, 1866.

STANLEY, H. M. ... ... How I found Livingstone in Central Africa. London, 1872.

STANLEY, H. M. ... ... Through the Dark Continent. London, 1878.
In Darkest Africa. London, 1890.
The Autobiography of. London, 1909.

STEERE, G. L. ... ... Judgment on German Africa. London, 1939.

STENTZLER, J. ... ... Deutsch-Ostafrika, Kriegs und Friedensbilder. Leipzig, 1906.

STEVENS, T. ... ... Scouting for Stanley in East Africa. London.

STEVENSON, J. ... ... The Civilization of South Eastern Africa. Glasgow, 1877.

STIGAND, C. H. ... ... The Land of Zinj. London, 1913.

STISTEAD, G. M. ... ... The True Life of Captain Sir Richard F. Burton. London, 1896.

STRANDES, J. ... ... Die Portugiesenzeit von Deutsch-und-Englisch Ost-Africa. Berlin, 1899.

STRONG, A. S. ... ... The History of Kilwa. *Journal of Royal Asiatic Society* (Reprint), 1895.

STUART-WATT, E. ... ... Africa's dome of mystery (Kilimanjaro). Marschall, Morgan & Scott Ltd., London.

STUHLMANN, F. ... ... Handwerk und Industrie in Ostafrika. Hamburg, 1910.
Mit Emin Pasha ins Herz von Afrika. Berlin, 1894.

SULIVAN, G. L. ... ... Dhow Chasing in Zanzibar Waters. London, 1873.

SWANN, A. J. ... ... Fighting the slave-hunters in Central Africa. Seeley & Co. Ltd., London, 1910.

SYMES, SIR STEWART ... ... Tour of Duty. London, 1946.

SYMONS, A. J. A. ... ... Emin, Governor of Equatoria. London, 1928.

Tanganyika—(Foreign Office Historical Handbook No. 113), H.M.S.O., 1920.

Tanganyika Notes and Records, published half-yearly by the Tanganyika Society, P.O. Box 511, Dar es Salaam.

TAYLOR, A. J. P. ... ... Germany's First Bid for Colonies (1884-1885). London, 1938.

The Tanganyika Guide. Public Relations Office, Dar es Salaam.

THEAL, G. M. ... ... The Portuguese in South Africa, Cape Town, 1896.
Records of South Eastern Africa, Vols. I to IX. Cape Town, 1898-1903.

THOMSON, J. ... ... To the Central African Lakes and Back. London, 1881.
Through Masailand. London, 1887.

THOMSON, J. B. ... ... Joseph Thomson, African Explorer. London, 1897.

TOWNSEND, M. E. ... ... The Rise and Fall of Germany's Colonial Empire. New York, 1930.

VAUSE, RICHARD ... ... Notes from the East Coast descriptive of a Trip to Zanzibar and back. Durban, 1877.

VELTEN, C. ... ... Prosa und Poetrie der Suaheli. Berlin, 1907.

VIERA, J. ... ... Mit Lettow-Vorbeck im Busch. Loewes Verlag Ferdinand Carl. Stuttgart, 1937.

VINCENT, M. ... ... The Periplus of the Erythraean Sea. London, 1800-05.

WALLER, H. ... ... Last Journals of David Livingstone. London, 1874.

WALMSLEY, L. ... ... Flying and sport in East Africa. William Blackwood & Sons, Edinburgh, 1920.

WASSERMANN, JAKOB ... ... H. M. Stanley, Explorer. London, 1932.

WELSH, S. R. ... ... South Africa under King Manuel. Cape Town, 1946.

WERTH, E. ... ... Das Deutsch-Ostafrikanishe Kustenland. Berlin, 1915.

WEULE, K. ... ... Native Life in East Africa. London, 1909.

WICHTERICH, Richard ... ... Carl Peters erobert Ostafrika. Stuttgart, 1941.

WILSON, C. J. ... ... The Story of the East African Mounted Rifles. Nairobi, 1938.

WINCKLER, H. and others ... Weltgeschichte: Vol. 3: Westasien und Africa. Bibliographisches Institut, Leipzig, 1901.

WISSMAN, H. VON ... ... Unter deutscher Flagge quer durch Afrika. Walther & Apolant, Berlin, 1902.

Afrika. Ernst Siegfried Mittler und Sohn. Berlin, 1895.

My Second Journey through Equatorial Africa. London, 1891.

WORSFOLD, W. B. ... ... Sir Bartle Frere. London, 1923.

YOUNG, E. D. ... ... Nyassa: a Journal of Adventures. London, 1876.

The Search after Livingstone, London, 1870.

YOUNGHUSBAND, E. ... ... Glimpses of East Africa and Zanzibar. London, 1910.

YULE, M. ... ... Mackay of Uganda. The Missionary Engineer. London.

ZIMMERMANN, A. ... ... Geschichte der deutschen Kolonialpolitik. E.S. Mittler & Sohn, Berlin, 1914.

Mit Dernburg nach Ostafrika. Berlin, 1909.

HISTORY AND PRE-HISTORY
Articles in Periodicals

ABDURRAHIM MOHAMED
JIDDAWI ... ... Extracts from an Arab account book, 1840-1954. *T.N.R.* 31, 1951, p.25.

ALLEN, J. W. T. ... ... Rhapta. *T.N.R.*, 17, 1944, p. 52.

The name "Dar es Salaam". *T.N.R.* 19, 1945. p. 67.

AMUR OMARI SAADI ... ... Mafia—history and traditions (transl. by D. W. I. Piggot) *T.N.R.* 12, 1945, p. 67.

ARKELL, A. J. ... ... An introduction to African prehistory. *Afr. Affairs* 49, 194, 56-67, Jan. 1950.

BAGSHAWE, F. J. ... ... Rock paintings of the Kangeju Bushmen. *Man.* 1923. 92, October, 1923.

BAKER, E. C. ... ... Notes on the Shirazi of East Africa. *T.N.R.* 11, 1941, p. 1.

Notes on the History of the Wasegeju. *T.N.R.* 27, 16-41, June, 1949.

BAX, S. N. ... ... The early Church Missionary Society Missions at Buzilima and Usambiro in the Mwanza District. *T.N.R.* 7, 1939 p. 39.

The grave of Fred Barker, one of Stanley's followers. *T.N.R.* 7, 1939, p. 56.

Doctor John Smith, 1852-1877. *T.N.R.* 14, 1941, p. 56.

BAXTER, H. C. ... ... Pangani: the trade centre of ancient history. *T.N.R.* 17. 1944, p. 15.

BEARDALL, W. ... ... Exploration of the Rufiji River. *Proceedings of the Royal Geographical Society*, 1881.

BELL, R. M. ... ... The Maji-Maji Rebellion in the Liwale District. *T.N.R.* 28, 1950, p. 38.

BRADSHAW, R. ... ... Darra Salaam, Africa. *Mercantile Magazine*, 1868.

BURTON, R. F. ... ... Description of a visit to Kilwa in 1859. *T.N.R.* 12. 1941, p. 45.

CADIZ, C. F. C. V. ... ... Dar es Salaam. *T.N.R.* 21, 1946, p. 77.

CANE, L. B. ... ... S.S. "Liemba". *T.N.R.* 23, 1947, p. 31.

CHRISTOPHER, W. ... ... Extract from Journal by, on the East Coast of Africa. *Journal of the Royal Geographical Society*, 1884.

COKE, C. M. ... ... The Livingstone Memorial, Ujiji. *T.N.R.* 25, 1948, p. 34.

CORY, HANS ... ... Buhaya and the African explorer (Extracts from a forthcoming book). *T.N.R.* 43. June 1956, 20-27.

CULWICK, A. T. ... ... Ritual Use of Rock Paintings at Bahi. *Man.* 1931. 41, London, 1931.

Some Rock Paintings in Central Tanganyika. *J.R.A.I.* Vol. LXI. July-December, 1931.

DAVEY, A. C. ... ... Church Missionary Society, Ngambo. *T.N.R.* 5, 1938, p. 68.

DIXON, J. W. ... ... Mikindani Bay, East Coast of Africa. *Nautical Mag.* 1874.

FORD, J. and HALL, R. DE Z. ... The history of Karagwe (Bukoba District). *T.N.R.* 24, 1947, p. 3.

FORSTER, N. ... ... A note on some ruins near Bagamoyo. *T.N.R.* 3, 1937, p. 106.

FOSBROOKE, H. A. ... ... Rift Valley ruins. *T.N.R.* 6, 1938, p. 58.

The Kondoa Rock Paintings: where they are and how to get there. *T.N.R.* 29, 1950, p. 30.

Rock Paintings in districts other than Kondoa. *T.N.R.* 29, 1950, p. 46.

The age and meaning of the Kondoa Rock Paintings. *T.N.R.* 29, 1950, p. 11.

Methods of preservation and reproduction (rock paintings). *T.N.R.* 29, 1950, p. 20.

Rock engravings or petroglyphs. *T.N.R.* 29, 1950, p. 27.

Kondoa Boma. *T.N.R.* 32, 1952, p. 50.

A Proto-Historic Burial. Naberera, Masai District, Tanganyika Territory. *S. African Archaeological Bulletin.* Vol. V.h. 105, 1950.

A Brief Review of Archaeological Remains in Tanganyika. *T.N.R.* No. 33, 1952.

FOSBROOKE, H. A. and
MAREALLE, P. I. ... ... The Engraved Rocks of Kilimanjaro. *Man.* 1952, 244 and 263.

FOSBROOKE, H. A. ... ... Further light on rock engravings in Northern Tanganyika. *Man.* 54, 157, 101-2, July, 1954.

FOSBROOKE, J. ... ... Some Kondoa Rock Paintings more fully described. *T.N.R.* 29, 1950, p. 39.

A prehistoric picturebook. *East Afr. Annual,* 1950.

FREEMAN-GRENVILLE, G. S. P.... A new Hoard and some Coins of the Sultans of Kilwa in the Dar es Salaam Museum. *Numismatic Chronicle.* 1954.

Ibn Batuta's visit to East Africa. A.D. 1332: A translation. *Uganda Journal*, Vol. 19. 1, 1955.

Chinese Porcelain in Tanganyika. *T.N.R.* No. 41, Dec. 1955, p. 62.

GALLOWAY, A. ... ... The Nebarara Skull. *South Afr. J. of Science*, Vol. XXX No. 585-596, 1933 (more usual spelling is Naberera).

GILLMAN, C. ... ... An annotated list of ancient and modern indigenous stone structures in Eastern Africa. *T.N.R.* 17, June, 1944, p. 44.

Supplementary note on stone structures in East Africa. *T.N.R.* 19, June, 1945, p. 64.

Dar es Salaam, 1860 to 1940: a story of growth and change. *T.N.R.*, 20, 1945, p. 1.

A short history of the Tanganyika Railways. *T.N.R.* 13, 1942, p. 14.

Indian elephants in Tanganyika. *T.N.R.* 12, 1941, p. 61.

GINNER, P. ... ... An artistic appreciation of the Kondoa rock paintings. *T.N.R.* 29, 1950, p. 3.

GRAY, SIR J. M. ... ... Portuguese Records relating to the Wasegeju. *T.N.R.* 29, July, 1950, pp. 85-97.

Stanley versus Tippoo Tib. *T.N.R.* 18, 1944, p. 11.

The Wadebuli and the Wadiba. *T.N.R.* 36, Jan. 1954.

Dar es Salaam under the Sultans of Zanzibar. *T.N.R.* 33, 1952.

Dar es Salaam in 1868. *T.N.R.* 24, 1947, p. 1.

Kilwa in 1812. *T.N.R.* 24, 1947, p. 24.

Mikindani Bay before 1887. *T.N.R.* 28, 1950, p. 29.

A History of Kilwa. *T.N.R.* 31, 1951, p. 1. and 32, 1952, p. 11.

The French at Kilwa, 1776-1784. *T.N.R.* No. 44, Sept. 1956.

HALL, R. DE Z. ... ... Angoni raids in the Rufiji District. *T.N.R.* 27, 1949, p. 74.

HARTNOLL, M. ... ... A story of the origin of the name of Bandar es Salaam, which in the old days was called Mzizima. *T.N.R.* 3, 1937, p. 117.

HARVEY, R. J. ... ... Mirambo, the Napoleon of Central Africa. *T.N.R.* 28, 1950, p. 10.

HATCHELL, G. W. ... ... The East African Campaign, 1914 to 1919. *T.N.R.* 21, 1946, p. 39.

Maritime Relics of the 1914-18 War. *T.N.R.* 16, 1943.

HEMEDI BIN ABDULLAH ... A history of Africa (transl. by E. C. Baker). *T.N.R.* 32, 1952, p. 65.

HOLMWOOD, F. ... ... Kingani River, East Africa. *Proceedings of the Royal Geographical Society*, 1877.

HOPWOOD, A. T. ... ... The age of Oldoway Man. *Man.* 1932, 226.

HUNTER, G. ... ... A Note on Some Tombs at Kaole. *T.N.R.* 37, July, 1954.

JACKSON, T. H. E. ... ... Some stone-built defences on Ukerewe Island. *T.N.R.* 25, 1948, p. 77.

JOHNSTON, P. H. ... ... Mtwara Bay. *T.N.R.*, 24 1947, p. 61.

KADI AHMUR OMAR SADDI ... Mafia, History and Traditions *T.N.R.* 12 23-3 Dec. 1941.

KENT, P. E. ... ... The recent history and Pleistocene deposits of the Plateau north of Lake Eyasi, Tanganyika. *Geol. Mag. Lond.*, vol. lxxviii, No. 3, 1941.

KOENIG, O. ... ... The ancient wells of Ngassumat in South Masailand. *T.N.R.* 31, 1951, p. 51.

LANE, L. P. ... ... Naval visit, Dar es Salaam—November, 1941. *T.N.R.* 16, 1943 p. 76.

The T.R.S. *Mwanza.* *T.N.R.* 6, 1938, p. 74.

LEAKEY, L. S. B. ... ... The Fossil Suidae of Oldoway. *J.E.Afr.Nat. His. Soc.* Vol. xvi, Nos. 4 an 1942.

Changes in the Physical Geography of E. Africa in Human Times. *Geographical Journal*, Vol. LXXXIV, No. 4, 1934.

A New Fossil Skull from Eyasi, East Africa. *Nature*, Vol. 138, Dec. 24th, 1936, p. 1084.

Preliminary report on examination of the Engaruka ruins. *T.N.R.* 1, 1936, p. 57.

The archaeological aspect of the Tanganyika Rock Paintings, *T.N.R.* 29, 1950, p. 15.

Report on a visit to the site of the Eyasi skull found by Dr. Kohl-Larsen. *J.E.A.N.H.S.*, June, 1946, pp. 185 and 186.

LEAKEY, L. S. B., HOPWOOD, A. T. and RICK, H. ... ... New Yields from the Oldoway Bone Beds, Tanganyika Territory. *Nature*, vol. 128, Dec. 26th, p. 1075, 1931.

LEAKEY, L. S. B. and others ... The Oldoway Human Skeleton. *Nature*, vol. 131, March 18th, 1933, p. 397.

LONGLAND, F. ... ... A note on the Tembe (Livingstone's) at Kwihara, Tabora. *T.N.R.* 1, 1936, p. 84.

MACKAY, A. ... ... A Boat Voyage along the Western Shores of Victoria Nyanza from Uganda to Kageye and Exploration of Jordan's Nullah. *P.R.G.S.*, 1884.

On the Kingani River. C.M.S. *Gleaner*, 1876.

MATHEW, A. G. ... ... A Medieval Islamic Kingdom off the Tanganyika Coast. *Illustrated London News*, Oct. 13, 1951.

Islamic Merchant Cities of East Africa. *The Times*, London, June, 26, 1951.

MOFFETT, J. P. ... ... One Hundred Years Ago in Tanganyika. *T.N.R.* 33, 1952.

MOFFETT, J. P. and MATHEW, A. G. ... ... Tanganyika's First Colonists—New Findings at Kilwa. *The East African Annual*, 1951-1952.

MNTAMBO, P. C. ... ... The Founding of King George V Memorial Museum, Dar es Salaam. *T.N.R.* 12, December, 1941.

OMARI BIN STAMBOUL ... ... An early history of Mombasa and Tanga. (trans. by E. C. Baker). *T.N.R.* 31, 1951, p. 32.

O'NEILL, H. E. ... ... The Ancient Civilisation, Trade and Commerce of Eastern Africa. *Scottish Geographical Magazine*, 1886.

PENNINGTON, A. L. ... ... Refugees in Tanganyika during the Second World War. *T.N.R.* 32, 1952, p. 50.

PIGGOTT, D. W. I. ... ... History of Mafia. *T.N.R.* 11, 1941, p. 35.

RANKIN, L. V. ... ... The Elephant Experiment in Africa: a brief account of the Belgian Elephant Expedition on the march from Dar es Salaam to Mpwapwa. *P.R.G.S.* (N.S.) (1882) IV. 273-289.

RECK, H.... ... ... Oldoway, die Schlucht des Urmenschen. *F.A. Brockhaus*, Leipzig, 1933.

Entdeckung von Stadt Trümmern in Ost Afrika. *P.M.* 1935, p. 458.

RECK, H. and KOHL-LARSEN, L. Erster Ueberblick über die jungdiluvialen Tier—und Menschenfunde im noroöstlichen Teil des Njarasa-Grabens. *Geol Mundschau*, No. 27, p. 401.

REEVE, W. H. ... ... Prehistory in Tanganyika. *T.N.R.* 6, 1938, p. 49.

Geological report on the site of Dr. Kohl-Larsen's discovery of a fossil human skull, Lake Eyasi, Tanganyika Territory. *J.E.A.N.H.S.* June, 1946.

REUSCH, R. ... ... How the Swahili People and Language came into existence. *T.N.R.*, 34, 1953.

The struggle of Mombasa for its freedom. *T.N.R.* 35, July, 1953, pp. 53-62.

REVINGTON, T. M. ... ... Some notes on the Mafia Island group (Mafia, Chole, Juani and Jibondo). *T.N.R.* 1, 1936, p.3.

RICHARDSON, R. B. ... ... Livingstone's *Tembe* at Kwihara, Tabora. *T.N.R.*, 9, June, 1940.

RIET LOWE, C. VAN ... ... A New African Acheul Stage IV Site in Tanganyika. *The South African Archaeological Bulletin.* Vol. VI, No. 24, December, 1951.

ROBINSON, A. E. ... ... Some historical notes on East Africa. *T.N.R.* 2, 1936, p. 21.

The Shirazi colonizations of East Africa. *T.N.R.* 3, 1937, p. 40, and 7, 1939, p. 92.

ROUSSEAU, M. ... ... En marge de l'histoire ancienne de l'Afrique. *Musée vivant*, 12, 36/37, 19-20, Nov. 1948.

SCHLICHTER, H. ... ... Ptolemy's Topography of Eastern Equatorial Africa. *Proceedings of Royal Geographical Society*, 1891.

SCOTT, R. R. ... ... The reefs of San Raphael, *T.N.R.* 14, 1942, p. 19.

SILLERY, A. ... ... Indian elephants in Tanganyika. *T.N.R.* 11, 1941, p. 64.

Maizan, *T.N.R.*, 10, 1940.

SMITH, G. SHERGOLD ... ... Letters. C.M.S. *Gleaner*, 1876-8.

SMUTS, GENERAL J. C. ... ... East Africa. *G.J.*, March, 1918.

STRONG, S. A. ... ... The History of Kilwa. *Journal of Royal Asiatic Society*, 1895.

STOWELL, R. F. ... ... Notes on some ruins at Tongoni, near Tanga. *T.N.R.* 4, 1937, p. 75.

TANNER, R. E. S. ... ... Some Chinese pottery found at Kilwa Kisiwani. *T.N.R.* 32, 1952, p. 83.

A Series of Rock Paintings near Mwanza. *T.N.R.* 34, 1953.

TAUTE, M. ... ... A German account of the medical side of the war in East Africa 1914-1918. *T.N.R.* 8, 1939, p. 1.

THOMAS, H. B. ... ... The Kionga triangle. *T.N.R.* 31, 1951, p. 47.

TOIT, P. J. DE ... ... Notes on the coinage of German East Africa (Tanganyika). *T.N.R.*, 31, 1951, p. 37.

Various sources (comp.) Some notes on Kilwa. *T.N.R.* 2, 1936, p. 92.

WADE, F. B. ... ... James Frederic Elton. *T.N.R.* 8, 1939, p. 98.

WALKER, J. ... ... The history and coinage of the Sultans of Kilwa. *Numismatic Chronicle*, 1936. Vol. XVI.

WALKER, DR. J. and FREEMAN-GRENVILLE, DR. G. S. P. ... The History and Coinage of the Sultans of Kilwa. *T.N.R.* No. 45, Dec. 1956, p. 33.

WETHERELL, M. A. ... ... The mysterious ruins of Engaruka. *East African Standard*, 11th Oct. 1935.

WHEELER, SIR MORTIMER ... Archaeology in East Africa. *T.N.R.* No. 40, Sept. 1955, p. 43.

WHITELEY, W. H. ... ... Southern Province rock paintings. *T.N.R.* 31, 1951, p. 58.

WORSLEY, P. M. and RUMBERGER, J. P. ... ... Remains of an Earlier People in Uhehe. *T.N.R.* 27, 1949.

WYNN-JONES, W. ... ... African Dugouts (caves) *T.N.R.* 11, 1941.

GEOGRAPHY AND TRAVEL
Books, Reports, Pamphlets

AHLEFELDT-BILLE, G. ... ... Tandalla. Routledge and Kegan Paul, London, 1948.

ALEXANDER, G. ... ... Tanganyika Memories. Blackie, London, 1936.

ARNING, W. ... ... Deutsch-Ostafrika. Dietrich Reimer, Berlin, 1936.

Atlas of Tanganyika. G.P.D.

BAKER, SIR S. W. ... ... Albert Nyanza, Great Basin of the Nile. London.

BARKER, DE LA BERE ... ... Rufiji, Hermit Hunter of Africa. London, 1955.

BAUMANN, O. ... ... Durch Massailand zur Nilquelle. Geographische Verlagshandlung, Dietrich Reimer, Berlin, 1894.

Die Kartographischen Ergebnisse der Massai-Expedition des deutschen Antisklaverei-Comites. Justus Perthes, Gotha, 1894.

BAUMANN, O. ... ... Usambara und seine Nachbargebiete. Geographische Verlagshandlung, Dietrich Reimer, Berlin, 1891.

BAUMGARTEN, J.... ... ... Deutsch-Afrika. Ferd. Dämmlers Verlagsbuchhandlung, Berlin, 1890.

BLANCHOD, F. ... ... Au paradis des grands fauves. Lausanne, 1947.

BROW ... ... Handbook of German East Africa. (Admiralty, I.D. 1055). H.M.S.O., 1914.

BULPIN, T. V. ... ... East Africa and the Islands (A book of photographs) London (Bailey Brothers) 1956. pp. 98. ill. map.

BURTON, R. F. ... ... Zanzibar, City, Island, and Coast. London, 1872.
The Lake Regions of Central Africa. 2 vols, London, 1860.

CAMPBELL, R. J.... ... ... Livingstone. Ernest Benn Ltd., London, 1920.

CAMERON, V. L. ... ... Across Africa. 2 vols. London, 1877.

CARNOCHAN, F. G. and
 ADAMSON, H. C. ... ... The Empire of the Snakes. London, 1935.

COUPLAND, R. ... ... Kirk on the Zambesi. Oxford, 1928.
Livingstone's Last Journey. Collins, 1945.

D'ALBERTIS, E. A. ... ... In Africa. Victoria Nyanza e Benadir, 3 maps, 2 panoramic plates and 185 illusts., roy. 8vo, Bergamo, 1906.

DEBENHAM, F. ... ... The Road to Ilala (Livingstone's Travels) London, 1956.

DECKEN, C. C. VON DER ... Reisen in Ostafrika. 6 vols. Leipzig and Heidelberg, 1869-1879.

DECLE, L. ... ... Three Years in Savage Africa. London, 1898.

DE HAAS, R. ... ... Der Wilderer von Deutsch-Ost, 12 drawings, Berlin, 1927.

DENBER, A. G. C. ... ... British East Africa. Overseas Economic Surveys. London, 1948.

DEPPE, C. & L. ... ... Um Ostafrika: Erinnerungen, illusts., ¼ cloth, Dresden, 1925.

DEUTSCH-OSTAFRIKA ... ... Berichte namhafter Reisender ueber Natur und Beschaffenheit von Deutsch-Ostafrika, 37 pp., Berlin, 1886.

DEVEREUX, W. C. ... ... A Cruise in the "Gorgon"—engaged in the suppression of the Slave Trade on the East Coast of Africa. London, 1869.

DUNDAS, A. ... ... Beneath African Glaciers. London, 1924.

DUNDAS, C. ... ... Kilimanjaro and its People. London, 1924.

East African Meteorological Department. Annual Summary of Rainfall. Part II, Tanganyika. Govt. Printer, Nairobi.

East African Statistical Department. African population of Tanganyika Territory (Geographical and Tribal Studies. Source: East African Population Census). Nairobi, 1950.

ELIOT, SIR C. ... ... The East Africa Protectorate. Edward Arnold, London, 1905.

ELLIOT, G. F. S. ... ... A Naturalist in mid-Africa. A. D. Innes & Co., London, 1896.

ELTON, J. F. and
COTTERILL, H. B. ... ... Travels and Researches among the Lakes and Mountains of Eastern and Central Africa. John Murray, London, 1879.

FALKENHORST, C. ... ... Deutsch Ost-Afrika. Stuttgart, Berlin, Leipzig 1890.

FARSON, N. ... ... Behind God's Back. London, 1940.

Last Chance in Africa. Gollancz, London, 1949.

FISCHER, G. A. ... ... Vorlaufiger Bericht uber die Expedition zur Auffindung Dr. Junkers. P.M. 1886.

FLATZ, J. ... ... Die Kulturen Ostafrikas, map, bibliography, Linz, 1936.

FONCK, H. ... ... Deutsch Ost-Afrika. Berlin, 1908-09.

Wildsteppen und Steppenwild in Ost-Afrika. Berlin, 1924.

FORAN, W. R. ... ... African Odyssey: the Life of Verney Lovett-Cameron, map and 59 illusts., 1937.

FORBES-WATSON, COL. R. ... Life and Wanderings in East Africa of Charles New (Early Travellers in E.A. Series—published by East African Literature Bureau). Nairobi, 1954.

GILLMAN, C. ... ... Report on Preliminary Surveys to open up South-West Tanganyika. Crown Agents, 1929.

A Reconnaissance Survey of the Hydrology of Tanganyika Territory in its geographical settings. Water Consultant's Report No. 6. G.P.D., 1940.

GIRAUD, V. ... ... Les Lacs de l'Afrique Equatoriale: Voyage d'Exploration, 1883-85, 2 maps and 161 illusts., Paris, 1890.

GOTZEN, G. A. GRAF VON ... Durch Afrika van Ost nach West. Berlin, 1899.

GOULER, A. ... ... Sur les bords du Victoria. Paris, 1949.

GRANT, A. ... ... A Walk across Africa. London, 1894.

GREGORY, J. W. ... ... The Rift Valleys and Geology of East Africa
Seeley Service & Co. Ltd., London, 1921.

GUILLAIN, M. ... ... Voyage ä la cöte orientale d'Afrique. Paris 1857

GUNTHER, J. ... ... Inside Africa. London, 1955.

HAAS, R. ... ... Piet Nieuwenhuizen der Pfadfinder. Safari
Verlag G.M.B.H. Berlin.

HAILEY, LORD ... ... An African Survey. O.U.P., London, 1957.

HAMILTON, G. ... ... In the Wake of Da Gama. London, 1951.

Handbook to German East Africa. Prepared on behalf of the Admiralty and
the War Office (I.D. 1055) 1914.

HAUER, A. ... ... Kumbuke. Erlebnisse eines arztes in
Deutsch-Ost-Afrika. Dom Verlag, Berlin,
1922.

HEMINGWAY, E. ... ... Green Hills of Africa. Cape, London, 1936.

HERTSLET, SIR E. ... ... The Map of Africa by Treaty. 2nd and
revised edition, 3 vols. London, 1896.

HOFFMAN, W. ... ... With Stanley in Africa. Cassell & Co.,
London, 1938.

HOHNEL, L. V. VON ... ... Discovery by Count Teleki of Lakes Rudolf
and Stefanie. 2 vols.

HORE, A. B. ... ... To Lake Tanganyika in a Bath-Chair, map
and 2 portraits, 1886.

HORE, E. C. ... ... Tanganyika: Eleven years in Central Africa.
Edward Stanford. London, 1892.

HOURANI, G. F. ... ... Arab Seafarers in the Indian Ocean in
Ancient and Early Medieval Times.
Princeton, 1951.

HUNTER, C. S. ... ... Victoria Nyanza. London, 1908.

HUNTER, J. A. ... ... Hunter (A Game Warden's life in East Africa).
London, 1952.

HUNTINGFORD, G. W. B. and
BELL, C. R. V. ... ... East African Background. London, 2nd
edition, 1950.

HUXLEY, E. ... ... The Sorcerer's Apprentice. London, 1948.

HUXLEY, J. S. ... ... Africa View. London, 1931.

IBN BATUTAH ... ... Travels in Asia and Africa, 1325-1354.
Translated by H. A. R. Gibb. Broadway
Travellers, London, 1929.

JOELSON, F. S. ... ... The Tanganyika Territory. T. Fisher Unwin
Ltd., London, 1920.

JOHNSON, W. P. ... ... Nyasa, the Great Water. O.U.P., London,
1922.

JOHNSTON, H. H. ... ... The Kilima-Njaro Expedition. Kegan Paul,
Trench & Co., London, 1886.

JOHNSTON, H. H. ... ... The Nile Quest. Lawrence & Bullen Ltd., London, 1903.
The Opening up of Africa. London, 1911.
British Central Africa. London, 1913.

JUNKER, W. ... ... Travels in East Africa during the years 1882-1886. Chapman & Hall Ltd., London, 1892.

KANDT, R. ... ... Caput Nili. D. Reimer, Berlin, 1905.

KERSTEN, O. ... ... Baron Carl Claus von der Decken's Reisen in Ost-Afrika. C.F. Wintersche Verlagshandlung, Leipzig, 1869.

KLAMROTH, M. ... ... Auf Bergpfaden in Deutsch Ost-Afrika. Berlin, 1907.

KOENIG, O. ... ... The Masai Story. London, 1956.
Pori Tupu. London, 1954.

KONDAZI, C. ... ... Indians Overseas, 1838-1949. London, 1952.

KRAPF, J. L. ... ... Reisen in Ostafrika. Kornthal, 1858.

LEUE, A. ... ... Dar es Salaam, Bilder aus dem Kolonialleben. Berlin, 1903.

LIGHT, R. U. ... ... Focus on Africa. Special Publ. No. 25, American Geographical Society, New York, 1941.

LINSCHOTEN, J. H. VAN ... Voyage to the East Indies. Hakluyt Society, 70-71, London, 1885.

LIVINGSTONE, D. ... ... First Expedition to Africa. London, 1912.
The Last Journals of D. Livingstone, 1874.

LOOFF, D. M. ... ... Kreuzerfahst und Buschkampf. Berlin, 1929.

LOVERIDGE, A. ... ... Tomorrow's a Holiday. London, 1951.

LUGARD, F. D. ... ... The Rise of our East African Empire. 2 vols. Edinburgh, 1893.

MACDONALD, S ... ... Tanganyika Safari. Angus and Robertson, Sydney, 1948.

MACMILLAN, M. ... ... Introducing East Africa. London, 1952.

MACNAIR, J. I. ... ... Livingstone's Travels (from his own diaries) London, 1954.

MALLETT, M. ... ... A White Woman among the Masai. London, 1923.

MAS'UDI, EL. ... ... Géographie (French transl. of Arabic Text, 14th Century). Paris 1861-77.

MAYER, A. ... ... Das Buch der deutschen Kolonien. Potsdam, Leipzig, Verlag Volf und Heimat.

MECKLENBURG, A. F. H. VON ... Ins innerste Afrika.

MEYER, H. ... ... Das deutsche Kolonialreich. Vol. 1: Ostafrika und Kamerun. Verlag des Bibiliographischen Instituts. Leipzig, 1909.

MEYER, H. ... ... Der Kilimanjaro. D. Reimer, Berlin, 1900.
Across East African Glaciers. George Philip
& Son, London, 1891.

MIGEOD, F. W. H. ... ... Across Equatorial Africa. Heath Cranton
Ltd., London, 1923.

MILLAIS, J. G. ... ... Life of Frederick Courtenay Selous, D.S.O.,
Capt. 25th Royal Fusiliers. Longmans,
Green & Co., London, 1918.

MONSON, R. A. ... ... Across Africa on foot. Elkin Mathews &
Marrot. London, 1936.

MOORE, AUDREY ... ... Serengeti. *Country Life*, London.

MUHAMMAD IBN MUHAMMAD
AL-IDRISI ... ... Géographie (transl. from Arabic by Jaubert)
Paris, 1836.

MUNZINGER, W. ... ... Die Deutsche Expedition in Ost-Afrika, 1861-
62, maps, (46 pp.), Gotha, 1864, Petermann's
Mittheilungen: Ergaenzungsheft, No. 13.

NEW, C. ... ... Wanderings in Eastern Africa. Hodder and
Stoughton, London, 1873.

NEWLYN, W. T. and ROWAN,
D. C. ... ... Money and Banking in British Colonial
Africa. London, 1954.

OBST, E. ... ... Das abflusslose Rumpfschollenland in nord-
östlichen. Hamburg, 1915.

OWEN, W. F. W. ... ... Narratives of voyages to explore the shores of
Africa, Arabia and Madagascar. London,
1933.

PAASCHE, H. ... ... Deutsch-Ostafrika. C.A. Schwetschke & Sohn,
Berlin, 1906.

PARKE, T. H. ... ... My Personal Experiences in Equatorial Africa.
London, 1891.

PEARCE, F. B. ... ... Zanzibar, the island Metroplis of Eastern
Africa. London, 1920.

PERHAM, M. and SIMMONS, J. ... African Discovery. Faber & Faber, London,
1942.

Permanent Committee on Geographical Names. First list of names in
Tanganyika Territory. Royal Geographical Society London, 1922, corrected
1926.

PETERS, C. ... ... Das deutsche Ostafrikanische Schutzgebiet.
Munich, 1895.

Die deutsche Emin Pascha Expedition in
ostlichen Mittel Afriken. Hamburg, 1907.

Die Gruendung von Deutsch-Ostafrika,
portrait, 14 illusts. and facsimile, Berlin,
1906.

PINTO, A. DE S. ... ... How I crossed Africa. London, 1881.

PRINCE, M. ... ... Eine deutsche Frau im Innern Deutsch-Ostafrikas. Berlin, 1905.

PRITTWITZ UND GAFFRON, G. VON ... ... Die Oberflachengestalt der Gebergslandschaft Utschungsen. Berlin, 1932.

RAVENSTEIN (ED) ... ... The first voyage of Vasco da Gama. Hakluyt Society, London, 1898.

RECK, I. ... ... Aufeinsamen määrschen im norden von Ost-Afrika. Berlin, 1925.

REHSE, H. ... ... Kisiba, Land und Leute. Stuttgart, 1910.

REID ... ... Tanganyika without Prejudice. East Africa & Rhodesia Ltd., London,

REICHS-MARINE-AMT ... ... Handbuch der Ostkuste Afrikas. E.S. Mittler & Sohn, Berlin, 1912.

ROUX, L. ... ... Des grands lacs à Zanzibar: l'est Africain Britannique. Paris, 1950.

SCHLIEBEN, H. J. ... ... Deutsch Ost-Afrika, einmal ganz anders, 2 maps and 182 illusts., Berlin, 1941.

SCHNEE, H. ... ... Deutsches Kolonial Lexikon. Quelle & Meyer. Leipzig, 1920.

SCHOELLER, M. ... ... Mitteilungen über meine reise nach Aquatorial-Ost-Africa. Berlih, 1901.

SCHOFF, W. H. ... ... The Periplus of the Erythraean Sea. Translated from the Greek. London, 1912.

SCHWARZE ... ... Deutsch-Ost-Afrika. Wilherlm Süsserott, Berlin, 1907.

SEIDEL, A. ... ... Deutsch-Ostafrika. Das Uberseeische Deutschland. Stuttgart, 1890.

SHARPE, A. ... ... The Backbone of Africa. H.F. & G. Witherby, London, 1921.

SHORTHOSE, W. T. ... ... Sport and Adventure in Africa. Seeley, Service & Co., Ltd. London, 1923.

SMITH, C. S. ... ... Explorations in Zanzibar Dominions. c.1884 (no publisher's name).

SPEKE, J. H. ... ... Journal of the Discovery of the Source of the Nile. William Blackwood and Sons, Edinburgh, 1863.

STANLEY, H. M. ... ... How I found Livingstone. London, 1872.
Through the Dark Continent. London, 1878.
In Darkest Africa. London, 1890.

STUART-WATT, E. ... ... Africa's Dome of Mystery. London, 1930.

STUHLMANN, F. ... ... Mit Emin Pascha ins Herz von Afrika. Berlin, 1894.
Beitrage zur Kulturgeschichte von Ostafrika.

SWANSON, G. H.   ...   ...   Touring Tanganyika. Augustana Book Concern, Rock Island, Illinois.

TELEKI, Count   ...   ...   Die Expedition des Grafen Teleki in das Gebiet des Kilimandscharo und Kenia, vorlauefiger Bericht, 2 foldg. plates, 118 pp., Vienna, 1888.

The Tanganyika Guide.   Public Relations Office, Dar es Salaam.

THOMSON, J.   ...   .   To the Central African Lakes and Back. Sampson Low, Marston, Searle & Rivington, London, 1881.

Through Masai Land.   London, 1881.

Notes on the basin of the River Rovuma. P.G.S. 1882.

WALLER, H.   ...   .   The last journals of David Livingstone. John Murray, London, 1874.

WATTEVILLE, V. DE   ...   ...   Speak to the Earth.   London, 1935.

WEHRMEISTER, P. C.   ...   ...   Vor dem Sturm. Eine Reise durch Deutsch-Ostafrika vor und bei dem Ausstande, 1905.

WEISS, K.   ...   .   Meine Reise nach dem Kilima-Ndjarogebiet im Auftrage der Deutsch-Ostafrikanischen Gesellschaft, foldg. map, 46 pp., Berlin, 1886.

WERTH, E.   ...   .   Das Deutsch-Ostafrikanische Kustenland und die vorgelagerten Inseln.   Berlin, 1915.

WERTHER, C. W.   ...   ...   Die mittleren Hochlander des nordlichen Deutsch Ostafrika. Herman Paetel, Berlin, 1898.

WILLOUGHBY, J. C.   ...   ...   East Africa and its Big Game—the narrative of a sporting trip from Zanzibar to the borders of the Masai.

WORTHINGTON, E. B.   ...   ...   Science in Africa.   London, 1938.

ZACHE, H.   ...   .   Deutsch-Ost-Afrika—Tanganyika Territorium Safari Verlag.   G.m.b.H. Berlin, 1926.

GEOGRAPHY AND TRAVEL
Articles in Periodicals

BARKER, R. DE LA B.   ...   ...   The delta of the Rufiji River. *T.N.R.* 2, 1936. p.1.

Some rivers of Southern Tanganyika. *T.N.R.* 24, 1947.   p.66.

The Rufiji River.   *T.N.R.* 4, 1937, p.10.

BARNS, T. A.   ...   .   Ngorongoro, the giant crater, and the gorilla, the giant ape.   *J.R.A.S.*, 1922-23, p.179.

BYATT, H.   ...   .   Tanganyika.   *J.R.A.S.* 1924-25, p.1.

Coss, D. K. ... ... Notes on the Country lying between Lake Nyassa and Tanganyika. *P.G.S.* Vol. XIII.

East African Statistical Department. *Quarterly Economic and Statistical Bulletin.* Nairobi.

Eliot, G. F. S. ... ... Expedition to Ruwenzori and Tanganyika. *G.J.* 1895. Vol. VI, p. 301.

Elliott, H. F. I. ... ... An island in Lake Victoria. *T.N.R.* 10, 1940, p. 28.

Some hints on climbing Masailand mountains. *T.N.R.* 26, 1948, p. 68.

Gilbert, E. W. and Steel, R. W. ... ... Social Geography and its place in colonial studies. *Geog. J.* 106, 3/4, 118-31, Sept.-Oct., 1945.

Gillman, C. ... ... An ascent of Kilimanjaro. *Geog. J.*, 61, 1 Jan. 1923, pp. 1-27.

A Bibliography of Kilimanjaro, 1944. *T.N.R.*, 18, Dec., 1944, p. 60.

Some geographical controls in East Africa. *S. Afr. Geog. J.*, 15, Dec. 1932, pp. 3-14.

South-west Tanganyika Territory. *G.J.*, Lond., Vol. 69, Feb. 1927, pp. 97-131.

A population map of Tanganyika. *G.Rev.*, New York, Vol. 26, No. 3, July, 1936, pp. 353-375 (Also published as Appendix 9 with accompanying maps, in the Report on the administration of Tanganyika Territory for the year 1935. Colonial No. 113. London, 1936.

A vegetation types map of Tanganyika Territory. *G. Rev.*, New York, Vol. 39, No. 1 Jan., 1949, pp. 7-37.

A synopsis of the geography of Tanganyika Territory. *T.N.R.* 1, 1936, p. 5.

Grant, C. H. B. ... ... Some Lakes and Waterfalls of Central and Western Tanganyika. *T.N.R.* 25, 1948, p. 63.

The Valley and Swamps of the Malagarasi River, Western Tanganyika Territory. *T.N.R.* 23, 1947, p. 29.

Uvinza, Tongwe and Ubende, Western Tanganyika. *T.N.R.* 27, 1949. p. 69,

The hot springs of Mtangata ("Boiling Water"). North-Western Tanganyika Territory. *T.N.R.* 24, 1947, p. 47.

GRIFFITHS, J. E. S. ... ... A visit to the island of Godziba in Lake Victoria. *T.N.R.* 28, 1950, p. 58.

GRIFFITH-JONES, T. ... ... Stanley's first and second expeditions through Mpwapwa. *T.N.R.* 25, 1948, p. 29.

GUEST, N. J. ... ... Climbing Oldonyo L'Engai. *T.N.R.* 31, 1951, p. 55.

HARRIS, J. H. ... ... Lake Manyara. *T.N.R.* 30, 1951, p. 6.

HATCHELL, G. W. ... ... San Raphael once again. *T.N.R.* 31, 1951, p. 51.

HOLMES-SIEDLE, J. ... ... Down Lake Tanganyika in the "Liemba". *T.N.R.* 25, 1949, p. 72.

JAEGER, F. ... ... Das Hochland der Riesenkrater. Mitt. aus den Deutsch. Schutzgeb. *Erganzheft*, 4, 1911 and 8, 1913.

Der Meru. *G.Z.* 1906.

LANE, L. P. ... ... Fungu Kizimkazi, or Latham Island. *T.N.R.* 18, Dec., 1944, p. 89.

To Utete by Ship. Rufiji River pilotage. *T.N.R.* 20, 1945, p. 55.

LEAKEY, E. A. and
ROUNCE, N. V. ... ... The human geography of the Kasulu District, Tanganyika: the land of the Abaha. *Geography*, London, Vol. 18, No. 4, Dec., 1933, pp. 293-305.

MEYER, HANS ... ... Die Ersteigung des Kilimandjaro, *V.G.E.B.* p. 90, 1890.

MOREAU, R. E. ... ... Kilimanjaro and Mount Kenya. *T.N.R.* 18, 1944, p. 26.

MOREAU, R. E. and
GREENWAY, P. J. ... ... A note on Longido and Ketumbeine Mountains. *T.N.R.* 3, 1937, p. 8.

MORGAN, J. C. ... ... The Machinga Caves (with a note on those on Songo-Songo Island, and the Tawa-Pondo Cave). *T.N.R.* 7, 1939, p. 59.

NTEMO, FINEHAS D. ... ... Some Notes on Ngulu. *T.N.R.* No. 45, Dec. 1956, p. 15.

O'HAGAN, C. C. ... ... Mkungwe Mountain. *T.N.R.* 9, 1940, p. 53.

PAGE-JONES, F. H. ... ... Water in Masailand. *T.N.R.* 26, 1948, p. 51.

PATTERSON, R. L. ... ... Ukara Island. *T.N.R.* No. 44, Sept. 1956, p. 54.

PIGGOTT, D. W. I. ... ... Magari. *T.N.R.* 11, 1941, p. 61.

POPPLEWELL, G. D. and
HARRIES, T. E. ... ... Notes on the geography of the Tunduru District of Tanganyika Territory. *Geog. J.*, London, Vol. 91, No. 1, Jan., 1938, pp. 31-43.

REIMERSCHMID, G. ... ... The intensity of solar radiation at various places in Tanganyika Territory. *T.N.R.* 20, 1945, p. 33.

ROSE, SISTER ... ... Voyage de Marseille au lac Tanganyika en 1902 via Mozambique et lac Nyasa. *T.N.R.* 3, 1937, p. 110.

SALT, GEORGE ... ... The Shira Plateau of Kilimanjaro. *T.N.R.* No. 39, June, 1955, p. 39.

SILLERY, A. ... ... Maizan, *T.N.R.* 10, 1940, p. 89.

SMITH, G. E. ... ... From the Victoria Nyanza to Kilimanjaro. *G.J.* 1907, vol. 29, p. 249.

Tanganyika Notes and Records: Published half-yearly by the Tanganyika Society, P.O. Box 511, Dar es Salaam.

TEALE, E. O. ... ... Geographical and geological problems in East Africa, with special reference to Tanganyika Territory. *J.A.S.* 1923-1924, p. 1.

TEALE, E. O. and HARVEY, E. ... A physiographical map of Tanganyika Territory. *Geog. Rev.*, New York, Vol. 23, No. 3, July, 1933, pp. 402-413., p. 1.

THOMAS, Fr. ... ... Un voyage de Marseille au lac Tanganyika en 1906. *T.N.R.* 5, 1938, p. 25.

THRELFALL, H. R. ... ... Some physical features of the Dar es Salaam District. *T.N.R.* 29, 1950, p. 68.

TULLOCH, W. ... ... Mafia Island. *Corona* 8, 6, 206-9, June 1955.

WALTER, A. ... ... A note on the seasonal rains in East Africa and their causation. *T.N.R.* 8, 1939, p. 21.

WATERMEYER, A. M. and
ELLIOTT, H. F. I. ... ... Lake Manyara. *T.N.R.* 15, 1943, p. 58.

ETHNOLOGY, SOCIOLOGY, ETC.

Books, Reports, Pamphlets

ANKERMANN, B. ... ... Das Eingeborenenrecht, Sitten und Gewohnheitsrechte der Eingeborenen des ehemaligen deutschen Kolonien in Afrika und in der Südsee. Strecker and Schröder, Stuttgart, 1929.

BAUMANN, O. ... ... Durch Masailand zur Nilquelle. Berlin, 1894. Usambara. Berlin, 1891.

BLOHM, WILHELM ... ... Die Nyamwezi: Gesellschaft und Weltbild. Hamburg: Friedrichseh, de Gruyter, 1933.

Die Nyamwezi: Land und Wirtschaft. Hamburg: Friedrichsen, de Gruyter, 1931.

BOESCH, F. ... ... Les Banyamwezi: peuple de l'Afrique Orientale. Anthropos Bibliothek, Münster, 1930.

BOHRENZ, W. ... ... Beitrage zur materiellen Kultur der Nyamwezi. H. Gildendruck. Hamburg, 1940.

BROWN, G. G. and HUTT, A. M. B. ... ... Anthropology in Action. (The Hehe tribe), Oxford, 1935.

CAROTHERS, J. C. ... ... The African mind in health and disease: a study in ethno-psychiatry. Geneva: World Health Organization, 1953. (Monograph series No. 17).

COLSON, E. ... ... Seven Tribes of British Central Africa. London, 1951.

CORY, H.... ... ... Ntemi—The Traditional Rites of a Sukuma Chief. Macmillan, London, 1951.

Sukuma Law and Custom. O.U.P., for Int. African Inst., 1953.

Wall-paintings by Snake Charmers in Tanganyika. Faber, London, 1953.

Sikilizeni: Mashairi na Picha (a book of new Swahili poems). East African Literature Bureau, 1954.

The Indigenous Political System of the Sukuma. Eagle Press, Nairobi, 1954.

African Figurines. London, 1956.

CORY, H. and HARTNOLL, M. M. The Customary Law of the Haya tribe. Laird Humphries, for International African Institute, London, 1945.

CULWICK, A. T. and G. M. ... Ubena of the Rivers. George Allen & Unwin Ltd., London, 1935.

DALE, G. ... ... The Peoples of Zanzibar. U.M.C.A., London, 1920.

DUNDAS, C. ... ... Kilimanjaro and its People. Witherby, 1924.

EVANS-PRITCHARD, E. E., FIRTH, R., MALINOWSKI, B. and SCHAPERA, I. (ed) ... ... Essays presented to C.G. Seligman. London. 1934.

FRAZER, J. G. (ed. DOWNIE, R. A.) ... ... The Native Races of Africa and Madagascar. London, 1938.

FUCHS, H. ... ... Sagen, Mythen und Sitten der Masai. Jena, 1910.

GUTMANN, B.	Das Recht der Dschagga. Arbeiten zur Entwicklung-psychologie. No. 7, Berlin, 1926.
	Volksbuch der Wadschagga. Leipzig, 1914.
HINDE, S. L.	The Last of the Masai. London, 1911.
HIRSCHBERG, W.	Die Arabisch-Persisch-Indische Kultur auf der Ostkuste Afrikas. M.A.G. LXL, 1931.
HOLLIS, A. C.	The Masai Language and Folklore. Oxford, 1905.
HUNTINGFORD, C. W. B. and BELL, C. R. V.	East African Background. Longmans, Green & Co., 1945.
GULLIVER, P. H.	Labour Migration in a Rural Economy; a study of the Ngoni and Ndendeule of Southern Tanganyika. Kampala (E.A. Institute of Social Research), 1955.
JERRARD, R. C.	The tribes of Tanganyika, their districts, usual dietary and pursuits. G.P.D., 1936.
JOHNSTON, H. H.	A comparative study of the Bantu and semi-Bantu languages. The Clarendon Press, Oxford, 1919.
KOLLMANN, P.	Victoria Nyanza. London, 1899.
LECHAPTOIS, P.	Aux rives du Tanganyika. Imprimerie des Missionaires d'Afrique, Alger, 1913.
KUCZYNSKI, R. R.	A demographic survey of the British Colonial Empire. Vol. II: South Africa, High Commission territories, East Africa, Mauritius, Seychelles. London: O.U.P., for Royal Institute of International Affairs, 1949.
KOENIG, O.	The Masai Story. London (Joseph), 1955.
MACKENZIE, D. R.	The spirit-ridden Konde. Seley, Service & Co., London, 1925.
MALCOLM, D. W.	Sukumaland: An African People and their Country. O.U.P., London, 1953.
MEINHOF, C.	Die Dichtung der Afrikaner. Buchhandlung der Berliner Evg. Missionsgesell., Berlin, 1911.
MERKER, M.	Die Masai. Ethnographische Monographie eins Ostafrikanischen Semitenvolkes. Berlin, 1904.
NIGMANN, E.	Dic Wahehe. E.S. Mittler & Sohn, Berlin, 1908.
NOTCUTT, L. A. and LATHAM, G. C.	The African and the Cinema. London, 1937.

ORDE-BROWNE, G. ST. J. ... The African Labourer. O.U.P., for International African Inst. London, 1933.

RADCLIFFE-BROWN, A. R. and
FORDE, D. ... ... African Systems of Kinship and Marriage. Oxford University Press, for International African Institute, London, 1950.

SCHMIDT, K. W.... ... ... Zanzibar, ein ostafrikanisches Bulturbild, Leipzig, 1888.

SELIGMAN, C. G. ... ... Races of Africa. London, 1939.

SHARP, E. ... ... The African Child. London, 1931.

STEERE, E. ... ... Swahili Tales. London, 1889.

STAHLMANN, F. ... ... Handwerk und Indstrie in Ostafrika. Hamburg, 1910.

The Tanganyika Guide. Public Relations Office, Dar es Salaam.

TEW, M. ... ... The Peoples of the Lake Nyasa region. Ethnographic Survey of Africa. O.U.P., London, 1950.

THURNWALD, R. C. ... ... Black and White in East Africa. London, 1935.

United Nations: Department of Social Affairs, Population Division. The population of Tanganyika. New York: 1949. (Reports on the population of trust territories, No. 2).

United Nations: Department of Social Affairs, Population Division. Additional information on the population of Tanganyika: supplement to the Population of Tanganyika New York: 1953. (Population studies, No. 14).

WEISS, M. ... ... Die Volkerstamme in Norden Deutsch Ostafrikas. Berlin, 1910.

WEULE, K. ... ... Native Life in East Africa. Sir Isaac Pitman & Sons, London, 1909.

WIDENMANN, A. ... ... Die Kilimandscharo-Bevoelkerung: Anthropologisches und Ethnographisches aus dem Dschaggalande, 11 plates and 75 illusts. in text, 104 pp., Gotha, 1899. Petermann's Mitteilungen: Ergaenzungsheft No. 129.

WILLOUGHBY, W. C. ... ... The Soul of the Bantu. S.C.M., London, 1928.

WILSON, G. ... ... The Nyakyusa, in "Seven tribes of British Central Africa", edited by Elizabeth Colson and Max Gluckman, 1951.

WILSON, M. ... ... Good Company: A study of Nyakyusa age-villages. O.U.P., for Int. African Inst., 1951.

Rituals of kinship among the Nyakyusa. Pp. 278, illus. London: Oxford University Press for International African Institute.

ETHNOLOGY, SOCIOLOGY, etc.
Articles in Periodicals

ABDULLAN BIN HEMEDI ... The story of Mbega. *T.N.R.* 1, 1936, p. 38; 2, 1936, p. 80; 3, 1937, p. 87.

ALEXANDER ... ... A history of the Wazinza. *Mambo Leo*, 1927/28.

ALLEN, J. W. T. ... ... Tenzi. *T.N.R.* 28, 1950, p. 81.

ARKELL, A. J. ... ... An introduction to African Pre-history. *Afr. Affairs* 49, 194, 56-7, Jan., 1950.

ARNING, W. ... ... Die Wahehe. *M.a.d.s.* 1896, p. 233.

ATKINSON, A. G, ... African Housing. *Afr. Affairs* 49, 196, 228-37 July, 1950.

BAGENAL, C. J. ... ... Mwariye: a Sacred Mountain of Tanganyika. *T.N.R.* 36, Jan., 1954.

BAKER, E. C. ... ... Notes on the Shirazi of East Africa. *T.N.R.* 11, April, 1941.

Mumiani. *T.N.R.* 21, 1946, p. 108.

A note on the Washomvi of Dar es Salaam. *T.N.R.* 23, 1947, p. 47.

Notes on the Waikizu and Wasizaki of Musoma. *T.N.R.* 23, 1947, p. 66.

History of the Wasegeju. *T.N.R.* 27, 1949, p. 47.

Age-grades in Musoma District, Tanganyika Territory. *Man.*, Jan., 1927, 1951.

Tribal Calendars *T.N.R.* 33, July, 1952.

BAKER, O. ... ... An Experiment in Applied Anthropology. *Africa.* Vol. VIII, No. 3, 1935.

BAKER, S. J. K. ... ... The distribution of native population over East Africa. *Africa*, 1937, p. 37.

BATES, D. J. P. ... ... Democracy among the Pare. *C.* 1950, p. 53.

BAUMANN, H. ... ... Nyama, the force of vengeance on some mana-like notions in Africa (Nyama die Rachemacht: Uber einige mana-artige Vorstellungen in Afrika). *Paideuma* 4, 191-230, 1950.

BAXTER, H. C. ... ... Pangani: The Trade Centre of Ancient History *T.N.R.* 17, 1944.

The religious practices of the pagan Wazigua. *T.N.R.* 15, 1943, p. 49.

Introduction to witchcraft in Africa. *T.N.R.* 18, 1944, p. 69.

BEHR, H. F. VON ... ... Die Völker zwischen Rufiji und Rowuma. *M.a.d.s.* 1892, p. 69.

BLAXLAND, R. W. ... ... Mass Education in Tanganyika. *Oversea Educ.* 22, 2, 52-7, 1951.

BLEEK, D. F. ... ... The Hadzapi or Watindega of Tanganyika Territory. *Africa*, 1931, Vol. IV, No. 3.

BOESCH, F. ... ... Le culte des ancetres chez les Banyamwezi. *Anth.*, 1925, p. 200.

Totemisme, exogamie et droit maternal des Banyamwezi. *Anth.*, 1929, p. 273.

BOULNOIS, J. ... ... La mystique de la fécondité et la symbolique de l'arbre, du serpent, de la pierre et de la déesse-mére dans le monde des Noirs. *Bull. IFAN* 7, 1/4, 115-47, 1945. (1949).

BOWIE, D. F. ... ... The lip plug, or "indonya" among the tribes of the Southern Province. *T.N.R.* 27, 1949, p. 75.

BRANDTSCHEN, A. ... ... Die ethnographische Literatur uber den Ulanga-Distrikt, Tanganyika-Territorium. *Acta tropica*, (Basel) Vol. 10, No. 2, 1953, p. 150.

BRIAULT, M. ... ... A travers les sorcelleries Africaines. *Grands lacs* 65, 1, 3-14, Oct., 1949.

BROOMFIELD, G. W. ... ... Development of the Swahili language. *Africa.* Vol. III, No. 4.

BROWN, E. F. ... ... Hehe grandmothers. *J.R.A.I.* 1935, p. 83.

BROWN, G. G. ... ... Bridewealth among the Hehe. *Africa*, Vol. 2, 1932.

Legitimacy and paternity among the Hehe. *J.A.S.* 1932/33.

CARNELL, W. J. ... ... Sympathetic magic among the Gogo of Mpwapwa District. *T.N.R.* 39, June, 1955, pp. 25-38.

Four Gogo folk tales. *T.N.R.* 40, pp. 30-42, Sept. 1955.

CESARD, E. ... ... Les Bahaya. *Anth.* 1935/37. Vol. 30 pp. 75 and 451; Vol. 31, pp. 97, 489 and 821 and Vol. 32; pp. 15.

Comment les Haya interpretent leurs origines. *Anth.*, 1927, p. 440.

Histoires des rois du Kyamtwara d'apres l'ensemble des traditions des familles regnantes. *Anth.*, 1931, p. 533.

Proverbes et contes Haya. *Anth.*, 1928, pp. 494 and 792; and 1929, p. 565.

Devinettes et observances supertitieuses des Haya. *Anth.* No. 29, 3.

CLARKE, J. C. ... ... A note on the *ntore* system in Bugufi, Biharamulo District. *T.N.R.* 5, 1938, p. 76.

CLEMENTS, P. ... ... Le forgeron en Afrique noire: Quelques attitudes du groupe à son egard. *Rev. Geogr. humaine et Ethnol* 1, 2, 35-58. Apr.-Jun. 1948 (14 fig.).

CONNOR, R. M. B. ... ... Nyakyusa pagan religion. *Int. Rev. Miss.* 43, 170-2, April, 1954.

COOPER, B. ... ... The Kindiga. *T.N.R.* 27, 1949, p. 8.

COPLAND, B. ... ... A note on the origin of the Mbugu. *Z.f.E.* 24, 4.

CORY, H.... ... ... Details of a native medical treatment. *T.N.R.* 2, 1936, p. 67.

Some East African native songs. *T.N.R.* 4, 1937, p. 51.

Sukuma twin ceremonies—Mbasa. *T.N.R.* 17, 1944, p. 34.

Land tenure in Bukuria. *T.N.R.* 23, 1947, p. 70.

Figurines used in the initiation ceremonies of the Nguu of Tanganyika Territory. *Africa*, 1944, p. 459.

The Buyeye: a secret society of snake-charmers in Sukumaland, Tanganyika Territory. *Africa*, 1946, p. 160.

The ingredients of magic medicines. *Africa* 19, 1, 1949, Jan. p. 13.

The necessity for the co-ordination of economic and political development. *T.N.R.* 30, Jan.-June, 1951, pp. 78-82.

The People of the Lake Victoria Region. *T.N.R.* 33, 1952.

Ngoma ya sheitani. An East African native treatment for psychical disorder. *J.R.A.I.*, 66, p. 209, 1936.

Jando. *J.R.A.I.* 77, July-Dec., 1947, d. 78, 1948.

The Buswezi. *Amer. Anthropologist*, 57, 5, 923-52, Oct. 1955.

CORY, H. (in collab. with HARTNOLL, M. M.) ... ... Tribal structure in Uhaya. *T.N.R.* 14, 1942, p. 1.

CORY, H. and MASALU, M. M. Place names in the Lake Province. *T.N.R.* 30, 1951, p. 53.

CULWICK, A. T.... ... ... Ritual use of rock paintings at Bahi, Tanganyika Territory. *Man.* 1931, p. 41.

Hippo hunting amongst the Wandamba of Tanganyika Territory. *Man.* 1932.

The hoe in Ulanga. *Man.* 1934, 5.

A Pogoro flute. *Man.* 1935, 39.

Ngindo honey-hunters. *Man.* 1936, 95 and *T.N.R.* 5, 1938.

Letter-writing in Ulanga. *T.N.R.* 5, 1938, p. 79.

The population trend. *T.N.R.* 11, April 1941, pp. 13-17.

CULWICK, A. T. and G. M. ... The functions of bride-wealth in Ubena of the Rivers. *Africa*, 1934, p. 140.

Religious and economic sanctions in a Bantu tribe. *B.J.P.* Oct., 1935.

Fostermothers in Ulanga. *T.N.R.* 1, 1936, p. 19.

Indonesian echoes in Central Tanganyika. *T.N.R.* 1, 1936, p. 60.

What the Wabena think of Indirect Rule. *J.A.S.* 1937, p. 176.

A Study of Population in Ulanga, Tanganyika Territory. *Sociological Rev.* 1938-39.

DEANE, PHYLLIS ... ... Problems of surveying village economics. *Human Problems Brit. Central Africa* 8, 42-9, 1949.

DEMPWOLFF, O. ... ... Die Sandawe. *Anth.* 1936, p. 375.

DE ROSAMOND, C. C. ... ... Iron smelting in the Kahama District. *T.N.R.* 16, Dec., 1953, pp. 79-84,

DOBSON, E. B. ... ... Land tenure of the Wasambara. *T.N.R.* 10, 1940, p. 1.

DORMAN, M. H.... ... ... Pottery among the Wangoni and Wandendeule, Southern Tanganyika. *Man.* 1938, 102.

DRESCH, JEAN ... ... Le Colonialisme économique en Afrique noire. *Musee vivant*, 36/37, 67-8 Nov., 1948.

DRIBERG, J. H. ... ... Primitive law in Eastern Africa. *Africa* Vol. 1, No. 1 Jan., 1928, p. 63.

DUDBRIDGE, B. J. and
GRIFFITHS, J. E. S. ... ... The development of local government in Sukumaland. *J. Afr. Admin.*, Vol. III No. 3 July, 1951.

DUNDAS, C. ... ... Native laws of some Bantu tribes of East Africa. *J.R.A.I.* 1921, p. 217.

DURAND-REVILLE, L. ... ... Les problémes de l'industrialisation des territoires d'outre. *Monde non chretien* 13, 27-47, Jan-Mar. 1950.

ELIAS, T. O. ... ... Insults as an offence in African customary law. *Afr. Affairs* 53, 210, 66-9. Jan. 1954.

ELLIOTT, H. F. I. ... ... An island in Lake Victoria. *T.N.R.* 10, Dec., 1940, pp. 28-33,

EVANS-PRITCHARD, E. E. ... Yao tribes and Clans. *Human Problems Brit. Central Afr.* 7, 24-40, 1949.

FORD, J. and HALL, R. DE Z. ... The history of Karagwe (Bukoba District) *T.N.R.* 24, Dec., 1947, pp. 1-27.

FOSBROOKE, H. A. ... ... The defensive measures of certain tribes in N.E. Tanganyika. *T.N.R.* 35, 1953, 36 and 37, 1954 and 39, 1955.

An administrative survey of the Masai social system. *T.N.R.* 26, 1948, p. 1.

Tanganyika rock paintings. *T.N.R.* 29, July, 1950 (ill.biblio), pp. 1-6.

Government Sociologists in Tanganyika. A sociological view. *J.Afr.Admin.* Vol. IV, No. 3, July, 1952.

A stone age tribe in Tanganyika (Hadzapi or Kindiga). *S.Afr.archaeol.Bull.* (Cape Town), 11, 1956, pp. 3-8, illus.

The Masai age-group system as a guide to tribal chronology. *Afr.Stud.*, 15, 4, 1956, pp. 188-204.

FRANK, C. N. ... ... Young pioneers in Tanganyika. *T.N.R.* 36, Jan., 1953, p. 16.

FREEMAN-GRENVILLE, G. S. P.... Mosques near Dar es Salaam. *T.N.R.* 36, Jan., 1954, p. 64.

GIBBONS, R. M. ... ... African good manners. *T.N.R.* 1, 1936, p. 81.

GILLMAN, C. ... ... A Bibliography of Kilimanjaro. *T.N.R.* 18, 1944.

GILLMAN, H. ... ... Bush Fallowing in the Makonde Plateau. *T.N.R.* 19, 1945.

GLUCKMAN, M. ... ... The nature of African marriage. *Anti-slavery Reporter* 9, 4, 65-6, May, 1954.

GOWER, R. H. ... ... Two views on the Masai. *T.N.R.* 26, 1948, p. 60.

The effect of a change of diet on Masai schoolboys. *T.N.R.* 26, 1948, p. 77.

GRANT, C. H. B. ... ... Some African Royal Burials and Coronations in Western Tanganyika. *A.S.* 10, 4, pp. 185-93, Dec., 1951.

GRAY, SIR JOHN... ... ... The Wadebuli and the Wadiba. *T.N.R.* 36, Jan., 1954, pp. 22-42.

GRAY, R. F. ... ... Positional succession among the Wambugwe. *Africa*, Vol. 23, No. 3, 1953, p. 233.

Notes on Irangi Houses. *T.N.R.* 35, 1953.

The Mbugwe Tribe: Origin and Development. *T.N.R.* 38, Mar. 1955.

GREIG, R. C. H. ... ... Iron smelting in Fipa. *T.N.R.* 4, 1937, p. 77.

GRIFFITH, A. W. M. ... ... Primitive native education in the Bukoba District. *T.N.R.* 1, 1936, ·p. 87.

GRIFFITHS, J. E. S. ... ... The Aba-Ha of the Tanganyika Territory—some aspects of their tribal organizations and sleeping sickness concentrations. *T.N.R.* 2, 1936, p. 72.

Notes on land tenure and land rights among the Sonjo of Tanganyika Territory. *T.N.R.* 9, 1940, p. 15.

GRIFFITHS, J. E. S. (Mrs.) ... Masai cattle auction. *T.N.R.* 6, 1938, p. 99.

GRIFFITHS, J. E. S. and
    DARLING, J. S. ... ... Snuff taking and the use of nose clips in Buha, Tanganyika Territory. *Man.* 1934, 210.

GULLIVER, P. H. ... ... A history of the Songea Ngoni. *T.N.R.* 41, Dec. 1955, pp. 16-30 (map).

GULLIVER, PAMELA ... ... Dancing clubs of the Nyasa. *T.N.R.* 41, Dec. 1955, pp. 58-59.

GUTMANN, B. ... ... Dichten und Denken der Dschagga-Neger. *Gl.* 1909.

The African standpoint. *Africa* VIII, 1.

HALL, R. DE Z. ... ... Irrigation in Bugufi, Tanganyika Territory. *Man.* 1939, 20.

Pottery in Bugufi, Tanganyika Territory. *Man.* 1939, 132.

The study of native court records as a method of ethnological enquiry. *Africa*, 1938, p. 412.

Nyakyusa law from court records. *A.S.* 1943, p. 153.

The dance societies of the Wasukuma as seen in the Maswa District. *T.N.R.* 1, 1936, p. 94.

Bao. *T.N.R.* 35, 1953.

Local migration in Tanganyika. *A.S.* June, 1945, p. 53.

HALL, R. DE Z. and CORY, H. A study of land tenure in Bugufi, 1925-1944. *T.N.R.* 24, 1947, p. 28.

HAMLYN, O. T. ... ... Provocation in the law of Tanganyika. *J. comp. legis and int. Law* 3rd Series 29, 3/4, 57-8, Nov. 1947.

HARRIES, L. ... ... Makua song-riddles from the initiation rites. *A.S.* March, 1942, p. 27.

Notes on the mythology of the Bantu in the Ruvuma District. *T.N.R.* 12, 1941, p. 38.

Swahili epic literature. *T.N.R.* 30, 1951, p. 73

Linguistic notes from the Southern Province. *T.N.R.* 19, 1945, p. 45.

The initiation rites of the Makonde tribe. *Communications from the Rhodes-Livingstone Institute* 1944, No. 3.

Some Riddles of the Mwere People. *African Studies* Vol. 6 Mar. 1947.

HARRIS, V. W. ... ... Some notes on insects as food. *T.N.R.* 9, 1940, p. 45.

HARRISON, H. S. ... ... Simeoni, H. ... ... A bolas-and-hoop game in East Africa. *Man.* 1947, 179.

HARTLEY, B. J. ... ... Land tenure in Usukuma. *T.N.R.* 5, 1938, p. 17.

HARTNOLL, A. V. ... ... Praying for rain in Ugogo. *T.N.R.* 13, 1942, p. 59.

HARTNOLL, M. M. ... ... Some African pastimes. *T.N.R.* 5, 1938, p. 31

HATCHELL, G. W. ... ... Fish-traps of Lake Tanganyika. *Man.* 1927, 135.

Some drums from Uruwira (Ukajala), Tanganyika Territory. *Man.* 1927, 19.

Vibangwa—a form of insignia used in the eastern hinterland of Lake Tanganyika. *Man.* 1928, 19.

The Angoni of Tanganyika Territory. *Man.* 1935, 73.

Some accounts of the people living under the protection of Mount Mkungwe. *T.N.R.* 11, 1941, p. 41.

The Angoni of Tanganyika Territory. *T.N.R.* 25, 1948, p. 69.

HECKEL, B. ... ... Yao tribe, their culture and their education. *Inst. of Education*, London, 1935, p. 7.

HELLIER, A. B. ... ... Swahili Prose Literature. *B.S.* 14, 3 pp. 247-257, Sept. 1940.

HOBLEY, C. W. ... ... Notes on the Dorobo people and other tribes. *Man.* 1906, 78, 2a.

HOLLIS, A. C. ... ... A note on the Masai system of relationship and other matters connected therewith. *J.R.A.I.* 1910, Vol. XL, July-Dec.

HORNELL, J. ... ... The sewn canoes of the Victoria-Nyanza: construction and origin. *T.N.R.* 15, 1943, p. 7.

The sea-going *mtepe* and *dau* of the Lamu Archipelago. *T.N.R.* 14, 1942, p. 27.

HUCKS, G. W. Y. ... ... Haya surnames. *T.N.R.* 7, 1939, p. 72.

HUGGINS, P. M.... ... ... Sukuma fables, *T.N.R.* 1, 1936, p. 90.

HUNTER, G. ... ... Hidden Drums in Singida District. *T.N.R.* 35, 1953.

A Note on some Tombs at Kaole. *T.N.R.* 37, July, 1954.

HUNTER-WILSON, M. ... ... Witch beliefs and social structure. *Amer. J. Social*, 156, 4, 307-13, Jan. 1951.

HUNTINGFORD, G. W. B. ... The boats of the Victoria Nyanza. *Man.* 1937, 177.

The social organization of the Dorobo. *A.S.* Sept. 1942, p. 183.

HUREL, E. ... ... Religion et vie domestique des Bakerewe. *Anth.* 1911, pp. 62 and 276.

Ikombe of Mwadui. The legend of Nkanda. *T.N.R.* 15, 1943, p. 72.

IONIDES, C. J. P. ... ... Stories of the Wangindo. *T.N.R.* 31, 1951, p. 81.

Some Native beliefs concerning animals. *J. E. Afr. Nat. Hist. Soc.* 19, 3/4, (87/8) 139-40, Dec. 1946.

JACKSON, C. H. N. ... ... The Mangati. *T.N.R.* 13, 1942, p. 6.

JEFFERIES, M. D. W. ... ... Circumcision: Its diffusion from Egypt among the Bantu. *Criteria* 1, 73-84, March, 1949.

Funary inversions in Africa. *Arch.f. volkerkde* 4, 24-37, 1949.

JERRARD, R. C. ... ... Three Swahili fables. *T.N.R.* 6, 1938, p. 93.

JOHNSON, F. ... ... Notes on Kimakonde. *Bulletin of the School of Orient. Studies, London Inst.* 1922, vol. II part 3.

Fifteen Makonde folk-tales. *Bulletin of the School of Orient. Studies, London Inst.* vol. III part 1.

Kiniramba folklore tales. *B.S.* No. 5.

JOHNSTON, P. H. ... ... Some notes on land tenure on Kilimanjaro and the *vihamba* of the Wachagga. *T.N.R.* 21, 1946, p. 1.

Some aspects of dhow building. *T.N.R.* 27, 1949, p. 47.

JONES, W. W. ... ... African Dug-Outs. *T.N.R.* 11, 1941.

KAYAMBA, H. M. T. ... ... The Kingdom of the Wakilindi. Prize-winning essay, *MS. Africa* IV/3, 1931.

Notes on the Wadigo. *T.N.R.* 23, 1947, p. 80.

KIMMENDDE, M. VAN DER ... Les Sandawe (Territorie du Tanganyika, Afrique). *Anth.* vol. XXXL, 1936.

KIMWANI, E. G.... ... ... A pictorial description of the manufacture of barkcloth in the Bukoba District. *T.N.R.* 30, 1951, p. 85.

KIRO ... ... Tribal History and Legend. (Zigua). *T.N.R.* 34, 1953.

KIRSCHSTEIN, E. F. ... ... Some tales of Tanganyika natives. *T.N.R.* 4, 1937, p. 82.

A note on native power of discernment. *T.N.R.* 6. 1938, p. 102.

Die Bewonner der Landschaft Uha. *D.K.Z.* 1936.

KORITSCHONER, H. and
HARTNOLL, M. M. ... ... Tribal structure in Uhaya. *T.N.R.* No. 14, Nov. 1942.

LAGERCRANTZ, S. ... ... Contribution to the ethnography of Africa. *Studia Ethnographica Upsaliensia*, I, 1950.

LAMBURN, R. G. P. ... ... Some notes on the Yao. *T.N.R.* 29, 1950, p. 73.

LAWMAN, P. ... ... Kilwa Island. *C.* Oct. 1952, p. 391.

LEAKEY, E. A. and
ROUNCE, N. V. ... ... The Human Geography of the Kasulu District *Geography*, Vol. 18, p. 292, 1933.

LEAKEY, L. S. B. ... ... Some notes on the Masai of Kenya Colony. *J.R.A.I.* Vol. LX pp. 185-209, 1930.

LEES, E. C. L. ... ... A note on the Wambulu. *T.N.R.* 2, 1936, p. 106.

LEHMANN, F. R.... ... ... Notes on the daily life of the Nyakyusa (Tanganyika Territory). *Sociologus* (Berlin) n.F. vol. 1, No. 2, 1951, p. 138.

Some field notes on the Nyakyusa (Tukuyu District). *Sociologus* n.F. vol. 1, No. 1, 1951, p. 53 and No. 2, p. 138, 1951.

Some field notes on the Chagga of Kilimanjaro. *B.S.* Dec. 1941, p. 385.

LUSSY, P. K. ... ... The Wapogoro: Notes on the Country and the People. *Anthropos.* 46, 3/4, pp. 431-41, May-Aug. 1951.

Some aspects of work and recreation among the Wapogoro of Southern Tanganyika. *Anthropological Quarterly* 26, 4, 109-28, Oct. 1953.

LUSSY, P. K. and
ENGELBERGER, A. ... ... Opinions et coutumes religieuses des Wapogoro. *Anthropos* 49, 103-22, 605-26, 1954.

MACKAY, D. ... ... A background for African psychiatry. *E.A. Med. J.* 25, 1, 2-4, Jan. 1948.

MACQUARIE, C. ... ... Water gipsies of the Malagarasi. *T.N.R.* 9, 1940, p. 61.

MAGUIRE, R. A. J. ... ... Il-Torobo. *J.A.S.* 1928, Vol. 27, pp. 127 and 249.

The Masai Penal Code. *J.A.S.* 1928, Oct. p. 12.

MAREALLE, T. L. M. ... ... The Wachagga of Kilimanjaro. *T.N.R.* 32, 1952, p. 57.

MARTIN, C. J. ... ... A demographic study of an immigrant community: the Indian population of British East Africa. *Population Studies*, 6, 3, March, 1953, pp. 233-47.

Some estimates of the general age distribution, fertility and rate of natural increase of the African population of British East Africa. *Population Studies*, 7, 2, Nov. 1953, pp. 181-99.

MAURICE, M. ... ... L'enfance, adolescence, le marriage chez les Bapimbwe. *B.A.* 1935, 5.

Le pays des Bapimbwe. *La Geographie* 1937, 64, 66, 67 and 69 and 1938, 5 and 6.

MEEK, C. A. ... ... A practical experiment in local Government. *J. Afr. Admin.* 2, 3, 21-8, July, 1950.

MEINHOF, C. ... ... Linguistische Studien in Ostafrika. *Mitt. des Sem fur Afr. und Orient. Spr.*, Berlin, 1906, Jahrg. lx.

Methods of direct taxation in British Tropical Africa (by the African Studies Branch, Colonial Office). *J. African Adm.* 2, 4, 3-12, Oct. 1950, 3, 1, 30-41, Jan.; 2, 77-87, Apr., 1951.

MEYER, E. H. ... ... Le Kirengo des Wadchagga. *Anth.* 1917/18. p. 187.

MOFFETT, J. P. ... ... Native courts in Tanganyika. *J. Afr. Admin.* 4, 1, 17-25, Jan. 1952.

Government Sociologists in Tanganyika: A Government View. *J. Afr. Admin.* 4, 3, July, 1952.

MONTAGUE, F. A. and
PAGE-JONES, F. H. ... ... Some difficulties in the democratization of Native Authorities in Tanganyika. *J. Afr. Admin.* 3, 1. 21-7, Jan. 1951.

MOREAU, R. E. ... ... Kilimanjaro and Mt. Kenya. *T.N.R.* 18, 1944.

Sacrosanct birds on islets near Mafia. *T.N.R.* 7, 1939, p. 114.

The joking relationships in Tanganyika. *Africa* 1943/44, p. 386.

The joking relationships (*utani*) in Tanganyika. *T.N.R.* 12, 1941, p. 1.

The *mtani* again as a sanitarian. *T.N.R.* 21, 1946, p. 106.

Suicide by "breaking the cooking pot". *T.N.R.* 12. 1941, p. 49.

MORGAN, J. C. ... ... The *ngalawa* of the Kilwa coast. *T.N.R.* 9, 1940, p. 27.

MORISON, T. ... ... The Wachagga of Kilimanjaro. *J.A.S.*, 1933, p. 140.

MORS, O. ... ... Bahaya twin ceremonies. *Anthropos.* 46, 3/4, 442-52, May-Aug. 1951.

Soothsaying among the Bahaya. *Anthropos.* 46, 5/6, Sept.-Dec. 1951.

Notes on hunting and fishing in Bahaya. *Anthropological Quarterly*, 26, 3, 88-93, July, 1953.

MTAWA, A. B. M. ... ... How the Wadoe got their name. *T.N.R.* 31, 1951, p. 79.

MUMFORD, W. B. ... ... Hehe-Bena-Sangu peoples of East Africa. *Am. Anthr.* 1934, vol. 36, p. 203.

MWAKOSYA, D. A. ... ... The Rule of Witchcraft among the Wasambaa. *Makerere* 1, 3, pp. 121-3, Sept. 1947.

MYLIUS, N. ... ... Marriage and children in the East African area of inland drainage. (Ehe und Kind im abflusslosen Gebiert Ostafrikas). *Arch. f. Volkerde* 3, 44-134, 1948; 4, 38-153, 1949 (biblio).

NDULA, S. and MAVELLA,
G. N. S. (ed Fosbrooke, H. A.). Hambageu, the God of the Wasonjo. *T.N.R.* 35, July, 1953, pp. 38-42.

NHONOLI, A. M. D. ... ... Ancient marriage ceremonies in Wilwana. *Makerere* 6, 141-5, Sept. 1948.

Some essentials of African witchcraft and superstitions. *Makerere* 3, 2, 30-2. June-Aug. 1949.

An inquiry into the infant mortality rate in rural areas of Unyamwezi. *E.Afr.Med.J.* 31, 1, 1-12, Jan. 1954.

NORTHCOTE, C ... ... The evolution of tribal control. *Africa*, 1933, Vol. VI, 3.

NTUNDU, Y. ... ... The position of rainmaker among the Wanyiramba. (trans. by J. W. T. Allen). *T.N.R.* 7, 1939, p. 84.

O'HAGAN, C. C. ... ... Mkungwe Mountain, *T.N.R.* June, 1940.

OLDEROGGE, D. A. ... ... The Hamitic problem in African studies. *Soviet Ethnogr.* 3, 156-70, 1949.

PELICHY, A. ... ... L'homme clanique et le proletaire en Afrique noire. *Economie et Humanism* 2/3, 38-51, Apr.-Jun. 1949.

PIKE, A. H. ... ... Soil conservation amongst the Matengo tribe. *T.N.R.* 6, 1938, p. 79.

POPPLEWELL, G. D. ... ... Notes on the Fipa. *T.N.R.* 3, 1937, p. 99.

RAUM, O. F. ... ... Some aspects of Indigenous Education among the Chagga. *J.R.A.I.* Vol. LXVIII Jan.-June, 1935.

Educational psychology in the speech of the Wachagga. *B.S.*, 1939, vol. 13, 3.

Language perversions in East Africa. *Africa* 1937, p. 221.

Female initiation among the Chagga. *Am. Anth.* 1939, Vol. 41, 4.

RAYMOND, W. D. ... ... Native *materia medica.* *T.N.R.* 2, 1936, p. 50 and 5, 1938, p. 72.

Tanganyika arrow poisons. *T.N.R.* 23, 1941. p. 49.

REUSCH, R. ... ... The Menelik legend. *T.N.R.* 2, 1936, p. 77.

REVINGTON, T. M. ... ... Concerning the Banangoma and Basumba Batale Societies of the Bukwimba Wasukuma. *T.N.R.* 5, 1938, p. 60.

ROBINSON, A. E. ... ... Some notes on ancient means of water transport in relation to the vessels of East Africa. *T.N.R.* 4, 1937, p. 65,

Arabic family and individual names. *T.N.R.* 5, 1938, p. 70.

ROBINSON, A. E. ... ... Notes on saucer and bowl decorations on houses, mosques and tombs. *T.N.R.* 10, 1940, p. 79.

ROEHL, K. ... ... The linguistic situation in East Africa. *Africa*, 1930, p. 191.

ROSEMOND, C. C. DE ... Iron smelting in the Kahama District. *T.N.R.* 16, 1943, p. 67.

ROUSSEAU, M. ... ... En marge de l'histoire ancienne de l'Afrique. *Musee vivant* 12, 36/37, 12-20, Nov. 1948.

ROUSSEAU, M. and LE CORNEUS, O. ... ... Quel sont les styles de l'art negre? *Musée vivant* 12, 36/37, 23-9, Nov. 1948.

ROUNCE, N. V. ... ... The development, expansion and re-habilitation of Sukumaland. *Emp. cotton growing Rev.* 26, 1, 32-41, Jan. 1949.

RUSHBY, G. G. ... ... Five fables. *T.N.R.* 27, 1949, p. 78.

SAADA SALIM BIN OMARI ... The Swahili life. *T.N.R.* 9, 1940, p. 20.

SCHEERDER, R. P. and TASTEVIN, R. ... ... Les Waluguru. *Anth.* 45, pp. 241-286, June, 1950.

SCRIVENOR, T. V. ... ... Some notes on *utani*, or the vituperative alliances existing between the clans in Masasi District. *T.N.R.* 4, 1937, p. 72.

SENIOR, H. S. ... ... Sukuma salt caravans to Lake Eyasi. *T.N.R.* 6, 1938, p. 87.

The Sukuma homestead. *T.N.R.* 9, 1940, p. 42.

SHANN, N. ... ... The Educational Development of the Chagga tribe. *Oversea Educ.* 26, 2, 47-65, July, 1954.

SILLERY, A. ... ... Note on learning tribal languages. *T.N.R.* 1, 1936, p. 14.

Musira and its burial caves. *T.N.R.* 13, 1942, p. 57.

A sketch of the Kikwaya lanuage. *B.S.* Dec. 1932. 6/4.

Notes for a grammar of the Kuria language. *B.S.* 1936, No. 10, p. 9.

SKENE, R. ... ... Arab and Swahili dances and ceremonies. *J.R.A.I.* 1917, p. 413.

SMITH, H. C. ... ... The Sukuma system of grazing rights. *E.A.A.J.* IV, 2, 9, 1938.

SPIES, E. ... ... Observations on *utani* customs among the Ngoni of Songea District. *T.N.R.* 16, 1943, p. 49.

41

STANNER, W. E. H. ... ... Sociological problems of the groundnut scheme in Tanganyika. *Colonial Review* Vol. 6 No. 2.

STEINER, F. B. ... ... Chagga truth: A note on Gutmann's account of the Chagga concept of truth in *Das Recht der Dschagga*, Africa, 24, 4, 364-9, Oct. 1954.

STIRLING, L. ... ... Ritual circumcision in Southern Tanganyika. *E. Afr. Med. J.* 18, 3, 81-9, June, 1941.

STONELEY, H. ... ... Power of the African Witch-Doctor. *Crown Colonist* 20, 222, p. 283, May, 1950.

SWYNNERTON, R. J. M. ... Some problems of the Chagga on Kilimanjaro. *E. Afr. Agric. J.* 1949 Vol. 14 No. 3.

Tanganyika Notes and Records, published half-yearly by the Tanganyika Society, P.O. Box 511, Dar es Salaam.

TANNER, R. E. S. ... ... Some Southern Province trees with their African names and uses. *T.N.R.* 31, July, 1951, pp. 61-70.

Some Chinese pottery found at Kilwa. *T.N.R.* 32, Jan. 1952, pp. 83-4.

Archery amongst the Sukuma. *T.N.R.* 35, 1953.

A Series of Rock Paintings near Mwanza. *T.N.R.* 35, 1953.

Law enforcement by communal action in Sukumaland. *J. Afr. Admin.* 7, 4, 159-65, Oct. 1955.

Hysteria in Sukuma medical practice. *Africa* 25, 3, 274-8, July, 1955.

Maturity and marriage among the Northern Basukuma of Tanganyika, *Afr.Stud.* 14, 3, 123-33, 4, 159-69, 1955.

Land tenure in northern Sukumaland, Tanganyika; an analysis of present-day trends in two parishes. *E. Afr. agric. J.* (Amani), 21, 2, Oct. 1955, 120-9.

Sukuma fertility: an analysis of 148 marriages in Mwanza district, Tanganyika. *E.Afr. med.J.* (Nairobi), 33, 3, Mar. 1956, 94-99.

An introduction to the northern Basukuma's idea of the Supreme Being. *Anthrop. Quart.* 29, 2, 45-56. Apr. 1956.

An introduction to the Spirit Beings of the northern Basukuma. *Anthrop.Quart.* 29, 3, 69-81. July 1956.

TANNER, R. E. S. ... ... A preliminary enquiry into Sukuma diet in the Lake Province, Tanganyika Territory. *E.Afr.med.J.* 33, 8, 305-24, Aug. 1956, (tables).

The sorcerer in northern Sukumaland, Tanganyika. *S.-W. J. Anthrop.* 12, 4, 437-43. Winter 1956.

TAWNEY, J. J. ... ... Insignia and ceremonies of the Heru Chiefdom of Buha, in the Kasulu District. *T.N.R.*, 18, 1944, p. 81.

Ugabire: a feudal custom amongst the Waha. *T.N.R.* 17, 1944, p. 6.

Election in Tanganyika. *C.* May, 1952, p. 181.

TEALE, E. ... ... An unusual place and form of burial. *T.N.R.* 31, 1951, p. 71.

TEW, M. A. ... ... A further note on funeral friendships. *Africa* 21, 2, 122-4, Apr. 1951.

THORNTON, D. and
 ROUNCE, N. V. ... ... Ukara Island and the agricultural practices of the Wakara. *T.N.R.* 1, 1936, p. 25.

THWAITES, D. H. ... ... Wanyakyusa agriculture. *E.A.A.J.* April, 1944, p. 236.

TRACEY, H. ... ... Recording tour in Tanganyika by team of the African Music Society. *T.N.R.* 32, 1952, p. 43.

TREVOR, J. C. ... ... The physical characteristics of the Sandawe. *J.R.A.I.* Vol. LXXVII, Part 1.

VAJDA, LASZLO ... ... Les fondements religieux et ethnologiques *Ethnog. Acad. Sci. Hungaricae*, 3, 1/4, 185-232, 1953.

VAN BUECK, V. ... ... Towards a classification of African Tribes (Naareen indeling van de Afrikaanse stammen). *Zaire* 2, 1, 15-24, Jan. 1948.

WALLIS, P. ... ... Waluguru sibs. *Primitive Man.*, 1935.

WHITEHOUSE, L. E. ... ... Masai social customs. *J.E.A. & U.N.H.S.* Oct. 1932 and Jan. 1933.

WHITELEY, W. H. ... ... Southern Province Rock Paintings. *T.N.R.* 31, July, 1951, pp. 58-60.

Modern local government among the Makua. *Africa* 24, 4, 349-58, Oct. 1954.

WILLIAMS, O. G. ... ... Village organization among the Sukuma. *Man.* 1935, 130.

WILSON, G. ... ... An introduction to Nyakyusa society. *B.S.* Sept. 1936, p. 253.

WILSON, G. ... ... An African morality. *Africa.* 1936 vol. 9.

Nyakyusa conventions of burial. *B.S.* March 1939, p. 1.

Introduction to Nyakyusa law. *Africa* 1937, p. 16.

The land rights of individuals among the Nyakyusa. *Rhodes-Livingstone Papers*, No. 1, 1939.

WILSON, G. McL. ... ... The Tatoga of Tanganyika. *T.N.R.* No. 33, 1952 and 34, 1953.

WILSON, M. ... ... Nyakyusa Kinship, in "African Systems of Kinship and Marriage", edited by A. R. Radcliffe Brown, 1951.

Nyakyusa age-villages. *J. Roy. Anthrop. Inst.* 79, 1/2, 21-5, 1949.

Nyakyusa ritual and symbolism. *Amer. Anthropologist*, 56, 1954, pp. 228-41.

Witchcraft beliefs and social structure. *Amer. J. Sociol.*, 56, 1951, pp. 307-13. (With reference to the Nyakyusa and Pondo).

WINNINGTON-INGRAM, C. ... Reforming Local Government in a Tanganyika District. *J. Afr. Admin.* 2, 2, 10-15, Apr. 1950.

WINTERBOTTOM, J. M. ... ... A note on the Angoni paramountcy. *Man.* 1937, p. 158.

WOODWARD, H. W. ... ... Makua Tales. *Bantu Studies*, Vols. 6 and 9.

WORSLEY, P. M. AND
RUMBERGER ... ... Remains of an earlier people in Uhehe. *T.N.R.* 1949.

WRIGHT, A. C. A. ... ... The Magical Importance of Pangolins among the Basukuma. *T.N.R.* 36, Jan. 1954.

Maize names as indicators of economic contacts. *Uganda J.* 13, 1, 61-81 Mar. 1949.

WYATT, A. W. ... ... The lion men of Singida. *T.N.R.* 28, Jan. 1950, pp. 3-9.

WYNN JONES, W. ... ... African Dugouts, *T.N.R.* 11, 1941, pp. 11-12.

MISSIONS
Books, Reports, Pamphlets

ACHTE, A. A. A. ... ... Le pére Auguste Achte des Missionaires d'Afrique (Péres Blancs). Alger, 1912.

ADOLPHI, H. AND SCHANZ ... Am Fusse der Bergriesen Ostafrikas. Geschichte der Lepziger Mission am Kilimandjaro und in den Nachtargebirgen Leipzig, 1912.

ANDERSON-MORSHEAD, E. M. ...   History of the Universities Mission to Central Africa, 1859-1909.   London, 1909.

ATTWATER, D. ...   .   The White Fathers in Africa.   London, 1937.

BARNES, B. H. ...   .   Johnson of Nyasaland.   London, 1933.

BECKER, J.   ...   .   Die Katholische Kircke in Neuen Afrika. Geneva, 1947.

BLOOD, A. G. ...   .   Dawn of a Diocese—Masasi.   London, 1935.

BOUNIOL, J.   ...   .   The White Fathers and their Missions. London, 1929.

BROOMFIELD, GERALD W.   ...   Towards freedom (History of U.M.C.A.) pp. 135.   London: Universities' Mission to Central Africa.   1957.

Catholic Handbook of East Africa.   Mombasa, 1932.

CHAMBERS, G. A.   ...   ...   Tanganyika's New Day.   London, 1931.

CLARKE, R. F. ...   .   Cardinal Lavigerie and Slavery in Africa. London, 1889.

DAWSON, E. C. ...   .   James Hannington.   London, 1886.

DORING, P.   ...   .   Morgendammerung in Deutsch Ostafrika. Berlin, 1901.

DE L'EPRENIER ...   .   Mére Marie Clare.   Paris, 1927.

EITNER, M.   ...   .   Berliner Mission in Nyassa-land (Deutsch-Ostafrika).   Berlin, 1897.

EVANS, GODFREY   ...   ...   Darkness or Light: Studies in the History of the U.M.C.A.   Westminster, 1912.

FRERE, H. B.   ...   .   East Africa as a Field for Missionary Labour. London, 1874.

GODWIN, H.   ...   .   A Memoir of Bishop Mackenzie.   London, 1864.

GOYAN, G.   ...   .   La Congregation du Saint Esprit.   Paris, 1937.

GROVES, C. P. ...   .   The Planting of Christianity in Africa.   Vol. II, 1840-78, Vol. III, 1878-1914.   London (Lutterworth), 1945-5

GROSCHEL, P. ...   .   Zehn Jahre Christlicher Kulturarbeit in Deutsch-ost-afrika.   Berlin, 1911.

GRUNDLER, W. ...   .   Hundert Jahre Berliner Mission.   Berlin, 1923.

GUTMANN, DR. B.   ...   ...   Das Dschaggaland und Seine Christen. Leipzig, 1925.

HARRISON, MRS. W. B. ...   ...   Mackay of Uganda.   London, 1890.

HARRIES, LYNDON, P. ...   ...   Islam in East Africa.   U.M.C.A., 1954.

HEANLEY, R. M.   ...   ...   A Memoir of Bishop Steere.   London, 1888.

HORE, E. C. ... ... Tanganyika, Eleven Years in Central Africa. London, 1892.

HORNER, A. ... ... Die Katholische Mission in Zanguebar.

JOHNSON, W. P. ... ... My African Reminiscences (U.M.C.A.). London, 1924.

KRAPF, J. L. ... ... Travels, Researches and Missionary Labours in Eastern Africa. London, 1860.

LATOURETTE, K. S. ... ... The History of the Expansion of Christianity. Vol. 5. London, 1947.

LECHAPTOIS ... ... Aux Rives du Tanganyika. Algiers, 1913.

LE ROY, A. ... ... Au Kilima-Ndjaro. Histoire d'une Mission Catholique en Afrique Orientale. Paris 1914.

Prés des Grands Lacs, par les Missionaires de S. Em. le Cardinal Lavigerie. Lyons, 1886.

LLOYD, T. E. ... ... African Harvest (Work of Africa Inland Mission). London, 1953.

LOVETT, R. ... ... A History of the London Missionary Society. London, 1899.

Mackay of Uganda by his Sister (Mrs. W. B. Harrison). London, 1890.

MACNAIR... ... ... Livingstone the Liberator. London.

MAPLES, CHAUNCY ... ... Letters and Journals. Longmans, London, 1897.

MAPLES, ELLEN ... ... Chauncy Maples—a Sketch. London, 1897.

NEW, C. ... ... Life, Wanderings and Labours in Eastern Africa. London, 1873.

NICQ, A. ... ... La Vie du vénérable Pére Siméon Lourdel. Paris, 1896.

OLIVER, R. ... ... The Missionary Factor in East Africa. London, 1952.

O'NEILL, T. ... ... Sketches of African Scenery from Zanzibar to Victoria Nyanza. C.M.S., 1878.

PIOLET, J. B. ... ... Les Missions Catholiques Francaises au XIXe Siecle. 5 Vols. Paris, 1902.

PLESSIS, J. DU ... ... The Evangelization of Pagan Africa. Cape Town, 1929.

REUSCH, R. ... ... Der Islam in Ost-Afrika. Leipzig, 1930.

RICHTER, JULIUS ... ... Geschichte der Evangelischen Mission in Africa. Guterslot, 1922.

ROWLEY, H. ... ... Twenty years in Central Africa.

The Story of the Universities Mission to Central Africa. London, 1867.

SCHMIDLIN, A. J. ... ... Die Katholischen Missionen in der Deutschen Schutzgebieten. Hamburg, 1914.

SCHNEIDER, G. ... ... Die Katholische Mission in Zanguebar. Georg Joseph Manz. Regensburg, 1877.

SMITH, H. M. ... ... Frank, Bishop of Zanzibar. 1926.

SMITH, E. W. ... ... The Christian Mission in Africa. London,

STOCK, E. ... ... The History of the Church Missionary Society. 4 Vols. London, 1899-1916.

SWANN, A. J. ... ... Fighting the Slave Hunters in Central Africa. London, 1910.

TUCKER, A. R. ... ... Eighteen Years in Uganda and East Africa. London, 1911.

WARD, G. ... ... Father Woodward of U.M.C.A. London. 1927.

WARD, GERTRUDE ... ... Letters of Bishop Tozer and his Sister, 1863-73. London, 1901.

WARD, GERTRUDE and
   RUSSELL, E. F. ... ... The Life of Charles Alan Smythies. U.M.C.A., London, 1898.

WEICHERT, LUDWIG ... ... Zehn Jahre Berliner Missionsarbeit in Dar es Salaam. Berlin, 1913.

WESTON, FRANK (Bishop of Zanzibar). Life of, by H. M. Smith. S.P.C.K. London, 1926.

WILSON, G. H. ... ... The History of the Universities Mission in Central Africa. London, 1936.

MISSIONS

Articles in Periodicals

BAX, S. N. ... ... The early Church Missionary Society missions at Buzilima and Usambiro in the Mwanza District. *T.N.R.*, 7, 1939.

Church Missionary Society's *The Gleaner*, 1876-1904.

DAVEY, A. C. ... ... Church Missionary Society, Ngambo, *T.N.R.* 5, 1938, p. 68.

FRANK, C. N. ... ... Young Pioneers in Tanganyika. *T.N.R.* 34, 1953.

GALLAND, J. ... ... Les Missions et l'evolution africain actuelle. *Tropiques*, 47, 316, 59-62. Dec. 1949.

GRIAULE, M. ... ... Reflexion sur les religions noires. *Tropiques*, 47, 316, 53-5, Dec. 1949.

LAMBURN, R. G. P. ... ... Zanzibar to Masasi in 1876: the Founding of the Masasi Mission. *T.N.R.* 31, 1951, p. 42.

AGRICULTURE, FORESTRY, BOTANY
Books, Reports, Pamphlets

Agriculture in Tanganyika. G.P.D. 1945.

Agricultural Extension and Advisory Work, with special reference to the Colonies. H.M.S.O. 1949.

Annual Reports of the Sisal Research Station, Ngomeni. G.P.D.

Department of Agriculture. Technical and Specialist Officers' Annual Reports. G.P.D.

Annual Reports of Government Chemist's Department, Tanganyika. G.P.D.

Annual Reports of the Forest Department, Tanganyika, 1921-22. G.P.D.

BALDOCK, W. F. ... ... Air Drying and Conditioning of Timber. 12 pp. 1936. G.P.D.

BURTT, B. D. ... ... A Field Key to the Savanna Genera and species of Trees, Shrubs and Climbing Plants of Tanganyika Territory.
Part 1, Genera and some Species. G.P.D. 1939, 53 pp.,

CARPENTER, G. D. H. ... ... A Naturalist on Lake Victoria. Clarendon Press, Oxford, 1925.
A Naturalist in East Africa. The Clarendon Press, Oxford, 1925.

Colonial Office: A plan for the mechanised production of groundnuts in East and Central Africa. H.M.S.O. London, 1947 (cmd. 7030).

The Cotton Industry 1939-1953. G.P.D. 1953.

DAVEY, J. BURTT ... ... Check Lists of the Forest Trees and Shrubs of the British Empire.
No. 5 Tanganyika Territory. In two volumes.
Part I compiled by F. Bayard Hora and P. J. Greenway.
Part II compiled by J. P. M. Brenan and P. J. Greenway.

DEBENHAM, FRANK ... ... Report on the water resources of the Bechuanaland Protectorate, Northern Rhodesia, the Nyasaland Protectorate, Tanganyika Territory, Kenya and the Uganda Protectorate. London: H.M.S.O. 1948. (Colonial Research Pubs. No. 2).

East Africa High Commission. Hydrology and water resources of British Eastern and Central Africa: proceedings of a conference held in Nairobi on 15th-17th November, 1950. Nairobi: East African Meteorological Department, for East Africa High Commission, 1951. (East Africa High Commission, Paper No. 3.).

East African Agricultural Journal: Numerous articles: E.A.A. & F.R.O. Box 21, Kikuyu, Kenya.

East African Industries Technical Committee and Substitutes Committee, Joint Bulletins of. G.P. Nairobi.

Forest Policy: Sessional Paper No. 1 of 1953, Legislative Council of Tanganyika. G.P.D. 1953.

GRANT, D. K. S. ... ... Some local Timbers (of Tanganyika Territory). G.P.D. 1924, 46 pp.

Forest Protection, Soil and Water Conservation in Tanganyika Territory, including an appendix of Trees recommended for planting in Tanganyika and on Nursery and Planting Practice. G.P.D., 1932, 24 pp.

HALL, SIR A. D. ... ... The Improvement of Native Agriculture in relation to Population and Public Health. Oxford, 1936.

Hints on Vegetable Growing in Tanganyika. G.P.D. 1943.

JACKS, G. V. and WHYTE, R. O. The Rape of the Earth—A World Survey of Soil Erosion.

JEX-BLAKE, A. J. ... ... Gardening in East Africa. Longmans, 1934.

LACEY, G. and WATSON, R. ... Report on rice production in East and Central African Territories: 1948. Col. No. 246, London, 1949.

MACKINNON, E. ... ... Report on the possibilities of Agricultural Development by Mechanization of the Bukindo Area of Uzinza Peninsula, Lake Province, Tanganyika Territory, 1951. Colonial Development Corporation, London.

MALCOLM, D. W. ... ... Report on Gum and Gum Arabic. G.P.D., 1936.

MANN, H. H. ... ... Report on tea cultivation in the Tanganyika Territory and its development. Crown Agents for the Colonies, 1933.

MATHESON, J. K. and
BOVILL, E. W. ... ... East African Agriculture. O.U.P., 1950.

MILNE, G. ... ... A Provisional Soil Map of East Africa. Crown Agents, London, 1936.

Report on Soil Salinity at Mazinde, Tanganyika. G.P.D., 1940.

MURRAY, S. S. ... ... Report on Tobacco with special reference to the prospects of increased production in Central and East Africa, 1949. H.M.S.O.

Notes on some Agricultural Development schemes in Africa, 1951. Colonial office.

Report on the analysis of the sample census of African agriculture 1950 (revised). Nairobi: 1953 (Duplicated).

Report of the Sorghum Mission to certain British African Territories. H.M.S.O. 1951.

Report of a survey of Problems in the Mechanization of Native Agriculture in Tropical African Territories. H.M.S.O. 1950.

Report of an enquiry into agricultural education at primary and middle schools. Dar es Salaam (Govt. Printer) 1956, Pp. 19.

Report on the possible extension of tea cultivation in Tanganyika. Dar es Salaam (Govt. Printer) 1956, Pp. 17.

A Review of the Position in Regard to Soil Conservation in the Colonial Empire, in 1937. Colonial Office.

ROUNCE, N. V. ... ... The Agriculture of the Cultivation Steppe of the Lake, Western and Central Provinces, 1949. Longmans Green, Cape Town.

SIEBENLIST, T. ... ... Forstwirtschaft in Deutsch-Ostafriken. Berlin, 1914.

STUHLMANN, DR. F. ... ... Deutsch OstAfrika, 3 Vols.

SWYNNERTON, R. J. M. and
BENNETT, A. L. B. ... ... All about K.N.C.U. Coffee (English and Swahili). Moshi Native Coffee Board, 1948.

Tanganyika Notes and Records, published half-yearly by the Tanganyika Society, P.O. Box 511, Dar es Salaam.

TEALE, E. O. and GILLMAN, C. Report on the Investigation of the Proper Control of Water and Reorganization of the Water Boards in the Northern Province of Tanganyika. Dar es Salaam, 1935, 47 pp.

TELFORD, A. M. ... ... Report on the Development of the Rufiji and Kilombero Valleys, Crown Agents, 1927.

THEIL, A. ... ... Deutsch Ost-Afrika. Die Pflanzenwelt. Berlin, 1895.

The Tanganyika Guide. Public Relations Office, Dar es Salaam.

TROUP, R. S. ... ... Report on Forestry in Tanganyika. G.D.P. 1936, 32 pp.

WOOD, A. ... ... The groundnut affair. London: Bodley Head 1950.

AGRICULTURE, FORESTRY, BOTANY
Articles in Periodicals

BALDWIN, R. R. ... ... Native authority afforestation on Kilimanjaro. *T.N.R.*, 21, 1946, p. 81.

BALLY, P. R. O.... ... ... East African Succulents. *J.E.A.N.H.S.* Aug. 1940, p. 6; Sept. 1941, p. 35, Feb. 1942, p. 119, June, 1942, p. 147 and June, 1945, p. 122.

BARKER, R. E. D. ... ... Report on a Visit to British East Africa to study the Cultivated and Wild Bananas, 1948. *I.C.T.A.* Trinidad.

BRASNETT, N. V. ... ... Some Problems of Sustained Yield Management in the Colonies (with a Note on the Steel Bros/Government Rondo Concession by W. MacF. Robertson) *Emp. For. Rev.* Vol. 29, No. 1 pp. 9-14, 1950.

BURTT, B. D. ... ... Some East African Vegetation Communities (ed. C. H. N. Jackson). *J. Ecol.* Vol. 30, No. 1 1942, pp. 65-146.

BUSSE, W. ... ... Die periodischen Grassbrände in tropischen Afrika. *Mitt. a.d. Deutsch. Schutzgebieten,* Vol. 21, No. 2 1908.

CHAMPION, F. W. ... ... Subsidiary Silvicultural Operations in Tanganyika. *E.A.A.J.* Vol. XVII, No. 1, July, 1951.

CHITTENDEN, A. E. and others Brachystegia Wood from Tanganyika as a Paper-making Material *Colonial Plant and Animal Products,* Vol. II, No. 1, 1951.

DUTHIE, D. W. ... ... (Matengo) Mound Cultivation. *E. Afr. Agri. J.* 16, 2, 63-64, Oct. 1950.

GILLMAN, C. ... ... A Vegetation-types Map of Tanganyika Territory, 1949. *American Geogr. Soc.* New York.

Bush fallowing on the Makonde plateau. *T.N.R.,* 19, 1945, p. 34.

Population Problems of Tanganyika Territory. *E. Afr. Agric. J.* 11, 2, 86-93, Oct. 1945.

GLOVER, H. M. ... ... Soil Conservation in parts of Africa and the Middle East. *Empire Forestry Review,* Vol. 32, No. 4 pp. 351-354, Dec. 1953.

GRANT, D. K. S. ... ... Forestry in Tanganyika. *Emp. For. J.* Vol. 3, No. 1 pp. 33-38, 1924.

Mangrove woods of Tanganyika Territory, their silviculture and dependent industries. *T.N.R.* 5, 1938, p. 5.

GREENWAY, P. J. ... ... The Vegetation of Mpwapwa, Tanganyika Territory. *Journal of Ecology,* 1933. Vol. XXI, No. 1.

GREENWAY, P. J.
and HARA, F. B. ... ... Check-lists of the forest trees and shrubs of the British Empire, No. 5: Tanganyika Territory. Part 1. *Imperial Forestry Institute,* Oxford, 1940.

GREENWAY, P. J. and
BRENAN, J. P. M. ... ... Check-lists of the forest trees and shrubs of the British Empire, No. 5; Tanganyika Territory, Part II. *Imperial Forestry Institute*, Oxford 1949.

GRIFFITH, A. L. ... ... East African Enumerations. The Rondo Plateau (S. Tanganyika) *Emp. For. Rev.* Vol. 30, No. 2 pp. 179-182, 1951.

East African Enumerations. *Pterocarpus angolensis* in Mixed Woodlands (Tanganyika). *Emp. For. Rev.*, Vol. 31, No. 2, pp. 146-149, June, 1952.

HARRIS, W. V. ... ... Native methods of food storage in Tanganyika *E. Afr. Agric. J.*, 6, 3 pp. 136-138, Jan. 1941.

HARTNOLL, A. V. and
FUGGLES COUCHMAN, N. R. The *Mashokora* Cultivations of the Coast. *T.N.R.* 3, 1937, p. 34.

HEDBERG, O. ... ... Vegetation Belts of the East African Mountains. *Svensk Botanisk Tidschrift.* Vol. 45, No. 1 pp. 141-202. 1951.

HOLTZ, W. ... ... Der Minsirowald in Deutsch-Buddu, seine Beschaffenheit, sein Wert und seine wirtschaftliche Bedeutung. *B.L.F.* Vol. 3, pp. 223-247 (Report submitted in 1906) 1909-11.

Bericht über Blackwattle-Wirtschaft in Sudafrika (with a section on Moglichkeit der Einfuhrung der Blackwattle-Wirtschaft in Deutsch-Ostafrika). *B.L.F.*, Vol. 3, pp. 1-14. 1906.

HORNBY, H. E. and R. M. ... A contribution to the study of the Vegetation of Mpwapwa. *T.N.R.* 15, 1943, p. 25.

HUGHES, J. F. ... ... Forests and Water Supplies in East Africa. *Forestry Abstracts.* Vol. II, No. 2 pp. 145-153; Vol. II No. 3 pp. 283-292, 1949.

Charcoal made in Forty-gallon Drums. *E.A. Agric. J.* Vol. 12, No. 3 pp. 195-196. 1947.

A Metal-lined Pit Charcoal Kiln. *E.A. Agric. J.* Vol. 14, No. 1 pp. 53-54, 1948.

Forests and Water Supplies in East Africa. *Emp. For. Rev.* Vol. 28, No. 4 pp. 314-323. 1949.

The Influence of Forests on Climate and Water Supply. *For. Abstracts*, Vol. 11, No. 2 pp. 145-153; Vol. 1, No. 3 pp. 283-292 1949-50.

IRVINE, F. R. ... ... Health and agriculture in Africa. *Afr. Affairs*, 53, 211, 132-42. April, 1954.

JACKSON, C. H. N. ... ... Field Notes on the Species of *Brachystegia* and *Isoberlinia* of Tanganyika Territory. *J.S.Afr.Bot.* 1940, pp. 33-40.

JEFFREYS, M. D. W. ... ... The history of maize in Africa. *S.Afr.J.Sc.* 50, 8, 197-200, March, 1954.

JERVIS, T. S. ... ... A History of *Robusta* Coffee in Bukoba. *T.N.R.* 8, 1939, p. 47.

KEMP, P. B. ... ... The Susceptibility of Wood to Termite Attack. *E.A.A.J.* Vol. XVII, No. 2, Oct. 1951.

KIRKPATRICK, T. W. ... ... Notes on Insect Damage to East African Timbers. E.A. War Supplies Board, Timber Control. *E.A. Standard*, Nairobi, 31 pp.

K.N.C.U. A Short Account of the Kilimanjaro Native Co-operative Union. *E.A.Agr.J.* 1, 45-8, July, 1946.

LUNAN, M. ... ... Mound Cultivation in Ufipa, Tanganyika. *E. Afr. Ag. J.* 16, 2, 88-9, Oct. 1950 (ill.).

MAIR, L. P. ... ... Agrarian policy in the British African Colonies (Summary of a paper read before the Land Tenure Conference at Amsterdam in Oct. 1950). *Col. Review* 7, 1, 9-12, March, 1951.

MARSLAND, H. ... ... *Mlau* cultivation in the Rufiji Valley. *T.N.R.* 5, 1938, p. 56.

MASEFIELD, G. B. ... ... The development of African agriculture. *Afr. Affairs* 53, 210, 41-51, Jan. 1954.

MEEK, K. O. ... ... Stock reduction in the Mbulu Highlands, Tanganyika. *J. Afr. Admin.* 5, 4, 158-66, Oct. 1953.

MILDBRAED, J. ... ... Die Vegetationsverhaltnisse der zentralafrikanischen Seenzone vom Viktoriasee bis zu den Kivu-Vulkanen, Abschnitt I. Das Gebiet der Kagera-Niederung, der Budduwald. *Sitz. der Kgl. Preuss Akad. Wiss*, Vol. 39, 1909.

MILNE, G. ... ... Essays in Applied Pedology:—

    1. Soil type and Soil Management in relation to Plantation Agriculture in East Usambara. *E.A. Agricultural Journal.* July, 1937, p. 7.

    2. Some factors in Soil Mechanics. *E.A. Agric. Journal.*, March, 1938, p. 350.

    3. Bukoba. High and low fertility on a laterised soil. *E.A. Agric. J.* July, 1938.

MILNE, G. ... ... Report on a reconnaissance in Western Province, Tanganyika Territory. *J. Ecol.* Vol. XXXV. Nos. 1 and 2. 1947 Dec.

A Soil Reconnaissance Journey through parts of Tanganyika Territory. *J. Ecol.* Vol. 35, Nos. 1 and 2, pp. 192-265, 1947.

MILNE, G. and CALTON, W. E. Mechanical Composition of E. African Soils. *E. Afr. Agric. J.* April, 1943.

Soil Salinity related to the clearing of Natural Vegetation. *E.A. Agric. J.* July, 1944 p. 10.

MOREAU, R. E. ... ... Pleistocene Climatic Changes and the Distribution of Life in East Africa. *J. Ecol.* Vol. 21, No. 2 pp. 415-435. 1933.

Some Eco-Climatic Data for Closed Evergreen Forest in Tropical Africa. *Linn. Soc. J. Zool.* Vol. 39, No. 8, pp. 285-293, 1935.

MUNGER, E. S. ... ... African Coffee on Kilimanjaro. *Economic Geography* (Concord, N.H.) XXVIII, 2, pp. 181-5, April, 1952.

NAUMANN, F. A. and
ABEL, HERBERT ... ... Contributions to the geography and ethnography of the Matengo Highlands (E.A.) 1. Results of the Matengo-Expedition, 1930-1933. *Dtsch. geog. Blatter* 46, 1, 33-46, 1951.

PARRY, M. S. ... ... Tree Planting in Tanganyika: *E. Afr. Agric. J.*

    1. Methods of Planting—Vol. XVIII, No. 3, pp. 102-115. Jan. 1953.

    2. Species for the Highlands Vol. XIX, No. 2, pp. 15-28, Oct. 1953.

    3. Species for Dry Areas. Vol. XIX. No. 3, pp. 154-160, Jan. 1954.

    4. Species for Coastal Areas. Vol. XX, No. 1, pp. 49-53, July, 1954.

PHILLIPS, J. F. V. ... ... Some Important Vegetation Communities in the Central Province of Tanganyika Territory. *J. Ecol.* Vol. 18, No. 2, pp. 193-234, 1930.

A Sketch of the Floral Regions of Tanganyika Territory. *Trans. Roy. Soc. S. Afr.* Vol. 19, pp. 363-372, 1931.

Fire: its influence on Biotic Communities and Physical Factors in South and East Africa. *S.A. Jour. Sci.* Vol. 27, pp. 352-367, 1930.

PIELOU, E. C. ... ... Notes on the vegetation of the Rukwa rift valley, Tanganyika. *J. Ecol.*, **40**, 2, Oct. 1952, pp. 383-92.

PITT, C. J. W. ... ... Planning for Fuel and Pole Plantations. *E.A. Agric. J.* Vol. 13, No. 4, pp. 195-202, 1948.

Pole and Fuel Plantations and Windbreaks, Kwimba District. *T.N.R.* 2, 1936, pp. 55-59.

PITT, J. ... ... Provisional Macroscopic Key to the Identification of Certain Timbers of Tanganyika Territory. *T.N.R.* 8 1939, pp. 27-46.

PITT-SCHENKEL, C. J. W. ... Windbreaks in Tanganyika, Kwimba District. *Emp. For. J.* Vol. 14, pp. 54-59, 1935.

Some Important Communities of Warm Temperature Rain Forest at Magamba, West Usambara, Tanganyika Territory. *J. Ecol.* Vol. 26, No. 1, pp. 50-81, 1938.

Pole and Fuel Plantations and Windbreaks, Kwimba District. *T.N.R.*, 2, 1936, p. 55.

RAYMOND, W. D. ... ... Native Materia Medica.

I. The Arrow Poisons. *T.N.R.* 1, Mar. 1936.

II. The Medicaments. *T.N.R.* 2, Oct. 1936.

III. The Deliriants. *T.N.R.* 5, Apr. 1938.

The Detection and Estimation of Ouabain and Strophanthin. *Analyst.* Vol. 63 No. 748, 1938 pp. 478-482.

Equivalent Quinine index and therapeutic efficiency of Totaquina. *E.A. Med. J.* 1944 (XXI) pp. 291-296.

Totaquina and its rivals. *E.A. Med. J.* 1946 XXIII pp. 301-311.

Notes on a Poisonous E. African Species of Wild Cucumber (Cucumis oculeatus). *E.A. Med. J.* XXIV. No. 12, 1947.

Tanganyika Arrow Poisons. *T.N.R.* 23, June, 1947.

The M-dinitro benzene reaction of ouabain and its application to the examination of East African Arrow poison. *Analyst* Vol. 64, p. 113, 1939.

Minimum Dietary Standard for East African natives. *E. A. Med. J.* Vol. XVII, No. 7, Oct. 1940 p. 249.

The poisonous effects of some local species of Euphorbia. *E.A. Med. J.* March, 1936.

RAYMOND, W. D. ... ... Nutrition and Tanganyika. *T.N.R.* 11, April, 1941, p. 18.

The Composition and Examination of Tanganyika Arrow Poisons. *Analyst.* Vol. 61 No. 719 pp. 100-103 1936.

RAYMOND, W. D. and
FRENCH, M. H. ... ... The Constants of Milk and Butter Fat in Tanganyika Territory. *Analyst.* Vol. 61, No. 728, 1936. pp. 750-751.

RAYMOND, W. D. and
JOJO, W. L. ... ... Nutritive value of Tanganyika Bananas. *E.A.A.J.* 1940 pp. 105-108.

RAYMOND, W. D. and JOJO,
W. L. AND NICODEMUS ... Nutritive value of some Tanganyika Foods (ii, Cassava). *E.A.A.J.* 1941.

RAYMOND, W. D. and
PADYE, V. P. ... ... A note on the possibility of the Stabilization of Pyrethrum. *E.A.A.J.* Vol. XIII, 1948 No. 3, pp. 162-163.

REA, R. J. A. ... ... The Forest types of Vegetation in Tanganyika Territory. *Emp. For. J.* Vol. 14, pp. 202-208, 1935.

ROUNCE, N. V. ... ... Technical Considerations in the Economic Development of Sukumaland. *Empire Journal of Experimental Agriculture*, Vol. XIX, No. 76, Oct. 1951.

The development, expansion and re-habilitation of Sukumalnd. *Emp. Cotton-growing Rev.* 26, 1, 32-41, Ja. 1949.

SALT, G. ... ... A Contribution to the Ecology of Upper Kilimanjaro. *J. Ecol.* Vol. 42, No. 2, July, 1954.

SAMPSON, D. N. ... ... Notes on the Flora of Kilimanjaro, *T.N.R.* 34, 1953.

SCOTT, J. D. ... ... The Ecology of Certain Plant Communities of the Central Province, Tanganyika Territory. *J. Ecol.* Vol. 22, No. 2, pp. 177-299, 1934.

SHEPSTONE, D. ... ... The Oil Palm in Western Tanganyika. *E.A.A.J.* Vol. XVI, No. 3, January, 1951.

SIEBENLIST, T. ... ... Forstwirtscnaft in Deutsch-Ostafrika. *Verlagsbuchhandlung Paul Parey*, Berlin, 1914.

STUHLMANN, F. ... ... Ubersicht über Land—und Forstwirtschaft in Deutsch Ostafrika im Berichstsjarhe 1, Juli 1900 bis 30.Juni 1901. *B.L.F.*, Vol. I pp. 1-23, 1903.

STURDY, D. ... ... Agricultural notes. *T.N.R.* 1, 1936, p. 52.

STURDY, D., CALTON, W. E.
and MILNE, G. ... ... A chemical Survey of the waters of Mount Meru, Tanganyika Territory. *J.E.A.U. Nat. Hist. Soc.* No. 45-46. May, 1933.

TANNER, R. E. S. ... ... Some Southern Province trees with their African names and uses. *T.N.R.* 31, 1951, p. 61.

THWAITES, D. H. ... ... Wanyakyusa Agriculture. *E.Afr.Agric.J.* 9, 4, 236-9, April, 1944.

WHYBROW, C. ... ... An English flower garden in the tropics. *T.N.R.* 2, 1936, p. 96.

WIGG, L. T. ... ... The Durability of Some East African Timbers. *E.Afr. Agric. J.* Vol. 12, No. 2, pp. 90-100, 1946.

Land Use in Tanganyika Territory. Appendix (pp. 17-22) to *Empire Forests and the War: Tanganyika Territory* (Statement presented to British Empire Forestry Conference, 1947). Dsm.

The Urgent Need for Uniformity in African Vegetation Description. *Emp. For. Rev.* Vol. 28, No. 1 pp. 14-17, 1949.

Problems of Dry Forest Silviculture in Tanganyika. *Emp. For. Rev.* Vol. 32, No. 3, pp. 212-221, Sept. 1953.

ZOOLOGY

Books, Reports, Pamphlets

GAME

AHLEFELD-BILLE, G. ... ... Tandalla. a Danish Game Warden's study of nature and wild life in Kenya and Tanganyika. Routledge and Kegan Paul, London, 1948.

Annual Reports of the Game Department. G.P.D.

Annual Reports of East African Tsetse and Trypanosomiasis Research and Reclamation Organization, 1949 to 1952. E.A. High Commission, Nairobi.

Annual Reports of Tsetse Survey and Reclamation Department. G.P.D.

BLUNT, D. ... ... The Elephant. East Africa Ltd., London, 1933.

BUXTON, P. A. ... ... Trypanosomiasis in East Africa. H.M.S.O. 1947.

DUGMORE, A. R. ... ... The Wonderland of Big Game. Arrowsmith, London, 1925.

East Africa High Commission (1948, 1952) Fauna of British East and Central Africa, Papers Nos. 1 and 4.

ELLERMAN, J. R., MORRISON-SCOTT, T. C. S. and HAYMAN, R. W. ... ... Southern African Mammals, 1758 to 1951: a Reclassification. London: British Museum. 1953.

FITZSIMONS, F. W. ... ... The Natural History of South Africa: Mammals. 4 vols. London: Longmans, Green & Co. 1919-20.

HAAGNER, A. ... ... South African Mammals. London: H.F. & G. Witherby, 1920.

LINDNER, E. ... ... Zoo-Safari: Bericht der Deutschen Zoologischen Ostafrika—Expedition 1951/52. Schweizerbartische Verlagsbuch Handlung, Stuttgart, 1954.

LONNBERG, E. ... ... Wissenschaftliche Ergebnisse der Schwedische Zoologischen Expedition nach dem Kilimanjaro, dem Meru, und den Umgebended Massaisteppen-Deutsch Ost-Afrika, 1905-6. Bd. 1, Abt. 1, Stockholm, 1910.

LYDEKKER, R. ... ... Catalogue of the Ungulate Mammals in the British Museum (Natural History). Vols. 1 4, 5. London: British Museum, 1913, 15 and 16.

The Game Animals of Africa. Rowland Ward, London, 1908.

LYDEKKER, R. and BLAINE, G. Catalogue of the Ungulate Mammals in the British Museum (Natural History). Vols. 2, 3. London: British Museum, 1914.

MATSCHIE, P. ... ... Säugetierwelt in Werther's: Die mittleren Hochländer des nordlichen Deutsch-Ost-Afrika. pp. 205, Berlin: Paetel, 1898.

MOEBINS, K. and others ... Die Tierwelt Deutsch-Ost-Afrikas und der nachbargebiete. Berlin, 1895-98.

MOORE, AUDREY ... ... Serengeti. *Country Life*, London, 1938.

MOORE, J. E. S. ... ... The Tanganyika Problem. Hurst & Blackett Ltd., London, 1903.

SCHILLINGS, C. G. ... ... In Wildest Africa. Hutchinson & Co. London, 1907.

With Flashlight and Rifle. London, 1906. 2 vols.

SIEDENTOPF, A. R. ... ... The Last Stronghold of Big Game. Hodder & Stoughton Ltd., London. 1947.

STIGAND, C. H. ... ... The Game of British East Africa. London, 1913.

SWYNNERTON, G. H. ... ... (1948) Notes on some mammals found in the Lake Rukwa catchment area, South-western Tanganyika Territory. Ann. Rep. Game Pres. Dept. Dar es Salaam, 1946, 8-43.

FISH

BERTRAM, BARLEY and
TREWAYAS ... ... Report on the Fish and Fisheries of Lake Nyasa. Crown Agents, 1942.

COPLEY, H. ... ... The Game Fishes of Africa. Witherby, London, 1952.

GRAHAM, M. ... ... (1929) The Victoria Nyanza and its Fisheries. Report on the fishing survey of Lake Victoria 1927-1928. Crown Agents for the Colonies, London.

RICARDO, C. K. ... ... Report on the Fish and Fisheries of Lake Rukwa in Tanganyika Territory and the Bangweulu Region in Northern Rhodesia. Crown Agents.

SWYNNERTON, G. H. ... ... Report of an Investigation of the Fisheries of Lake Rukwa.

INSECTS

HARRIS, W. V. ... ... The Red Locust. Agric. Department Pamphlet No. 10. G.P.D. 1933.

SWYNNERTON, R. J. M. ... The Tsetse Flies of East Africa. The transactions of the Royal Entomological Society of London. Vol. 84, 1936.

AMPHIBIANS AND REPTILES

LONNBERG, E. ... ... (1910) Reptilia and Batrachia in Sjöstedt's Kilimanjaro—Meru Expedition 1905/06. Bd. 1 Abt 4. p. 17.

LOVERIDGE, A. ... ... To-morrow's a Holiday. (Collecting snakes, etc.) London, 1957.

MATSCHIE, P. ... ... (1892) Uber eine kleine Sammlung von Saugetieren und Reptilien welche Herr L. Conradt aus Usambara (Deutsch-Ost-Afrika) heimgebracht hat. Sb. Ges. Naturf. Fr. Berlin 1892, 101-110.

ZOOLOGY

Articles in Periodicals

CUNNINGTON, W. A. ... ... The fauna of the African lakes: a study in comparative limnology, with special reference to Tanganyika. *P.Z.S.* London, 1920, 507-622.

DAVID, L. ... ... Contribution à l'étude de la faune ichthyologique du lac Tanganyika. *Rev. Zool. Bot. Afr.* 28, 149-160.

DOLLMAN, G. ... ... The occurrence of the chimpanzee in Tanganyika Territory. *Proc. Linn. Soc. Lond.* 1935, 15.

FRASER, H. ... ... The introduction of trout into Tanganyika. *T.N.R.* 4, 1937.

FRENCH, M. H. ... ... The Liveweight Development of Certain Shorthorned Zebu Cattle in Tanganyika Territory. *Trop. Agric.* 16. 51.

The Development of Livestock in Tanganyika; Skeletal Measurements of Local fat-tailed and grade Blackhead Persian Sheep. *Emp. J.Exp. Agric.* 1938.

FORCART, L. ... ... Beiträge zur Kenntnis der Insectivorenfamilie Chrysochloridae. *Rev. Suisse Zool.* 49 1-6.

GILLMAN, C. ... ... Indian elephants in Tanganyika. *T.N.R.* 12, 1941, pp. 61-63.

FUGGLES-COUCHMAN, N. R. ... Notes on the nesting habits of some Tanganyika birds. *T.N.R.* 1, 1936, p. 61.

The Habitat-Distribution of Birds of Northern, Eastern and Central Tanganyika, with Field Keys, Part I, *T.N.R.* No. 33 July 1952, Part II, No. 35, July 1953, Part III, No. 37, July 1954.

GRANT, C. H. B. ... ... The distribution of the chimpanzee in Tanganyika Territory. *T.N.R.* 21, 1946, p. 110.

GRANT, D. K. S. ... ... Introduction of trout into Tanganyika Territory. *J.E.A.N.H.S.*, April-July, 1933, p. 197.

GUEST, N. J. and LEEDAL, G. P. Notes on the Fauna of Kilimanjaro. *T.N.R.* 36, Jan. 1954.

GUNN, D. L. ... ... A history of Lake Rukwa and the red locust. *T.N.R.* 42, Mar. 1956, 1-18, ill. map.

HALDANE, L. A. ... ... Butterflies of the Njombe Highlands. *T.N.R.* No. 43, June 1956.

HALDANE, L. A. ... ... Birds of the Njombe District. *T.N.R.* No. 44, Sept. 1956.

HARRISON, H. ... ... The Shinyanga game experiment; a few of the early observations. *J. Anim. Ecol.* 1936, 271.

HATCHELL, G. W. ... ... Some Notes on Sea-Fishing near Tanga. *T.N.R.* 5, April, 1938.

Further Notes on Fishing near Tanga. *T.N.R.* 9, June, 1940.

Sea Fishing on the Tanganyika Coast. *T.N.R.* 37, July, 1954.

Giant fish in Lake Tanganyika. *T.N.R.* 36, 1954. pp. 73-74.

HATT, R. T. ... ... Mammals collected by the Rockefeller-Murphy expedition to Tanganyika Territory and the eastern Belgian Congo. *Amer. Mus. Novit.* 1940. 1070, 1.

HARVEY, W. O. ... ... The East African Pitta (*Pitta angolensis longipennis Reichenow*). *Ibis*, 1938, pp. 335-337.

HOLLOWAY, J. W. T. ... ... Destocking and culling in Tanganyika. *E. Afr. Agric. J.* 19, 3, 161-3, Jan. 1954.

HONE, E. ... ... African game protection. An outline of the existing game reserves and national parks of Africa with notes on certain species of big game nearing extinction, or needing additional protection. *Amer. C'ttee Int. Wild Life Prot. Sp. Publ.* 1(3) 1933. 1-45.

HUTCHISON, H. G. and
MABON, R. M. ... ... Studies on the Environmental Physiology of Cattle in Tanganyika. *J. Agric. Sc.* 44. 121.

IONIDES, C. J. P. ... ... Pages from a Tanganyika Game Ranger's Notebook. *T.N.R.* 29, 1950, p. 62 and 30, 1951.

Snakes of the Southern Province. *T.N.R.* 29, 1950, p. 98.

JACKSON, C. H. N. and
LOVERIDGE, A. ... ... The Vernacular Names of East African Mammals. *Trans. R. Ent. Soc.* Lond. 84, 547.

JERRARD, R. C. ... ... Anti-locust measures memoirs. *T.N.R.* 3, 1937, p. 114.

JOERGENS, W. ... ... Crocodile gall. *T.N.R.* 18, 1944, p. 99.

JOHNSTON, H. H. ... ... General observations on the fauna of Kilima-Ndjaro. *P.Z.S.* London, 1885, 214.

Journal of the Society for the Preservation of the Fauna of the Empire. Papers on Tanganyika mammals.

LANE, L. P.	Fishing in Lake Tanganyika. *T.N.R.* 7, 1939, p. 3.
	Fungu Kizimkasi, or Latham Island. *T.N.R.* 18, 1944, p. 89.
LEWIS, E.	A further note on chimpanzees in the Kigoma District. *T.N.R.* 19, 1945, p. 68.
LOCKLEY, G. J.	The Families of Freshwater Fishes of Tanganyika Territory with a Key to their identification. *E.A.A.J.* Vol. XIV, No. 4, April, 1949.
LOVERIDGE, A.	The crocodiles of Tanganyika Territory. *T.N.R.* 10. 1940, p. 41.
	Some geckos of Tanganyika Territory. *T.N.R.* 12, 1941, p. 32.
	Comments on the reptiles and amphibians of Lindi. *T.N.R.* 14, 1942, p. 38.
	The green and black mambas of East Africa. *J.E.A.N.H.S.* 1947-8, vol. XIX, No. 5 (89).
	On lemurs at Morogoro. G.E.A. *P.Z.S.* Lond. 1922, 313-315.
	New reptiles and amphibians from Tanganyika Territory and Kenya Colony. *B.M.C.Z.* Harvard, 72, 1932. 375-387.
	Scientific results of an expedition to rain forest regions in eastern Africa. 1. New reptiles and amphibians from East Africa. *B.M.C.Z.* Harv. 79, 1935, 1-19.
	Reports on the scientific results of an expedition to the southwestern highlands of Tanganyika Territory. 1. Introduction and Zoogeography. *B.M.C.Z.* Harv. 75, 1933 1-43.
	On a Third Collection of Reptiles taken in Tanganyika by C. J. P. Ionides, Esq. *T.N.R.* No. 43, June 1956.
McCONNELL, R. B.	A further note on chimpanzees in the Kigoma District. *T.N.R.* 19, 1945, p. 68.
MICHELMORE, A. P. G. ...	Th Internationa Red Locust Control. *T.N.R.*, 20, 1945, p. 48.
MOCQUARD, M. F.	Note sur quelques reptiles de Tanga, don de M. Gierra. *Bull. Mus. Hist. Nat.* Paris, 1897, 122.

MOREAU, R. E. ... ... Migrant birds in Tanganyika Territory. *T.N.R.* 4, 1937, p. 17.

Bird-names used in coastal North-eastern Tanganyika Territory. *T.N.R.* 10, 1940, p. 47 and 11, 1941, p. 47.

The distribution of the chimpanzee in Tanganyika Territory. *T.N.R.*, 14, 1942, p. 52.

Kilimanjaro and Mount Kenya: some comparisons with special reference to the mammals and birds: and with a note on Mount Meru. *T.N.R.*, 18, 1944, p. 28.

The dwarf parrots (*Agapornis*) of Tanganyika. *T.N.R.* 19, 1945, p. 23.

Ornithology in Tanganyika. *T.N.R.* 28, 1950, p. 64 (contains bibliography).

MOREAU, R. E. and
PAKENHAM, R. H. W. ... The land vertebrates of Pemba, Zanzibar and Mafia: a zoo-geographical study. *P.Z.S.* Lond. 110, pp. 97-128.

MOREAU, R. E. and
SCLATER, W. L. ... ... The avifauna of the mountains along the Rift Valley in north central Tanganyika Territory (Mbulu District). *Ibis* 1937, pp. 760-786; 1938, pp. 1-32.

MYERS, G. S. ... ... Report on the fishes collected by H. C. Raven in Lake Tanganyika in 1920. *Proc. U.S. Nat. Mus.* 84, 1936. p. 15.

NICKEL, E. ... ... Die Kriechtiere Deutsch-Ostafrikas. *Helios,* 18, 1901, 65-73.

NIEDENA, F. ... ... (1913, 1915) Neues Verzeichnis der Kriechtiere (auber den Schlangen) von Deutsch-Ostafrika. *Mitt. Zool. Mus Berlin* 7, 53-100 (Reptilia); 345-390 (Amphibia.)

PIGGOTT, D. W. I. ... ... Spoonfishing in the Mafia group. *T.N.R.* 12, 1941, pp. 11-19; No. 37, Mar. 1954, p. 39.

POCOCK, R. I. ... ... The Races of the Striped and Brown Hyaenas. *Proc. Zool. Soc. Lond.* 1934.

POTTS, W. H. ... ... The Distribution of tsetse flies in Tanganyika. *Bull. Ent. Res.* 28, 129-148.

POTTS, W. H. and
JACKSON, C. H. N. ... ... The Shinyanga game destruction experiment. *Bull. Ent. Res.* 43, 1952 pp. 365-374.

RICARDO, G. K. ... ... The fish of Lake Rukwa. *J. Linn. Soc.* (Zool.) 40, 1939, pp. 625-657.

REGAN, C. T. ... ... The cichlid fishes of Lake Nyasa. *P.Z.S.* Lond. 1921, 675-727.

RUSHBY, G. G. ... ... The African elephant and its hunters. *T.N.R.* 17, 1944, p. 59.

Pan Satyrus (chimpanzee). *T.N.R.*, 16, 1943, p. 99.

Game in relation to tsetse. *T.N.R.*, 18, 1944, p. 77.

RUSHBY, G. G. and
  SWYNNERTON, G. H. ... Notes on some game animals of Tanganyika Territory. *T.N.R.* 22, 1946, p. 14.

SALT, G. ... ... A contribution to the ecology of upper Kilimanjaro. *J. Ecol.* 42, 1954. pp. 375-423.

SCHWARZ, E. ... ... Notes on the classification of the African monkeys in the genus *Cercopithecus*, Erxleben. *Ann. Mag. N.H.* 1, 1928, 649.

SILLERY, A. ... ... Indian elephants in Tanganyika. *T.N.R.* 11, 1941, pp. 64-65.

SMITH, A. and others ... Zoological results of the Third Tanganyika Expedition, conducted by W. A. Cunnington. *Proc. Zool. Soc.* London, 1906, I and II.

SMITH, F. G. ... ... Preliminary Report on Trigon Wax. *E.A.A.J.* Vol. XVI, No. 4, April, 1951.

Beekeeping Observations in Tanganyika 1950/51. *E.A.A.J.* Vol. XVII No. 2, October, 1951.

STEINDACHNER, F. ... ... Beitrage zur Kenntniss der Fischfauna des Tanganyikasees und des Kongogebietes. *Sb. Akad. Wiss.* Wien, 120, 1911, 1-16.

STERNFELD, R. ... ... Zur Reptilienfauna Deutsch Ostafrikas. *Sb. Ges. naturf. Fr.* Berlin, 1911, 250.

STUBBINGS, B. J. J. ... ... Notes on native methods of fishing in the Mafia islands. *T.N.R.* 19, 1945, pp. 49-53.

SWYNNERTON, G. H. ... ... A revision of the type-localities of mammals occurring in the Tanganyika Territory. *P.Z.S.* Lond. 115, 49.

Vernacular names for some of the better known mammals in the Central Province, Tanganyika Territory. *T.N.R.* 21, 1946, p. 21.

SWYNNERTON, G. H. and
  HAYMAN, R. W. ... ... A checklist of the land mammals of the Tanganyika Territory and the Zanzibar Protectorate. *J.E.A.N.H.S.*, Vol. XX, 1950, No. 6 and 7 (90) p. 274.

SWYNNERTON, B. ... ... A key to the recognition in the field of two hundred and sixty of the commoner birds of Tanganyika. *T.N.R.* 6, 1938, p. 5.

THOMAS, O. ... ... Report on the mammals obtained and observed by Mr. H. H. Johnston on Mount Kilima-Ndjaro. *P.Z.S.* Lond. 1885, 219.

Descriptions of two new rodents from the Victoria Nyanza. *Ann. Mag. N.H.* 12, 1893, 267.

List of mammals from Mount Kilimanjaro, obtained by Mr. Robin Kemp, and presented to the British Musuem by Mr. C. D. Rudd. *Ann Mag. N.H.* 6, 1910, 308.

TORNIER, G. ... ... Reptilien and Amphibien in Zur Faunistik Deutsch-Ost-Afrikas. *Arch. Naturg.* 43, 1897, 63-66.

TREWAYAS, E. ... ... A synopsis of the cichlid fishes of Lake Nyasa. *Ann. Mag. N.H.* (10(16)), 1935, 65-118.

Nyasa fishes of the genus *Tilapia. Ann. Mag. N.H.* (11) 7, 1941, 294-306.

TRUE, F. W. ... ... An Annotated Catalogue of the Mammals collected by Dr. W. L. Abbott in the Kilima-Ndjaro Region, East Africa. *Proc. U.S. Nat. Mus.* 13, 1890, 227.

VERDCOURT, B. ... ... Observations on the Ecology of the Land and Freshwater Mollusca of North-East Tanganyika. *T.N.R.* 33, 1952 and 35, 1953.

Veterinary Department, Kabete. Notes on animal diseases. Various volumes of the *East African Agricultural Journal* from 1949 onwards.

WILLIAMS, C. B. ... ... Record of butterfly migration in East Africa. *J.E.A.N.H.* Jan. & June, 1929, No. 35, p. 9.

WORTHINGTON, E. B. and RICARDO, C. K. (1937) ... The fish of Lake Tanganyika (other than the Cichlidae). *P.Z.S.* Lond. 1936, 1061-1112.

WORTHINGTON, E. B. ... ... The fishes of Lake Nyasa other than the Cichlidae. *P.Z.S.* Lond. 1933, 285-316.

WHYBROW, C. ... ... Preliminary list of some butterflies taken near Malangali—with notes. *T.N.R.* 9, 1940, p. 37.

Some Sukuma bird names. *T.N.R.* 25, 1948, p. 56.

GEOLOGY

Books, Reports, Pamphlets

Annual Reports of the Geological Survey of Tanganyika. G.P.D.

BORNHARDT, W.... ... ... Zur Oberflächengestaltung und Geologie Deutsch-Ostafrikas. D. Reimer, Berlin.

EADES, N. W. ... ... The Geology of the Iramba Plateau. Short Paper Geological Survey, No. 15. G.P.D.

GILLMAN, C. ... ... A Reconnaissance Survey of the Hydrology of Tanganyika Territory in its Geographical Settings. Water Consultant's Report, No. 6. G.P.D.

The Geography and Hydrography of the Tanganyika part of the Ruvuma Basin. G.P.D.

GRANTHAM, D. R. ... ... Lupa Goldfield. Short Paper Geol. Survey No. 2. G.P.D.

The Eastern Extension of the Lupa Goldfield, Ipogolo-Sengambi-Shoga. Short Pap. Geol. Surv. Tanganyika No. 11, 1933. G.P.D.

GRANTHAM, D. R. and
  B. N. TEMPERLEY ... ... Preliminary Report of the Geology and Gold Occurrences of the Kahama region. Short pap. geol. Surv. Tanganyika 21. G.P.D., 1939.

GREGORY, J. W. ... ... The Rift Valleys and Geology of East Africa. Seeley Service, London, 1921.

HARKIN, D. A. ... ... The Geology of the Mhukuru Coalfield, (Songea District). Short Pap. geol. Surv. Tanganyika, 28, G.P.D. 1953.

KLUTE, F. ... ... Ergebnisse der Forschungen am Kilimanjaro. Berlin, 1920.

KRENKEL, E. ... ... Geologie Afrikas. Borutraeger. Berlin, 1925.

LEAKEY, L. S. B. ... ... Stone Age Africa. O.U.P., 1936.

Olduvai Gorge. A Report on the Evolution of the Hand-axe Culture. O.U.P., 1951.

MEYER, H. ... ... Der Kilimanjaro: Reisen und Studien. Berlin, 1900.

McCONNELL, R. B. ... ... Preliminary Report on the Mining Geology of the Iramba-Sekenke Goldfield. Short Pap. geol. Surv. Tanganyika, 25, G.P.D. 1945.

MCCONNELL, R. B. ... ... The Geology of the Namwele-Mkomolo Coalfield, Ufipa District, with Notes on Underground Exploration carried out by the Tanganyika Government. With appendices by the Imperial Institute, J. H. Harris, A. Caperle and F. Oates. Short Pap. geol. Surv. Tanganyika 27, G.P.D. 1947,

PARKINSON, J. ... ... The Dinosaur in East Africa. Witherby, London, 1930.

A note on the Geology of the Country around Tendaguru (Lindi District), Tanganyika Territory. Short Pap. geol. Surv. Tanganyika, 6, G.P.D. 1930.

OATES, F. ... ... The Microscope as an Aid in Metallurgical Testing of Gold Ores. Pamphl. geol. Div. Tanganyika, 7, G.P.D. 1937.

Notes on the Sampling and Testing of Mineral Deposits in Tanganyika. Pamphl. geol. Div. Tanganyika, 1, G.P.D. 1939,

OATES, F. and HARRIS, J. H. ... War-time Manufacture of Abrasives in Tanganyika Territory. Short Pap. geol. Surv. Tanganyika 26, G.P.D. 1950.

ORR, D. and GRANTHAM, D. R. Some Salt Lakes of the Northern Rift Zone. Short Pap. geol. Surv. Tanganyika, 8, G.P.D. 1931,

RECK, H. ... ... Oldoway. Leipzig, 1933.

RAED, F. R. C. ... ... The Geology of the British Empire, London, 1950.

SKERL, A. C. and OATES, F. The Geology of the North Ilunga area. Short paper, Geol. Surv. 18, G.P.D. 1938.

STOCKLEY, G. M. ... ... The Kigugwe Copper Deposit near Brandts. Short Pap. geol. Surv. Tanganyika 3, G.P.D. 1928.

Notes on the Mineral Deposits in the Newala-Lindi Area. Short Pap. geol. Surv. Tanganyika, 7, G.P.D. 1931.

Outline of the Geology of the Musoma District. Bull. geol. Div. Tanganyika, 7, G.P.D. 1935.

Geology of the South and South-Eastern Regions of the Musoma District. Short. Pap. geol. Surv. Tanganyika, 13, G.P.D. 1936.

STOCKLEY, G. M. ... ... The Geology of Parts of the Tabora, Kigoma and Ufipa Districts, North-west Lake Rukwa. Short Pap. geol. Surv. Tanganyika 20, G.P.D. 1938.

The Geology of the Country around Mwanza Gulf. Short Pap. geol. Surv. Tanganyika, 29, G.P.D. 1947.

STROMER, VON REICHENBACH, E. Die Geologie der Deutschen Schutzgebiete in Afrika. 1896. Munich.

TEALE, E. O. ... ... The Soil and Agricultural Development in Relation to the Geology of Portions of the Northern Kigoma and Southern Bukoban Provinces. Short Pap. geol. Surv. Tanganyika 4, G.P.D. 1929.

Shinyanga Diamond Fields. Short Pap. geol. Surv. Tanganyika 9, G.P.D. 1931.

The Kimberlite and Associated Occurrences of the Iramba Plateau. Short Pap. geol. Surv. Tanganyika, 10, G.P.D. 1932.

Geological Survey of Tanganyika Territory. Final Report with guide map to specimens. Waterlow & Sons., London, 1922.

TEMPERLEY, B. N. ... ... The Geology of the Country around Mpwapwa. Short Pap. geol. Surv. Tanganyika, 19, G.P.D. 1938.

VALLEE POUSSIN, J. DE LA, and
R. B. McCONNELL ... ... The Mpanda Mineral Field of Western Tanganyika. Short Pap. geol. Surv. Tanganyika, 30, G.P.D. 1950.

WADE, F. B. ... ... Water Supplies in the Region between Tabora and the Speke Gulf. Bull. geol. Surv. Tanganyika, 1, G.P.D. 1927.

Water Supplies for Cattle along the Kondoa-Irangi—Handeni Stock Route. Short Pap. geol. Surv. Tanganyika, 5, G.P.D. 1930.

WADE, F. B. and OATES, F. ... The Saragura and Associated Gold Occurrences of the Mwanza Area. Short Pap. geol. Surv. Tanganyika, 12, G.P.D. 1934.

An explanation of Degree Sheet No. 52 (Dodoma) Short Pap. geol. Surv. Tanganyika, 17, G.P.D. 1938.

WILLIS, B. ... ... Living Africa. McCraw-Hill Book Co. Inc. London and New York, 1930.

GEOLOGY

Articles in Periodicals

AITKEN, W. G. ... ... 1950. Geomorphology of Parts of the Kondoa District. *T.N.R.* 29, pp. 55-58.

ASTRUP, J. ... ... 1939. Galula coal field and its relation to the coal-bearing series of the Karroo system. *Trans. R. geol. Soc. Cornwall*, XVII, 11.

BEHREND, F. and E. LEHMANN 1924. Das Vulkangebiet am Nordende des Nyassa als magmatische Provinz. *Z. Vulkanol.*, Bd. IV.

BISSET, C. B. ... ... 1955. Minerals and Industry in Tanganyika. *Colon. Geol. min. Resour.*, Vol. 5, No. 1, pp. 40-50.

BOONSTRA, L. D. ... ... 1953. A Note on some Rhynchosaurian Remains from Tanganyika Territory. *Ann. S. Afr. Mus.*, Vol. XLII, pp. 1-4.

1953. A Report on a Collection of Fossil Reptilian Bones from Tanganyika Territory. *Ann. S. Afr. Mus.*, Vol. XLII, pp. 5-18.

BRENNICH, G. ... ... 1937. Neuere Ergebnisse der geologischen Erforschung von Ostafrika. *Geol. Rdsch.* Bd. XXVIII, Heft 3/4, pp. 298-327.

BRIDGES, R. J. ... ... 1935. On a suite of igneous rocks near Kidete, Tanganyika, and associated development of copper ore. *Trans. geol. Soc. S. Afr.*, Vol. XXXVIII, pp. 1-28.

BULLARD, E. C. ... ... 1935. Gravity Measurements in East Africa. *Bull. geol. Surv. Uganda*, 2, pp. 28-29.

COX, L. R. ... ... 1932. Lamellibranchia from the Karroo Beds of the Ruhuhu Coalfields, Tanganyika Territory. *Quart. J. geol. Soc. Lond.*, Vol. 88.

1936. Karroo Lamellibranchia from Tanganyika Territory and Madagascar. *Quart. J. geol. Soc. Lond.*, 92, Pt. 1, pp. 32-57.

1939. Notes on Jurassic Lamellibranchia, III. On a New Trigonia and other species from Tanganyika. *Proc. malac. Soc. Lond.*, Vol. XXII, Pt. IV, pp. 190-203.

1939. Mollusca from the Quaternary Deposits of Lake Rukwa (Tanganyika Territory). *Proc. malac. Soc. Lond.*, Vol. XXIII, Pt. IV, pp. 242-252.

DIETRICH, W. O. ... ... 1914. Die Gastropoden der Tendaguruschichten, der Aptstufe und der Oberkreide in südlichen Deutsch-Ostafrika. *Arch. Biontol., Berl.*, Bd. III, Heft 4, pp. 99-152.

1925. Uber eine dem mittleren Sauriermergel am Tendaguru äquivalent, rein marine Kimmeridgebildung in Mahokondo, Deutsch-Ostafrika. *Palaeontographica*, Suppl. Bd. VII, II Reihe, Teil I, L.f.g. 1.

1925. Zur Kenntnis der Urgongesteine im südlichen Deutsch-Ostafrika nebst Beschreibung der darin vorkommenden Orbitolinen. *Palaeontographica*, Suppl. Bd. VII, II Reihe, Teil I, Lfg. 1.

1933. Zur Stratigraphie der Tendaguruschichten in Deutsch-Ostafrika. *Zbl. Miner. Paläont.*, Abt. B, 7, pp. 423-8.

DIXEY, F. ... ... 1928. The Dinosaur Beds of Lake Nyasa. *Trans. roy. Soc. S. Afr.*, Vol. XVI.

ELLIOTT, G. F. S. and J. GREGORY ... ... 1895. The Geology of Mount Ruwenzori and some adjoining regions of Equatorial Africa. *Quart. J. geol. Soc. Lond.*, Vol. 51, pp. 669-80.

FAHRION, H. ... ... 1937. Die Foraminiferen der Kreide-und Tertiärschichten im südlichen Deutsch-Ostafrika. *Palaeontographica*, Suppl. VII, II Reihe, Teil II, Lfg. 2.

FUCHS, V. E. ... ... 1934. The Geological Work of the Cambridge Expedition to the East African Lakes, 1930-31. *Geol. Mag.*, Vol. LXXI, No. 3, pp. 97-112, No. 4, pp. 145-166.

GEILINGER, W. ... ... 1936. The Retreat of the Kilimanjaro Glaciers. *T.N.R.* 2, pp. 7-20.

GILLMAN, C. ... ... 1927. South-west Tanganyika Territory. *Geogr. J.*, Vol. LXIX, pp. 97-126.

1933. The Hydrology of Lake Tanganyika. *Bull. geol. Surv. Tanganyika*, 5.

1936. A Synopsis of the Geography of Tanganyika Territory. *T.N.R.* 1, pp. 5-13.

GRACE, G. and G. M. STOCKLEY 1931. Geology of the Usongo area, Tanganyika Territory. *J. E. Afr. Ug. nat. Hist. Soc.*, Vol. 37, p. 185.

GRANT, C. H. B. ... ... 1947. The Hot Springs of Mtagata ("Boiling Water"), North Western Tanganyika. *T.N.R.* 24, pp. 47-48.

GRANTHAM, D. R. ... ... 1932. Lupa Goldfield. *Bull. geol. Surv., Tanganyika*, 3.

1955. The Geology and Ecology of the Nachingwea Region, Southern Province. *Bull. geol. Surv. Tanganyika*, 26.

GRANTHAM, D. R., B. N. TEMPERLEY and R. B. MCCONNELL ... ... 1945. Explanation of the Geology of Degree Sheet No. 17 (Kahama). *Bull. geol. Surv. Tanganyika*, 15.

GRANTHAM, D. R. and F. OATES 1931. The Mbosi meteoric iron, Tanganyika Territory. With a note on the structure by Dr. L. J. Spencer. *Min. Mag.*, London., Vol. XXII, 133, pp. 487-493.

GREIG, R. C. H. ... ... Iron Smelting in Fipa. *T.N.R.* 4, pp. 77-81.

GROSEMANS, P. ... ... 1949. Le district aurifére du Tanganyika. *Ann. Serv. Mines Katanga*, T. 14, pp. 53-70.

GUEST, N. J. ... ... 1951. Climbing Oldonyo L'Engai. *T.N.R.* 31, pp. 55-57.

HARKIN, D. A. ... ... 1948. The Mbamba Bay Coalfield, Tanganyika Territory. *Min. Mag.*, Lond., 78, p. 265.

1955. The Geology of the Songwe-Kiwira Coalfield, Rungwe District. *Bull. geol. Surv. Tanganyika*, 27.

HARKIN, D. A., A. C. M. MCKINLAY and J. SPENCE ... 1954. The Karroo System of Tanganyika. *C.R. XIX Congr. géol. Int.*, Fasc. XXI, pp. 93-101.

HARPUM, J. R. ... ... 1949. The Origin of Limestone Caves with special reference to those of Cheddar and Amboni. *T.N.R.* 27, pp. 1-7.

1952. The Titanium-Bearing Iron Occurrences of the Njombe District, South-West Tanganyika. (With a note on the metallurgy of the Liganga iron ores by J. H. Harris.) *C.R. XIX Congr. géol. Int.*, Symposium sur les Gisements de Fer du Monde, T. I, pp. 193-209.

1954. Some Problems of Pre-Karroo Geology in Tanganyika. *C.R. XIX Congr. géol. Int.*, Fasc. XX, pp. 209-239.

1954. Formation of Epidote in Tanganyika. *Bull. geol. Soc. Amer.*, Vol. 65, pp. 1075-92.

HARPUM, J. R. ... ... 1955. Recent Investigations in Pre-Karroo Geology in Tanganyika. *Proc. Ass. Servs. géol. Afr.*, Nairobi, 1954. (In the press.).

HARRIS, J. H. ... ... 1951. Lake Manyara. *T.N.R.* 30, pp. 6-14.

HAUGHTON, S. H. ... ... 1924. Reptilian Remains from the Karroo Beds of East Africa. *Quart. J. geol. Soc. Lond.*, Vol. 80, pp. 1-11.

1932. On a Collection of Karroo Vertebrates from Tanganyika Territory. *Quart. J. geol. Soc. Lond.*, Vol. 88, pp. 634-71.

1936. On some Karroo Fishes from East Africa. *Quart. J. geol. Soc. Lond.*, Vol. 92, pp. 58-61.

HOPWOOD, A. T. ... ... 1931. Pleistocene Mammalia from Nyasaland and Tanganyika Territory. *Geol. Mag.*, Vol. 68, pp. 133-135.

1932. The Olduvai Expedition, 1931. *Nat. Hist. Mag.*, Vol. III, No. 23, pp. 214-225.

1934. New Fossil Mammals from Tanganyika Territory. *Ann. Mag. nat. Hist.*, Series 10, 14.

1936. New and little-known fossil Mammals from the Pleistocene of Kenya Colony and Tanganyika Territory. *Ann. Mag. nat. Hist.*, 17.

HUENE, F. VON ... ... 1939. Die Karroofauna im ostafrikanischen Ruhuhu-Gebiet. *Zbl. Miner. Geol. Paläont.*, B, pp. 69-71.

1944. The Age and Tectonic Relationship of East African Volcanic Rocks. *Geol. Mag.*, Vol. 81, pp. 15-27.

1944. Kilimanjaro: An Active Volcano. *Nature*, Lond., Vol. 153, pp. 454-455.

KENT, P. E. ... ... 1941. The Recent History and Pleistocene Deposits of the Plateau North of Lake Eyasi, Tanganyika. *Geol. Mag.*, Vol. 78, No. 3, pp. 173-184.

1942. A Note on Pleistocene Deposits near Lake Manyara, Tanganyika. *Geol. Mag.*, Vol. 79, pp. 72-77.

KITCHIN, F. L. ... ... 1929. On the age of the Upper and Middle Dinosaur Deposits at Tendaguru, Tanganyika Territory. *Geol. Mag.*, Vol. LXVI, pp. 193-220.

LEAKEY, L. S. B. ... ... 1934. Changes in the Physical Geography of East Africa in Human Times. *Geogr. J.*, Vol. LXXXIV, No. 4, pp. 296-310.

MACKAY, R. A. .. ... 1936. The Lupa Goldfield. *J. chem. Soc. S. Afr.* Vol. XXXVI, No. 3, pp. 98-108.

MATHEW, W. D. ... ... 1924. Jurassic Dinosaurs of Utah and East Africa. *Bull. geol. Soc. Amer.*, 24.

MAUFE, H. B. ... ... 1915. The Coastal Series of Sediments in East Africa. *Geol. Mag.*, Vol. III, pp. 274-277.

McCONNELL, R. B. ... ... 1950. Outline of the Geology of Ufipa and Ubende. *Bull. geol. Surv. Tanganyika*, 19.

1951. Rift and Shield Structure in East Africa. *Rep. XXXVIII Int. geol. Congr. (A.S.G.A.)*, Pt. XIV, pp. 199-207.

McKINLAY, A. C. M. ... ... 1954. The Geology of the Ketewaka-Mchuchuma Coalfield, Njombe District. *Bull. geol. Surv. Tanganyika*, 21.

MENNELL, F. P. ... ... 1930. The Karroo System in East and Central Africa. *C.R. XV Int. geol. Congr.*, Vol. II, pp. 263-87.

NOPCSA, F. ... ... 1924. On the Systematic Position of Tangasaurus and Saurosternon. *S. Afr. J. Sci.*, Vol. 21, pp. 206-7.

NOWACK, E. ... ... 1937. Zur Kenntnis der Karruformation im Ruhuhu-Graben. *Neues Jb. Min. Geol. Paläont.*, Bd. 78, pp. 380-412.

Geologische Forschungen im Ostafrika. *Geol. Rdsch.*, XXI, p. 294.

OATES, F. ... ... 1930. A note on the Turoka Series of East Africa and the Nachipere Beds of Nyasland. *Geol. Mag.*, Vol. 67, pp. 521-5.

1932. A Note on the Gneiss of the Ufipa Plateau, Tanganyika Territory. *Geol. Mag.*, Vol. LXIX, pp. 326-7.

1933. The Limestone Deposits of Tanganyika Territory. *Bull. geol. Surv. Tanganyika*, 4.

1936. The Meteoric Iron at Mbosi. *T.N.R.* 2, pp. 44-49.

1941. A Record of the Meteorites of Tanganyika Territory. *T.N.R.* 12, pp. 28-31.

43

OATES, F. AND B. N.
TEMPERLEY ... ...   1937. A Contribution to the Geology of the Lower Division Basement Complex of Tanganyika Territory. *Rep. XVII Int. geol. Congr.*, Vol. II, pp. 225-46.

PAGE-JONES, F. H. ... ...   1948. Water in Masailand. *T.N.R.* 26, pp. 51-59.

PARKINSON, J. ... ...   1928. The Dinosaurs of Tendaguru. *Nat. Hist. Mag.*, Vol. 1, No. 8.

1929. The Dinosaur Deposits at Tendaguru, Tanganyika Territory. *Geol. Mag.*, Vol. LXVI, pp. 558-60.

PASSARGE, S. ... ...   1922. Die Inselberglandschaft der Massai-Steppe. *Petermanns Mitt.*, pp. 205-9.

QUENNELL, A. M. ... ...   1951. The Lupa Goldfield, Tanganyika Territory. *Min. Mag.*, Lond., Vol. 85, pp. 341-7.

RECK, H.... ... ...   1921. Uber eine neue Faunula im Juragebiet der Deutsch-Ostafrikanischen Mittellbahn. *Zbl. Miner. Geol. Paläont.*, p. 431.

1930-1931. Pluvial geology, Landscape and Man in the East African Rift Valley. *J.E. Afr. Ug. nat. Hist. Soc.*, Vol. 40-41.

RECK, H. and W. O.
DIETRICH ... ...   1921. Ein Beiträge zur geologisch Kenntnis der Landschaft Usaramo in Deutsch-Ostafrika. *Zbl. Miner. Geol. Paläont.*, p. 372.

1925. Grabungen auf fossile Wirbetiere in Deutsch-Ostafrika. *Geol. Charakterb.*, Pt. 31.

RECK, H. and G. SCHULZE ...   1921. Ein Beiträge zur Kenntnis des Baues und der jüngsten Veränderungen des l' Engai Vulkans im nördlichen Deutsch-Ostafrika. *Z. Vulkanol.*, 6, pp. 47-71.

REEVE, W. H. ... ...   1937. Sandstone "Dykes" in the Dodoma District of Tanganyika Territory. *Geol. Mag.*, Vol. LXXIV, pp. 468-75.

1938. Prehistory in Tanganyika. *T.N.R.* 6, pp. 49-57.

RICHARD, J. J. ... ...   1942. Volcanological observations in East Africa. Oldonyo L'Engai. The 1940-41 Eruption. *J.E. Afr. Ug. nat. Hist. Soc.*, Vol. XVI, Nos. 2 and 3.

RICHARD, J. J. ... ... 1944. Volcanological Observations in East Africa, II. Kilimanjaro. Kibo's fumarolic activity in 1942-1943. *J.E. Afr. Ug. nat. Hist. Soc.*, Vol. XVIII, Nos. 1-3.

1945. Crater Fumaroles of Kibo and Seismic Activity during 1942-5. *Nature*, Lond., Vol. 156, p. 352.

1945. The Mudvolcanoes of Moa, near Tanga. *T.N.R.* 19, pp. 3-8.

ROBERTS, R. O. ... ... 1939. Mwanza Goldfield Geology. *Min. Mag.*, Lond., Vol. 60, pp. 137-147.

ROBERTSON, L. S. ... ... 1934. Report on some fossil plants collected in Tanganyika Territory. *Quart. J. geol. Soc. Lond.*, 90, Pt. I, pp. 1-6.

ROSE, C. ... ... 1929. The Geology of the Kalambo Gorge. *Geogr. J.*, Vol. 74, pp. 38-46.

SALT, G. ... ... 1951. The Shira Plateau of Kilimanjaro. *Geogr. J.*, CXA4II, pp. 150-166.

SAMPSON, D. N. ... ... 1954. Notes for Mica Prospectors in Tanganyika. *Bull. geol. Surv. Tanganyika*, 23.

SCHLUTER, W. ... ... 1911. Mining in the German Protectorate. *Min. J.*, Lond., January, pp. 78-9.

SCHOLZ, E. ... ... 1911. Beittäge zur Kenntnis der deutschost-afrikanischen Tertiärablagerungen. *Z. dtsch. geol. Ges.*, Bd. LXII, pp. 368-79.

1914. Vulkanologische Beobachtungen an der Deutsch-Ost-afrikanischen Mitteiland-hahn. *Z. dtsch. geol. Ges.*, Bd. 66, pp. 330-5.

1912. The Karroo Formation West of the Uluguru Mts. *Pflanzer*, Bd. 8, June.

1912. Coal West of the Uluguru Mts. *Pflanzer*, Bd. 8, August.

1912. Coal at Nyasa. *Pflanzer*, Bd. 8, Sept.

1914. Beiträge zur Geologie des Südlichen Teiles Deutsch-Ostafrikas. *Mitt. dtsch. Schutzgeb.*, Bd. 27, pp. 49-67.

1914. Beiträge zur Geologie der südwest-lichen Graben-Gebiete Deutsch-Ostafrikas. *Pflanzer*, Bd. 10, pp. 80-6.

SCHUEHERT, C. ... ... 1918. The Age of the American Morrison and East African Tendaguru Formations. *Bull. geol. Soc. Amer.*, 29, pp. 245-80.

1934. Upper Jurassic Age of the Tendaguru Dinosaur Beds. *Amer. J. Sci.*, Vol. XXVII, pp. 463-6.

SCOTT-ELLIOT, G. F. and J. W. GREGORY ... ... 1895. The Geology of Mount Ruwenzori and some adjoining Regions of Equatorial Africa. *Quart. J. geol. Soc. Lond.*, 51.

SEWARD, A. C. ... ... 1934. Some Early Mesozoic Plants from the Tanganyika Territory. *Geol. Mag.*, Vol. 71, pp. 385-92.

SIMPSON, G. G. ... ... 1926. The Age of the Morrison Formation. *Amer. J. Sci.*, Vol. XVII.

SMITH, G. E. ... ... 1907. From the Victoria Nyanza to Kilimanjaro. *Geogr. J.*, Vol. XXIX, pp. 249-72.

SPATH, L. F. ... ... 1920. Jurassic Ammonites from East Africa. *Geol. Mag.*, Vol. LVII, pp. 311-20; 351-62.

SPENCE, J. ... ... 1954. The Geology of the Galula Coalfield, Mbeya District. *Bull. geol. Surv. Tanganyika*, 25.

SPENCER, L. J. ... ... 1906. Phenacite and other minerals from German East Africa. *Min. Mag.*, Lond., 24, p. 178.

SPINK, P. C. ... ... 1943. Glaciers in Kilimanjaro Crater. *Quart. J.R. met. Soc.*, Oct.

SPURR, A. M. M. ... ... 1955. The Soils of Mbozi. *Bull. geol. Surv. Tanganyika*, 24.

STANLEY, G. H. ... ... 1931. On the Meteorite at M'bozi, Tanganyika. *S. Afr. J. Sci.*, Vol. XXVIII, pp. 88-91.

STOCKLEY, G. M. ... ... 1936. A Further Contribution on the Karroo Rocks of Tanganyika Territory. *Quart. J. geol. Soc. Lond.*, 92, pp. 1-31.

1937. Geological notes on the Coastal Region of Tanganyika. *T.N.R.* 3, pp. 82-6.

1939. Outline of the Geology of the Uruwira Mineral Field. *Short Pap. geol. Surv. Tanganyika*, 22,

1943. The Geology of the Rufiji District including a small portion of the Northern Kilwa District (Matumbi Hills). *T.N.R.* 16, pp. 7-28.

STOCKLEY, G. M. ... ... 1943. The Pre-Karroo Stratigraphy of Tanganyika. *Geol. Mag.*, 80, pp. 161-70.

1946. Phosphate Deposits in Tanganyika Territory. With Special Reference to the Zizi Apatite-Limestone, South of Kisaki. *E. Afr. agric. J.*, Vol. XII, pp. 118-24.

1947. New Coal Discoveries in Tanganyika and Coal Resources of East and Central Africa. *Min. Mag.*, Lond., Vol. 76, p. 329. (May.)

1947. The Coal Resources of East and Central Africa. *Min. Mag.*, Lond., Vol. 76. (June.)

1948. Geology of North, West and Central Njombe District, Southern Highlands Province. *Bull. geol. Surv. Tanganyika*, 18.

1948. The Geology and Mineral Resources of Tanganyika Territory. *Bull. geol. Surv. Tanganyika*, 20.

STOCKLEY, G. M. and F. OATES 1931. Report on the Geology of the Ruhuhu Coalfields, Njombe-Songea Districts: Being a Preliminary Geological Survey of the Karroo Rocks, East of Lake Nyasa. *Bull. geol. Surv. Tanganyika*, 2.

1931. The Ruhuhu Coalfields, Tanganyika Territory. *Min. Mag.*, Lond., 45, pp. 73-91.

STOCKLEY, G. M. and J. WALTON ... ... 1932. The Geology of the Ruhuhu Coalfields Tanganyika Territory, with a Report on some Fossil Plants from Karroo Rocks in the Ruhuhu River Depression. *Quart J. geol. Soc. Lond.*, Vol. 88, pp. 610-622.

STOCKLEY, G. M. and G. J. WILLIAMS ... ... 1938. Explanation of the Geology, Degree Sheet No. 1 (Karagwe Tinfields). *Bull. geol. Surv. Tanganyika.* 10.

SUTTON, J., J. WATSON and T. C. JAMES ... ... 1954. A Study of the Metamorphic Rocks of Karema and Kungwe Bay, Western Tanganyika. *Bull. geol. Surv. Tanganyika*, 22.

SWEET, C. T. ... ... 1945. The Kyerwa Tin Deposits, Tanganyika Territory, and their Beneficiation by Dry Blower. *Trans. Instn. Min. Metall.*, Lond., Vol. LIV, pp. 115-40.

TEALE, E. O. ... ... 1923. Geographical and Geological Problems in East Africa. *J.E. Afr. Ug. nat. Hist. Soc.* 23, pp. 6-18.

1923. Some non-foliated igneous rocks in Tanganyika Territory and their bearing on tectonic problems in that region. *Geol. Mag.*, Vol. 60, pp. 74-88.

1928. Tanganyika Territory; Its Geology and Mineral Resources. *Min. Mag.*, Lond., Vol. 38, pp. 331-8; Vol. 39, pp. 9-17;

1930. A Consideration of the term Tanganyika System with special reference to Ujiji and Uha regions. *C.R. XV Int. geol. Congr.*, Vol. II, pp. 210-21.

1933. A Physiographical Map of Tanganyika Territory. *Geogr. Rev.*, XXIII, pp. 402-13.

1933. Provisional Geological Map of Tanganyika with Explanatory Notes. *Bull. geol. Surv. Tanganyika*, 6. (Revised 1936).

1936. Provisional Geological Map of Tanganyika with Explanatory Notes. (1933, revised 1936). *Bull. geol. Surv. Tanganyika*,

1942. East African Mining. *Min. Mag.*, Lond., Vol. LXVI, pp. 53-62.

TEALE, E. O., N. W. EADES and F. OATES ... ... 1935. The Eastern Lupa Goldfield. *Bull. geol. Surv. Tanganyika*, 8.

TEALE, E. O. and F. OATES ... 1935. The Limestone Caves and Hot Springs of the Songwe River (Mbeya) Area, with notes on the Associated Guano Deposits. *J.E. Afr. Ug. nat. Hist. Soc.*, XII, 3/4, pp. 130-7.

1947. The Mineral Resources of Tanganyika Territory. *Bull. geol. Surv. Tanganyika*, 16. 6.

TEALE, E. O. and F. B. WADE 1937. A Stratigraphical Classification and Table of Tanganyika Territory. *Bull. geol. Surv. Tanganyika*, 9.

TEMPERLEY, B. N. ... ... 1942. Some problems of the Archaean rocks of Tanganyika Territory. *Geol. Mag.* Vol. 79, pp. 67-71.

TEMPERLEY, B. N. ... ... 1945. Piezo-electric quartz in Tanganyika. *T.N.R.* 19, pp. 9-22.

THRELFALL, H. R. ... ... 1950. Some Physical Features of the Dar es Salaam District. *T.N.R.*, 29, pp. 68-72.

VALLEE POUSSIN, J. DE LA. ... 1937. L'age du systéme de L'Uha (Tanganyika Territory). *Bull. Soc. belge Géol. Pal. Hydr.* XLVI.

1937. Un graben transversal Tanganyika-Rukwa au Tanganyika Territory. *Bull. Soc. belge Géol. Pal. Hydr.*, XLVI.

WADE, F. B. ... ... 1937. A Stratigraphical Classification and Table of Tanganyika Territory. *Bull. geol. Surv. Tanganyika*, 9.

WATERMEYER, A. M. and H. F. I. ELLIOTT ... ... 1943. Lake Manyara. *T.N.R.* 15, pp. 58-71.

WILCOCKSON, W. H. ... ... Preliminary notes on the geology of Kilimanjaro. London. *Geological Magazine* 1956. Pp. 13, ill. map.

WILLIAMS, G. J. ... ... 1939. The Kimberlite Province and Associated Diamond Deposits of Tanganyika Territory. *Bull. geol. Surv. Tanganyika*, 12.

WILLIAMS, G. J. and N. W. EADES ... ... 1939. Explanation of the Geology of Degree Sheet No. 18 (Shinyanga). *Bull. geol. Surv. Tanganyika*, 13.

WILLIAMS, G. J. and A. F. SKERL ... ... 1940. Mica in Tanganyika Territory. *Bull. geol. Surv. Tanganyika*, 14.

WILLIS, B. ... ... 1933. Peneplains of East Africa. *Geogr. J.*, Vol. 82.

1936. East African Plateaux and Rift Valleys. Studies in Comparative Seismology. Carnegie Inst., Washington, Publ. No. 470.

WOHLTMANN, F. ... ... 1897. Die Ergebnisse der Chemischen Untersuchung Deutsch-Ostafrikanischer Böden. *Tropenpflanzer*, Bd. 1, pp. 129-133.

WYATT, A. W. ... ... 1943. Earthquake at Songea. *T.N.R.*, 16, pp. 91-5.

ZWIERZYCKI, J. ... ... 1941. Die Cephalopodenfauna der Tendaguru-schichten in Deutsch-Ostafrika. *Arch. Biontol.*, *Berl.*, Bd. III, Heft 4, pp. 7-96.

ORNITHOLOGY

Books, Reports, Pamphlets

BELCHER, C. F. ... ... The Birds of Nyasaland. London, 1930.

BANNERMANN, D. A. ... ... The Birds of West and Equatorial Africa. Edinburgh. 1950.

BENSON, C. W. ... ... A Check List of the Birds of Nyasaland. Blantyre, 1953.

CAVE, F. O. and
  MACDONALD, J. D. ... ... The Birds of the Sudan. Edinburgh.

CHAPIN, J. P. ... ... The Birds of the Belgian Congo, 4 vols. *Bull. Amer. Mus. Nat. Hist.*, New York. (Reprinted in book form).

GILL, E. L. ... ... A First to South African Birds. Cape Town, 1945.

JACKSON, Sir F. J. ... ... The Birds of Kenya Colony and the Uganda Protectorate. 3 vols. Gurney and Jackson, London, 1938.

MACKWORTH-PRAED, C. W. and
  GRANT, CAPT. C. H. B. ... Birds of Eastern and North-Eastern Africa, 2 vols. Longmans, London, 1953 and 1955.

PRIEST, CAPT. C. D. ... ... A Guide to the Birds of Southern Rhodesia. London, 1929.

  Eggs of Birds Breeding in Southern Africa. Glasgow, 1948.

REICHENOW, A. ... ... Die Vögel Deutsch-Ost-Afrikas. Berlin, 1894.

  Die Vögel Afrikas. Neudamm, 1902-3.

  Die Fauna der deutschen Kolonien. Reihe III. Deutsch Ostafrika, heft 1. Die jagbdaren vögel. Berlin, 1909.

ROBERTS, AUSTIN ... ... The Birds of South Africa. London and Johannesburg, 1940.

RUGGLES-BRISE, C. J. ... ... Notes on Some Birds of Dar es Salaam. Norwich, undated.

SCLATER, W. L. ... ... Systema Avium Aethiopicarum. 2 vols. London, 1924-30.

VAN SOMEREN, DR. V. G. L. ... The Birds of Kenya, and Uganda. Reprinted from *J.E.A.N.H.S.* in book form.

WHITE, C. M. N. and
  WINTERBOTTOM, J. M. ... A Check List of the Birds of Northern Rhodesia. Lusaka, 1949.

ORNITHOLOGY

Articles in Periodicals*

BANGS, O. and LOVERIDGE, A. ... Reports on the scientific results of an expedition to the Southwestern Highlands of Tanganyika Territory. III. Birds. *Bull. Mus. Comp. Zool.* Harvard, 75: 143-221. (Includes also specimens from Ukerewe, Mwanza and the east shore of Lake Tanganyika.) (1933).

BANNERMAN, D. A. ... ... On a collection of birds made by A. B. Percival in British East Africa. *Ibis* (9) 4: 676-710. (Includes some with locality "Kilimanjaro", but none are montane. (1910).

BENSON, C. W. and F. M. ... Notes in birds from northern Nyasaland and Adjacent Tanganyika Territory. *Ann. Tramsvaal Mus.* 21: 155-177. (1949).

BOULTON, R. ... ... New species and sub-species of African Birds. *Ann. Carnegie Mus.* Pittsburgh 21: 43-56. (1931).

BOWEN, W. W. ... ... East African Birds collected during the Gray African Expedition—1929. *Proc. Acad. Nat. Sci.* Philadelphia 83: 11-79. (Includes 245 speciemens from south-west of Ikoma.) (1931).

BOXBERGER, L. ... ... Short description of nests and eggs at Dar es Salaam. *Zoologie* 18: 178-180. 19: 21-22, 51-52. *Orn. Mber.* (1909-10).

DUDBRIDGE, B. J. ... ... Some notes on the ducks and geese of Usukuma. *T.N.R.* 31; 74-78 (1951).

ELLIOTT, H. F. I. ... ... An island in Lake Victoria. *T.N.R.* 10: 28-40. (Kaserazi Is., Buchosa. Birds listed, 130 spp., pp. 34-37.) (1940).

ELLIOTT, H. F. and FUGGLES-COUCHMAN, N. R. ... ... An ecological survey of the birds of the Crater Highlands of Rift Lakes, Northern Tanganyika Territory. *Ibis* 90: 394-425. (1948).

FRIEDMANN, H. ... ... A collection of birds from the Uluguru and Usambara Mountains, Tanganyika Territory. *Ibis* (12) 4: 74-99. (1928).

---

*Compiled largely from R. E. Moreau's bibliography in *Tanganyika Notes and Records* No. 28, pp. 64-79.

FRIEDMANN, H. and
LOVERIDGE, A. ... ... Notes on the ornithology of tropical Africa. *Bull. Mus. Comp. Zool.* Harvard 81: 1-413. (Many of the notes refer to records and observations in Tanganyika. They cannot, however, be accepted implicitly: see *Ibis* 1938: 591-597.) (1937).

FUGGLES-COUCHMAN, N. R. ... Notes on the nesting habits of some Tanganyika birds. *T.N.R.* 1; 61-76 (1936).

Some obervations on birds raiding rice fields in Kilosa District, T.T. *E. Africa. Agric. J.* 2: 54-59. (1936).

The habitat distribution of the birds of northern, eastern and central Tanganyika, with field keys. *T.N.R.*, 33; 48-59 (1952); 35, 14-37 (1953); 37, 71-114 (1954).

Notes on some birds of the Eastern Province of Tanganyika Territory. *Ibis* (14) 3: 76-106. (1939).

The ornithology of Mt. Hanang in northern-central Tanganyika Territory. *Ibis* 95; 468-482. (1953).

Further notes on nesting habits and the breeding seasons of some Tanganyika birds. *T.N.R.* 21; 85-103. (1946).

FUGGLES-COUCHMAN, N. R. and
ELLIOTT, H. F. I. ... ... Some records and field-notes from north-eastern Tanganyika Territory. *Ibis* 88: 327-347. (1946).

GROTE, H. ... ... Beiträgezur Ornis des sudostlechen Deutsch-Ostafrika. (Mikindani). *J. Orn.* 61: 125-142. (1912-1913).

Uber einige Vogel der deutschostafrika-nischen Sudkuste. *J. Orn.* 67: 298-302. (1919).

HALDANE, L. A. ... ... Birds of the Rufiji. *T.N.R.* 22; 27-54. (1946) (Contains ki-Rufiji names).

LOVERIDGE, A. ... ... Notes on East African birds (chiefly nesting habits and stomach contents) collected 1915-1919. *Proc. Zool. Soc.* London, 1922: 837-862. (Includes some T.T. Records, mostly from the Central Line.) (1923).

LOVERIDGE, A. ... ... Notes on East African birds (chiefly nesting habits and endo-parasites) collected 1920-1923. *Proc. Zool. Soc.* London, 1923: 899-921. (T.T. records, mostly Central Line and Mwanza.) (1923).

Notes on East African birds (chiefly nesting-habits and stomach contents) collected in 1926. *Proc. Zool. Soc.* London, 1928: 71-79. (Refers to Uluguru and Usambara.) (1928).

Field notes on vertebrates collected by the Smithsonian Chrysler East African Expedition of 1926. *Proc. U.S. Nat. Mus.* 73 (17): 1-69, (pp. 28-48 deal with birds in Central T.T., mainly near Dodoma, and mainly from the point of view of their behaviour in captivity.) (1928).

LYNES, H. ... ... Contributions to the ornithology of Southern Tanganyika Territory. *J. Orn.* 82: Sondtrh. (1934).

MEIKLEJOHN, M. F. M. ... Notes on migratory birds from the southern shores of Lake Victoria, etc. *Ostrich* II: 33-40. (1940).

MEISE, W. ... ... Zur Vogelwelt des Matengo-Hochlandes nahe dem Nordende des Njassasees. *Mitt Zoolog. Mus.* Berlin, 22: 86-160. (1937).

MOREAU, R. E. ... ... A contribution to tropical bird ecology. *J. Anim. Ecol.* 3: 41-69. (1934).

A synecological study of Usambara, Tanganyika Territory, with particular reference to birds. *J. Ecol.* 23: 1-43. (1935).

A critical analysis of the distribution of birds in a tropical African area. *J. Anim. Ecol.* 4: 167-191. (1935).

A contribution to the ornithology of Kilimanjaro and Mt. Meru. *Proc. Zool. Soc.* London, 1953: 843-891. (1936).

Bird-insect nesting associations. *Ibis* (13) 6: 460-471. (1936).

Breeding seasons of birds in East African evergreen forest. *Proc. Zool. Soc.* London. 1936: 631-653. (1936).

MOREAU, R. E. ... ... Migrant birds in Tanganyika Territory. *T.N.R.* 4; 17-50. (1937).

The avifauna of the mountains along the Rift Valley in North Central Tanganyika Territory (Mbulu District). *Ibis* (14) 1: 760-786. (14)2: 1-32. (1937-38).

Contributions to the ornithology of the East African islands. *Ibis* (14)4: 48-91. (1940).

Distributional notes on East African birds. *Ibis* (14)4: 454-463. (Extensions of range). (1940).

Bird Names used in Central North-Eastern Tanganyika Territory. *T.N.R.* 10; 47-72. (1940); 11, 47-60. (1941).

The nesting of African birds in association with other living things. *Ibis* (14)6: 240-263. (1942).

A contribution to the ornithology of the east side of Lake Tanganyika. *Ibis* 85: 377-412. (1943).

Additions to the ornithology of the Mafia group of islands. *Ibis* 86: 33-37. (1944).

Relations between number in brood, feeding-rate and nesting period in nine species of birds in Tanganyika Territory. *J. Anim. Ecol.* 6: 205-209. (1947).

A contribution to the faunistics of Tanganyika Territory. *Ibis* 89: 216-234. (Chiefly east side of Lake Tanganyika and Matengo Highlands.) (1947).

Ecological isolation in rich tropical avifauna (Usambara). *J. Anim. Ecol.* 17: 113-126. (1948).

Ornithology in Tanganyika. *T.N.R.* 28; 64-79 (1950). (Gives a full bibliography from 1900-1950).

MOREAU, R. E. and
   GREENWAY, J. P. ... ... A note on Longido and Ketumbeine Mountains. *T.N.R.* 3: 8-14. (1937).

MOREAU, R. E. and
   MOREAU, W. M. ... ... Biological and other notes on some East African birds. *Ibis* (14)1: 152-174, 321-345. (1937).

Observations on some East African Birds. *Ibis* (14)3: 296-323. (1939).

MOREAU, R. E. and
MOREAU, W. M. ... ... A supplementary contribution to the ornithology of Kilimanjaro. *Rev. Zool. Bot. Afr.* 33: 1-15. (1939).

Incubation and fledging periods of African birds. *Auk.* 14.

Incubation and fledging periods of African birds. *Auk.* 57: 313-325; 60: 608. (1940).

PETERS, J. L. and
LOVERIDGE, A. ... ... Scientific results of a fourth expedition to forested areas in East and Central Africa. II. Birds. *Bull. Mus. Comp.* Harvard 89: 217-275. (Includes some specimens from Mikindani, Lindi and Tanga Districts.) (1942).

REICHENOW, A. ... ... List of birds in C. G. Schillings "Mit Blitzlicht und Buchse." (North-west of Kilimanjaro). Leipzig. (1905).

Die Fauna der Deutschen Kolonien. 3: Deutsch—Ostafrica. (1) Die jagdbaren Vogel. Berlin iv 109. (1909).

Die vogelfauna des mittelafrikanischen Seengebietes in "Wiss Ergeb. Deutsch. Zentral-Africa Expedition 1907-1908" 3(8). Leipzig. (Includes collection by Stegmann, Kandt and Grauer.) (1910).

SALVADORI, T. ... ... Uccelli reccolti da S.A.R. la Duchessa D'Aosta nella regione dei grandi laghi dell' Africa equatoriale. *Napoli Ann. Mus. Zool.* 4: 1-29. (Usambara to Bukoba and near Mwanza.) (1914).

SASSI, M.... ... ... Liste der von A. Horn (Wien) in Zentralafrika gesammelten Vogelbalge. *Orn. Mber.* 17: 106-109. (Mwanza—Tabora—Ujiji and back more directly.) (1908).

Beiträge zur Ornis Zentralafrikas. *Ann. Naturalist Mus. Wien,* 26: 347-393. (Includes Bukoba records.) (1912).

SASSI, M. and ZIMMER, F. ... Beiträge zur Kenntnis der Vogelwelt des Songea Distriktes mit besonderer Berücksichtigung des Matengo-Hochlandes (D.O.A.) (einschl. einigd Arten aus dem nordl—D.O.A.). *Ann. Natruhist. Mus. Wien* 51: 236-346. (1941).

SCHUSTER, L. ... ... Oologisches aus Deutsch-Ostafrika. *J. Orn.* 61: 540-546. (1913).

Uber Ruf, Gesang, Paarungflug und Gelege einige ostafrikanischer Vogel. *Orn. Mber.* 22: 44-48. (1914).

SCHUSTER, L. ... ... Ornithologische Beobachtungen auf eine Reise durch Uhehe und Ubena. *Orn. Mber.* 22: 173-179. (1914).

Eimasse, Eischalen—. Ei—und gelegegewichte einiger ostafrikanischer Vogel. *Beitr. Fortfl. Vogel* Berlin 1: 69-74. (1925).

Beiträge zur Verbreitungund Biologie der Vogel Deutsch-Ostafrikas. *J. Orn.* 74: 138-167, 521-541, 709-742. (1926).

Notizen. *Orn. Mber.* 19: 93-98, 165-166, 193-196. 21: 133-138. (1911-1913).

SCLATER, W. L., and
MOREAU, R. E. ... ... Taxonomic and field-notes on some birds of north-eastern Tanganyika Territory. *Ibis* (13)2: 487-522, (1932-1933).

SJOSTEDT, Y. ... ... Wissenschaftliche Ergebnisse der schwedischen Expedition nach Kilimanjaro, dem Meru und den umgebenden Masai-steppen Deutsch Ostafrikas, 1905-1906. (399-440). Stockholm. (1910).

SWYNNERTON, B. ... ... A key to the recognition in the field of 260 of the commoner birds of Tanganyika. *T.N.R.* 6: 5-48. (1938).

VERHEYEN, R. ... ... Notes sur la faune ornithologique de l'Afrique centrale. *Bull. Mus. Hist. Nat. Belge.* 15(61); 1-8. 15 (62): 1-7. (A collection from Rukwa.) (1939).

WATERMEYER, A. M. and
ELLIOT, H. F. I. ... ... Lake Manyara. *T.N.R.* 15: 58-71. (Pp. 66-68 and 71 deal with the birds.) (1943).

WHYBROW, C. ... ... Some Sukuma bird names. *T.N.R.* 25: 56-62. (1948).

WOLTAG ... ... Einiges uber die Vogelfauna Ostafrikas. *Konigsberg Schr. Physik. Ges.* 50: 55-56. (1909).

LINGUISTICS*

Books, Reports, Pamphlets

ANONYMOUS ... ... Outline of a Sukuma Grammar. Catholic Mission, Mwanza—No date.

Sitte und Rechte der Wazaramo. Berlin Mission—No date.

BAUMANN, O. ... ... Durch Masailand zur Nilquelle. Berlin, 1894.

BETBEDER, P. and JONES, J. ... Handbook of the Haya Language, 1949.

BUTTNER, C. I. ... ... Anthologie aus der Swahili Literatur. Berlin, 1894.

---

*This section has been compiled very largely from "A Linguistic Bibliography of East Africa" by W. H. Whiteley and A. E. Gutkind, Makerere College, Uganda.

CLARK, G. J. ... ... Vocabulary of the Chigogo Language, 1877.

CORDELL, O. T. ... ... Gogo Grammar (Exercises). Dar es Salaam, 1941.

DEMPWOLFF ... ... Die Sandawe. Linguistisches und Ethnographisches Material aus Deutsch-Ostafrika. Hamburg, 1916.

DOKE, C. M. ... ... Bantu. Modern Grammatical, Phonetical and Lexicographical Studies, since 1860. London, 1945.

ELMSLIE, W. A. ... ... Introductory Grammar of the Ngoni Language, 1891.

Table of Concords and Paradigms of the Ngoni Language, 1891.

ERHARDT, J. ... ... Vocabulary of the Enguduk Iloigob, as spoken by the Masai tribes in East Africa. Ed. J. L. Krapf, Ludwigsburg, 1857.

GUTHRIE, MALCOLM and
TUCKER, A. N. (Supervisors) Linguistic survey of the northern Bantu borderland. Part II. Oubangui to Great Lakes, by G. Van Bulck and Peter Hackett. Part III. Great Lakes to Indian Ocean, by A. N. Tucker and M. A. Bryan. Pp. 146 (maps). London: Oxford University Press for International African Institute.

HARRIES, L. ... ... A Grammar of Mwera. Witwatersrand Univ. Press, 1950.

HETHERWICK, A. ... ... Introductory Handbook and Vocabulary of the Yao Language, 1889.

A Handbook of the Yao Language, London, 1902 (2nd Ed.)

HINDE, H. ... ... The Masai Language. Cambridge, 1901.

HOLLIS, A. C. ... ... The Masai, their Language and Folklore. Clarendon Press, Oxford, 1905.

HYNDE, R. S. ... ... Second Yao-English Primer, 1894.

JOHNSTON, H. H. ... ... The Kilimanjaro Expedition. London, 1886.

JONES, D. P. ... ... Grammar and Vocabulary of Mambwe. L.M.S., 1890.

KIMMENADE, M. VAN DER ... Essai de Grammaire et Vocabulaire de la langue Sandawe. Posieux, Switzerland, 1954.

KISBEY, W. H. ... ... Zigula Exercises, 1896. 2nd ed. 1906.

KOLLMANN, P. ... ... Victoria Nyanza (Vocabulary of "Ha"). London, 1890.

KUIJPERS, E. M.... ... ... Grammaire de la langue Haya. Boxtel, Holland, 1922.

LAST, J. T. ... ... Poluglotta Africana Orientalis. London, 1885.

MAPLES, C. ... ... Collections for a Handbook of the Makua Language. London, 1879.

Yao-English Vocabulary. 1888.

MEINHOF, C. (TR. N. H. VON WARMELO) ... ... Introduction to the Phonology of the Bantu Languages. Berlin, 1932.

MÜLLER, R. P. F. ... ... Grammatik der Kinyamwesi-Sprache. Salzburg, 1904.

REIMER, H. ... ... Die Sprache der Wapogoro. Berlin, 1907.

SANDERSON, M. ... ... A Yao Grammar. 1916, 1917 (?) 2nd revised Edition, 1922.

SCOTT, R. R. ... ... A Glossary of some Scientific Terms used in Sanitary Practice by Swahili-speaking Africans. Dar es Salaam, 1929.

SEIDEL, A. ... ... Grammatik der Sprache von Irangi. Die Mittleren Hochlander des Nordlichen D. Ost-Afrika, Ed. C. W. Werther, 1898.

STEERE, E. ... ... Collections for a Handbook of the Yao Language, 1871.

Collections for a Handbook of the Shambala Language, 1867. Revised by H. W. Woodward, 1905.

TAYLOR, W. E. ... ... African Aphorisms or Saws from Swahililand. London, 1924.

TUCKER, A. N. ... ... Distribution of the Nilotic and Nilo-Hamitic Languages of Africa. O.U.P., London, 1948.

TUCKER, A. N. and MPAAYEI, J. T. O. ... ... A Masai Grammar with vocabulary. (Publications of the African Institute, Leyden, No. 2). London (Longmans), 1955.

VELTEN, C. ... ... Prosa und Poesie der Suaheli. Berlin, 1907. Desturi za Wasueheli. Göttingen, 1903.

WERNER, A. ... ... Introductory Sketch of the Bantu Languages. London, 1919.

WOODWARD, H. W. ... ... Collections for a Handbook of the Zigula Language, 1902.

LINGUISTICS

Articles in Periodicals

ALLEN, J. W. T.... ... ... Tenzi. *T.N.R.* 28, 81-3, Jan. 1950.

BLEEK, D. F. ... ... The Hadzapi or Watindiga of Tanganyika Territory. *Africa*, Vol. IV, 1931.

BLOHM, W. ... ... Die Nyamwesi: Texte unde Mitteilungen. *Z.E.S.* No. III, Hamburg, 1934.

BOSCH, R. P. ... ... Die Wanyamwezi. (Notes on language.) *Anthropos*, 1930.

BOURQUIN, W. ... ... Clickwords which Xhosa, Zulu and Sotho have in common. *Afr. Studies.* 10, 2, 59-81, June 1951.

BURTT, B. D. ... ... List of Plant Names in Vernaculars. *T.R.E.S.*, Vol. 84. Covers the following languages: Sukuma, Nyamwezi, Swahili, Nyaturu, Luguru.

CAPUS, A. ... ... Grammaire de Shi-Sumbwa. *Z.A.O.S.* Vol. IV, 1898 (Available in the Dar es Salaam Museum).

CORY, H. and MASALU, M. M. Place names in the Lake Province. *T.N.R.* 30, 53-72, 1951.

DAMMANN, E., tr. by
TATTERSALL, A. ... ... German contributions to Swahili studies in recent decades. *J. E. Afr. Swahili Committee*, 26, June, 1956, 9-17.

DEMPWOLFF, O. ... ... Beiträge zur Kenntnis der Sprachen in Deutsch-Ostafrika No. 7. *Z.F.K.* Vol. VI, 1915-16.

Beiträge zur Kenntnis der Sprachen in Deutsch-Ostafrika. No. 5. *Z.F.K.* Vol. V, 1914-15 (Available in the Dar es Salaam Museum).

DREXEL, A. ... ... Gliederung Afrikanischer Sprachen. *Anthropos*. Vols. XVI-XVII, XVIII-XIX and XX, 1921-2, 1923-4 and 1925.

East African Swahili Committee. Proposed supplement to the standard Swahili-English dictionary. *J.E. Afr. Swahili Committee*, 26, June 1956. 53-81.

GREENWAY, P. J. ... ... A Veterinary Glossary. *E.A.A.J.*, April, 1947 Covers the following languages: Arusha, Barabaig, Bena, Burunge, Chagga, Fipa, Gogo, Gorowa, Ha, Haya, Hehe, Iraqw, Jaruo (Luo), Jita, Kinga, Kizu, Koma

GREENWAY, P. J.—(*contd.*)   (Ikoma), Kuria, Luri (Ruri), Masai, Mbungwe, Meru, Nata, Ngureme, Nguu (Ngulu), Nyakyusa, Nyamwanga, Nyamwezi, Nyaturu (Remi), Nyiha, Nyiramba, Pimbwe, Rangi, Safwa, Sandawe Sangi, Sukuma, Tusi, Wanda, Zanaki.

GUTHRIE, MALCOLM ... ...   Gender, number and person in Bantu Languages. *Bull. School Orient. and Afr. Studies.* 12, 3/4, 847-56, 1948.

HADDON, E. B. ... ...   Some notes on the initial vowel pre-prefix. *J.E. Afr. Swahili Committee*, 26, June 1956. Pp. 32-48.

HARRIES, L. ... ...   Linguistic Notes from Southern Province. *T.N.R.* 1945.

Swahili Epic Literature. *Africa* 20, 1, 55-9, Jan. 1950.

An outline of Mawiha Grammar. *Bantu Stud.* 14, 2, 91-146, June 1940.

Some riddles of the Mwere people. *Afr. Stud.* 6, 1, 21-34, March 1947.

Cultural verse-forms in Swahili. *Afr. Stud.*, 15, 4, 1956, 176-87.

Swahili in the Belgian Congo. *T.N.R.* No. 39, June 1955. p. 12.

Congo Swahili. *T.N.R.* No. 44, Sept. 1956. p. 50.

HEESE, P. ... ...   Die Sango-Sprache. *Z.E.S.* Vol. X, 1919-20.

HELLIER, A. B. ... ...   Swahili prose literature. *Bantu Stud.* 14, 3, 247-257, Sept. 1940.

HENDEL, P. G. ... ...   Die Sprache der Wapogoro. *A.S.D.K.* Vol. VI, 1907 (Available in the Dar es Salaam Museum).

HERMANN, C. ... ...   Kisukuma. *M.S.O.S.*, Vol. I, 1898. (Available in the Dar es Salaam Museum.)

JACKSON, C. H. N. ... ...   Vernacular Names of East African Mammals. *T.R.E.S.*, Vol. 84. Covers the following languages: Masai, Swahili, Sukuma, Nyamwezi, Nyaturu (Remi), Rangi, Sandawe, Gogo, Zigua, Sagara, Sungwa, Haya.

KOOTZ-KRETSCHMER, E. ...   Safwa—und Nyiha Texte. *Z.E.S.* Vol. XXII, 1932.

LANGHEINRICH, F. ... ...   Schambala-Wörterbuch. *A.H.K.I.*, Vol. XXXIII, 1921.

MEINHOF, C.	Linguistische Studien in Ostafrika. No. II. *M.S.O.S.*, Vol. VII, 1904.
MEYER, E.	The Interrogative in Bantu languages (Das Fragewert in der Bantusprachen). *Z. Eing.—Sprachen*, 33, 2, 81, 106, Nov. 1949.
MOREAU, R. E.	Bird Names used in Coastal North East Tanganyika. *T.N.R.* 10/11, 1940/1941. Covers the following languages: Zigua, Digo, Bondei, Sambaa, Zaramu, Kami, Swahili.
	Bird Nomenclature in an East African area. (Tanganyika). *Bull. School Orient. and Afr. Stud.*, 10, 4, 998-1006, 1942.
PRINS, A. H. J.	An analysis of Swahili kinship terminology. *J.E. Afr. Swahili Committee* (Kampala), 26, June 1956, 20-27 (To be continued).
REHSE, H.	Eigentümlichkeiten in der Sprache der Bazinza in Deutsch-Ostafrika. *Z.F.K.* Vol. IV, 1913-14.
	Die Sprache der Baziba in Deutsch-Ostafrika. *Z.F.K.*, Vol. III, 1912-13.
	Wörtersammlung des Ruziba. Mitteilungen, Seminar fur Kolonial sprachen. Hamburg, 1914.
ROSLER, O.	Schambala-Grammatik. *A.S.D.K.* Vol. XIII, 1912.
SCHLOBACCH, ...	Die Volksstämme der Deutschen Ostküste des Victoria Nyansa *M.D.S.*, Vol. XIV, 1901.
SCHUMANN, C.	Grundriss einer Grammatik der Kondsprache *M.S.O.S.*, Vol. II, 1899.
SEIDEL, A.	Die Sprache von Ufiome in Deutsch-Ostafrika *Z.A.O.S.*, Vol. V, 1900.
SOWA, R. VON	Skizze der Grammatik des Ki-Mwere in Deutsch-Ostafrika. *Z.A.O.S.*, Vol. II, 1896. (Available in the Dar es Salaam Museum.)
SPISS, C.	Kihehe-Wörter-Sammlung. *M.S.O.S.*, Vol. III, 1900 (Available in the Dar es Salaam Museum.)
STERN, R.	Eine Kinyamwezi-Grammatik. *M.S.O.S.*, Vol. IX, 1906. (Available in the Dar es Salaam Museum.)

STRUCK, B. ... ... Fipa Vocabulary. *J.A.S.* Supplement, 1908.

Uber die Sprachen du Tatoga und Irakuleute. *M.D.S.*, Suppl. IV, 1911.

SWYNNERTON, G. H. ... ... Vernacular Names for some of the Better Known Mammals of Central Province. *T.N.R.* 21, 1946. Covers the following languages: Swahili, Gorowa, Asi, Burungi, Sandawe, Rangi, Masai, Gogo, Hehe, Sangu, Kimbu, Nyamwezi, Yanzi, Taturu (three dialects), Nyaturu (two dialects), Iramba, Iambi, Isanzu, Kindiga, Sukuma.

TAGLIARINI, C. ... ... On some words for "pupil" (of the eye). A study in "onomasiology" with special reference to the Hamito-semitic and Negro-African languages. *Am. Inst. univ. orient. Napoli.*, m.s. 3, 341-78, 1949.

TEMPELO, P. ... ... L'étude des langues Bantoues a la lumiére de la philosophie bantoue. *Presence afr.* 5, 755-60, 1948.

TUCKER, A. N. ... ... African Orthography. *Makerere* 1, 1, 22-6, Nov. 1946.

VAN BULCK, V. ... ... Westermann's classification of African Languages. (Classification des groupes des langues en Afrique selon Westermann). *Zaire*, 4, 2, 189-201, fév. 1950.

VELTEN, C. ... ... Kikami, die Sprache der Wakami in Deutsch-Ostafrika. *M.S.O.S.*, Vol. III, 1900. (Available in the Dar es Salaam Museum).

Die Sprache der Wahehe. *M.S.O.S.*, Vol. II, 1899. (Available in the Dar es Salaam Museum).

WESTERMANN, D. ... ... Linguistic relationships in Africa (Sprache beziehungen und sprach-oerwandtschaft in Afrika) Sitz-Beridtsch: *Akad. Wiss. Berlin, phil. hist. Kl.* pp. 27, 1948 (1949).

WERNER, A. ... ... Notes on the Shambala Language. *J.A.S.*, Vol. V, No. XVIII, 1906.

Specimens of East African Bantu Dialects. *B.St.*, Vol. III, 1927.

Specimens of East African Bantu Dialects. *B.St.*, Vol. III, 1927.

WILSON, G. McL. ... ... The Tatoga of Tanganyika. *T.N.R.*, 33, 1952. (For distribution and nomenclature.)

WOODWARD, H. W. ... ... An Outline of Makua Grammar. *B.St.*, Vol. II, 1926. (Available in the Dar es Salaam Museum.)

WORMS, A. ... ... Grundzüge der Grammatik des Kizaramo. *Z.A.O.S.* Vol. III, 1897. (Available in the Dar es Salaam Museum.)

WRIGHT, A. C. A. ... ... Maize names as indicators of economic contacts. *Uganda J.*, 13, 1, 61-81, March 1949.